THE BRIEF

American Pageant

A History of the Republic

SIXTH EDITION

David M. Kennedy
Stanford University

Lizabeth Cohen
Harvard University

Thomas A. Bailey

Mel Piehl
Valparaiso University

Houghton Mifflin Company   Boston   New York

Publisher: Charles Hartford
Editor-in-Chief: Jean Woy
Sponsoring Editor: Mary Dougherty
Development Editor: Leah R. Strauss
Senior Project Editor: Rosemary R. Jaffe
Senior Production/Design Coordinator: Jill Haber
Senior Manufacturing Coordinator: Jane Spelman
Senior Marketing Manager: Sandra McGuire

Cover image: *Flags, Beacon Street, Boston*, 1918, Dodge MacKnight, American, 1860–1950, watercolor over graphite pencil on paper. Copyright © 2002 Museum of Fine Arts, Boston. Bequest of Mrs. Edward Jackson Holmes, Edward Jackson Holmes Collection; 64.2114.

Printed in the U.S.A.

Library of Congress Control Number: 2002115905

ISBN: 0-618-33268-5

1 2 3 4 5 6 7 8 9-VH-07 06 05 04 03

Contents

Maps, Graphs, and Tables

Preface

This *Brief American Pageant* shares the reputation of its parent text, *The American Pageant*, as one of the most accessible, popular, and effective textbooks in the field of American history. Its authors, David Kennedy, Lizabeth Cohen, and Mel Piehl, have sustained and enhanced the key features that strongly distinguish the *Pageant* and the *Brief Pageant* from other American history textbooks, and make them appealing and useful to countless students: clarity, concreteness, a consistent chronological narrative, strong emphasis on major themes, avoidance of clutter, access to a variety of interpretive perspectives, and a colorful writing style leavened, as appropriate, with wit.

This Sixth Edition maintains these outstanding attributes in a format especially suitable for one-semester courses in American history, as well as for courses that rely heavily on supplementary readings in secondary historical works or primary sources. Like the longer Twelfth Edition from which it is drawn, *The Brief American Pageant* incorporates its authors' combined strengths in political, economic, social, and cultural history. This edition is especially concerned with integrating the rich recent scholarship in social history into *The Brief American Pageant's* core political narrative. It maintains a commitment to telling the story of the American past as vividly and clearly as possible, without sacrificing a sense of the often-sobering seriousness of history, and of its sometimes challenging complexity.

The essays that introduce the six parts are a key feature of *The Brief American Pageant* and are designed to encourage students to think coherently about six eras in American history. Newly revised for this edition, the essays seek to demonstrate that the study of history is not just a matter of piling up mountains of facts, but is principally concerned with discovering complex patterns of change over time, and organizing seemingly disparate events, actions, and ideas into meaningful chains of cause and consequences.

This edition also contains seven new "Makers of America" essays. These new essays discuss the Loyalists during and after the American Revolution, the settlers of the Old Northwest in the early nineteenth century, the radical Oneida Community, the Knights of Labor who anticipated American unionism, the environmentalists who pioneered the conservation of American natural resources in the early twentieth century, the suburbanites who created new communities and lifestyles in the post–World War II era, and the nineteenth- and twentieth- century feminists who founded movements committed to securing equal rights for women. In addition to the "Makers of America" essays included in most chapters, "Varying Viewpoints" essays appear at the close of many chapters. These essays summarize different historians' interpretations of the chapter topic.

Readers will find other new features in this edition of *The Brief American Pageant* as well: enriched discussion at many points of the experiences and contributions of women; expanded treatment of the environment, the West, and the Indians; deeper analysis of the ideological origins of the American Revolution and the enduring commitment to republicanism after it; updated discussion of the War of 1812; and exploration of how the market revolution in the antebellum period transformed American life. The Jacksonian era is now considered within the context of the "Rise of a Mass Democracy," in a freshly conceived Chapter 13. The material on U.S. expansionism at the turn of the twentieth century has been amplified into two chapters on "The Path of Empire" and "America on the World Stage." The text also covers the terrorist attacks of September 11, 2001, and their aftermath, including a brief discussion in Chapter 41 of the significance of these attacks within the larger context of American history.

The Sixth Edition also features a new design, many new or revised maps and charts, and additional illustrations. Updated bibliographies are now located at the end of the book, along with a revised Appendix, containing abundant statistical data on many aspects of the American historical experience.

Supplements Available with *The Brief American Pageant,* Sixth Edition

FOR STUDENTS:

Online Student Guidebook assists students by focusing their attention on the central themes and major historical developments of each chapter through a variety of interactive exercises, flashcards of key historical terms, and numerous study review questions designed to reinforce comprehension of the text. This website for students features ACE self-quizzes, online primary sources with activities, and annotated links to history websites.

The American Pageant **@history CD-ROM**, student version, contains over 1,000 searchable primary sources (text and graphic), video, and audio, many of which are accompanied by introductory headnotes, writing activities and questions.

American History Geoquest CD-ROM contains thirty interactive historical maps.

Rand McNally Atlas of American History

FOR INSTRUCTORS:

HM Class Prep CD-ROM with HM Testing is a complete instructional resource for instructors that features the Instructor's Resource Guide, test items, and maps and graphics in Powerpoint for presentations. **HMTesting**, the computerized test bank for Macintosh and Windows, allows instructors to create customized tests by editing and adding questions. It includes identification, multiple choice, and essay questions for the instructor's use. Most electronic resources can be customized to complement the way you teach your course.

Online Instructor's Resource Guide features summaries of chapter themes, chapter outlines, suggestions for lecture and discussion topics, and other resources including online primary sources with instructor notes, and annotated links to history websites.

The American Pageant **@history CD-ROM** contains over 1,000 searchable primary sources (text and graphic), video, and audio, many of which are accompanied by introductory headnotes, writing activities and questions that can be used to analyze, interpret, and discuss primary sources; to enhance collaborative learning; and to create multimedia lecture presentations.

American History Map Transparencies, available in two-volume sets upon adoption, provides over 150 full-color maps.

Please visit us on the web at **http://college.hmco. com** or contact your local Houghton Mifflin representative for more information about the ancillary items or to obtain desk copies.

Acknowledgments

Many people have contributed to this and past editions of *The Brief American Pageant.* We would especially like to thank the following colleagues who reviewed its parent text, *The American Pageant,* Twelfth Edition: Matthew Booker, Stanford University; Kurk Dorsey, University of New Hampshire; Junelle Harris, Harvard University; Robert Henry, Skyline College; Donna Kumler, Grayson County College; Sean Mallow, Stanford University; Drew R. McCoy, Clark University; Robert MacDougall, Harvard University; G. Kay Pulley, Trinity Valley Community College; Jack Rakove, Stanford University; Rosalind Rosenberg, Barnard College; Shirley Teresa Wajda, Kent State University; and Richard White, Stanford University.

Like its predecessors, this edition of *The Brief American Pageant* tries to cultivate in its readers the capacity for balanced judgment and informed understanding about American society by holding up to the present the mirror and measuring rod that is the past. The book's goal is not to teach the art of prophecy but the much subtler and more difficult arts of seeing things in context, of understanding the roots and direction and pace of change, and of distinguishing what is truly new under the sun from what is not. The study of history, it has been rightly said, does not make one smart for the next time, but wise forever.

We hope that the *Brief Pageant* will help to develop those intellectual assets in its readers, and that those who use the book will take from it both a fresh appreciation of what has gone before and a seasoned perspective on what is to come. And we hope, too, that readers will take as much pleasure in reading *The Brief American Pageant* as we have in writing it.

D. M. K.
L. C.
M. P.

Sail, sail thy best, ship of Democracy,
Of value is thy freight, 'tis not the Present only,
The Past is also stored in thee,
Thou holdest not the venture of thyself alone, not of
   the Western continent alone,
Earth's résumé entire floats on thy keel,
   O ship, is steadied by thy spars,
With thee Time voyages in trust, the antecedent
   nations sink or swim with thee,
With all their ancient struggles, martyrs, heroes,
   epics, wars, thou bear'st the other continents,
Theirs, theirs as much as thine, the destination-port
   triumphant. . . .

WALT WHITMAN

Thou Mother with Thy Equal Brood, 1872

PART ONE

FOUNDING THE NEW NATION

—◦◦◦—

c. 33,000 B.C.–A.D. 1783

The European explorers who followed Christopher Columbus to North America in the sixteenth century had no notion of founding a new nation. Neither did the first European settlers who peopled the thirteen English colonies on the eastern shores of the continent in the seventeenth and eighteenth centuries. These original colonists may have fled poverty or religious persecution in the Old World, but they continued to view themselves as Europeans, and as subjects of the English king. They regarded America as but the western rim of a transatlantic European world.

Yet life in the New World made the colonists different from their European cousins, and eventually, during the American Revolution, the Americans came to embrace a vision of their country as an independent nation. How did this epochal transformation come about? How did the colonists overcome the conflicts that divided them, unite against Britain, and declare themselves at great cost to be an "American" people?

They had much in common to begin with. Most were English-speaking. Most came determined to create an agricultural society modeled on English customs. Conditions in the New World deepened their common bonds. Most learned to live lives unfettered by the tyrannies of royal authority, official religion, and social hierarchies that they had left behind. They grew to cherish ideals that became synonymous with American life—individual liberty, self-government, religious tolerance, and economic opportunity. They also commonly displayed a willingness to subjugate outsiders—first Indians, who were nearly annihilated through war and disease, and then Africans, who were brought in chains to serve as slave labor, especially on the tobacco, rice, and indigo plantations of the southern colonies.

But if the settlement experience gave people a common stock of values, both good and bad, it also divided them. The thirteen colonies were quite different from one another. Puritans carved tight, pious, and relatively democratic communities of small family farms out of rocky-soiled New England. Theirs was a homogeneous world in comparison with most of the southern colonies, where large landholders, mostly Anglicans, built plantations along the coast from which they lorded over a labor force of black slaves and looked down on the poor white farmers who settled the backcountry. Different still were the middle colonies stretching from New York to Delaware. There diversity reigned. Well-to-do merchants put their stamp on New York City, as Quakers did on Philadelphia, while out in the countryside sprawling estates were interspersed with modest homesteads. Within individual colonies, conflicts festered over economic interests, ethnic rivalries, and religious practices. All those clashes made it difficult for colonists to imagine that they were a single people with a common destiny, much less that they ought to break free from Britain.

The American colonists in fact had little reason to complain about Britain. Each of the thirteen colonies enjoyed a good deal of self-rule. Many colonists profited from trade within the British Empire. But by the 1760s this stable arrangement began to crumble, a victim of the imperial rivalry between France and Britain. Their struggle for supremacy in North America began in the late seventeenth century and finally dragged in the colonists during the French and Indian War from 1756 to 1763. That war in one sense strengthened ties with Britain,

since colonial militias fought triumphantly alongside the British army against their mutual French and Indian enemies. But by driving the French from the North American continent, the British made themselves less indispensable to the American colonies. More important still, after 1763 a financially overstretched British government made the fateful choice of imposing taxes on colonies that had been accustomed to answering mainly to their own colonial assemblies. By the 1770s issues of taxation, self-rule, and trade restrictions brought the crisis of imperial authority to a head. Although as late as 1775 most people in the colonies clung to the hope of some kind of accommodation short of outright independence, royal intransigence soon thrust the colonists into a war of independence that neither antagonist could have anticipated just a few years before.

Eight years of revolutionary war did more than anything in the colonial past to bring Americans together as a nation. Comradeship in arms and the struggle to shape a national government forced Americans to subdue their differences as best they could. But the spirit of national unity was hardly universal. One in five colonists sided with the British as "Loyalists," and a generation would pass before the wounds of this first American "civil war" fully healed. Yet in the end, Americans won the Revolution, with no small measure of help from the French, because in every colony people shared a belief that they were fighting for the "unalienable rights" of "life, liberty, and the pursuit of happiness," in the words of Thomas Jefferson's magnificent Declaration of Independence. Almost two hundred years of living a new life had prepared Americans to found a new nation.

3

1

New World Beginnings

⎯⎯⎯ ✤ ⎯⎯⎯

33,000 B.C.–A.D. 1769

*I have come to believe that this is a mighty conti-
nent which was hitherto unknown. . . .
Your Highnesses have an Other World here.*

CHRISTOPHER COLUMBUS, 1498

About six thousand years ago—only a minute ago in geological time—recorded history began among certain peoples of the ancient Middle East. Just five hundred years ago the first Europeans stumbled on the American continents. This dramatic achievement opened breathtaking new vistas and forever altered the future of both the Old World and the New, and of Africa and Asia as well.

Of the numerous new republics that eventually appeared in the Americas, the most influential has been the United States. Born a weakling, it grew to be a giant whose liberal democratic ideals, robust economy, and achievements in science, technology, and the arts shaped people's lives in every corner of the planet.

The Shaping of North America

Planet earth took on its present form slowly. Some 225 million years ago, a single supercontinent contained all the world's dry land. Then enormous chunks of terrain began to drift away from this colossal continent, opening the Atlantic and Indian oceans, narrowing the Pacific Ocean, and forming the great landmasses of Eurasia, Africa, Australia, Antarctica, and the Americas.

Continued shifting and folding of the earth's crust thrust up mountain ranges. The Appalachians were probably formed even before continental separation, perhaps 350 million years ago. The majestic

4

A Rocky Mountain Lake near Aspen, Colorado *The geologically young Rockies form the rugged backbone of the North American continent.*

ranges of western North America—the Rockies, the Sierra Nevada, the Cascades, and the Coast Range—arose much more recently, geologically speaking, some 135 million to 25 million years ago.

By about 10 million years ago, nature had sculpted the basic geological shape of North America (see the map at the end of the book). The continent was anchored in its northeastern corner by the massive Canadian Shield—a zone undergirded by ancient rock, probably the first part of what became the North American landmass to have emerged above sea level. A narrow eastern coastal plain, or "tidewater" region, creased by many valleys, sloped gently upward to the timeworn ridges of the Appalachians. Those ancient mountains slanted away on their western side into the huge midcontinental basin that rolled downward to the Mississippi Valley bottom and then rose relentlessly to the towering peaks of the Rockies. From the Rocky Mountain crest—the "roof of America"—the land fell off jaggedly into the intermountain Great Basin, bounded by the Rockies on the east and the Sierra and Cascade ranges on the west. The valleys of the Sacramento and San Joaquin rivers and the Willamette–Puget Sound trough

seamed the interiors of present-day California, Oregon, and Washington. The land at last met the foaming Pacific, where the Coast Range rose steeply from the sea.

Beginning about 2 million years ago, two-mile-thick ice sheets crept across much of northern Europe, Asia, and the Americas. In North America, the glaciers spread as far southward as a line stretching from Pennsylvania through the Ohio country and the Dakotas to the Pacific Northwest.

When the glaciers finally retreated about ten thousand years ago, they left the North American landscape transformed and much as we know it today. The grinding and flushing action of the moving and melting ice pitted the rocky surface of the Canadian Shield with thousands of shallow depressions, into which the melting glaciers flowed to form lakes. The same glacial action scooped out and filled the Great Lakes. When the Great Lakes eventually found an outlet to the Atlantic Ocean through the St. Lawrence River, they left the Missouri-Mississippi-Ohio river system to drain the enormous midcontinental basin between the Appalachians and the Rockies.

Similarly, in the west, water from the melting glaciers filled sprawling Lake Bonneville, covering much of present-day Utah, Nevada, and Idaho. Eventually deprived of both inflow and drainage as the glaciers retreated, the giant lake became a shrinking inland sea. It grew increasingly saline and slowly evaporated, leaving an arid, mineral-rich desert, with only the Great Salt Lake as a relic of its former vastness. Today Lake Bonneville's ancient beaches are visible on mountainsides up to a thousand feet above the dry floor of the Great Basin.

Peopling the Americas

The Great Ice Age shaped more than the geological history of North America. It also contributed to the origins of the continent's human history. Some 35,000 years ago, the Ice Age congealed much of the world-ocean into massive ice-pack glaciers, lowering the level of the sea. As the waters dropped, a land bridge connecting Eurasia with North America was exposed. Across that bridge spanning the present-day Bering

The First Discoverers of America *For some twenty-five thousand years, people crossed the Bering Strait land bridge from Eurasia to North America. Gradually, they dispersed southward down ice-free valleys, populating both of the American continents.*

- Area of land bridge c. 35,000–10,000 years ago
- Extent of ice cap c. 10,000 years ago
- Migratory path
- Earliest discovered Indian sites

Sea between Siberia and Alaska ventured small bands of nomadic Asian hunters—the "immigrant" ancestors of the Native Americans. They continued to trek from Siberia to Alaska for some 250 centuries, slowly peopling the Americas.

As the Ice Age ended and the glaciers melted, the sea level rose again, inundating the land bridge about ten thousand years ago. Nature thus barred the door to further immigration for many thousands of years, leaving this part of the human family to develop its separate existence on the American continents.

Time did not stand still for these original Americans. Roaming slowly through this awesome wilderness, they eventually reached the far tip of South America, some 15,000 miles from Siberia. By the time the Europeans arrived in America in 1492, perhaps 54 million people inhabited the two American continents. Over the centuries they split into numerous tribes, evolved more than two thousand separate languages, and developed many diverse religions, cultures, and ways of life.

Incas in Peru, Mayans in Central America, and Aztecs in Mexico shaped stunningly sophisticated civilizations. Their advanced agricultural practices, based primarily on the cultivation of maize, which is Indian corn, fed large populations—perhaps as many as 20 million in Mexico alone. Though lacking such technologies as the wheel, these peoples built elaborate cities and carried on far-flung commerce. Talented mathematicians, they made strikingly accurate astronomical observations. The Aztecs also sought the favor of their gods by offering human sacrifices, sometimes cutting the hearts out of the chests of living victims.

The Earliest Americans

Agriculture, especially corn growing, accounted for the size and sophistication of the Native American civilizations in Mexico and South America. About 5000 B.C. hunter-gatherers in highland Mexico developed a wild grass into the staple of corn, which became the foundation of the complex, large-scale, centralized Aztec and Incan nation-states. As cultivation of corn spread across the Americas from the Mexican heartland, it slowly transformed nomadic hunting bands into settled, agricultural villagers.

Corn planting reached the present-day American Southwest by about 1200 B.C. and powerfully molded Pueblo culture. The Pueblo peoples in the Rio Grande Valley constructed intricate irrigation systems to water their cornfields, and they built villages of terraced, multistory buildings. Corn cultivation reached other parts of North America considerably later, and the timing of its arrival explains the relative rates of development of different Native American peoples. North and east of the Pueblos, elaborately developed "societies" in the modern sense of the word scarcely existed. The lack of dense concentrations of population or complex nation-states was one of the reasons for the relative ease with which the European colonizers subdued the native North Americans.

The Mound Builders of the Ohio River valley, the Mississippian culture of the lower Midwest, as well as the desert-dwelling Anasazi peoples of the Southwest, did sustain some large settlements after the incorporation of corn-planting into their way of life during the first millennium A.D. The Mississippian settlement at Cahokia, near present-day East St. Louis, was at one time home to as many as 25,000 people. The Anasazis built an elaborate pueblo of more than six hundred inter-connected rooms in Chaco Canyon in modern-day New Mexico. But mysteriously, perhaps due to prolonged drought, all those ancient cultures had fallen into decline by about 1300.

Maize cultivation reached the southeastern Atlantic seaboard region of North America about A.D. 1000, along with high-yielding strains of beans and squash. The rich diet provided by these three crops produced some of the highest population densities on the continent, among them the Creek, Choctaw, and Cherokee peoples. In the northeastern woodlands, the Iroquois, inspired by their legendary leader Hiawatha, created in the sixteenth century perhaps the closest North American approximation to the great nation-states of Mexico and Peru. The Iroquois Confederacy developed the political and organizational skills to sustain a robust military alliance that menaced its neighbors, Native American and European alike, for well over a century (see "Makers of America: The Iroquois," pp. 26–27).

North American Indian Tribes at the Time of European Colonization *This map illustrates the great diversity of the Indian population—and suggests the inappropriateness of identifying all the Native American peoples with the single label* Indian. *The more than two hundred tribes were deeply divided by geography, language, and lifestyle. The heavy lines identify geographical areas that are similar in climate and terrain.*

Cahokia   *This artist's rendering of Cahokia, based on archaeological excavations, shows the huge central square and the imposing Monk's Mound, which rivaled in size the pyramids of Egypt.*

But for the most part, native North Americans on the eve of the Europeans' arrival lived in scattered and impermanent settlements. Loosely defined tribes often encamped along rivers in the spring and then dispersed in small family bands for the winter's hunting. In more settled agricultural groups, women tended the crops while men hunted, fished, gathered fuel, and cleared fields for planting. This pattern of life frequently conferred substantial authority on women, and many North American native peoples, including the Iroquois, developed matrilinear cultures, in which power and possessions passed down the female side of the family.

Unlike the Europeans, who would soon arrive with the presumption that humans had dominion over the earth and with technologies to alter the very face of the land, Native Americans had neither the desire nor the means to manipulate nature aggressively. They revered the physical world and endowed nature with spiritual properties. Yet they did sometimes ignite massive forest fires, deliberately torching trees to create better hunting habitats, especially for deer. This practice accounted for the open, parklike appearance of the eastern woodlands that so amazed early European explorers.

But in a broad sense the Native Americans did not lay heavy hands on the continent because they were so few in number. In the fateful year 1492, probably no more than 4 million Native Americans padded through the whispering primeval forests and paddled across the sparkling, virgin waters of North America. They were blissfully unaware that the historic isolation of the Americas was about to end forever, as both the land and the native peoples alike felt the full shock of the European "discovery."

Indirect Discoverers of the New World

Europeans were equally unaware of the existence of the Americas. Blond-bearded Norse seafarers from Scandinavia had visited northeastern North America about 1000 A.D., and briefly settled near L'Anse aux Meadows in present-day Newfoundland. But no strong nation-state yearning to expand supported these venturesome voyagers. Their flimsy settlements consequently were soon abandoned, and their discovery was forgotten, except in Viking saga and song.

For several centuries thereafter, other restless Europeans, with the growing power of ambitious governments behind them, sought contact with a wider world, whether for conquest or trade. They thus set in motion the chain of events that led to a drive toward Asia, the exploitation of Africa, and the completely accidental discovery of the New World.

Christian crusaders of the eleventh to the four-teenth centuries rank high among America's indirect discoverers. Though ultimately foiled in their military assaults on the Holy Land, they acquired a taste for the exotic delights of Asia—silk for clothing, drugs for aching flesh, perfumes for unbathed bodies, colorful draperies for gloomy castles, and sugar and spices for preserving and flavoring food. The Italian adventurer Marco Polo further whetted European appetites for Asian luxury goods when he returned from China in 1295 with news of its golden pagodas and rose-tinted pearls.

But the distance and difficulties of transporta-tion, for which Muslim and Italian middlemen charged dearly, made European consumers and dis-tributors eager to find a less expensive route to the riches of Asia. Their hopes for an ocean route to Asia were long frustrated. Before the mid-fifteenth cen-tury, European sailors refused to sail southward along the coast of West Africa because they could not beat their way home again against the prevailing northerly winds and south-flowing currents.

Europeans Enter Africa

About 1450, Portuguese mariners overcame these obstacles by developing the caravel, a ship that could sail even with crossing winds. They also learned that they could return to Europe by way of the Azores islands, whose prevailing westward breezes carried them home.

The new world of sub-Saharan Africa, previously remote and mysterious to Europeans, came within their questing grasp. African gold, perhaps two-thirds of Europe's supply, crossed the Sahara on camelback, and tales may have reached Europe about the flour-ishing West African kingdom of Mali in the Niger River valley, with its impressive Islamic university at Timbuktu. But Europeans had no direct access to sub-Saharan Africa until the Portuguese mariners began to creep down the West African coast in the mid-fifteenth century.

The Portuguese promptly set up trading posts along the African shore for the purchase of gold—and slaves. Arab and African merchants had traded slaves for centuries before the Europeans arrived. They rou-tinely charged higher prices for slaves from distant sources, who could not flee to their native villages. Slave brokers also deliberately separated persons from the same tribes to frustrate organized resistance.

The Portuguese adopted these long-standing slave practices in the sugar plantations that they, and later the Spanish, established on the African coastal islands of Madeira, the Canaries, São Tomé, and Principe. The Portuguese appetite for slaves was enormous, and slave trading became big business. Some forty thousand Africans were carried away to the Atlantic sugar islands in the last half of the fif-teenth century. Millions more would be wrenched from their home continent after the discovery of the Americas. These fifteenth-century Portuguese adven-tures in Africa contained the origins of the modern plantation system, based on large-scale commercial agriculture and the wholesale exploitation of slave labor. This kind of plantation economy would shape the destiny of much of the New World.

After years of cautious exploration, the Por-tuguese mariner Bartholomeu Días finally rounded the southernmost tip of Africa in 1488. Ten years later Vasco da Gama reached India and returned home with a small but tantalizing cargo of jewels and spices. Meanwhile, the kingdom of Spain was united as a result of the marriage of two sovereigns, Ferdi-nand of Aragon and Isabella of Castile. After the bru-tal expulsion of the Muslim Moors from Spain, the new Spanish nation was eager to outstrip its Por-tuguese rivals in the race to tap the wealth of the Indies. Because Portugal controlled the round-Africa route to India, Spain of necessity looked westward.

Columbus Comes upon a New World

The stage was now set for a cataclysmic shift in the course of history—the history not only of Europe but of all the world. Europeans clamored for more and cheaper products from the lands beyond the Mediterranean. Africa had been established as a source of cheap slave labor for plantation agriculture. The Portuguese voyages had demonstrated the feasi-bility of long-range ocean navigation. In Spain a modern national state was taking shape, with the unity, wealth, and power to shoulder the formidable tasks of discovery, conquest, and colonization. The dawn of the Renaissance in the fourteenth century nurtured an ambitious spirit of optimism and adventure. Printing presses, introduced about 1450, facilitated the spread of scientific knowledge. The mariner's compass, possibly borrowed from the Arabs, eliminated some of the uncertainties of travel.

Onto this stage stepped Christopher Columbus. This skilled Italian seafarer persuaded the Spanish monarchs to outfit him with three tiny but seaworthy ships. Columbus sailed westward into the oceanic unknown, and after six weeks at sea his fearful sailors grew increasingly mutinous. But on October 12, 1492, the crew sighted land—an island in the Bahamas. A new world thus came onto the horizon of Europeans.

Only gradually did Europeans realize that sprawling new continents had been discovered. For decades explorers tried to get through or around the "islands" that, they assumed, blocked the ocean pathway to Asia. Columbus himself was at first so certain that he had skirted the rim of the "Indies" that he called the native peoples Indians, a gross geographical misnomer that somehow stuck.

Columbus's discovery would eventually convulse four continents—Europe, Africa, and the two Americas. Thanks to his epochal voyage, an interdependent global economic system emerged on a scale undreamed of before he set sail. Its workings touched every shore washed by the Atlantic Ocean. Europe provided the markets, the capital, and the technology; Africa furnished the labor; and the New World offered its raw materials—especially its precious metals and its soil for the cultivation of sugar cane. For Europeans, as well as for Africans and Native Americans, the world after 1492 would never be the same, for better or worse.

When Worlds Collide

Two ecosystems—the fragile, naturally evolved networks of relations among organisms in a stable environment—commingled and clashed when Columbus waded ashore. The flora and fauna of the Old and New Worlds had been separated for thousands of years. European explorers marveled at the strange sights that greeted them, including exotic beasts such as iguanas and "snakes with castanets" (rattlesnakes).

Native New World plants such as tobacco, maize, beans, tomatoes, and especially the lowly potato eventually revolutionized the international economy and fed the rapidly growing population of the Old World. These foodstuffs were among the most important Indian gifts to the Europeans and the rest of the world. Ironically, the introduction into Africa of New World staples like maize, manioc, and sweet potatoes may have fed an African population boom that numerically, though not morally, more than offset the losses inflicted by the slave trade.

In exchange the Europeans introduced Old World crops and animals, such as cattle and horses, to the Americas. Horses reached the North American mainland through Mexico. North American tribes like the Apaches, Sioux, and Blackfoot swiftly adopted the horse, transforming their cultures into highly mobile, wide-ranging hunter societies that pursued the shaggy buffalo across the Great Plains. Columbus also brought sugar cane. Thriving in the warm Caribbean climate, it prompted a "sugar revolution" in the European diet that fueled the forced migration of millions of Africans to work the canefields and sugar mills of the New World.

Unwittingly, the Europeans also brought the germs that caused smallpox, yellow fever, and malaria—diseases that quickly devastated the Native Americans. During the Indians' millennia of separate existence in the Americas, most of the Old World's killer maladies had disappeared from among them. Devoid of natural resistance to Old World sicknesses, Indians died in droves. Within fifty years of the Spanish arrival, the population of the Taino natives in Hispaniola dwindled from some 1 million people to about two hundred. The lethal germs spread among New World peoples with the speed and force of a hurricane, swiftly sweeping far ahead of the human invaders; most of those afflicted never laid eyes on a European. In the centuries after Columbus's landfall, as many as 90 percent of Native Americans perished, a demographic catastrophe without parallel in human history. Depopulation was so severe that entire cultures and ancient ways of life were extinguished forever. Perhaps it was poetic justice that the Indians unintentionally infected the early explorers with syphilis, injecting that lethal sexually transmitted disease for the first time into Europe.

Trade Routes with the East
Goods on the early routes passed through so many hands along the way that their ultimate source remained mysterious to Europeans.

The Spanish *Conquistadores*

Gradually, Europeans realized that the American continents held rich prizes, especially the gold and silver of the advanced civilizations in Mexico and Peru. Spain secured its title to Columbus's discoveries in the Treaty of Tordesillas (1494), dividing with Portugal the "heathen lands" of the New World.

Spain became the dominant exploring and colonizing power of the 1500s. Seeking both the glitter of gold and the glory of God, Spanish *conquistadores* (conquerors) fanned out across the Caribbean and eventually onto the mainland of the American continents (see "Makers of America: The Spanish *Conquistadores*," pp. 14–15). Some early explorers, among them Ponce de León, Coronado, and de Soto, ventured into territory that eventually became part of the United States. But the permanent Spanish conquests of Peru and Mexico were by far the most consequential achievements of the *conquistadores*.

In South America, the ironfisted conqueror Francisco Pizarro crushed the Incas of Peru in 1532 and added a huge horde of booty, especially silver, to Spanish coffers. This flood of precious metal touched off a price revolution in Europe that increased con-

sumer costs by as much as 500 percent in the hundred years after the mid-sixteenth century. Some scholars see in this ballooning European money supply the fuel that fed the growth of the economic system known as capitalism.

The conquest of Mexico was engineered by Hernán Cortés, who set sail from Cuba in 1519 with sixteen horses and several hundred men. From an island near the coast of Mexico, he picked up a female Indian slave named Malinche, who knew both Mayan and Nahuatl, the language of the powerful Aztecs. Aided by Malinche and another interpreter, Cortés learned of the unrest among subordinate peoples within the Aztec empire, and of the gold and other wealth in its capital of Tenochtitlán. "We Spanish suffer from a strange disease of the heart," Cortés allegedly told ambassadors of the Aztec ruler Moctezuma, "for which the only known remedy is gold." The emissaries reported this comment to Moctezuma, along with the astonishing fact that the newcomers rode on the backs of "deer" (horses). Believing that Cortés was the god Quetzalcoatl, whose return from the eastern sea was predicted in Aztec legends, Moctezuma allowed the *conquistadores* to approach his capital unopposed.

The Spaniards were amazed by the beauty and wealth of Tenochtitlán, with its 300,000 inhabitants

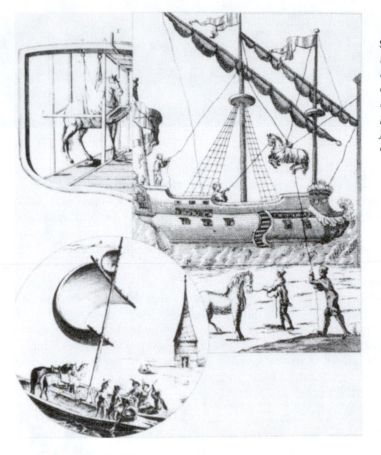

Seafaring Horses Come to America *The horse was first brought to the New World by the Spanish but quickly spread across both American continents. These drawings show how horses were lowered onto Spanish ships by pulleys* (right), *suspended by slings to avoid falls on rough seas* (upper left), *and ferried ashore in smaller craft* (lower left).

and marvelous temples, aqueducts, and floating gardens. Moctezuma received Cortés hospitably at first, but soon the Spanish were unable to contain their lust for gold. After warfare broke out on June 30, 1520, Cortés laid siege to the city. It capitulated on August 13, 1521.

The Aztec empire thus gave way to three centuries of Spanish rule. Its people suffered not only from the armed conquest but from smallpox and other epidemics that burned through the Valley of Mexico. The native population shrank from more than 20 million to fewer than 2 million people in less than a century. The temples of Tenochtitlán were destroyed to make way for the Christian cathedrals of Mexico City, built on the site of the ruined Aztec capital.

Yet the invader brought more than conquest and death. He brought his language, laws, customs, and religion, all of which proved adaptable to the peoples of Mexico. He intermarried with the surviving Mexi-

cans, creating a distinctive culture of *mestizos,* people of mixed Indian and European heritage. To this day Mexican civilization remains a unique blend of the Old World and New, producing both ambivalence and pride among people of Mexican heritage. Cortés's translator Malinche, for example, has given her name to the Mexican language in the word *malinchista,* or "traitor." But Mexicans also celebrate Columbus Day as the Dia de la Raza—the birthday of a wholly new race of people.

The Spread of Spanish America

Spain's colonial empire grew swiftly and impressively. Within about half a century of Columbus's landfall, hundreds of Spanish cities and towns flourished in the Americas. Majestic cathedrals dotted the land, printing presses turned out books, and scholars stud-

The Spanish *Conquistadores*

In 1492, the same year that Columbus sighted America, the great Moorish city of Grenada fell after a ten-year siege. For five centuries the Christian kingdoms of Spain had tried to drive the North African Muslim Moors off the Iberian peninsula, and with the fall of Grenada this "Reconquista" succeeded. Centuries of religious war nurtured an obsession with status and honor, bred religious zealotry and intolerance, and created a large class of men who regarded manual labor and commerce contemptuously. With the Reconquista ended, some of these men turned their restless gaze to Spain's New World frontier.

Between 1519 and 1540, Spanish *conquistadores* swept across the Americas in two wide arcs of conquest—one driving from Cuba through Mexico into what is now the southwestern United States, the other starting from Panama, previously conquered by Vasco Balboa, and pushing south into Peru. The military conquest of this vast region was achieved by just ten thousand men, organized in a series of private expeditions. Hernán Cortés, Francisco Pizarro, and other aspiring conquerors signed contracts with the Spanish monarch, raised money from investors, and then proceeded to recruit private armies. Only a minority of the *conquistadores* were nobles. About half were professional soldiers or sailors; the rest

Indians Bearing Gifts of Gold to Balboa, by Theodore de Bry *This European painting portrays Indians happily welcoming the* conquistadores *to their land; real relationships were seldom so harmonious.*

comprised peasants, artisans, and members of the middling classes. Most were in their twenties and early thirties.

Some of these motley adventurers hoped to win royal titles or favors. Others sought to assure God's favor by spreading Christianity to the pagans. Some men aspired to escape dubious pasts, while others sought the kind of historical adventure experienced by heroes of classical antiquity. Nearly all shared a lust for gold.

But most never achieved their dreams of glory or riches. Even when an expedition captured exceptionally rich booty, the spoils were unevenly divided: men from the commander's home region often received more, and men on horseback generally got two shares to the infantryman's one. The *conquistadores* lost still more power as the crown tightened its control in the New World. By the 1550s the day of the *conquistador* had ended.

Nevertheless, the *conquistadores* achieved a kind of immortality. Because of a scarcity of Spanish women in the early days of the conquest, many *conquistadores* married Indian women. Their offspring, the "new race" of *mestizos*, formed a cultural and biological bridge between Latin America's European and Indian races.

ied at distinguished universities, including those at Mexico City and Lima, Peru, both founded in 1551, eighty-five years before Harvard, the first college established in the English colonies.

But how secure were these imperial possessions? Other powers were already sniffing around the edges of the Spanish domain, eager to bite off their share of the promised wealth of the new lands. The upstart English sent Giovanni Caboto (known in English as John Cabot) to explore the northeastern coast of North America in 1497 and 1498. The French king dispatched Giovanni da Verrazano to probe the eastern seaboard in 1524 and Jacques Cartier to explore the St. Lawrence River in 1534. To protect sea lanes and secure their northern borderlands against such encroachments, the Spanish erected a fortress at St. Augustine, Florida,

The Devastation of Disease *This engraving of a burial service records the horrendous impact of Old World diseases on the vulnerable Native Americans.*

in 1565, thus founding the oldest continually inhabited European settlement in the future United States.

In Mexico, the tales of Francisco Coronado's expedition of the 1540s beckoned *conquistadores* northward from Mexico into the Rio Grande and Colorado River regions. A Spanish expedition led by Don Juan de Oñate entered the Rio Grande Valley in 1598 and cruelly abused the Pueblo peoples they encountered. In the battle of Acoma in 1599, the Spanish severed one foot of each survivor. The Spaniards proclaimed the area to be the province of New Mexico in 1609 and founded its capital at Santa Fe the following year. The Spanish settlers found precious little gold, but missionaries did discover a wealth of souls to be harvested for the Christian religion. Their efforts to suppress Pueblo religious customs provoked an uprising called Popé's Rebellion in 1680. The Pueblo rebels destroyed every Catholic church in the province and killed a score of priests and hundreds of Spanish settlers. It took nearly half a century for the Spanish to reclaim New Mexico from the insurrectionary Indians.

Meanwhile, as a further hedge against the ever-threatening French, who had sent an expedition under Robert La Salle down the Mississippi River in the 1680s, the Spanish began around 1716 to establish a few weak settlements and missions in Texas, including the one at San Antonio later known as the Alamo. To the west, in California, no serious foreign threat loomed, and Spain directed its attention there only belatedly. Juan Rodriguez Cabrillo had explored the California coast in 1542, but for some two centuries thereafter California slumbered undisturbed by European intruders.

Then in 1769, Spanish missionaries led by Father Junipero Serra founded at San Diego the first of a chain of twenty-one missions that wound up the coast as far as Sonoma, north of San Francisco Bay. Father Serra's brown-robed Franciscan friars toiled with zealous devotion to Christianize three hundred thousand native Californians and to teach them horticulture and crafts. These "mission Indians" did adopt Christianity, but they lost their native cultures and often lost their lives as well, as the white man's diseases doomed these biologically vulnerable peoples.

The misdeeds of the Spanish in the New World obscured their substantial achievements and helped give birth to the "Black Legend." This false concept held that the conquerors merely tortured and butchered the Indians, stole their gold, infected them with smallpox, and left little but misery behind. The Spanish invaders did indeed kill, enslave, and infect countless natives, but they also grafted their culture, laws, religion, and language onto a vast array of native societies, laying the foundations for a score of Spanish-speaking nations.

Principal Early Spanish Explorations and Conquests *Notice that Coronado traversed northern Texas and Oklahoma. In present-day eastern Kansas he found, instead of the great golden city he sought, a drab encampment, probably of Wichita Indians.*

Clearly, the Spanish, who had more than a century's head start over the English, were genuine empire builders and cultural innovators in the New World. Compared with their Anglo-Saxon rivals, their colonial establishment was larger and richer, and it was destined to endure more than a quarter of a century longer. And in the last analysis, the Spanish paid the Native Americans the high compliment of fusing with them through marriage and incorporating indigenous culture into their own, rather than shunning and eventually isolating the Indians as their English adversaries would do.

Chronology

c. 33,000–8000 B.C.	First humans cross over to the Americas from Asia.
c. 5000 B.C.	Corn is developed as a staple crop in highland Mexico.
c. 4000 B.C.	First civilized societies develop in the Middle East.
c. 1200 B.C.	Corn planting reaches present-day American Southwest.
c. A.D. 1000	Norse voyagers discover and briefly settle in North America. Corn cultivation reaches Midwest and southeastern Atlantic seaboard.
c. A.D. 1100	Height of Mississippian settlement at Cahokia.
c. A.D. 1100–1300	Christian crusades arouse European interest in Asia.
1295	Marco Polo returns to Europe.
late 1400s	Spain becomes united.
1488	Días rounds southern tip of Africa.
1492	Columbus lands in the Bahamas.
1494	Treaty of Tordesillas between Spain and Portugal.
1498	Vasco da Gama reaches India. Cabot explores northeastern coast of North America for England.
1513, 1521	Ponce de León explores Florida.
1519–1521	Cortés conquers Mexico for Spain.
1532	Pizarro crushes Incas.
1540–1542	Coronado explores present-day Southwest.
1542	Cabrillo explores California coast for Spain.
1565	Spanish build fortress at St. Augustine.
late 1500s	Iroquois Confederacy founded, according to Iroquois legend.
1609	Spanish found New Mexico.
1680	Popé's rebellion in New Mexico.
1680s	French expedition down Mississippi River under La Salle.
1769	Serra founds first California mission, at San Diego.

For further reading, see the Appendix. For web resources, go to **http://college.hmco.com**.

2

The Planting of English America

1500–1733

. . . For I shall yet live to see it [Virginia] an Inglishe nation.

SIR WALTER RALEIGH, 1602

As the seventeenth century dawned, scarcely a hundred years after Columbus's momentous landfall, the face of much of the New World had already been profoundly transformed. European crops and livestock had begun to alter the very landscape, touching off an ecological revolution that would reverberate for centuries to come. From Tierra del Fuego in the south to Hudson's Bay in the north, disease and armed conquest had cruelly winnowed and disrupted the native peoples. Several hundred thousand Africans toiled on Caribbean and Brazilian sugar plantations. From Florida and New Mexico southward, most of the New World lay firmly in the grip of imperial Spain.

But *North* America in 1600 remained largely unexplored and effectively unclaimed by Europeans.

Then, as if to herald the coming century of colonization and conflict in the northern continent, three European powers planted primitive outposts in three distant corners of the continent within three years of one another: the Spanish in Santa Fe in 1610, the French at Quebec in 1608, and, most consequentially for the future United States, the English at Jamestown, Virginia, in 1607.

England's Imperial Stirrings

Feeble indeed were England's efforts in the 1500s to compete with the sprawling Spanish Empire. As Spain's ally in the first half of the century, England took little interest in establishing its own overseas colonies. But in 1558 the Protestant Elizabeth ascended to the English throne and solidified her father King Henry VIII's break with the Roman Catholic Church (see Ch. 3, p. 30). Protestantism became dominant in England, and rivalry with Catholic Spain intensified.

An early scene of that rivalry was Ireland, where the Catholic Irish sought help from Catholic Spain to throw off the yoke of Protestant English rule. In crushing the Irish uprising of the 1570s and 1580s with terrible ferocity, many English developed a sneering contempt for the "savage" natives, an attitude they brought with them to the New World.

Encouraged by the ambitious Queen Elizabeth, hardy English buccaneers swarmed out on the shipping lanes to plunder Spanish treasure ships and raid Spanish settlements. The most famous of these semi-piratical "sea dogs" was the courtly Francis Drake, who in 1577 began to loot his way around the globe and returned three years later, his flagship laden with Spanish gold.

The first English attempt at colonization, in bleak Newfoundland, collapsed when its promoter, Sir Humphrey Gilbert, lost his life at sea in 1583. Gilbert's gallant half-brother, Sir Walter Raleigh, then organized a group of settlers who landed in 1585 on North Carolina's Roanoke Island. But the hapless Roanoke colony mysteriously vanished, swallowed up by the wilderness.

These pathetic English failures at colonization contrasted embarrassingly with the glories of the Spanish Empire, whose profits were fabulously enriching Spain. Philip II of Spain, self-anointed foe of the Protestant Reformation, used part of his imperial gains to amass an "Invincible Armada" of ships for an invasion of England in 1588. But the skillful

The *Mary Rose*, a Sixteenth-Century English Navy Ship   *Typical of English Royal Navy ships of the sixteenth century was the* Mary Rose, *a 700-ton, 41-gun ship built by King Henry VIII in 1509–1510. The* Mary Rose *was sunk during a battle with a French fleet in 1545 off the coast of Portsmouth, England, where the ship had been built. The wreck was discovered by pioneer divers in 1836 and yielded many artifacts revealing the lives and work of English sailors in the age of the Tudor monarchy.* (Above left) *From the painting by W. H. Bishop entitled "The Warship* Mary Rose *leaving Portsmouth Harbor—Summer 1545" showing in detail how the ship actually looked.* (Above right) *Personal items recovered from the* Mary Rose, *including a thimble-ring, clasp, pocket sundial, whistle, purse-hanger, comb, coins, knife-handle, seal, and rosary.*

English sea dogs inflicted heavy damage on the armada, and a devastating storm (the "Protestant wind") scattered the crippled Spanish ships.

The rout of the Spanish Armada marked the beginning of the end of Spanish imperial dreams, though Spain's New World empire would not fully collapse for three more centuries. England's victory also started that country on its way to becoming master of the world oceans—a fact of enormous importance to the American people. Indeed England now possessed many of the strengths that Spain had displayed on the eve of its colonizing adventure a century earlier: a strong, unified national state under a popular monarch; a measure of religious unity after a protracted struggle between Protestants and Catholics; and a vibrant sense of nationalism.

This new sense of national pride blossomed in the Elizabethan golden age of culture and politics. Shakespeare, who made occasional poetic references to England's American colonies, was only one of many contemporary patriots who expressed boundless faith in the future of the English nation.

But England's scepter'd isle, as Shakespeare called it, also throbbed with social and economic tension as the seventeenth century opened. Its population was mushrooming, from some 3 million people in 1550 to about 4 million in 1600. In the ever-green English countryside, landlords were "enclosing" croplands for sheep grazing, forcing many small farmers into precarious tenancy or off the land altogether. It was no accident that the woolen districts of eastern and western England—where Puritanism had taken strong root—supplied many of the earliest immigrants to America. When economic depression hit the woolen trade in the late 1500s, thousands of unemployed farmers took to the roads, often ending up as beggars and paupers in cities like Bristol and London.

At the same time, laws of primogeniture decreed that only eldest sons were eligible to inherit landed estates. Landholders' ambitious younger sons, among them Gilbert, Raleigh, and Drake, were forced to seek their fortunes elsewhere. By the early 1600s the unsuccessful lone-wolf ventures of such courtiers were replaced by the joint-stock company, which enabled a considerable number of investors to pool their capital.

Peace with a chastened Spain provided the opportunity for English colonization. Population growth provided the workers. Unemployment, as well as a thirst for adventure, for markets, and for religious freedom, provided the motives. Joint-stock companies provided the financial means. The stage was set for a historic effort to establish an English beachhead in the still uncharted North American wilderness.

England Plants the Jamestown Seedling

In 1606, two years after peace with Spain, the hand of destiny beckoned toward Virginia. A joint-stock company, the Virginia Company of London, received a charter from King James I, who had assumed the English throne in 1603, for a settlement in the New World. The main attractions were the promise of gold and the desire to find a passage through America to the Indies. Like most joint-stock companies of the day, the Virginia Company was intended to endure

Sir Walter Raleigh (c. 1552–1618)   *Here shown "drinking tobacco," as smoking was first called, he is credited with introducing both tobacco and the potato into England. A dashing courtier, he launched important colonizing failures in the New World. After seducing (and marrying) one of Queen Elizabeth's maids of honor, he fell out of favor and ultimately was beheaded for treason.*

for only a few years, after which its stockholders hoped to liquidate it for a profit. This arrangement put severe pressure on the luckless colonists, who were threatened with abandonment in the wilderness if they did not quickly strike it rich on the company's behalf. Few of the investors thought in terms of long-term colonization. Apparently no one even faintly suspected that the seeds of a mighty nation were being planted.

The charter of the Virginia Company is a significant document in American history. It guaranteed to the overseas settlers the same rights of Englishmen that they would have enjoyed if they had stayed at home. This precious boon was gradually extended to the other English colonies, helping to reinforce the colonists' sense that even on the far shore of the Atlantic they remained comfortably within the embrace of traditional English institutions. But ironically, a century and a half later, the colonists' insistence on the "rights of Englishmen"—rights denied, they claimed—fed their hot resentment against an increasingly meddlesome mother country and nourished their appetite for independence.

Setting sail in late 1606, the colonists arrived in Virginia and chose a site for their settlement on the wooded and malarial banks of a swampy river. There, on May 24, 1607, about a hundred English settlers, all men, disembarked. They called the place Jamestown and the river the James.

The early years of Jamestown proved to be a nightmare for all concerned—except the buzzards. Once ashore, the settlers died by the dozens from disease, malnutrition, and starvation. The woods rustled with game and the rivers flopped with fish, but the greenhorn settlers, many of them self-styled "gentlemen" unaccustomed to fending for themselves, wasted valuable time grubbing for nonexistent gold when they should have been gathering provisions.

Virginia was saved from utter collapse at the start largely by the leadership and resourcefulness of an intrepid young adventurer, Captain John Smith. Taking over in 1608, he whipped the gold-hungry colonists into line with the rule "He who shall not work shall not eat." He had been kidnapped in December 1607 and subjected to a mock execution by the Indian chieftain Powhatan, whose daughter Pocahontas "saved" Smith by dramatically interpos-

ing her head between his and the war clubs of his captors. Pocahontas became an intermediary between the Indians and the settlers, helping to preserve a shaky peace and provide needed food.

Still, the colonists died in droves, and living skeletons were driven to desperate acts. They were reduced to eating "Dogges, Catts, Ratts, and Myce" and even to digging up corpses for food. One hungry man killed, salted, and ate his wife, for which misbehavior he was executed. Of the four hundred settlers who managed to make it to Virginia by 1609, only sixty survived the "starving time" winter of 1609–1610. Diseased and despairing, the remaining colonists were ready to return to England in the spring of 1610 when a relief party suddenly arrived, headed by a new governor, Lord De La Warr.

De La Warr ordered the settlers to stay in Jamestown, imposed a harsh military regime on the colony, and soon undertook aggressive military action against the Indians. But disease continued to reap a gruesome harvest. By 1625 Virginia contained only some twelve hundred hard-bitten survivors of the nearly eight thousand adventurers who had tried to start life anew in the precarious colony.

Cultural Clash in the Chesapeake

When the English landed in 1607, the chieftain Powhatan dominated the few dozen small tribes in the James River area. Powhatan at first may have considered the English potential allies in his struggle to extend his power over his Indian rivals, and he tried to be conciliatory. But relations between the Indians and the English remained tense, especially as the starving colonists took to raiding Indian food supplies.

The atmosphere grew even more strained after Lord De La Warr arrived in 1610. He carried orders from the Virginia Company that amounted to a declaration of war against the Indians in the Jamestown region. A veteran of the vicious campaigns against the Irish, De La Warr introduced "Irish tactics" against the Indians. His troops raided their villages, burned houses, confiscated provisions, and torched cornfields. A peace settlement ended this First Anglo-Powhatan War in 1614, sealed by the marriage of

Pocahontas (c. 1595–1617) (detail) *Taken to England by her husband, she was received as a princess. She died when preparing to return to Virginia. Her infant son ultimately reached Virginia, where hundreds of his descendants have lived, including the second Mrs. Woodrow Wilson.*

Pocahontas to the colonist John Rolfe—the first known interracial union in Virginia.

A fragile peace prevailed for eight years. But the Indians, pressed by the land-hungry whites and ravaged by European diseases, struck back in 1622. A series of Indian attacks left 347 settlers dead, including John Rolfe. Pushed westward by retaliatory settler raids, the Indians made one last effort to dislodge the Virginians in the Second Anglo-Powhatan War in 1644. They were again defeated. The peace treaty of 1646 repudiated any hope of assimilating the native peoples into Virginian society or of peacefully coexisting with them. Instead it effectively banished the Chesapeake Indians from their ancestral lands and formally separated Indian from white areas of settlement—the origins of the later reservation system. By 1669 an official census revealed that only about two thousand Indians remained in Virginia, perhaps 10

percent of the population the original English settlers had encountered in 1607. By 1685 the English considered the Powhatan peoples extinct.

It had been the Powhatans' calamitous misfortune to fall victim to three Ds: disease, disorganization, and disposability. Like native peoples throughout the New World, they were struck down by European epidemics of smallpox and measles. They also lacked the unity to oppose the relatively well-organized and militarily disciplined whites. Finally, the Powhatans served no economic function for the Virginia colonists, having no gold, labor, or valuable goods to offer in commerce. Indeed the Indian presence frustrated the colonists' desire for a local commodity the Europeans desperately wanted: land.

The Indians' New World

The fate of the Powhatans foreshadowed the destinies of indigenous peoples throughout the continent as the process of European settlement went forward. Native Americans, of course, were no strangers to change, adaptation, and even catastrophe throughout their history, well before Columbus's arrival. But the shock of extensive European colonization disrupted Native American life on a vast scale, inducing unprecedented demographic and cultural transformations.

Some changes were fairly benign. Horses acquired from the Spanish catalyzed a substantial migration of previously sedentary forest-dwelling peoples, like the Lakota (Sioux) onto the Great Plains in the eighteenth century. There they thrived impressively, adopting an entirely new way of life as mounted nomadic hunters. But the effects of contact with Europeans proved less salutary for most other native peoples.

Disease was by far the biggest disrupter, as Old World pathogens licked lethally through biologically defenseless Indian populations. Disease took more than human life; it extinguished entire cultures—and occasionally helped to shape new ones. Epidemics robbed native peoples of the elders who preserved their oral traditions, and the survivors then faced the daunting task of literally re-inventing themselves without benefit of accumulated wisdom or kin networks. The decimation and forced migration of native peoples sometimes scrambled them together in wholly new ways. The Catawba nation of the southern piedmont region, for example, was formed from the remnants of several different groups uprooted by the Europeans.

Trade also transformed Indian life, as traditional barter-and-exchange networks gave way to the temptations of European commerce. The drive to acquire European firearms in exchange for fur pelts fueled competition for prime hunting grounds and led to an escalating cycle of Indian-on-Indian violence.

Indians along the Atlantic seaboard felt the most ferocious effects of European contact. Further inland, native peoples had the advantages of time, space, and numbers as they sought to adapt to the European incursion. The Algonquians in the Great Lakes area, for instance, became a substantial regional power, able to deal from a position of strength with the few Europeans who managed to penetrate the interior. As a result, a British or French trader wanting to do business with the inland tribes had little choice but to conform to Indian ways, often taking an Indian wife. Thus was created a "middle ground," a zone where both Europeans and Native Americans were compelled to accommodate one another—at least until the Europeans arrived in large numbers.

Virginia: Child of Tobacco

John Rolfe, the husband of Pocahontas, became the father of the tobacco industry and an economic savior of the Virginia colony. By 1612 he had perfected methods of raising and curing the pungent weed. A tobacco rush swept over Virginia as crops were planted in the streets of Jamestown and even between the numerous graves. Colonists who had once hungered for food now hungered for ever more land on which to plant ever more tobacco. Relentlessly, they pressed the frontier of settlement up the river valleys to the west, abrasively edging against the Indians.

Virginia's prosperity was finally built on tobacco smoke. This "bewitching weed" played a vital role in putting the colony on firm economic foundations. But tobacco—King Nicotine—was something of a tyrant. It was ruinous to the soil when greedily planted in successive years, and it chained Virginia's

fortunes to the fluctuating price of a single crop. Tobacco also promoted the broad-acred plantation system and with it a brisk demand for slave labor.

In 1619, the year before the Plymouth Pilgrims landed in New England, what was described as a Dutch warship appeared off Jamestown and sold some twenty Africans. The scanty record does not reveal whether they were purchased as lifelong slaves or as servants committed to limited years of servitude. This commercial transaction planted the seeds of the North American slave system. Yet blacks were too costly for most of the hard-pinched white colonists to acquire, and for decades few were brought to Virginia. In 1650 Virginia counted but three hundred blacks, although by the end of the century blacks, most of them enslaved, made up approximately 14 percent of the colony's population.

Representative self-government was also born in primitive Virginia, in the same cradle with slavery and in the same year—1619. The London Company authorized the settlers to summon an assembly, known as the House of Burgesses. A momentous precedent was thus feebly established, for this assemblage was the first of many miniature parliaments to mushroom from the soil of America.

As time passed, James I grew increasingly hostile to Virginia. He detested tobacco and he distrusted the representative House of Burgesses, which he branded a "seminary of sedition." In 1624 he revoked the charter of the bankrupt Virginia Company, thus making Virginia a royal colony directly under his control.

Maryland: Catholic Haven

Maryland—the second plantation colony but the fourth English colony to be planted—was founded in 1634 by Lord Baltimore, of a prominent English Catholic family. He embarked on the venture partly to reap financial profits and partly to create a refuge for his fellow Catholics, who were harshly persecuted in Protestant England.

Absentee proprietor Lord Baltimore hoped that the two hundred settlers who founded Maryland at St. Marys, on Chesapeake Bay, would be the vanguard of a vast new feudal domain. Huge estates were to be awarded to his largely Catholic relatives, and gracious manor houses, modeled on those of England's

Early Maryland and Virginia

(Map labels: Susquehanna R., Delaware R., Potomac R., MARYLAND, DELAWARE BAY, CHESAPEAKE BAY, St. Marys (1634), VIRGINIA, York R., James R., Jamestown (1607), Roanoke Island (1580s))

Limit of original grant to Lord Baltimore
Present boundary of Maryland

aristocracy, were intended to sprout from the fertile forests. As in Virginia, colonists proved willing to come only if offered the opportunity to acquire land of their own. Soon they were dispersed around the Chesapeake region on modest farms, and the haughty land barons, mostly Catholic, were surrounded by resentful backcountry planters, mostly Protestant. Resentment flared into open rebellion near the end of the century, and the Baltimore family for a time lost its proprietary rights.

Despite these tensions Maryland prospered. Like Virginia, it blossomed forth in acres of tobacco. Also like Virginia, it depended for labor in its early years mainly on white indentured servants—penniless persons who bound themselves to work for a number of years to pay their passage. In both colonies it was only in the later years of the seventeenth century that black slaves began to be imported in large numbers.

Lord Baltimore permitted unusual freedom of worship for his fellow Catholics and for Protestant settlers in Maryland. But when the heavy tide of Protestants threatened to submerge the Catholics, the Catholic settlers sought legal guarantees for their religious practice in the famed Act of Toleration, passed in 1649 by the local representative assembly. This statute guaranteed toleration to all Christians, but it decreed the death penalty for anyone who denied the divinity of Jesus. While falling far short of later standards of religious liberty, the statute did extend a temporary cloak of protection to the uneasy Catholic minority.

The West Indies: Way Station to Mainland America

While the English were nursing the first frail colonial shoots in the Chesapeake, they were also busily colonizing the West Indies. By the mid-seventeenth century, England had secured its claim to several West Indian islands, including the large prize of Jamaica in 1655.

Sugar formed the foundation of the West Indian economy. What tobacco was to the Chesapeake, sugar cane was to the Caribbean—with one crucial difference. Tobacco was a poor man's crop that could be planted and processed easily. Sugar cane was a rich man's crop, requiring extensive planting and an elaborate refining process in a mill. Because of the need for land, and for the labor to clear it and to run the mills, sugar cultivation was a capital-intense business. Only wealthy growers with abundant resources to invest could succeed in sugar.

The sugar lords extended their dominion over the West Indies in the seventeenth century. To work their sprawling plantations, they imported enormous numbers of African slaves—more than a quarter of a million in the five decades after 1640. By about 1700, black slaves outnumbered white settlers in the English West Indies by nearly four to one, and the region's population has remained predominantly black ever since. West Indians thus take their place among the numerous children of the African diaspora—the vast scattering of African peoples throughout the New World in the three and a half centuries following Columbus's discovery.

To control this large and potentially restive population of slaves, English authorities devised formal "codes" that defined the slaves' legal status and the masters' prerogatives. The notorious Barbados slave code of 1661 denied even the most fundamental rights to slaves and gave masters virtually complete control over their laborers.

English settlers from Barbados arrived in Carolina in 1670, bringing with them a few African slaves, as well as the model of the Barbados code. In 1696 Carolina officially adopted a version of the code, which eventually inspired statutes governing slavery throughout the mainland colonies. The Caribbean islands thus served as a staging area for the slave system that would take root elsewhere in British North America.

Colonizing the Carolinas

Civil war convulsed England in the 1640s. King Charles I had dismissed Parliament in 1629, and when he recalled it in 1640, the members were mutinous. Finding their great champion in the Puritan soldier Oliver Cromwell, they ultimately beheaded Charles in 1649, and Cromwell ruled England for nearly a decade. Finally, Charles II, son of the decapitated king, was restored to the throne in 1660.

Colonization had been interrupted during this period of bloody unrest. Now, in the so-called Restoration period, empire building resumed with even greater intensity—and royal involvement. Carolina was formally created in 1670, after King Charles II granted to eight of his court favorites, the Lords Proprietors, an expanse of wilderness ribboning across the continent to the Pacific. These aristocratic founders hoped to grow foodstuffs to provision the sugar plantations in Barbados and to export non-English products like wine, silk, and olive oil.

Carolina prospered by developing close economic ties with the flourishing sugar islands of the English West Indies. Among the colonists' ventures was the capture and sale of inland Indians, which they turned into a thriving export business. As many as ten thousand Indians were dispatched to lifelong labor in the West Indies, and others were sold to New England. A war with the Savannah Indians that began in 1707 ended this deplorable commerce. By 1715, after a series of bloody conflicts, the Indian tribes of coastal Carolina were all but extinct.

After much experimentation, rice emerged as the principal export crop in Carolina. Since rice was grown in Africa, the Carolinians were soon paying premium prices for West African slaves experienced in rice cultivation. The Africans' agricultural skill and their relative immunity to malaria made them ideal laborers on the hot and swampy rice plantations. By 1710 they constituted a majority of Carolinians.

Moss-festooned Charles Town—named for King Charles II—rapidly became the busiest seaport in the South. Many high-spirited sons of English landed families, deprived of an inheritance, came to the Charleston area and gave it a rich aristocratic flavor. The village became a colorfully diverse community, to which French Protestant refugees and others were attracted by religious toleration.

Nearby, in Florida, the Catholic Spaniards bitterly resented the intrusion of these Protestant heretics. Carolina's frontier was often aflame. Armorclad Spanish soldiers, often aided by their Indian allies, attacked English settlements during the successive Anglo-Spanish wars. But by 1700 Carolina was too strong to be wiped out.

The wild northern expanse of the huge Carolina grant bordered on Virginia. From the older colony a ragtag group of poverty-stricken outcasts and religious dissenters drifted down, many of them repelled by the rich planters of Virginia, who belonged to the established Church of England. These small farmers, who were often "squatters" without legal right to the soil, raised their tobacco and other crops on small farms with little need for slaves. Regarded as riffraff by their snobbish neighbors, the North Carolinians earned a reputation for being resistant to authority, hostile to religion, and hospitable to pirates. Their location between aristocratic Virginia and aristocratic South Carolina caused the area to be dubbed "a vale of humility between two mountains of conceit." North Carolina was officially separated from South Carolina in 1712, and subsequently each segment became a royal colony.

North Carolina, unlike its sister colony, did not at first import large numbers of African slaves. But both Carolinas shared in the ongoing tragedy of bloody relations between Indians and Europeans. After Tuscarora Indians fell upon the fledgling settlement of Newbern in 1711, North and South Carolinians retaliated by crushing the Tuscaroras in battle and selling hundreds of them into slavery. In another ferocious encounter four years later, the South Carolinians defeated and scattered the Yamasees, thereby devastating the last of

The Iroquois

Well before the crowned heads of Europe turned their eyes and their dreams of empire toward North America, a great military power had emerged in the Mohawk Valley of what is now New York State. The Iroquois Confederacy, dubbed by whites the "League of the Iroquois," bound together five Indian nations—the Mohawks, the Oneidas, the Onondagas, the Cayugas, and the Senecas. According to Iroquois legend, the alliance was founded in the late 1500s by two leaders, Deganawidah and Hiawatha. This proud and potent league vied with neighboring Indians for territorial supremacy, then with invading Europeans for control of the fur trade. Ultimately, decimated by the white man's diseases, whiskey, and muskets, the Iroquois struggled for their very survival as a people.

The building block of Iroquois society was the longhouse. Twenty-five feet wide and up to two hundred feet long, these wooden structures sheltered several closely related nuclear families, their connections of blood running exclusively through the maternal line. The oldest woman in a clan was the honored matriarch. Men dominated the society, but they owed their positions of prominence to their mothers' families.

As if sharing one great longhouse, the five nations joined in the Iroquois Confederacy but kept their own separate fires. Although they celebrated together and shared a common policy toward out-

The Longhouse (reconstruction) *Bent saplings and sheets of elm bark made for sturdy, weathertight shelters.*

siders, they remained essentially independent of one another. On the eastern flank, the Mohawks, known as the Keepers of the Eastern Fire, specialized as middlemen with European traders, whereas the outlying Senecas, the Keepers of the Western Fire, became fur suppliers. In the early 1700s, the Tuscaroras from the Carolina region gained affiliation with the Iroquois Confederacy.

Throughout the seventeenth and eighteenth centuries the Iroquois allied alternately with the British against the French and vice versa, for a time successfully working this perpetual rivalry to their advantage. But the confederacy divided during the American Revolution, with most tribes siding with the British. Their ultimate defeat left the Iroquois Confederacy in tatters. Most Iroquois moved to British Canada or were relegated to reservations in western New York.

Reservation life proved unbearable to the proud Iroquois, who fell into feuding and alcoholism. But in 1799 an Iroquois prophet named Handsome Lake arose, warning his people to mend their ways, affirm family values, and revive their old Iroquois customs. Handsome Lake died in 1813, but his teachings, in the form of the Longhouse religion, survive to this day.

---

the coastal Indian tribes in the southern colonies. In the interior Appalachian Mountains, however, the powerful Cherokees, Creeks, and Iroquois remained (see "Makers of America: The Iroquois," pp. 26–27). Stronger and more numerous than their coastal cousins, they managed for half a century more to contain British settlement on the coastal plain east of the mountains.

Late-Coming Georgia: The Buffer Colony

Pine-forested Georgia, with the harbor of Savannah nourishing its chief settlement, was formally founded in 1733. It proved to be the last of the thirteen colonies to be planted—126 years after the first, Virginia, and 52 years after the twelfth, Pennsylvania.

The British crown intended Georgia to function chiefly as a buffer. It would serve to protect the more valuable Carolinas from inroads by vengeful Spaniards from Florida and against the hostile French from Louisiana. Georgia indeed suffered much buffeting, especially when wars broke out between Spain and Britain in the European arena.

Named in honor of King George II of Britain, Georgia was launched by a high-minded group of philanthropists. Besides producing silk and wine and strengthening the empire, they were also determined to create a haven for wretched souls imprisoned for debt. The ablest of the founders was the dynamic soldier-statesman James Oglethorpe, who became keenly interested in prison reform after one of his friends died in a debtors' jail. As an able military leader, Oglethorpe repelled Spanish attacks. As an imperialist and a philanthropist, he saved "the Charity Colony" by his energetic leadership and by heavily mortgaging his own personal fortunes.

The hamlet of Savannah, like Charleston, was a melting-pot community that included German Lutherans and Scottish Highlanders, among others. All Christian worshipers except Catholics enjoyed religious toleration. Many Bible-carrying missionaries arrived to work among debtors and Indians, including young John Wesley, who later returned to Britain and founded the Methodist church.

Georgia grew with painful slowness and at the end of the colonial era was perhaps the least populous of the colonies. The development of a plantation economy was thwarted by an unhealthful climate, by early restrictions on black slavery, and by demoralizing Spanish attacks.

The Plantation Colonies

Certain distinctive features were shared by all of Britain's southern mainland colonies: Maryland, Virginia, North Carolina, South Carolina, and Georgia. Broad-acred, these outposts of empire were all to some degree devoted to exporting commercial agricultural crops like tobacco, rice, and indigo. Slavery was established in all the plantation colonies, though

Early Carolina and Georgia Settlements

only after 1750 in reform-minded Georgia. Immense acreage in the hands of a favored few fostered a strong aristocratic atmosphere, except in North Carolina and to some extent in debtor-tinged Georgia. The wide scattering of plantations and farms, often along stately rivers, retarded the growth of cities and made the establishment of churches and schools both difficult and expensive.

Although the tax-supported Church of England became the dominant faith, all the plantation colonies permitted some religious toleration. The plantation colonies were to some degree expansionary. "Soil butchery" by excessive tobacco growing drove settlers westward, and the long, lazy rivers invited penetration of the continent—and continuing confrontation with Native Americans.

Chronology

1558	Elizabeth I becomes queen of England.
c. 1565–1590	English crush Irish uprising.
1577–1580	Drake circumnavigates the globe.
1585	Raleigh founds Roanoke colony.
1588	England defeats Spanish Armada.
1603	James I becomes king of England.
1607	Virginia colony founded at Jamestown.
1612	Rolfe perfects tobacco culture in Virginia.
1614	First Anglo-Powhatan War ends.
1619	First Africans arrive in Jamestown. Virginia House of Burgesses established.
1624	Virginia becomes a royal colony.
1634	Maryland colony founded.

1640s	Large-scale slave-labor system established in English West Indies.
1644	Second Anglo-Powhatan War.
1649	Act of Toleration established in Maryland. Charles I beheaded; Cromwell rules England.
1660	Charles II restored to English throne.
1661	Barbados slave code adopted.
1670	Carolina colony created.
1711–1713	Tuscarora War in North Carolina.
1712	North Carolina officially separates from South Carolina.
1715–1716	Yamasee War in South Carolina.
1733	Georgia colony founded.

3

Settling the Northern Colonies

❧

1619–1700

God hath sifted a Nation that he might send
Choice Grain into this Wilderness.

WILLIAM STOUGHTON [OF MASSACHUSETTS BAY], 1669

Though colonists both north and south were bound together by a common language and a common allegiance to Mother England, they established different patterns of settlements, different economies, different political systems, and even different sets of values—defining distinctive regional characteristics that would persist for generations. The promise of riches—especially from golden-leafed tobacco—drew the first settlers to the southern colonies. But to the north, in the fertile valleys of the mid-Atlantic region and especially along the rocky shores of New England, it was not worldly wealth but religious devotion that principally shaped the earliest settlements.

The Protestant Reformation Produces Puritanism

Little did the German monk Martin Luther suspect, when he nailed his protests against Catholic doctrines to the door of Wittenberg's castle church in 1517, that he was shaping the destiny of a yet unknown nation. Denouncing the authority of priests and popes, Luther declared that the Bible alone was the source of God's word. He ignited a fire of religious reform (the "Protestant Reformation") that licked its way across Europe for more than a century, dividing people, toppling sovereigns, and kindling the spiritual fervor of millions of men and women—some of whom helped to found America.

The reforming flame burned especially brightly in the bosom of John Calvin of Geneva. This somber and severe religious leader elaborated Martin Luther's ideas in ways that profoundly affected the thought and character of generations of Americans yet unborn. Calvinism became the dominant theological credo not only of the New England Puritans but of other American settlers as well, including Scottish Presbyterians, French Huguenots, and the Dutch Reformed.

Calvin argued in the *Institutes of the Christian Religion* (1536) that God was all-powerful and all-good. Humans, because of the corrupting effect of original sin, were weak and wicked. God was also all-knowing and since the first moment of creation had destined some souls—the elect—for eternal bliss and others for eternal torment. Good works could not save those whom predestination had marked for the infernal fires.

But neither could the elect count on their determined salvation and lead lives of wild, immoral abandon. For one thing, no one could be certain of his or her status in the heavenly ledger. Gnawing doubts about their eternal fates caused Calvinists to seek signs of "conversion," or the receipt of God's free gift of saving grace. Those who had the intense personal experience of conversion were expected to lead "sanctified" lives, demonstrating by their holy behavior that they were among the "visible saints."

These doctrines swept into England just as King Henry VIII was breaking his ties with the Roman Catholic Church in the 1530s, making himself the head of the Church of England. Henry would have been content to retain Roman rituals and creeds, but some English religious reformers sought a total purification of English Christianity. As they grew increasingly unhappy with the snail-like progress of the Protestant Reformation in England, these "Puritans" burned with pious zeal to see the Church of England wholly de-Catholicized.

The most devout Puritans—including those who eventually settled New England—believed that only "visible saints" (that is, persons who felt the stirrings of grace in their souls and could demonstrate its presence to their fellow Puritans) should be admitted to church membership. The Church of England enrolled all the king's subjects, which meant that the "saints" had to share pews and communion rails with the "damned." Appalled by this unholy fraternizing, a tiny group of dedicated Puritans, known as Separatists, vowed to break away entirely from the Church of England. King James I, who was head of both the church and the state in England, threatened to harass the more bothersome Separatists out of the land.

The Pilgrims End Their Pilgrimage at Plymouth

The most famous congregation of Separatists, fleeing royal wrath, departed for Holland in 1608. During the ensuing twelve years of toil and poverty, they were increasingly distressed by the "Dutchification" of their children. They longed to find a haven where they could live and die as English men and women—and as purified Protestants. America was the logical refuge.

A group of the Separatists in Holland, after negotiating with the Virginia Company, at length secured rights to settle under its jurisdiction. But their crowded *Mayflower*, sixty-five days at sea, missed its destination and arrived off the rocky coast of New England in 1620, with a total of 102 persons.

The Pilgrims chose for the site of their settlement the shore of inhospitable Plymouth Bay. This area was outside the domain of the Virginia Company, and consequently the settlers became squatters. They were without legal right to the land, and without specific authority to establish a government.

Before disembarking, the Pilgrim leaders drew up and signed the brief Mayflower Compact. Though setting an invaluable precedent for later written constitutions, this document was not a constitution at all. It was a simple agreement to form a crude government and to submit to the will of the majority under the regulations agreed upon. The compact was signed by forty-one adult males, eleven of them with the exalted rank of "mister," though not by the servants and two seamen. The pact was a promising step toward genuine self-government, for soon the adult male settlers were assembling to make their own laws in open-discussion town meetings—a great laboratory of liberty.

Plymouth Plantation
Carefully restored, the modest village at Plymouth looks today much as it did nearly four hundred years ago.

The Pilgrims' first winter, in 1620–1621, took a grisly toll. Only 44 out of the 102 survived. Yet when the *Mayflower* sailed back to England in the spring, not a single one of the courageous band of Separatists left. As one of them wrote, "It is not with us as with other men, whom small things can discourage."

God caused his children to prosper, so the Pilgrims believed. The next autumn, that of 1621, brought bountiful harvests and with them the first Thanksgiving Day in New England. In time the frail colony found sound economic legs in fur, fish, and lumber. The beaver and the Bible were the early mainstays: the one for the sustenance of the body, the other for the sustenance of the soul. The Pilgrims were also extremely fortunate in their leaders, especially William Bradford, a self-taught scholar who read Hebrew, Greek, Latin, French, and Dutch.

Quiet and quaint, the little colony of Plymouth was never important economically or numerically. Its population numbered only seven thousand souls by 1691, when, still charterless, it merged with its giant neighbor, the Massachusetts Bay Colony. But the tiny settlement of Pilgrims was big both morally and spiritually.

The Bay Colony Bible Commonwealth

The Separatist Pilgrims were dedicated extremists—the purest Puritans. More moderate Puritans sought to reform the Church of England from within. But their efforts faced catastrophe when Charles I dismissed Parliament in 1629 and sanctioned the anti-Puritan persecutions of the reactionary Archbishop William Laud.

In 1629 an energetic group of non-Separatist Puritans, fearing for their faith and for England's future, secured a royal charter to form the Massachusetts Bay Company. Stealing a march on both king and church, the newcomers brought their charter with them when they emigrated to the Massachusetts area. For many years they used it as a kind of constitution, out of easy reach of royal authority.

The Massachusetts Bay enterprise was singularly blessed. The well-equipped expedition of 1630, with eleven vessels carrying nearly a thousand immigrants, started the colony off on a larger scale than any of the other English settlements. Continuing turmoil in England tossed up additional enriching waves of Puritans on the shores of Massachusetts in the following decade

The English

During the late Middle Ages, the Black Death and other epidemics that ravaged England kept the island's population in check. But by 1500 increased resistance to such diseases allowed the population to soar; and a century later the island nation was bursting at the seams. This population explosion, combined with economic depression and religious repression, sparked the first major European migration to England's New World colonies.

Some of those who voyaged to Virginia and Maryland in the seventeenth century were independent artisans or younger members of English gentry families. But roughly three-quarters of the English migrants to the Chesapeake during this period came as servants, signed to "indentures" ranging from four to seven years. One English observer described such indentured servants as "idle, lazie, simple people," and another complained that many of those taking ship for the colonies "have been pursued by hue-and-cry for robberies, burglaries, or breaking prison."

Whereas English immigration to the Chesapeake was spread over nearly a century, most English voyagers to New England arrived within a single decade. In the twelve years between 1629 and 1642, some twenty thousand Puritans swarmed to the Massachusetts Bay Colony. Fleeing a sustained economic depression and the cruel religious repression of Charles I, the Puritans came to plant a godly commonwealth in New England's rocky soil.

In contrast to the single indentured servants of the Chesapeake, the New England Puritans migrated in family groups, and in many cases whole communities were transplanted from England to America.

Although they remained united by the common language and common Puritan faith they carried to New England, their English baggage was by no means uniform. Most New Englanders were farmers, but some towns recreated the specialized economies of particular localities in England. Marblehead, Massachusetts, for example, became a fishing village because most of its settlers had been fishermen in Old England. The townsfolk of Rowley, Massachusetts, brought from Yorkshire their distinctive way of life revolving around textile manufacturing.

Political practices, too, reflected the towns' variegated English roots. In Ipswich, Massachusetts, settled by East Anglian Puritans, the ruling selectmen served long terms and ruled with an iron hand. By contrast, local politics in the town of Newbury was

Land Use in Rowley, Massachusetts, c. 1650 *Notice the small private plots and large common fields.*

often contentious and turnovers among officeholders high; the town's founders were from western England, a region with little tradition of local government. Although the Puritans' imperial masters in London eventually circumscribed such precious local autonomy, this diverse heritage of fiercely independent New England towns endured, reasserting itself during the American Revolution.

(see "Makers of America: The English," pp. 32–33). During the "Great Migration" of the 1630s, about seventy thousand refugees left England. But not all of them were Puritans, and only about twenty thousand came to Massachusetts. Many were more attracted to the warm and fertile West Indies, especially Barbados.

Many fairly affluent, educated persons emigrated to the Bay Colony, including John Winthrop, a well-to-do pillar of English society. A successful attorney and manor lord in England, Winthrop eagerly accepted the offer to become the first governor of the Massachusetts Bay Colony, believing that he had a "calling" from God to lead the new religious experiment. He served as governor or deputy governor for nineteen years. The resources and skills of talented settlers like Winthrop helped Massachusetts prosper, and the Bay Colony rapidly shot to the fore as the biggest and the most influential of the New England outposts.

Massachusetts also benefited from a shared sense of purpose among most of the first settlers. "We shall be as a city upon a hill," a beacon to humanity, declared Governor Winthrop. The Puritan bay colonists believed that they had a covenant with God, an agreement to build a holy society that would be a model for humankind.

Building the Bay Colony

These common convictions deeply shaped the infant colony's life. Soon after arrival the settlers extended the franchise to all "freemen"—adult males who belonged to the Puritan congregations, which in time came to be called collectively the Congregational Church. On this basis about two-fifths of adult males enjoyed the franchise in provincial affairs, a far larger proportion than in contemporary England. Town governments, which conducted much important business, were even more inclusive. There all male property holders, and in some cases other residents as well, discussed and voted on public issues.

Yet the provincial government, liberal by the standards of the time, was not a democracy. "If the people be governors," asked one Puritan clergyman, "who shall be the governed?" True, the freemen annually elected the governor and his assistants, as well as a representative assembly called the General Court. But only Puritans—the "visible saints" who were alone eligible for church membership—could be freemen. And according to the doctrine of the covenant, the whole purpose of government was to enforce God's laws—which applied to believers and nonbelievers alike. Moreover, nonbelievers as well as believers paid taxes for the government-supported church.

Religious leaders thus wielded enormous influence in the Massachusetts "Bible commonwealth." They powerfully influenced admission to church membership, by conducting public interrogations of persons claiming to have experienced conversions. But the power of preachers, such as the eminent and learned John Cotton, was not absolute. Because Puritans had suffered so much at the hands of a "political" Anglican clergy, they barred clergymen from holding formal political office. In a limited way, the bay colonists thus endorsed the idea of the separation of church and state.

The Puritans were a worldly lot, despite—or even because of—their spiritual intensity. Like John Winthrop, they believed in the doctrine of a "calling" to do God's work on this earth. They shared in what was later called the "Protestant ethic," which involved serious commitment to work and to engagement in worldly pursuits. Legend to the contrary, they also enjoyed simple pleasures; they ate plentifully, drank heartily, sang songs occasionally, and made love monogamously.

Yet life was serious business, and hellfire was real—a hell where sinners shriveled and shrieked in vain and forever for divine mercy. Puritan clergyman Michael Wigglesworth's poem "Day of Doom" (1662) described the horrifying fate of the damned:

> They cry, they roar for anguish sore,
>   and gnaw their tongues for horrour,
> But get away without delay,
>   Christ pitties not your cry:
> Depart to hell, there may you yell,
>   and roar Eternally.

Trouble in the Bible Commonwealth

The Bay Colony in its early years enjoyed a high degree of social harmony, stemming from common beliefs. But even in this tightly knit community, dissension soon appeared. Quakers, who flouted the authority of the Puritan clergy, were persecuted with fines, floggings, and banishment. In one extreme case, four Quakers were hanged on Boston Common for their beliefs.

A sharp challenge to Puritan orthodoxy came from Anne Hutchinson. An exceptionally intelligent, strong-willed, and talkative woman, she claimed that the truly saved need not bother to obey the law of either God or man. This assertion, known as *antinomianism* (from the Greek, "against the law"), was high heresy. Brought to trial in 1638, the quick-witted Hutchinson bamboozled her clerical inquisitors for days, until she eventually stated that she had come by her beliefs through a direct revelation from God. This was even higher heresy. After the Puritan magistrates banished her, she traveled on foot to Rhode Island, and finally moved to New York, where she and all but one of her household were killed by Indians.

More threatening to the Puritan leaders was a personable and popular Salem minister, Roger Williams. An extreme Separatist with an unrestrained tongue, Williams demanded a clean break with the corrupt Church of England and challenged the legality of the Bay Colony's charter, which he condemned for its unfairness to the Indians. As if all this were not enough, he went on to deny the authority of civil gov-

Anne Hutchinson, Dissenter *Mistress Hutchinson (1591–1643) held unorthodox views that challenged the authority of the clergy and the very integrity of the Puritan experiment in the Massachusetts Bay Colony.*

ernment to regulate religious behavior—a seditious blow at the Puritan idea of government's very purpose. Their patience exhausted by 1635, the Bay Colony authorities found Williams guilty of disseminating "newe & dangerous opinions" and ordered him banished.

New England Spreads Out

Aided by friendly Indians, Roger Williams fled to the Rhode Island area in 1636, where he built a Baptist church. He established complete freedom of religion, even for Jews and Catholics, a degree of toleration far ahead of the other English settlements in the New World. He demanded no oaths regarding religious beliefs, no compulsory attendance at worship, and no taxes to support a state church. He even sheltered the abused Quakers, although disagreeing sharply with their views.

Those outcasts who clustered about Roger Williams also enjoyed additional blessings. They exercised simple manhood suffrage from the start, though this broad-minded practice was later narrowed by a property qualification. Opposed to special privilege of any sort, the malcontents and exiles who largely populated "Rogues' Island" had little in common with Roger Williams—except being unwelcome anywhere else. The Puritan clergy back in Boston sneered at Rhode Island as "that sewer" in which the "Lord's debris" had collected and rotted. Stubbornly individualistic, the squatters in "Little Rhody" finally established rights to the soil when they secured a charter from Parliament in 1644. A huge bronze statue of the "Independent Man" appropriately stands today on the dome of the state house in Providence.

The fertile valley of the Connecticut River had meanwhile attracted a different type of Dutch and English settlers. Hartford was founded in 1635, and the next year an energetic group of Boston Puritans, led by the Reverend Thomas Hooker, swarmed into the area. In 1639 the settlers of the new Connecticut River colony drafted a trailblazing document known as the Fundamental Orders, which established a regime controlled by the "substantial" citizens.

Another flourishing Connecticut settlement began to spring up at New Haven in 1638. It was a prosperous community, founded by Puritans who contrived to set up an even closer church-government alliance than in Massachusetts. The colonists dreamed of making New Haven a bustling seaport, but they fell into disfavor with Charles II because they sheltered two of the judges who had condemned his father, Charles I, to death. In 1662 the crown granted a charter that merged New Haven with the more democratic outposts in the Connecticut Valley.

Two smaller settlements grew up north of Massachusetts Bay. The fishermen and fur traders who had settled along the coast of Maine even before the founding of Plymouth were absorbed by Massachusetts Bay in 1677. The Maine territory remained part of Massachusetts for nearly a century and a half before becoming a separate state. In 1641 the Bay Colony also annexed its immediate northern neigh-

bor, New Hampshire, under a strained interpretation of the Massachusetts charter. The king, annoyed by this display of greed, separated New Hampshire from Massachusetts in 1679 and made it a royal colony.

Puritans Versus Indians

The spread of English settlements inevitably led to clashes with the Indians, who were particularly weak in New England. Shortly before the Pilgrims arrived at Plymouth in 1620, an epidemic, probably triggered by contact with English fishermen, had swept through the coastal tribes and killed more than three-fourths of the native people. The deserted fields that greeted the Plymouth settlers provided grim evidence of the impact of the disease.

In no position to resist the English incursion, the local Wampanoag Indians at first befriended the settlers. Cultural accommodation was facilitated by

Seventeenth-Century New England Settlements *The Massachusetts Bay Colony was the hub of New England. All earlier colonies grew into it; all later colonies grew out of it.*

Squanto, a Wampanoag who had learned English from the ship's captain who had kidnapped him some years earlier. The Wampanoag chieftain Massasoit signed a treaty with the Plymouth Pilgrims in 1621 and helped them celebrate the first Thanksgiving after the autumn harvests that same year.

As more English settlers arrived and pushed inland into the Connecticut River valley, confrontations between Indians and whites ruptured these peaceful relations. Hostilities exploded in 1637 between the settlers and the powerful Pequot tribe. In a brutal war the English militiamen virtually annihilated the Pequots.

During the ensuing four decades of tense peace, the Puritans made some feeble efforts to convert the remaining Indians to Christianity. But their missionary zeal never equaled that of the Spanish and French Catholics, and a mere handful of Indians were gathered into Puritan "praying towns."

The Indians' only hope for resisting English encroachment lay in intertribal unity—a pan-Indian alliance against the swiftly spreading settlements. In 1675 Massasoit's son Metacom, called King Philip by the English, forged such an alliance and mounted a series of coordinated assaults on English villages throughout New England. When the war ended in 1676, fifty-two Puritan towns had been attacked, and twelve destroyed entirely. Hundreds of colonists and many more Indians lay dead. Metacom was captured, beheaded, and drawn and quartered. His head was carried on a pike back to Plymouth, where it was displayed for years.

King Philip's War slowed the westward march of English settlement in New England for several decades. But the setback to settlers was temporary; it was New England's Indians who suffered a lasting defeat in the war. Drastically reduced in numbers, dispirited, and disbanded, they thereafter posed only sporadic threats to the New England colonists.

Seeds of Colonial Unity and Revolt

A path-breaking experiment in union was launched in 1643, when four colonies banded together to form the New England Confederation. The confederation was intended to provide defense against foes like the Indians, French, and Dutch, as well as to solve intercolonial problems like runaway servants and criminals. Each member colony, regardless of size, wielded two votes.

Weak though it was, the confederation was the first notable milestone on the long and rocky road toward colonial unity. The delegates took tottering but long-overdue steps toward acting together on matters of intercolonial importance.

English monarchs had paid little attention to the American colonies in the early years of settlement. This benign neglect allowed the colonies, in effect, to become semiautonomous commonwealths. But when Charles II was restored to the throne in 1660, the royalists and their Church of England allies determined to take an aggressive hand in the management of the colonies. The king's agents took particular aim at proud and stubborn Massachusetts in 1662 by extending rival Connecticut's charter and granting a charter to the outcasts in Rhode Island. Another crushing blow fell on the stiff-necked Bay Colony in 1684, when royal authorities revoked its own previous charter.

Massachusetts suffered further humiliation in 1686, when the royal government created the Dominion of New England, which was soon extended to include New York and East and West Jersey. Unlike the homegrown New England Confederation, the Dominion was imposed from London and designed primarily to stitch England's overseas possessions more tightly to the motherland by throttling American trade with countries not ruled by the British crown.

The new Dominion's governor was Sir Edmund Andros, an able but tactless English soldier who established his headquarters in Puritan Boston and promptly outraged the colonials with his profane soldiers and ironhanded tactics. Andros ruthlessly curbed the cherished town meetings, restricted the courts, and taxed the people without the consent of their popular assemblies.

On the verge of revolt, liberty-loving colonials were spared the need by the people of old England. In the Glorious Revolution of 1688–1689 they overthrew the despotic Catholic King James II and then invited the Dutch Protestant rulers William III and Mary to assume the English throne. When news of the Glorious Revolution reached America, a Boston mob attacked the existing regime, and the ramshackle Dominion of New England collapsed like a house of cards. Sir Edmund Andros attempted to flee in women's clothing but was betrayed by boots protruding beneath his dress. The rebels then dispatched the captured Andros to England as a traitor.

Though rid of Andros, Massachusetts did not gain as much from the upheaval as it had hoped. In 1691 it was arbitrarily made a royal colony, and the proud Puritans were forced to yield the privilege of voting—once a monopoly of church members—to all qualified male property holders.

The new English monarchs relaxed the royal grip on colonial trade and inaugurated a period of "salutary neglect" in which the much-resented Navigation Laws were only weakly enforced. Yet residues remained of Charles II's effort to assert tighter administrative control over his empire. More English officials—judges, clerks, customs officials—staffed the courts and strolled the wharves of English America. Many were incompetent, corrupt hacks who knew little and cared less about American affairs. Aggrieved Americans viewed them with mounting contempt and resentment as the eighteenth century wore on.

New Netherland Becomes New York

Late in the sixteenth century, the oppressed people of the Netherlands unfurled the standard of rebellion against Catholic Spain. After bloody and protracted fighting, they finally succeeded, with the aid of Protestant England, in winning their independence. This vigorous little lowland nation quickly emerged as a major commercial and naval power that ungratefully challenged the supremacy of its former benefactor, England.

The Dutch Republic also became a leading colonial power through the activities of the enterprising Dutch East India Company. The company's vast riches came mostly from the East Indies, where it maintained an enormous and profitable empire for over three hundred years. In 1609 it employed an English explorer, Henry Hudson, who ventured into Delaware Bay and New York Bay and then ascended the Hudson River, hoping that he had at last chanced upon the coveted shortcut through the continent. But the exploration proved that there was no transcontinental waterway, so Hudson merely filed a Dutch claim to the magnificently watered and wooded area.

New Netherland was permanently planted in 1623–1624 by the Dutch West India Company, the less

New Amsterdam, c. 1653 *The site of latter-day New York, this colonial village was still in Dutch hands in 1653, as shown by the Dutch-style windmill on the left in the background.*

wealthy counterpart of the East India Company. Never more than a secondary interest of the founders, the colony was exploited for its quick-profit fur trade. The company's most brilliant stroke was to buy Manhattan Island from the Indians (who did not actually "own" it) for trinkets—22,000 acres of what is now perhaps the most valuable real estate in the world for pennies per acre.

New Amsterdam—later New York City—was a company town. It was run by and for the Dutch company, in the interests of the stockholders. The investors had no enthusiasm for religious toleration, free speech, or democratic practices; and the governors appointed by the company were usually harsh and despotic.

Although picturesque, the whole Dutch colony of New Netherland soon took on a strongly aristocratic tinge and retained it for generations. Vast feudal estates fronting the Hudson River, known as "patroonships," were granted to promoters who agreed to settle fifty people on them. One patroonship in the Albany area was slightly larger than the later state of Rhode Island.

A threat to New Netherland soon came from the Swedes, who trespassed on Dutch preserves by planting the colony of New Sweden on the Delaware River in 1638. Resenting the Swedish intrusion, the Dutch dispatched a small military expedition in 1655, led by the able but despotic director-general Peter Stuyvesant. The Swedish fort fell easily and the colony came to an abrupt end, leaving behind only a sprinkling of Swedish place-names and Swedish log cabins (the first log cabins in America), as well as an admixture of Swedish blood.

Just as New Netherland absorbed New Sweden, it was soon the turn of the Dutch to be swallowed up by the English. In 1664, after Charles II had granted the area to his brother, the Duke of York, a strong English squadron appeared off the decrepit defenses of New Amsterdam. A fuming Peter Stuyvesant, short of all munitions except courage, was forced to surrender without firing a shot. New Amsterdam was thereupon renamed New York, in honor of the Duke of York. England won a splendid harbor, strategically located in the middle of the mainland colonies, and the stately Hudson River penetrating the interior. With the removal of this foreign wedge, the English banner waved triumphantly over a solid stretch of territory from Maine to the Carolinas.

The conquered Dutch province tenaciously retained many of the illiberal features of earlier days. An autocratic spirit survived, and the aristocratic element gained strength when certain corrupt English governors granted immense acreage to their favorites. Influential landowning families—such as the Livingstons and the De Lanceys—wielded disproportionate power in the affairs of colonial New York. These monopolistic land policies, combined with the lordly atmosphere, discouraged many European immigrants from coming. The physical growth of New York was correspondingly retarded.

Penn's Holy Experiment in Pennsylvania

A remarkable group of dissenters, commonly known as Quakers, arose in England during the mid-1600s. Their name derived from the report that they "quaked" when touched by deep religious emotion. Officially they were known as the Religious Society of Friends.

Quakers were especially offensive to the authorities, both religious and civil. They refused to support the established Church of England with taxes. They built simple meetinghouses, without a paid clergy, and "spoke up" themselves in meetings when moved. Believing that all were equal as children in the sight of God, Quakers kept their broad-brimmed hats on in the presence of their "betters" and addressed others with simple "thee's" and "thou's," rather than with conventional titles. They would take no oaths because Jesus had commanded, "Swear not at all." This peculiarity often embroiled them with government officials, for "test oaths" were still required to establish the fact that a person was not a Roman Catholic.

The Quakers, beyond a doubt, were a people of deep conviction. They abhorred strife and warfare and refused military service. As advocates of passive resistance, they would turn the other cheek and rebuild their meetinghouses on the sites where their enemies had torn them down. Their courage and devotion to principle finally triumphed. Though at times they seemed stubborn and unreasonable, they were a simple, devoted, democratic people, contending in their own way for religious and civic freedom.

William Penn, a well-born and athletic young Englishman, was attracted to the Quaker faith in 1660, when only sixteen years old. His father, disapproving, administered a sound flogging. After various adventures in the army (the best portrait of the peaceful Quaker has him in armor), the youth firmly embraced the despised faith and suffered much persecution.

Penn felt keenly the plight of his fellow Quakers, thousands of whom were executed, flogged, or cast into "nasty stinking prisons." Penn's thoughts naturally turned to the New World, where a sprinkling of Quakers had already fled, notably to Rhode Island, North Carolina, and New Jersey. Eager to establish an asylum for his people, he also hoped to experiment with liberal ideas in government and at the same time make a profit. Finally, in 1681, he managed to secure from the king an immense grant of fertile land, in consideration of a monetary debt that the crown owed to his deceased father. The king called the area Pennsylvania ("Penn's Woodland") in honor of the father.

Pennsylvania was by far the best advertised of all the colonies. Its founder sent out paid agents and distributed countless pamphlets printed in English, Dutch, French, and German. Unlike the lures of many an American real estate promoter, then and later, Penn's inducements were generally truthful. His liberal land policy, which encouraged substantial holdings of land, was instrumental in attracting a heavy inflow of immigrants.

Penn formally launched his colony in 1681. He farsightedly bought land along the Delaware River from the Indians for his town of Philadelphia ("brotherly love" in Greek). His treatment of the native people was so fair that the Quaker "broad brims" went among them unarmed and even employed them as babysitters. For a brief period, Pennsylvania seemed the promised land of amicable Indian-white relations. Some southern tribes even migrated there, seeking the Quaker haven. But ironically, Quaker tolerance proved the undoing of Quaker Indian policy. As non-Quaker European immigrants flooded into the welcoming province, they undermined the Quakers' own benevolent policy toward the Indians. The feisty Scots-Irish were particularly unpersuaded by Quaker idealism.

Penn's Treaty, by Edward Hicks *The peace-loving Quaker founder of Pennsylvania made a serious effort to live in harmony with the Indians, but the westward thrust of white settlement eventually caused friction, as in other colonies.*

Among other noteworthy features, no provision was made by the Quakers of Pennsylvania for a military defense. No restrictions were placed on immigration, and naturalization was made easy. The humane Quakers early developed a strong dislike of black slavery, and in the genial glow of Pennsylvania some progress was made toward social reform.

With its many liberal features, Pennsylvania attracted a rich mix of ethnic groups. They included numerous religious misfits who were repelled by the harsh practices of neighboring colonies. The Quaker haven boasted a surprisingly modern atmosphere in an unmodern age, and to an unusual degree it afforded economic opportunity, civil liberty, and religious freedom. Even so, certain "blue laws" targeted "ungodly revelers," stage plays, playing cards, dice, games, and excessive hilarity.

Under such generally happy auspices, Penn's brainchild grew lustily. The Quakers were shrewd businesspeople, and in a short time the settlers were exporting grain and other foodstuffs. Within two years Philadelphia claimed 300 houses and 2,500 people. Within nineteen years—by 1700—the colony was surpassed in population and wealth only by long-established Virginia and Massachusetts.

William Penn spent only about four years in the colony and eventually died full of sorrows back in England. But Pennsylvania, his enduring monument, was not only a noble experiment in government but also a new commonwealth. Based on civil and religious liberty, and dedicated to freedom of conscience and worship, it held aloft a hopeful torch to a world of semidarkness.

Small Quaker settlements flourished next door to Pennsylvania. New Jersey was started in 1664, when two noble proprietors received the area from the Duke of York. One of the proprietors sold West New Jersey in 1674 to a group of Quakers, and Quakers also acquired East New Jersey a few years later. In 1702 the crown combined the two Jerseys in a royal colony.

Swedish-tinged Delaware consisted of only three counties—two at high tide, the witticism goes—and was named after Lord De La Warr, the harsh military governor who had arrived in Virginia in 1610. Harboring some Quakers, and closely associated with Penn's flourishing colony, Delaware was granted its own assembly in 1703. But until the American Revolution it remained under the governor of Pennsylvania.

The Middle Way in the Middle Colonies

The middle colonies—New York, New Jersey, Delaware, and Pennsylvania—enjoyed certain features in common. In general, the soil was fertile and the expanse of land was broad, unlike rock-strewn New England. Pennsylvania, New York, and New Jersey came to be known as the "bread colonies" because of their heavy exports of grain.

Rivers also played a vital role. Broad, languid streams—notably the Susquehanna, the Delaware, and the Hudson—tapped the fur trade of the interior and beckoned adventuresome spirits into the backcountry. The rivers, unlike New England's, had few cascading waterfalls and hence presented little inducement to manufacturing with water-wheel power.

A surprising amount of industry nonetheless flourished in the middle colonies. Virginal forests abounded for lumbering and shipbuilding. The presence of deep river estuaries and landlocked harbors stimulated both commerce and the growth of seaports, such as New York and Philadelphia. Even Albany, more than a hundred miles up the Hudson, was a port of some consequence in colonial days.

The middle colonies stood midway between New England and the southern plantation group in many respects besides geography. Except in aristocratic New York, the landholdings were generally intermediate in size—smaller than in the big-acreage South but larger than in small-farm New England. Local government lay somewhere between the personalized town meeting of New England and the diffused county government of the South. There were fewer industries in the middle colonies than in New England, but more than in the South.

Yet the middle colonies could claim certain distinctions in their own right. Generally speaking, the population was more ethnically mixed than that of other settlements. The people were blessed with an unusual degree of religious toleration and democratic control. Earnest and devout Quakers, in particular, made a contribution to human freedom out of all proportion to their numbers. Desirable land was more easily acquired in the middle colonies than in New England or in the tidewater South. One result was that a considerable amount of economic and social democracy prevailed, though less so in aristo-

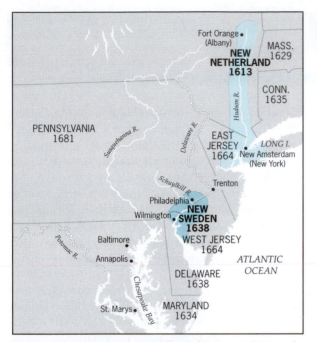

Early Settlements in the Middle Colonies, with Founding Dates

Chronology

1517	Martin Luther begins Protestant Reformation.
1536	John Calvin of Geneva publishes *Institutes of the Christian Religion.*
1620	Pilgrims sail on the *Mayflower* to Plymouth Bay.
1624	Dutch found New Netherland.
1629	Charles I dismisses Parliament and persecutes Puritans.
1630	Puritans found Massachusetts Bay Colony.
1635–1636	Roger Williams convicted of heresy and founds Rhode Island colony.
1635–1638	Connecticut and New Haven colonies founded.
1637	Pequot War.
1638	Anne Hutchinson banished from Massachusetts colony.
1639	Connecticut's Fundamental Orders drafted.
1642–1648	English Civil War.
1643	New England Confederation formed.
1655	New Netherland conquers New Sweden.
1664	England seizes New Netherland from Dutch. East and West Jersey colonies founded.
1675–1676	King Philip's War.
1681	William Penn founds Pennsylvania colony.
1686	Royal authority creates Dominion of New England.
1688–1689	Glorious Revolution overthrows King James II and Dominion of New England.

cratic New York. Thus in some ways the mid-Atlantic region was the most American part of America.

Modern-minded Benjamin Franklin, often regarded as the most representative American personality of this era, was a child of the middle colonies. Although it is true that Franklin was born a Yankee in puritanical Boston, he entered Philadelphia as a seventeen-year-old in 1720 with a loaf of bread under each arm and immediately found a congenial home in the urbane, open atmosphere of what was then North America's biggest city. One Pennsylvanian later boasted that Franklin "came to life, at seventeen, in Philadelphia."

By the time Franklin arrived in the City of Brotherly Love, the American colonies themselves were "coming to life." Population was growing robustly. Transportation and communication were improving. For the most part, the British left the colonists to fashion their own local governments, run their own churches, and develop networks of intercolonial trade. As people and products crisscrossed the colonies with increasing frequency and increasing volume, Americans began to realize that—far removed from Mother England—they were not merely surviving but truly thriving.

VARYING   VIEWPOINTS

Europeanizing America or Americanizing Europe?

The history of discovery and the earliest colonization raises perhaps the single most fundamental question about all American history. Should it be understood as the extension of European civilization into the New World or as the gradual development of a uniquely "American" culture? One school of thought tended to emphasize the Europeanization of America. Historians of that persuasion paid close attention to the situation in Europe, particularly in England and Spain, in the fifteenth and sixteenth centuries. They also focused on the various means by which the values and institutions of the mother continent were exported to the new lands in the western sea. Some European writers varied this general question by asking what transforming effect the discovery of America had on Europe itself. Both of these approaches are Eurocentric. More recently, historians have concentrated on the distinctiveness of America. The concern with European origins has evolved into a comparative treatment of English, Spanish, Dutch, and French settlements in the New World. The newest trend to emerge is a transatlantic history that views European empires and their American colonies as players in a process of cultural cross-fertilization affecting not only the colonies but Europe and Africa as well.

This less Eurocentric approach has changed the way historians explain the colonial development of America. Historians increasingly view the colonial period as one of "contact" and "adaptation" between European, African, and Native American ways of life.

Scholars including Richard White, Alfred W. Crosby, William Cronon, Karen Kupperman, and Timothy Silver have enhanced understanding of the cultural as well as physical transformations that resulted from contact.

The variety of American societies that emerged out of the interaction of Europeans, Africans, and Native Americans has also become better appreciated. Studies such as Richard S. Dunn's *Sugar and Slaves* (1972) emphasize the importance of the Caribbean in early English colonization efforts. Similarly, Edmund S. Morgan's *American Slavery, American Freedom* (1975) stresses the role of economic ambition in explaining the English peopling of the Chesapeake and the eventual importation of African slaves to that region. Studies by Bernard Bailyn and David Hackett Fischer demonstrate that there was scarcely a "typical" English migrant to the New World. English colonists migrated both singly and in families, and for economic, social, political, and religious reasons.

The picture of colonial America that is emerging from all this new scholarship is of a society unique—and diverse—from its inception. No longer simply Europe transplanted, American colonial society by 1700 is now viewed as an outgrowth of many intertwining roots—of different European and African heritages, of varied encounters with native peoples, and of complicated mixtures of settler populations, each with its own distinctive set of ambitions.

For further reading, see the Appendix. For web resources, go to **http://college.hmco.com**.

American Life in the Seventeenth Century

1607–1692

Being thus passed the vast ocean, and a sea of troubles before in their preparation . . . , they had now no friends to wellcome them, nor inns to entertaine or refresh their weatherbeaten bodys, no houses or much less towns to repaire too, to seeke for succore.

WILLIAM BRADFORD, OF PLYMOUTH PLANTATION, 1622

As the seventeenth century wore on, the crude encampments of the first colonies slowly gave way to permanent settlements. Durable and distinctive ways of life emerged, as Europeans and Africans adapted to their new conditions. Even the rigid doctrines of Puritanism softened somewhat in response to the circumstances of life in America. And though all the colonies remained tied to England and stitched tightly into the fabric of an Atlantic economy, regional differences continued to crystallize, notably the increasing importance of slavery to the southern way of life.

The Unhealthy Chesapeake

Life in the American wilderness was nasty, brutish, and short for the earliest Chesapeake settlers. Malaria, dysentery, and typhoid took a cruel toll, cutting ten years off the life expectancy of newcomers from England. Half the people born in early Virginia and Maryland did not survive to celebrate their twentieth birthdays. Few of the remaining half lived to see their fiftieth—or even their fortieth, if they were women.

The disease-ravaged settlements of the Chesapeake grew only slowly in the seventeenth century, mostly through fresh immigration from England. The great majority of immigrants were single men in their late teens and early twenties, and most perished soon after their arrival. Surviving males competed for the affections of the extremely scarce women, whom they outnumbered nearly six to one in 1650 and still outnumbered by three to two at the end of the century. Eligible women did not remain single for long.

Families were few and fragile in this ferocious environment. Most men could not find mates. Most marriages were destroyed by the death of a partner within seven years. Weak family ties were reflected in the many pregnancies among unmarried young girls. In one Maryland county, more than a third of all brides were already pregnant when they wed.

Yet despite these hardships, the Chesapeake colonies struggled on. The native-born inhabitants eventually acquired immunity to the killer diseases that had ravaged the original immigrants. In time, the presence of more women allowed more families to form, and by the end of the seventeenth century the white population of the Chesapeake was growing on the basis of its own birthrate. As the eighteenth century opened, Virginia, with some fifty-nine thousand people, was the most populous colony. Maryland, with about thirty thousand, was the third largest (after Massachusetts).

The Tobacco Economy

Although unhealthy for human life, the Chesapeake was immensely hospitable to tobacco cultivation. Profit-hungry settlers often planted tobacco to sell before they planted corn to eat. But intense tobacco cultivation quickly exhausted the soil, creating a nearly insatiable demand for virgin land. Relentlessly seeking fresh fields to plant to tobacco, commercial growers plunged ever farther up the river valleys, provoking ever more Indian attacks.

This continual expansion created tobacco yields that reached almost 40 million pounds a year by the end of the seventeenth century. The enormous production depressed prices for the crop, but colonial Chesapeake tobacco growers responded to falling prices by planting still more acres in tobacco and bringing still more product to market.

More tobacco meant more labor, but where was it to come from? Families procreated too slowly to provide it by natural population increase. Indians died too quickly on contact with whites, and African slaves cost too much money. But England still had a "surplus" of displaced farmers desperate for employment. Many of them, as indentured servants, voluntarily mortgaged the sweat of their bodies for several years to Chesapeake masters. In exchange they received transatlantic passage and eventual "freedom dues," including a few barrels of corn, a suit of clothes—and perhaps a small parcel of land.

Both Virginia and Maryland employed the "head-right" system to encourage the importation of servant workers. Under its terms, any master who paid the passage of a laborer received the right to acquire fifty acres of land. Taking advantage of this system, some masters soon parlayed their investments in servants into huge fortunes in real estate. They became the great merchant-planters who came to dominate the agriculture and commerce of the southern colonies. Chesapeake planters brought some 100,000 indentured servants to the region by 1700. These "white slaves" represented more than three-quarters of all European immigrants to Virginia and Maryland in the seventeenth century.

Indentured servants led a hard but hopeful life in the early days of the Chesapeake settlements. They looked forward to becoming free and acquiring land of their own after completing their terms of servitude. But as the century wore on, prime land became scarcer and the servants' lot grew harsher. Masters became increasingly resistant to including land grants in "freedom dues." Even after formal freedom was granted, penniless freed workers often had little choice but to hire themselves out for pitifully low wages to their former masters.

Frustrated Freemen and Bacon's Rebellion

An accumulating mass of footloose, impoverished freemen was drifting discontentedly about the Chesapeake region by the late seventeenth century. Mostly single young men, they were frustrated by their broken hopes of acquiring land as well as by their gnawing failure to find single women to marry.

The swelling number of these wretched bachelors rattled the established planters. Led by Governor William Berkeley, the Virginia assembly in 1670 disenfranchised most of the landless knockabouts. About a thousand Virginians then broke out of control in 1676, led by a twenty-nine-year-old planter, Nathaniel Bacon. Angered by Berkeley's mild Indian policies as well as economic grievances, Bacon and his followers first attacked Indians on the frontier. They then chased Berkeley from Jamestown and put the torch to the capital. Chaos swept the raw colony as frustrated freemen and resentful servants—

described as "a rabble of the basest sort of people"—went on a rampage of plundering and pilfering.

As this civil war in Virginia ground on, Bacon suddenly died of disease. Berkeley thereupon crushed the uprising with brutal cruelty, hanging more than twenty rebels. Back in England Charles II complained, "That old fool has put to death more people in that naked country than I did here for the murder of my father."

The distant English king could scarcely imagine the depths of passion and fear that Bacon's Rebellion excited in Virginia. Bacon had ignited the smoldering unhappiness of landless former servants, and he had pitted the hard-scrabble backcountry frontiersmen against the haughty gentry of the tidewater plantations. The rebellion was suppressed, but the tensions that provoked it remained. Lordly planters, surrounded by a still-seeting sea of malcontents, anxiously looked about for less troublesome laborers to toil in the restless tobacco kingdom. Their eyes soon lit on Africa.

Colonial Slavery

Perhaps 10 million Africans came in chains to the New World in the three centuries or so after Columbus's landing. Only about 400,000 ended up in North America. Most were carried to Spanish and Portuguese South America or the sugar-rich West Indies. Africans had been brought to Jamestown as early as 1619, but as late as 1670 they numbered only about 7 percent of the 50,000 people in the southern plantation colonies as a whole. For hard-pinched colonists, white servants were far less costly than high-priced slaves.

Drastic change came in the 1680s. Rising prices in England shrank the pool of penniless indentured servants, while large planters grew increasingly fearful of the potentially mutinous former servants in their midst. By the mid-1680s, for the first time, black slaves outnumbered white servants among the plantation colonies' new arrivals. In 1698 the Royal African Company, first chartered in 1672, lost its

Main Sources of African Slaves, c. 1500 to c. 1800 *The three centuries of the African diaspora scattered blacks all over the New World, with about 400,000 coming to North America. Boundaries shown are those of modern African states.*

The "Middle Passage" *Human cargo in the hold of a slave ship.*

crown-granted monopoly on carrying slaves to the colonies. Enterprising Americans, especially Rhode Islanders, rushed to cash in on the lucrative slave trade, and the supply of slaves rose steeply. By 1750 blacks accounted for nearly half the population of Virginia; in South Carolina they outnumbered whites two to one.

Most slaves who reached North America came from the west coast of Africa, including the area stretching from present-day Senegal to Angola. They were originally captured by African coastal tribes, who traded them in crude markets to itinerant European—and American—flesh merchants. Usually branded and bound, the captives were herded aboard sweltering ships for the gruesome "middle passage," on which death rates ran as high as 20 percent. Terrified survivors were eventually shoved onto auction blocks in New World ports like Newport, Rhode Island, or Charleston, South Carolina, where a giant slave market traded in human misery for more than a century.

A few of the earliest African immigrants gained their freedom, and some even became slaveowners themselves. But as the number of Africans in their midst increased dramatically toward the end of the seventeenth century, white colonists reacted remorselessly to this supposed racial threat. Beginning in Virginia in 1662, the iron conditions of bondage were spelled out in slave codes that made blacks and their children the property (or "chattels") for life of their white masters. Not even conversion to Christianity could qualify a slave for freedom. Slavery might have begun in America for economic reasons, but by the end of the seventeenth century, it was clear that racial discrimination also powerfully molded the American slave system.

Africans in America

In the deepest South, slave life was especially severe. The climate was hostile to health, and the labor was life draining. The widely scattered South Carolina rice and indigo plantations were lonely hells on earth where gangs of mostly male Africans toiled and perished. Only fresh imports could sustain the slave population under these loathsome conditions.

Blacks in the tobacco-growing Chesapeake region had a somewhat easier lot. Tobacco was a less physically demanding crop than the crops of the deeper South. Tobacco plantations were smaller and closer to one another than rice plantations. By about 1720 the proportion of females in the Chesapeake slave population had begun to rise, making family life possible. The captive black population of the Chesapeake area soon began to grow not only through new imports but also through its own fertility—making it one of the few slave societies in history to perpetuate itself by its own natural reproduction.

Native-born African-Americans contributed to the growth of a stable and distinctive slave culture, a mixture of African and American elements of speech, religion, and folkways (see "Makers of America: From African to African-American," pp. 48–49). On the sea islands off South Carolina's coast, blacks evolved a unique language, Gullah, that blended English with several African languages, including Yoruba, Ibo, and Hausa. The "ringshout," a West African religious dance, was brought to colonial America by slaves and eventually contributed to the development of jazz.

Slaves also helped mightily to build the country with their labor. A few became skilled artisans—carpenters, bricklayers, and tanners. But chiefly they performed the sweaty toil of clearing swamps, grubbing out trees, and other menial tasks. Condemned to life under the lash, slaves naturally pined for freedom. Slave revolts erupted in New York City in 1712, and again in South Carolina in 1739. But in the end the slaves in the South proved to be a more manageable labor force than the white indentured servants they gradually replaced. No slave uprising in American history matched the scale of Bacon's Rebellion.

Southern Society

As slavery spread, the gaps in the South's social structure widened. The rough equality of poverty and disease of the early days was giving way to a defined hierarchy of wealth and status in the early eighteenth century. At the top of this southern social ladder perched a small but powerful covey of great planters. Owning gangs of slaves and vast domains of land, the planters ruled the region's economy and virtually monopolized political power. Yet, legend to the contrary, these great seventeenth-century merchant-planters were not silk-swathed cavaliers gallantly imitating the ways of English country gentlemen. For the most part they were a hard-working, businesslike lot, laboring long hours over the problems of plantation management.

Far beneath the planters in wealth, prestige, and political power were the small farmers, the largest social group. They lived a ragged, hand-to-mouth existence on their modest plots. Still lower on the social scale were landless whites and, below them, indentured servants still serving out their terms. The oppressed black slaves, of course, remained enchained in society's basement.

Few cities sprouted in the colonial South, and consequently an urban professional class, including lawyers and financiers, was slow to emerge. Southern life revolved around the great plantations, distantly isolated from one another. Waterways, rather than the wretched roads, provided the principal means of transportation from one plantation to another.

The New England Family

Nature smiled more benignly on pioneer New Englanders than on their disease-plagued fellow colonists to the south. Clean water and cool temperatures, which retarded the spread of microbes, created healthier living conditions that enabled settlers in seventeenth-century New England to add ten years to their life spans by migrating from the Old World, in stark contrast to the fate of Chesapeake immigrants. The first generations of Puritan colonists enjoyed, on the average, about seventy years on this earth—not very different from the life expectancy of present-day Americans.

In further contrast with the Chesapeake, New Englanders tended to migrate not as single individuals but as families, and the family remained at the center of New England life. Early marriage and prolific childbearing enabled New England's population to grow from natural reproductive increase almost from the outset. Women typically wed by their early twenties and produced babies about every two years thereafter until menopause. A married woman could expect to experience up to ten pregnancies and rear as many as eight surviving children. A New England woman might well have dependent children living in her household from the earliest days of her marriage until the day of her death, and child raising became virtually her full-time occupation.

The longevity of the New Englanders contributed to family stability. Children received nurturing love and guidance not only from their parents but from their grandparents as well. Family stability was reflected in low premarital pregnancy rates (again in contrast with the Chesapeake) and in the generally strong, tranquil social structure characteristic of colonial New England.

Oddly enough, the strength of New England families actually weakened the economic independence of women in that region compared with women in the South. In the southern colonies, men frequently died

MAKERS OF AMERICA

From African to African-American

Dragged in chains from West African shores, the first African-Americans struggled to preserve their diverse heritages from the ravages of slavery. Their children, the first generation of American-born slaves, melded these various traditions—Guinean, Ibo, Yoruba, Angolan—into a distinctive African-American culture. Their achievement sustained them during the cruelties of enslavement and has endured to this day to enrich American life.

With the arrival of the first Africans in the seventeenth century, a cornucopia of African traditions poured into the New World: handicrafts and skills in numerous trades; a plethora of languages, musics, and cuisines; even rice-planting techniques that conquered the inhospitable soil of South Carolina. It was North America's rice paddies, tilled by experienced West Africans, that introduced the staple rice into the English diet.

These first American slaves were mostly males who lived on small, isolated farms. But by the beginning of the eighteenth century, a settled slave society was emerging in the southern colonies. Laws tightened; slave traders stepped up their deliveries of human cargo; large plantations formed. Most signifi-

(left) **Yarrow Mamout, by Charles Willson Peale, 1819** *When Peale painted this portrait, Mamout was over 100 years old. A devout Muslim brought to Maryland as a slave, he eventually bought his freedom and settled in Georgetown.*
(right) **The Emergence of an African-American Culture** *In this scene from the mid-nineteenth century, African-Americans play musical instruments of European derivation, like the fiddle, as well as instruments of African origin, like the bones and banjo—a vivid illustration of the blending of the two cultures in the crucible of the New World.*

cantly, a new generation of American-born slaves joined their forebears at labor in the fields. By 1740 large groups of slaves lived together on sprawling plantations, the American-born outnumbered the African-born, and the importation of African slaves slowed.

Plantation life was an endless cycle of miserable toil for the slaves. After a day's backbreaking work, women were expected to sit up for hours spinning, weaving, or sewing clothes for themselves and their families. Enslaved women also lived in constant fear of sexual exploitation by conscienceless masters.

Slave religion illustrates how new ideas were combined with a traditional heritage. Most slaves became Christians but fused elements of African and Western traditions and drew their own conclusions from Scripture. White Christians might encourage slaves to "stay in their place," but black Christians emphasized God's role in freeing the Hebrews from slavery and saw Jesus as the Messiah who would deliver them from bondage.

At their Sunday and evening prayer meetings, slaves also patched African remnants onto conventional Christian ritual. Black Methodists, for example, evaded the traditional Methodist ban on dancing by practicing the "ringshout." Some worshipers clapped their hands and beat time in a circle while others walked around the ring, singing in unison. Christian slaves also often used outwardly religious songs as encoded messages about escape or rebellion. The hymn "Wade in the Water," for instance, taught fleeing slaves one way of covering their trails. The "Negro spirituals" that took shape as a distinctive form of American music thus had their origins in both Christianity and slavery. Indeed, much American music was born in the slave quarters from African importations. But this rich cultural harvest came at the cost of generations of human agony.

young, leaving widows with small children to support. The law therefore allowed married women to retain separate titles to their property, and it gave widows the right to inherit their husband's estates. But in New England, Puritan lawmakers worried that recognizing women's separate property rights would undercut family unity. Thus New England women usually gave up their property rights when they married.

"A true wife accounts subjection her honor," one Massachusetts Puritan leader declared, expressing a sentiment then common in Europe as well as America. But in the New World, a rudimentary conception of women's rights as individuals was beginning to appear in the seventeenth century. Women still could not vote, and the popular attitude persisted that they were morally weaker than men. But a husband's power over his wife was not absolute. The New England authorities could and did intervene to restrain abusive spouses, and women had some spheres of autonomy. Midwifery—assisting with childbirths—was a virtual female monopoly, and midwives often fostered networks of women bonded by the common travails of motherhood.

Above all, the laws of Puritan New England sought to defend the integrity of marriage. Divorce was exceedingly rare: outright abandonment and adultery were among the few permissible grounds for divorce. Convicted adulterers—especially if they were women—were whipped in public and forced forever after to wear the capital letter "A" cut out in cloth and sewn on their outer garments—the basis for Nathaniel Hawthorne's famous 1850 tale, *The Scarlet Letter*.

Life in the New England Towns

Sturdy New Englanders evolved a tightly knit society, the basis of which was small farming villages. Puritanism especially made for unity of purpose—and for concern about the moral health of the whole community.

Even territorial expansion occurred in orderly, communal fashion, in contrast to the Chesapeake's normal mode of expansion by lone-wolf planters. New towns were legally chartered by the colonial authorities, and the distribution of land was

Mrs. Elizabeth Freake and Baby Mary   *This portrait of a Boston mother and child in about 1674 suggests the strong family ties that characterized early New England society.*

Puritans ran their own churches, and democracy in Congregational church government led logically to democracy in political government. The town meeting, in which the adult males met together and each man voted, was a showcase and a classroom for democracy. The town meeting, observed Thomas Jefferson, was "the best school of political liberty the world ever saw."

The Changing New England Way of Life

Yet worries plagued the God-fearing pioneers of these tidy New England settlements. The pressure of a growing population was gradually dispersing the Puritans onto outlying farms, far from the control of church and neighbors. And although the core of Puritan belief still burned brightly, the passage of time was dampening the first generation's religious zeal. About the middle of the seventeenth century, earnest preachers began scolding parishioners for their waning piety in a new form of sermon—the "jeremiad." In response to the apparent decline in conversions, troubled ministers in 1662 announced a new formula for church membership, the "Half-Way Covenant." This new arrangement admitted to baptism, but not to "full communion," the as-yet unconverted children of existing members. By conferring partial membership rights in the once-exclusive Puritan congregations, the Half-Way Covenant weakened the distinction between the "elect" and other members of society. In effect, strict religious purity was sacrificed somewhat to the cause of wider religious participation. Interestingly, from about this time onward women were in the majority in the Puritan congregations.

Women also played a prominent role in one of New England's most frightening religious episodes. A group of adolescent girls in Salem, Massachusetts, claimed to have been bewitched by certain older women. A hysterical "witch hunt" ensued, leading to the execution in 1692 of twenty persons. The reign of horror in Salem grew not only from the superstitions and prejudices of the age but also from the unsettled social and religious conditions of the rapidly evolving Massachusetts village. Most of the accused witches came from families associated with Salem's burgeoning market economy; their accusers came largely

entrusted to the steady hands of sober-minded town fathers, or "proprietors." After receiving a grant of land from the colonial legislature, the proprietors usually laid out their town around a meetinghouse, which served as both the place of worship and the town hall. Also marked out was a village green, where the militia could drill. Each family received several parcels of land.

Towns of more than fifty families were required to provide elementary education, and a majority of adults knew how to read and write. As early as 1636, just six years after the colony's founding, the Massachusetts Puritans established Harvard College to train local boys for the ministry. Only in 1693, eighty-six years after the founding of Jamestown, did the Virginians establish their first college, William and Mary.

from the ranks of subsistence farming families in Salem's hinterland. The episode thus reflected the widening social stratification of New England, as well as the anxieties of many religious traditionalists that the Puritan heritage was being eclipsed by Yankee commercialism. The Salem witchcraft delusion marked an all-time low in America's experience of popular passions run wild.

New England soil, like New England religion, was hard and unyielding. Scratching a living from the rock-strewn land put a premium on industry and penny-pinching frugality, for which New Englanders became famous. The grudging land also left colonial New England less ethnically mixed than its southern neighbors. European immigrants were not attracted in great numbers to a site where the soil was so stony—and the sermons so sulfurous.

Yet the harsh climate and unproductive soil of New England eventually encouraged a diversified agriculture and industry. Staple products like tobacco did not flourish, as in the South. Black slavery, although attempted, could not exist profitably on small farms. Turning away from the land, New Englanders more and more looked to the sea for a living. Hacking timber from their dense forests, they became experts in shipbuilding and commerce. They also ceaselessly exploited the self-perpetuating codfish lode off the coast of Newfoundland—the fishy "gold mines of New England." As a reminder of the importance of fishing, a handsome replica of the "sacred cod" is proudly displayed to this day in the Massachusetts State House in Boston.

Just as the land shaped New Englanders, so they shaped the land. In contrast with Native Americans, who used the land but recognized no right to own it, European settlers felt a virtual duty to "improve" the land by clearing woodlands for pasturage and tillage, building roads and fences, and laying out permanent settlements. The introduction of livestock also led colonists to clear ever more forests for pastureland, while the animals' voracious appetites and heavy hooves compacted the soil, speeding erosion and flooding.

The combination of Calvinism, clay, and climate in New England made for energy, purposefulness, sternness, stubbornness, self-reliance, and resourcefulness. Righteous New Englanders prided them-

selves on being God's chosen people. They long boasted that Boston was "the hub of the universe"—at least in spirit. A famous jingle of later days ran:

> I come from the city of Boston
> The home of the bean and the cod
> Where the Cabots speak only to Lowells
> And the Lowells speak only to God.

New England has had an incalculable impact on the rest of the nation. Ousted by their sterile soil, thousands of New Englanders scattered from Ohio to Oregon and even Hawaii. The democratic town meeting, the tidy schoolhouse, and "Yankee ingenuity," all originally fostered in the towns and fields of New England, came to be claimed by all Americans as part of their national heritage. And the fabled "New England conscience," born of the steadfast Puritan heritage, left a legacy of high idealism in the national character and inspired many later reformers.

The Early Settlers' Days and Ways

The cycles of the seasons and the sun set the schedules of all the earliest American colonists—men as well as women and blacks as well as whites. The overwhelming majority of colonists were farmers. They planted in the spring, tended their crops in the summer, harvested in the fall, and prepared in the winter to begin the cycle anew. They usually rose at dawn and went to bed at dusk. Chores might be performed after nightfall only if they were "worth the candle," a phrase that has persisted in American speech.

Women, slave or free, on southern plantations or northern farms, cooked, cleaned, and cared for children. Men worked the land, cut firewood, and butchered livestock as needed. Children helped with all these tasks, while picking up such schooling as they could.

Life was humble but comfortable by contemporary standards. Compared with most seventeenth-century Europeans, Americans lived in affluent abundance. Land was relatively cheap, though somewhat less available in the planter-dominated South than elsewhere.

"Dukes don't emigrate," the saying goes, for if people enjoy wealth and security, they are not likely to risk exposing their lives in the wilderness. Similarly, the very poorest members of a society may not possess even the modest means needed to pull up stakes and seek a fresh start in life. Accordingly, most white migrants to early colonial America came neither from the aristocracy nor from the dregs of European society—with the partial exception of the impoverished indentured servants.

Seventeenth-century society in all the colonies had a certain simple sameness to it, especially in the more egalitarian New England and middle colonies. Yet many settlers who considered themselves to be of the "better sort" tried to re-create on a modified scale the social structure they had known in the Old World. Resentment against such upper-class pretensions helped to spark outbursts like Bacon's Rebellion in Virginia in 1676, the uprising of Maryland's Protestants toward the end of the seventeenth century, and Leisler's Rebellion in New York City from 1689 to 1691.

For their part, would-be American blue bloods resented the pretensions of the "meaner sort" and passed laws to try to keep them in their place. Massachusetts in 1651 prohibited poorer folk from "wearing gold or silver lace," and in eighteenth-century Virginia a tailor was fined and jailed for arranging to race his horse—"a sport only for gentlemen." But these efforts to reproduce the finely stratified societies of Europe proved feeble in the early American wilderness, where equality and democracy found fertile soil—at least for white people.

Chronology

1619	First Africans arrive in Virginia.
1636	Harvard College founded.
1662	Half-Way Covenant for Congregational church membership established.
1670	Virginia assembly disfranchises landless freemen.
1676	Bacon's Rebellion in Virginia.
1680s	Mass expansion of slavery in colonies.
1689–1691	Leisler's Rebellion in New York.
1692	Salem witch trials in Massachusetts.
1693	College of William and Mary founded.
1698	Royal African Company slave trade monopoly ended.
1712	New York City slave revolt.
1739	South Carolina slave revolt.

5

Colonial Society on the Eve of Revolution

1700–1775

Driven from every other corner of the earth, freedom of thought and the right of private judgment in matters of conscience direct their course to this happy country as their last asylum.

SAMUEL ADAMS, 1776

The common term *thirteen original colonies* is misleading. Britain ruled thirty-two colonies in North America by 1775, including Canada, the Floridas, and various Caribbean islands. But only thirteen of them unfurled the standard of rebellion. A few of the nonrebels, such as Canada and Jamaica, were larger, wealthier, or more populous than some of the revolting thirteen. Why, then, did some British colonies eventually strike for their independence, while others did not? Part of the answer is to be found in the distinctive social, economic, and political structures of the thirteen Atlantic seaboard colonies—and in the halting, gradual appearance of a recognizably *American* way of life.

Conquest by the Cradle

Among the distinguishing characteristics that the eventually rebellious settlements shared was lusty population growth. In 1700 they contained fewer than 300,000 souls, about 20,000 of whom were black. By 1775, 2.5 million people inhabited the thirteen colonies, of whom about half a million were black. White immigrants made up nearly 400,000 of the increased number, and black "forced immigrants" accounted for almost as many again. But most of the spurt stemmed from the remarkable natural fertility of all Americans, white and black. The youthful

Americans, whose average age in 1775 was about sixteen, were doubling their numbers every twenty-five years. Dr. Samuel Johnson, back in Britain, growled that the Americans were multiplying like their own rattlesnakes.

This population boom had political consequences. In 1700 there were twenty Britons for each American colonist. By 1775 the British advantage in numbers had fallen to three to one—setting the stage for a momentous shift in the balance of power between the colonies and Britain.

The bulk of the population was cooped up east of the Alleghenies. The most populous colonies in 1775 were Virginia, Massachusetts, Pennsylvania, North Carolina, and Maryland—in that order. Only four communities could properly be called cities: Philadelphia, including suburbs, ranked first with about thirty-four thousand residents, trailed by New York, Boston, and Charleston. About 90 percent of the people lived in rural areas.

A Potpourri of Peoples

Colonial America was a melting pot and had been from the outset. The population, although basically English in stock and language, was picturesquely mottled with numerous foreign groups.

Heavy-accented Germans constituted about 6 percent of the total population, or 150,000, by 1775. Fleeing religious persecution, economic oppression, and the ravages of war, they had flocked to America in the early 1700s and had settled chiefly in Pennsylvania. They belonged to several different Protestant groups—primarily Lutheran—and thus further enhanced the religious diversity of the colony. Known popularly but erroneously as the Pennsylvania Dutch (a corruption of the German word *Deutsch*, for "German"), they totaled about one-third of the colony's population. In parts of Philadelphia, street signs were painted in both German and English. In the Pennsylvania backcountry, where many of them moved, German immigrants clung tenaciously to their language and customs.

The Scots-Irish, who in 1775 numbered about 175,000, or 7 percent of the population, were an important non-English group, although they spoke English (see "Makers of America: The Scots-Irish," pp. 56–57). They were not Irish at all but turbulent Scots Lowlanders. Over many decades, they had first been transplanted to Northern Ireland, where they had not prospered. The Irish Catholics already there, hating Scottish Presbyterianism, resented the intruders (and still do). Early in the 1700s tens of thousands of embittered Scots-Irish finally abandoned Ireland and came to America, chiefly to tolerant and deep-soiled Pennsylvania.

Finding the best acres already taken by Germans and Quakers, the Scots-Irish pushed out onto the frontier. There many of them illegally but defiantly squatted on the unoccupied lands and quarreled with both Indian and white owners. It was said, somewhat unfairly, that the Scots-Irish kept the Sabbath—and all else they could lay their hands on. Pugnacious, lawless, and individualistic, they brought with them the Scottish secrets of whiskey distilling and dotted the Appalachian hills and hollows with their stills. They cherished no love for the British government that had uprooted them, and many of them—including the young Andrew Jackson—eventually joined the embattled American revolutionists.

Approximately 5 percent of the colonial population consisted of other European groups, including French, Welsh, Dutch, Swedes, Jews, Irish, Swiss, and Scots Highlanders. Except for the Scots Highlanders, these ethnic groups felt little loyalty to the British crown. By far the largest single non-English group was African, accounting for nearly 20 percent of the colonial population in 1775 and heavily concentrated in the South.

The population of the thirteen colonies, though mainly Anglo-Saxon, was perhaps the most mixed to be found anywhere in the world. The South, holding about 90 percent of the slaves, already displayed its historic black-and-white racial composition. New England, mostly staked out by the original Puritan migrants, showed the least ethnic diversity. The middle colonies, especially Pennsylvania, received the great majority of later white immigrants and boasted an astonishing variety of people. Outside New England, about half of the population was non-English in 1775.

As these various immigrant groups mingled and intermarried, they laid the foundations for a new

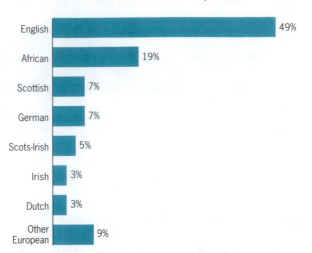

Ethnic and Racial Composition of the American People, 1790 *Based on surnames. (Source: Adapted from the American Council of Learned Societies, "Report of Committee on Linguistic and National Stocks in the Population of the United States," 1932. Percentages total more than 100 percent due to rounding.)*

Immigrant Groups in 1775 *America was already a nation of diverse ethnic groups in the colonial period. This map shows the great variety of immigrant groups, especially in Pennsylvania and New York. It also illustrates the tendency of later arrivals, particularly the Scots-Irish, to push into the backcountry. The basic ethnic makeup of many of these colonial settlements persists even today, each with distinct cultural patterns and attitudes.*

multicultural American national identity unlike anything known in Europe. White colonists were not alone in creating new societies out of diverse ethnic groups. The African slave trade long had mixed peoples from many different tribal backgrounds, giving birth to an African-*American* community far more variegated in its cultural origins than anything to be found in Africa itself. Similarly, in the New England "praying towns" where Indians were gathered to be Christianized, and in Great Lakes villages like Detroit, home to dozens of different displaced indigenous peoples, polyglot Native American communities emerged, blurring the boundaries of individual tribal identities.

The Structure of Colonial Society

In contrast with contemporary Europe, eighteenth-century America was a shining land of equality and opportunity—with the notorious exception of slavery. No titled nobility dominated society from on high, and no pauperized underclass threatened it from below. Most white Americans, and even some

The Scots-Irish

As the British Empire spread its dominion across the seas in the seventeenth and eighteenth centuries, great masses of people poured into its ever-widening realms. Their migration unfolded in stages. They journeyed from farms to towns, from towns to great cities such as London and Bristol, and eventually from the seaports to Ireland, the Caribbean, and North America. Among these intrepid wanderers, few were more restless than the Scots-Irish, the settlers of the first American West. Never feeling at home in the British Empire, these perennial outsiders always headed for its most distant outposts. They migrated first from their native Scottish Lowlands to Northern Ireland and from there to the New World. But even in North America, the Scots-Irish remained on the periphery, ever distancing themselves from the reach of the English crown and the Church of England.

The Scottish migration from Scotland itself was driven by severe poverty. Always forced to struggle with a harsh and unyielding land, poorer Scots were oppressed further in the 1600s by merciless rent increases at the hands of the landowning lairds. Adding insult to injury, the British authorities repeatedly persecuted the Presbyterian Scots, squeezing taxes from their barren purses to support the hated Church of England.

Not surprisingly, then, some 200,000 Scots immigrated to neighboring Ireland in the 1600s. So great was the exodus that Protestant Scots eventually outnumbered Catholic natives in the several northern Irish counties that compose the province of Ulster. But soon the Scots discovered that their migration had not freed them from their ancient woes. Their

Irish landlords raised rents just as ruthlessly as their Scottish lairds had done. Under such punishing pressures, waves of these already once-transplanted Scots, now known as Scots-Irish, fled again, this time to America.

Most debarked in Pennsylvania, seeking the religious tolerance and abundant land of William Penn's commonwealth. But these unquiet people did not stay put for long. They fanned out from Philadelphia into the farmlands of western Pennsylvania. Blocked temporarily by the Allegheny Mountains, they migrated south along the backbone of the Appalachian range, slowly filling the backcountry of Virginia, the Carolinas, and Georgia.

This Scottish Presbyterian church, built in 1794, still stands in Alexandria, Virginia.

Almost every Scots-Irish community, however isolated or impermanent, maintained a Presbyterian church. Religion was the bond that yoked these otherwise fiercely independent folk. In backcountry towns, churches were erected before law courts, and clerics were pounding their pulpits before civil authorities had the chance to raise their gavels. But despite their intense faith, the Scots-Irish were not theocrats or advocates of religious rule. Their bitter struggles with the Church of England made them stubborn opponents of established religions in the United States, just as their seething resentment against the king of England ensured that they would be well represented among the Patriots in the American Revolution.

free blacks, were small farmers. In the cities lived a small class of skilled artisans, as well as a few shopkeepers, tradespeople, and unskilled casual laborers. The most remarkable feature of the social ladder was the rags-to-riches ease with which an ambitious colonist might rise from a low rung to a higher one.

Yet in contrast with seventeenth-century America, colonial society on the eve of the Revolution was beginning to show signs of stratification and barriers to mobility that raised worries about the "Europeanization" of America. A new class of merchant princes in New England and the middle colonies, many of whom had made their fortunes as military suppliers in the colonial wars, roosted regally atop the social ladder. They sported imported clothing and dined at tables laid with English china and gleaming silverware. Prominent individuals came to be seated in churches and schools according to their social rank.

Poverty and diminished opportunity also began to appear at the bottom of society. Both Philadelphia and New York built almshouses in the 1730s to care for the destitute, although the numbers of poor people remained tiny compared with the numbers in England. In the New England countryside the descendants of the original settlers faced more limited prospects than had their pioneering forebears. As families grew and existing landholdings were repeatedly divided, the average size of farms shrank drastically. Younger sons as well as daughters were forced to hire out as wage laborers. By 1750 Boston contained a large number of homeless poor, who were supported by public charity and forced to wear a large red "P" on their clothing.

In the South the power of the great planters continued to be bolstered by their disproportionate ownership of slaves. Wealth was concentrated in the hands of the largest slaveowners, widening the gap between the prosperous gentry and the "poor whites," who were more and more likely to become tenant farmers. In all the colonies the ranks of the lower classes were further swelled by the continuing stream of indentured servants. Far less fortunate than the voluntary indentured servants were the paupers and convicts involuntarily shipped to America. Altogether, about fifty thousand "jayle birds"—including robbers, rapists, and murderers—were dumped on the colonies by the London authorities. But many of the convicts were the hapless victims of a viciously unfair British penal code, and some eventually became highly respectable citizens.

Least fortunate of all, of course, were the black slaves. Oppressed and downtrodden, the slaves were America's closest approximation to Europe's volatile lower classes, and fears of black rebellion plagued the white colonists. Some colonial legislatures, notably South Carolina's in 1760, attempted to restrict or halt the importation of slaves, but British authorities vetoed all such efforts. Thomas Jefferson, himself a slaveholder, assailed such vetoes in an early draft of the Declaration of Independence but was forced to withdraw the proposed clause by a torrent of protest from southern slavemasters.

Clergy, Physicians, and Jurists

Most honored of the professions was the Christian ministry. In 1775 the clergy wielded less influence than in the early days of Massachusetts, when piety had burned more warmly. But they still occupied a position of high prestige.

Most physicians, in contrast, were poorly trained and not highly esteemed. Not until 1765 was the first medical school established, although European centers attracted some students. Aspiring young doctors served for a while as apprentices to older practitioners and were then turned loose on their "victims." Bleeding was a favorite and often fatal remedy; when the physician was not available, a barber was often summoned.

Epidemics were a constant nightmare. Especially dreaded was smallpox, which afflicted one out of five persons, including the heavily pock-marked George Washington. A crude form of inoculation was introduced in 1721 despite the objections of many physicians and some of the clergy, who opposed tampering with the will of God. Powdered dried toad was a favorite prescription for smallpox. Diphtheria was also a deadly killer, especially of young people. One epidemic in the 1730s took the lives of thousands.

At first the law profession was not favorably regarded. In this pioneering society, which required much honest manual labor, the parties to a dispute often presented their own cases in court. Lawyers were commonly regarded as noisy windbags or troublemaking rogues; an early Connecticut law classed them with drunkards and brothel keepers.

Workaday America

Agriculture was the leading industry, involving about 90 percent of the people. Tobacco continued to be the staple crop in Maryland and Virginia, though wheat cultivation also spread in the Chesapeake, often on lands depleted by the over-growth of tobacco. The fertile middle ("bread") colonies produced large quantities of grain, and by 1759 New York alone was exporting eighty thousand barrels of flour a year. Seemingly the farmer had only to tickle the soil with a hoe and it would laugh with a harvest. Overall, Americans probably enjoyed a higher average standard of living than the masses of any country in history up to that time.

Fishing (including whaling), though ranking far below agriculture, was rewarding. Pursued in all the colonies, this harvesting of the sea was a major industry in New England, which exported smelly shiploads of dried cod to the Catholic countries of Europe. The fishing fleet also stimulated shipbuilding and served as a nursery for the seamen who manned the navy and merchant marine.

Yankee seamen were famous in many climes not only as skilled mariners but as tightfisted traders. They provisioned the Caribbean sugar islands with food and forest products. They hauled Spanish and Portuguese gold, wine, and oranges to London, to be exchanged for industrial goods, which were then sold for a juicy gain in America.

The so-called triangular trade was infamously profitable, though small in relation to total colonial commerce. A skipper would leave a New England port with a cargo of rum and sail to the Gold Coast of Africa. Bartering the fiery liquor with African chiefs for captured African slaves, he would proceed to the West Indies with his suffocating cargo sardined below deck. There he would exchange the slaves for molasses, which he would then carry to New England, where it would be distilled into rum. He would then repeat the trip, making a handsome profit on each leg of the triangle.

Manufacturing in the colonies was of only secondary importance, although there was a surprising variety of small enterprises. Huge quantities of "kill devil" rum were distilled in Rhode Island and Massachusetts, and even some of the "elect of the Lord" developed an overfondness for it. Beaver hats, iron forges, and household goods spun and woven by women constituted other colonial manufactures. As in all colonies, strong-backed laborers and skilled craftspeople were scarce and highly prized.

Lumbering was perhaps the most important single manufacturing activity. Countless cartloads of virgin timber were consumed by shipbuilders, who by 1770 were sending four hundred new vessels splashing into the sea each year. Colonial naval stores—such as tar, pitch, resin, and turpentine—were highly valued. Towering trees, ideal as masts for His Majesty's Navy, were marked with the king's broad arrow for future use. The luckless lumberman who was caught cutting down this reserved timber was subject to a fine.

Americans held an important flank of a thriving, many-sided Atlantic economy by the dawn of the eighteenth century. Yet strains appeared in this com-

Colonial Trade Patterns, c. 1770 *Future president John Adams noted about this time that "the commerce of the West Indies is a part of the American system of commerce. They can neither do without us, nor we without them. The Creator has placed us upon the globe in such a situation that we have occasion for each other."*

plex network as early as the 1730s. Fast-breeding Americans demanded more and more British products—but the slow-growing British population early reached the saturation point for absorbing imports from America. How, then, could the colonists sell the goods to make the money to buy what they wanted in Britain? The answer was obvious: by seeking foreign (non-British) markets.

By the eve of the Revolution the bulk of Chesapeake tobacco was filling pipes in France and other European countries, though it passed through the hands of British re-exporters, who took a slice of the profits. More important was the trade with the West Indies, especially the French islands. West Indian purchases of North American timber and foodstuffs provided the crucial cash for the colonists to continue to make their own purchases in Britain. But in 1733, bowing to pressure from influential British West Indian planters, Parliament passed the Molasses Act, aimed at squelching North American trade with the French West Indies. If successful, this scheme would have struck a crippling blow to American international trade and to the colonists' standard of living.

American merchants responded by bribing and smuggling their way around the law. Thus was foreshadowed the impending imperial crisis, when headstrong Americans would revolt rather than submit to the dictates of a far-off Parliament apparently bent on destroying their very livelihood.

Horsepower and Sailpower

As a sprawling and sparsely populated pioneer territory, America was cursed with oppressive problems of transportation. Not until the 1700s did roads connect even the major cities, and these dirt thoroughfares were treacherously deficient.

Roads were often clouds of dust in summer and quagmires of mud in winter. Stagecoach travelers braved additional dangers such as fallen trees, rickety bridges, carriage overturns, and runaway horses. Travel was so slow that it actually took twenty-nine days after the Fourth of July in 1776 for the news of the Declaration of Independence to reach Charleston from Philadelphia.

Estimated Religious Census, 1775

Name	Number	Chief Locale
Congregationalists	575,000	New England
Anglicans	500,000	N.Y., South
Presbyterians	410,000	Frontier
German churches (incl. Lutheran)	200,000	Pa.
Dutch Reformed	75,000	N.Y., N.J.
Quakers	40,000	Pa., N.J., Del.
Baptists	25,000	R.I., Pa., N.J., Del.
Roman Catholics	25,000	Md., Pa.
Methodists	5,000	Scattered
Jews	2,000	N.Y., R.I.
EST. TOTAL MEMBERSHIP	1,857,000	
EST. TOTAL POPULATON	2,493,000	
PERCENTAGE CHURCH MEMBERS	74%	

Where roads were wretched, heavy reliance was placed on waterways. Population tended to cluster along the banks of navigable rivers. There was also much coastwise traffic, which was cheap and pleasant but slow.

Taverns sprang up along the main routes of travel as well as in the cities. Along with such attractions as bowling alleys, pool tables, and gambling equipment, taverns provided plentiful information, rumors, and gossip—frequently stimulated by alcoholic refreshment and impassioned political talk. Before a cheerful, roaring log fire all social classes would mingle, including the village loafers and drunks. Taverns were important in crystallizing public opinion, and alehouses like Boston's Green Dragon proved to be hotbeds of agitation as the revolutionary movement gathered momentum.

Dominant Denominations

Two "established," or tax-supported, churches were conspicuous in 1775: the Church of England and the Congregational Church. The Church of England, or the "Anglican" Church, became the official faith in Georgia, North and South Carolina, Virginia, Maryland, and part of New York. British officials made vigorous attempts to impose it on additional colonies but ran into a stone wall of opposition. On the eve of the American Revolution, there was serious talk of creating a resident Anglican bishop in North America, but this scheme was also violently opposed by non-Anglicans, who feared a tightening of the royal reins.

Secure, self-satisfied, and often worldly, the Anglican Church itself fell distressingly short of its promise. So dismal was the reputation of the Anglican clergy in seventeenth-century Virginia that the College of William and Mary was founded in 1693 to train a better class of clerics.

The influential Congregational Church, which had grown out of the Puritan Church, was formally established in all the New England colonies except independent-minded Rhode Island. Presbyterianism, though closely associated with Congregationalism, was never the official church of any colony. Sometimes turning from the Bible to worldly politics, many Congregationalist and Presbyterian ministers of the gospel joined in stirring up opposition to the British crown in the 1760s and 1770s. But most Anglican clergymen, aware of which side their tax-provided bread was buttered on, naturally supported the king.

Despite the presence of established churches, religious toleration had made enormous strides in America. Roman Catholics were still generally discriminated against, as in Britain, though the anti-papist laws were less severe and less strictly enforced. In general, people could worship—or not worship—as they pleased.

The Great Awakening

In all the colonial churches, religion was less fervid in the early eighteenth century than it had been a century earlier, when the colonies were first planted. The Puritan churches in particular sagged under the weight of two burdens: their elaborate theological doctrines and their compromising efforts to liberalize membership requirements. Churchgoers increasingly complained about the "dead dogs" who droned out tedious sermons from the pulpit. For their part, many ministers worried that their parishioners had gone soft and no longer embraced orthodox Calvinism. These twin trends toward clerical rigidity and lay indifference were sapping the spiritual vitality of many denominations.

The stage was thus set for a rousing religious revival. Known as the "Great Awakening," it exploded in the 1730s and 1740s and swept through the colonies like a fire through prairie grass. The Awakening was first ignited in Northampton, Massachusetts, by a tall, delicate, and intellectual pastor, Jonathan Edwards. Perhaps the deepest theological mind ever nurtured in America, Edwards proclaimed with burning righteousness the need for complete dependence on God's grace. His preaching style was learned and closely reasoned, but his stark doctrines sparked a warmly sympathetic reaction among his parishioners in 1734.

Four years later, the itinerant English parson George Whitefield loosed a different style of evangelical preaching on America and touched off a conflagration of religious ardor that revolutionized the spiritual life of the colonies. A former alehouse attendant, Whitefield was a magnificent orator whose voice boomed sonorously over thousands of enthralled listeners in many an open field. Triumphantly touring the colonies, Whitefield displayed an eloquence that reduced Jonathan Edwards to tears and even caused the skeptical and thrifty Benjamin Franklin to empty his pockets into the collection plate. During Whitefield's roaring revival meetings, countless sinners professed conversion, while hundreds of the "saved" groaned, shrieked, or rolled in the snow from religious excitement. Soon, American imitators took up Whitefield's electrifying new style of preaching and shook enormous audiences with emotional appeals.

Orthodox clergymen, known as "old lights," were deeply skeptical of the emotionalism and the theatrical antics of the revivalists. But "new light" ministers defended the Awakening for its role in revitalizing American religion. The Awakening left many lasting effects. Its emphasis on direct, emotive spirituality seriously undermined the older clergy, whose authority had derived from their education and erudition. The schisms the Awakening set off in many denominations increased the numbers and competitiveness of American churches. The Awakening also encour-

George Whitefield Preaching *Americans of both genders and all races and regions were spellbound by Whitefield's fervent oratory.*

aged a fresh wave of missionary work among the Indians and black slaves, many of whom attended open-air revivals. It also led to the founding of "new light" centers of higher learning such as Dartmouth, Brown, Rutgers, and Princeton. Perhaps most significant, the Great Awakening was the first spontaneous mass movement of the American people. By breaking down sectional boundaries and denominational lines, it contributed to the Americans' growing sense of themselves as a single people united by a common history and shared experience.

Schools and Colleges

Only slowly and painfully did American colonists break away from the English idea that education should be reserved for the aristocratic few. In Puritan

New England, education was dominated by the Congregational Church, which stressed the need for Bible reading by the individual worshiper. Education, principally for boys, flourished almost from the outset in New England, which boasted an impressive number of graduates from the British universities, especially Cambridge. New Englanders, at a relatively early date, established primary and secondary schools, which varied widely in the quality of instruction and in the length of time their doors remained open each year.

Fairly adequate elementary schools were also hammering knowledge into the heads of reluctant "scholars" in the middle colonies and in the South. Some of these institutions were tax supported; others were privately operated. The South, with its white and black populations diffused over wide areas, was severely handicapped in attempting to establish an effective school system. Wealthy families leaned heavily on private tutors.

The general atmosphere in the colonial schools and colleges continued grim and gloomy. Emphasis was placed on religion and on the classical languages, Latin and Greek. Independence of thinking was discouraged, and severe discipline was often administered with a switch cut from a birch tree. But by 1750 a distinct trend had emerged toward "live" languages and other modern subjects in the nine small colonial colleges. A significant contribution was made by Benjamin Franklin, who played a major role in launching what became the University of Pennsylvania, the first American college free from denominational control.

A Provincial Culture

When it came to art and culture, colonial Americans were still in thrall to European tastes, especially British. The simplicity of pioneer life had not yet bred many homespun patrons of the arts, nor artists either. One aspiring painter, John Trumbull of Connecticut (1756–1843), was discouraged in his youth by his father's chilling remark, "Connecticut is not Athens." Trumbull, as well as his talented artistic contemporaries Charles Willson Peale (1741–1827), Ben-

Colonial Craftsmanship   *In the "Pennsylvania Dutch" country, parents gave daughters painted wooden chests to hold their precious dowry linens at marriage. The horsemen, unicorns, and flower patterns on this dower chest confirm its origins in Berks County, Pennsylvania.*

jamin West (1738–1820), and John Copley (1738–1815), all eventually succeeded in their ambition to become famous painters. But they had to go to Britain to complete their training and find patrons to support them.

Colonial architecture, too, was largely imported from the Old World. The red-brick Georgian style, so common in the pre-Revolutionary decades, was introduced about 1720 and is best exemplified by the beauty of now-restored Williamsburg, Virginia.

Colonial literature, like art, was generally undistinguished, but a few outstanding individuals produced original and enduring work. Precocious black poet Phillis Wheatley (c. 1753–1784) was an uneducated slave girl who was brought to Boston at age eight and then taken to London when she was twenty. She overcame her disadvantages and produced polished poems that revealed the influence of Alexander Pope.

Versatile Benjamin Franklin, often called "the first civilized American," also shone as a literary light. His autobiography was his greatest literary achievement, but he was best known to his contemporaries for *Poor Richard's Almanack*, which he edited from 1732 to 1758. Emphasizing the homespun virtues of thrift, industry, and common sense, "Poor Richard" was most famous for his pithy sayings: "Plough deep while sluggards sleep"; "Fish and visitors stink in three days." *Poor Richard's* was well known in Europe and was more widely read in America than anything except the Bible. As a teacher of both old and young, Franklin had an incalculable influence in shaping the American character.

Franklin's scientific efforts, including his spectacular kite-flying experiments with electricity, made him the colonies' only first-rate scientist and won him numerous honors in Europe. Among the inventions produced by his practical mind were bifocal spectacles, the Franklin stove, and the lightning rod.

Pioneer Presses

Stump-grubbing Americans were generally too poor to buy quantities of books and too busy to read them. A few fine private libraries, like that of the Byrd family in Virginia, could be found. Bustling Benjamin Franklin established in Philadelphia the first privately supported circulating library, and by 1776 about fifty other communities had set up subscription-supported public libraries.

On the eve of the Revolution colonial presses churned out about forty newspapers, chiefly weeklies that consisted of a single large sheet folded once. The "news," especially from overseas, often lagged many weeks behind the event, and the papers devoted much column space to somber essays. Nevertheless, newspapers proved to be a powerful agency for airing colonial grievances and rallying opposition to British control.

A celebrated legal case in 1734–1735 involved John Peter Zenger, a newspaper printer. Significantly, the case arose in New York, reflecting the tumultuous give-and-take of politics in the middle colonies, where so many different ethnic groups jostled against one another. Zenger's newspaper had assailed the corrupt royal governor. Charged with seditious libel, the accused was hauled into court, where he was defended by a former indentured servant, now a distinguished Philadelphia lawyer, Andrew Hamilton. Zenger argued that he had printed the truth, but the royal chief justice ruled that the mere fact of printing, regardless of the truth, was enough to convict. But the jury, swayed by Hamilton's eloquence, defied the bewigged judge and daringly returned a verdict of not guilty. Cheers burst from the spectators.

The Zenger decision was a banner achievement for freedom of the press and the health of democracy. It pointed the way to the kind of open public discussion required by the diverse society that colonial New York already was and that all America was to become. Although contrary to existing law and not immediately accepted by other judges and juries, in time the ruling helped establish the doctrine that true statements about public officials could not be prosecuted as libel. Newspapers were thus eventually free to print responsible criticisms of powerful officials, though full freedom of the press was unknown during the pre-Revolutionary era.

The Great Game of Politics

American colonists may have been backward in natural or physical science, but they were making noteworthy contributions to political science.

The thirteen colonial governments took a variety of forms. By 1775 eight of the colonies had royal governors appointed by the king. Three—Maryland, Pennsylvania, and Delaware—were under proprietors who themselves chose the governors. And two—Connecticut and Rhode Island—elected their own governors under self-governing charters.

Practically every colony utilized a two-house legislative body. The upper house, or council, was normally appointed by the crown in the royal colonies and by the proprietor in the proprietary colonies. It was chosen by the voters in the self-governing colonies. The lower house, as the popular branch, was elected by the people—or rather by those who owned enough property to qualify as voters. In several of the colonies, the backcountry settlers were seriously underrepresented, and they hated the ruling colonial clique perhaps more than they did kingly authority. Legislatures, in which the people enjoyed direct representation, voted such taxes as they deemed necessary for the expenses of colonial government. Self-taxation through representation was a precious privilege that Americans had come to cherish above most others.

Governors appointed by the king were generally able men. Some, unfortunately, were incompetent or corrupt—broken-down politicians badly in need of jobs. The worst of the group was probably impoverished Lord Cornbury, first cousin of Queen Anne, who was made governor of New York and New Jersey in 1702. He proved to be a drunkard, a spendthrift, a grafter, an embezzler, a religious bigot, and a vain fool. He was also accused (probably inaccurately) of dressing as a woman. Even the best appointees had trouble with the colonial legislatures, basically because every royal governor embodied a bothersome transatlantic authority some three thousand miles away.

The colonial assemblies found various ways to assert their authority and independence. Some of them employed the trick of withholding the governor's salary unless he yielded to their wishes. Because he was normally in need of money, the power of the purse usually forced him to terms.

Administration at the local level was also varied. County government remained the rule in the plantation South; town-meeting government predominated in New England; and a modification of the two developed in the middle colonies. In the town meeting, with its open discussion and open voting, direct democracy functioned at its best. In this unrivaled cradle of self-government, Americans learned to cherish their privileges and exercise their duties as citizens of the New World commonwealths.

Yet the ballot was by no means a birthright. Religious or property qualifications for voting, with even stiffer qualifications for officeholding, existed in all the colonies in 1775. The privileged upper classes, fearful of democratic excesses, were unwilling to grant the ballot to every "biped of the forest." Perhaps half of the adult white males were thus disfranchised. But because of the ease of acquiring land and thus satisfying property requirements, the right to vote was not beyond the reach of most industrious and enterprising colonists.

By 1775 America was not yet a true democracy—socially, economically, or politically. But it was far more democratic than Britain and the European continent. Colonial institutions were giving freer rein to the democratic ideals of tolerance, educational advantages, equality of economic opportunity, freedom of speech, freedom of the press, freedom of assembly, and representative government. And these democratic seeds, planted in rich soil, were to bring forth a lush harvest in later years.

Colonial Folkways

Everyday life in the colonies may now seem quaint, especially as reflected in antique shops. But judged by modern standards, it was drab and tedious. For most people, the labor was heavy and constant—from "can see" to "can't see."

Basic comforts now taken for granted were lacking. Food was plentiful, though the diet could be coarse and monotonous. Churches were unheated except for charcoal foot-warmers that the women carried. There was no running water in the houses, no plumbing, and probably not a single bathtub in all colonial America. Candles and whale-oil lamps provided faint and flickering illumination. Garbage disposal was primitive. Long-snouted hogs customarily ranged the streets to consume refuse, while buzzards, protected by law, flapped greedily over tidbits of waste.

Amusement was eagerly pursued where time and custom permitted. Militia "musters," house-raisings, quilting bees, funerals, and weddings everywhere afforded opportunities for social gatherings, which customarily involved the swilling of much strong liquor. Winter sports were common in the North, whereas the South favored hunting, horse racing, dancing, stage plays, card playing, and cockfighting. George Washington, not surprisingly, was equally skilled at riding and dancing.

Lotteries were universally approved, even by the clergy, and were used to raise money for churches and colleges, including Harvard. Holidays were celebrated everywhere, but Christmas was frowned upon in New England as an offensive reminder of "Popery." Thanksgiving Day came to be a truly American festival, for it combined gratitude to God with an opportunity for jollification, gorging, and guzzling.

By the mid-eighteenth century Britain's several North American colonies, despite their differences, revealed some striking similarities. All were basically English in language and customs and Protestant in religion, and the widespread presence of other peoples and faiths compelled every colony to cede at least some degree of ethnic and religious toleration. Compared with contemporary Europe, they afforded unusual opportunities for economic advancement and a measure of self-government, though by no means complete democracy. British North America by 1775 looked like a patchwork quilt—each section slightly different but stitched together by common origins, common ways of life, and common beliefs in toleration, economic development, and, above all, self-rule. Fatefully, all the colonies were also separated from the seat of imperial authority by a vast ocean moat some three thousand miles wide. These simple facts of shared history, culture, and geography set the stage for the colonists' struggle to unite as an independent people.

Chronology

1693	College of William and Mary founded.
1701	Yale College founded.
1721	Smallpox inoculation introduced.
1732	First edition of Franklin's *Poor Richard's Almanack*.
1734	Jonathan Edwards begins Great Awakening.
1734–1735	Zenger free-press trial in New York.
1738	George Whitefield spreads Great Awakening.
1746	Princeton College founded.
1760	Britain vetoes South Carolina anti–slave trade measures.
1764	Brown College founded.
1766	Rutgers College founded.
1769	Dartmouth College founded.

VARYING VIEWPOINTS

Colonial America: Communities of Conflict or Consensus?

The earliest historians of colonial society portrayed close-knit, homogeneous, and hierarchical communities. Richard Bushman in *From Puritan to Yankee* (1967) challenged that traditional view. He described colonial New England as an expanding, open society in which the colonists gradually lost the religious discipline and social structure of the founding generations. Rhys Isaac viewed the Great Awakening in the South as similar evidence of erosion in the social constraints and deference that once held colonial society together.

Some scholars dispute that a loss of common faith and morals undermined colonial communities. Christine Heyrmann in particular argued in *Commerce and Culture* (1984) that the decline of traditional mores was overstated and that religious beliefs and commercial activities coexisted throughout the late seventeenth and early eighteenth centuries. Similarly, colonial historian Jack Greene has suggested that the obsession with the decline of deference obscures the fact that colonies outside New England, like Virginia and Maryland, actually experienced a consolidation of religious and social authority throughout the seventeenth and eighteenth centuries, becoming more hierarchical and paternalistic, not less.

Since the 1970s, some historians have also attacked the traditional idea that New England was the home of American freedom and that the South spawned hierarchical, aristocratic communities. They argue that not only did the South produce many of the founders—Washington, Jefferson, and Madison—but that republican principles were actually strongest in Virginia. Some scholars, notably Edmund

S. Morgan in *American Slavery, American Freedom* (1975), consider the willingness of wealthy planters to concede the equality and freedom of all white males a device to ensure racial solidarity and to mute class conflict.

Few historians still argue that the colonies offered boundless opportunities for inhabitants, white or black. Whether one accepts Morgan's arguments that "Americans bought their independence with slave labor" or those interpretations that point to the rising social conflict between whites as the salient characteristic of colonial society on the eve of the Revolution, the once-common assumption that America was a world of equality and consensus no longer reigns undisputed. Yet because one's life chances were still unquestionably better in America than in Europe, immigrants who viewed America as a land of opportunity continued to pour in.

For further reading, see the Appendix. For web resources, go to **http://college.hmco.com.**

6

The Duel for North America

1608–1763

*A torch lighted in the forests of
America set all Europe in conflagration.*

VOLTAIRE, C. 1756

As the seventeenth century neared its sunset, a titanic struggle was shaping up for mastery of the North American continent. The contest involved three Old World nations—Britain, France, and Spain—and it unavoidably swept up Native American peoples as well. From 1688 to 1763, four bitter wars convulsed Europe. All four of those conflicts were world wars. Fought on the waters and on the soil of two hemispheres, they amounted to a death struggle for domination in Europe as well as in the New World. Counting these first four clashes, nine world wars have been waged since 1688. The American people, whether as British subjects or as American citizens, proved unable to stay out of a single one of them. And one of those wars—known as the Seven Years' War in Europe and the French and Indian War in America—set the stage for America's independence.

France Finds a Foothold in Canada

Like England and Holland, France was a latecomer in the scramble for New World real estate, and for basically the same reasons. It was convulsed during the 1500s by foreign wars and domestic strife, including frightful clashes between Roman Catholics and Protestant Huguenots.

A new era dawned in 1598 when the Edict of Nantes, issued by the crown, granted limited toleration to French Protestants. Religious wars ceased, and in the new century France blossomed into the mightiest and most feared nation in Europe.

Success finally rewarded the exertions of France in the New World. In 1608, the year after Jamestown, the permanent beginnings of a vast empire were established at Quebec, a granite sentinel commanding the St. Lawrence River. The leading figure was Samuel de Champlain, an intrepid soldier and explorer whose energy and leadership fairly earned him the title "Father of New France."

Champlain entered into friendly relations—a fateful friendship—with the nearby Huron Indian tribes. At their request, he joined them in battle against their foes, the federated Iroquois tribes of the upper New York area. Two volleys from the "lightning sticks" of the whites routed the Iroquois, who left behind three dead and one wounded. France, to its sorrow, thus earned the lasting enmity of the Iroquois tribes, who thereafter hampered French penetration of the Ohio Valley, sometimes ravaging French settlements, and frequently serving as allies of the British in the prolonged struggle for supremacy on the continent.

The government of New France (Canada) finally fell under the direct control of the king after various commercial companies had faltered or failed. This royal regime was almost completely autocratic. The people elected no representative assemblies, as the English colonies did; nor did they enjoy the right of trial by jury.

Population in Catholic New France grew at a listless pace. As late as 1750 only sixty thousand or so whites inhabited New France. Landowning French peasants, unlike the dispossessed English tenant farmers who embarked for the British colonies, had little economic motive to move. Protestant Huguenots, who might have had a religious motive to migrate, were denied a refuge in this raw colony. The French government, in any case, favored its Caribbean island colonies, rich in sugar and rum, over the snow-cloaked wilderness of Canada.

New France Fans Out

New France did contain one valuable resource: the beaver. To adorn the heads of fashionable Europeans, French fur trappers ranged over the woods and waterways of North America in pursuit of beaver. These colorful *coureurs des bois* (runners of the woods) were also runners of risks—two-fisted drinkers, free spenders, free livers and lovers. They littered the land with scores of place names, including Baton Rouge (red stick), Terre Haute (high land), Des Moines (some monks), and Grand Teton (big breast).

Singing, paddle-swinging French voyageurs also recruited Indians into the fur business. But the Indians were decimated by the white man's diseases and debauched by his alcohol. Slaughtering beaver by the boatload also violated many Indian religious beliefs and sadly demonstrated the shattering effect that contact with Europeans wreaked on traditional Indian ways of life.

Pursuing the sleek-furred beaver ever deeper into the heart of the continent, French trappers and their Indian partners covered amazing distances. They trekked in a huge arc across the Great Lakes, into present-day Saskatchewan and Manitoba, along the valleys of the Platte, the Arkansas, and the Missouri, west to the Rockies, and south to the border of Spanish Texas. In the process, they all but extinguished the beaver population in many areas, inflicting incalculable ecological damage.

French Catholic missionaries, notably the Jesuits, labored zealously to save the Indians for

Quebec Scene, by Jean-Baptiste-Louis Franquelin, c. 1699 (detail) *The metal cooking pot and the Indians' clothing and blankets show the Native Americans' growing reliance on European trade goods.*

Christ and from the fur trappers. But though they made few permanent converts, the Jesuits played a vital role as explorers and geographers.

Other explorers sought neither souls nor pelts, but empire. To check Spanish penetration into the region around the Gulf of Mexico, ambitious Robert La Salle floated down the Mississippi in 1682 to the point where it mingles with the gulf. Three years later he tried to return to the territory he had named "Louisiana," but he failed to find the Mississippi delta. He landed instead in Spanish Texas and in 1687 was murdered by his mutinous men.

Persistent French officials planted several fortified posts in what is now Mississippi and Louisiana, the most important of which was New Orleans (1718). Commanding the mouth of the Mississippi River, this strategic semitropical outpost also tapped the fur and grain trade of the huge interior valley, especially the fertile Illinois country.

The Clash of Empires

The earliest contests among the European powers for control of North America, the War of the League of Augsburg and the War of Spanish Succession, known to the British colonists respectively as King William's War (1689–1697) and Queen Anne's War (1702–1713), mostly pitted British colonists against the French *coureurs des bois*, with both sides recruiting whatever Indian allies they could. Neither France nor Britain considered America worth the commitment of large detachments of regular troops, so the combatants in these conflicts waged a kind of guerrilla warfare. France's Indian allies ravaged with torch and tomahawk the British colonial frontiers from New York to Massachusetts. Spain, eventually allied with France, probed from its Florida base at outlying South Carolina settlements. For their part, the British colonists failed miserably in sallies against Quebec and Montreal but did temporarily seize the stronghold of Port Royal in Acadia (present-day Nova Scotia).

In the Peace of Utrecht (1713), victorious Britain acquired French-populated Acadia and the wintry wastes of Newfoundland and Hudson Bay. These immense tracts pinched the St. Lawrence settlements of France. The British also won limited trading rights

in Spanish America, but these later created much friction over smuggling. Ill feeling between Britain and Spain led to war in 1739, when the British captain Robert Jenkins, whose ear had been sliced off by a Spanish sword, returned to London with a tale of woe on his tongue and a shriveled ear in his hand. The War of Jenkins's Ear was confined to the Caribbean Sea and to the much-buffeted buffer colony of Georgia.

This small-scale scuffle with Spain in America soon merged with the large-scale War of Austrian Succession in Europe (called King George's War in America). Once again, France allied itself with Spain. And once again, a rustic force of New Englanders, with the help of the British fleet, captured the reputedly impregnable French fortress of Louisbourg on Cape Breton Island, which commanded the approaches to the St. Lawrence River. When the peace treaty of 1748 handed Louisbourg back to their French foe, the victorious New Englanders were outraged. The glory of their arms seemed tarnished by the wiles of Old World diplomats. Worse, Louisbourg was still a cocked pistol pointed at the heart of the American continent. France, powerful and unappeased, still clung to its vast holdings in North America.

George Washington Inaugurates War with France

As the dogfight intensified in the New World, the Ohio Valley became the chief bone of contention between the French and British. The Ohio country was the critical area into which the westward-pushing British would inevitably penetrate. It was the key to the continent that the French had to retain, particularly if they were going to link their Canadian holdings with those of the lower Mississippi Valley. By the mid-1700s the British colonists, painfully aware of these basic truths, were no longer so reluctant to bear the burdens of empire. Alarmed by French land-grabbing and cutthroat fur-trade competition in the Ohio Valley, they were determined to fight for their economic security and for the supremacy of their way of life in North America.

Rivalry for the lush lands of the upper Ohio Valley brought tensions to the snapping point. In 1749 a group of British colonial speculators, chiefly influential

Virginians, including the Washington family, had secured rights to some 500,000 acres in this region. In the same disputed wilderness, the French were in the process of erecting a chain of forts commanding the strategic Ohio River, including Fort Duquesne on the site of present-day Pittsburgh.

In 1754 the governor of Virginia ushered George Washington, a twenty-one-year-old surveyor and fellow Virginian, onto the stage of history. Washington was sent to the Ohio country as a lieutenant colonel in command of about 150 Virginia militiamen. Encountering a small detachment of French troops in the forest about forty miles from Fort Duquesne, the Virginians fired the first shots of the globe-girdling new war. The French leader was killed, and his men retreated. An exultant Washington wrote: "I heard the bullets whistle, and believe me, there is something charming in the sound." It soon lost its charm.

The French promptly returned with reinforcements, who surrounded Washington's hastily constructed bastion, Fort Necessity. After a ten-hour siege he was forced to surrender his entire command in July 1754—ironically on the fourth of July.

Global War and Colonial Disunity

The first three Anglo-French colonial wars had all started in Europe, but the tables were now reversed. The fourth struggle, known as the French and Indian War, began in America. Touched off by George Washington in the wilds of the Ohio Valley in 1754, it rocked along on an undeclared basis for two years and then widened into the most far-flung conflict the world had yet seen—the Seven Years' War. It was fought not only in America but in Europe, in the West Indies, in the Philippines, in Africa, and on the ocean. The Seven Years' War was a seven-seas war.

In Europe, Britain liberally subsidized Frederick the Great of Prussia to fight against his traditional enemy, France. The French wasted so much strength in the European bloodbath that they were unable to throw an adequate force into the New World. "America was conquered in Germany," declared British statesman William Pitt.

In previous colonial clashes, the Americans had revealed an astonishing lack of unity. Colonists who were nearest to hotspots had responded much more generously with volunteers and money than those enjoying the safety of remoteness. Now, with musketballs already whining in the Ohio country, the crisis demanded concerted action.

In 1754 the British government summoned an intercolonial congress to Albany, New York, near the Iroquois country. Travel-weary delegates from only seven of the thirteen colonies showed up. The immediate purpose was to keep the Iroquois chiefs loyal to the British in the spreading war.

The longer-range purpose at Albany was to achieve greater colonial unity and thus bolster the common defense against France. Leading this effort was wise and witty Benjamin Franklin. Before the Albany Congress had assembled, Franklin published the famous cartoon showing the separate colonies as parts of a disjointed snake, with the slogan, "Join, or die." Franklin gained the congress's approval for his well-devised but premature scheme of colonial home rule, but the individual colonies and the London regime both spurned it. To the colonists it did not seem to give enough independence; to the British officials, it seemed to give too much.

Braddock's Blundering and Its Aftermath

Led by haughty and stubborn General Edward Braddock, the British stumbled badly in their opening

Famous Cartoon by Benjamin Franklin   *Delaware and Georgia were omitted.*

clashes with the French and Indians. Braddock set out from Virginia in 1755 with a mixed force of two thousand British regulars and ill-disciplined colonial militiamen to capture Fort Duquesne. Experienced in European warfare, "Bulldog" Braddock was professionally contemptuous of colonial "buckskins" and their behind-the-trees method of fighting Indians.

Dragging heavy artillery through the dense forest, Braddock's expedition crept slowly to within a few miles of Fort Duquesne. There it encountered a much smaller French and Indian army. At first the enemy force was repulsed, but it quickly melted into the thickets and poured a murderous fire into the ranks of the redcoats. Braddock's energetic and fearless aide, George Washington, had two horses shot from under him and four bullet holes in his coat, and Braddock himself was mortally wounded. The entire British force was routed with appalling losses.

Inflamed by this easy victory, the Indians took to a wider warpath. The whole frontier from Pennsylvania to North Carolina, left virtually naked by Braddock's bloody defeat, felt their fury. Scalping forays occurred within eighty miles of Philadelphia, and in desperation the local authorities offered bounties for Indian scalps: $50 for a woman's and $130 for a warrior's.

The British launched a full-scale invasion of Canada in 1756, now that the undeclared war in America had at last merged into a world conflict. But they unwisely tried to attack a number of exposed wilderness posts simultaneously, instead of throwing all their strength at Quebec and Montreal. Ignoring such sound strategy, the British armies experienced defeat after defeat, both in America and in Europe.

Pitt's Palms of Victory

In the hour of crisis, Britain brought forth, as it repeatedly would, a superlative leader—William Pitt. A tall and imposing figure, whose flashing eyes were set in a hawklike face, Pitt was popularly known as the "Great Commoner." He drew much of his strength from the common people, who admired him so greatly that on occasion they kissed his horses.

In 1757 Pitt became the foremost leader in the London government. He wisely decided to concentrate the war effort on the vitals of Canada—the Quebec-Montreal area. Pitt first dispatched a powerful expedition in 1758 against Louisbourg. The frowning fortress, though greatly strengthened by the French, fell after a blistering siege. Wild rejoicing swept Britain, for this was the first significant British victory of the entire war.

Quebec was next on Pitt's list. For this crucial expedition he chose thirty-two-year-old James Wolfe, who had been an officer since the age of fourteen. In a daring move, Wolfe sent a detachment up a poorly guarded part of the rocky eminence protecting Quebec. This vanguard scaled the cliff, pulling itself upward by the bushes and showing the way for the others. In the morning the two armies faced each other on the Plains of Abraham just beyond the citadel walls, the British under Wolfe and the French under the Marquis de Montcalm. Both commanders fell fatally wounded, but the French were defeated and the city surrendered (see "Makers of America: The French," pp. 72–73).

The Battle of Quebec ranks as one of the most significant engagements in British and American history. When Montreal fell in 1760, the French flag had fluttered in Canada for the last time. By the peace settlement at Paris (1763), French power was thrown completely off the continent of North America, leaving behind a fertile French population that is to this day a strong minority in Canada. Great Britain thus emerged as the dominant power in North America, while taking its place as the leading naval power of the world.

Restless Colonists

Britain's colonists, baptized in fire, emerged with increased confidence in their military strength. They had borne the brunt of battle at first; they had fought bravely alongside the crack British regulars; and officers and men alike had gained valuable experience. In the closing days of the conflict some twenty thousand American recruits were under arms.

The French and Indian War, while bolstering colonial self-esteem, simultaneously shattered the myth of British invincibility. On Braddock's bloody field the "buckskin" militia had seen the demoralized regulars huddling helplessly together or fleeing their unseen enemy.

Ominously, friction had developed during the war between arrogant British officers and the raw

The French

King Louis XIV's dream of a bountiful empire in New France flickered out like a candle after the British conquered his French colonies in the eighteenth century. His former subjects in Quebec and the maritime provinces of Acadia had to suffer foreign governance in the aftermath of the French defeats in 1713 and 1763. Over the course of the next two centuries many eventually found their way to the United States.

The first French to leave Canada were the Acadians, the settlers of the seaboard region that now comprises Nova Scotia, New Brunswick, Prince Edward Island, and part of Maine. In 1713 the French crown ceded this territory to the British, who demanded that the Acadians either swear allegiance to Britain or withdraw to French territory. At first doing neither, they managed to escape reprisals until Le Grand Dérangement ("The Great Displacement") in 1755, when the British expelled them from the region at bayonet point. The Acadians fled far south to the French colony of Louisiana, where they settled among the sleepy bayous, planted sugar cane and sweet potatoes, practiced Roman Catholicism, and spoke the French dialect that came to be called Cajun (a corruption of the English word *Acadian*). The Cajun settlements were tiny and secluded, many of them accessible only by small boat.

For generations these insular people were scarcely influenced by developments outside their

Modern-Day Quebec *A bit of the Old World in the New.*

tight-knit communities. Not until the twentieth century did Cajun parents surrender their children to public schools and submit to a state law restricting French speech. Only in the 1930s, with a bridge-building spree engineered by Governor Huey Long, was the isolation of the bayou communities broken.

In 1763, as the French settlers of Quebec fell under British rule, a second group began to leave Canada. By 1840 what had been an irregular southward trickle of Quebecois swelled to a steady stream of people who were driven away mostly by lean harvests.

Most of them emigrated to work in New England's lumberyards and textile mills, gradually establishing permanent settlements in the northern woods. Like the Acadians, these later migrants from Quebec stubbornly preserved their Roman Catholicism. Both groups shared a passionate love of their French language, believing it to be the cement that bound them, their religion, and their culture together. As one French-Canadian explained: "Let us worship in peace and in our own tongue. All else may disappear but this must remain our badge."

Today, almost all Cajuns and New England French Canadians speak English. But their ethnic communities and traditions eloquently testify to the continued vitality of French culture in North American history.

colonial "boors." Displaying the professional soldier's scorn for amateurs, the British refused to recognize any American militia commission above the rank of captain—a demotion humiliating to "Colonel" George Washington. They also showed the usual condescension of snobs from the civilized Old Country toward the "scum" who had confessed failure by fleeing to the "outhouses of civilization." Energetic and hard-working American settlers, by contrast, believed themselves to be on the cutting edge of British civilization. They felt that they deserved credit rather than contempt for risking their lives to erect a New World empire.

British officials were further distressed by the reluctance of the colonists to support the common cause wholeheartedly. American shippers developed a reasonable but lucrative trade with the Spanish and French West Indies at the very time the British navy was trying to subdue them. Other self-centered colonists refused to provide troops and money for the conflict until Pitt reimbursed the colonies for their mounting expenditures.

The curse of intercolonial disunity, present from early days, had continued throughout the recent hostilities. It had been caused mainly by enormous distances and geographical barriers; by conflicting

Events of 1755–1760

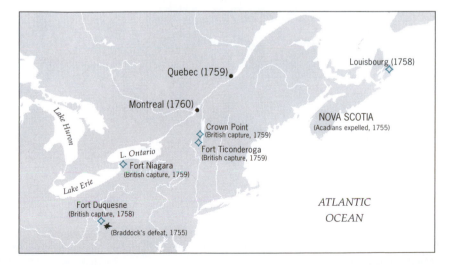

religions, from Catholic to Quaker; by various nation-alities, from German to Irish; by differing types of colonial governments; by scores of boundary dis-putes; and by the resentment that the crude back-country settlers felt against the aristocratic bigwigs.

Yet unity received some encouragement during the French and Indian War. When soldiers and states-men from widely separated colonies met around common campfires and council tables, they were often agreeably surprised to discover that they were all fellow Americans who generally spoke the same language and shared common ideals. Barriers of dis-unity began to melt, although a long and rugged road lay ahead before a coherent nation would emerge.

Americans: A People of Destiny

The removal of the French menace in Canada pro-foundly affected American attitudes. While the French hawk had been hovering in the North and West, the colonial chicks had been forced to cling close to the wings of their British mother hen. Now that the hawk was killed, they could range far afield with a new spirit of independence.

The French, humiliated by the British and sad-dened by the fate of Canada, consoled themselves with one wishful thought. Perhaps the loss of their American empire would one day result in Britain's loss of its American empire. In a sense the history of the United States began with the fall of Quebec and Montreal; the infant republic was conceived on the Plains of Abraham.

The Spanish and Indian menaces were also sub-stantially reduced. Spain was eliminated from Florida, although entrenched in Louisiana and New Orleans. As for the Indians, the Treaty of Paris dealt a harsh blow to the Creeks, Delawares, and other inte-rior tribes. Sensing the newly precarious position of the Indian peoples, the Ottawa chief Pontiac in 1763 led several tribes in a violent campaign to drive the British out of the Ohio country. Pontiac's warriors

North America Before 1754

North America After 1763   *(after French losses)*

seized Detroit in the spring of 1763 and eventually overran all but three British outposts west of the Appalachians.

The British retaliated swiftly and cruelly. Waging a primitive version of biological warfare, one British commander ordered blankets infected with smallpox to be distributed among the Indians. Such tactics crushed the uprising, and Pontiac's subsequent death brought an uneasy truce to the frontier. The bloody episode convinced the British of the need to stabilize relations with the western Indians and to station regular troops along the restless frontier, a measure for which they soon asked the colonists to foot the bill.

Land-hungry American colonists were now free to burst over the dam of the Appalachian Mountains and flood out over the verdant western lands. A tiny rivulet of pioneers like Daniel Boone had already trickled into Tennessee and Kentucky. Other courageous pioneers made their preparations for the long, dangerous trek over the mountains.

Then, out of a clear sky came a thunderbolt. The London government issued its Proclamation of 1763, which flatly prohibited settlement in the area beyond the Appalachians, pending further adjustments. The truth is that this hastily drawn document was not designed to oppress the colonists at all, but to work out the Indian problem fairly and prevent another bloody eruption like Pontiac's uprising.

But countless Americans, especially land speculators, were dismayed and angered. Was not the land beyond the mountains their birthright? Had they not, in addition, bought it with their blood in the recent war? In complete defiance of the proclamation, they clogged the westward trails. In 1765 an estimated one thousand wagons rolled through the town of Salisbury, North Carolina, on their way "up west." This wholesale flouting of royal authority boded ill for the longevity of British rule in America.

The French and Indian War caused the colonists to develop a new vision of their destiny. With the path cleared for the conquest of a continent, with their birthrate high and their energy boundless, they sensed that they were a potent people on the march.

Lordly Britons, whose suddenly swollen empire had tended to produce swollen heads, were in no mood for back talk. Puffed up over their recent victories, they were already annoyed with their unruly colonial subjects. The stage was thus set for a violent family quarrel.

Chronology

1598	Edict of Nantes.
1608	Champlain colonizes Quebec for France.
1682	La Salle explores Mississippi River to the Gulf of Mexico.
1689–1697	King William's War (War of the League of Augsburg).
1702–1713	Queen Anne's War (War of Spanish Succession).
1718	French found New Orleans.
1739	War of Jenkins's Ear.
1740–1748	King George's War (War of Austrian Succession).
1754	Washington battles French on frontier. Albany Congress.
1754–1763	French and Indian War (Seven Years' War).
1755	Braddock's defeat.
1757	Pitt emerges as leader of British government.
1759	Battle of Quebec.
1763	Peace of Paris. Pontiac's uprising. Proclamation of 1763.

For further reading, see the Appendix. For web resources, go to **http://college.hmco.com.**

7

The Road to Revolution

ᐭᕈ

1763–1775

The Revolution was effected before the war commenced.
The Revolution was in the minds and hearts of the people.

JOHN ADAMS, 1818

Victory in the Seven Years' War made Britain the master of a vastly enlarged imperial domain in North America. But victory—including the subsequent need to garrison ten thousand troops along the sprawling American frontier—was painfully costly. The London government therefore struggled after 1763 to compel the American colonists to shoulder some of the financial costs of empire. This change in British colonial policy reinforced an emerging sense of American political identity and helped to precipitate the American Revolution.

The eventual conflict was by no means inevitable. Indeed, given the tightening commercial, military, and cultural bonds between the colonies and mother country since the first crude settlements a century and a half earlier, it might be considered remarkable that the Revolution happened at all. The truth is that Americans were reluctant revolutionaries. Until late in the day, they sought only to claim the "rights of Englishmen," not to separate from the mother country. But what began as a squabble about economic policies soon exposed irreconcilable differences between Americans and Britons over cherished political principles. The ensuing clash gave birth to a new nation.

The Deep Roots of Revolution

In a broad sense, America was a revolutionary force from the day of its discovery. The New World nurtured new ideas about the nature of society, citizen, and government. In the Old World many humble folk had long lived in the shadow of graveyards that contained the bones of their ancestors for a thousand years past. Few people born into such changeless surroundings dared to question their superiors. But in the American wilderness ordinary people encountered a world that was theirs to make afresh.

Two ideas in particular had taken root in the minds of the American colonists by the mid-eighteenth century: One was what historians call *republicanism.* Looking to the models of the ancient Greek and Roman republics, exponents of republicanism defined a just society as one in which all citizens willingly subordinated their private, selfish interests to the common good. The stability of society and the authority of government thus depended on the virtue of the citizenry, especially its appetite for civic involvement.

A second idea that fundamentally shaped American political thought derived from a group of British political commentators known as the "radical Whigs." Widely read by the colonists, the Whigs feared the threat to liberty posed by the arbitrary power of the monarch and his ministers, especially the "corruption" revealed by patronage and bribes. Whigs warned citizens to be eternally vigilant against corruption and possible conspiracies to denude them of their hard-won liberties. Together, republican and Whig ideas predisposed the American colonists to be on hair-trigger alert against any threat to their rights.

The circumstances of colonial life had done much to bolster those attitudes. Dukes and princes, barons and bishops were unknown in the colonies, while property ownership and political participation were relatively widespread. The Americans had also grown accustomed to running their own affairs, largely unmolested by remote officials in London. Distance weakens authority; great distance weakens authority greatly. So it came as an especially jolting shock when Britain after 1763 tried to enclose its American colonists more snugly in its grip.

Mercantilism and Colonial Grievances

Britain's empire was acquired in a "fit of absentmindedness," an old saying goes, and there is much truth in the jest. Not one of the original thirteen colonies except Georgia was formally planted by the British government. All the others were haphazardly founded by trading companies, religious groups, or land speculators.

The British authorities nevertheless embraced a theory, called "mercantilism," that justified their control of the colonies. Mercantilists believed that wealth was power and that a country's economic wealth could be measured by the amount of gold or silver in its treasury. In order to amass gold or silver, a country needed to export more than it imported. Possessing colonies thus conferred distinct advantages, since the colonies could both supply raw materials to the mother country (thereby reducing the need for foreign imports) and provide a guaranteed market for exports.

The London government therefore looked on the American colonists more or less as tenants. They were expected to furnish raw products needed in the mother country; refrain from making finished products like cloth or beaver hats for export; buy imported manufactured goods exclusively from Britain; and not indulge in dangerous dreams of economic independence or, worse, self-government.

From time to time Parliament passed laws to regulate the mercantile system. The first of these, the Navigation Law of 1650, required that all commerce flowing to and from the colonies must be transported only in British (including colonial) vessels. Subsequent laws stipulated that European goods destined for America had to be landed first in Britain, where tariff duties could be collected and British middlemen would take a slice of the profits. American merchants also had to ship certain "enumerated" products, notably tobacco, exclusively to Britain, even though prices might be better elsewhere.

British policy also inflicted a currency shortage on the colonies. Since the colonists bought more from Britain than they sold there, the difference had to be made up in hard cash. Every year gold and silver coins, mostly from the Spanish and French West Indies, drained out of the colonies, creating an acute money shortage. To facilitate everyday purchases, the colonists resorted to using butter, nails, pitch, and feathers for purposes of exchange.

Currency issues came to a boil when dire financial need finally forced many of the colonies to issue paper money, which swiftly depreciated. British merchants and creditors squawked so loudly that Parliament prohibited the colonial legislatures from printing paper currency and from passing indulgent bankruptcy laws—practices that might harm British merchants.

The British crown also reserved the right to nullify any colonial legislation that might work mischief with the mercantile system. This royal veto was in fact used rather sparingly—just 469 times in connection with 8,563 laws. But the colonists nevertheless fiercely resented its very existence—another example of how principle could weigh more heavily than practice in fueling colonial grievances.

The Merits and Menace of Mercantilism

In theory, the British mercantile system was thoroughly selfish and deliberately oppressive. But the truth is that until 1763 the various Navigation Laws imposed no intolerable burden, mainly because they were loosely enforced. Enterprising colonial merchants early learned to disregard or evade troublesome restrictions. Some of the first American fortunes, like that of John Hancock, were amassed by wholesale smuggling.

Americans also reaped direct benefits from the mercantile system. If the colonies existed for the benefit of the mother country, it was hardly less true that Britain existed for the benefit of the colonies. London paid liberal bounties to colonial producers of ships' parts, over the protests of British competitors. Virginia tobacco planters enjoyed a monopoly in the British market. The colonists also benefited from the protection of the world's mightiest navy and a strong, seasoned army of redcoats—all without a penny of cost.

But even when painted in its rosiest colors, the mercantile system burdened the colonists with annoying liabilities. Mercantilism stifled economic initiative and imposed a rankling dependency on British agents and creditors. Most grievously, many Americans simply found the mercantilist system debasing. They felt used, kept in a state of perpetual economic adolescence, and never allowed to come of age. As Benjamin Franklin wrote in 1775:

Paul Revere, by John Singleton Copley, c. 1768   *This painting of the famed silversmith-horseman challenged convention—and reflected the new democratic spirit of the age—by portraying an artisan in working clothes. Notice how Copley has depicted the serene confidence of the master craftsman and Revere's quiet pride in his work.*

We have an old mother that peevish is grown;
She snubs us like children that scarce walk
    alone;
She forgets we're grown up and have sense of
    our own.

Revolution broke out, as Theodore Roosevelt later remarked, because Britain failed to recognize an emerging nation when it saw one.

The Stamp Tax Uproar

Victory-flushed Britain emerged from the Seven Years' War holding one of the biggest empires in the world—

and also, less happily, the biggest debt, some £140 million, about half of which had been incurred defending the American colonies. To justify and service that debt, British officials now moved to redefine their relationship with their North American colonies.

Prime Minister George Grenville first aroused the resentment of the colonists in 1763 by ordering the British navy to enforce the Navigation Laws. He also secured from Parliament the so-called Sugar Act of 1764, the first law ever passed by that body for raising tax revenue in the colonies for the crown. Among various provisions, it increased the duty on foreign sugar imported from the West Indies. After bitter protests from the colonists, the duties were lowered substantially, and the agitation died down. But resentment was kept burning by the Quartering Act of 1765. This measure required certain colonies to provide food and quarters for British troops.

Then in the same year, 1765, Grenville proposed the most odious measure of all: a stamp tax, to raise revenues to support the new military force. The Stamp Act mandated the use of stamped paper or the affixing of stamps certifying payment of tax. Stamps were required on bills of sale for about fifty trade items as well as on certain types of commercial and legal documents, including playing cards, pamphlets, newspapers, diplomas, bills of lading, and marriage licenses.

Grenville regarded all these measures as reasonable and just. He was simply asking the Americans to pay their fair share of the costs for their own defense, through taxes that were already familiar in Britain. In fact, Englishmen for two generations had endured a stamp tax far heavier than that passed for the colonies.

Yet the Americans were angrily aroused at what they regarded as Grenville's fiscal aggression. The new laws did not merely pinch their pocketbooks; far more ominously, Grenville seemed also to be striking at the local liberties they had come to assume as a matter of right. Thus some colonial assemblies defiantly refused to comply with the Quartering Act, or voted for only a fraction of the supplies that it called for.

Worst of all, Grenville's noxious legislation seemed to jeopardize the basic rights of the colonists as Britons. Both the Sugar Act and the Stamp Act provided for trying offenders in the hated admiralty courts, where juries were not allowed. The burden of proof was on the defendants, who were assumed to be guilty unless they could prove themselves innocent. Trial by jury and the precept of "innocent until proved guilty" were ancient privileges that British people everywhere, including the American colonists, held most dear.

And why was a British army needed at all in the colonies, now that the French were expelled from the continent and Pontiac's warriors crushed? Could its real purpose be to whip rebellious colonists themselves into line? Many Americans, weaned on the radical Whigs' suspicion of all authority, began to sniff the strong scent of a conspiracy to strip them of their historic liberties. They lashed back violently, and the Stamp Act became the target that drew their most ferocious fire.

Angry throats raised the cry, "No taxation without representation." There was some irony in the slogan, because the seaports and tidewater towns that were most wrathful against the Stamp Act had long denied full representation to their own backcountry pioneers. But now the aggravated colonists took the high ground of principle.

The Americans made a distinction between "legislation" and "taxation." They conceded the right of Parliament to legislate about matters that affected the entire empire, including the regulation of trade. But they steadfastly denied the right of Parliament, in which no Americans were seated, to impose taxes on Americans. Only their own elected colonial legislatures, the Americans insisted, could legally tax them.

Grenville dismissed these American protests as hairsplitting absurdities. The power of Parliament was supreme and undivided, he asserted, and in any case the Americans were represented in Parliament. Elaborating the theory of "virtual representation," Grenville claimed that every member of Parliament represented all British subjects, even those Americans in Boston or Charleston who had never voted for a member of the London Parliament. The Americans scoffed at the notion of virtual representation.

Thus the principle of no taxation without representation was supremely important, and the colonists clung to it with tenacious consistency. When the British replied that the sovereign power of government could not be divided between "legislative" authority in London and "taxing" authority in the colonies, they forced the Americans to deny the authority of Parliament altogether and to begin to consider their own political independence. This chain of logic eventually led to revolutionary consequences.

Parliament Forced to Repeal the Stamp Act

Among colonial outcries against the hated stamp tax, the most conspicuous was the Stamp Act Congress, held in New York City in 1765. Twenty-seven distinguished delegates from nine colonies petitioned the king and Parliament to repeal the repugnant legislation. The Stamp Act Congress made little splash in America at the time, but it was one more significant step toward intercolonial unity.

More effective than the congress was the widespread adoption of nonimportation agreements against British goods. Homespun woolen garments became fashionable, and the eating of lamb chops was discouraged so that the wool-bearing sheep would be allowed to mature. Nonimportation agreements were in fact a promising stride toward union; they spontaneously united the American people for the first time in common action.

Mobilizing in support of nonimportation gave ordinary men and women new opportunities to participate in colonial protests. Joining consumer boycotts, groups of women assembled in public to hold spinning bees and make homespun cloth as a replacement for shunned British textiles. Such public defiance helped spread revolutionary fervor throughout American colonial society.

Sometimes violence accompanied colonial protests. Crying, "Liberty, property, and no stamps," ardent Sons and Daughters of Liberty enforced the nonimportation agreements against violators, often with a generous coat of tar and feathers. Patriot mobs ransacked the houses of unpopular officials and hanged stamp agents on liberty poles, albeit in effigy.

Shaken by colonial commotion, the machinery for collecting the tax broke down. On that dismal day in 1765 when the new act was to go into effect, the stamp agents had all been forced to resign, and there was no one to sell the stamps. While flags flapped at half-mast, the law was openly and flagrantly defied—or rather, nullified.

Britain was hard hit. Merchants, manufacturers, and shippers suffered from the colonial nonimportation agreements, and hundreds of laborers were thrown out of work. Loud demands converged on Parliament for repeal of the Stamp Act. But many of the members could not understand why 7.5 million Britons had to pay heavy taxes to protect the colonies, whereas some 2 million colonists refused to pay for only one-third of the cost of their own defense.

After a stormy debate, Parliament in 1766 grudgingly repealed the Stamp Act. But virtually in the same breath, it provocatively passed the Declaratory Act, reaffirming Parliament's right "to bind" the colonies "in all cases whatsoever." The British government thereby drew its line in the sand. It defined the constitutional principle it would not yield: absolute and unqualified sovereignty over its North American colonies. The colonists had already drawn their own battle line by making it clear that they wanted a measure of sovereignty of their own, and would undertake drastic action to secure it. The stage was set for a continuing confrontation.

The Townshend Tea Tax and the Boston "Massacre"

Control of the British ministry was now seized by the gifted but erratic "Champagne Charley" Townshend, a man who could deliver brilliant speeches in Parliament even while drunk. Rashly promising to pluck feathers from the colonial goose with a minimum of squawking, he persuaded Parliament in 1767 to pass the Townshend Acts. The most important of these new regulations was a light import duty on glass, white lead, paper, paint, and tea. Townshend made this tax, unlike the Stamp Act, an indirect customs duty payable at American ports.

Flushed with their recent victory over the stamp tax, the colonists were in a rebellious mood. The impost on tea was especially irksome, for an estimated 1 million people drank the refreshing brew twice a day.

Hardest to swallow, the new Townshend revenues would be used to pay the salaries of the royal governors and judges in America. The ultrasuspicious

Americans, who had long beaten the royal governors into line by controlling the purse, regarded Townshend's tax as another attempt to enchain them. Their worst fears took on a greater reality when the London government, after passing the Townshend taxes, suspended the New York legislature in 1767 for failure to comply with the Quartering Act.

Nonimportation agreements, previously potent, were quickly revived against the Townshend Acts. But they proved less effective than those devised against the Stamp Act. The colonists, again enjoying prosperity, took the new tax less seriously than might have been expected, largely because it was light and indirect. They found, moreover, that they could secure smuggled tea at a cheap price, and consequently smugglers increased their activities, especially in Massachusetts.

British officials, faced with a breakdown of law and order, landed two regiments of troops in Boston in 1768. With liberty-loving colonists mercilessly taunting the redcoats, a clash between citizens and soldiers was inevitable. On the evening of March 5,

1770, a crowd of some sixty townspeople set upon a squad of about ten "bloody backs," one of whom was hit by a club and another of whom was knocked down. Acting apparently without orders but under extreme provocation, the troops opened fire and killed or wounded eleven "innocent" citizens. One of the first to die was Crispus Attucks, described by contemporaries as a "mulatto" and a leader of the mob. Both sides were in some degree to blame, and in the subsequent trial only two of the soldiers were found guilty of manslaughter.

The Seditious Committees of Correspondence

By 1770 King George III was strenuously attempting to assert the power of the British monarchy. Earnest, industrious, stubborn, and lustful for power, he surrounded himself with cooperative "yes men," notably his corpulent Tory prime minister, Lord North.

The Boston Massacre, 1770
This widely reprinted engraving by Paul Revere was both art and propaganda.

The ill-timed Townshend Acts, though producing near-rebellion, had failed to produce revenue. Net proceeds from the tax in one year were a paltry £295, and during that time the annual military costs to Britain in the colonies had mounted to £170,000. Nonimportation agreements, though feebly enforced, were pinching British manufacturers. The government of Lord North, bowing to various pressures, finally persuaded Parliament to repeal the Townshend revenue duties. But the three-pence tax on tea was retained to keep alive the principle of parliamentary taxation.

Flames of discontent in America, fanned by periodic incidents involving British officials, were further kindled by a master propagandist and engineer of rebellion, Samuel Adams. This cousin of John Adams was so unimpressive in appearance that his friends had to buy him a presentable suit of clothes when he left Massachusetts on intercolonial business. Zealous, tenacious, and courageous, Samuel Adams cherished a deep faith in the common people.

Samuel Adams's signal contribution was to organize in Massachusetts the local committees of correspondence. After he had formed the first one in Boston during 1772, some eighty towns in the colony speedily set up similar organizations. Their chief function was to spread the spirit of resistance by exchanging letters and thus keep alive opposition to British policy.

Intercolonial committees of correspondence were the next logical step. Virginia led the way in 1773 by creating such a body as a standing committee of the House of Burgesses. Within a short time every colony had established a central committee through which it could exchange ideas and information with other colonies. These intercolonial groups were supremely significant in stimulating and disseminating sentiment in favor of united action. They evolved directly into the first American congresses.

Tea Parties at Boston and Elsewhere

Thus far—that is, by 1773—nothing had happened to make rebellion inevitable. Nonimportation was weakening. Increasing numbers of colonists were reluctantly paying the tea tax because the legal tea was cheaper than the smuggled tea.

A new ogre entered the picture in 1773. The powerful British East India Company, overburdened with 17 million pounds of unsold tea, was facing bankruptcy. If it collapsed, the London government would lose heavily in tax revenue. The ministry therefore decided to assist the company by awarding it a complete monopoly of the American tea business. The giant corporation would now be able to sell the coveted leaves more cheaply than ever before, even with the three-pence tax tacked on. But to the stubborn Americans, principle remained far more important than price.

Fatefully, the British officials decided to enforce the letter of the law. Once more, the colonists rose up in wrath to defy it. Not a single one of the thousands of chests of tea shipped by the East India Company ever reached the hands of the consignees. In Philadelphia and New York, mass demonstrations forced the tea-bearing ships to return to Britain. At Annapolis, Marylanders burned both cargo and vessel, while proclaiming "Liberty and Independence or death in pursuit of it."

Only in Boston did a British official stubbornly refuse to be cowed. Massachusetts governor Thomas Hutchinson agreed that the tea tax was unjust, but believed even more strongly that the colonists had no right to flout the law. Hutchinson further inflamed the situation when he declared that "an abridgement of what are called English liberties" was necessary for the preservation of law and order in the colonies—apparently confirming the darkest conspiracy theories of the American radicals. Provoked beyond restraint, a band of Bostonians, clumsily disguised as Indians, boarded the docked tea ships on December 16, 1773. They smashed open 342 chests and dumped the contents into Boston harbor. A silent crowd watched approvingly from the wharves as salty tea was brewed for the fish.

Reactions varied. Radicals exulted in the people's zeal for liberty. Conservatives complained that the destruction of private property violated the fundamental norms of civil society. As Hutchinson fled to Britain, the British authorities determined to whip the upstart colonists into line. Granting the Americans a measure of home rule at this stage might still have prevented rebellion, but few Britons of that era were blessed with such wisdom. Among those who were

The Boston Tea Party, December 16, 1773 *Crying "Boston harbor a tea-pot this night," Sons of Liberty disguised as Indians hurled chests of tea into the sea to protest the tax on tea and to make sure that the tea's cheap price did not prove an "invincible temptation" to the people.*

was Edmund Burke, the great conservative political theorist and stout champion of the American cause. "To tax and to please, no more than to love and be wise," he stoically remarked, "is not given to men."

Parliament Passes the "Intolerable Acts"

An irate Parliament responded speedily to the Boston Tea Party with measures that brewed a revolution. By huge majorities in 1774 it passed a series of acts designed to chastise Boston in particular, and Massachusetts in general.

Most drastic of all was the Boston Port Act. It closed the tea-stained harbor until damages were paid and order could be ensured. By other "Intolerable Acts"—as they were called in America—many of the chartered rights of colonial Massachusetts were swept away. Restrictions were likewise placed on the precious town meetings. Contrary to previous practice, enforcing officials who killed colonists in the line of duty could now be sent to Britain for trial. There, suspicious Americans assumed, they would be likely to get off scot-free.

By a fateful coincidence, the "Intolerable Acts" were accompanied in 1774 by the Quebec Act. Passed at the same time, it was erroneously regarded in English-speaking America as part of the British reaction to the turbulence in Boston. Actually, the Quebec Act was a good law in bad company. For many years the British government had debated how it should administer the sixty thousand or so conquered French subjects in Canada, and it had finally framed this farsighted and statesmanlike measure. The French Canadians were guaranteed their Catholic religion. They were also permitted to retain many of their old customs and institutions, which did not include a representative assembly or trial by jury in civil cases. In addition, the old boundaries of the Province of Quebec were extended southward all the way to the Ohio River.

The Quebec Act, from the viewpoint of the French Canadians, was a shrewd and conciliatory measure. If Britain had only shown as much foresight in dealing with its English-speaking colonies, it might not have lost them.

But from the viewpoint of the British-American colonists, the Quebec Act was especially noxious. All the other "Intolerable Acts" slapped directly at Massachusetts, but this one had a much wider range. It seemed to set a dangerous precedent in America against jury trials and popular assemblies. It alarmed land speculators, who were distressed to see the huge trans-Allegheny area snatched from their grasp. It aroused anti-Catholics, who were shocked by the extension of Roman Catholic jurisdiction southward into a huge territory once earmarked for Protestantism—a region about as large as the thirteen original colonies.

The Continental Congress and Bloodshed

American dissenters, chafing over the Quebec Act and the other "Intolerable Acts," responded sympathetically to the plight of Massachusetts. Their most memorable step was the summoning of a Continental Congress, which met in Philadelphia from September 5 to October 26, 1774. John Adams played a stellar role at this First Continental Congress. Eloquently swaying his colleagues to a revolutionary course, he helped defeat by the narrowest of margins a proposal by moderates for a species of American home rule under British direction.

The most significant action of the Congress was the creation of The Association. Unlike previous nonimportation agreements, this one called for a *complete* boycott of British goods: nonimportation, nonexportation, and nonconsumption. Yet it is important to note that the delegates were not yet calling for independence. They sought merely to repeal the offensive legislation and return to the happy days before parliamentary taxation. Resistance had not yet ripened into open rebellion.

But the fatal drift toward war continued. Parliament rejected the Continental Congress's petitions. In America, chickens squawked and tar kettles bubbled as violators of The Association were tarred and feathered. Muskets were gathered, men began to drill openly, and a clash seemed imminent.

In April 1775, the British commander in Boston sent a detachment of troops to nearby Lexington and Concord. They intended to seize stores of colonial gunpowder and also to bag the "rebel" ringleaders, Samuel Adams and John Hancock. At Lexington the colonial "Minute Men" refused to disperse rapidly enough, and shots were fired that killed eight Americans and wounded several more. The redcoats

pushed on to Concord, whence they were forced to retreat by the rough-and-ready Americans, whom Emerson immortalized:

> By the rude bridge that arched the flood,
> Their flag to April's breeze unfurled,
> Here once the embattled farmers stood,
> And fired the shot heard round the world.*

The bewildered British, fighting off murderous fire from militiamen crouched behind thick stone walls, finally regained the sanctuary of Boston. Licking their wounds, they could count about three hundred casualties, including some seventy killed. Britain now had a war on its hands.

Imperial and Colonial Strengths and Weaknesses

Aroused Americans had brashly rebelled against a mighty empire. The population odds were about three to one against the rebels—some 7.5 million Britons to 2.5 million colonists. The odds in monetary wealth and naval power overwhelmingly favored the mother country.

Britain boasted a professional army of some fifty thousand men, as compared with the numerous but wretchedly trained American militia. King George III, in addition, hired some thirty thousand German soldiers—so-called Hessians. The British also enlisted the services of about fifty thousand American Loyalists and many Indians, who inflamed long stretches of the frontier.

Yet Britain was weaker than it seemed at first glance. British troops had to be detached to monitor the smoking volcano of oppressed Ireland. Recently defeated France was bitterly awaiting an opportunity to stab Britain in the back. The London government, under stubborn George III and his pliant Tory prime minister, Lord North, was confused and inept.

Many earnest and God-fearing Britons had no desire to kill their American cousins. Many British Whigs actually believed that the battle for their own

---

*Ralph Waldo Emerson, Concord Hymn.

Quebec Before and After 1774   *Young Alexander Hamilton voiced the fears of many colonists when he warned that the Quebec Act of 1774 would introduce "priestly tyranny" into Canada, making that country another Spain or Portugal. "Does not your blood run cold," he asked, "to think that an English Parliament should pass an act for the establishment of arbitrary power and Popery in such a country?"*

Map labels: Quebec, QUEBEC, Montreal, NOVA SCOTIA, NEW YORK, PENNSYLVANIA, VIRGINIA, Mississippi R., Ohio R.

Legend: Quebec before 1774 / Quebec after 1774

liberties was being fought in America. If George III triumphed there, his rule at home might become more tyrannical. This outspoken sympathy in Britain, though plainly a minority voice, greatly encouraged the Americans. If they continued their resistance long enough, the Whigs might come to power and deal generously with them.

Britain's army in America had to operate under endless difficulties. The generals were second-rate; the soldiers, though on the whole capable, were brutally treated. Provisions were often scarce, rancid, and wormy.

Other handicaps loomed. The redcoats had to conquer the Americans; simply restoring the pre-1763 status quo would be a victory for the colonists. Britain was operating some 3,000 miles from its home base, and distance added greatly to the delays and uncertainties arising from storms and other mishaps.

America's geographical expanse was enormous: roughly 1,000 by 600 miles. The united colonies had no urban nerve center like France's Paris. In the war, British armies captured every city of any size, yet like a boxer punching a feather pillow, they made little more than a dent in the entire country. The Americans wisely traded space for time.

The revolutionists were also blessed with outstanding leadership. George Washington was a giant among men. Master diplomat Benjamin Franklin eventually secured open foreign aid from France. In a class by himself was Marquis de Lafayette, a wealthy young French noble who loved glory and liberty. Lafayette became a major general in the colonial army at age nineteen, and the services of the teenage "French gamecock" helped secure further aid from France.

Other conditions aided the Americans. They were fighting defensively on their own terrain. In agriculture, the colonies were mainly self-sustaining, like a kind of Robinson Crusoe's island. The Americans also enjoyed the moral advantage that came from belief in a just cause.

Yet the American rebels were badly organized for war. Almost fatally lacking in unity, the new nation lurched forward uncertainly like an uncoordinated centipede. Even the Continental Congress, which directed the conflict, was hardly more than a debating society, and it grew feebler as the struggle dragged on. Disorganized colonists fought almost the entire war before adopting a written constitution—the Articles of Confederation—in 1781.

Economic difficulties were nearly insuperable. With metallic money drained away and taxation an explosive issue, the Continental Congress was forced to print "Continental" paper money in great amounts. As this currency poured from the presses, it depreciated until the expression "not worth a Continental" became current. Inflation of the currency inevitably skyrocketed prices, hitting the families of soldiers at the front especially hard. Debtors easily acquired handfuls of the quasi-worthless money and gleefully paid their debts "without mercy."

A Thin Line of Heroes

Basic military supplies in the colonies were dangerously scanty, especially firearms. Legend to the contrary, colonial Americans were not a well-armed people. Not a single gun factory existed in the colonies, and an imported musket cost the equivalent of two months' salary for a skilled artisan. Small wonder that Benjamin Franklin seriously proposed arming American troops with bows and arrows

Other shortages bedeviled the rebels. At Valley Forge, Pennsylvania, shivering American soldiers went without bread for three successive days in the cruel winter of 1777–1778. In one southern campaign, some men fainted for lack of food.

Manufactured goods were generally in short supply in agricultural America, and clothing and shoes were appallingly scarce. The path of the Patriot fighting men was often marked by bloody snow. At frigid Valley Forge, during one anxious period, twenty-eight hundred men were barefoot or nearly naked.

American militiamen were numerous but also highly unreliable. Able-bodied American males—perhaps several hundred thousand of them—had received rudimentary training, and many of these recruits served for short terms in the rebel armies. But poorly trained plowboys could not stand up in the open field against professional British troops advancing with bare bayonets. Many of these undisciplined warriors would, in the words of Washington, "fly from their own shadows."

A few thousand regulars—perhaps seven or eight thousand at war's end—were finally whipped into shape by stern drillmasters. Notable among them was an organizational genius, the salty German Baron von Steuben. He spoke no English when he reached America, but he soon taught his men that bayonets were not for broiling beefsteaks over open fires. As they gained experience, these soldiers of the Continental line could hold their own in open battle against crack British troops.

Blacks also fought and died for the American cause. Although many states initially barred them from militia service, by war's end more than five thousand blacks, most from the northern states, had enlisted in the American armed forces. Blacks fought at Trenton, Brandywine, Saratoga, and other important battles.

African-Americans also served on the British side. Lord Dunmore, royal governor of Virginia, issued a proclamation offering freedom to any enslaved black in Virginia who joined the British army. In time, thousands of blacks fled plantations in response to these promises of emancipation. The British kept their word, to some at least, evacuating as many as fourteen thousand "Black Loyalists" to Nova Scotia, Jamaica, and England after the war.

Morale in the Revolutionary army was badly undermined by American profiteers. Putting profits before patriotism, these speculators sold supplies to the British and made profits of 50 to 200 percent on army garb while the American army was freezing at Valley Forge. The faltering of revolutionary zeal meant that Washington never had as many as twenty thousand effective troops in one place at one time.

The brutal truth is that only a select minority of colonists attached themselves to the cause of independence with a spirit of selfless devotion. These were the dedicated souls who bore the burden of battle and the risks of defeat; these were the freedom-loving Patriots who deserved the gratitude and esteem of generations yet unborn. Seldom have so few done so much for so many.

Chronology

1650	First Navigation Laws to control colonial commerce.
1763	French and Indian War (Seven Years' War) ends.
1764	Sugar Act.
1765	Quartering Act. Stamp Act. Stamp Act Congress.
1766	Declaratory Act.
1767	Townshend Acts passed. New York legislature suspended by Parliament.
1768	British troops occupy Boston.
1770	Boston Massacre. All Townshend Acts except tea tax repealed.
1772	Committees of correspondence formed.
1773	British East India Company granted tea monopoly. Governor Hutchinson's actions provoke Boston Tea Party.
1774	"Intolerable Acts." Quebec Act. First Continental Congress. The Association boycotts British goods.
1775	Battles of Lexington and Concord.

VARYING VIEWPOINTS

Whose Revolution?

Historians once assumed that the American Revolution was just another chapter in the unfolding story of human liberty—a kind of divinely ordained progress toward perfection in human affairs. This approach is often called the Whig view of history.

By the early twentieth century, the concept was sharply challenged by so-called progressive historians, who argued that not divine destiny but a sharp struggle among different social groups brought about change. For example, Carl Becker saw the Revolution as stemming from class conflict and ending in a truly transformed social order. As one of them put it, the Revolution was not only about "home rule" within the British Empire but about "who should rule at home" in America.

In the 1950s, the progressive historians fell out of favor as the political climate became more conservative. Historians such as Robert Brown and Edmund Morgan downplayed the role of class conflict in the Revolutionary era, but emphasized that colonists of all ranks shared a commitment to certain fundamental political principles.

Since the 1950s, two broad interpretations have contended with each other and perpetuated controversy over whether political ideals or economic and social realities were most responsible for the Revolution. The first, articulated most prominently by Bernard Bailyn, has emphasized inherent ideological and psychological factors. Bailyn argued that the colonists, incited by their reading of earlier English theorists, were extraordinarily suspicious of any attempts to tighten the imperial reins. When confronted with new taxes and imperial regulations, they took up armed insurrection in defense of their intellectual commitment to liberty.

A second school of historians, inspired by the social movements of the turbulent 1960s and 1970s, has revived the progressive interpretation of the Revolution. Gary Nash in *An Urban Crucible* (1979) and Edward Countryman in *A People in Revolution* (1981)

see attacks by laborers on political elites as evidence of a society breeding revolution from within, quite aside from British provocations. The neoprogressives argue that the varying material circumstances of American participants gave the Revolution a less unified and more complex ideological underpinning than the idealistic historians had previously suggested. The dialogue between proponents of "ideas" and "interests" is gradually leading to a more nuanced meeting of the two views.

America Secedes from the Empire

1775–1783

These are the times that try men's souls. The summer soldier and the sunshine patriot will, in this crisis, shrink from the service of their country; but he that stands it now, deserves the love and thanks of man and woman.

THOMAS PAINE, DECEMBER 1776

Bloodshed at Lexington and Concord in April 1775 was a clarion call to arms. About twenty thousand musket-bearing "Minute Men" swarmed around Boston, there to coop up the outnumbered British.

The Second Continental Congress met in Philadelphia the next month, on May 10, 1775; and this time the full slate of thirteen colonies was represented. The conservative element in the Congress was still strong, despite the bloodshed in Massachusetts. There was still no well-defined sentiment for independence—merely a desire to continue fighting in the hope that king and Parliament would consent to a redress of grievances. Congress hopefully drafted new appeals to the British people and king—appeals that were spurned. Anticipating a possible rebuff, the delegates also adopted measures to raise money and to create an army and a navy. The British and the Americans now teetered on the brink of all-out warfare.

Congress Drafts George Washington

Perhaps the most important single action of the Congress was to select George Washington, one of its members already in officer's uniform, to head the hastily improvised army besieging Boston. This choice was made with considerable misgivings. The tall, powerfully built, dignified, blue-eyed Virginia planter, then forty-three, had never risen above the rank of colonel in the militia. His largest command had numbered only twelve hundred men, and that had been some twenty years earlier. Falling short of true military genius, Washington would actually lose more pitched battles than he won.

But the distinguished Virginian was gifted with outstanding powers of leadership and immense strength of character. He radiated patience, courage, self-discipline, and a sense of justice. He was a great moral force rather than a great military mind—a symbol and a rallying point. People instinctively trusted him. As a man of wealth, by inheritance and by marriage, Washington could not be accused of being a fortune seeker. He insisted on serving without pay, though he would keep a careful wartime expense account amounting to more than $100,000.

The Continental Congress initially selected Washington more for political reasons than for his leadership qualities. Americans from other sections distrusted the large New England army gathering around Boston, and prudence suggested a commander from Virginia.

Bunker Hill and Hessian Hirelings

The clash of arms continued on a strangely contradictory basis. On the one hand, the Americans were emphatically affirming their loyalty to the king and earnestly voicing their desire to patch up existing difficulties. On the other hand, they were raising armies and shooting down His Majesty's soldiers. This curious war of inconsistency was fought for fourteen long months—from April 1775 to July 1776—before the fateful plunge into independence was taken.

Gradually the tempo of warfare increased. In May 1775 a tiny American force, under Ethan Allen and Benedict Arnold, surprised and captured the British garrisons at Ticonderoga and Crown Point, on the scenic lakes of upper New York. A priceless store of gunpowder and artillery for the siege of Boston was thus secured.

In June 1775 the colonists seized a hill, now known as Bunker Hill (actually Breed's Hill), from which they menaced the enemy in Boston. The British blundered bloodily when they launched a frontal attack up its slopes with three thousand men. Sharpshooting Americans, numbering fifteen hundred and strongly entrenched, mowed down the advancing redcoats in a frightful slaughter. But the

colonists' scanty store of gunpowder finally gave out, and they were forced to abandon the hill in disorder. With two more such victories, remarked the French foreign minister, the British would have no army left in America.

Following Bunker Hill, the king slammed the door on all hope of reconciliation. In August 1775 he formally proclaimed the colonies in rebellion. The next month he widened the chasm by hiring thousands of German troops, shocking colonists who feared the so-called Hessians' exaggerated reputation for butchery. Actually, the Hessian hirelings turned

Washington at Verplanck's Point, New York, 1782, Reviewing the French Troops After the Victory at Yorktown, by John Trumbull, 1790 *This noted American artist accentuated Washington's height (6 feet, 2 inches) by showing him towering over his horse. Washington so appreciated this portrait of himself that he hung it in his dining room at his home at Mount Vernon, Virginia.*

out to be more interested in booty than in duty. Hundreds of them finally deserted and remained in America as respected citizens.

The Abortive Conquest of Canada

The unsheathed sword continued to take its toll. In October 1775, on the eve of a cruel winter, the British burned Falmouth (Portland), Maine. In that same autumn the rebels daringly undertook a two-pronged invasion of Canada. American leaders believed, erroneously, that the conquered French were explosively restive under the British yoke. A successful assault on Canada would add a fourteenth colony while depriving Britain of a valuable base for striking at the colonies in revolt. But this large-scale attack, involving some two thousand American troops, contradicted the claim of the colonists that they were merely fighting defensively for a redress of grievances. Invasion northward was undisguised offensive warfare.

This bold stroke for Canada narrowly missed success. One invading column under the Irish-born General Richard Montgomery pushed up the Lake Champlain route and captured Montreal. He was joined at Quebec by the bedraggled army of General Benedict Arnold, whose men had been reduced to eating dogs and shoe leather during their grueling march through the Maine woods. An assault on Quebec, launched on the last day of 1775, was beaten off. The able Montgomery was killed; the dashing Arnold was wounded in one leg. Scattered remnants under his command retreated up the St. Lawrence River, reversing Montgomery's route. French-Canadian leaders, who had been generously treated by the British in the Quebec Act of 1774, showed no real desire to welcome the plundering anti-Catholic invaders.

Bitter fighting persisted in the colonies, though the Americans still continued to disclaim all desire for independence. In January 1776 the British set fire to the Virginia town of Norfolk. In March they were finally forced to evacuate Boston, taking with them the leading friends of the king. In the South the rebellious colonists won two victories in 1776: one in February against some fifteen hundred Loyalists at Moore's Creek Bridge, in North Carolina, and the other in June against an invading British fleet in Charleston harbor.

Thomas Paine Preaches Common Sense

Why did Americans continue to deny any intention of independence? Loyalty to the empire was deeply ingrained; many Americans continued to consider themselves part of a transatlantic community in which the mother country played a leading role; colonial unity was poor; and open rebellion was dangerous, especially against a formidable Britain. Irish rebels of that day were customarily hanged, drawn, and quartered. American rebels might have fared no better. As late as January 1776—five months before independence was declared—the king's health was being toasted by the officers of Washington's mess near Boston. "God save the king" had not yet been replaced by "God save the Congress."

Gradually the Americans were shocked into an awareness of their inconsistency. Their eyes were opened by harsh British acts such as the burning of Falmouth and Norfolk, and especially by the hiring of the Hessians. Then in 1776 came the publication of *Common Sense*, one of the most influential pamphlets ever written. Its author was the radical Thomas Paine, once an impoverished corset-maker's apprentice, who had come over from Britain a year earlier. His tract became a whirlwind bestseller and within a few months reached the astonishing total of 120,000 copies in circulation.

Paine flatly branded the shilly-shallying of the colonists as contrary to "common sense." Why not throw off the cloak of inconsistency? Nowhere in the physical universe did the smaller heavenly body control the larger one. Then why should the tiny island of Britain control the vast continent of America? As for the king, whom the Americans professed to revere, he was nothing but "the Royal Brute of Great Britain."

Paine's passionate protest was as compelling as it was eloquent and radical—even doubly radical. It called not simply for independence but for the creation of a new kind of political society, a *republic*, where power flowed from the people themselves, not

Thomas Paine   *Engraving from a portrait by Charles Willson Peale*

Most Americans considered citizen "virtue" fundamental to any successful republican government. Because political power no longer rested with the king, individuals in a republic needed to sacrifice their personal self-interest to the public good. The collective good of "the people" mattered more than the private rights and interests of individuals. Paine inspired his contemporaries to view America as fertile ground for the cultivation of such civic virtue.

Some more conservative American patriots, however, thought that Paine's ultra-democratic republicanism went too far. Republicanism for them meant an end to hereditary aristocracy but not an end to all social hierarchy. These more conservative republicans feared that the fervor for liberty would overwhelm the stability of the social order. They watched with trepidation as the "lower orders" of society—poorer farmers, tenants, and laboring classes in towns and cities—seemed to embrace a kind of runaway republicanism that amounted to radical "leveling." The contest to define the nature of American republicanism would noisily continue for the next hundred years.

Jefferson's "Explanation" of Independence

Members of the Philadelphia Congress, instructed by their respective colonies, gradually edged toward a clean break. On June 7, 1776, fiery Richard Henry Lee of Virginia moved that "These United Colonies are, and of right ought to be, free and independent states. . . ." After considerable debate, the motion was adopted nearly a month later, on July 2, 1776.

The passing of Lee's resolution was the formal "declaration" of independence by the American colonies, and technically this was all that was needed to cut the British tie. John Adams wrote confidently that ever thereafter July 2 would be celebrated annually with fireworks. But something more was required. An epochal rupture of this kind called for some formal explanation to "a candid world." An inspirational appeal was also needed to enlist other British colonies in the Americas, to invite assistance from foreign nations, and to rally resistance at home.

from a corrupt and despotic monarch. In language laced with biblical imagery familiar to common folk, Paine argued that all government officials—governors, senators, and judges, not just representatives in a house of commons—should derive their authority from popular consent.

The colonists' experience with governance had prepared them well for Paine's summons to create a republic. Many settlers, particularly New Englanders, had practiced a kind of republicanism in their democratic town meetings and annual elections, while the popularly elected committees of correspondence during 1774 and 1775 had demonstrated the feasibility of republican government. The absence of a hereditary aristocracy and the relative equality of condition enjoyed by landowning farmers meshed well with the republican repudiation of a fixed hierarchy of power.

Shortly after Lee made his memorable motion on June 7, Congress appointed a committee to prepare an appropriate statement. The task of drafting it fell to Thomas Jefferson, a tall, freckled, sandy-haired Virginia lawyer of thirty-three. Despite his youth, he was already recognized as a brilliant writer, and he measured up splendidly to the awesome assignment. After some debate and amendment, the Declaration of Independence was formally approved by the Congress on July 4, 1776.

Jefferson's pronouncement, couched in a lofty style, was magnificent. He gave his appeal universality by invoking the "natural rights" of humankind—not just British rights. He argued persuasively that because the king had flouted these rights, the colonists were justified in cutting their connection. He then set forth a long list of the presumably tyrannous misdeeds of George III. The overdrawn bill of indictment included imposing taxes without consent, dispensing with trial by jury, abolishing valued laws, establishing a military dictatorship, maintaining standing armies in peacetime, cutting off trade, burning towns, hiring mercenaries, and inciting hostility among the Indians.*

The formal declaration of independence cleared the air as a thundershower does on a muggy day. Foreign aid could be solicited with greater hope of success. Those patriots who defied the king were now rebels, not loving subjects shooting their way into reconciliation. They must all hang together, Franklin is said to have grimly remarked, or they would all hang separately. Or, in the eloquent language of the great declaration, "We mutually pledge to each other our lives, our fortunes and our sacred honor."

Patriots and Loyalists

The War of Independence was a civil war between two factions of Americans as well as a war between Americans and the British. Besides battling the British redcoats, the American rebels, called Patriots or "Whigs," fought Americans loyal to the king, called Loyalists or "Tories" (see "Makers of America: The Loyalists," pp. 94–95).

Like many revolutions, the American Revolution was a minority movement. Many colonists were apathetic or neutral, including the Byrds of Virginia, who sat on the fence. The opposing forces contended not only against each other but also for the allegiance and support of the civilian population. In this struggle for the hearts and minds of the people, the Patriot militia proved far more successful than the inept British. The British military managed to control only those areas where it could maintain a massive military presence. Elsewhere, as soon as the redcoats had marched on, the rebel militiamen appeared and took up the task of "political education"—sometimes by coercive means. Often lacking bayonets but always loaded with political zeal, the ragtag militia units convinced many colonists, even those indifferent to independence, that the British army was an unreliable friend and that they had better throw in their lot with the Patriot cause.

Loyalists, numbering perhaps 15 percent of the American people, remained true to their king. Some fifty thousand Loyalist volunteers at one time or another bore arms for the British. They also helped the king's cause by serving as spies, by inciting the Indians, and by keeping Patriot soldiers at home to protect their families.

Many people of education and wealth, of culture and caution, remained loyal. Loyalists were more numerous among the older generation, for young people make revolutions. They also included the king's officers and other beneficiaries of the crown—people who knew where their daily bread came from. Loyalists were most numerous where the Anglican Church was strongest, except in Virginia, where debt-burdened Anglican aristocrats flocked into the rebel camp. The king's followers were well entrenched in aristocratic New York City and Charleston, and also in Quaker Pennsylvania and New Jersey, where General Washington felt that he was fighting in "the enemy's country." Loyalists were least numerous in New England, where Presbyterianism and Congregationalism flourished, producing strong support for rebellion.

Before the Declaration of Independence in 1776, persecution of the Loyalists was relatively mild. But once independence was declared, Loyalists were

---

*For an annotated text of the Declaration of Independence, see the Appendix.

The Loyalists

In late 1776 Catherine Van Cortlandt wrote to her husband, a New Jersey merchant fighting in a Loyalist brigade, about the Patriot troops who had quartered themselves in her house. "They were the most disorderly of species," she complained, "and their officers were from the dregs of the people."

Like the Van Cortlandts, many Loyalists thought of themselves as "the better sort of people." Conservative, wealthy, and well-educated, Loyalists of this breed thought a break with Britain would invite anarchy. But Loyalism was hardly confined to the well-to-do. It also appealed to many people of modest means who identified strongly with Britain or who had reason to fear a Patriot victory. They included British veterans of the Seven Years' War who had received land grants from the crown, and recent immigrants from Scotland and Ireland who had settled the backcountry of Georgia or the Carolinas. Resenting the plantation elites who ran these colonies, they filled the ranks of Tory brigades organized by the British army.

Other ethnic minorities found their own reasons to support the British. Some Dutch, German, and French religious sects believed that religious tolerance would be greater under the British than under the Americans. Encouraged by British officials, thousands of African-Americans joined the Loyalist ranks in hopes that their service might bring an escape from bondage. Many of them joined black regiments that specialized in making small sorties against Patriot militia.

As the war drew to an end in 1783, the fate of black Loyalists varied enormously. Many thousands who came to Loyalism as fugitive slaves managed to find a way to freedom, especially in Nova Scotia. Other African-American Loyalists suffered betrayal. British general Lord Cornwallis abandoned over four thousand former slaves in Virginia, and others found themselves sold back into slavery in the West Indies.

White Loyalists faced no threat of enslavement, but they did often suffer arrest, exile, confiscation of property, and loss of legal rights. Faced with such retribution, some eighty thousand Loyalists fled abroad, mostly to Britain or Canada. Some settled contentedly as exiles, but many, especially in Britian, had difficulty becoming accepted and lived lonely and diminished lives.

Most Loyalists, though, remained in America, despite the daunting burden of reestablishing themselves in a society that viewed them as traitors. Some succeeded remarkably, such as Hugh Gaine, a New York City printer who reopened his business and even won printing contracts from the new government. Gaine reintegrated himself into public life by siding with the Federalist call for a strong central government and a powerful executive. When New York ratified the Constitution in 1788, Gaine rode the float at the head of the city's celebration parade. He had, like many other former Loyalists, become an American.

more roughly handled. A Patriot definition of a Tory betrayed the bitterness many felt: "A Tory is a thing whose head is in England, and its body in America, and its neck ought to be stretched." A few noncombatant Loyalists were hanged, and others were imprisoned. About eighty thousand loyal supporters of George III were driven out or fled the country, and their estates were confiscated to finance the war. But no reign of terror comparable to that of the later French and Russian revolutions occurred. Confiscation often worked great economic hardship, but most Loyalists did not regret their stand. Ardent Loyalists had their hearts in their cause, and a major blunder of the haughty British was not to make full use of them in the fighting.

General Washington at Bay

With Boston evacuated in March 1776, the British concentrated on New York as a base of operations. Here was a splendid seaport, centrally located, where the king could count on cooperation from the numerous Loyalists. An awe-inspiring British fleet appeared off New York in July 1776. It consisted of some five hundred ships and 35,000 men—the largest armed force to be seen in America until the Civil War. General Washington, dangerously outnumbered, could muster only 18,000 ill-trained troops with which to meet the crack army of the invader.

Disaster befell the Americans in the summer and fall of 1776. Outgeneraled and outmaneuvered, they were routed at the Battle of Long Island, where panic seized the raw recruits. By the narrowest of margins, and thanks to a favoring wind and fog, Washington escaped to Manhattan Island. Retreating northward, he crossed the Hudson River to New Jersey and finally reached the Delaware River with the British close at his heels. Tauntingly, enemy buglers sounded the fox-hunting call so familiar to Virginians of Washington's day. The Patriot cause was at low ebb when the rebel remnants fled across the river after collecting all available boats to forestall pursuit.

The wonder is that Washington's adversary, General William Howe, did not speedily crush the demoralized American forces. But he was no military genius, and he well remembered the horrible slaugh-

ter at Bunker Hill, where he had commanded. The country was rough, supplies were slow in coming, and as a professional soldier Howe did not relish the rigors of winter campaigning.

Washington, who was now almost counted out, stealthily recrossed the ice-clogged Delaware River. At Trenton, on December 26, 1776, he surprised and captured a thousand Hessians who were sleeping off the effects of their Christmas celebration. A week later, leaving his campfires burning as a ruse, he slipped away and inflicted another sharp defeat on a smaller British detachment at Princeton.

Burgoyne's Blundering Invasion

London officials adopted an intricate scheme for capturing the vital Hudson River Valley in 1777. If successful, the British would sever New England from the rest of the states and paralyze the American cause. The main invading force, under an actor-playwright-soldier, General John ("Gentleman Johnny") Burgoyne, would push down the Lake Champlain route from Canada. General Howe's troops in New York planned to advance up the Hudson River to meet Burgoyne near Albany. A third and much smaller British force, commanded by Colonel Barry St. Leger, would come in from the west by way of Lake Ontario and the Mohawk Valley.

British planners did not reckon with General Benedict Arnold. Retreating slowly from Quebec, Arnold had heroically kept his army in the field and assembled a small fleet on Lake Champlain. The British finally constructed a fleet that defeated Arnold's tiny flotilla. But by now winter was descending and the British were forced to retire back to Canada. This delay was critical to the American cause.

Compelled to start over in the spring of 1777, General Burgoyne began his fateful invasion with seven thousand regular troops, a heavy baggage train, and many officers' wives. Progress was painfully slow, for sweaty axmen had to chop a path through the forest, while American militiamen began to swarm like hornets on Burgoyne's flanks.

Meanwhile, astonished eyebrows rose as General Howe marched the main British army toward

Washington Crossing the Delaware, by Emanuel Gottlieb Leutze, 1851 *On Christmas Day, 1776, George Washington set out from Pennsylvania with twenty-four hundred men to surprise the British forces, chiefly Hessians, in their quarters across the river in New Jersey. The subsequent British defeat proved to be a turning point in the Revolution, as it checked the British advance toward Philadelphia and restored American morale. Seventy-five years later, Leutze, a German-born American painter, mythologized the heroic campaign in this painting.*

Philadelphia at a time when it seemed obvious he should be starting up the Hudson River from New York to meet the advancing Burgoyne. As scholars now know, Howe wanted to engage and destroy Washington's army, apparently assuming he had ample time to assist Burgoyne directly should he be needed.

General Washington, keeping a wary eye on the British in New York, hastily transferred his army to the vicinity of Philadelphia. There, late in 1777, he was defeated in two pitched battles, at Brandywine Creek and Germantown. Pleasure-loving General Howe then settled down comfortably in the lively capital, leaving Burgoyne to flounder through the wilds of

upstate New York. Benjamin Franklin, recently sent to Paris as an envoy, truthfully jested that Howe had not captured Philadelphia but that Philadelphia had captured Howe. Washington finally retired to winter quarters at Valley Forge, a strong hilly position some twenty miles northwest of Philadelphia. There his frostbitten and hungry men were short of about everything except misery. This rabble was nevertheless whipped into a professional army by the recently arrived Prussian drillmaster, the profane but patient Baron von Steuben.

Burgoyne, meanwhile, had begun to bog down north of Albany, while a host of American militiamen,

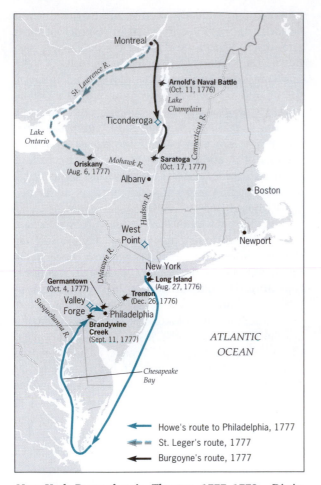

New York–Pennsylvania Theater, 1777–1778 *Distinguished members of the Continental Congress fled from Philadelphia in near-panic as the British army approached. Thomas Paine reported that at three o'clock in the morning the streets were "as full of Men, Women, and Children as on a Market Day." John Adams had anticipated that "I shall run away, I suppose, with the rest," since "we are too brittle ware, you know, to stand the dashing of balls and bombs." Adams got his chance to decamp with the others into the interior of Pennsylvania and tried to put the best face on things. "This tour," he commented, "has given me an opportunity of seeing many parts of this country which I never saw before."*

scenting the kill, hounded him on all sides. After a series of sharp engagements, the British army was trapped. Meanwhile, the Americans had driven back St. Leger's force at Oriskany, New York. Unable to

advance or retreat, Burgoyne was forced to surrender his entire command at Saratoga, on October 17, 1777, to the American general Horatio Gates.

Saratoga ranks high among the decisive battles of both American and world history. The victory immensely revived the faltering colonial cause. Even more important, it made possible the urgently needed foreign aid from France, which in turn helped ensure American independence.

The Colonial War Becomes a World War

France, thirsting for revenge against Britain, was eager to inflame the quarrel that had broken out in America. After the shooting at Lexington in April 1775, French agents undertook to blow on the embers. They secretly provided the Americans with life-saving supplies of firearms and gunpowder. About 90 percent of all the gunpowder used by the Americans during the first two and a half years of the war came from French arsenals.

Secrecy enshrouded all these French schemes. Open aid to the American rebels might provoke Britain into a declaration of war; and France, still weakened by its recent defeat, was not ready to fight. It feared that the American rebellion might fade out, for the colonies were still proclaiming their desire to patch up differences. But the Declaration of Independence in 1776 showed that the Americans really meant business, and the smashing victory at Saratoga seemed to indicate that they had an excellent chance of winning their freedom.

After the humiliation at Saratoga in 1777, the British Parliament belatedly passed a measure that in effect offered the Americans home rule within the empire. This was essentially all that the colonists had ever asked for—except independence. If the French were going to break up the British Empire, they would have to bestir themselves. Wily and bespectacled old Benjamin Franklin, whose simple fur cap and witty sayings had captivated the French public, played skillfully on France's fears of reconciliation.

Seeing an opportunity to undo the victor's peace of 1763, and dreading a British-American rapprochement, France offered the Americans a treaty of alliance in 1778. This was the first entangling military alliance in the experience of the Republic, and one that later caused prolonged trouble.

Britain and France thus came to blows in 1778, and the shot fired at Lexington rapidly widened into a global conflagration. Spain entered the fray against Britain in 1779, as did Holland. Catherine the Great of Russia lined up the remaining European neutrals into the "Armed Neutrality," which assumed an attitude of passive hostility toward Britain.

To Britain, now struggling for its very life, the scuffle in the New World became secondary. The Americans deserve credit for having kept the war going, with secret French aid, until 1778. But they did not achieve their independence until the conflict erupted into a multipower world war that was too big for Britain to handle. From 1778 to 1783, France provided the rebels with guns, money, immense amounts of equipment, about one-half of America's regular armed forces, and practically all of the new nation's naval strength.

France's entrance into the conflict forced the British to change their basic strategy in America. With powerful French fleets in American waters, Britain could no longer blockade the colonial coast and command the seas. To shorten their lines of supply, the British evacuated Philadelphia and escaped to New York City after the indecisive Battle of Monmouth in June 1778. Washington followed them to the New York area and hemmed them in.

Blow and Counterblow

In the summer of 1780 a powerful French army of six thousand regular troops, commanded by the Comte de Rochambeau, arrived in Newport, Rhode Island. Preparations began for a Franco-American attack on New York.

Improving American morale was staggered later in 1780 when General Benedict Arnold turned traitor. A leader of undoubted dash and brilliance, he was ambitious, greedy, and unscrupulous, and suffered from a well-grounded but petulant feeling that his valuable services were not fully appreciated. He plotted with the British to sell out the key stronghold of West Point, which commanded the Hudson River, for

£6,300 and an officer's commission. By the sheerest accident the plot was detected in the nick of time, and Arnold fled to the British. "Whom can we trust now?" cried General Washington in anguish.

The British meanwhile had devised a plan to roll up the colonies, beginning with the South, where the Loyalists were numerous. Georgia was ruthlessly overrun in 1778–1779. Charleston, South Carolina, fell in 1780. The surrender of that city to the British involved the capture of five thousand men and four hundred cannon, and was a heavier loss to the Americans, in relation to existing strength, than Burgoyne's was to the British.

Warfare now intensified in the Carolinas, where Patriots bitterly fought their Loyalist neighbors. It was not uncommon for prisoners on both sides to be butchered in cold blood after they had thrown down their arms. The tide turned later in 1780 and early in 1781, when American riflemen wiped out a British detachment at King's Mountain and then defeated a smaller force at Cowpens. In the Carolina campaign of 1781, General Nathanael Greene, a Quaker-reared tactician, distinguished himself by his strategy of delay. Standing and then retreating, he exhausted his foe, General Cornwallis, in vain pursuit. By losing

War in the South, 1780–1781

battles but winning campaigns, the "Fighting Quaker" finally succeeded in clearing most of Georgia and South Carolina of British troops.

The Land Frontier and the Sea Frontier

The West was ablaze during much of the war. Indian allies of George III, hoping to protect their land, were busy attacking and burning frontier settlements. They were egged on by British agents, branded as "hair buyers" because they allegedly paid bounties for American scalps. Although two nations of the Iroquois Confederacy, the Oneidas and the Tuscaroras, sided with the Americans, the Senecas, Mohawks, Cayugas, and Onondagas joined the British. They were led by Mohawk chief Joseph Brant, a convert to Anglicanism who believed that a victorious Britain would restrain American expansion into the West. Brant and the British ravaged large areas of back-country Pennsylvania and New York until checked by an American force in 1779.

In the wild Illinois country the British were especially vulnerable to attack, for they held only scattered posts that they had captured from the French. An audacious frontiersman, George Rogers Clark, conceived the idea of seizing these forts by surprise. In 1778–1779 he floated down the Ohio River with about 175 men and captured in quick succession Forts Kaskaskia, Cahokia, and Vincennes.

America's infant navy, commanded by daring officers like the hard-fighting Scotsman John Paul Jones, was more successful in destroying British merchant shipping than in engaging Britain's powerful fleets. More numerous and damaging than ships of the regular American navy were swift privateers—privately owned armed ships authorized by Congress to prey on enemy shipping. Over a thousand of these legalized pirates captured some six hundred British prizes. Although they diverted manpower from the main war effort and involved Americans in speculation and graft, privateers brought in urgently needed gold, harassed the enemy, and raised American morale. Unhappy British shippers and manufacturers brought increasing pressure on Parliament to end the war on honorable terms.

Yorktown and the Final Curtain

One of the darkest periods of the war for the American Patriots was 1780–1781, just before the last decisive victory. Inflation of the currency continued at full gallop, and the government was virtually bankrupt. Despair prevailed; the sense of unity withered; and mutinous sentiments infected the army.

But meanwhile the British General Cornwallis was blundering into a trap. After futile operations in Virginia, he had fallen back to Chesapeake Bay at Yorktown to await seaborne supplies and reinforcements. He assumed Britain would continue to control the sea. But these few fateful weeks just happened to be one of the brief periods during the war when British naval superiority slipped away.

The French were now prepared to cooperate energetically in a brilliant stroke. Admiral de Grasse, operating with a powerful fleet in the West Indies, sent word to the Americans that he was free to join with them in an assault on Cornwallis at Yorktown. Quick to seize this opportunity, General Washington made a swift march of more than three hundred miles to the Chesapeake from the New York area. Accompanied by Rochambeau's French army, Washington beset the British by land, while de Grasse blockaded them by sea after beating off the British fleet. Completely cornered, Cornwallis surrendered his entire force of seven thousand men on October 19, 1781, as his band appropriately played "The World Turn'd Upside Down." The triumph was no less French than American: France provided essentially all the seapower and about half of the regular troops in the besieging army of some sixteen thousand men.

Stunned by news of the disaster, Prime Minister Lord North cried, "Oh God! It's all over! It's all over!" But it was not. George III stubbornly planned to continue the struggle, for Britain was far from being crushed. It still had 54,000 troops in North America, including 32,000 in the United States. Washington returned with his army to New York, there to continue keeping a vigilant eye on a British force of 10,000 men.

Fighting actually continued for more than a year after Yorktown, with Patriot-Loyalist warfare in the

South especially savage. "No quarter for Tories" was the common battle cry. One of Washington's most valuable contributions was to keep the languishing cause alive, the army in the field, and the states together during these critical months. Otherwise, a satisfactory peace treaty might never have been signed.

Peace at Paris

After Yorktown, the war-weary British were increasingly ready to come to terms. They had suffered heavy reverses in India and in the West Indies. Lord North's Tory ministry collapsed in March 1782, temporarily ending the personal rule of George III, and was replaced by a Whig ministry rather favorable to the Americans.

Three American peace negotiators had meanwhile gathered at Paris: the aging but astute Benjamin Franklin; the flinty John Adams, vigilant for New England interests; and the impulsive John Jay of New York, deeply suspicious of Old World intrigue. The three envoys had explicit instructions from Congress to make no separate peace and to consult with their French allies at all stages of the negotiations. But the American representatives chafed under this directive. They well knew that it had been written by a subservient Congress, with the French Foreign Office indirectly guiding the pen.

France was in a painful position. It had induced Spain to enter the war on its side, and the Spanish coveted the immense trans-Appalachian area for itself. Wanting an America that would be independent but feeble, the French therefore joined the scheme to keep the new republic cooped up east of the Appalachian Mountains.

But John Jay was unwilling to play France's game. Suspiciously alert, he perceived that the French could not satisfy the conflicting ambitions of both Americans and Spaniards. He saw signs—or thought he did—indicating that the Paris Foreign Office was about to betray America's trans-Appalachian interests to satisfy those of Spain. He therefore secretly made separate overtures to London, contrary to his instructions from Congress. The hard-pressed British, eager to entice one of their enemies from the alliance, speedily came to terms with the Americans. A prelim-

inary treaty of peace was signed in 1782, and the final treaty the next year.

By the Treaty of Paris of 1783, the British formally recognized the independence of the United States. In addition, they granted generous boundaries, stretching majestically to the Mississippi on the west, to the Great Lakes on the north, and to Spanish Florida on

Benjamin Franklin (1706–1790), by Charles Willson Peale, 1789   *He left school at age ten, and became a wealthy businessman, a journalist, an inventor, a scientist, a legislator, and preeminently a statesman-diplomat. He was sent to France in 1776 as the American envoy at age seventy, and he remained there until 1785, negotiating the alliance with the French and helping to negotiate the treaty of peace. His fame had preceded him, and when he discarded his wig for the fur cap of a simple "American agriculturist," he took French society by storm. French aristocratic women, with whom he was a great favorite, honored him by adopting the high* coiffure à la Franklin *in imitation of his cap.*

the south. (Spain had recently captured Florida from Britain.)

The Americans, on their part, had to yield important concessions. Loyalists were not to be further persecuted, and Congress was to recommend to the state legislatures that confiscated Loyalist property be restored. As for the debts long owed to British creditors, the states were bound to put no lawful obstacles in the way of their collection. Unhappily for future harmony, the assurances regarding both Loyalists and debts were not honored in the manner hoped for by London.

A New Nation Legitimized

Britain's terms were liberal almost beyond belief. The enormous trans-Appalachian area was thrown in as a virtual gift, for George Rogers Clark had captured only a small segment of it. Why the generosity? Had the United States beaten Britain to its knees?

The key to the riddle may be found in the Old World. At the time the peace terms were drafted, Britain was trying to entice the United States out of the French-American alliance, so it made the terms as alluring as possible. The shaky Whig ministry, hanging

on by its fingernails for only a few months, was more friendly to the Americans than were the Tories. It was determined, by a policy of liberality, to salve recent wounds, reopen old trade channels, and prevent future wars over the coveted trans-Appalachian region. This far-visioned policy was regrettably not followed by the successors of the Whigs.

In spirit, the Americans made a separate peace—contrary to the French alliance. In fact, they did not. The Paris Foreign Office, though disturbed by the lone-wolf course of its American ally, formally approved the terms of peace. France was immensely relieved by the prospect of bringing the costly conflict to an end, and of freeing itself from its embarrassing promises to the Spanish crown.

America alone gained from the world-girdling war. The British, though soon to stage a comeback, were battered and beaten. The French savored sweet revenge but plunged headlong down the slippery slope to bankruptcy and revolution. In truth, fortune smiled benignly on the Americans. Snatching their independence from the furnace of world conflict, they began their national career with a splendid territorial birthright and a priceless heritage of freedom. Seldom, if ever, have any people been so favored.

Chronology

1775	Battles of Lexington and Concord. Second Continental Congress. Battle of Bunker Hill. King George III formally proclaims colonies in rebellion. Failed invasion of Canada.
1776	Paine's *Common Sense*. Declaration of Independence. Battle of Trenton.
1777	Battle of Brandywine. Battle of Germantown. Battle of Saratoga.
1778	Formation of French-American alliance. Battle of Monmouth.
1778–1779	Clark's victories in the West.
1781	Battle of King's Mountain. Battle of Cowpens. Greene leads Carolina campaign. French and Americans force Cornwallis to surrender at Yorktown.
1782	North's ministry collapses in Britain.
1783	Treaty of Paris.

For further reading, see the Appendix. For web resources, go to **http://college.hmco.com**.

PART TWO

BUILDING THE NEW NATION

—⦿—

1776–1860

By 1783 Americans had won their freedom. Now they had to build their country. To be sure, they were blessed with a vast and fertile land, and they inherited from their colonial experience a proud legacy of self-rule. But history provided scant precedent for erecting a democracy on a national scale. No law of nature guaranteed that the thirteen rebellious colonies would stay glued together as a single nation, or that they would preserve, not to mention expand, their democratic way of life. New institutions had to be created, new habits of thought cultivated. Who could predict whether the American experiment in government by the people would succeed?

The ramshackle national government cobbled together under the Articles of Confederation during the Revolutionary War soon proved woefully inadequate to the task of nation building. Less than ten years after the war's conclusion, the Articles were replaced by a new constitution, but even its adoption did not end the debate over what form American democracy should take. Would the president, or the congress, or the courts be the dominant branch of government? What should be the proper division of authority between the federal government and the states? How could the rights of individuals be protected against a potentially powerful government? What economic policies would best serve the infant Republic? How should the nation defend itself against foreign foes? What principles should guide foreign policy? Was America a nation at all, or was it merely a geographic expression, destined to splinter into several bitterly quarreling sections, as had happened to so many other would-be countries?

After a shaky start under George Washington and John Adams in the 1790s, buffeted by foreign troubles and domestic crises, the new Republic passed a major test when power was peacefully transferred from the conservative Federalists to the more liberal

Jeffersonians in the election of 1800. A confident President Jefferson proceeded boldly to expand the national territory with the landmark Louisiana Purchase in 1803. But before long Jefferson, and then his successor, James Madison, were embroiled in what eventually proved to be a fruitless effort to spare the United States from the ravages of the war then raging in Europe.

America was dangerously divided during the War of 1812 and suffered a humiliating defeat. But a new sense of national unity and purpose was unleashed in the land thereafter. President Monroe, presiding over this "Era of Good Feelings," proclaimed in the Monroe Doctrine of 1823 that both of the American continents were off-limits to further European intervention.The foundations of a continental-scale economy were laid, as a "transportation revolution" stitched the country together with canals and railroads and turnpikes. Settlers flooded over those new arteries into the burgeoning West, often brusquely shouldering aside the native peoples. Immigrants, especially from Ireland and Germany, flocked to American shores. The combination of new lands and new labor fed the growth of a market economy, including the commercialization of agriculture and the beginnings of the factory system of production. Old ways of life withered as the market economy drew women as well as men, children as well as adults, blacks as well as whites, into its embrace. Ominously, the slave system grew robustly as cotton production, mostly for sale on European markets, exploded into the booming Southwest.

Meanwhile, the United States in the era of Andrew Jackson gave the world an impressive lesson in political science. Between roughly 1820 and 1840 Americans virtually invented mass democracy, creating huge political parties and enormously expanding political participation by enfranchising nearly all adult white males. Nor was the spirit of innovation confined to the political realm. A wave of reform and cultural vitality swept through many sectors of American society. Utopian experiments proliferated. Religious revivals and even new religions, like Mormonism, flourished. A national literature blossomed. Crusades were launched for temperance, prison reform, women's rights, and the abolition of slavery.

By the second quarter of the nineteenth century, the outlines of a distinctive American national character had begun to emerge. Americans were a diverse, restless people, tramping steadily westward, eagerly forging their own nascent industrial revolution, proudly exercising their democratic political rights, impatient with the old, in love with the new, testily asserting their superiority over all other peoples—and increasingly divided, in heart, in conscience, and in politics, over the single greatest blight on their record of nation making and democracy building: slavery.

The Confederation and the Constitution

1776–1790

This example of changing the constitution by assembling the wise men of the state, instead of assembling armies, will be worth as much to the world as the former examples we have given it.

THOMAS JEFFERSON

The American Revolution did not usher in a radical or total change. It did not suddenly and violently overturn an entire political and social framework, as later occurred in the French and Russian revolutions. What happened was accelerated evolution rather than outright revolution.

Yet some striking changes were ushered in, affecting social customs, political institutions, and ideas about society and government and even gender roles. The exodus of some eighty thousand substantial Loyalists after the war robbed the new ship of state of conservative ballast. This weakening of the aristocratic upper crust, with all its culture and elegance, paved the way for new, Patriot elites to emerge. It also cleared the field for more egalitarian ideas to sweep across the land.

The Pursuit of Equality

"All men are created equal," the Declaration of Independence proclaimed, and equality was everywhere the watchword. Most states reduced (but usually did not elminate altogether) property-holding requirements for voting. Ordinary men and women demanded to be addressed as "Mr." and "Mrs."—titles once reserved for the wealthy and highborn. Most Americans ridiculed the lordly pretensions of Continental Army officers who formed an exclusive hereditary order, the Society of the Cincinnati. Social democracy was further stimulated by the growth of trade organizations for artisans and laborers.

A protracted fight for separation of church and state resulted in notable gains. The well-entrenched Congregational Church continued to be legally established in some New England states, but the Anglican Church, tainted by association with the British crown, was humbled. De-Anglicized, it re-formed as the Protestant Episcopal Church and was everywhere disestablished. The fierce struggle for divorce between religion and government in Virginia was prolonged to 1786, when free-thinking Thomas Jefferson and his co-reformers, including the Baptists, won a complete victory with the passage of the Virginia Statute for Religious Freedom.

The egalitarian sentiments unleashed by the war likewise challenged the institution of slavery.

Elizabeth "Mumbet" Freeman (c. 1744–1829), by Susan Anne Livingston Ridley Sedgwick, 1811 *In 1781, having overheard Revolutionary-era talk about the "rights of man," Mumbet sued her Massachusetts master for her freedom from slavery. She won her suit and lived the rest of her life as a paid domestic servant in the home of the lawyer who had pleaded her case.*

Philadelphia Quakers in 1775 founded the world's first antislavery society. The Continental Congress in 1774 called for the complete abolition of the slave trade, a summons to which most of the states responded positively. Several northern states went further and either abolished slavery outright or provided for the gradual emancipation of blacks. Even on the plantations of Virginia, a few idealistic masters freed their human chattels—the first frail sprouts of the later abolitionist movement.

But this revolution of sentiments was sadly incomplete. No states south of Pennsylvania abolished slavery, and in both north and south the law discriminated harshly against freed blacks and slaves alike. Emancipated African-Americans could be barred from purchasing property, holding certain jobs, or educating their children. Laws against interracial marriage also sprang up at this time.

Why in this dawning democratic age did abolition not go further and clearly blot the evil of slavery from the fresh face of the new nation? The sorry truth is that the fledgling idealism of the Founding Fathers was sacrificed to political expedience. A fight over slavery would have fractured the fragile national unity that was so desperately needed. "Great as the evil [of slavery] is," the young Virginian James Madison wrote in 1787, "a dismemberment of the union would be worse."

Likewise incomplete was the extension of the doctrine of equality to women. Some women (disguised as men) did serve in the military, and New Jersey's new constitution in 1776 even for a time enabled women to vote. But though Abigail Adams teased her husband John in 1776 that "the ladies" were determined "to foment a rebellion" of their own if they were not given political rights, most of the women in the Revolutionary era were still doing traditional women's work.

Yet women did not go untouched by revolutionary ideals. Republican ideology advanced the concept of "civic virtue"—the idea that democracy depended on the unselfish commitment of each citizen to the public good. Mothers, to whom society entrusted the education of the young, were often cited as the very models of proper republican behavior. The idea of "republican motherhood" thus took root, elevating women to a newly prestigious role as special keepers of the nation's conscience. Educational opportunities for women expanded, in the expectation that educated wives and mothers could better cultivate the virtues demanded by the Republic in their husbands, daughters, and sons. Republican women now bore crucial responsibility for the survival of the nation.

Constitution Making in the States

The Continental Congress in 1776 called on the colonies to draft new constitutions. In effect, Congress was actually asking the colonies to summon themselves into being as new states, whose sovereignty, according to the theory of republicanism, would rest on the authority of the people. In most of the states, constitution writers worked tirelessly to capture on black-inked parchment the republican spirit of the age.

Massachusetts contributed one especially noteworthy innovation when it called a special convention to draft its constitution and then submitted the final draft directly to the people for ratification. This procedure was later imitated in the drafting and ratification of the federal Constitution.

The newly penned state constitutions enjoyed many features in common. As written documents, they were intended to represent a fundamental law, superior to the transient whims of ordinary legislation. Most of these documents included bills of rights, specifically guaranteeing long-prized liberties against later legislative encroachment. All of them deliberately created weak executive and judicial branches. A generation of quarreling with His Majesty's officials had implanted a deep distrust of despotic governors and arbitrary judges. But the legislatures, presumably the most democratic branch of government, were given sweeping powers.

The democratic character of the new state legislatures was vividly reflected in the presence of many members from the recently enfranchised poorer western districts. Their influence was powerfully felt in their several successful movements to relocate state capitals from the haughty eastern seaports into the less pretentious interior. These geographical shifts portended political shifts that deeply discomfited many more conservative Americans.

Economic Crosscurrents

Economic changes begotten by the war were likewise noteworthy, but not overwhelming. States seized control of former crown lands, and although rich speculators had their day, many of the large Loyalist holdings were confiscated and eventually cut up into small farms. Roger Morris's huge estate in New York, for example, was sliced into 250 parcels—thus accelerating the spread of economic democracy. The frightful excesses of the French Revolution were avoided, partly because cheap land was easily available. People do not chop off heads so readily when they can chop down trees. It is significant that in the United States economic democracy, broadly speaking, preceded political democracy.

A sharp stimulus was given to manufacturing by the prewar nonimportation agreements and later by the war itself. Goods that formerly had been imported from Britain were mostly cut off, and the ingenious Yankees were forced to make their own. Ten years after the Revolution the tumbling Brandywine Creek, south of Philadelphia, was turning the waterwheels of numerous mills along an eight-mile stretch. Yet America remained overwhelmingly a nation of soil-tillers.

Economically speaking, independence had drawbacks. Much of the coveted commerce of Britain was still reserved for the loyal parts of the empire. American ships were now barred from British and British West Indian harbors. But new commercial outlets, fortunately, compensated partially for the loss of old ones. Americans could now trade freely with foreign nations, subject to local restrictions—a boon they had not enjoyed in the old days of mercantilism. Enterprising Yankee shippers ventured boldly—and profitably—into the Baltic and China Seas.

Yet the general economic picture was far from being rosy. War had spawned demoralizing extravagance, speculation, and profiteering, with profits for some as indecently high as 300 percent. Runaway inflation had been ruinous to many citizens, and Congress had failed in its feeble political attempts to restrain the inevitable laws of economics. The average citizen was probably worse off financially at the end of the shooting than before.

A Shaky Start Toward Union

What would the Americans do with the independence they had so dearly won? Prospects for erecting a lasting regime were far from bright. It is always difficult to set up a new government, doubly difficult to set up a new type of government. The picture was further clouded in America by leaders preaching "natural rights" and looking suspiciously at all persons clothed with authority. America was more a name than a nation, and unity ran little deeper than the color on the map.

Disruptive forces stalked the land. The departure of the conservative Loyalists left the political system inclined toward experimentation and innovation. Patriots had fought the war with a high degree of disunity, but they at least had concurred on allegiance to a common cause. Now even that was gone. It would have been almost a miracle if any government fashioned in all this confusion had long endured.

Hard times, the bane of all regimes, set in shortly after the war and hit bottom in 1786. As if other troubles were not enough, British manufacturers, with dammed-up surpluses, began flooding the American market with cut-rate goods. War-baby American industries, in particular, suffered industrial colic from such ruthless competition.

Yet hopeful signs could be discerned. The thirteen sovereign states were basically alike in governmental structure and functioned under similar constitutions. Americans enjoyed a rich political inheritance, derived partly from Britain and partly from their own homegrown devices for self-government. Finally, they were blessed with political leaders of a high order in men like George Washington, James Madison, John Adams, Thomas Jefferson, and Alexander Hamilton.

Creating a Confederation

The Second Continental Congress of revolutionary days was little more than a conference of ambassadors from the thirteen states. In nearly all respects the states were sovereign, for they coined money, raised armies and navies, and erected tariff barriers.

Shortly before declaring independence in 1776, Congress appointed a committee to draft a written constitution for the new nation. The finished product was the Articles of Confederation. Adopted by Congress in 1777, it was translated into French after the Battle of Saratoga so as to convince France that America had a genuine government in the making. The articles were not ratified by all thirteen states until 1781, less than eight months before the victory at Yorktown.

The chief apple of discord was western lands. Six of the jealous states, including Pennsylvania and Maryland, had no holdings beyond the Appalachian Mountains. Seven, notably New York and Virginia, were favored with enormous acreage on the basis of earlier sea-to-sea charter grants. The six land-hungry states argued that the more fortunate states would not have retained possession of this splendid prize if all the other states had not fought for it also. Why not turn the whole western area over to the central government?

Unanimous approval of the Articles of Confederation by the thirteen states was required, and land-starved Maryland stubbornly held out until March 1, 1781. Maryland at length gave in when New York surrendered its western claims and Virginia seemed about to do so. To sweeten the pill, Congress pledged itself to dispose of these vast areas for the "common benefit." It further agreed to carve from the new public domain not colonies but a number of "republican" states, which in time would be admitted to the Union on terms of complete equality with all the others. This extraordinary commitment faithfully reflected the anticolonial spirit of the Revolution, and the pledge was later fully redeemed in the famed Northwest Ordinance of 1787.

Fertile public lands thus transferred to the central government proved to be an invaluable bond of union. The states that had thrown their heritage into the common pot had to remain in the Union if they were to reap their share of the advantages from the land sales. An army of westward-moving pioneers purchased their farms from the federal government, directly or indirectly, and they learned to look to the national capital, rather than to the state capitals—with a consequent weakening of local influence. Finally, a uniform national land policy was made possible.

Western Land Cessions to the United States, 1782–1802

The Articles of Confederation: America's First Constitution

The Articles of Confederation provided for a loose confederation or "firm league of friendship." Thirteen independent states were thus linked together for joint action in dealing with common problems, such as foreign affairs. A clumsy Congress was to be the chief agency of government. There was no executive branch—George III had left a bad taste—and the vital judicial arm was left almost exclusively to the states.

Congress, though dominant, was closely hobbled by the suspicious states. All bills dealing with subjects of importance required the support of nine states; any amendment of the Articles themselves required unanimous ratification. Purposely designed to be weak, Congress was crippled by its lack of power to regulate commerce, which left the states free to establish conflicting laws regarding tariffs and navigation. With no power to enforce its tax-collection program, Congress set a tax quota for the individual states and then asked them please to contribute their shares on a voluntary basis.

In spite of their defects, the anemic Articles of Confederation were a significant steppingstone toward the present Constitution. They clearly outlined the general powers that were to be exercised by the central government, such as making treaties and establishing a postal service. As the first written constitution of the Republic, the Articles kept alive the flickering ideal of union and held the states together—until such time as they were ripe for the establishment of a strong constitution by peaceful, evolutionary methods. Without this intermediary jump, the states probably would never have consented to the breathtaking leap from the old boycott Association of 1774 to the Constitution of the United States.

Landmarks in Land Laws

Handcuffed though the Congress of the Confederation was, it succeeded in passing supremely farsighted pieces of legislation. These related to an immense part of the public domain recently acquired from the states, commonly known as the Old Northwest. This area of land lay north of the Ohio River, east of the Mississippi River, and south of the Great Lakes.

The first of these red-letter laws was the Land Ordinance of 1785. It provided that the acreage of the Old Northwest should be sold and that the proceeds should be used to help pay off the national debt. The vast area was to be surveyed before sale and settlement, thus forestalling endless confusion and lawsuits. It was to be divided into townships six miles square, each of which in turn was to be split into thirty-six sections of one square mile each. The sixteenth section of each township was set aside to be sold for the benefit of the public schools—a priceless gift to education in the Old Northwest.

Even more noteworthy was the Northwest Ordinance of 1787, which established governments for the Old Northwest. This law came to grips with the problem of how a nation should deal with its colonies—the same problem that had bedeviled the king and Parliament in London. The solution provided by the Northwest Ordinance was a judicious compromise: temporary tutelage, then permanent equality. First, there would be two evolutionary territorial stages, during which the area would be subordinate to the federal government. Then, when a territory could boast sixty thousand inhabitants, it might be admitted by Congress as a state, with all the privileges of the thirteen charter members. The ordinance also forbade slavery in the Old Northwest—a path-breaking gain for freedom.

The wisdom of Congress in handling this explosive problem deserves warm praise. If it had attempted to chain the new territories in permanent subordination, a second American Revolution almost certainly would have erupted in later years, fought this time by the West against the East. Congress thus neatly solved the seemingly insoluble problem of empire. The scheme worked so well that its basic principles were ultimately carried over from the Old Northwest to other frontier areas.

Surveying the Old Northwest   Sections of a township under the Land Ordinance of 1785.

The World's Ugly Duckling

Foreign relations, especially with London, continued troubled during these anxious years of confederation. Britain flatly declined to send a minister to America, to make a commercial treaty, or to repeal its ancient Navigation Laws. A British lord argued that Britain would win back America's trade anyhow, as commerce would naturally return to old channels. London also shut off its profitable West Indian trade from the United States.

Along the northern frontier, British agents intrigued with the disgruntled Allen brothers to annex Vermont to Canada. Redcoats continued to hold a chain of trading posts on American soil, maintaining their fur trade and keeping the Indians lined up on the side of the king as a barrier against future American attacks on Canada.

Maddened by these grievances, some patriotic Americans demanded that the United States force the British into line by imposing restrictions on their imports to America. But Congress could not control commerce, and the states refused to adopt a uniform tariff policy.

Spain, though recently an enemy of Britain, was openly unfriendly to the new Republic. It controlled the mouth of the all-important Mississippi, down which the pioneers of Tennessee and Kentucky were forced to float their produce. In 1784 Spain closed the river to American commerce, threatening the West with strangulation. Spain likewise claimed a large area north of the Gulf of Mexico, including Florida, granted to the United States by the British in 1783. At Natchez, on disputed soil, Spain held an important fort. Spain and Britain together, radiating their influence out among resentful Indian peoples, prevented America from exercising effective control over about half of its total territory.

Even France, America's wartime ally, demanded the repayment of money loaned during the war and restricted trade with its bustling West Indies ports. North African pirates, including the arrogant Dey of Algiers, ravaged America's Mediterranean commerce and enslaved Yankee sailors. The British purchased protection for their subjects, but as an independent nation the United States was too weak to fight and too poor to bribe. John Jay, secretary for foreign affairs, hoped that these insults would at least humiliate the American people into framing a new government at home that would be strong enough to command respect abroad.

The Horrid Specter of Anarchy

Economic storm clouds continued to hang low in the mid-1780s. Interest on the public debt was piling up at home, and the nation's credit was evaporating abroad. An alarming uprising, known as Shays's Rebellion, flared up in western Massachusetts in 1786 and set off widespread fear of further insurrection. Impoverished backcountry farmers, many of them Revolutionary War veterans, were losing their farms through mortgage foreclosures and tax delinquencies. Led by Captain Daniel Shays, a veteran of the Revolution, these desperate debtors demanded cheap paper money, lighter taxes, and a suspension of mortgage foreclosures. Hundreds of angry agitators, again seizing their muskets, attempted to enforce their demands.

Massachusetts authorities responded with drastic action. Supported partly by contributions from wealthy citizens, they raised a small army. After a few skirmishes the revolt collapsed. Daniel Shays, who believed that he was fighting anew against tyranny, was condemned to death but later pardoned.

Shays's followers were crushed—but the nightmarish memory lingered on. The outbursts of these and other distressed debtors struck fear in the hearts of the propertied class, who began to suspect that the Revolution had raised up a Frankenstein's monster of "mobocracy." Unbridled republicanism, it seemed to many of the elite, had fed an insatiable appetite for liberty that was fast becoming license. Civic virtue was no longer sufficient to rein in self-interest and greed. It had become "undeniably evident," one skeptic sorrowfully lamented, "that some malignant disorder has seized upon our body politic." If republicanism was too shaky a ground on which to construct a new nation, a stronger central government would provide the needed foundation. A few panicky citizens even whispered of importing a European monarch to carry on where George III had failed.

How critical were conditions under the Confederation? Conservatives, anxious to safeguard their wealth and position, naturally exaggerated the seriousness of the nation's plight. They were eager to persuade their fellow citizens to amend the Articles of Confederation in favor of a muscular central government. But the poorer states' rights people pooh-poohed the talk of anarchy. Many of them were debtors who feared that a powerful federal government would force them to pay their creditors.

Yet friends and critics of the Confederation agreed that it needed strengthening. Popular toasts were "Cement to the Union" and "A hoop to the barrel." The chief differences arose over how this goal should be attained and how a maximum amount of states' rights could be reconciled with a strong central government.

A Convention of "Demi-Gods"

Control of commerce touched off the chain reaction that led to a constitutional convention. Interstate squabbling over this issue had become so alarming by 1786 that Virginia issued a call for a convention at Annapolis, Maryland. When delegates from only five states showed up, nothing could be done about the ticklish question of commerce. A charismatic thirty-one-year-old New Yorker, Alexander Hamilton, brilliantly saved the convention from failure by engineering a call for another convention to meet the next year in Philadelphia to bolster the entire fabric of the Articles of Confederation.

Congress was reluctant to take a step that might lead to signing its own death warrant. But after six states appointed delegates anyhow, Congress belatedly issued the call for a convention "for the sole and express purpose of revising" the Articles of Confederation.

Every state chose representatives, except independent-minded Rhode Island, a stronghold of paper-moneyites. These leaders were all appointed by the state legislatures, whose members had been elected by voters who could qualify as property holders. This double distillation inevitably brought together a select group of propertied men.

A quorum of the fifty-five emissaries from twelve states finally convened at Philadelphia on May 25, 1787, in the imposing red-brick statehouse. The smallness of the assemblage facilitated intimate acquaintance and hence compromise. Sessions were held in complete secrecy, with armed sentinels posted at the doors. Delegates knew that they would generate heated differences, and they did not want to advertise their own dissensions or put crippling arguments into the mouths of the opposition.

The caliber of the participants was extraordinarily high—"demi-gods," Jefferson called them. The crisis was such as to induce the ablest men to drop their personal pursuits and come to the aid of their country. Most of the members were lawyers, and most of them fortunately were old hands at constitution making in their own states.

George Washington, towering austere and aloof among the "demi-gods," was unanimously elected

Statehouse in 1778, from a drawing by Charles Willson Peale, by William L. Breton, c. 1830 *Originally built in the 1730s as a meeting place for the Pennsylvania colonial assembly, this building witnessed much history: here Washington was given command of the Continental Army, the Declaration of Independence was signed, and the Constitution was hammered out. The building began to be called "Independence Hall" in the 1820s.*

chairman. His enormous prestige as "the Sword of the Revolution" served to quiet overheated tempers. Benjamin Franklin, then eighty-one, added the urbanity of an elder statesman, though he was inclined to be indiscreetly talkative in his declining years. Concerned for the secrecy of their deliberations, the convention assigned chaperones to accompany Franklin to dinner parties and make sure he held his tongue. James Madison, then thirty-six and a profound student of government, made contributions so notable that he has been dubbed "the Father of the Constitution." Alexander Hamilton, then only thirty-two, was present as an advocate of a super-powerful central government. His five-hour speech in behalf of his plan, though the most eloquent of the convention, left only one delegate convinced—himself.

Most of the fiery revolutionary leaders of 1776 were absent. Thomas Jefferson, John Adams, and Thomas Paine were in Europe; Samuel Adams and John Hancock were not elected by Massachusetts. Patrick Henry, ardent champion of states' rights, was chosen as a delegate from Virginia but declined to serve, declaring that he "smelled a rat." It was perhaps well that these architects of revolution were absent. The time had come to yield the stage to leaders interested in fashioning solid political systems.

Patriots in Philadelphia

The fifty-five delegates were a conservative, well-to-do body: lawyers, merchants, shippers, land speculators, and moneylenders. Not a single spokesperson was present from the poorer debtor groups. Nineteen of the fifty-five owned slaves. They were young (the average age was about forty-two) but experienced statesmen. Above all, they were nationalists, more interested in preserving and strengthening the young Republic than in further stirring the roiling cauldron of popular democracy.

The delegates hoped to crystallize the evaporating pools of revolutionary idealism into a stable political structure that would endure. They strongly desired a firm, dignified, and respected government. They believed in republicanism but sought to protect the American experiment from its weaknesses abroad and excesses at home. They aimed to clothe the central authority with genuine power, especially in controlling tariffs, so that the United States could wrest satisfactory commercial treaties from foreign nations.

Other motives were present in the stately Philadelphia hall. Delegates were determined to preserve the Union, forestall anarchy, and ensure security of life and property against dangerous uprisings by the "mobocracy." Above all, they sought to curb the unrestrained democracy rampant in the various states. The specter of the recent outburst in Massachusetts was especially alarming, and in this sense, Daniel Shays was a Founding Father. Grinding necessity extorted the Constitution from a reluctant nation. There were fifty-five delegates; fear occupied the fifty-sixth chair.

Hammering Out a Bundle of Compromises

Some of the travel-stained delegates, when they first reached Philadelphia, decided on a daring step. They would completely scrap the old Articles of Confederation, despite explicit instructions from Congress to revise. Technically, these bolder spirits were determined to overthrow the existing government of the United States by peaceful means.

A scheme proposed by populous Virginia, and known as "the large-state plan," was first pushed forward as the framework of the Constitution. Its essence was that representation in both houses of a bicameral Congress should be based on population—an arrangement that would naturally give the larger states an advantage. Tiny New Jersey, suspicious of Virginia, countered with "the small-state plan." This provided for equal representation in a unicameral Congress by states, regardless of size and population.

After bitter and prolonged debate, the "Great Compromise" of the convention was hammered out and agreed upon. The larger states were conceded representation by population in the House of Representatives (Art. I, Sec. II, para. 3; see the Appendix at the end of this book), and the smaller states were appeased by equal representation in the Senate (see Art. I, Sec. III, para. 1). Each state, no matter how poor or small, would have two senators. The big states obviously yielded more. As a sop to them, the delegates agreed that every tax bill or revenue measure had to originate in the House, where population counted more heavily (see Art. I, Sec. VII, para. 1). This critical compromise broke the logjam, and from then on success seemed within reach.

The Constitution as drafted was a bundle of compromises; they stand out in every section. A vital compromise was the method of electing the president indirectly by the Electoral College, rather than by direct means (see Art. II, Sec. I, para. 2). While the large states would have the advantage in the first round of popular voting, the small states would gain a larger voice if no candidate got a majority of electoral votes and the election was thrown to the House of Representatives, where each state had only one vote (see Art. II, Sec. I, para. 2). Although the framers of the Constitution expected election by the House to occur frequently, it has happened only twice, in 1800 and 1824.

Sectional jealousy also intruded. Should the voteless slave of the southern states count as a person in apportioning direct taxes and also representation in the House of Representatives? The South, not wishing to be deprived of influence, answered "yes." The North replied "no," arguing that slaves were not citizens. As a compromise between total representation and none at all, it was decided that a slave might count as three-fifths of a person. Hence the memorable, if arbitrary, "three-fifths compromise" (see Art. I, Sec. II, para. 3).

Most of the states wanted to shut off the African slave trade. But slave-holding South Carolina and Georgia raised vehement protests. In another compromise the convention stipulated that the slave trade might continue until the end of 1807, at which time Congress could end the importation of slaves (see Art. I, Sec. IX, para. 1). It did so as soon as the prescribed interval had elapsed. Meanwhile all the new state constitutions except Georgia's forbade overseas slave trade.

Safeguards for Conservatism

Heated clashes among the delegates have been overplayed. The area of agreement was actually large; otherwise the convention would have speedily disbanded. Economically, the members of the Constitutional Convention generally saw eye to eye; they demanded sound money and the protection of private property. Politically, they were in basic agreement; they favored a stronger government, with three

Strengthening the Central Government

Under Articles of Confederation	Under Federal Constitution
A loose confederation of states	A firm union of people
1 vote in Congress for each state	2 votes in Senate for each state; representation by population in House (see Art. I, Secs. II, III)
Vote of 9 states in Congress for all important measures	Simple majority vote in Congress, subject to presidential veto (see Art. I, Sec. VII, para. 2)
Laws administered loosely by committees of Congress	Laws executed by powerful president (see Art. II, Secs. II, III)
No congressional power over commerce	Congress to regulate both foreign and interstate commerce (see Art. I, Sec. VIII, para. 3)
No congressional power to levy taxes	Extensive power in Congress to levy taxes (see Art. I, Sec. VIII, para. 1)
Limited federal courts	Federal courts, capped by Supreme Court (see Art. III)
Unanimity of states for amendment	Amendment less difficult (see Art. V)
No authority to act directly upon individuals and no power to coerce states	Ample power to enforce laws by coercion of individuals and to some extent of states

branches and with checks and balances among them—what critics called a "triple-headed monster." Finally, the convention was virtually unanimous in believing that manhood-suffrage democracy—government by "democratick babblers"—was something to be feared and fought.

Daniel Shays, the prime bogeyman, still frightened the conservative-minded delegates. They deliberately erected safeguards against the excesses of the "mob," and they made these barriers as strong as they dared. The awesome federal judges were to be appointed for life. The powerful president was to be elected *indirectly* by the Electoral College. The lordly senators were to be chosen *indirectly* by state legislatures (see Art. I, Sec. III, para. 1). Only in the case of one-half of one of the three great branches—the House of Representatives—were qualified (propertied) citizens permitted to choose their officials by *direct* vote (see Art. I, Sec. II, para. 1).

Yet the new charter also contained democratic elements. Above all, it stood foursquare on the two great principles of republicanism: that the only legitimate government was one based on the consent of the governed, and that the powers of the government should be limited. The virtue of the people, not the authority of the state, was to be the ultimate guarantor of liberty, justice, and order. "We the people," the preamble began, in a ringing affirmation of these republican doctrines.

At the end of seventeen muggy weeks—May 25 to September 17, 1787—only forty-two of the original fifty-five members remained to sign the Constitution. Three of the forty-two, refusing to do so, returned to their states to resist ratification. The remainder, adjourning to the City Tavern, appropriately celebrated the occasion.

The Clash of Federalists and Antifederalists

The Framing Fathers early foresaw that nationwide acceptance of the Constitution would not be easy to obtain. A formidable barrier was unanimous ratification by all thirteen states, as required for amendment by the still-existent Articles of Confederation. But since absent Rhode Island was certain to veto the Constitu-

tion, the delegates boldly adopted a different scheme. They stipulated that when nine states had registered their approval through specially elected conventions, the Constitution would become the supreme law of the land in those states ratifying (see Art. VII).

This was extraordinary, even revolutionary. It was in effect an appeal over the heads of Congress, which had called the convention, and over the heads of the legislatures that had chosen its members, to the people—or those of the people who could vote. In this way the framers could claim greater popular sanction for their handiwork. A divided Congress submitted the document to the states on this basis, without recommendation of any kind.

The American people were somewhat shocked, so well had the secrets of the convention been kept. The public had expected the old Articles of Confederation to be patched up; now it was handed a startling new document in which, many thought, the precious jewel of state sovereignty was swallowed up. One of the hottest debates of American history forthwith erupted. The antifederalists, who opposed the stronger federal government, were arrayed against the federalists, who obviously favored it.

A motley crowd gathered in the antifederalist camp. Its leaders included prominent revolutionaries such as Samuel Adams, Patrick Henry, and Richard Henry Lee. Their followers consisted primarily, though not exclusively, of the states' rights devotees, the backcountry dwellers, the one-horse farmers, and people in debt—in general, the poorer classes. Many antifederalists saw in the Constitution a plot by the upper crust to steal power from the common folk.

Silver-buckled federalists had power and influence on their side. They enjoyed the support of such commanding figures as George Washington and Benjamin Franklin. Most of them lived along the seaboard. Overall, they were wealthier, better educated, and more organized than the antifederalists. They also controlled the press. Of about a hundred newspapers published in America in the 1780s, only a dozen supported the antifederalist cause.

Antifederalists voiced vehement objections to the "gilded trap" known as the Constitution. They cried with much truth that it had been drawn up by the aristocratic elements and hence was antidemocratic. They likewise charged that the sovereignty of

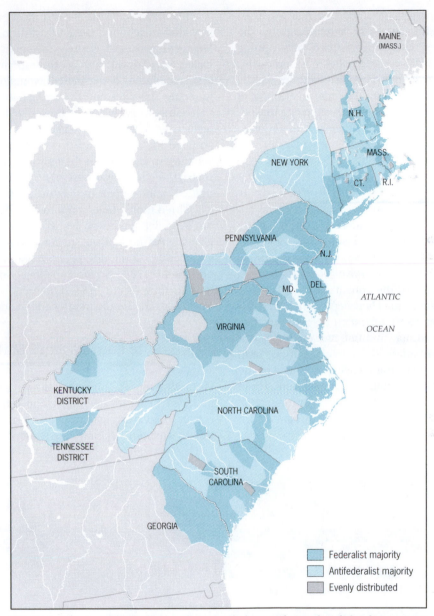

The Struggle over Ratification   *This mottled map shows that federalist support tended to cluster around the coastal areas, which had enjoyed profitable commerce with the outside world, including the export of grain and tobacco. Impoverished frontiersmen, suspicious of a powerful new central government under the Constitution, were generally antifederalists.*

the states was being submerged and that the freedoms of the individual were jeopardized by the absence of a bill of rights. They decried the dropping of annual elections for congressional representatives, the erecting of a federal stronghold ten miles square (later the District of Columbia), the creation of a standing army, the omission of any reference to God, and the highly questionable procedure of ratifying with only two-thirds of the states.

The Great Debate in the States

Special elections, some apathetic but others hotly contested, were held in the various states for members of the ratifying conventions. The candidates—federalist or antifederalist—were elected on the basis of pledges for or against the Constitution.

Four small states quickly accepted the Constitution, for they had come off much better than they expected. Pennsylvania, number two on the list of ratifiers, was the first large state to act, but not until high-handed irregularities had been employed by the federalist legislature in calling a convention. These included the forcible seating of two antifederalist members, their clothes torn and their faces red with rage, in order to complete a quorum.

Massachusetts, the second most populous state, provided an acid test. If the Constitution had failed in Massachusetts, the entire movement might easily have bogged down. The Boston ratifying convention at first contained an antifederalist majority, including grudging Shaysites and the aging Samuel Adams, as suspicious of government power in 1787 as he had been in 1776. The absence of a bill of rights especially alarmed the antifederalists, but the federalists gave solemn assurances that the new Congress would add such a safeguard by amendment. Massachusetts then ratified by the narrow margin of 187 to 168.

Three more states fell into line. Nine states—all but Virginia, New York, North Carolina, and Rhode Island—had now taken shelter under the "new federal roof," and the document was officially adopted on June 21, 1788. But federalist rejoicing was premature so long as the four dissenters, conspicuously New York and Virginia, remained outside the fold.

The Four Laggard States

Proud Virginia, the biggest and most populous state, provided fierce antifederalist opposition. There the college-bred federalist orators, for once, encountered worthy antagonists, including the fiery Patrick Henry.

A Triumphant Cartoon　*It appeared in the* Massachusetts Centinel *on August 2, 1788. Note the two laggards, especially the sorry condition of Rhode Island.*

Hamiltonian Frigate *This victory parade in New York City honors Alexander Hamilton and the ratification of the Constitution. At the key New York ratifying convention at Poughkeepsie, Hamilton, by sheer eloquence and cogent argument, turned a two-thirds majority against the Constitution into a majority of three in favor of it.*

He professed to see in the fearsome parchment the death warrant of liberty. George Washington, James Madison, and John Marshall, on the federalist side, lent influential support. The new Union was going to be formed anyhow, and Virginia could not very well continue comfortably as an independent state. After exciting debate in the state convention, ratification carried, 89 to 79.

New York also experienced an uphill struggle, burdened as it was with its own heavily antifederalist state convention. Alexander Hamilton at heart favored a much stronger central government than that under debate, but he contributed his sparkling personality and persuasive eloquence to whipping up support for federalism as framed. He also joined John Jay and James Madison in penning a masterly series of articles for the New York newspapers. Though designed as propaganda, these essays remain the most penetrating commentary ever written on the Constitution and are still widely sold in book form as *The Federalist*. Probably the most famous of these is Madison's *Federalist* No. 10, which brilliantly refuted the conventional wisdom that a republic could not extend over a large territory.

New York finally yielded. Realizing that the state could not prosper apart from the Union, the convention ratified the document by the close count of 30 to 27.

Last-ditch dissent developed in only two states. A hostile convention met in North Carolina, then adjourned without taking a vote. Rhode Island did not even summon a ratifying convention, rejecting the Constitution by popular referendum. The two most ruggedly individualist centers of the colonial era—homes of the "otherwise minded"—thus ran true to form. They were to change their course, albeit unwillingly, only after the new government had been in operation for some months.

The race for ratification was close and extremely bitter in some localities. No lives were lost, but riotous disturbances broke out in New York and Pennsylvania, involving bruises and bloodshed. There was much behind-the-scenes pressure on delegates who had promised their constituents to vote against the Constitution. The last four states ratified not because they wanted to but because they had to. They could not survive as lone wolves.

A Conservative Triumph

The minority had triumphed—twice. A militant minority of American radicals had engineered the military Revolution that cast off the unwritten British constitution. A militant minority of conservatives—now embracing many of the earlier radicals—had engineered the peaceful revolution that overthrew the inadequate constitution known as the Articles of Confederation. Eleven states, in effect, had seceded from the Confederation, leaving the two still in actually out in the cold.

A majority had not spoken. Only about one-fourth of the adult white males in the country, chiefly the propertied people, had voted for delegates to the ratifying conventions. Careful estimates indicate that if the new Constitution had been submitted to a manhood-suffrage vote, as in New York, it would have encountered much more opposition, probably defeat.

Conservatism was victorious. Safeguards had been erected against mob-rule excesses, while the republican gains of the Revolution were conserved. Radicals like Patrick Henry, who had ousted British rule, saw themselves upended in turn by American conservatives. The federalists were convinced that by setting the drifting ship of state on a steady course they could restore economic and political stability.

Yet if the architects of the Constitution were conservative, it is worth emphasizing that they conserved the principle of republican government through a redefinition of popular sovereignty. Unlike the antifederalists, who believed that the sovereignty of the people resided in a single branch of government—the legislature—the federalists contended that every branch—executive, judiciary, and legislature—effectively represented the people. By ingeniously embedding the doctrine of self-rule in a self-limiting system of checks and balances, the Constitution reconciled the potentially conflicting principles of liberty and order. It elevated the ideals of the Revolution even while setting boundaries to them. One of the distinctive—and enduring—paradoxes of American history was thus revealed: conservatives and radicals alike have championed the heritage of republican revolution.

Chronology

1774   First Continental Congress calls for abolition of slave trade.

1775   Philadelphia Quakers found world's first anti-slavery society.

1776   New Jersey constitution temporarily gives women the vote.

1777   Articles of Confederation adopted by Second Continental Congress.

1780   Massachusetts adopts first constitution drafted in convention and ratified by popular vote.

1781   Articles of Confederation put into effect.

1783   Military officers form Society of the Cincinnati.

1785   Land Ordinance of 1785.

1786   Virginia Statute for Religious Freedom.
Shays's Rebellion.
Meeting of five states to discuss revision of the Articles of Confederation.

1787   Northwest Ordinance.
Constitutional Convention in Philadelphia.

1788   Ratification by nine states guarantees a new government under the Constitution.

VARYING VIEWPOINTS

The Constitution: Revolutionary or Counterrevolutionary?

Although the Constitution has endured over two centuries as the basis of American government, historians have differed sharply over how to interpret its origins and meaning. Early nationalist historians viewed the Constitution as the logical culmination of the Revolution, and a crucial step in saving the young nation from internal chaos and foreign threats.

By the early twentieth century, however, the progressive historians had turned a more critical eye to the Constitution. For historians like Carl Becker and Charles Beard, the Constitution was part of a revolutionary struggle between the lower classes (small farmers, debtors, and laborers) and the upper classes (merchants, financiers, and manufacturers). Beard's *An Economic Interpretation of the Constitution of the United States* (1913) argued that the Articles of Confederation had protected debtors and displeased wealthy elites heavily invested in trade, the public debt, and manufacturing. Reviewing the economic holdings of the Framing Fathers, Beard argued that the Constitution represented a successful attempt by conservative elites to buttress their own economic supremacy at the expense of less fortunate Americans.

Beard's economic interpretation of the Constitution held sway through the 1940s. In the 1950s, however, it fell victim to "consensus" historians such as Robert Brown and Forrest McDonald, who disputed Beard's evidence and argued that the Constitution derived from an emerging consensus that the country needed a stronger central government.

Scholars since the 1950s have searched for new ways to understand the origins of the Constitution. The most influential work has been Gordon Wood's *The Creation of the American Republic* (1969). Wood reinterpreted the ratification controversy as a struggle to define the true essence of republicanism. While antifederalists feared human corruption and, consequently, a strong central government, federalists believed that a strong, balanced government would rein in selfish human instincts and channel them toward the common good. James Madison and the other Founding Fathers argued that an "extensive republic" would achieve stability by virtue of its great size and diversity. In this sense, Wood argued, the Constitution represented a bold experiment and the fulfillment of the most advanced revolutionary ideas—even though it emanated from traditional elites determined to curtail dangerous disruptions to the social order.

For further reading, see the Appendix. For web resources, go to **http://college.hmco.com.**

10

Launching the New Ship of State

◦◦◦

1789–1800

I shall only say that I hold with Montesquieu, that a government must be fitted to a nation, as much as a coat to the individual; and, consequently, that what may be good at Philadelphia may be bad at Paris, and ridiculous at Petersburg [Russia].

ALEXANDER HAMILTON, 1799

America's new ship of state did not spread its sails to the most favorable breezes. Within twelve troubled years the American people had risen up and thrown overboard both the British yoke and the Articles of Confederation. A decade of lawbreaking and constitution smashing was not the best training for government making. Americans had come to regard central authority, replacing that of George III, as a necessary evil—something to be distrusted, watched, and curbed.

Finances of the infant government were likewise precarious. The revenue had declined to a trickle, whereas public debt, with interest heavily in arrears, was mountainous. Worthless paper money, both state and national, was as plentiful as metallic money was scarce. Nonetheless, the Americans were brashly trying to erect a republic on an immense scale, something that no other people had attempted and that traditional political theory deemed impossible. The eyes of a skeptical world were on the upstart United States.

Growing Pains

When the Constitution was launched in 1789, the Republic was continuing to grow at an amazing rate. Population was still doubling about every twenty-five years, and the first official census, in 1790, recorded almost 4 million people. Cities had blossomed proportionately: Philadelphia numbered 42,000; New York, 33,000; Boston, 18,000; Charleston, 16,000; and Baltimore, 13,000.

America's population was still about 90 percent rural, despite the flourishing cities. All but 5 percent of the people lived east of the Appalachian Mountains. The trans-Appalachian overflow was concentrated chiefly in Kentucky, Tennessee, and Ohio, all of which were welcomed as states within fourteen years. (Vermont had preceded them, becoming the fourteenth state in 1791.) Foreign visitors to the new Republic looked down their noses at the roughness and crudity resulting from ax-and-rifle pioneering life.

Washington for President

General Washington, the esteemed war hero, was unanimously drafted as president by the Electoral College in 1789—the only presidential nominee ever to be honored by unanimity.

Washington Honored *This idealized portrait symbolized the reverential awe in which Americans held "the Father of the Country."*

His presence was imposing: 6 feet, 2 inches tall and 175 pounds, with broad and sloping shoulders, strongly pointed chin, and pockmarks (from smallpox) on nose and cheeks. Much preferring the quiet of Mount Vernon to the turmoil of politics, he was perhaps the only president who did not in some way angle for this exalted office. Balanced rather than brilliant, he commanded his followers by strength of character rather than by the arts of the politician.

Washington's long journey from Mount Vernon to New York City, the temporary capital, was a triumphal procession. He was greeted by roaring cannon, pealing bells, flower-carpeted roads, and singing and shouting citizens. With appropriate ceremony, he solemnly and somewhat nervously took the oath of office on April 30, 1789, on a crowded balcony overlooking Wall Street.

Washington soon put his stamp on the new government by establishing the cabinet. The Constitution does not mention a cabinet; it merely provides that the president "may require" written opinions of the heads of the executive branch departments (see Art. II, Sec. II, para. 1). But this system proved so cumbersome that cabinet meetings gradually evolved during the Washington administration. At first only three department heads served under the president: Secretary of State Thomas Jefferson, Secretary of the Treasury Alexander Hamilton, and Secretary of War Henry Knox.

The Bill of Rights

The new nation faced some unfinished business. Many antifederalists had sharply criticized the Constitution drafted at Philadelphia for its failure to provide guarantees of individual rights such as freedom of religion and trial by jury. Many states had ratified the federal Constitution with the understanding that it would soon be amended to include such guarantees. Drawing up a bill of rights headed the list of tasks requiring immediate attention.

The proposed amendments were drafted and submitted to Congress by James Madison, whose intellectual and political skills were quickly making him the leading figure in the new body. Adopted by the necessary number of states in 1791, the first ten

Evolution of the Cabinet

Position	Date Established	Comments
Secretary of state	1789	
Secretary of treasury	1789	
Secretary of war	1789	Loses cabinet status, 1947
Attorney general	1789	Not head of Justice Dept. until 1870
Secretary of navy	1798	Loses cabinet status, 1947
Postmaster general	1829	Loses cabinet status, 1970
Secretary of interior	1849	
Secretary of agriculture	1889	
Secretary of commerce and labor	1903	Office divided in 1913
Secretary of commerce	1913	
Secretary of labor	1913	
Secretary of defense	1947	Subordinate to this secretary, without cabinet rank, are secretaries of army, navy, and air force
Secretary of health, education, and welfare	1953	Office divided in 1979
Secretary of housing and urban development	1965	
Secretary of transportation	1966	
Secretary of energy	1977	
Secretary of health and human services	1979	
Secretary of education	1979	
Secretary of veterans affairs	1989	
Secretary of homeland security	2002	

amendments to the Constitution, popularly known as the Bill of Rights, safeguard some of the most precious American principles. Among these are protections for freedom of religion, speech, and the press; the right to bear arms and to be tried by a jury; and the right to assemble and petition the government for redress of grievances. The Bill of Rights also prohibits cruel and unusual punishments and arbitrary government seizure of private property.

To guard against the danger that enumerating such rights might lead to the conclusion that they were the only ones protected, Madison inserted the crucial Ninth Amendment. It declares that specifying certain rights "shall not be construed to deny or disparage others retained by the people." To reassure states' righters, he included the equally significant Tenth Amendment, which reserves all rights not

explicitly delegated or prohibited by the federal Constitution "to the States respectively, or to the people." By preserving a strong central government while specifying certain protections for minority and individual liberties, Madison's amendments partially swung the federalist pendulum back in an antifederalist direction. (See Amendments I–X, in the Appendix.)

The first Congress also nailed other newly sawed governmental planks into place. It created effective federal courts under the Judiciary Act of 1789. The act organized the Supreme Court, with a chief justice and five associates, as well as federal district and circuit courts, and established the office of attorney general. New Yorker John Jay, Madison's collaborator on *The Federalist* papers, became the first chief justice of the United States.

Hamilton Revives the Corpse of Public Credit

The key figure in the new government was thirty-four-year-old Treasury Secretary Alexander Hamilton, a native of the British West Indies. Hamilton's genius was unquestioned, but critics claimed he loved his adopted country more than he loved his countrymen. Doubt about his character and his loyalty to the republican experiment always swirled about his head. Hamilton regarded himself as a kind of prime minister in Washington's cabinet, and on occasion he thrust his hands into the affairs of other departments, including that of his archrival, Secretary of State Thomas Jefferson.

A financial wizard, Hamilton set out immediately to correct the economic vexations that had crippled the Articles of Confederation. His plan was to shape the fiscal policies of the administration in such a way as to favor the wealthier groups. They, in turn, would gratefully lend the government monetary and political support. The new federal regime would flourish, the propertied classes would fatten, and prosperity would trickle down to the masses.

The youthful financier's first objective was to bolster the national credit. Without public confidence in the government, Hamilton could not secure the funds with which to float his risky schemes. He therefore boldly urged Congress to "fund" the entire national debt "at par" and to assume completely the debts incurred by the states during the recent war.

"Funding at par" meant that the federal government would pay off its debts at face value, plus accumulated interest—a then-enormous total of more than $54 million. So many people believed the infant Treasury incapable of meeting those obligations that government bonds had depreciated to ten or fifteen cents on the dollar. Yet speculators held fistfuls of them, and when Congress passed Hamilton's measure in 1790, they grabbed for more. Some of them galloped into rural areas ahead of the news, buying for a song the depreciated paper holdings of farmers, war veterans, and widows.

Hamilton was willing, even eager, to have the new government shoulder additional obligations. While pushing the funding scheme, he urged Congress to assume the debts of the states, totaling some $21.5 million. The secretary made a convincing case for "assumption." The state debts could be regarded as a proper national obligation, for they had been incurred in the war for independence. But foremost in Hamilton's thinking was the belief that assumption would chain the states more tightly to the "federal chariot." Thus, the secretary's maneuver would shift the attachment of wealthy creditors from the states to the federal government. The support of the rich for the national administration was a crucial link in Hamilton's political strategy of strengthening the central government.

States burdened with heavy debts, such as Massachusetts, were delighted by Hamilton's proposal. States with small debts, such as Virginia, were less charmed. The stage was set for some old-fashioned horse trading. Virginia did not want the state debts assumed, but it did want the forthcoming federal district*—now the District of Columbia—to be located on the Potomac River. Hamilton persuaded a reluctant Jefferson to line up enough votes in Congress for assumption. In return, Virginia would have the federal district in its backyard. The bargain was carried through in 1790.

Customs Duties and Excise Taxes

The new ship of state thus set sail dangerously overloaded. The national debt had swelled to $75 million owing to Hamilton's insistence on honoring the outstanding federal and state obligations alike. But Hamilton, the "Father of the National Debt," was not greatly worried. His objectives were as much political as economic. He believed that, within limits, a national debt was a "national blessing"—a kind of cement of union. The more creditors to whom the government owed money, the more people there would be with a personal stake in the success of his ambitious enterprise.

Where was the money to come from to pay interest on this huge debt and to run the government? Hamilton's first answer was customs duties, derived

---

*Authorized by the Constitution, Art. I, Sec. VIII, para. 17.

from a tariff. Tariff revenues, in turn, depended on a vigorous foreign trade, another crucial link in Hamilton's overall economic strategy for the new Republic.

The first tariff law, which imposed a low tariff of about 8 percent on dutiable imports, was speedily passed by Congress in 1789. Revenue was by far the main goal, but the measure was also designed to erect a low protective wall around infant industries, which bawled noisily for more shelter than they received. Hamilton had the vision to see that the Industrial Revolution would soon reach America, and he argued strongly in favor of more protection for the well-to-do manufacturing groups—another vital element in his economic program. But Congress was still dominated by agricultural and commercial interests, and it voted only two slight increases in the tariff during Washington's presidency.

Hamilton, with characteristic vigor, sought additional internal revenue and in 1791 secured from Congress an excise tax on a few domestic items, notably whiskey. The new levy of seven cents a gallon was borne chiefly by the distillers who lived in the mountains and backcountry. Whiskey flowed so freely on the frontier that it was used for money.

Alexander Hamilton, Secretary of the Treasury *Everyone recognized Hamilton's talents and leadership, but many feared his fierce ambition and disdain for popular government.*

Hamilton Battles Jefferson for a Bank

As the capstone for his financial system, Hamilton proposed a Bank of the United States. With the Bank of England as his model, he envisioned a private institution with the government as its major stockholder. The bank would provide a convenient strongbox for surplus federal funds, stimulate business by keeping money in circulation, and print an urgently needed sound paper currency.

Jefferson, whose written opinion Washington requested, argued vigorously against the bank. The Constitution, he insisted, provided no specific authorization for such a financial octopus. He was convinced that all powers not specifically granted to the central government were reserved to the states, as provided in the about-to-be-ratified Bill of Rights (see Amendment X). He therefore concluded that the states, not Congress, had the power to charter banks. Believing that the Constitution should be interpreted "literally" or "strictly," Jefferson and his states' rights

disciples zealously embraced the theory of "strict construction."

Hamilton, also at Washington's request, prepared a brilliantly reasoned reply to Jefferson's arguments. He boldly invoked the clause of the Constitution that stipulates that Congress may pass any laws "necessary and proper" to carry out the powers vested in the various governmental agencies (see Art. I, Sec. VIII, para. 18). The government was explicitly empowered to collect taxes and regulate trade. In carrying out these basic functions, Hamilton argued, a national bank would be not only "proper" but "necessary." By inference or by implication—that is, by virtue of "implied powers"—Congress would be fully justified in establishing the Bank of the United States. In short, Hamilton contended for a "loose" or "broad" interpretation of the Constitution. He and his federalist followers thus evolved the theory of "loose construction" by invoking the "elastic clause" of the Constitution—a precedent for enormous federal powers.

Hamilton's financial views prevailed. Washington accepted his eloquent and realistic arguments and reluctantly signed the bank measure into law. This explosive issue had been debated with much heat in Congress, where the old North-South cleavage still lurked ominously. The most enthusiastic support for the bank naturally came from the commercial and financial centers of the North; the strongest opposition arose from the agricultural South.

The Bank of the United States, as created by Congress in 1791, was chartered for twenty years. Located in Philadelphia, it was to have capital of $10 million, one-fifth of it owned by the federal government, the rest by private investors.

Mutinous Moonshiners in Pennsylvania

The Whiskey Rebellion, which flared up in southwestern Pennsylvania in 1794, sharply challenged the new national government. Hamilton's excise bore harshly on these homespun pioneer folk. They regarded it not as a tax on a luxury but as a burden on an economic necessity and a medium of exchange. Even preachers of the gospel were paid in "Old Monongahela rye." Defiant distillers finally erected whiskey poles, similar to the liberty poles of anti–stamp tax days in 1765, and raised the cry "Liberty and No Excise." Boldly tarring and feathering revenue officers, they brought collections to a halt.

President Washington, once a revolutionist, was alarmed by what he called these "self-created societies." With the hearty encouragement of Hamilton, he summoned the militia of several states. An army of about thirteen thousand men rallied to the colors, and two widely separated columns marched briskly forth in a gorgeous, leaf-tinted Indian summer. When the troops reached the hills of western Pennsylvania, they found no insurrection. The "Whiskey Boys" were overawed, dispersed, or captured.

The Whiskey Rebellion was minuscule—some three rebels were killed—but its consequences were mighty. George Washington's government, now substantially strengthened, commanded a new respect. Yet the foes of the administration condemned its brutal display of force, charging it had used a sledgehammer to crush a gnat.

The Emergence of Political Parties

Almost overnight Hamilton's fiscal feats established the government's sound credit rating. The Treasury could now borrow needed funds in the Netherlands on favorable terms. But Hamilton's financial successes—funding, assumption, the excise, the bank, suppression of the Whiskey Rebellion—created some political liabilities. All these schemes encroached sharply on states' rights. Many Americans, dubious about the Constitution in the first place, might never have approved it if they had foreseen how the states were going to be overshadowed by the federal colossus. Now, out of resentment against Hamilton's revenue-raising and centralizing policies, an organized opposition began to build. What once was a personal feud between Hamilton and Jefferson developed into a full-blown and frequently bitter political rivalry.

National political parties, in the modern sense, were unknown to America when George Washington took the inaugural oath. There had been Whigs and Tories, federalists and antifederalists, but these groups were factions rather than parties. They had sprung into existence over hotly contested special issues; they had faded away when their cause had triumphed or fizzled.

The Founders at Philadelphia had not envisioned the existence of permanent political parties. Organized opposition to the government seemed tainted with disloyalty, an affront to the spirit of national unity that the glorious cause of the Revolution had inspired.

The notion of a formal party apparatus was thus a novelty in the 1790s, and when Jefferson and Madison first organized their opposition to the Hamiltonian program, they did not anticipate creating a long-lived and popular party. But as their antagonism toward Hamilton endured, and as the boisterous newspapers spread their political message, and Hamilton's, primitive semblances of political parties emerged.

Republicanism Triumphant   *Artists often used classical motifs to celebrate the triumph in America of republicanism—a form of government they traced back to ancient Greece and Rome.*

The two-party system has existed in the United States since that time. Ironically, in light of the early suspicions about the very legitimacy of parties, their competition for power has actually proved to be among the indispensable ingredients of a sound democracy.

The Impact of the French Revolution

When Washington's first administration ended, early in 1793, domestic controversies had already formed two political camps—Hamiltonian Federalists and Jeffersonian Democratic-Republicans. As Washington's second term began, foreign-policy issues brought the differences between them to a fever pitch.

Only a few weeks after Washington's inauguration in 1789, the curtain had risen on the first act of the French Revolution. Twenty-six years were to pass before the seething continent of Europe settled back into a peace of exhaustion. Few non-American events have left a deeper scar on American political and social life. In a sense the French Revolution was misnamed: it was a revolution that sent tremors through much of the civilized world.

Most Americans, except a few ultraconservative Federalists, cheered the early, peaceful stages of the French Revolution, involving as it did a successful attempt to impose constitutional shackles on King Louis XVI. The Revolution entered a more ominous phase in 1792, when France declared war on hostile Austria. Late that year the electrifying news reached America that French citizen armies had hurled back the invading foreigners, and that France had proclaimed itself a republic, endorsing "liberty, equality, and fraternity." Americans enthusiastically sang the rousing revolutionary anthem "The Marseillaise" and renamed roads "Liberty Street" and "Equality Lane."

But centuries of pent-up poison could not be purged without baleful results. The guillotine was set up, the king was beheaded in 1793, the Roman Catholic Church was attacked, and the head-rolling Reign of Terror was begun. Back in America, God-fearing Federalist aristocrats nervously fingered their tender white necks and eyed the Jeffersonian masses apprehensively. Lukewarm Federalist approval of the early Revolution turned, almost overnight, to heated complaints about "blood-drinking cannibals."

Sober-minded Jeffersonians regretted the bloodshed. But they felt, with Jefferson, that one could not expect to be carried from "despotism to liberty in a feather bed," and that a few thousand aristocratic heads were a cheap price to pay for human freedom.

Such approbation was shortsighted, for peril loomed ahead. The earlier battles of the French Revolution had not hurt America directly, but now Britain was sucked into the contagious conflict. The conflagration speedily spread to the New World, where it vividly affected the expanding young American republic.

Washington's Neutrality Proclamation

Ominously, the Franco-American alliance of 1778 was still on the books, and many Jeffersonian Democratic-Republicans favored honoring the pact.

Aflame with the liberal ideals of the French Revolution, Jeffersonians were eager to enter the conflict against Britain (the recent foe) at the side of France (the recent friend).

But level-headed President Washington was not swayed by the clamor of the crowd. Backed by Hamilton, he believed that war had to be avoided at all costs. Accordingly, Washington boldly issued his Neutrality Proclamation in 1793, shortly after the outbreak of war between Britain and France. This epochal document not only proclaimed the government's official neutrality in the widening conflict but sternly warned American citizens to be impartial toward both armed camps. As America's first formal declaration of aloofness from Old World quarrels, Washington's Neutrality Proclamation proved to be a major prop of the spreading isolationist tradition.

The pro-French Jeffersonians were enraged by the Neutrality Proclamation; the pro-British Federalists were heartened. Debate intensified when an impetuous, thirty-year-old representative of the French republic, Citizen Edmond Genêt, landed at Charleston, South Carolina. With unrestrained zeal, he undertook to outfit privateers and otherwise take advantage of the existing Franco-American alliance. Swept away by his enthusiastic reception by the Jeffersonian Democratic-Republicans, Genêt foolishly came to believe that the Neutrality Proclamation did not reflect the true wishes of the American people. He consequently embarked on an outrageously unneutral campaign to appeal over the head of "Old Washington" to the sovereign voters. The president quickly demanded Genêt's withdrawal, and the Frenchman was replaced by a less impulsive emissary.

Embroilments with Britain

President Washington's far-visioned policy of neutrality was sorely tried by the British. For ten years they had been retaining the chain of northern frontier posts on United States soil, all in defiance of the peace treaty of 1783. British agents openly sold firearms to the Miami Confederacy, an alliance of eight Indian nations who attacked Americans invading their lands northwest of the Ohio River. In 1790 and 1791 Little Turtle's braves repulsed armies led by

American Posts Held by the British After 1783

Generals Josiah Harmer and Arthur St. Clair, handing the United States what remains one of its worst military defeats in the history of the frontier. But in 1794 General "Mad Anthony" Wayne's army routed the Miamis at the Battle of Fallen Timbers. In the Treaty of Greenville, signed in August 1795, the confederacy gave up most of the present-day states of Ohio and Indiana. In exchange the Indians received monetary compensation, the right to hunt on the lands they had ceded, and what they understood to be recognition of their sovereign status.

On the sea frontier, the British were eager to starve out the French West Indies and naturally expected the United States to defend them under the Franco-American alliance. Hard-boiled commanders of the Royal Navy, acting under instructions from London in 1793, struck savagely. They seized about three hundred American merchant ships in the West Indies, impressed scores of seamen into service on British vessels, and threw hundreds of others into foul dungeons. A mighty outcry arose, chiefly from incensed Jeffersonians, that America should once again fight George III in defense of its liberties.

President Washington, in a last desperate gamble to avert war, sent Chief Justice John Jay to London in 1794. The Jeffersonians were acutely unhappy over the choice, partly because they feared that so notorious a Federalist and Anglophile would sell out his country.

Unhappily, Jay entered the negotiations with weak cards and could win only a few concessions.

The British did promise to evacuate the chain of posts on U.S. soil—a pledge that inspired little confidence, since it had been made before in Paris (to the same John Jay!) in 1783. In addition, Britain consented to pay damages for the recent seizures of American ships. But the British stopped short of pledging anything about future maritime seizures and impressments or about supplying arms to Indians. And they forced Jay to give ground by binding the young nation to pay the debts still owed to British merchants on pre-Revolutionary accounts.

When the Jeffersonians learned of Jay's concessions, their rage was fearful to behold. The treaty seemed like an abject surrender to Britain, as well as a betrayal of the Jeffersonian South. Jeffersonian mobs hanged, burned, and guillotined in effigy that "damn'd archtraitor, Sir John Jay." His unpopular pact, more than any other issue, vitalized the newborn Democratic-Republican party of Thomas Jefferson.

Jay's Treaty had other unforeseen consequences. Fearing that the treaty foreshadowed an Anglo-American alliance, Spain moved hastily to strike a deal with the United States. Pinckney's Treaty of 1795 with Spain granted the Americans virtually everything they demanded, including free navigation of the Mississippi and the large disputed territory north of Florida.

Exhausted after the diplomatic and partisan battles of his second term, President Washington decided to retire. His choice contributed powerfully to establishing a two-term tradition for American presidents.* In his Farewell Address to the nation in 1796, Washington strongly advised the avoidance of "permanent alliances" like the still-vexatious French treaty of 1778. Contrary to general misunderstanding, Washington did not oppose all alliances, but rather favored only "temporary alliances" for "extraordinary emergencies."

Washington's contributions as president were enormous, even though the sparkling Hamilton at times seemed to outshine him. The central government, its fiscal feet now under it, was solidly established. The West was expanding. The merchant marine was plowing the seas. Above all, Washington had kept the nation out of both overseas entanglements and foreign wars. The experimental stage had passed, and the presidential chair could now be turned over to a less impressive figure. But republics are notoriously ungrateful. When Washington left office in 1797, he was showered with the brickbats of partisan abuse, quite in contrast with the bouquets that had greeted his arrival.

John Adams Becomes President

Who should succeed the exalted "Father of His Country"? Alexander Hamilton was the best-known Federalist leader now that Washington had bowed out. But his financial policies, some of which had fattened speculators, had made him so unpopular that he could not hope to be elected president. The Federalists were forced to turn to Washington's experienced but ungracious vice president John Adams, a rugged chip off old Plymouth Rock. The Democratic-Republicans naturally rallied behind their master organizer and leader, Thomas Jefferson.

Political passions ran feverishly high in the presidential campaign of 1796. The lofty presence of Washington had hitherto imposed some restraints on partisan attacks; now the lid was off. Cultured Federalists referred to the Jeffersonians as "fire-eating salamanders, poison-sucking toads." Federalists and Democratic-Republicans even drank their ale in separate taverns. The Jeffersonians again assailed the too-forceful crushing of the Whiskey Rebellion and, above all, the negotiation of Jay's hated treaty.

John Adams, with most of his support in New England, squeezed through by the narrow margin of 71 votes to 68 in the Electoral College. Jefferson, as runner-up, became vice president.* One of the ablest statesmen of his day, Adams at sixty-two was bald, short, and thickset ("His Rotundity"). He impressed observers as a man of stern principles who did his duty with stubborn devotion. Although learned and upright, he was a tact-

---

* This tradition, not broken until 1940 by Franklin D. Roosevelt, was made part of the Constitution in 1951 by the Twenty-second Amendment.

* The possibility of such an inharmonious two-party combination in the future was removed by the Twelfth Amendment to the Constitution in 1804. (See text in the Appendix.)

less and prickly intellectual aristocrat with no appeal to the masses and no desire to cultivate any. Many citizens regarded him with "respectful irritation."

The crusty New Englander suffered from other handicaps. He had stepped into Washington's shoes, which no successor could hope to fill. In addition, Adams was hated by Hamilton, who now headed the pro-war faction of the Federalist party. The famed financier even secretly plotted with certain members of the cabinet against the new president, who soon had a conspiracy rather than a cabinet on his hands. Most ominous of all, Adams inherited a violent quarrel with France—a quarrel whose gunpowder lacked only a spark.

Unofficial Fighting with France

The Jeffersonians were not the only ones infuriated by Jay's Treaty. The French condemned it as the initial step toward an American alliance with Britain, their perpetual foe. French warships, in retaliation, seized about three hundred defenseless American merchant vessels by mid-1797.

President Adams kept his head, temporarily, even though the nation was mightily aroused. Trying to reach an agreement with the French, he appointed a diplomatic commission of three men, including John Marshall, the future chief justice. When Adams's envoys reached Paris in 1797, they were secretly approached by three French go-betweens, later referred to as X, Y, and Z in the published dispatches. The French spokesmen demanded an unneutral loan of 32 million florins, plus what amounted to a bribe of $250,000, for the privilege of merely talking with Talleyrand, the French foreign minister.

These terms were intolerable. The American trio knew that bribes were standard diplomatic devices in Europe, but they gagged at paying a quarter of a million dollars for mere talk, without any assurances of a settlement. Negotiations quickly broke down.

War hysteria swept through the United States, catching up even President Adams. The slogan of the hour became "Millions for defense, but not one cent for tribute." Despite considerable Jeffersonian opposition in Congress, war preparations were pushed along at a feverish pace. The Navy Department was created; the three-ship navy was expanded; the United States Marine Corps was established.

Bloodshed was confined to the sea, principally in the West Indies. In two and a half years of undeclared hostilities (1798–1800), American privateers and men-of-war of the new navy captured over eighty armed vessels flying the French colors, though several hundred Yankee merchant ships were lost to the enemy. Only a slight push, it seemed, might plunge both nations into a full-dress war.

Adams Puts Patriotism Above Party

Embattled France, its hands full in Europe, wanted no war. An outwitted Talleyrand realized that to fight the United States would add one more foe to his enemy roster. He therefore let it be known, through roundabout channels, that if the Americans would send a new minister, he would be received with proper respect.

Despite the popular acclaim that he might have enjoyed by leading the nation into a full-fledged war, Adams early in 1799 submitted to the Senate the name of a new minister to France. Hamilton and his war-hawk faction were enraged. But public opinion—Jeffersonian and reasonable Federalist alike—was favorable to one last try for peace.

America's new envoys found the political skies brightening when they reached Paris early in 1800. The ambitious "Little Corporal," the Corsican Napoleon Bonaparte, had recently seized dictatorial power. He was eager to free his hands of the American squabble so that he might continue to redraw the map of Europe—and perhaps create a New World empire in Louisiana. The afflictions and ambitions of the Old World were again working to America's advantage.

After a great deal of haggling, a memorable treaty known as the Convention of 1800 was signed in Paris. France agreed to annul the twenty-two-year-old marriage of (in)convenience, but as a kind of alimony the United States agreed to pay the damage claims of American shippers. So ended the nation's only peacetime military alliance for a century and a half. Its troubled history does much to explain the traditional antipathy of the American people to foreign entanglements.

Preparation for War to Defend Commerce: The Building of the Frigate *Philadelphia* *In 1803 this frigate ran onto the rocks near Tripoli harbor, and about three hundred officers and men were imprisoned by the Tripolitans. The ship was refloated for service against the Americans, but Stephen Decatur led a party of men that set it afire.*

John Adams, flinty to the end, deserves immense credit for his belated push for peace, even though moved in part by jealousy of Hamilton. Adams not only avoided the hazards of war but unwittingly smoothed the path for the peaceful purchase of Louisiana three years later. If America had drifted into a full-blown war with France in 1800, Napoleon would not have sold Louisiana to Jefferson on any terms in 1803.

President Adams, the bubble of his popularity pricked by peace, was aware of his signal contribution to the nation. He later suggested as the epitaph for his tombstone (not used): "Here lies John Adams, who took upon himself the responsibility of peace with France in the year 1800."

The Federalist Witch Hunt

Exulting Federalists had meanwhile capitalized on the anti-French frenzy to drive through Congress in 1798 a sheaf of laws designed to reduce or gag their Jeffersonian foes.

The first of these oppressive laws was aimed at supposedly pro-Jeffersonian "aliens." The Federalist Congress, hoping to discourage the "dregs" of Europe, erected a disheartening barrier. They raised the residence requirements for aliens who desired to become citizens from a tolerable five years to an intolerable fourteen. This drastic new law violated the traditional American policy of open-door hospitality and speedy assimilation.

Two additional Alien Laws struck heavily at undesirable immigrants. The president was empowered to deport dangerous foreigners in time of peace and to deport or imprison them in time of hostilities. This was an arbitrary grant of executive power contrary to American tradition and to the spirit of the Constitution, even though the stringent Alien Laws were never enforced.

The "lockjaw" Sedition Act, the last measure of the harsh Federalist clampdown, was a direct slap at two priceless freedoms guaranteed in the Constitution by the Bill of Rights in the First Amendment—freedom of speech and freedom of the press. This law provided that anyone who impeded the policies of the government or falsely defamed its officials, including the president, would be liable to a heavy fine and imprisonment.

Many outspoken Jeffersonian editors were indicted under the Sedition Act and ten were brought to trial, most in front of prejudiced Federalist judges. All of them were convicted, including Vermont congressman Matthew Lyon (the "Spitting Lion"), who had gained fame by spitting in the face of a Federalist and fighting on the floor of Congress.

The Sedition Act seemed to be in direct conflict with the Constitution. But the Supreme Court, dominated by Federalists, was of no mind to declare this Federalist law unconstitutional (the law expired in March 1801). This attempt by the Federalists to crush free speech and silence the opposition party undoubtedly made many converts for the Jeffersonian cause.

Yet the Alien and Sedition Acts, despite pained outcries from the Jeffersonians, commanded widespread popular support. Anti-French hysteria played directly into the hands of witch-hunting conservatives. In the congressional elections of 1798–1799, the Federalists, riding a wave of popularity, scored the most sweeping victory of their entire history.

The Virginia (Madison) and Kentucky (Jefferson) Resolutions

Resentful Jeffersonians naturally refused to take the Alien and Sedition Acts lying down. Jefferson himself feared that if the Federalists managed to choke free speech and free press, they would then wipe out other precious constitutional guarantees. His own fledgling political party might even be stamped out of existence.

Fearing prosecution for sedition, Jefferson secretly wrote a series of resolutions, which the Kentucky legislature approved in 1798 and 1799. His friend and fellow Virginian James Madison drafted a similar but less extreme statement, which was adopted by the Virginia legislature in 1798.

Both Jefferson and Madison stressed the compact theory—a theory popular among English political philosophers in the seventeenth and eighteenth centuries. As applied to America by the Jeffersonians,

this concept meant that the thirteen sovereign states, in creating the federal government, had entered into a "compact," or contract, regarding its jurisdiction. The national government was consequently the agent or creation of the states. Since water can rise no higher than its source, the individual states were the final judges of whether their agent had broken the "compact" by overstepping the authority originally granted. Invoking this logic, Jefferson's Kentucky resolutions concluded that the federal regime had exceeded its constitutional powers and that, with regard to the Alien and Sedition Acts, "nullification" was the "rightful remedy."

The Virginia and Kentucky resolutions were a brilliant formulation of the extreme states' rights view of the Union—indeed more sweeping in their implications than their authors had intended. They were later used by southerners to support nullification—and ultimately secession. Yet neither Jefferson nor Madison, as Founding Fathers of the Union, had any intention of breaking it up: they were groping for ways to preserve it. Their resolutions were basically campaign documents designed to crystallize opposition to the Federalist party and to unseat it in the upcoming presidential election of 1800. The only real nullification that Jefferson had in view was the nullification of Federalist abuses.

Federalists Versus Democratic-Republicans

As the presidential contest of 1800 approached, the differences between Federalists and Democratic-Republicans were sharply etched. As might be expected, most federalists of the pre-Constitutional period (1787–1789) became Federalists in the 1790s. Largely welded by Hamilton into an effective group by 1793, they openly advocated rule by the "best people." "Those who own the country," remarked John Jay, "ought to govern it." With their intellectual arrogance and Tory tastes, Hamiltonians distrusted full-blown democracy as the fountain of all mischiefs and feared the "swayability" of the untutored common folk.

Hamiltonian Federalists also advocated a strong central government with the power to crush democratic excesses like Shays's Rebellion, protect the lives and estates of the wealthy, and subordinate the sovereignty-loving states. They believed the national government should support private enterprise, not interfere with it. This attitude came naturally to the seaboard merchants, manufacturers, and shippers who made up the majority of Federalist support. Farther inland, few Hamiltonians dwelled.

Federalists were also pro-British in foreign affairs. Some of them still harbored mildly Loyalist sentiments from pre-Revolutionary days and saw foreign trade with Britain as a key to the success of Hamilton's financial policies.

Leading the anti-Federalists, who eventually came to be known as Democratic-Republicans or sometimes simply Republicans, was Thomas Jefferson. Lanky and relaxed in appearance, lacking oratorical skills and personal aggressiveness, he became a master political organizer through his ability to lead people rather than drive them. His strongest appeal was to the middle class and to the underprivileged—the "dirt" farmers, the laborers, the artisans, and the small shopkeepers.

Liberal-thinking Jefferson, with his aristocratic head set on a farmer's frame, was a bundle of inconsistencies. By one set of tests he should have been a Federalist, for he was a Virginia aristocrat and slave-owner who lived in an imposing hilltop mansion at Monticello. A so-called traitor to the upper class, Jefferson cherished uncommon sympathy for the common people, especially the downtrodden, the oppressed, and the persecuted. As he wrote in 1800, "I have sworn upon the altar of God eternal hostility against every form of tyranny over the mind of man."

The Jeffersonian Democratic-Republicans demanded a weak central regime. They believed that the best government was one that governed least, and that the bulk of power should be retained by the states. There the people could keep a more vigilant eye on their public servants. The national debt should be paid off, and government should provide no special privileges for special classes, especially manufacturers. Agriculture, to Jefferson, was the favored branch of the economy. He regarded farming as essentially ennobling; it kept people away from wicked cities and close to the sod. Most of his followers naturally came from the agricultural South and West.

Monticello, Jefferson's Self-Designed Architectural Marvel

Above all, Jefferson advocated the rule of the people. But he did not propose thrusting the ballot into the hands of every adult white male; he favored government *for* the people but not *by all* the people. Since the ignorant were incapable of self-government, only people literate enough to inform themselves about citizenship should have the ballot. Universal education would have to precede universal suffrage. Jefferson had a profound faith in the reasonableness and teachableness of the masses and in their collective wisdom when taught.

Landlessness among American citizens threatened popular democracy as much as illiteracy, in Jefferson's eyes. He feared that propertyless dependents would be political pawns in the hands of their landowning superiors. How could the emergence of a landless class of voters be avoided? The answer, in part, was by slavery. A system of black slave labor ensured that southern white yeoman farmers would remain independent landowners and not be forced to labor for low wages in others' tobacco and rice fields. Jefferson thus tortuously reconciled slaveholding—his own included—with his more democratic impulses.

Yet for his time, Jefferson's belief that white, free men could become responsible and knowledgeable citizens was open-minded. He also championed their free speech, for without free speech and a free press, the misdeeds of tyranny could not be exposed. Although Jefferson suffered much foul abuse from editorial pens, he said that he would choose "newspapers without a government" rather than "a government without newspapers."

Jeffersonian Democratic-Republicans, unlike the Federalist "British boot lickers," were basically pro-French. They believed that it was to America's advantage to support the liberal ideals of the French Revolution rather than applaud the reaction of the British Tories.

So as the young Republic's first full decade of nationhood came to a close, the Founders' hopes seemed already imperiled. Conflicts over domestic politics and foreign policy undermined the unity of the Revolutionary era and called into question the very viability of the American experiment in democracy. As the presidential election of 1800 approached, the danger loomed that the fragile and battered American ship of state would founder on the rocks of controversy. The shores of history are littered with the wreckage of nascent nations torn asunder before they could grow to stable maturity. Why should the United States expect to enjoy a happier fate?

Chronology

1789	Constitution formally put into effect. Judiciary Act of 1789. Washington elected president. French Revolution begins.
1790	First official census.
1791	Bill of Rights adopted. Vermont becomes fourteenth state. Bank of the United States created. Excise tax passed.
1792	Washington reelected president.
1792–1793	Federalist and Democratic-Republican parties formed.
1793	Louis XVI beheaded; radical phase of French Revolution. Washington's Neutrality Proclamation. Citizen Genêt affair.
1794	Whiskey Rebellion. Battle of Fallen Timbers. Jay's Treaty with Britain.
1795	Treaty of Greenville: Indians cede Ohio. Pinckney's Treaty with Spain.
1796	Washington's Farewell Address.
1797	Adams becomes president. XYZ affair.
1798	Alien and Sedition Acts.
1798–1799	Kentucky and Virginia resolutions.
1798–1800	Undeclared war with France.
1800	Convention of 1800: peace with France.

For further reading, see the Appendix. For web resources, go to **http://college.hmco.com**.

The Triumphs and Travails of the Jeffersonian Republic

<hr/>

1800–1812

Timid men . . . prefer the calm of despotism to the boisterous sea of liberty.

THOMAS JEFFERSON, 1796

In the critical presidential election of 1800, the first in which Federalists and Democratic-Republicans functioned as two national political parties, John Adams and Thomas Jefferson again squared off against each other. The choice seemed clear and dramatic. Adams's Federalists waged a defensive struggle for a strong central government and public order. Their Jeffersonian opponents presented themselves as the guardians of agrarian purity, liberty, and states' rights.

The next dozen years, however, would turn what seemed like a clear-cut choice in 1800 into a messier reality, as the Jeffersonians in power were confronted with a series of opportunities and crises requiring the assertion of federal authority. As the first challengers successfully to rout a reigning party, the Republicans were also the first to learn that it is far easier to condemn from the stump than to govern consistently.

Federalist and Republican Mudslingers

In fighting for their survival, the Federalists labored under heavy handicaps. Their Alien and Sedition Acts had aroused a host of enemies, although most of these critics were dyed-in-the-wool Jeffersonians. The Hamiltonian wing of the Federalist party, robbed of its glorious war with France, split openly with President Adams, and Hamilton himself attacked the president.

The most damaging blow to the Federalists, however, was the refusal of Adams to give them a rousing fight with France. Their feverish war preparations had swelled the public debt and required disagreeable new taxes, including a stamp tax. After all these unpopular measures, the war scare had petered out, and the country was left with an all-dressed-up-but-no-place-to-go feeling.

Thrown on the defensive, the Federalists concentrated their fire on Jefferson himself, who became the victim of one of America's earliest "whispering campaigns." He was accused of having robbed a widow and her children of a trust fund and of having fathered numerous mulatto children by his own slave women. (Jefferson's long-rumored intimacy with his slave Sally Hemings has recently been confirmed by DNA testing.) As a liberal in religion, Jefferson had earlier incurred the wrath of the orthodox clergy, largely through his successful struggle to separate church and state in Virginia. From the New England stronghold of Federalism and Congregationalism, preachers thundered against his alleged atheism. Old ladies of Federalist families, fearing Jefferson's election, even buried their Bibles or hung them in wells.

The Jeffersonian "Revolution of 1800"

Jefferson won by a majority of 73 electoral votes to 65. In defeat, the colorless and presumably unpopular Adams polled more electoral strength than he had gained four years earlier—except for New York. The Empire State fell into the Jeffersonian basket, and with it the election, largely because Aaron Burr, a master wire-puller, turned New York to Jefferson by the narrowest of margins. The Virginian polled the bulk of his strength in the South and West, particularly in those states where universal white manhood suffrage had been adopted.

Jeffersonian joy was dampened by an unexpected deadlock. Through a technicality Jefferson, the presidential candidate, and Burr, his vice-presidential running mate, received the same number of electoral votes for the presidency. Under the Constitution the tie could be broken only by the House of Representatives (see Art. II, Sec. I, para. 2). This body would be controlled for several more months by the lame duck Federalists, who preferred Burr to the hated Jefferson.*

---

* A "lame duck" has been humorously defined as a politician whose political goose has been cooked at the recent elections. The possibility of another such tie was removed by the Twelfth Amendment in 1804 (for text, see the Appendix). Before then, each elector had two votes, and the second-place finisher became vice president.

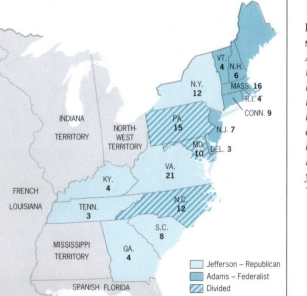

Presidential Election of 1800 (with electoral vote by state) *New York was the key state in this election, and Aaron Burr helped to swing it away from the Federalists with tactics that anticipated the political machines of a later day. Federalists complained that Burr "travels every night from one meeting of Republicans to another, haranguing . . . them to the most zealous exertions. [He] can stoop so low as to visit every low tavern that may happen to be crowded with his dear fellow citizens." But Burr proved that the price was worth it. "We have beat you," Burr told kid-gloved Federalists after the election, "by superior Management."*

Voting in the House moved slowly to a climax as exhausted representatives snored in their seats. The agonizing deadlock was broken at last when a few Federalists, despairing of electing Burr and hoping for moderation from Jefferson, refrained from voting. The election then went to the rightful candidate. John Adams, as fate would have it, was the last Federalist president of the United States. His party sank slowly into the mire of political oblivion and ultimately disappeared completely in the days of Andrew Jackson.

Jefferson later claimed that the election of 1800 was a "revolution" comparable to that of 1776. But it was no revolution in the sense of a massive popular upheaval or an upending of the political system. Jefferson had only narrowly squeaked through to victory. Jefferson meant that his election represented a return to what he considered the original spirit of the Revolution. In his eyes, Hamilton and Adams had betrayed the ideals of 1776 and 1787. Jefferson's mission, as he saw it, was to restore the republican experiment, to check the growth of government, and to halt the decay of virtue that had set in under Federalist rule.

No less "revolutionary" was the peaceful and orderly transfer of power on the basis of an election whose results all parties accepted. This was a remarkable—indeed even revolutionary—achievement for a raw young nation, especially after all the partisan bitterness that had agitated the country during Adams's presidency. After a decade of division and doubt, Americans could take justifiable pride in the vigor of their experiment in democracy.

Responsibility Breeds Moderation

"Long Tom" Jefferson was inaugurated president on March 4, 1801, in the swampy village of Washington, the crude new national capital. Tall (6 feet, 2.5 inches), with large hands and feet, red hair ("the Red Fox"), and prominent cheekbones and chin, he was an arresting figure. Believing that the customary pomp did not befit his democratic ideals, he spurned a horse-drawn coach and strode to the Capitol from his boardinghouse.

Jefferson's inaugural address, beautifully phrased, was a classic statement of democratic principles.

Seeking to allay Federalist fears of a bull-in-the-china-shop overturn, Jefferson ingratiatingly intoned, "We are all Republicans, we are all Federalists." As for foreign affairs, he pledged "honest friendship with all nations, entangling alliances with none."

With its rustic setting, Washington lent itself admirably to the simplicity and frugality of the Jeffersonian Republicans. In this respect, it contrasted sharply with the elegant atmosphere of New York City, the former temporary capital.

As president, Jefferson was shockingly unconventional. He often received callers in sloppy attire—

Jefferson in Casual Attire *As befitted a champion of the new democracy, Jefferson typically dressed casually, shunning the sartorial pretensions affected by many Federalists.*

once in a dressing gown and slippers. He started the precedent, unbroken until Woodrow Wilson's presidency 112 years later, of sending messages to Congress to be read by a clerk. Personal appearances, in the Federalist manner, suggested too strongly a monarchical speech from the throne.

As if plagued by an evil spirit, Jefferson was forced to reverse many of the political principles he had so vigorously championed. There were in fact two Thomas Jeffersons. One was the scholarly private citizen who philosophized in his study. The other was the harassed public official, who made the disturbing discovery that bookish theories worked out differently in the noisy arena of practical politics. The open-minded Virginian was therefore consistently inconsistent; it is easy to quote one Jefferson to refute the other.

As a practical politician, Jefferson proved able and successful. He was especially effective in the informal atmosphere of a dinner party, where he would woo congressional representatives while personally pouring imported wines and serving French food.

In part, Jefferson had to rely on his charm because his party was so weak-jointed. Denied the power to dispense patronage, the Republicans could not build a political following. Opposition to the Federalists was the chief glue holding them together, and as the Federalists faded, so did Republican unity. The era of well-developed, well-disciplined political parties still lay in the future.

At the outset, Jefferson was determined to undo the Federalist abuses begotten by the anti-French hysteria. The hated Alien and Sedition Acts had already expired. The incoming president speedily pardoned the "martyrs" serving sentences under the Sedition Act, and the government returned many fines. Shortly after Congress met, the Jeffersonians enacted the new naturalization law of 1802, which reduced the unreasonable requirement of fourteen years of residence to five years.

Jefferson actually kicked away only one substantial prop of the Hamiltonian economic system. He hated the excise tax, which bred bureaucrats and bore heavily on his farmer following, and he early persuaded Congress to repeal it. But except for excising the excise tax, the Jeffersonians left the Hamiltonian framework essentially intact. They launched no attack on the Bank of the United States, nor did they repeal the mildly protective Federalist tariff.

Paradoxically, Jefferson's moderation thus further cemented the gains of the "Revolution of 1800." By shrewdly absorbing many major Federalist programs, Jefferson showed that a change of regime need not be disastrous for the defeated group. His restraint pointed the way toward the two-party system that was later to become a characteristic feature of American politics.

The "Dead Clutch" of the Judiciary

The "deathbed" Judiciary Act of 1801 was one of the last important laws passed by the expiring Federalist Congress. It created sixteen new federal judgeships and other judicial offices. President Adams remained at his desk until nine o'clock in the evening on his last day in office, supposedly signing the commissions of the Federalist "midnight judges."

This Federalist-sponsored Judiciary Act, though a long-overdue reform, aroused bitter resentment. "Packing" of these lifetime posts with anti-Jeffersonian partisans was, in Republican eyes, a brazen attempt by the ousted party to entrench itself in one of the three powerful branches of government. Jeffersonians condemned the midnight judges in violent language.

The newly elected Republican Congress bestirred itself to repeal the Judiciary Act of 1801 in the year after its passage. Jeffersonians thus swept sixteen benches from under their recently appointed midnight judges.

Jeffersonians likewise had their knives sharpened for the scalp of Chief Justice John Marshall, whom Adams had appointed to the Supreme Court in the dying days of his term. The strong-willed Marshall, with his rasping voice and steel-trap mind, was a cousin of Thomas Jefferson. As a Federalist and fervent advocate of a powerful central government, Marshall was cordially disliked by the states' rights Jeffersonians. The Federalist party died out, but Marshall lived on, handing down Federalist decisions serenely for thirty-four years under Democratic-Republican administrations. For over three decades, the ghost of Alexander Hamilton spoke through the lanky, black-robed judge.

One of the midnight judges of 1801 presented John Marshall with a historic opportunity. When obscure William Marbury, whom President Adams had named a justice of the peace for the District of Columbia, learned that his commission was being shelved by Secretary of State James Madison, he sued for its delivery. Chief Justice John Marshall knew that his Jeffersonian rivals, entrenched in the executive branch, would hardly spring forward to enforce a writ to deliver the commission to his fellow Federalist Marbury. He therefore dismissed Marbury's suit, avoiding a direct showdown. But the wily Marshall snatched victory from the jaws of this judicial defeat. In explaining his ruling, Marshall said that the part of the Judiciary Act of 1789 on which Marbury tried to base his appeal was unconstitutional. The act had attempted to assign to the Supreme Court powers that the Constitution had not foreseen.

In this self-denying opinion, Marshall greatly magnified the authority of the Court—and slapped at the Jeffersonians. Until the case of *Marbury* v. *Madison* (1803), controversy had clouded the question of who had the final authority to determine the meaning of the Constitution. Jefferson in the Kentucky resolutions (1798) had tried to assign that right to the individual states. But now his cousin on the Court had cleverly promoted the contrary principle of "judicial review"—the idea that the Supreme Court alone had the last word on the question of constitutionality. In this landmark case, Marshall inserted the keystone into the arch that supports the tremendous power of the Supreme Court in American life.*

Jefferson: A Reluctant Warrior

One of Jefferson's first actions as president was to reduce the military establishment to a mere 2,500 officers and men. Jefferson's reluctance to spend money for soldiers and ships was less about money than about republican ideals. He fondly hoped that America would transcend Europe's bloody wars and set an example for the world by winning friends through "peaceful coercion." The Republicans also distrusted standing armies as standing invitations to dictatorships. Even navies, the farm-loving Jeffersonians feared, might embroil the Republic in costly and corrupting wars far from America's shores.

But harsh realities forced Jefferson's principles to bend. Pirates of the North African Barbary States had long made a national industry of blackmailing and plundering merchant ships that ventured into the Mediterranean. Preceding Federalist administrations had been forced to buy protection. At the time of the French crisis of 1798, when Americans were shouting, "Millions for defense, but not one cent for tribute," twenty-six barrels of blackmail dollars were being shipped to Algiers.

War across the Atlantic was not part of the Jeffersonian vision—but neither was paying tribute to a pack of pirate states. The showdown came in 1801. The pasha of Tripoli, dissatisfied with his share of protection money, informally declared war on the United States by cutting down the flagstaff of the American consulate. A gauntlet was thus thrown squarely into the face of Jefferson—the noninterventionist, the critic of a big-ship navy, and the political foe of Federalist shippers. He reluctantly rose to the challenge by dispatching the infant navy to "the shores of Tripoli," as related in the song of the U.S. Marine Corps. After four years of intermittent fighting, Jefferson succeeded in exacting a treaty of peace from Tripoli in 1805 in which the United States paid $60,000 for captured Americans.

The Louisiana Godsend

A secret pact, fraught with peril for America, was signed in 1800. Napoleon Bonaparte induced the king of Spain to cede to France, for attractive considerations, the immense trans-Mississippi region of Louisiana, which included the New Orleans area. Then, in 1802, the right of deposit at New Orleans, guaranteed to America by the treaty of 1795, was withdrawn. Deposit (warehouse) privileges were vital to

---

* The next invalidation of a federal law by the Supreme Court came fifty-four years later with the explosive *Dred Scott* decision (see p. 258).

frontier farmers who floated their produce down the Mississippi to its mouth, there to await oceangoing vessels. A roar of anger rolled up the mighty river and into its tributary valleys. American pioneers talked wildly of descending on New Orleans, rifles in hand.

Thomas Jefferson was again on the griddle. Louisiana in the senile grip of Spain posed no real threat; America could seize the territory when the time was ripe. But Louisiana in the iron fist of Napoleon, the preeminent military genius of his age, foreshadowed a dark and blood-drenched future.

Hoping to quiet the clamor of the West, Jefferson moved decisively. Early in 1803 he sent James Monroe to Paris to join forces with the regular minister there, Robert R. Livingston. The two envoys were instructed to buy New Orleans and as much land to the east as they could get for a maximum of $10 million.

At this critical juncture, Napoleon suddenly abandoned his dream of a New World empire and decided to sell all Louisiana. Two developments prompted his change of mind. First, he had failed to reconquer the sugar-rich island of Santo Domingo, for which Louisiana was to serve as a source of foodstuffs. Infuriated ex-slaves, ably led by the gifted Toussaint L'Ouverture, had put up a stubborn resistance. Santo Domingo could not be reconquered, except perhaps at a staggering cost. Second, Bonaparte was about to end the twenty-month lull in his deadly conflict with Britain. Because the British controlled the seas, he feared that he might be forced to make them a gift of Louisiana. Rather than drive America into the arms of Britain by attempting to hold the area, he decided to sell the huge wilderness to the Americans and pocket the money for his schemes nearer home. The predicaments of France in Europe were again paving the way for America's diplomatic successes.

Events now unrolled dizzily. Suddenly, out of a clear sky, the French foreign minister asked the American minister Livingston how much he would give for all Louisiana. Scarcely able to believe his ears (he was partially deaf anyhow), Livingston nervously entered upon the negotiations. After about a week of haggling, the treaties were signed on April 30, 1803, ceding Louisiana to the United States for about $15 million.

When news of the bargain reached America, Jefferson was startled. He had authorized his envoys to offer not more than $10 million for New Orleans, and

as much to the east in the Floridas as they could get. Instead, they had signed three treaties that pledged $15 million for New Orleans and a vast wilderness entirely to the west—an area that would more than double the United States. They had bought a wilderness to get a city.

Once again the two Jeffersons wrestled with each other: the theorist and former strict constructionist versus the realist and public official. Where in his beloved Constitution was the president authorized to negotiate treaties incorporating a huge new expanse into the Union—an expanse containing tens of thousands of Indian, white, and black inhabitants? There was no such clause. So Jefferson shamefacedly submitted the treaties to the Senate while privately admitting that the purchase was unconstitutional.

The senators were less finicky than Jefferson. Reflecting enthusiastic public support, they registered their prompt approval of the transaction. Land-hungry Americans were not disposed to split constitutional hairs when confronted with perhaps the most magnificent real estate bargain in history—828,000 square miles at about three cents an acre.

Jefferson's bargain with France was epochal. By scooping up Louisiana, America secured at one bloodless stroke the western half of the richest river valley in the world and further laid the foundations of a future major power. The ideal of a great agrarian democracy, as envisioned by Jefferson, would have elbowroom in the vast "Valley of Democracy." At the same time, the transfer established a precedent that was to be followed repeatedly: the acquisition of foreign territory and peoples by purchase.

The extent of the huge new area was more fully unveiled by a series of explorations under the direction of Jefferson. In the spring of 1804, Jefferson sent Meriwether Lewis and William Clark up the "Great Muddy" Missouri River, through the Rockies, and down the Columbia River to the Pacific coast. This hazardous venture into the uncharted western wilderness yielded a rich harvest of scientific observations, bolstered America's claim to Oregon, and further opened the West to trade and exploration. Other explorers also pushed into the uncharted West. Zebulon M. Pike, in 1805–1806, explored the headwaters of the Mississippi River and in 1807 ventured into the southern portion of the Louisiana territory.

The Aaron Burr Conspiracies

In the long run, the Louisana Purchase greatly expanded the fortunes of the United States and the power of the federal government. In the short term, the vast expanse of territory and the government's questionable ability to control it raised fears of secession and foreign intrigue.

Aaron Burr, Jefferson's first-term vice president, played no small part in provoking—and justifying—such fears. Dropped from the ticket for Jefferson's second term, Burr joined an extremist Federalist plot aimed at the secession of New England and New York. Alexander Hamilton, though no friend of Jefferson, exposed and foiled this conspiracy. Incensed, Burr challenged his foe to a duel, and Hamilton reluctantly accepted. Hamilton was shot to death by Burr after refusing to fire his own weapon.

His political career as dead as Hamilton's, Burr now turned his disunionist plottings to the trans-Mississippi West. Burr and the unscrupulous military governor of Louisiana, General James Wilkinson, developed a scheme to lead the West in seceding from the United States and then, apparently, to expand their new confederacy by invading Spanish Mexico and Florida. But at the last minute Wilkinson betrayed Burr, and the former vice president was arrested and tried for treason. Chief Justice Marshall ruled that there was insufficient proof that Burr had committed overt acts of treason according to the Constitution (see Art. III, Sec. III), and Burr then fled to Europe. His insurrectionary brashness demonstrated that purchasing a large expanse of western territory was far easier than controlling it.

America: A Nutcrackered Neutral

Jefferson was triumphantly reelected in 1804, with 162 electoral votes to only 14 for his Federalist opponent. But the laurels of Jefferson's first administration soon withered under the blasts of the new storm that broke in Europe. After unloading Louisiana in 1803, Napoleon deliberately provoked a renewal of his war with Britain, an awesome conflict that raged for eleven long years.

Exploring the Louisiana Purchase and the West
Seeking to avert friction with France by purchasing all of Louisiana, Jefferson bought trouble because of the vagueness of the boundaries. The disputants included Spain in the Floridas, Spain and later Mexico in the Southwest, and Great Britain in Canada.

Meriwether Lewis   *This painting portrays him as he looked on his return from the great expedition through the Louisiana Purchase and the West.*

After the Battle of Trafalgar in 1805, Britain's navy controlled the seas while Napoleon's armies ruled the European continent. Like the tiger and the shark, France and Britain were supreme in their chosen elements.

Unable to hurt each other directly, the two antagonists were forced to strike indirect blows. Britain ruled the waves and waived the rules. The London government, beginning in 1806, issued a series of Orders in Council. These edicts closed the ports under French continental control to foreign shipping, including American, unless the vessels first stopped at a British port.

Napoleon struck back, ordering the seizure of all merchant ships, including American, that entered British ports. There was no way to trade with either nation without facing the other's guns. American vessels were, quite literally, caught between the devil and the deep blue sea.

Even more galling to American pride than the seizure of wooden ships was the seizure of flesh-and-blood American seamen. Impressment—the forcible enlistment of sailors—was a crude form of conscription that the British, among others, had employed for over four centuries. Clubs and stretchers (for men knocked unconscious) were standard equipment of press-gangs from His Majesty's crew-hungry ships. Some six thousand bona fide U.S. citizens were impressed by the "piratical man stealers" of Britain from 1808 to 1811 alone.

Britain's determination was spectacularly highlighted in 1807 when a British warship, seeking deserters, fired on a U.S. frigate, the *Chesapeake*, killing three Americans and wounding eighteen. A roar of national wrath went up from infuriated Americans. Jefferson, the peace lover, could easily have had war if he had wanted it.

The Hated Embargo

National honor would not permit a slavish submission to British and French mistreatment. Yet a large-scale foreign war was contrary to the settled policy of the new Republic—and in addition it would be futile. The navy was weak, thanks largely to Jefferson's anti-navalism; and the army was even weaker. A disastrous defeat would not improve America's plight.

The warring nations in Europe depended heavily on the United States for raw materials and foodstuffs. In his eager search for an alternative to war, Jefferson seized on this essential fact. He reasoned that if America voluntarily cut off its exports, the offending powers would be forced to come, hat in hand, and agree to respect U.S. rights. Responding to the presidential lash, Congress hastily passed the Embargo Act late in 1807. This rigorous law forbade the export of all goods from the United States, whether in American or in foreign ships. More than just a compromise between submission and shooting, the embargo embodied Jefferson's idea of "peaceful coercion." If it worked, the embargo would vindicate the rights of neutral nations and point to a new way of conducting foreign affairs.

The American economy staggered under the effect of the embargo long before Britain or France began to bend. Forests of dead masts gradually filled once-flourishing harbors; docks that had once rumbled were deserted (except for illegal trade); and soup kitchens cared for hordes of the hungry unemployed. Jeffersonian Republicans probably hurt the commerce of New England, which they avowedly were trying to protect, far more than Britain and France together were doing.

Farmers of the South and West, the strongholds of Jefferson, suffered no less disastrously than New England. They were alarmed by the mounting piles of exportable cotton, grain, and tobacco. Jefferson in truth seemed to be waging war on his fellow citizens rather than on the offending belligerents.

An enormous illicit trade mushroomed in 1808, especially along the Canadian border, where bands of armed Americans on loaded rafts overawed or overpowered federal agents. Irate citizens cynically transposed the letters of "embargo" to read "o grab me," "go bar 'em," and "mobrage," while they heartily denounced the "dambargo."

Jefferson nonetheless induced Congress to pass iron-toothed enforcing legislation. It was so inquisitorial and tyrannical as to cause some Americans to think more kindly of George III, whom Jefferson had berated in the Declaration of Independence. One indignant New Hampshirite denounced the president with this ditty:

> Our ships all in motion,
> Once whiten'd the ocean;
>   They sail'd and return'd with a cargo;
> Now doom'd to decay
> They are fallen a prey,
>   To Jefferson, worms, and EMBARGO.

The embargo even had the effect of reviving the moribund Federalist party. Gaining new converts, its leaders hurled their nullification of the embargo into the teeth of the "Virginia lordlings" in Washington. In 1804 the discredited Federalists had polled only 14 electoral votes out of 176; in 1808, the embargo year, the figure rose to 47 out of 175. New England seethed with talk of secession, and Jefferson later admitted that he felt the foundations of government tremble under his feet.

An alarmed Congress, yielding to the storm of public anger, finally repealed the embargo on March

The Ograbme (Embargo)   *As a snapping turtle, it halts overseas shipments.*

1, 1809, three days before Jefferson's retirement. A half-loaf substitute was provided by the Non-Intercourse Act. This measure formally reopened trade with all the nations of the world, except the two most important, Britain and France. Though thus watered down, economic coercion continued to be the policy of the Jeffersonians from 1809 to 1812, when the nation finally plunged into war.

Why did the embargo, Jefferson's most daring act of statesmanship, collapse after fifteen dismal months? First of all, the president underestimated the bulldog determination of the British, as others have, and overestimated the dependence of both belligerents on America's trade. Bumper grain crops blessed the British Isles during these years, and the revolutionary Latin American republics unexpectedly threw open their ports for compensating commerce. With most of Europe under his control, Napoleon simply tightened his belt and went without American trade while cynically continuing to seize American ships and cargo.

More critically, perhaps, Jefferson miscalculated the unpopularity of such a self-crucifying weapon and the difficulty of enforcing it. The hated embargo was not continued long enough or tightly enough to achieve the desired results—and a leaky embargo was perhaps more costly than none at all.

Curiously enough, New England plucked a new prosperity from the ugly jaws of the embargo. With shipping tied up and imported goods scarce, the resourceful Yankees reopened old factories and erected new ones. The real foundations of modern America's industrial might were laid behind the protective wall of the embargo, followed by nonintercourse and the War of 1812. Jefferson, the avowed critic of factories, may have unwittingly done more for American manufacturing than Alexander Hamilton, industry's outspoken friend.

Madison's Gamble

Following Washington's precedent, Jefferson left the presidency after two terms, happy to escape what he called the "splendid misery" of the highest office in the land. As his successor, he strongly supported his friend and fellow Virginian, the quiet, intellectual, and unassuming James Madison.

Madison took the presidential oath on March 4, 1809, as the awesome conflict in Europe was roaring to its climax. The scholarly Madison was small of stature, light of weight, bald of head, and weak of voice. Despite a distinguished career as a legislator, as president he was crippled by factions within his party and his cabinet. Unable to dominate Congress as Jefferson had done, Madison often found himself "holding the bag" for risky foreign policies not of his own making.

The Non-Intercourse Act of 1809—a diluted embargo aimed solely at Britain and France—was due to expire in 1810. To Madison's dismay, Congress dismantled the embargo completely with a bargaining measure known as Macon's Bill No. 2. While reopening American trade with all the world, it dangled what Congress hoped was an attractive lure. If either Britain or France repealed its commercial restrictions, America would restore its embargo against the nonrepealing nation.

Madison glumly recognized that this measure only emphasized America's economic weakness, by leaving the determination of who would be America's trading partner to the potentates of London and Paris.

The crafty Napoleon saw his chance. Without actually promising to do so, he signaled in August 1810 that France might repeal its trade restrictions if Britain in turn lifted its Orders in Council. Madison knew better than to trust Napoleon, but he gambled that by accepting the French offer as evidence of repeal, he could lead the British to re-open neutral trade. But in fact they did not. Madison's gamble had failed. He saw no choice but to reestablish the embargo against Britain alone—a decision that meant the end of American neutrality and a dangerous step toward war.

Tecumseh and the Prophet

Not all of Madison's party were reluctant to fight. The complexion of the Twelfth Congress, which met late in 1811, differed markedly from that of its predecessor. Recent elections had swept away many of the older "submission men" and replaced them with young hotheads, many from the South and West. Dubbed "war hawks" by their Federalist opponents, the newcomers were indeed on fire for a new war with the old enemy—actually two old enemies. The war hawks detested the British for their manhandling of American sailors and their Orders in Council that dammed the flow of American trade, especially western farm products headed for Europe. They also yearned to wipe out the Indian threat to the flood of pioneer settlers then washing into the trans-Appalachian West.

Two remarkable Shawnee brothers, Tecumseh and Tenskwatawa, known to non-Indians as "the Prophet," concluded that the time had come to stop this onrushing tide. They began to weld together a far-flung confederacy of all the tribes east of the Mississippi, inspiring a vibrant movement of Indian unity and cultural renewal. Their followers gave up textile clothing for traditional buckskin garments. Their warriors foreswore alcohol, the better to fight a last-ditch battle with the white invaders. Tecumseh urged his supporters never to cede land to whites unless all Indians agreed.

White frontierspeople and their war-hawk spokesmen in Congress were convinced that British "scalp buyers" in Canada were nourishing the Indians' growing strength. In the fall of 1811 General William Henry Harrison, governor of the Indiana Territory, gathered an army and advanced on Tecumseh's headquarters at the junction of the Wabash and Tippecanoe Rivers in present-day Indiana. Tecumseh was absent, recruiting supporters in the South, but the Prophet attacked Harrison's army—foolishly, in Tecumseh's eyes—with a small band of Shawnees. The Shawnees were routed and their settlement burned.

The battle of Tippecanoe made Harrison a national hero. It also discredited the Prophet and drove Tecumseh into an alliance with the British. When war with Britain came, Tecumseh fought fiercely for the redcoats until his death in 1813 at the Battle of the Thames. With him perished the dream of an Indian confederacy.

Mr. Madison's War

By the spring of 1812 Madison believed war with Britain to be inevitable. The British arming of hostile Indians pushed him toward this decision, as did the

Tecumseh (1768?–1813) *A Shawnee Indian born in the Ohio country, he was probably the most gifted organizer and leader of his people in U.S. history. A respected warrior, he fought the tribal custom of torturing prisoners and opposed the practice of permitting any one tribe to sell land that, he believed, belonged to all Indians.*

whoops of the war hawks in his own party who believed the only way to remove the menace of the Indians was to wipe out their Canadian base. "On to Canada, on to Canada" was the war hawks' chant. Southern expansionists, less vocal, cast a covetous eye on Florida, then held by Britain's ally Spain.

But above all, Madison turned to war to restore confidence in the republican experiment. For five years the Republicans had nobly tried to steer between submission and battle with the warring European powers. But the only result was international derision and internal strife. Madison and the Republicans came to believe that only a vigorous assertion of American rights could demonstrate the viability of American nationhood—and of democracy as a form of government. If America could not fight to protect itself, its experiment in republicanism would be discredited in the eyes of a scoffing world.

Madison asked Congress to declare war on June 1, 1812. Congress obliged him two weeks later. The vote in the House was 79 to 49 for war, in the Senate 19 to 13. The close tallies revealed deep divisions over the wisdom of fighting. The split was both emotional and party-based. Support for war came from the South and West, but also from Republicans in the populous middle states like Pennsylvania and Virginia. Federalists in both North and South damned the conflict, but their stronghold was New England, which greeted the declaration of war with muffled bells, flags at half-mast, and public fasting.

Why should seafaring New England oppose the war for a free sea? The answer is that Federalists in the Northeast sympathized with Britain and resented the Republicans' sympathy with Napoleon, whom they regarded as the "Corsican butcher" and the "anti-Christ of the age."

The Federalists also opposed the acquisition of Canada—one of the hawks' war aims—because it would only add more agrarian states and increase Jeffersonian Republican voting strength

The bitterness of New England Federalists against "Mr. Madison's War" led them to treason or near-treason. They were determined, charged one Republican versifier,

> To rule the nation if they could,
> But see it damned if others should.

New England gold holders probably lent more dollars to the British than to the federal Treasury. Federalist farmers sent huge quantities of supplies and foodstuffs to Canada, enabling British armies to invade New York. New England governors stubbornly refused to permit their militias to serve outside their own states. In a sense America had to fight two enemies simultaneously, Old England and New England.

Thus perilously divided, the barely united states plunged into armed conflict against Britain, then the world's most powerful empire. No sober American could have had much reasonable hope of victory—but by 1812 the Jeffersonian Republicans saw no other choice.

Chronology

1800	Jefferson defeats Adams for presidency.
1801	Judiciary Act of 1801.
1801–1805	Naval war with Tripoli.
1802	Revised naturalization law. Judiciary Act of 1801 repealed.
1803	*Marbury* v. *Madison.* Louisiana Purchase.
1804	Jefferson reelected president.
1804–1806	Lewis and Clark expedition.
1805	Peace treaty with Tripoli.
1805–1807	Pike's explorations.
1806	Burr treason trial.
1807	*Chesapeake* affair. Embargo Act.
1809	Non-Intercourse Act replaces Embargo Act.
1810	Macon's Bill No. 2. Napoleon announces (falsely) repeal of blockade decrees. Madison reestablishes nonimportation against Britain.
1811	Battle of Tippecanoe.
1812	United States declares war on Britain.

For further reading, see the Appendix. For web resources, go to **http://college.hmco.com.**

12

The Second War for Independence and the Upsurge of Nationalism

1812–1824

The American continents . . . are henceforth not to be considered as subjects for future colonization by any European powers.

JAMES MONROE, DECEMBER 2, 1823

The War of 1812 ranks as one of America's worst-fought wars. Instead of the solidarity born of a burning national anger, as there had been in 1807 following the *Chesapeake* outrage, Americans showed a widespread disunity. The supreme lesson of the conflict was the folly of leading a divided and apathetic people into war.

And yet, despite the unimpressive military outcome and the even less decisive negotiated peace, Americans came out of the war with a renewed sense of nationhood. For the next dozen years an awakened spirit of nationalism would inspire activities ranging from protecting manufacturing to building roads to defending the authority of the federal government over the states.

On to Canada over Land and Lakes

On the eve of the War of 1812, the regular army was ill-trained, ill-disciplined, and widely scattered. It had to be supplemented by the even more poorly trained militia, who were sometimes distinguished by their speed of foot in leaving the battlefield. Some of the ranking generals were semisenile heirlooms from the Revolutionary War, rusting on their laurels and lacking in vigor and vision.

The offensive strategy against Canada was especially poorly conceived. Had the Americans captured Montreal, the center of population and transportation, everything to the west might have died, just as the leaves of a tree wither when the trunk is girdled. But instead of laying ax to the trunk, the Americans frittered away their strength in the three-pronged invasion of 1812. The trio of invading forces that set out from Detroit, Niagara, and Lake Champlain were all beaten back shortly after they crossed the Canadian border.

By contrast, the British and Canadians displayed energy from the outset. Early in the war they captured the American fort of Michilimackinac, which commanded the upper Great Lakes and the Indian-inhabited area to the south and west. Their brilliant defensive operations were led by the inspired British General Isaac Brock, assisted (in the American camp) by "General Mud" and "General Confusion."

When several American land invasions of Canada were again hurled back in 1813, Americans looked for success on water. Man for man and ship for ship, the American navy did better than the army. Compared to the larger British navy, American craft on the whole were more skillfully handled, had better gunners, and were manned by non–press-gang sailors who were burning to avenge numerous indignities. The American frigates, notably the *Constitution* ("Old Ironsides"), had thicker sides, heavier firepower, and larger crews, of which one sailor in six was a free black.

Control of the Great Lakes was vital, and an energetic American naval officer, Oliver Hazard Perry, managed to build a fleet of green-timbered ships on the shores of Lake Erie, manned by even greener seamen. When Perry captured a British fleet in a furious engagement on Lake Erie, he reported to his superior, "We have met the enemy and they are ours." Perry's victory and his slogan infused new life into the drooping American cause. Forced to withdraw from Detroit and Fort Malden, the retreating redcoats were overtaken by General Harrison's army and beaten at the Battle of the Thames in October 1813.

Despite these successes, the Americans by late 1814, far from invading Canada, were grimly defending their own soil against the invading British. In Europe the diversionary power of Napoleon was destroyed in mid-1814, and the dangerous despot was marooned on the Mediterranean isle of Elba. The United States, which had so brashly provoked war behind the protective skirts of Napoleon, was now left to face the music alone. Thousands of victorious veteran redcoats began to pour from the continent into Canada.

Assembling some ten thousand crack troops, the British prepared in 1814 for a crushing blow into New York, along the familiar lake-river route. In the absence of roads, the invader was forced to bring supplies over

The Three U.S. Thrusts of 1812 *The thin green line denotes the Canadian boundary.*

Campaigns of 1813 *The thin green line denotes the Canadian boundary.*

Constitution **and** ***Guerrière,*** **1812** *The* Guerrière *was heavily outweighed and outgunned, yet its British captain eagerly—and foolishly—sought combat. His ship was totally destroyed. Historian Henry Adams later concluded that this duel "raised the United States in one half hour to the rank of a first-class Power in the world." Today, the* U.S.S. Constitution, *berthed in Boston harbor, remains the oldest actively commissioned ship in the U.S. Navy.*

the Lake Champlain waterway. A weaker American fleet, commanded by thirty-year-old Thomas Macdonough, challenged the British. The ensuing battle was desperately fought near Plattsburgh, on September 11, 1814, on floating slaughterhouses. The American flagship at one point was in grave trouble. But Macdonough, unexpectedly turning his ship about with cables, confronted the enemy with a fresh broadside and snatched victory from the fangs of defeat.

The results of this heroic naval battle were momentous. The invading British army was forced to retreat. Macdonough thus saved at least upstate New York from conquest, New England from further disaffection, and the Union from possible dissolution. He also profoundly affected the concurrent negotiations of the Anglo-American peace treaty in Europe.

Despite its success on the Great Lakes, the American navy could not match the powerful British fleet on the Atlantic. Its wrath aroused, the Royal Navy finally retaliated by throwing a ruinous naval blockade along America's coast and by landing raiding parties almost

at will. American economic life, including fishing, was crippled. Customs revenues were choked off, and near the end of the war the bankrupt Treasury was unable to meet its maturing obligations.

Washington Burned and New Orleans Defended

A second formidable British force, numbering about four thousand, landed in the Chesapeake Bay area in August 1814. Advancing rapidly on Washington, it easily dispersed some six thousand panicky militia at Bladensburg ("the Bladensburg races"). The invaders then entered the capital and set fire to most of the public buildings, including the Capitol and the White House. But while Washington burned, the Americans at Baltimore held firm. The British fleet hammered Fort McHenry with their cannons but could not capture the city. Francis Scott Key, a detained American anxiously watching the bombardment from a British ship, was inspired to write the words of "The Star-Spangled Banner." Set to the tune of a saucy English tavern refrain, the song quickly attained popularity.

A third British blow of 1814, aimed at New Orleans, menaced the entire Mississippi Valley. Gaunt and hawk-faced Andrew Jackson, fresh from crushing the southwest Indians at the Battle of Horseshoe Bend, was placed in command. His hodgepodge force consisted of seven thousand sailors, regulars, pirates, and Frenchmen, as well as militiamen from Louisiana, Kentucky, and Tennessee. Among the defenders were two Louisiana regiments of free black volunteers, numbering about four hundred men. The Americans threw up their entrenchment, and in the words of a popular song:

> Behind it stood our little force—
> None wished it to be greater;
> For ev'ry man was half a horse,
> And half an alligator.

The overconfident British, numbering some eight thousand battle-seasoned veterans, blundered badly. They made the mistake of launching a frontal assault, on January 8, 1815, on the entrenched American riflemen and cannoneers. The attackers suffered the most devastating defeat of the entire war, losing over two thousand killed and wounded in half an hour, compared with seventy for the Americans. It was an astonishing victory for Jackson and his men.

News of the victory struck the country "like a clap of thunder," according to one contemporary. Andrew Jackson became a national hero, as poets and politicians lined up to sing the praises of the defenders of New Orleans. It hardly mattered when word arrived that a peace treaty had been signed at Ghent, Belgium, ending the war two weeks before the battle. The United States had fought for honor as much as material gain. The Battle of New Orleans restored that honor, at least in American eyes, and unleashed a wave of nationalism and self-confidence.

The Treaty of Ghent

Tsar Alexander I of Russia, hard-pressed by Napoleon's army and not wanting his British ally to fritter away its strength in America, proposed mediation between the clashing Anglo-Saxon cousins in 1812. The tsar's feeler eventually set in motion the machinery that brought five American peacemakers to the quaint Belgian city of Ghent in 1814. The bickering group was headed by early rising, puritanical John Quincy Adams, son of John Adams, who deplored the late-hour card playing of his high-living colleague Henry Clay.

Confident after their military successes, Britain's envoys made sweeping demands for a neutralized Indian buffer state in the Great Lakes region, control of the Great Lakes, and a substantial part of conquered Maine. The Americans flatly rejected these terms, and the talks appeared stalemated. But news of British reverses in upstate New York and at Baltimore, and increasing war-weariness in Britain, made London more willing to compromise. Preoccupied with the Congress of Vienna that concluded the Napoleonic wars, and with still-dangerous France, the British lion resigned itself to licking its wounds.

The Treaty of Ghent, signed on Christmas Eve in 1814, was essentially an armistice. Both sides simply agreed to stop fighting and to restore conquered territory. No mention was made of those grievances for which America had ostensibly fought: Indian relations, search and seizure, Orders in Council, impressment, and confiscations. With neither side able to impose its will, the treaty negotiations—like the war itself—ended as a virtual draw. Relieved Americans boasted, "Not One Inch of Territory Ceded or Lost"— a watchword that contrasted strangely with the "On to Canada" rallying cry at the war's outset.

Federalist Grievances and the Hartford Convention

Defiant New England remained a problem. It was by far the most prosperous section during the conflict, owing largely to illicit trade with the enemy in Canada and to the absence of a British blockade until 1814. But the embittered opposition of the Federalists to the war continued unabated.

The most spectacular manifestation of Federalist discontent was the ill-omened Hartford Convention. Late in 1814, when the British capture of New Orleans seemed imminent, Massachusetts issued a call for a convention at Hartford, Connecticut. The states of Massachusetts, Connecticut, and Rhode Island dispatched full delegations, and New Hampshire and

Vermont sent partial representation. This group of prominent men, twenty-six in all, met in complete secrecy for about three weeks—December 15, 1814, to January 5, 1815—to discuss their grievances and to seek redress for their wrongs. The convention's final report was actually quite moderate; it included demands for financial compensation for lost trade, abolition of the "three-fifths" clause of the Constitution, and a single-term limit for the presidency. These and other measures reflected Federalist fears that a once-proud New England was falling subservient to an agrarian South and West.

Bearing these demands, three special envoys from Massachusetts journeyed to the burned-out capital of Washington. The trio arrived just in time to be overwhelmed by the glorious news from New Orleans, followed by that from Ghent. As the rest of the nation congratulated itself on a glorious victory, New England's wartime complaints seemed petty at best, and treasonous at worst. Pursued by the sneers and jeers of the press, they sank away into obscurity.

The Hartford resolutions, as it turned out, were the death song of the Federalist party. In 1816, the next year, the Federalists nominated their last presidential candidate. He was handily trounced by James Monroe, yet another Virginian.

Federalist doctrines of disunity, which long survived the party, blazed a fateful trail. Until 1815 there was far more talk of nullification and secession in New England than in any other section, including the South. The outright flouting of the Jeffersonian embargo and the later crippling of the war effort were the two most damaging acts of nullification in America prior to the events leading to the Civil War.

The Second War for American Independence

The War of 1812 was a small war, involving about six thousand Americans killed or wounded. It was but a footnote to the mighty European conflagration. In 1812, when Napoleon invaded Russia with about 500,000 men, Madison tried to invade Canada with about 5,000. But if the American conflict was globally unimportant, its results were highly important to the United States.

The Republic had shown that it would resist, sword in hand, what it regarded as grievous wrongs. Other nations developed a new respect for America's fighting prowess. America's emissaries abroad were henceforth treated with less scorn. In a diplomatic sense, if not in a military sense, the conflict could be called the Second War for American Independence.

A new nation, moreover, was welded in the fiery furnace of armed conflict. Sectionalism, now identified with discredited New England Federalists, was given a black eye. The painful events of the war glaringly revealed, as perhaps nothing else could have done, the folly of sectional disunity. In a sense, the most conspicuous casualty of the war was the Federalist party.

War heroes emerged, especially the two Indian-fighters, Andrew Jackson and William Henry Harrison. Both of them were to become president.

Left in the lurch by their British friends at Ghent, the Indians were forced to make such terms as they could. They reluctantly consented, in a series of treaties, to relinquish vast areas of forest land north of the Ohio River.

Manufacturing increased behind the fiery wooden wall of the British blockade. Not only in a diplomatic sense but in an economic sense as well, the War of 1812 may be regarded as the Second War for American Independence. The industries that were thus stimulated by the fighting rendered America less dependent on Europe's workshops.

Canadian patriotism and nationalism also received a powerful stimulus from the clash. Many Canadians felt betrayed by the Treaty of Ghent. They were especially aggrieved by the failure to secure an Indian buffer state or even mastery of the Great Lakes. Canadians fully expected the frustrated Yankees to return, and for a time the Americans and British engaged in a naval armaments race on the Great Lakes. But in 1817 the Rush-Bagot agreement between Britain and the United States severely limited rival flotillas on the lakes. Better relations brought the last border fortifications down in the 1870s, with the happy result that the United States and Canada now share the world's longest unfortified boundary—stretching 5,527 miles.

After Napoleon's final defeat at Waterloo in 1815, Europe slumped into a peace of exhaustion. Deposed monarchs returned to battered thrones, as the Old

World took the rutted road back to conservatism, illiberalism, and reaction. Largely unaffected by these European developments, the American people turned their backs on the Old World and faced resolutely toward the untamed West—and toward the task of building democracy.

Nascent Nationalism

The most impressive by-product of the War of 1812 was heightened nationalism—the spirit of nation-consciousness or national oneness. America may not have fought the war as one nation, but it emerged as one nation.

The changed mood even manifested itself in the birth of a distinctively national literature. Washington Irving and James Fenimore Cooper attained international recognition in the 1820s, significantly as the nation's first writers of importance to use American scenes and themes. School textbooks, often British in an earlier era, were now being written by Americans for Americans. In the world of magazines, the highly intellectual *North American Review* began publication in 1815—the year of the triumph at New Orleans. Even American painters increasingly celebrated their native landscapes on their canvases.

A fresh nationalistic spirit could be recognized in many other areas as well. A more handsome capital began to rise from the ashes of Washington. The army was expanded to ten thousand men. The navy covered itself with glory in 1815 when it administered a thorough beating to the piratical plunderers of North Africa. Stephen Decatur, naval hero of the War of 1812 and of the Barbary Coast expeditions, pungently captured the country's nationalist mood in a famous toast made on his return from the Mediterranean campaigns: "Our country, right or wrong!"

The American System

Nationalism likewise manifested itself in manufacturing and finance. A revived Bank of the United States was voted by Congress in 1816. Patriotic Americans took pride in the factories that had recently

Washington, D.C., 1824   *This view of the Capitol building, much smaller than it is today, reveals the rustic conditions of the early days in the nation's capital.*

mushroomed, largely as a result of the self-imposed embargoes and the war.

When hostilities ended in 1815, British competitors began to dump the contents of their bulging warehouses on the United States, often cutting their prices below cost in an effort to strangle the American war-baby factories in the cradle. The infant industries bawled lustily for protection.

A nationalist Congress, out-federalizing the old Federalists, responded by passing the path-breaking Tariff of 1816—the first tariff in American history instituted primarily for protection, not revenue. Its rates—roughly 20 to 25 percent on the value of dutiable imports—were not high enough to provide completely adequate safeguards, but the law was a bold beginning. A strongly protective trend was started that stimulated the appetites of the protected for more protection.

Nationalism was further highlighted by Henry Clay's grandiose plan for developing a profitable home market. Still radiating the nationalism of war-hawk days, Clay threw himself behind an elaborate scheme known by 1824 as the American System. It began with a strong banking system and a protective tariff, behind which eastern manufacturing would flourish. Revenues gushing from the tariff would provide funds for roads and canals, especially in the burgeoning Ohio Valley. Through these new arteries of transportation would flow foodstuffs and raw materials from the South and West to the North and East. In exchange, a stream of manufactured goods would flow in the return direction, knitting the country together economically and politically.

Persistent and eloquent demands by Henry Clay and others for internal improvements struck a responsive chord with the public, especially in the road-poor West. The recent attempts to invade Canada had all failed partly because of oath-provoking roads—or no roads at all.

But attempts to secure federal funding for roads and canals stumbled on Republican constitutional scruples. Congress voted in 1817 to distribute $1.5 million to the states for internal improvements. But President Madison sternly vetoed the measure as unconstitutional, forcing the individual states to undertake building programs on their own, including the Erie Canal, completed by New York in 1825. Jeffersonian Republicans, who had gulped down Hamiltonian loose construction on other important problems, choked on the idea of direct federal support for intrastate internal improvements. New England also opposed federally constructed roads and canals because such outlets would further drain away population and create competing states beyond the mountains.

The So-Called Era of Good Feelings

James Monroe—6 feet tall, somewhat stooped, courtly, and mild mannered—was nominated for the presidency in 1816 by the Republicans. They thus undertook to continue the so-called Virginia dynasty of Washington, Jefferson, and Madison. The fading Federalists ran a candidate for the last time in their checkered history, and he was crushed by 183 electoral votes to 34. The vanquished Federalist party was gasping its dying breaths, leaving the field to the triumphant Republicans and one-party rule.

In James Monroe, the man and the times auspiciously met. As the last president to wear an old-style cocked hat, he straddled two generations: the bygone age of the Founding Fathers and the emergent age of nationalism. Never brilliant, the serene Virginian with gray-blue eyes was in intellect and personal force among the least distinguished of the first eight presidents. But the times called for sober administration, not heroics. And Monroe was an experienced, level-headed executive, with an ear-to-the-ground talent for interpreting popular rumblings.

President Monroe further cemented emerging nationalism with a goodwill tour in 1817 that took him deep into Federalist New England. The heartwarming welcome he received even in "the enemy's country" ushered in the "Era of Good Feelings," as the Monroe administrations commonly have been called.

"Era of Good Feelings," unfortunately, was something of a misnomer. Considerable tranquillity and prosperity did in fact smile on the early years of Monroe, but the period was a troubled one. The acute issues of the tariff, the bank, internal improvements, and the sale of public lands were being hotly contested. Sectionalism was crystallizing, and the conflict over slavery was beginning to raise its hideous head.

The Panic of 1819 and the Curse of Hard Times

Much of the goodness went out of the good feelings in 1819, when a paralyzing economic panic descended. It brought deflation, depression, bankruptcies, bank failures, unemployment, soup kitchens, and overcrowded pesthouses known as debtors' prisons.

This was the first national financial panic since President Washington took office. Many factors contributed to the catastrophe of 1819, but looming large was overspeculation in frontier lands. The Bank of the United States, through its western branches, had become deeply involved in this popular type of outdoor gambling.

Financial paralysis from the panic, which lasted in some degree for several years, dealt a rude setback to the nationalistic ardor. The West was especially hard hit. When the pinch came, the Bank of the United States forced the speculative ("wildcat") western banks to the wall and foreclosed mortgages on countless farms. All this was technically legal but politically unwise. In the eyes of the western debtor, the nationalist Bank of the United States soon became a kind of financial devil.

The panic of 1819 also created backwashes in the political and social world. The poorer classes—the one-suspender men and their families—were severely strapped and in their troubles was sown the seedbed of Jacksonian democracy. Hard times also directed attention to the inhumanity of imprisoning debtors. In extreme cases, often overplayed, mothers were torn from their infants for owing a few dollars. Mounting agitation against imprisonment for debt bore fruit in remedial legislation in an increasing number of states.

Growing Pains of the West

The onward march to the West continued. Nine frontier states had joined the original thirteen between 1791 and 1819. With an eye to preserving the North-South sectional balance, most of these commonwealths had been admitted alternately, free or slave. (See Admission of States in the Appendix.)

Why this explosive expansion? In part, it was simply a continuation of the generations-old westward movement, which had been going on since early colonial days. In addition, the siren call of cheap lands—"the Ohio fever"—had a special appeal to European immigrants. Eager newcomers from abroad were beginning to stream down the gangplanks in impressive numbers, especially after the war of boycotts and bullets. Land exhaustion in the older tobacco states, where the soil was "mined" rather than cultivated, likewise drove people westward. Glib speculators accepted small down payments, making it easier to buy new holdings.

The western boom was stimulated by additional developments. Acute economic distress during the embargo years turned many pinched faces toward the setting sun (see "Makers of America: Settlers of the Old Northwest," p. 154). The crushing of the Indians in the Northwest and South by General Harrison and General Jackson pacified the frontier and opened up vast virgin tracts of land. The building of highways improved the land routes to the Ohio Valley. Noteworthy was the Cumberland Road, begun in 1811, which ran ultimately from western Maryland to Illinois. The use of the first steamboat on western waters, also in 1811, heralded a new era of upstream navigation.

But the West, despite the inflow of settlers, was still weak in population and influence. To make its voice heard, it was forced to ally itself with other sections. Thus strengthened, it demanded cheap federal land, cheap transportation, and cheap money issued by its own "wildcat" banks. After 1820 it made significant headway in achieving all these goals.

Slavery and Sectional Balance

Sectional tensions were stunningly revealed in 1819, when the territory of Missouri knocked on the doors of Congress for admission as a slave state. This fertile area contained sufficient population to warrant statehood. But the House of Representatives stymied the plans of the Missourians by passing the incendiary Tallmadge amendment. It stipulated that no more slaves should be brought into Missouri and also provided for the gradual emancipation of children born to slave parents already there. A roar of anger burst from slaveholding southerners.

Settlers of the Old Northwest

The Old Northwest beckoned to settlers after the War of 1812. The withdrawal of the British protector weakened the Indians' grip on the territory. Then the canal and highway boom of the 1820s opened broad arteries along which the westward movement flowed.

The first wave of newcomers came mainly from Kentucky, Tennessee, and the upland regions of Virginia and the Carolinas. Most migrants were rough-hewn white farmers who had been pushed from good land to bad by an expanding plantation economy. Some settlers acquired land for the first time. John Palmer, whose family left Kentucky for Illinois in 1831, recalled his father telling him "of land so cheap that we could all be landholders, where men were *equal*." Migrants from the South settled mainly in the southern portions of Ohio, Indiana, and Illinois.

Having escaped from a lowly social position in a slaveholding society, many of these new immigrants sought to prevent the spread of slavery by enacting Black Codes in their new territories that prevented blacks from following them. They wanted their own democratic communities, free of rich planters and African-Americans alike.

If southern "Butternuts," as these settlers were called, dominated settlement in the 1820s, the next decade brought equally land-starved Yankees from the Northeast. Yankee settlers came especially to the northern parts of Ohio, Indiana, and Illinois. Unlike the Butternuts who wanted to quit forever the imposing framework of southern society, northerners hoped to re-create the world they had left behind.

Conflict soon emerged between Yankees and southerners. As self-sufficient farmers who did not produce for the market, southerners viewed the northern newcomers as inhospitable, greedy, and excessively ambitious. Northerners, in turn, viewed the southerners as uncivilized, a "coon dog and butcher knife tribe" with no interest in education, self-improvement, or agricultural innovation. While Yankees advocated taxes to establish public schools and fund roads and canals, southerners opposed such efforts, especially public schooling. Religion also divided settlers. Northerners typically embraced denominations like Congregationalism and Presbyterianism that supported a learned ministry. Southerners preferred the more revivalist Methodists and Baptists, and preferred humble, uneducated preacher-farmers who would, in their eyes, stay closer to the Lord and his people.

As the population swelled and the region acquired its own character, the stark contrasts between northerners and southerners started to fade. Some residents like Abraham Lincoln, with roots in Kentucky, came to adopt views more akin to those of the Yankees than the southerners. Railroads and Great Lakes shipping tied the region economically ever more tightly to the Northeast. Yankees and southerners sometimes allied as new kinds of economic, ethnic, and religious cleavages emerged.

Still, echoes of the clash between Yankees and Butternuts persisted. During the Civil War, the southern counties of Ohio, Indiana, and Illinois, where southerners had first settled, harbored sympathizers with the South and served as a key area for Confederate military infiltration into the North. Decades later these same counties became a stronghold of the Ku Klux Klan. The Old Northwest may have become firmly anchored to the economy of the Northeast, but vestiges of its early dual personality persisted.

Wagons West   *This busy scene on the Frederick Road, leading westward from Baltimore, was typical as pioneers flooded into the newly secured West in the early 1800s.*

Southerners saw in the Tallmadge amendment, which they eventually managed to defeat in the Senate, an ominous threat to the sectional balance. When the Constitution was adopted in 1788, the North and South were running neck and neck in wealth and population. But with every passing decade, the North was becoming wealthier and also more thickly settled—an advantage reflected in an increasing northern majority in the House of Representatives. Yet in the Senate, with eleven states free and eleven slave, the southerners had maintained equality. They were therefore in a good position to thwart any northern effort to interfere with the expansion of slavery, and they did not want to lose this neutralizing veto.

The future of the slave system caused southerners profound concern. Missouri was the first state entirely west of the Mississippi River to be carved out of the Louisiana Purchase, and the Missouri emancipation amendment might set a damaging precedent for all the rest of the area. Even more disquieting was another possibility. If Congress could abolish the "peculiar institution" in Missouri, might it not attempt to do likewise in the older states of the South? The wounds of the Constitutional Convention of 1787 were once more ripped open.

Burning moral questions also protruded, even though the main issue was political and economic balance. A small but growing group of antislavery agitators in the North seized the occasion to raise an outcry against the evils of slavery. They were determined that the plague of human bondage should not spread farther into the virgin territories.

The Uneasy Missouri Compromise

Deadlock in Washington was at length broken in 1820 by the time-honored American solution of compromise—actually a bundle of three compromises. Congress, despite abolitionist pleas, agreed to admit Missouri as a slave state. But at the same time, free-soil Maine, which until then had been part of Massachusetts, was admitted as a separate state. The balance between North and South was thus kept at twelve states each and remained there for fifteen years. Although Missouri was permitted to retain slaves, all future bondage was prohibited in the remainder of the Louisiana Purchase north of the line of 36° 30′—the southern boundary of Missouri.

Neither North nor South was acutely displeased, although neither was completely happy. Fortunately, the Missouri Compromise lasted thirty-four years—a vital formative period in the life of the young Republic—and during that time it preserved the shaky compact of the states. Yet the embittered dispute over slavery heralded the future breakup of the Union. Ever after, the morality of the South's peculiar institution was an issue that could not be swept under the rug. The Missouri Compromise only ducked the question—it did not resolve it. Sooner or later, Thomas Jefferson predicted, it will "burst on us as a tornado."

The Missouri Compromise and the concurrent panic of 1819 should have dimmed the political star of President Monroe. Certainly both unhappy events had a dampening effect on the Era of Good Feelings. But smooth-spoken James Monroe was so popular, and the Federalist opposition so weak, that he received every electoral vote except one in the election of 1820. Unanimity remained an honor reserved for George Washington.

John Marshall and Judicial Nationalism

The upsurging nationalism of the post-Ghent years, despite the ominous setbacks concerning slavery, was further reflected and reinforced by the Supreme Court. The high tribunal continued to be dominated by the tall, thin, and aggressive Chief Justice John Marshall. One group of his decisions—perhaps the most famous—bolstered the power of the federal government at the expense of the states.

A notable case in this category was *McCulloch* v. *Maryland* (1819). The suit involved an attempt by the state of Maryland to destroy a branch of the Bank of the United States by imposing a tax on its notes. John Marshall, speaking for the Court, declared the bank constitutional by invoking the Hamiltonian doctrine of implied powers (see p. 124). At the same time, he strengthened federal authority and slapped at state infringements when he denied the right of Maryland to tax the bank.

Marshall's ruling in this case gave the doctrine of "loose construction" its most famous formulation. The Constitution, he said, derived from the consent of the people and thus permitted the government to act for their benefit. He further argued that the Constitution was "intended to endure for ages to come and, consequently, to be adapted to the various crises of human affairs." Finally, he declared, "Let the end be legitimate, let it be within the scope of the Constitution, and all means which are appropriate, which are plainly adapted to that end, which are not prohibited, but consist with the letter and spirit of the Constitution, are constitutional."

The Missouri Compromise and Slavery, 1820–1821   *In the 1780s Thomas Jefferson had written of slavery in America: "Indeed I tremble for my country when I reflect that God is just; that his justice cannot sleep forever; that . . . the Almighty has no attribute which can take side with us in such a contest." Later, at the time of the Missouri Compromise, Jefferson feared that his worst forebodings were coming to pass. "I considered it at once," he said of the Missouri question, "as the knell of the Union."*

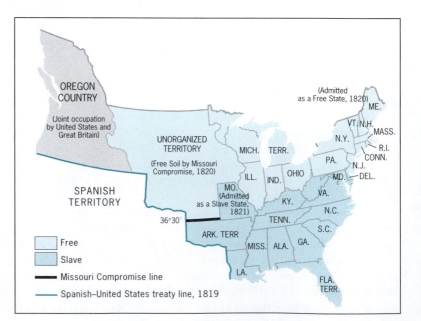

Another set of Marshall's decisions bolstered judicial barriers against democratic or demagogic attacks on property rights. The notorious case of *Fletcher* v. *Peck* (1810) arose when a Georgia legislature, swayed by bribery, granted 35 million acres in the Yazoo River country (present-day Mississippi) to private speculators. The next legislature, yielding to an angry public outcry, canceled the crooked transaction. But the Supreme Court, with Marshall presiding, decreed that the legislative grant was a contract (even though fraudulently secured) and that the Constitution forbids state laws "impairing" contracts (see Art. I, Sec. X, para. 1). The decision is perhaps most noteworthy for further protecting property rights against popular pressures. It is also one of the earliest clear assertions of the right of the Court to invalidate state laws conflicting with the federal Constitution.

A similar principle was upheld in the case of *Dartmouth College* v. *Woodward* (1819), perhaps the best-remembered of Marshall's decisions. The college had been granted a charter by King George III in 1769, but the democratic New Hampshire state legislature had seen fit to change it. Marshall put the states firmly in their place when he ruled that the original charter must stand. It was a contract, and the Constitution protected contracts against state encroachments. The *Dartmouth* decision had the fortunate effect of safeguarding business enterprise from domination by the states. But it had the unfortunate effect of creating a precedent that enabled chartered corporations, in later years, to escape the handcuffs of needed public control.

Marshall's decisions are felt even today. In this sense his nationalism was the most tenaciously enduring of the era. He buttressed the federal Union and helped to create a stable, nationally uniform environment for business. In an age when white manhood suffrage was flowering and America was veering toward popular control, Marshall almost single-handedly shaped the Constitution along conservative, centralizing lines that ran somewhat counter to the dominant spirit of the new country. Through him the conservative Hamiltonians triumphed from the tomb.

Sharing Oregon and Acquiring Florida

The robust nationalism of the years after the War of 1812 was likewise reflected in foreign policy. To this

John Marshall (1755–1835) *Born in a log cabin on the Virginia frontier, he attended law lectures for just a few weeks at the College of William and Mary—his only formal education.*

end, the nationalistic President Monroe teamed with his nationalistic secretary of state, John Quincy Adams, the cold and scholarly son of the frosty and bookish ex-president. The younger Adams, a statesman of the first rank, happily rose above the ingrown Federalist sectionalism of his native New England and proved to be one of the great secretaries of state.

To its credit, the Monroe administration negotiated the much-underrated Treaty of 1818 with Britain. This multisided agreement permitted Americans to share the coveted Newfoundland fisheries with their Canadian cousins. It also fixed the vague northern limits of Louisiana along the forty-ninth parallel from the Lake of the Woods (Minnesota) to the Rocky Mountains. The treaty further provided for a ten-year joint occupation of the untamed Oregon country, without a surrender of the rights or claims of either America or Britain.

To the south lay semitropical Spanish Florida, which many Americans believed geography and providence had destined to become part of the United States. Americans already claimed West Florida, where uninvited American settlers had torn down the hated Spanish flag in 1810. Congress ratified this grab in 1812, and during the War of 1812 a small American army seized the Mobile region. But the bulk of Florida remained under Spanish rule.

When an epidemic of revolutions broke out in South America, Spain was forced to denude Florida of troops to fight the rebels. General Andrew Jackson, idol of the West and scourge of the Indians, saw opportunity in the undefended swamplands. On the pretext that hostile Seminole Indians and fugitive slaves were using Florida as a refuge, Jackson secured a commission to enter Spanish territory, punish the Indians, and recapture the runaways. But he was to respect all posts under the Spanish flag.

Early in 1818 Jackson swept across the Florida border with all the fury of an avenging angel. He hanged two Indian chiefs without ceremony and, after hasty military trials, executed two British subjects for assisting the Indians. He also seized the two most important Spanish posts in the area, St. Marks and Pensacola, where he deposed the Spanish governor.

Jackson had clearly exceeded his instructions from Washington. Alarmed, President Monroe consulted his cabinet. Its members were for disavowing or disciplining the overzealous Jackson—all except

the lone wolf John Quincy Adams, who refused to howl with the pack. An ardent patriot and nationalist, the flinty New Englander took the offensive and demanded huge concessions from Spain.

In the mislabeled Florida Purchase Treaty of 1819, Spain ceded Florida as well as shadowy Spanish claims to Oregon, in exchange for America's abandonment of equally murky claims to Texas, soon to become part of independent Mexico. The hitherto vague western boundary of Louisiana was made to run zigzag along the Rockies to the forty-second parallel and then to turn due west to the Pacific, dividing Oregon from Spanish holdings.

The Menace of Monarchy in America

After the Napoleonic nightmare, the rethroned autocrats of Europe banded together in a kind of monarchical protective association. Determined to restore the good old days, they undertook to stamp out the democratic tendencies that had sprouted from soil they considered richly manured by the ideals of the French Revolution. The world must be made safe from democracy.

The crowned despots acted promptly. With complete ruthlessness, they smothered the embers of rebellion in Italy (1821) and in Spain (1823). According to the European rumor factory, they were also gazing across the Atlantic. Russia, Austria, Prussia,

U.S.-British Boundary Settlement, 1818 *Notice that the United States gained considerable territory by securing a treaty boundary rather than the natural boundary of the Missouri River watershed. The line of 49° was extended westward to the Pacific Ocean under the Treaty of 1846 with Britain.*

and France, acting in partnership, would presumably send powerful fleets and armies to the revolted colonies of Spanish America and there restore the autocratic Spanish king to his ancestral domains.

Many Americans were alarmed. Sympathetic to democratic revolutions everywhere, they had cheered when the Latin American republics rose from the ruins of monarchy. Americans feared that if the European powers intervened in the New World, the cause of republicanism would suffer irreparable harm. The physical security of the United States—the mother lode of democracy—would be endangered by the proximity of powerful and unfriendly forces.

The southward push of the Russian bear, from the chill region now known as Alaska, had already publicized the menace of monarchy to North America. In 1821 the tsar of Russia issued a decree extending Russian jurisdiction over one hundred miles of the open sea down to the line of 51°, an area that embraced most of the coast of present-day British Columbia.

Great Britain, still Mistress of the Seas, was beginning to play a single-handed role on the complicated international stage. In particular, Britain recoiled from joining with the continental European powers in crushing the newly won liberties of the Spanish-Americans. Those revolutionists had thrown open their monopoly-bound ports to outside trade, and British shippers, as well as Americans, had found the profits sweet. Accordingly, in August 1823, George Canning, the haughty British foreign secretary, approached the American minister in London with a startling proposition. Would not the United States join with Britain in a joint declaration and specifically warn the European despots to keep their harsh hands off the Latin American republics? The American minister, lacking instructions, referred this fateful scheme to his superiors in Washington.

Monroe and His Doctrine

The lone-wolf nationalist, Secretary of State John Quincy Adams, was hardheaded enough to beware of Britons bearing gifts. Why should the lordly British, with the mightiest navy afloat, need America as an ally—an America that had neither naval nor military strength? Such a union, argued Adams, was undignified—like a tiny American "cockboat" sailing "in the wake of the British man-of-war."

Adams, ever alert, thought that he detected a joker in the Canning proposal. If Canning could seduce the United States into supporting existing territorial arrangements in the New World, America's hands would be morally tied against expansion. He suspected—correctly—that European powers had no definite plans for invading the Americas. In any event the British navy would prevent hostile fleets from interfering with South American markets, so Adams decided it was safe for Uncle Sam to blow a defiant nationalistic blast at all Europe.

The Monroe Doctrine was born late in 1823, when the nationalistic Adams won the nationalistic Monroe over to his way of thinking. The president, in his regular annual message to Congress on December 2, 1823, incorporated a stern warning to the European powers. Its two basic features were (1) noncolonization and (2) nonintervention.

Monroe first directed his verbal blast primarily at Russia in the Northwest. He proclaimed, in effect, that the era of colonization in the Americas had ended and that henceforth the hunting season was permanently closed. What the great powers had they might keep, but neither they nor any other Old World governments could seize or otherwise acquire more.

At the same time Monroe trumpeted a warning blast against foreign intervention. He was clearly concerned with regions to the south, where the fledgling Latin American republics were extremely vulnerable. Monroe bluntly directed the crowned heads of Europe to keep their hated monarchical systems out of the Western Hemisphere. For its part, the United States would not intervene in the war that the Greeks were then fighting against the Turks for their independence.

Monroe's Doctrine Appraised

The ermined monarchs of Europe were angered at Monroe's doctrine. Having resented the incendiary American experiment from the beginning, they were deeply offended by Monroe's high-flown pronouncement—all the more so because of the gulf between America's loud pretensions and weak military strength. But though offended by the upstart Yankees, the European powers found their hands tied, and their frustration increased their annoyance. Even if they had worked out plans for invading the Americas, they would have been helpless before the booming broadsides of the British navy.

Monroe's solemn warning, when issued, made little splash in the newly hatched republics to the south. Anyone could see that Uncle Sam was only secondarily concerned about his neighbors; he was primarily concerned about defending himself against future invasion. Only a relatively few educated Latin Americans knew of the message, and they generally recognized that the British navy—not the paper pronouncement of James Monroe—stood between them and a hostile, greedy Europe.

In truth, Monroe's message actually did not have very much contemporary significance. Americans applauded it and then forgot it as they turned back to such activities as felling trees and fighting Indians. Not until 1845 did President James Polk revive it, and not until midcentury did it become an important national dogma.

The Monroe Doctrine might more accurately have been called the Self-Defense Doctrine. President Monroe was concerned mainly with the security of his own country—not of Latin America. The United States has never willingly permitted a powerful foreign nation to secure a foothold near its strategic Caribbean vitals. Yet in the absence of the British navy or other allies, the strength of the Monroe Doctrine has never been greater than America's power to eject the trespasser.

The Monroe Doctrine has had a long career of ups and downs. It was never law—domestic or international. It was not, technically speaking, a pledge or an agreement. It was merely a simple, personalized statement of the policy of President Monroe. And Monroe's presidential successors have ignored, revived, distorted, or expanded the original version. But in 1823 the Monroe Doctrine was largely an expression of the post-1812 nationalism energizing the United States. Although it was directed at a specific menace in 1823 and hence is a kind of period piece, the doctrine proved to be the most famous of all the long-lived offspring of that nationalism. While giving vent to a spirit of patriotism, it simultaneously deepened the American sense of isolation from European dangers.

Chronology

1812	United States declares war on Britain. Madison elected president.
1812–1813	American invasions of Canada fail.
1813	Battle of the Thames. Battle of Lake Erie.
1814	Battle of Plattsburgh. British burn Washington. Battle of Horseshoe Bend. Treaty of Ghent signed.
1814–1815	Hartford Convention.
1815	Battle of New Orleans.
1816	Second Bank of the United States founded. Monroe elected president.
1817	Rush-Bagot agreement limits naval armament on Great Lakes.
1818	Treaty of 1818 with Britain. Jackson invades Florida.
1819	Panic of 1819. Spain cedes Florida to United States. *McCulloch* v. *Maryland* case. *Dartmouth College* v. *Woodward* case.
1820	Missouri Compromise. Missouri and Maine admitted to Union. Monroe reelected.
1823	Secretary of State Adams proposes Monroe Doctrine.
1825	Erie Canal completed.

For further reading, see the Appendix. For web resources, go to **http://college.hmco.com**.

13

The Rise of a Mass Democracy

1824–1840

In the full enjoyment of the gifts of Heaven and the fruits of superior industry, economy, and virtue, every man is equally entitled to protection by law; but when the laws undertake to add to those natural and just advantages artificial distinctions . . . and exclusive privileges . . . the humble members of society— the farmers, mechanics, and laborers . . . have a right to complain of the injustice of their government.

ANDREW JACKSON, 1832

The so-called Era of Good Feelings was never entirely tranquil, but even the illusion of national consensus was shattered by the panic of 1819 and the Missouri Compromise of 1820. Economic distress and the slavery issue raised the political stakes in the 1820s and 1830s. Vigorous political conflict, once feared, came to be celebrated as necessary for the health of democracy. New political parties emerged. New styles of campaigning took hold. A new chapter opened in the history of American politics. The political landscape of 1824 was similar, in its broad outlines, to that of 1796. By 1840 it would be almost unrecognizable.

The deference, apathy, and virtually nonexistent party organizations of the Era of Good Feelings yielded to the boisterous democracy, frenzied vitality, and strong political parties of the Jacksonian era. The old suspicion of political parties as illegitimate disrupters of society's natural harmony gave way to an acceptance of the sometimes wild contentiousness of political life.

In 1828 an energetic new party, the Democrats, captured the White House. By the 1830s the Democrats faced an equally vigorous opposition party in the form of the Whigs. This two-party system institutionalized divisions that had vexed the Revolutionary generation and came to constitute an important part of the nation's checks and balances on political power.

New forms of politicking emerged in this era, as candidates used banners, badges, parades, barbecues, free drinks, and baby kissing to "get out the vote." Voter turnout rose dramatically; only about one-quarter of eligible voters cast a ballot in the presidential election of 1824, but that proportion doubled in 1828, and in the election of 1840 it reached 78 percent. Everywhere the people flexed their political muscles.

The "Corrupt Bargain" of 1824

The last of the old-style elections was marked by the controversial "corrupt bargain" of 1824. The woods were full of presidential timber as James Monroe, last of the Virginia dynasty, completed his second term. Four candidates towered above the others: John Quincy Adams of Massachusetts, highly intelligent, experienced, and aloof; Henry Clay of Kentucky, the gamy and gallant "Harry of the West"; William H. Crawford of Georgia, an able though ailing giant of a man; and Andrew Jackson of Tennessee, the gaunt and gutsy hero of New Orleans.

All four rivals professed to be "Republicans." Well-organized parties had not yet emerged; their identities were so fuzzy, in fact, that John C. Calhoun appeared as the vice-presidential candidate on both the Adams and the Jackson tickets.

The results of the noisy campaign were interesting but confusing. Jackson, the war hero, clearly had the strongest personal appeal, especially in the West, where his campaign against the forces of corruption and privilege in government resonated deeply. He polled almost as many popular votes as his next two rivals combined, but he failed to win a majority of the electoral vote. In such a deadlock the House of Representatives, as directed by the Twelfth Amendment (see the Appendix), must choose among the top three candidates. Clay was thus eliminated, yet as Speaker of the House he presided over the very chamber that had to pick the winner.

The influential Clay was in a position to throw the election to the candidate of his choice. He reached the decision by a process of elimination. Crawford, recently felled by a paralytic stroke, was out of the picture. Clay hated the "military chieftain" Jackson, who in turn bitterly resented Clay's public denunciation of his Florida foray in 1818. The only candidate left was the puritanical Adams, with whom Clay—a free-living gambler and duelist—had never established cordial personal relations. But the two men had much in common politically: both were fervid nationalists and advocates of the American System. Shortly before the final ballot in the House, Clay met privately with Adams and assured him of his support.

Decision day came early in 1825. The House of Representatives met amid tense excitement, with sick members being carried in on stretchers. On the first ballot, thanks largely to Clay's behind-the-scenes maneuvering, Adams was elected president. A few days later, the victor announced that Henry Clay would be the new secretary of state.

Masses of angered Jacksonians, most of them common folk, roared in protest against this "corrupt bargain." Jackson condemned Clay as the "Judas of the West," and John Randolph of Virginia declared that Clay "shines and stinks like . . . a rotten mackerel by moonlight." No positive evidence has ever been unearthed to prove that Adams and Clay entered into a formal bargain. Clay was a natural choice for secretary of state,

Election of 1824

Candidates	Electoral Vote	Popular Vote	Popular Percentage
Jackson	99	153,544	42.16%
Adams	84	108,740	31.89
Crawford	41	46,618	12.95
Clay	37	47,136	12.99

and Adams was scrupulously honest—and not one given to patronage. But the outcry over Adams's election showed that change was in the wind. What had once been common practice was now condemned as furtive, elitist, and subversive of democracy. The next president would not be chosen behind closed doors.

A Yankee Misfit in the White House

John Quincy Adams was a chip off the old family glacier. Short, thickset, and billiard-bald, he was even more frigidly austere than his president-father, John Adams. Shunning people, he often went for early morning swims, sometimes stark naked, in the then-pure Potomac River. Essentially a closeted thinker rather than a politician, he was irritable, sarcastic, and tactless. Yet few individuals have ever come to the presidency with a more brilliant record in statecraft, especially in foreign affairs. He ranks as one of the most successful secretaries of state, yet one of the least successful presidents.

A man of puritanical honor, Adams entered upon his four-year "sentence" in the White House smarting under charges of "bargain," "corruption," and "usurpation." Fewer than one-third of the voters had voted for him. As the first "minority president," he would have found it difficult to win popular support even under the most favorable conditions. He possessed almost none of the arts of the politician and scorned those who did. He had achieved high office by commanding respect rather than by courting popularity. In the dawning age of back-slapping and baby-kissing democracy, the cold fish John Quincy Adams could hardly hope for success at the polls.

Adams's nationalistic views contributed to his woes in the White House. Much of the nation was turning away from post-Ghent nationalism toward states' rights and sectionalism. But Adams swam against the tide. The new president urged upon Congress in his first annual message the construction of a national network of roads and canals. He renewed George Washington's proposal for a national university and went so far as to advocate federal support for an astronomical observatory.

The public reaction to these proposals was prompt and unfavorable. To many workaday Ameri-

President John Quincy Adams (1767–1848), daguerreotype by Phillip Haas, 1843 *Adams wrote in his diary, in June 1819, nearly six years before becoming president, "I am a man of reserved, cold, austere, and forbidding manners: my political adversaries say, a gloomy misanthropist, and my personal enemies an unsocial savage."*

cans grubbing out stumps, astronomical observatories seemed like a scandalous waste of public funds. The South in particular bristled. If the federal government could meddle in local concerns like education and roads, it might even try to lay its hand on the "peculiar institution" of black slavery.

Going "Whole Hog" for Jackson in 1828

The presidential campaign for Andrew Jackson had started early—on February 9, 1825, the day of John Quincy Adams's controversial election by the House. It continued noisily for nearly four years.

Even before the election of 1828, the temporarily united Republicans of the Era of Good Feelings had split into two camps. One was the National Republicans, with Adams as their standard-bearer. The other was the Democratic-Republicans, with the fiery Jackson heading their ticket.

Chanting "All hail, Old Hickory" and planting hickory poles for their hickory-tough hero, Jackson's zealots argued that the will of the voters had been thwarted in 1825 by the backstairs "corrupt bargain" between Adams and Clay. The only way to right the wrong was to seat Jackson, who would then bring about "reform" by sweeping out the "dishonest" Adams gang.

Mudslinging reached a disgraceful level, and the electorate developed a taste for bare-knuckle politics. Adams would not stoop to gutter tactics, but many of his backers were less squeamish. They described Jackson's mother as a prostitute and his wife as an adulteress, and they recounted "Old Hickory's" numerous duels and his hanging of six militiamen.

Jackson men also hit below the belt. A billiard table that President Adams had purchased with his own money became, in the mouths of rabid Jacksonites, "gambling tables" in the "presidential palace." Jackson campaigners mocked Adams's long service on the federal payroll and even accused him of having served as a pimp for the tsar while serving as minister to Russia.

On voting day, the electorate split on largely sectional lines. Jackson's strongest support came from the West and South. The middle Atlantic states and the Old Northwest were divided, while Adams won the backing of his own New England as well as the propertied "better elements" of the Northeast. But when the popular vote was converted to electoral votes, General Jackson's triumph could not be denied. Old Hickory had trounced Adams by an electoral count of 178 to 83. Although a considerable part of Jackson's support was lined up by machine politicians in eastern cities, particularly in New York and Pennsylvania, the political center of gravity clearly had shifted away from the conservative eastern seaboard toward the emerging states across the mountains.

The Advent of Old Hickory Jackson

The new president cut a striking figure—tall, lean, with bushy iron-gray hair brushed high above a

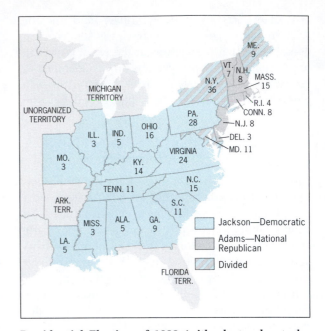

Presidential Election of 1828 (with electoral vote by state) *Jackson swept the South and West, while Adams retained the old Federalist stronghold of the Northeast. Yet Jackson's inroads in the Northeast were decisive. He won twenty of New York's electoral votes and all twenty-eight of Pennsylvania's. If those votes had gone the other way, Adams would have been victorious—by a margin of one vote.*

prominent forehead, craggy eyebrows, and blue eyes. His irritability and emaciated condition resulted in part from long-term bouts with dysentery, malaria, tuberculosis, and lead poisoning from two bullets that he carried in his body from near-fatal duels. His autobiography was written in his lined face.

Jackson's upbringing had shortcomings. Born in the Carolinas and early orphaned, "Mischievous Andy" grew up without parental restraints. As a youth, he displayed much more interest in brawling and cockfighting than in his scanty opportunities for reading and spelling. Although he eventually learned to express himself in writing with vigor and clarity, his grammar was always rough-hewn and his spelling original.

The youthful Carolinian shrewdly moved "up West" to Tennessee, where fighting was prized above writing. There—through native intelligence, force of

Andrew Jackson (1767–1845), by Thomas Sully, 1845 *A self-taught and popularly elected major general of the Tennessee militia, Andrew Jackson became a major general of the U.S. Army in 1814. He was noted for his stern discipline, iron will ("Old Hickory"), and good luck.*

Jackson's inauguration symbolized the ascendancy of the masses. "Hickoryites" poured into Washington from far places, sleeping on hotel floors and in hallways. They were curious to see their hero take office—and perhaps to pick up a well-paying office for themselves. Nobodies mingled with notables as the White House, for the first time, was thrown open to the multitude. A milling crowd of clerks, shopkeepers, hobnailed artisans, and grimy laborers surged in, wrecking the china and furniture and threatening the "people's champion" with cracked ribs. Jackson was hastily spirited through a side door, and the White House miraculously emptied itself when the word was passed that huge bowls of well-spiked punch had been placed on the lawns. Such was the "inaugural brawl."

To conservatives, this orgy seemed like the end of the world. "King Mob" reigned triumphant as Jacksonian vulgarity replaced Jeffersonian simplicity. Faint-hearted traditionalists shuddered, drew their blinds, and recalled the opening scenes of the French Revolution.

Jackson Nationalizes the Spoils System

Once in power, the Democrats, famously suspicious of the federal government, demonstrated they were not above striking some bargains of their own. Under Jackson the spoils system—that is, rewarding political supporters with public office—was introduced into the federal government on a large scale. Its name came from Senator William Marcy's remark in 1832, "To the victors belong the spoils of the enemy." The system had already secured a firm hold in New York and Pennsylvania, where well-greased machines ladled out the "gravy" of office.

Jackson defended the spoils system on democratic grounds. "Every man is as good as his neighbor," he declared—perhaps "equally better." As this was believed to be so, and as the routine of office was thought to be simple enough for any upstanding American to learn quickly, why encourage the development of an aristocratic, bureaucratic, officeholding class? But the spoils system was less about qualifications than about rewarding old cronies. The questions asked of each appointee were not "What can he

personality, and powers of leadership—he became a judge and a member of Congress. Afflicted with a violent temper, he early became involved in numerous duels, stabbings, and bloody frays. His passions were so profound that on occasion he would choke into silence when he tried to speak.

The first president from the West, the first nominated in a formal party convention (in 1832), and only the second without a college education (Washington was the first), Jackson was unique. His university was adversity. He had risen from the masses but was not one of them, except insofar as he shared many of their prejudices. Essentially a frontier aristocrat, he owned many slaves, cultivated broad acres, and lived in one of the finest mansions in America—the Hermitage, near Nashville, Tennessee.

do for the country?" but "What has he done for the party?" or "Is he loyal to Jackson?"

Scandal inevitably accompanied the new system. Men who had openly bought their posts by campaign contributions were appointed to high office. Illiterates, incompetents, and plain crooks were given positions of public trust; scoundrels lusted for the spoils—rather than the toils—of office. Samuel Swartwout, despite ample warnings of his untrustworthiness, was awarded the lucrative post of collector of customs for the port of New York. Nearly nine years later he "Swartwouted out" for Britain, leaving his accounts more than a million dollars short—the first person to steal a million from the Washington government.

But despite its undeniable abuses, the spoils system was an important element of the emerging two-party order, cementing as it did loyalty to party over competing claims from economic class or geographic region. The promise of patronage provided a compelling reason for Americans to pick a party and stick with it through thick and thin.

The Tricky "Tariff of Abominations"

The touchy tariff issue had been one of John Quincy Adams's biggest headaches. Now Andrew Jackson felt his predecessor's pain.

In 1824 Congress had increased the general tariff significantly. But wool manufacturers bleated for still-higher barriers. Ardent Jacksonites now played a cynical political game. They promoted a high-tariff bill, expecting it to be defeated, which would give a black eye to then President Adams. To their surprise the tariff passed, and Andrew Jackson inherited the political hot potato.

Southerners, as heavy consumers of manufactured goods with little manufacturing of their own, were hostile to tariffs, particularly to the high rates of this Tariff of 1828. Hotheads branded it the "Black Tariff" and the "Tariff of Abominations." Several southern states adopted formal protests, and in South Carolina flags were lowered to half-mast.

Why did the South react so angrily to the tariff? Southerners believed, not illogically, that the "Yankee tariff" discriminated against them. But the fact is that while other regions prospered, the Old South was falling on hard times, and the tariff provided a convenient scapegoat. Southerners who sold their cotton in an unprotected world market were forced to buy from Yankee and middle state manufacturers heavily protected by tariffs. The farmers and planters of the Old South felt they were stuck with the bill.

But much deeper issues underlay the southern outcry—in particular, a growing anxiety about possible federal interference with the institution of slavery. The congressional debate on the Missouri Compromise had kindled those anxieties, and they were further fanned by an abortive slave rebellion in Charleston in 1822, led by a free black, Denmark Vesey. At the same time, British West Indian slaveholders were feeling the pressures of British abolitionism on the London government, and southerners feared that American abolitionists might similarly use the power of the Washington government to suppress slavery. If so, now was the time, and the tariff was the issue, for making a strong stand against all federal encroachments on states' rights.

South Carolinians took the lead in protesting the "Tariff of Abominations." Vice President John C. Calhoun secretly authored a pamphlet known as the "South Carolina Exposition" that was endorsed by the state legislature. Going a stride beyond the Kentucky and Virginia resolutions of 1798, it bluntly and explicitly proposed that the states should nullify the tariff—that is, they should declare it null and void within their borders.

"Nullies" in South Carolina

The stage was set for a showdown. Through Jackson's first term the South Carolina nullifiers—"nullies" they were called—tried strenuously to muster the necessary two-thirds vote in the legislature, but they were blocked by a determined minority of Unionists. Congress sought resolution by passing the new, lower Tariff of 1832, but it was still frankly protectionist and fell far short of satisfying southern demands.

South Carolina was now nerved for drastic action. After the "nullies" won a commanding majority in the state election of 1832, the legislature called for a special convention. Meeting in Columbia, the delegates solemnly declared the existing tariff null and void, and threatened to take South Carolina out of the Union if Washington attempted to collect the customs duties by force.

Such tactics might have intimidated John Quincy Adams. But Andrew Jackson was the wrong president to stare down. The cantankerous general was not a diehard supporter of the tariff, but he would not permit defiance or disunion. Privately threatening to invade the state and hang the nullifiers, he publicly dispatched naval and military forces to the Palmetto State and issued a ringing proclamation against nullification. Governor Robert Hayne responded with a counter-proclamation, and the lines were drawn. If civil war was to be avoided, one side would have to surrender, or both would have to compromise.

Conciliatory Senator Henry Clay of Kentucky stepped forward. Although himself a supporter of tariffs, he had no desire to see his old enemy Andrew Jackson win laurels by crushing the South Carolinians and John C. Calhoun. He thus pushed through Congress a compromise bill that would gradually reduce the Tariff of 1832 by about 10 percent over eight years, to the mildly protective level of 1816.

South Carolinians welcomed this opportunity to extricate themselves from a dangerously tight corner without loss of face. To the consternation of the Calhounites, no other southern states had sprung to their support, and an appreciable Unionist minority within South Carolina was gathering guns and nailing the Stars and Stripes to flagpoles. Faced with civil war within and invasion from without, the Columbia convention met again and repealed the ordinance of nullification.

Neither Jackson nor the "nullies" won a clear-cut victory in 1833. Clay was the true hero of the hour, hailed in Charleston and Boston alike for saving the country. Armed conflict had been avoided, but the fundamental issues had not been resolved. When next the "nullies" and the Union clashed, compromise would prove more elusive.

The Trail of Tears

Jackson's Democrats were committed to western expansion. But such expansion necessarily meant confrontation with the current inhabitants of the land. More than 125,000 Native Americans lived in the forests and prairies east of the Mississippi in the 1820s. Federal policy toward them varied. Beginning in the 1790s the Washington government ostensibly recognized the tribes as separate nations and agreed to acquire land from them through formal treaties. The Indians were shrewd and determined negotiators, but this availed them little when Americans routinely violated their own covenants as white settlement pushed west.

Many white Americans felt respect and admiration for the Indians and believed that the Native Americans could be assimilated into white society. Much energy was therefore devoted to "civilizing" and Christianizing the Indians. Many denominations sent missionaries into Indian villages, and in 1793 Congress appropriated $20,000 for Indian literacy programs and agricultural instruction.

Although many tribes violently resisted white encroachment, others followed the path of accommodation. The Cherokees of Georgia made especially remarkable efforts to learn white ways. They adopted a written legal code, developed a system of settled agriculture, opened schools on their lands, and one of them, Sequoyah, devised a Cherokee alphabet. Some Cherokees became prosperous cotton planters and even turned to slaveholding. Nearly 1,300 black slaves toiled for their Native American masters in the Cherokee nation in the 1820s. For these efforts, the Cherokees—along with the Creeks, Choctaws, Chickasaws, and Seminoles—were numbered by the whites among the "Five Civilized Tribes."

All this embrace of "civilization" apparently was not good enough for the whites. In 1828 the Georgia legislature declared the Cherokee tribal council illegal and asserted its own jurisdiction over Indian affairs and Indian lands. The Cherokees appealed this move to the Supreme Court, which thrice upheld the rights of the Indians. But President Jackson, who clearly wanted to open Indian lands to white settlement, refused to recognize the Court's decisions. In a callous jibe at the Indians' defender, Jackson reportedly snapped, "John Marshall has made his decision; now let him enforce it."

Feeling some obligation, though, to rescue "this much injured race," Jackson proposed a bodily removal of the "Five Civilized Tribes" of the southeast to beyond the Mississippi. Emigration was supposed to be voluntary because it would be "cruel and unjust to compel the aborigines to abandon the graves of their fathers," Jackson declared.

Jackson's policy, passed by Congress as the Indian Removal Act of 1830, led to the forced uprooting of more than 100,000 Indians. In the ensuing decade, countless Indians died on the "Trail of Tears" to the newly established Indian Territory (present-day Oklahoma). The Bureau of Indian Affairs was established in 1836 to administer relations with America's original inhabitants, but as land-hungry "palefaces" pushed rapidly west, the government's guarantee of a "permanent" Indian homeland went up in smoke.

Suspicious of white intentions from the start, Black Hawk, the leader of the Sac and Fox Indians, mobilized resistance to eviction from Illinois and Wisconsin. His braves were bloodily crushed in 1832 by regular troops, including Lieutenant Jefferson Davis of Mississippi, and by military volunteers, including Captain Abraham Lincoln of Illinois. In Florida the Seminoles, under the leadership of Osceola, retreated into the swampy Everglades, and for seven years (1835–1842) waged a bitter guerrilla war that took the lives of some fifteen hundred soldiers. It proved to be the costliest Indian conflict in the American experience. After their defeat, some Seminoles fled deeper into the Everglades, where their descendants now live, but about four-fifths of them were moved to Oklahoma, where several thousand of the tribe survive.

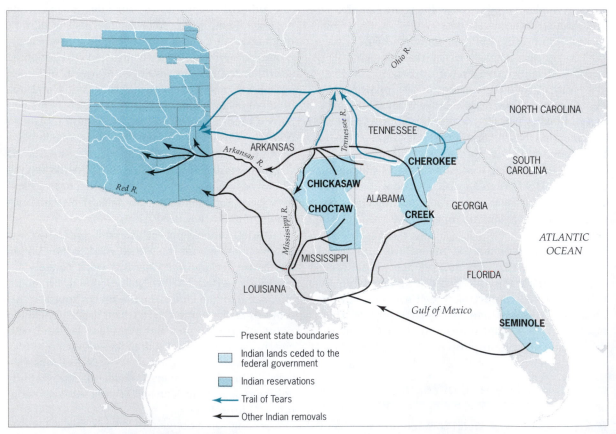

The Removal of the Southern Tribes to the West

The "Trail of Tears" *In the fall and winter of 1838–1839, the U.S. Army forcibly removed about 15,000 Cherokees, some of them in manacles, from their ancestral homelands in the southeastern United States and marched them to the "Indian Territory" of present-day Oklahoma. Freezing weather and inadequate food supplies led to unspeakable suffering. The escorting troops refused to slow the forced march so that the ill could recover, and some four thousand Cherokees died on the 116-day journey.*

The Bank War

President Jackson did not hate all banks and all businesses, but he distrusted monopolistic banking and overbig business, as did his followers. A man of virulent dislikes, he came to share the prejudices of his own West against the "moneyed monster" known as the Bank of the United States.

What made the bank a monster in Jackson's eyes? The national government minted gold and silver coins in the mid-nineteenth century but did not issue paper money. Paper notes issued by private banks in effect functioned as money, giving private bankers considerable power over the nation's economy.

No bank in America had more power than the Bank of the United States. In many ways, the bank acted like a branch of government. It was the principal depository for the funds of the Washington government and controlled much of the nation's gold and silver. A source of credit and stability, the bank was an important and useful part of the nation's expanding economy.

But the Bank of the United States was a private institution, accountable not to the people but only to its elite circle of moneyed investors. Its president, the brilliant but arrogant Nicholas Biddle—dubbed "Czar Nicholas I" by his enemies—held an immense amount of power over the nation's financial affairs.

To some, the bank's very existence seemed to sin against the egalitarian credo of American democracy. That conviction formed the deepest source of Jackson's opposition. The bank also won no friends by foreclosing on many western farms and draining "tribute" into eastern coffers. Profit, not public service, was its first priority.

The Bank War erupted in 1832, when Daniel Webster and Henry Clay presented Congress with a bill to renew the Bank of the United States' charter. The charter was not set to expire until 1836, but Clay pushed for renewal four years early to make it an election issue in 1832. As Jackson's leading rival for the presidency, Clay, with fateful blindness, looked upon the bank issue as a surefire winner.

The recharter bill slid through Congress on greased skids, as planned, but was killed by a scorching veto from Jackson. The "Old Hero" declared the monopolistic bank to be unconstitutional, ignoring the Supreme Court's earlier declaration upholding its constitutionality in *McCulloch* v. *Maryland* (1819). The grizzled general growled privately, "The Bank . . . is trying to kill me, but I will kill it." Jackson's veto message not only squashed the bank bill, but vastly amplified the powers of the presidency. If the legislative and executive branches were partners in government, Jackson implied, the president was unmistakably the senior partner.

Delighted with the veto message's financial fallacies, but blind to its political appeal to the common people, Henry Clay arranged to have thousands of copies printed as a campaign document. The bank issue was now thrown into the noisy arena of the presidential contest of 1832.

"Old Hickory" Wallops Clay in 1832

Clay and Jackson were the chief gladiators in the fierce electoral combat of 1832. The grizzled old gen-

Henry Clay (1777–1852), daguerreotype by Mathew Brady, 1849 *A glamorous, eloquent, and ambitious member of the House and Senate for many years, Clay was thrice an unsuccessful candidate for the highest office in the land. "Sir," he declared in the Senate in 1850, "I would rather be right than be President." But it was his inability to straddle the growing conflict over slavery, rather than his conscience, that kept him from attaining the highest office.*

eral's supporters again raised hickory poles and shouted "Jackson Forever: Go the Whole Hog!" Clay's admirers called for "Freedom and Clay," while his detractors harped on his dueling, gambling, cockfighting, and fast living.

Novel features made the campaign of 1832 especially memorable. For the first time, a third party entered the field—the newborn Anti-Masonic party, which opposed the influence and fearsome secrecy of the Masonic order. Energized by the mysterious disappearance and probable murder in 1826 of a New Yorker who was threatening to expose the Masons' secret rituals, the Anti-Masonic party quickly became a potent political force throughout the middle Atlantic and New England states. The Anti-Masons appealed to Americans' democratic suspicions of secret societies, and even attacked Jackson, himself a proud Mason. The Anti-Masonic party also attracted support from many evangelical Protestants seeking to use political power to effect moral and religious reforms, such as prohibiting mail deliveries on Sunday.

A further novelty of the presidential contest in 1832 was the calling of national nominating conventions (three of them) to name candidates. The Anti-Masons and a group of National Republicans added still another innovation when they adopted formal platforms, articulating and publicizing their positions on the issues.

Henry Clay and his overconfident National Republicans sailed into the campaign with rich financial support, much of it from the Bank of the United States, and strong newspaper backing, also "bought" with Biddle's bank loans. Yet Jackson, idol of the masses, easily defeated the big-money Kentuckian. A Jacksonian wave again swept over the West and South, surged into Pennsylvania and New York, and even washed into rock-ribbed New England. The popular vote stood at 687,502 to 530,189 for Jackson; the electoral count a lopsided 219 to 49.

Burying Biddle's Bank

Its charter denied, the Bank of the United States was due to expire in 1836. But Jackson was not one to let the financial octopus die in peace. He was convinced that he now had a mandate from the voters for its extermination, and he feared that the slippery Biddle might try to manipulate the bank (as he did) so as to force its recharter. Jackson therefore proposed to bury the bank for good by removing all federal deposits from its vaults, thereby bleeding the bank dry and ensuring its demise.

Even the president's closest advisers opposed this vindictive and possibly unconstitutional move. His dander up, Jackson was forced to reshuffle his cabinet twice before he could find a secretary of the treasury who would bend to his iron will. Hoping to demonstrate the bank's importance, the desperate Biddle called in its loans, thereby generating a minor financial crisis—"Biddle's Panic." But Jackson's resolution was firm. If anything, the vengeful conduct of the dying "monster" seemed to justify the earlier accusations of its adversaries.

But the death of the Bank of the United States left a financial vacuum in the American economy and kicked off a lurching cycle of booms and busts. Surplus federal funds were placed in several dozen pro-Jackson state banks, the so-called pet banks. Without a sober central bank in control, the pet banks and smaller "wildcat" banks—fly-by-night operations that often consisted of little more than a few chairs and a suitcase full of printed notes—flooded the country with unsound paper money.

Jackson tried to rein in the runaway economy in 1836, the year Biddle's bank breathed its last. "Wildcat" currency had become so unreliable, especially in the West, that Jackson authorized the Treasury to issue a Specie Circular—a decree that required all public lands to be purchased with "hard," or metallic, money. This drastic step slammed the brakes on the speculative boom, a neck-snapping change of direction that contributed to a financial panic, and crash, in 1837.

But by then Jackson had retired to his Nashville home, hailed as the hero of his age. His successor would have to deal with the damage.

The Birth of the Whigs

New political parties were gelling as the 1830s lengthened. As early as 1828, the Democratic-Republicans of Jackson had unashamedly adopted the once-tainted name of "Democrats." Jackson's opponents condemned him as "King Andrew I" and began to coalesce as Whigs—a name deliberately chosen to recollect eighteenth-century British and Revolutionary American opposition to the monarchy.

The Whig party contained so many diverse elements that it was mocked at first as "an organized incompatibility." Hatred of Jackson and his "executive usurpation" was its only apparent cement in its formative days. The Whigs first emerged as an identifiable group in the Senate, where Clay, Webster, and Calhoun joined forces in 1834 in opposition to Jackson's bank policies. Thereafter, the Whigs rapidly evolved into a potent national political force by attracting other groups alienated by Jackson: supporters of Clay's American System; southern states' righters offended by Jackson's stand on nullification; the larger northern industrialists and merchants; and eventually many of the evangelical Protestants associated with the Anti-Masonic party.

Whigs thought of themselves as conservatives, yet they were progressive in their support of active government programs and reforms. Instead of boundless territorial acquisition, they called for internal improvements like canals, railroads, and telegraph lines, and they supported institutions like prisons, asylums, and public schools. The Whigs welcomed the market economy, drawing support from manufacturers in the North, planters in the South, and merchants and bankers in all sections. But they were not simply a party of wealthy fat cats, however dearly the Democrats wanted to paint them as such. By absorbing the egalitarian Anti-Masonic party, the Whigs blunted much of the Democratic appeal to the common man. Turning Jacksonian rhetoric on its head, the Whigs portrayed Jackson and his successor, Martin Van Buren, as imperious aristocrats, and the Democrats as the party of cronyism and corruption.

The Election of 1836

The smooth-tongued and keen-witted secretary of state, Martin Van Buren of New York, was Jackson's choice for "appointment" as his successor in 1836. Jackson was too old and ailing to consider a third term, but he was not loath to try to serve a third term through Van Buren, something of a "yes man." Leaving nothing to chance, Jackson carefully rigged the nominating convention and rammed his favorite down the throats of the delegates. Van Buren was supported by the Jacksonites without wild enthusiasm, even though he had promised "to tread generally" in the military-booted footsteps of his predecessor.

As the election neared, the still-ramshackle organization of the Whigs showed in their inability to nominate a single presidential candidate. Their long-shot strategy was instead to run several prominent "favorite sons" from different regions, hoping thereby to scatter the vote and throw the election into the House of Representatives. With Henry Clay elbowed aside, the leading Whig "favorite son" was heavy-jawed General William Henry Harrison, hero of the Battle of Tippecanoe (see p. 144). The fine-spun schemes of the Whigs availed nothing, however. Van Buren, the dapper "Little Magician," squirmed into office by the close popular vote of 765,483 to 735,795, but by the comfortable margin of 170 votes to 124 (for all the Whigs combined) in the Electoral College.

Big Woes for the "Little Magician"

Martin Van Buren, the eighth president, was the first to be born under the American flag. Short and slender, bland and bald, the adroit little New Yorker has been described as "a first-class second-rate man." An accomplished strategist and spoilsman—"the wizard of Albany"—he was also a statesman of wide experience in both legislative and administrative life. The myth of his mediocrity sprouted mostly from a series of misfortunes over which he had little control.

From the outset, the new president labored under severe handicaps. As a machine-made candidate, he incurred the resentment of many Democrats. Jackson, the master showman, had been the dynamic type of chief executive whose administration had resounded with furious quarrels and cracked heads. Mild-mannered Martin Van Buren seemed to tiptoe quietly behind his bull-in-the-china shop predecessor. The people felt let down. Inheriting Jackson's mantle without his popularity, Van Buren also inherited the ex-president's numerous and vengeful enemies.

Van Buren's four years overflowed with toil and trouble. Ugly incidents along the Canadian border threatened to trigger war with Britain. Antislavery agitators in the North were in full cry. Among other grievances, they were condemning the prospective annexation of Texas.

Worst of all, Jackson bequeathed to Van Buren the makings of a searing depression. Much of Van Buren's energy had to be devoted to the purely negative task of battling the panic, and there were not enough rabbits in the "Little Magician's" tall silk hat. Hard times ordinarily blight the reputation of a president—and Van Buren was no exception.

Depression Doldrums and the Independent Treasury

The panic of 1837 was a symptom of the financial sickness of the times. Its basic cause was rampant speculation prompted by a mania of get-rich-quick-ism. Gamblers in western lands were doing a "land-office business" on borrowed capital, much of it in the shaky currency of "wildcat" banks. The speculative craze spread to canals, roads, railroads, and slaves.

But speculation alone did not cause the crash. Jacksonian finance, including the Bank War and the Specie Circular, gave an additional jolt to an already teetering structure. The collapse of two British banks caused investors to call in loans in the United States. Failures of wheat crops deepened the distress. Grain prices were forced so high that three weeks before Van Buren took the oath of office, mobs in New York City stormed warehouses and broke open flour barrels.

Soon the depression's full fury burst about Van Buren's bewildered head. Hardship was acute and widespread. American banks collapsed by the hundreds, including some of the pet banks, which carried down with them several millions in government funds. Commodity prices drooped, sales of public lands fell off, and customs revenues dried to a rivulet. Factories closed their doors, and unemployed workers milled in the streets.

The Whigs came forward with proposals for active government remedies for the economy's ills. They called for the expansion of bank credit, higher tariffs, and subsidies for internal improvements. But

Van Buren, shackled by the Jacksonian philosophy of keeping the government's paws off the economy, spurned all such ideas.

The beleaguered Van Buren tried to apply vintage Jacksonian medicine to the ailing economy through his controversial "Divorce Bill." Convinced that some of the financial fever was fed by the injection of federal funds into private banks, he championed the principle of "divorcing" the government from banking altogether. By establishing a so-called independent treasury, the government could lock its surplus money in vaults. Government funds would thus be safe, but they would also be denied to the banking system as reserves, thereby shriveling available credit resources.

Van Buren's "divorce" scheme was never highly popular. His fellow Democrats, many of whom longed for the risky but lush days of the pet banks, supported it only lukewarmly. The Whigs condemned it outright, primarily because it would dampen the likelihood of a revived Bank of the United States. After a prolonged struggle, the Independent Treasury Bill passed Congress in 1840. Repealed the next year by the victorious Whigs, the scheme was reenacted by the triumphant Democrats in 1846 and then continued until merged with the Federal Reserve System in the next century.

Gone to Texas

Americans, greedy for land, continued to covet the vast expanse of Texas, which the United States had abandoned to Spain when acquiring Florida in 1819. The Spanish authorities wanted to populate this virtually unpeopled area, but before they could carry through their contemplated plans, the Mexicans won their independence. A new regime in Mexico City thereupon concluded arrangements in 1823 for granting a huge tract of land to Stephen Austin, with the understanding that he would bring into Texas three hundred American families. Immigrants were to be of the established Roman Catholic faith and upon settlement were to become properly Mexicanized.

Those two stipulations were largely ignored. Hardy Texan pioneers remained Americans at heart, resenting the trammels imposed by a "foreign" government. They were especially annoyed by the presence of Mexican soldiers, many of whom were ragged ex-convicts.

Energetic and prolific, Texan-Americans numbered about thirty thousand by 1835 (see "Makers of America: Mexican or Texican?" pp. 174–175). Most of them were law-abiding, God-fearing people, but some of them had left the "states" only one or two jumps ahead of the sheriff. "G.T.T." (Gone To Texas) became current descriptive slang. Among the adventurers were Davy Crockett, the famous rifleman and former Congressman, and James Bowie, the presumed inventor of the murderous knife that bears his name. A distinguished latecomer and leader was an ex-governor of Tennessee, Sam Houston. His life had been temporarily shattered in 1829 when his bride of a few weeks left him and he took up transient residence with the Arkansas Indians, who dubbed him "Big Drunk."

These pioneer individualists who came to Texas were not easy to push around. Friction rapidly increased between Mexicans and Texans over such issues as slavery, immigration, and local rights. Slavery was a particularly touchy issue. Mexico emancipated its slaves in 1830 and prohibited their further importation into Texas, as well as further colonization by troublesome Americans. The Texans refused to honor this decree. They kept their slaves in bondage, and new American settlers kept bringing more slaves into Texas. The explosion finally came in 1835, when Mexican dictator Santa Anna wiped out all local rights and started to raise an army to suppress the upstart Texans.

The Lone Star Rebellion

Early in 1836 the Texans unfurled their Lone Star flag and declared their independence—with Sam Houston as commander in chief. Santa Anna, at the head of about six thousand men, stormed ferociously into Texas. Trapping a band of nearly two hundred pugnacious Texans at the Alamo in San Antonio, he wiped them out to a man after a thirteen-day siege. A short time later a band of about four hundred surrounded and defeated American volunteers, having thrown down their arms at Goliad, were butchered as "pirates."

Mexican or Texican?

Moses Austin, born a Connecticut Yankee in 1761, was determined to be Spanish—if that's what it took to acquire cheap land and freedom from pesky laws. In 1798 he tramped into untracked Missouri, still part of Spanish Louisiana, and pledged his allegiance to the king of Spain. He was not pleased when the Louisiana Purchase of 1803 restored him to American citizenship. In 1820, with his old Spanish passport in his saddlebag, he rode into Spanish Texas and asked for permission to establish a colony of three hundred families.

The Spanish authorities had repeatedly stamped out previous attempts at American settlement in Texas. But the governor somewhat reluctantly allowed Austin's colonists to enter the territory, hoping that they might "civilize" the land and wrest it from the Indians. Upon Moses Austin's death in 1821, the task of realizing his dream fell to his twenty-seven-year-old son, Stephen. "I bid an everlasting farewell to my native country," Stephen Austin said, and he crossed into Texas on July 15, 1821, "determined to fulfill rigidly all the duties and obligations of a Mexican citizen." (Mexico declared its independence from Spain in early 1821.) Soon he learned fluent Spanish and was signing his name as "Don Estévan F. Austin."

Austin fell just three families short of recruiting the three hundred households that his father had contracted to bring to Texas. The original settlers were nevertheless dubbed "the Old Three Hundred," the Texas equivalent of New England's Mayflower Pilgrims or the "First Families of Virginia." Mostly Scots-Irish southerners from the trans-Appalachian frontier, the Old Three Hundred were cultured folk by frontier standards; all but four of them were literate. Other settlers followed, from Europe as well as America. Within ten years the "Anglos" (many of them French and German) outnumbered the Mexican residents, or *tejanos*, ten to one. They soon evolved a distinctive "Texican" culture, which included the mounted Texas Rangers, and planters and cattle ranchers who ran huge operations on the limitless prairies. The original Anglo-Texans brought with them the old Scots-Irish frontiersman's hostility to officialdom and authority. When the Mexican government tried to impose its will on the Anglo-Texans in the 1830s, they protested. Like the American revolutionaries of the 1770s, who at first demanded only the rights of Englishmen, the Texans began by asking simply for Mexican recognition of their rights as guaranteed by the Mexican constitution of 1824. But bloodshed at the Alamo in 1836, like that at Lexington in 1775, transformed protest into rebellion.

Texas lay—and still lies—along the frontier where Latino and Anglo-American cultures met, mingled, and clashed. In part, the Texas revolution was a contest between those two cultures. But it was also a contest about philosophies of government, pitting liberal frontier ideals of freedom against the conservative concept of centralized control. Stephen Austin sincerely tried to "Mexicanize" himself and his followers—until the Mexican government grew too arbitrary and authoritarian. Some of those who adhered to this philosophy were not "Anglos" but *tejanos*. Seven *tejanos* died at the Alamo, and several others signed the Texas declaration of independence, including José Antonio Navarro and Francisco Ruiz. Lorenzo de Zavala, an ardent Mexican liberal who had long resisted the centralizing tendencies of Mexico's dominant political party, was designated vice president of the Texas republic's interim government in 1836. Like the Austins, these *tejanos* and Mexicans had sought in Texas an escape from overbearing governmental authority. Their role in the revolution underscores the fact that the uprising was a struggle between defenders of local rights and agents of central authority as much as it was a fight between Anglo and Mexican cultures.

Slain heroes like Jim Bowie and Davy Crockett, well known in life, became legendary in death. Texan war cries—"Remember the Alamo!" "Remember Goliad!" and "Death to Santa Anna!"—swept up into the United States. Scores of vengeful Americans seized their rifles and rushed to the aid of relatives, friends, and compatriots.

General Sam Houston's small army retreated to the east, luring Santa Anna to San Jacinto, near the site of the city that now bears Houston's name. The Mexicans numbered about thirteen hundred men, the Texans about nine hundred. Suddenly, on April 21, 1836, Houston turned, wiping out the pursuing force. The captured Santa Anna was forced to sign two treaties in which he agreed to withdraw Mexican troops and to recognize the Rio Grande as the extreme southwestern boundary of Texas. When released, he repudiated the whole agreement as illegal because it was extorted under duress.

These events put the United States government in a sticky situation. As the Mexicans bitterly complained, the Washington government's weak enforcement of neutrality laws had permitted American men and supplies to leak across the border and aid the Texans. But American public opinion, overwhelmingly favorable to the Texans, left the federal authorities powerless to act. On the day before he left office in 1837, President Jackson extended the right hand of recognition to the Lone Star Republic, led by his old comrade-in-arms against the Indians, Sam Houston.

Mexican Forces Assault the Alamo   *The defenders fought bravely but were overwhelmed by Santa Anna's army. Among those who died defending the historic mission were Colonel William Travis, Captain James Bowie, and former congressman David Crockett.*

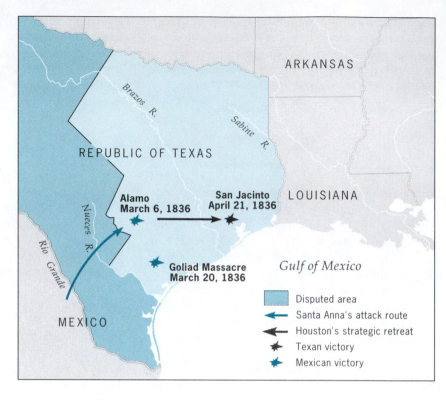

The Texas Revolution, 1835–1836 *General Houston's strategy was to retreat and use defense in depth. His line of supply from the United States was shortened as Santa Anna's lengthened. The Mexicans were forced to bring up supplies by land because the Texas navy controlled the sea. This force consisted of only four small ships, but it was big enough to do the job.*

Many Texans wanted not just recognition of their independence, but outright union with the United States. The radiant Texan bride, officially petitioning for annexation in 1837, presented herself for marriage. But the expectant groom, Uncle Sam, was jerked back by the black hand of the slavery issue. Antislavery crusaders in the North were opposing annexation with increasing vehemence; they contended that the whole scheme was merely a conspiracy cooked up by the southern "slavocracy" to bring new slave pens into the Union.

At first glance, a "slavery plot" charge seemed plausible. Most of the early settlers in Texas, as well as American volunteers during the revolution, had come from slaveholding states of the South and Southwest. But scholars have concluded that the settlement of Texas was merely the normal and inexorable march of the westward movement. The explanation was proximity rather than conspiracy. Yet the fact remained that many Texans were slaveholders, and admitting Texas to the Union inescapably meant enlarging American slavery.

Log Cabins and Hard Cider of 1840

Martin Van Buren was renominated by the Democrats in 1840, albeit without terrific enthusiasm. The party had no acceptable alternative to what the Whigs called "Martin Van Ruin."

The Whigs, hungering for the spoils of office, scented victory in the breeze. Pangs of the panic were still being felt, and voters blamed their woes on the party in power. Learning from their mistake in 1836, the Whigs united behind one candidate, Ohio's William Henry Harrison. He was not their ablest statesman—that would have been Webster or Clay— but he was believed to be their ablest vote-getter.

The aging hero, nearly sixty-eight when the campaign ended, was known for his successes against Indians and the British at the Battles of Tippecanoe (1811) and the Thames (1813). Harrison's views on current issues were only vaguely known. "Old Tippecanoe" was nominated primarily because he was issueless and enemyless—a tested recipe for electoral success that still appeals today. John Tyler of Virginia, an afterthought, was selected as his vice-presidential running mate.

The Whigs, eager to avoid offense, published no official platform, hoping to sweep their hero into office with a frothy huzza-for-Harrison campaign reminiscent of Jackson's triumph in 1828. A dull-witted Democratic editor played directly into Whig hands. Stupidly insulting the West, he lampooned Harrison as an impoverished old farmer who should be content with a pension, a log cabin, and a barrel of hard cider—the poor westerner's champagne. Whigs gleefully adopted honest hard cider and the sturdy log cabin as symbols of their campaign. Harrisonites portrayed their hero as the poor "Farmer of North Bend" who had been called from his cabin and his plow to drive corrupt Jackson spoilsmen from the "presidential palace." They denounced Van Buren as a supercilious aristocrat, a simpering dandy who wore corsets and ate French food from golden plates. As a jeering Whig campaign song proclaimed,

> Old Tip, he wears a homespun shirt,
> He has no ruffled shirt, wirt, wirt.
> But Matt, he has the golden plate,
> And he's a little squirt, wirt, wirt.

The Whig campaign was a masterpiece of inane hoopla. Log cabins were dished up in every conceivable form. Bawling Whigs, stimulated by fortified cider, rolled huge balls from village to village and state to state, representing the snowballing majority for "Tippecanoe and Tyler too." In truth, Harrison was not lowborn but from one of the FFV's ("First Families of Virginia"). He was not the poverty-stricken inhabitant of a one-room log cabin, but rather lived in a sixteen-room mansion on a three-thousand acre estate. He did not swill down gallons of hard cider (he evidently preferred whiskey). And he did not plow his fields with his own "huge paws." But such details had not mattered when General Jackson rode to victory, and they did not matter now.

The Democrats who hurrahed Jackson into the White House in 1828 now discovered to their chagrin that whooping it up for a backwoods Westerner was a game two could play. Harrison won by the surprisingly close margin of 1,275,016 popular votes to 1,129,102, but by an overwhelming electoral count of 234 to 60. With hardly a real issue debated, though with hard times blighting the incumbent's fortunes, Van Buren was washed out of Washington in a wave of apple juice. The hard ciderites had apparently received a mandate to tear down the White House and erect a log cabin.

Politics for the People

The election of 1840 conclusively demonstrated two major changes in American politics since the Era of Good Feelings. The first was the triumph of a populist democratic style. Democracy had been something of a taint in the days of the lordly Federalists. But by the 1840s, aristocracy was the taint and democracy respectable. Politicians were forced to unbend and curry favor with the voting masses. Lucky indeed was the aspiring office seeker who could boast of birth in a log cabin. In 1840 Daniel Webster publicly apologized for not being able to claim so humble a birthplace, though he quickly added that his brothers could. The semiliterate frontiersman Davy Crockett of Tennessee had been elected to Congress mainly on the basis of his bear-hunting prowess. Hopelessly handicapped was the candidate who appeared too well dressed, too grammatical, too high-browishly intellectual. In truth, most high political offices continued to be filled by "leading citizens," but now these prominent men had to cultivate the common touch if they hoped to win elections.

Snobbish bigwigs sneered at the "coonskin Congressmen" elected by newly enfranchised "bipeds of the forest." But these critics protested in vain. The common man was moving to the center of the national political stage: the sturdy American who donned plain trousers rather than silver-buckled knee breeches, who sported a plain haircut and a coonskin cap rather than a powdered wig. Instead of the old divine right of kings, America was now bowing to the divine right of the people.

The Two-Party System

The second dramatic change was the formation of a vigorous and durable two-party system. The Jefferso-

The County Election, by George Caleb Bingham, 1851–1852
The artist here gently satirizes the drinking and wheeler-dealing that sometimes marred the electoral process in the boisterous age of Jacksonian politics.

nians of an earlier day had been so successful in absorbing the programs of their Federalist opponents that a full-blown two-party system had never truly emerged in the subsequent Era of Good Feelings. The idea had prevailed that parties of any kind smacked of conspiracy and "faction" and were injurious to the health of the body politic in a virtuous republic. By 1840 political parties had fully come of age, a lasting legacy of Andrew Jackson's tenaciousness.

Both national parties, the Democrats and the Whigs, grew out of the rich soil of Jeffersonian republicanism, and each laid claim to different aspects of the republican inheritance. Jacksonian Democrats glorified the liberty of the individual and were fiercely on guard against the inroads of "privilege" into government. Whigs trumpeted the natural harmony of society and the value of community, and were willing to use government to realize their objectives. Whigs also berated those leaders—and they considered Jackson to be one—whose appeals to self-interest fostered conflict among individuals, classes, or sections.

Democrats clung to states' rights and federal restraint in social and economic affairs as their basic doctrines. Whigs tended to favor a renewed national bank; protective tariffs; internal improvements; public schools; and, increasingly, moral reforms such as the prohibition of liquor and eventually the abolition of slavery.

The two parties were thus separated by real differences of philosophy and policy. But they also had much in common. Both were mass-based "catchall" parties that tried deliberately to mobilize as many voters as possible for their cause. Although it is true that Democrats tended to be more humble folk and Whigs more prosperous, both parties nevertheless commanded the loyalties of all kinds of Americans, from all social classes and in all sections. The social diversity of the two parties fostered horse-trading compromises within each party that prevented either from assuming extreme or radical positions. By the same token, the geographical diversity of the two parties retarded the emergence of purely sectional political parties—temporarily suppressing, through compromise, the ultimately uncompromisable issue of slavery. When the two-party system began to creak in the 1850s, the Union was mortally imperiled.

Chronology

1822	Vesey slave rebellion in Charleston, South Carolina.
1823	Mexico opens Texas to American settlers.
1824	Lack of electoral majority for presidency throws election into the House of Representatives.
1825	House elects John Quincy Adams president.
1828	Tariff of 1828 ("Tariff of Abominations"). Jackson elected president.
1829	Indian Removal Act.
1832	"Bank War"—Jackson vetoes bill rechartering Bank of the United States. Tariff of 1832. Jackson defeats Clay for presidency. Black Hawk War.
1832–1833	South Carolina nullification crisis.
1833	Compromise Tariff of 1833. Jackson removes federal deposits from Bank of the United States.
1836	Bank of the United States expires. Specie Circular issued. Bureau of Indian Affairs established. Battle of the Alamo. Battle of San Jacinto. Texas wins independence from Mexico. Van Buren elected president.
1837	Seminole Indians defeated and most eventually removed from Florida. Panic of 1837. United States recognizes republic of Texas but refuses annexation.
1838–1839	Cherokee Indians removed on "Trail of Tears."
1840	Independent Treasury established. Harrison defeats Van Buren for presidency.

VARYING VIEWPOINTS

What Was Jacksonian Democracy?

Aristocratic, eastern-born historians of the nineteenth century damned Jackson as a backwoods barbarian and Jacksonianism as democracy run riot. In the late nineteenth and early twentieth centuries, another generation of historians, many of them midwesterners, rejected the elitist views of their predecessors. Frederick Jackson Turner and his disciples saw the western frontier as the fount of democratic virtue, and they hailed Jackson as a true popular hero battling for the people against the moneyed interests.

When Arthur M. Schlesinger, Jr., published *The Age of Jackson* in 1945, however, the debate on Jacksonianism shifted dramatically. Schlesinger cast the Jacksonian era not as a sectional conflict but as a class conflict between poor farmers, laborers, and noncapitalists on the one hand and the business community on the other. Soon after Schlesinger's book appeared, the discussion again shifted ground and entirely new interpretations of Jacksonianism emerged. Richard Hofstadter argued in *The American Political Tradition and the Men Who Made It* (1948) that Jacksonian democracy was not a rejection of capitalism, as Schlesinger insisted, but rather the effort of aspiring entrepreneurs to serve their own interests against their entrenched, monopolistic, eastern competitors. Lee Benson contended in *The Concept of Jacksonian*

Democracy (1961) that the political conflicts of the Jacksonian era were rooted not in class but in different ethnic and religious splits within American society.

In the 1980s, Sean Wilentz and other scholars began to resurrect some of Schlesinger's arguments about the importance of class to Jacksonianism. In *Chants Democratic* (1984), Wilentz maintained that Jacksonian politics cannot be understood without reference to the changing national economy. Artisans and small producers believed that impersonal institutions and large-scale employers threatened the very existence of a republic founded on virtuous self-sufficiency, Wilentz said. Jackson symbolized the antagonism these individuals felt toward the emerging capitalist economy. This interpretation is conspicuous in Charles Sellers's *The Market Revolution: Jacksonian America, 1815–1846* (1991), which raised a fascinating question: What was the relationship between American democracy and free-market capitalism? Often assumed to be twins, they were really adversaries, Sellers suggested, with Jacksonians inventing mass democracy in order to hold capitalist expansion in check. Yet if this interpretation is correct, what explains the phenomenal growth of the capitalist economy in the years immediately following the triumphs of Jacksonianism?

For further reading, see the Appendix. For web resources, go to **http://college.hmco.com**.

14

Forging the National Economy

∾

1790–1860

*The progress of invention is really a threat [to monarchy].
Whenever I see a railroad I look for a republic.*

RALPH WALDO EMERSON, 1866

The new nation went bounding into the nineteenth century in a burst of movement. New England Yankeees, Pennsylvania farmers, and southern yeomen all pushed west in search of cheap land and prodigious opportunity, soon to be joined by vast numbers of immigrants from Europe, who also made their way to the country's fast-growing cities. But not only people were in motion. Newly invented machinery quickened the cultivating of crops and the manufacturing of goods, while workers found themselves laboring under new, more demanding expectations for their pace of work. Better roads, faster steamboats, farther-reaching canals, and tentacle-stretching railroads all helped move people, raw materials, and manufactured goods from coast to hinterland and Gulf to Great Lakes by the mid-nineteenth century. The momentum gave rise to a more dynamic, market-oriented economy.

The Westward Movement

The rise of Andrew Jackson, the first president from beyond the Appalachian Mountains, exemplified the inexorable westward march of the American people. The West, with its raw frontier, was the most typically American part of the nation. As Ralph Waldo Emerson wrote in 1844, "Europe stretches to the Alleghenies; America lies beyond."

The Republic was young, and so were the people—as late as 1850, half of Americans were under the age of thirty. They were also restless and energetic,

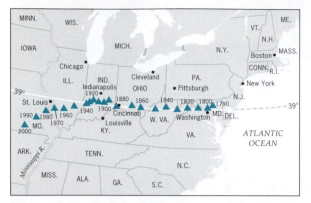

Westward Movement of the Center of Population, 1790–2000   *Notice the remarkable equilibrium of the north-south pull from 1790 onward, and the strong spurt west and south after 1940. The 1980 census revealed that the nation's center of population had at last moved west of the Mississippi River.*

seemingly always on the move, and always westward. By 1840 the "demographic center" of the American population had crossed the Alleghenies. On the eve of the Civil War, it had marched beyond the Ohio River.

Legend portrays an army of muscular axmen triumphantly carving civilization out of the western woods. But in reality life was downright grim for most pioneer families. Poorly fed, ill clad, housed in hastily erected shanties, they were perpetual victims of disease, depression, and premature death. Above all, unbearable loneliness haunted them, especially the women, who were often cut off from human contact, even their neighbors, for days or even weeks, while confined to the cramped orbit of a dark cabin erected in a secluded clearing. Breakdowns and even madness were all too frequently the "opportunities" that the frontier offered to pioneer women.

Frontier life could be tough and crude for men as well. No-holds-barred wrestling, which permitted such niceties as the biting off of noses and the gouging out of eyes, was a popular entertainment. Pioneering Americans, marooned by geography, were often ill informed, superstitious, provincial, and fiercely individualistic. Emerson's popular lecture-essay "Self-Reliance" struck a deeply responsive chord. Popular literature of the period abounded with portraits of heroically unique, isolated figures such as James Feni-

A Pioneer Homestead in Wisconsin, c. 1847   *This frontier family felled trees both to build a crude cabin and to provide fuel for cooking. After the remaining stumps were burned, the cleared fields were ready for planting. Cooking outdoors (weather permitting) spared the rough shelter from smoke and odors.*

more Cooper's courageous Natty Bumppo and Herman Melville's restless Captain Ahab—just as Jacksonian politics aimed to emancipate the lone-wolf, enterprising businessperson. Yet even in this heyday of "rugged individualism," there were important exceptions. Pioneers, in tasks clearly beyond their own individual resources, would call upon neighbors for logrolling and barn raising and upon their governments for help in building internal improvements.

Shaping the Western Landscape

The westward movement also molded the physical environment. Pioneers in a hurry often exhausted the land and then pushed on, leaving behind barren and rain-gutted fields. In the Kentucky bottomlands, settlers discovered that they could burn off the native cane and plant "Kentucky bluegrass," which made ideal pasture for livestock.

The American West felt the pressure of civilization in additional ways. By the 1820s American fur-trappers were setting their trap-lines all over the vast Rocky Mountain region. Each summer, trappers came down from the mountains and swapped their beaver pelts for manufactured goods from the East. This trade thrived for some two decades; by the time beaver hats had gone out of fashion, the hapless beavers had all but disappeared from the region. Trade in buffalo robes also flourished, until the massive bison herds were virtually annihilated. On the California coast, other traders pursued sea-otter pelts, driving the once-bountiful otters nearly to extinction. Some historians have called this aggressive and often heedless exploitation of the West's natural bounty "ecological imperialism."

Yet Americans in this period also reverenced nature and admired its beauty. Indeed the spirit of nationalism fed the growing appreciation of the uniqueness of the American wilderness. Searching for the United States' distinctive characteristics in this nation-conscious age, many observers found the wild land of the West to be among the young nation's defining attributes. Devotion to the pristine, natural beauty of the American wilderness became in time a national mystique, inspiring literature and painting and eventually kindling a conservation movement.

George Catlin, a painter and student of Native American life, was among the first Americans to advocate the preservation of nature as a deliberate national policy. Appalled at the reckless slaughter of the buffalo, Catlin proposed the creation of a national park to preserve nature and wildlife. His idea later bore fruit with the establishment of Yellowstone National Park in 1872.

The March of the Millions

As the American people moved west, they also multiplied at an amazing rate. By midcentury the population was still doubling approximately every twenty-five years, as in fertile colonial days. By 1860 the original thirteen states had more than doubled in number: thirty-three stars graced the American flag. And the United States was the fourth most populous nation in the Western world, exceeded only by three European countries—Russia, France, and Austria.

Urban growth continued explosively. In 1790 only two American cities could boast 20,000 or more souls: Philadelphia and New York. By 1860 there were forty-three, and about three hundred other places claimed over 5,000 inhabitants apiece. New York was the metropolis; New Orleans, the "Queen of the South"; and Chicago, the swaggering lord of the Midwest, destined to be "hog butcher for the world."

Such overrapid urbanization unfortunately brought undesirable by-products. It intensified the problems of smelly slums, feeble street lighting, inadequate policing, impure water, foul sewage, ravenous rats, and improper garbage disposal. Hogs poked their scavenging snouts about many city streets as late as the 1840s. Boston in 1823 pioneered with a sewage system, and New York in 1842 abandoned wells for a piped-in water supply. The city thus unknowingly eliminated many of the breeding places of disease-carrying mosquitoes.

A continuing high birthrate accounted for most of the increase in population, but by the 1840s the tides of immigration were adding hundreds of thousands more. Before this decade, immigrants had been flowing in at the rate of about 60,000 a year, but suddenly the influx tripled in the 1840s and then quadrupled in the 1850s. During these two feverish decades, over a

Irish and German Immigration by Decade, 1830–1900

Years	Irish	Germans
1831–1840	207,381	152,454
1841–1850	780,719	434,626
1851–1860	914,119	951,667
1861–1870	435,778	787,468
1871–1880	436,871	718,182
1881–1890	655,482	1,452,970
1891–1900	388,416	505,152
TOTAL	3,818,766	5,000,519

million and a half Irish, and nearly as many Germans, swarmed down the gangplanks. Why did they come?

The immigrants came partly because Europe seemed to be running out of room. The population of the Old World more than doubled in the nineteenth century, and Europe began to generate a great seething pool of apparently "surplus" people. They were displaced and footloose in their homelands before they felt the tug of the American magnet. Indeed, at least as many people moved about within Europe as crossed the Atlantic.

Yet America still beckoned most strongly to the struggling masses of Europe. About 35 million of the nearly 60 million who abandoned Europe in the century after 1840 headed for "the land of freedom and opportunity," where no aristocratic caste or state church oppressed the individual. Much-read letters sent home by immigrants—"America letters"—often described in glowing terms the richer life: low taxes, no compulsory military service, and "three meat meals a day." The introduction of transoceanic steamships also meant that the immigrants could come speedily, in a matter of ten or twelve days instead of ten or twelve weeks. On board, they were still jammed into unsanitary quarters, thus suffering an appalling death rate, but the nightmare was more endurable because it was shorter.

The Emerald Isle Moves West

Ireland, already groaning under the heavy hand of British overlords, was prostrated in the mid-1840s. A terrible rot attacked the potato crop, on which the people had become dangerously dependent, and about one-fourth of them were swept away by disease and hunger. People dead from starvation were found by the roadsides with grass in their mouths. All told, about 2 million perished.

Tens of thousands of destitute souls, fleeing the Land of Famine for the Land of Plenty, flocked to America in the "Black Forties." Ireland's great export has been population, and the Irish take their place beside the Africans and the Jews as a dispersed people (see "Makers of America: The Irish," pp. 186–187). These uprooted newcomers swarmed into the larger seaboard cities, such as Boston and New York (which rapidly became the largest Irish city in the world). Before many decades, more people of Irish descent lived in America than on the "ould sod" of Erin's isle.

The luckless Irish immigrants received no red-carpet treatment. They were scorned by the older American stock, especially "proper" Protestant Bostonians, who regarded the scruffy Catholic arrivals as a social menace. Barely literate "Biddies" (Bridgets) took jobs as kitchen maids. Broad-shouldered "Paddies" (Patricks) were pushed into pick-and-shovel drudgery on canals and railroads, where thousands left their bones as victims of disease and accidental explosions. It was said that an Irishman lay buried under every railroad tie. As wage-depressing competitors for jobs, the Irish were hated by native workers. "No Irish Need Apply" was a sign commonly posted at factory gates—and was often abbreviated to NINA. The Irish, for similar reasons, fiercely resented the blacks, with whom they shared society's basement. Race riots between black and Irish dockworkers flared up in several port cities, and the Irish were generally cool to the abolitionist cause.

The friendless "famine Irish" were forced to fend for themselves. The Ancient Order of Hibernians, a semisecret society founded in Ireland to fight rapacious landlords, served in America as a benevolent society, aiding the downtrodden. It also helped to spawn the "Molly Maguires," a shadowy Irish miners' union that rocked the Pennsylvania coal districts in the 1860s and 1870s.

The Irish tended to remain in low-skill occupations but gradually improved their lot, usually by acquiring modest amounts of property. The education of children was cut short as families struggled to save money to purchase a home. But for humble Irish peasants, cruelly cast out of their homeland, property ownership counted as a grand "success."

Politics quickly attracted these gregarious Gaelic newcomers. They soon began to gain control of powerful city machines, notably New York's Tammany Hall, and reaped the patronage rewards. Before long, beguilingly brogued Irishmen dominated police departments in many big cities, where they drove the "Paddy wagons" that had once carted their brawling forebears to jail.

The German Forty-Eighters

The influx of refugees from Germany between 1830 and 1860 was hardly less spectacular than that from Ireland. During these troubled years, over a million and a half thrifty Germans stepped onto American soil (see "Makers of America: The Germans," pp. 190–191). Most of them were uprooted farmers, displaced by crop failures and by other hardships. But a strong sprinkling were liberal political refugees. Saddened by the collapse of the democratic revolutions of 1848, they had decided to leave the autocratic fatherland and flee to America—the brightest hope of democracy. Germany's loss was America's gain. Zealous German liberals like the lanky and public-spirited Carl Schurz, a relentless foe of slavery and public corruption, contributed richly to the elevation of American political life.

Unlike the Irish, many of the German newcomers possessed a modest amount of material goods. Most of them pushed out to the lush lands of the Midwest, notably Wisconsin, where they settled and established model farms.

The hand of Germans in shaping American life was widely felt in other ways. They had fled from the militarism and wars of Europe and consequently came to be a bulwark of isolationist sentiment in the upper Mississippi Valley. Better educated on the whole than the dirt-farming Americans, they strongly supported public schools, including their *Kindergarten* ("children's garden"). They likewise did much to stimulate art and music. As outspoken champions of freedom, they became relentless enemies of slavery during the fevered years before the Civil War.

Yet the Germans—often dubbed "damned Dutchmen"—were occasionally regarded with suspicion by their old-stock American neighbors. Seeking to preserve their language and culture, they sometimes settled in compact "colonies" and kept aloof from the surrounding community. Accustomed to the "Continental Sunday" and uncurbed by Puritan tradition, they made merry on the Sabbath and drank huge quantities of beer, which dates its real popularity in America to their coming. Their Old World drinking habits, like those of the Irish newcomers, spurred advocates of temperance in the use of alcohol to redouble their reform efforts.

Flare-ups of Antiforeignism

The invasion by this so-called immigrant "rabble" in the 1840s and 1850s inflamed the hates of American "nativists." Not only did the newcomers take jobs from "native" Americans, but most of the displaced Irishmen were Roman Catholics, as were a substantial minority of the Germans. The Church of Rome was still widely regarded by many old-line Americans as a "foreign" church.

Roman Catholics were now on the move. Seeking to protect their children from Protestant indoctrination in the public schools, they began in the 1840s to construct an entirely separate Catholic school system—an enormously expensive undertaking for a poor immigrant community but one that revealed the strength of its religious commitment. A negligible minority during colonial days, Catholics became a powerful religious group with the enormous influx of the Irish and Germans in the 1840s and 1850s. In 1840 they had ranked fifth, behind the Baptists, Methodists, Presbyterians, and Congregationalists. By 1850, with some 1.8 million communicants, they had bounded into first place—a position they have never lost.

Older-stock Americans were alarmed by these mounting figures. They professed to believe that in due time the "alien riffraff" would "establish" the Catholic Church at the expense of Protestantism and would introduce "popish idols." The noisier American "nativists" rallied for political action. In 1849 they formed the Order of the Star-Spangled Banner, which soon developed into the formidable American, or

The Irish

During the wars that ravaged Europe from 1793 to 1815, Irish tenant farmers temporarily prospered by planting every available acre with wheat and potatoes to feed ravenous armies. But when peace came, wheat prices plummeted and hard-pressed landlords, aided by British police, forced their tenants off the land. Many displaced Irish farmers sought work in England; some went to America. Then in 1845, a blight that ravaged the potato crop sounded the final knell for the Irish peasantry. The resultant famine spread desolation throughout the island. In five years, more than a million people died. Another million sailed for America.

Of the emigrants, most were young and literate in English. Families typically pooled money to send strong young sons to the New World, where they would earn wages to pay the fares for those who remained behind. These "famine Irish" mostly remained in the port cities of the Northeast, abandoning the farmer's life for the dingy congestion of the urban metropolis.

The disembarking Irish were poorly prepared for urban life. They found progress up the economic ladder painfully slow. Their work as domestic servants or construction laborers was dull and arduous, and mortality rates were astoundingly high. Escape from the potato famine hardly guaranteed a long life to an Irish-American; a gray-bearded Irishman was a rare sight in nineteenth-century America.

But it was their Roman Catholicism, even more than their penury and their perceived fondness for alcohol, that earned the Irish the distrust and resentment of their native-born, Protestant American

Just off the Boat *Most poverty-stricken Irish peasants arrived in America with no more than the few goods they could carry on their backs. Yet within a few generations Irish-Americans were playing a prominent role in America's cities, politics, and Catholic Church life.*

neighbors. The cornerstone of social and religious life for Irish immigrants was the parish. Worries about safeguarding their children's faith inspired the construction of parish schools, financed by the pennies of struggling working-class Irish parents.

If Ireland's green fields scarcely equipped Irish sons and daughters for the scrap and scramble of economic life in America's cities, life in the Old Country had instilled in them an aptitude for politics. Irish-Catholic resistance against centuries of English-Anglican domination had instructed many Old-Country Irish in the ways of mass politics. That political experience readied them for the boss system of the political "machines" in America's northeastern cities. Irish voters soon became a bulwark of the Democratic party, reliably supporting the party of Jefferson and Jackson in cities like New York and Boston. As Irish-Americans like New York's "Honest John" Kelly themselves became bosses, white-collar jobs in government service opened up to the Irish. They became building inspectors, aldermen, and even policemen—an astonishing irony for a people driven from their homeland by the nightsticks and bayonets of the British police.

"Know-Nothing" party—a name derived from its secretiveness. "Nativists" agitated for rigid restrictions on immigration and naturalization and for laws authorizing the deportation of alien paupers. They also promoted a lurid anti-Catholic literature, most of it pure fiction. The authors, sometimes posing as "escaped nuns," described shocking sins they imagined the cloisters concealed—including the secret burial of babies. One of these books—Maria Monk's *Awful Disclosures* (1836)—sold over 300,000 copies.

Even uglier was occasional mass violence. As early as 1834 a Catholic convent near Boston was burned by a howling mob, and in ensuing years a few scattered attacks fell upon Catholic schools and churches. The most frightful flare-up occurred during 1844 in Philadelphia, where the Irish Catholics fought back against the threats of the "nativists." The City of Brotherly Love did not quiet down until two Catholic churches had been burned and some thirteen citizens had been killed and fifty wounded in several days of fighting. These outbursts of intolerance, though infrequent and generally localized in the larger cities, remain an unfortunate blot on the record of America's treatment of minority groups.

Immigrants were undeniably making America a more pluralistic society—one of the most ethnically and racially varied in the history of the world. Why, in fact, were such episodes not even more frequent and more violent? Part of the answer lies in the robust American economy. The vigorous growth of the economy in these years ensured that immigrants could claim their share of American wealth without jeopardizing the wealth of others. Their hands and brains, in fact, helped fuel economic expansion. Immigrants and the American economy, in short, needed one another. Without the newcomers, a preponderantly agricultural United States might have been condemned to watch in envy as the Industrial Revolution swept through nineteenth-century Europe.

Crooked Voting *A bitter "nativist" cartoon charging Irish and German immigrants with "stealing" elections.*

The March of Mechanization

A group of gifted British inventors, beginning about 1750, perfected a series of machines for the mass production of textiles. This enslavement of steam multiplied the power of human muscles some ten-thousandfold and ushered in the modern factory system—and with it the so-called Industrial Revolution.

The factory system gradually spread from Britain—"the world's workshop"—to other lands. It took a generation or so to reach western Europe, and then the United States. Why was the youthful American Republic, destined to be an industrial giant, so slow to embrace the machine?

For one thing, virgin soil in America was cheap. Land-starved descendants of land-starved peasants were not going to coop themselves up in smelly factories when they might till their own acres in God's fresh air and sunlight. Labor was therefore generally scarce, and enough nimble hands to operate the machines were hard to find—until immigrants began to pour ashore in the 1840s. Money for capital investment, moreover, was not plentiful in pioneering America. Raw materials lay undeveloped, undiscovered, or unsuspected.

Just as labor was scarce, so were consumers. The young country at first lacked a domestic market large enough to make factory-scale manufacturing profitable.

Long-established British factories, which provided cutthroat competition, posed another problem. Their superiority was attested by the fact that a few unscrupulous Yankee manufacturers, out to make a dishonest dollar, stamped their own products with faked English trademarks.

The British also enjoyed a monopoly of the textile machinery, whose secrets they were anxious to hide from foreign competitors. Parliament enacted laws, in harmony with the mercantilistic system, forbidding the export of the machines or the emigration of mechanics able to reproduce them.

Although a number of small manufacturing enterprises existed in the early Republic, the future industrial colossus was still snoring. Not until well past the middle of the nineteenth century did the value of the output of the factories exceed that of the farms.

Whitney Ends the Fiber Famine

Samuel Slater has been acclaimed the "Father of the Factory System" in America, and seldom can the paternity of a movement more properly be ascribed to one person. A skilled British mechanic of twenty-one, he was attracted by bounties being offered to English workers familiar with the textile machines. After memorizing the plans for the machinery, he escaped in disguise to America, where he won the backing of Moses Brown, a Quaker capitalist in Rhode Island. Laboriously reconstructing the essential apparatus with the aid of a blacksmith and a carpenter, he put into operation in 1791 the first efficient American machinery for spinning cotton thread.

The ravenous mechanism was now ready, but where was the cotton fiber? Handpicking one pound of lint from three pounds of seed was a full day's work for one slave, and this process was so expensive that cotton cloth was relatively rare.

Another mechanical genius, Massachusetts-born Eli Whitney, now made his mark. After graduating from Yale, he journeyed to Georgia to serve as a private tutor while preparing for the law. There he was told that the poverty of the South would be relieved if someone could only invent a workable device for separating the seed from the short-staple cotton fiber. Within ten days, in 1793, he built a crude machine called the cotton gin (short for *engine*), which was fifty times more effective than the hand-picking process.

Few machines have ever wrought so wondrous a change. The gin affected not only the history of America but that of the world. Almost overnight the raising of cotton became highly profitable, and the South was tied hand and foot to the throne of King Cotton. Human bondage had been dying out, but the insatiable demand for cotton reriveted the chains on the limbs of the downtrodden southern blacks.

South and North both prospered. Slave-driving planters cleared more acres for cotton, pushing the Cotton Kingdom westward off the depleted tidewater plains, over the Piedmont, and onto the black loam bottomlands of Alabama and Mississippi. Humming gins poured out avalanches of snowy fiber for the spindles of the Yankee machines. The American phase of the Industrial Revolution, which first blossomed in cotton textiles, was well on its way.

Factories at first flourished most actively in New England, with its poor soil and easy access to water power. By 1860 more than 400 million pounds of southern cotton were pouring annually into the gaping maws of more than a thousand mills. Factories eventually branched out into New York, New Jersey, and Pennsylvania. But the South, increasingly wedded to the production of cotton, could boast of comparatively little manufacturing. Its capital was bound up in slaves; its local consumers for the most part were desperately poor.

Marvels in Manufacturing

America's factories spread slowly until about 1807, when there began the fateful sequence of the embargo, nonintercourse, and the War of 1812. The stoppage of European commerce drove both capital and labor from the waves onto the factory floor. Generous bounties were offered by local authorities for homegrown goods. "Buy American" and "Wear American" became popular slogans, and patriotism prompted the wearing of baggy homespun garments. President Madison donned some at his inauguration, where he was said to have been a walking argument for the better processing of native wool.

But the manufacturing boomlet broke abruptly with the peace of Ghent in 1815, as British competitors unloaded their dammed-up surpluses at ruinously low prices. Responding to pained outcries, Congress provided some relief when it passed the mildly protective Tariff of 1816—among the earliest political contests to control the shape of the economy.

As the factory system flourished, it embraced numerous other industries in addition to textiles. Prominent among them was the manufacturing of firearms, and here the wizardly Eli Whitney again appeared with an extraordinary contribution. Frustrated in his earlier efforts to monopolize the cotton gin, he turned to the mass production of muskets for the U.S. Army. Up to this time each part of a firearm had been hand-tooled, and if the trigger of one broke, the trigger of another might or might not fit. About 1798 Whitney seized upon the idea of having

machines make each part, so that all the triggers, for example, would be as much alike as the successive imprints of a copperplate engraving. Journeying to Washington, he reportedly dismantled ten of his new muskets in the presence of skeptical officials, scrambled the parts together, and then quickly reassembled ten different muskets.

The principle of interchangeable parts was widely adopted by 1850, and it ultimately became the basis of modern mass-production, assembly-line methods. Ironically, the Yankee Eli Whitney, by perfecting the cotton gin, gave slavery a renewed lease on life, and thus perhaps made inevitable the Civil War. At the same time, by popularizing the principle of interchangeable parts, the same Whitney helped factories to flourish in the North, giving the Union a decided advantage when that showdown came.

The sewing machine, invented by Elias Howe in 1846 and perfected by Isaac Singer, gave another strong boost to industrialization. The sewing machine became the foundation of the ready-made clothing industry, which took root about the time of the Civil War. It drove many a seamstress from the shelter of the private home to the factory where, like a human robot, she tended the clattering mechanism.

Each momentous new invention seemed to stimulate still more imaginative inventions. For the decade ending in 1800 only 306 patents were registered in Washington; but the decade ending in 1860 saw the amazing total of 28,000. Yet in 1838 the clerk of the Patent Office had resigned in despair, complaining that all worthwhile inventions had been discovered.

Technical advances spurred equally important changes in the form and legal status of business organizations. The principle of limited liability aided the concentration of capital by permitting the individual investor, in cases of legal claims or bankruptcy, to risk no more than his or her own share of the corporation's stock. Laws of "free incorporation," first passed in New York in 1848, meant that businesspeople could create corporations without applying for individual charters from the legislature.

Samuel F. B. Morse's telegraph was among the inventions that tightened the sinews of an increasingly complex business world. A distinguished but poverty-stricken portrait painter, Morse finally

The Germans

Between 1820 and 1920, a sea of Germans lapped at America's shores and seeped into its very heartland. Their numbers surpassed those of any other immigrant group, even the prolific and often detested Irish. Yet this Germanic flood, unlike its Gaelic equivalent, stirred little panic in the hearts of native-born Americans because the Germans largely stayed to themselves, far from the madding crowds and nativist fears of northeastern cities.

These "Germans" actually hailed from many different Old World lands, because there was no unified nation of Germany until 1871, when the ruthless and crafty Prussian Otto von Bismarck assembled the German state out of a mosaic of independent principalities, kingdoms, and duchies. Until that time, "Germans" came to America as Prussians, Bavarians, Hessians, Rhinelanders, Pomeranians, and Westphalians. They arrived at different times and for many different reasons. Some, particularly the so-called Forty-Eighters—refugees from the abortive democratic revolution of 1848—hungered for the democracy they had failed to win in Germany. Others, particularly Jews, Pietists, and Anabaptist groups like the Amish and the Mennonites, coveted religious freedom.

Typical German immigrants arrived with fatter purses than their Irish counterparts. Small landowners or independent artisans in their native countries, they did not have to settle for bottom-rung industrial employment in the grimy factories of the Northeast and instead could afford to push on to the open spaces of the West.

In Wisconsin these immigrants found a home away from home, a place with a climate, soil, and geography much like central Europe's. Milwaukee, a crude frontier town before their arrival, became the "German Athens." It boasted a German theater, German beer gardens, a German volunteer fire company, and a German-English academy. In distant Texas, German settlements like New Braunfels and Friedrichsburg flourished. When the famous landscape architect and writer Frederick Law Olmsted stumbled upon these prairie outposts of Teutonic culture in 1857, he was shocked to be "welcomed by a figure in a blue flannel shirt and pendant beard, quoting Tacitus."

These German colonizers of America's heartland also formed religious communities, none more distinctive or durable than the Amish settlements of Pennsylvania, Indiana, and Ohio. The Amish took their name from their founder and leader, the Swiss Anabaptist Jacob Ammann. Like other Anabaptist groups, they shunned extravagance and reserved bap-

"Little Germany" *Cincinnati's "Over-the-Rhine" district in 1887.*

tism for adults, repudiating the tradition of infant baptism practiced by most Europeans. For this they were persecuted, even imprisoned, in Europe. Seeking escape from their oppression, some five hundred Amish ventured to Pennsylvania in the 1700s, followed by three thousand in the years from 1815 to 1865.

In America they formed enduring religious communities—isolated enclaves where they could shield themselves from the corruption and the conveniences of the modern world. To this day the German-speaking Amish travel in horse-drawn buggies and farm without heavy machinery. The Amish remain a stalwart, traditional community in a rootless, turbulent society, a living testament to the religious ferment and social experiments of the antebellum era.

secured from Congress, to the accompaniment of the usual jeers, an appropriation of $30,000 to support his experiment with "talking wires." In 1844 Morse strung a wire forty miles from Washington to Baltimore and tapped out the historic message, "What hath God wrought?" The invention brought fame and fortune to Morse, as he put distantly separated people in almost instant communication with one another. By the eve of the Civil War, a web of singing wires spanned the continent, revolutionizing news gathering, diplomacy, and finance.

Workers and "Wage Slaves"

One ugly outgrowth of the factory system was an increasingly acute labor problem. Hitherto manufacturing had been done in the home, or in the small shop, where the master craftsman and his apprentice, rubbing elbows at the same bench, could maintain an intimate and friendly relationship. The Industrial Revolution submerged this personal association in the impersonal ownership of stuffy factories in "spindle cities." Around these, like tumors, the slumlike hovels of the "wage slaves" tended to cluster.

Clearly the early factory system did not shower its benefits evenly on all. While many owners waxed fat, workingpeople often wasted away at their workbenches. Hours were long, wages were low, and meals were skimpy and hastily gulped. Workers were forced to toil in unsanitary buildings that were poorly ventilated, lighted, and heated. They were forbidden by law to form labor unions to raise wages, for such cooperative activity was regarded as a criminal conspiracy. Not surprisingly, only twenty-four recorded strikes occurred before 1835.

Especially vulnerable to exploitation were child workers. In 1820 half the nation's industrial toilers were children under ten years of age. Victims of factory labor, many children were mentally blighted, emotionally starved, physically stunted, and even brutally whipped in special "whipping rooms." In Samuel Slater's mill of 1791, the first machine tenders were seven boys and two girls, all under twelve years of age.

By contrast, the lot of most adult wage workers improved markedly in the 1820s and 1830s. In the full flush of Jacksonian democracy, many of the states granted the laboring man the vote. Brandishing the ballot, workers pushed for such goals as the ten-hour workday, better wages and working conditions, public education for their children, and an end to the inhumane practice of imprisonment for debt.

Employers, abhorring the rise of the "rabble" in politics, fought the ten-hour day to the last ditch. But labor registered a red-letter gain in 1840 when President Van Buren established the ten-hour day for federal employees on public works. In ensuing years a number of states gradually fell into line by reducing the hours for workingpeople.

Day laborers at last learned that their strongest weapon was to lay down their tools, even at the risk of prosecution under the law. Dozens of strikes erupted in the 1830s and 1840s, most of them for higher wages, some for the ten-hour day. The workers usually lost more strikes than they won, for the employer could resort to such tactics as importing strikebreakers—often derisively called "scabs" or "rats," and often fresh off the boat from the Old World. Labor long raised its voice against the unrestricted inpouring of wage-depressing and union-busting immigrant workers.

Labor's early and painful efforts at organization had netted some 300,000 trade unionists by 1830. But such encouraging gains were dashed on the rock of hard times following the severe depression of 1837. Yet toilers won a promising legal victory in 1842. The Massachusetts Supreme Court ruled in the case of *Commonwealth* v. *Hunt* that labor unions were not illegal conspiracies, provided that their methods were "honorable and peaceful." This enlightened decision did not legalize the strike overnight throughout the country, but it was a significant signpost of the times. Trade unions still had nearly a century to go before they could meet management on relatively even terms.

Women and the Economy

Women were also sucked into the clanging mechanism of factory production. Farm wives and daughters had an important place in the preindustrial economy, spinning yarn, weaving cloth, and making candles, soap, butter, and cheese. New factories undermined these activities, cranking out manufactured goods faster than they could be made by hand at home. Yet these factories also offered employment to the very same young women they were displacing. Factory jobs promised greater economic independence for women, as well as the means to buy the manufactured products of the market economy.

"Factory girls" typically toiled six days a week, earning a pittance for dreary stints of twelve or thirteen hours—"from dark to dark." The Boston Associates' textile mills at Lowell, Massachusetts, employed New England farm girls, carefully supervised on and off the job by watchful matrons who escorted them to church from their company boardinghouses.

But factory jobs of any kind were still unusual for women. Opportunities for women to be economically self-supporting were scarce and consisted mainly of nursing, domestic service, and especially teaching. The dedicated Catharine Beecher, daughter of a famous preacher and sister of Harriet Beecher

Stowe, tirelessly urged women to enter the teaching profession. She eventually succeeded beyond her dreams, as men left teaching for other lines of work and schoolteaching became a thoroughly "feminized" occupation. By 1850 about 10 percent of white women were working for pay outside their own homes, and estimates are that about 20 percent of all women had been employed at some time prior to marriage.

The vast majority of working women were single. Upon marriage, they left their paying jobs and took up their new work (without wages) as wives and mothers. In the home they were enshrined in a "cult of domesticity," a widespread cultural creed that glorified the traditional functions of the homemaker. From their pedestals, married women commanded immense moral power, and they increasingly made decisions that altered the character of the family itself.

Women's changing roles and the spreading Industrial Revolution brought some important changes in the life of the nineteenth-century home—the traditional "women's sphere." Love, not parental "arrangement," more and more frequently determined the choice of a spouse—yet parents often retained the power of veto. Families thus became more closely knit and affectionate, providing the emotional refuge that made the threatening impersonality of big-city industrialism tolerable to many people.

Most striking, families grew smaller. The average household had nearly six members at the end of the eighteenth century but fewer than five members a century later. The "fertility rate," or number of births to women age fourteen to forty-five, dropped sharply among white women in the years after the Revolution and, in the course of the nineteenth century as a whole, fell by half. Birth control was still a taboo topic for polite conversation, and contraceptive technology was primitive, but clearly some form of family limitation was being practiced quietly and effectively in countless families, rural and urban alike. Women undoubtedly played a large part—perhaps the leading part—in decisions to have fewer children. This newly assertive role for women has been called "domestic feminism" because it signified the growing power and independence of women, even while they remained trapped in the "cult of domesticity."

The Sewing Floor of Thompson's Skirt Factory, 1859 *The burgeoning textile industry provided employment for thousands of women in antebellum America—and also produced the clothes that women wore. This view of a New York City shop in 1859 illustrates the transition from hand-sewing (on the right) to machine-stitching (on the left). It also vividly illustrates the contrast between the kinds of "sewing circles" in which women had traditionally sought companionship and the impersonal mass-production line of the modern manufacturing plant. Notice the stark exhortation on the wall: "Strive to Excel."*

Smaller families, in turn, meant child-centered families, since where children are fewer, parents can lavish more care on them individually. European visitors to the United States in the nineteenth century often complained about the unruly behavior of American "brats." But though American parents may have increasingly spared the rod, they did not spoil their children. What Europeans saw as permissiveness was in reality the consequence of an emerging new idea of child-rearing, in which the child's will was not to be simply broken, but shaped.

In the little republic of the family, as in the Republic at large, good citizens were raised not to be meekly obedient to authority, but to be independent individuals who could make their own decisions on the basis of internalized moral standards. Thus, the outlines of the "modern" family were clear by midcentury: it was small, affectionate, and child-centered, and provided a special arena for the talents of women. Feminists of a later day might decry the stifling atmosphere of the nineteenth-century home, but to many women of the time it seemed a big step upward from the conditions of grinding toil—often alongside men in the fields—in which their mothers had lived.

Western Farmers Reap a Revolution in the Fields

As smoke-belching factories altered the eastern skyline, flourishing farms were changing the face of the West. The trans-Allegheny region—especially the Ohio-Indiana-Illinois tier—was fast becoming the nation's breadbasket. Before long, it would become a granary to the world.

Pioneer farmers first hacked a clearing out of the forest and then planted their painfully furrowed fields to corn. The yellow grain was amazingly versatile. It could be fed to hogs ("corn on the hoof") or distilled into liquor ("corn in the bottle"). Both these products could be transported more easily than the bulky grain itself, and they became the early western farmer's staple market items. So many corn-fed hogs were butchered, traded, or shipped at Cincinnati that the city was known as the "Porkopolis" of the West.

Most western produce was at first floated down the Ohio-Mississippi river system to feed the booming Cotton Kingdom. Spurred on by the easy availability of the seemingly boundless acres, these farmers continuously sought ways to bring more and more acres into cultivation. They were frustrated by the thickly matted soil of the West that snagged and snapped fragile wooden plows. John Deere in 1837 finally produced a sharp steel plow light enough to be pulled by horses, rather than oxen.

In the 1830s Virginia-born Cyrus McCormick contributed the most wondrous contraption of all: a mechanical mower-reaper. The clattering cogs of McCormick's horse-drawn machine were to the western farmers what the cotton gin was to the southern planters. Seated on his red-chariot reaper, a single harvester could do the work of five men with sickles and scythes.

No other American invention cut so wide a swath. It made ambitious capitalists out of humble plowmen, who now scrambled for more acres on which to plant more fields of billowing wheat. Large-scale ("extensive"), specialized, cash-crop agriculture came to dominate the West. With it followed mounting indebtedness, as farmers bought more land and more machinery to work it. Soon hustling farmer-businesspeople were annually harvesting a larger crop than the South could devour. They began to dream of markets elsewhere—in the mushrooming factory towns of the East, or across the faraway Atlantic. But they were still largely landlocked. Commerce moved north and south on the river systems. Before it could begin to move east-west in bulk, a transportation revolution would have to occur.

Highways and Steamboats

In 1789, when the Constitution was launched, primitive methods of travel were still in use. Waterborne commerce, whether along the coast or on the rivers, was slow, uncertain, and often dangerous. Stagecoaches and wagons lurched over bone-shaking roads. Passengers would be rousted out to lay nearby fence rails across muddy stretches, and occasionally horses would drown in muddy pits while wagons sank slowly out of sight.

Cheap and efficient carriers were imperative if raw materials were to be transported to the factories, and if the finished product was to be delivered to consumers. A promising improvement came in the 1790s, when a private company completed the Lancaster turnpike, a broad, hard-surfaced highway that thrust sixty-two miles westward, from Philadelphia to Lancaster, Pennsylvania. The highly successful Lancaster turnpike returned dividends as high as 15 percent annually to its stockholders, attracted a rich trade to Philadelphia, and touched off the westward migration of the canvas-covered Conestoga wagons.

Westerners scored a notable triumph in 1811 when the federal government began to construct the elongated National Road, or Cumberland Road. When finally completed in 1852, after interruptions caused by the War of 1812 and states' rights shackles on internal improvements, the highway stretched 591 miles from Cumberland, Maryland, to Vandalia, Illinois.

The steamboat craze, which overlapped the turnpike-building era, was touched off by an ambitious painter-engineer named Robert Fulton. In 1807 he installed a powerful steam engine in the *Clermont*, dubbed "Fulton's Folly" by a dubious public. Belching sparks from its single smokestack, the quaint little ship steadily churned up the Hudson River from New York City to Albany, making the run of 150 miles in thirty-two hours.

The success of the steamboat was sensational. People could now in large degree defy wind, wave, tide, and downstream current. Within a few years Fulton had changed all of America's navigable streams into two-way arteries, thereby doubling their carrying capacity. Hitherto, keelboats had been pushed up the Mississippi, with quivering poles and raucous profanity, at less than one mile an hour—a process that was prohibitively expensive. The steamboats could churn rapidly against the current, ultimately attaining speeds in excess of ten miles an hour. The mighty Mississippi had finally met its master. By 1820 there were some sixty steamboats on the Mississippi and its tributaries; by 1860 about a thousand of them were luxurious river palaces.

The Railroad Revolution   *Notice the explosion of new railroad construction in the 1850s, and its heavy concentration in the North.*

Canals and the Iron Horse

A canal-cutting craze paralleled the boom in turnpikes and steamboats. Blessed with the driving leadership of Governor DeWitt Clinton, New York State started the trend when it dug the Erie Canal linking the Hudson River to the Great Lakes.

Begun in 1817, the canal eventually ribboned 363 miles. On its completion in 1825, a garland-bedecked canal boat glided from Buffalo, on Lake Erie, to the Hudson River and on to New York harbor. There, with colorful ceremony, Governor Clinton emptied a cask of water from the lake to symbolize "the marriage of the waters."

The water from Clinton's keg baptized the Empire State. Mule-drawn passengers and bulky freight could now be handled with cheapness and dispatch at the dizzying speed of five miles an hour. The cost of shipping a ton of grain from Buffalo to New York City fell from $100 to $5, and the time of transit from about twenty days to six.

Ever-widening economic ripples followed the completion of the Erie Canal. The value of land along the route skyrocketed, and new cities—such as Rochester and Syracuse—blossomed. Industry in the state boomed. The new profitability of farming in the Old Northwest—notably in Ohio, Michigan, Indiana, and Illinois—attracted thousands of European immigrants to the unaxed and untaxed lands now available. Flotillas of steamships soon plied the Great Lakes, connecting with waiting canal barges at Buffalo. Interior waterside villages such as Cleveland, Detroit, and Chicago exploded into mighty cities.

Canals greatly reduced transportation costs for people and goods, thereby expanding national markets. But the greatest contribution to the developing continental economy proved to be the railroad. It was fast, reliable, cheaper than canals to construct, and not frozen over in winter. Able to go almost anywhere,

The Stourbridge Lion *On August 8, 1829, at Honesdale, Pennsylvania, this smoke-belching beast made the first successful trip in America by a steam locomotive.*

even through the Appalachian barrier, it defied terrain and weather. The first railroad appeared in the United States in 1828. By 1860, only thirty-two years later, the United States boasted thirty thousand miles of railroad track, three-fourths of it in the rapidly industrializing North.

At first the railroad faced strong opposition from vested interests, especially canal backers. Anxious to protect its investment in the Erie Canal, the New York legislature in 1833 prohibited the railroads from carrying freight—at least temporarily. Early railroads were also considered a dangerous public menace, for flying sparks could set fire to haystacks and houses, and appalling railway accidents could turn the wooden "miniature hells" into flaming funeral pyres for their riders.

Railroad pioneers had to overcome other obstacles as well. Arrivals and departures were conjectural, and numerous differences in gauge (the distance between the rails) meant frequent changes of trains for passengers. In 1840 there were seven transfers between Philadelphia and Charleston. But gauges gradually became standardized, safety devices were adopted, and the Pullman "sleeping palace" was introduced in 1859. America at long last was being bound together with ribs of iron, later to be made of steel.

Cables, Clippers, and Pony Riders

A new pattern of American foreign trade emerged in the antebellum years. Abroad as at home, cotton was king and regularly accounted for more than half the value of all American exports. After the repeal of the British exclusionary Corn Laws in 1846, the wheat gathered by McCormick's reapers began to play an increasingly important role in trade with Britain. Americans generally exported agricultural products and imported manufactured goods—and they generally imported more than they exported.

A crucial step came in 1858 when Cyrus Field, called "the greatest wire puller in history," stretched a telegraph cable under the deep North Atlantic waters from Newfoundland to Ireland. Although this initial cable went dead after three weeks of public rejoicing, a heavier cable laid in 1866 permanently linked the American and European continents.

The United States merchant marine encountered rough sailing during much of the early nineteenth century. American vessels were repeatedly laid up by the embargo, the War of 1812, and the panics of 1819 and 1837. American naval designers made few contributions to maritime progress. A pioneer American steamer, the *Savannah*, crept across the Atlantic in 1819, but it used sail most of the time and was pursued for a day by a British captain who thought it afire.

In the 1840s and 1850s, a golden age dawned for American shipping. Yankee naval yards, notably Donald McKay's at Boston, began to send down the ways sleek new crafts called clipper ships. Long, narrow, and majestic, they glided across the sea under towering masts and clouds of canvas. In a fair breeze they could outrun any steamer. The stately clippers sacrificed cargo space for speed, and their captains made killings by hauling high-value cargoes in record times. They wrested much of the tea-carrying trade between East Asia and Britain from their slower-sailing British competitors, and they sped thousands of impatient adventurers to the gold fields of California and Australia.

But the hour of glory for the clipper was relatively brief. On the eve of the Civil War the British had clearly won the world race for maritime ascendancy with their iron tramp steamers ("teakettles"). Although slower and less romantic than the clipper, these vessels were steadier, roomier, more reliable, and hence more profitable.

No story of rapid American communication would be complete without including the Far West. By 1858 horse-drawn overland stages, immortalized in Mark Twain's *Roughing It*, were a familiar sight. Their dusty tracks stretched from the banks of the muddy Missouri River clear to California.

Even more dramatic was the Pony Express, established in 1860 to carry mail speedily the two thousand lonely miles from St. Joseph, Missouri, to Sacramento, California. Daring, lightweight riders, leaping onto wiry ponies saddled at stations approximately ten miles apart, could make the trip in an amazing ten days. These unarmed horsemen galloped on, summer or winter, day or night, through dust or snow, past Indians and bandits. The speeding postmen missed only one trip, though the whole enterprise lost money heavily and folded after only eighteen legend-leaving months.

Just as the clippers had succumbed to steam, so were the Pony Express riders unhorsed by Morse's clacking keys, which began tapping messages to California in 1861. The swift ships and the fleet ponies ushered out a dying technology of wind and muscle. In the future, machines would be in the saddle.

The Transport Web Binds the Union

More than anything else, the desire of the East to tap the West stimulated the "transportation revolution." Until about 1830, the produce of the western region drained southward to the cotton belt or to the heaped-up wharves of New Orleans. The steamboat vastly aided the reverse flow of finished goods up the watery western arteries and helped bind the West and South together. But the truly revolutionary changes in commerce and communication came in the three decades before the Civil War, as canals and railroad tracks radiated out from the East, across the Appalachians, and into the blossoming heartland. The ditch-diggers and tie-layers were attempting nothing less than a conquest of nature itself. They would offset the "natural" flow of trade on the interior rivers by laying down an impressive grid of "internal improvements."

The builders succeeded beyond their wildest dreams. The Mississippi was increasingly robbed of its traffic, as goods moved eastward on chugging trains, puffing lake boats, and mule-tugged canal barges. Governor Clinton had in effect picked up the mighty Father of Waters and flung it over the Appalachians, forcing it to empty into the sea at New York City. By the 1840s Buffalo was handling more western produce than New Orleans. Between 1836 and 1860, grain shipments through Buffalo increased a staggering sixtyfold. New York City became the seaboard queen of the nation, a gigantic port through which a vast hinterland poured its wealth and to which it daily paid economic tribute.

By the eve of the Civil War, a truly continental economy had emerged. The principle of division of labor, which spelled productivity and profits in the factory, applied on a national scale as well. Each region now specialized in a particular type of economic activity. The South raised cotton for export to New England and Old England; the West grew grain and livestock to feed factory workers in the East and Europe; the East made machines and textiles for the South and West.

The economic pattern thus woven had fateful political and military implications. Many southerners regarded the Mississippi as a silver chain that naturally linked together the upper valley states and the Cotton Kingdom. They were convinced, as secession approached, that some or all of these states would have to secede with them or be strangled. But they overlooked the man-made links that now bound the upper Mississippi Valley to the East in intimate commercial union. Southern rebels would have to fight not only northern armies but the tight bonds of an interdependent continental economy. Economically, the two northerly sections were Siamese twins.

The Market Revolution

No less revolutionary than the political upheavals of the antebellum era was the "market revolution" that transformed a subsistence economy of scattered farms and tiny workshops into a national network of industry and commerce. As more and more Americans linked their economic fates to the burgeoning market economy, the self-sufficient households of colonial days were transformed. Most families had once raised all their own food, spun their own wool, and bartered with their neighbors for the few necessities they could not make themselves. In growing numbers, they now scattered to work for wages in the mills, or they planted just a few crops for sale at market and used the money to buy goods made by strangers in far-off factories.

As store-bought fabrics, candles, and soap replaced homemade products, a quiet revolution occurred in the household division of labor and status. Traditional women's work was rendered superfluous and devalued. The home itself, once a center of economic production in which all family members cooperated, grew into a place of refuge from the world of work, a refuge that became increasingly the special and separate sphere of women.

Revolutionary advances in manufacturing and transportation brought increased prosperity to all Americans, but they also widened the gulf between the rich and the poor. Millionaires had been rare in the early days of the Republic, but by the eve of the Civil War, several specimens of colossal financial success were strutting across the national stage. Spectacular was the case of fur-trader and real estate speculator John Jacob Astor, who left an estate of $30 million on his death in 1848.

Cities bred the greatest extremes of economic inequality. Unskilled workers, then as always, fared worst. Many of them came to make up a floating mass of "drifters," buffeted from town to town by the shifting prospects for menial jobs. These wandering workers accounted at various times for up to half the population of the brawling industrial centers. Although their numbers were large, they left little behind them but the homely fruits of their transient labor. Largely unstoried and unsung, they are among the forgotten men and women of American history.

Many myths about "social mobility" grew up over the buried memories of these luckless day laborers. Mobility did exist in industrializing America—but not in the proportions that legend often portrays. Rags-to-riches success stories were relatively few.

Yet America, with its dynamic society and its wide open spaces, undoubtedly provided more "opportunity" than did the contemporary countries of the Old World—which is why millions of immigrants packed their bags and headed for New World shores. Moreover, a rising tide lifts all boats, and the improvement in overall standards of living was real. Wages for unskilled workers in labor-hungry America rose about 1 percent a year from 1820 to 1860. This general prosperity helped to defuse the potential class conflict that otherwise might have exploded—and that did explode in many European countries.

Chronology

c. 1750   Industrial Revolution begins in Britain.

1791   Samuel Slater builds first U.S. textile factory.

1793   Eli Whitney invents the cotton gin.

1798   Whitney develops interchangeable parts for muskets.

1807   Robert Fulton's first steamboat.
Embargo spurs American manufacturing.

1811   Cumberland Road construction begins.

1817   Erie Canal construction begins.

1825   Erie Canal completed.

1828   First railroad in United States.

1830s   Cyrus McCormick invents mechanical mower-reaper.

1834   Anti-Catholic riot in Boston.

1837   John Deere develops steel plow.

1840   President Van Buren establishes ten-hour day for federal employees.

1842   Massachusetts declares labor unions legal in *Commonwealth* v. *Hunt*.

1844   Samuel Morse invents telegraph.
Anti-Catholic riot in Philadelphia.

1845– 1849   Potato famine in Ireland.

1846   Elias Howe invents sewing machine.

1848   First general incorporation laws in New York.
Democratic revolutions collapse in Germany.

1849   Order of the Star-Spangled Banner (Know-Nothing party) formed.

1852   Cumberland Road completed.

1858   Cyrus Field lays first transatlantic cable.

1860   Pony Express established.

1861   First transcontinental telegraph.

1866   Permanent transatlantic cable established.

For further reading, see the Appendix. For web resources, go to **http://college.hmco.com**.

15

The Ferment of Reform and Culture

1790–1860

*We [Americans] will walk on our own feet; we will
work with our own hands; we will speak our own minds.*

RALPH WALDO EMERSON, "THE AMERICAN SCHOLAR," 1837

A third revolution accompanied the reformation of American politics and the transformation of the American economy in the mid-nineteenth century. This was a diffuse yet deeply felt commitment to improve the character of ordinary Americans, to make them more upstanding, God-fearing, and literate. Some high-minded souls were disillusioned by the rough-and-tumble realities of democratic politics. Others, notably women, were excluded from the political game altogether. As the young Republic grew, increasing numbers of Americans poured their considerable energies into religious revivals and reform movements.

Reform campaigns of all types flourished in sometimes bewildering abundance. There was not "a reading man" who was without some scheme for a new utopia in his "waistcoat pocket," claimed Ralph Waldo Emerson. Reformers promoted better public schools and rights for women, as well as miracle medicines, polygamy, celibacy, rule by prophets, and guidance by spirits. Societies were formed against alcohol, tobacco, profanity, and the transit of mail on the Sabbath. Eventually overshadowing all other reforms was the great crusade against slavery (see pp. 225–228). Many reformers drew their crusading zeal from religion. Beginning in the late 1790s and boiling over into the early nineteenth century, a Second Great Awakening swept through America's Protestant churches, transforming the place of religion in American life and sending a generation of believers out on anointed missions to perfect the world.

Reviving Religion

Church attendance was still a regular ritual for about three-fourths of the 23 million Americans in 1850. Alexis de Tocqueville declared that there was "no country in the world where the Christian religion retains a greater influence over the souls of men than in America." Yet the old Calvinist rigor had long been seeping out of the nation's churches.

The rationalist ideas of the French Revolutionary era had done much to soften the older orthodoxy. Many of the Founders, including Paine, Jefferson, and Franklin, embraced the liberal doctrines of Deism, which relied on reason rather than revelation, on science rather than the Bible. Deists rejected the concept of original sin and denied Christ's divinity. Yet they believed in a Supreme Being who had endowed human beings with a capacity for moral behavior.

Deism helped to inspire an important spinoff from Puritanism—the Unitarian faith, which began to gather momentum in New England at the end of the eighteenth century. Unitarians held that God existed in only *one* person (hence *uni*tarian) and not in the orthodox Trinity. Denying the deity of Jesus, Unitarians stressed the essential goodness of human nature, the possibility of salvation through good works, and God as a loving Father rather than a stern Creator. Embraced by many leading thinkers (including Ralph Waldo Emerson), the Unitarian movement appealed mostly to intellectuals whose rationalism and optimism contrasted sharply with the Calvinist doctrines of predestination and human depravity.

A boiling reaction against the growing liberalism in religion set in about 1800. A fresh wave of roaring revivals, beginning on the southern frontier but soon rolling even into the cities of the Northeast, sent another Great Awakening surging across the land. The Second Awakening was one of the most momentous episodes in the history of American religion, a tidal wave of spiritual fervor that left in its wake countless converted souls, shattered and reorganized churches, and numerous new sects.

The Second Great Awakening was spread to the masses on the frontier by huge "camp meetings" where as many as twenty-five thousand people would gather for an encampment of several days. In the East, many converts were moved to engage in missionary work among the Indians, in Hawaii, and in Asia. Everywhere the Second Awakening encouraged

A Camp Meeting at Sing Sing, New York *The preacher stands with hands uplifted under the canopy at the left. A British visitor wrote in 1839 of a revival meeting, "In front of the pulpit there was a space railed off and strewn with straw, which I was told was the anxious seat, and on which sat those who were touched by their consciences."*

an effervescent evangelicalism that bubbled up into innumerable areas of American life—including prison reform, the temperance cause, the women's movement, and the crusade to abolish slavery.

Methodists and Baptists reaped the most abundant harvest of souls from the fields fertilized by revivalism. Both sects stressed personal conversion (contrary to predestination), a relatively democratic control of church affairs, and a rousing emotionalism. As a frontier jingle ran,

> The devil hates the Methodist
> Because they sing and shout the best.

Powerful Peter Cartwright (1785–1872), was the best known of the Methodist "circuit riders," or traveling frontier preachers. He ranged for a half-century from Tennessee to Illinois, calling upon sinners to repent. Bell-voiced Charles Grandison Finney, the greatest of the revival preachers, abandoned his career as a lawyer to become an evangelist after a deeply moving conversion experience as a young man. Finney held huge crowds spellbound with the power of his oratory. He led massive revivals in Rochester and New York City in 1830 and 1831. Holding out the promise of a perfect Christian kingdom on earth, Finney denounced both alcohol and slavery. He eventually served as president of Oberlin College in Ohio, which he helped to make a hotbed of revivalist activity and abolitionism.

A key feature of the Second Great Awakening was the feminization of religion, both in terms of church membership and theology. Middle-class women, the wives and daughters of businessmen, were the first and most fervent enthusiasts of religious revivalism. They made up the majority of new church members, and they were most likely to stay within the fold when the tents were packed up and the traveling evangelist left town. Perhaps women's greater ambivalence than men about the changes wrought by the expanding market economy made them such eager converts to piety. It helped as well that evangelicals preached a gospel of female spiritual worth and offered women an active role in bringing their husbands and families back to God. That accomplished, many women turned to saving the rest of society. They formed a host of benevolent and charitable organizations and spearheaded crusades for most, if not all, of the era's ambitious reforms.

Denominational Diversity

Revivals also furthered the fragmentation of religious faiths. Western New York, where many descendants of New England Puritans had settled, was so blistered by sermonizers preaching "hellfire and damnation" that it came to be known as the "Burned-Over District." Millerites, or Adventists, who mustered several hundred thousand adherents, rose from the superheated soil of the Burned-Over region in the 1830s. The failed prophecy of their eloquent leader, William Miller, that Jesus would return in 1844 dampened but did not destroy the movement.

Like the First Great Awakening, the Second Great Awakening tended to widen the lines between classes and regions. The more prosperous and conservative denominations in the East were little touched by revivalism, and Episcopalians, Presbyterians, Congregationalists, and Unitarians continued to rise mostly from the wealthier, better-educated levels of society. Methodists, Baptists, and members of the new denominations spawned by the swelling evangelistic fervor tended to come from less prosperous, less "learned" communities in the rural South and West.

Religious diversity further reflected social cleavages when the churches faced up to the slavery issue. By 1844–1845 both the southern Baptists and the southern Methodists had split with their northern brethren over human bondage. In 1857 the Presbyterians, North and South, parted company. The secession of the southern churches foreshadowed the secession of the southern states. First the churches split, then the political parties split, and then the Union split.

A Desert Zion in Utah

The smoldering spiritual embers of the Burned-Over District kindled one especially ardent flame in 1830. In that year Joseph Smith—a rugged visionary, proud of his prowess at wrestling—reported that he had received some golden plates from an angel. When deciphered, they constituted the Book of Mormon, and the Church of Jesus Christ of Latter-Day Saints (Mormons) was launched. It was a native American

Columbia R.

Missouri R.

Fort Hall

Fort Bridger

(Fort Laramie)

North Platte R.

Winter Quarters

Nauvoo

Salt Lake City

Council Bluffs

Carthage

Mormon Station

Platte R.

Colorado R.

Beaver

Moab

Parowan

Mountain Meadow

Cedar City

St. George

Las Vegas

Littlefield

Lee's Ferry

Barstow

Tuba City

Arkansas R.

San Bernardino

Holbrook

Rio Grande

Red R.

Tempe

Luna

Mississippi R.

Mesa

Thatcher

Pomerene

St. David

→ Mormon trek, 1846–1847
← California Trail
→ Mormon Corridor
Proposed state of Deseret

• Mormon settlements
( ) Non-Mormon settlement
— Current state boundaries

The Mormon World *After the murder of Joseph Smith in 1844, the Mormons abandoned their thriving settlement at Nauvoo, Illinois (which had about twenty thousand inhabitants in 1845), and set out for the valley of the Great Salt Lake, then still part of Mexico. When the Treaty of Guadalupe Hidalgo in 1848 brought the vast Utah Territory into the United States, the Mormons rapidly expanded their desert colony, which they called Deseret, especially along the "Mormon Corridor" that stretched from Salt Lake to southern California.*

product, a new religion, destined to spread its influence worldwide.

After establishing a religious oligarchy, Smith ran into serious opposition from his non-Mormon neighbors, first in Ohio and then in Missouri and Illinois. His cooperative sect rasped rank-and-file Americans, who were individualistic and dedicated to free enterprise. The Mormons aroused further antagonism by voting as a unit and by openly but understandably drilling their militia for defensive purposes. Accusations of polygamy likewise arose and increased in

intensity, for Joseph Smith was reputed to have several wives.

Continuing hostility finally drove the Mormons to desperate measures. In 1844 Joseph Smith and his brother were murdered and mangled by a mob in Carthage, Illinois, and the movement seemed near collapse. The falling torch was seized by a remarkable Mormon Moses named Brigham Young, an aggressive leader, an eloquent preacher, and a gifted administrator. Determined to escape further persecution, Young in 1846–1847 led his oppressed and despoiled

Latter-Day Saints over vast rolling plains to Utah as they sang "Come, Come, Ye Saints."

Overcoming pioneer hardships, the Mormons soon made the desert bloom like a new Eden by means of ingenious and cooperative methods of irrigation. The crops of 1848, threatened by hordes of crickets, were saved when flocks of gulls appeared, as if by a miracle, to gulp down the invaders. (A monument to the sea gulls stands in Salt Lake City today.)

Semiarid Utah grew remarkably. By the end of 1848 some five thousand settlers had arrived, and other large bands were to follow them. Many dedicated Mormons in the 1850s actually made the 1,300-mile trek across the plains pulling two-wheeled carts.

Under the rigidly disciplined management of Brigham Young, the community became a prosperous frontier theocracy and a cooperative commonwealth. Young married as many as twenty-seven women—some of them wives in name only—and begot fifty-six children.

A crisis developed when the Washington government was unable to control the hierarchy of Brigham Young, who had been made territorial governor in 1850. A federal army marched in 1857 against the Mormons, who harassed its lines of supply and rallied to die in their last dusty ditch. Fortunately, the quarrel was finally adjusted without serious bloodshed. The Mormons later ran afoul of the anti-polygamy laws passed by Congress in 1862 and 1882, and their marital customs delayed statehood for Utah until 1896.

Free Schools for a Free People

Tax-supported primary schools were scarce in the early years of the Republic. They had the odor of pauperism about them, since they existed chiefly to educate the children of the poor—the so-called ragged schools. Advocates of "free" public education met stiff opposition.

Between 1825 and 1850, the spread of Jeffersonian democratic ideals gradually won acceptance for the public schools. But most of the one-room, one-teacher "little red schoolhouses" of the time were poor training grounds for democracy. The schools stayed open only a few months of the year, and

schoolteachers, most of them men in this era, were too often ill trained, ill tempered, and ill paid. These knights of the blackboard often "boarded around" in the community, and some knew scarcely more than their older pupils. They usually taught only the "three Rs—readin', 'ritin', and 'rithmetic."

Reform was urgently needed. Into the breach stepped Horace Mann (1796–1859), a brilliant and idealistic graduate of Brown University. As secretary of the Massachusetts Board of Education, he campaigned effectively for more and better schoolhouses, longer school terms, higher pay for teachers, and an expanded curriculum. His influence radiated out to other states, and impressive improvements were chalked up. Yet education remained an expensive luxury for many communities. As late as 1860 the nation counted only a few hundred public secondary schools—and nearly a million white adult illiterates. Black slaves in the South were legally forbidden to receive instruction in reading or writing, and even free blacks, in the North as well as the South, were usually excluded from the schools.

Educational advances were aided by improved textbooks, notably those of Noah Webster (1758–1843), a Yale-educated Connecticut Yankee who was known as the "Schoolmaster of the Republic." Webster devoted twenty years to his famous dictionary, published in 1828, which helped to standardize the American language.

Equally influential was Ohioan William H. McGuffey (1800–1873), a teacher-preacher of rare power. His grade-school readers, first published in the 1830s, sold 122 million copies in the following decades. *McGuffey's Readers* hammered home lasting lessons in morality, patriotism, and idealism.

Higher Goals for Higher Learning

Higher education was likewise stirring. The religious zeal of the Second Great Awakening led to the planting of many small, denominational, liberal arts colleges, chiefly in the South and West.

The first state-supported universities sprang up in the South, beginning with North Carolina in 1795. Federal land grants nourished the growth of state institutions of higher learning. Conspicuous among

School Days *Schoolteaching in the early nineteenth century was a poorly paid occupation that was often pursued by single men who were not very well educated themselves. This drawing depicts John Pounds (1766–1839), who taught school and supplemented his income by mending shoes.*

the early group was the University of Virginia, founded in 1819 by Thomas Jefferson, who also designed its beautiful architecture.

Women's higher education was frowned upon in the early decades of the nineteenth century. A woman's place was believed to be in the home, and training in needlecraft seemed more important than training in algebra. In an era when the clinging-vine bride was the ideal, coeducation was regarded as frivolous. Prejudices also prevailed that too much learning injured the feminine brain, undermined health, and rendered a young lady unfit for marriage. The teachers of Susan B. Anthony, the future feminist, refused to instruct her in long division.

Women's schools at the secondary level began to attain some respectability in the 1820s, thanks in part to the dedicated work of Emma Willard (1787–1870). In 1821 she established the Troy (New York) Female Seminary. Oberlin College in Ohio shocked tradition-

alists in 1837 when it opened its doors to women as well as men. (Oberlin had already created shock waves by admitting black students.) In the same year, Mary Lyon established an outstanding women's school, Mount Holyoke Seminary (later College), in South Hadley, Massachusetts.

For those without access to higher education, traveling lecturers made learning available through the lyceum lecture associations, which numbered about three thousand by 1835. The lyceums provided platforms for speakers in such areas as science, literature, and moral philosophy. Talented talkers like Ralph Waldo Emerson journeyed thousands of miles on the lyceum circuits, casting their pearls of civilization before appreciative audiences.

Magazines flourished in the pre–Civil War years, but most of them withered after a short life. The *North American Review*, founded in 1815, was the long-lived leader of the intellectuals. *Godey's Lady's*

Book, a women's magazine founded in 1830, survived until 1898 and attained the enormous circulation (for those days) of 150,000. It was devoured devotedly by millions of women, many of whom read the dog-eared copies of their relatives and friends.

An Age of Reform

Some of the reformers touched by the fire of evangelical religion were simply cranks, but most were intelligent, inspired idealists. The optimistic fervor of the Second Great Awakening inspired countless souls to do battle against earthly evils. These modern idealists dreamed anew the old Puritan vision of a perfected society: free from cruelty, war, intoxicating drink, discrimination, and—ultimately—slavery. Women were particularly prominent in these reform crusades, especially in their own struggle for suffrage. For many middle-class women, the campaigns provided a unique opportunity to escape the confines of home and enter the arena of public affairs.

In part, the practical, activist Christianity of these reformers resulted from their desire to reaffirm traditional values as they plunged ever further into a world disrupted and transformed by the turbulent forces of a market economy. Often blissfully unaware that they were witnessing the dawn of the industrial era, they either ignored the factory workers or blamed their problems on bad habits. Reformers sometimes applied conventional virtue to refurbishing an older order—while events hurtled them headlong into the new.

Imprisonment for debt continued to be a nightmare. As late as 1830 hundreds of penniless people were languishing in filthy holes. The poorer working classes were especially hard hit by this merciless practice. But state legislators gradually abolished the debtors' prison and softened the criminal codes. The number of capital offenses was reduced, and brutal punishments, such as whipping and branding, were slowly eliminated. A refreshing idea began taking hold that prisons should reform as well as punish—hence "reformatories," "houses of correction," and "penitentiaries" (for penance).

Sufferers from so-called insanity were still being treated with incredible cruelty. The mentally deranged were considered willfully perverse and depraved, and often were treated like beasts in jails or poorhouses. A formidable New England teacher-author, Dorothea Dix (1802–1887) spent eight years observing these conditions at first hand and then presented her damning reports to the Massachusetts legislature in 1843. Deploying both facts and compassion, she described cells so foul that visitors were driven back by the stench. Her persistent prodding resulted in improved conditions and in a gain for the concept that the demented were not willfully perverse but mentally ill.

Agitation for peace also gained momentum in the pre–Civil War years. In 1828 the American Peace Society was formed, with a ringing declaration of war on war. The American peace crusade, linked with a European counterpart, was making promising progress by midcentury, but it was set back by the bloodshed of the Crimean War in Europe and the Civil War in America.

Demon Rum: The "Old Deluder"

The ever-present drink problem also attracted dedicated reformers. Weddings and funerals all too often became disgraceful brawls, and occasionally a drunken mourner would fall into the open grave with the corpse. Heavy drinking decreased labor efficiency and increased the danger of accidents on the job. Drunkenness also fouled the sanctity of the family, threatening the spiritual welfare—and physical safety—of women and children.

After earlier and feebler efforts, the American Temperance Society was formed at Boston in 1826. Within a few years about a thousand local groups sprang into existence. They implored drinkers to sign the temperance pledge and organized children's clubs, known as the "Cold Water Army."

The most popular anti-alcohol tract of the era was T. S. Arthur's melodramatic novel, *Ten Nights in a Barroom and What I Saw There* (1854). It described in shocking detail how a once-happy village was ruined by Sam Slade's tavern. The book was second only to Harriet Beecher Stowe's *Uncle Tom's Cabin* as a bestseller in the 1850s, and it enjoyed a highly successful run on the stage.

Early foes of Demon Drink adopted two major lines of attack. One was to stiffen the individual's will to resist the wiles of the little brown jug. The moderate reformers thus stressed temperance rather than "teetotalism," or the total elimination of intoxicants. But less patient zealots came to believe that temptation should be removed by legislation. Prominent among this group was Neal S. Dow of Maine, a blue-nosed reformer who, as mayor of Portland and an employer of labor, had often witnessed the debauching effect of alcohol.

Dow—the "Father of Prohibition"—sponsored the so-called Maine Law of 1851. This drastic new statute, hailed as "the law of Heaven Americanized," prohibited the manufacture and sale of intoxicating liquor. Other states in the North followed Maine's example, and by 1857 about a dozen had passed various prohibitory laws.

By the eve of the Civil War the prohibitionists had registered inspiriting gains. There was much less drinking among women than earlier in the century and probably much less per capita consumption of hard liquor.

Women in Revolt

When the nineteenth century opened, it was still a man's world, both in America and in Europe. A wife was supposed to immerse herself in her home and subordinate herself to her husband. Like black slaves, she could not vote; like black slaves, she could be legally beaten by her overlord "with a reasonable instrument." When she married, she could not retain title to her property; it passed to her husband. Women in America were still the "submerged sex" in the early part of the century, though their position was somewhat better than that of their European cousins. French visitor Alexis de Tocqueville noted that in his native France rape was punished only lightly, whereas in America it was one of the few crimes punishable by death.

But as the decades unfolded, American women increasingly yearned to breathe fully the fresh air of freedom and self-determination. In contrast to colonial times, many women avoided marriage altogether—about 10 percent of adult women were unmarried at the time of the Civil War.

Gender differences were strongly emphasized in nineteenth-century America, largely because the burgeoning market economy was increasingly separating women and men into sharply distinct economic roles. Women were thought to be physically and emotionally weak but also artistic and refined. Endowed with finely tuned moral sensibilities, they were the keepers of society's conscience, with special responsibility to teach the young how to be good citizens of the Republic. Men were considered strong but crude, always in danger of slipping into some savage or beastly way of life if not guided by the gentle hands of their loving ladies.

The home was woman's special sphere. Prominent leaders like Catharine Beecher endlessly celebrated the role of the good homemaker. But some women increasingly felt that the glorified sanctuary

Stellar Suffragists *Elizabeth Cady Stanton (left) and Susan B. Anthony (right) were two of the most persistent battlers for women's rights. Their National Woman Suffrage Association fought for women's equality in courts and workplaces as well as at the polls.*

of the home was in fact a gilded cage. They yearned to tear down the bars that separated the private world of women from the public world of men.

Clamorous female reformers, most of them white and well-to-do, began to gather strength as the century neared its halfway point. Most were broad-gauge battlers; while demanding rights for women, they joined in the general reform movement of the age, fighting for temperance and the abolition of slavery. Like men, they had been touched by the evangelical spirit that offered the alluring promise of earthly reward for human endeavor. Neither foul eggs nor foul words, when hurled by disapproving men, could halt women heartened by these doctrines.

The women's rights movement was mothered by some arresting characters. Prominent among them was Lucretia Mott, a sprightly Quaker whose ire had been aroused when she and her fellow female delegates to the London antislavery convention of 1840 were not recognized. Elizabeth Cady Stanton, a mother of seven who had insisted on leaving "obey" out of her marriage ceremony, shocked fellow feminists by going so far as to advocate suffrage for women. Quaker-reared Susan B. Anthony, a militant lecturer for women's rights, fearlessly exposed herself to rotten garbage and vulgar epithets.

Other feminists challenged the man's world. Dr. Elizabeth Blackwell, a pioneer in a previously forbidden profession for women, was the first female graduate of a medical college. Precocious Margaret Fuller edited a transcendentalist journal, *The Dial*, and took part in the struggle to bring unity and republican government to Italy. The talented Grimké sisters, Sarah and Angelina, championed antislavery. Lucy Stone retained her maiden name after marriage—hence the latter-day "Lucy Stoners," who follow her example. Amelia Bloomer revolted against the current "street-sweeping" female attire by donning a short skirt with Turkish trousers—"bloomers," they were called—amid much bawdy ridicule about "Bloomerism" and "loose habits." A jeering male rhyme of the times jabbed

> Gibbey, gibbey gab
> The women had a confab
> And demanded the rights
> To wear the tights
> Gibbey, gibbey gab.

Fighting feminists met at Seneca Falls, New York, in a memorable Woman's Rights Convention (1848). The defiant Stanton read a "Declaration of Sentiments," which in the spirit of the Declaration of Independence declared that "all men and women are created equal." One resolution formally demanded the ballot for females. Amid scorn and denunciation from press and pulpit, the Seneca Falls meeting launched the modern women's rights movement.

The crusade for women's rights was eclipsed by that against slavery in the decade before the Civil War. Still, any white male over twenty-one could vote, whereas no woman could. Yet women were being gradually admitted to colleges, and some states, beginning with Mississippi in 1839, were even permitting wives to own property after marriage.

Wilderness Utopias

Bolstered by the utopian spirit of the age, various reformers, ranging from the high-minded to the "lunatic fringe," set up more than forty communities of a cooperative, communistic, or "communitarian" nature. Seeking human betterment, a wealthy and idealistic Scottish textile manufacturer, Robert Owen, founded in 1825 a communal society of about a thousand people at New Harmony, Indiana. Little harmony prevailed in the colony, which, in addition to hard-working visionaries, attracted a sprinkling of radicals, work-shy theorists, and outright scoundrels. The colony sank in a morass of contradiction and confusion.

Brook Farm in Massachusetts, comprising two hundred acres of grudging soil, was started in 1841 with the brotherly and sisterly cooperation of about twenty intellectuals committed to the philosophy of transcendentalism. They prospered reasonably well until 1846, when they lost by fire a large new communal building shortly before its completion. The whole venture in "plain living and high thinking" then collapsed in debt. The Brook Farm experiment inspired Nathaniel Hawthorne's classic novel *The Blithedale Romance* (1852), whose main character was modeled on the feminist writer Margaret Fuller.

A more radical experiment was the Oneida Colony, founded in New York in 1848. It practiced free love ("complex marriage"), birth control, and the eugenic selection of parents to produce superior offspring. This curious enterprise flourished for more than thirty years, largely because its artisans made superior steel traps and Oneida Community (silver) Plate. In 1879–1880 the group embraced monogamy and abandoned communism (see "Makers of America: The Oneida Community, " pp. 210–211).

Among the longest-lived communitarian sects were the Shakers. Led by Mother Ann Lee, they began in the 1770s to set up a score or so of religious communities. The Shakers attained a membership of about six thousand in 1840, but since their monastic customs prohibited both marriage and sexual relations, they were virtually extinct by 1940.

Artistic Achievements

Architecturally, America contributed little of note in the first half of the century. The rustic Republic, still under pressure to erect shelters in haste, was continuing to imitate European models. Public buildings and other important structures followed Greek and Roman lines, which seemed curiously out of place in a wilderness setting. A remarkable Greek revival came between 1820 and 1850. About midcentury strong interest developed in a revival of Gothic forms, with their emphasis on pointed arches and large windows.

Talented Thomas Jefferson, architect of revolution, was probably the ablest American architect of his generation. He brought a classical design to his Virginia hilltop home, Monticello—perhaps the most stately mansion in the nation. The quadrangle of the University of Virginia at Charlottesville, another of Jefferson's creations, remains one of the finest examples of classical architecture in America.

Painting, like the theater, suffered from the Puritan prejudice that art was a sinful waste of time—and often obscene. When Edward Everett, the eminent Boston scholar and orator, placed a statue of Apollo in his home, he had its naked limbs draped. Competent painters nevertheless emerged.

Gilbert Stuart (1775–1828) wielded his brush in Britain, in competition with the best artists. He produced several portraits of Washington, all of them somewhat idealized and dehumanized. Charles Will-

son Peale (1741–1827) painted some sixty portraits of Washington, who patiently sat for about fourteen of them. John Trumbull (1756–1843), who had fought in the Revolutionary War, recaptured its scenes and spirit on scores of striking canvases.

During the nationalistic upsurge after the War of 1812, American painters turned increasingly from human subjects to romantic mirrorings of local landscapes. The Hudson River School excelled in this type of art. At the same time, portrait painters gradually encountered some unwelcome competition from the invention of a crude photograph known as the daguerreotype, perfected about 1839 by a Frenchman, Louis Daguerre.

The Blossoming of a National Literature

"Who reads an American book?" sneered a British critic in 1820. The painful truth was that the nation's rough-hewn, pioneering civilization gave little encouragement to imaginative literature. America produced political essays, sermons, and autobiographies, but imported or plagiarized much of its reading matter from England.

A genuinely American literature received a strong boost from the wave of nationalism that followed the Revolutionary War and especially the War of 1812. By 1820 the older seaboard areas were sufficiently removed from the survival mentality of tree chopping and butter churning so that literature could be supported as a profession. The Knickerbocker Group in New York blazed brilliantly across the literary heavens, enabling America for the first time to boast of a literature to match its magnificent landscapes.

Washington Irving (1783–1859), born in New York City, was the first American to win international recognition as a literary figure. Steeped in the traditions of New Netherland, he published in 1809 his *Knickerbocker's History of New York*, with its amusing caricatures of the Dutch. Irving won fame at home and abroad with his *Sketch Book* (1819–1820) and later published such popular Dutch-American tales as "Rip Van Winkle" and "The Legend of Sleepy Hollow." Europe was amazed to find at last an American with a feather in his hand, not in his hair.

The Oneida Community

John Humphrey Noyes (1811–1886), the founder of the Oneida Community, repudiated the old Puritan doctrines that God was vengeful and that sinful mankind was doomed to dwell in a vale of tears. Noyes believed in a benign deity, in the sweetness of human nature, and in the possibility of a perfect Christian community on earth. "The more we get acquainted with God," he declared, "the more we shall find it our special duty to be happy."

That sunny thought was shared by many early-nineteenth-century American utopians (a word derived from Greek that slyly combines the meanings of "a good place" and "no such place"). But Noyes added some wrinkles of his own. The key to happiness, he taught, was the suppression of selfishness. True Christians should possess no private property— nor should they indulge in exclusive emotional relationships, which bred jealousy, quarreling, and covetousness. Material things and sexual partners alike, Noyes preached, should be shared. Marriage should not be monogamous. Instead all members of the community should be free to love one another in "complex marriage." Noyes called his system "Bible Communism."

Tall and slender, with piercing blue eyes and reddish hair, the charismatic Noyes began voicing these ideas in his hometown of Putney, Vermont, in the 1830s. He soon attracted a group of followers who called themselves the Putney Association, a kind of extended family whose members farmed five hundred acres by day and sang and prayed together in the evenings.

The Putney Association also indulged in sexual practices that outraged the surrounding community's sense of moral propriety. Indicted for adultery in 1847, Noyes led his followers to Oneida, in the supposedly more tolerant region of New York's Burned-Over District, the following year.

The Oneidans struggled in New York until the manufacture of steel animal traps and other goods put the Community on a sound financial footing. By the 1860s Oneida was a flourishing commonwealth of some three hundred people. Men and women shared equally in all the community's tasks, from field to factory to kitchen. Children at the age of three were removed from direct parental care and raised communally until the age of thirteen or fourteen, when they took up jobs in the community's industries. They imbibed their religious doctrines with their school lessons:

> I-spirit
> With me never shall stay,
> We-spirit
> Makes us happy and gay.

Oneida's apparent success fed the utopian dreams of others, and for a time it became a great tourist attraction. Visitors from as far away as Europe came to picnic on the shady lawns, speculating on the sexual secrets that the Community guarded, while their hosts fed them strawberries and cream and entertained them with music.

But eventually the same problems that had driven Noyes and his band from Vermont began to shadow their lives at Oneida. Their New York neighbors grew increasingly horrified at the Oneidans' licentious sexual practices, including the selective breeding program by which the community matched mates and gave permission—or orders—to procreate, without regard to the niceties of matrimony.

Yielding to their neighbors' criticisms, the Oneidans gave up complex marriage in 1879. Soon other "communistic" practices withered away as well. In 1880 the Oneidans abandoned communism altogether and became a joint-stock company specializing in the manufacture of silver tableware. Led by Noyes's son Pierrepont, Oneida Community, Ltd., grew into the world's leading manufacturer of stainless steel knives, forks, and spoons, with annual sales by the 1990s of some half a billion dollars. Ironically, what grew from Noyes's religious vision was not utopia but a mighty capitalist corporation.

The novelist James Fenimore Cooper (1789–1851) gained world fame and made New World themes internationally respectable. He made his initial reputation in 1821 with his novel *The Spy*—an absorbing tale of the American Revolution. His fame rests most enduringly on the *Leatherstocking Tales*. A deadeye rifleman named Natty Bumppo, one of nature's noblemen, meets with Indians in stirring adventures like *The Last of the Mohicans*. Some Europeans who read Cooper's novels came to think of all Americans as born with a tomahawk in hand. Actually Cooper was exploring the viability and destiny of America's republican experiment by contrasting the values of "natural men" from the wilderness with the artificiality of modern civilization.

A third member of the Knickerbocker Group in New York was the belatedly Puritan William Cullen Bryant (1794–1878), transplanted from Massachusetts. At age sixteen he wrote the meditative and melancholy "Thanatopsis" (1817), one of the first high-quality poems produced in the United States. Critics could hardly believe that it had been written on "this side of the water."

Trumpeters of Transcendentalism

A golden age in American literature dawned in the second quarter of the nineteenth century, when an amazing outburst shook New England. One of the mainsprings of this literary flowering was transcendentalism, especially around Boston, which preened itself as "the Athens of America."

The transcendentalist movement of the 1830s resulted in part from a liberalizing of the straitjacket Puritan theology. It also owed much to foreign influences, including the German romantic philosophers and the religions of Asia. The transcendentalists rejected the prevailing theory, derived from John Locke, that all knowledge comes to the mind through the senses. Truth, rather, "transcends" the senses: it cannot be found by observation alone. Every person possesses an inner light that can illuminate the highest truth and put him or her in direct touch with God, or the "Oversoul."

These mystical doctrines of transcendentalism defied precise definition, but they underlay concrete beliefs. Foremost was a stiff-backed individualism in matters religious as well as social. Closely associated was a commitment to self-reliance, self-culture, and self-discipline. These traits naturally bred hostility to authority and to formal institutions of any kind, as well as to all conventional wisdom. Finally came exaltation of the dignity of the individual, whether black or white—the mainspring of a whole array of humanitarian reforms.

Best known of the transcendentalists was Boston-born Ralph Waldo Emerson (1803–1882). Tall, slender, and intensely blue-eyed, he mirrored serenity in his noble features. Trained as a Unitarian minister, he early forsook his pulpit and ultimately reached a wider audience by pen and platform. He was a never-failing favorite as a lyceum lecturer and for twenty years took a western tour every winter. Perhaps his most thrilling public effort was a Phi Beta Kappa address, "The American Scholar," delivered at Harvard College in 1837. This brilliant appeal was an intellectual Declaration of Independence, for it urged American writers to throw off European traditions and delve into the riches of their own backyards.

Hailed as both a poet and a philosopher, Emerson was not of the highest rank as either. He was more influential as a practical philosopher and through his fresh and vibrant essays enriched thousands of humdrum lives. Catching the individualistic mood of the Republic, he stressed self-reliance, self-improvement, optimism, and freedom. The secret of Emerson's popularity lay largely in the fact that his ideals reflected those of an expanding America. By the 1850s he was an outspoken critic of slavery, and he ardently supported the Union cause in the Civil War.

Henry David Thoreau (1817–1862) was Emerson's close associate—a poet, a mystic, a transcendentalist, and a nonconformist. Condemning a government that supported slavery, he refused to pay his Massachusetts poll tax and was jailed for a night.* A gifted prose writer, he is well known for *Walden: Or Life in the Woods* (1854). The book is a record of Thoreau's two years of simple existence in a hut that he built on the edge of Walden Pond, near Concord, Massachusetts. A stiff-necked individualist, he believed that he should reduce his bodily wants so as to gain time for a pursuit of truth through study and meditation. Thoreau's *Walden* and his essay *On the Duty of Civil Disobedience* exercised a strong influence in furthering idealistic thought, both in America and abroad. His writings later encouraged Mohandas Gandhi to resist British rule in India and, still later, inspired the development of American civil rights leader Martin Luther King Jr.'s thinking about nonviolence.

Bold, brassy, and swaggering was the open-collared figure of Brooklyn's Walt Whitman (1819–1892). In his famous collection of poems, *Leaves of Grass* (1855), he gave free rein to his gushing genius with what he called a "barbaric yawp." Highly romantic, emotional, and unconventional, he dispensed with titles, stanzas, rhymes, and at times even regular meter. He handled sex with shocking frankness, and his book was banned in Boston.

Whitman's *Leaves of Grass* was at first a financial failure. The only three enthusiastic reviews that it received were written by the author himself—anonymously. But in time the once-withered *Leaves of Grass*, revived and honored, won for Whitman an enormous following in both America and Europe.

Leaves of Grass gained for Whitman the informal title "Poet Laureate of Democracy." Singing with tran-

Walt Whitman *This portrait of the young poet appeared in the first edition of* Leaves of Grass *(1855).*

scendental abandon of his love for the masses, he caught the exuberant enthusiasm of an expanding America that had turned its back on the Old World:

> All the Past we leave behind;
> We debouch upon a newer, mightier world,
>   varied world;
> Fresh and strong the world we seize—world of
>   labor and the march—
> Pioneers! O Pioneers!

Here at last was the native art for which critics had been crying.

Two women writers whose work remains enormously popular today were also leaders of the New England literary world. Louisa May Alcott (1832–1888) grew up in Concord, Massachusetts, in the

---

* The story (probably apocryphal) is that Emerson visited Thoreau at the jail and asked, "Why are you here?" The reply came, "Why are you not here?"

bosom of transcendentalism, alongside neighbors Emerson, Thoreau, and Fuller. Her philosopher father Bronson Alcott occupied himself more devotedly to ideas than to earning a living, leaving his daughter to write *Little Women* (1868) and other books to support her mother and sisters. Not far away in Amherst, Massachusetts, poet Emily Dickinson (1830–1886) lived as a recluse but created her own original world through precious gems of poetry. In deceptively spare language and simple rhyme schemes, she explored universal themes of nature, love, death, and immortality. Although she refused during her lifetime to publish any of her poems, when she died, nearly two thousand of them were found among her papers and eventually made their way into print.

Literary Individualists and Dissenters

Not all writers in these years believed so keenly in human goodness and social progress as Whitman and the New England transcendentalists. Edgar Allan Poe (1809–1849), who spent much of his youth in Virginia, was an eccentric genius. Orphaned at an early age, cursed with ill health, and married to a child-wife of thirteen who fell fatally ill of tuberculosis, he suffered hunger, cold, poverty, and debt. Poe was a gifted lyric poet, as "The Raven" attests. If he did not invent the modern detective novel, he at least set new high standards in tales like "The Gold Bug." A master stylist, he also excelled in the short story, especially of the horror genre, in which he shared his fantastic nightmares with fascinated readers.

Gripped by the ghostly and ghastly, in "The Fall of the House of Usher" and other stories, Poe reflected a dark sensibility distinctly at odds with the usually optimistic tone of American culture. Perhaps for this reason, Poe has been even more prized by Europeans than by Americans. His brilliant career was cut short when he was found drunk in a Baltimore gutter and shortly thereafter died.

Two other writers reflected the continuing Calvinist obsession with original sin and with the never-ending struggle between good and evil. In somber Salem, Massachusetts, Nathaniel Hawthorne grew up in an atmosphere heavy with the memories of his Puritan forebears and the tragedy of his father's premature death on an ocean voyage. His masterpiece was *The Scarlet Letter* (1850), which described the Puritan practice of forcing an adulteress to wear a scarlet A on her clothing. In *The Marble Faun* (1860), Hawthorne dealt with a group of young American artists who witness a mysterious murder in Rome. The book explores the concepts of the omnipresence of evil and the dead hand of the past weighing on the present.

Herman Melville (1819–1891), an orphaned and ill-educated New Yorker, went to sea as a youth and served eighteen adventuresome months on a whaler. "A whale ship was my Yale College and my Harvard," he wrote. Jumping ship in the South Seas, he lived among cannibals, from whom he providentially escaped uneaten. His masterpiece, *Moby Dick* (1851), is a complex allegory of good and evil, told in terms of the conflict between a whaling captain, Ahab, and a giant white whale, Moby Dick. Captain Ahab, having lost a leg to the marine monster, lives only for revenge. His pursuit finally ends when Moby Dick rams and sinks his ship, leaving only one survivor. The whale's exact identity and Ahab's motives remain obscure. In the end the sea, like the terrifyingly impersonal and unknowable universe of Melville's imagination, simply rolls on.

Moby Dick was widely ignored at the time of its publication; people were accustomed to more straightforward and upbeat prose. A disheartened Melville continued to write unprofitably for some years, part of the time eking out a living as a customs inspector, and then died in relative obscurity and poverty. His brooding masterpiece about the mysterious white whale had to wait until the more jaded twentieth century for readers and for proper recognition.

Portrayers of the Past

A distinguished group of American historians was emerging at the same time that other writers were winning distinction. Energetic George Bancroft (1800–1891), who as secretary of the navy helped found the Naval Academy at Annapolis in 1845, has deservedly received the title "Father of American History." He published a spirited, superpatriotic history of the United States to 1789 in six volumes (1834–

1876), a work that grew out of his vast researches in dusty archives in Europe and America.

Two other historians are read with greater pleasure and profit today. William H. Prescott (1796–1859) published classic accounts of the conquest of Mexico (1843) and Peru (1847). Francis Parkman (1823–1893) penned a brilliant series of volumes beginning in 1851. In epic style he chronicled the struggle between France and Britain in colonial times for the mastery of North America.

Early American historians of prominence were almost without exception New Englanders, largely because the Boston area provided well-stocked libraries and a stimulating literary tradition. These writers numbered abolitionists among their relatives and friends and hence were disposed to view unsympathetically the slavery-cursed South. The writing of American history for generations to come was to suffer from an antisouthern bias perpetuated by this early "made in New England" interpretation.

Chronology

1770s First Shaker communities formed.

1795 University of North Carolina founded.

1800 Second Great Awakening begins.

1819 Jefferson founds University of Virginia.

1821 Cooper publishes *The Spy*, his first successful novel.
Emma Willard establishes Troy (New York) Female Seminary.

1825 New Harmony commune established.

1826 American Temperance Society founded.

1828 American Peace Society founded.
Noah Webster publishes dictionary.

1830 Joseph Smith founds Mormon church.
Godey's Lady's Book first published.

1830–1831 Charles Finney conducts revivals in eastern cities.

1835 Lyceum movement flourishes.

1837 Emerson delivers "The American Scholar" address.
Mary Lyon establishes Mount Holyoke Seminary.
Oberlin College admits female students.

1841 Brook Farm commune established.

1843 Dorothea Dix petitions Massachusetts legislature on behalf of the insane.

1846–1847 Mormon migration to Utah.

1848 Seneca Falls Woman's Rights Convention held.
Oneida community established.

1850 Hawthorne publishes *The Scarlet Letter*.

1851 Melville publishes *Moby Dick*.
Maine passes first law prohibiting liquor.

1855 Whitman publishes *Leaves of Grass*.

VARYING VIEWPOINTS

Reform: Who? What? How? and Why?

Early chronicles of the antebellum period universally lauded the era's reformers, portraying them as idealistic, altruistic crusaders intent on improving American society. After World War II, however, some historians began to detect selfish and even conservative motives underlying the apparent benevolence of the reformers. They described reforms like temperance, asylums, prison, and mandatory public education as efforts by anxious upper-class men and women to assert "social control" over the ferment of antebellum life.

The wave of reform activity in the 1960s prompted a reevaluation of the reputations of the antebellum reformers. These more recent interpretations found much to admire in the authentic religious commitments of the reformers and especially in the participation of women, who sought various social improvements as an extension of their function as protectors of the home and family.

Abolitionism, for example, which had once been blamed by some historians for the Civil War, received new favorable treatment as the racial climate began to change by the mid-twentieth century. Similarly, historians like Nancy Cott, Kathryn Sklar, and Mary Ryan began to look more closely at women's reform activity. They argued that what Cott called "the bonds of womanhood" inspired many female reformers to leave the confines of their homes and seek to purify society of male dominance as well as particular social evils. More recently, historians Nancy Hewitt and Lori Ginzburg have challenged the idea of a single female reform identity, pointing to class-based tensions within female ranks and detecting a shift from moral uplift to social control.

Historians of the suffrage movement like Ellen DuBois have also discovered that after a brief alliance with the abolitionist movement, many female suffrage reformers abandoned the cause of black liberation in order to achieve their own goal. Whatever they conclude about the liberating or leashing character of the impulse to "improve" American society, historians now find that they have to contend with the ways in which class, gender, and race divided the multitude of reform movements—in the plural.

For further reading, see the Appendix. For web resources, go to **http://college.hmco.com**.

PART THREE

TESTING THE NEW NATION

—⬤—

1820–1877

The Civil War of 1861–1865 was the awesome trial by fire of American nationhood and of the American soul. All Americans knew, said Abraham Lincoln, that slavery "was somehow the cause of this war." The war tested, in Lincoln's ringing phrase at Gettysburg, whether any nation "dedicated to the proposition that all men are created equal . . . can long endure." How did this great and bloody conflict come about? And what were its results?

American slavery was by any measure a "peculiar institution." It was rooted in both racism and economic exploitation and depended for its survival on brutal repression. Yet the American slave population was the only enslaved population in history that grew by means of its own biological reproduction—a fact that suggests to many historians that conditions under slavery in the United States were somehow less punitive than in other slave societies. Indeed, a distinctive and durable African-American culture managed to flourish under slavery, further suggesting that the slave regime provided some "space" for African-American cultural development. But however benignly it might be painted, slavery remained a cancer in the heart of American democracy, a moral outrage that mocked the nation's claim to be a model of social and political enlightenment. As time went on, more and more voices called more and more stridently for its abolition.

The nation lived uneasily with slavery from the outset. Thomas Jefferson was only one among many in the founding generation who felt acutely the conflict between the high principle of equality and the ugly reality of slavery. The federal government in the early Republic took several steps to check the growth of slavery. It banned slavery in the Old Northwest in 1787, prohibited the further importation of slaves after 1808, and declared in the Missouri Compromise of 1820 that the vast western territories secured in the Louisiana Purchase were forever closed to slavery north of the state of Missouri. Antislavery sentiment even abounded in the South in the immediate post-Revolutionary years. But as time progressed, and especially after Eli Whitney's invention of the cotton gin in the 1790s, the southern planter class became increasingly dependent on slave labor to wring profits from the sprawling plantations that carpeted the South. As cotton cultivation spread westward, the South's stake in slavery grew deeper, and the abolitionist outcry grew louder.

The controversy over slavery significantly intensified following the war with Mexico in the 1840s. "Mexico will poison us," predicted the philosopher Ralph Waldo Emerson, and he proved distressingly prophetic. The lands acquired from Mexico—most of the present-day American Southwest, from Texas to California—reopened the question of extending slavery into the western territories. The decade and a half following the Mexican War—from 1846 to 1861—witnessed a series of ultimately ineffective efforts to come to grips with that question, including the ill-starred Compromise of 1850, the conflict-breeding Kansas-Nebraska Act of 1854, and the Supreme Court's inflammatory decision in the *Dred Scott* case

of 1857. Ultimately, the slavery question was settled by force of arms, in the Civil War itself.

The Civil War, as Lincoln observed, was assuredly about slavery. But as Lincoln also repeatedly insisted, the war was about the viability of the Union as well and about the strength of democracy itself. Could a democratic government, built on the principle of popular consent, rightfully deny some of its citizens the same right to independence that the American Revolutionaries had exercised in seceding from the British Empire in 1776? Southern rebels, calling the conflict "The War for Southern Independence," asked that question forcefully, but ultimately it, too, was answered not in the law courts or in the legislative halls but on the battlefield.

The war unarguably established the supremacy of the Union, and it ended slavery as well. But as the victorious Union set about the task of "reconstruction" after the war's end in 1865, a combination of weak northern will and residual southern power frustrated the goal of making the emancipated blacks full-fledged American citizens. The war in the end brought nothing but freedom—but over time, freedom proved a powerful tool indeed.

16

The South and the Slavery Controversy

1793–1860

If you put a chain around the neck of a slave,
the other end fastens itself around your own.

RALPH WALDO EMERSON, 1841

At the dawn of the Republic, slavery faced an uncertain future. Touched by Revolutionary idealism, some southern leaders, including Thomas Jefferson, were talking openly of freeing the slaves. Others predicted that the iron logic of economics would eventually expose slavery's unprofitability, speeding its demise.

But the introduction of Eli Whitney's cotton gin in 1793 scrambled all those predictions. Whitney's invention made possible the wide-scale cultivation of short-staple cotton. The white fiber rapidly became the dominant southern crop, eclipsing tobacco, rice, and sugar. The explosion of cotton cultivation created an insatiable demand for labor, chaining the slave to the gin, and the planter to the slave. As the nineteenth century opened, the reinvigoration of southern slav-ery carried fateful implications for blacks and whites alike—and threatened the survival of the nation itself.

"Cotton Is King!"

As time passed, the Cotton Kingdom developed into a huge agricultural factory, pouring out avalanches of the fluffy fiber. Quick profits drew planters to the virgin bottomlands of the Gulf states. As long as the soil was still vigorous, the yield was bountiful and the rewards were high. Caught up in an economic spiral, the planters bought more slaves and land to grow more cotton, so as to buy still more slaves and land.

Northern shippers reaped a large part of the profits from the cotton trade. They would load bulging bales of cotton at southern ports, transport them to Britain, sell their fleecy cargo for pounds sterling, and buy needed manufactured goods for sale in the United States. To a large degree, the prosperity of both North and South rested on the bent backs of southern slaves.

Cotton accounted for half the value of all American exports after 1840. It even held foreign nations in partial bondage. Britain's most important single manufacture in the 1850s was cotton cloth, from which about one-fifth of the British people, directly or indirectly, drew their livelihood. About 75 percent of this precious supply of fiber came from the white-carpeted acres of the South.

Southern leaders were fully aware that Britain was tied to them by cotton threads, and this dependence gave them a heady sense of power. In their eyes "Cotton Was King," the gin was his throne, and the black slaves were his henchmen. If war should ever break out between North and South, northern warships would presumably cut off the outflow of cotton. Fiber-famished British factories would then close their gates, starving mobs would force the London government to break the blockade, and the South would triumph. Cotton was a powerful monarch indeed.

Slaves of the Slave System

Before the Civil War the South was in some respects not so much a democracy as an oligarchy—a government by the few, in this case heavily influenced by a planter aristocracy. In 1850 only 1,733 families owned more than one hundred slaves each, and this select group provided the cream of the political and social leadership of the section and nation. Here was the mint-julep South of the tall-columned and white-painted plantation mansion—the "big house," where dwelt the "cottonocracy."

The planter aristocrats, with their blooded horses and Chippendale chairs, enjoyed the lion's share of southern wealth. They could educate their children in the finest schools, often in the North or abroad. Their money provided the leisure for study,

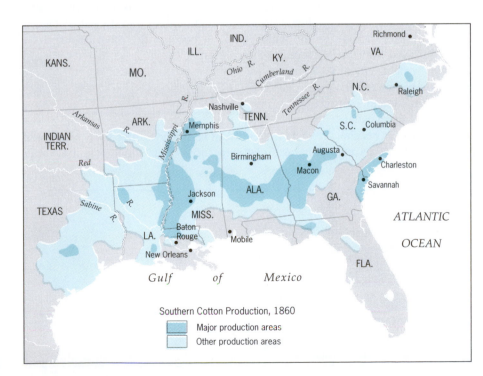

Southern Cotton Production, 1860
The concentration of cotton-growing was in the "black belt" stretching from South Carolina to Louisiana.

reflection, and statecraft, as was notably true of men like John C. Calhoun (a Yale graduate) and Jefferson Davis (a West Point graduate).

The plantation system also shaped the lives of southern women. The mistress of a great plantation commanded a sizable household staff of mostly female slaves. She gave daily orders to cooks, maids, seamstresses, laundresses, and personal servants. Some mistresses showed tender regard for their bondswomen, while others treated their slaves atrociously. But virtually no slaveholding women believed in abolition, and relatively few protested when the husbands and children of their slaves were sold.

Despite the occasional benevolent relations between owners and slaves, the moonlight-and-magnolia tradition concealed much that was worrisome, distasteful, and sordid. Plantation agriculture was wasteful, largely because King Cotton and his money-hungry subjects despoiled the good earth. Quick profits led to excessive cultivation or "land butchery," which in turn caused a heavy leakage of population to the West and Northwest.

The economic structure of the South became increasingly monopolistic. As the land wore thin, many small farmers sold their holdings to more prosperous neighbors. The big got bigger and the small got smaller. When the Civil War finally erupted, a large percentage of southern farms had passed from the hands of the families that had originally cleared them.

Another cancer in the bosom of the South was the financial instability of the plantation system. The temptation to overspeculate in land and slaves caused many planters, including Andrew Jackson in his later years, to plunge in beyond their depth. The slaves rep-

resented a heavy investment of capital, perhaps $1,200 each in the case of "prime field hands"; and they might deliberately injure themselves or run away.

Dominance by King Cotton likewise led to a dangerous dependence on one crop, whose price level was at the mercy of world conditions. The whole system discouraged the healthy diversification of agriculture and particularly of manufacturing.

Southern planters resented watching the North grow fat at their expense. They were pained by the heavy outward flow of commissions and interest to northern middlemen, bankers, agents, and shippers. True souls of the South, especially by the 1850s, deplored the fact that when they were born they were wrapped in Yankee-made swaddling clothes, that they spent the rest of their lives in servitude to Yankee manufacturing, and that when they died they were laid in coffins made with Yankee nails and were buried in graves dug with Yankee shovels. The South furnished only the corpse and the hole in the ground.

The Cotton Kingdom also repelled large-scale European immigration, which added so richly to the manpower and wealth of the North. In 1860 only 4.4 percent of the southern population was foreign-born, compared with 18.7 percent for the North. The diverting of non-English immigration to the North caused the white South to become the most Anglo-Saxon section of the nation.

The White Majority

Only a handful of southern whites lived in pillared mansions. Below those 1,733 families in 1850 who

Slaveowning Families, 1850   *More than half of all slaveholding families owned fewer than four slaves. In contrast, 2 percent of slaveowners owned more than fifty slaves each. A tiny slaveholding elite held a majority of slave property in the South. The great majority of white southerners owned no slaves at all.*

1,733 own **100** or more slaves
6,196 own **50–99**
29,733 own **20–49**
54,595 own **10–19**
80,765 own **5–9**
105,683 own **2–4**
68,820 own **1** each

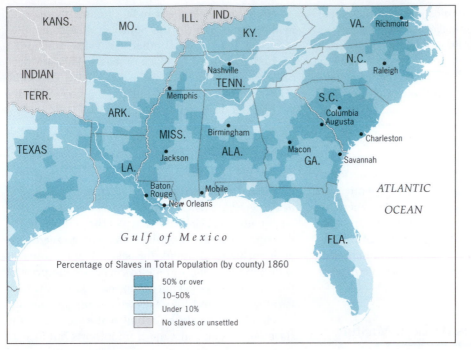

Percentage of Slaves in Total Population (by county) 1860

- 50% or over
- 10–50%
- Under 10%
- No slaves or unsettled

owned one hundred or more slaves were the less wealthy slaveowners. They totaled in 1850 some 345,000 families, representing about 1,725,000 white persons. Over two-thirds of these families—255,268 in all—owned fewer than ten slaves each. All told, only about one-fourth of white southerners owned slaves or belonged to a slaveowning family.

The smaller slaveowners did not own a majority of the slaves, but they made up a majority of the masters. With the striking exception that their households contained a slave or two, or perhaps an entire slave family, the style of their lives resembled that of small farmers in the North more than it did that of the southern planter aristocracy. They lived in modest farmhouses and sweated beside their bondsmen in the cotton fields, laboring callus for callus just as hard as their slaves.

Beneath the slaveowners was the great body of whites who owned no slaves at all. By 1860 their numbers had swelled to 6,120,825—three-quarters of all southern whites. Shouldered off the richest bottomlands by the mighty planters, they scratched a simple living from the thinner soils of the backcountry and the mountain valleys. These red-necked farmers participated in the market economy scarcely at all. As subsistence farmers, they raised corn and hogs, not cotton, and often lived isolated lives, punctuated by extended socializing and sermonizing at religious revival meetings. Some of the least prosperous nonslaveholding whites were scorned even by slaves as "poor white trash," "hillbillies," or "crackers."

All these whites without slaves had no direct stake in the preservation of slavery, yet they were among the stoutest defenders of the system. Why? The answer is not hard to find.

The carrot on the stick ever dangling before their eyes was the hope of buying a slave or two and of parlaying their holdings into riches—all in accord with the American dream of upward social mobility. They also took fierce pride in their presumed racial superiority, which would be watered down if the slaves were freed. Many of the poorer whites were hardly better off economically than the slaves, but even the most wretched whites could take perverse comfort from the knowledge that they outranked someone in status: the still more wretched African-American slave.

Thus did the logic of economics join with the illogic of racism in buttressing the slave system.

In a special category among white southerners were the mountain whites, more or less marooned in the valleys of the Appalachian range that stretched from western Virginia to northern Georgia and Alabama. As independent small farmers, hundreds of miles distant from the heart of the Cotton Kingdom and rarely if ever in sight of a slave, these mountain whites had little in common with the whites of the flatlands. Many of them, including future president Andrew Johnson of Tennessee, hated both the haughty planters and their gangs of blacks. When the Civil War came, the tough-fibered mountain men constituted a vitally important peninsula of Unionism jutting down into the secessionist southern sea. They ultimately played a significant role in crippling the Confederacy.

Free Blacks: Slaves Without Masters

Precarious in the extreme was the standing of the South's free blacks, who numbered about 250,000 by 1860. In the Upper South, the free black population traced its origins to a wavelet of emancipation inspired by the idealism of Revolutionary days. In the deeper South, many free blacks were mulattoes, usually the emancipated children of a white planter and his black mistress. Throughout the South were some free blacks who had purchased their freedom with earnings from labor after hours.

These free blacks in the South were a kind of "third race." They were prohibited from certain occupations and always were vulnerable to being hijacked back into slavery by unscrupulous slave traders. As free men and women, they were walking examples of what might be achieved by emancipation. Defenders of the slave system resented and detested them.

Free blacks were also unpopular in the North, where about another 250,000 of them lived. Several states forbade their entrance, most denied them the right to vote, and some barred blacks from public schools. Much of the agitation in the North against the spread of slavery into the new territories in the 1840s and 1850s grew out of race prejudice, not humanitarianism.

Antiblack feeling was in fact frequently stronger in the North than in the South. It was sometimes observed that white southerners, who were often suckled and reared by black nurses, liked black people as individuals but despised the race. The white northerner, on the other hand, often professed to like the race but disliked individual blacks.

Plantation Slavery

In society's basement in the South of 1860 were nearly 4 million black human chattels. Their numbers had quadrupled since the dawn of the century, as the booming cotton economy created a seemingly unquenchable demand for slave labor. Congress ended the legal slave trade in 1808, but the price of "black ivory" was so high in the years before the Civil War that thousands of slaves were smuggled illegally into the South. Yet the huge bulk of the increase in the slave population came not from imports but instead from natural reproduction—a fact that distinguished slavery in America from slavery in other New World societies and implied much about the tenor of the regime and the conditions of family life under slavery.

Above all, the planters regarded the slaves as investments, into which they had sunk nearly $2 billion by 1860. Slaves were the primary form of wealth in the South, and as such they were cared for as any asset is cared for by a prudent capitalist. Masters sometimes hired cheap Irish wage laborers to perform dangerous work like tunnel blasting or swamp draining, rather than risk the life of a valuable slave, worth $1,800 by 1860 (a price that had quintupled since 1800).

Slavery was profitable for the great planters, though it hobbled the economic development of the region as a whole. The profits from the cotton boom sucked ever more slaves from the Upper to the Lower South. Thousands of blacks from the soil-exhausted states of the Old South, especially Virginia, were "sold down the river" to the cotton frontier of the lower Mississippi Valley. By 1860 the Deep South states of South Carolina, Florida, Mississippi, Alabama, and Louisiana each had a majority or near-majority of blacks and accounted for about half of all slaves in the South.

The forced "breeding" of slaves was not openly encouraged. But white masters all too frequently forced their attention on female slaves, fathering a sizable mulatto population, most of which remained enchained.

Slave auctions were brutal sights. The open selling of human flesh under the hammer was among the most revolting aspects of slavery. On the auction block, families were separated with distressing frequency, usually for economic reasons such as bankruptcy or the division of "property" among heirs. The sundering of families in this fashion was perhaps slavery's greatest psychological horror. Abolitionists decried the practice, and Harriet Beecher Stowe seized on the emotional power of this theme by putting it at the heart of the plot of *Uncle Tom's Cabin*.

Life Under the Lash

White southerners often romanticized about the happy life of their singing, dancing, banjo-strumming, joyful "darkies." But how did the slaves actually live? There is no simple answer to this question. Conditions varied greatly from region to region, from large plantation to small farm, and from master to master. Everywhere, of course, slavery meant hard work, ignorance, and oppression. The slaves—both men and women—usually toiled from dawn to dusk in the fields, under the watchful eyes and ready whip-hand of a white overseer or black "driver." They had no civil or political rights, and even minimal protection from murder or unusually cruel punishment was difficult to enforce. Slaves were forbidden to testify in court, and their marriages were not legally recognized.

Floggings were common, for the whip was the substitute for the wage-incentive system and the most visible symbol of the planter's mastery. Strong-willed slaves were sometimes sent to "breakers," whose technique consisted mostly in lavish laying on of the lash. As an abolitionist song of the 1850s lamented,

> To-night the bond man, Lord
> Is bleeding in his chains;
> And loud the falling lash is heard
> On Carolina's plains!

But savage beatings made sullen laborers, and lash marks hurt resale values. There are, to be sure, sadis-

Slave Nurse and Young White Master *Southern whites would not allow slaves to own property or exercise civil rights, but, paradoxically, they often entrusted them with the raising of their own precious children. Many a slave "mammy" served as a surrogate mother for the offspring of the planter class.*

tic monsters in any population, and the planter class contained its share. But the typical planter had too much of his own prosperity riding on the backs of his slaves to beat them bloody on a regular basis.

By 1860 most slaves were concentrated in the "black belt" of the Deep South that stretched from South Carolina and Georgia into the new southwest states of Alabama, Mississippi, and Louisiana. A majority of blacks lived on larger plantations that harbored communities of twenty or more slaves. In some counties of the Deep South, especially along the lower Mississippi River, blacks accounted for more than 75 percent of the population. There the family life of slaves tended to be relatively stable, and a distinctive African-American culture developed. Forced separation of spouses, parents, and children was evidently more common on smaller plantations and in the Upper South. Slave marriage vows sometimes proclaimed, "Until death or *distance* do you part."

With impressive resilience, blacks managed to sustain family life in slavery, and most slaves were raised in stable two-parent households. Continuity of family identity across generations was evidenced in the widespread practice of naming children for grandparents or adopting the surname not of a current master but of a forebear's master. African-Americans also displayed their African cultural roots when they avoided marriage between first cousins, a practice the ingrown planter aristocracy allowed.

African roots were also visible in the slaves' religious practices. Though heavily Christianized by itinerant evangelists of the Second Great Awakening, blacks in slavery molded their own distinctive religious forms from a mixture of Christian and African elements. They emphasized those aspects of the Christian heritage that seemed most pertinent to their own situation—especially the captivity of the Israelites in Egypt. One of the most haunting spirituals implored,

> Tell old Pharaoh,
> "Let my people go."

And another lamented,

> Nobody knows de trouble I've seen
> Nobody knows but Jesus.

African practices also persisted in the "responsorial" style of preaching, in which the congregation frequently punctuates the minister's remarks with assents and amens—an adaptation of the give-and-take between caller and dancers in the African ring-shout dance.

The Cruelty of Slavery *(left) Held captive in a net, a slave sits on the Congo shore, waiting to be sold and shipped. (above) This device was riveted around a slave's neck. Its attached bells, like a cow bell, made it impossible for the wearer to hide from his or her owner.*

The Burdens of Bondage

Slavery was intolerably degrading to the victims. They were deprived of the dignity and sense of responsibility that come from independence and the right to make choices. Slaves were denied an education, because reading brought ideas, and ideas brought discontent. Many states passed laws forbidding their instruction, and perhaps nine-tenths of adult slaves at the beginning of the Civil War were illiterate. For all slaves—indeed for virtually all blacks, slave or free—the "American dream" of bettering one's lot through study and hard work was a cruel and empty mockery.

Not surprisingly, victims of the "peculiar institution" devised countless ways to throw sand in its gears. Slaves often slowed the pace of their labor to the barest minimum that would spare them the lash, thus fostering the myth of black "laziness" in the minds of whites. They filched food from the "big house" and pilfered other goods that had been produced by their labor. They sometimes sabotaged expensive equipment and occasionally even poisoned their master's food.

The slaves also universally pined for freedom. Many took to their heels as runaways, frequently in search of a separated family member. Others rebelled, though never successfully. In 1800 an armed insurrection led by a slave named Gabriel in Richmond, Virginia, was foiled by informers, and in 1822 Denmark Vesey, a free black, organized another ill-fated rebellion in Charleston. In both cases the rebels were betrayed by informers and hanged. In 1831 Nat Turner, a visionary black preacher, led an uprising that slaughtered about sixty Virginians, mostly women and children. Reprisals were swift and bloody.

The dark taint of slavery also left its mark on the whites. It fostered the brutality of the whip, the bloodhound, and the branding iron. White southerners increasingly lived in a state of imagined siege, surrounded by potentially rebellious blacks inflamed by abolitionist propaganda from the North. Their fears bolstered an intoxicating theory of biological racial superiority and turned the South into a reactionary backwater in an era of progress. The defenders of slavery were forced to degrade themselves, along with their victims. As Booker T. Washington, a distinguished black leader and former slave, later observed, whites could not hold blacks in a ditch without getting down there with them.

Early Abolitionism

The inhumanity of the "peculiar institution" gradually caused antislavery societies to sprout forth. Abolitionist sentiment first stirred at the time of the Revolution, especially among Quakers. Because of the widespread loathing of blacks, some of the earliest abolitionist efforts focused on transporting blacks back to Africa. The American Colonization Society was founded for this purpose in 1817, and in 1822 the Republic of Liberia was established for former slaves on the West African coast. But only fifteen thousand blacks were transported there over the next four decades.

In the 1830s the abolitionist movement took on new energy and momentum, mounting to the proportions of a crusade. American abolitionists took heart in 1833 when their British counterparts unchained the slaves in the West Indies. Most important, the religious spirit of the Second Great Awakening inflamed the hearts of many abolitionists against the sin of slavery.

Prominent among them was lanky, tousle-haired Theodore Dwight Weld, who had been evangelized by Charles Grandison Finney in the 1820s. In 1832 Weld enrolled at Lane Theological Seminary in Cincinnati, which was presided over by the formidable Lyman Beecher, father of novelist Harriet Beecher Stowe, reformer Catharine Beecher, and preacher-abolitionist Henry Ward Beecher. Expelled along with several other students in 1834 for organizing an eighteen-day debate on slavery, Weld and his fellow "Lane Rebels"—full of the energy and idealism of youth—fanned out across the Old Northwest preaching the antislavery gospel. Weld also assembled a potent propaganda tract, *American Slavery As It Is* (1839), which greatly influenced Harriet Beecher Stowe's *Uncle Tom's Cabin*.

Radical Abolitionism

On New Year's Day, 1831, a shattering abolitionist blast came from the bugle of William Lloyd Garrison, a mild-looking reformer of twenty-six. A spiritual child of the Second Great Awakening, Garrison published in Boston the first issue of his militantly anti-slavery newspaper the *Liberator*. With this mighty paper broadside, Garrison triggered a thirty-year war of words and in a sense fired one of the opening barrages of the Civil War.

Stern and uncompromising, Garrison proclaimed in strident tones that under no circumstances would he tolerate the poisonous weed of slavery:

> I will be as harsh as truth and as uncompromising as justice. . . . I am in earnest—I will not equivocate—I will not excuse—I will not retreat a single inch—and I WILL BE HEARD!

Other dedicated abolitionists rallied to Garrison's standard, and in 1833 they founded the American Anti-Slavery Society. Prominent among them was eloquent Wendell Phillips, a Boston patrician known as "abolition's golden trumpet."

Black abolitionists distinguished themselves as living monuments to the cause of African-American freedom. Their ranks included the incendiary David Walker, who advocated violent revolt against white supremacy. Also noteworthy were Sojourner Truth, a freed black woman who fought tirelessly for black emancipation and women's rights, and Martin Delany, one of the few black leaders to take seriously the notion of black recolonization in Africa.

The greatest of the black abolitionists was Frederick Douglass. Escaping from bondage in 1838 at the age of twenty-one, Douglass was "discovered" by the abolitionists three years later when he gave a stunning impromptu speech at an antislavery meeting in Massachusetts. Thereafter he lectured widely for the cause, despite frequent beatings and threats against his life. In 1845 he published his autobiography, *Narrative of the Life of Frederick Douglass.*

Douglass was as flexibly practical as Garrison was stubbornly principled. Garrison often appeared to be more interested in his own righteousness than in the substance of the slavery evil itself. He repeatedly demanded that the "virtuous" North secede from

Frederick Douglass (c. 1817–1895) *Born a slave in Maryland, Frederick Douglass escaped to the North and became the most prominent of the black abolitionists. A gifted orator, writer, and editor, he continued to battle for the civil rights of his people after emancipation. Near the end of a distinguished career, he served as U.S. minister to Haiti.*

the "wicked" South. Renouncing politics, on the Fourth of July 1854, he publicly burned a copy of the Constitution as "a covenant with death and an agreement with hell." Douglass, on the other hand, along with other abolitionists, increasingly looked to politics to end the blight of slavery. These political abolitionists backed the Liberty party in 1840, the Free Soil party in 1848, and eventually the Republican party in the 1850s. In the end, most abolitionists, including even the pacifist Garrison himself, followed out the logic of their beliefs and supported a frightfully costly fratricidal war as the price of emancipation.

High-minded and courageous, the abolitionists were men and women of goodwill and various colors who faced the cruel choice that people in many ages have had thrust upon them: When is evil so enormous that it must be denounced, even at the risk of precipitating bloodshed and butchery?

The South Lashes Back

Antislavery sentiment was not unknown in the South, but after about 1830 the voice of white southern abolitionism was silenced. Nat Turner's rebellion in 1831 sent a wave of hysteria sweeping over the snowy cotton fields, and planters in growing numbers slept with pistols by their pillows.

The nullification crisis of 1832 further implanted haunting fears in white southern minds, conjuring up nightmares of black incendiaries and abolitionist devils. Jailings, whippings, and lynchings now greeted rational efforts to discuss the slavery problem in the South.

Proslavery whites responded to the abolitionist groundswell by launching a massive defense of slavery as a positive good. In doing so they forgot their own section's previous doubts about the morality of the "peculiar institution." Slavery, they claimed, was supported by the authority of the Bible and the wisdom of Aristotle. It was good for the Africans, who were lifted from the "barbarism of the jungle" and clothed with the blessings of Christian civilization.

Slavemasters did indeed encourage religion in the slave quarters, emphasizing those teachings that encouraged obedience. White apologists also contended that master-slave relationships really resembled those of a family. Southern whites were quick to contrast the "happy" lot of their "servants" with that of the overworked northern wage slaves, including exploited women and stunted children. The blacks mostly toiled in the fresh air and sunlight, not in dark and stuffy factories. They did not have to worry about slack times or unemployment, as did the "hired hands" of the North. Provided with a jail-like form of social security, slaves were cared for in sickness and old age, unlike the northern workers, who were set adrift when they outlived their usefulness.

These curious proslavery arguments only widened the chasm between a backward-looking South and a forward-looking North—and indeed much of the rest of the Western world. Southerners reacted defensively to the pressure of their own fears and the merciless nagging of the northern abolitionists. Increasingly the white South turned in upon itself and grew hotly intolerant of any embarrassing questions about the status of slavery.

Regrettably, also, the controversy over free people endangered free speech in the entire country. Piles of petitions poured into Congress from the antislavery reformers, and in 1836 sensitive southerners drove through the House the so-called Gag Resolution. It required all such antislavery appeals to be tabled without debate. This attack on the right of petition aroused the aged ex-president, Representative John Quincy Adams, who waged a successful eight-year fight for its repeal.

Southern whites likewise resented the flooding of their mails with incendiary abolitionist literature. In 1835 a mob in Charleston, South Carolina, looted the local post office and burned a pile of abolitionist propaganda. Capitulating to southern pressures, the Washington government in 1835 ordered southern postmasters to destroy abolitionist material and called on southern state officials to arrest federal postmasters who did not comply. Such was "freedom of the press" as guaranteed by the Constitution.

The Abolitionist Impact in the North

Abolitionists—especially the extreme Garrisonians—were for a long time unpopular in many parts of the North. Northerners had been brought up to revere the Constitution and to regard the clauses on slavery as a lasting bargain. The ideal of Union, hammered home by the thundering eloquence of Daniel Webster and others, had taken deep root; and Garrison's wild talk of secession grated harshly on northern ears.

The North also had a heavy economic stake in Dixieland. By the late 1850s, southern planters owed northern bankers and other creditors about $300 million, and much of this immense sum would be lost—as, in fact, it later was—if the Union dissolved. New England textile mills were fed with cotton raised by the slaves, and a disrupted labor system might cut off this vital supply and bring unemployment. The Union during these critical years was partly bound together with cotton threads, tied by lords of the loom in collaboration with the so-called lords of the lash. It was not surprising that strong hostility developed in the North against the boat-rocking tactics of the radical antislaveryites.

Repeated tongue-lashings by the extreme abolitionists provoked many mob outbursts in the North, some led by respectable gentlemen. A gang of young toughs broke into abolitionist Lewis Tappan's New York house in 1834 and demolished its interior, while a crowd in the street cheered. In 1835 Garrison, with a rope tied around him, was dragged through the streets of Boston by the so-called Broadcloth Mob but escaped almost miraculously. Reverend Elijah P. Lovejoy, of Alton, Illinois, not content to assail slavery, impugned the chastity of Catholic women. His printing press was destroyed four times. In 1837 he was killed by a mob and became "the martyr abolitionist." So unpopular were the antislavery zealots that ambitious politicians, like Abraham Lincoln, usually avoided the taint of Garrisonian abolition like the plague.

Yet by the 1850s the abolitionist outcry had made a deep dent in the northern mind. Many citizens had come to see the South as the land of the unfree and the home of a hateful institution. Few northerners were prepared to abolish slavery outright, but a growing number, including Lincoln, opposed extending it to the western territories. People of this stamp, commonly called "free-soilers," swelled their ranks as the Civil War approached.

Chronology

1793	Whitney's cotton gin transforms southern economy.
1800	Gabriel slave rebellion in Virginia.
1808	Congress outlaws slave trade.
1817	American Colonization Society formed.
1820	Missouri Compromise.
1822	Republic of Liberia established in Africa. Vesey slave rebellion in Charleston.
1831	Garrison begins publishing the *Liberator*. Nat Turner slave rebellion in Virginia.
1833	British abolish slavery in the West Indies. American Anti-Slavery Society founded.
1834	Abolitionist students expelled from Lane Theological Seminary.
1835	U.S. Post Office orders destruction of abolitionist mail. "Broadcloth Mob" attacks Garrison.
1836	House of Representatives passes "Gag Resolution."
1837	Mob kills abolitionist Lovejoy in Alton, Illinois.
1839	Weld publishes *American Slavery As It Is*.
1845	Douglass publishes *Narrative of the Life of Frederick Douglass*.

VARYING VIEWPOINTS

What Was the True Nature of Slavery?

By the early twentieth century, the predictable accounts of slavery written by partisans of the North or South had receded in favor of a romantic vision of the Old South. A scholarly version of this vision was Ulrich Bonnell Phillips's landmark study, *American Negro Slavery* (1918), which portrayed a dying, unprofitable institution where benevolent masters treated their slaves with kindly paternalism and blacks submissively accepted the system that enslaved them.

Phillips's claim that slavery was unprofitable has been decisively refuted by economic historians who have shown that it was a viable, profitable, expanding system. Beginning in the late 1950s, historians came increasingly to emphasize the harshness of the slave system. One study, Stanley Elkins's *Slavery* (1959), went so far as to compare the "peculiar institution" to the Nazi concentration camps of World War II. More recently, scholars such as Eugene Genovese have contended that slavery did indeed embrace a strange form of paternalism, one reflecting not slaveholders' benevolence but their need to control and coax work out of their reluctant and often recalcitrant "investments." Furthermore, within this paternalist system, black slaves were able to make reciprocal demands of their white owners and to protect a "cultural space" of their own in which family and religion particularly could flourish.

Other historians also debate the extent to which blacks were able to maintain personal and cultural autonomy within the repressive slave system. Kenneth Stampp rejected Stanley Elkins's view that slaves were "infantilized" like concentration camp inmates, and stressed the frequency and variety of slave resistance. In another perspective, Lawrence Levine imaginatively argues in *Black Culture and Black Consciousness* (1977) that the "Sambo" image whites perceived was an act, a role that slaves played to confound their masters without incurring punishment. More recently, historians have attempted to avoid the polarity of repression versus autonomy. Their challenge is to capture the vibrancy of slave culture and its legacy for African-American society after emancipation, without diminishing the brutality of life under the southern slave regime.

New sensitivity to gender, spurred by the growing field of women's history, has also expanded the horizons of slavery studies. Historians such as Elizabeth Fox-Genovese, Jacqueline Jones, and Catherine Clinton focus on the ways in which slavery differed for men and women, both slaves and slaveholders. Enslaved black women, for example, had the unique task of negotiating an identity out of their dual responsibilities as plantation laborer, even sometimes caretaker of white women and children, and anchor of the black family. By tracing the interconnectedness of race and gender in the American South, these historians also show how slavery shaped conceptions of masculinity and femininity within southern society, further distinguishing its culture from that of the North.

For further reading, see the Appendix. For web resources, go to **http://college.hmco.com.**

17

Manifest Destiny and Its Legacy

—◦&◦—

1841–1848

Our manifest destiny [is] to overspread the continent allotted by Providence for the free development of our yearly multiplying millions.

JOHN L. O'SULLIVAN, 1845*

Territorial expansion dominated American diplomacy and politics in the 1840s. Settlers swarming into the still-disputed Oregon country aggravated relations with Britain, which had staked its own claims in the Pacific Northwest. The clamor to annex Texas to the Union provoked bitter tension with Mexico, which continued to regard Texas as a Mexican province in revolt. And when Americans began casting covetous eyes on Mexico's northernmost province, the great prize of California, open warfare erupted between the United States and its southern neighbor. Victory over Mexico added vast new domains to the United States, but it also raised thorny questions about the status of slavery in the newly acquired territories—questions that would be answered in blood in the Civil War of the 1860s.

The Accession of "Tyler Too"

A horde of hard-ciderites descended on Washington in 1841, thirsty for the spoils of office. The real leaders of the Whig party regarded President William Henry Harrison, "Old Tippecanoe," as little more than an impressive figurehead. Daniel Webster, as secretary of state, and Henry Clay, the uncrowned king of the Whigs and their ablest spokesman in the Senate, would grasp the helm.

Unluckily for Clay and Webster, their schemes soon hit a fatal snag. Before the new term had fairly

---

* This is the earliest known use of the term *Manifest Destiny*.

started, Harrison contracted pneumonia and died after only four weeks in the White House—by far the shortest administration in American history.

The "Tyler too" part of the Whig ticket, hitherto only a rhyme, now claimed the spotlight. Tall, slender, blue-eyed, and fair-haired, with classical features and a high forehead, John Tyler was a Virginia gentleman of the old school—gracious and kind, yet stubbornly attached to principle. He had earlier resigned from the Senate, quite unnecessarily, rather than accept distasteful instructions from the Virginia legislature. Still a lone wolf, he had forsaken the Jacksonian Democratic fold for that of the Whigs, largely because he could not stomach the dictatorial tactics of Jackson.

Tyler's enemies accused him of being a Democrat in Whig clothing, but this charge was only partially true. The Whig party, like the Democratic party, was something of a catchall, and the accidental president belonged to the minority wing, which embraced a number of Jeffersonian states' righters. Tyler had in fact been put on the ticket partly to attract the vote of this influential group.

It was true, however, that on virtually every major issue the obstinate Virginian was at odds with the majority of his Whig party, which was pro-bank, pro–protective tariff, and pro–internal improvements. "Tyler too" rhymed with "Tippecanoe," but there the harmony ended. As events turned out, President Harrison, the Whig, served for only 4 weeks, whereas Tyler, the ex-Democrat who was still largely a Democrat at heart, served for 204 weeks.

John Tyler: A President Without a Party

After their hard-won, hard-cider victory, the Whigs brought their not-so-secret platform out of Clay's waistcoat pocket. To the surprise of no one, it outlined a strongly nationalistic program.

Financial reform came first. The Whig Congress hastened to pass a law ending the independent treasury system, and President Tyler, disarmingly agreeable, signed it. Clay next drove through Congress a bill for a "Fiscal Bank," which would establish a new Bank of the United States.

Tyler's hostility to a centralized bank was notorious, and Clay—the "Great Compromiser"—would

have done well to conciliate him. But the Kentuckian, robbed repeatedly of the presidency by lesser men, was in an imperious mood and riding for a fall. When the bank bill reached the presidential desk, Tyler flatly vetoed it on both practical and constitutional grounds. A drunken mob gathered late at night near the White House and shouted insultingly, "Huzza for Clay!" "A bank! A bank!" "Down with the Veto!"

Whig extremists, seething with indignation, condemned Tyler as "His Accidency" and as an "Executive Ass." To the delight of Democrats, the stiff-necked Virginian was formally expelled from his party by a caucus of Whig congressmen, and a serious attempt to impeach him was broached in the House of Representatives. His entire cabinet resigned in a body, except Secretary of State Webster, who was in the midst of delicate negotiations with Britain.

The proposed Whig tariff also felt the prick of the president's well-inked pen. Tyler vetoed a tariff bill that included a scheme for distributing to the states revenues from the sale of public land. But he reluctantly signed the revised Clay-sponsored Tariff of 1842, pushing rates back down to the moderately protective level of 1832, about 32 percent.

Manipulating the Maine Maps

Hatred of Britain during the nineteenth century periodically came to a head and had to be lanced by treaty settlement or by war. The sore festered ominously in the late 1830s, especially because of private American involvement in an unsuccessful Canadian rebellion in 1837. When an American steamer, the *Caroline*, attempted to deliver supplies to Canadian insurgents, British troops sank the ship in the Niagara River, killing one American.

Anglo-American controversy then exploded in the early 1840s over the disputed Maine boundary. Hoping to bypass the icebound St. Lawrence River, the British planned to build a road westward from the seaport of Halifax to Quebec. But the proposed route ran through territory claimed also by Maine under the treaty of 1783. Tough-knuckled lumberjacks from both Maine and Canada commenced fighting in the disputed no-man's-land of the tall-timbered Aroostook River valley. When both sides summoned the local militias, the small-scale lumberjack clash, dubbed the "Aroostook War," threatened to widen into a full-dress shooting war.

As the crisis deepened in 1842, the London Foreign Office sent to Washington a conciliatory diplomat, Lord Ashburton, who had married a wealthy American woman. He speedily established cordial relations with Secretary Webster, who had recently been lionized during a visit to England. After protracted and nerve-wracking negotiations in the heat of a Washington summer, the two statesmen finally agreed to compromise on the Maine boundary. On the basis of a rough, split-the-difference arrangement, the Americans were to retain some 7,000 square miles of the 12,000 square miles of wilderness in dispute. The British got less land but won the desired Halifax-Quebec route.

A rich bonus sneaked into the small print of the same treaty; the British, in adjusting the U.S.-Canadian boundary to the west, surrendered 6,500 square miles. The area was later found to contain the priceless Mesabi iron range of Minnesota.

Old Glory Adds the Lone Star of Texas

During the uncertain eight years since 1836, Texas had led a precarious existence. Mexico, refusing to recognize Texas's independence, regarded the Lone Star Republic as a province in revolt, to be reconquered in the future. Mexican officials loudly threatened war if the American eagle gathered the fledgling republic under its protective wings.

Confronted with such perils, Texas was driven to open negotiations with Britain and France in the hope of securing the defensive shield of a protectorate. In 1839 and 1840 the Texans concluded treaties with France, the Dutch Republic, and Belgium.

Britain was intensely interested in an independent Texas. Such a republic would check the southward surge of the American colossus, whose bulging biceps posed a constant threat to nearby British possessions in the New World.

British abolitionists were also busily intriguing in Texas, hoping that gaining freedom for blacks there

A Texas Party, Early Nineteenth Century   *Texas was a meeting ground of Latino and Anglo-American cultures, creating a unique way of life that has been called "Texican."*

would inflame the nearby slaves of the South. In addition, British merchants regarded Texas as a potentially important free-trade area—an offset to the tariff-walled United States. British textile manufacturers believed that an independent Texas, with its vast cotton-producing plains, would relieve British looms of their dependence on American fiber—a supply that might be cut off by embargo or war.

Partly because of the fears aroused by these British schemers, Texas became a leading issue in the presidential campaign of 1844. The pro-expansion Democrats under James K. Polk finally triumphed over the Whigs under Henry Clay, the hardy perennial candidate. Lame duck President Tyler thereupon interpreted the narrow Democratic victory, with dubious accuracy, as a "mandate" to acquire Texas.

Eager to crown his troubled administration with this splendid prize, Tyler quickly shepherded Texas into the fold. Many "conscience Whigs" feared that Texas in the Union would be red meat to nourish the lusty "slave power." Tyler despaired of securing the needed two-thirds vote for a treaty in the Senate, and he therefore arranged for annexation by a joint resolution. This solution required only a simple majority in both houses of Congress. After a spirited debate, the resolution passed early in 1845, and Texas was formally invited to become the twenty-eighth star on the American flag.

Mexico angrily charged that the Americans had despoiled it of Texas. This was to some extent true in 1836 but hardly true in 1845, for the area was no longer Mexico's to be despoiled of. As the years stretched out, realistic observers could see that the Mexicans would not be able to reconquer their lost province. Yet Mexico left the Texans dangling by denying their right to dispose of themselves as they chose.

By 1845 the Lone Star Republic had become a danger spot, inviting foreign intrigue that menaced the American people. The continued existence of Texas as an independent nation threatened to involve the United States in a series of ruinous wars, both in America and in Europe.

What other power would have spurned the imperial domain of Texas? The bride was so near, so rich, so fair, so willing. Whatever the peculiar circumstances of the Texas revolution, the United States can hardly be accused of unseemly haste in achieving annexation. Nine long years were surely a decent wait between the beginning of the courtship and the consummation of the marriage.

Oregon Fever Populates Oregon

The Oregon Country was an enormous wilderness. It sprawled magnificently west of the Rockies to the Pacific Ocean, and north of California to the line of 54°40'—the present southern tip of the Alaska panhandle. All or substantial parts of this immense area were claimed at one time or another by four nations: Spain, Russia, Britain, and the United States.

Two claimants dropped out of the scramble. Spain, though the first to raise its banner in Oregon, bartered away its claims to the United States in the Florida Treaty of 1819. Russia retreated to the line of 54°40' by the treaties of 1824 and 1825 with America and Britain. These two remaining rivals now had the field to themselves.

British claims to Oregon were strong—at least to that portion north of the Columbia River. They were based squarely on prior discovery and exploration, on treaty rights, and on actual occupation. The most important colonizing agency was the far-flung Hudson's Bay Company, which was trading profitably with the Indians of the Pacific Northwest for their furs.

Americans, for their part, could also point pridefully to exploration and occupation. Captain Robert Gray in 1792 had stumbled upon the majestic Columbia River, which he named after his ship; and the famed Lewis and Clark expedition of 1804–1806 had ranged overland through the Oregon Country to the Pacific. This shaky American toehold was ultimately strengthened by the presence of missionaries and other settlers, a sprinkling of whom reached the grassy Willamette River valley, south of the Columbia, in the 1830s. These men and women of God were instrumental in saving the soil of Oregon for the United States. They stimulated interest in a faraway domain that Americans had earlier assumed would not be settled for centuries.

Scattered American and British pioneers in Oregon continued to live peacefully side by side. At the

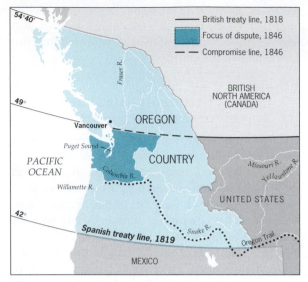

The Oregon Controversy, 1846

time of negotiating the Treaty of 1818, the United States had sought to divide the vast domain by the forty-ninth parallel. But the British, who regarded the Columbia River as the St. Lawrence of the West, were unwilling to yield this vital artery. A scheme for peaceful "joint occupation" was thereupon adopted, pending future settlement.

The handful of Americans in the Willamette Valley was suddenly multiplied in the early 1840s, when "Oregon fever" seized hundreds of restless pioneers. In increasing numbers their creaking covered wagons jolted over the two-thousand-mile Oregon Trail as the human rivulet widened into a stream. By 1846 about five thousand Americans had settled south of the Columbia River.

The British, in the face of this rising torrent of humanity, could muster only seven hundred or so subjects north of the Columbia. Losing out lopsidedly in the population race, they were beginning to see the wisdom of arriving at a peaceful settlement before being engulfed by their neighbors.

A curious fact is that only a relatively small segment of the Oregon Country was in actual controversy by 1845. The area in dispute consisted of the rough quadrangle between the Columbia River on the south and east, the forty-ninth parallel on the north, and the Pacific Ocean on the west (most of the

present state of Washington). Britain had repeatedly offered the line of the Columbia; America had repeatedly offered the forty-ninth parallel. The whole fateful issue was now tossed into the presidential election of 1844, where it was largely overshadowed by the question of annexing Texas.

A Mandate (?) for Manifest Destiny

The two major parties nominated their presidential standard-bearers in May 1844. Ambitious but often-frustrated Henry Clay, easily the most popular man in the country, was enthusiastically chosen by the Whigs at Baltimore. The Democrats, meeting later in the same city, nominated James K. Polk of Tennessee, America's first "dark horse," or "surprise," presidential candidate. Speaker of the House of Representatives for four years and governor of Tennessee for two terms, Polk was a determined, industrious, ruthless, and intelligent public servant. Whigs attempted to jeer him into oblivion with the taunt, "Who is James K. Polk?" They soon found out.

The campaign of 1844 was in part an expression of the mighty emotional upsurge known as "Manifest Destiny." Countless citizens in the 1840s and 1850s, feeling a sense of mission, believed that Almighty God had "manifestly" destined the American people for a hemispheric career. They would irresistibly spread their uplifting and ennobling democratic institutions over at least the entire continent, and possibly over South America as well. Land greed and ideals—"empire" and "liberty"—were thus conveniently conjoined.

Expansionist Democrats were strongly swayed by the intoxicating spell of Manifest Destiny. They came out flat-footedly in their platform for the "Re-annexation of Texas"* and the "Reoccupation of Oregon," all the way to 54°40'. The Whigs countered with such slogans as "Hooray for Clay" and "Polk, Slavery, and Texas, or Clay, Union, and Liberty."

On the crucial issue of Texas, the acrobatic Clay tried to ride two horses at once. The "Great Compro-

---

* The United States had given up its claims to Texas in the Florida Purchase Treaty with Spain in 1819 (see p. 158). The slogan "Fifty-four forty or fight" was evidently not coined until two years later, in 1846.

miser" compromised away the presidency when he stated that he favored annexing slave-holding Texas (an appeal to the South) but that he also favored postponement (an appeal to the North). By straddling the issue this way, Clay alienated ardent antislaveryites.

In the stretch drive, "Dark Horse" Polk nipped Henry Clay at the wire, 170 to 105 votes in the Electoral College and 1,338,464 to 1,300,097 in the popular column. Clay would have won if he had not lost New York by a scant 5,000 votes. There the tiny antislavery Liberty party absorbed nearly 16,000 votes, many of which would otherwise have gone to the unlucky Kentuckian. Ironically, the anti-Texas Liberty party, by helping to elect the pro-Texas Polk, hastened the annexation of Texas. The victorious Democrats proclaimed that they had received a mandate from the voters to take Texas, and three days before leaving office President Tyler signed the joint resolution of annexation.

Polk the Purposeful

"Young Hickory" Polk, unlike "Old Hickory" Jackson, was not an impressive figure. Of medium height, lean, white-haired, gray-eyed, and stern-faced, he took life seriously and drove himself mercilessly into a premature grave. His burdens were increased by an unwillingness to delegate authority. Methodical and hard-working but not brilliant, he was shrewd, narrow-minded, conscientious, and persistent. "What he went for he fetched," wrote a contemporary. Purposeful in the highest degree, he developed a positive four-point program and with remarkable success achieved it completely in less than four years.

Polk's first goal was a lower tariff. Robert Walker, his secretary of the treasury, lobbied through Congress a tariff bill that reduced the average rates of the Tariff of 1842 from about 32 percent to 25 percent. The Walker Tariff of 1846 proved to be an excellent revenue producer.

A second objective of Polk was restoration of the independent treasury, unceremoniously dropped by the Whigs in 1841. Pro-bank Whigs in Congress raised a storm of opposition, but victory at last rewarded the president's efforts in 1846. The third and fourth

President James K. Polk (1795–1849), by George P. A. Healy, 1858 *Distinguished for both determination and deviousness, Polk added more territory to the United States (by questionable means) than any other president. In tenaciously pursuing his goals, he broke himself down with overwork and died 103 days after his single term ended. His somewhat priggish wife (and secretary) banned all drinking and dancing in the White House.*

points on Polk's "must list" were the settlement of the Oregon dispute and the acquisition of California.

"Reoccupation" of the "whole" of Oregon had been promised northern Democrats in the campaign of 1844. But southern Democrats, once they had annexed Texas, rapidly cooled off. Polk, himself a southerner, had no intention of insisting on the 54°40' pledge of his own platform. But feeling bound by the offers of his predecessors to London, he again proposed the compromise line of 49°.

Fortunately for peace, British anti-expansionists ("Little Englanders") were now persuaded that the Columbia River after all was not the St. Lawrence of the West. Early in 1846 the British came around and proposed the line of 49° themselves. The senators speedily accepted the offer and approved the subsequent treaty, despite a few diehard shouts of "Fifty-four forty forever!"

Satisfaction with the Oregon settlement among Americans was not unanimous. The northwestern states, hotbed of Manifest Destiny and "fifty-four forty-ism," joined the antislavery forces in condemning what they regarded as a base betrayal by the South. Why all of Texas and not all of Oregon? Because, retorted expansionist Senator Thomas Hart Benton of Missouri, "Great Britain is powerful and Mexico is weak."

So Polk, despite all the campaign bluster, got neither "fifty-four forty" nor a fight. But he did get something that in the long run was better: a reasonable compromise without a rifle being raised.

Misunderstandings with Mexico

Faraway California was Polk's final concern. He and other disciples of Manifest Destiny had long coveted its verdant valleys and especially the spacious bay of San Francisco. This splendid harbor was widely regarded as America's future gateway to the Pacific Ocean.

The population of California in 1845 was curiously mixed. It consisted of perhaps 13,000 sun-blessed Spanish-Mexicans and as many as 75,000 dispirited Indians. There were fewer than a thousand "foreigners," mostly Americans, some of whom had "left their consciences" behind them as they rounded Cape Horn. Given time, these transplanted Yankees might bring California into the Union by "playing the Texas game."

Polk was eager to buy California from Mexico. But relations with Mexico City were dangerously embittered, partly over unpaid damage claims by U.S. citizens, but mostly over Texas. After threatening war if the United States acquired the Lone Star Republic, the Mexican government completely severed diplomatic relations following annexation.

Deadlock with Mexico over Texas was further tightened by a question of boundaries. During the long era of Spanish-Mexican occupation, the southwestern boundary of Texas had been the Nueces River. But the expansive Texans, on rather far-fetched grounds, were claiming the more southerly Rio Grande instead. Polk, for his part, felt a strong obligation to defend Texas in its claim, once it was annexed.

The Mexicans were far less concerned about this boundary quibble than the United States. In their eyes all of Texas was still theirs, although temporarily in revolt, and a dispute over the two rivers seemed pointless. Yet Polk was careful to keep American troops out of virtually all of the explosive no-man's-land between the Nueces and the Rio Grande, as long as there was any real prospect of peaceful adjustment.

The golden prize of California continued to cause Polk much anxiety. Disquieting rumors (now known to have been ill founded) were circulating that Britain was about to buy or seize California—a grab that Americans could not tolerate under the Monroe Doctrine. In a last desperate throw of the dice, Polk dispatched John Slidell to Mexico City as minister late in 1845. The new envoy, among other alternatives, was instructed to offer a maximum of $25 million for California and territory to the east. But the proud Mexican people would not even permit Slidell to present his "insulting" proposition.

American Blood on American (?) Soil

A frustrated Polk was now prepared to force a showdown. On January 13, 1846, he ordered four thousand men, under General Zachary Taylor, to march from the Nueces River to the Rio Grande, provocatively near Mexican forces. Polk's presidential diary reveals that he expected at any moment to hear of a clash. When none occurred after an anxious wait, he informed his cabinet on May 9, 1846, that he proposed to ask Congress to declare war on the basis of (1) unpaid claims and (2) Slidell's rejection. These, at best, were rather flimsy pretexts. Two cabinet members spoke up and said that they would feel better satisfied if Mexican troops should fire first.

That very evening, news of bloodshed arrived. On April 25, 1846, Mexican troops had crossed the Rio Grande and attacked General Taylor's command, with a loss of sixteen Americans killed or wounded.

Polk, further aroused, sent a vigorous war message to Congress. He declared that despite "all our efforts" to avoid a clash, hostilities had been forced upon the country by the shedding of "American blood on the American soil." A patriotic Congress overwhelmingly voted for war, and enthusiastic volunteers cried, "Ho for the Halls of the Montezumas!"

and "Mexico or Death!" Inflamed by the war fever, even antislavery Whig bastions joined with the rest of the nation, though they later condemned "Jimmy Polk's war." As James Russell Lowell of Massachusetts lamented,

> Massachusetts, God forgive her,
> She's akneelin' with the rest.

In his message to Congress, Polk was making history—not writing it. If he had been a historian, he would have explained that American blood had been shed on soil that the Mexicans had good reason to regard as their own. A gangling, rough-featured Whig congressman from Illinois, one Abraham Lincoln, introduced certain resolutions that requested information as to the precise "spot" on American soil where American blood had been shed. He pushed his "spot" resolutions with such persistence that he came to be known as the "spotty Lincoln" who could die of "spotted fever."

Did Polk provoke war? California was an imperative point in his program, and Mexico would not sell it at any price. The only way to get it was to use force or wait for an internal American revolt. But in 1846, patience had ceased to be a virtue as far as Polk was concerned. Bent on grasping California by fair means or foul, he pushed the quarrel to a bloody showdown.

Both sides, in fact, were spoiling for a fight. Feisty Americans, especially southwestern expansionists, were eager to teach the Mexicans a lesson. The Mexicans, in turn, were burning to humiliate the "Bullies of the North." Possessing a considerable standing army, heavily overstaffed with generals, they boasted of invading the United States, freeing the black slaves, and lassoing whole regiments of Americans. They were hoping that the quarrel with Britain over Oregon would blossom into a full-dress war, as it came near doing, and further pin down the hated *yanquis.* Fired by indignation, Mexicans and Americans each believed the other was the aggressor.

The Mastering of Mexico

Polk wanted California—not war. But when war came, he hoped to fight it on a limited scale and then pull out when he had captured the prize. The dethroned Mexican dictator Santa Anna, then exiled in Cuba, let it be known that if the American blockading squadron would permit him to slip into Mexico, he would sell out his country. Incredibly, Polk agreed to this discreditable intrigue. But the double-crossing Santa Anna, once he returned to Mexico, proceeded to rally his countrymen to a desperate defense of their soil.

American operations in the Southwest and in California were completely successful. In 1846 General Stephen W. Kearny led a detachment of seventeen hundred troops over the famous Santa Fe Trail from Fort Leavenworth to Santa Fe. This sunbaked outpost, with its drowsy plazas, was easily captured. But before Kearny could reach California, the fertile province was won. When war broke out, Captain John C. Frémont, the dashing explorer, just "happened" to be there with several dozen well-armed men. In helping to overthrow Mexican rule in 1846, he collaborated with American naval officers and with the local Americans, who had hoisted the banner of the short-lived California Bear Flag Republic.

General Zachary Taylor meanwhile had been spearheading the main thrust. Known as "Old Rough and Ready" because of his iron constitution and incredibly unsoldierly appearance—he sometimes wore a Mexican straw hat—he fought his way across the Rio Grande into Mexico. After several gratifying victories, he reached Buena Vista. There, on February 22–23, 1847, his weakened force of 5,000 men was attacked by some 20,000 march-weary troops under Santa Anna. The Mexicans were finally repulsed with extreme difficulty, and overnight Zachary Taylor became the "Hero of Buena Vista."

Sound American strategy now called for a crushing blow at the enemy's vitals—Mexico City. General Taylor, though a good leader of modest-sized forces, could not win decisively in the semideserts of northern Mexico. The command of the main expedition, which pushed inland from the coastal city of Vera Cruz early in 1847, was entrusted to General Winfield Scott. A handsome giant of a man, Scott had emerged as a hero from the War of 1812 and later earned the nickname "Old Fuss and Feathers" because of his resplendent uniforms and strict discipline. Scott succeeded in battling his way up to Mexico City by September 1847 in one of the most brilliant campaigns in American military annals. He proved to be the most distinguished general produced by his country between 1783 and 1861.

Fighting Mexico for Peace

Polk was anxious to end the shooting as soon as he could secure his territorial goals. Accordingly, he sent along with Scott's invading army the chief clerk of the State Department, Nicholas P. Trist. Grasping a fleeting opportunity to negotiate, Trist signed the Treaty of Guadalupe Hidalgo on February 2, 1848, and forwarded it to Washington.

The terms of the treaty were breathtaking. They confirmed the American title to Texas and yielded the enormous area stretching northward to Oregon and west to the ocean, embracing coveted California. This total expanse, including Texas, was about one-half of Mexico. The United States agreed to pay $15 million for the land and to assume the claims of its citizens against Mexico in the amount of $3,250,000 (see "Makers of America: The Californios," pp. 240–241).

Polk submitted the treaty to the Senate. Speed was imperative. The antislavery Whigs in Congress— dubbed "Mexican Whigs" or "conscience Whigs"— were condemning this "damnable war" with increasing heat. Having secured control of the House

Major Campaigns of the Mexican War

in 1847, they were even threatening to vote down supplies for the armies in the field. If they had done so, Scott probably would have been forced to retreat, and the fruits of victory might have been tossed away.

Another peril impended. A swelling group of expansionists, intoxicated by Manifest Destiny, was clamoring for all of Mexico. If America had seized it, the nation would have been saddled with a vexatious problem. Farseeing southerners like Calhoun, alarmed by the mounting anger of antislavery agitators, realized that the South would do well not to be too greedy. The treaty was finally approved by the Senate, 38 to 14. Oddly enough, it was condemned both by opponents who wanted all of Mexico and by opponents who wanted none of it.

Profit and Loss in Mexico

As wars go, the Mexican War was small. It cost some thirteen thousand American lives, most of them taken by disease. But the fruits of the fighting were enormous.

America's total expanse, already vast, was increased by about one-third (counting Texas)—an addition even greater than that of the Louisiana Purchase. A sharp stimulus was given to the spirit of Manifest Destiny for, as the proverb has it, the appetite comes with eating.

As fate ordained, the Mexican War was the blood-spattered schoolroom of the Civil War. The campaigns provided priceless field experience for most of the officers destined to become leading generals in the forthcoming conflict, including Captain Robert E. Lee and Lieutenant Ulysses S. Grant. The Military Academy at West Point, founded in 1802, fully justified its existence through the well-trained officers. Useful also was the navy, which did valuable work in throwing a crippling blockade around Mexican ports. The Marine Corps, in existence since 1798, won new laurels and to this day sings, in its stirring hymn, about the "Halls of Montezuma."

The army waged war without defeat and without a major blunder, despite formidable obstacles and a half-dozen or so achingly long marches. Chagrined British critics, as well as other foreign skeptics, reluctantly revised upward their estimate of Yankee military prowess. Opposing armies, moreover, emerged with increased respect for each other. The Mexicans, though poorly led, fought heroically. At Chapultepec, near Mexico City, the teenage lads of the military academy there (*los niños*) perished to a boy.

Long-memoried Mexicans have never forgotten that their northern enemy tore away about half of their country. The argument that they were lucky not to lose all of it, and that they had been paid something for their land, scarcely lessened their bitterness. The war also marked an ugly turning point in the relations between the United States and Latin America as a whole. Hitherto, Uncle Sam had been regarded with some complacency, even friendliness. Henceforth, he was increasingly feared as the "Colossus of the North." Suspicious neighbors to the south condemned him as a greedy and untrustworthy bully, who might next despoil them of their soil.

Most ominous of all, the war rearoused the snarling dog of the slavery issue, and the beast did not stop yelping until drowned in the blood of the Civil War. Abolitionists assailed the Mexican conflict as one provoked by the southern "slavocracy" for its own evil purposes.

Quarreling over slavery extension also erupted on the floors of Congress. In 1846, shortly after the shooting started, Polk requested an appropriation of $2 million with which to buy peace. Representative David Wilmot of Pennsylvania, fearful of the southern "slavocracy," introduced a fateful amendment. It stipulated that slavery should never exist in any of the territory wrested from Mexico.

The disruptive Wilmot amendment twice passed the House but not the Senate. Southern members, unwilling to be robbed of prospective slave states, fought the restriction tooth and nail. Antislavery forces, in Congress and out, battled no less bitterly for the exclusion of slaves. The "Wilmot Proviso" soon came to symbolize the burning issue in the territories.

In a broad sense, the opening shots of the Mexican War were the opening shots of the Civil War. President Polk left the nation the splendid physical heritage of California and the Southwest but also the ugly moral heritage of an embittered slavery dispute. Mexicans could later take some satisfaction in knowing that the territory wrenched from them had proved to be a venomous apple of discord that could well be called Santa Anna's revenge.

MAKERS OF AMERICA

The Californios

When the United States acquired the Mexican Cession in 1848, it took in a vast land that stretched from the arid desert Southwest to the fruited valleys and port cities of California. There, at the conclusion of the Mexican War, dwelled some thirteen thousand Californios—descendants of the Spanish and Mexican conquerors who had once ruled California.

The Spanish had first arrived in California in 1769, extending their New World empire and out-racing Russian traders to bountiful San Francisco Bay. Father Junipero Serra, an enterprising Franciscan friar, soon established twenty-one missions along the coast. Indians in the iron grip of the missions were encouraged to adopt Christianity and often forced to toil endlessly as farmers and herders, in the process suffering disease and degradation. These frequently maltreated mission Indians occupied the lowest rungs on the ladder of Spanish colonial society.

Upon the loftiest rungs perched the Californios. Pioneers from the Mexican heartland of New Spain, they had trailed Serra to California, claiming land and civil offices in their new home. Yet even the proud Californios had deferred to the all-powerful Franciscan missionaries until Mexico threw off the Spanish colonial yoke in 1826 and began transferring power from the missions to secular (that is, governmental) authorities.

This "secularization" program attacked and eroded the immense power of the Franciscans, who had self-confidently commanded their rich fiefdoms and resisted even minor efforts to reform their harsh

California Indians Dancing at the Mission in San José, by Sykes, 1806

treatment of the Indians. But during the 1830s much of their land and many of their assets were confiscated by the Californios, who established vast *ranchos* (ranches) that they ruled until the Mexican War.

The Californios' glory faded in the wake of the American victory. Overwhelmed by the inrush of Anglo gold-diggers after the discovery at Sutter's Fort in 1848, the Californios saw their recently acquired lands and political power slip through their fingers. When the Civil War broke out in 1861, so harshly did the word *Yankee* ring in their ears that many Californios supported the South.

By 1870 the Californios' brief ascendancy had utterly vanished—a short and sad tale of riches to rags in the face of the Anglo onslaught. Half a century later, beginning in 1910, hundreds of thousands of young Mexicans would flock into California and the Southwest. They would enter a region liberally endowed with Spanish architecture and artifacts, bearing the names of Spanish missions and Californios' ranchos. But they would find it a land dominated by Anglos, a place far different from that which their Californio ancestors had settled so hopefully in earlier days.

Chronology

1841 Harrison dies after four weeks in office. Tyler assumes presidency.

1842 "Aroostook War" over Maine boundary. Webster-Ashburton Treaty.

1844 Polk defeats Clay in "Manifest Destiny" election.

1845 United States annexes Texas.

1846 United States settles Oregon dispute with Britain.

1846 United States and Mexico clash over Texas boundary.
Kearny takes Santa Fe.
Frémont conquers California.
"Wilmot Proviso" passes House of Representatives.

1846–1848 Mexican War.

1847 Battle of Buena Vista.
Scott takes Mexico City.

1848 Treaty of Guadalupe Hidalgo.

For further reading, see the Appendix. For web resources, go to **http://college.hmco.com**.

18

Renewing the Sectional Struggle

⚮

1848–1854

*Secession! Peaceable secession! Sir, your eyes
and mine are never destined to see that miracle.*

DANIEL WEBSTER, 1850

The year 1848, highlighted by a rash of revolutions in Europe, was filled with unrest in America. The Treaty of Guadalupe Hidalgo officially ended the war with Mexico but initiated a new and perilous round of political warfare in the United States. The vanquished Mexicans were forced to relinquish an enormous tract of real estate, including Texas, California, and all the area between. The acquisition of this huge domain raised anew the burning issue of extending slavery into the territories. Northern antislaveryites had rallied behind the Wilmot Proviso, which flatly prohibited slavery in any territory acquired in the Mexican War. Southern senators had blocked the passage of the proviso, but the issue did not die. Ominously, debate over slavery in the area of the Mexican Cession threatened to disrupt the ranks of both Whigs and Democrats and split national politics along North-South sectional lines.

The Popular Sovereignty Panacea

Each of the two great political parties was a vital bond of national unity, for each enjoyed powerful support in both North and South. If they were replaced by two purely sectional groupings, the Union would be in peril. To politicians, the wisest strategy seemed to be to sit on the lid of the slavery issue and ignore the boiling beneath. Even so, the cover bobbed up and down in response to the agitation of zealous northern abolitionists and impassioned southern "fire-eaters."

President Polk, broken in health, did not seek a second term. The Democratic National Convention in Baltimore turned to aging General Lewis Cass, an experienced but pompous senator whose enemies dubbed him "General Gass." The Democratic platform was silent on the burning issue of slavery in the territories. But Cass himself was a well-known advocate of "popular sovereignty," the doctrine that the people of a territory, under the principles of the Constitution, should themselves determine the status of slavery.

Popular sovereignty had a persuasive appeal. The public liked it because it accorded with the democratic tradition of self-determination. Politicians liked it because it seemed a comfortable compromise between the abolitionist bid for a ban on slavery in the territories and southern demands that Congress protect slavery in the territories. Popular sovereignty tossed the slavery problem into the laps of the people in the various territories. Advocates of the principle thus hoped to dissolve the most stubborn national issue of the day into a series of local issues. Yet popular sovereignty had one fatal defect: it might serve to spread the blight of slavery.

Meeting in Philadelphia, the Whigs turned away from controversial Henry Clay and nominated Zachary Taylor, the "Hero of Buena Vista," who had never held civil office or even voted for president. As usual, the Whigs pussyfooted in their platform. Eager to win at any cost, they dodged all troublesome issues and merely extolled the homespun virtues of their candidate. Taylor had not committed himself on the issue of slavery extension, but as a wealthy Louisiana sugar planter he owned scores of slaves.

Aroused by the conspiracy of silence in the Democratic and Whig platforms, ardent antislavery northerners organized the Free Soil party. It stood foursquare for the Wilmot Proviso and against slavery in the territories. The new party nominated ex-president Van Buren and marched into the fray shouting, "Free soil, free speech, free labor, and free men."

Those freedoms provided the bedrock on which the Free-Soilers built their party. Free-Soilers condemned slavery not so much for enslaving blacks but for destroying the chances of free white workers to rise up from wage-earning dependence to the esteemed status of self-employment. Free-Soilers argued that only with free soil in the West could a traditional American commitment to upward mobility continue to flourish. If forced to compete with slave labor, more costly wage labor would inevitably wither away, and with it the chance for the American worker to own property. As the first widely inclusive party organized around the issue of slavery and confined to a single section, the Free Soil party foreshadowed the emergence of the Republican party six years later.

With the slavery issue officially shoved under the rug by the two major parties, politicians on both sides were happy to focus on personalities. The amateurish Taylor had to be carefully watched, lest his indiscreet pen puncture his puffed-up military reputation. Taylor won with 1,360,967 popular and 163 electoral votes, compared with Cass's 1,222,342 popular and 127 electoral votes. Free-Soiler Van Buren, although winning no state, polled 291,263 votes and apparently diverted enough Democratic strength from Cass in the crucial state of New York to throw the election to Taylor.

Sectional Balance and the Underground Railroad

The South of 1850 was relatively well off. It had seated in the White House the war hero Zachary Taylor, a Virginia-born, slaveowning planter from Louisiana. It boasted a majority in the cabinet and on the Supreme Court. If outnumbered in the House, the South had equality in the Senate, where it could at least neutralize northern maneuvers. Its cotton fields were expanding, and cotton prices were profitably high. Few sane people, North or South, believed that slavery was seriously threatened where it already existed below the Mason-Dixon line. The fifteen slave states could easily veto any proposed constitutional amendment.

Yet the South was deeply worried, as it had been for several decades, by the ever-tipping political balance. There were then fifteen slave states and fifteen free states. But the discovery of gold in California immediately after the Mexican War drew tens of thousands of "forty-niners" to the area. Soon the newcomers were clamoring for the direct admission of California to the Union. California's admission as a free state would destroy the delicate equilibrium in the Senate, perhaps forever. With New Mexico and Utah also lining up for future entry into the Union, the fate of California might well establish a precedent for the rest of the Mexican Cession territory.

Texas nursed an additional grievance of its own. It claimed a huge area east of the upper Rio Grande and north to the forty-second parallel, part of present New Mexico. The federal government was proposing to detach this prize, while hot-blooded Texans were threatening to descend on Santa Fe and seize what they regarded as rightfully theirs. The explosive quarrel foreshadowed shooting.

Many southerners were also angered by the nagging agitation in the North for the abolition of slavery in the District of Columbia. They looked with alarm on the prospect of a ten-mile-square oasis of free soil thrust between slaveholding Maryland and slaveholding Virginia.

Even more disagreeable to the South was the loss of runaway slaves, many of whom were assisted north by the Underground Railroad. This virtual freedom train consisted of an informal chain of "stations" (antislavery homes), through which scores of "passengers" (runaway slaves) were spirited by "conductors" (usually white and black abolitionists) from the slave states to the free-soil sanctuary of Canada.

The most amazing of these "conductors" was a runaway slave from Maryland, fearless Harriet Tubman. During nineteen forays into the South, she rescued more than three hundred slaves, including her aged parents, and deservedly earned the title "Moses." Lively imaginations later exaggerated the role of the Underground Railroad, but its existence is a fact.

By 1850 southerners were demanding a new and more stringent fugitive-slave law. The old one, passed by Congress in 1793, had proved inadequate to cope with runaways, especially since unfriendly state authorities failed to cooperate.

Estimates indicate that the South in 1850 was losing perhaps a thousand runaways a year out of its total of some 4 million slaves. In fact, more blacks probably gained their freedom by self-purchase or voluntary emancipation than ever escaped. But the moral judgment implied by the Underground Railroad infuriated slaveowners, and the new fugitive-slave law was a militant assertion of their belief in the rightness of slavery.

Twilight of the Senatorial Giants

Southern fears were such that Congress was confronted with catastrophe in 1850. Free-soil California was clamoring for admission, and "fire-eaters" in the South were voicing ominous threats of secession. The crisis brought into the congressional forum the most distinguished assemblage of statesmen since the Constitutional Convention of 1787—the Old Guard of the dying generation and the young gladiators of the new. That "immortal trio"—Clay, Calhoun, and Webster—appeared together for the last time on the public stage.

Resurrection of Henry "Box" Brown   *Brown, a slave, was shipped to Philadelphia abolitionists from Virginia in a box.*

Compromise of 1850

Concessions to the North	Concessions to the South
California admitted as a free state	The remainder of the Mexican Cession area to be formed into the territories of New Mexico and Utah, without restriction on slavery, hence open to popular sovereignty
Territory disputed by Texas and New Mexico to be surrendered to New Mexico	Texas to receive $10 million from the federal government as compensation
Abolition of the domestic slave trade (but not slavery) in the District of Columbia	A more stringent fugitive-slave law, going beyond that of 1793

Henry Clay, then seventy-three, played a crucial role by proposing a series of compromises. Ably seconded by thirty-seven-year-old Senator Stephen A. Douglas of Illinois, the "Little Giant," Clay persuasively urged both North and South to make concessions.

Senator John C. Calhoun, then sixty-eight and dying of tuberculosis, championed the South in his last formal speech. Too weak to deliver it himself, he sat bundled up in the Senate chamber, his eyes glowing within a stern face, while a younger colleague read his fateful words. Rejecting Clay's proposed concessions, Calhoun's passionate plea was to leave slavery alone, return runaway slaves, give the South its rights as a minority, and restore the political balance. Calhoun died in 1850, before the debate was over, murmuring the sad words, "The South! The South! God knows what will become of her."

Daniel Webster, sixty-eight years old and also ailing, next took the Senate spotlight to uphold Clay's compromise measures in his own last great speech. Webster urged all reasonable concessions to the South, including a new fugitive-slave law with teeth. Because climate and topography would prevent the spread of cotton production to the Mexican Cession territory, Webster argued, it was unnecessary to legislate on slavery there.* The grand old orator's eloquent plea visibly strengthened Union sentiment and especially pleased northern banking and commercial centers, which stood to lose millions of dollars by secession. But the abolitionists, who had mistakenly assumed Webster was one of them, upbraided him as a traitor.

The stormy congressional debate of 1850 was not finished, for the Young Guard from the North were yet to have their say. Led by the wiry freshman senator William Seward of New York, this new generation of antislavery leaders was more interested in purifying the Union than in patching and preserving it. Seward unequivocally opposed further concessions to the South, appealing to a moral "higher law" than the Constitution to exclude slavery from the territories.

As the great debate in Congress ran its heated course, deadlock seemed certain, and President Taylor pledged to veto any compromise. In response to the threats of Texas to seize Santa Fe, the crusty soldier-president seemed ready to lead an army into Texas and hang all the "damned traitors." If troops had marched, the South probably would have rallied to the defense of Texas, and the Civil War might have erupted in 1850.

Breaking the Congressional Logjam

At the height of the controversy in 1850, President Taylor unknowingly made compromise possible by dying suddenly. The colorless vice president, Millard Fillmore, took the reins. As presiding officer of the Senate, he had been impressed with the arguments

---

* Webster was wrong here; within one hundred years California had become one of the great cotton-producing states of the Union.

A Seward Caricature *He later became Lincoln's foremost rival for the presidency, and still later his secretary of state.*

for conciliation, and he gladly signed the series of compromise measures that passed Congress after seven long months of stormy debate.

The struggle to get these measures accepted by the country was hardly less heated than in Congress. In the northern states, "Union savers" like Senators Clay, Webster, and Douglas orated on behalf of the compromise. The ailing Clay himself delivered more than seventy speeches. Their cause was strengthened by a growing feeling of goodwill and by an upsurge of prosperity.

But the southern "fire-eaters" were still violently opposed to concessions. In mid-1850 an assemblage of southern extremists met in Nashville, Tennessee, to condemn the compromise. But the convention proved to be a dud, and southern opinion reluctantly came to accept the verdict of compromise.

Like the calm after a storm, a second Era of Good Feelings dawned. Peace-loving people in both the North and South were determined that the compromises should finally bury the explosive issue of slavery. But this placid period of reason proved all too brief.

Balancing the Compromise Scales

Who got the better deal in the Compromise of 1850? The answer is clearly the North. California, as a free state, tipped the Senate balance permanently against the South. The territories of New Mexico and Utah were open to slavery on the basis of popular sovereignty. But the iron law of nature—the "highest law" of all—had loaded the dice in favor of free soil. The southerners urgently needed more slave territory to restore the "sacred balance." If they could not carve new states out of the recent conquests from Mexico, where else could they get them? In the Caribbean, was one answer.

Even the apparent gains of the South rang hollow. Disgruntled Texas was to be paid $10 million toward discharging its indebtedness, but in the long run this was a modest sum. The immense area in dispute had been torn from the side of slaveholding Texas and was almost certain to be free. The South had halted the drive toward abolition in the District of Columbia, at least temporarily, by permitting the termination of the slave trade in the federal district. But even this move was an entering wedge toward complete emancipation in the nation's capital.

Most alarming of all, the drastic new Fugitive Slave Law of 1850—"the Bloodhound Bill"—stirred up a storm of opposition in the North. The fleeing slaves could not testify on their own behalf, and they were denied a jury trial. These harsh practices threatened to create dangerous precedents for white Americans. Freedom-loving northerners who aided the slave to escape were liable to heavy fines and jail sentences. They might even be ordered to join the slave-catchers, and this possibility rubbed salt into old sores.

So savage was this "Man-Stealing Law" that it touched off an explosive chain reaction in the North. Many shocked moderates, hitherto passive, were driven into the swelling ranks of the antislaveryites.

The Underground Railroad stepped up its timetable, and infuriated northern mobs rescued slaves from their pursuers. Massachusetts, in a move toward nullification suggestive of South Carolina in 1832, made it a penal offense for any state official to enforce the new federal statute. Other states passed "personal liberty laws," which denied local jails to

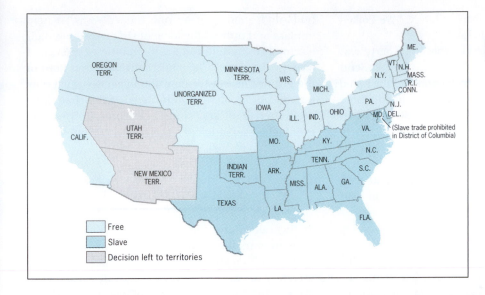

Slavery After the Compromise of 1850

federal officials and otherwise hampered enforcement. The abolitionists rent the heavens with their protests against the man-stealing statute. A meeting presided over by William Lloyd Garrison in 1851 declared, "We execrate it, we spit upon it, we trample it under our feet."

Beyond question, the Fugitive Slave Law was an appalling blunder on the part of the South. No single irritant of the 1850s was more persistently galling to both sides, and none did more to awaken in the North a spirit of antagonism against the South. The southerners in turn were embittered because the northerners would not in good faith execute the law—the one real and immediate southern "gain" from the Great Compromise. Slave-catchers, with some success, redoubled their efforts.

Should the shooting showdown have come in 1850? From the standpoint of the secessionists, yes; from the standpoint of the Unionists, no. Time was fighting for the North. With every passing decade this huge section was forging further ahead in population and wealth—in crops, factories, foundries, ships, and railroads.

Delay also added immensely to the moral strength of the North—to its will to fight for the Union. In 1850 thousands of northern moderates were unwilling to pin the South to the rest of the nation with bayonets. But the inflammatory events of the 1850s did much to bolster the Yankee will to resist secession, whatever the cost. This one feverish decade gave the North time to accumulate the material and moral strength that provided the margin of victory. Thus the Compromise of 1850, from one point of view, won the Civil War for the Union.

Defeat and Doom for the Whigs

Meeting in Baltimore, the deadlocked Democratic convention of 1852 eventually nominated an obscure New Hampshire lawyer-politician, Franklin Pierce, the second "dark horse" candidate in American history. Weak and indecisive, Pierce was called the "Fainting General" by his opponents because he had fallen off a horse during the Mexican War. As a prosouthern northerner, Pierce was acceptable to the slavery wing of the Democratic party. His platform came out for the finality of the Compromise of 1850, Fugitive Slave Law and all.

The Whigs, also convening in Baltimore, foolishly bypassed figures associated with the Compromise of 1850, such as President Fillmore and Senator Webster. Having won in the past only with military heroes, they turned to another, "Old Fuss and Feathers," Winfield Scott. Although Scott was the ablest American general of his generation, his haughty personality repelled the masses, and Democrats cried exultantly, "We Polked 'em in '44; we'll Pierce 'em in '52."

Luckily for the Democrats, the Whig party was hopelessly split. Antislavery Whigs swallowed Scott but deplored his platform, which endorsed the hated Fugitive Slave Law. Southern Whigs, who doubted Scott's loyalty to the Compromise of 1850 and especially to the Fugitive Slave Law, accepted the platform but spat on the candidate. Stabbed in the back by his fellow Whigs in the South, Scott received only 42 electoral votes. The pliant Pierce won in a landslide with 254 electoral votes, although the popular vote was closer, 1,601,117 to 1,385,453.

The election of 1852 was fraught with frightening significance, though it seemed tame at the time. It marked the effective end of the disorganized Whig party and, within a few years, its complete death. The Whigs were governed at times by the crassest opportunism, and they won only two presidential elections in their colorful career (1840 and 1848), both with war heroes. They finally choked to death trying to gag down the Fugitive Slave Law. But their great contribu-tion—and a noteworthy one indeed—was to help implant and uphold the ideal of Union through their electoral strength in the South and the eloquence of leaders like Henry Clay and Daniel Webster. Both of these statesmen, by unhappy coincidence, died dur-ing the 1852 campaign. But the good they had done lived after them and contributed powerfully to the eventual preservation of a united United States.

The Expansionist Legacy of the Mexican War

At the outset the Pierce administration displayed vigor in pursuing expansion. The new president's cabinet contained aggressive southerners, including Secretary of War Jefferson Davis, future president of the Confederacy. The people of Dixie were deter-mined to acquire more slave territory, and the com-pliant Pierce was their willing tool.

The intoxicating victories of the Mexican War stimulated the spirit of Manifest Destiny and a lust

A Ride for Liberty, by East-man Johnson *In this famous painting, Johnson, a New England artist, bril-liantly evokes the anxiety of fleeing slaves.*

for new slave territory among "slavocrats." Many Americans were also looking for potential canal routes across Central America in Nicaragua and Panama, and favored expansion into the islands flanking them, notably Spain's Cuba. Proslavery expansionists imagined a southern republic that would stretch from the Mason-Dixon line to the Caribbean islands and Central America.

Southerners took a special interest in Nicaragua. A brazen American adventurer, William Walker, tried repeatedly to grab control of this Central American country in the 1850s. Backed by an armed force recruited largely in the South, he installed himself as president in July 1856 and promptly legalized slavery. One southern newspaper proclaimed to the planter aristocracy that Walker—the "gray-eyed man of destiny"—"now offers Nicaragua to you and your slaves." But a coalition of Central American nations formed an alliance to overthrow him. President Pierce withdrew diplomatic recognition, and the gray-eyed man's destiny was to crumple before a Honduran firing squad in 1860.

Nicaragua was also of vital concern to Britain. Fearing that the grasping Yankees would monopolize trade there, the British seized a solid foothold at Greytown, the eastern end of the proposed Nicaraguan canal route, and an ugly armed clash threatened. But the crisis was surmounted in 1850 by the Clayton-Bulwer Treaty, which stipulated that neither America nor Britain would secure exclusive control over any future isthmian waterway.

America had become a Pacific power with the acquisition of California and Oregon. American shippers already traded with China, and they urged Washington to push for commercial intercourse with Japan, which had been closed to the European world for over two hundred years.

The Washington government, now eager to pry open the bamboo gates of Japan, responded in 1853 by dispatching a fleet of awesome, smoke-belching warships commanded by Commodore Matthew C. Perry. By a judicious display of force and tact, Perry persuaded the Japanese in 1854 to sign a memorable treaty that proved to be the beginning of an epochal relationship between the two nations.

Sugar-rich Cuba, lying off the nation's southern doorstep, was the prime objective of Manifest Destiny in the 1850s. Supporting a large population of enslaved blacks, it was coveted by the South as the most desirable slave territory available. Carved into several states, it would once more restore the political balance in the Senate.

Cuba was a kind of heirloom—the most important remnant of Spain's once-mighty New World empire. Polk, the expansionist, had offered the Spanish $100 million for Cuba, but they had replied that they would see it sunk into the ocean before they would sell it to the Americans at any price. With purchase out of the question, seizure was apparently the only way to pluck the ripening fruit.

Private adventurers from the South now undertook to shake the tree of Manifest Destiny. During 1850–1851, two "filibustering" expeditions, each numbering several hundred armed men, descended on Cuba. Both feeble efforts were repelled, and fifty of the invaders were summarily shot or strangled.

When Spanish officials in Cuba seized an American steamer in 1854, southern-dominated President Pierce decided to provoke a war with Spain and seize Cuba. An incredible cloak-and-dagger episode followed. The secretary of state instructed the American ministers to Spain, Britain, and France to meet in Ostend, Belgium, and draw up a plan to acquire Cuba. Their top-secret dispatch, known as the "Ostend Manifesto," urged the administration to offer $120 million for Cuba; if Spain refused to sell, the United States would "be justified in wresting" the island from the Spanish.

When the secret Ostend Manifesto leaked out, northern free-soilers rose in an outburst of wrath against the "manifesto of brigands." The red-faced Pierce administration was forced to drop its brazen schemes for Cuba. The shackled black hands of Harriet Beecher Stowe's Uncle Tom, whose plight had already stung the conscience of the North, now held the South back from Cuba.

Pacific Railroad Promoters and the Gadsden Purchase

Acute transportation problems were another legacy of the Mexican War. The newly acquired prizes of California and Oregon might just as well have been islands some eight thousand miles west of the nation's capital. The sea routes to and from the isthmus of Panama, to say nothing of those around South America, were too long. Covered-wagon travel past bleaching animal bones was possible but slow and dangerous. A popular song recalled the formidable trek.

> They swam the wide rivers and crossed the
>   tall peaks,
> And camped on the prairie for weeks upon
>   weeks.
> Starvation and cholera and hard work and
>   slaughter,
> They reached California spite of hell and high
>   water.

Feasible land transportation was imperative—or the newly won possessions on the Pacific Coast might break away. Camels were even introduced to the West as an answer, but a transcontinental railroad was clearly the only real solution to the problem. The South, losing the economic race with the North, was eager to extend a railroad through adjacent southwestern territory all the way to California. The best route across the Southwest ran slightly south of the Mexican border. Secretary of War Jefferson Davis therefore appointed South Carolina railroad man James Gadsden as minister to Mexico. He negotiated a treaty in 1853 that ceded to the United States the Gadsden Pur-

chase area for $10 million. The transaction aroused northern criticism, but the Senate approved the pact.

Southerners now argued that because their proposed rail line ran through the organized New Mexico Territory, the southern route should be built first. Northern railroad boosters quickly replied that if organized territory was the test, then Nebraska, site of the proposed northern route, should also be organized. But southerners in Congress greeted all schemes for organizing Nebraska with apathy or hostility. Why should the South help create new free-soil states and thus cut its own throat by facilitating a northern railroad?

Douglas's Kansas-Nebraska Scheme

At this point in 1854, Senator Stephen A. Douglas of Illinois delivered a counterstroke to offset the Gadsden thrust for southern expansion westward. A squat, bull-necked, and heavy-chested figure, the "Little Giant" radiated the energy and breezy optimism of the self-made man. An ardent booster for the West, he longed to break the North-South deadlock over westward expansion and stretch a line of settlements across the continent. He also had invested heavily in Chicago real estate and in railway stock and was

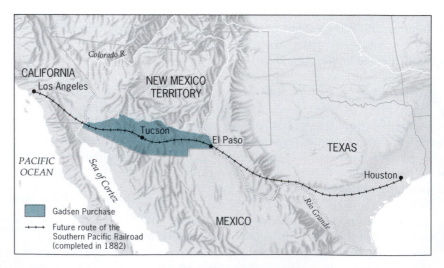

Gadsden Purchase, 1853 *The purchase made possible a southern rail route to the West Coast. But the Southern Pacific railroad (whose route is shown here) was not built until 1882, after the Civil War.*

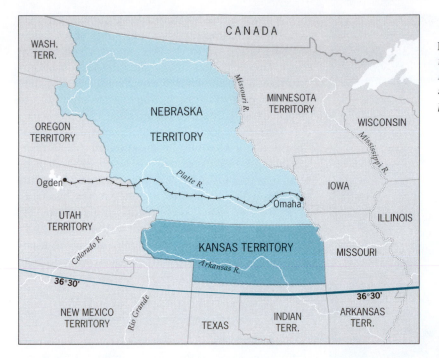

Kansas and Nebraska, 1854 *The route of the future Union Pacific Railroad (completed in 1869) is shown. Notice the Missouri Compromise line of 36°30' (1820).*

eager to have the Windy City become the eastern terminus of the proposed Pacific railroad. He would thus endear himself to Illinois voters, benefit his section, and enrich his own purse.

A veritable "steam engine in breeches," Douglas threw himself behind a legislative scheme that would enlist the support of a reluctant South. The proposed Territory of Nebraska would be carved into two territories, Kansas and Nebraska. Their status regarding slavery would be settled by popular sovereignty—a democratic concept to which Douglas and his western constituents were deeply attached. Kansas, which lay due west of slaveholding Missouri, would presumably choose to become a slave state. But Nebraska, lying west of free-soil Iowa, would presumably become a free state.

Douglas's Kansas-Nebraska scheme ran headlong into a formidable political obstacle. The Missouri Compromise of 1820 had forbidden slavery in the proposed Nebraska Territory, which lay north of the sacred 36° 30' line. The only way to open the region to popular sovereignty was to repeal the ancient compact outright. This bold step Douglas

was prepared to take, even at the risk of shattering the uneasy truce patched together by the Compromise of 1850.

Many southerners, who had not conceived of Kansas as slave soil, rose to the bait. Here was a chance to gain one more slave state. The pliable President Pierce, under the thumb of southern advisers, threw his full weight behind the Kansas-Nebraska Bill.

But the Missouri Compromise, now thirty-four years old, could not be brushed aside lightly. Whatever Congress passes it can repeal, but by this time the North had come to regard the sectional pact as almost as sacred as the Constitution itself. Free-soil members of Congress struck back with a vengeance. They met their match in the violently gesticulating Douglas, who was the ablest rough-and-tumble debater of his generation. Employing twisted logic and oratorical fireworks, he rammed the bill through Congress with strong support from many southerners. So heated were political passions that bloodshed was barely averted. Some members carried a concealed revolver or a bowie knife—or both.

Stephen A. Douglas (1813–1861) *Despite having stirred up sectional bitterness, Douglas was so devoted to the Union that he warmly supported his rival, Lincoln, when war broke out. He attended the inauguration and reportedly held Lincoln's stovepipe hat while the president spoke.*

Douglas's motives in prodding anew the snarling dog of slavery have long puzzled historians. His personal interests have already been mentioned. In addition, his foes accused him of angling for the presidency in 1856. Yet his admirers have argued in his defense that if he had not championed the ill-omened bill, someone else would have.

The truth seems to be that Douglas acted somewhat impulsively and recklessly. His heart did not bleed over the issue of slavery, and he declared repeatedly that he did not care whether it was voted up or down in the territories. What he failed to perceive was that hundreds of thousands of his fellow citizens in the North *did* feel deeply on this moral issue. They regarded the repeal of the Missouri Compromise as an intolerable breach of faith, and they would henceforth resist to the last trench all future southern demands for slave territory.

Genuine leaders, like skillful chess players, must foresee all the possible effects of their moves. Douglas predicted a "hell of a storm," but he grossly underestimated its proportions. His critics in the North, branding him a "Judas" and a "traitor," greeted his name with frenzied boos, hisses, and "three groans for Doug." But he still enjoyed a high degree of popularity among his following in the Democratic party, especially in Illinois, a stronghold of popular sovereignty.

Congress Legislates a Civil War

The Kansas-Nebraska Act—curtain raiser to a terrible drama—was one of the most momentous measures ever to pass Congress. By one way of reckoning, it greased the slippery slope to civil war.

Antislavery northerners were angered by what they condemned as an act of bad faith by the "Nebrascals" and their "Nebrascality." All future compromise with the South would be immeasurably more difficult, and without compromise there was bound to be conflict.

Henceforth the Fugitive Slave Law of 1850, previously enforced in the North only halfheartedly, was a dead letter. The Kansas-Nebraska Act wrecked two compromises: that of 1820, which it repealed specifically, and that of 1850, which northern opinion repealed indirectly. Emerson wrote, "The Fugitive [Slave] Law did much to unglue the eyes of men, and now the Nebraska Bill leaves us staring."

Northern abolitionists and southern "fire-eaters" alike saw less and less they could live with. The growing legion of antislaveryites gained numerous recruits, who resented the grasping move by the "slavocracy" for Kansas. The southerners, in turn, became inflamed when the free-soilers attempted to control Kansas, contrary to the presumed "deal."

The proud Democrats—a party now over half a century old—were shattered by the Kansas-Nebraska

Act. They did elect a president in 1856, but he was the last one they were to boost into the White House for twenty-eight long years.

Undoubtedly the most durable offspring of the Kansas-Nebraska blunder was the new Republican party. It sprang up spontaneously in the Midwest, notably in Wisconsin and Michigan, as a mighty moral protest against the gains of slavery. Gathering together dissatisfied elements, it soon included disgruntled Whigs (among them Abraham Lincoln), Democrats, Free-Soilers, Know-Nothings, and other foes of the Kansas-Nebraska Act. The hodgepodge party spread eastward with the swiftness of a prairie fire and with the zeal of a religious crusade. Unheard of and unheralded at the beginning of 1854, it elected a Republican Speaker of the House of Representatives within two years. Never really a third-party movement, it erupted with such force as to become almost overnight the second major political party—and a purely sectional one at that.

At long last the dreaded sectional rift had appeared. The new Republican party would not be allowed south of the Mason-Dixon line. Countless southerners subscribed wholeheartedly to the sentiment that it was "a nigger stealing, stinking, putrid, abolition party." The Union was in dire peril.

Chronology

1848 Treaty of Guadalupe Hidalgo ends Mexican War.
Taylor defeats Cass and Van Buren for presidency.

1849 California gold rush.
Fillmore assumes presidency after Taylor's death.
Compromise of 1850, including Fugitive Slave Law.
Clayton-Bulwer Treaty with Britain.

1852 Pierce defeats Scott for presidency.

1853 Gadsden Purchase from Mexico.

1854 Commodore Perry "opens" Japan.
"Ostend Manifesto" proposes seizure of Cuba.
Kansas-Nebraska Act.
Republican party organized.

1856 William Walker becomes president of Nicaragua and legalizes slavery.

19

Drifting Toward Disunion

1854–1861

*A house divided against itself cannot stand.
I believe this government cannot endure
permanently half slave and half free.*

ABRAHAM LINCOLN, 1858

The slavery question continued to churn the cauldron of controversy throughout the 1850s. As moral temperatures rose, prospects for a peaceful political solution to the slavery issue simply evaporated. Kansas Territory erupted in violence between pro- and antislavery factions in 1855. Two years later the Supreme Court's *Dred Scott* decision invalidated the Missouri Compromise of 1820, which had imposed a shaky lid on the slavery problem for more than a generation. Attitudes on both sides progressively hardened. When the newly formed Republican party in 1860 elected to the presidency Abraham Lincoln, an outspoken opponent of the further expansion of slavery, the stage was set for all-out civil war.

Stowe and Helper: Literary Incendiaries

Sectional tensions were further strained in 1852, and later, by an inky phenomenon. Harriet Beecher Stowe, a wisp of a woman and the mother of a half-dozen children, published her heart-rending novel *Uncle Tom's Cabin*. Dismayed by the passage of the Fugitive Slave Law, she was determined to awaken the North to the wickedness of slavery by laying bare its terrible inhumanity, especially the cruel splitting of families. Her book was distinguished by powerful imagery and touching pathos. "God wrote it," she explained in later years—a reminder that the sources

Cover of Children's Edition of *Uncle Tom's Cabin*, 1853
Harriet Beecher Stowe's antislavery novel was the all-time bestseller in nineteenth-century America, and the stage version became equally popular.

of her antislavery sentiments lay in the evangelical religious crusades of the Second Great Awakening.

The success of the novel at home and abroad was sensational. Several hundred thousand copies were published in the first year, and the totals soon ran into the millions as the tale was translated into more than a score of languages. It was also put on the stage in "Tom shows" for lengthy runs. No other novel in American history—perhaps in all history—can be compared with it as a political force. To millions of people it made slavery appear almost as evil as it really was.

When Mrs. Stowe was introduced to President Lincoln in 1862, he reportedly remarked, "So you're the little woman who wrote the book that made this great war." The truth is that *Uncle Tom's Cabin* did help start the Civil War—and win it.

Uncle Tom, endearing and enduring, left a profound impression on the North. Thousands of read-ers swore that henceforth they would have nothing to do with the enforcement of the Fugitive Slave Law. The tale was devoured by millions of impressionable youths in the 1850s—some of whom later became the Boys in Blue who volunteered to fight the Civil War through to its grim finale. The memory of a beaten and dying Uncle Tom helped sustain their determination to wipe out the plague of slavery.

Another trouble-brewing book appeared in 1857, five years after the debut of *Uncle Tom*. Entitled *The Impending Crisis of the South*, it was written by Hinton R. Helper, a nonaristocratic white from North Carolina. Hating both slavery and blacks, he attempted to prove by an array of statistics that indirectly the non-slaveholding whites were the ones who suffered most from the millstone of slavery. Helper's book, with its "dirty allusions," was banned in the South, where book-burning parties were held. But in the North thousands of copies, many in condensed form, were distributed as campaign literature by the Republicans.

The North-South Contest for Kansas

The rolling plains of Kansas had meanwhile been providing a horrible example of the worst possible workings of popular sovereignty. Newcomers who ventured into Kansas were a motley lot. Most of the northerners were just ordinary westward-moving pioneers. But a small part of the inflow was financed by groups of northern abolitionists or free-soilers, especially the New England Emigrant Aid Company, which sent about two thousand people to the troubled area to forestall the South—and also to make a profit. Shouting "Ho for Kansas!" many of them carried the deadly new breech-loading Sharps rifles, nicknamed "Beecher's Bibles" after the Reverend Henry Ward Beecher (Harriet Beecher Stowe's brother), who had helped raise money for their purchase. Many of the Kansas-bound pioneers sang Whittier's marching song (1854):

> We cross the prairie as of old
>   The pilgrims crossed the sea,
> To make the West, as they the East,
>   The homestead of the free!

Southern spokesmen, now more than ordinarily touchy, raised furious cries of betrayal. They had supported the Kansas-Nebraska scheme of Douglas with the unspoken understanding that Kansas would become slave and Nebraska free. The northern "Nebrascals" were now apparently out to "abolitionize" both Kansas and Nebraska.

A few southern hotheads, quick to respond in kind, attempted to "assist" small groups of well-armed slaveowners to Kansas. But despite such efforts slavery never took hold in Kansas. The census of 1860 found only 2 slaves among 107,000 souls in all Kansas, and only 15 in Nebraska. There was much truth in the charge that the whole quarrel over slavery in the territories revolved around "an imaginary Negro in an impossible place."

Crisis conditions in Kansas rapidly worsened. When the day came in 1855 to elect members of the first territorial legislature, proslavery "border ruffians" poured in from Missouri to vote early and often. The slavery supporters triumphed and then set up their own puppet government at Shawnee Mission. The free-soilers, unable to stomach this fraudulent conspiracy, established an extralegal regime of their own in Topeka. Confused Kansans thus had their choice between two governments—one based on fraud, the other on illegality. Tensions reached the breaking point in 1856 when a gang of proslavery raiders shot up and burned a part of the free-soil town of Lawrence. This outrage was but the prelude to a bloodier tragedy.

Kansas in Convulsion

The fanatical figure of John Brown now stalked upon the Kansas battlefield. Spare, gray-bearded, and iron-willed, he was obsessively dedicated to the abolitionist cause. The power of his glittering gray eyes was such, so he claimed, that his stare could force a dog or cat to slink out of a room. Brooding over the recent attack on Lawrence, "Old Brown" of Osawatomie led a band of his followers to Pottawatomie Creek, in May 1856. There they literally hacked to pieces five surprised men, presumed to be proslaveryites. This fiendish butchery brought vicious retaliation from proslavery forces. Civil war in Kansas thus flared forth in 1856 and continued intermittently until it merged with the large-scale Civil War of 1861–1865.

The proslavery forces intensified the conflict in 1857 when they attempted to bring Kansas into the Union under a tricky document known as the Lecompton Constitution. Although the majority of

Bleeding Kansas, 1854–1860   *"Enter every election district in Kansas . . . and vote at the point of a bowie knife or revolver,"* one proslavery agitator exhorted a Missouri crowd. Proslavery Missouri senator David Atchison declared that *"there are 1,100 men coming over from Platte County to vote, and if that ain't enough we can send 5,000— enough to kill every Goddamned abolitionist in the Territory."*

SOUTHERN CHIVALRY — ARGUMENT versus CLUB'S.

Sumner Beaten by Brooks
Notice that the cartoonist has two of the senators smiling or laughing and one of them preventing interference with his cane. Notice also that Sumner is defending himself with a quill pen while Brooks is wielding a club.

Kansans were free-soilers, the vote on the proposed constitution was arranged so that it was impossible to prohibit all black bondage and still obtain statehood. With infuriated free-soilers boycotting the election, the slaveryites approved the constitution with slavery late in 1857.

The new president, James Buchanan, was just as much under southern influence as President Pierce had been, and he threw the weight of his administration behind the notorious Lecompton Constitution. But Senator Douglas, who had championed true popular sovereignty, would have none of this semipopular fraudulency. Deliberately tossing away his strong support in the South for the presidency, he fought courageously to obtain a fair popular vote on the entire Lecompton Constitution. The free-soil voters thereupon snowed it under at the polls, ending Kansas's hopes for statehood until 1861, when the southern secessionists left Congress.

President Buchanan, by antagonizing the numerous Douglas Democrats in the North, hopelessly divided the once-powerful Democratic party. Until then, it had been the only remaining national party, for the Whigs were dead and the Republicans were sectional. With the disruption of the Democrats came the snapping of one of the last important strands in the rope that was barely binding the Union together.

"Bully" Brooks and His Bludgeon

"Bleeding Kansas" also splattered blood on the floor of the Senate in 1856. Tall and imposing Senator Charles Sumner of Massachusetts delivered a blistering speech entitled "The Crime Against Kansas," in which he condemned proslavery men as "hirelings picked from the drunken spew and vomit of an uneasy civilization." The speech also insulted white-haired Senator Andrew Butler of South Carolina.

Butler's hot-tempered distant cousin, South Carolina congressman Preston Brooks, took vengeance into his own hands. On May 22, 1856, he approached Sumner, then sitting at his Senate desk, and pounded the orator with an eleven-ounce cane until it broke. The victim fell bleeding and unconscious to the floor, suffering serious injuries to his head and nervous system.

Bleeding Sumner was thus joined with bleeding Kansas as a political issue. South Carolina triumphantly reelected Brooks, and Massachusetts defiantly did the same for Sumner, even though the battered abolitionist was unable to take his seat for over three years. Meanwhile, Sumner's abusive speech sold by the thousands in the North, while southern admirers deluged Brooks with canes to replace the one he had broken over Sumner's head.

The Sumner-Brooks clash and the ensuing reactions revealed how dangerously inflamed passions were becoming, North and South. It was ominous that the cultured Sumner should have used the language of a barroom bully and that the gentlemanly Brooks should have employed the tactics and tools of a thug. Emotion was displacing thought. The blows rained on Sumner's head were, broadly speaking, among the first blows of the Civil War.

"Old Buck" Versus "The Pathfinder"

With bullets whining in Kansas, Democrats met in Cincinnati to nominate their presidential standard-bearer of 1856. Both weak-kneed President Pierce and dynamic Senator Douglas were too indelibly tainted by the Kansas-Nebraska Act, so the delegates finally turned to a well-to-do Pennsylvania lawyer, James Buchanan, who had been serving as minister to London during the recent Kansas-Nebraska uproar. Although his "Kansasless" neutrality made him acceptable to the party, "Old Buck" was mediocre, irresolute, and confused.

The fast-growing Republican party, meeting in Philadelphia, passed over "Higher Law" Senator William Seward, their most conspicuous leader, and instead chose John C. Frémont, a dashing but erratic explorer-soldier-surveyor. Republicans hoped that the "Pathfinder of the West" would blaze them a path to the White House. Vigorously condemning the extension of slavery into the territories, Republicans sang,

> Arise, arise ye brave!
> And let our war-cry be
> Free speech, free press, free soil, free men,
> Fré-mont and victory!

The bland Buchanan, although polling less than a majority of the popular vote, won handily. His tally in the Electoral College was 174 to 114 for Frémont, with former president Millard Fillmore garnering 8 on the anti-immigrant American party ticket. The popular vote was 1,832,955 for Buchanan to 1,339,932 for Frémont, with 871,731 for Fillmore.

Democrats had carried the hapless "Old Buck" into office, but the Republicans could rightfully claim a "victorious defeat" in 1856. The new party—a mere two-year-old toddler—had made an astonishing showing against the well-oiled Democratic machine. John Greenleaf Whittier pointedly asked,

> Then sound again the bugles,
> Call the muster-roll anew;
> If months have well-nigh won the field,
> What may not four years do?

That question cast a long shadow forward, as politicians, North and South, peered anxiously toward 1860.

The *Dred Scott* Bombshell

The *Dred Scott* decision, handed down by the Supreme Court on March 6, 1857, abruptly ended the two-day presidential honeymoon of the unlucky bachelor, James Buchanan. Basically, the case was simple. Dred Scott, a black slave, had lived with his master for five years in Illinois and Wisconsin Territory. Backed by interested abolitionists, he sued for freedom on the basis of his long residence on free soil.

The Supreme Court proceeded to turn a simple legal case into a complex political issue. It ruled, not surprisingly, that Dred Scott was a black slave and not a citizen, and hence could not sue in federal courts.* The tribunal could then have thrown out the case on these technical grounds alone. But a majority decided to go further, under the leadership of Chief Justice Roger Taney from the slave state of Maryland.

Taney's sweeping judgment on the larger question of slavery rocked the free-soilers back on their heels. A majority of the Court decreed that because a slave was private property, he or she could be taken into *any* territory and legally held there in slavery. The reasoning was that the Fifth Amendment clearly forbade Congress to deprive people of their property without due process of law. The Court, to be consistent, went further. The 1820 Missouri Compromise,

---

* This part of the ruling, denying blacks their citizenship, seriously menaced the precarious position of the South's quarter-million free blacks.

banning slavery north of 36° 30', had been repealed three years earlier by the Kansas-Nebraska Act, but its spirit was still venerated in the North. Now the Court ruled that the Compromise of 1820 had been unconstitutional all along: Congress had no power to ban slavery from the territories, regardless even of what the territorial legislatures might want.

Southerners were delighted with this unexpected victory. Champions of popular sovereignty, including Senator Douglas and most northern Democrats, were aghast. Another lethal wedge was thus driven between the northern and southern wings of the once-united Democratic party.

Foes of slavery extension, led by the Republicans, were infuriated by the *Dred Scott* setback. Especially because a majority of the Supreme Court justices were southerners, Republicans considered the opinion purely political and declared it no more binding than the views of a "southern debating society." Southerners in turn wondered how long they could remain joined to a section that refused to honor the Supreme Court, to say nothing of the constitutional compact that had established it.

The Financial Crash of 1857

Bitterness caused by the *Dred Scott* decision was deepened by hard times, which dampened a period of feverish prosperity. Late in 1857, a financial panic burst about Buchanan's harassed head. The crisis was not so bad economically as the panic of 1837, but psychologically it was probably the worst of the nineteenth century.

The North, including its grain growers, was hardest hit. The South, enjoying favorable cotton prices abroad, rode out the storm with flying colors. Panic conditions seemed further proof that cotton was king, and that its economic kingdom was stronger than that of the North. This fatal delusion helped drive the overconfident southerners closer to a shooting showdown.

Financial distress in the North, especially in agriculture, gave new vigor to the demand for free farms of 160 acres from the public domain. Overcoming the objections of both eastern industrialists and southern slaveholders, Congress in 1860 finally passed a home-stead act that made public lands available at the nominal sum of twenty-five cents an acre. But it was stabbed to death by the veto pen of Buchanan, near whose elbows sat leading southern sympathizers.

The panic of 1857 also created a clamor for higher tariff rates. The Tariff of 1857 had lowered duties to about 20 percent, but hardly had the revised rates been placed on the books when the financial distress descended like a black pall. Northern manufacturers noisily blamed their misfortunes on the low tariff and clamored for increased protection. Thus the panic of 1857 gave the Republicans two surefire issues for 1860: protection for the unprotected and farms for the farmless.

An Illinois Rail-Splitter Emerges

The Illinois senatorial election of 1858 now claimed the national spotlight. Senator Douglas's term was about to expire, and the Republicans decided to run against him a rustic Springfield lawyer, one Abraham Lincoln. The Republican candidate—6 feet, 4 inches in height and 180 pounds in weight—presented an awkward but arresting figure. Lincoln's legs, arms, and neck were grotesquely long; his head was crowned by coarse, black, and unruly hair; and his face was sad, sunken, and weather-beaten.

Lincoln was no silver-spoon child of the elite. Born in 1809 in a Kentucky log cabin to impoverished parents, he attended a frontier school for not more than a year; being an avid reader, he was mainly self-educated. All his life he said "git," "thar," and "heered." Although narrow-chested and somewhat stoop-shouldered, he shone in his frontier community as a wrestler and weight lifter, and spent some time, among other pioneering pursuits, as a splitter of logs for fence rails. A superb teller of earthy and amusing stories, he would oddly enough plunge into protracted periods of melancholy.

Lincoln's private and professional life was not especially noteworthy. He married "above himself" socially, into the influential Todd family of Kentucky. After reading a little law, he gradually emerged as one of the dozen or so better-known trial lawyers in Illinois, although still accustomed to carrying important papers in his stovepipe hat. He was widely referred to as "Honest Abe," partly because he would refuse cases that he had to suspend his conscience to defend.

The rise of Lincoln as a political figure was less than rocketlike. After making his mark in the Illinois legislature as a Whig politician of the logrolling variety, he served one undistinguished term in Congress, 1847–1849. Until 1854, when he was forty-five years of age, he had done nothing to establish a claim to statesmanship. But the passage of the Kansas-Nebraska Act in that year lighted within him unexpected fires. After mounting the Republican bandwagon, he emerged as one of the foremost politicians and orators of the Northwest. At the Philadelphia convention of 1856, where Frémont was nominated, Lincoln actually received 110 votes for the vice-presidential nomination.

The Great Debate: Lincoln Versus Douglas

Lincoln, as Republican nominee for the Senate seat, boldly challenged Douglas to a series of joint debates. This was a rash act because the stumpy senator was probably the nation's most devastating debater. Douglas promptly accepted Lincoln's challenge, and seven meetings were arranged from August to October 1858.

The most famous debate came at Freeport, Illinois, where Lincoln neatly impaled his opponent on the horns of a dilemma. Suppose, he queried, the people of a territory should vote slavery down? The Supreme Court in the *Dred Scott* decision had decreed that they could not. Who would prevail, the Court or the people?

Douglas's reply, which came to be known as the "Freeport Doctrine," was that no matter how the Supreme Court ruled, slavery would stay down if the people voted it down. Laws to protect slavery would have to be passed by the territorial legislatures. These would not be forthcoming in the absence of popular approval, and black bondage would soon disappear.

The upshot was that Douglas defeated Lincoln for the Senate seat. The "Little Giant's" loyalty to popular sovereignty, which still had a powerful appeal in Illinois, probably was decisive. But Douglas, in winning Illinois, had further split his splintering Democratic party. After his opposition to the Lecompton Constitution for Kansas, and his further defiance of the Supreme Court at Freeport, southern Democrats were determined to break up the party (and the Union) rather than accept him. For his part, Lincoln lost the election but shambled into the national limelight as a leading northern spokesman and potential Republican nominee for president. The Lincoln-Douglas debate platform thus proved to be one of the preliminary battlefields of the Civil War.

John Brown: Murderer or Martyr?

The gaunt, grim figure of John Brown of Kansas infamy now appeared again in an even more terrible way. His crackbrained scheme was to invade the South secretly with a handful of followers, call upon the slaves to rise, furnish them with arms, and establish a kind of black free state as a sanctuary. Brown secured several thousand dollars for firearms from

Lincoln and Douglas Debate, 1858
Thousands attended each of the seven Lincoln-Douglas debates. Douglas is shown here sitting to Lincoln's right in the debate at Charleston, Illinois, in September. On one occasion, Lincoln quipped that Douglas's logic would prove that a horse chestnut was a chestnut horse.

northern abolitionists and finally arrived in hilly western Virginia with some twenty men. He seized the federal arsenal at scenic Harpers Ferry in October 1859, incidentally killing seven innocent people, including a free black, and injuring ten or so more. But the slaves failed to rise, and the wounded Brown and the remnants of his tiny band were quickly captured by U.S. Marines. "Old Brown" was convicted of murder and treason, after a hasty but legal trial.

But Brown—"God's angry man"—was given every opportunity to pose and to enjoy martyrdom. Though probably of unsound mind, he was clever enough to see that he was worth much more to the abolitionist cause dangling from a rope than in any other way. So the hangman's trap was sprung, and Brown plunged not into oblivion but into world fame. A memorable marching song of the impending Civil War ran,

> John Brown's body lies a-mould'ring in the
> grave,
> His soul is marching on.

The effects of Harpers Ferry were calamitous. In the eyes of the South, already embittered, "Osawatomie Brown" was a wholesale murderer and an apostle of treason. Many southerners asked how they could possibly remain in the Union while a "murderous gang of abolitionists" were financing armed bands to "Brown" them. Moderate northerners, including Republican leaders, openly deplored this mad exploit. But the South naturally concluded that the violent abolitionist view was shared by the entire North, dominated by "Brown-loving" Republicans.

Abolitionists and other ardent free-soilers were infuriated by Brown's execution. On the day of his hanging, free-soil centers in the North tolled bells, fired guns, lowered flags, and held mass meetings. Some spoke of "Saint John" Brown, and Ralph Waldo Emerson compared the new martyr-hero with Jesus. The gallows became a cross. E. C. Steman wrote,

> And Old Brown,
> Osawatomie Brown,
> May trouble you more than ever
> When you've nailed his coffin down!

The ghost of the martyred Brown would not be laid to rest.

Democrats Divide and Republicans Rise

Beyond question the presidential election of 1860 was the most fateful in American history. Deeply divided, the Democrats met in Charleston, South Carolina. Northern Democrats looked to Douglas as their leader, but southern "fire-eaters" regarded him as a traitor. After a bitter platform fight, cotton-state delegates walked out of the convention. The southerners' departure from the Democratic convention was the first tragic act of secession. Departure became habit forming.

The Democrats tried again in Baltimore. With northern Douglas Democrats firmly in the saddle, the cotton-state delegates again took a walk, and the rest of the convention enthusiastically nominated their hero. Angered southern Democrats promptly organized a rival convention in Baltimore and selected as their nominee the stern-jawed vice president, John C. Breckinridge, from the border state of Kentucky. Their platform favored the extension of slavery into the territories and the annexation of slave-populated Cuba.

A middle-of-the-road group, fearing for the Union, hastily organized the Constitutional Union party. It consisted mainly of former Whigs and Know-Nothings. This "gathering of graybeards" met in Baltimore and nominated John Bell of Tennessee for the presidency on a platform of "the Union, the Constitution, and the enforcement of the law."

With their opponents hopelessly split into three factions, elated Republicans scented victory in the breeze. The best known of the contenders at their convention in Chicago was William H. Seward. But Seward's radical utterances, including his "irrepressible conflict" speech at Rochester in 1858,* had ruined his prospects. Lincoln, the favorite son of Illinois, was a stronger candidate because he had made fewer enemies than Seward. Overtaking Seward on the third ballot, he was nominated amid scenes of wild excitement.

---

* Seward had referred to an "irrepressible conflict" between slavery and freedom, though not necessarily a bloody one.

The Republican platform had a seductive appeal for almost every important nonsouthern group: for the free-soilers, the nonextension of slavery; for northern manufacturers, a protective tariff; for immigrants, no abridgment of rights; and for westerners and farmers, internal improvements and free homesteads at federal expense.

Southern secessionists promptly served notice that the election of the "baboon" Lincoln would split the Union. In fact, "Honest Abe," though hating slavery, was no outright abolitionist. He campaigned quietly and issued no new statements in response to these threats. The most active opposition to southern extremism came from the "Little Giant" Douglas, who waged a vigorous speaking campaign, even in the South, and threatened to put the rope with his own hands around the neck of the first secessionist.

The returns, breathlessly awaited, proclaimed a sweeping victory for Lincoln (see map, p. 263).

The Electoral Upheaval of 1860

Awkward "Abe" Lincoln had run a curious race. To a greater degree than any other holder of the nation's highest office (except John Quincy Adams), he was a minority president. Sixty percent of the voters preferred some other candidate. He was also a sectional president, for in ten southern states, where he was not allowed on the ballot, he polled no popular votes. The election of 1860 was virtually two elections: one in the North, the other in the South. South Carolinians rejoiced over Lincoln's victory; they now had their excuse to secede. In winning the North the "rail-splitter" had split off the South.

Douglas, though scraping together only twelve electoral votes, made an impressive showing. He drew important strength from all sections and ranked a fairly close second in the popular-vote column. In fact, the Douglas Democrats and the Breckinridge Democrats together amassed 366,484 more popular votes than did Lincoln. But contrary to myth, Lincoln's electoral vote victory did not occur because his opponents were divided. Even if all the Democrats and Constitutional Unionists had united behind Douglas, Lincoln would have carried the populous northern states and therefore would still have won the electoral vote 169 to 134 instead of 180 to 123.

Significantly, the verdict of the ballot box did not indicate a strong sentiment for secession. Breckinridge, while favoring the extension of slavery, was no disunionist. Although the candidate of the "fire-eaters," he polled fewer votes in the slave states than Douglas and Bell combined. Despite its electoral defeat, the South was not badly off. Southerners still controlled the Supreme Court, both houses of Congress, and more than enough states to block any attempt to end slavery by constitutional amendment.

The Secessionist Exodus

But a tragic chain reaction of secession now began to erupt. South Carolina had threatened to go out if the "Illinois baboon" were elected, and in December 1860 a special convention called by the legislature carried out the threat by voting unanimously to secede. During the next six weeks, six other states of the Lower South followed the leader over the precipice: Alabama, Mississippi, Florida, Georgia, Louisiana, and Texas. Four more were to join them later, bringing the total to eleven.

With the eyes of destiny upon them, the seven seceders, formally meeting in Montgomery, Alabama, in February 1861, created a government known as the Confederate States of America. As their president they chose Jefferson Davis, a dignified and austere former secretary of war and recent U.S. senator from Mississippi.

The crisis, already critical enough, was deepened by the "lame duck"* interlude. Lincoln, although elected president in November 1860, could not take office until four months later, March 4, 1861. During this protracted period, when he was still a private citizen, Lincoln watched seven of the deserting states pull out of the Union.

---

*The lame duck period was shortened to ten weeks in 1933 by the Twentieth Amendment (see the Appendix).

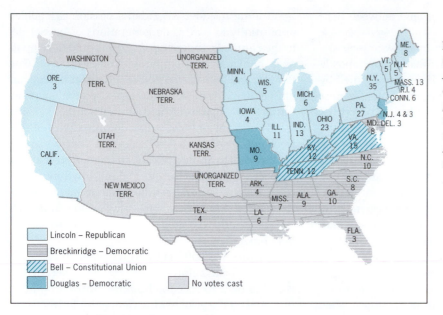

Presidential Election of 1860 (with electoral vote by state) *A surprising fact is that Lincoln, often rated among the greatest presidents, ranks near the bottom in percentage of popular votes. In all eleven states that seceded, he received only a scattering of one state's votes—about 1.5 percent in Virginia.*

Map legend:
- Lincoln – Republican
- Breckinridge – Democratic
- Bell – Constitutional Union
- Douglas – Democratic
- No votes cast

Meanwhile, aging President Buchanan chose to wring his hands rather than secessionist necks. Surrounded by prosouthern advisers, Buchanan found constitutional and practical justifications for inaction. One reason for not resorting to force was that the tiny standing army of fifteen thousand men was widely scattered, fighting Indians in the West. Public opinion in the North, at that time, was far from willing to unsheathe the sword. Fighting would merely shatter all prospects of adjustment, and until the guns began to boom, there was still a flickering hope of reconciliation rather than a contested divorce. The weakness lay not so much in Buchanan as in the Constitution and in the Union itself. Ironically, when Lincoln became president in March, he essentially continued Buchanan's wait-and-see policy.

A Failed Compromise and Secession

Impending bloodshed spurred final and frantic attempts at compromise, most notably by Senator James Henry Crittenden of Kentucky. Crittenden proposed several constitutional amendments designed to appease the South. Slavery in the territories was to be prohibited north of 36°30', but south of that line it was to be given federal protection in all territories existing or "hereafter to be acquired" (such as Cuba). Future states, north or south of 36°30', could come into the Union with or without slavery, as they should choose. In short, the slavery supporters were to be guaranteed full rights in the southern territories, as long as they were territories, regardless of the wishes of the majority under popular sovereignty. Federal protection in a territory south of 36°30' might conceivably, though improbably, turn the entire area permanently to slavery.

Lincoln flatly rejected the Crittenden scheme, which offered some slight prospect of success, and all hope of compromise evaporated. For this refusal he must bear a heavy responsibility. Yet he had been elected on a platform that opposed the extension of slavery, and he felt that as a matter of principle he could not afford to yield, even though gains for slavery in the territories might be only temporary. Larger gains might come later in Cuba and Latin America. Crittenden's proposal, said Lincoln, "would amount to a perpetual covenant of war against every people, tribe, and state owning a foot of land between here and Tierra del Fuego."

Secessionists who parted company with their sister states left for a number of avowed reasons, mostly relating in some way to slavery. They were alarmed by the inexorable tipping of the political balance against them—"the despotic majority of numbers." The "crime" of the North, observed James Russell Lowell, was the census returns. Southerners were also dismayed by the triumph of the new sectional Republican party, which seemed to threaten their rights as a slaveholding minority. They were weary of free-soil criticism, abolitionist nagging, and northern interference, ranging from the Underground Railroad to John Brown's raid. "All we ask is to be let alone," declared President Jefferson Davis in an early message to his congress.

Many southerners supported secession because they felt sure that their departure would be unopposed, despite "Yankee yawp" to the contrary. They were confident that the clodhopping and codfishing Yankee would not or could not fight. They also believed that northern manufacturers and bankers, so heavily dependent on southern cotton and markets, would not dare to cut their own economic throats with their own swords.

Southern leaders regarded secession as a golden opportunity to cast aside generations of "vassalage" to the North. An independent Dixie could develop its own banking and shipping, trade directly with Europe, and forever rid itself of the threat of high tariffs. For decades these issues had pitted the manufacturing North against the agricultural South.

The principles of self-determination—of the Declaration of Independence—seemed to many southerners to apply perfectly to them. Few, if any, of the seceders felt that they were doing anything wrong or immoral. The thirteen original states had voluntarily entered the Union and now seven—ultimately eleven—southern states were voluntarily withdrawing from it.

Historical parallels ran even deeper. In 1776 thirteen American colonies, led by the rebel George Washington, had seceded from the British Empire by throwing off the yoke of King George III. In 1860–1861 eleven American states, led by the rebel Jefferson Davis, were seceding from the Union by throwing off the yoke of "King" Abraham Lincoln. With that burden gone, the South was confident that it could work out its own peculiar destiny more quietly, happily, and prosperously.

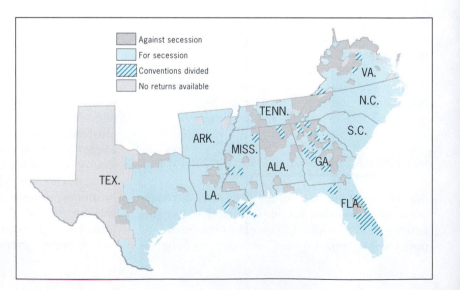

Southern Opposition to Secession, 1860–1861 (showing vote by county)   *This county vote shows the opposition of the antiplanter, antislavery mountain whites in the Appalachian region. There was also considerable resistance to secession in Texas, where Governor Sam Houston, who led the Unionists, was deposed by secessionist hotheads.*

Against secession
For secession
Conventions divided
No returns available

VA.
N.C.
TENN.
ARK.
S.C.
MISS.
ALA.
GA.
TEX.
LA.
FLA.

Chronology

1852 Harriet Beecher Stowe publishes *Uncle Tom's Cabin*.

1854 Kansas-Nebraska Act.
Republican party forms.

1856 Buchanan defeats Frémont and Fillmore for presidency.
Sumner beaten by Brooks in Senate chamber.
Brown's Pottawatomie massacre.

1856–1860 Civil war in "bleeding Kansas."

1857 *Dred Scott* decision.
Lecompton Constitution rejected.
Panic of 1857.
Hinton R. Helper publishes *The Impending Crisis of the South*.

1858 Lincoln-Douglas debates.

1859 Brown raids Harpers Ferry.

1860 Lincoln wins four-way race for presidency.
South Carolina secedes from the Union.
Crittenden Compromise fails.

1861 Seven seceding states form the Confederate States of America.

VARYING VIEWPOINTS

The Civil War: Repressible or Irrepressible?

Few topics have generated as much controversy among American historians as the causes of the Civil War. Interpretations of the great conflict have naturally differed according to section and have been charged with emotional and moral fervor. Yet despite long and keen interest in the origins of the conflict, the causes of the Civil War remain as passionately debated today as they were a century ago.

In the early twentieth century, progressive historians like Charles and Mary Beard challenged the dominant nationalist school that believed slavery caused the Civil War. The Beards argued that the war was not fought over slavery per se but rather was a deeply rooted economic struggle between an industrial North and an agricultural South. Anointing the Civil War "the Second American Revolution," the Beards claimed that the war transferred the dominant class power in America from the southern plantation aristocracy to the rising class of northern industrialists.

Shaken by the disappointing results of World War I, a new wave of historians argued that the Civil War, too, had actually been a big mistake. James G. Randall and Avery Craven asserted that the war had been a "repressible conflict," and they attributed the bloody confrontation to overzealous reformers and blundering political leaders.

After the Second World War, however, historians again began depicting the Civil War as an unavoidable conflict between two societies, one slave and one free. For Allan Nevins and David M. Potter, irreconcilable differences in morality, politics, culture, social values, and economic systems increasingly eroded the ties between the sections and set the United States on the road to Civil War. Going further, Eric Foner and Eugene Genovese emphasize each section's nearly paranoid fear that the survival of its way of life was threatened by the other section. Foner emphasizes that most northerners detested slavery not because it enslaved blacks but because it threatened the position of free white laborers. Genovese argues that the South, convinced that its labor system was superior to the northern factory system, believed the North had designs to destroy its way of life.

More recently, historians of the "ethnocultural school," especially Michael Holt, offer a new analysis of how the collapse of the two established political parties caused the Civil War. They note that the two great political parties had earlier muted sectional differences over slavery by focusing on issues such as the tariff, banking, and internal improvements. According to this argument, it was the temporary consensus on almost all national issues other than slavery that enabled the slavery issue to dominate politics. Slavery fueled the rise of purely regional parties that saw their political opponents as threats to their way of life and to the Republic itself.

20

Girding for War: The North and the South

1861–1865

*I consider the central idea pervading this struggle is the
necessity that is upon us, of proving that popular government
is not an absurdity. We must settle this question now, whether in
a free government the minority have the right to break up the
government whenever they choose. If we fail it will go far to
prove the incapability of the people to govern themselves.*

ABRAHAM LINCOLN, MAY 7, 1861

Abraham Lincoln solemnly took the presidential oath of office on March 4, 1861, after having slipped into Washington at night, partially disguised to thwart assassins. He thus became president not of the *United* States of America, but of the *disunited* states of America. Seven had already departed; eight more teetered on the edge. The girders of the unfinished Capitol dome loomed nakedly in the background, as if to symbolize the imperfect state of the Union. Before the nation was restored—and the slaves freed at last—the American people would endure four years of anguish and bloodshed, and Lincoln would face tortuous trials of leadership such as have been visited on few presidents.

The Menace of Secession

Lincoln's inaugural address was firm yet conciliatory: there would be no conflict unless the South provoked it. Secession, the president declared, was wholly impractical because, "Physically speaking, we cannot separate."

Here Lincoln put his finger on a profound geographical truth. The North and South were bound inseparably together. If they had been divided by the Pyrenees Mountains or the Danube River, a sectional divorce might have been more feasible. But the Appalachian Mountains and the mighty Mississippi River both ran the wrong way.

The Stink of Secession *Passions ran high in the North against the crime of "secesh."*

"Whew! That Old Hen, JEFF DAVIS, has been trying to hatch a Rotten Egg."

Uncontested secession would create new controversies. What share of the national debt should the South be forced to take with it? What portion of the jointly held federal territories, if any, should the Confederate states be allotted—areas largely won with Southern blood? How would the fugitive-slave issue be resolved? The Underground Railroad would certainly redouble its activity, and it would have to transport its passengers only across the Ohio River, not all the way to Canada. Was it conceivable that all such problems could have been solved without ugly armed clashes?

A united United States had hitherto been the paramount republic in the Western Hemisphere. If this powerful democracy broke into two hostile nations, the European nations would be delighted. They could gleefully transplant to America their ancient concept of the balance of power. Playing the no less ancient game of divide and conquer, they could incite one snarling fragment of the dis–United States against the other. The colonies of the European powers in the New World, notably those of Britain, would thus be made safer against the rapacious Yankees. And European imperialists, with no unified republic to stand across their path, could more easily defy the Monroe Doctrine and seize territory in the Americas.

South Carolina Assails Fort Sumter

The issue of the divided Union came to a head over the matter of federal forts in the South. As the seceding states left, they seized the United States arsenals, mints, and other public property within their borders. When Lincoln took office, only two significant forts in the South still flew the Stars and Stripes. The more important of the pair was square-walled Fort Sumter, in Charleston harbor, with fewer than a hundred men.

Ominously, the choices presented to Lincoln by Fort Sumter were all bad. This stronghold had provisions that would last only a few weeks—until the middle of April 1861. If no supplies were forthcoming, its commander would have to surrender without firing a shot. Lincoln, quite understandably, did not feel that such a weak-kneed course squared with his obligation to protect federal property. But if he sent reinforcements, the South Carolinians would undoubtedly fight back; they could not tolerate a federal fort blocking the mouth of their most important Atlantic seaport.

After agonizing indecision, Lincoln adopted a middle-of-the-road solution. He notified the South Carolinians that an expedition would be sent to provision the garrison, though not to reinforce it. But to Southern eyes "provision" spelled "reinforcement."

A Union naval force next started on its way to Fort Sumter—a move that the South regarded as an act of aggression. On April 12, 1861, the cannon of the Carolinians opened fire on the fort while crowds in Charleston applauded and waved handkerchiefs. After a thirty-four-hour bombardment, which took no lives, the dazed garrison surrendered.

The shelling of the fort electrified the North, which at once responded with cries of "Remember Fort Sumter!" and "Save the Union!" Earlier, countless Northerners had been saying that if the Southern states wanted to go, they should not be pinned to the rest of the nation with bayonets. "Wayward sisters, depart in peace" was a common sentiment. But the assault on Fort Sumter provoked the North to a fighting pitch: the fort was lost, but the Union was saved.

Lincoln had turned a tactical defeat into a strategic victory. Southerners had wantonly fired on the glorious Stars and Stripes, and honor demanded an armed response. Lincoln promptly (April 15) issued a call to the states for seventy-five thousand militiamen; and volunteers sprang to the colors in such enthusiastic numbers that many were turned away— a mistake not often repeated. On April 19 and 27 the president proclaimed a leaky blockade of Southern seaports.

The call for troops, in turn, aroused the South much as the attack on Fort Sumter had aroused the North. Lincoln was now waging war—from the Southern view an aggressive war—on the Confederacy. Virginia, Arkansas, and Tennessee, all of which had earlier voted down secession, reluctantly joined their embattled sister states, as did North Carolina. Thus the seven states became eleven as the "submissionists" and "Union shriekers" were overcome. Richmond, Virginia, replaced Montgomery, Alabama, as the Confederate capital.

Brothers' Blood and Border Blood

The only slave states left were the crucial Border States. This group consisted of Missouri, Kentucky, Maryland, Delaware, and later West Virginia—the "mountain white" area that somewhat illegally uprooted itself from Virginia in mid-1861. If the North had fired the first shot, some or all of these doubtful states probably would have seceded, and the South might well have succeeded. The Border group actually boasted a white population more than half that of the entire Confederacy. Lincoln reportedly said that he *hoped* to have God on his side but he *had* to have Kentucky.

In dealing with the Border States, President Lincoln used methods of dubious legality. In Maryland he declared martial law where needed and sent in troops because this state threatened to cut off Washington from the North. Lincoln also deployed Union soldiers in western Virginia and notably in Missouri, where they fought beside Unionists in a local civil war within the larger Civil War.

Any official statement of the North's war aims was profoundly influenced by the teetering Border States. At the very outset, Lincoln was obliged to declare publicly that he was not fighting to free the blacks. An antislavery declaration would no doubt have driven the Border States into the welcoming arms of the South. Lincoln insisted repeatedly—even though undercutting his high moral ground—that his paramount purpose was to save the Union at all costs. Thus the war began not as one between slave soil and free soil, but one for the Union—with slaveholders on both sides and many proslavery sympathizers in the North.

Slavery also colored the character of the war in the West. In the Indian Territory (present-day Oklahoma), most of the Five Civilized Tribes—the Cherokees, Creeks, Choctaws, Chickasaws, and Seminoles—sided with the Confederacy. Some of these Indians, notably the Cherokees, owned slaves and thus felt themselves to be making common cause with the slaveowning South. These Native Americans sent delegates to the Confederate congress and supplied troops to the Confederate army. A rival faction of Cherokees and most of the Plains Indians, however, sided with the Union.

Unhappily, the conflict between "Billy Yank" and "Johnny Reb" was a brothers' war. There were many Northern volunteers from the Southern states, and many Southern volunteers from the Northern states. The "mountain whites" of the South sent north some 50,000 men, and the loyal slave states contributed some 300,000 soldiers to the Union. In many a family

Seceding States (with dates and order of secession)

Notice the long interval—nearly six months—between the secession of South Carolina, the first state to go, and that of Tennessee, the last state to leave the Union. These six months were a time of terrible trial for moderate Southerners. When a Georgia statesman pleaded for restraint and negotiations with Washington, he was rebuffed with the cry, "Throw the bloody spear into this den of incendiaries!"

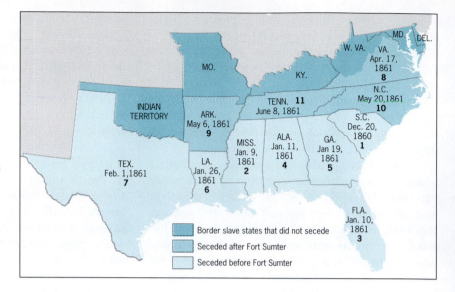

- Border slave states that did not secede
- Seceded after Fort Sumter
- Seceded before Fort Sumter

of the Border States, one brother rode north to fight with the Blue, another south to fight with the Gray. Senator Crittenden of Kentucky, who fathered the abortive Crittenden Compromise, fathered two sons: one became a general in the Union army, the other a general in the Confederate army.

The Balance of Forces

When war broke out, the South seemed to have great advantages. The Confederacy could fight defensively behind interior lines. The North had to invade the vast territory of the Confederacy, conquer it, and drag it bodily back into the Union. In fact, the South did not have to win the war in order to win its independence. If it merely fought the invaders to a draw and stood firm, Confederate independence would be won. Fighting on their own soil for self-determination and preservation of their way of life, Southerners at first enjoyed an advantage in morale as well.

Militarily, the South from the opening volleys of the war had the most talented officers. Most conspicuous among a dozen or so first-rate commanders was gray-haired General Robert E. Lee, whose knightly bearing and chivalric sense of honor embodied the Southern ideal. Lincoln had unofficially offered him the command of the Northern armies, but when Vir-

ginia seceded Lee felt honor-bound to go with his native state. Lee's chief lieutenant for much of the war was black-bearded Thomas J. ("Stonewall") Jackson, a gifted tactical theorist and a master of speed and deception.

Besides their brilliant leaders, ordinary Southerners were also bred to fight. Accustomed to managing horses and bearing arms from boyhood, they made excellent cavalrymen and foot soldiers. Their high-pitched rebel yell ("yeeeahhh") was designed to strike terror into the hearts of fuzz-chinned Yankee recruits.

As one immense farm, the South seemed to be handicapped by the scarcity of its factories. Yet by seizing federal weapons, running Union blockades, and developing their own ironworks, Southerners managed to obtain sufficient weaponry. "Yankee ingenuity" was not confined to Yankees.

Nevertheless, as the war dragged on, grave shortages of shoes, uniforms, and blankets afflicted the South. Even with immense stores of food on Southern farms, civilians and soldiers often went hungry because of supply problems. "Forward, men! They have cheese in their haversacks," cried one Southern officer as he attacked the Yankees. Much of the hunger was caused by a breakdown of the South's rickety transportation system, especially where the railroad tracks were cut or destroyed by the Yankee invaders.

The economy was the greatest Southern weakness; it was the North's greatest strength. The North was not only a huge farm but a sprawling factory as well. Yankees boasted about three-fourths of the nation's wealth, including three-fourths of the thirty thousand miles of the railroads.

The North also controlled the sea. With its vastly superior navy, it established a blockade that, though a sieve at first, soon choked off Southern supplies and eventually shattered Southern morale. Sea power also enabled the North to exchange huge quantities of grain for munitions and supplies from Europe, thus adding the factories of Europe to its own.

The Union also enjoyed a much larger reserve of manpower. The loyal states had a population of some 22 million; the seceding states had 9 million people, including about 3.5 million slaves. Adding to the North's overwhelming supply of soldiery were ever more immigrants from Europe, who continued to pour into the North even during the war. Over 800,000 newcomers arrived between 1861 and 1865, most of them British, Irish, and German. Large numbers of them were induced to enlist in the Union armies. Altogether about one-fifth of the Union forces were foreign-born, and in some units military commands were given in four different languages.

Whether immigrant or native, ordinary Northern boys were much less prepared than their Southern counterparts for military life. Yet the Northern "clodhoppers" and "shopkeepers" eventually adjusted themselves to soldiering and became known for their discipline and determination.

The North was much less fortunate in its higher commanders. Lincoln was forced to use a costly trial-and-error method to sort out effective leaders from the many incompetent political officers, until he finally uncovered a general, Ulysses Simpson Grant, who would crunch his way to victory.

In the long run, as Northern strengths were brought to bear, they outweighed the strengths of the South. But when the war began, the chances for Southern independence were unusually favorable— certainly better than the prospects for success of the thirteen colonies in 1776. The turn of a few events could easily have produced a different outcome.

The might-have-beens are fascinating. *If* the Border States had seceded, or *if* the uncertain states of the upper Mississippi Valley had turned against the Union, or *if* a wave of Northern defeatism had demanded an armistice, or *if* Britain and/or France had broken the naval blockade, the South might well have won. All of these possibilities almost became realities, but none of them actually occurred, and lacking their impetus, the South could not hope to win.

Friendly Enemies   *The man on the right is George Armstrong Custer. The youngest general in the Union army, this brilliant young officer survived the Civil War only to lose his life and that of every soldier under his command to Sioux warriors at the battle of the Little Bighorn River in 1876—"Custer's Last Stand." The man on the left is a Southern soldier and prisoner of war. He and Custer were classmates at West Point.*

Dethroning King Cotton

Successful revolutions, including the American Revolution of 1776, have generally succeeded because of foreign intervention. The South counted on it, did not get it, and lost. Of all the Confederacy's potential assets, none counted more weightily than the prospect of assistance from abroad. Europe's ruling classes, which had long abhorred the incendiary example of American democracy, were openly sympathetic to the semifeudal, aristocratic South.

In contrast, the masses of workingpeople in Britain, and to some extent in France, were pulling and praying for the North. Many of them had read *Uncle Tom's Cabin*, and they sensed that the war—though at the outset officially fought only over the question of union—might extinguish slavery if the North emerged victorious. The hostility of British common folk to any official intervention evidently had a sobering effect on the British government. Yet the fact remained that British textile mills depended on the American South for 75 percent of their cotton supplies. Humanitarian sympathies aside, Southerners counted on hard economic need to bring Britain to their aid. Why did King Cotton fail them?

He failed in part because he had been so lavishly productive in the immediate prewar years of 1857–1860. Enormous exports of cotton in those years had piled up surpluses in British warehouses. When the shooting started in 1861, British manufacturers had on hand a hefty oversupply of fiber. The real pinch did not come until about a year and a half later, when thousands of hungry operatives were thrown out of work. But by this time Lincoln had announced his slave-emancipation policy, and the "wage slaves" of Britain were not going to demand a war to defend the slaveowners of the South.

The direst effects of the "cotton famine" in Britain were relieved in several ways. Hunger among unemployed workers was partially eased when certain kindhearted Americans sent over several cargoes of foodstuffs. As Union armies penetrated the South, they captured or bought considerable supplies of cotton and shipped them to Britain; and the Confederates also ran a limited quantity through the blockade. In addition, the cotton growers of Egypt and India, responding to high prices, increased their output. Finally, booming war industries in Britain, which supplied both North and South, relieved unemployment.

King Wheat and King Corn—the monarchs of Northern agriculture—proved to be more potent potentates than King Cotton. Blessed with ideal weather and the efficient harvesting of McCormick's mechanical reaper, the North produced bountiful crops during the war years. The grain was purchased by Britain, which suffered a series of bad harvests in the same period. If the British had broken the blockade to gain cotton, they would have provoked the North to war and would have lost this precious granary.

Foreign Flare-ups

America's diplomatic front has seldom been so critical as during the Civil War. The South never wholly abandoned its dream of foreign intervention, and Europe's rulers schemed to take advantage of America's distress.

The first major crisis with Britain came over the *Trent* affair, late in 1861. A Union warship cruising on the high seas north of Cuba stopped a British mail steamer, the *Trent*, and forcibly removed two Confederate diplomats bound for Europe.

Britons were outraged: upstart Yankees could not do this kind of thing to the mistress of the seas. War preparations buzzed, and red-coated troops embarked for Canada with bands blaring "I Wish I Was in Dixie." The London Foreign Office prepared an ultimatum demanding surrender of the prisoners and an apology. But luckily, slow communications gave passions on both sides a chance to cool. Lincoln came to see the *Trent* prisoners as "white elephants" and reluctantly released them.

Another major crisis in Anglo-American relations arose over the unneutral building in Britain of Confederate commerce-raiders, notably the *Alabama*. These vessels were not warships within the meaning of loopholed British law because they left their shipyards unarmed and picked up their guns elsewhere. The *Alabama* escaped in 1862 to the Portuguese Azores and there took on weapons and a crew from two British ships that followed it.

The *Alabama* lighted the skies from Europe to East Asia with the burning hulks of Yankee merchantmen. All told, this "British pirate" captured over sixty vessels. Competing British shippers were delighted, while an angered North had to divert naval strength from its blockade for wild goose chases. The barnacled *Alabama* was finally sunk by a Union cruiser off the coast of France in 1864.

A final Anglo-American crisis was touched off in 1863 by the Laird rams—two Confederate warships being constructed in Great Britain. Designed to destroy the wooden ships of the Union navy with their iron rams and large-caliber guns, they were far more dangerous than the swift and lightly armed *Alabama*. If delivered to the South, they probably would have sunk the blockading squadrons and then brought Northern cities under their fire. In retaliation, the North doubtless would have invaded Canada, and a full-dress war with Britain would have erupted. But America's envoy, Minister Charles Francis Adams, took a hard line, warning that "this is war" if the rams were released. At the last minute the London government relented and bought the two ships for the Royal Navy. Everyone seemed satisfied—except the disappointed Confederates.

Emperor Napoleon III of France, taking advantage of America's preoccupation with its own internal problems, dispatched a French army to occupy Mexico City in 1863. The following year he installed on the ruins of the crushed republic his puppet, Austrian Archduke Maximilian, as emperor of Mexico. Both sending the army and enthroning Maximilian were flagrant violations of the Monroe Doctrine. Napoleon was gambling that the Union would collapse and thus America would be too weak to enforce its "hands-off" policy in the Western Hemisphere.

The North, as long as it was convulsed by war, pursued a walk-on-eggs policy toward France. But when the shooting stopped in 1865, Secretary of State Seward, speaking with the authority of nearly a million war-tempered bayonets, prepared to march south. Napoleon realized that his costly gamble was doomed. He reluctantly took "French leave" of his ill-starred puppet in 1867, and Maximilian soon crumpled ingloriously before a Mexican firing squad.

President Davis Versus President Lincoln

The Confederate government, like King Cotton, betrayed fatal weaknesses. Its constitution, borrowing liberally from that of the Union, had one deadly defect. Created by secession, it could not logically deny future secession to its constituent states. Jefferson Davis, while making his bow to states' rights, had in view a well-knit central government. But determined states' rights supporters fought him bitterly to the end. The Richmond regime encountered difficulty even in persuading certain state troops to serve outside their own borders.

Sharp-featured President Davis—tense, humorless, legalistic, and stubborn—was repeatedly in hot water. Although an eloquent orator and an able administrator, he at no time enjoyed real personal popularity and was often at loggerheads with his congress. At times there was serious talk of impeachment. Unlike Lincoln, Davis was somewhat imperious and inclined to defy rather than shape public opinion. Suffering acutely from neuralgia and other nervous disorders (including a tic), he overworked himself with the details of both civil government and military operations. No one could doubt his courage, sincerity, integrity, and devotion to the South, but the task proved beyond his powers.

Lincoln also had his troubles, but on the whole they were less prostrating. The North enjoyed the prestige of a long-established government, financially stable and fully recognized both at home and abroad. Lincoln, the inexperienced prairie politician, proved superior to the more experienced but less flexible Davis. Able to relax with droll stories at critical times, "Old Abe" grew as the war dragged on. Tactful, quiet, patient, yet firm, he developed a genius for interpreting and leading a fickle public opinion. Holding aloft the banner of Union with inspiring utterances, he revealed charitableness toward the South and forbearance toward backbiting colleagues. "Did [Secretary of War Edwin] Stanton say I was a damned fool?" he reportedly replied to a talebearer. "Then I dare say I must be one, for Stanton is generally right and he always says what he means."

Volunteers and Draftees: North and South

Ravenous, the gods of war demanded men—lots of men. Northern armies were at first manned solely by volunteers, with each state assigned a quota based on population. But in 1863, after volunteering had slackened off, Congress passed a federal conscription law for the first time on a nationwide scale in the United States. The provisions were grossly unfair to the poor. Rich boys, including young John D. Rockefeller, could hire substitutes to go in their places or purchase exemption outright by paying $300.

The draft was especially damned in the Democratic strongholds of the North, notably in New York City. A frightful riot broke out in 1863, touched off largely by underprivileged and antiblack Irish-Americans who shouted "Down with Lincoln!" and "Down with the draft!" For several days the city was at the mercy of a burning, drunken, pillaging mob. Scores of lives were lost, the victims including many lynched blacks. Elsewhere in the North, conscription met with resentment and an occasional minor riot.

More than 90 percent of the Union troops were volunteers, since social and patriotic pressures to enlist were strong. As able-bodied men became scarcer, generous bounties for enlistment were offered by federal, state, and local authorities. With money flowing so freely, an unsavory crew of "bounty brokers" and "substitute brokers" sprang up at home and abroad. They combed the poorhouses of the British Isles and western Europe; and many an Irishman or German was befuddled with whiskey and induced to enlist.

Like the North, the South at first relied mainly on volunteers. But since the Confederacy was much less populous, it scraped the bottom of its manpower barrel much more quickly. The Richmond regime, robbing both "cradle and grave" (ages seventeen to fifty), was forced to resort to conscription as early as April 1862, nearly a year earlier than the Union.

Confederate draft regulations also worked serious injustices. As in the North, a rich man could hire a substitute or purchase exemption. Slaveowners or overseers with twenty slaves might also claim exemption. These special privileges, later modified, made for bad feelings among the less prosperous, many of whom complained that this was "a rich man's war and a poor man's fight." No large-scale draft riots broke out in the South, as in New York City. But Confederate conscription agents often found it prudent to avoid areas inhabited by sharpshooting mountain whites, who were branded "Tories," "traitors," and "Yankee lovers."

The Dollar Goes to War

Blessed with the lion's share of the wealth, the North rode through the financial breakers much more smoothly than the South. Excise taxes on tobacco and alcohol were substantially increased by Congress. An income tax was levied for the first time in the nation's experience.

Customs receipts likewise proved to be important revenue raisers. Early in 1861, after enough antiprotection Southern members had seceded, Congress passed the Morrill Tariff Act. It increased the existing duties some 5 to 10 percent, but these modest rates were soon pushed sharply upward by the necessities of war. The increases were designed partly to raise additional revenue and partly to provide more protection for the prosperous manufacturers who were being plucked by the new internal taxes. A protective tariff thus became identified with the Republican party, as American industrialists, mostly Republicans, waxed fat on these welcome benefits.

The Washington Treasury also issued greenback paper money totaling nearly $450 million at face value. This printing-press currency was inadequately supported by gold, and hence its value was determined by the nation's credit. Greenbacks thus fluctuated with the fortunes of Union arms and at one low point were worth only 39 cents on the gold dollar.

Borrowing far outstripped both greenbacks and taxes as a money raiser. The federal Treasury netted $2,621,916,786 through the sale of bonds, which bore interest and were payable at a later date. A financial landmark of the war was the National Banking System, authorized by Congress in 1863. Launched partly as a stimulant to the sale of government bonds, it was also designed to establish a standard bank-note currency. (The country was then flooded with depreciated "rag money" issued by unreliable bankers.) Banks that joined the National Banking System could buy government bonds and issue sound paper money backed by them. The war-born National Banking System thus turned out to be the first significant step taken toward a unified banking network since 1836, when the "monster" Bank of the United States was killed by Andrew Jackson. Spawned by the war, this new system continued to function for fifty years, until replaced by the Federal Reserve System in 1913.

The impoverished South was beset by different financial woes. Customs duties were choked off as the coils of the Union blockade tightened. Large issues of Confederate bonds were sold at home and abroad, amounting to nearly $400 million. The Richmond regime also increased taxes sharply and imposed a 10 percent levy on farm produce. But in general, the states' rights Southerners were vigorously opposed to heavy direct taxation by the central authority: only about 1 percent of the total income was raised this way.

As revenue began to dry up, the Confederate government was forced to print blueback paper money with complete abandon. "Runaway inflation" occurred as Southern presses continued to grind out the poorly backed treasury notes, totaling in all more than $1 billion. The Confederate paper dollar finally sank to the point where it was worth only 1.6 cents when Lee surrendered. Overall, the war inflicted a 9,000 percent inflation rate on the Confederacy, contrasted with 80 percent for the Union.

"Shoddy" Millionaires in the North

Wartime prosperity in the North was little short of miraculous. New factories, sheltered by the friendly umbrella of the new protective tariffs, mushroomed forth. Soaring prices, resulting from inflation, unfortunately pinched the day laborer and the white-collar worker to some extent, but manufacturers and businesspeople raked in "the fortunes of war." The Civil War bred a millionaire class for the first time in American history.

Yankee "sharpness" appeared at its worst. Dishonest agents, putting profits above patriotism, palmed off aged and blind horses on government purchasers. Unscrupulous Northern manufacturers supplied shoes with cardboard soles and fast-disintegrating uniforms of reprocessed or "shoddy" wool, rather than virgin wool. Hence the reproachful term "shoddy millionaires" was doubly fair.

Newly invented laborsaving machinery enabled the North to expand economically, even though the cream of its manpower was being drained off to the fighting front. The sewing machine wrought wonders in fabricating uniforms and military footwear. Clattering mechanical reapers, which numbered about 250,000 by 1865, proved hardly less potent than thundering guns. They not only released tens of thousands of farm boys for the army but fed them their field rations.

Other industries were humming. The discovery of petroleum gushers in 1859 had led to a rush of "Fifty-Niners" to Pennsylvania. The result was the birth of a new industry, with its "petroleum plutocracy" and "coal oil Johnnies." Pioneers continued to push westward during the war, altogether an estimated 300,000 people. Major magnets were free gold nuggets and free lands under the Homestead Act of 1862.

The Civil War was a woman's war, too. The protracted conflict opened new opportunities for women. When men departed in uniform, women often took their jobs. In Washington, D.C., five hundred women clerks ("government girls") became government workers, with over one hundred in the Treasury Department alone. The booming military demand for shoes and clothing, combined with technological marvels like the sewing machine, likewise drew countless women into industrial employment. Before the war, one industrial worker in four had been female; during the war, the ratio rose to one in three.

Women on both sides stepped up to the fighting front—or close behind it. More than four hundred women accompanied husbands and sweethearts into battle by posing as male soldiers. Other women took on dangerous spy missions. One woman was executed for smuggling gold to the Confederacy. Dr. Elizabeth Blackwell, America's first female physician, helped organize the U.S. Sanitary Commission to assist Union armies in the field. The commission trained nurses, collected medical supplies, and equipped hospitals. Commission work helped many women to acquire the organizational skills and the self-confidence that would propel the women's movement forward after the war. Heroically energetic Clara Barton and dedicated Dorothea Dix, superintendent of nurses for the Union army, helped transform nursing from a lowly service into a respected profession—and in the process opened up another major sphere of employment for women in the postwar era. Equally renowned in the South was Sally Tompkins, who ran a Richmond infirmary for wounded Confederate soldiers and was awarded the rank of captain by Confederate president Jefferson Davis. Still other women, North as well as South, organized bazaars and fairs that raised millions of dollars for the relief of widows, orphans, and disabled soldiers.

A Crushed Cotton Kingdom

The South fought to the point of exhaustion. The suffocation caused by the blockade, together with the

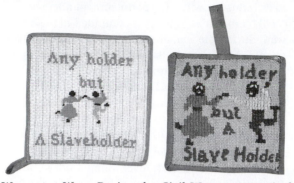

Women at War *During the Civil War women raised money to help soldiers and their families by making handicrafts like these potholders sold at the Northwestern Sanitary Fair in Chicago in 1865.*

replaced dishes; pins became so scarce that they were loaned with reluctance.

To the brutal end, the South mustered remarkable resourcefulness and spirit. Women buoyed up their menfolk, many of whom had seen enough of war at first hand to be heartily sick of it. A proposal was made by a number of women that they cut off their long hair and sell it abroad. But the project was not adopted, partly because of the blockade. The self-sacrificing women took pride in denying themselves the silks and satins of their Northern sisters.

At war's end, the Northern Captains of Industry had conquered the Southern Lords of the Manor. A crippled South left the capitalistic North free to work its own way, with high tariffs and other benefits. The manufacturing moguls of the North, ushering in the full-fledged Industrial Revolution, were destined for increased dominance over American economic and political life. In the past the agrarian "slavocracy" of the South had partially checked the rising plutocracy of the North, but now cotton capitalism lost out to industrial capitalism. The South of 1865 was to be rich in little but amputees, war heroes, ruins, and memories.

destruction wrought by invaders, took a terrible toll. Possessing 30 percent of the national wealth in 1860, the South claimed only 12 percent in 1870. Transportation collapsed. The South was even driven to the economic cannibalism of pulling up rails from the less-used lines to repair the main lines. Window weights were melted down into bullets; gourds

Chronology

1861	Confederate government formed.
	Lincoln takes office (March 4).
	Fort Sumter fired upon (April 12).
	Four Upper South states secede (April–June).
	Morrill Tariff Act passed.
	Trent affair.
	Lincoln declares martial law in Maryland.
1862	Confederacy enacts conscription.
	Homestead Act.

1862–	
1864	*Alabama* raids Northern shipping.
1863	Union enacts conscription.
	New York City draft riots.
	National Banking System established.
1863–	Napoleon III installs Archduke Maximilian as
1864	emperor of Mexico.
1864	*Alabama* sunk by Union warship.

21

The Furnace of Civil War

1861–1865

My paramount object in this struggle is to save the Union, and is not either to save or to destroy slavery.

ABRAHAM LINCOLN, 1862

When President Lincoln issued his call to the states for seventy-five thousand militiamen on April 15, 1861, he envisioned them serving for only ninety days. Reaffirming his limited war aims, he declared that he had "no purpose, directly or indirectly, to interfere with slavery in the States where it exists." With a swift flourish of federal force, he hoped to show the folly of secession and rapidly return the rebellious states to the Union. But the war was to be neither brief nor limited. When the guns fell silent four years later, hundreds of thousands of soldiers on both sides lay dead, slavery was ended forever, and the nation faced the challenge of reintegrating the defeated but still recalcitrant South into the Union.

Bull Run Ends the "Ninety-Day War"

Northern newspapers, at first sharing Lincoln's expectation of quick victory, raised the cry "On to Richmond!" In this yeasty atmosphere, a Union army of some thirty thousand men drilled near Washington in the summer of 1861. It was ill prepared for battle, but the press and the public clamored for action. Lincoln eventually concluded that an attack on a smaller Confederate force at Bull Run (Manassas Junction), some thirty miles southwest of Washington, might be worth a try. If successful, it would demonstrate the superiority of Union arms. It might even lead to the capture of the Confederate capital at Richmond, one hundred miles to the south. If Richmond fell, secession would be thoroughly discredited, and the Union could be restored without damage to the economic and social system of the South.

Raw Yankee recruits swaggered out of Washington toward Bull Run on July 21, 1861, as if they were headed for a sporting event. Congressmen and spectators trailed along with their lunch baskets to witness the fun. At first the battle went well for the Yankees. But "Stonewall" Jackson's gray-clad warriors stood like a stone wall (here he won his nickname), and Confederate reinforcements arrived unexpectedly. Panic seized the green Union troops, many of whom fled in shameful confusion. The Confederates, too exhausted or disorganized to pursue, feasted on captured lunches.

The "military picnic" at Bull Run, though not decisive militarily, had significant psychological and political consequences. Victory was worse than defeat for the South because it inflated an already dangerous overconfidence. Many of the Southern soldiers promptly deserted, feeling that the war was now surely over. Southern enlistments fell off sharply, and preparations for a protracted conflict slackened. Defeat was better than victory for the Union because it dispelled all illusions of a one-punch war and caused the Northerners to buckle down to the staggering task at hand. It also set the stage for a war that would be waged not merely for the cause of Union but also, eventually, for the abolitionist ideal of emancipation.

"Tardy George" McClellan and the Peninsula Campaign

Northern hopes brightened later in 1861, when General George B. McClellan was given command of the Army of the Potomac, as the major Union force near Washington was now called. Red-haired and red-mustached, strong and stocky, McClellan was a brilliant, thirty-four-year-old West Pointer who had seen plenty of fighting in the Mexican War.

Cocky George McClellan embodied a curious mixture of virtues and defects. He was a superb organizer and drillmaster, and he injected splendid morale into the Army of the Potomac. Hating to sacrifice his troops, he was idolized by his men, who affectionately called him "Little Mac." But he was a perfectionist who seems not to have realized that an army is never ready to the last button, and that wars cannot be won without running some risks. He consistently but erroneously believed that the enemy outnumbered him, partly because his intelligence reports from the head of Pinkerton's Detective Agency were unreliable. He was overcautious—Lincoln once accused him of having "the slows"—and he addressed the president in an arrogant tone that a less forgiving person than Lincoln would never have tolerated. Privately the general referred to his chief as a "baboon." After threatening to "borrow" the army if it was not going to be used, Lincoln finally issued firm orders to move.

A reluctant McClellan at last decided on a waterborne approach to Richmond. Moving up the narrow peninsula formed by the James and York Rivers, McClellan warily inched toward the Confederate capital in the spring of 1862 with about 100,000 men. After taking a month to capture historic Yorktown, which bristled with imitation wooden cannon, he finally came within sight of the spires of Richmond. Aided by "Jeb" Stuart's Confederate cavalry, General Robert E. Lee suddenly launched a devastating counterattack—the Seven Days' Battles—June 26–July 2, 1862. The Confederates slowly drove McClellan back to the sea. The Union forces abandoned the Peninsula Campaign as a costly failure, and Lincoln temporarily abandoned McClellan as commander of the Army of the Potomac—though Lee's army had suffered some twenty thousand casualties to McClellan's ten thousand.

Lee had achieved a brilliant, if bloody, triumph. Yet the ironies of his accomplishment are striking. If McClellan had succeeded in taking Richmond and ending the war in mid-1862, the Union would probably have been restored with minimal disruption of slavery, which would have survived at least for a time. By his successful defense of Richmond and defeat of McClellan, Lee had in effect ensured that the war would endure until slavery was uprooted and the Old South thoroughly destroyed. Lincoln himself now declared that the rebels "cannot experiment for ten years trying to destroy the government and if they fail

Main Thrusts, 1861–1865
Northern strategists at first believed that the rebellion could be snuffed out quickly by a swift, crushing blow. But the stiffness of Southern resistance to the Union's early probes revealed that the conflict would be a war of attrition, long and bloody.

still come back into the Union unhurt." He began to draft an emancipation proclamation.

Union strategy now turned toward total war. As finally developed, the Northern military plan had six components: first, slowly suffocate the South by blockading its coasts; second, liberate the slaves and hence undermine the economic foundations of the Old South; third, cut the Confederacy in half by seizing control of its Mississippi River backbone; fourth, chop the Confederacy to pieces by sending troops through Georgia and the Carolinas; fifth, decapitate it by capturing its capital at Richmond; and sixth (this was Ulysses Grant's idea, especially), try everywhere to engage the enemy's main strength and grind it into submission.

The War at Sea

The blockade started leakily; it was not clamped down all at once but extended by degrees. Blockading was simplified by concentrating on the principal ports and inlets, where dock facilities were available for loading bulky bales of cotton. The blockade was

further strengthened when Britain recognized it as binding and warned its shippers that they ignored it at their peril.

Blockade-running soon became riskily profitable, as the growing scarcity of Southern goods drove prices skyward. A leading rendezvous for successful runners was the West Indies port of Nassau, in the British Bahamas, where at one time thirty-five of the speedy ships rode at anchor. But the lush days of blockade-running finally passed as Union squadrons gradually pinched off the leading Southern ports, from New Orleans to Charleston.

The most alarming Confederate threat to the blockade came in 1862. Resourceful Southerners raised and reconditioned a former wooden United States warship, the *Merrimack*, and plated its sides with old iron railroad rails. Renamed the *Virginia*, this clumsy but powerful monster easily destroyed two wooden ships of the Union navy in the Virginia waters of Chesapeake Bay; it also threatened the entire Yankee blockading fleet.

A tiny Union ironclad, the *Monitor*, built in about one hundred days, arrived on the scene in the nick of time. For four hours, on March 9, 1862, the little "Yankee cheesebox on a raft" fought the wheezy Merrimack to a standstill. Britain and France had already built several powerful ironclads, but the first battle test of these new craft heralded the doom of wooden warships.

The Pivotal Point: Antietam

Robert E. Lee, having broken the back of McClellan's assault on Richmond, next moved northward. Emboldened by a victory at the Second Battle of Bull Run (August 29–30, 1862), Lee daringly thrust into Maryland. He hoped to strike a blow that would not only encourage foreign intervention but also seduce the still wavering Border State and its sisters from the Union. The Confederate troops sang lustily,

> Thou wilt not cower in the dust,
>   Maryland! my Maryland!
> Thy gleaming sword shall never rust,
>   Maryland! my Maryland!

But the Marylanders did not respond to the siren song. The presence among the invaders of so many blanketless, hatless, and shoeless soldiers dampened the state's ardor.

Events finally converged toward a critical battle at Antietam Creek, Maryland. Lincoln, yielding to popular pressure, hastily restored "Little Mac" to active command of the main Northern army. His soldiers tossed their caps skyward and hugged his horse as they hailed his return. McClellan succeeded in halting Lee at Antietam on September 17, 1862, in one of the bloodiest and most bitter days of the war. Antietam was more or less a draw militarily. But Lee, finding his thrust parried, retired across the Potomac.

The landmark Battle of Antietam was one of the most decisive engagements of world history—probably the most decisive of the Civil War. Jefferson Davis was perhaps never again so near victory as on that fateful summer day. The British and French governments were on the verge of diplomatic mediation, a form of interference sure to be angrily resented by the North. But both Paris and London cooled off when the Union displayed unexpected power at Antietam, and their chill deepened with the passing months.

Bloody Antietam also provided Lincoln with the long-awaited opportunity to launch his Emancipation Proclamation. The abolitionists were growing increasingly impatient. Congress had already passed "Confiscation Acts" punishing "traitors" by declaring their slaves "captives of war" who "shall be forever free." By the summer of 1862 Lincoln was ready for bolder action. All four Border States had now come safely into the Union fold. With a solid victory of arms, he could proclaim emancipation from a position of military strength. With keen anticipation, the president awaited the outcome of Lee's invasion.

The halting of Lee's offensive was just enough of a victory to justify Lincoln's issuing, on September 23, 1862, the preliminary Emancipation Proclamation. This hope-giving document announced that on January 1, 1863, the president would issue a final proclamation. On the scheduled date he fully redeemed his promise, and the Civil War became more of a moral crusade and more of what Lincoln called a "remorseless revolutionary struggle." After January 1, 1863, Lincoln said, "The character of the war will be changed. It will be one of subjugation. . . . The [Old] South is to be destroyed and replaced by new propositions and ideas."

A Proclamation Without Emancipation

Lincoln's Emancipation Proclamation of 1863 declared "forever free" the slaves in those Confederate states still in rebellion. Bondsmen in the loyal Border States were not affected, nor were those in specific conquered areas in the South—all told, about 800,000. The tone of the document was dull and legalistic. But if Lincoln stopped short of a clarion call for a righteous war to achieve freedom, he pointedly concluded his historic document by declaring that the proclamation was an "act of justice."

The presidential pen did not formally strike the shackles from a single slave. Where Lincoln could presumably free the slaves—that is, in the loyal Border States—he refused to do so, lest he spur disunion. Where he could not—that is, in the Confederate states—he tried to. In short, where he could he would not, and where he would he could not. Thus the

The Killing Fields of Antietam
These Confederate corpses testify to the awful slaughter of the battle. The twelve-hour fight at Antietam Creek ranks as the bloodiest single day of the war, with more than ten thousand Confederate casualties and even more on the Union side. "At last the battle ended," one historian wrote, "smoke heavy in the air, the twilight quivering with the anguished cries of thousands of wounded men."

Emancipation Proclamation was stronger on proclamation than emancipation.

Yet much unofficial do-it-yourself liberation did take place. Thousands of jubilant slaves, learning of the proclamation, flocked to the invading Union armies, stripping already rundown plantations of their work forces. But many fugitives would have come anyhow, as they had from the war's outset. Lincoln's immediate goal was not only to liberate the slaves but also to strengthen the moral cause of the Union at home and abroad. This he succeeded in doing. At the same time, Lincoln's proclamation clearly foreshadowed the ultimate doom of slavery. This was legally achieved by actions of the individual states and by their ratification of the Thirteenth Amendment in 1865, eight months after the Civil War had ended. (For text, see the Appendix.)

Public reactions to the long-awaited proclamation of 1863 were varied. "God bless Abraham Lincoln," exulted the antislavery editor Horace Greeley in his *New York Tribune*. But many ardent abolitionists complained that Lincoln had not gone far enough. On the other hand, formidable numbers of Northerners, especially in the Old Northwest and the

Border States, felt that he had gone too far. A Democratic rhymester sneered,

> Honest old Abe, when the war first began,
> Denied abolition was part of his plan;
> Honest old Abe has since made a decree,
> The war must go on till the slaves are all free.
> As both can't be honest, will someone tell how,
> If honest Abe then, is he honest Abe now?

Opposition mounted in the North against supporting an "abolition war." Many Boys in Blue, especially from the Border States, had volunteered to fight for the Union, not against slavery. Desertions increased sharply. The crucial congressional elections in the autumn of 1862 went heavily against the administration, particularly in New York, Pennsylvania, and Ohio. Democrats even carried Lincoln's Illinois, although they did not secure control of Congress.

The Emancipation Proclamation caused an outcry to rise from the South that "Lincoln the fiend" was trying to stir up the "hellish passions" of a slave insurrection. European aristocrats, noting that the proclamation applied only to rebel slaveholders, were inclined to sympathize with Southern protests. But the Old World working classes, especially in Britain, reacted otherwise. They sensed that the proclamation spelled the ultimate doom of slavery, and many laborers were more determined than ever to oppose intervention. Gradually the diplomatic position of the Union improved.

The North now had much the stronger moral cause. In addition to preserving the Union, it had committed itself to freeing the slaves. The moral position of the South was correspondingly diminished.

Blacks Battle Bondage

As Lincoln moved to emancipate the slaves, he also took steps to enlist blacks in the armed forces. Although some African-Americans had served in the Revolution and the War of 1812, the regular army contained no blacks at the war's outset, and the War Department refused to accept those free Northern blacks who tried to volunteer. (The Union navy, however, enrolled many blacks, mainly as cooks, stewards, and firemen.)

But as manpower ran low and emancipation was proclaimed, black enlistees were accepted, sometimes over ferocious protests from Northern as well as Southern whites. By war's end some 180,000 blacks served in the Union armies, most of them from the slave states but many from the free-soil North. Blacks accounted for about 10 percent of the total enlistments in the Union forces, on land and sea, and included two black Massachusetts regiments raised largely through the efforts of ex-slave Frederick Douglass.

Black fighting men unquestionably had their hearts in the war against slavery that the Civil War had become after Lincoln proclaimed emancipation. Participating in about five hundred engagements, they received twenty-two Congressional Medals of Honor—the highest military award. Their casualties were extremely heavy; more than thirty-eight thousand died, whether from battle, sickness, or reprisals from vengeful masters. Many were put to death as slaves in revolt, for not until 1864 did the South recognize them as prisoners of war. In one notorious case, several black soldiers were massacred after they had formally surrendered at Fort Pillow, Tennessee. Thereafter angrily aroused black units cried "Remember Fort Pillow!" as they swung into battle, and vowed to take no prisoners.

For reasons of pride, prejudice, and principle, the Confederacy could not bring itself to enlist slaves until a month before the war ended, and then it was too late. Meanwhile tens of thousands were impressed into labor battalions, the building of fortifications, the supplying of armies, and other war-connected activities. Slaves moreover were "the stomach of the Confederacy," for they kept the farms going while the white men fought.

Through the grapevine, blacks learned of Lincoln's Emancipation Proclamation. The bulk of them did not immediately cast off their chains. But tens of thousands *did* eventually revolt "with their feet" when they abandoned their plantations at the

Black Union Soldiers   *These former slaves, recruited into the Union army in Tennessee, helped to man an artillery battery during the Battle of Nashville.*

approach or arrival of Union armies, with or without emancipation proclamations. About twenty-five thousand joined Sherman's march through Georgia in 1864, and their presence in such numbers created problems of supply and discipline.

Lee's Last Lunge at Gettysburg

After Antietam, Lincoln replaced McClellan as commander of the Army of the Potomac with General A. E. Burnside, whose ornate side-whiskers came to be known as "burnsides" or "sideburns." Protesting his unfitness for this responsibility, Burnside proved it when he launched a rash frontal attack on Lee's strong position at Fredericksburg, Virginia, on December 13, 1862. A chicken could not have lived in the line of fire, remarked one Confederate officer. More than ten thousand Northern soldiers were killed or wounded in "Burnside's Slaughter Pen."

A new slaughter pen was prepared when General Burnside yielded his command to "Fighting Joe" Hooker, an aggressive officer but a headstrong subordinate. At Chancellorsville, Virginia, May 2–4, 1863, Lee daringly divided his numerically inferior force and sent "Stonewall" Jackson to attack the Union flank. The strategy worked. Hooker, temporarily dazed by a near-hit from a cannonball, was badly beaten but not crushed. This victory was probably Lee's most brilliant, but it was dearly bought. Jackson was mistakenly shot by his own men in the gathering dusk and died a few days later. "I have lost my right arm," lamented Lee. Southern folklore relates how Jackson outflanked the angels while galloping into Heaven.

Lee prepared to follow up his brilliant victory by invading the North again, this time through Pennsylvania. A decisive blow would add strength to the increasingly noisy peace prodders in the North and would also encourage foreign intervention—still a Southern hope. Quite by accident, the Northern army, now under General George G. Meade, took its stand on the rolling hills near quiet little Gettysburg, Pennsylvania. There his 92,000 men in blue locked horns in furious combat with Lee's 76,000 gray-clad warriors. The battle seesawed across the green slopes

for three agonizing days, July 1–3, 1863, and the outcome was in doubt until the very end. The failure of General George Pickett's magnificent but futile charge finally broke the back of the Confederate attack—and broke the heart of the Confederate cause.

Pickett's charge has been called the "high tide of the Confederacy." It defined both the northernmost point reached by any significant Southern force and the last real chance for the Confederacy to win the war. After Gettysburg, Lincoln spurned Southern efforts to reach a negotiated peace settlement between the parties. From then on the Southern

The Battle of Gettysburg, 1863 *With the failure of Pickett's charge, the fate of the Confederacy was sealed—though the Civil War dragged on for almost two more bloody years.*

cause was doomed. Yet the men of Dixie fought for nearly two years longer, through sweat, blood, and weariness of spirit.

Later, in the dreary autumn of 1863, with the graves still fresh, Lincoln journeyed to Gettysburg to dedicate the cemetery. He read a two-minute address, following a two-hour speech by the orator of the day. Lincoln's noble remarks were branded by the *London Times* as "ludicrous" and by Democratic editors as "dishwatery" and "silly." The address attracted relatively little attention at the time, but the president was speaking for the ages.

The War in the West

Events in the western theater of the war at last provided Lincoln with an able general who did not have to be shelved after every reverse. Ulysses S. Grant had been a mediocre student at West Point, although he did do well in mathematics and horsemanship. After fighting creditably in the Mexican War, he was stationed at isolated frontier posts, where boredom and loneliness drove him to drink. Resigning from the army to avoid a court-martial for drunkenness, he failed at various business ventures and when war came was working in his father's leather store in Illinois for $50 a month.

Grant did not cut much of a figure. The shy and silent shopkeeper was short, stooped, awkward, stubble-bearded, and sloppy in dress. He managed with some difficulty to secure a colonelcy in the volunteers. From then on his military experience—combined with his boldness, resourcefulness, and doggedness—catapulted him on a meteoric rise.

Grant's first notable success came in the northern Tennessee theater. After heavy fighting, he captured Fort Henry and Fort Donelson on the Tennessee and Cumberland Rivers in February 1862. When the Confederate commander at Fort Donelson asked for terms, Grant bluntly demanded "an unconditional and immediate surrender."

Grant's triumph in Tennessee was crucial. It not only riveted Kentucky more securely to the Union but also opened the gateway to the strategically important region of Tennessee, as well as to Georgia and the

heart of Dixie. Grant next attempted to exploit his victory by capturing the junction of the main Confederate north-south and east-west railroads in the Mississippi Valley at Corinth, Mississippi. But a Confederate force foiled his plans in a gory battle at Shiloh, just over the Tennessee border from Corinth, on April 6–7, 1862.

Lincoln resisted all demands for the removal of "Unconditional Surrender" Grant, insisting, "I can't spare this man; he fights." When talebearers later told Lincoln that Grant drank too much, the president allegedly replied, "Find me the brand, and I'll send a barrel to each of my other generals."

Other Union thrusts were in the making. In the spring of 1862, a flotilla commanded by David G. Farragut joined with a Northern army to strike the South a staggering blow by seizing New Orleans. With Union gunboats both ascending and descending the Mississippi, the eastern part of the Confederacy was left with a precarious back door. Through this narrowing entrance, between Vicksburg and Port Hudson, flowed herds of vitally needed cattle and quantities of

The Mississippi River and Tennessee, 1862–1863

other provisions from Louisiana and Texas. The fortress of Vicksburg, located on a hairpin turn of the Mississippi, was the South's sentinel protecting the lifeline to the western sources of supply.

General Grant was given command of the Union forces attacking Vicksburg, and in the teeth of grave difficulties he displayed rare skill and daring. The siege of Vicksburg was his best-fought campaign of the war. The beleaguered city at length surrendered, on July 4, 1863, with the garrison reduced to eating mules and rats. Five days later came the fall of Port Hudson, the last southern bastion on the Mississippi. The spinal cord of the Confederacy was severed and, in Lincoln's quaint phrase, the Father of Waters at last flowed "unvexed to the sea."

The Union's victory at Vicksburg came the day after the Confederate defeat at Gettysburg. The political significance of these back-to-back military successes was momentous. Reopening the Mississippi helped to quell strong peace agitation in southern Ohio, Indiana, and Illinois. Confederate control of the Mississippi had cut off that region's usual trade routes down the Ohio-Mississippi river system to New Orleans, thus adding economic pain to that border section's already shaky support for the "abolition war." The twin victories also conclusively tipped the diplomatic scales in favor of the North, as Britain stopped delivery of the Laird rams to the Confederates and as France killed a deal for the sale of six naval vessels to the Richmond government. By the end of 1863 all Confederate hopes for foreign help were irretrievably lost.

Sherman Scorches Georgia

General Grant, the victor of Vicksburg, was now transferred to the east Tennessee theater. There he won a series of desperate engagements in November 1863 in the vicinity of besieged Chattanooga, including Missionary Ridge and Lookout Mountain ("the Battle Above the Clouds"). Chattanooga was captured, the state was cleared of Confederates, and the way was thus opened for an invasion of Georgia. Grant was rewarded by being made general in chief.

Georgia's conquest was entrusted to General William Tecumseh Sherman. Red-haired and red-

Sherman's March, 1864–1865

bearded, grim-faced and ruthless, he captured Atlanta in September 1864 and burned the city in November of that year. He then daringly left his supply base, lived off the country for some 250 miles, and emerged at Savannah on the sea.

Sherman's hated "Blue Bellies," sixty thousand strong, cut a sixty-mile-wide swath of destruction through Georgia. They burned buildings, leaving only the blackened chimneys ("Sherman's Sentinels"). They tore up railroad rails, heated them red-hot, and twisted them into "iron doughnuts" and "Sherman's hairpins." They bayoneted family portraits and ran off with valuable "souvenirs." "War . . . is all hell," admitted Sherman later, and he proved it by his efforts to "make Georgia howl." His major purposes were to destroy supplies destined for the Confederate army and to weaken the morale of the men at the front by waging war on their homes.

Sherman was a pioneer practitioner of total war. His success in "Shermanizing" the South was attested by increasing numbers of Confederate desertions. Although effective, his methods were unquestionably brutal. At times the discipline of his army broke down, as roving riffraff (Sherman's "bummers") engaged in an orgy of pillaging. "Sherman the Brute" was universally damned in the South.

After seizing Savannah as a Christmas present for Lincoln, Sherman's army veered north into South Carolina, where the destruction was even more vicious. Many Union soldiers believed that this state, the "hell-hole of secession," had wantonly provoked the war. The capital city, Columbia, burst into flames, in all probability the handiwork of the Yankee invader. Crunching northward, Sherman's conquering army had rolled deep into North Carolina by the time the war ended.

The Politics of War

Presidential elections come by the calendar, not by the crisis. The election of 1864 fell most inopportunely in the midst of war.

Political infighting in the North added greatly to Lincoln's cup of woe. Factions within his own party, distrusting his ability or doubting his commitment to abolition, sought to tie his hands or even remove him from office. Conspicuous among his critics was a group led by the overambitious secretary of the treasury, Salmon Chase. Especially burdensome to Lincoln was the creation of the Congressional Committee on the Conduct of the War, formed in late 1861. It was dominated by "radical" Republicans who pressed Lincoln zealously on emancipation.

Most dangerous of all to the Union cause were the Northern Democrats. Deprived of the talent that had departed with the Southern wing of the party, those Democrats remaining in the North were left with the taint of association with the seceders. Tragedy befell the Democrats—and the Union— when their gifted leader, Stephen A. Douglas, died of typhoid fever seven weeks after the war began. Unshakably devoted to the Union, he probably could have kept much of his following on the path of loyalty.

Lacking a leader, the Democrats divided. A large group of "War Democrats" patriotically supported the Lincoln administration, but tens of thousands of "Peace Democrats" did not. At the extreme were the so-called Copperheads, named for the poisonous snake that strikes without a warning rattle. Copperheads openly obstructed the war through attacks against the draft, against Lincoln, and especially, after 1863, against emancipation. They denounced the president as the "Illinois Ape" and condemned the "Nigger War."

Notorious among the Copperheads was a some-time congressman from Ohio, Clement L. Vallandigham. This tempestuous character possessed brilliant oratorical gifts and unusual talents for stirring up trouble. A Southern partisan, he publicly demanded an end to the "wicked and cruel" war. In 1863 he was convicted and sentenced to prison by a military tribunal for treasonable utterances. Lincoln decided that if Vallandigham liked the Confederates so much, he ought to be banished to their lines. This was done. But Vallandigham was not so easily silenced. Working his way to Canada, he ran for the governorship of Ohio on foreign soil and polled a substantial but insufficient vote.

The Election of 1864

As the election of 1864 approached, Lincoln's precarious authority depended on his retaining Republican support while spiking the threat from the Peace Democrats and the Copperheads. Fearing defeat, the Republican party executed a clever maneuver. Joining with the War Democrats, it proclaimed itself to be the Union party. Thus the Republican party passed temporarily out of existence.

Lincoln's renomination at first encountered surprisingly strong opposition. Hostile factions whipped up considerable agitation to shelve him in favor of Secretary of the Treasury Chase. Lincoln was accused of lacking force, of being overready to compromise, of not having won the war, and of having shocked many sensitive souls by his ill-timed and earthy jokes. ("Prince of Jesters," one disapproving journal called him.) But the "ditch Lincoln" move collapsed, and he was nominated by the Union party without serious dissent.

Lincoln's running mate was ex-tailor Andrew Johnson, a loyal War Democrat from Tennessee who had been a small slaveowner when the conflict began. He was placed on the Union party ticket to "sew up" the election by attracting War Democrats and voters in the Border States and, sadly, with no proper regard for the possibility that Lincoln might die in office.

Embattled Democrats—regulars and Copperheads—nominated the deposed and overcautious war hero, General McClellan. The Copperheads managed to force into the Democratic platform a plank denouncing the prosecution of the war as a failure. But McClellan, who could not otherwise have faced his old comrades-in-arms, repudiated this defeatist declaration.

The campaign was noisy and nasty. Lincoln's reelection was at first gravely in doubt. The war was going badly, and Lincoln himself gave way to despondency, fearing that political defeat was imminent. But the atmosphere of gloom was changed electrically, as balloting day neared, by a succession of Northern victories. Admiral Farragut captured Mobile, Alabama, after defiantly shouting the now famous order, "Damn the torpedoes! Go ahead." General Sherman seized Atlanta. General ("Little Phil") Sheridan laid

waste the verdant Shenandoah Valley of Virginia so thoroughly that in his words, "A crow could not fly over it without carrying his rations with him."

The president pulled through, but nothing more than necessary was left to chance. At election time many Northern soldiers were furloughed home to support Lincoln at the polls. Other soldiers were permitted to cast their ballots at the front.

Bolstered by the so-called bayonet vote, Lincoln vanquished General McClellan by 212 electoral votes to 21, losing only Kentucky, Delaware, and New Jersey. But "Little Mac" ran a much closer race than the electoral count indicates. He netted a healthy 45 percent of the popular vote, 1,803,787 to Lincoln's 2,206,938, piling up much support in the Southerner-infiltrated states of the Old Northwest, in New York, and also in his native state of Pennsylvania.

One of the most crushing defeats suffered by the South was the defeat of the Northern Democrats in 1864. The removal of Lincoln was the last ghost of a hope for a Confederate victory, and the Southern soldiers would wishfully shout, "Hurrah for McClellan!" When Lincoln triumphed, desertions from the sinking Southern ship increased sharply.

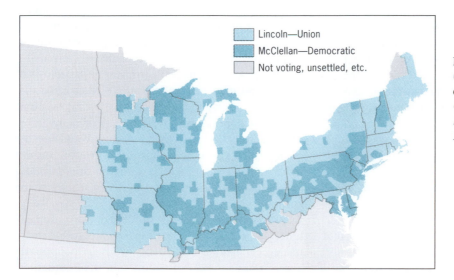

Presidential Election of 1864 (showing popular vote by county) *Lincoln also carried California, Oregon, and Nevada, but there was a considerable McClellan vote in each.*

Legend:
- Lincoln—Union
- McClellan—Democratic
- Not voting, unsettled, etc.

General Ulysses S. Grant and General Robert E. Lee *Trained at West Point, Grant (left) proved to be a better general than a president. Oddly, he hated the sight of blood and recoiled from rare beef. Lee (right), a gentlemanly general in an ungentlemanly business, remarked when the Union troops were bloodily repulsed at Fredericksburg, "It is well that war is so terrible, or we should get too fond of it."*

Grant Outlasts Lee

After Gettysburg, Grant was brought in from the West over Meade, who was blamed for failing to pursue the defeated but always dangerous Lee. Lincoln needed a general who, employing the superior resources of the North, would have the intestinal stamina to drive straight ahead, regardless of casualties. A soldier of bulldog tenacity, Grant was the man for this meat-grinder type of warfare. His overall basic strategy was to assail the enemy's armies simultaneously, so that they could not assist one another and hence could be destroyed piecemeal. His personal motto was "When in doubt, fight." Lincoln urged him "to chew and choke, as much as possible."

A grimly determined Grant, with more than 100,000 men, struck for Richmond. He engaged Lee in a series of furious battles in the Wilderness of Virginia, during May and June 1864, notably in the leaden hurricane of the "Bloody Angle" and "Hell's Half Acre." In this Wilderness Campaign Grant suf-

fered about fifty thousand casualties, or nearly as many men as Lee had commanded at the start. But Lee lost about as heavily in proportion.

In a ghastly gamble, on June 3, 1864, Grant ordered a frontal assault on the impregnable position of Cold Harbor. Union soldiers advanced to almost certain death with papers pinned on their backs bearing their names and addresses. In a few minutes, about seven thousand men were killed or wounded.

Public opinion in the North was appalled by this "blood and guts" type of fighting. Critics cried that "Grant the Butcher" had gone insane. But his basic strategy of hammering ahead seemed brutally necessary; he could trade two men for one and still beat the enemy to its knees. "I propose to fight it out on this line," he wrote, "if it takes all summer." It did—and it also took all autumn, all winter, and a part of the spring.

In February 1865 the Confederates, tasting the bitter dregs of defeat, tried desperately to negotiate for peace between the "two countries." But Lincoln could accept nothing short of Union, and the Southerners could accept nothing short of independence. So the tribulation wore on—amid smoke and agony—to its terrible climax.

The end came with dramatic suddenness. Rapidly advancing Northern troops captured Richmond and cornered Lee at Appomattox Courthouse in Virginia, in April 1865. Grant—stubble-bearded and informally dressed—met with Lee on the ninth, Palm Sunday, and granted generous terms of surrender. Among other concessions, the hungry Confederates were allowed to keep their own horses for spring plowing. Tattered Southern veterans—"Lee's Ragamuffins"—wept as they took leave of their beloved commander. Elated Union soldiers cheered but were silenced by Grant's stern admonition, "The war is over; the rebels are our countrymen again."

Lincoln traveled to conquered Richmond and sat in Jefferson Davis's evacuated office just forty hours after the Confederate president had left it. As he walked the blasted streets of the city, crowds of freed slaves gathered to see and touch "Father Abraham." One black man fell to his knees before the Emancipator, who said to him, "Don't kneel to me. This is not

right. You must kneel to God only, and thank Him for the liberty you will enjoy hereafter." Sadly, as many freed slaves would discover, the hereafter of their full liberty was a long time coming.

The Martyrdom of Lincoln

On the night of April 14, 1865 (Good Friday), only five days after Lee's surrender, Ford's Theater in Washington witnessed its most sensational drama. A half-crazed, fanatically pro-Southern actor, John Wilkes Booth, slipped behind Lincoln as he sat in his box and shot him in the head. After lying unconscious all night, the Great Emancipator died the following morning.

Lincoln expired in the arms of victory at the very pinnacle of his fame. From the standpoint of his reputation, his death could not have been better timed if he had hired the assassin. A large number of his countrymen had not suspected his greatness, and many others had even doubted his ability. But his dramatic death helped to erase the memory of his

The Assassination of Abraham Lincoln at Ford's Theater, 1865
John Wilkes Booth (left) shot Lincoln (top center) from behind, then leaped to the stage and escaped. Many heard him shout, "Sic Semper Tyrannis!" ("Thus Ever to Tyrants!"), the state motto of Virginia.

shortcomings and caused his nobler qualities to stand out in clearer relief.

The full impact of Lincoln's death was not at once apparent to the South. Hundreds of bedraggled ex-Confederate soldiers cheered, as did some Southern civilians and Northern Copperheads, when they learned of the assassination. But as time wore on, increasing numbers of Southerners perceived that Lincoln's death was a calamity for them. Belatedly they recognized that his kindliness and moderation would have been the most effective shields between them and vindictive treatment by the victors. The assassination unfortunately increased the bitterness of the North, partly because of the fantastic rumor that Jefferson Davis had plotted it.

A few historians have argued that if the rail-splitter had lived, he would have suffered Andrew Johnson's fate of being impeached by the embittered members of his own party who demanded harshness, not forbearance, toward the South. Lincoln no doubt would have clashed with Congress; in fact, he had already found himself in some hot water. But the surefooted and experienced Lincoln could hardly have blundered into the same quicksands that engulfed Johnson. Lincoln was a victorious president, and there is no arguing with victory. In addition to his powers of leadership refined in the war crucible, Lincoln possessed in full measure tact, sweet reasonableness, and an uncommon amount of common sense. Andrew Johnson, hot-tempered and impetuous, lacked all of these priceless qualities. Ford's Theater, with its tragic murder of Lincoln, set the stage for the wrenching ordeal of Reconstruction.

The Aftermath of the Nightmare

The Civil War took a grisly toll in gore, about as much as all of America's subsequent wars combined. Over 600,000 men died in action or of disease, and in all, over a million were killed or seriously wounded. To its lasting hurt, the nation lost the cream of its young manhood and potential leadership.

Direct monetary costs of the conflict totaled about $15 billion. But this colossal figure does not include continuing expenses, such as pensions and interest on the national debt. The intangible costs—

dislocations, disunities, wasted energies, lowered ethics, blasted lives, bitter memories, and burning hates—cannot be calculated.

The greatest constitutional decision of the century, in a sense, was written in blood and handed down at Appomattox Courthouse, where Lee surrendered. The extreme states' righters were crushed. The national government, tested in the fiery furnace of war, emerged unbroken. Nullification and secession, those twin nightmares of previous decades, were laid to rest.

Beyond doubt the Civil War—the nightmare of the Republic—was the supreme test of American democracy. It finally answered the question, in the words of Lincoln at Gettysburg, whether a nation dedicated to such principles "can long endure." The preservation of democratic ideals, though not an officially announced war aim, was subconsciously one of the major objectives of the North.

Victory for Union arms also provided inspiration to the champions of democracy and liberalism the world over. The great English Reform Bill of 1867, under which Britain became a true political democracy, was passed two years after the Civil War ended. American democracy had proved itself, and its success was an additional argument used by the disfranchised British masses in securing similar blessings for themselves.

The "lost cause" of the South was lost, but few Americans today would argue that the end result was not for the best. The shameful cancer of slavery was sliced away by the sword, and African-Americans were at last in a position to claim their rights to life, liberty, and the pursuit of happiness. The nation was again united politically, though for many generations it was still divided spiritually by the passions of the war. Grave dangers were averted by a Union victory, including the indefinite prolongation of the "peculiar institution," the unleashing of the "slave power" on weak Caribbean neighbors, and the transformation of the area from Panama to Hudson's Bay into an armed camp, with several hostile states constantly snarling and sniping at one another. America still had a long way to go to make the promises of freedom a reality for all its citizens, black and white. But emancipation laid the necessary groundwork, and a united and democratic United States was free to fulfill its destiny as the dominant republic of the hemisphere—and eventually of the world.

Chronology

VARYING   VIEWPOINTS

What Were the Consequences of the Civil War?

With the end of the Civil War in 1865, the United States was permanently altered despite the reunification of the Union and the Confederacy. Slavery was officially banned, secession was a dead issue, and industrial growth surged forward. With the Union's victory, power rested firmly with the North, and it would orchestrate the future development of the country.

According to historian Eric Foner, the war redrew the economic and political map of the country. For example, the first twelve amendments to the Constitution had all served to limit government power. In contrast, the Thirteenth Amendment, which abolished slavery, and the revolutionary Fourteenth Amendment, which conferred citizenship on and guaranteed civil rights to all those born in the United States, marked unprecedented expansions of federal power.

Historian James M. McPherson has noted still other ways in which the Civil War extended the authority of the central government. It expanded powers of taxation, developed a national banking system, bolstered federal courts, and established the first federal social welfare agency—the Freedmen's Bureau—to aid former slaves.

Some scholars have disputed whether the Civil War marked an absolute watershed in American history. They correctly note that racial inequality scandalously persisted after the Civil War despite the supposed protections extended by federal civil rights legislation. Others note that industrial growth had begun in the Jacksonian era, and that regional differences between North and South endured, even down to the present day.

Yet the argument that the Civil War launched a modern America remains convincing. The lives of Americans, white and black, North and South, were transformed by the war experience. Industry entered a period of unprecedented growth. The emergence of new, national legal and governmental institutions marked the birth of the modern American state. All considered, it is hard to deny that the end of the Civil War brought one chapter of the nation's history to a close while opening another.

For further reading, see the Appendix. For web resources, go to **http://college.hmco.com.**

The Ordeal of Reconstruction

1865–1877

*With malice toward none, with charity for all, with firmness
in the right as God gives us to see the right, let us strive on to
finish the work we are in, to bind up the nation's wounds, to care
for him who shall have borne the battle and for his widow and
orphan, to do all which may achieve and cherish a just and
lasting peace among ourselves and with all nations.*

ABRAHAM LINCOLN, SECOND INAUGURAL ADDRESS, MARCH 4, 1865

The battle was done, the buglers silent. Bone-weary and bloodied, the American people, North and South, now faced the staggering challenges of peace. Four questions loomed large: How would the South, physically devastated by war and socially revolutionized by emancipation, be rebuilt? How would the liberated blacks fare as free men and women? How would the Southern states be reintegrated into the Union? And who would direct the process of Reconstruction—the Southern states themselves, the president, or Congress?

The Problems of Peace

Other questions also clamored for answers. What should be done with the captured Confederate ring-leaders? During the war a popular Northern song had been "Hang Jeff Davis to a Sour Apple Tree." Davis was clapped into prison for two years, but no treason trials were ever held. President Andrew Johnson pardoned all "rebel" leaders as a sort of Christmas present in 1868. Congress removed their civil disabilities thirty years later.

Dismal indeed was the picture presented by the war-wracked South when the rattle of musketry faded. Not only had an age perished, but a civilization had collapsed, in both its economic and its social structure. The moonlight-and-magnolia Old South, largely imaginary in any case, had forever gone with the wind.

Handsome cities of yesteryear, like Charleston and Richmond, were rubble strewn and weed choked. An Atlantan returned to his once-fair home-town and remarked, "Hell has laid her egg, and right here it hatched." Economic life had creaked to a halt. Banks and business houses had locked their doors, ruined by runaway inflation. Factories were smokeless, silent, dismantled. The transportation system had broken down completely. Efforts to untwist the rails corkscrewed by Sherman's soldiers proved bumpily unsatisfactory.

Agriculture—the economic lifeblood of the South—was almost hopelessly crippled. Once-white cotton fields yielded a lush harvest of nothing but green weeds. The slave-labor system had collapsed, seed was scarce, and livestock had been driven off by plundering Yankees. Pathetic instances were reported of men hitching themselves to plows, while women and children gripped the handles.

The princely planter aristocrats were humbled by the war—at least temporarily. Reduced to proud poverty, they faced charred and gutted mansions, lost investments, and almost worthless land. Their investment of more than $2 billion in slaves, their primary form of wealth, had evaporated with emancipation.

Beaten but unbent, many high-spirited white Southerners remained dangerously defiant. They cursed the "damnyankees" and spoke of "your government" in Washington instead of "our government." Conscious of no crime, these former Confederates continued to believe that their view of secession was correct and that the "lost cause" was still a just war. One popular anti-Union song ran,

I'm glad I fought agin her, I only wish we'd won,
And I ain't axed any pardon for anything I've done.

Such attitudes boded ill for the prospects of painlessly binding up the Republic's wounds.

Freedmen Define Freedom

Confusion abounded in the still-smoldering South about the precise meaning of "freedom" for blacks. Emancipation took effect haltingly and unevenly in different parts of the conquered Confederacy, and in some regions planters stubbornly protested that slavery was legal until state legislatures or the Supreme Court might act. For many slaves, the shackles of bondage were not struck off in a single mighty blow; long-suffering blacks often had to pry off their chains link by link.

The variety of responses to emancipation, by whites as well as blacks, illustrated the sometimes startling complexity of the master-slave relationship. Loyalty to the plantation master prompted some slaves to resist the liberating Union armies. Other slaves' pent-up bitterness burst violently forth on the day of liberation. In one instance, a group of Virginia slaves laid twenty lashes on the back of their former master—a painful dose of his own favorite medicine.

Richmond Devastated *Charleston, Atlanta, and other Southern cities looked much the same, resembling bombed-out Berlin and Dresden in 1945.*

Prodded by the bayonets of Yankee armies of occupation, all masters were eventually forced to recognize their slaves' permanent freedom. The once-commanding planter would assemble his former human chattels in front of the porch of the "big house" and announce their liberty. Though some blacks initially responded to news of their emancipation with suspicion and uncertainty, they soon celebrated their newfound freedom. Many took new names in place of the ones given by their masters and demanded that whites formally address them as "Mr." or "Mrs."

Tens of thousands of emancipated blacks took to the roads, some to test their freedom, others to search for long-lost spouses, parents, and children. Emancipation thus strengthened the black family, and many newly freed men and women formalized "slave marriages" for personal and pragmatic reasons, including the desire to make their children legal heirs.

Whole communities sometimes moved together in search of opportunity. From 1878 to 1880, some twenty-five thousand blacks from Louisiana, Texas, and Mississippi surged in a mass exodus to Kansas. The westward flood of these "Exodusters" was stemmed only when steamboat captains refused to transport more black migrants across the Mississippi River.

The church became the focus of black community life in the years following emancipation. As slaves, blacks had worshiped alongside whites, but now they formed their own churches pastored by their own ministers. The black churches grew robustly. The 150,000-member black Baptist Church of 1850 reached 500,000 by 1870, while the African Methodist Episcopal Church quadrupled in size from 100,000 to 400,000 in the first decade after emancipation. These churches formed the bedrock of black community life, and they soon gave rise to other benevolent, fraternal, and mutual aid societies. All these organizations helped blacks protect their newly won freedom.

Emancipation also meant education for many blacks. Learning to read and write had been a privilege generally denied to them under slavery. Freedmen wasted no time establishing societies for self-improvement, which undertook to raise funds to purchase land, build schoolhouses, and hire teachers. With black teachers in short supply, they turned to white women sent by the American Missionary Association for help, and to the federal government.

The Freedmen's Bureau

Abolitionists had long preached that slavery was a degrading institution. Now the emancipators had to face the brutal truth that the former slaves were overwhelmingly unskilled, unlettered, without property or money, and with scant knowledge of how to survive as free people. To cope with this problem throughout the conquered South, Congress created the Freedmen's Bureau in 1865.

Primary School for Freedmen in Vicksburg, Mississippi, 1866 Top: *Outdoor recess at school.* Bottom: *Teaching the pupils; notice the wide range of ages.*

On paper at least, the bureau was intended to be a kind of primitive welfare agency. It was to provide food, clothing, and education both to freedmen and to white refugees. It was also authorized to distribute up to forty acres of abandoned or confiscated land to black settlers. Headed by General O. O. Howard, who later founded Howard University, the bureau achieved its greatest successes in education. It taught an estimated 200,000 blacks how to read. Many former slaves had a passion for learning, partly because they wanted to close the gap between themselves and the whites and partly because they longed to read the Word of God.

But in other areas the bureau's accomplishments were meager—or even mischievous. Little confiscated Confederate land actually passed into black hands, as had been promised. Instead, local administrators often collaborated with planters in expelling blacks from towns and cajoling them into signing labor contracts to work for their former masters. Still, the white South resented the bureau as a meddlesome federal interloper that threatened to upset white racial dominance. President Andrew Johnson, who shared the white-supremacist views of most white Southerners, repeatedly tried to kill it, and it expired in 1872.

Johnson: The Tailor President

Few presidents have ever been faced with a more perplexing sea of troubles than that confronting Andrew Johnson. What manner of man was this medium-built, dark-eyed, black-haired Tennessean, chief executive by virtue of the bullet that killed Lincoln?

No citizen, not even Lincoln, ever reached the White House from humbler beginnings. Born to impoverished parents in North Carolina and early orphaned, Johnson never attended school but was apprenticed to a tailor at age ten. Ambitious to get ahead, he taught himself to read, and later his wife taught him to write and do simple arithmetic. Like many a self-made man, he was inclined to overpraise his maker.

Johnson early became active in politics in Tennessee, where he had moved when seventeen years old. He shone as an impassioned champion of the poor whites against the planter aristocrats and as a two-fisted stump speaker before angry and heckling crowds. Elected to Congress, he refused to secede with his own state and was then appointed war governor after Tennessee was partially recovered for the Union by federal armies.

Political exigency next thrust Johnson into the vice presidency. Lincoln's Union party in 1864 needed to attract support from the War Democrats and other pro-Southern elements, and Johnson, a Democrat, seemed to be the ideal man.

"Old Andy" Johnson was no doubt a man of parts—unpolished parts. He was intelligent, able, forceful, and steadfastly devoted to duty and the Constitution. Yet the man who had raised himself from the tailor's bench to the president's chair was a misfit. A Southerner who did not understand the North, a Tennessean who had earned the distrust of the South, a Democrat who had never been accepted by the Republicans, a president who had never been elected to the office, he was not at home in a Republican White House. Hotheaded, contentious, and stubborn, he was the wrong man in the wrong place at the wrong time. A Reconstruction policy devised by the angels might well have failed in his tactless hands.

Presidential Reconstruction

Even before the shooting war had ended, the political war over Reconstruction had begun. Abraham Lincoln believed that the withdrawal of the Southern states from the Union had never been legal. Their formal restoration to the Union would therefore be relatively simple. Accordingly, Lincoln in 1863 proclaimed his "10 percent" Reconstruction plan. It decreed that a state could be reintegrated into the Union when 10 percent of its voters—based on the 1860 presidential election numbers—had taken an oath of allegiance to the United States and pledged to abide by emancipation. The next step would be formal erection of a state government. Lincoln would then recognize the purified regime.

Lincoln's proclamation provoked a sharp reaction in Congress, where Republicans feared the restoration of the planter aristocracy to power and the possible re-enslavement of the blacks. Republicans therefore rammed through Congress in 1864 the Wade-Davis Bill. It required that 50 percent of a state's voters take the oath of allegiance and demanded stronger safeguards for emancipation than Lincoln's as the price of readmission. Republicans were outraged when Lincoln "pocket-vetoed" this bill by refusing to sign it after Congress had adjourned.

The controversy surrounding the Wade-Davis Bill revealed deep differences between the president and Congress. Unlike Lincoln, many in Congress insisted that the seceders had indeed left the Union—had "committed suicide" as republican states—and had therefore forfeited all their rights. They could be readmitted only as "conquered provinces" on such conditions as Congress should decree.

The episode further revealed differences among two emerging Republican factions, moderates and radicals. The majority moderate group tended to agree with Lincoln that the seceded states should be restored to the Union as simply and swiftly as reasonable—though on Congress's terms, not the president's. The minority radical group believed that before the South could be restored, its social structure should be uprooted, the haughty planters punished, and the newly emancipated blacks protected by federal power.

After the assassination of President Lincoln in April 1865, some radicals hoped that spiteful Andy Johnson, who shared their hatred for the planter aristocracy, would also share their desire to reconstruct the South with a rod of iron. But Johnson soon disillusioned them. He quickly recognized several of Lincoln's 10 percent governments, and on May 29, 1865, he issued his own Reconstruction proclamation. It disfranchised certain leading Confederates and called for special state conventions, which were required to repeal secession, repudiate all Confederate debts, and ratify the slave-freeing Thirteenth Amendment.

Johnson, savoring his dominance over the high-toned aristocrats who now begged his favor, granted pardons in abundance. Bolstered by the political resurrection of the planter elite, the recently rebellious states moved rapidly in the second half of 1865 to organize governments. But as the pattern of the new governments became clear, Republicans of all stripes grew furious.

The Baleful Black Codes

Among the first acts of the new Southern regimes sanctioned by Johnson was the passage of the iron-toothed Black Codes. These laws were designed to regulate the affairs of the emancipated blacks, much as the slave statutes had done in pre–Civil War days. The Black Codes aimed, first of all, to ensure a stable and subservient labor force. Dire penalties were therefore imposed on blacks who "jumped" their labor contracts, which usually committed them to work for the same employer for one year, generally at pittance wages.

The codes also sought to restore as nearly as possible the pre-emancipation system of race relations. Freedom was legally recognized, as were some other privileges, such as the right to marry. But all the codes forbade a black to serve on a jury or vote, and some even barred blacks from renting or leasing land.

These oppressive laws mocked the ideal of freedom, so recently purchased by buckets of blood. The Black Codes imposed terrible burdens on the unfettered blacks, struggling against mistreatment and poverty to make their way as free people. Thousands of impoverished former slaves slipped into virtual peonage as sharecropper farmers, as did many landless whites.

The Black Codes made an ugly impression in the North. If the former slaves were being re-enslaved, people asked one another, had not the Boys in Blue spilled their blood in vain? Had the North really won the war?

Congressional Reconstruction

These questions grew more insistent when the congressional delegations from the newly reconstituted Southern states presented themselves in the Capitol in December 1865. To the shock and disgust of the Republicans, many former Confederate leaders were on hand to claim their seats.

The appearance of these ex-rebels was a natural but costly blunder. Voters of the South, seeking able representatives, had turned instinctively to their experienced statesmen. But most of the Southern leaders were tainted by active association with the "lost cause." Among them were four former Confederate generals, five colonels, and various members of the Richmond cabinet and Congress. Worst of all, there was the shrimpy but brainy Alexander Stephens, ex–vice president of the Confederacy, still under indictment for treason but now representing Georgia in the House.

The presence of these "whitewashed rebels" infuriated the Republicans in Congress. The war had been fought to restore the Union, but not on these kinds of terms. Most Republicans balked at giving up the political advantage they had enjoyed while the South had been "out" from 1861 to 1865. On the first day of the congressional session, December 4, 1865, they banged shut the door in the face of the newly elected Southern delegations.

Looking to the future, the Republicans were alarmed to realize that a restored South would be stronger than ever in national politics. Before the war a black slave had counted as three-fifths of a person in apportioning congressional representation. But now, owing to full counting of free blacks, the eleven rebel states were entitled to twelve more votes in Congress, and twelve more presidential electoral votes, than they had previously enjoyed. Again, angry voices in the North raised the cry, Who won the war?

Republicans had good reason to fear that ultimately they might be elbowed aside. Southerners might join hands with Democrats in the North and win control of Congress or maybe even the White House. If this happened, they could perpetuate the Black Codes, virtually re-enslaving the blacks. They could dismantle the economic program of the Republican party and possibly even repudiate the national debt. President Johnson thus deeply disturbed the congressional Republicans when he announced on December 6, 1865, that the recently rebellious states had satisfied his conditions and that in his view the Union was now restored.

Johnson Clashes with Congress

A clash between president and Congress was now inevitable. It exploded into the open in February 1866, when the president vetoed a bill (later repassed) extending the life of the controversial Freedmen's Bureau.

Aroused, the Republicans swiftly struck back. In March 1866 they passed the Civil Rights Bill, which conferred on the blacks the privileges of American citizenship and struck at the Black Codes. President Johnson resolutely vetoed this forward-looking measure, but in April congressmen steamrollered it over his veto—something they repeatedly did henceforth. The hapless president, dubbed "Sir Veto" and "Andy Veto," had his presidential wings clipped short, as Congress increasingly assumed the dominant role in running the government.

The Republicans undertook to rivet the principles of the Civil Rights Bill into the Constitution as the Fourteenth Amendment. The proposed amendment, as approved by Congress and sent to the states in June 1866, was sweeping. It (1) conferred civil rights, including citizenship but excluding the franchise, on the freedmen; (2) reduced proportionately the representation of a state in Congress and in the Electoral College if it denied blacks the ballot; (3) disqualified from federal and state office former Confederates who as federal officeholders had once sworn to "support the Constitution of the United States"; and (4) guaranteed the federal debt, while repudiating all Confederate debts. (See text of the Fourteenth Amendment in the Appendix.)

The radical faction was disappointed that the Fourteenth Amendment did not grant the right to vote, but all Republicans agreed that no state should be welcomed back into the Union fold without first ratifying it. Yet President Johnson advised the Southern states to reject it, and all of the "sinful eleven," except Tennessee, defiantly spurned the amendment.

Swinging 'Round the Circle with Johnson

As 1866 lengthened, the battle intensified between Congress and the president. Now the issue was whether Reconstruction was to be carried on with or without the drastic Fourteenth Amendment. The Republicans would settle for nothing less.

The crucial congressional elections of 1866— more crucial than some presidential elections—were fast approaching. Johnson was naturally eager to escape from the clutches of Congress by securing a majority favorable to his soft-on-the-South policy. Invited to dedicate a Chicago monument to Stephen A. Douglas, he undertook to speak at various cities en route in support of his views.

Johnson's famous "swing 'round the circle," beginning in the late summer of 1866, was a serio-comedy of errors. The president delivered a series of "give 'em hell" speeches, in which he accused the radicals in Congress of having planned large-scale antiblack riots and murder in the South. As he spoke, hecklers hurled insults at him. Reverting to his stump-speaking days in Tennessee, he shouted back angry retorts, amid cries of "You be damned" and "Don't get mad, Andy." The dignity of his high office sank to a new low.

As a vote-getter, Johnson was highly successful—for the opposition. His inept speechmaking heightened the cry "Stand by Congress" against the "Tailor of the Potomac." When the ballots were counted, the Republicans had rolled up more than a two-thirds majority in both houses of Congress.

Republican Reconstruction

The Republicans had a veto-proof Congress and virtually unlimited control of Reconstruction policy. But moderates and radicals still disagreed over the best course to pursue in the South.

The radicals in the Senate were led by courtly and principled Charles Sumner, and in the House by crusty and vindictive Thaddeus Stevens, both devoted not only to black freedom but to racial equality. Still opposed to rapid restoration of the Southern states, the radicals wanted to keep them out as long as possible, and to apply federal power to bring about a drastic social and economic transformation in the South.

But moderate Republicans, more attuned to time-honored Republican principles of states' rights and self-government, preferred policies that restrained the states from abridging citizens' rights, rather than policies that directly involved the federal government in individual lives. The actual policies adopted by Congress showed the influence of both these schools of thought, though the moderates, as the majority faction, had the upper hand. And one thing both groups had come to agree on by 1867 was the necessity to enfranchise black voters, even if it took federal troops to do it.

Against a backdrop of vicious and bloody race riots that had erupted in several Southern cities, Congress passed the Reconstruction Act on March 2, 1867. This drastic legislation divided the South into five military districts, each commanded by a Union general and policed by blue-clad soldiers, about twenty thousand all told.

Congress additionally laid down stringent requirements for the readmission of the seceded states. The wayward states were required to ratify the Fourteenth Amendment, giving the former slaves their rights as citizens, and to guarantee in their state constitutions full suffrage for their former adult male slaves. Yet the act, reflecting moderate sentiment, stopped short of giving the freedmen land or education at federal expense. The overriding purpose of the moderates was to create an electorate in Southern states that would vote those states back into the Union on acceptable terms and thus free the federal government from direct responsibility for the protection of black rights. As later events would demonstrate, this approach proved woefully inadequate to the cause of justice for the blacks.

The radical Republicans still worried that once the unrepentant states were readmitted, they would amend their constitutions to withdraw the ballot from the blacks. They therefore sought the ironclad safeguard of black suffrage in the federal Constitution. This goal was finally achieved by the Fifteenth Amendment, passed by Congress in 1869 and ratified by the required number of states in 1870. (For text, see the Appendix.)

Military Reconstruction of the South not only usurped certain functions of the president as commander in chief but set up a martial regime of dubious legality. The Supreme Court had already ruled, in the case *Ex parte Milligan* (1866), that military tribunals could not try civilians, even during wartime, in areas where the civil courts were open. Peacetime military rule seemed starkly contrary to the spirit of the Constitution, but for the time being the Supreme Court avoided offending the Republican Congress.

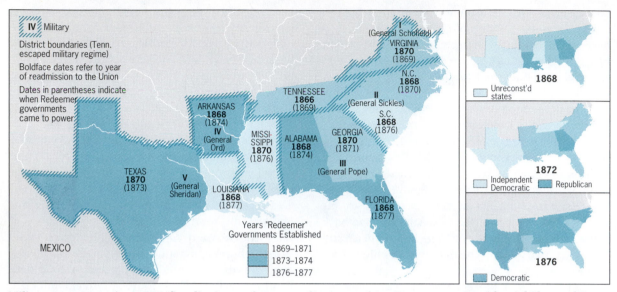

Military Reconstruction, 1867 (five districts and commanding generals) *For many white Southerners, military Reconstruction amounted to turning the knife in the wound of defeat. An often-repeated story of later years had a Southerner remark, "I was sixteen years old before I discovered that* damnyankee *was two words."*

Presidential Electoral Vote by Party

Prodded into line by federal bayonets, the Southern states got on with the task of constitution making. By 1870 all of them had reorganized their governments and had been accorded full rights. The hated "Blue Bellies" remained until the new regimes—usually called "radical" regimes—appeared to be firmly entrenched. Yet as soon as the last federal muskets were removed from state politics in 1877, the all-white regimes, the so-called "redeemer" governments, swiftly returned to power, and the "solid" Democratic South congealed.

The passage of the three Reconstruction Amendments—the Thirteenth, Fourteenth, and Fifteenth—delighted former abolitionists but deeply disappointed advocates of women's rights. Women had played a prominent part in the prewar abolitionist movement, and in the eyes of many women the struggle for black freedom and the crusade for women's rights were one and the same. Now, feminist leaders reeled with shock when the Fourteenth Amendment, which defined equal national citizenship, for the first time inserted the word *male* into the Constitution in referring to a citizen's right to vote.

When the Fifteenth Amendment proposed to prohibit denial of the vote on the basis of "race, color, or previous condition of servitude," women's rights leaders Susan B. Anthony and Elizabeth Cady Stanton wanted the word *sex* added to the list. They lost this battle, too. Fifty years would pass before the Constitution granted women the right to vote.

The Realities of Radical Reconstruction in the South

Blacks now had freedom, of a sort. By 1867 Republican hesitation over black voting had given way to a hard determination to enfranchise the former slaves wholesale and immediately, while thousands of white Southerners were being denied the right to vote. By glaring contrast most of the Northern states, before ratification of the Fifteenth Amendment in 1870, withheld the ballot from their tiny black minorities. White Southerners naturally concluded that the Republicans were hypocritical in insisting that blacks in the South be allowed to vote.

Having gained their right to suffrage, Southern black men seized the initiative and began to organize politically. Their primary vehicle became the Union League, originally a pro-Union organization based in the North. Assisted by Northern blacks, freedmen turned the League into a network of political clubs that educated members in their civic duties and campaigned for Republican candidates. The League's mission soon expanded to include building black churches and schools, representing black grievances before local employers and governments, and recruiting militias to protect black communities from white retaliation.

Though African-American women did not obtain the right to vote, they too assumed new political roles. Black women faithfully attended the parades and rallies common in black communities during the early years of Reconstruction and helped assemble mass meetings in the newly constructed black churches. They even showed up at the constitutional conventions held throughout the South in 1867, monitoring the proceedings and participating in informal votes outside the convention halls.

But black men elected as delegates to the state constitutional conventions held the greater political authority. They formed the backbone of the black political community. At the conventions, they sat down with whites to hammer out new state constitutions, which most importantly provided for universal male suffrage.

The sight of former slaves holding office deeply offended their onetime masters, who lashed out with fury at the freedmen's white allies, labeling them "scalawags" and "carpetbaggers." The so-called scalawags were Southerners, often former Unionists, whom former Confederates wildly accused of plundering the treasuries of the Southern states through their political influence in the radical governments. The carpetbaggers were supposedly sleazy Northerners who had packed all their worldly goods into a carpetbag suitcase at war's end and come south to seek personal power and profit. In fact, most were former Union soldiers and Northern businessmen and professionals who wanted to play a role in modernizing the "New South."

How well did the radical regimes rule? Black voters made up a majority of the electorate in five states, but only in South Carolina did blacks predominate in the lower house of the legislature. Many of the newly

Freedmen Voting, Richmond, Virginia, 1871 *The exercise of democratic rights by former slaves constituted a political and social revolution in the South, and was bitterly resented by whites.*

elected black legislators were literate and able; more than a few came from the ranks of the prewar free blacks who had acquired considerable education. More than a dozen black congressmen and two black United States senators, Hiram Revels and Blanche K. Bruce, both of Mississippi, did creditable work in the national capital.

In some radical regimes, there was truth to the charges of graft and corruption. This was especially true in South Carolina and Louisiana, where conscienceless promoters and other pocket-padders used politically inexperienced blacks as cat's-paws. The worst "black-and-white" legislatures purchased as "legislative supplies" such "stationery" items as hams, perfumes, suspenders, bonnets, corsets, champagne, and a coffin. Yet this kind of corruption was no more outrageous than the scams and felonies being perpetrated in the North at the same time, especially in Boss Tweed's New York.

The radical legislatures also passed much desirable legislation. For the first time in Southern history, steps were taken toward establishing adequate public schools. Tax systems were streamlined; public works were launched; and property rights were guaranteed to women. Many of these reforms were so welcome that they were retained by the all-white "redeemer" governments that later returned to power.

The Ku Klux Klan

Deeply embittered, some Southern whites resorted to savage measures against "radical rule." Many whites resented the success and ability of black legislators as much as they resented alleged "corruption."

A number of secret organizations mushroomed forth, the most notorious of which was the "Invisible Empire of the South," or Ku Klux Klan, founded in Tennessee in 1866. Besheeted nightriders, their horses' hoofs muffled, would approach the cabin of an "upstart" black and hammer on the door. In ghoulish tones one thirsty horseman would demand a bucket of water. Then, under pretense of drinking, he would pour the whole bucket into a rubber attachment concealed beneath his mask and gown, smack his lips, and declare that this was the first water he had tasted since he was killed at the Battle of Shiloh.

If fright did not produce the desired effect of intimidating black voters, force was employed. Such terror tactics proved partially effective. Many ex-bondsmen and white "carpetbaggers," quick to take a hint, shunned the polls. Those stubborn souls who persisted in their "upstart" ways were flogged, mutilated, or even murdered.

Congress, outraged by this night-riding lawlessness, passed the harsh Force Acts of 1870 and 1871. Federal troops were able to stamp out much of the "lash law," but by this time the Invisible Empire had already done its work of intimidation.

White resistance undermined attempts to empower the blacks politically. The white South for many decades openly flouted the Fourteenth and Fifteenth Amendments. Wholesale disfranchisement of the blacks, starting conspicuously about 1890, was achieved by intimidation, fraud, and trickery. Among various underhanded schemes were the literacy tests, unfairly administered by whites to the advantage of illiterate whites. In the eyes of white Southerners, the goal of white supremacy fully justified these dishonorable devices.

Impeachment and Acquittal for Johnson

Radicals meanwhile had been sharpening their hatchets for President Johnson. Not content with curbing his authority, they decided to remove him altogether by constitutional processes.*

As an initial step, Congress in 1867 passed the Tenure of Office Act—as usual over Johnson's veto. Contrary to precedent, the new law required the president to secure the consent of the Senate before he could remove his appointees, including the secretary of war, Edwin M. Stanton. Originally a Lincoln appointee and outwardly professing loyalty to Johnson, Stanton was secretly serving as a spy and informer for the radicals.

Johnson, sensing Stanton's secret hostility, took the bait when he abruptly dismissed the war secre-

---

* For impeachment, see Art. I, Sec. II, para. 5; Art. I, Sec. II, paras. 6, 7; Art. II, Sec. IV, in the Appendix.

tary early in 1868. The House of Representatives immediately voted 126 to 47 to impeach Andrew Johnson for "high crimes and misdemeanors," as provided for by the Constitution. They charged him with various violations of the Tenure of Office Act. Two additional articles related to Johnson's verbal assaults on the Congress, involving "disgrace, ridicule, hatred, contempt, and reproach."

The radical-led Senate sat as a court to try Johnson on these dubious impeachment charges, with the House conducting the prosecution. The trial aroused intense public interest and, with only one thousand seats available for spectators, proved to be the hottest ticket in Washington. Johnson kept his dignity and maintained a discreet silence. His able battery of attorneys argued that the president had merely fired Stanton in order to test the Tenure of Office Act before the Supreme Court. The House prosecutors, including oily-tongued Benjamin F. Butler and embittered Thaddeus Stevens, had a harder time building a case for impeachment.

On May 16, 1868, the day for voting in the Senate, the tension was electric, and heavy breathing could be heard in the galleries. By a margin of only one vote, the radicals failed to muster the two-thirds majority for Johnson's removal.

Die-hard radicals were infuriated. "The Country is going to the Devil!" cried the crippled Stevens as he was carried from the hall. But the nation, though violently aroused, accepted the verdict with a good tem-per and an absence of street violence that did credit to its political maturity.

The nation thus narrowly avoided a bad precedent that would have gravely weakened one of the three branches of the federal government. Johnson was clearly guilty of bad speeches, bad judgment, and bad temper, but not of "high crimes and misdemeanors." From the standpoint of the radicals, his greatest crime had been to stand inflexibly in their path.

The Purchase of Alaska

Johnson's administration, though largely reduced to a figurehead, achieved its most enduring success in the field of foreign relations. The Russians by 1867 were in a mood to sell the vast and chilly expanse of land now known as Alaska. The region had been ruthlessly "furred out" and was a growing economic liability. The Russians were therefore eager to unload their "frozen asset." And by dealing with the Americans, they could score twice, further strengthening the Republic as a barrier against their ancient enemy, Britain.

In 1867 Secretary of State William Seward, an ardent expansionist, signed a treaty with Russia that transferred Alaska to the United States for the bargain price of $7.2 million. But Seward's enthusiasm for these frigid wastes was not shared by his thrifty and anti-expansionist countrymen, who jeered at "Seward's Folly," "Seward's Icebox," "Frigidia," and "Walrussia."

Impeachment Drama *The impeachment proceedings against President Andrew Johnson, among the most severe constitutional crises in the Republic's history, were high political theater, and tickets were in sharp demand.*

Then why did Congress and the American public sanction the purchase? For one thing Russia, alone among the great powers, had been conspicuously friendly to the North during the recent Civil War. Americans did not feel that they could offend their good friend the tsar by hurling his walrus-covered icebergs back into his face. Besides, the territory was rumored to be still teeming with furs, fish, and gold, and it might yet "pan out" profitably—as it later did, with natural resources, including oil and gas.

The Heritage of Reconstruction

Many white Southerners regarded Reconstruction as a more grievous wound than the war itself. It left a festering scar that would take generations to heal. They resented the upending of their social and racial system, the political empowerment of blacks, and the insult of federal intervention in their local affairs. Yet given the explosiveness of the issues that had caused the war, and the bitterness of the fighting, the wonder is that Reconstruction was not far harsher than it was. Northern policymakers groped for the right policies, influenced as much by Southern responses to defeat and emancipation as by any specific plans of their own.

The Republicans acted from a mixture of idealism and political expediency. They wanted both to protect the freed slaves and to promote the fortunes of the Republican party. In the end their efforts backfired badly. Reconstruction conferred only fleeting benefits on the blacks, and it virtually extinguished the Republican party in the South for nearly one hundred years.

Moderate Republicans never fully appreciated the efforts necessary to make the freed slaves completely independent citizens, or the lengths to which Southern whites would go to preserve their system of racial dominance. Had Thaddeus Stevens's radical program of drastic economic reforms and heftier protection of political rights been enacted, things might well have been different. But deep-seated racism, ingrained American resistance to tampering with property rights, and rigid loyalty to the principle of local self-government, combined with spreading in-difference in the North to the plight of the blacks, formed too formidable an obstacle. Despite good intentions by Republicans, the Old South was in many ways more resurrected than reconstructed.

Chronology

1863 Lincoln announces "10 percent" Reconstruction plan.

1864 Lincoln vetoes Wade-Davis Bill.

1865 Lincoln assassinated.
Johnson issues Reconstruction proclamation.
Congress refuses to seat Southern congressmen.
Freedmen's Bureau established.
Southern states pass Black Codes.

1866 Congress passes Civil Rights Bill over Johnson's veto.
Fourteenth Amendment (citizenship for blacks) passed.
Johnson-backed candidates lose congressional election.
Ex parte Milligan case.
Ku Klux Klan founded.

1867 Reconstruction Act.
Tenure of Office Act.
United States purchases Alaska from Russia.

1868 Johnson impeached and acquitted.
Johnson pardons Confederate leaders.

1870 Fifteenth Amendment (black suffrage) ratified.

1870–1871 Force Acts.

1872 Freedmen's Bureau ended.

1877 Reconstruction ends.

VARYING VIEWPOINTS

How Radical Was Reconstruction?

Few topics have triggered as much intellectual warfare as the "dark and bloody ground" of Reconstruction. The period provoked questions—sectional, racial, and constitutional—about which people felt deeply and remain deeply divided even today. Scholarly argument goes back to a Columbia University historian, William A. Dunning, who wrote about Reconstruction as a kind of national disgrace, foisted on a prostrate region by vindictive and self-seeking radical Republican politicians.

In the 1920s, widespread suspicion that the Civil War itself had been a tragic and unnecessary blunder shifted attention to Northern politicians. Scholars like Howard Beale argued that the radical Republicans had masked a ruthless desire to exploit Southern resources and expand Republican power in the South behind a false "front" of concern for the freed slaves.

After World War II, Kenneth Stampp, among others, turned this view on its head. Influenced by the modern civil rights movement, he argued that Reconstruction was a noble attempt to extend American principles of equity and justice. By the early 1970s, this view had become orthodoxy, and it generally holds sway today. Yet some scholars such as Michael Benedict and Leon Litwack claimed to discover that Reconstruction was never really very radical, and they argued that the Freedmen's Bureau and other agencies merely allowed white planters to maintain local political and economic control.

More recently, Eric Foner has powerfully reasserted the argument that Reconstruction was a truly radical and noble attempt to establish an interracial democracy. Drawing on the work of black scholar W. E. B. Du Bois, Foner emphasizes that Reconstruction allowed blacks to form political organizations and churches and to establish some measure of economic independence. Many of the benefits of Reconstruction were erased by white Southerners during the Gilded Age, but in the twentieth century, constitutional principles and organizations developed during Reconstruction provided the foundation for the modern civil rights movement—which some have called the Second Reconstruction.

For further reading, see the Appendix. For web resources, go to **http://college.hmco.com**.

PART FOUR

FORGING AN INDUSTRIAL SOCIETY

1865–1899

A nation of farmers fought the Civil War in the 1860s. By the time the Spanish-American War broke out in 1898, America was an industrial nation. For generations Americans had plunged into the wilderness and plowed their fields. Now they settled in cities and toiled in factories. Between the Civil War and the century's end, economic and technological change came so swiftly and massively that it seemed to many Americans that a whole new civilization had emerged.

In some ways it had. The sheer scale of the new industrial civilization was dazzling. Transcontinental railroads knit the country together from sea to sea. New industries like oil and steel grew to staggering size—and made megamillionaires out of entrepreneurs like oilman John D. Rockefeller and steelmaker Andrew Carnegie.

Drawn by the allure of industrial employment, Americans moved to the city. In 1860 only about 20 percent of the population were city dwellers. By 1900 that proportion doubled, as rural Americans and European immigrants alike flocked to mill town and metropolis in search of steady jobs.

These sweeping changes challenged the spirit of individualism that Americans had celebrated since the seventeenth century. Even on the western frontier, that historic bastion of rugged loners, the hand of government was increasingly felt, as large armies were dispatched to subdue the Plains Indians and federal authority was invoked to regulate the use of natural resources. The rise of powerful monopolies called into question the government's traditional hands-off policy toward business, and a growing band of reformers increasingly clamored for government regulation of private enterprise. The mushrooming cities, with their needs for transport systems, schools, hospitals, sanitation, and fire and police protection, required bigger governments and budgets than an earlier generation could have imagined. As never before, Americans struggled to adapt old ideals of private autonomy to the new realities of industrial civilization.

With economic change came social and political turmoil. Labor violence brought bloodshed to places such as Chicago and Homestead, Pennsylvania. Small farmers, squeezed by debt and foreign competition, rallied behind the People's, or "Populist," party, a radical movement of the 1880s and 1890s that attacked the power of Wall Street, big business, and the banks. Anti-immigrant sentiment swelled. Bitter disputes over tariffs and monetary policy deeply divided the country, setting debtors against lenders, farmers against manufacturers, the West and South against the Northeast. And in this unfamiliar era of big money and expanding government, corruption flourished, from town hall to Congress, fueling loud cries for political reform.

The bloodiest conflict of all pitted Plains Indians against the relentless push of westward expansion. As railroads drove their iron arrows through the heart of the West, the Indians lost their land and life-sustaining buffalo herds. By the 1890s, after three decades of fierce fighting with the U.S. Army, the Indians who had once roamed across the vast rolling prairies were confined to the open-air prisons called reservations.

The South remained the one region largely untouched by the Industrial Revolution sweeping the rest of America. A few sleepy southern hamlets did become boomtowns; but for the most part, the South's rural way of life, and its peculiar system of race relations, were largely unperturbed by the changes happening elsewhere. On African-Americans, the vast majority of whom continued to live in the Old South, the post-emancipation era inflicted new forms of racial injustice. State legislatures systematically deprived black Americans of their political rights, including the right to vote. Segregation of schools, housing, and all kinds of public facilities made a mockery of African-Americans' Reconstruction-era hopes for equality before the law.

The new wealth and power of industrial America nurtured a growing sense of national self-confidence. Literature flowered, and a golden age of philanthropy dawned. The reform spirit spread. So did a restless appetite for overseas expansion. In a brief war against Spain in 1898, the United States, born in a revolutionary war of independence and long the champion of colonial peoples yearning to breathe free, seized control of the Philippines and itself became an imperial power. Uncle Sam's venture into empire touched off a bitter national debate about America's role in the world and ushered in a long period of argument over the responsibilities, at home and abroad, of a modern industrial state.

23

Political Paralysis in the Gilded Age

1869–1896

*Grant . . . had no right to exist. He should have been extinct
for ages. . . . That, two thousand years after Alexander the
Great and Julius Caesar, a man like Grant should be called—
and should actually and truly be—the highest product of the
most advanced evolution, made evolution ludicrous. . . . The
progress of evolution, from President Washington to President
Grant, was alone evidence enough to upset Darwin. . . .
Grant . . . should have lived in a cave and worn skins.*

HENRY ADAMS, THE EDUCATION OF HENRY ADAMS, 1907

The population of the post–Civil War Republic
continued to vault upward by vigorous leaps,
despite the awful bloodletting in both Union and
Confederate ranks. Census takers reported over 39
million people in 1870, a gain of 26.6 percent over the
preceding decade, as the immigrant tide surged
again. The United States was now the third largest
nation in the Western world, ranking behind Russia
and France.

But the civic health of the United States did not
keep pace with its physical growth. The Civil War and
its aftermath spawned waste, extravagance, speculation, and graft. Disillusionment ran deep among idealistic Americans in the postwar era. They had spilled
their blood for the Union, emancipation, and Abraham Lincoln, who had promised "a new birth of freedom." Instead, they got a bitter dose of corruption and
political stalemate—beginning with Ulysses S. Grant,
a great soldier but an utterly inept politician.

The "Bloody Shirt" Elects Grant

Wrangling between Congress and Andrew Johnson had
soured the people on professional politicians, and the
notion still prevailed that a good general was bound to

make a good president. Stubbily bearded General Grant was by far the most popular northern hero to emerge from the war. Grateful citizens of Philadelphia, Washington, and New York showered him with gifts of houses and cash, which the general, silently puffing on his cigar, unapologetically accepted.

Grant was a hapless greenhorn in the political arena. His one presidential vote had been cast for the Democratic ticket in 1856. A better judge of horse-flesh than of humans, his cultural background was breathtakingly narrow. He once reportedly remarked that Venice, Italy, would be a fine city if only it were drained.

The Republicans, freed from the Union party coalition of war days, enthusiastically nominated Grant for the presidency in 1868. The party's platform sounded a clarion call for continued Reconstruction of the South under the glinting steel of federal bayonets. Yet Grant, always a man of few words, coined a popular campaign slogan in his letter of acceptance when he said, "Let us have peace."

Expectant Democrats, meeting in their own nominating convention, denounced military Reconstruction but could agree on little else. Wealthy eastern delegates demanded that federal war bonds be redeemed in gold, while the poorer midwesterners backed the "Ohio Idea" calling for redemption in greenbacks. Debt-burdened agrarian Democrats thus hoped to keep more money in circulation and to keep interest rates lower. This dispute introduced a bitter contest over monetary policy that continued to convulse the Republic until the century's end.

Midwestern delegates got the platform but not the candidate. The nominee, former New York governor Horatio Seymour, scuttled the Democrats' faint hope for success by repudiating the Ohio Idea plank. Republicans whipped up enthusiasm for Grant by energetically "waving the bloody shirt"—that is, reviving gory memories of the Civil War—which became for the first time a prominent feature of a presidential campaign. "Vote as You Shot" was a powerful Republican slogan aimed at Union army veterans.

Grant won, with 214 electoral votes to 80 for Seymour. But despite his great popularity, the former general scored a majority of only 300,000 in the popular vote (3,013,421 to 2,706,829). Most white voters apparently supported Seymour, and the ballots of three still-unreconstructed southern states (Mississippi, Texas, and Virginia) were not counted at all. An estimated 500,000 former slaves gave Grant his margin of victory. To remain in power, the Republican party somehow had to continue to control the South—and to keep the ballot in the hands of the grateful freedmen. Republicans could not take future victories "for Granted."

The Era of Good Stealings

A few skunks can pollute a large area. Although the great majority of businesspeople and government officials continued to conduct their affairs with decency and honor, the whole postwar atmosphere was fetid. The Man in the Moon, it was said, had to hold his nose when passing over America. Freewheeling railroad promoters sometimes left gullible bond buyers with only "two streaks of rust and a right of way." Unscrupulous stock-market manipulators were a cinder in the public eye. Too many judges and legislators put their power up for hire. Cynics defined an honest politician as one who, when bought, would stay bought.

Notorious in the financial world were two millionaire partners, "Jubilee Jim" Fisk and Jay Gould. The corpulent and unscrupulous Fisk provided the "brass," while the undersized and cunning Gould provided the brains. The crafty pair concocted a plot in 1869 to corner the gold market. Their slippery game would work only if the federal Treasury refrained from selling gold. The conspirators worked on President Grant directly, and also through his brother-in-law, who received $25,000 for his complicity. On "Black Friday" (September 24, 1869), Fisk and Gould madly bid the price of gold skyward, while scores of honest businesspeople were driven to the wall. The bubble finally broke when the Treasury, contrary to Grant's supposed assurances, was compelled to release gold. A congressional probe concluded that Grant had done nothing crooked, though he had acted stupidly and indiscreetly.

The infamous Tweed Ring in New York City vividly displayed the ethics (or lack of ethics) typical of the age. Burly "Boss" Tweed—240 pounds of rascality—employed bribery, graft, and fraudulent elections to milk the metropolis of as much as $200 million. Honest citizens were cowed into silence. Protesters found their tax assessments raised.

Tweed's luck finally ran out. The *New York Times* secured damning evidence in 1871 and courageously published it, though offered $5 million not to do so. Gifted cartoonist Thomas Nast pilloried Tweed mercilessly, after spurning a heavy bribe to desist. New York attorney Samuel J. Tilden headed the prosecution, gaining fame that later paved the path to his presidential nomination. Unbailed and unwept, Tweed died behind bars.

More serious than Boss Tweed's peccadilloes were the misdeeds of the federal government. Presi-

Can the Law Reach Him? 1872 *Cartoonist Thomas Nast attacked "Boss" Tweed in a series of cartoons like this one that appeared in* Harper's Weekly *in 1872. Here Nast depicts the corrupt Tweed as a powerful giant, towering over a puny law force.*

dent Grant's cabinet was a rodent's nest of grafters and incompetents. Favor seekers haunted the White House, plying Grant himself with cigars, wine, and horses. Several dozen of his in-laws attached themselves to the public payroll.

The easygoing Grant was first tarred by the Crédit Mobilier scandal, which erupted in 1872. Union Pacific Railway insiders had formed the Crédit Mobilier construction company and then cleverly hired themselves at inflated prices to build the railroad line, earning dividends as high as 348 percent. Fearing that Congress might blow the whistle, the company furtively distributed shares of its valuable stock to key congressmen. A newspaper exposé and congressional investigation of the scandal led to the formal censure of two congressmen and the revelation that the vice president of the United States had also accepted payments from Crédit Mobilier.

The breath of scandal in Washington also reeked of alcohol. In 1874–1875 a sprawling Whiskey Ring robbed the Treasury of millions in excise tax revenues. When President Grant's own private secretary turned up among the culprits, the president volunteered a written statement to a jury that helped exonerate the thief. Further rottenness in the Grant administration came to light in 1876, forcing Secretary of War William Belknap to resign after pocketing bribes from suppliers to the Indian reservations. Grant, ever loyal to his crooked cronies, accepted Belknap's resignation "with great regret."

The Liberal Republican Revolt of 1872

By 1872 a powerful wave of disgust with Grantism was beginning to build up throughout the nation, even before some of the worst scandals had been exposed. Reform-minded citizens banded together in the Liberal Republican party. Voicing the slogan "Turn the Rascals Out," they urged purification of the Washington administration as well as an end to military Reconstruction.

The Liberal Republicans muffed their chance when their Cincinnati nominating convention astounded the country by nominating the brilliant but erratic Horace Greeley for the presidency. Although Greeley was a fearless editor of the *New*

York Tribune, he was dogmatic, emotional, petulant, and notoriously unsound in his political judgments.

More astonishing still was the action of the office-hungry Democrats, who foolishly proceeded to endorse Greeley's candidacy. In swallowing Greeley the Democrats "ate crow" in large gulps, for the eccentric editor had long blasted them as traitors, slave whippers, saloon keepers, horse thieves, and idiots. Yet Greeley pleased the Democrats, North and South, when he pleaded with the party faithful to clasp hands across "the bloody chasm." The Republicans dutifully renominated Grant. The voters were thus presented with a choice between two candidates who had made their careers in fields other than politics and who were both eminently unqualified, by temperament and lifelong training, for high political office.

In the mud-spattered campaign that followed, Republicans denounced Greeley as an atheist, a free-lover, and a vegetarian, while Democrats derided Grant as a drunken swindler. But the regular Republicans, chanting "Grant us another term," pulled the president through. The count in the electoral column was 286 to 66, in the popular column 3,596,745 to 2,843,446.

Liberal Republican agitation frightened the regular Republicans into cleaning their own house before they were thrown out of it. The Republican Congress in 1872 passed a general amnesty act, removing political disabilities from all but some five hundred former Confederate leaders. Congress also moved to reduce high Civil War tariffs and to fumigate the Grant administration with mild civil-service reform. Like many American third parties, the Liberal Republicans left some enduring footprints, even in defeat.

Depression and Demands for Inflation

Grant's woes deepened in the paralyzing economic panic that broke in 1873. Bursting with startling rapidity, the crash was one of those periodic plummets that roller-coastered the economy in this age of unbridled capitalist expansion. Boom times became gloom times as more than fifteen thousand businesses went bankrupt. In New York City, an army of unemployed riotously battled the police.

Black Americans were hard hit. The Freedman's Savings and Trust Company had made unsecured loans to several companies that went under. Black depositers, who had entrusted over $7 million to the bank, lost their savings, and black economic development and black confidence in savings institutions likewise evaporated.

Hard times inflicted the worst punishment on debtors, who intensified their clamor for inflationary policies. Proponents of inflation breathed new life into the issue of greenbacks. During the war $450 million of the "folding money" had been issued, but it had depreciated under a cloud of popular mistrust and dubious legality.* By 1868 the Treasury had already withdrawn $100 million of the "battle-born currency" from circulation, and "hard-money" people everywhere looked forward to its complete disappearance. But now afflicted agrarian and debtor groups—"cheap-money" supporters—pressed for a reissuance of the greenbacks. With a crude but essentially accurate grasp of monetary theory, they reasoned that more money meant cheaper money and, hence, rising prices and easier-to-pay debts. Creditors, of course, reasoning from the same premises, advocated precisely the opposite policy.

The hard-money advocates carried the day. In 1874 they persuaded a confused Grant to veto a bill to print more paper money. They scored another victory in the Resumption Act of 1875, which pledged the government to the further withdrawal of greenbacks from circulation and to the redemption of all paper currency in gold at face value, beginning in 1879.

Down but not out, debtors looked for relief to another precious metal, silver. The "sacred white metal," they claimed, had received a raw deal. In the early 1870s, the Treasury had so undervalued silver that Congress formally dropped the coinage of silver dollars in 1873. Fate then played a sly joke when new silver discoveries later in the 1870s shot production up and forced silver prices down. Westerners from

---

* The Supreme Court in 1870 declared the Civil War Legal Tender Act unconstitutional. With the concurrence of the Senate, Grant thereupon added to the bench two justices who could be counted on to help reverse that decision, which happened in 1871. This is how the Court grew to its current size of nine justices.

silver-mining states joined with debtors in assailing the "Crime of '73," demanding a return to the "Dollar of Our Daddies." Like the demand for more greenbacks, the demand for the coinage of more silver was nothing more nor less than another scheme to promote inflation.

Hard-money Republicans resisted this scheme and counted on Grant to hold the line against it. He did not disappoint them. The Treasury began to accumulate gold stocks against the appointed day for resumption of metallic-money payments. Coupled with the reduction of greenbacks, this policy was called "contraction." It had a noticeable deflationary effect—the amount of money per capita in circulation actually decreased between 1870 and 1880, from $19.42 to $19.37. Contraction probably worsened the impact of the depression. But the new policy did restore the government's credit rating, and it brought the embattled greenbacks up to their full face value. When Redemption Day came in 1879, few greenback holders bothered to exchange the lighter and more convenient bills for gold.

Republican hard-money policy had a political backlash. It helped elect a Democratic House of Representatives in 1874, and in 1878 it spawned the Greenback Labor party, which polled over a million votes and elected fourteen members of Congress. The contest over monetary policy was far from over.

Pallid Politics in the Gilded Age

The political seesaw was delicately balanced throughout most of the Gilded Age (a sarcastic name given to the post–Civil War era by Mark Twain in 1873). Even a slight nudge could tip the teeter-totter to the advantage of the opposition party. Every presidential election was a squeaker, and the majority party in the House of Representatives switched six times in the eleven sessions between 1869 and 1891. Wobbling in such shaky equilibrium, politicians tiptoed timidly, producing a political record that was often trivial and petty.

Few significant economic issues separated the major parties. Democrats and Republicans saw very nearly eye-to-eye on questions like the tariff and civil-service reform, and majorities in both parties substantially agreed even on the much-debated currency question. Yet despite their rough agreement on these national matters, the two parties were ferociously competitive with each other. They were tightly and efficiently organized, and they commanded fierce loyalty from their members. Nearly 80 percent of eligible voters cast their ballots in presidential elections in the three decades after the Civil War. On election days droves of the party faithful tramped behind marching bands to the polling places, and "ticket splitting," or failing to vote the straight party line, was as rare as a silver dollar.

How can this apparent paradox of political consensus and partisan fervor be explained? The answer lies in the sharp ethnic and cultural differences in the membership of the two parties—in distinctions of style and tone, and especially of religious sentiment. Republican voters tended to adhere to those creeds that traced their lineage to Puritanism. They stressed strict codes of personal morality and believed that government should play a role in regulating both the economic and the moral affairs of society. Democrats, among whom immigrant Lutherans and Roman Catholics figured heavily, were more likely to adhere to faiths that took a less stern view of human weakness. Their religions professed toleration of differences in an imperfect world, and they spurned government efforts to impose a single moral standard on the entire society. These differences in temperament and religious values often produced raucous political contests at the local level, where issues like prohibition and education loomed large.

Democrats had a solid electoral base in the South and in the northern industrial cities, teeming with immigrants and controlled by well-oiled political machines. Republican strength lay largely in the Midwest and the rural and small-town Northeast. Grateful freedmen in the South continued to vote Republican in significant numbers. Another important bloc of Republican ballots came from the members of the Grand Army of the Republic (GAR)—a politically potent organization of several hundred thousand Union veterans

The lifeblood of both parties was patronage—disbursing jobs by the bucketful in return for votes, kickbacks, and party service. Boisterous infighting over patronage beset the Republican party in the 1870s and 1880s. A "Stalwart" faction, led by the handsome and imperious Senator Roscoe ("Lord Roscoe") Conkling of New York, unblushingly embraced the time-honored system of swapping jobs for votes. Opposed to the Conklingites were the so-called Half-Breeds, who flirted coyly with civil-service reform, but whose real quarrel with the Stalwarts was over who should grasp the ladle that dished out the spoils. The champion of the Half-Breeds was James G. Blaine, a radiantly personable congressman from Maine with a fine physical presence, a thrilling speaking voice, and an elastic conscience. A perennial contender for the presidency, Blaine was inclined to demagoguery in his pursuit of the office. But despite all the color of their personalities, Conkling and Blaine succeeded only in stalemating each other and deadlocking their party.

The Hayes-Tilden Standoff, 1876

Hangers-on around Grant, like fleas urging their ailing dog to live, begged the "Old Man" to try for a third term in 1876. The general, blind to his own ineptitudes, showed a disquieting willingness. But the House, by a lopsided bipartisan vote of 233 to 18, spiked the third-term boom. It passed a resolution that sternly reminded the country—and Grant—of the antidictator implications of the two-term tradition.

With Grant out of the running, and with the Conklingites and Blaineites neutralizing each other, the Republicans turned to a compromise candidate, Rutherford B. Hayes, who was obscure enough to be dubbed "the Great Unknown." His foremost qualification was having served as three-term governor of the potent "swing" state of Ohio, so crucial to the cliffhanging electoral contests of the day that it regularly produced presidential candidates.

Pitted against the humdrum Hayes was the Democratic nominee, Samuel J. Tilden, who had risen to fame as the man who bagged Boss Tweed in New York. Campaigning against Republican scandal, Tilden racked up 184 electoral votes of the needed 185, with 20 votes in four states doubtful because of irregular returns. Oregon eventually fell completely to Hayes, but surely Tilden could pick up at least one of the other three, especially in view of the fact that he had polled 247,448 more popular votes than Hayes, 4,284,020 to 4,036,572.

Both parties scurried to send "visiting statesmen" to the still-contested southern states of Louisiana, South Carolina, and Florida. All three disputed states submitted two sets of returns, one Democratic and one Republican. As the weeks drifted by, the paralysis tightened, generating a dramatic constitutional crisis. The Constitution merely specifies that the electoral returns from the states shall be sent to Congress, and in the presence of the House and Senate they shall be opened by the president of the Senate (see the Twelfth Amendment). But who should count them? On this point the Constitution was silent. If counted by the president of the Senate (a Republican), the Republican returns would be selected. If counted by the Speaker of the House (a Democrat), the Democratic returns would be chosen. How could the impasse be resolved?

The Compromise of 1877 and the End of Reconstruction

Clash or compromise was the stark choice. The danger loomed that there would be no president on inauguration day, March 4, 1877. "Tilden or Blood!" cried Democratic hotheads, and some of their "Minute Men" began to drill with arms. But behind the scenes, frantically laboring statesmen gradually hammered out an agreement in the Henry Clay tradition—the Compromise of 1877.

The election deadlock itself was to be broken by the Electoral Count Act, which passed Congress early in 1877. It set up an electoral commission consisting of fifteen men selected from the Senate, the House, and the Supreme Court.

In February 1877, about a month before Inauguration Day, the Senate and House met together in an electric atmosphere to settle the dispute. The roll of the states was tolled off alphabetically. When Florida was reached, the disputed documents were referred to the electoral commission, which sat in a nearby chamber. After prolonged discussion the members agreed, by the partisan vote of eight Republicans to seven Democrats, to accept the Republican returns. Outraged Democrats in Congress, smelling defeat, undertook to launch a filibuster "until hell froze over."

Hayes-Tilden Disputed Election of 1876 (with electoral vote by state) *Nineteen of the twenty disputed votes composed the total electoral count of Louisiana, South Carolina, and Florida. The twentieth was one of Oregon's three votes, cast by an elector who turned out to be ineligible because he was a federal officeholder (a postmaster), contrary to the Constitution (see Art. II, Sec. I, para. 2).*

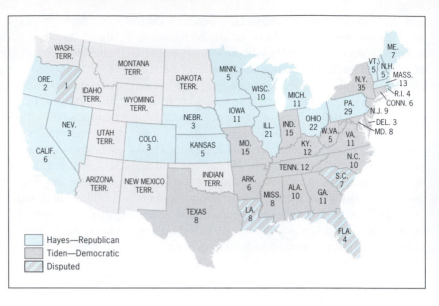

Renewed deadlock was avoided by the rest of the complex Compromise of 1877, already partially concluded behind closed doors. The Democrats reluctantly agreed that Hayes might take office in return for his withdrawing intimidating federal troops from the two states in which they remained, Louisiana and South Carolina. Among various concessions, the Republicans assured the Democrats a place at the presidential patronage trough and support for a bill subsidizing the Texas and Pacific Railroad's construction of a southern transcontinental line. Not all of these promises were kept in later years, including the Texas and Pacific subsidy. But the deal held together long enough to break the dangerous electoral standoff.

The compromise bought peace at a price. Violence was averted by sacrificing the black freedmen in the South. With the Hayes-Tilden deal, the Republican party quietly abandoned its commitment to black equality. That commitment had been weakening, in any case. The Civil Rights Act of 1875 was in a sense the last feeble gasp of the congressional radical Republicans. The act supposedly guaranteed equal accommodations in public places and prohibited racial discrimination in jury selection, but the law was born toothless and stayed that way for nearly a century. The Supreme Court pronounced much of the act unconstitutional in the *Civil Rights Cases*

(1883), declaring that the Fourteenth Amendment prohibited only *government* violations of civil rights, not the denial of civil rights by *individuals*. Hayes clinched the bargain by withdrawing the last federal troops that were propping up carpetbag governments. The bayonet-backed Republican regimes collapsed as the blue-clad soldiers departed.

The Birth of Jim Crow in the South

Relying shamelessly on fraud and intimidation, white Democrats ("Redeemers") swiftly suppressed the now-friendless blacks. For generations to come, blacks (as well as poor whites) would be forced into sharecropping and tenant farming under conditions scarcely better than slavery. Through the "crop-lien" system, storekeepers extended credit to small farmers for food and supplies and in return took a lien on their customers' harvests. Shrewd merchants manipulated the system so that farmers remained in perpetual debt.

With white southerners back in the political saddle, daily discrimination against blacks grew increasingly oppressive. What had started as the informal separation of blacks and whites in the immediate postwar years developed by the 1890s into systematic state-level codes of segregation known as Jim Crow laws. Southern states also enacted literacy requirements, voter-registration laws, and poll taxes to ensure full-scale disfranchisement of the South's black population. The Supreme Court validated the South's segregationist social order in the case of *Plessy* v. *Ferguson* (1896). It ruled that "separate but equal" facilities were constitutional under the "equal protection" clause of the Fourteenth Amendment.

But in reality the quality of African-American life was grotesquely unequal to that of whites. Segregated in inferior schools and separated from whites in virtually all public facilities, blacks were assaulted daily by reminders of their second-class citizenship. To ensure the stability of this political and economic "new order," southern whites dealt harshly with any black who dared to violate the South's racial code of conduct. A record number of blacks were lynched during the 1890s, most often for the "crime" of asserting themselves as equals. It would take a second Reconstruction, nearly a century later, to redress the racist imbalance of southern society.

Class Conflicts and Ethnic Clashes

The year 1877 marked more than the end of Reconstruction. As the curtains officially closed on regional warfare, they opened on scenes of class warfare. The explosive atmosphere was largely a by-product of the long years of depression and deflation following the panic of 1873. Railroad workers faced particularly hard times. When the presidents of the nation's four largest railroads collectively decided in 1877 to cut employees' wages by 10 percent, the workers struck back. President Hayes's decision to call in federal troops to quell the unrest brought the striking laborers an outpouring of working-class support. Work stoppages spread like wildfire in cities from Baltimore to St. Louis. When the battling between workers and soldiers ended after several weeks, over one hundred people had died.

The failure of the great railroad strike exposed the weakness of the labor movement. Racial and ethnic fissures among workers fractured labor unity and were particularly acute between the Irish and Chinese in California (see "Makers of America: The Chinese," pp. 316–317). By 1880 the Golden State

counted seventy-five thousand Asian newcomers, about 9 percent of its entire population.

Mostly single males from southern China, these newcomers had originally come to dig in the gold fields and to sledgehammer the tracks of the transcontinental railroads across the West. When those jobs ended, the Chinese who remained worked at the most menial jobs, often as cooks, laundrymen, or domestic servants. Without women or families, the Chinese male laborers lived lonely lives, bereft of the children who in other communities eased their parents' assimilation into the United States through their exposure to the English language and American customs in school.

In San Francisco, Irish-born demagogue Denis Kearney incited his followers, many of them recently arrived European immigrants, to violent abuse of the

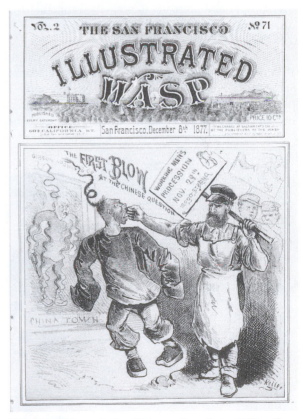

The First Blow at the Chinese Question, 1877 *Caucasian workers, seething with economic anxiety and ethnic prejudice, savagely mistreated the Chinese in California in the 1870s.*

The Chinese

In the late nineteenth century the burgeoning industries and booming frontier towns of the United States' Pacific Coast hungered for laborers. In faraway Asia the Chinese answered the call. Contributing their muscle to the building of the West, they dug in the gold mines and helped to lay the transcontinental railroads that stitched together the American nation.

The first major wave of Chinese came in response to the discovery of gold in California in 1848. The fortune-hungry immigrants who sailed into San Francisco named the city the "golden mountain."

The California boom coincided with the culmination of years of tumult and suffering in China. As the once-great Chinese Empire disintegrated, the European imperial powers forced their way into the unstable country. Faced with economic hardship and political turmoil, more than 2 million Chinese left their homeland between 1840 and 1900, for destinations as diverse as Southeast Asia, Peru, Hawaii, and Cuba. More than three hundred thousand entered the United States. Although their numbers included a few merchants and artisans, most were unskilled country folk.

The Chinese-America of the late-nineteenth-century West was overwhelmingly a bachelor society. Women of good repute rarely made the passage. Of the very few Chinese women who did venture to California at this time, most became prostitutes.

Although a stream of workers returned to China, many Chinese stayed. "Chinatowns" sprang up wher-

Chinese Butcher Shop, San Francisco, California, c. 1890

ever economic opportunities presented themselves. Chinese in these settlements spoke their own language, enjoyed the fellowship of their own compatriots, and sought safety from prejudice and violence. Many immigrant clubs and associations were American adaptations of Chinese traditions of loyalty to clan. The poorest and most alienated immigrants also established *tongs*—literally, "meeting halls"—secret societies that acquired a sinister reputation among non-Chinese.

After 1882 the Chinese Exclusion Act barred nearly all Chinese from the United States for six decades. Many of the bachelors died or returned home. Slowly, however, those men and the few women who remained raised families and reared a new generation of Chinese-Americans. Like their immigrant parents, this second generation suffered from discrimination. They had to eke out a living in jobs despised by Caucasian laborers or take daunting risks in small entrepreneurial ventures. Yet many hard-working Chinese did manage to open their own restaurants, laundries, and other small businesses. Such enterprises formed a solid economic foundation for their small community and remain a source of livelihood for many Chinese-Americans even today.

hapless Chinese. Taking to the streets, gangs of Kearneyites terrorized the Asians by shearing off precious pigtails. Some victims were murdered outright.

Seeing the Chinese, not their tormentors, as the problem, Congress finally slammed the door on Chinese immigrant laborers when it passed the Chinese Exclusion Act in 1882, prohibiting all further immigration from China. The door stayed shut until 1943. Some exclusionists even tried to strip native-born Chinese-Americans of their citizenship, but the Supreme Court ruled in *U.S.* v. *Wong Kim Ark* in 1898 that the Fourteenth Amendment guaranteed citizenship to all persons born in the United States. This doctrine of "birthright citizenship" provided important protections to Chinese-Americans as well as to other immigrant communities.

Garfield and Arthur

As the presidential campaign of 1880 approached, "Rutherfraud" Hayes was a man without a party, repudiated by the Republican Old Guard. Seeking a new standard-bearer, the Republicans finally settled on a "dark-horse" candidate, James A. Garfield of Ohio. His vice-presidential running mate was a notorious Stalwart henchman, Chester A. Arthur of New York.

Energetically waving the bloody shirt, Garfield barely squeaked out a victory over the Democratic candidate, Civil War hero Winfield Scott Hancock. Garfield polled only 39,213 more votes than Hancock—4,453,295 to 4,414,082—but his margin in the electoral column was a comfortable 214 to 155.

The new president was an energetic and able man, but he was immediately ensnared in political conflict between his new secretary of state, James G. Blaine, and Blaine's Stalwart nemesis, Senator Roscoe Conkling. Then, as the Republican factions dueled, tragedy struck. A disappointed and mentally deranged office seeker, Charles J. Guiteau, shot President Garfield in the back in a Washington railroad station. Garfield died eleven weeks later, on September 19, 1881, and Chester Arthur assumed the presidency.

Garfield's death did have one positive outcome: it shocked politicians into reforming the shameful spoils system. The unlikely instrument of reform was Chester Arthur. Arthur's record of cronyism and fondness for fine wines and elegant clothing (including eighty pairs of trousers) suggested that he was little more than a foppish dandy. But Arthur surprised his critics by prosecuting several fraud cases and giving his former Stalwart pals the cold shoulder.

Disgust with Garfield's murder gave the Republican party itself a previously undetected taste for reform. The medicine finally applied to the long-suffering federal government was the Pendleton Act of 1883—the so-called Magna Carta of civil-service reform. It made compulsory campaign contributions from federal employees illegal, and it established the Civil Service Commission to make appointments to federal jobs on the basis of competitive examinations rather than party pull.

Although at first covering only about 10 percent of federal offices, civil service did rein in the most blatant political abuses. Yet like many well-intentioned reforms, it bred unintended problems of its own. With the "plum" federal posts now beyond their control, politicians were forced to look elsewhere for money, the "mother's milk of politics." Increasingly, they turned to the bulging coffers of the big corporations. A new breed of boss emerged—less skilled at mobilizing small armies of immigrants and other voters on election day, but more adept at milking dollars from manufacturers and lobbyists.

President Arthur's surprising display of integrity offended too many powerful Republicans. His ungrateful party turned him out to pasture, and in 1886 he died of a cerebral hemorrhage.

The Blaine-Cleveland Mudslingers of 1884

James G. Blaine's persistence in pursuit of the presidential nomination finally paid off in 1884. The dashing Maine politician, blessed with almost every asset except a reputation for honesty, was clearly the choice of the Republican convention in Chicago. But many reform-minded Republicans gagged on Blaine's candidacy.

Blaine's enemies publicized Blaine's fishy-smelling "Mulligan letters" to a Boston businessman. These damning documents linked Blaine to a corrupt deal involving federal favors to a southern railroad, and one of them ended with the furtive warning "Burn this letter." Some reformers, unable to swallow Blaine, bolted to the Democrats. They were sneeringly dubbed Mugwumps, a word of Indian derivation meant to suggest that they were sanctimonious or "holier than thou."

Victory-starved Democrats turned enthusiastically to a noted reformer, Grover Cleveland. A burly bachelor with a soup-straining mustache and a taste for chewing tobacco, Cleveland was a solid but not brilliant lawyer of forty-seven. He had rocketed from the Buffalo mayor's office to the governorship of New York and the presidential nomination in three short years. Known as "Grover the Good," he enjoyed a well-deserved reputation for probity in office.

But Cleveland's admirers soon got a shock. Resolute Republicans, digging for dirt in the past of

"I Want My Pa!" *Malicious anti-Cleveland cartoon.*

bachelor Cleveland, unearthed the report that he had been involved in an amorous affair with a Buffalo widow, to whom an illegitimate son, now eight years old, had been born. Demoralized Democratic elders hurried to Cleveland and urged him to lie like a gentleman, but their ruggedly honest candidate insisted, "Tell the truth."

The campaign of 1884 sank to perhaps the lowest level in American experience, as the two parties grunted and shoved for the hog trough of office. Few fundamental differences separated them. Even the bloody shirt had faded to pale pink.* Personalities, not principles, claimed the headlines. Crowds of Democrats surged through city streets, chanting—to the rhythm of left, left, left, right, left—"Burn, burn, burn this letter!" Republicans taunted in return, "Ma, ma, where's my pa?" Defiant Democrats shouted back, "Gone to the White House, ha, ha, ha!"

The contest hinged on the state of New York, where Blaine blundered badly in the closing days of the cam-

---

*Neither candidate had served in the Civil War. Cleveland had hired a substitute to go in his stead while he supported his widowed mother and two sisters. Blaine was the only candidate nominated by the Republicans from Grant through McKinley (1868–1900) who had not been a Civil War officer.

paign. A witless Republican clergyman damned the Democrats as the party of "Rum, Romanism, and Rebellion"—insulting with one swift stroke the recreational habits, faith, and patriotism of New York's numerous Irish-Americans. Blaine was present but lacked the presence of mind to repudiate the statement immediately. The pungent phrase, shortened to "RRR," stung and stuck. Blaine's silence seemed to give assent, and the wavering Irishmen who then deserted his camp helped to account for Cleveland's paper-thin plurality of about a thousand votes in New York State, enough to give him the presidency. Cleveland swept the solid South and squeaked into office with 219 to 182 electoral votes and 4,879,507 to 4,850,293 popular votes.

"Old Grover" Takes Over

Bull-necked Cleveland in 1885 was the first Democrat to take the oath of presidential office since Buchanan, twenty-eight years earlier. Huge question marks hung over his portly frame (5 feet, 11 inches, 250 pounds). Could the "party of disunion" be trusted to govern the Union? Would desperate Democrats, ravenously hungry after twenty-four years of exile, trample the frail sprouts of civil-service reform in a stampede to the patronage trough? Could Cleveland restore a measure of respect and power to the maligned and enfeebled presidency?

Cleveland was a man of principles, most of them safely orthodox by the standards of the day. A staunch apostle of the hands-off creed of laissez-faire, the new president summed up his political philosophy in 1887 when he vetoed a bill to provide seeds for drought-ravaged Texas farmers. "Though the people support the government," he declared, "the government should not support the people." As tactless as a mirror and as direct as a bulldozer, Cleveland was outspoken, unbending, and profanely hot-tempered.

At the outset Cleveland narrowed the North-South chasm by naming to the cabinet two former Confederates. As for the civil service, Cleveland was whipsawed between the demands of the Democratic faithful for jobs and the demands of the Mugwumps, who had helped elect him, for reform. Believing in the merit system, Cleveland at first favored the cause of the reformers, but he eventually caved in to the carpings of Democratic bosses and fired almost two-thirds of the 120,000 federal employees, including 40,000 incumbent (Republican) postmasters, to make room for "deserving Democrats."

Military pensions gave Cleveland some of his most painful political headaches. The politically powerful Grand Army of the Republic (GAR) routinely lobbied hundreds of often questionable private pension bills through a compliant Congress. A nonveteran, Cleveland was in an awkward position to fight the pension grabbers, but he conscientiously read each bill and ended up vetoing several hundred of them.

Cleveland also risked his political welfare by prodding the hornet's nest of the tariff issue. Jacked up to new high levels during the Civil War, the tariff duties were producing embarassing surplus revenues while sheltering American industry. Congress could reduce the surplus by squandering it on pensions or other "pork-barrel" bills, or by lowering the tariff—something big industrialists vehemently opposed.

Impressed by the arguments for reduction, Cleveland bluntly tossed an appeal for lower tariffs like a bombshell into the lap of Congress in late 1887. The response was electric. Democrats were deeply distressed at the obstinacy of their chief. Republicans rejoiced at his apparent recklessness. The old warrior Blaine gloated, "There's one more president for us in [tariff] protection." For the first time in years, a real issue divided the two parties as the 1888 presidential election loomed.

Dismayed Democrats dejectedly nominated Cleveland at their St. Louis convention, while eager Republicans turned to Benjamin Harrison of Indiana, the grandson of former president William Henry ("Tippecanoe") Harrison. The tariff was the prime issue, and the two parties flooded the country with some 10 million pamphlets on the subject. Republicans raised an unprecedented $3 million war chest, largely by "frying the fat" out of nervous industrialists. The money was widely used to line up corrupt "voting cattle," known as "repeaters" or "floaters," especially in crucial swing states like Indiana.

On election day, Harrison nosed out Cleveland, 233 to 168 electoral votes. A change of about 7,000 ballots in New York would have reversed the outcome. Cleveland actually polled more popular votes, 5,537,857 to 5,447,129, but he nevertheless became the first sitting president to be voted out of his chair since Martin Van Buren in 1840.

Republicans Return Under Harrison

After a four-year famine, the Republicans under Harrison licked their lips hungrily for federal offices to lavish upon the party faithful. But in the House of Representatives they had only three votes more than the necessary quorum of 163 members, and the Democrats were preparing to obstruct all House business by refusing to answer roll calls, demanding roll calls to determine the presence of a quorum, and employing other delaying tactics.

Into this tense cockpit stepped the new Republican Speaker of the House, Thomas B. Reed of Maine. A hulking figure who towered 6 feet, 3 inches, he was renowned as a master debater. He spoke with a harsh nasal drawl and wielded a verbal harpoon of sarcasm. To one congressman who quoted Henry Clay that he would "rather be right than president," Reed caustically retorted that he "would never be either." Opponents cringed at the crack of his quip.

Employing clever parliamentary tactics to the fullest, "Czar" Reed utterly dominated the "Billion-Dollar" Congress—the first in history to appropriate that sum. Congress showered pensions on Civil War veterans and increased government purchases of silver. To keep the revenues flowing in—and to protect Republican industrialists from foreign competition—the Billion-Dollar Congress also passed the McKinley Tariff Act of 1890, boosting rates to their highest peacetime level ever (an average of 48.4 percent on dutiable goods).

Sponsored in the House of Representatives by rising Republican star William McKinley of Ohio, the new tariff act brought fresh woes to farmers. Debt-burdened farmers had no choice but to buy high-priced manufactured goods from protected American industrialists, but they were compelled to sell their own agricultural products into highly competitive, unprotected world markets. Mounting discontent against Bill McKinley and his McKinley Bill caused many rural voters to rise in wrath. In the congressional elections of 1890, Republicans lost their precarious majority and were reduced to just 88 seats, compared with 235 Democrats. Ominously for

conservatives, the new Congress also included nine members of the Farmers' Alliance, a militant organization of southern and western farmers.

The Drumbeat of Discontent

Politics was no longer "as usual" in 1892, when the newly formed People's party, or "Populists," burst upon the scene. Rooted in the Farmers' Alliances of the great agricultural belts of the West and South, the Populists met in Omaha and adopted a scorching platform that denounced the "prolific womb of governmental injustice." They demanded inflation through free and unlimited coinage of silver at the ratio of sixteen ounces of silver to one ounce of gold. They further called for a graduated income tax; government ownership of the railroads, telephone, and telegraph; the direct election of U.S. senators; a one-term limit on the presidency; the adoption of the initiative and referendum to allow citizens to shape legislation more directly; a shorter workday; and immigration restrictions. As their presidential candidate the Populists uproariously nominated an eloquent old veteran of the Greenback Labor party, General James B. Weaver.

An epidemic of nationwide strikes in the summer of 1892 raised the prospect that the Populists could weld together a coalition of aggrieved workers and indebted farmers in a revolutionary joint assault on the capitalist order. At Andrew Carnegie's Homestead steel plant near Pittsburgh, company officials called in three hundred armed Pinkerton detectives in July to crush a strike by steelworkers angry over pay cuts. Defiant strikers, armed with rifles and dynamite, forced their assailants to surrender after a vicious battle that left ten people dead and some sixty wounded. Troops were eventually summoned, and both the strike and the union were broken. That same month, federal troops bloodily smashed a strike among silver miners in Idaho's Coeur d'Alene district.

The Populists made a remarkable showing in the 1892 presidential election. Singing "Good-bye, Party Bosses," they rolled up 1,029,846 popular votes and 22 electoral votes for General Weaver. They thus became one of the few third parties in U.S. history to break into the electoral column. But they fell far short of an electoral majority. Industrial laborers, especially in the urban East, did not rally to the Populist banner in appreciable numbers. Populist electoral votes came from only six midwestern and western states, four of which (Kansas, Colorado, Idaho, and Nevada) fell completely into the Populist basket.

The South, although a hotbed of agrarian agitation, proved especially unwilling to throw in its lot with the new party. Race was the reason. The more than one million southern black farmers, organized in the Colored Farmers' National Alliance, shared a host of complaints with poor white farmers, and for a time their common economic goals promised to overcome their racial differences. Recognizing the crucial edge that black votes could give them in the South, Populist leaders like Georgia's Tom Watson reached out to the black community. Watson was a wiry redhead who could "talk like the thrust of a Bowie knife." He declared, "There is no reason why the black man should not understand that the law that hurts me, as a farmer, hurts him, as a farmer." Many blacks were disillusioned enough with the Republican party to respond. Alarmed, the conservative white "Bourbon" elite in the South played cynically upon historic racial antagonisms to counter the Populists' appeal for interracial solidarity and woo back poor whites.

Southern blacks were heavy losers. The Populist-inspired reminder of potential black political strength led to the near-total extinction of what little African-American suffrage remained in the South. White southerners more aggressively than ever used literacy tests and poll taxes to deny blacks the ballot. The notorious "grandfather clause" exempted from those requirements anyone whose forebear had voted in 1860—when, of course, black slaves had not voted at all. More than half a century would pass before southern blacks could again vote in considerable numbers. Accompanying this disfranchisement were more severe Jim Crow laws designed to enforce racial segregation in public places, including hotels and restaurants, and backed up by atrocious lynchings and other forms of intimidation.

The conservative crusade to eliminate the black vote also had dire consequences for the Populist party itself. Even Tom Watson abandoned his interracial appeals and, in time, became a vociferous racist himself. After 1896 the Populist party lapsed increasingly into vile racism and staunchly advocated black disfranchisement. Such were the bitterly ironic fruits of the Populist campaign in the South.

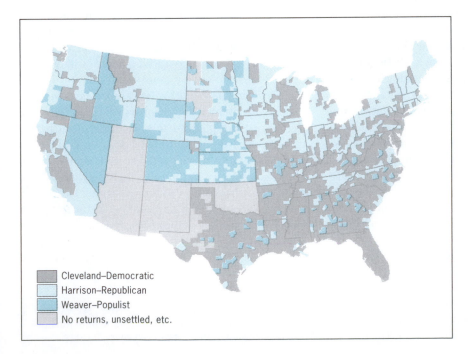

Presidential Election of 1892 (showing vote by county) *Notice the concentration of Populist strength in the semiarid farming regions of the western half of the country. People living in territories (unsettled areas—see key) could not vote.*

- Cleveland–Democratic
- Harrison–Republican
- Weaver–Populist
- No returns, unsettled, etc.

Grover, Grim Times, and Gold

With the Populists divided and the Republicans discredited, Grover Cleveland took office once again in 1893, the only president ever reelected after defeat. He was the same old bull-necked and bull-headed Cleveland, with a little more weight, polish, conservatism, and self-assertiveness.

But if it was the same old Grover, it was not the same old country. Debtors were up in arms, workers were restless, and the advance shadows of panic were falling. Hardly had Cleveland seated himself back in the presidential chair when the devastating panic of 1893 burst about his burly frame. Lasting for about four years, it was the most punishing economic downturn of the nineteenth century. Contributing causes were the splurge of overbuilding and speculation, labor disorders, and the ongoing agricultural depression.

Distress ran deep and far. About eight thousand American businesses collapsed in six months, and dozens of railroad lines went into receivership. Business executives "died like flies under the strain," wrote Henry Adams. Soup kitchens fed the unemployed, while gangs of hoboes ("tramps") wandered aimlessly about the country. Local charities did their feeble best, but the federal government, bound by the let-nature-take-its-course philosophy of the times, saw no legitimate way to relieve the suffering masses.

Cleveland, who had earlier been bothered by a surplus, now faced a growing deficit. Owners of the paper currency issued under the Sherman Silver Purchase Act of 1890, which had greatly expanded the government's silver holdings, were presenting the notes for gold. By law the notes had to be reissued, and the new holders would then repeat the process, draining away gold in an "endless chain" operation.

Alarmingly, the gold reserve in the Treasury dropped below the $100 million regarded as the safe minimum for supporting about $350 million in outstanding paper money. Cleveland saw no alternative but to halt the bleeding away of gold by asking Congress to repeal the Sherman Silver Purchase Act of 1890.

The Congressional debate was heated. A silver-tongued young Democratic congressman from Nebraska, thirty-three-year-old William Jennings Bryan, held the galleries spellbound for three hours as he championed the cause of free silver. The friends of silver announced that "hell would freeze over" before Congress passed the repeal measure. But an angered Cleveland railroaded the measure through, alienating Democratic silverites like Bryan and dividing his party at the very outset of his administration.

Repeal of the Sherman Silver Purchase Act only partially stopped the hemorrhaging of gold from the Treasury. In February 1894 the gold reserve sank to a dismaying $41 million. The United States was now in grave danger of going off the gold standard—a move that could make the nation's currency dangerously unreliable and mortally cripple America's international trade.

Early in 1895 Cleveland turned in desperation to J. P. Morgan, "the bankers' banker" and the head of a Wall Street syndicate. After tense negotiations at the White House, Morgan and his fellow bankers agreed to lend the government $65 million in gold. They were obviously in business for profit, so they charged a commission amounting to about $7 million. The loan, at least temporarily, helped restore confidence in the nation's finances.

The gold loan stirred up a storm. In the eyes of the silverites and other debtors, Wall Street represented all that was wicked and grasping in American politics. Cleveland's secretive dealings with the mighty "Jupiter" Morgan were savagely condemned as a "sellout" of the national government. But Cleveland was certain that he had done no wrong. Sarcastically denying that he was "Morgan's errand boy," Cleveland asserted, "Without shame and without repentance I confess my share of the guilt."

Cleveland suffered further embarrassment with the passage of the Wilson-Gorman Tariff in 1894. The Democrats had pledged to lower tariffs, but by the time the measure got through Congress, it had been so loaded with special-interest protection that it made scarcely a dent in the high McKinley Tariff rates. An outraged Cleveland grudgingly let the bill, which also contained a 2 percent tax on incomes over $4,000, become law without his signature. When the Supreme Court struck down the income-tax provision in 1895,* the Populists and other disaffected

---

*It violated the "direct tax" clause. See Art. I, Sec. IX, para. 4, in the Appendix. The Sixteenth Amendment to the Constitution, adopted in 1913, permitted an income tax.

groups found proof that the courts were only the tools of the plutocrats.

Democratic political fortunes naturally suffered in the face of these setbacks. The tariff dynamite that had blasted the Republicans out of the House in 1890 now dislodged the Democrats, with a strong helping hand from the depression. The revitalized Republicans, singing "Times Are Mighty Hard," won the congressional elections of 1894 in a landslide—244 seats to 105 for the Democrats. Republicans looked forward to the 1896 presidential elections with unconcealed glee.

Despite his gruff integrity and occasional courage, Grover Cleveland failed utterly to cope with the serious economic crisis that befell the country in 1893. He was tied down in office by the same threads that held all the presidents of the day to Lilliputian levels. Grant, Hayes, Garfield, Arthur, Harrison, and Cleveland are often referred to as the "forgettable presidents." Bewhiskered and bland in person, they left mostly blanks—or blots—on the nation's political record, as issues like the tariff, the money question, and the rights of labor continued to fester. What little political vitality existed in Gilded Age America was to be found in local settings or in Congress, which overshadowed the White House for most of this period. But before the century ended, down-and-out debtors and disgruntled workers would make one last titanic effort to wring reform out of the political system—in the momentous election of 1896.

Chronology

1868	Grant defeats Seymour for the presidency.
1869	Fisk and Gould corner the gold market.
1871	Tweed scandal in New York.
1872	Crédit Mobilier scandal exposed. Liberal Republicans break with Grant. Grant defeats Greeley for presidency.
1873	Panic of 1873.
1875	Whiskey Ring scandal. Civil Rights Act of 1875. Resumption Act passed.
1876	Hayes-Tilden election standoff and crisis.
1877	Compromise of 1877. Reconstruction ends. Railroad strikes paralyze nation.
1880	Garfield defeats Hancock for presidency.
1881	Garfield assassinated; Arthur assumes presidency.
1882	Chinese Exclusion Act.
1883	*Civil Rights Cases.* Pendleton Act sets up Civil Service Commission.
1884	Cleveland defeats Blaine for presidency.
1888	Harrison defeats Cleveland for presidency.
1890	"Billion Dollar" Congress. McKinley Tariff Act. Sherman Silver Purchase Act of 1890.
1892	Homestead steel strike. People's party candidate James B. Weaver wins 22 electoral votes. Cleveland defeats Harrison and Weaver for presidency.
1893	Depression of 1893 begins.
1894	Wilson-Gorman Tariff (income-tax provision is declared unconstitutional in 1895). Republicans regain House of Representatives.
1895	J.P. Morgan's banking syndicate loans $65 million in gold to federal government.
1896	*Plessy* v. *Ferguson* legitimizes "separate but equal" doctrine.

VARYING VIEWPOINTS

The Populists: Radicals or Reactionaries?

Taking their cue from contemporary satirical commentaries like Mark Twain and Charles Dudley Warner's *The Gilded Age* (1873), the first historians who wrote about the post–Civil War era judged it harshly. They condemned its politicians as petty and corrupt, lamented the emergence of a new plutocratic class, and railed against the arrogance of corporate power. Such a view is conspicuous in Charles and Mary Beard's *The Rise of American Civilization* (4 vols., 1927–1942) and in Vernon Louis Parrington's classic *Main Currents in American Thought* (3 vols, 1927–1930).

The Beards and Parrington were leaders of the so-called progressive school of historical writing that flourished in the early years of the twentieth century, whose political sympathies were anti-business and pro-reform. Progressive historians identified Populism as virtually the only organized opposition to the social, economic, and political order that took shape in the last decades of the nineteenth century. The Populists thus became heroes to historians like John D. Hicks, whose work *The Populist Revolt* (1931) is the classic portrayal of the Populists as embattled farmers hurling defiance at Wall Street and the robber barons in defense of their simple, honest way of life. Though bowed by the defeat of their great champion, William Jennings Bryan, in the election of 1896, the Populists, Hicks claimed, left a reformist legacy that flourished again in the Progressive era and the New Deal.

Hicks's point of view was the dominant one until the 1950s, when it was sharply criticized by Richard Hofstadter in *The Age of Reform* (1955). The city-born-and-bred Hofstadter argued that the Populists were best understood not as picturesque protesters, but as "harassed little country businessmen" with provincial prejudices not just against Wall Street, but also against urbanism, immigrants, the East, and modernity itself. Hofstadter thus exposed an irrational "dark side" of Populism that contained elements of backwoods anti-intellectualism, paranoia, and even anti-Semitism.

In the 1960s several scholars, inspired by the work of C. Vann Woodward as well as by sympathy with the protest movements of that turbulent decade, began to rehabilitate the Populists as authentic reformers with genuine grievances. Especially notable in this vein was Lawrence Goodwyn's *Democratic Promise: The Populist Moment in America* (1976), which portrayed the Populists as the last gasp of popular political revolt against urban industrialism and finance capitalism, a democratic "moment" in American history that expired with the Populists' absorption into the Democratic party.

Two subsequent works, Edward L. Ayers's *Promise of the New South* (1992) and Robert C. McMath's *American Populism* (1993), synthesized many of the older perspectives and presented a balanced view of the Populists as radical in many ways but also limited by their nostalgia for a lost agrarian past.

For further reading, see the Appendix. For web resources, go to **http://college.hmco.com**.

Industry Comes of Age

— ∘⌒∘ —

1865–1900

The wealthy class is becoming more wealthy, but the poorer class is becoming more dependent. The gulf between the employed and the employer is growing wider; social contrasts are becoming sharper; as liveried carriages appear, so do barefooted children.

HENRY GEORGE, 1879

As the nineteenth century drew toward a close, observers were asking, "Why are the best men not in politics?" One answer was that they were being lured away from public life by the lusty attractions of the booming private economy. As America's Industrial Revolution slipped into high gear, talented men ached for profits, not the presidency. They dreamed of controlling corporations, not the Congress. What the nation lost in civic leadership, it gained in an astounding surge of economic growth. Although in many ways still a political dwarf, the United States was about to stand up before the world as an industrial colossus—and the lives of millions of working Americans would be transformed in the process.

The Iron Colt Becomes an Iron Horse

The government-business entanglements that increasingly shaped politics after the Civil War also undergirded the industrial development of the nation. The unparalleled outburst of railroad construction was a crucial case. When Lincoln was shot in 1865, there were only 35,000 miles of steam railways in the United States, mostly east of the Mississippi. By 1900 the figure had spurted up to 192,556 miles, or more than the total for all Europe combined.

Transcontinental railroad building was so costly and risky as to require governmental subsidies. Congress began to advance liberal money loans to two favored cross-continent companies in 1862 and added enormous donations of acreage paralleling the tracks. Granting land was a "cheap" way to subsidize a much-desired transportation system because it avoided new taxes to cover direct cash grants. All told, Washington rewarded the railroads with 155,504,994 acres, and the western states contributed 49 million more—a total area larger than Texas.

Deadlock in the 1850s over the location of the proposed transcontinental railroad was broken when the

South seceded, leaving the field to the North. In 1862, the year after the guns first spoke at Fort Sumter, Congress made provision for starting the long-awaited line. One weighty argument for action was the urgency of bolstering the Union, already disrupted, by binding the Pacific Coast more securely to the rest of the Republic.

The Union Pacific Railroad—note the word *Union*—was thus commissioned by Congress to thrust westward from Omaha, Nebraska. The laying of rails began in earnest after the Civil War ended in 1865; and with juicy loans and land grants available, the "groundhog" promoters made all possible haste.

Sweaty construction gangs, containing many Irish "Paddies" (Patricks), worked at a frantic pace. On one record-breaking day, a sledge-and-shovel army of some five thousand men laid ten miles of track. A favorite song was

Then drill, my Paddies, drill;
Drill, my heroes, drill;
Drill all day,
No sugar in your tay [tea]
Workin' on the U.P. Railway.

When hostile Indians attacked, the laborers would drop their picks and seize their rifles. At rail's end, workers tried to find relaxation and conviviality in tented towns known as "hells on wheels," sometimes numbering as many as ten thousand men and a sprinkling of painted prostitutes.

Rail laying at the California end was undertaken by the Central Pacific Railroad. This line pushed boldly eastward from boomtown Sacramento, over and through the towering, snow-clogged Sierra Nevada. Four farseeing men—the so-called Big Four—were the chief financial backers of the enterprise. The quartet included the heavyset, enterprising ex-governor Leland Stanford of California, who had useful political connections, and the burly, energetic Collis P. Huntington, an adept lobbyist.

The Central Pacific, which was granted the same princely subsidies as the Union Pacific, had the same incentive to rush construction. Some ten thousand Chinese laborers sweated from dawn to dusk under their basket hats. Hundreds lost their lives in premature explosions and other mishaps. The towering Sierra Nevada presented a formidable barrier; and the nerves of the Big Four were strained when their workers could chip only a few inches a day through solid rock, while the Union Pacific was sledgehammering westward across the plains.

Snow Sheds on the Central Pacific Railroad in the Sierra Nevada Mountains, by Joseph H. Becker, c. 1869 *Formidable obstacles of climate and terrain confronted the builders of the Central Pacific Railroad in the mountainous heights of California. Note the Chinese laborers in the foreground.*

Federal Land Grants to Railroads *The heavy green lines indicate areas within which the railroads might be given specific parcels of land. As shown in the inset, land was reserved in belts of various widths on either side of a railroad's right of way. Until the railroad selected the individual mile-square sections it chose to possess, all such sections within the belt were withdrawn from eligibility for settlement. The "time zones" were introduced in 1883 (see p. 328), and their boundaries have since been adjusted.*

A "wedding of the rails" was finally consummated near Ogden, Utah, in 1869, as the cowcatchers of two locomotives gently kissed. The colorful ceremony included the breaking of champagne bottles and the driving of a last ceremonial (golden) spike, with ex-governor Stanford clumsily wielding a silver sledgehammer.* In all, the Union Pacific built 1,086 miles, and the Central Pacific 689 miles.

Completion of the transcontinental line welded the West Coast more firmly to the Union and facilitated a flourishing trade with Asia. It penetrated the arid barrier of the deserts, paving the way for the phe-nomenal growth of the Great West. Americans compared this great achievement with the Declaration of Independence and the emancipation of the slaves; jubilant Philadelphians again rang the cracked bell of Independence Hall.

Binding the Country with Railroad Ties

With the westward trail now blazed, four other transcontinental lines were completed before the century's end. None of them secured monetary loans from the federal government, as did the Union Pacific and the Central Pacific. But all of them except the Great Northern received generous grants of land.

---

* The spike was promptly removed and is now exhibited at the Stanford University Museum.

The Northern Pacific Railroad, stretching from Lake Superior to Puget Sound, reached its terminus in 1883. The Atchison, Topeka, and Santa Fe, stretching through the southwestern deserts to California, was completed in 1884. The Southern Pacific ribboned from New Orleans to Los Angeles and was consolidated in the same year.

The last of the five nineteenth-century transcontinental railroads, the Great Northern, ran north of the Northern Pacific from Duluth to Seattle. Its creator was James J. Hill, a far-visioned Canadian-American who perceived that the prosperity of his railroad depended on the prosperity of the area that it served. Hill's sound organization enabled his railroad to ride through later financial storms with flying colors.

Yet the romance of the rails was not without its sordid side. Pioneer builders were often guilty of gross overoptimism, laying down rails that went "from nowhere to nothing" in order to get the lavish federal land bounties. When prosperity failed to smile, they went into bankruptcy, carrying down with them the savings of trusting investors. Many of the large railroads in the post–Civil War decades passed through seemingly endless bankruptcies, mergers, or reorganizations.

Revolution by Railways

The metallic fingers of the railroads intimately touched countless phases of American life. For the first time, a sprawling nation became united in a physical sense, bound with ribs of iron and steel. By stitching North America together from sea to sea, the transcontinental lines created an enormous market for American raw materials and manufactured goods—a huge empire of commerce that beckoned to foreign and domestic investors alike.

The railroad network, more than any other single factor, spurred the amazing industrialization of the post–Civil War years. The puffing locomotives opened up fresh markets for manufactured goods and sped raw materials to the factory. The forging of the rails themselves provided the largest single source of orders for the adolescent steel industry.

The screeching iron horse likewise stimulated mining and agriculture, especially in the West. It took farmers out to their land, carried the fruits of their toil to market, and brought them their manufactured necessities. Clusters of farm settlements paralleled the railroads, just as earlier they had followed the rivers.

Railways were a boon for cities and played a leading role in the great cityward movement of the last decades of the century. The iron monsters could carry food to enormous concentrations of people and at the same time ensure them a livelihood by providing both raw materials and markets.

Railroad companies also stimulated the mighty stream of immigration. Seeking settlers to whom their land grants might be sold at a profit, they advertised seductively in Europe and sometimes offered to transplant the newcomers free to their farms.

The land also felt the impact of the railroad—especially the broad, ecologically fragile midsection of the continent. Settlers following the railroads plowed up the tallgrass prairies of Iowa, Illinois, Kansas, and Nebraska and planted well-drained, rectangular cornfields. On the shortgrass prairies of the high plains in the Dakotas and Montana, range-fed cattle rapidly displaced the buffalo, which were hunted to near-extinction. The white pine forests of Michigan, Wisconsin, and Minnesota disappeared into lumber that was rushed by rail to prairie farmers who used it to build houses and fences.

Time itself was bent to the railroads' needs. Until the 1880s every town in the United States had its own "local" time, dictated by the sun's position. When it was noon in Chicago, it was 11:50 a.m. in St. Louis and 12:18 p.m. in Detroit. For railroad operators worried about keeping schedules and avoiding wrecks, this patchwork of local times was a nightmare. Thus on November 18, 1883, the major rail lines decreed that the continent would henceforth be divided into four "time zones." Most communities quickly adopted railroad "standard" time.

Finally, the railroad, more than any other single factor, was the maker of millionaires. A raw new aristocracy, consisting of "lords of the rail" like Cornelius Vanderbilt and "palace car" inventor George Pullman, replaced the old southern "lords of the lash." The multi-webbed lines became the playthings of Wall Street; and colossal wealth was amassed by stock speculators and corporate railroad manipulators.

Wrongdoing in Railroading

Corruption lurks nearby when fabulous fortunes can materialize overnight. The fleecings administered by the railroad construction companies, such as the Crédit Mobilier, were but the first of the bunco games that the railroad promoters learned to play. Methods soon became more refined, as fast-fingered financiers executed multimillion-dollar maneuvers beneath the noses of a bedazzled public. Jay Gould was the most adept of these ringmasters of rapacity. For nearly thirty years he boomed and busted the stocks of the Erie, the Kansas Pacific, the Union Pacific, and the Texas and Pacific in an incredible circus of speculative skullduggery.

One of the favorite devices of the moguls of manipulation was "stock watering." The term originally referred to the practice of making cattle thirsty by feeding them salt, and then having them bloat themselves with water before they were weighed in for sale. Using a variation of this technique, railroad stock promoters grossly inflated their claims about a given line's assets and profitability and sold stocks and bonds far in excess of the railroad's actual value. "Promoters' profits" were often the tail that wagged the iron horse itself. Railroad managers were forced to charge extortionate rates and wage ruthless competitive battles in order to pay off the exaggerated financial obligations with which they were saddled.

The public interest was frequently trampled underfoot as the railroad titans waged their brutal wars. Crusty old Cornelius Vanderbilt, when told that the law stood in his way, reportedly exclaimed: "Law! What do I care about the law? Hain't I got the power?" His son, William H. Vanderbilt, when asked in 1883 about the discontinuance of a fast mail train, reportedly snorted, "The public be damned!"

While abusing the public, the railroaders blandly bought and sold people in public life. They bribed judges and legislatures, elected their own agents to high office, and showered free passes on journalists and politicians.

Railroad kings were, for a time, virtual industrial monarchs. As manipulators of a huge natural monopoly, they exercised more direct control over the lives of more people than did the president of the

The Modern Colossus of Railroads, 1879 *William H. Vanderbilt, flanked by Cyrus Field (left) and Jay Gould (right), towers over the scene. With the Interstate Commerce Act in 1887, the government began to weaken the magnates' grip over the nation's transportation system.*

United States—and their terms were not limited to four years. They increasingly shunned the crude bloodletting of cutthroat competition and began to cooperate with one another to rule the railroad dominion. Sorely pressed to show at least some returns on their bloated investments, they entered into defensive alliances to protect precious profits.

The earliest form of combination was the "pool"—an agreement to divide the business in a given area and share the profits. Other rail barons granted secret rebates or kickbacks to powerful shippers in return for steady and assured traffic. Often they slashed their rates on competing lines, but they more than made up the difference on noncompeting ones, where they might actually charge more for a short haul than for a long one.

Government Bridles the Iron Horse

It was neither healthy nor politically acceptable that so many people should be at the mercy of so few. Impoverished farmers, especially in the Midwest, began to wonder if the nation had not escaped from the slavery power only to fall into the hands of the money power, as represented by the railroad plutocracy.

But the American people, though quick to respond to political injustice, were slow to combat economic injustice. Dedicated to free enterprise and to the principle that competition is the soul of trade, they remembered that Jefferson's ideals were hostile to governmental interference with business. Above all, there shimmered the "American dream": the hope that in a catch-as-catch-can economic system, *anyone* might become a millionaire.

The depression of the 1870s finally goaded the farmers into protesting against being "railroaded" into bankruptcy. Under pressure from organized agrarian groups like the Grange (see p. 371), many midwestern legislatures tried to regulate the railroad monopoly. The scattered state efforts screeched to a halt in 1886. The Supreme Court, in the *Wabash* case, decreed that individual states had no power to regulate *inter*state commerce. If the mechanical monster were to be corralled, the federal government would have to do the job.

Congress ignored President Cleveland's grumbling indifference to the problem and passed the Interstate Commerce Act in 1887. It prohibited rebates and pools and required the railroads to publish their rates openly. It also forbade unfair discrimination against shippers and outlawed charging more for a short haul than for a long one over the same line. Most important, it set up the Interstate Commerce Commission (ICC) to enforce and administer the new legislation.

Despite acclaim, the Interstate Commerce Act emphatically did not represent a popular victory over corporate wealth. One of the leading corporation lawyers of the day, Richard Olney, shrewdly noted

that the new commission "can be made of great use to the railroads. It satisfies the popular clamor for a government supervision of railroads, at the same time that such supervision is almost entirely nominal. . . . The part of wisdom is not to destroy the Commission, but to utilize it."

What the new legislation did do was provide an orderly forum where competing business interests could resolve their conflicts in peaceable ways. The country could now avoid ruinous rate wars among the railroads, and outraged, "confiscatory" attacks on the lines by pitchfork-prodded state legislatures were deflected. This was a modest accomplishment but by no means an unimportant one. The Interstate Commerce Act tended to stabilize, not revolutionize, the existing business system.

Yet the act still ranks as a red-letter law. It was the first large-scale attempt by Washington to regulate business in the interest of society at large. It foreshadowed the doom of freewheeling, buccaneering business practices and served full notice that there was a public interest in private enterprise that the government was bound to protect.

Miracles of Mechanization

Postwar industrial expansion, partly a result of the railroad network, rapidly began to assume mammoth proportions. When Lincoln was elected in 1860, the Republic ranked only fourth among the manufacturing nations of the world. By 1894 it had bounded into first place. Why the sudden upsurge?

Liquid capital, previously scarce, was becoming abundant. The word *millionaire* had not been coined until the 1840s, and in 1861 only a handful of individuals composed this class. But the Civil War, partly through profiteering, created immense fortunes; and these accumulations could now be combined with the customary borrowings from foreign capitalists.

The amazing natural resources of the nation, including coal, oil, and iron, were about to be fully exploited. Massive immigration helped make unskilled labor cheap and plentiful. Steel, the keystone industry, built its strength largely on the sweat of low-priced immigrant labor, working in two twelve-hour shifts, seven days a week.

American ingenuity at the same time played a vital role in the second American Industrial Revolution. American inventiveness flowered luxuriantly in the postwar years: between 1860 and 1890 some 440,000 patents were issued. Business operations were facilitated by the cash register, the stock ticker, and the typewriter ("literary piano"), which attracted women to industry. Urbanization was speeded by the refrigerator car, the electric dynamo, and the electric railway, which displaced animal-drawn cars.

The ingenious telephone was introduced in 1876 by Alexander Graham Bell, a teacher of the deaf who said that if he could make the mute talk, he could make iron speak. His invention had a great social impact on the nation, especially when it attracted many women from the home to become the "number, please" operators in the gigantic communications network.

The most versatile inventor of all was Thomas Alva Edison (1847–1931), who as a boy had been considered so dull-witted that he was taken out of school. Edison was a gifted tinkerer and a tireless worker, not a pure scientist. "Genius," he said, "is one percent inspiration and ninety-nine percent perspiration." Wondrous devices poured out of his "invention factory" in New Jersey—the phonograph, the mimeograph, the dictaphone, and the moving picture. He is probably best known for his perfection in 1879 of the electric light bulb. The electric light turned night into day and transformed ancient human habits as well. People had previously slept an average of nine hours a night; now they slept just a bit more than seven hours.

The Trust Titan Emerges

Despite pious protests to the contrary, competition was the bugbear of most business leaders of the day. Tycoons such as Andrew Carnegie, the steel king, John D. Rockefeller, the oil baron, and J. Pierpont Morgan, the bankers' banker, exercised their genius in devising ways to circumvent competition. Carnegie developed the "vertical integration" of production by directly controlling every phase of his steel-making operation. His miners scratched ore from the earth in Minnesota's Mesabi range; Carnegie

ships floated it across the Great Lakes; Carnegie railroads delivered it to blast furnaces at Pittsburgh. When the molten metal finally poured from the glowing crucibles into the waiting ingot molds, no other hands but those in Carnegie's employ had touched the product.

Rockefeller pursued the less economically justifiable technique of "horizontal integration," which simply meant consolidating with competitors to monopolize a given market. He perfected a device for controlling bothersome rivals—the "trust." Stockholders in various smaller oil companies assigned their stock to the board of directors of Rockefeller's Standard Oil Company. It then consolidated and concerted the operations of the previously competing enterprises. "Let us prey" was said to be Rockefeller's unwritten motto. Ruthlessly wielding vast power, Standard Oil soon cornered virtually the entire world petroleum market. Weaker competitors, left out of the trust agreement, were forced to the wall. Rockefeller's stunning success inspired many imitators, and the word *trust* came to be generally used to describe any large-scale business combination.

The imperial Morgan devised still other schemes for eliminating "wasteful" competition. The depression of the 1890s drove into his welcoming arms many bleeding businesspeople, wounded by cutthroat competition. His prescribed remedy was to consolidate rival enterprises and to ensure future harmony by placing officers of his own banking syndicate on their various boards of directors. These came to be known as "interlocking directorates."

The Supremacy of Steel

"Steel is king!" might well have been the exultant war cry of the new industrialized generation. The mighty metal ultimately held together the new civilization, from skyscrapers to coal scuttles, while providing it with food, shelter, and transportation. Steel making, notably rails for railroads, typified the dominance of heavy industry, which concentrated on making "capital goods," as distinct from the production of "consumer goods" such as clothes and shoes.

Today taken for granted, steel was a scarce commodity in the wood-and-brick America of Abraham

Lincoln. Yet within an amazing twenty years after 1870, the United States outdistanced all foreign competitors and was pouring out more than one-third of the world's supply of steel. By 1900 the Americans were producing as much as Britain and Germany combined.

What wrought the transformation? Chiefly the invention in the 1850s of a method of making cheap steel—the Bessemer process. It was named after a derided British inventor, although an American had stumbled on it a few years earlier. William Kelly, a Kentucky manufacturer of iron kettles, discovered that cold air blown on red-hot iron caused the metal to become white-hot by igniting the carbon and thus eliminating impurities.

Kingpin among steelmasters was Andrew Carnegie, an undersized, charming Scotsman. As a towheaded lad of thirteen, he was brought to America by his impoverished parents in 1848 and got a job as a bobbin boy at $1.20 a week. Mounting the ladder of success so fast that he was said to have scorched the rungs, he forged ahead by working hard, doing extra chores, cheerfully assuming responsibility, and smoothly cultivating influential people.

After accumulating some capital, Carnegie entered the steel business in the Pittsburgh area. By 1900 he was producing one-fourth of the nation's Bessemer steel, and his partners were dividing the profits of $40 million a year, with the "Napoleon of the Smokestacks" himself receiving a cool $25 million. These were the pre–income-tax days, when millionaires made real money and profits represented take-home pay.

Into the picture now stepped the financial giant of the age, J. Pierpont Morgan. "Jupiter" Morgan had made a legendary reputation for himself and his Wall Street banking house by financing the reorganization of railroads, insurance companies, and banks. An impressive figure of a man, with massive shoulders, shaggy brows, piercing eyes, and a bulbous, acne-cursed red nose, he had established an enviable reputation for integrity. He did not believe that "money power" was dangerous, except when in dangerous hands—and he did not regard his own hands as dangerous.

The force of circumstances brought Morgan and Carnegie into collision. By 1900 the canny little Scots-man, weary of turning steel into gold, was eager to sell his holdings. Morgan had meanwhile plunged heavily into the manufacture of steel pipe tubing. Carnegie, cleverly threatening to invade the same business, was ready to ruin his rival if he did not receive his price. The steelmaster's agents haggled with the imperious Morgan for eight agonizing hours, and the financier finally agreed to buy out Carnegie for over $400 million. Fearing that he would die "disgraced" with so much wealth, Carnegie dedicated the remaining years of his life to giving it away for public libraries, pensions for professors, and other such philanthropic purposes—in all disposing of about $350 million.

Morgan moved rapidly to expand his new industrial empire. He took the Carnegie holdings, added others, "watered" the stock liberally, and in 1901 launched the enlarged United States Steel Corporation. Capitalized at $1.4 billion, it became America's first billion-dollar corporation—a larger sum than the total estimated wealth of the nation in 1800. The Industrial Revolution, with its hot Bessemer breath, had come into its own.

Rockefeller Grows an American Beauty Rose

Another new industry was born almost overnight when in 1859 the first oil well—"Drake's Folly" in Pennsylvania—poured out its liquid "black gold." Kerosene, derived from petroleum, was the first major product of the infant oil industry. Replacing whale oil as the fuel for America's lamps, kerosene became the country's fourth most valuable export by the 1870s.

But what technology gives, technology takes away. By 1885 Thomas Edison's new electric light bulbs had rendered kerosene largely obsolete. Oil might thus have remained a modest, even a shrinking industry but for yet another turn of the technological tide—the invention of the automobile. By 1900 the gasoline-burning internal combustion engine had clearly bested its rivals, steam and electricity, and the oil business got a new, long-lasting, and hugely profitable lease on life.

John D. Rockefeller—lanky, shrewd, ambitious, abstemious (he neither drank, smoked, nor swore)—

came to dominate the oil industry. Born to a family of precarious income, he became a successful business-man at age nineteen. One upward stride led to another, and in 1870 he organized the Standard Oil Company of Ohio, nucleus of the great trust formed in 1882.

In the jungle world of big business, a kind of primitive savagery prevailed. Rockefeller—"Reckafel-low," as Carnegie once called him—showed little mercy to his competitors. His son later explained that the giant American Beauty rose could be produced "only by sacrificing the early buds that grew up around it." His father pinched off the small buds with complete ruthlessness. By 1877 Rockefeller con-trolled 95 percent of all the oil refineries in the coun-try. Employing spies and extorting secret rebates from the railroads, he even forced the lines to pay him rebates on the freight bills of his competitors!

Rockefeller thought he was simply obeying a law of nature. "The time was ripe" for aggressive consoli-dation, he later reflected. "It had to come, though all we saw at the moment was the need to save ourselves from wasteful conditions. . . . The day of combination is here to stay. Individualism has gone, never to return."

On the other side of the ledger, Rockefeller's oil monopoly did turn out a superior product at a rela-tively cheap price. It achieved important economies, both at home and abroad, by its large-scale methods of production and distribution. This, in truth, was the tale of the other trusts as well. The efficient use of expensive machinery called for bigness, and consoli-dation proved more profitable than ruinous price wars.

Other trusts blossomed along with the American Beauty of oil. These included the sugar trust, the tobacco trust, the leather trust, and the harvester trust, which amalgamated some two hundred com-petitors. The meat industry arose on the backs of bawling western herds, and meat kings like Gustavus F. Swift and Philip Armour took their places among the new royalty. Wealth was coming to dominate the commonwealth.

These untrustworthy trusts, and the "pirates" who captained them, were disturbingly new. They eclipsed an older American aristocracy of modestly successful merchants and professionals. An arrogant class of "new rich" was now elbowing aside the patri-cian families in the mad scramble for power and prestige. Not surprisingly, the ranks of the antitrust crusaders were frequently spearheaded by the "best men"—genteel old-family do-gooders who were not radicals but conservative defenders of their own van-ishing influence.

The Gospel of Wealth

Monarchs of yore invoked the divine right of kings, and America's industrial plutocrats took a somewhat similar stance. Some candidly credited heavenly help and justified their social position with what came to be known as the "Gospel of Wealth." "Godliness is in league with riches," preached the Episcopal bishop of Massachusetts, and hard-fisted John D. Rockefeller piously acknowledged that "the good Lord gave me my money." But most defenders of wide-open capi-talism relied more heavily on the survival-of-the-fittest theories of Charles Darwin. "The millionaires are a product of natural selection," concluded Yale professor William Graham Sumner. "They get high wages and live in luxury, but the bargain is a good one for society." Despite plutocracy and deepening class divisions, the captains of industry provided wide-spread material progress.

Self-justification by the wealthy inevitably involved contempt for the poor. Many of the rich, especially the newly rich, had pulled themselves up by their own bootstraps; hence they concluded that those who stayed poor must be lazy and lacking in enterprise. The Reverend Russell Conwell of Philadel-phia became rich by delivering his lecture "Acres of Diamonds" thousands of times. In it he said, "There is not a poor person in the United States who was not made poor by his own shortcomings." Such attitudes were a formidable roadblock to social reform.

Plutocracy, like the earlier slavocracy, took its stand firmly on the Constitution. The clause that gave Congress sole jurisdiction over interstate commerce was a godsend to the monopolists; their high-priced lawyers used it time and again to thwart controls by the state legislatures. Giant trusts likewise sought refuge behind the Fourteenth Amendment, which had been originally designed to protect the rights of ex-slaves as persons. The courts ingeniously interpreted a corporation to be a legal "person" and decreed that, as such, it could not be deprived of its property by a state without "due process of law" (see Art. XIV, para. 1).

Great industrialists likewise sought to incorporate in "easy states," like New Jersey, where the restrictions on big business were mild or nonexistent. For example, the Southern Pacific Railroad, with much of its trackage in California, was incorporated in Kentucky.

Government Tackles the Trust Evil

At long last the masses of the people began to mobilize against monopoly. They first tried to control the trusts through state legislation, as they had earlier attempted to curb the railroads. Failing here, as before, they were forced to appeal to Congress. After prolonged pulling and hauling, the Sherman Anti-Trust Act of 1890 was finally signed into law.

The Sherman Act flatly forbade combinations in restraint of trade, without making any distinction between "good" trusts and "bad" trusts. Bigness, not badness, was the sin. The law proved ineffective, largely because it had only baby teeth or no teeth at all, and because it contained legal loopholes through which clever corporation lawyers could wriggle. But it was unexpectedly effective in one respect. Contrary to its original intent, it was used to curb labor unions or labor combinations that were deemed to be restraining trade.

Early prosecutions of the trusts by the Justice Department under the Sherman Act of 1890, as it turned out, were neither vigorous nor successful. Not until 1914 were the paper jaws of the Sherman Act fitted with reasonably sharp teeth. Until then, there was some question as to whether the government would control the trusts or the trusts the government.

But the iron grip of monopolistic corporations was being threatened. A revolutionary new principle had been written into the law books by the Sherman Anti-Trust Act of 1890, as well as by the Interstate Commerce Act of 1887. Private greed must henceforth be subordinated to public need.

The South in the Age of Industry

The industrial tidal wave that washed over the North after the Civil War caused only feeble ripples in the backwater of the South. The plantation system had degenerated into a pattern of absentee landownership.

Washington as Seen by the Trusts, 1900   *"What a funny little government," John D. Rockefeller observes in this satirical cartoon. His own wealth and power are presumed to dwarf the resources of the federal government.*

White and black sharecroppers tilled the soil for a share of the crop, or they became tenants, in bondage to landlords who controlled needed credit and supplies.

Southern agriculture received a welcome boost in the 1880s, when machine-made cigarettes replaced the roll-your-own variety and tobacco consumption shot up. James Buchanan Duke took full advantage of the new technology to mass-produce the dainty "coffin nails." In 1890, in what was becoming a familiar pattern, he absorbed his main competitors into the American Tobacco Company. The cigarette czar later showed such generosity to Trinity College, near his birthplace in Durham, North Carolina, that the trustees gratefully changed its name to Duke University.

Industrialists tried to coax the agricultural South out of the fields and into the factories, but with only modest success. The region remained overwhelmingly rural. Prominent among the boosters of a "new South" was silver-tongued Henry W. Grady, editor of the *Atlanta Constitution*. He tirelessly exhorted the ex-Confederates to become "Georgia Yankees" and outplay the North at the commercial and industrial game.

Yet formidable obstacles lay in the path of southern industrialization. One was the paper barrier of regional rate-setting systems imposed by the northern-dominated railroad interests. Railroads gave preferential rates to manufactured goods moving southward from the North, but in the opposite direction they discriminated in favor of southern raw materials. The net effect was to keep the South in a kind of "Third World" servitude to the Northeast—as a supplier of raw materials to the manufacturing metropolis, unable to develop a substantial industrial base of its own.

A bitter example of this economic discrimination against the South was the "Pittsburgh plus" pricing system in the steel industry. Rich deposits of coal and iron ore near Birmingham, Alabama, worked by low-wage southern labor, should have given steel manufacturers there a competitive edge, especially in southern markets. But the steel lords of Pittsburgh brought pressure to bear on the compliant railroads. As a result, Birmingham steel, no matter where it was delivered, was charged a fictional fee, as if it had been shipped from Pittsburgh. This stunting of the South's natural economic advantages throttled the growth of the Birmingham steel industry.

In manufacturing cotton textiles, the South fared considerably better. Southerners had long resented shipping their fiber to New England, and now their cry was, "Bring the mills to the cotton." Beginning about 1880, northern capital began to erect cotton mills in the South, largely in response to tax benefits and the prospect of cheap and nonunionized labor.

The textile mills proved a mixed blessing to the economically blighted South. Cheap labor was the South's major attraction for potential investors, and keeping labor cheap became almost a religion among southern industrialists. The mills took root in the chronically depressed Piedmont region of southern Appalachia. Blacks were excluded from the mills, so rural southern whites, often derided as "hillbillies" or "lint-heads," worked from dawn to dusk amid the whirring spindles. Paid at half the rate of their northern counterparts, most were perpetually in debt to the company store. But despite their depressed working conditions and poor pay, many southerners saw employment in the mills as their salvation. With many mills anxious to tap the cheap labor of women and children, mill work often offered destitute farm-fugitive families their only chance to remain together.

The Impact of the New Industrial Revolution on America

Economic miracles wrought during the decades after the Civil War enormously increased the wealth of the Republic. The standard of living rose sharply, and well-fed American workers enjoyed more physical comforts than their counterparts in any other powerful nation. Urban centers mushroomed as the insatiable factories demanded more American labor, and as immigrants swarmed like honeybees to the new jobs.

Early Jeffersonian ideals were withering before the smudgy blasts from the smokestacks. As agriculture declined in relation to manufacturing, America could no longer aspire to be a nation of small freehold farms. Jefferson's concepts of free enterprise, with neither help nor hindrance by Washington, were being thrown out the factory window.

Older ways of life also wilted in the heat of the factory furnaces. The very concept of time was revolutionized. Rural American migrants and peasant European immigrants, used to living by the languid clock of nature, had to regiment their lives by the factory whistle. The seemingly arbitrary discipline of industrial labor did not come easily and sometimes was forcibly taught by corporate managers.

Probably no single group was more profoundly affected by the new industrial age than women. Propelled into industry by recent inventions, chiefly the typewriter and the telephone switchboard, millions of stenographers and "hello girls" discovered new economic and social opportunities. The "Gibson Girl," a magazine image of an independent and athletic "new woman" created in the 1890s by Charles Dana Gibson, became the romantic ideal of the age. For middle-class women, careers often meant delayed marriages and smaller families. Most women workers, however, toiled neither for independence nor for glamour but out of economic necessity. They faced the same long hours and dangerous working conditions as did their mates and brothers, and they earned less because wages for "women's jobs" were usually set below men's.

The clattering machine age likewise accentuated class division. "Industrial buccaneers" flaunted bloated fortunes, and their rags-to-riches spouses displayed glittering diamonds. Such extravagances evoked bitter criticism. Some of it was envious, but much of it rose from the small and increasingly vocal group of socialists and other radicals, many of whom were recent European immigrants. The existence of an oligarchy of money was amply demonstrated by the fact that in 1900 about one-tenth of the people owned nine-tenths of the nation's wealth.

Finally, strong pressures for foreign trade developed as the tireless industrial machine threatened to saturate the domestic market. American products radiated out all over the world—notably the five-gallon kerosene can of the Standard Oil Company. The flag follows trade, and empire tends to follow the flag—a harsh lesson that America was soon to learn.

In Unions There Is Strength

Sweat of the laborer lubricated the vast new industrial machine. Yet wage workers did not share propor-

tionately with their employers the benefits of the age of big business.

The worker, suggestive of the Roman galley slave, was becoming a lever-puller in a giant mechanism. Individual originality and creativity were being stifled, and less value than ever before was being placed on manual skills. Before the Civil War, the worker might have toiled in a small plant whose owner hailed the employee in the morning by first name and inquired after the family's health. But now the factory hand was employed by a corporation—depersonalized, bodiless, soulless, and often conscienceless. The vast new railroad network could bring unemployed workers, including blacks and immigrants, into areas where wages were high and thus beat down wage levels. During the 1880s and 1890s and later, the labor market also had to absorb the several hundred thousand unskilled immigrant workers who poured in from Europe each year.

Individual workers were powerless to battle single-handedly against giant industry. The corporation could dispense with the individual worker much more easily than the worker could dispense with the corporation. Employers could pool vast wealth through thousands of stockholders, import strikebreakers ("scabs"), and employ thugs to beat up labor organizers. In 1886 Jay Gould reputedly boasted, "I can hire one-half of the working class to kill the other half."

Corporations had still other weapons in their arsenals. They could call upon conservative federal judges to issue injunctions against strikers, and if defiance continued, could then request state or federal authorities to send in troops. Employers could lock the doors of their plants—a procedure called the "lockout"—and starve rebellious workers into submission. They could compel them to sign "ironclad oaths" or "yellow dog contracts," both of which were solemn agreements not to join a labor union, as a condition of employment. They could put the names of labor agitators on a "black list" and circulate it among fellow employers. A corporation might even own the "company town," which often sank workers into perpetual debt—a status that strongly resembled serfdom.

The public, annoyed by recurrent strikes, grew deaf to the outcry of the worker. Carnegie and Rockefeller had battled their way to the top, and the view was common that the laborer could do likewise. Somehow the strike seemed like a foreign importation—socialistic and hence unpatriotic. Big business might combine into trusts to raise prices, but the worker must not combine into unions to raise wages. Unemployment seemed to be an act of God, who somehow would take care of the laborer.

Labor Limps Along

Labor unions, which had been few and disorganized in 1861, were given a strong boost by the Civil War. By 1872 several hundred thousand organized workers had formed some thirty-two national unions, representing such crafts as the bricklayers, typesetters, and shoemakers.

The National Labor Union, organized in 1866, represented a giant bootstride by the workers. The union lasted six years and attracted the impressive total of some 600,000 members, including the skilled, unskilled, and farmers, though it excluded the Chinese and made only nominal efforts to include women and blacks. Black workers organized their own Colored National Labor Union, but persistent white racism prevented the two national unions from working together. The National Labor Union agitated for the eight-hour workday and the arbitration of industrial disputes. It finally succeeded in winning an eight-hour day for government workers, but the devastating depression of the 1870s dealt the union a knockout blow. Wage reductions in 1877 touched off such disruptive strikes on the railroads that nothing short of federal troops could restore order.

A new organization—the Knights of Labor—seized the torch dropped by the defunct National Labor Union (see "Makers of America: The Knights of Labor," p. 338). Officially known as the Noble and Holy Order of the Knights of Labor, it began inauspiciously in 1869 as a secret society, with a private ritual, passwords, and a secret grip.

The Knights of Labor, like the National Labor Union, sought to include all workers in "one big union." Their slogan was "An injury to one is the concern of all." A welcome mat was rolled out for the skilled and unskilled, for men and women, for whites and underprivileged blacks, some ninety thousand of whom joined. The Knights barred only liquor dealers, professional gamblers, lawyers, bankers, and stockbrokers.

Setting up broad goals, the embattled Knights campaigned for economic and social reform, including producers' cooperatives and codes for safety and health. The ordinary workday was then ten hours or more, and the Knights waged a determined campaign for the eight-hour stint.

Under the eloquent but often erratic leadership of Terence V. Powderly, an Irish-American of nimble wit and fluent tongue, the Knights won a number of strikes for the eight-hour day. When the Knights staged a successful strike against Jay Gould's Wabash Railroad in 1885, membership mushroomed to about three-quarters of a million workers.

Unhorsing the Knights of Labor

Despite their outward success, the Knights were riding for a fall. They became involved in a number of May Day strikes in 1886, about half of which failed. A focal point was Chicago, home to about eighty thousand Knights. The city was also honeycombed with a few hundred anarchists, many of them foreign-born, who were advocating a violent overthrow of the American government.

Tensions rapidly built up to the bloody Haymarket Square episode. Labor disorders had broken out, and on May 4, 1886, the Chicago police advanced on a meeting called to protest alleged brutalities by the authorities. Suddenly a dynamite bomb was thrown that killed or injured several dozen persons, including police.

Hysteria swept the Windy City. Eight anarchists were rounded up. Although nobody proved that they had anything to do directly with the bomb, a judge and jury held that since they had preached incendiary doctrines, they could be charged with conspiracy. Five were sentenced to death: one of these men committed suicide, and four were executed. The other three anarchists were given stiff prison terms. They were eventually pardoned in 1892 by Illinois governor John P. Altgeld, a German-born Democrat of strong liberal tendencies.

The Haymarket Square bomb helped blow the props from under the Knights of Labor. They were

The Knights of Labor

It was 1875. The young worker was guided into a room, where his blindfold was removed. Surrounding him were a dozen men, their faces covered by hoods. One of the masked figures solemnly asked three questions: "Do you believe in God?" "Do you gain your bread by the sweat of your brow?" "Are you willing to take a solemn vow, binding you to secrecy, obedience, and mutual assistance?" Yes, came the reply. The men doffed their hoods and joined hands in a circle. Their leader, the Master Workman, declared, "On behalf of the toiling millions of earth, I welcome you to this Sanctuary, dedicated to the service of God, by serving humanity." Then the entire group burst into song:

> Storm the fort, ye Knights of Labor,
> Battle for your cause;
> Equal rights for every neighbor,
> Down with tyrant laws!

The carefully staged pageantry then drew to a close. The worker was now a full-fledged member of the Knights of Labor.

He had just joined a loose-knit organization of some 100,000 workingpeople, soon to swell to nearly one million following several successful strikes in the 1880s. The first women Knights joined in 1881, and there were female organizers, too. Fiery Mary Harris ("Mother") Jones got her start agitating for the Knights in the Illinois coalfields. The first all-black local was founded among coal miners in Ottumwa, Iowa. The Knights preached tolerance and the solidarity of all working men and women, and they meant it, though they supported restrictions on immigration, including the Chinese Exclusion Act of 1882.

Terence V. Powderly, born to Irish immigrant parents in Carbondale, Pennsylvania, in 1849, became the Grand Master Workman of the Knights. He had dropped out of school at age thirteen to take a job guarding railroad track switches and rose to mayor of Scranton, Pennsylvania. A complex, colorful, and sometimes cynical man, he denounced the "multimillionaires [for] laying the foundation for their colossal fortunes on the bodies and souls of living men." In the eyes of Powderly and the Knights, only the economic and political independence of American workers could preserve republican traditions and institutions from corruption by monopolists and other "parasites."

Powderly denounced "wage-slavery" and dedicated the Knights to achieving the "cooperative commonwealth." Shunning socialism, Powderly urged laborers to save enough from their wages to purchase mines, factories, railroads, and stores. Because labor would own and operate these enterprises, the conflict between labor and capital would evaporate in a kind of toilers' utopia.

Powderly's vision of the cooperative commonwealth reflected the persistent dream of many nineteenth-century American workers that they would all one day become producers. As expectant capitalists, they lacked "class consciousness"—that is, a sense of themselves as a permanent working class that must organize to coax what benefits it could out of the hostile capitalist system. Samuel Gompers followed that conservative strategy, and his American Federation of Labor, not Powderly's utopian dream, eventually carried the day. The swift decline of the Knights in the 1890s underscored the obsolescence of their unrealistic view that a bygone age of independent producers could be restored. Yet the Knights' commitment to unifying all workers in one union—regardless of race, gender, ethnicity, or skill level—produced a blueprint for the eventual success of similarly committed unions like the Congress of Industrial Organizations in the 1930s.

associated in the public mind, though mistakenly, with the anarchists. The eight-hour movement suffered correspondingly, and subsequent strikes by the Knights met with scant success. By the 1890s the Knights had melted away to 100,000 members, and these gradually fused with other protest groups of that decade.

The AF of L to the Fore

The elitist American Federation of Labor, born in 1886, was largely the brainchild of squat, square-jawed Samuel Gompers. This colorful Jewish cigar maker, born in a London tenement and removed from school at age ten, was brought to America when thirteen. Taking his turn at reading informative literature to his fellow cigar makers in New York, he was pressed into overtime service because of his strong voice. Rising spectacularly in the labor ranks, he was elected president of the American Federation of Labor every year except one from 1886 to 1924.

Gompers adopted a down-to-earth approach, soft-pedaling attempts to engineer sweeping social reform. A bitter foe of socialism, he shunned politics for economic strategies and goals. Gompers had no quarrel with capitalism, but he demanded a fairer share for labor. All he wanted, he said simply, was "more." Promoting what he called "pure and simple" unionism, he sought better wages, hours, and working conditions.

The AF of L thus established itself on solid but narrow foundations. Although attempting to speak for all workers, it fell far short of being representative of them. Composed of skilled craftsmen, like the carpenters and bricklayers, it was willing to let unskilled laborers, including women and especially blacks, fend for themselves. The AF of L weathered the panic

The Strike, by Robert Koehler, 1886   *Scenes like this were becoming more typical of American life in the late nineteenth century as industrialism advanced spectacularly and sometimes ruthlessly. Here Koehler (1850–1917) shows an entire community of men, women, and children—many of them apparently immigrant newcomers—challenging the power of the "boss." The scene is tense but orderly, though violence seems to be imminent as one striker reaches for a rock.*

of 1893 reasonably well, and by 1900 it could boast a membership of 500,000.

Labor disorders continued, peppering the years from 1881 to 1900 with an alarming total of over 23,000 strikes. These disturbances involved 6,610,000 workers, with a total loss to both employers and employees of $450 million. The strikers lost about half their strikes and won or compromised the remainder. Perhaps the gravest weakness of organized labor was that it still embraced only a small minority of all working people—about 3 percent in 1900.

But attitudes toward labor had begun to change perceptibly by 1900. The public was beginning to concede the right of workers to organize, to bargain collectively, and to strike. As a sign of the times, Labor Day was made a legal holiday by act of Congress in 1894. A few enlightened industrialists had come to perceive the wisdom of avoiding costly economic warfare by bargaining with the unions and signing agreements. But the vast majority of employers continued to fight organized labor, which achieved its grudging gains only after recurrent strikes and frequent reverses. Several trouble-fraught decades were to pass before labor was to gain a position of relative equality with capital. If the age of big business had dawned, the age of big labor was still some distance over the horizon.

Chronology

1862	Congress authorizes a transcontinental railroad.
1866	National Labor Union organized.
1869	Transcontinental railroad joined near Ogden, Utah. Knights of Labor organized.
1870	Standard Oil Company organized.
1876	Bell invents the telephone.
1879	Edison invents the electric light.
1886	Haymarket Square bombing. *Wabash* case. American Federation of Labor formed.
1887	Interstate Commerce Act.
1890	Sherman Anti-Trust Act.
1901	United States Steel Corporation formed.

VARYING VIEWPOINTS

Industrialization: Boon or Blight?

The capitalists who forged an industrial America in the late nineteenth century were once called "captains of industry"—a respectful title that bespoke the awe inspired by their wondrous material accomplishments. But these economic innovators have never been universally admired. During the Great Depression of the 1930s, when the entire industrial order they had created seemed to have collapsed utterly, it was fashionable to speak of them as "robber barons"—a term implying scorn for their highhanded methods. This sneer often issued from the lips and pens of leftist critics like Matthew Josephson,

who sympathized with the working classes allegedly brutalized by the factory system.

Criticism has also come from writers nostalgic for the preindustrial past. These critics believe that industrialization stripped away the traditions, values, and pride of native farmers and immigrant craftspeople. Conceding that economic development elevated the material standard of living for working Americans, this interpretation contends that the Industrial Revolution diminished their spiritual "quality of life." Accordingly, historians like Herbert Gutman and David Montgomery portray labor's struggle for control of the workplace as the central drama of industrial expansion.

In the 1960s, historians led by Stephan Thernstrom began to test this long-standing belief. Looking at such factors as occupation, wealth, and geographic mobility, they tried to gauge the nature and extent of social mobility in the United States. Most of these historians concluded that although relatively few Americans made rags-to-riches leaps, large numbers experienced small improvements in their economic and social status. Few sons of laborers became corporate tycoons, but many more became line bosses and white-collar clerks.

In recent years such studies have been criticized by historians who point out the difficulties involved in defining "social status." For instance, some white-collar clerical workers received lower wages than manual laborers did. But were they higher or lower on the social scale? Furthermore, as James Henretta points out, different groups defined success differently: whereas Jewish immigrants often struggled to give their sons professional educations, the Irish put more emphasis on acquiring land, and Italians, on building small family-run businesses.

Meanwhile, leftist historians such as Michael Katz maintain that the degree of social mobility in America has been overrated. These historians argue that industrial capitalism created two classes: a working class that sold its labor, and a business class that controlled resources and bought labor. Although most Americans took small steps upward, they generally remained within the class in which they began. Thus, say these historians, the inequality of a capitalistic class system persisted in America's seemingly fluid society.

25

America Moves to the City

1865–1900

What shall we do with our great cities? What will our great cities do with us . . . ? [T]he question . . . does not concern the city alone. The whole country is affected . . . by the condition of its great cities.

LYMAN ABBOT, 1891

Born in the country, America moved to the city in the decades following the Civil War. By the year 1900 the United States' upsurging population had nearly doubled from the 40 million people enumerated in the census of 1870. Yet in the very same period the population of American cities *tripled*. This cityward drift affected not only the United States but most of the Western world. European peasants, pushed off the land in part by competition from cheap American foodstuffs, were pulled into cities—in both Europe and America—by the new lure of industrial jobs. A revolution in American agriculture thus fed the industrial and urban revolution in Europe, as well as in the United States.

The Urban Frontier

The growth of American metropolises was spectacular. In 1860 no city in the United States could boast a million inhabitants; by 1890 New York, Chicago, and Philadelphia had spurted past the million mark. By 1900 New York, with some 3.5 million people, was the second largest city in the world, outranked only by London.

Cities grew both up and out. Cloud-brushing skyscrapers allowed more people and workplaces to be packed onto a parcel of land. Appearing first as a ten-story building in Chicago in 1885, the skyscraper

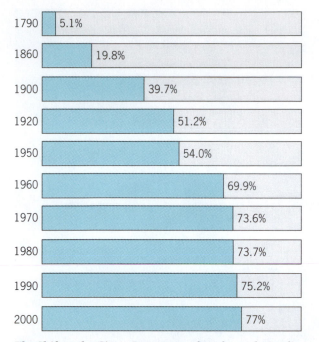

1790	5.1%
1860	19.8%
1900	39.7%
1920	51.2%
1950	54.0%
1960	69.9%
1970	73.6%
1980	73.7%
1990	75.2%
2000	77%

The Shift to the City *Percentage of total population living in cities of twenty-five hundred or more. Notice the slowing pace of the cityward trend since the 1970s.*

was made usable by the perfecting of the electric elevator. An opinionated Chicago architect, Louis Sullivan (1856–1924), contributed formidably to the further development of the skyscraper with his famous principle that "form follows function."

Cities also spread out, turning many Americans into commuters who were carted daily by mass-transit electric trolleys between urban job and suburban home. The compact and communal "walking city" gave way to the immense and impersonal megalopolis, carved into distinctly different districts for business, industry, and residential neighborhoods—which in turn were segregated by race, ethnicity, and social class.

Rural America could not compete with the siren song of the city. Industrial jobs, above all, drew country folks off the farms and into factory centers. But the urban lifestyle also held powerful attractions. The predawn milking of cows had little appeal when compared with the late-night glitter of city lights. Electricity, indoor plumbing, and telephones all made life in the big city more alluring. Engineering marvels like

the skyscraper and New York's awesome Brooklyn Bridge, a harplike suspension span dedicated in 1883, further added to the seductive glamour of the gleaming cities.

Cavernous department stores such as Macy's in New York and Marshall Field's in Chicago attracted urban shoppers and heralded the dawning era of consumerism. They also accentuated widening class divisions. When Carrie Meeber, novelist Theodore Dreiser's fictional heroine in *Sister Carrie* (1900), escapes from rural boredom to Chicago, the city's dazzling department stores awaken her to a richer, more elegant way of life.

The move to the city also introduced Americans to new ways of living. Household products sold in bulk at the local store, without wrapping, gave way to city goods that came in throwaway bottles, boxes, bags, and cans. Apartment houses had no adjoining barnyards where residents might toss garbage to the hogs. Waste disposal, in short, was an issue new to the urban age.

The jagged skyline of America's perpendicular civilization could not fully conceal the canker sores of feverish growth. Criminals flourished like lice in the teeming asphalt jungles. Impure water, uncollected garbage, unwashed bodies, and droppings from draft animals enveloped many cities in a satanic stench.

The cities were monuments of contradiction. They represented "humanity compressed," remarked one observer, "the best and the worst combined, in a strangely composite community." They harbored merchant princes and miserable paupers, stately banks and sooty factories, green-grassed suburbs and stinking tenements. The glaring contrasts that assaulted the eye in New York reminded one visitor of "a lady in ball costume, with diamonds in her ears, and her toes out at the boots."

Worst of all were the human pigsties known as slums. They seemed to grow ever more crowded, more filthy, and more rat infested, especially after the perfection in 1879 of the "dumbbell" tenement. So named because of the outline of its floor plan, the dumbbell was usually seven or eight stories high, with shallow, sunless, and ill-smelling air shafts providing minimal ventilation. Several families were sardined onto each floor of the barrackslike structures, and they shared a malodorous toilet in the hall. Small

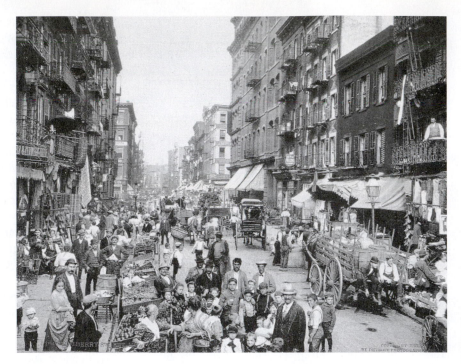

New York's Mulberry Street, c. 1900 *Outside the teeming tenement buildings, crowded city streets became places of work, play, and rough-and-tumble Americanization for many of the nation's recent immigrants.*

wonder that slum dwellers strove mightily to escape their wretched surroundings—as many of them did. The slums remained foul places, inhabited by successive waves of newcomers, but to a remarkable degree hard-working people moved up and out of them. The wealthiest left the cities altogether and headed for the semirural suburbs. These leafy "bedroom communities" eventually ringed the brick-and-concrete cities with a greenbelt of affluence.

The New Immigration

The powerful pull of the American urban magnet was felt even in faraway Europe. A brightly colored stream of immigrants continued to pour in from the old "mother continent." In each of the three decades from the 1850s through the 1870s, more than 2 million migrants had stepped onto America's shores. By the 1880s the stream had swelled to a rushing torrent, as more than 5 million cascaded into the country.

Until the 1880s, most immigrants had come from the British Isles and western Europe, chiefly Germany and Scandinavia. They were usually Protestant, except for the Catholic Irish and many Catholic Germans. They boasted a comparatively high rate of literacy and fitted relatively easily into American society.

But in the 1880s the character of the immigrant stream changed drastically. The so-called New Immigrants—Italians, Croats, Slovaks, Greeks, Poles—came from southern and eastern Europe. Many of them worshiped in Roman Catholic or Eastern Orthodox churches or in Jewish synagogues. Largely illiterate and impoverished, most New Immigrants hived together in the "Little Italys" and "Little Polands" of the jam-packed cities. These new peoples totaled only 19 percent of newcomers in the 1880s; but by the first decade of the twentieth century, they constituted an astonishing 66 percent of the total inflow. (See "Makers of America: The Italians," p. 346.)

Why were these bright-shawled and quaint-jacketed strangers hammering on the gates? In part, they left their old countries because Europe seemed to have no room for them. Rapid population growth, American food imports, and European industrialization shook the peasantry loose from its ancient habitats and customary occupations, creating a vast, foot-loose army of the unemployed. Europeans by the millions drained out of the countryside and into European cities. Most stayed there, but some kept moving and left Europe altogether. About 60 million Europeans abandoned the old continent in the nineteenth and early twentieth centuries. More than half of them moved to the United States. But that striking fact should not obscure the important truth that masses of people were already in motion in Europe before they felt the tug of the American magnet. Immigration to America was, in many ways, a by-product of the urbanization of Europe.

"America fever" proved highly contagious in Europe. The United States was often painted as a land of fabulous opportunity in the "America letters" sent by friends and relatives already transplanted.

The land of the free was also blessed with freedom from military conscription and religious persecution. Beginning in the 1880s, savage treatment of minorities in Europe, especially Russian Jews, drove tens of thousands of battered refugees to American shores. Virtually unique among the New Immigrants, Jews had experienced city life in Europe, and many of them brought their urban skills of tailoring and shopkeeping to American cities.

The New Immigrants struggled heroically to preserve their traditional cultures. Catholics expanded their parochial school system and Jews established Hebrew schools. Foreign-language newspapers, parishes, theaters, restaurants, and social clubs all attested to the desire to keep old ways alive. Yet time took its toll on these efforts to conserve the customs of the Old World in the New. The children of the immigrants grew up speaking fluent English, sometimes mocking the broken grammar of their parents. They often rejected the Old Country manners of their mothers and fathers in their desire to plunge headlong into the mainstream of American life.

Reactions to the New Immigration

America's government system, nurtured in wide-open spaces, was ill suited to the cement forests of the great cities. Beyond minimal checking to weed out criminals and the insane, the federal government did virtually nothing to ease the assimilation of immigrants into American society. State governments, usually dominated by rural representatives, did even less. City governments, overwhelmed by the sheer scale of rampant urban growth, proved woefully inadequate to the task. By default, the business of ministering to the immigrants' needs fell to the unofficial "governments" of the urban political machines, led by "bosses" such as New York's notorious Boss Tweed.

Taking care of the immigrants was big business, indeed. Trading jobs and services for votes, a powerful boss might claim the loyalty of thousands of followers. In return for their support at the polls, the boss provided employment on the city's payroll, found housing for new arrivals, tided over the needy with gifts of food and clothing, patched up minor scrapes with the law, and helped get schools, parks, and hospitals built in immigrant neighborhoods. Reformers gagged at this cynical exploitation of the immigrant vote, but the political boss gave valuable assistance that was forthcoming from no other source.

The nation's social conscience gradually awakened to the plight of the cities and their immigrant masses. Prominent in this awakening were Protestant clergymen such as Walter Rauschenbusch of New York City and Washington Gladden of Columbus, Ohio, both of whom sought to apply the lessons of Christianity to the slums and factories. Preaching the "social gospel," they insisted that churches tackle the burning social issues of the day.

One middle-class woman who was deeply dedicated to uplifting the urban masses was Jane Addams (1860–1935). Born into a prosperous Illinois family, Addams was one of the first generation of college-educated women and sought suitable outlets for her large talents. Inspired by a visit to England, in 1889 she established Hull House in Chicago as the most prominent American settlement house. Located in a poor immigrant neighborhood of Greeks, Italians, Russians, and Germans, Hull House offered instruction in English, counseling to help newcomers cope with American big-city life, child care for working mothers, and cultural activities of all kinds for neighborhood residents.

Following Jane Addams's lead, women founded settlement houses in other cities as well—notably

The Italians

Who were the "New Immigrants"? Who were these southern and eastern European birds of passage that flocked to the United States between 1880 and 1920? Prominent and typical among them were Italians, some 4 million of whom sailed to the United States during the four decades of the New Immigration.

They came from the southern provinces of their native land, the heel and toe of the Italian boot. These areas had lagged behind the prosperous, industrial region of northern Italy. Unification had raised hopes of similar progress in the downtrodden south, but it was slow in coming. Southern peasants tilled their fields without fertilizer or machinery, using hand plows and rickety hoes that had been passed down for generations.

From such disappointing and demeaned conditions, southern Italians set out for the New World. Almost all of them were young men who intended to spend only a few months in America, stuff their pockets with dollars, and return home. Almost half of Italian immigrants did indeed repatriate—as did comparable numbers of the other New Immigrants, with the conspicuous exception of the Jews, who had fled their native lands to escape religious persecution. Almost all Italian immigrants sailed through New York harbor, sighting the Statue of Liberty as they debarked from crowded ships. Many soon moved on to other large cities, but so many remained that, in the early years of the twentieth century, more Italians resided in New York than in Florence, Venice, and Genoa combined.

Although Italian immigrants huddled in the cities, they did not abandon their rural upbringings entirely. Much to their neighbors' consternation, they often kept chickens in vacant lots and raised vegetables in small garden plots nestled between decaying tenement houses.

Those who bade a permanent farewell to Italy clustered in tightly knit communities that boasted opera clubs, Italian-language newspapers, and courts for playing *bocci*—a version of lawn bowling imported from the Old Country. Pizza emerged from the hot wood-burning ovens of these Little Italys, its aroma and flavor wafting its way into the hearts and stomachs of all Americans.

Italians typically earned their daily bread as industrial laborers—most famously as longshoremen and construction workers. They owed their prominence in the building trades to the "padrone system." The *padrone,* or labor boss, met immigrants upon arrival and secured jobs for them in New York, Chicago, or wherever there was an immediate demand for industrial labor.

Lacking education, the Italians, as a group, remained in blue-collar jobs longer than some of their fellow New Immigrants. Many of them, valuing vocation over schooling, sent their children off to work as early in their young lives as possible. Before World War I, less than 1 percent of Italian children were enrolled in high school. Over the next fifty years, Italian-Americans and their offspring gradually prospered, moving out of the cities into the more affluent suburbs. Many served heroically in World War II and availed themselves of the GI Bill to finance the college educations and professional training their immigrant forebears had lacked.

Lillian Wald's Henry Street Settlement in New York, which opened its doors in 1893. The settlement houses became centers of women's activism and social reform on behalf of women, children, blacks, and consumers. The women of Hull House, for example, successfully lobbied in 1893 for an Illinois anti-sweatshop law that protected women workers and prohibited child labor. They were led by Florence Kelley, a guerrilla warrior in the urban jungle who battled for decades on behalf of the underprivileged at both Hull House and the Henry Street Settlement.

The pioneering work of Addams, Wald, and Kelley vividly demonstrated that the city was the frontier of opportunity for women, just as the wilderness had been for men. The urban frontier opened new possibilities for women—as social workers and secretaries, store clerks and seamstresses, telephone operators and bookkeepers. More than a million women joined the work force in the single decade of the 1890s. As America moved to the city, women moved nearer to economic and social independence.

Narrowing the Welcome Mat

Antiforeignism, or "nativism," earlier touched off by the Irish and German arrivals in the 1840s and 1850s,

bared its ugly face in the 1880s with fresh ferocity. The so-called New Immigrants had come for much the same reasons as the Old—to escape the poverty and squalor of Europe and to seek new opportunities in America. But "nativists" viewed the eastern and southern Europeans as culturally and religiously exotic hordes and often gave them a rude reception. The newest newcomers aroused widespread alarm. Their high birthrate, common among people with a low standard of living and sufficient youth and vigor to pull up stakes, raised worries that the original Anglo-Saxon stock would soon be outbred and outvoted. Still more horrifying was the prospect that it would be mongrelized by a mixture of "inferior" southern European blood and that the fairer Anglo-Saxon types would disappear. One New England writer cried out in anguish,

> O Liberty, white Goddess! is it well
> To leave the gates unguarded?

"Native" Americans voiced additional fears. They blamed the immigrants for the degradation of urban government. Trade unionists assailed the alien arrivals for their willingness to work for "starvation" wages, which seemed like princely sums to the immigrants themselves, and for importing in their intellectual baggage such dangerous doctrines as socialism,

Looking Backward
Older immigrants, trying to keep their own humble arrival in America "in the shadows," sought to close the bridge that had carried them and their ancestors across the Atlantic.

communism, and anarchism. Many business leaders had welcomed the flood of cheap manual labor but now began to fear that they had embraced a Franken-stein's monster.

Antiforeign organizations, reminiscent of the "Know-Nothings" of antebellum days, were revived in a different guise. Notorious among them was the American Protective Association (APA), which was created in 1887 and soon claimed a million members. In pursuing its nativist goals, the APA urged voting against Roman Catholic candidates for office and sponsored the publication of lustful fantasies about runaway nuns.

Organized labor was quick to throw its growing weight behind the move to choke off the rising tide of foreigners. Frequently used as strikebreakers, the wage-depressing immigrants were hard to unionize because of the language barrier. Labor leaders argued, not illogically, that if American industry was entitled to protection from foreign goods, the American worker was entitled to protection from foreign laborers.

Congress finally nailed up partial bars against the inpouring immigrants. The first restrictive law, in 1882, banged the gate shut in the faces of paupers, criminals, and convicts, all of whom had to be returned at the expense of the greedy or careless shipper. Congress further responded to pained outcries from organized labor when in 1885 it prohibited the importation of workers under contract—usually for substandard wages.

In later years other federal laws lengthened the list of undesirables to include the insane, polygamists, prostitutes, alcoholics, anarchists, and persons carrying contagious diseases. A proposed literacy test, long a favorite of "nativists" because it favored the Old Immigrants over the New, met vigorous opposition. It was not enacted until 1917, after three presidents had vetoed it on the grounds that literacy was more a measure of opportunity than of intelligence.

The year 1882 brought forth, in addition to the first federal restrictions on immigration, a law to bar completely one ethnic group—the Chinese (see "Makers of America: The Chinese," pp. 316–317). Previously America had embraced the oppressed and underprivileged of all races and creeds. Now the gates were padlocked against defective undesirables—plus the Chinese.

Four years later, in 1886, the Statue of Liberty arose in New York harbor, a gift from the people of France. On its base were inscribed the words of Emma Lazarus:

> Give me your tired, your poor,
> Your huddled masses yearning to breathe free,
> The wretched refuse of your teeming shore.

To many "nativists," those noble words described only too accurately the "scum" washed up by the New Immigrant tides. Yet the uprooted immigrants, unlike "natives" lucky enough to have had parents who caught an earlier ship, became American citizens the hard way. These new immigrants stepped off the boat ready to put their shoulders to the nation's industrial wheels. The Republic owes much to these latecomers—for their brawn, their brains, their courage, and the diversity they brought to American society.

Churches Confront the Urban Challenge

The swelling size and changing character of the urban population posed sharp challenges to American churches, which, like other national institutions, had grown up in the countryside. Protestant churches in particular suffered heavily from the shift to the city, where many of their traditional doctrines and pastoral approaches seemed irrelevant.

As they lost their bearings in the new urban world, some churches were tending to become merely sacred diversions or amusements. Reflecting the wealth of their prosperous parishioners, many of the old-line churches were distressingly slow to raise their voices against social and economic vices. John D. Rockefeller was a pillar of the Baptist church; J. Pierpont Morgan, of the Episcopal church. Cynics remarked that the Episcopal church had become "the Republican party at prayer." The mounting emphasis was on materialism; too many devotees worshiped at the altar of avarice. Money was the accepted measure of achievement, and the new "Gospel of Wealth" proclaimed that God caused the righteous to prosper.

Into this spreading moral vacuum stepped a new generation of urban revivalists. Most conspicuous was a former Chicago shoe salesman, Dwight Lyman Moody. Proclaiming a gospel of kindness and forgiveness, Moody was a modern urban circuit rider who took his message to countless American cities in the

1870s and 1880s. Clad in a dark business suit, the bearded and rotund Moody held huge audiences spellbound. He contributed powerfully to adapting the old-time religion to the realities of city life. The Moody Bible Institute, founded in Chicago in 1889, carried on his work after his death in 1899.

Simultaneously, the Roman Catholic and Jewish faiths were gaining enormous strength from the New Immigration. By 1900 the Roman Catholics had increased their lead as the largest single denomination, numbering nearly 9 million communicants. Roman Catholics and Jewish groups kept the common touch better than many of the leading Protestant churches. Cardinal James Gibbons (1834–1921) of Baltimore, an urban Catholic leader devoted to American unity, was immensely popular with Roman Catholics and Protestants alike. Acquainted with every president from Andrew Johnson to Warren Harding, he employed his liberal sympathies to assist the American labor movement.

By 1890 the variety-loving American could choose from 150 religious denominations, 2 of them newcomers. One was the band-playing Salvation Army, whose soldiers without swords invaded America from England in 1879 and established a beachhead on the street corners. Appealing frankly to the down-and-outers, the boldly named Salvation Army did much practical good, especially with free soup.

The other important new faith was the Church of Christ, Scientist (Christian Science), founded by Mary Baker Eddy in 1879, after she had suffered much ill health. Preaching that the true practice of Christianity heals sickness, she set forth her views in a book entitled *Science and Health with Key to the Scriptures* (1875), which sold an amazing 400,000 copies before her death. Appealing especially to America's hurried, nerve-wracked urban residents, Christian Science embraced several hundred thousand worshipers in the early twentieth century.

Although immigrant churches and new faiths managed to grow, traditional theology received serious blows from modern books on comparative religion and historical criticism of the Bible. Most unsettling of all was *On the Origin of Species* (1859), in which the English naturalist Charles Darwin set forth the sensational theory that humans had slowly evolved from lower forms of life. Evolution cast serious doubt on a literal interpretation of the Bible,

which relates how God created the heavens and the earth in six days.

Darwinism eventually created rifts in the churches and colleges of the post–Civil War era. Conservative believers, or "Fundamentalists," stood firmly on the Scripture as the inspired and infallible Word of God, whereas "Modernists" refused to accept the Bible as either history or science. "Modernist" clergymen were removed from their pulpits; teachers of biology who embraced evolution were dismissed from their chairs. As time wore on, an increasing number of liberal thinkers were able to reconcile Darwinism with Christianity by interpreting evolution as a newer and grander revelation of the ways of the Almighty. But Darwinism undoubtedly did much to loosen religious moorings and promote unbelief.

The Lust for Learning

Public education continued its upward climb. The ideal of tax-supported elementary schools was still gathering strength. Beginning about 1870, more and more states were making at least a grade-school education compulsory, and this gain, incidentally, helped check the frightening abuses of child labor.

Spectacular indeed was the spread of the high schools, especially by the 1880s and 1890s. By 1900 some six thousand high schools were educating teenage boys and girls. In addition, the taxpayers of the states were providing free textbooks in increasing numbers during the last two decades of the century.

Other trends were noteworthy. Teacher training schools, then called "normal schools," experienced a striking expansion after the Civil War. In 1860 only twelve normal schools were operating; in 1910, over three hundred. Kindergartens, earlier borrowed from Germany, also began to gain strong support. The New Immigration in the 1880s and 1890s brought vast new strength to the private Catholic parochial schools, which were fast becoming a major pillar of the nation's educational structure.

Public schools, though showering benefits on children, excluded millions of adults. This deficiency was partially remedied by the Chautauqua movement, launched in 1874 on the shores of Lake Chautauqua in New York. The organizers achieved gratifying success through nationwide public lectures, often held in tents and featuring such well-known speakers as Mark Twain. In addition, Chautauqua offered extensive home study courses, for which 100,000 people enrolled in 1892 alone.

Crowded cities, despite their drawbacks, generally provided better educational facilities than the old one-room, one-teacher red schoolhouse. The success of the public schools is confirmed by the falling of the illiteracy rate from 20 percent in 1870 to 10.7 percent in 1900. Americans were developing a profound faith, often misplaced, in formal education as the sovereign remedy for their ills.

Booker T. Washington and Education for Black People

War-torn and impoverished, the South lagged far behind other regions in public education, and African-Americans suffered most severely from the school drought. A staggering 44 percent of nonwhites were illiterate in 1900. Some help came from northern philanthropists, but the foremost champion of black education was an ex-slave, Booker T. Washington, who had slept under a board sidewalk to save pennies for his schooling. Called in 1881 to head the black normal and industrial school at Tuskegee, Alabama, he began with forty students in a tumbledown shanty. Undaunted, he taught black students useful trades so that they could gain self-respect and economic security. But he stopped short of advocating social equality with whites.

Washington's commitment to training young blacks in agriculture and the trades guided the curriculum at Tuskegee Institute and made it an ideal place for slave-born George Washington Carver to teach and research. After Carver joined the faculty in 1896, he became an internationally famous agricul-

Booker T. Washington in His Office at Tuskegee Institute, c. 1902 *In a famous speech in Atlanta, Washington accepted social separateness for blacks: "In all things that are purely social, we can be as separate as the fingers, yet one as the hand in all things essential to mutual progress."*

W. E. B. Du Bois *At the end of a long lifetime of struggle for racial justice in the United States, Du Bois renounced his American citizenship in 1961, at the age of 93, and took up residence in the newly independent African state of Ghana.*

tural chemist who helped the economy of the South by discovering hundreds of new uses for the lowly peanut (shampoo, axle grease), sweet potato (vinegar), and soybean (paints).

Other black leaders, notably Dr. W. E. B. Du Bois, assailed Booker T. Washington as an "Uncle Tom" who was condemning their race to manual labor and perpetual inferiority. Born in Massachusetts, Du Bois was a mixture of African, French, Dutch, and Indian blood ("Thank God, no Anglo-Saxon," he would add). After a determined struggle, he earned a Ph.D. at Harvard, the first of his race to achieve this goal. He demanded complete equality for blacks, social as well as economic, and helped to found the National Association for the Advancement of Colored People (NAACP) in 1910. Rejecting Washington's gradualism and separatism, he demanded that the "talented tenth" of the black community be given full and immediate access to the mainstream of American life. An exceptionally skilled historian, sociologist, and poet, he died as a self-exile in Africa in 1963, at the age of ninety-five.

The Hallowed Halls of Ivy

Colleges and universities also shot up like lusty young saplings in the decades after the Civil War. The educational battle for women, only partially won before the war, turned into a rout of masculine diehards. Women's colleges, such as Vassar, were gaining ground; and universities open to both genders were blossoming forth, notably in the Midwest. By 1900 every fourth college graduate was a woman. Also by the turn of the century the black institutes and academies planted during Reconstruction had blossomed into a crop of southern black colleges. Howard University in Washington, D.C., Hampton Institute in Virginia, Atlanta University, and numerous others nurtured higher education for blacks until the civil rights movement of the 1960s made attendance at white institutions possible.

The truly phenomenal growth of higher education owed much to the Morrill Act of 1862. This enlightened law, passed after the South had seceded, provided a generous grant of the public lands to the states for support of education. "Land-grant col-

leges," most of which became state universities, in turn bound themselves to provide certain services, such as military training. The Hatch Act of 1887, extending the Morrill Act, provided federal funds for the establishment of agricultural experiment stations in connection with the land-grant colleges.

Private philanthropy richly supplemented federal grants to higher education. Many of the new industrial millionaires, developing tender social consciences, donated immense fortunes to educational enterprises. In the twenty years from 1878 to 1898 these money barons gave away about $150 million. Noteworthy among the new private universities of high quality to open their doors were Cornell (1865) and Leland Stanford Junior (1891), the latter founded in memory of the deceased fifteen-year-old only child of a builder of the Central Pacific Railroad. The University of Chicago, opened in 1892, speedily forged into a front-rank position, owing largely to the lubricant of Rockefeller's oil millions.

Towering among the new professionalized institutions of higher education was Johns Hopkins University, opened in 1876, which developed the nation's first high-grade graduate school. Several generations of American scholars, repelled by snobbish English cousins and attracted by painstaking European methods, had attended German universities. Now reputable scholars no longer had to go abroad for a gilt-edged graduate degree; Dr. Woodrow Wilson, among others, received his Ph.D. from Johns Hopkins.

The old cut-and-dried classical curriculum in the colleges was on the way out, as the new industrialization brought insistent demands for "practical" courses and specialized training in the sciences. The elective system, which permitted students to choose more courses in cafeteria fashion, was gaining popularity. It received a powerful boost in the 1870s, when Dr. Charles W. Eliot, a vigorous young chemist, became president of Harvard College and embarked on a lengthy career of educational statesmanship.

One of America's most brilliant intellectuals, the slight and sickly William James (1842–1910), served for thirty-five years on Eliot's Harvard faculty. Through his numerous writings he made a deep mark on many fields. His *Principles of Psychology* (1890) helped to establish the modern discipline of psychology. In *The Will to Believe* (1897) and *Varieties of Reli-*

gious Experience (1902), he explored the philosophy and psychology of religion. In his most famous work, *Pragmatism* (1907), he colorfully described America's greatest contribution to the history of philosophy. The concept of pragmatism held that truth was to be tested, above all, by the practical consequences of an idea, by action rather than theories. This kind of reasoning aptly expressed the philosophical temperament of a nation of doers.

The Appeal of the Press

Well-stocked public libraries—the poor people's university—were making encouraging progress, especially in Boston and New York. The magnificent Library of Congress building, which opened its doors in 1897, provided thirteen acres of floor space in the largest and costliest edifice of its kind in the world. A new era was inaugurated by the generous gifts of Andrew Carnegie. This open-handed Scotsman, book-starved in his youth, contributed $60 million for the construction of public libraries all over the country. By 1900 there were about nine thousand free circulating libraries in America, each with at least three hundred books.

Roaring newspaper presses, spurred by the invention of the Linotype in 1885, more than kept pace with the demands of a word-hungry public. But the heavy investment in machinery and plant was accompanied by a growing fear of offending advertisers and subscribers. Bare-knuckle editorials were, to an increasing degree, being supplanted by feature articles and noncontroversial syndicated material. The day of slashing journalistic giants like Horace Greeley was passing.

Sensationalism, at the same time, was beginning to debase the public taste. The semiliterate immigrants, combined with straphanging urban commuters, created a profitable market for news that was

Educational Levels, 1870–2000

Year	Number Graduating from High School	Number Graduating from College	Median School Years Completed Completed (Years)*	High School Graduates as a Percentage of 17-Year-Old Population
1870	16,000	9,371		2.0%
1880	24,000	12,896		2.5
1890	44,000	15,539		3.5
1900	95,000	27,410		6.4
1910	156,000	37,199	8.1[†]	8.8
1920	311,000	48,622	8.2[†]	16.8
1930	667,000	122,484	8.4[†]	29.0
1940	1,221,000	186,500	8.6	50.8
1950	1,199,700	432,058	9.3	59.0
1960	1,858,000	392,440	10.5	69.5
1970	2,889,000	792,656	12.2	76.9
1980	3,043,000	929,417	12.5	71.4
1990	2,503,000	1,048,631	12.7	74.2
2000	2,875,000 (est.)	1,173,000 (est.)	N.A.	N.A.

* People twenty-five years and over.

[†] 1910–1930 based on retrogressions of 1940 data; 1940 was the first year measured (Folger and Nam, *Education of the American Population*, a 1960 Census Monograph).

(Sources: *Digest of Education Statistics*, 1992, a publication of the National Center for Education Statistics, and *Statistical Abstract of the United States*, relevant years.)

simply and punchily written. Stories of sex, scandal, and other titillating subjects burst into the headlines as a vulgarization of the press accompanied the growth of circulation. Critics complained in vain about these "presstitutes."

Two new journalistic tycoons emerged. Joseph Pulitzer, Hungarian-born and near-blind, was a leader in the techniques of sensationalism in St. Louis and especially with the *New York World.* His use of the colored comic supplements, featuring the "Yellow Kid," gave the name *yellow journalism* to his lurid sheets. A close and ruthless competitor was youthful William Randolph Hearst, who had been expelled from Harvard College for a crude prank. Able to draw on his California father's mining millions, he built up a powerful chain of newspapers, beginning with the *San Francisco Examiner* in 1887.

Unfortunately, the influence of Pulitzer and Hearst was not altogether wholesome. Although both championed many worthy causes, both prostituted the press in their struggle for increased circulation; both "stooped, snooped, and scooped to conquer."

Apostles of Reform

Magazines partly satisfied the public appetite for good reading, notably old standbys like *Harper's,* the *Atlantic Monthly,* and *Scribner's Monthly.* Possibly the most influential journal was the liberal and highly intellectual *Nation,* which was read by its small (10,000 circulation) readership of professors, preachers, and publicists as "the weekly Day of Judgment." Launched in 1865 by the Irish-born Edwin L. Godkin, a merciless critic, it crusaded for civil-service reform, honesty in government, and a moderate tariff.

Another journalist-author, Henry George, was an original thinker who left an enduring mark. Poor in formal schooling, he was rich in idealism and in the milk of human kindness. After seeing poverty at its worst in India, and land grabbing at its greediest in California, he took pen in hand. His classic treatise, *Progress and Poverty* (1879), undertook to solve "the great enigma of our times"—"the association of progress with poverty." According to George, property owners unjustifiably profited from the pressure of growing population on a fixed supply of land. A single 100 percent tax on these

windfall profits would eliminate unfair inequalities and stimulate economic growth.

George soon became a most controversial figure. His book broke into the best-seller lists and ultimately sold some 3 million copies. George also lectured widely in America, where he influenced thinking about the maldistribution of wealth, and in Britain, where he left an indelible mark on Fabian socialism.

Edward Bellamy, a quiet Massachusetts Yankee, was another journalist-reformer of remarkable power. In 1888 he published a socialistic novel, *Looking Backward,* in which the hero, falling into a hypnotic sleep, awakens in the year 2000. He "looks backward" and finds that the social and economic injustices of 1887 have melted away under an idyllic government, which has nationalized big business to serve the public interest. To a nation already alarmed by the trust evil, the book had a magnetic appeal and sold over a million copies. Scores of Bellamy Clubs sprang up to discuss this mild utopian socialism, and they heavily influenced American reform movements near the end of the century.

Postwar Writing

As literacy increased, so did book reading. Post–Civil War Americans devoured millions of "dime novels," usually depicting the wilds of the West. Paint-bedaubed Indians and quick-triggered gunmen like "Deadwood Dick" shot off vast quantities of gunpowder, and virtue invariably triumphed. These lurid "paperbacks" were frowned on by parents, but goggle-eyed youths read them in haylofts or in schools behind the broad covers of geography books. The king of dime novelists was Harlan F. Halsey, who made a fortune by dashing off about 650 novels, often one in a day.

General Lewis Wallace—lawyer, soldier, and author—was a colorful figure. Having fought with distinction in the Civil War, he sought to combat the prevailing wave of Darwinian skepticism with his novel *Ben Hur: A Tale of the Christ* (1880). A phenomenal success, the book sold an estimated 2 million copies in many languages, including Arabic and Chinese, and later was adapted for stage and screen. It was the *Uncle Tom's Cabin* of the anti-Darwinists, who found in it support for the Holy Scriptures.

An even more popular writer was Horatio ("Holy Horatio") Alger, a Puritan-reared New Englander, who in 1866 forsook the pulpit for the pen. He wrote more than a hundred volumes of juvenile fiction that sold over 100 million copies.

In poetry Walt Whitman was one of the few luminaries of yesteryear who remained active. Although shattered in health by service as a Civil War nurse, he brought out successive—and purified—revisions of his hardy perennial, *Leaves of Grass*. The assassination of Lincoln inspired him to write two of the most moving poems in American literature, "O Captain! My Captain!" and "When Lilacs Last in the Dooryard Bloom'd."

The curious figure of Emily Dickinson, one of America's most gifted lyric poets, did not emerge until 1886, when she died and her poems were discovered. A Massachusetts recluse, she wrote over a thousand short lyrics on odd scraps of paper. Only two were published during her lifetime, and those without her consent. As she wrote,

> How dreary to be somebody!
> How public, like a frog
> To tell your name the livelong day
> To an admiring bog!

Literary Landmarks

In novel writing, the romantic sentimentality of a youthful era was giving way to a rugged realism that reflected more faithfully the materialism of an industrial society. American authors turned increasingly to the coarse human comedy and tragedy of the world around them to find their subjects.

Two Missouri-born authors with deep connections to the South brought altogether new voices to the late-nineteenth-century literary scene. The daring feminist author Kate Chopin (1851–1904) wrote candidly about adultery, suicide, and women's ambitions in *The Awakening* (1899). Largely ignored in her own day, Chopin was rediscovered by later readers who cited her work as suggestive of the feminist yearnings that stirred beneath the surface of "respectability" in the Gilded Age.

Mustachioed Mark Twain (1835–1910) leapt to fame with *The Celebrated Jumping Frog of Calaveras County* (1867) and *The Innocents Abroad* (1869). He teamed up with Charles Dudley Warner in 1873 to write *The Gilded Age*. An acid satire on post–Civil War politicians and speculators, the book gave a name to an era. With his scanty formal schooling in frontier Missouri, Twain typified a new breed of American authors in revolt against the elegant refinements of the old New England school of writing. Christened Samuel Langhorne Clemens, he had served for a time as a Mississippi riverboat pilot and later took his pen name, Mark Twain, from the boatman's cry that meant "two fathoms." After a brief stint in the armed forces, Twain journeyed to California, a trip he described, with a mixture of truth and tall tales, in *Roughing It* (1872).

Many other books flowed from Twain's busy pen. *The Adventures of Tom Sawyer* (1876) and *The Adventures of Huckleberry Finn* (1884) rank among American masterpieces. His later years were soured by bankruptcy growing out of unwise investments, and he was forced to take to the lecture platform and amuse what he called "the damned human race." Twain made his most enduring contribution in recapturing frontier realism and humor in the authentic American dialect.

William Dean Howells (1837–1920), a printer's son from Ohio, could boast of little schoolhouse education, but his busy pen carried him high into the literary circles of the East. In 1871 he became the editor of the prestigious Boston-based *Atlantic Monthly* and was subsequently presented with honorary degrees from six universities, including Oxford. He wrote about ordinary people and about contemporary and sometimes controversial social themes. *A Modern Instance* (1882) deals with the once-taboo subject of divorce; *The Rise of Silas Lapham* (1885) describes the trials of a newly rich paint manufacturer caught up in the caste system of Brahmin Boston. *A Hazard of New Fortunes* (1890) portrays the reformers, strikers, and socialists in Gilded Age New York.

Stephen Crane (1871–1900), the fourteenth son of a Methodist minister, also wrote about the seamy underside of life in urban, industrial America. His *Maggie: A Girl of the Streets* (1893), a brutal tale about a poor prostitute driven to suicide, was too grim to find a publisher. Crane had to have it printed privately. He rose quickly to prominence with *The Red*

Badge of Courage (1895), the stirring story of a blood-ied young Civil War recruit under fire. Crane himself had never seen a battle and wrote entirely from the printed Civil War records. He died of tuberculosis in 1900, when only twenty-nine.

Henry James (1843–1916), brother of Harvard philosopher William James, was a New Yorker who turned from law to literature. Taking as his dominant theme the confrontation of innocent Americans with subtle Europeans, James penned a remarkable number of brilliant novels, including *Daisy Miller* (1879), *The Portrait of a Lady* (1881), and *The Wings of the Dove* (1902). In *The Bostonians* (1886) he wrote one of the first novels about the rising feminist movement. James frequently made women his central characters, exploring their inner reactions to complex situations with a deftness that marked him as a master of "psychological realism." Long resident in England, he became a British subject shortly before his death.

Candid portrayals of contemporary life and social problems were the literary order of the day by the turn of the century. Jack London (1876–1916), famous as a nature writer of such books as *The Call of the Wild* (1903), turned to depicting a possible fascistic revolution in *The Iron Heel* (1907). Frank Norris (1870–1902), like London a Californian, wrote *The Octopus* (1901), an earthy saga of the stranglehold of the railroad and corrupt politicians on California wheat ranchers.

Conspicuous among the new "social novelists" rising in the literary firmament was Theodore Dreiser (1871–1945), a homely, gangling writer from Indiana. He burst on the literary scene in 1900 with *Sister Carrie*, a graphically realistic narrative of a poor working girl in Chicago and New York. She becomes one man's mistress, then elopes with another, and finally strikes out on her own to make a career on the stage. The fictional Carrie's disregard for prevailing moral standards so offended Dreiser's publisher that the book was soon withdrawn from circulation—though it later re-emerged as an acclaimed American classic.

The New Morality

Victoria Woodhull, who was real flesh and blood, also shook the pillars of conventional morality when she publicly proclaimed her belief in free love in 1871. Woodhull was a beautiful and eloquent divorcée, sometime stockbroker, and tireless feminist propagandist. Together with her sister Tennessee Claflin she published a far-out periodical, *Woodhull and Claflin's Weekly*. The sisters again shocked "respectable" society in 1872 when their journal struck a blow for the new morality by charging that Henry Ward Beecher, the most famous preacher of his day, had for years been carrying on an adulterous affair.

Pure-minded Americans sternly resisted these affronts to their moral principles. Their foremost champion was a portly crusader, Anthony Comstock, who made lifelong war on the "immoral." Armed after 1873 with a federal statute—the notorious Comstock Law—this self-appointed defender of sexual purity boasted that he had confiscated no fewer than 202,679 "obscene pictures and photos"; 4,185 "boxes of pills, powders, etc., used by abortionists"; and 26 "obscene pictures, framed on walls of saloons."

The antics of the Woodhull sisters and Anthony Comstock exposed to daylight the battle going on in late-nineteenth-century America over sexual attitudes and the place of women. Switchboards and typewriters in the booming cities became increasingly the tools of women's liberation. Economic freedom encouraged sexual freedom, and the "new morality" began to be reflected in soaring divorce rates, the spreading practice of birth control, and increasingly frank discussion of sexual topics. By 1913, said one popular magazine, the chimes had struck "sex o'clock in America."

Families and Women in the City

The new urban environment was hard on families. Paradoxically, the crowded cities were emotionally isolating places. Urban families had to go it alone, separated from clan, kin, and village. Many families cracked under the strain of providing the virtually exclusive arena for intimate companionship and emotional satisfaction. The late-nineteenth-century urban era launched the "divorce revolution" that transformed the United States' social landscape in the twentieth century.

Urban life also dictated changes in work habits and even in family size. Not only fathers but mothers and even children as young as ten years old often worked, and usually in widely scattered locations. In the city more children meant more mouths to feed, more crowding in sardine-tin tenements, and more human baggage to carry in the uphill struggle for social mobility. Not surprisingly, birthrates were still dropping and family size continued to shrink as the nineteenth century lengthened. Marriages were being delayed, and more couples learned the techniques of birth control.

Women were growing more independent in the urban environment, and in 1898 they heard the voice of a major feminist prophet, Charlotte Perkins Gilman. In that year the freethinking and original-minded Gilman published *Women and Economics*. In this classic of feminist literature, Gilman called on women to abandon their dependent status and contribute to the larger life of the community through productive involvement in the economy. Rejecting all claims that biology gave women a fundamentally different character from men, she argued that "our highly specialized motherhood is not so advantageous as believed." She advocated centralized nurseries and cooperative kitchens to facilitate women's participation in the work force—anticipating by more than half a century the day-care centers and convenience-food services of a later day.

Fiery feminists also continued to insist on the ballot. They had been demanding the vote since before the Civil War, but many high-minded female reformers had temporarily shelved the cause of women to battle for the rights of blacks. In 1890 militant suffragists formed the National American Woman Suffrage Association. Its founders included aging pioneers like Elizabeth Cady Stanton, who had helped organize the first women's rights convention in 1848, and her long-time comrade Susan B. Anthony, the radical Quaker who had courted jail by trying to cast a ballot in the 1872 presidential election.

By 1900 a new generation of women had taken command of the suffrage battle. Their most effective leader was Carrie Chapman Catt, a pragmatic and businesslike reformer of relentless dedication. Significantly, under Catt the suffragists de-emphasized the argument that women deserved the vote as a matter of right, because they were in all respects the equals of men. Instead Catt stressed the desirability of giving women the vote if they were to continue to discharge their traditional duties as homemakers and mothers in the increasingly public world of the city.

By thus linking the ballot to a traditional definition of women's role, suffragists registered encouraging gains as the new century opened, despite continuing showers of rotten eggs and the jeers of male critics. Women were increasingly permitted to vote in local elections, particularly on issues related to the schools. Wyoming Territory—later called "the Equality State"—granted the first unrestricted suffrage to women in 1869. This important breach in the dike once made, many states followed Wyoming's example. Paralleling these triumphs, most of the states by 1890 had passed laws to permit wives to own or control their property after marriage.

The reborn suffrage movement and other women's organizations excluded black women from their ranks. Fearful that an integrated campaign would handicap its efforts to get the vote, the National American Woman Suffrage Association limited membership to whites. Black women, however, created their own associations. Journalist and teacher Ida B. Wells inspired black women to mount a nationwide antilynching crusade. She also helped launch the black women's club movement, which culminated in the establishment of the National Association of Colored Women in 1896.

Artistic Triumphs

John Adams had anticipated that his generation's preoccupation with nation-building would allow art to flourish in the future, but the results long proved unspectacular. Portrait painting continued to appeal, as it had since the colonial era, but many of America's finest painters made their livings abroad. James Whistler (1834–1903) did much of his work, including the celebrated portrait of his mother, in England. This eccentric and quarrelsome Massachusetts Yankee had earlier been dropped from West Point after failing chemistry. "Had silicon been a gas," he later jested, "I would have been a major general." Another gifted portrait painter, likewise self-exiled in England, was

John Singer Sargent (1856–1925). His flattering but somewhat superficial likenesses of the British nobility were highly prized. Mary Cassatt, an American-in-exile in Paris, painted sensitive portrayals of women and children that earned her a place in the pantheon of the French impressionist painters.

Other brush wielders, no less talented, brightened the artistic horizon. Self-taught George Inness (1825–1894), who looked like a fanatic with his long hair and piercing gaze, became America's leading landscapist. Thomas Eakins (1844–1916) attained a high degree of realism in his paintings, a quality not appreciated by portrait sitters who wanted their blemishes overlooked. Boston-born Winslow Homer (1836–1910), who as a youth had secretly drawn sketches in school, was perhaps the greatest painter of the group. Earthily American and largely resistant to foreign influences, he revealed rugged realism and boldness of conception. His canvases of the sea and of fisherfolk were masterly, and probably no American artist has excelled him in portraying the awesome power of the ocean.

Probably the most gifted sculptor yet produced by America was Augustus Saint-Gaudens (1848–1907). Born in Ireland of an Irish mother and a French father, he became an adopted American. Among his most moving works is the Robert Gould Shaw memorial, erected in Boston in 1897. It depicts Colonel Shaw, a young white "Boston Brahmin" officer, leading his black troops into battle in the Civil War.

Music, too, was gaining popularity. America of the 1880s and 1890s was assembling high-quality symphony orchestras, notably in Boston and Chicago. The famed Metropolitan Opera House of New York was erected in 1883. In its fabled "Diamond Horseshoe" the newly rich, often under the pretense of enjoying the imported singers, would flaunt their jewels, gowns, and furs. While symphonies and operas were devoted to bringing European music to elite American audiences, new strains of homegrown American music were sprouting in the South. Black folk traditions like spirituals and "ragged music" were evolving into the blues, ragtime, and jazz that would transform American popular music in the twentieth century.

A marvelous discovery was the reproduction of music by mechanical means. The phonograph, though a squeakily imperfect instrument when invented by the deaf Edison, had by 1900 reached over 150,000 homes. Americans were rapidly being dosed with "canned music," as the parlor piano increasingly gathered dust.

In addition to skyscraper builder Louis Sullivan, a famous American architect of the age was Henry H. Richardson. Born in Louisiana and educated at Harvard and in Paris, Richardson settled in Boston and from there spread his immense influence throughout the eastern half of the United States. He popularized a distinctive, ornamental style that came to be known as "Richardsonian." High-vaulted arches, like those on Gothic churches, were his trademark. His masterpiece and most famous work was the Marshall Field Building (1885) in Chicago.

The Business of Amusement

Fun and frolic were not neglected by the workaday American. The legitimate stage still flourished, as appreciative audiences responded to the lure of the footlights. Vaudeville, with its coarse jokes and graceful acrobats, continued to be immensely popular during the 1880s and 1890s.

The circus—high-tented and multiringed—finally emerged full-blown. Phineas T. Barnum, the master showman who had early discovered that "the public likes to be humbugged," joined hands with James A. Bailey in 1881 to stage the "Greatest Show on Earth."

Colorful "Wild West" shows, first performed in 1883, were even more distinctively American. Headed by the knightly, goateed, and free-drinking William F. ("Buffalo Bill") Cody, the troupe included war-whooping Indians, live buffalo, and deadeye sharpshooters. Among them was the girlish Annie Oakley. Rifle in hand, at thirty paces she could perforate a tossed-up card half a dozen times before it fluttered to the ground.

Baseball, already widely played before the Civil War, was clearly emerging as the national pastime, if not a national mania. A league of professional players was formed in the 1870s, and in 1888 an all-star baseball team toured the world, using the pyramids as a backstop while in Egypt. The trend toward spectator sports was well exemplified by football, a rugged

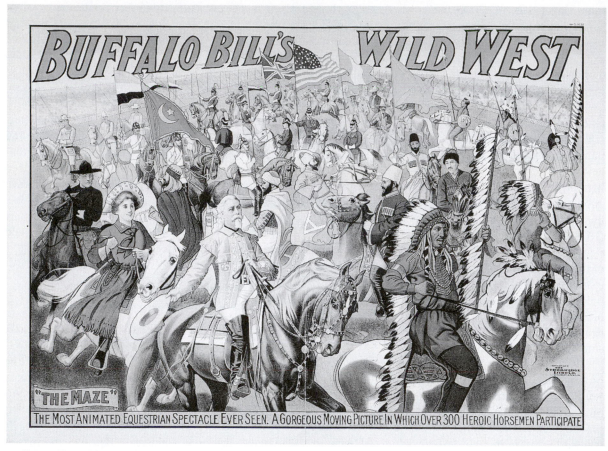

Buffalo Bill's Wild West Show, c. 1907 *By the late 1800s, the "wild" West was already passing into the realm of myth—and popular entertainment. Famed frontiersman William F. ("Buffalo Bill") Cody made his fortune showing off his tame cowboys and Indians to urban audiences.*

game that used the dangerous flying wedge formation. The Yale-Princeton game of 1893 drew fifty thousand cheering fans, while foreigners jeered that the nation was getting "sports on the brain."

Even boxing, with its unsavory reputation for bareknuckle brutality, gained a new and gloved respectability in 1892. Agile "Gentleman Jim" Corbett wrested the world championship from the aging and alcoholic John L. Sullivan, the fabulous "Boston Strong Boy."

Basketball was invented in 1891 by James Naismith, a YMCA instructor in Springfield, Massachusetts. Designed as an active indoor sport that could be played during the winter months, it spread rapidly and enjoyed enormous popularity in the next century.

Two crazes swept the country in the closing decades of the century. Croquet became enormously popular, though condemned by moralists of the "naughty nineties" because it exposed feminine ankles and promoted flirtation. The low-framed "safety" bicycle replaced the high-seated model. By 1893 a million bicycles were in use.

The land of the skyscraper was plainly becoming more standardized, owing largely to the new industrialization. To an increasing degree, Americans shared a common culture—playing, reading, shopping, and talking alike. As the century drew to a close, the explosion of cities paradoxically made Americans more diverse and more similar at the same time.

Chronology

1859 Charles Darwin publishes *On the Origin of Species*.

1862 Morrill Act provides public land for higher education.

1869 Wyoming Territory grants women the right to vote.

1871 *Woodhull and Claflin's Weekly* published.

1873 Comstock Law passed.

1876 Johns Hopkins University graduate school established.

1879 Henry George publishes *Progress and Poverty*.
Dumbbell tenement introduced.
Mary Baker Eddy establishes Christian Science.
Salvation Army begins work in America.

1881 Booker T. Washington becomes head of Tuskegee Institute.

1882 First immigration-restriction laws passed.

1883 Brooklyn Bridge completed.

1884 Mark Twain publishes *The Adventures of Huckleberry Finn*.

1885 Louis Sullivan builds the first skyscraper, in Chicago.

1886 Statue of Liberty erected in New York harbor.

1887 American Protective Association (APA) formed.

1888 Edward Bellamy publishes *Looking Backward*.

1889 Jane Addams founds Hull House in Chicago.
Moody Bible Institute established in Chicago.

1890 National American Woman Suffrage Association formed.

1891 Basketball invented.

1893 Lillian Wald opens Henry Street Settlement in New York.

1897 Library of Congress opens.

1898 Charlotte Perkins Gilman publishes *Women and Economics*.

1899 Kate Chopin publishes *The Awakening*.

1900 Theodore Dreiser publishes *Sister Carrie*.

1910 National Association for the Advancement of Colored People (NAACP) founded.

26

The Great West and the Agricultural Revolution

1865–1896

Up to our own day American history has been in a large degree the history of the colonization of the Great West. The existence of an area of free land, its continuous recession, and the advance of American settlement westward, explain American development.

FREDERICK JACKSON TURNER, 1893

When the Civil War crashed to a close, the frontier line was still wavering westward. A long fringe of settlement, bulging outward here and there, ran roughly north through central Texas and on up to the Canadian border. Between this jagged line and the settled areas on the Pacific slope, there were virtually no white people. The few exceptions were the islands of Mormons in Utah, occasional trading posts and gold camps, and several scattered Spanish-Mexican settlements throughout the Southwest.

Sprawling in expanse, the Great West was a rough square that measured about a thousand miles on each side. Embracing mountains, plateaus, deserts, and plains, it was the habitat of the Indian, the buffalo, the wild horse, the prairie dog, and the coyote. Twenty-five years later—that is, by 1890—the entire

domain had been carved into states and the four territories of Utah, Arizona, New Mexico, and "Indian Territory," or Oklahoma. Pioneers flung themselves greedily on this enormous prize, as if to ravish it. Probably never before in human experience had so huge an area been transformed so rapidly.

The Clash of Cultures in the West

Native Americans numbered about 360,000 in 1860, many of them scattered about the vast grasslands of the trans-Missouri West. But to their misfortune, the Indians stood in the path of the advancing white pioneers. An inevitable clash loomed between an acquisitive, industrializing civilization and the Indians' highly evolved lifeways, adapted over centuries to the demanding environment of the sparsely watered western plains.

Migration and conflict—and sometimes dramatic cultural change—were no strangers to the arid West, even before the whites began to arrive. The Comanches had driven the Apaches off the central plains into the upper Rio Grande valley in the eighteenth century. Harried by the Mandans and Chippewas, the Cheyenne had abandoned their villages along the upper reaches of the Mississippi and Missouri Rivers in the century before the Civil War. In the late eighteenth century, the Sioux had left the Great Lakes woodlands for the plains, where they battled the Crows, Kiowas, and Pawnees. Mounted on Spanish-introduced horses, peoples like the Cheyenne and the Sioux became wide-ranging nomadic traders and deadly efficient buffalo hunters.

When white soldiers and settlers edged onto the plains in the decades just before the Civil War, they accelerated a fateful cycle that exacerbated already fierce enmities among the Indians and ultimately undermined the foundations of Native American culture. White intruders unwittingly spread cholera, typhoid, and smallpox among the native peoples of the plains, with devastating results. Equally harmful, whites put further pressure on the shrinking bison population by hunting and by grazing their own livestock on the prairie grasses. As the once-mammoth buffalo herds dwindled, warfare intensified among the Plains tribes for ever-scarcer hunting grounds.

The federal government tried to sign treaties with the "chiefs" of various tribes at Fort Laramie in 1851, but the white treaty makers misunderstood both Indian government and Indian society. Living in scattered bands, Native Americans usually recognized no authority outside their immediate family, or perhaps a village elder, and resisted white attempts to confine them to a defined territory. In the 1860s the federal government tried to herd the Plains Indians onto smaller confines like the "Great Sioux Reservation" in the Dakotas and the Indian Territory of present-day Oklahoma, into which dozens of southern Plains tribes were forced. Promises that they would be left alone and provided with food, clothing, and other supplies were often violated by corrupt federal agents who regularly cheated the Indians.

For more than a decade after the Civil War, fierce warfare between Indians and the U.S. Army raged in various parts of the West. Army troops, many of them recent immigrants, met formidable adversaries in the Plains Indians, whose superb horsemanship gave them baffling mobility. Fully one-fifth of all U.S. Army personnel on the frontier were African-American—dubbed "Buffalo Soldiers" by the Indians, supposedly because of the resemblance of their hair to the bison's furry coat.

Receding Native Population

The Indian wars in the West were often brutal affairs. Aggressive whites sometimes shot peaceful Indians on sight. At Sand Creek, Colorado, in 1864, Colonel J. M. Chivington's militia massacred in cold blood some four hundred Indians who apparently thought they had been promised immunity. Women were shot praying for mercy, children had their brains dashed out, and braves were tortured, scalped, and mutilated.

Cruelty begot cruelty. In 1866 a Sioux war party ambushed Captain William Fetterman's command of eighty-one soldiers and civilians in Wyoming's Bighorn Mountains, killing every man and mutilating the corpses. As the cycle of ferocious warfare intensified, the federal government in 1868 abandoned its attempt to construct the Bozeman Trail through Montana. The sprawling "Great Sioux Reservation" was guaranteed to the Sioux tribes.

But in 1874 a new round of warfare with the Plains Indians began when Colonel George Armstrong Custer, a famed Civil War officer, led a "scientific" expedition into the Black Hills of South Dakota (part of the Sioux reservation) and announced that he had discovered gold. Hordes of greedy gold-seekers swarmed into the Sioux lands. The aggrieved Sioux took to the warpath, led by the influential and wily Sitting Bull.

Colonel Custer's Seventh Cavalry set out to suppress the Indians and force them onto the reservation. Attacking what turned out to be a superior force of some 2,500 well-armed warriors camped along the Little Bighorn River in present-day Montana, the "White Chief with Yellow Hair" and his 264 officers and men were completely wiped out in 1876 when two supporting columns failed to come to their

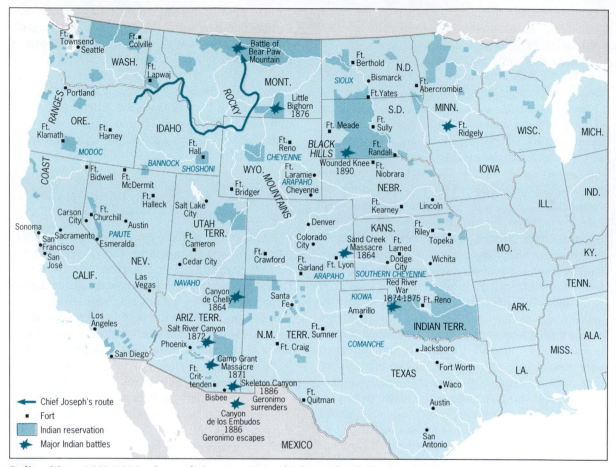

Indian Wars, 1860–1890   *Surrendering in 1877, Chief Joseph of the Nez Percés declared: "Our chiefs are killed. . . . The old men are all dead. . . . The little children are freezing to death. . . . I want to have time to look for my children. . . . Hear me, my chiefs. My heart is sick and sad. From where the sun now stands I will fight no more forever."*

rescue.* But in a series of battles across the northern plains in the ensuing months, the U.S. Army relentlessly hunted down the Indians who had humiliated Custer.

The Nez Percé Indians of northeastern Oregon were goaded into warfare in 1877, when U.S. authorities tried to herd them onto a reservation. Chief Joseph finally surrendered his band after a tortuous, seventeen-hundred-mile, three-month trek across the Continental Divide toward Canada. There Chief Joseph hoped to rendezvous with Sitting Bull, who had taken refuge north of the border after the Battle of Little Bighorn. Betrayed into believing that they would be returned to their ancestral lands in Idaho, the Nez Percés instead were sent to a dusty reservation in Kansas, where 40 percent of them perished from disease. The survivors eventually returned to Idaho.

Fierce Apache tribes of Arizona and New Mexico were the most difficult to subdue. Led by Geronimo,

---

* When whites annihilated Indians, the engagement (in white history books) was usually a "battle"; when Indians slaughtered whites, it was a "massacre." "Strategy," when practiced by Indians, was "treachery."

whose eyes blazed hatred of the whites, they were pursued into Mexico by federal troops. Scattered remnants of the warriors were finally persuaded to surrender after the Apache women had been exiled to Florida.

This relentless fire-and-sword policy of the whites at last shattered the spirit of the Indians. The vanquished Native Americans were finally ghettoized on reservations, where they were compelled to eke out an existence as wards of the government.

The defeat of the Indians was engineered by a number of factors. Of cardinal importance was the railroad, which shot an iron arrow through the heart of the West. The Indians were also ravaged by the white people's diseases and liquor, to which they showed little resistance.

Above all, the virtual extermination of the buffalo doomed the Plains Indians' nomadic way of life. When the white Americans ventured onto the Great Plains after the Civil War, some 15 million buffalo, or American bison, still blackened the prairies. These huge, shaggy, lumbering beasts were the staff of life for the Native Americans (see "Makers of America: The Plains Indians," pp. 364–365). Their flesh provided food; their dried dung provided fuel ("buffalo chips"); their hides provided clothing, lariats, and harnesses.

But the building of the railroad meant doom for the buffalo. In 1868 a Kansas Pacific locomotive had to wait eight hours for a herd to amble across the tracks. Soon the creatures were being slain for their hides, for a few choice cuts of meat, or simply for amusement. William "Buffalo Bill" Cody killed over four thousand buffalo in eighteen months while employed by the Kansas Pacific. "Sportsmen" on lurching railroad trains would lean out the windows and blaze away at the animals to satisfy their lust for slaughter or excitement. Such wholesale butchery left fewer than a thousand buffalo by 1885, and the once-numerous beasts were barely saved from extinction. The whole story is a shocking example of the greed and waste that accompanied the conquest of the North American continent.

The End of the Trail

By the 1880s the national conscience began to stir uneasily over the plight of the Indians. Helen Hunt Jackson, a Massachusetts writer of children's literature, pricked the moral sense of Americans in 1881 when she published *A Century of Dishonor*. The book chronicled the sorry record of governmental ruthlessness and chicanery in dealing with the Indians. Her later novel *Ramona* (1884), a story of injustice to the California Indians, sold some 600,000 copies and further inspired sympathy for the Indians.

Debate seesawed. Humanitarians wanted to treat the Indians kindly and persuade them thereby to "walk the white man's road." Yet hard-liners insisted on the current policy of forced containment and brutal punishment. Neither side showed much respect for Native American culture. Christian reformers, who often administered educational facilities on the reservations, sometimes withheld food to force the Indians to give up their tribal religions and assimilate to white society. In 1884 these zealous white souls joined with military men in successfully persuading the federal government to outlaw the sacred Sun Dance. When the "Ghost Dance" cult later spread to the Dakota Sioux, the army bloodily stamped it out in 1890 at the so-called Battle of Wounded Knee. In the fighting thus provoked, an estimated two hundred Indian men, women, and children were killed, as well as twenty-nine invading soldiers.

The misbegotten offspring of the movement to reform Indian policy was the Dawes Severalty Act of 1887. Reflecting the forced-civilization views of the reformers, the act dissolved many tribes as legal entities, wiped out tribal ownership of land, and set up individual Indian family heads with 160 free acres. If the Indians behaved themselves like "good white settlers," they would get full title to their holdings, as well as citizenship, in twenty-five years. The probationary period was later extended, but full citizenship was granted to all Indians in 1924.

The federal efforts at forced assimilation included boarding schools for Indian children, beginning in 1879 with the Carlisle Indian School in Pennsylvania. "Kill the Indian and save the man" was the motto for these schools, where Native American children, separated from their tribes, were taught English and inculcated with white values and customs. The government also sent "field matrons" to the reservations to teach Native American women the art of

The Plains Indians

The last of the native peoples of North America to bow before the military might of the whites, the Indians of the northern Great Plains long defended their lands and their ways of life against the American cavalry. After the end of the Indian wars, toward the close of the nineteenth century, the Plains tribes struggled on, jealously guarding their communities against white encroachment.

Before Europeans first appeared in North America in the sixteenth century, the vast plain from northern Texas to Saskatchewan was home to some thirty different tribes. There was no typical Plains Indian; each tribe spoke a distinct language, practiced its own religion, and formed its own government.

Indians had first trod the arid plains to pursue sprawling herds of antelope, elk, and especially buffalo, but they were not exclusively hunters. The women were expert farmers, coaxing lush gardens of pumpkins, squash, corn, and beans from the dry but fertile soil. Still, the shaggy pelt and heavy flesh of the buffalo constituted the staff of life on the plains. Hunted by men, the great bison were butchered by women, who made use of every part of the beast.

The nomadic Plains Indians dispersed in small bands to find shelter throughout the winter, gathering together in the summer for larger-scale religious ceremonies, socializing, and communal buffalo hunts. Then in the sixteenth century, the mounted Spanish *conquistadores* ventured into the New World, and their steeds quickly spread over the plains. The horse revolutionized Indian societies, turning the Plains tribes into efficient hunting machines that promised to banish hunger from the prairies. But the

Arapaho Chief Hail Wearing Ghost Dance Shirt, c. 1890
The Ghost Dance cult originated among the Paiute Indians in the 1870s and spread swiftly throughout the western tribes. It held out the promise of a revival of traditional Indian culture and revenge on the invading whites, but it was ruthlessly suppressed by the U.S. authorities. Ghost Dance shirts like this one were thought by their wearers to be impermeable to bullets.

plains pony also ignited a furious competition for grazing land and for ever more horses, so that wars became increasingly bitter and frequent.

The European invasion soon eclipsed the short-lived era of the horse. After many battles the Plains Indians found themselves crammed together on tiny reservations, clinging with tired but determined fingers to their traditions. Although much of Plains Indian culture persists to this day, the Indians' free-ranging way of life passed into memory. As Black Elk, an Oglala Sioux, put it, "Once we were happy in our own country and we were seldom hungry, for then the two-leggeds and the four-leggeds lived together like relatives, and there was plenty for them and for us. But then the Wasichus [white people] came, and they made little islands for us . . . and always these islands are becoming smaller, for around them surges the gnawing flood of Wasichus."

sewing and to preach the virtues of chastity and hygiene.

The Dawes Act struck directly at tribal organization and tried to make rugged individualists out of the Indians. This legislation ignored the inherent reliance of traditional Indian culture on tribally held land. The Dawes Act remained the cornerstone of the government's official Indian policy until 1934, when the Indian Reorganization Act ("the Indian New Deal") reversed the individualistic approach and belatedly tried to restore the tribal basis of Indian life (see p. 477).

Under these new federal policies, defective though they were, the Indian population started to mount slowly. The total number had been reduced by 1887 to about 243,000—the result of bullets, bottles, and bacteria—but the census of 2000 counted nearly 4.7 million Native Americans, urban and rural.

Mining: From Dishpan to Ore-Breaker

The conquest of the Indians and the coming of the railroad were life-giving boons to the mining frontier. The golden gravel of California continued to yield "pay dirt," and in 1858 an electrifying discovery convulsed Colorado. Avid "fifty-niners" or "Pike's Peakers" rushed west to rip at the ramparts of the Rockies. Many miners failed and returned "busted" and weary to the East. But bearded fortune seekers stayed on in Colorado to strip silver or develop nonmetallic wealth in the form of golden grain.

"Fifty-niners" also poured feverishly into Nevada in 1859, after the fabulous Comstock lode had been uncovered. A fantastic amount of gold and silver, worth more than $340 million, was mined by the "Kings of the Comstock" from 1860 to 1890. The scantily populated state of Nevada, "child of the Comstock lode," was prematurely railroaded into the Union in 1864, partly to provide three electoral votes for President Lincoln.

Smaller "lucky strikes" drew frantic gold and silver seekers into Montana, Idaho, and other western states. Boomtowns, known as "Helldorados," sprouted from the desert sands like magic. Every third cabin was a saloon, where sweat-stained miners drank adulterated liquor ("rotgut") in the company of accommodating women. Lynch law and vigilante justice, as in early California, preserved a crude semblance of order. And when the "diggings" petered out, the gold seekers decamped, leaving picturesque "ghost towns," such as Virginia City, Nevada, silhouetted in the desert. Begun with a boom, these towns ended with a whimper.

Once the loose surface gold was gobbled up, ore-breaking machinery was imported to smash the gold-bearing quartz. This operation was so expensive that it could ordinarily be undertaken only by corporations pooling the wealth of stockholders. Gradually the age of big business came to the mining industry. Dusty, bewhiskered miners, dishpans in hand, were replaced by impersonal corporations with their costly machinery and trained engineers.

Yet the mining frontier had played a vital role in subduing the continent. Magnetlike, it attracted population and wealth while advertising the wonders of the Wild West. The amassing of precious metals helped finance the Civil War, facilitated the building

Dance-Hall Girl, Virginia City, Nevada, c. 1890   *Women as well as men sought their fortunes in the frontier West—especially in wide-open mining towns like Virginia City.*

of railroads, enabled the Treasury to resume specie payments in 1879, and injected the silver issue into American politics. "Silver senators," representing the thinly peopled "acreage states" of the West, used their disproportionate influence to promote the interests of the silver miners. Finally, the mining frontier added to American folklore and literature, as the writings of Mark Twain so colorfully attest.

Beef Bonanzas and the Long Drive

When the Civil War ended, the grassy plains of Texas supported several million tough, longhorn cattle.

These scrawny beasts were killed primarily for their hides. There was no way to get their meat profitably to market.

The problem of marketing was neatly solved when the transcontinental railroads thrust their iron fingers into the West. Cattle could now be shipped bodily to the stockyards and, under "beef barons" like the Swifts and Armours, the highly industrialized meatpacking business sprang into existence as a main pillar of the economy. Drawing on the gigantic stockyards at Kansas City and Chicago, the packers could ship their fresh products to the East Coast in the newly perfected refrigerator cars.

A spectacular feeder of the new slaughterhouses was the "Long Drive." Texas cowboys—black, white, and Mexican—drove herds numbering from one thousand to ten thousand head slowly over the unfenced and unpeopled plains until they reached a railroad terminal. The bawling beasts grazed en route on the free government grass. Favorite terminal points were fly-specked "cow towns" like Dodge City and Abilene (Kansas), Ogallala (Nebraska), and Cheyenne (Wyoming). From 1866 to 1888, bellowing herds totaling over 4 million steers were driven northward from the beef bowl of Texas.

What the Lord giveth, the Lord also can take away. The railroad made the Long Drive; and the railroad unmade the Long Drive, primarily because the locomotives ran both ways. The same rails that bore the cattle from the open range to the kitchen range brought out the homesteader and the sheepherder. Both of these intruders, sometimes amid flying bullets, built barbed-wire fences that were too numerous to be cut down by the cowboys. Furthermore, the terrible winter of 1886–1887, with blinding blizzards reaching 68° below zero, left thousands of dazed cattle starving and freezing. Overexpansion and overgrazing likewise took their toll, as the cowboys slowly gave way to plowboys.

The only escape for the stockman was to make cattle-raising a big business and avoid the perils of overproduction. Breeders learned to fence their ranches, lay in winter feed, import blooded bulls, and produce fewer and meatier animals. They also learned to organize. The Wyoming Stock-Growers' Association, especially in the 1880s, virtually controlled the territory and its legislature.

Nebraska Homesteaders in Front of Their Sod House, 1887 *These two brothers and their families had escaped to Canada from the slave South during the Civil War. Returning to the United States in the 1880s, they took advantage of the Homestead Act to stake out farms in Custer County, Nebraska.*

This was the heyday of the cowboy. The equipment of the lone cowhand—from "shooting irons" and ten-gallon hat to chaps and high-heeled boots—served a useful, not an ornamental, function. A "genuwine" gun-toting cowpuncher, riding where men were men and smelled like horses, could justifiably boast of his toughness.

These bowlegged Knights of the Saddle, with colorful trappings and cattle-lulling songs, became an authentic part of American folklore. Many of them, perhaps five thousand, were blacks, who especially enjoyed the newfound freedom of the open range.

The Farmers' Frontier

Miners and cattlemen created the romantic legend of the West, but it was the sober sodbuster who wrote the final chapter of frontier history. A fresh day dawned for western farmers with the Homestead Act of 1862. The new law allowed a settler to acquire as much as 160 acres of land (a quarter-section) by living on it for five years, improving it, and paying a nominal fee of about $30.

The Homestead Act marked a drastic departure from previous policy. Before the act, public land had been sold primarily for revenue; now it was to be given away to encourage a rapid filling of empty spaces and to provide a stimulus to the family farm—"the backbone of democracy." During the forty years after its passage, about half a million families took advantage of the Homestead Act to carve out new homes in the vast open stretches. Yet five times that many families *purchased* their land from the railroads, land companies, or the states.

The Homestead Act often turned out to be a cruel hoax. The standard 160 acres, quite adequate in the well-watered Mississippi basin, frequently proved pitifully inadequate on the rain-scarce Great Plains. Thousands of homesteaders, perhaps two out of three, were forced to give up the one-sided struggle against drought.

Naked fraud was spawned by the Homestead Act and similar laws. Perhaps ten times more of the public domain wound up in the clutches of land-grabbing promoters than in the hands of bona fide farmers. Unscrupulous corporations would use "dummy" homesteaders—often their employees or immigrants bribed with cash or beer—to grab the best properties, containing timber, minerals, and oil. Settlers would later swear that they had "improved" the property by erecting a "twelve-by-fourteen" dwelling, which turned out to measure twelve by fourteen *inches*.

The railways also played a major role in developing the agricultural West, largely through the profitable marketing of crops. Some railroad companies induced Americans and European immigrants to buy the cheap lands earlier granted by the government. The Northern Pacific Railroad at one time had nearly a thousand paid agents in Europe distributing leaflets in various languages.

Agriculture expanded once the myth of the Great American Desert was shattered. Pioneer explorers had assumed that the soil must be barren, simply because it was not heavily watered and did not support immense forests. But once the prairie sod was broken with heavy iron plows pulled by four yokes of oxen, the earth proved astonishingly fruitful.

Lured by higher wheat prices resulting from crop failures elsewhere in the world, settlers in the 1870s rashly pushed still farther west, onto the poor, marginal lands beyond the 100th meridian. Geologist John Wesley Powell, explorer of the Colorado River's Grand Canyon, warned in 1874 that beyond the 100th meridian so little rain fell that agriculture was impossible without massive irrigation. Ignoring Powell's advice, farmers heedlessly chewed up the crusty earth in western Kansas, eastern Colorado, and Montana. They quickly went broke as a six-year drought in the 1880s further desiccated the already dusty region. In the wake of the drought, some pioneers tried the "dry farming" technique of frequent shallow cultivation. But over time this practice pulverized the surface soil and contributed to the "Dust Bowl" several decades later (see p. 477).

Other adaptations to the western environment were more successful. Tough strains of wheat, resistant to cold and drought, were imported from Russia and blossomed into billowing yellow carpets. Barbed wire, perfected by Joseph F. Glidden in 1874, solved the problem of how to build fences on the treeless prairies. Eventually, federally financed irrigation projects on a colossal scale caused the Great American Desert to bloom. In the long run, hydraulic engi-

neers had more to do with shaping the modern West than all the trappers, miners, cavalrymen, and cowboys there ever were.

The Great West experienced a fantastic growth in population from the 1870s to the 1890s. A parade of new western states proudly joined their eastern sisters. Boomtown Colorado, offspring of the Pike's Peak gold rush, was greeted in 1876 as the "Centennial State." In 1889–1890 a Republican Congress, eagerly seeking more Republican electoral and congressional votes, admitted in a wholesale lot six new states: North Dakota, South Dakota, Montana, Washington, Idaho, and Wyoming. The Mormon church formally banned polygamy in 1890, but not until 1896 was Utah deemed worthy of admission. Only Oklahoma, New Mexico, and Arizona remained to be formed into states from contiguous territory on the mainland of North America.

In a last gaudy fling, the federal government made available to settlers vast stretches of fertile plains formerly occupied by the Indians in the district of Oklahoma ("the beautiful land"). Scores of overeager and well-armed "sooners," illegally jumping the gun, had entered Oklahoma Territory. They had to be evicted repeatedly by federal troops, who on occasion would shoot the intruders' horses. On April 22, 1889, all was in readiness for the legal opening, and some 50,000 "boomers" were poised expectantly on the boundary line. At high noon the bugle shrilled, and a horde of "eighty-niners" poured in on lathered horses or careening vehicles. That night a lonely spot on the prairie had mushroomed into the tented city of Guthrie, with over 10,000 people. By the end of the year Oklahoma boasted 60,000 inhabitants, and Congress made it a territory. In 1907 it became the "Sooner State."

The Fading Frontier

In 1890—a watershed date—the superintendent of the census announced that for the first time in America's experience a frontier line was no longer discernible. All the unsettled areas had been invaded by isolated bodies of settlement. The "closing" of the frontier inspired one of the most influential essays ever written about American history—Frederick Jackson Turner's "The Significance of the Frontier in American History," in 1893.

As the nineteenth century neared its sunset, the westward-tramping American people were disturbed to find that their fabled free land was going or had gone. The secretary of war had prophesied in 1827 that five hundred years would be needed to fill the West. But as the nation learned that its land was not inexhaustible, seeds were planted to preserve the vanishing resource. The government set aside lands for national parks—first Yellowstone in 1872 and Sequoia in 1890.

The frontier was more than a place: it was also a state of mind and a symbol of opportunity. Its passing ended a romantic phase of the nation's internal development and created new economic and psychological problems. Traditionally footloose, Americans were notorious for their mobility. The nation's farmers, unlike the peasants of Europe, seldom remained rooted to their soil.

Much has been said about the frontier as a "safety valve." The theory is that when hard times came, the unemployed who cluttered the city pavements merely moved west, took up farming, and prospered. In truth, relatively few city dwellers, at least in the populous eastern centers, migrated to the frontier during depressions. Most of them did not know how to farm; few of them could raise enough money to transport themselves west and then pay for livestock and expensive machinery.

But the safety valve theory does have some validity. Free acreage did lure to the West a host of immigrants, who otherwise might have remained in the eastern cities to clog the job markets and crowd the slums. And the very *possibility* of westward migration may have induced urban employers to maintain wage rates high enough to discourage workers from leaving.

But the real safety valve by the late nineteenth century was in western cities like Denver, San Francisco, and Seattle, where failed farmers, busted miners, and displaced easterners found the best places to seek their fortunes. Indeed, after about 1880 the area from the Rocky Mountains to the Pacific Coast, measured by the percentage of people living in cities, was the most urbanized region in America.

United States history cannot be properly understood unless it is viewed in light of the westward-moving experience. As Frederick Jackson Turner wrote, "American history has been in a large degree the history of the colonization of the Great West." The story of settling and taming the trans-Mississippi West in the late nineteenth century was but the last chapter in the saga of the colonizing of various American "wests" since Columbus.

Yet the trans-Mississippi West formed a distinct chapter in that saga and retains its uniqueness today. There the Native American peoples made their last struggle against colonization, and there most Native Americans live today. There "Anglo" culture collided most directly with Hispanic culture, and the Southwest remains the most Hispanicized region in America. There America faced Asia across the Pacific, and there most Asian-Americans dwell today. There the scale and severity of the environment posed their greatest challenges to human ambitions, and there the environment continues to mold social and political life, as well as the American imagination, as in no other part of the nation.

The westward-moving pioneers and the country they confronted have assumed mythic proportions in the American mind. For better or worse, those pioneers planted the seeds of civilization in the immense western wilderness. The life we live, they dreamed of; the life they lived, we can only dream.

The Farm Becomes a Factory

The situation of American farmers, once Jacks-and-Jills-of-all-trades, was rapidly changing. They had once raised their own food, fashioned their own clothing, and bartered for other necessities with neighbors. Now high prices persuaded farmers to concentrate on growing single "cash" crops, such as wheat or corn, and use their profits to buy foodstuffs at the general store and manufactured goods in town or by mail order. The Chicago firm of Aaron Montgomery Ward sent out its first catalogue—a single sheet—in 1872.

Large-scale farmers were now both specialists and businesspeople. As cogs in the vast industrial machine, they were intimately tied in with banking, railroading, and manufacturing. They had to buy expensive machinery to plant and to harvest their crops. A powerful steam engine could drag behind it simultaneously the plow, seeder, and harrow. The speed of harvesting wheat was immensely increased in the 1870s by the twine binder and then in the 1880s by the "combine"—the combined reaper-thresher, which was drawn by twenty to forty horses and both reaped and bagged the grain.

This amazing mechanization of agriculture in the postwar years was almost as striking as the mechanization of industry. As the rural population steadily decreased, those who remained achieved miracles of production, making America the world's breadbasket and butcher shop. The farm was attaining the status of a factory—an outdoor grain factory. Bonanza wheat farms of the Minnesota–North Dakota area, for example, were enormous. By 1890 at least a half-dozen of them were larger than fifteen thousand acres, with communication by telephone from one part to another. These bonanza farms foreshadowed the gigantic agribusinesses of the next century.

Agriculture was a big business from the outset in California's phenomenally productive (and phenomenally irrigated) Central Valley. California farms, carved out of giant Spanish-Mexican land grants and the railroads' huge holdings, were from the outset more than three times larger than the national average. With the advent of the railroad refrigerator car in the 1880s, California fruits and vegetable crops, raised on sprawling tracts by ill-paid Mexican and Chinese farmhands, sold at a handsome profit in the rich urban markets of the East.

Deflation Dooms the Debtor

Once the grain farmers became chained to a one-crop economy—wheat or corn—they were in the same leaky boat as southern cotton growers. They were no longer the masters of their own destinies. American grain growers found themselves engaged in one of the most fiercely competitive businesses because the price of their product was determined in a world market by the world output. If the wheat fields of Argentina, Russia, and other foreign countries smiled, the price of the farmers' grain would fall and American sodbusters would face ruin, as they did in the 1880s and 1890s.

Low prices and a deflated currency were the chief worries of the frustrated farmers—North, South, and West. If a family had borrowed $1,000 in 1855, when wheat was worth about a dollar a bushel, they expected to pay back the equivalent of 1,000 bushels, plus interest, when the mortgage fell due. But if they let their debt run to 1890, when wheat had fallen to about fifty cents a bushel, they would have to pay back the price of 2,000 bushels for the $1,000 they had borrowed, plus interest. This unexpected burden struck them as unjust, though their steely-eyed creditors often branded the complaining farmers as slippery and dishonest rascals.

The deflationary pinch on the debtor flowed partly from the static money supply. There were simply not enough dollars to go around, and as a result, prices were forced down. In 1870 the currency in circulation for each person was $19.42; in 1890 it had risen only to $22.67. Yet during these twenty years, business and industrial activity, increasing manyfold, had intensified the scramble for available currency.

The forgotten farmers were caught on a treadmill. Despite unremitting toil, they operated year after year at a loss. In a vicious circle, their farm machinery increased their output of grain, lowered the price, and drove them even deeper into debt. Mortgages engulfed homesteads at an alarming rate; by 1890 Nebraska alone reported more than 100,000 farms blanketed with mortgages. The repeated crash of the sheriff-auctioneer's hammer kept announcing to the world that another sturdy American farmer had become landless in a landed nation.

Ruinous rates of interest, running from 8 to 40 percent, were charged on mortgages, largely by agents of eastern loan companies. The windburned sons and daughters of the sod, who felt that they deserved praise for developing the country, cried out in despair against the loan sharks and the Wall Street octopus.

Farm tenancy rather than farm ownership was spreading like stinkweed. The trend was especially marked in the sharecropping South, where cotton prices also sank dismayingly. By 1880 one-fourth of all American farms were operated by tenants. The United States was ready to feed the world, but under the new industrial feudalism the farmers were sinking into a status suggesting Old World serfdom.

Unhappy Farmers

Even Mother Nature ceased smiling as her powerful forces conspired against agriculture. Mile-wide clouds of grasshoppers, leaving "nothing but the mortgage," periodically ravaged prairie farms. The terrible cotton-boll weevil was also wreaking havoc by the early 1890s.

The good earth was going sour. Floods added to the waste of erosion, which had already washed the topsoil off millions of once-lush southern acres. A long succession of droughts seared the trans-Mississippi West, beginning in the summer of 1887. Whole towns were abandoned. "Going home to the wife's folks" and "in God we trusted, in Kansas we busted" were typical laments of many impoverished farmers as they fled their weather-beaten shacks and sun-baked sod houses.

To add to their miseries, the soil-tillers were gouged by their government—local, state, and national. Their land was overassessed, and they paid painful local taxes, whereas wealthy easterners could conceal their stocks and bonds in safe-deposit boxes. High protective tariffs in these years poured profits into the pockets of manufacturers. Farmers, on the other hand, had no choice but to sell their low-priced products in a fiercely competitive world market, while buying high-priced manufactured goods in a protected home market.

The farmers were also "farmed" by the corporations. Trusts raised prices on farmers' machinery and supplies to extortionate levels, while storage rates for their grain at warehouses and elevators were pushed up by the operators. The railroad octopus often pushed freight rates so high that the farmers sometimes lost less if they burned their corn for fuel than if they shipped it.

Farmers still made up nearly one-half of the population in 1890, but they were hopelessly disorganized. The manufacturers and the railroad barons knew how to combine to promote their own interests, and so, increasingly, did industrial workers. But the farmers were by nature independent and individualistic—dead set against consolidation or regimentation. They never did organize successfully to restrict production until forced to by the federal government nearly half a century later, in Franklin Roosevelt's New Deal days. What they did manage to organize was a monumental political uprising.

The Farmers Take Their Stand

Agrarian unrest had flared forth earlier, in the Greenback movement shortly after the Civil War. Prices sagged in 1868, and a host of farmers unsuccessfully sought relief from low prices and high indebtedness by demanding an inflation of the currency with paper money.

The National Grange of the Patrons of Husbandry—better known as the Grange—was organized in 1867. Its leading spirit was Oliver H. Kelley, a shrewd and energetic Minnesota farmer then working as a clerk in Washington. Kelley's first objective was to enhance the lives of isolated farmers through social, educational, and fraternal activities. The Grange spread like an old-time prairie fire and by 1875 claimed some 800,000 members, chiefly in the Midwest and South.

The Grangers gradually raised their goals from self-improvement to improvement of the farmers' collective plight. In a determined effort to escape the clutches of the trusts, they established cooperative stores, grain elevators, and warehouses, and even made a failed attempt to manufacture harvesting machinery.

Embattled Grangers also went into politics, enjoying their most gratifying success in the grain-growing regions of the upper Mississippi Valley, chiefly in Illinois, Wisconsin, Iowa, and Minnesota. There, through state legislation, they strove to regulate railway rates and the storage fees charged by railroads and by the operators of warehouses and grain elevators. Many of the state courts, notably in Illinois, were disposed to recognize the principle of public control of private business for the general welfare. A number of the so-called Granger Laws, however, were bitterly fought through the high courts by the well-paid lawyers of the "interests." Following judicial reverses, most severely at the hands of the Supreme Court in the *Wabash* decision of 1886 (see p. 330), the Grangers' influence faded.

Farmers' grievances likewise found a vent in the Greenback Labor party, which combined the inflationary appeal of earlier Greenbackers with a program for improving the lot of labor. In 1878, the high-water mark of the movement, the Greenback-Laborites polled over a million votes and elected fourteen members of Congress. In the presidential election of 1880 the Greenbackers ran General James B. Weaver, an old Granger who spoke to perhaps a half-million citizens but polled only 3 percent of the popular vote.

Prelude to Populism

A striking manifestation of rural discontent came through the Farmers' Alliance, founded in Texas in the late 1870s (see p. 320). Farmers came together in the Alliance to socialize, but more importantly they hoped to break the strangling grip of the railroads and manufacturers through cooperative buying and selling. Local chapters spread throughout the South and the Great Plains during the 1880s, until by 1890 members numbered more than a million hard-bitten souls.

Unfortunately, the Alliance weakened itself by ignoring the plight of landless tenant farmers, sharecroppers, and farmworkers. Even more debilitating was the Alliance's exclusion of blacks, who counted for nearly half the agricultural population of the South. In the 1880s a separate Colored Farmers' National Alliance emerged to attract black farmers, and by 1890 membership numbered more than 250,000. The long history of racial division in the South, however, made it difficult for white and black farmers to work together in the same organization.

Out of the Farmers' Alliances a new political party emerged in the early 1890s—the People's party. Better known as the Populists, these frustrated farmers attacked Wall Street and the "money trust." They called for nationalizing the railroads, telephones, and telegraph; instituting a graduated income tax; and building government-owned warehouses where they could store their grain until market prices rose. They also wanted the free and unlimited coinage of silver— yet another of the debtors' demands for inflation that echoed continuously throughout the Gilded Age.

Numerous fiery prophets leapt forward to trumpet the Populist cause. William Hope Harvey produced an enormously popular pamphlet called *Coin's Financial School.* Illustrated by clever woodcuts, the booklet showed how "Coin" Harvey overwhelmed the bankers and professors of economics with his brilliant arguments on behalf of free silver. Another noto-

rious spellbinder was red-haired Ignatius Donnelly of Minnesota, three times elected to Congress. The queen of the Populist "calamity howlers" was Mary Elizabeth ("Mary Yellin'") Lease, a tall, athletic woman known as "the Kansas Pythoness." She reportedly advised Kansans to raise "less corn and more hell." The big-city *New York Evening Post* snarled, "We don't want any more states until we can civilize Kansas." To many easterners, complaint, not corn, was becoming rural America's staple crop.

Yet the Populists, despite their oddities, were not to be laughed away. They were leading a deadly earnest and impassioned campaign to relieve the farmers' many miseries. Smiles faded from Republican and Democratic faces alike as countless thousands of Populists began to sing "Good-bye, My Party, Good-bye."

In 1892 the Populists had jolted the traditional parties by winning several congressional seats and polling more than 1 million votes for their presidential candidate, James B. Weaver. Racial divisions continued to hobble the Populists in the South, but in the West their ranks were swelling. Could the People's party now reach beyond its regional bases in agrarian America, join hands with urban workers, and mount a successful assault on the northeastern citadels of power?

Coxey's Army and the Pullman Strike

The panic of 1893 and severe ensuing depression strengthened the Populists' argument that farmers and laborers alike were being victimized by an oppressive economic and political system. Ragged armies of the unemployed began marching to protest their plight. In the growing hordes of displaced industrial toilers, the Populists saw potential political allies.

The most famous marcher was "General" Jacob S. Coxey, a wealthy Ohio quarry owner, who set out for Washington in 1894 with a few score supporters. His platform included a demand that the government relieve unemployment by an inflationary $500 million federal public works program. Coxey himself rode in a carriage with his wife and infant son, while his tiny "army" tramped along behind, singing:

> We're coming, Grover Cleveland,
>   500,000 strong.
> We're marching on to Washington
>   to right the nation's wrong.

The "Commonweal Army" of Coxeyites finally straggled into the nation's capital, but the "invasion" took on the aspects of a comic opera when "General" Coxey and his "lieutenants" were arrested for walking on the grass.

Elsewhere, violent flare-ups accompanied labor protests, notably in Chicago. Most dramatic was the crippling Pullman strike of 1894. Eugene V. Debs, a charismatic labor leader, had helped organize the American Railway Union of about 150,000 members. The Pullman Palace Car Company, which maintained a model town near Chicago for its employees, was hit hard by the depression and cut wages by about one-third, while holding the line on rent for company houses. The workers finally struck—in some places overturning Pullman cars—and paralyzed railway traffic from Chicago to the Pacific Coast.

The turmoil in Chicago was serious but not completely out of hand. At least this was the judgment of Governor John Peter Altgeld of Illinois, a friend of the downtrodden, who had pardoned the Haymarket Square anarchists the year before (see p. 337). But U.S. Attorney General Richard Olney, an archconservative and an ex-railroad attorney, urged the dispatch of federal troops on the legal grounds that the strikers were interfering with the transit of the United States mail. President Cleveland supported Olney with the ringing declaration, "If it takes the entire army and navy to deliver a postal card in Chicago, that card will be delivered."

To the delight of conservatives, federal troops, bayonets fixed, crushed the Pullman strike. Debs was sentenced to six months' imprisonment for contempt of court because he had defied a federal court injunction to cease striking. Ironically, the lean labor agitator spent much of his enforced leisure reading radical literature, which led to his later leadership of the socialist movement in America.

Embittered cries of "government by injunction" now burst from organized labor. This was the first time that such a legal weapon had been used conspicuously by Washington to break a strike, and it was all the more distasteful because defiant workers who were held in contempt could be imprisoned without jury trial. Signs multiplied that employers were striving to smash labor unions by court action. Nonlabor elements of the country, including the Populists and other debtors, were likewise incensed. They saw in the brutal Pullman episode further proof of an unholy alliance between business and the courts.

Golden McKinley and Silver Bryan

The smoldering grievances of the long-suffering farmers and depression-plagued laborers gave ominous significance to the election of 1896. Conservatives of all stripes feared an impending upheaval, while down-and-out husbandmen and discontented workers cast about desperately for political salvation. Increasingly, monetary policy—whether to maintain the gold standard or inflate the currency by monetizing silver—loomed as the issue on which the election would turn.

The leading candidate for the Republican presidential nomination in 1896 was former Congressman William McKinley of Ohio, sponsor of the ill-starred tariff bill of 1890 (see p. 320). He had established a record as a Civil War officer; he hailed from the electorally potent state of Ohio; and he could point to long years of honorable service in Congress, where he had made a great many friends by his kindly and conciliatory manner.

As a presidential candidate, McKinley was largely the creature of a fellow Ohioan, Marcus Alonzo Hanna, who had made his fortune in the iron business and now coveted the role of president-maker. As a wholehearted Hamiltonian, Hanna believed that a prime function of government was to aid business. He further believed that in some measure prosperity "trickled down" to the laborer, whose dinner pail was full when business flourished. Critics assailed this idea as equivalent to feeding the horses in order to feed the sparrows.

The hardheaded Hanna, although something of a novice in politics, organized his preconvention campaign for McKinley with consummate skill and with a liberal outpouring of his own money. The convention steamroller, well lubricated with Hanna's dollars, nominated McKinley on the first ballot at St. Louis in June 1896. The Republican platform condemned Democratic incapacity in hard times and declared for the gold standard, even though McKinley's voting record in Congress had been embarrassingly friendly to silver.

Dissension riddled the Democratic camp. Cleveland no longer led his party; dubbed "the Stuffed Prophet," he was undeniably the most unpopular man in the country. Labor-debtor groups remembered too vividly his intervention in the Pullman strike, the backstairs Morgan bond deal, and especially his stubborn hard-money policies. Ultraconservative in finance, Cleveland now looked more like a Republican than a Democrat on the money issue.

Rudderless, the Democratic convention met in Chicago in July 1896, with the silverites lusting for victory. Shouting insults at the absent Cleveland, the delegates refused even to endorse their own administration. They had the enthusiasm and the numbers; all they lacked was a leader.

A new Moses suddenly appeared in the person of William Jennings Bryan of Nebraska. Then only thirty-six years of age and known as "the Boy Orator of the Platte,"* he stepped confidently onto the platform before fifteen thousand people. His masterful presence was set off by a peninsular jaw, and raven-black hair. He radiated honesty, sincerity, and energy.

The convention-hall setting was made to order for a magnificent oratorical effort. A hush fell over the delegates as Bryan stood before them. With an organ-like voice that rolled into the outer corners of the huge hall, he delivered a fervent plea for silver. Rising to supreme heights of eloquence, he thundered, "We will answer their demands for a gold standard by saying to them: 'You shall not press down upon the brow of labor this crown of thorns, you shall not crucify mankind upon a cross of gold.'"

The Cross of Gold speech was a sensation. Swept off its feet in a tumultuous scene, the Democratic convention nominated Bryan the next day on the fifth ballot. The platform demanded inflation through the unlimited coinage of silver at the ratio of 16 ounces of silver to 1 of gold, though the market ratio was about 32 to 1. This meant that the silver in a dollar would be worth about fifty cents.

Democratic "Gold Bugs," unable to swallow Bryan, bolted their party over the silver issue. A conservative senator from New York, when asked if he was a Democrat still, reportedly replied, "Yes, I am a Democrat still—very still." The Democratic minority, including Cleveland, charged that the Populist-silverites had stolen both the name and the clothes of their party. Many of them, including Cleveland, not too secretly hoped for a McKinley victory.

The Populists now faced a dilemma because the Democratic majority had appropriated their main plank—"16 to 1," that "heaven-born ratio." The bulk of the Populists, fearing a hard-money McKinley victory, endorsed both "fusion" with the Democrats and Bryan for president, sacrificing their identity in the mix. Singing "The Jolly Silver Dollar of the Dads," they became in effect the "Demo-Pop" or "Popocratic" party, though a handful of the original Populists refused to support Bryan and went down with their colors nailed to the mast.

Class Conflict: Plowholders Versus Bondholders

Mark Hanna smugly assumed that he could make the tariff the focus of the campaign. But Bryan, a dynamo of energy, forced the free-trade issue into a back seat when

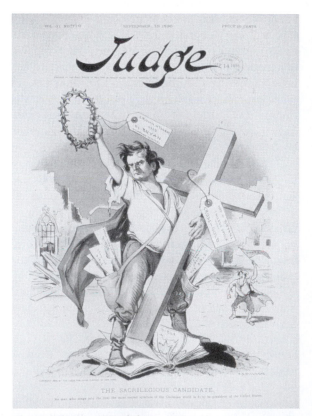

The Sacrilegious Candidate *A hostile cartoonist makes sport of Bryan's flamboyant Cross of Gold speech in 1896.*

---

*One contemporary sneered that Bryan, like the Platte River, was "six inches deep and six miles wide at the mouth."

singing "No Crown of Thorns, No Cross of Gold," hailed Bryan as the messiah to lead them out of the wilderness of debt.

Bryan created panic among eastern conservatives with his threat of converting their holdings overnight into fifty-cent dollars. "In God we trust, with Bryan we bust," the Republicans sneered, while one clergyman cried, "That platform was made in Hell." Widespread fear of Bryan and the "silver lunacy" enabled "Dollar Mark" Hanna, now chairman of the Republican National Committee, to shine as a money-raiser. He "shook down" the trusts and plutocrats and piled up an enormous "slush fund" for a "campaign of education"—or of propaganda, depending on one's point of view. Republicans appealed to the "belly vote" with their prize slogan, "McKinley and the full dinner pail." The McKinleyites amassed the most formidable political campaign chest thus far in American history—about $16 million, contrasted with about $1 million for the poorer Democrats (roughly "16 to 1"). With some justification, the Bryanites accused Hanna of "buying" the election and of floating McKinley into the White House on a tidal wave of money and mud.

Bryan's cyclonic campaign began to lose velocity as the weeks passed. Fear was probably the strongest ally of Hanna, as it was Bryan's worst enemy. Some Republican businesspeople threatened wage reductions or told their workers not to come to work on Wednesday morning if Bryan won. Such were some of the "dirty tricks" of the "Stop Bryan, Save America" crusade.

Hanna's campaign methods paid off. On election day McKinley triumphed decisively. The vote was 271 to 176 in the Electoral College, and 7,102,246 to 6,492,559 in the popular election. Driven by fear, hope, and excitement, an unprecedented outpouring of voters flocked to the polls. McKinley ran strongly in the populous East, where he carried every county of New England, and in the upper Mississippi Valley. Bryan's states, concentrated in the debt-burdened South and the trans-Mississippi West, involved more acreage than McKinley's but less population.

The free-silver election of 1896 was probably the most significant political turning point since Lincoln's

William Jennings Bryan, 1896   *The premier orator of his day, the spellbinding speaker was the presidential candidate of both the Democratic and Populist parties in 1896.*

he took to the stump in behalf of free silver. Sweeping through twenty-seven states and traveling 18,000 miles, he made nearly 600 speeches—36 in one day—and even invaded the East, "the enemy's country." Vachel Lindsay caught the spirit of his oratorical orgy:

Prairie avenger, mountain lion,
Bryan, Bryan, Bryan, Bryan,
Gigantic troubadour, speaking like a siege
    gun,
Smashing Plymouth rock with his boulders
    from the West.*

Free silver became almost as much a religious as a financial issue. Hordes of fanatical free-silverites,

* Reprinted with permission of Macmillan Publishing Company, Inc., from *Collected Poems*, by Vachel Lindsay. Copyright 1920 by Macmillan Publishing Company, Inc., renewed 1948 by Elizabeth C. Lindsay.

Presidential Election of 1896 (with electoral vote by state) *This election tolled the death knell of the Gilded Age political system, with its razor-close elections, strong party loyalties, and high voter turnouts. For years after 1896, Republicans predominated, and citizens showed declining interest in either joining parties or voting.*

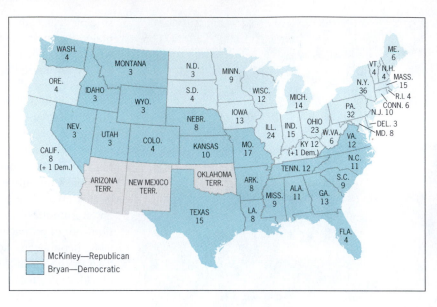

WASH. 4
MONTANA 3
N.D. 3
MINN. 9
ME. 6
VT. 4
N.H. 4
MASS. 15
N.Y. 36
R.I. 4
CONN. 6
ORE. 4
IDAHO 3
S.D. 4
WISC. 12
MICH. 14
PA. 32
N.J. 10
DEL. 3
MD. 8
WYO. 3
IOWA 13
OHIO 23
W.VA. 6
VA. 12
NEV. 3
UTAH 3
NEBR. 8
ILL. 24
IND. 15
KY 12 (+1 Dem.)
CALIF. 8 (+ 1 Dem.)
COLO. 4
KANSAS 10
MO. 17
N.C. 11
TENN. 12
ARIZONA TERR.
NEW MEXICO TERR.
OKLAHOMA TERR.
ARK. 8
S.C. 9
MISS. 9
ALA. 11
GA. 13
TEXAS 15
LA. 8
FLA. 4

☐ McKinley—Republican
☐ Bryan—Democratic

victories in 1860 and 1864. Despite Bryan's strength in the South and West, the results vividly demonstrated his lack of appeal to the unmortgaged farmer and especially to the eastern urban laborer. Many wage earners in the East, threatened as they were by free silver, free trade, and fireless factories, voted for their jobs and full dinner pails. Living precariously on fixed wages, the factory workers had no reason to favor inflation, which was the heart of the Bryanites' program.

The Bryan-McKinley battle heralded the advent of a new era in American politics. The outcome was a resounding victory for big business, the big cities, middle-class values, and financial conservatism. Bryan's defeat marked the last serious effort to win the White House with mostly agrarian votes. The future of presidential politics lay not on the farms, with their dwindling populations, but in the mushrooming cities, with their growing throngs of freshly arriving immigrants.

The smashing Republican victory of 1896 also heralded a Republican grip on the White House for sixteen consecutive years—indeed, for all but eight of the next thirty-six years. McKinley's election thus imparted a new character to the American political system. The long reign of Republican political dominance that it ushered in was accompanied by diminishing voter participation in elections, the weakening of party organizations, and the fading away of issues like the money question and civil-service reform, which came to be replaced by concern for industrial regulation and the welfare of labor. Scholars have dubbed this new political era the period of the "fourth party system."*

Republican Stand-pattism Enthroned

An eminently "safe" McKinley took the inaugural oath in 1897. Though a man of considerable ability, he was an ear-to-the-ground politician who seldom got far out of line with majority opinion. His cautious, conservative nature caused him to shy away from the flaming banner of reform. Business was given a free rein, and the trusts, which had trusted him in 1896, were allowed to develop more mighty muscles without serious restraints.

---

* The so-called first party system, marked by doubts about the very legitimacy of parties, embraced the Federalist-Republican clashes of the 1790s and early 1800s. The second party system took shape with the emergence of mass-based politics in the Jacksonian era, pitting Democrats against Whigs. The third party system was characterized by the precarious equilibrium between Republicans and Democrats, as well as the high electoral participation, that lasted from the end of the Civil War to McKinley's election. The fourth party system is described above. The fifth party system emerged in Franklin Roosevelt's New Deal, which initiated a long period of Democratic ascendancy. Each "system," except the fifth, lasted about forty years. Debate continues as to whether the nation has entered or is about to enter the era of the sixth party system.

Almost as soon as McKinley took office, the tariff issue, which had played second fiddle to silver in the "Battle of '96," quickly forced itself to the fore. Eventually the Dingley Tariff Bill was jammed through the House in 1897 under the pounding gavel of the rethroned "Czar" Reed. The proposed new rates were high, but not high enough to satisfy the paunchy lobbyists, who once again descended upon the Senate. Over 850 amendments were tacked onto the overburdened bill. The resulting piece of patchwork finally established the average rates at 46.5 percent, substantially higher than the Democratic Wilson-Gorman Act of 1894 and in some categories even higher than the McKinley Act of 1890. (See the chart in the Appendix.)

With the return of prosperity under McKinley in 1897, the money issue that overshadowed politics since the Civil War gradually faded away. The Gold Standard Act of 1900, passed over last-ditch silverite opposition, provided that paper currency was to be freely redeemed in gold. Electrifying discoveries of new gold deposits in Canada's fabled Klondike, as well as in Alaska, South Africa, and Australia, brought huge new quantities of gold onto world markets. Moderate inflation thus took care of the currency needs of an explosively expanding nation, as its circulatory system greatly improved. The tide of "silver heresy" rapidly receded, and the "Popocratic" fish were left gasping high and dry on a golden-sanded beach.

Chronology

1858	Pike's Peak gold rush.
1859	Nevada Comstock lode discovered.
1862	Homestead Act.
1864	Sand Creek massacre. Nevada admitted to the Union.
1867	National Grange organized.
1876	Battle of Little Bighorn. Colorado admitted to the Union.
1877	Nez Percé Indian war.
1881	Helen Hunt Jackson publishes *A Century of Dishonor*.
1884	Federal government outlaws Indian Sun Dance.
1885–1890	Local chapters of Farmers' Alliances formed.
1887	Dawes Severalty Act.
1889	Oklahoma opened to settlement.
1889–1890	North Dakota, South Dakota, Montana, Washington, Idaho, and Wyoming admitted to the Union.
1890	Census Bureau declares frontier line ended. Emergence of People's party (Populists). Battle of Wounded Knee.
1892	Populist party candidate James B. Weaver polls more than 1 million votes in presidential election.
1893	Frederick Jackson Turner publishes "The Significance of the Frontier in American History."
1894	"Coxey's Army" marches on Washington. Pullman strike.
1896	McKinley defeats Bryan for presidency. Utah admitted to the Union.
1897	Dingley Tariff Act.
1900	Gold Standard Act.
1907	Oklahoma admitted to the Union.
1924	Indians granted U.S. citizenship.
1934	Indian Reorganization Act.

VARYING VIEWPOINTS

Was the West Really "Won"?

For more than half a century, the Turner thesis dominated historical writing about the West. In his essay, "The Significance of the Frontier in American History," historian Frederick Jackson Turner argued that the American national character had been uniquely shaped by the westward movement. The struggle to overcome the hazards of the western wilderness had transformed Europeans into tough, inventive, and self-reliant Americans.

Written just three years after the superintendent of the census declared the frontier closed, Turner's hypothesis is surely among the most provocative statements ever made about formative influences on the nation's development and character. But as the frontier era recedes ever further into the past, scholars are less persuaded that Turner's thesis adequately explains the character of American society and its differences from Europe.

Modern historians such as David Weber challenge Turner's assumptions by suggesting that the line of the frontier did not define the quavering edge of "civilization," but rather marked the boundary between diverse and equally legitimate cultures. The frontier should therefore be understood as the principal site of the interaction between those cultures.

Several so-called New Western historians take this argument still further. Scholars such as Patricia Nelson Limerick, Richard White, and Donald Worster suggest that the cultural and ecological damage inflicted by advancing "civilization" must be reckoned with in any final accounting of what these pioneers accomplished. These same scholars insist that the West did not lose its regional identity after 1890 and is still a unique part of the national mosaic, a region whose history, culture, and identity remain every bit as distinctive as those of New England or the Old South.

But where Turner saw the frontier as the principal shaper of the region's character, the New Western historians emphasize the effects of ethnic and racial confrontation, topography, climate, and the roles of government and big business as the factors that have made the modern West. The pioneer "conquests" of Native Americans and Hispanics were less than complete, they contend, and the West therefore remains, uniquely among American regions, an unsettled arena of commingling and competition among these groups. Moreover, in these accounts the West's distinctively challenging climate and geography yielded to human habitation not through the efforts of heroic individual pioneers, but only through massive corporate—and especially federal government—investments in projects like the transcontinental railroads and irrigation systems. Such developments still give western life its special character today.

27

The Path of Empire

1890–1899

We assert that no nation can long endure half republic and half empire, and we warn the American people that imperialism abroad will lead quickly and inevitably to despotism at home.

DEMOCRATIC NATIONAL PLATFORM, 1900

In the years immediately following the Civil War, Americans remained astonishingly indifferent to the outside world. Enmeshed in struggles over Reconstruction policies and absorbed in efforts to heal the wounds of war, build an industrial economy, make their cities habitable, and settle the sprawling West, most citizens took little interest in international affairs. But the sunset decades of the nineteenth century witnessed a momentous shift in U.S. foreign policy. America's new diplomacy reflected the far-reaching changes that were reshaping agriculture, industry, and the social structure. American statesmen also responded to the intensifying scramble of several other nations for international advantage in the dawning "age of empire." By century's end America itself would become an imperial power, an astonishing departure from its venerable anticolonial traditions.

Imperialist Stirrings

Many developments fed the nation's ambition for overseas expansion. Both farmers and factory owners began to look beyond American shores as agricultural and industrial production boomed. Many Americans believed that the United States had to expand or explode. Their country was bursting with a new sense of power generated by the robust growth in population, wealth, and productive capacity—and it was trembling with the hammer blows of labor violence and agrarian unrest. Overseas markets might provide a safety valve to relieve those pressures.

Other forces whetted the popular appetite for overseas involvement. The lurid "yellow press" of Joseph Pulitzer and William Randolph Hearst described foreign exploits as manly adventures, the kind of dashing derring-do that was the stuff of young boys' dreams. Pious missionaries, inspired by books like the Reverend Josiah Strong's *Our Country: Its Possible Future and Its Present Crisis*, looked overseas for new fields to till. Strong trumpeted the superiority of Anglo-Saxon civilization and summoned Americans to spread their religion and their values to "backward" peoples. At the same time, aggressive Americans like Theodore Roosevelt and Congressman Henry Cabot Lodge were interpreting Darwinism to mean that the earth belonged to the strong and the fit—that is, to Uncle Sam. This view was strengthened as latecomers to the colonial scramble scooped up leavings from the banquet table of earlier diners in Africa and elsewhere. If America was to survive in the competition of modern nation-states, perhaps it, too, would have to become an imperial power.

The development of a new steel navy also focused attention overseas. Captain Alfred Thayer Mahan's book of 1890, *The Influence of Sea Power upon History, 1660–1783*, argued that control of the sea was the key to world dominance. Mahan helped stimulate the naval race among the great powers that gained momentum around the turn of the century. Red-blooded Americans joined in the demands for a mightier navy and for an American-built isthmian canal between the Atlantic and the Pacific.

America's new international interest manifested itself in a number of diplomatic crises or near-wars in the late 1880s and early 1890s. The American and German navies nearly came to blows in 1889 over the far-away Samoan Islands in the South Pacific. The lynching of eleven Italians in New Orleans in 1891 brought America and Italy to the brink of war, until the United States agreed to pay compensation. In the ugliest affair, American demands on Chile after the deaths of two American sailors in the port of Valparaiso in 1892 made hostilities between the two countries seem inevitable. The threat of attack by Chile's modern navy spread alarm on the Pacific Coast, until American power finally forced the Chileans to pay an indemnity. A simmering argument between the United States and Canada over seal hunting near the Pribilof Islands off the coast of Alaska was resolved by arbitration in 1893. The willingness of Americans to risk war over such distant and minor disputes demonstrated the aggressive new national mood.

This new American belligerence combined with old-time anti-British feeling to create a serious crisis between the United States and Britain in 1895–1896. The jungle boundary between British Guiana and Venezuela had long been in dispute, but the discovery of gold in the contested area brought the conflict between Britain and Venezuela to a head. President Cleveland and his pugnacious secretary of state, Richard Olney, stepped into the affair with a combative note to Britain that invoked the Monroe Doctrine. British officials, unimpressed, shrugged off Olney's lengthy salvo as just another twist of the lion's tail and declared that the affair was none of Uncle Sam's business. President Cleveland—"mad clear through," as he put it—sent a bristling special message to Congress that called for a U.S. commission to determine where the line ought to go, and he implied that, if the British would not accept this boundary, the United States would fight for it.

The entire country, irrespective of political party, was swept off its feet in an outburst of hysteria. War seemed inevitable. Fortunately, sober second thoughts prevailed on both sides of the Atlantic. Shifts in the European balance of power had left Britain in a state of insecure isolation, and an American war would be a disaster. London backed off and consented to arbitrate the Venezuelan dispute. The chastened British, their eyes wide open to the European peril, inaugurated an era of "patting the Eagle's head," which replaced a century or so of America's "twisting the lion's tail." Sometimes called the Great Rapprochement—or reconciliation—between the United States and Britain, the new Anglo-American cordiality became a cornerstone of both nations' foreign policies as the twentieth century opened.

Spurning the Hawaiian Pear

Enchanted Hawaii had early attracted the attention of Americans. In the morning years of the nineteenth century, the breeze-brushed islands were a way station and provisioning point for Yankee shippers, sailors, and whalers. In 1820 came the first New England missionaries, who preached the twin blessings of Protestant Christianity and protective calico. Americans gradually came to regard the Hawaiian

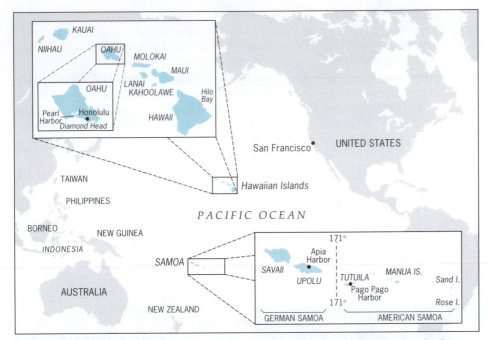

The Pacific   *The enlargements show the Hawaiian Islands and the Samoas, both areas of American imperialistic activity in the late nineteenth century.*

Islands as a virtual extension of their own coastline. The State Department, beginning in the 1840s, sternly warned other powers to keep their hands off the islands. America's grip was further tightened in 1887 by a treaty with the native government guaranteeing priceless naval-base rights at spacious Pearl Harbor.

But economic and political trouble was brewing in the insular paradise. Sugar cultivation went sour in 1890 when the McKinley Tariff Act erected barriers against the Hawaiian product. White American planters' ambitions for annexation by the United States were blocked by Queen Liliuokalani, who insisted that Hawaiians should control the islands. Desperate whites, though only a tiny minority, then organized a successful revolt early in 1893. The coup was openly assisted by American troops, who landed under the unauthorized orders of the expansionist American minister to Honolulu. "The Hawaiian pear is now fully ripe," he wrote exultantly to his superiors in Washington, "and now is the golden hour for the United States to pluck it."

A treaty of annexation was rushed to Washington, but before it could be railroaded through the Senate,

Republican President Harrison's term expired and Democratic President Cleveland came in. Suspecting that his powerful nation had gravely wronged the deposed Queen Liliuokalani, "Old Grover" abruptly withdrew the treaty. When the subsequent probe revealed the damning fact that a majority of the Hawaiian natives did not favor annexation at all, the sugar-coated move for annexation had to be abandoned. The Hawaiian pear continued to ripen until 1898.

War with Spain over Cuba

Cuba's masses, frightfully misgoverned, again rose against their Spanish oppressors in 1895. The roots of their revolt were partly economic. Sugar production—the backbone of the island's prosperity—was crippled when the American tariff of 1894 restored high duties on the toothsome product.

Driven to desperation, the insurgents adopted a scorched-earth policy, torching canefields and sugar mills and even dynamiting passenger trains. American sympathies went out to the Cuban underdogs. Aside from pure sentiment, the United States had an investment stake of about $50 million in Cuba and an annual trade stake of about $100 million.

Fuel was added to the Cuban conflagration in 1896 with the coming to power of the Spanish General ("Butcher") Weyler. He undertook to crush the rebellion by herding many civilians into barbed-wire reconcentration camps, where they could not give assistance to the armed *insurrectos*. Lacking proper sanitation, these enclosures turned into deadly pest-holes; the victims died like dogs.

The atrocities in Cuba were made to order for the sensational new yellow journalism. William R. Hearst and Joseph Pulitzer, then engaged in a titanic duel for circulation, attempted to outdo each other with screeching headlines and hair-raising "scoops." Lesser competitors zestfully followed suit. Where atrocity stories did not exist, they were invented.

Hearst sent the gifted artist Frederic Remington to Cuba to draw sketches, and when the latter reported that conditions were not bad enough to warrant hostilities, Hearst is alleged to have replied, "You furnish the pictures and I'll furnish the war." Among other outrages, Remington depicted Spanish customs officials brutally disrobing and searching an American woman. Most readers of Hearst's *Journal*, their indignation soaring, had no way of knowing that such tasks were performed by female attendants.

Early in 1898 Washington sent the battleship *Maine* to Cuba, ostensibly for a "friendly visit," but actually to protect and evacuate Americans if a dangerous flare-up should again occur. Tragedy struck on February 15, 1898, when the *Maine* mysteriously blew up in Havana harbor, with a loss of 260 officers and men.

The Explosion of the *Maine*, February 15, 1898 *Encouraged and amplified by the "yellow press," the outcry over the tragedy of the* Maine *helped drive the country into an impulsive war against Spain.*

Two investigations of the iron coffin were undertaken, one by U.S. naval officers, the other by Spanish officials. The Spanish commission stated that the explosion had been internal and presumably accidental; the American commission reported that the blast had been caused by a submarine mine. Not until 1976 did Admiral Hyman G. Rickover, under U.S. Navy auspices, present overwhelming evidence that the initial explosion had resulted from spontaneous combustion in one of the coal bunkers adjacent to a powder magazine. Ironically, this is essentially what the Spanish commission had deduced in 1898.

But Americans in 1898, now war-mad, blindly accepted the unlikely explanation of Spanish government treachery. The battle cry of the hour became

Remember the *Maine*!
To hell with Spain!

Nothing would do but to hurl the "dirty" Spanish flag from the hemisphere.

The national war fever burned higher, even though American diplomats had already gained Madrid's agreement to Washington's two basic demands: a revocation of reconcentration and an armistice with the Cuban rebels. The cautious McKinley did not want hostilities. Neither did Mark Hanna and Wall Street, for war might unsettle business. As "Wobbly Willy" McKinley hesitated, the jingoistic yellow press and the frenzied public denounced him. Fight-hungry Theodore Roosevelt snarled that the "white-livered" occupant of the White House did not have "the backbone of a chocolate eclair." Encouraged and amplified by the rabid headlines trumpeting alleged Spanish atrocities, other politicians and agitators joined in beating the drums for war.

The president, recognizing the inevitable, finally yielded and gave the people what they wanted. McKinley also perceived that the Democrats would make political capital out of his resistance to war, and it seemed to him better to break up the remnants of Spain's empire than to break up the Grand Old Party. On April 11, 1898, McKinley sent his war message to Congress, urging armed intervention to free the oppressed Cubans. The legislators responded uproariously with what was essentially a declaration of war. In a burst of self-righteousness, they likewise adopted the hand-tying Teller Amendment. This proviso proclaimed to the world that when America had over-thrown Spanish misrule, it would give the Cubans their freedom—a declaration that caused imperialistic Europeans to smile skeptically.

Dewey's May Day Victory at Manila

The American people plunged into the war light-heartedly, like schoolchildren off to a picnic. Bands blared incessantly "There'll Be a Hot Time in the Old Town Tonight" and "Hail, Hail, the Gang's All Here," thus leading foreigners to believe that those were the national anthems.

But such jubilation seemed premature to European observers. Except for ally-seeking Britain, the Old World powers generally favored Spain in the war, and they looked with disdain on America's unprepared army and small navy. But the new American steel navy, now fifteen years old and ranking fifth among the fleets of the world, was in fairly good trim, though the war was to lay bare serious defects.

The war got off to a splendid start for American forces. On February 25, 1898, while navy secretary John Long was away for a weekend, assistant secretary of the navy Theodore Roosevelt cabled Commodore George Dewey to send the American Asian squadron to Spain's Philippines in the event of war. Dewey carried out his orders magnificently on May 1, 1898. Sailing boldly with his six warships at night into the fortified harbor of Manila, he trained his guns the next morning on the Spanish fleet. The entire collection of antiquated and overmatched vessels was quickly destroyed, with a loss of nearly four hundred Spaniards killed and wounded and without the loss of a single life in Dewey's fleet.

Taciturn George Dewey became a national hero overnight. An amateur poet blossomed forth with

Oh, dewy was the morning
Upon the first of May,
And Dewey was the Admiral
Down in Manila Bay.
And dewy were the Spaniards' eyes,
Them orbs of black and blue;
And dew we feel discouraged?
I dew not think we dew!

Yet Dewey was in a perilous position. He had destroyed the enemy fleet, but he could not storm the forts of Manila with his sailors. His nerves frayed, he was forced to wait in the steaming-hot bay while troop reinforcements were slowly assembled in America. The appearance of German warships in Manila harbor added to the tension.

Long-awaited American troops, finally arriving in force, captured Manila on August 13, 1898. They collaborated with the Filipino insurgents, commanded by their well-educated leader, Emilio Aguinaldo. Dewey, to his later regret, had brought this shrewd and magnetic revolutionist from exile in Asia so that he might weaken Spanish resistance.

These thrilling events in the Philippines had meanwhile focused attention on Hawaii. An impression spread that America needed the archipelago as a coaling and provisioning way station in order to send supplies and reinforcements to Dewey. A joint resolution of annexation was rushed through Congress and approved by McKinley on July 7, 1898.

The Confused Invasion of Cuba

Shortly after the outbreak of war, the Spanish government ordered a fleet of warships to Cuba. Panic seized the eastern seaboard of the United States. American vacationers abandoned their seaside cottages, while nervous investors moved their securities to inland depositories. The Spanish commander, Admiral Cervera, was soon forced into Santiago harbor, where he was blockaded by the much more powerful American fleet.

Sound strategy seemed to dictate that an American army be sent in from the rear to drive out Cervera. Leading the invading force was the grossly overweight General William R. Shafter, a leader so blubbery that he had to be carried about on a door.

The "Rough Riders," a part of the invading army, now charged onto the stage of history. This colorful regiment of volunteers, short on discipline but long on dash, consisted largely of western cowboys and other hardy characters, with a sprinkling of ex–polo players and ex-convicts. Commanded by Colonel Leonard Wood, the group was organized principally by the glory-hungry Theodore Roosevelt, who had resigned from the Navy Department to serve as a lieutenant colonel.

About the middle of June a bewildered American army of seventeen thousand men finally embarked from Tampa, Florida, amid scenes of indescribable confusion. Shafter's landing near Santiago, Cuba, was made without serious opposition. Brisk fighting broke out on July 1 at El Caney and San Juan Hill, up which Colonel Roosevelt and his Rough Riders charged, with strong support from two crack black regiments. They suffered heavy casualties, but the colorful colonel, having the time of his life, shot a Spaniard with his revolver and rejoiced to see his victim double up like a jackrabbit. He later wrote a book on his exploits, which, humorist Finley Peter Dunne's fictional "Mr. Dooley" remarked, ought to have been entitled *Alone in Cubia* [sic].

The American army, fast closing in on Santiago, spelled doom for the Spanish fleet. After a running chase, on July 3, the Spanish fleet was entirely destroyed as wooden decks caught fire and the blazing infernos were beached. About five hundred Spaniards were killed, compared with one American. "Don't cheer, men," admonished Captain Philip of the *Texas*, "the poor devils are dying." Shortly thereafter Santiago surrendered.

Hasty preparations were then made for a descent on Puerto Rico before the war ended. There the American army met little resistance. By this time Spain had satisfied its honor and on August 12, 1898, signed an armistice.

If the Spanish had held out a few months longer in Cuba, U.S. forces might have melted away. The inroads of malaria, typhoid fever, dysentery, and yellow fever became so severe that hundreds were incapacitated—"an army of convalescents." Others suffered from eating spoiled canned meat known as "embalmed beef." The various diseases, which were especially rampant in unsanitary American training camps, took a terrible death toll. All told, nearly four hundred men lost their lives to bullets, and over five thousand succumbed to bacteria and other causes.

America's Course (Curse?) of Empire

Late in 1898 Spanish and American negotiators met in Paris. War-racked Cuba, as expected, was freed from its Spanish overlords. The Americans had little diffi-

Colonel Theodore Roosevelt with Some of the "Rough Riders" *Roosevelt later described his first encounter with the Spanish enemy: "Soon we came to the brink of a deep valley. There was a good deal of cracking of rifles way off in front of us, but as they used smokeless powder we had no idea as to exactly where they were, or who they were shooting at. Then it dawned on us that we were the target. The bullets began to come overhead, making a sound like the ripping of a silk dress, with sometimes a kind of pop. . . . We advanced, firing at them, and drove them off."*

culty in securing the remote Pacific island of Guam, which they had captured early in the conflict. They also picked up Puerto Rico, the last remnant of what had been Spain's vast New World empire. In the decades to come, American investment in the island and Puerto Rican immigration to the United States would make this acquisition one of the weightier consequences of this somewhat carefree war (see "Makers of America: The Puerto Ricans," pp. 386–387).

Knottiest of all was the problem of the Philippines, a veritable apple of discord. These lush islands not only embraced an area larger than the British Isles but also contained a completely alien population of some 7 million souls. McKinley was confronted with a devil's dilemma. He did not feel that America could honorably give the islands back to Spanish misrule, especially after it had fought a war to free Cuba. And America would be turning its back on its responsibilities, he believed, if it simply pulled up anchor and sailed away.

McKinley viewed other alternatives open to him as trouble-fraught. The Filipinos, if left to govern themselves, might fall into anarchy. One of the major powers, possibly aggressive Germany, might seize them, and the result might be a world war into which the United States would be sucked. Seemingly the

least of the evils consistent with national honor and safety was to acquire all the Philippines and then perhaps give the Filipinos their freedom later.

President McKinley, ever sensitive to public opinion, kept a carefully attuned ear to the ground. The rumble that he heard seemed to call for the entire group of islands. Zealous Protestant missionaries were eager for new converts from Spanish Catholicism.* Wall Street had generally opposed the war; but awakened by the booming of Dewey's guns, it was clamoring for profits in the Philippines.

Tormented, McKinley later confessed that he finally went down on his knees seeking divine guidance. An inner voice seemed to tell him to take all the Philippines and Christianize and civilize them. Accordingly, he decided for outright annexation of the islands. The deed was accomplished by negotiators in Paris after the Americans agreed to pay Spain $20 million for the Philippine Islands—the last great Spanish haul from the New World.

The signing of the pact of Paris touched off one of the most impassioned debates of American

---

* The Philippines had been substantially Christianized by Catholics before the founding of Jamestown in 1607.

The Puerto Ricans

At dawn on July 26, 1898, the U.S. warship *Gloucester* steamed into Puerto Rico's Guanica harbor, fired at the Spanish blockhouse, and landed some thirty-three hundred troops. Within days, the Americans had taken possession of the militarily strategic Caribbean island a thousand miles southeast of Florida. In so doing they set in motion changes on the island that ultimately brought a new wave of immigrants to U.S. shores.

Puerto Rico had been a Spanish possession since Christopher Columbus claimed it for Castile in 1493. The Spaniards enslaved many of the island's forty thousand Taino Indians and set them to work on farms and in mines. Many Tainos died of exhaustion and disease, and in 1511 the Indians rebelled. The Spaniards crushed the uprising, killed thousands of Indians, and began importing African slaves—thus establishing the basis for Puerto Rico's multiracial society.

The first Puerto Rican immigrants to the United States arrived as political exiles in the nineteenth century. From their haven in America, they agitated for the island's independence from Spain. In 1897 Spain finally granted the island local autonomy; ironically, however, the Spanish-American War the following year placed it in American hands. Puerto Rican political émigrés in the United States returned home, but they were soon replaced by poor islanders looking for work.

When Congress granted Puerto Ricans U.S. citizenship in 1917, thereby eliminating immigration hurdles, many islanders hurried north to find jobs. Over the ensuing decades, Puerto Ricans went to work in Arizona cotton fields, New Jersey soup factories, and Utah mines. The majority, however, clus-tered in New York City and found work in the city's cigar factories, shipyards, and garment industry. Migration slowed somewhat after the 1920s as the Great Depression shrank the job market on the mainland and as World War II made travel hazardous.

When World War II ended in 1945, the sudden advent of cheap air travel sparked an emigration explosion. As late as the 1930s, the tab for a boat trip to the mainland exceeded the average Puerto Rican's yearly earnings. But with an airplane surplus after World War II, the six-hour flight from Puerto Rico to New York cost under fifty dollars. The Puerto Rican population on the mainland quadrupled between

The First Puerto Ricans *The Spanish* conquistadores *treated the native Taino Indian peoples in Puerto Rico with extreme cruelty, and the Indians were virtually extinct by the mid-1500s.*

1940 and 1950 and tripled again by 1960. In 1970, 1.5 million Puerto Ricans lived in the United States, one-third of the island's total population.

U.S. citizenship and affordable air travel made it easy for Puerto Ricans to return home. Thus to a far greater degree than most immigrant groups, Puerto Ricans kept one foot in the United States and the other on their native island. By some estimates, 2 million people a year journeyed to and from the island during the postwar period. Puerto Rico's gubernatorial candidates sometimes campaigned in New York for the thousands of voters who were expected to return to the island in time for the election.

Puerto Ricans have fared better economically in the United States than on the island, where, in 1970, 60 percent of all inhabitants lived below the poverty line. In recent years Puerto Ricans have attained more schooling, and many have attended college. Invigorated by the civil rights movement of the 1960s, Puerto Ricans also have become more politically active, electing growing numbers of congressmen and state and city officials.

history. Except for glacial Alaska, coral-reefed Hawaii, and a handful of Pacific atolls, the Republic had hitherto acquired only contiguous territory on the continent. All previous acquisitions had been thinly peopled and capable of ultimate statehood. But in the Philippines the nation had on its hands a distant tropical area, thickly populated by Asians of a different race, tongue, and government institutions.

The Anti-Imperialist League sprang into being to fight the McKinley administration's expansionist moves. The organization counted among its members some of the most prominent people in the United States, including the presidents of Stanford and Harvard Universities, the philosopher William James, and the novelist Mark Twain. The anti-imperialist blanket even stretched over such strange bedfellows as labor leader Samuel Gompers and steel titan Andrew Carnegie. "Goddamn the United States for its vile conduct in the Philippine Isles!" burst out the usually mild-mannered Professor James. The Harvard philosopher could not believe that the United States could "puke up its ancient soul in five minutes without a wink of squeamishness."

Anti-imperialists had still other arrows in their quiver. The Filipinos panted for freedom; and to annex them would violate the "consent of the governed" philosophy of the Declaration of Independence. Finally, annexation would propel the United States into the political and military cauldron of East Asia.

Yet the expansionists or imperialists could sing a seductive song. They appealed to patriotism and played up possible trade profits. Manila, in fact, might become another Hong Kong. Rudyard Kipling, the British poet laureate of imperialism, urged America down the slippery path:

> Take up the White Man's burden—
> Ye dare not stoop to less—
> Nor call too loud on Freedom
> To cloak your weariness.

In short, the wealthy Americans must help to uplift (and exploit) the underprivileged, underfed, and underclad of the world.

In the Senate the Spanish treaty ran into such heated opposition that it seemed doomed to defeat. But it received last-minute support from a surprising source—William Jennings Bryan. Bryan argued that the war would not officially end until America ratified the pact, and the sooner it accepted the document, the sooner it could give the Filipinos their independence. After Bryan had used his personal influence with certain Democratic senators, the treaty was approved, on February 6, 1899, with only one vote to spare. But the responsibility, as Bryan had foreseen, rested primarily with the Republicans.

Perplexities in Puerto Rico and Cuba

Many of Puerto Rico's 1 million inhabitants lived in poverty. The island's population grew faster than its economy. By the Foraker Act of 1900, Congress accorded the Puerto Ricans a limited degree of popular government, and in 1917 the islanders were granted

The Imperial Menu *A pleased Uncle Sam gets ready to place his order with headwaiter William McKinley. Swallowing some of these possessions eventually produced political indigestion. (Sandwich Islands was an earlier European name for Hawaii.)*

U.S. citizenship. Although the American regime worked wonders in education, sanitation, good roads, and other tangible improvements, many of the inhabitants still aspired to independence. Great numbers of Puerto Ricans moved to New York City, where they added to the complexity of the melting pot.

A thorny legal problem was posed by the annexations: Did the Constitution follow the flag? Did American laws, including tariff laws and the Bill of Rights, apply with full force to the newly acquired possessions? Beginning in 1901 with the *Insular Cases*, a badly divided Supreme Court decreed, in effect, that the flag outran the Constitution and that the outdistanced document did not necessarily extend with full force to the new windfalls. The Filipinos and Puerto Ricans might be subject to American rule, but they did not enjoy all American rights.

Cuba, scorched and chaotic, presented another headache. An American military government, set up under the administrative genius of General Leonard Wood of Rough Rider fame, wrought miracles in government, finance, education, agriculture, and public health. Under his leadership and that of Colonel William C. Gorgas, a frontal attack was launched on yellow fever. Spectacular experiments were performed by Dr. Walter Reed and others upon American soldiers, who volunteered as human guinea pigs; and the stegomyia mosquito was proved to be the lethal carrier.

The United States, honoring its self-denying Teller Amendment of 1898, withdrew from Cuba in 1902. Old World imperialists could scarcely believe their eyes. But the Washington government could not turn this rich and strategic island completely loose on the international sea; a grasping power like Germany might secure dangerous lodgment near America's soft underbelly. The Cubans were therefore forced to write into their own constitution of 1901 the so-called Platt Amendment.

The hated restriction severely hobbled the Cubans. They reluctantly bound themselves not to impair their independence by treaty or by contracting a debt beyond their resources. They further agreed that the United States might intervene with troops to restore order and to provide mutual protection. Finally, the Cubans promised to sell or lease needed coaling or naval stations, ultimately two and then only one (Guantanamo), to their powerful "benefactor." The United States still occupies the base under an agreement that can be revoked only by the consent of both parties.

New Horizons in Two Hemispheres

In essence the Spanish-American War was a kind of colossal coming-out party. Dewey's thundering guns merely advertised the fact that the nation was already a world power. The war itself was short (113 days), spectacular, low in casualties, and successful—despite the bungling. American prestige rose sharply, and the European powers grudgingly accorded the Republic more respect.

An exhilarating new spirit thrilled America, buoyed along by the newly popular military marching-band music of John Philip Sousa. National pride was touched and cockiness was swelled by what John Hay called a "splendid little war."* America did not start the war with imperialistic motives, but after falling through the cellar door of imperialism in a drunken fit of idealism, it wound up with imperialistic and colonial fruits in its grasp.

---

* Anti-imperialist William James called it "our squalid war with Spain."

By taking on the Philippine Islands, the United States became a full-fledged East Asian power. Hereafter these distant islands were to be a "heel of Achilles"—a kind of indefensible hostage given to Japan, as events proved in 1941. With singular shortsightedness, the Americans assumed dangerous commitments that they were later unwilling to defend by proper naval and military outlays.

But the lessons of unpreparedness were not altogether lost. Captain Mahan's big-navyism seemed vindicated, and popular support grew for more and better battleships. A masterly organizer, Elihu Root, took over the reins at the War Department. He established a general staff and founded the War College in Washington.

One of the happiest results of the conflict was the further closing of the "bloody chasm" between North and South. Thousands of patriotic southerners had flocked to the Stars and Stripes, and gray-bearded General Joseph ("Fighting Joe") Wheeler—a Confederate cavalry hero—was given a command in Cuba. He allegedly cried, in the heat of battle, "To hell with the Yankees! Dammit, I mean the Spaniards."

Chronology

1820 New England missionaries arrive in Hawaii.	**1898** *Maine* explosion in Havana harbor. Spanish-American War. Teller Amendment. Dewey's victory at Manila Bay. Hawaii annexed.
1889 Samoa crisis with Germany.	
1890 Mahan publishes *The Influence of Sea Power upon History.*	**1899** Senate ratifies treaty acquiring the Philippines.
1891 New Orleans crisis with Italy.	**1900** Hawaii receives full territorial status. Foraker Act for Puerto Rico.
1892 Valparaiso crisis with Chile.	
1893 White planter revolt in Hawaii. Cleveland refuses Hawaii annexation. Pribilof Islands dispute with Canada	**1901** Supreme Court *Insular Cases.* Platt Amendment.
1895 Cubans revolt against Spain.	**1902** U.S. troops leave Cuba.
1895–1896 Venezuelan boundary crisis with Britain.	**1917** Puerto Ricans granted U.S. citizenship.

For further reading, see the Appendix. For web resources, go to **http://college.hmco.com.**

PART FIVE

STRUGGLING FOR JUSTICE AT HOME AND ABROAD

—◈—

1899–1945

The new century brought astonishing changes to America. Victory in the Spanish-American War made it clear that the United States was a world power. Industrialization ushered in giant corporations, sprawling factories, sweatshop labor, and the ubiquitous automobile. A huge wave of immigration was altering the face of the nation, especially the cities, where a majority of Americans lived by 1920. With bigger cities came bigger fears—of crime, vice, poverty, and disease.

Changes of such magnitude raised vexing questions. What role should the United States play in the world? How could the enormous power of industry be controlled? How would the millions of new immigrants make their way in America? What should the country do about poverty, disease, and the continuing plague of racial inequality? All these issues turned on a fundamental point: Should government remain narrowly limited in its powers, or did the times require a more potent government that would actively shape society and secure American interests abroad?

The progressive movement represented the first attempt to answer those questions. Reform-minded men and women from all walks of life and from both major parties shared in the progressive crusade for greater government activism. Buoyed by this outlook, Presidents Theodore Roosevelt, William Howard Taft, and Woodrow Wilson enlarged the capacity of government to fight graft, "bust" business trusts, regulate corporations, and promote fair labor practices, child welfare, conservation, and consumer protection. Progressive reformers, convinced that women would bring greater morality to politics, bolstered the decades-long struggle for female suffrage. Women finally secured the vote in 1920 with the ratification of the Nineteenth Amendment.

The progressive-era presidents also challenged America's tradition of isolationism in foreign policy.

They felt the country had a moral obligation to spread democracy and an economic opportunity to reap profits in foreign markets. Roosevelt and Taft launched diplomatic initiatives in the Caribbean, Central America, and East Asia. Wilson aspired to "make the world safe for democracy" by rallying support for American intervention in the First World War.

The progressive spirit waned, however, as the United States retreated during the 1920s into what President Harding called "normalcy." Isolationist sentiment revived with a vengeance. Blessed with a booming economy, Americans turned their gaze inward to baseball heroes, radio, jazz, movies, and the first mass-produced American automobile, the Model T Ford. Presidents Harding, Coolidge, and Hoover backed off from the economic regulatory zeal of their predecessors.

"Normalcy" also had a brutal side. Thousands of suspected radicals were jailed or deported in the red scare of 1919 and 1920. Anti-immigrant passions flared until immigration quotas in 1924 squeezed the flow of newcomers to a trickle. Race riots scorched several northern cities in the summer of 1919, a sign of how embittered race relations had become in the wake of the "great migration" of southern blacks to wartime jobs in northern industry. A reborn Ku Klux Klan staged a comeback, not just in the South but in the North and West as well.

"Normalcy" itself soon proved short-lived, a casualty of the stock market crash of 1929 and the Great Depression that followed. As Americans watched banks fail, businesses collapse, and millions of people lose their jobs, they asked with renewed urgency what role the government should play in rescuing the nation. President Franklin D. Roosevelt's answer was the "New Deal"—an ambitious array of relief programs, public works, and economic regulations that failed to cure the depression but furnished an impressive legacy of social reforms.

Most Americans came to accept an expanded federal governmental role at home under FDR's leadership in the 1930s, but they still clung stubbornly to isolationism. The United States did little in the 1930s to check the rising military aggression of Japan and Germany. By the early 1940s events forced Americans to reconsider. Once Hitler's Germany had seized control of most of Europe, Roosevelt, who had long opposed the isolationists, found ways to aid a beleaguered Britain. When Japan attacked the American naval base at Pearl Harbor in December 1941, isolationists at last fell silent. Roosevelt led a stunned but determined nation into the Second World War, and victory in 1945 positioned the United States to assume a commanding position in the postwar world order.

The Great Depression and the Second World War brought to a head a half-century of debate over the role of government and the place of the United States in the world. In the name of a struggle for justice, FDR established a new era of government activism at home and internationalism abroad. The New Deal's legacy set the terms of debate in American political life for the rest of the century.

America on the World Stage

--- ◈ ---

1899–1909

I never take a step in foreign service policy unless I am assured that I shall be able eventually to carry out my will by force.

THEODORE ROOSEVELT, 1905

Liberty-loving Filipinos assumed that they, like the Cubans, would be granted their freedom after the Spanish-American War. They were tragically deceived. The Senate refused to pass a resolution granting Filipino independence. Bitterness toward the American troops mounted. It finally erupted into open insurrection on February 4, 1899, under Emilio Aguinaldo.

The war with the Filipinos, unlike the "splendid" little set-to with Spain, was sordid and prolonged. It involved more savage fighting, more soldiers killed, and far more scandal. Anti-imperialists redoubled their protests. In their view the United States, having plunged into war with Spain to free Cuba, was now fighting ten thousand miles away to rivet shackles on a people who asked for nothing but liberty—in the American tradition.

"Little Brown Brothers" in the Philippines

As the ill-equipped Filipino armies were defeated, they melted into the jungle to wage a vicious guerrilla warfare. Many of the outgunned Filipinos used barbarous methods, and the infuriated American troops responded in kind.

Atrocity tales shocked and rocked the United States, for such methods did not reflect America's better self. Uncle Sam's soldiers resorted to such extremes as the painful "water cure"—that is, forcing water down victims' throats until they yielded information or died. Reconcentration camps were even established that strongly suggested those of "Butcher" Weyler in

Cuba. America, having begun the Spanish war with noble ideals, now dirtied its hands. One New York newspaper published a reply to Rudyard Kipling's famous poem:

> We've taken up the white man's burden
>> Of ebony and brown;
> Now will you kindly tell us, Rudyard,
>> How we may put it down?

The backbone of the Filipino insurrection was finally broken in 1901, when American soldiers captured Aguinaldo at a guerrilla camp. But sporadic fighting dragged on for many dreary months.

In 1899 President McKinley appointed a Philippine Commission to develop a government for the islands and the next year named future president William H. Taft as its head. An amiable lawyer-judge from Ohio who weighed about 350 pounds, Taft formed a strong attachment to the Filipinos, calling them his "little brown brothers." But among American soldiers combing the jungles, a different view of the insurgent prevailed:

> He may be a brother of Big Bill Taft,
> But he ain't no brother of mine.

McKinley's "benevolent assimilation" of the Philippines proceeded with painful slowness. Millions of American dollars were poured into the islands to improve roads, sanitation, and public health. Important economic ties, including trade in sugar, developed between the two peoples. American teachers—"pioneers of the blackboard"—set up an unusually good school system and helped make English a second language. But all this vast expenditure, which profited America little, was ill received. The Filipinos, who hated compulsory civilization, preferred less sanitation and more liberty. Like caged hawks, they beat against their gilded bars until they finally got their freedom, on the Fourth of July, 1946. In the meantime, thousands of Filipinos emigrated to the United States (see "Makers of America: The Filipinos," p. 394).

Hinging the Open Door in China

Exciting events had meanwhile been brewing in China. After its defeat by Japan in 1894–1895, the imperialistic European powers, notably Russia and Germany, moved in. Like vultures descending on a wounded whale, they began to tear away valuable leaseholds and economic spheres of influence from the Manchu government.

A growing group of Americans viewed the vivisection of China with alarm. Churches were worried about their missionary strongholds; manufacturers and exporters feared that Chinese markets would be monopolized by Europeans. An alarmed American public, prodded by the press and by certain free-trade Britons, demanded that Washington do something. Secretary of State John Hay finally decided on a dramatic move.

In the summer of 1899, Hay dispatched to all the great powers a communication soon known as the Open Door note. He urged them to announce that in their leaseholds or spheres of influence they would respect certain Chinese rights and the ideal of fair competition. The phrase *Open Door* quickly caught the public's fancy and gained wide acceptance. Hay's proposal caused much squirming in the leading world capitals, but all the great powers eventually acquiesced, though subject to the condition that the others sign on unconditionally.

Open Door or not, patriotic Chinese did not care to be used as a doormat by the Europeans. In 1900 a superpatriotic group known as the "Boxers" broke loose with the cry, "Kill Foreign Devils." Over two hundred missionaries and other ill-fated whites were murdered, and a number of foreign diplomats were besieged in the capital, Beijing (Peking).

A multinational rescue force of some eighteen thousand soldiers, including some twenty-five hundred Americans, arrived in the nick of time and quelled the rebellion. Such participation in a joint military operation, especially in Asia, was plainly contrary to the nation's time-honored principles of nonentanglement and noninvolvement.

The victorious allied invaders acted angrily and vindictively. They assessed prostrate China an excessive indemnity of $333 million, of which America's share was to be $24.5 million. When Washington discovered that this sum was much more than enough to pay damages and expenses, it remitted about $18 million. The Beijing government, appreciating this gesture of goodwill, set aside the money to educate a

The Filipinos

At the beginning of the twentieth century, the United States, its imperial muscles just flexed in the war with Spain, found itself in possession of the Philippines. Uncertain of how to manage this empire, which seethed resentfully against its new masters, the United States promised to build democracy in the Philippines and to ready the islanders for home rule. Almost immediately after annexation, the American governor of the archipelago sent a corps of Filipino students to the United States, hoping to forge future leaders steeped in American ways who would someday govern an independent Philippines. Yet this small student group found little favor in their adopted country, although in their native land many went on to become respected citizens and leaders.

Most Filipino immigrants to the United States in these years, however, came not to study but to toil. With Chinese immigration banned, Hawaii and the Pacific Coast states turned to the Philippines for cheap agricultural labor. Beginning in 1906, the Hawaiian Sugar Planters Association aggressively recruited Filipino workers. Enlistments grew slowly at first, but by the 1920s thousands of young Filipino men had reached the Hawaiian Islands and been assigned to sugar plantations or pineapple fields.

Those Filipinos venturing as far as the American mainland found work less arduous but also less certain than did their countrymen on Hawaiian plantations. Many mainlanders worked seasonally—in winter as domestic servants, busboys, or bellhops; in summer journeying to the fields to harvest lettuce, strawberries, sugar beets, and potatoes. Eventually, Filipinos, along with Mexican immigrants, shared the dubious honor of making up California's agricultural work force.

By 1930, with Filipino male immigrants outnumbering women by fourteen to one, the issue of intermarriage became acutely sensitive. In California and many other states, demeaning laws that remained on the books until 1948 prohibited the intermarriage of Asians and Caucasians. Undeterred by hostility and the vigilante violence sometimes directed at them, especially in Washington and California, Filipinos continued to challenge restrictive state laws even though they did not attain U.S. citizenship until 1946.

After World War II, Filipino immigration accelerated. Between 1950 and 1970, the number of Filipinos in the United States nearly doubled. Many of these recent arrivals were solidly middle class and sought in America a better life for their children. Today, the perpetually depressed and politically unstable Philippine archipelago sends more immigrants to American shores than does any other Asian nation.

selected group of Chinese students in the United States. These bright young people later played a significant role in the westernization of Asia.

Secretary Hay let fly another paper broadside in 1900, announcing that henceforth the Open Door would embrace the territorial integrity of China. Defenseless China was spared partition during these troubled years. But its salvation was probably due not to Hay's fine phrases but to the strength of the competing powers. None of them could trust the others not to seek their own advantage.

Imperialism or Bryanism in 1900?

President McKinley's renomination by the Republicans in 1900 was a foregone conclusion. He had piloted the country through a victorious war; he had acquired rich, though burdensome, real estate; he had established the gold standard; and he had brought the promised prosperity of the full dinner pail.

An irresistible vice-presidential boom had developed for "Teddy" Roosevelt (TR), the cowboy-hero of San Juan Hill. Capitalizing on his war-born popularity, he had been elected governor of New York, where the local political bosses had found him headstrong and difficult to manage. They therefore devised a scheme to kick the colorful colonel upstairs into the vice presidency.

This plot to railroad Roosevelt worked beautifully. Gesticulating wildly, he attended the nominating convention, where his western-style cowboy hat made him stand out like a white crow. Yielding to the cries of "We Want Teddy!" he accepted the nomination, receiving a unanimous vote, except for his own. A frantic Hanna reportedly moaned that there would be only one heartbeat between "that damned cowboy" and the presidency of the United States.

William Jennings Bryan was the odds-on choice of the Democrats, meeting at Kansas City. The Democratic platform proclaimed, as did Bryan, that the "paramount" issue was Republican overseas imperialism.

McKinley, the soul of dignity, sat safely on his front porch during the campaign of 1900 as he had in 1896. Also as before, Bryan took to the stump in a cyclonic campaign, assailing both imperialism and Republican-fostered trusts. Lincoln, he charged, had abolished slavery for 3.5 million Africans; McKinley had reestablished it for 7 million Filipinos.

Republicans responded that "Bryanism," not imperialism, was the paramount issue. By this accusation they meant that Bryan would rock the boat of prosperity once he got into office with his free-silver lunacy and other dangerous ideas. The voters were much less concerned about imperialism than about "Four Years More of the Full Dinner Pail."

McKinley triumphed by a much wider margin than in 1896: 7,218,491 to 6,356,734 popular votes, and 292 to 155 electoral votes. Victory for the Republicans was not a mandate for or against imperialism. If there was any mandate at all it was for the two Ps: prosperity and protection.

TR: Brandisher of the Big Stick

Kindly William McKinley had scarcely served another six months when, in September 1901, he was murdered by a deranged anarchist. Roosevelt became president at age forty-two, the youngest thus far in American history.

What manner of man was Theodore Roosevelt, the red-blooded blueblood? Born into a wealthy and distinguished New York family, he had fiercely built up his spindly, asthmatic body by a stern and self-imposed routine of exercise. Graduating from Harvard with Phi Beta Kappa honors, he published at the age of twenty-four the first of some thirty volumes of muscular prose. Then came busy years, which involved duties as a ranch owner and bespectacled cowboy ("Four Eyes") in the Dakotas, followed by various political posts. When fully developed, he was a barrel-chested 5 feet, 10 inches, with prominent teeth, squinty eyes, droopy mustache, and piercing voice.

The Rough Rider's high-voltage energy was electrifying. Believing that it was better to wear out than to rust out, he would shake the hands of some six thousand people at one stretch or ride horseback many miles in a day as an example for portly cavalry officers. Incurably boyish and bellicose, Roosevelt never ceased to preach the virile virtues and to denounce civilized softness, with its pacifists and other "flubdubs" and "mollycoddles." An ardent champion of military and naval preparedness, he adopted as his pet proverb, "Speak softly and carry a big stick, [and] you will go far."

Wherever Roosevelt went, there was a great stir. At a wedding he eclipsed the bride; at a funeral, the corpse. Shockingly unconventional, he loved to break hoary precedents—the hoarier the better. He loved people and mingled with those of all ranks—from Catholic cardinals to professional prizefighters, one of whom blinded a Rooseveltian eye in a White House bout.

An outspoken moralizer and reformer, Roosevelt preached virtue from the White House pulpit. Yet he was an opportunist who would compromise rather than butt his head against a stone wall. He was, in reality, much less radical than his blustery actions would indicate. A middle-of-the-roader, he stood just a little left of center and bared his mulelike molars at liberals and reactionaries alike.

Roosevelt rapidly developed into a master politician with an idolatrous personal following. A magnificent showman, he was always front-page copy; and his cowboyism, his bear shooting, his outsize teeth, and his pince-nez glasses were ever the delight of cartoonists.

Above all, Roosevelt was a direct-actionist. He believed that the president should lead. He had no real respect for the delicate checks and balances among the three branches of government. The president, he felt, may take any action in the general interest that is not specifically forbidden by the laws or the Constitution.

Building the Panama Canal

Foreign affairs absorbed much of Roosevelt's bullish energy. Having traveled extensively in Europe, he enjoyed a far more intimate knowledge of the outside world than most of his predecessors.

The Spanish-American War had emphasized the need for the long-talked-about canal across the Central American isthmus. An isthmian canal would plainly augment the strength of the navy by increas-

ing its mobility. Such a waterway would also make easier the defense of such recent acquisitions as Puerto Rico, Hawaii, and the Philippines, while facilitating the operations of the American merchant marine.

Initial obstacles in the path of the canal builders were legal rather than geographical. By the terms of the ancient Clayton-Bulwer Treaty, concluded with Britain in 1850, the United States could not secure exclusive control over such a route. But by 1901 America's British cousins were willing to yield ground. Confronted with an unfriendly Europe and bogged down in the South African Boer War, they consented to the Hay-Pauncefote Treaty in 1901. It not only gave the United States a free hand to build the canal but conceded the right to fortify it as well.

Legal barriers now removed, the next question was, Where should the canal be dug? Many American experts favored the Nicaraguan route, but agents of an old French canal company were eager to salvage something from their costly failure at S-shaped Panama. Represented by a young, energetic, and unscrupulous engineer, Philippe Bunau-Varilla, the New Panama Canal Company suddenly dropped the price of its holdings from $109 million to the fire sale price of $40 million.

After much debate, Congress in June 1902 finally decided on the Panama route. The scene now shifted to Colombia, of which Panama was an unwilling part. A treaty providing a perpetual lease on a six-mile-wide zone for $10 million plus an annual payment was negotiated between Washington and the Bogota government. But the Colombian senate rejected the treaty, putting a higher value on this precious isthmian strip. Roosevelt was infuriated by this setback at the hands of what he called "those dagoes." Anxious to "make the dirt fly" and impress the voters, he reportedly cried in private, "Damn the law. I want the canal built!"

Impatient Panamanians, who had rebelled numerous times, were ripe for another revolt. They had counted on a wave of prosperity to follow construction of the canal, and they feared that the United States would now turn to the Nicaraguan route. The scheming Bunau-Varilla was no less disturbed by the prospect of losing the company's $40 million. Working hand in glove with the Panama revolutionists, he helped incite a rebellion on November 3, 1903. Colombian troops were gathered to crush the uprising, but U.S. naval forces would not let them cross the isthmus.

Roosevelt moved rapidly to make steamy Panama a virtual outpost of the United States. Three days after the uprising, he hastily extended the right hand of recognition. Fifteen days later, Bunau-Varilla, who was now the Panamanian minister despite his French citizenship, signed the Hay–Bunau-Varilla Treaty in Washington. The price of the canal strip was left the same, but the zone was widened from six to ten miles. The French company gladly pocketed its $40 million from the U.S. Treasury.

Roosevelt, it seems clear, did not actively plot to tear Panama from the side of Colombia. Yet the

Roosevelt in Panama *When he visited the Panama Canal construction site in 1906 to see "the dirt fly," Roosevelt was the first president to leave the United States for foreign soil.*

Rough Rider became so indiscreetly involved in the Panama affair as to create the impression that he had been a secret party to the intrigue.

Unhappily, the United States suffered a black eye as a result of Roosevelt's "cowboy diplomacy." European imperialists, who were old hands at this kind of thing, could now raise their eyebrows in scorn at America's superior moral pretensions. Roosevelt heatedly defended himself against charges of evildoing. He claimed that he had received a "mandate from civilization" to start the canal and that Colombia had wronged the United States by not permitting itself to be benefited.

Active work was begun on "making the dirt fly" in 1904, but grave difficulties were encountered, ranging from labor troubles to landslides. The organization was finally perfected under an energetic but autocratic West Point engineer, Colonel George Washington Goethals. At the outset, sanitation proved to be more important than excavation. Colonel William C. Gorgas, the quiet and determined exterminator of yellow fever in Havana, ultimately made the Canal Zone "as safe as a health resort."

Americans finally succeeded where Frenchmen had failed. In 1914 the colossal canal project was completed at an initial cost of about $400 million.

TR's Perversion of Monroe's Doctrine

Latin American debt defaults created the conditions for further Rooseveltian involvement in affairs south of the border. Nations such as Venezuela and the Dominican Republic were chronically in arrears in their payments to European creditors, particularly Britain and Germany. Roosevelt feared that if the Germans or British got their feet in the door as bill collectors, they might remain in Latin America. He therefore devised a devious policy of "preventive intervention," better known as the Roosevelt Corollary to the Monroe Doctrine. In 1904 he declared that in the event of future financial malfeasance by the Latin American nations, the United States itself would intervene, take over the customshouses, pay off the debts, and keep the troublesome powers on the other side of the Atlantic. In short, no outsiders

Big Stick in the Caribbean   *In 1901 Roosevelt declared: "If a man continually blusters . . . a big stick will not save him from trouble; and neither will speaking softly avail, if back of the softness there does not lie strength, power. . . . If the boaster is not prepared to back up his words his position becomes absolutely contemptible."*

could push the Latin nations around except Uncle Sam, Policeman of the Caribbean.

This new brandishing of the Big Stick in the Caribbean became effective in 1905. It was formalized in a treaty with the Dominican Republic two years later giving the United States supervisory powers over Dominican tariff collections.

Roosevelt's rewriting of Monroe's doctrine did more than any other single step to promote the "Bad Neighbor" policy begun in these years. As time wore on, the new corollary was used to justify wholesale interventions and repeated landings of the U.S. Marines, all of which helped turn the Caribbean into a "Yankee pond." To Latin Americans it seemed as though the Monroe Doctrine, far from providing a shield, was a cloak behind which the United States sought to strangle them.

Roosevelt on the World Stage

Booted and spurred, Roosevelt charged into international affairs far beyond Latin America. The outbreak

of war between Russia and Japan in 1904 gave him a chance to perform as a global statesman. With the Russians threatening permanent occupation of China's Manchuria, the Japanese suddenly began a war in 1904 with a devastating surprise attack on the Russian fleet at Port Arthur. They proceeded to administer a humiliating series of beatings to the inept Russians. But as the war dragged on, Japan began to run short of men and yen—a weakness it did not want to betray to the enemy. Tokyo officials therefore approached Roosevelt in the deepest secrecy and asked him to help sponsor peace negotiations.

Roosevelt agreed and shepherded the delegates of the two sides together at Portsmouth, New Hampshire, in 1905. The Japanese presented stern demands for a huge indemnity and the entire strategic island of Sakhalin, while the Russians stubbornly refused to admit the depths of their defeat. Blustering at both sides behind the scenes, Roosevelt forced through an accord in which the Japanese received no indemnity and only the southern half of Sakhalin.

For achieving this agreement, as well as for helping arrange an international conference at Algeciras,

Theodore Roosevelt and His Big Stick in the Caribbean, 1904 *Roosevelt's policies seemed to be turning the Caribbean into a Yankee pond.*

Spain, in 1906 to mediate North African disputes, Roosevelt received the Nobel Peace Prize in 1906. But the price of TR's diplomatic glory was high for U.S. foreign relations. Two historic friendships withered on the windswept plains of Manchuria. America's relations with Russia, once friendly, soured as the Russians implausibly accused Roosevelt of robbing them of military victory. Japan, once America's protégé, felt robbed of its due compensation. Both newly powerful, Japan and America now became rivals in Asia, as fear and jealousy between them grew.

Japanese Laborers in California

Adding to tensions between America and Japan was the issue of Japanese migration to America's Pacific Coast. The Japanese government prohibited emigration of its citizens until 1884, when it began allowing temporary laborers to work on sugar plantations in Hawaii. From there thousands of Japanese were recruited to work in California as farm laborers, railroad workers, and servants. Like the Chinese before them, Japanese immigrants did the nation's most arduous, dangerous work but were banned from becoming citizens. And like the Chinese, Japanese immigrants confronted racist hostility. Although Japanese residents never amounted to more than 3 percent of the state's population, white Californians ranted about a new "yellow peril" and feared being drowned in an Asian sea.

A showdown on the Japanese influx came in 1906 when San Francisco's school board, coping with the aftermath of a frightful earthquake and fire, ordered the segregation of Chinese, Japanese, and Korean schoolchildren to free more space for whites. The people of Japan, who were highly sensitive on questions of race, regarded this discrimination as an insult to them and their beloved children. On both sides of the Pacific, irresponsible war talk sizzled in the yellow press—the real "yellow peril." Roosevelt, who as a Rough Rider had relished shooting, was less happy over the prospect that California might stir up a war that all the other states would have to fight. He therefore invited the entire San Francisco Board of Education to come to the White House.

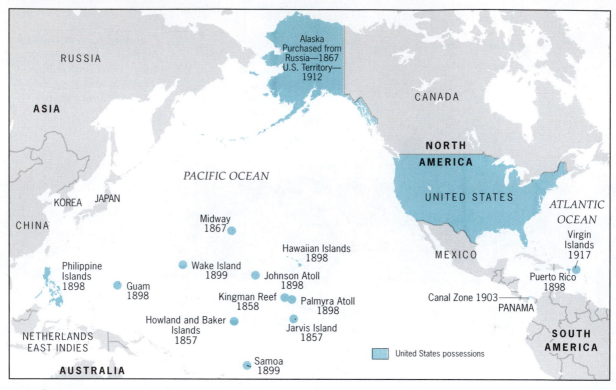

RUSSIA

Alaska
Purchased from
Russia—1867
U.S. Territory—
1912

CANADA

ASIA

NORTH
AMERICA

PACIFIC OCEAN

UNITED STATES

ATLANTIC
OCEAN

KOREA JAPAN

CHINA

Midway
1867

Hawaiian Islands
1898

MEXICO

Virgin
Islands
1917

Philippine
Islands
1898

Wake Island
1899

Johnson Atoll
1898

Puerto Rico
1898

Guam
1898

Kingman Reef
1858

Palmyra Atoll
1898

Canal Zone 1903

PANAMA

Howland and Baker
Islands
1857

Jarvis Island
1857

NETHERLANDS
EAST INDIES

SOUTH
AMERICA

United States possessions

AUSTRALIA

Samoa
1899

United States Possessions to 1917

TR finally broke the deadlock, but not until he had brandished his big stick and bared his teeth. The Californians were induced to repeal the offensive school order and to accept what came to be known as the "Gentlemen's Agreement." This secret understanding was worked out during 1907–1908 by an exchange of diplomatic notes between Washington and Tokyo. The Japanese agreed to stop the flow of laborers to the American mainland by withholding passports.

Roosevelt worried that his intercession between California and Japan might be interpreted in Tokyo as prompted by fear of the Japanese. Accordingly, he hit upon a dramatic scheme to impress the Japanese with the heft of his big stick. He daringly decided to send the entire U.S. battleship fleet on a highly visible voyage around the world.

Late in 1907, sixteen smoke-belching battleships started from Virginia waters. Their commander

pointedly declared that he was ready for "a feast, a frolic, or a fight." The Great White Fleet—saluted by cannonading champagne corks—received tumultuous welcomes in Latin America, Hawaii, New Zealand, and Australia. The high point of the trip was an overwhelming reception in Japan, as tens of thousands of kimonoed schoolchildren turned out to wave tiny American flags and sing "The Star Spangled Banner."

In the warm diplomatic atmosphere created by the visit of the fleet, the Root-Takahira agreement of 1908 was reached with Japan. The United States and Japan solemnly pledged themselves to respect each other's territorial possessions in the Pacific and to uphold the Open Door in China. The once fight-thirsty Theodore Roosevelt, who thus went out of his way to avoid a war with Japan, regarded the battleship cruise as his most important contribution to peace.

Japanese Workers Building a Road in California, c. 1910

Chronology

1899 Aguinaldo launches rebellion against the United States in the Philippine Islands.
First American Open Door note.

1900 Boxer Rebellion and U.S. expedition to China.
Second Open Door note.
McKinley defeats Bryan for presidency.

1901 McKinley assassinated; Roosevelt assumes presidency.
Filipino rebellion defeated.
Hay-Pauncefote Treaty.

1903 Panamanian revolution against Colombia.
Hay–Bunau-Varilla Treaty.

1904 Roosevelt Corollary to the Monroe Doctrine.

1904–1914 Construction of the Panama Canal.

1905 Roosevelt mediates Russo-Japanese peace treaty.
United States takes over Dominican Republic customs.

1906 San Francisco Japanese education crisis.
Roosevelt arranges Algeciras conference.

1906–1909 U.S. Marines occupy Cuba.

1907 Great White Fleet.

1907–1908 "Gentlemen's Agreement" with Japan.

1908 Root-Takahira agreement.

VARYING   VIEWPOINTS

Why Did America Become a World Power?

American imperialism has long been an embarrassing topic for students of American history who remember the Republic's own revolutionary origins and anticolonial tradition. Perhaps for that reason, many historians have tried to explain the dramatic overseas expansionism of the 1890s as some kind of aberration—a sudden, singular, and short-lived departure from time-honored American principles and practices. Various explanations have been offered to account for this spasmodic lapse. Scholars such as Julius Pratt pointed to the irresponsible behavior of the yellow press. Richard Hofstadter ascribed America's imperial fling to the "psychic crisis of the 1890s," a crisis brought on, he argued, by the strains of the decade's economic depression and the Populist upheaval. Howard K. Beale emphasized the contagious scramble for imperial possessions by the European powers, as well as Japan, in these years.

In Beale's argument, the United States—and Theodore Roosevelt in particular—succumbed to a kind of international peer pressure: if other countries were expanding their international roles and even establishing colonies around the globe, could the United States safely refrain from doing the same?

Perhaps the most controversial interpretation of American imperialism has come from the so-called New Left school of writers, inspired by William Apple-man Williams (and before him by V. I. Lenin's 1916 book *Imperialism: The Highest Stage of Capitalism*). Historians such as Williams and Walter LaFeber argue that the explanation for political and military expansion abroad is to be found in economic expansion at home. That "revisionist" interpretation, in turn, has been sharply criticized by scholars who point out that foreign trade accounted for only a tiny share of American output and that the diplomacy of this period was far too complex to be reduced to "economic need."

Most recently, historians have highlighted the importance of race and gender in the march toward empire. Roosevelt and other imperialists perceived their world in gendered terms, and many feared American society was growing soft and "feminine," losing touch with "masculine" virtues. Imperialists also saw the world in terms of a strict racial hierarchy, with "primitive" blacks and Indians at the bottom and "civilized" Anglo-Saxons at the top. In this world-view the conquest of "inferior" peoples seemed a natural tonic to restore the nation's virility. Scholars who emphasize these explanations of imperialism are less likely to see the expansionism of the 1890s as an aberration. Instead, they argue, these overseas adventures were part of a long tradition of race-fueled militarism throughout American history.

For further reading, see the Appendix. For web resources, go to **http://college.hmco.com**.

29

Progressivism and the Republican Roosevelt

1901–1912

*When I say I believe in a square deal I do not mean . . .
to give every man the best hand. If the cards do not come
to any man, or if they do come, and he has not got the power
to play them, that is his affair. All I mean is that there shall
be no crookedness in the dealing.*

THEODORE ROOSEVELT, 1905

Nearly 76 million Americans greeted the new century in 1900. Of them, almost one in seven was foreign-born. In the fourteen years of peace that remained before the Great War of 1914 engulfed the globe, 13 million more migrants would carry their bundles down the gangplanks to the land of promise.

Hardly had the twentieth century dawned on the ethnically and racially mixed American people than they were convulsed by a reform movement, the likes of which the nation had not seen since the 1840s. The new crusaders, who called themselves "progressives," waged war on many evils, notably monopoly, corruption, inefficiency, and social injustice. The progressive army was large, diverse, and widely deployed, but the real heart of the movement, explained one progressive reformer, was to "use the government as an agency of human welfare."

Progressive Roots

The groundswell of the new reformist wave went far back—to the Greenback Labor party of the 1870s and the Populists of the 1890s, to the mounting unrest throughout the land as grasping industrialists concentrated more and more power in fewer and fewer hands. An outworn philosophy of hands-off individualism seemed increasingly out of place in the modern machine age. Progressive theorists were insisting that society could no longer afford the luxury of a limitless "let-alone" (laissez-faire) policy. The people, through government, must substitute mastery for drift.

Well before 1900, perceptive politicians and writers had begun to pinpoint targets for the progressive attack. Bryan, Altgeld, and the Populists loudly branded the "bloated trusts" with the stigma of corruption and wrongdoing. In 1894 Henry Demarest Lloyd charged headlong into the Standard Oil Company with his book entitled *Wealth Against Commonwealth.* Eccentric Thorstein Veblen assailed the new rich with his prickly pen in *The Theory of the Leisure Class* (1899), a savage attack on "predatory wealth" and "conspicuous consumption."

Other pen-wielding knights likewise entered the fray. The keen-eyed and keen-nosed Danish immigrant Jacob A. Riis, a reporter for the *New York Sun,* shocked middle-class Americans in 1890 with *How the Other Half Lives.* His account was a damning indictment of the dirt, disease, vice, and misery of those rat-gnawed human rookeries known as the New York slums. Novelist Theodore Dreiser used his blunt prose to batter promoters and profiteers in *The Financier* (1912) and *The Titan* (1914).

Socialists, many of whom were European immigrants, began to register appreciable strength at the ballot box. High-minded messengers of the social gospel used Christian teachings to demand better housing and living conditions for the poor. Feminists in multiplying numbers added social justice to suffrage on their list of needed reforms. With urban pioneers like Jane Addams blazing the way, women entered the fight to improve the lots of families living and working in the festering cities.

Raking Muck with the Muckrakers

Beginning about 1902 the exposing of evil became a flourishing industry among American publishers. A group of aggressive ten- and fifteen-cent popular magazines surged to the front, notably *McClure's, Cosmopolitan, Collier's,* and *Everybody's.* Waging fierce circulation wars, they dug deep for the dirt that the public loved to hate. Enterprising editors financed extensive research and encouraged pugnacious writing by their bright young reporters, whom President Roosevelt branded as "muckrakers" in 1906.

In 1902 a brilliant New York reporter, Lincoln Steffens, launched a series of articles in *McClure's* entitled "The Shame of the Cities." He fearlessly unmasked the corrupt alliance between big business

Child Workers   *Two young girls tend a thread-winding machine. The boy is already a veteran coal miner.*

and municipal government. Steffens was followed in the same magazine by Ida M. Tarbell, a pioneering woman journalist who published a devastating factual exposé of the Standard Oil Company.

Muckrakers also assailed the malpractices of life insurance companies and tariff lobbies. They roasted the beef trust, the "money trust," the railroad barons, and the corrupt amassing of American fortunes. David G. Phillips shocked an already startled nation by his series in *Cosmopolitan* entitled "The Treason of the Senate" (1906). He boldly charged that seventy-five of the ninety senators did not represent the people at all but the railroads and trusts.

Some of the most effective fire of the muckrakers was directed at social evils. The ugly list included the immoral "white slave" traffic in women, the rickety slums, and the appalling number of industrial accidents. The sorry subjugation of America's 9 million blacks was spotlighted in Ray Stannard Baker's *Following the Color Line* (1908). The abuses of child labor were brought luridly to light by John Spargo's *The Bitter Cry of the Children* (1906).

Vendors of potent patent medicines (often heavily spiked with alcohol) likewise came in for bitter criticism. These conscienceless vultures sold incredible quantities of adulterated or habit-forming drugs. Muckraking attacks in *Collier's* were substantiated by Dr. Harvey W. Wiley, chief chemist of the Department of Agriculture, who even performed experiments on himself.

Full of sound and fury, the muckrakers signified much about the nature of the progressive reform movement. They were long on lamentation and short on sweeping remedies. To right social wrongs they counted on publicity and an aroused public conscience, not drastic political change. They sought not to overthrow capitalism but to cleanse it. The cure for the ills of American democracy, they earnestly believed, was more democracy.

Political Progressivism

Progressive reformers were mainly middle-class men and women who felt themselves squeezed from above and below. They sensed pressure from the new giant corporations, the restless immigrant hordes, and the aggressive labor unions. The progressives simultaneously sought two goals: to use state power to curb the trusts, and to stem the socialist threat by generally improving the common person's conditions of life and labor. Progressives emerged in both major parties, in all regions, and at all levels of government. The truth is that progressivism was less a minority movement and more a majority mood.

One of the first objectives of progressives was to regain the power that had slipped from the hands of the people into those of the "interests." These ardent reformers pushed for direct primary elections so as to undercut power-hungry party bosses. They favored the "initiative" so that voters could directly propose legislation themselves, thus bypassing the boss-bought state legislatures. Progressives also agitated for the "referendum." This device would place laws on the ballot for final approval by the people, especially laws that had been railroaded through a compliant legislature by free-spending agents of big business. The "recall" would enable the voters to remove faithless elected officials, particularly those who had been bribed by bosses or lobbyists. The secret Australian ballot was likewise being introduced more widely in the states to counteract boss rule.

Direct election of U.S. senators became a favorite goal of progressives, especially after muckrakers had exposed the scandalous intimacy between greedy corporations and Congress. Direct election was finally achieved by the Seventeenth Amendment to the Constitution, approved in 1913 (see the Appendix). But the expected improvement in caliber was slow in coming.

Woman suffrage, the goal of feminists for many decades, likewise received powerful new support from the progressives early in the 1900s. The political reformers believed that women's votes would elevate the political tone, and the foes of the saloon felt that they could count on the support of enfranchised females. Many of the states, especially the more liberal ones in the West, gradually extended the vote to women. But by 1910 nationwide female suffrage was still a decade away.

Progressivism in the Cities and States

Progressives scored some of their most impressive gains in the cities. Frustrated by the inefficiency and corruption of machine-oiled city government, many

Suffragists Put the Pressure on Washington *Success finally crowned their effort with the ratification of the Nineteenth Amendment in 1920.*

localities followed the pioneering example of Galveston, Texas. In 1901 it had appointed expert-staffed commissions to manage urban affairs. Other communities adopted the city manager system, also designed to take politics out of municipal administration. Some of these "reforms" obviously valued efficiency more highly than democracy, as control of civic affairs was further removed from the people's hands.

Urban reformers likewise attacked "slumlords," juvenile delinquency, and wide-open prostitution (vice-at-a-price), which flourished in red-light districts unchallenged by bribed police. Public-spirited city dwellers also moved to halt the corrupt sale of franchises for streetcars and other public utilities.

Progressivism naturally bubbled up to the state level, notably in Wisconsin, which became a yeasty laboratory of reform. Pompadoured Governor Robert M. ("Fighting Bob") La Follette was an undersized but overbearing crusader who emerged as the most militant of the progressive Republican leaders. Elected governor in 1901 after a desperate fight with the railroad and timber interests, he perfected a scheme for regulating public utilities while laboring in close association with experts on the faculty of the University of Wisconsin at Madison.

Other states marched steadily toward the progressive camp, as they undertook to regulate railroads and trusts, chiefly through public utilities commissions. Oregon was not far behind Wisconsin, and California made giant bootstrides under the stocky Hiram W. Johnson. Elected Republican governor in 1910, this dynamic prosecutor of grafters helped break the dominant grip of the Southern

Pacific Railroad on California politics and then, like La Follette, set up a political machine of his own.

Progressive Women

Women proved themselves an indispensable part of the progressive army. A crucial focus for women's activism was the settlement house movement (see p. 345). At a time when women could neither vote nor hold political office, settlement houses offered a side-door entry to public life. They exposed middle-class women to the numerous problems plaguing American cities and gave them the skill and confidence to tackle those evils. The women's club movement also turned from literary self-improvement to engagement with social issues and current events. "Dante has been dead for several centuries," observed the president of the General Federation of Women's Clubs in 1904. "I think it is time that we dropped the study of his *Inferno* and turned attention to our own."

Nineteenth-century notions of "separate spheres" dictated that a woman's place was in the home, so most female progressives defended their new activities as an extension—not a rejection—of the traditional roles of wife and mother. Thus they were often drawn to moral and "maternal" issues like keeping children out of sweatshops or ensuring safe food products. Female activists agitated through organizations like the Women's Trade Union League and the National Consumers League, as well as through two new federal agencies, the Children's Bureau (1912) and the Women's Bureau (1920), both in the Department of Labor.

Campaigns for factory reform and temperance particularly attracted women foot soldiers. Unsafe and unsanitary sweatshops—factories where workers toiled long hours for low wages—were a public scandal in many cities. Florence Kelley, a former resident of Jane Addams's Hull House, became the state of Illinois's first chief factory inspector and one of the leading advocates for improved factory conditions. In 1899 Kelley took control of the newly founded National Consumers League, which mobilized female consumers to press for laws safeguarding women and children in the workplace. In the landmark case *Muller* v. *Oregon* (1908), crusading attorney Louis D.

Brandeis persuaded the Supreme Court to accept the constitutionality of laws protecting women workers by presenting evidence of the harmful effects of factory labor on women's bodies. Although this argument seems discriminatory by later standards, progressives at the time hailed Brandeis's achievement as a triumph. The American welfare state that emerged from female activism focused more on protecting women and children than on granting benefits to everyone, as was the case in much of western Europe with its stronger labor overtones.

Crusaders for these humane measures did not always have smooth sailing. One dismaying setback came in 1905, when the Supreme Court in *Lochner* v. *New York* invalidated a New York law establishing a ten-hour day for bakers. Yet the reformist progressive wave finally washed up into the judiciary, and in 1917 the Court upheld a ten-hour law for factory workers.

Laws regulating factories were worthless if not enforced, a truth horribly demonstrated by a lethal fire in 1911 at the Triangle Shirtwaist Company in New York City. Locked doors and other flagrant violations of the fire code turned the factory into a death trap, incinerating one hundred forty-six workers, most of them young immigrant women. Lashed by the public outcry, the legislature of New York and later other legislatures passed much stronger laws regulating the hours and conditions of sweatshop toil. By 1917 thirty states had workers' compensation laws on their books, providing insurance to workers injured in industrial accidents. Gradually, the concept of the employer's responsibility to society was replacing the old dog-eat-dog philosophy of unregulated free enterprise.

Corner saloons, with their shutter doors, naturally attracted the ire and fire of progressives. By 1900 cities such as New York and San Francisco had one saloon for about every two hundred people. Antiliquor campaigners received powerful support from several militant organizations, notably the Woman's Christian Temperance Union (WCTU). Founder Frances E. Willard, who would fall on her knees in prayer on saloon floors, mobilized nearly 1 million women to "make the world homelike" and built the WCTU into the largest organization of women in the world. She found a vigorous ally in the

Anti-Saloon League, which was aggressive, well organized, and well financed.

Caught up in the crusade, some states and numerous counties passed "dry" laws, which controlled, restricted, or abolished alcohol. The big cities were generally "wet," for they had a large immigrant vote accustomed in the Old Country to the free flow of wine and beer. When World War I erupted in 1914, nearly one-half of the population lived in "dry" territory. Demon Rum was groggy and was to be floored—temporarily—by the Eighteenth Amendment in 1919.

TR's Square Deal for Labor

Theodore Roosevelt, although something of an imperialistic busybody abroad, was touched by the progressive wave at home. Like other reformers, he feared that the "public interest" was being submerged in the drifting seas of indifference. Everybody's interest was nobody's interest. Roosevelt decided to make it his. His sportsman's instincts spurred him into demanding a "square deal" for capital, labor, and the public at large. Broadly speaking, his program embraced three C's: control of the corporations, consumer protection, and conservation of natural resources.

The Square Deal for labor received its acid test in 1902, when a crippling strike broke out in the anthracite coal mines of Pennsylvania. Some 140,000 besooted workers, many of them illiterate immigrants, had long been frightfully exploited and accident plagued. They demanded, among other improvements, a 20 percent increase in pay and a reduction in the workday from ten to nine hours.

Unsympathetic mine owners, confident that a chilled public would react against the miners, refused to arbitrate or even negotiate. One of their spokesmen, multimillionaire George F. Baer, wrote that workers would be cared for "not by the labor agitators, but by the Christian men to whom God in his infinite wisdom has given the control of the property interests of this country."

As coal supplies dwindled, factories and schools were forced to shut down, and even hospitals felt the icy grip of winter. Desperately seeking a solution, Roosevelt threatened to seize the mines and operate them with federal troops. Faced with this first-time-ever threat to use federal bayonets against capital, rather than labor, the owners grudgingly consented to arbitration. A compromise decision ultimately gave the miners a 10 percent pay boost and a workday of nine hours. But their union was not officially recognized as a bargaining agent.

Keenly aware of the mounting antagonisms between capital and labor, Roosevelt urged Congress to create a new Department of Commerce and Labor. This goal was achieved in 1903. (Ten years later the agency was split into two.) An important arm of the newly born Department of Commerce and Labor was the Bureau of Corporations, which was authorized to probe businesses engaged in interstate commerce. The bureau was highly useful in helping to break the stranglehold of monopoly and in clearing the road for the era of "trustbusting."

TR Corrals the Corporations

The sprawling railroad octopus sorely needed restraint. The Interstate Commerce Commission, created in 1887 as a feeble sop to the public, had proved woefully inadequate. Railroad barons could simply appeal the commission's decisions on rates to the federal courts—a process that might take ten years.

Spurred by the former-cowboy president, Congress passed effective railroad legislation, beginning with the Elkins Act of 1903. This curb was aimed primarily at the rebate evil. Heavy fines could now be imposed both on the railroads that gave rebates and on the shippers that accepted them.

Still more effective was the Hepburn Act of 1906. Free passes, with their hint of bribery, were severely restricted. The once-infantile Interstate Commerce Commission was expanded, and its reach was extended to include express companies, sleeping-car companies, and pipelines. For the first time, the commission was given real bite when it was authorized, on complaint of shippers, to nullify existing rates and stipulate maximum rates.

Roosevelt, as a trustbuster, first burst into the headlines in 1902 with an attack on the Northern Securities Company, a railroad holding company organized by financial titan J. P. Morgan and empire builder James J. Hill. These moguls of money sought to achieve a virtual monopoly of the railroads in the Northwest. Roosevelt was therefore challenging the most regal potentates of the industrial aristocracy.

The railway promoters appealed to the Supreme Court, which in 1904 upheld Roosevelt's antitrust suit and ordered the Northern Securities Company to be dissolved. The *Northern Securities* decision jolted Wall Street and angered big business but greatly enhanced Roosevelt's reputation as a trust smasher. Roosevelt's big stick crashed down on other giant monopolies, as he initiated over forty legal proceedings against the beef, sugar, fertilizer, harvester, and other monopolies.

Much mythology, however, has inflated Roosevelt's reputation as a trustbuster. The Rough Rider understood the political popularity of monopoly smashing, but he did not consider it sound economic policy. Combination and integration, he felt, were the hallmarks of the age, and to try to stem the tide of economic progress by political means he considered the rankest folly. Bigness was not necessarily badness, so why punish success? Roosevelt's real purpose in assaulting the Goliaths of industry was symbolic: to prove conclusively that the government, not private business, ruled the country. He believed in regulating, not fragmenting, the big business combines. The threat of dissolution, he felt, might make the sultans of the smokestacks more amenable to federal regulation—and it did.

In truth, Roosevelt never swung his trust-crushing stick with maximum force. His successor, William Howard Taft, actually "busted" more trusts than TR did. In one celebrated instance in 1907, Roosevelt even gave his personal blessing to J. P. Morgan's plan to have United States Steel Corporation absorb the Tennessee Coal and Iron Company, without fear of antitrust reprisals. When Taft then launched a suit against United States Steel in 1911, the political reaction from TR was explosive (see p. 414).

Caring for the Consumer

Roosevelt backed a noteworthy measure in 1906 that benefited both corporations and consumers. Big meatpackers were being shut out of certain European markets because some American meat—from the small packinghouses, claimed the giants—had been found to be tainted. Foreign governments were even threatening to ban all American meat imports by throwing out the good beef with the bad botulism.

At the same time, American consumers hungered for safer canned products. Their appetite for reform was whetted by Upton Sinclair's sensational novel *The Jungle*, published in 1906. Sinclair intended his revolting tract to focus attention on the plight of the workers in the big canning factories, but instead he appalled the public with his description of disgustingly unsanitary food products. (As he put it, he aimed for the nation's heart but hit its stomach.) The book described in noxious detail the filth, disease, and putrefaction in Chicago's damp, ill-ventilated slaughterhouses. A cynical jingle of the time ran

> Mary had a little lamb,
>   And when she saw it sicken,
> She shipped it off to Packingtown,
>   And now it's labeled chicken.

Backed by a nauseated public, Roosevelt induced Congress to pass the Meat Inspection Act of 1906. It decreed that the preparation of meat shipped over state lines would be subject to federal inspection from corral to can. Although the largest packers resisted certain features of the act, they accepted it as an opportunity to drive their smaller, fly-by-night competitors out of business. At the same time, they could receive the government's seal of approval on their exports. As a companion to the Meat Inspection Act, the Pure Food and Drug Act of 1906 was designed to prevent the adulteration and mislabeling of foods and pharmaceuticals.

Earth Control

Wasteful Americans, assuming that their natural resources were inexhaustible, had looted and polluted their incomparable domain with unparalleled speed and greed. Western ranchers and timbermen were especially eager to accelerate the destructive process, for they panted to build up the country, and the environmental consequences be hanged. But even before the end of the nineteenth century, far-visioned leaders saw that such a squandering of the nation's birthright would have to be halted or America would sink from resource richness to despoiled squalor.

A first serious step toward conservation was the Forest Reserve Act of 1891, authorizing the president to set aside public forest land as national forests and other reserves. Under this statute some 46 million acres of magnificent trees were rescued from the lumberman's saw in the 1890s and preserved for posterity.

A new day in the history of conservation dawned with the advent of Roosevelt. Huntsman, naturalist, rancher, lover of the great outdoors, he was appalled by the pillaging of timber and other natural resources. Other dedicated conservationists, notably Gifford Pinchot, head of the federal Division of Forestry, had broken important ground before him. But Roosevelt seized the banner of leadership and charged into the fray with all the weight of his prestige, his energy, his firsthand knowledge, and his slashing invective.

Congress responded to the whip of the Rough Rider by passing the landmark Newlands Act of 1902. Washington was authorized to collect money from the sale of public lands in the sun-baked western states and then use these funds for the development of irrigation projects. Settlers repaid the cost of reclamation from the fruits of their now-productive soil, and the money was put into a fund to finance more such enterprises.

Roosevelt pined to preserve the nation's shrinking forests. By 1900 only about a quarter of the once-vast virgin timberlands remained standing. Lumbermen had already logged off most of the virgin timber from Maine to Michigan, and the sharp thud of their axes was beginning to split the silence in the great fir forests of the Pacific slope. Roosevelt proceeded to set aside in federal reserves some 125 million acres, or almost three times the acreage thus saved from the saw by his three predecessors. He similarly earmarked millions of acres of coal deposits, as well as water resources useful for irrigation and power.

Conservation, including reclamation, may have been Roosevelt's most enduring tangible achievement. The superactive president took conservation out of the conversation stage, threw the force of his colorful personality behind it, dramatized it, and

High Point for Conservation *Conservationist Roosevelt and famed naturalist-conservationist John Muir visit Glacier Point, on the rim of Yosemite Valley, California. In the distance is Yosemite Falls; a few feet behind Roosevelt is a sheer drop of 3,254 feet (992 meters).*

aroused public opinion to a constructive crusade. He was buoyed in this effort by an upwelling national mood of concern about the disappearance of the frontier. City dwellers snapped up Jack London's *Call of the Wild* (1903) and other books about nature. Groups like the outdoor-oriented Boy Scouts of America and the Sierra Club, founded in 1892, dedicated themselves to preserving the wildness of the western landscape.

Conservationist forces were not all of one mind. The building of a dam in the Hetch Hetchy Valley in Yosemite National Park in 1913 laid bare a deep division that persists to this day. To the preservationists of the Sierra Club, including famed naturalist John Muir, Hetch Hetchy was a "temple" of nature that should be held inviolable by the civilizing hand of humanity. But other conservationists, among them President Roosevelt's chief forester, Gifford Pinchot, believed that "wilderness was waste." Pinchot and Roosevelt wanted to use their nation's natural endowment intelligently. They sought to combine recreation, sustained-yield logging, watershed protection, and summer stock grazing on the same expanse of federal land (see "Makers of America: The Environmentalists," p. 412).

At first many westerners resisted the federal management of natural resources, but they soon learned how to take advantage of new agencies like the Forest Service and especially the Bureau of Reclamation. The largest ranches and timber companies in particular figured out how to work hand in glove with federal conservation programs devoted to the rational, large-scale, and long-term use of natural resources. The one-man-and-a-mule logger or the one-man-and-a-dog sheepherder had little clout in the new resources bureaucracy. Solitary enterprises were shouldered aside, in the interest of efficiency, by the combined bulk of big business and big government.

The Rough Rider's Second Term

Roosevelt was handily elected president in his own right in 1904 and entered his new term buoyed up by his enormous personal popularity. Yet the conservative Republican bosses grew increasingly restive as Roosevelt in his second term called ever more loudly for regulating the corporations, taxing incomes, and protecting workers. Roosevelt, meanwhile, had partly defanged himself after his election in 1904 by announcing that under no circumstances would he be a candidate for a third term.

Roosevelt suffered a sharp setback in 1907, when a short but punishing panic descended on Wall Street. The financial flurry featured frightened "runs" on banks, suicides, and criminal indictments against speculators. The financial world hastened to blame Roosevelt for the storm. It cried that this "quack" had unsettled industry with his boat-rocking tactics and branded the current distress the "Roosevelt panic." The hot-tempered president angrily lashed back at his critics when he accused "certain malefactors of great wealth" of having deliberately engineered the monetary crisis to force the government to relax its assaults on trusts.

Still warmly popular in 1908, Roosevelt could easily have won a second presidential nomination

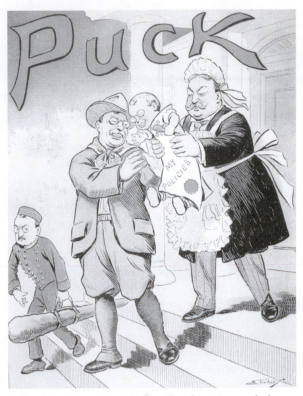

Baby, Kiss Papa Good-bye *Theodore Roosevelt leaves his baby, "My Policies," in the hands of his chosen successor, William Howard Taft. Friction between Taft and Roosevelt would soon erupt, however, prompting Roosevelt to return to politics and challenge Taft for the presidency.*

and almost certainly the election. But he felt bound by his impulsive postelection promise after his victory in 1904. The departing president thus naturally sought a successor who would carry out "my policies." The man of his choice was amiable, ample-girthed, and huge-framed William Howard Taft, secretary of war and a mild progressive.

As heir apparent, Taft had often been called upon in Roosevelt's absence to "sit on the lid"—all 350 pounds of him. At the Republican convention of 1908 in Chicago, Roosevelt used his control of the party machinery—the "steamroller"—to push through Taft's nomination on the first ballot. Three weeks later, in mile-high Denver, in the heart of silver country, the Democrats nominated twice-beaten William Jennings Bryan.

The Environmentalists

Humans have long been awed by nature, but they have also yearned to be its masters. The earliest European colonists saw North America as a "howling wilderness" and toiled mightily with ax and plow to tame it. By the mid-nineteenth century, Americans commanded powerful new technologies that promised unbridled dominion over the natural world. Only then did voices begin to be heard in defense of the wounded earth—the first faint stirrings of what would come to be called "environmentalism."

In a pattern that would often be repeated, nature's earliest defenders tended to be well-off townsfolk and city dwellers like Henry David Thoreau and Ralph Waldo Emerson. The Americans most likely to appreciate the value of pristine wilderness, it seemed, were those who had ceased to struggle against it. For the loggers, miners, and farmers who continued to sweat their living out of nature's grudging embrace, concern for environmental niceties often seemed like the sanctimonious piety of a privileged elite.

By the dawn of the twentieth century, many genteel, urban Americans had come to romanticize their pioneer forebears. Preservationists like John Muir waxed lyrical about the mystic allure of unspoiled nature. Theodore Roosevelt deliberately constructed an image of himself as a manly outdoorsman and hunter. Roosevelt also pioneered the progressive conservation movement, which believed that nature must neither be uncritically reverenced nor wastefully exploited. Thus the same TR who admired the wonders of Yosemite Valley in the company of John Muir promoted the "rational use" philosophy that justified the systematic harvesting of trees in order to provide lumber for homebuilders. This attitude toward nature triumphed in the New Deal era of the 1930s, when the federal government initiated colossal projects—like the Tennessee Valley Authority,

the Soil Conservation Service, and the Shelterbelt tree-planting on the Great Plains—that actually reengineered the face of the continent.

The rise of ecological science in the post–World War II era fundamentally changed the debate about the relation of nature to civilization. Ecologists charged that the apparent "rationality" of the earlier conservationists dangerously neglected the stunningly complex interrelationships that linked together seemingly unrelated organisms, and the perils of tampering even slightly with biological fabrics. Rachel Carson helped to popularize this new outlook in her sensational 1962 exposé, *Silent Spring*, about the far-reaching effects of pesticides on birds, plants, and animals—including humans.

The advent of ecological studies coincided with a revival of preservationist sentiment, especially in the swelling suburbs. Membership in environmental organizations such as the Sierra Club and the Audubon Society soared, as a generation infatuated with nature demanded a clean and green world. The year 1970 saw the first Earth Day, marking the maturation of modern-day environmentalism, and the creation of the federal Environmental Protection Agency (EPA), which signaled a new governmental commitment to regulating the relationship between humans and nature.

At the outset of the twenty-first century, developments like global warming served dramatic notice that planet earth was an ecological system that did not recognize national boundaries. Yet who were Americans, who had long ago consumed their timberlands and dammed their rivers, to tell the Brazilians not to cut down their Amazon forest or the Chinese not to construct dams? For the peoples of the developing world, struggling to match America's standard of living, environmentalists often seemed like spoiled spoilers, preaching the same privileged pieties that had infuriated generations of working Americans.

The dull campaign of 1908 featured the rotund Taft and the now-balding "Boy Orator" trying to claim the progressive Roosevelt mantle. The solid Judge Taft read cut-and-dried speeches while Bryan griped that Roosevelt had stolen his policies from the Bryanite camp. A majority of voters chose stability with Roosevelt-endorsed Taft, who polled 321 electoral votes to 162 for Bryan. The victor's popular count was 7,675,320 to 6,412,294. The election's only surprise came from the Socialists, who amassed 420,793 votes for Eugene V. Debs, the hero of the Pullman strike of 1894.

Roosevelt, ever in the limelight, left soon after the election for a lion hunt in Africa. His numerous enemies clinked glasses while toasting "Health to the lions," and a few irreverently prayed that some big cat would "do its duty." But TR survived, still bursting with energy at the age of fifty-one in 1909.

Roosevelt was branded by his adversaries as a wild-eyed radical, but his reputation as an eater of errant industrialists now seems inflated. He fought many a sham battle, and the number of laws that he inspired was certainly not in proportion to the amount of noise he emitted. He was often under attack from the reigning business lords, but the more enlightened of them knew that they had a friend in the White House. Roosevelt should be remembered first and foremost as the cowboy who started to tame the bucking bronco of adolescent capitalism, thus ensuring it a long adult life.

TR's enthusiasm and perpetual youthfulness, like an overgrown Boy Scout's, appealed to the young of all ages. "You must always remember," a British diplomat cautioned his colleagues, "that the president is about six." He served as a political lightning rod to protect capitalists against popular indignation—and against socialism, which Roosevelt regarded as "ominous." He strenuously sought the middle road between unbridled individualism and paternalistic collectivism. His conservation crusade, which tried to mediate between the romantic wilderness-preservationists and the rapacious resource-predators, was probably his most typical and his most lasting achievement.

Several other contributions of Roosevelt lasted beyond his presidency. First, he greatly enlarged the power and prestige of the presidential office—and masterfully developed the technique of using the big stick of publicity as a political bludgeon. Second, he

helped shape the progressive movement and beyond it the liberal reform campaigns later in the century. His Square Deal, in a sense, was the grandfather of the New Deal later launched by his fifth cousin, Franklin D. Roosevelt. Finally, to a greater degree than any of his predecessors, TR opened the eyes of Americans to the fact that they shared the world with other nations. As a great power they had fallen heir to great responsibilities—and had been seized by great ambitions—from which there was no escaping.

Taft: A Round Peg in a Square Hole

William Howard Taft, with his ruddy complexion and upturned mustache, at first inspired widespread confidence. "Everybody loves a fat man," the saying goes, and the jovial Taft, with "mirthquakes" of laughter bubbling up from his abundant abdomen, was personally popular. He had graduated second in his class at Yale and established an admirable reputation as a lawyer and judge, though widely regarded as hostile to labor unions. He had been a trusted administrator under Roosevelt—in the Philippines, at home, and in Cuba, where he had served capably as a troubleshooter.

But "good old Will" suffered from lethal political handicaps. Roosevelt had led the conflicting elements of the Republican party by the sheer force of his personality. Taft, in contrast, had none of the arts of a dashing political leader, and none of Roosevelt's zest for the fray. Recoiling from the clamor of controversy, he generally adopted an attitude of passivity toward Congress. He was a poor judge of public opinion, and his candor made him a chronic victim of "foot-in-mouth" disease.

"Peaceful Bill" was no doubt a mild progressive, but at heart he was more wedded to the status quo than to change. Significantly, his cabinet did not contain a single representative of the party's "insurgent" wing, which was on fire for reform of current abuses, especially the tariff.

The Dollar Goes Abroad as a Diplomat

Though ordinarily lethargic, Taft bestirred himself to use the lever of American investments to boost American political interests abroad. Washington warmly encouraged Wall Street bankers to sluice their surplus dollars into foreign areas of strategic concern to the United States, especially in East Asia and in the regions critical to the security of the Panama Canal. New York bankers would thus strengthen American defenses and foreign policies while bringing further prosperity to their homeland—and to themselves. The almighty dollar thereby supplanted the big stick.

China's Manchuria was the object of Taft's most spectacular effort to inject the reluctant dollar into the East Asian theater. Newly ambitious Japan and imperialistic Russia, recent foes, controlled the railroads of this strategic province. President Taft saw in the Manchurian railway monopoly a possible strangulation of Chinese economic interests and a consequent slamming of the Open Door in the faces of U.S. merchants. An American attempt to persuade foreign investors to invest in Manchurian railroads ran into stiff Japanese and Russian opposition.

Another dangerous new trouble spot was the revolution-riddled Caribbean—now virtually a Yankee lake. Hoping to head off trouble, Washington urged Wall Street bankers to pump dollars into the financial vacuums in Honduras and Haiti to keep out foreign funds. But dollar diplomacy did not bring an end to armed Caribbean intervention. Sporadic disorders in palm-fronded Cuba, Honduras, and the Dominican Republic brought American forces to these countries to restore order. A revolutionary upheaval in Nicaragua, perilously close to the nearly completed canal, resulted in the landing of twenty-five hundred U.S. Marines in 1912.

Taft the Trustbuster

Taft managed to gain some fame as a smasher of monopolies. The ironic truth is that the colorless Taft brought ninety suits against the trusts during his four years in office, compared with some forty-four for Roosevelt in seven and a half years.

By fateful happenstance the most sensational judicial actions during the Taft regime came in 1911. In that year the Supreme Court ordered dissolution of the mighty Standard Oil Company, which was judged to be a combination in restraint of trade in violation of the Sherman Anti-Trust Act of 1890. At the same time the Court handed down its famous "rule of reason." This doctrine held that only those combinations that "unreasonably" restrained trade were illegal. This fine-point proviso ripped a huge hole in the government's antitrust net.

Even more explosively, in 1911 Taft decided to press an antitrust suit against United States Steel Corporation. This initiative infuriated Roosevelt, who had personally been involved in one of the mergers that prompted the suit. Once Roosevelt's protégé, President Taft was increasingly taking on the role of his antagonist. The stage was being set for a bruising confrontation.

Taft Splits the Republican Party

Lowering the barriers of the high protective tariff—the "Mother of Trusts"—was high on the agenda of the progressive members of the Republican party, and they at first thought they had a friend and ally in Taft. When the president called Congress into special session in March 1909, the House passed a moderately reductive bill. But senatorial reactionaries, led by Senator Nelson Aldrich of Rhode Island, tacked on hundreds of upward tariff revisions. Only such items as hides, sea moss, and canary-bird seed were left on the duty-free list.

After much handwringing, Taft signed the Payne-Aldrich Bill, thus betraying his campaign promises and outraging the progressive wing of his party, heavily drawn from the Midwest. Taft rubbed salt in the wound by proclaiming it "the best bill that the Republican party ever passed."

Taft revealed a further knack for shooting himself in the foot in his handling of conservation. The portly president was a dedicated conservationist, and his contributions actually equaled or surpassed those of Roosevelt. He set up the Bureau of Mines to control mineral resources, rescued millions of acres of western coal lands from exploitation, and protected water-power sites from private development. But those praiseworthy accomplishments were largely erased in the public mind by the noisy Ballinger-Pinchot quarrel that erupted in 1910.

When Secretary of the Interior Richard Ballinger opened public lands in Wyoming, Montana, and

Alaska to corporate development, he was sharply criticized by Gifford Pinchot, chief of the Agriculture Department's Division of Forestry and a stalwart Rooseveltian. When Taft dismissed Pinchot on the narrow grounds of insubordination, a storm of protest arose from conservationists and from Roosevelt's friends, who were legion. The whole unsavory episode further widened the growing rift between the president and the former president, one-time close political partners.

The reformist wing of the Republican party was up in arms, as Taft was increasingly drawn into the embrace of the stand-pat Old Guard. By the spring of 1910, the Grand Old Party was split wide open, owing largely to the clumsiness of Taft. A suspicious Roosevelt returned triumphantly to New York in June 1910 and shortly thereafter stirred up a tempest. In a flaming speech at Osawatamie, Kansas, he proclaimed a doctrine—popularly known as the "New Nationalism"—that urged the national government to increase its power to remedy economic and social abuses.

Weakened by these internal divisions, the Republicans lost badly in the congressional elections of 1910. The Democrats emerged from their landslide victory with 228 seats to only 161 for the once-dominant Republicans. In a further symptom of the reforming temper of the times, a Socialist representative, Austrian-born Victor L. Berger, was elected from Milwaukee.* The Republicans, by virtue of holdovers,

---

* Berger was eventually denied his seat in 1919, during a wave of anti-red hysteria.

retained the Senate, 51 to 41, but the insurgents in their midst were numerous enough to make that hold precarious.

The Taft-Roosevelt Rupture

The sputtering uprising in Republican ranks now blossomed into a full-fledged revolt. Early in 1911 the National Progressive Republican League was formed, with the fiery, white-maned Senator Robert La Follette of Wisconsin its leading candidate for the Republican presidential nomination. The assumption was that Roosevelt would not permit himself to be "drafted."

But the restless Rough Rider began to change his views about third terms as he saw Taft coming under the thumb of the hated Old Guard and discarding "my policies." In February 1912 Roosevelt formally wrote to seven state governors that he was willing to accept the Republican nomination. His reasoning was that the third-term tradition applied to three consecutive elective terms. Exuberantly he cried, "My hat is in the ring!" and "The fight is on and I am stripped to the buff!"

Roosevelt forthwith seized the Progressive banner, while La Follette, who had served as a convenient pathbreaker, was protestingly elbowed aside. Girded for battle, the Rough Rider clattered into the presidential primaries then being held in many states. He shouted through half-clenched teeth that the president had fallen under the thumb of the reactionary

Roosevelt the Take-Back Giver

bosses and that although Taft "means well, he means well feebly." The once-genial Taft, now in a fighting mood, branded Roosevelt supporters as "emotionalists and neurotics."

A Taft-Roosevelt explosion was near in June 1912, when the Republican convention met in Chicago. The Rooseveltites, who were about 100 delegates short of winning the nomination, challenged the right of some 250 Taft delegates to be seated. Most of these contests were arbitrarily settled in favor of Taft, whose supporters held the throttle of the convention juggernaut. The Roosevelt adherents, crying "fraud" and "naked theft," in the end refused to vote, and Taft triumphed.

Roosevelt, the supposedly good sportsman, refused to quit the game. Having tasted for once the bitter cup of defeat, he was now on fire to lead a third-party crusade.

Chronology

1901 Commission system established in Galveston, Texas.
Progressive Robert La Follette elected governor of Wisconsin.

1902 Lincoln Steffens and Ida Tarbell publish muckraking exposés.
Anthracite coal strike.
Newlands Act.

1903 Department of Commerce and Labor established.
Elkins Act.

1904 *Northern Securities* case.
Roosevelt defeats Alton B. Parker for presidency.

1905 *Lochner* v. *New York*.

1906 Hepburn Act.
Upton Sinclair publishes *The Jungle*.
Meat Inspection Act.
Pure Food and Drug Act.

1907 "Roosevelt panic."

1908 *Muller* v. *Oregon*.
Taft defeats Bryan for presidency.

1909 Payne-Aldrich Tariff.

1910 Ballinger-Pinchot affair.

1911 Triangle Shirtwaist Company fire.
Standard Oil antitrust case.
U.S. Steel Corporation antitrust suit.

1912 Taft wins Republican nomination over Roosevelt.

1913 Seventeenth Amendment passed (direct election of U.S. senators).

For further reading, see the Appendix. For web resources, go to **http://college.hmco.com**.

Wilsonian Progressivism at Home and Abroad

1912–1916

American enterprise is not free; the man with only a little capital is finding it harder and harder to get into the field, more and more impossible to compete with the big fellow. Why? Because the laws of this country do not prevent the strong from crushing the weak.

WOODROW WILSON, THE NEW FREEDOM, 1913

Office-hungry Democrats—the "outs" since 1897—were jubilant over the disruptive Republican brawl at Chicago. If they could come up with an outstanding reformist leader, they had an excellent chance to win the White House. Such a leader appeared in Dr. Woodrow Wilson, once a mild conservative but now a militant progressive. Beginning professional life as a brilliant academic lecturer on government, he rose in 1902 to the presidency of Princeton University, where he achieved some sweeping educational reforms.

Wilson entered politics in 1910 when New Jersey bosses, needing a respectable "front" candidate for the governorship, offered him the nomination. They expected to lead the academic novice by the nose, but to their surprise, Wilson waged a passionate reform campaign in which he assailed the "predatory" trusts and promised to return state government to the people. Riding the crest of the progressive wave, the "Schoolmaster in Politics" was swept into office.

Once in the governor's chair, Wilson drove through the legislature a sheaf of forward-looking measures that made reactionary New Jersey one of the more liberal states. Filled with righteous indignation, Wilson revealed irresistible reforming zeal, burning eloquence, superb powers of leadership, and a refreshing habit of appealing over the heads of the scheming bosses to the sovereign people. Now a figure of national eminence, Wilson was being widely mentioned for the presidency.

The "Bull Moose" Campaign of 1912

When the Democrats met at Baltimore in 1912, Wilson was nominated on the forty-sixth ballot, aided by William Jennings Bryan's switch to his side. The Democrats gave Wilson a strong progressive platform to run on, including calls for antitrust legislation, banking reform, and tariff reductions.

Surging events had meanwhile been thrusting Roosevelt to the fore as a candidate for the presidency on a third-party Progressive Republican ticket. The fighting ex-cowboy, angered by his recent rebuff, was eager to lead the charge. A pro-Roosevelt Progressive convention, with about two thousand delegates from forty states, assembled in Chicago during August 1912. Dramatically symbolizing the rising political status of women, as well as Progressive support for the cause of social justice, settlement-house pioneer Jane Addams placed Roosevelt's name in nomination for the presidency.

Fired-up Progressives entered the campaign with righteousness and enthusiasm. Roosevelt boasted that he felt "as strong as a bull moose," so the bull moose took its place with the donkey and the elephant in the American political zoo. As one poet whimsically put it,

> I want to be a Bull Moose,
> And with the Bull Moose stand
> With antlers on my forehead
> And a Big Stick in my hand.

Roosevelt and Taft were bound to slit each other's political throats: by dividing the Republican vote they virtually guaranteed a Democratic victory. The two antagonists tore into each other as only former friends can. "Death alone can take me out now," cried the once-jovial Taft, as he branded Roosevelt a "dangerous egotist" and a "demagogue." Roosevelt, fighting mad, assailed Taft as a "fathead" with the brain of a "guinea pig."

Beyond the clashing personalities, the overshadowing question of the 1912 campaign was which of two varieties of progressivism would prevail—Roosevelt's New Nationalism or Wilson's New Freedom. Both men favored a more active government role in economic and social affairs, but they disagreed sharply over specific strategies. Roosevelt preached the theories spun out by the progressive thinker Herbert Croly in his book *The Promise of American Life* (1910). Croly and TR both favored continued consolidation of trusts and labor unions, paralleled by the growth of powerful regulatory agencies in Washington. Roosevelt and his "bull moosers" also campaigned for woman suffrage and a broad program of social welfare, including minimum-wage laws and social insurance. Clearly, the bull moose Progressives looked forward to the kind of activist welfare state that Franklin Roosevelt's New Deal would one day make a reality.

Wilson's New Freedom, by contrast, favored small enterprise, entrepreneurship, and the free functioning of unregulated and unmonopolized markets. The Democrats shunned social welfare propos-

GOP Divided by Bull Moose Equals Democratic Victory, 1912

als and pinned their economic faith on competition—on the "man on the make," as Wilson put it. The keynote of Wilson's campaign was not regulation but fragmentation of the big industrial combines, chiefly by means of vigorous enforcement of the antitrust laws. The election of 1912 thus offered the voters a choice not merely of policies but of political and economic philosophies—a rarity in United States history.

The heat of the campaign cooled a bit when, in Milwaukee, Roosevelt was shot in the chest by a fanatic. The Rough Rider suspended active campaigning for more than two weeks after delivering, with bull moose gameness and a bloody shirt, his scheduled speech.

Woodrow Wilson: A Minority President

Former professor Wilson won handily, with 435 electoral votes and 6,296,547 popular votes. The "third-party" candidate, former president Roosevelt, finished second, with 88 electoral votes and 4,118,571 popular votes. Taft won only 8 electoral votes and 3,486,720 popular votes.

The election figures are fascinating. Wilson, with only 41 percent of the popular vote, was clearly a minority president, though his party won a majority in Congress. Wilson's popular total was actually smaller than Bryan's in any of his three defeats, despite the increase in population. Taft and Roosevelt together polled over a million and a quarter more votes than the Democrats. Progressivism rather than Wilson was the runaway winner. Although the Democratic total obviously included many conservatives in the solid South, the combined progressive vote for Wilson and Roosevelt still exceeded the tally of the more conservative Taft. To the progressive totals must be added some support for the Socialist candidate, persistent Eugene V. Debs, who rolled up 900,672 votes, or more than twice as many as he had netted four years earlier. Starry-eyed Socialists dreamed of being in the White House within eight years.

Roosevelt's lone-wolf course was tragic both for himself and for his former Republican associates. The Progressive party, which was primarily a one-man show, had no future because it had elected few candidates to state and local offices. Without patronage plums to hand out to the faithful workers, death by slow starvation was inevitable. Yet the Progressives made a tremendous showing for a hastily organized third party and helped spur the enactment of many of their pet reforms by the Wilsonian Democrats.

As for the Republicans, they were thrust into unaccustomed minority status in Congress for the next six years and were frozen out of the White House for eight years. Taft himself had a fruitful old age. He taught law for eight pleasant years at Yale University and in 1921 became chief justice of the Supreme Court—a job for which he was far more happily suited than the presidency.

Wilson: The Idealist in Politics

(Thomas) Woodrow Wilson, the second Democratic president since 1861, looked like the ascetic intellectual he was, with clean-cut features, pinched-on eyeglasses, and trim figure. Born in Virginia shortly before

The Presidential Vote, 1912

Candidate	Party	Electoral Vote	Popular Vote	Approximate Percentage
Woodrow Wilson	Democratic	435	6,296,547	41%
Theodore Roosevelt	Progressive	88	4,118,571	27
William H. Taft	Republican	8	3,486,720	23
Eugene V. Debs	Socialist	—	900,672	6
E. W. Chafin	Prohibition	—	206,275	1
A. E. Reimer	Socialist-Labor	—	28,750	0.2

the Civil War and reared in Georgia and the Carolinas, the professor-politician was the first man from one of the seceded southern states to reach the White House since Zachary Taylor, sixty-four years earlier.

Son of a Presbyterian minister, Wilson was reared in an atmosphere of fervent piety. He later used the presidential pulpit to preach his inspirational political sermons. A moving orator, Wilson could rise on the wings of spiritual power to soaring eloquence. Skillfully using a persuasive voice, he relied not on arm waving but on sincerity and moral appeal. As a lifelong student of finely chiseled words, he turned out to be a "phraseocrat" who coined many noble epigrams. Someone remarked that he was born halfway between the Bible and the dictionary and never strayed far from either.

Splendid though Wilson's intellectual equipment was, he suffered from serious defects of personality. Though jovial and witty in private, he could be cold and standoffish in public. Incapable of unbending and acting the showman, like "Teddy" Roosevelt, he lacked the common touch. He loved humanity in the mass rather than the individual in person. His academic background caused him to feel most at home with scholars, although he had to work with politicians. An austere and somewhat arrogant intellectual, he looked down his nose through pince-nez glasses upon lesser minds, including journalists. He was especially intolerant of stupid senators, whose "bungalow" minds made him "sick."

Wilson's burning idealism—especially his desire to reform ever-present wickedness—drove him forward faster than lesser spirits were willing to go. His sense of moral righteousness was such that he often found compromise difficult: black was black, wrong was wrong, and one should never compromise with wrong. Wilson's Scottish Presbyterian ancestors had passed on to him an inflexible stubbornness. When convinced that he was right, he would break before he would bend, unlike the pragmatic Roosevelt.

Wilson Attacks the "Triple Wall of Privilege"

Few presidents have arrived at the White House with a clearer program than Wilson's or one destined to be so completely achieved. The new president called for an all-out assault on what he called the "triple wall of privilege": the tariff, the banks, and the trusts.

Wilson tackled the tariff first. In a precedent-shattering move, he appeared in person before a joint session of Congress in 1913 and presented his appeal with stunning eloquence and effectiveness. Moved by Wilson's aggressive leadership, the House swiftly passed the Underwood Tariff Bill, which provided for a substantial reduction of rates. It was also a landmark in tax legislation. Under authority granted by the recently ratified Sixteenth Amendment, Congress enacted a graduated income tax, beginning with a modest levy on incomes over $3,000 (then considerably higher than the average family's income). By 1917 revenue from the income tax shot ahead of receipts from the tariff. This gap has since been vastly widened.

A second bastion of the "triple wall of privilege" was the antiquated and inadequate banking and currency system, long since outgrown by the Republic's lusty economic expansion. The most serious shortcoming of the country's financial structure, as exposed by the panic of 1907, was the inelasticity of the currency. Banking reserves were heavily concentrated in New York and a handful of other large cities and could not be mobilized in times of financial stress into areas that were badly pinched.

In 1911 a special commission headed by ultra-conservative Republican Senator Nelson Aldrich recommended a gigantic bank with numerous branches—in effect, a third Bank of the United States. Democratic banking reformers preferred the findings of a House committee chaired by Congressman Arsene Pujo, which traced the tentacles of the "money monster" into the hidden vaults of American banking and business. President Wilson's confidant, progressive-minded Massachusetts attorney Louis D. Brandeis, further fanned the flames of reform with his incendiary though scholarly book *Other People's Money and How the Bankers Use It* (1914).

In June 1913, in a second dramatic personal appearance before Congress, the president ringingly endorsed sweeping Democratic proposals for a decentralized bank in government hands, as opposed to Republican demands for a huge private bank. Again appealing to the sovereign people, Wilson scored another triumph. In 1913 he signed the Federal Reserve Act, the most important piece of economic legislation between the Civil War and the New Deal.

The new Federal Reserve Board, appointed by the president, oversaw a nationwide system of twelve regional reserve districts, each with its own central bank. Although these regional banks were actually bankers' banks, owned by member financial institutions, the final authority of the Federal Reserve Board guaranteed a substantial measure of public control. The board was also empowered to issue paper money—"Federal Reserve notes"—backed by commercial paper, such as the promissory notes of businesspeople. Thus the amount of money in circulation could be swiftly increased as needed for the legitimate requirements of business.

The Federal Reserve Act was a red-letter achievement. It carried the nation with flying banners through the financial crises of the World War of 1914–1918. Without it, the Republic's progress toward the modern economic age would have been seriously retarded.

Without pausing for breath, Wilson pushed toward the last remaining rampart in the "triple wall of privilege"—the trusts. A third personal appearance before Congress in 1914 led to the Federal Trade Commission Act of 1914. The new law empowered a presidentially appointed commission to turn a searchlight on industries engaged in interstate commerce, such as the meatpackers. The commissioners were expected to crush monopoly in the cradle by rooting out unfair trade practices, including unlawful competition, false advertising, mislabeling, adulteration, and bribery.

The knot of monopoly was further cut by the Clayton Anti-Trust Act of 1914. It lengthened the shopworn Sherman Act's list of business practices that were deemed objectionable, including price discrimination and interlocking directorates (whereby the same individuals served as directors of supposedly competing firms).

The Clayton Act also conferred long-overdue benefits on labor. The law exempted labor and agricultural organizations from antitrust prosecutions under the Sherman Act, while explicitly legalizing strikes and peaceful picketing. Union leader Samuel Gompers hailed the act as the Magna Carta of labor because it legally lifted human labor out of the category of "a commodity or article of commerce." But the rejoicing was premature, as conservative judges in later years continued to clip the wings of the union movement.

Wilsonian Progressivism at High Tide

Energetically scaling the "triple wall of privilege," Woodrow Wilson had treated the nation to a dazzling demonstration of vigorous presidential leadership. He proved nearly irresistible in his first eighteen months in office. For once, a political creed was matched by deed as the progressive reformers racked up victory after victory.

Standing at the peak of his powers at the head of the progressive forces, Wilson pressed ahead with further reforms. The Federal Farm Loan Act of 1916 made credit available to farmers at low rates of interest—as long demanded by the Populists. Sweaty laborers also made gains as the progressive wave foamed forward. Sailors, treated brutally from cat-o'-nine-tails days onward, were given relief by the La Follette Seamen's Act of 1915. It required decent treatment and a living wage on American merchant ships.

Wilson further helped workers with the Workingmen's Compensation Act of 1916, granting assistance to federal civil-service employees during periods of disability. In the same year the president approved an act restricting child labor on products flowing into interstate commerce, though the stand-pat Supreme Court soon invalidated the law. The Adamson Act of 1916 established an eight-hour workday for all employees on trains in interstate commerce, with extra pay for overtime.

Wilson earned the enmity of businesspeople and bigots but endeared himself to progressives when in 1916 he nominated for the Supreme Court the prominent reformer Louis D. Brandeis—the first Jew to be called to the high bench. Yet even Wilson's progressivism had its limits, and it clearly stopped short of better treatment for blacks. The southern-bred Wilson actually presided over accelerated segregation in the federal bureaucracy. When a delegation of black leaders personally protested to him, the schoolmasterish president virtually froze them out of his office.

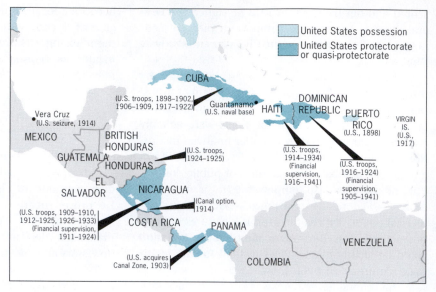

The United States in the Caribbean   *This map explains why many Latin Americans accused the United States of turning the Caribbean Sea into a Yankee lake. It also suggests that Uncle Sam was much less "isolationist" in his own backyard than he was in faraway Europe or Asia.*

Despite these limitations, Wilson knew that to be reelected in 1916, he needed to identify himself clearly as the candidate of progressivism. Wilson's election in 1912 had been something of a fluke, owing largely to the Taft-Roosevelt split in the Republican ranks. To remain in the White House, the president would have to woo the bull moose voters into the Democratic fold.

New Directions in Foreign Policy

In one important area, Wilson chose not to answer the trumpet call of the bull moosers. In contrast to Roosevelt and even Taft, Wilson recoiled from an aggressive foreign policy. Hating imperialism, he was repelled by TR's big stickism. Suspicious of Wall Street, he detested the so-called dollar diplomacy of Taft.

In office only a week, Wilson declared war on dollar diplomacy. He proclaimed that the government would no longer offer special support to American investors in Latin America and China. Shivering from this Wilsonian bucket of cold water, American bankers pulled out of the Taft-engineered six-nation loan to China the next day. Wilson's anti-imperialism also produced the Jones Act of 1916, which granted territorial status and promised eventual independence for the Philippines.

Events in the Caribbean soon forced Wilson to eat some of his anti-imperialist words. In response to dis-

orders in Haiti in 1914–1915, the president reluctantly dispatched marines to protect American lives and property. In 1916 he stole a page from the Roosevelt Corollary to the Monroe Doctrine and concluded a treaty with Haiti providing for U.S. supervision of finances and police. In the same year, Wilson sent the leathernecked marines to the riot-rocked Dominican Republic, which came under the shadow of the American eagle's wings. In 1917 Wilson purchased from Denmark the Virgin Islands in the West Indies. Increasingly the Caribbean Sea, with its vital approaches to the now-completed Panama Canal, was taking on the earmarks of a Yankee preserve.

Moralistic Diplomacy in Mexico

Rifle bullets whining across the southern border served as a constant reminder that all was not quiet in Mexico. For decades Mexico had been sorely exploited by foreign investors in oil, railroads, and mines. By 1913 American capitalists had sunk about a billion dollars into the underdeveloped but richly endowed country. But if Mexico was rich, the Mexicans were poor. Fed up with their miserable lot, they at last revolted.

Their revolution took an ugly turn in 1913, when a conscienceless clique murdered the popular new revolutionary president and installed General Victoriano Huerta, an Indian, in the president's chair. All this chaos accelerated a massive migration of Mexicans to the United States. More than a million Spanish-speaking newcomers tramped across the southern border in the first three decades of the twentieth century. Settling mostly in Texas, New Mexico, Arizona, and California, they helped to create a unique borderland culture that blended Mexican and American folkways. The revolutionary bloodshed also menaced American lives and property in Mexico. Cries for intervention burst from the lips of American jingoes like publisher William Randolph Hearst, owner of a Mexican ranch larger than Rhode Island.

Wilson stood firm against demands to step in. He also refused to recognize the murderous government of "that brute" Huerta. "I am going to teach the South American republics to elect good men," the former professor declared. He put his munitions where his mouth was in 1914, when he allowed American arms to flow to Huerta's principal rivals, white-bearded Venustiano Carranza and the firebrand Francisco ("Pancho") Villa.

The Mexican volcano erupted at the Atlantic seaport of Tampico in April 1914, when a small party of American sailors was arrested. The Mexicans promptly released the captives and apologized, but they refused the hotheaded American admiral's demand for a salute of twenty-one guns. Wilson then ordered the navy to seize the Mexican port of Vera Cruz. Huerta as well as Carranza hotly condemned this high-handed Yankee intervention.

Just as a full-dress shooting conflict seemed inevitable, Wilson was rescued by an offer of mediation from the ABC powers—Argentina, Brazil, and Chile. Huerta collapsed in July 1914 under pressure from within and without. He was succeeded by his archrival, Venustiano Carranza, still fiercely resentful of Wilson's military meddling. The whole sorry episode did not augur well for the future of United States–Mexican relations.

"Pancho" Villa, a combination of bandit and Robin Hood, had meanwhile emerged as the chief rival of President Carranza, whom Wilson now reluctantly supported. Villa punished the "gringos" by killing sixteen young American mining engineers who were traveling through northern Mexico in January 1916. A month later Villa's men murdered nineteen more Americans during a raid across the border into Columbus, New Mexico.

General John J. ("Black Jack"*) Pershing, a ramrod-erect veteran of the Cuban and Philippine campaigns, was ordered to break up the bandit band. His hastily organized force of several thousand mounted troops penetrated deep into rugged Mexico with surprising speed. They clashed with Carranza's forces and mauled the Villistas but missed capturing Villa himself. As the threat of war with Germany loomed larger, the invading army was withdrawn in January 1917.

A Precarious Neutrality

Europe's powder magazine, long smoldering, blew up in the summer of 1914, when the flaming pistol of a Serb patriot killed the heir to the throne of Austria-Hungary in Sarajevo. An outraged Vienna government, backed by Germany, forthwith presented a stern ultimatum to Serbia.

An explosive chain reaction followed. Russian mobilization in support of Serbia threatened Germany in the east, even as the tsar's ally, France, confronted Germany in the west. In alarm, the Germans struck suddenly at France through unoffending Belgium. Great Britain in turn was sucked into the conflagration on the side of France.

Almost overnight most of Europe was locked in a fight to the death. On one side were arrayed the Central Powers: Germany and Austria-Hungary, and later Turkey and Bulgaria. On the other side were the Allies, principally France, Britain, and Russia, and later Japan and Italy. Americans thanked God for the ocean moats and self-righteously congratulated themselves on having had ancestors wise enough to have abandoned the hell pits of Europe. Americans felt strong, snug, smug, and secure—but not for long.

President Wilson sorrowfully issued the routine neutrality proclamation and called on Americans to be neutral in thought as well as deed. But such scrupulous evenhandedness proved difficult. Both sides wooed the United States, the great neutral to the west. The British enjoyed the boon of close cultural, linguistic, and economic ties with America and had the added advantage of controlling most of the

---

* So called from his earlier service as an officer with the crack black Tenth Cavalry.

transatlantic cables. Their censors sheared away war stories harmful to the Allies and drenched the United States with tales of German bestiality.

Some German-American immigrants expressed noisy sympathy for the fatherland, but most Americans were anti-German from the outset. With his villainous upturned mustache, Kaiser Wilhelm II seemed the embodiment of arrogant autocracy, an impression strengthened by Germany's ruthless strike at neutral Belgium. Inept German plans for industrial sabotage in the United States further inflamed opinion against the kaiser and Germany. Yet the great majority of Americans earnestly hoped to stay out of the horrible war.

America Earns Blood Money

When Europe burst into flames in 1914, the United States was bogged down in a worrisome business recession. But as fate would have it, British and French war orders soon pulled American industry out of the morass of hard times and onto a peak of war-born prosperity. Part of this boom was financed by American bankers, notably the Wall Street firm of J. P. Morgan and Company, which eventually advanced to the Allies the enormous sum of $2.3 billion during the period of American neutrality. The Central Powers protested bitterly against the immense trade between America and the Allies, but this traffic did not in fact violate international neutrality laws. Germany was technically free to trade with the United States, but the tight British naval blockade prevented it from doing so.

Hard-pressed Germany did not tamely consent to being starved out. In retaliation for the British blockade, in February 1915 Berlin announced a submarine war area around the British Isles. The submarine was a weapon so new that existing international law could not be made to fit it. The old rule that a warship must stop and board a merchantman could hardly apply to submarines, which could easily be rammed or sunk if they surfaced.

The cigar-shaped marauders posed a dire threat to the United States—as long as Wilson insisted on maintaining America's neutral rights. Berlin officials declared that they would try not to sink neutral shipping, but they warned that mistakes would probably occur. Wilson now determined on a policy of calcu-

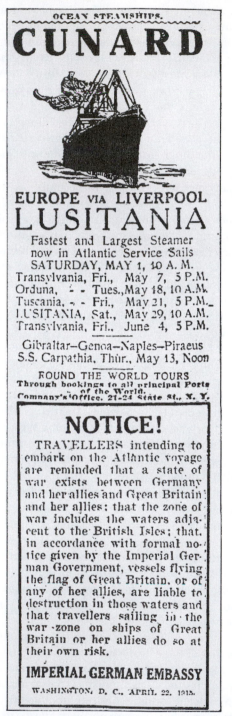

Advertisement from the New York *Herald*, **May 1, 1915**
Six days later the Lusitania *was sunk. Notice the German warning.*

lated risk. He would continue to claim profitable neutral trading rights while hoping that no high-seas incident would force his hand to grasp the sword of war. He emphatically warned Germany that it would be held to "strict accountability" for any attacks on American vessels or citizens.

The German submarines meanwhile began their deadly work. In the first months of 1915, they sank about ninety ships in the war zone. Then the submarine issue became acute when the British passenger liner *Lusitania* was torpedoed and sank off the coast of Ireland on May 7, 1915, with the loss of 1,198 lives, including 128 Americans.

The *Lusitania* was carrying forty-two hundred cases of small-arms ammunition, a fact the Germans used to justify the sinking. But Americans were swept by a wave of shock and anger at this act of "mass murder" and "piracy." The eastern United States, closer to the war, seethed with talk of fighting, but the rest of the country showed a strong distaste for hostilities. The peace-loving Wilson had no stomach for leading a disunited nation into war and instead relied on a series of increasingly strong notes to bring the German warlords sharply to book. "There is such a thing," he said, "as a man being too proud to fight."

Yet Wilson, sticking to his verbal guns, made some diplomatic progress. After another British liner, the *Arabic,* was sunk in August 1915, with the loss of two American lives, Berlin reluctantly agreed not to sink unarmed and unresisting passenger ships *without warning.*

This pledge appeared to be violated in March 1916, when the Germans torpedoed a French passenger steamer, the *Sussex.* The infuriated Wilson informed the Germans that unless they renounced the inhuman practice of sinking merchant ships without warning he would break diplomatic relations—an almost certain prelude to war.

Germany reluctantly knuckled under to President Wilson's *Sussex* ultimatum, agreeing not to sink passenger ships and merchant vessels without giving warning. But the Germans attached a long string to their *Sussex* pledge: the United States would have to persuade the Allies to modify what Berlin regarded as their illegal blockade. This, obviously, was something that Washington could not do. Wilson promptly accepted the German pledge, without accepting the "string." He thus

won a temporary but precarious diplomatic victory—precarious because Germany could pull the string whenever it chose, and the president might suddenly find himself hauled over the cliff of war.

Wilson Wins Reelection in 1916

Against this ominous backdrop, the presidential campaign of 1916 gathered speed. Both the bull moose Progressives and the Republicans met in Chicago. The Progressives uproariously renominated Theodore

Wilson Campaign Poster, 1916 *This poster presents Wilson's campaign theme of patriotism.*

Roosevelt, but the Rough Rider, who loathed Wilson and all his works, had no stomach for splitting the Republicans again and ensuring the reelection of his hated rival. In refusing to run, he sounded the death knell of the Progressive party.

Roosevelt's Republican admirers also clamored for "Teddy," but the Old Guard detested the renegade who had ruptured the party in 1912. Instead, they drafted Supreme Court Justice Charles Evans Hughes, a cold intellectual who had achieved a solid record as governor of New York. The Republican platform condemned the Democratic tariff, assaults on the trusts, and Wilson's wishy-washiness in dealing with both Mexico and Germany.

The thick-whiskered Hughes ("an animated feather duster") left the bench for the campaign stump, where he was not at home. In anti-German areas of the country, he assailed Wilson for not standing up to the kaiser, whereas in isolationist areas he took a softer line. This fence-straddling operation led to the jeer "Charles Evasive Hughes."

Hughes was further plagued by Roosevelt, who was delivering a series of skin-'em-alive speeches against "that damned Presbyterian hypocrite Wilson."

Frothing for war, TR privately sneered at Hughes as a "whiskered Wilson." The only difference between the two, he said, was "a shave."

Wilson, nominated by acclamation at the Democratic convention in St. Louis, ignored Hughes on the theory that one should not try to murder a man who is committing suicide. His campaign was built on the slogan "He Kept Us Out of War." And Democratic orators warned that by electing Charles Evans Hughes, the nation would be electing a fight—with a certain frustrated Rough Rider leading the charge. A Democratic advertisement appealing to American workers read,

> You are Working;
> —Not Fighting!
> Alive and Happy;
> —Not Cannon Fodder!
> Wilson and Peace with Honor?
> or
> Hughes with Roosevelt and War?

On election day, Hughes swept the East and looked like a surefire winner. Wilson went to bed that night prepared to accept defeat, while New York newspapers displayed huge portraits of "The Presi-

Presidential Election of 1916 (with electoral vote by state)   *Wilson was so worried about being a lame duck president in a time of great international tensions that he drew up a plan whereby Hughes, if victorious, would be appointed secretary of state, Wilson and the vice president would resign, and Hughes would thus succeed immediately to the presidency.*

dent-Elect—Charles Evans Hughes." But the rest of the country turned the tide. Midwesterners and westerners, attracted by Wilson's progressive reforms and antiwar policies, flocked to the polls for the president. The final result, in doubt for several days, hinged on California, which Wilson carried by some 3,800 votes out of about a million cast.

Wilson barely squeaked through, with a final vote of 277 to 254 in the Electoral College and 9,127,695 to 8,533,507 in the popular column. The pro-labor Wilson received strong support from the working class and from renegade bull moosers, whom Republicans failed to lure back into their camp. Wilson had not specifically promised to keep the country out of war, but probably enough voters relied on such implicit assurances to ensure his victory. Their hopeful expectations were soon rudely shattered.

Chronology

1912 Wilson defeats Taft and Roosevelt for presidency.

1913 Underwood Tariff Act.
Sixteenth Amendment (income tax) passed.
Federal Reserve Act.
Huerta takes power in Mexico.

1914 Clayton Anti-Trust Act.
Federal Trade Commission established.
U.S. occupation of Vera Cruz, Mexico.
World War I begins in Europe.

1915 La Follette Seamen's Act.
Lusitania torpedoed and sunk by German U-boat.
U.S. Marines sent to Haiti.

1916 *Sussex* ultimatum and pledge.
Workingmen's Compensation Act.
Federal Farm Loan Act.
Adamson Act.
Jones Act.
Pancho Villa raids New Mexico.
Brandeis appointed to Supreme Court.
U.S. Marines sent to Dominican Republic.
Wilson defeats Hughes for presidency.

1917 United States buys Virgin Islands from Denmark.

VARYING VIEWPOINTS

Who Were the Progressives?

Debate about progressivism has revolved mainly around a question that is simple to ask but devilishly difficult to answer: Who were the progressives? It was once taken for granted that progressive reformers were simply the heirs of the Jeffersonian-Jacksonian-Populist reform crusades; they were the oppressed and downtrodden common folk who finally erupted in wrath and demanded their due. But in his influential *Age of Reform* (1955), Richard Hofstadter astutely challenged that view.

Progressive leaders, Hofstadter argued, were not drawn from the ranks of society's poor and marginalized. Rather, they were middle-class people threatened from above by the emerging power of new corporate elites and from below by a restless working class. It was not economic deprivation, but "status anxiety," Hofstadter insisted, that prompted these people to become reformers. Their psychological motivation, he concluded, rendered many of their reform efforts quirky and ineffectual.

By contrast, New Left historians, notably Gabriel Kolko, argue that progressivism was dominated by established business leaders who successfully directed "reform" to their own conservative ends. In this view, government regulation (as embodied in new agencies like the Federal Reserve Board and the Federal Tariff Commission, and in legislation like the Meat Inspection Act) simply accomplished what two generations of private efforts had failed to accomplish: dampening cutthroat competition, stabilizing markets, and making America safe for monopoly capitalism.

Still other scholars, notably Robert H. Wiebe and Samuel P. Hays, argue that the progressives were neither the psychologically or economically disadvantaged, nor the old capitalist elite, but rather were members of a rapidly emerging , self-confident social class possessed of the new techniques of scientific management, technological expertise, and organizational know-how. This "organizational school" of historians does not see progressivism as a struggle of the "people" against the "interests," or as a confused and nostalgic campaign by status-threatened reformers, or as a conservative coup d'état. The progressive movement, in this view, was by and large an effort to rationalize and modernize many social institutions by introducing the wise and impartial hand of government regulation.

This view has much to recommend it. Yet despite its widespread acceptance among historians, it is an explanation that cannot adequately account for the titanic political struggles of the progressive era over the very reforms that the "organizational school" regards as simple adjustments to modernity. Recently, scholars such as Robyn Muncy, Linda Gordon, and Theda Skocpol have stressed the role of women in advocating progressive reforms. Building the American welfare state in the early twentieth century, they argue, was fundamentally a gendered activity inspired by a "female dominion" of social workers and "social feminists." Moreover, in contrast to many European countries where labor movements sought a welfare state to benefit the working class, American female reformers promoted welfare programs specifically to protect women and children.

The War to End War

---cๆ---

1917–1918

*The world must be made safe for democracy. Its peace
must be planted upon the tested foundations of political liberty.
We have no selfish ends to serve. We desire no conquest, no
dominion. We seek no indemnities for ourselves, no material
compensation for the sacrifices we shall freely make.*

WOODROW WILSON, WAR MESSAGE, APRIL 2, 1917

Destiny dealt cruelly with Woodrow Wilson. The lover of peace, as fate would have it, was forced to lead a hesitant and peace-loving nation into war. As the last days of 1916 slipped through the hourglass, the president made one final, futile attempt to mediate between the embattled belligerents. On January 22, 1917, he delivered one of his most moving addresses, restating America's conviction that only a negotiated "peace without victory" would prove durable.

Germany's warlords responded with a blow of the mailed fist. On January 31, 1917, they announced to an astonished world that they intended to wage *unrestricted* submarine warfare, sinking *all* ships, including America's, in the war zone.

Why this rash act? War with America was the last thing Germany wanted. But after three ghastly years

in the trenches, Germany's leaders decided that making distinctions between combatants and noncombatants was a luxury they could no longer afford. Thus they jerked on the string they had attached to their *Sussex* pledge in 1916, desperately hoping to bring Britain to its knees before the United States entered the war. Wilson, his bluff called, broke diplomatic relations with Germany but refused to move closer to war unless the Germans undertook "overt" acts against American lives.

War by Act of Germany

To defend American interests short of war, the president asked Congress for authority to arm American merchant ships. When a band of midwestern senators launched a filibuster to block the measure, Wilson denounced them as a "little group of willful men" who were rendering a great nation "helpless and contemptible." But their obstructionism was a powerful reminder of the continuing strength of American isolationism.

Meanwhile, the sensational Zimmermann note was intercepted and published on March 1, 1917, infuriating Americans, especially westerners. German foreign secretary Arthur Zimmermann had secretly proposed a German-Mexican alliance, tempting anti-Yankee Mexico with thoughts of recovering Texas, New Mexico, and Arizona.

On the heels of this provocation came the long-dreaded "overt" acts in the Atlantic, where German U-boats sank four unarmed American merchant vessels in the first two weeks of March. As one Philadelphia newspaper observed, "the difference between war and what we have now is that now we aren't fighting back." Simultaneously came the rousing news that a revolution in Russia had toppled the cruel regime of the tsars. America could now fight foursquare for democracy on the side of the Allies without the black sheep of Russian despotism in the Allied fold.

Subdued and solemn, Wilson at last stood before a hushed joint session of Congress on the evening of April 2, 1917, and asked for a declaration of war. He had lost his gamble that America could pursue the profits of neutral trade without being sucked into the ghastly maelstrom. A myth developed in later years that America was dragged unwittingly into war by munitions makers and Wall Street bankers, desperate to protect their profits and loans. Yet the weapons merchants and financiers were already thriving, unhampered by wartime government restrictions and heavy taxation. Their slogan might well have been "Neutrality Forever." The simple truth is that British harassment of American commerce had been galling but endurable; Germany had resorted to the mass killing of civilians. President Wilson had drawn a clear, if risky, line against the depredations of the submarine. The German high command, in a last desperate throw of the dice, chose to cross it. In a figurative sense, America's war declaration of April 6, 1917, bore the unambiguous trademark "Made in Germany."

Wilsonian Idealism Enthroned

"It is a fearful thing to lead this great peaceful people into war," Wilson said in his war message. It was fearful indeed, not least of all because of the formidable challenge it posed to Wilson's leadership skills. Ironically, it fell to the scholarly Wilson, deeply respectful of American traditions, to shatter one of the most sacred of those traditions by entangling America in a distant European war.

How could the president arouse the American people to shoulder this unprecedented burden? Isolationism remained strong, and no fewer than six senators and fifty representatives (including the first congresswoman, Jeannette Rankin of Montana) had voted against the war resolution. Wilson could whip up no enthusiasm, especially in the landlocked Midwest, for fighting to make the world safe from the submarine.

To galvanize the country, Wilson would have to proclaim more glorified aims. Radiating the spiritual fervor of his Presbyterian ancestors, he declared the twin goals of "a war to end war" and a crusade "to make the world safe for democracy." Brandishing the sword of righteousness, Wilson virtually hypnotized the nation with his lofty ideals. He contrasted the selfish war aims of the other belligerents, Allied and enemy alike, with America's shining altruism. America, he preached, did not fight for the sake of riches or territorial conquest. The Republic sought only to shape an international order in which democracy could flourish without fear of power-crazed autocrats and militarists.

In Wilsonian idealism, the personality of the president and the necessities of history were perfectly matched. The high-minded Wilson genuinely believed in the principles he so eloquently intoned. And probably no other appeal could have successfully converted the American people from their historic hostility to involvement in European squabbles. Americans, it seemed, could be either isolationists or crusaders, but nothing in between.

Wilson's appeal worked—perhaps too well. Holding aloft the torch of idealism, the president fired up the public mind to a fever pitch. "Force, force to the utmost, force without stint or limit," he cried, while the country responded less elegantly with, "Hang the kaiser!" Lost on the gale was Wilson's earlier plea for "peace without victory."

Wilson's Fourteen Potent Points

Wilson quickly came to be recognized as the moral leader of the Allied cause. He scaled a summit of inspiring oratory on January 8, 1918, when he delivered his famed Fourteen Points Address to an enthusiastic Congress. One of Wilson's primary purposes in this speech was to keep reeling Russia, now led by a new revolutionary government, in the war. His eloquence also inspired all the drooping Allies to make mightier efforts and demoralized the enemy governments by holding out alluring promises to their dissatisfied minorities.

The first five of the Fourteen Points were broad in scope: (1) A proposal to abolish secret treaties pleased liberals of all countries. (2) Freedom of the seas appealed to the Germans, as well as to Americans who distrusted British sea power. (3) A removal of economic barriers among nations was comforting to Germany, which feared postwar vengeance. (4) Reduction of armament burdens was gratifying to taxpayers everywhere. (5) An adjustment of colonial claims in the interests of both native peoples and the colonizers was reassuring to the anti-imperialists.

Other points among the fourteen proved to be no less seductive. They held out the promise of independence ("self-determination") to oppressed minority groups, such as the Poles, millions of whom lay under the heel of Germany and Austria-Hungary. The capstone point, number fourteen, foreshadowed the League of Nations—an international organization that Wilson dreamed would provide a system of collective security. Wilson earnestly prayed that this new scheme would effectively guarantee the political independence and territorial integrity of all countries, whether large or small.

Yet Wilson's appealing points, though raising hopes the world over, were not everywhere applauded. Certain leaders of the Allied nations, with an eye to territorial booty, were less than enthusiastic. Hard-nosed Republicans at home grumbled, and some of them openly mocked the "fourteen commandments" of "God Almighty Wilson."

Creel Manipulates Minds

Mobilizing the mind for war, both in America and abroad, was an urgent task facing the Washington authorities. For this purpose the Committee on Public Information was created. It was headed by a youngish journalist, George Creel, who, though outspoken and tactless, was gifted with zeal and imagination. His job was to sell America on the war and sell the world on Wilsonian war aims. The Creel organization, employing 150,000 workers at home and overseas, proved that words were indeed weapons. It sent out an army of 75,000 "four-minute men"—often

Anti-German Propaganda *The government relied extensively on emotional appeals and hate propaganda to rally support for the First World War, which most Americans regarded as a distant "European" affair.*

longer-winded than that—who delivered countless speeches full of "patriotic pep."

Creel's propaganda took varied forms. Posters were splashed on billboards in the "Battle of the Fences," as artists "rallied to the colors." Millions of leaflets and pamphlets, which contained the most pungent Wilsonisms, were showered like confetti upon the world. Propaganda booklets with red-white-and-blue covers were printed by the millions. Hang-the-kaiser movies, carrying such titles as *The Kaiser, the Beast of Berlin* and *To Hell with the Kaiser,* revealed the "Hun" at his bloodiest. Arm-waving conductors by the thousands led huge audiences in songs that poured scorn on the enemy and glorified the "boys" in uniform.

Creel typified American war mobilization, which relied more on aroused passion and voluntary compliance than on formal laws. But he oversold the ideals of Wilson and led the world to expect too much. When the president proved to be a mortal and not a god, the resulting disillusionment at home and abroad was disastrous.

Enforcing Loyalty and Stifling Dissent

German-Americans numbered over 8 million, counting those with at least one parent foreign-born, out of a total population of 100 million. As emotion mounted, hate hysteria against Germans and things Germanic swept the nation. Orchestras found it unsafe to present German-composed music, such as that of Wagner and Beethoven. German books were removed from library shelves, and German classes were cancelled in high schools and colleges. Sauerkraut became "liberty cabbage," hamburger "liberty steak." Even beer became suspect, as patriotic Americans fretted over the loyalty of breweries with names like Schlitz or Pabst. A few German-Americans were tarred, feathered, and beaten; in one extreme case a German Socialist in Illinois was lynched by a drunken mob.

Both the Espionage Act of 1917 and the Sedition Act of 1918 reflected current fears about Germans and antiwar Americans. Especially visible among the nineteen hundred prosecutions undertaken under these laws were antiwar Socialists and members of the radical union Industrial Workers of the World (IWW). Kingpin Socialist Eugene V. Debs was convicted under the Espionage Act in 1918 and sentenced to ten years in a federal penitentiary. IWW leader William D. ("Big Bill") Haywood and ninety-nine associates were similarly convicted. Some leftist journals like *The Masses* were denied use of the mails.

Virtually any criticism of the government could be censored and punished. Some critics claimed the new laws were bending, if not breaking, the First Amendment. But in *Schenck* v. *United States* (1919), the Supreme Court affirmed their legality, arguing that freedom of speech could be revoked when such speech posed a "clear and present danger" to the nation.

These prosecutions form an ugly chapter in the history of American civil liberty. With the dawn of peace, presidential pardons were rather freely granted, including President Harding's to Eugene Debs in 1921. Yet a few victims lingered behind bars into the 1930s.

Factories and Workers in Wartime

Victory was no foregone conclusion, especially since the Republic, despite ample warning, was caught flat-footedly unready for its leap into global war. Wilson had only belatedly backed some mild preparedness measures beginning in 1915, including a shipbuilding program and a civilian Council of National Defense. It would take a herculean effort to mobilize America's daunting but disorganized resources and throw them into the field quickly enough to bolster the Allied war effort.

Towering obstacles confronted economic mobilizers. Sheer ignorance was among the biggest roadblocks, as knowledge of such basics as the country's capacity for manufacturing steel or explosives was lacking. Traditional fears of big government hamstrung efforts to orchestrate the economy from Washington.

Only late in the war did Wilson succeed in imposing some order on this economic confusion. In March 1918 he appointed Wall Street's Bernard Baruch to head the War Industries Board, but that agency had only feeble formal powers. Even in a globe-girdling crisis, the American preference for laissez-faire and a weak central government proved amazingly strong.

Spurred by the slogan "Labor Will Win the War," American workers sweated their way to victory. In 1918 the War Department threatened to draft any unemployed male, but for the most part the government tried to treat labor fairly. The National War Labor Board, chaired by former president Taft, pressed employers to pay higher wages and adopt the eight-hour workday.

Samuel Gompers and his American Federation of Labor (AF of L) loyally supported the war, though some smaller and more radical labor organizations like the Industrial Workers of the World, which represented many downtrodden workers in the lumber and fruit industries, did not.

Still, labor harbored grievances. Recognition of the basic right to organize still eluded labor's grasp. Strikes broke out during and after the war, culminating in the great steel strike of 1919, the largest strike in American history. A quarter of a million workers walked off the job to demand the right to organize and bargain collectively. The strike was broken only after violent confrontations and the use of thirty thousand African-American strikebreakers.

Many thousands more southern blacks were drawn to the North by the magnet of war-industry employment. Their sudden appearance in previously all-white areas sometimes sparked interracial violence. An explosive riot in East St. Louis, Illinois, in July 1917 left nine whites and at least forty blacks dead. An equally gruesome riot ripped through Chicago in July 1919, fanned by tensions between white working-class neighborhoods and African-Americans who had found jobs as strikebreakers in meatpacking plants. Fifteen whites and twenty-three blacks were killed during nearly two weeks of terror.

Suffering Until Suffrage

Women also heeded the call of patriotism and opportunity. Thousands of female workers flooded into factories and fields, taking up jobs vacated by men who left the assembly line for the front line. But the war split the women's movement deeply. Many progressive feminists were pacifists, inclined to oppose both the participation of America in the war and women in the war effort. This group found a voice in the National Woman's party, led by Quaker activist Alice Paul, which demonstrated against "Kaiser Wilson" with marches and hunger strikes.

But the larger part of the suffrage movement, represented by the National American Woman Suffrage Association, supported Wilson's war. Leaders echoed Wilson's justification for fighting by arguing

Women Ordnance Plant Workers with Pneumatic Hammers, 1918
A minority of women had long been in the work force, but World War I drew more of them into heavy industrial labor.

that women must take part in the war effort to earn a role in shaping the peace. The fight for democracy abroad was women's best chance for winning true democracy at home.

War mobilization gave new momentum to the suffrage fight. Impressed by women's war work, President Wilson endorsed woman suffrage as "a vitally necessary war measure." In 1917 New York voted for suffrage at the state level, followed by Michigan, Oklahoma, and South Dakota. Eventually the groundswell could no longer be contained. In 1920— eighty years after the first calls for suffrage at Seneca Falls—the Nineteenth Amendment was ratified, giving all American women the right to vote. (For text, see the Appendix).

Despite political victory, women's wartime economic gains proved fleeting. When peace arrived, most women workers soon gave up their war jobs. Meanwhile, Congress reaffirmed its support for women's traditional role as mothers when it passed the Sheppard-Towner Maternity Act of 1921, providing federally financed instruction in maternal and infant health care.

Forging a War Economy

Mobilization relied more on the heated emotions of patriotism than on the cool majesty of the laws. The largely voluntary and somewhat haphazard character of economic war organization testified eloquently to ocean-insulated America's safe distance from the fighting—as well as to the still-modest scale of government power in the progressive-era Republic.

As the larder of democracy, America had to feed itself and its allies. By a happy inspiration, the man chosen to head the Food Administration was the Quaker humanitarian Herbert C. Hoover, already a hero for his successful charitable drive to feed the starving people of war-racked Belgium.

In common with other American war administrators, Hoover preferred to rely on voluntary compliance rather than on formal edicts. Instead of rationing food supplies, he waged a whirlwind propaganda campaign through posters, billboards, newspapers, pulpits, and movies. To save food for export, Hoover proclaimed wheatless Wednesdays and meatless Tuesdays—all on

a voluntary basis. Even children, when eating apples, were urged to be "patriotic to the core."

The country soon broke out in a rash of backyard "victory gardens." Congress severely restricted the use of foodstuffs for manufacturing alcoholic beverages. The wartime drive against German-descended brewers aided in the passage of the Eighteenth Amendment in 1919, which—temporarily—prohibited all alcoholic drinks.

Thanks to the fervent patriotic wartime spirit, Hoover's voluntary approach worked. Farm production increased by one-fourth, and food exports to the Allies tripled in volume. Hoover's methods were widely imitated in other war agencies. The Fuel Administration exhorted Americans to save fuel with "heatless Mondays" and "gasless Sundays." The Treasury Department sponsored huge parades and invoked slogans such as "Halt the Hun" to promote four great Liberty Loan drives, followed by a Victory Loan campaign in 1919. Together, these efforts netted the then-fantastic sum of about $21 billion, or two-thirds of the cost of the war to the United States. The remainder was raised by increased taxes.

Despite the Wilson administration's preference for voluntary means of mobilizing the economy, the government on occasion reluctantly exercised its sovereign formal power, notably when it took over the nation's railroads following indescribable traffic snarls in late 1917. Washington also launched a gigantic shipbuilding program, though it was slow to get under way.

Making Plowboys into Doughboys

Most citizens, at the outset, did not dream of sending a mighty force to France. They expected America to use its navy to uphold freedom of the seas, ship war materials to the Allies, and supply them with loans. But in April and May of 1917, the European associates confessed that they were scraping the bottom not only of their money chests but, more ominously, of their manpower barrels. A huge American army would have to be raised, trained, and transported, or the whole western front would collapse.

Conscription was the only answer to the need for raising an immense army with all possible speed. Wilson disliked a draft, but he eventually accepted and eloquently supported conscription as a disagreeable and temporary necessity. After six weeks of criticism and debate, Congress grudgingly passed conscription.

The draft act required the registration of all males between the ages of eighteen and forty-five. The draft machinery, on the whole, worked effectively. No draftee could purchase an exemption or hire a substitute, as in the days of the Civil War. Within a few frantic months the army grew to over 4 million men. For the first time, women were admitted to the armed forces: some 11,000 to the navy and 269 to the marines.

Recruits were supposed to receive six months of training in America and two more months overseas. But so great was the urgency that many "doughboys" were swept swiftly into battle scarcely knowing how to handle a rifle, much less a bayonet.

America Helps Hammer the Hun

Russia's collapse underscored the need for haste. As the communistic Bolsheviks withdrew their beaten country from the war, Germany moved its forces to the western front in France. The Germans hoped to deliver the knockout blow to the Allies in about six months, long before American reinforcements could arrive.

Berlin's calculations as to American tardiness were surprisingly accurate. No really effective American fighting force reached France until about a year after Congress declared war. Nevertheless, France gradually began to bustle with American doughboys. The first trainees to reach the front were used as replacements in the Allied armies. The newcomers soon made friends with the French girls—or tried to—and one of the most sung-about women in history was the fabled "Mademoiselle from Armentières." One of the printable stanzas ran

> She was true to me, she was true to you,
> She was true to the whole damned army, too.

The dreaded German drive on the western front exploded in the spring of 1918. Spearheaded by about half a million troops, the enemy rolled forward with terrifying momentum. So dire was the peril that the Allies for the first time united under a supreme commander, the quiet Frenchman Marshal Ferdinand Foch.

Over There *American troops ("doughboys") man a machine gun in a bomb-blasted forest.*

At last the ill-trained "Yanks" were coming—and not a moment too soon. Late in May 1918, the forward-rolling Germans, smashing to within forty miles of Paris, threatened to knock out France. Newly arrived American troops, numbering fewer than thirty thousand, were thrown into the breach at Château-Thierry, right in the teeth of the German advance. This was a historic moment—the first significant engagement of American troops in a European war. With their arrival, it was clear that a new American giant had arisen in the West to replace the dying Russian titan in the East.

By July 1918 the awesome German drive had spent its force, and keyed-up American boys participated in a Foch counteroffensive in the Second Battle of the Marne. This engagement marked the beginning of a German withdrawal that was never effectively reversed. In September 1918 nine American divisions (about 243,000 men) joined four French divisions to push the Germans from the St. Mihiel salient, a German dagger in France's flank.

The Americans, dissatisfied with merely bolstering the British and French, demanded and got their own army under General John J. ("Black Jack") Pershing. Pershing was finally assigned a front stretching from the Swiss border to meet the French lines. As part of the last mighty Allied assault, involving several million men, Pershing's army undertook the Meuse-Argonne offensive, from September 26 to November 11, 1918. This battle, the most gargantuan thus far in American history, lasted forty-seven days and engaged 1.2 million American troops. With especially heavy fighting in the rugged Argonne Forest, the killed and wounded mounted to 120,000, or 10 percent of the Americans involved.

Victory was in sight—and fortunately so. The slowly advancing American armies in France were eating up their supplies so rapidly that they were in grave danger of running short. But the battered Germans were reeling under the sledgehammer blows of the Allies and suffering from critical food shortages caused by the British blockade. Propaganda leaflets contain-

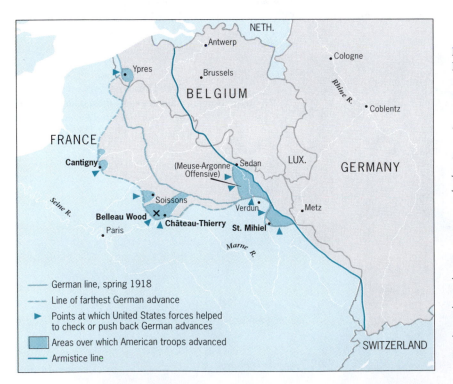

Major U.S. Operations in France, 1918 *One doughboy recorded in his diary his baptism of fire at St. Mihiel: "Hiked through dark woods. No lights allowed, guided by holding on the pack of the man ahead. Stumbled through underbrush for about half mile into an open field where we waited in soaking rain until about 10:00 P.M. We then started on our hike to the St. Mihiel front, arriving on the crest of a hill at 1:00 A.M. I saw a sight which I shall never forget. It was the zero hour and in one instant the entire front as far as the eye could reach in either direction was a sheet of flame, while the heavy artillery made the earth quake."*

ing seductive Wilsonian promises rained upon their crumbling lines from balloons, shells, and rockets.

Berlin was now ready to hoist the white flag. The Germans first sought a peace based on the Fourteen Points in October 1918. But a stern Wilson made it clear that the kaiser must be thrown overboard before an armistice could be negotiated. The war-weary Germans then forced the disgraced kaiser to flee to Holland.

The exhausted Germans laid down their arms at eleven o'clock on the eleventh day of the eleventh month of 1918, and an eerie, numbing silence fell over the western front. War-taut America burst into a delirium of around-the-clock rejoicing, as streets were jammed with laughing, whooping, milling, dancing masses. The war to end wars had ended.

The United States' main contribution to the ultimate victory had been foodstuffs, munitions, credits, oil, and manpower—but not battlefield victories. The Yanks fought only two major battles, at St. Mihiel and the Meuse-Argonne. It was the prospect of endless U.S. troop reserves, rather than America's actual military performance, that eventually demoralized the Germans.

Ironically enough, General Pershing in some ways depended more on the Allies than they depended on him. Most of his army's supplies and weapons were purchased from the British and French. The United States was no arsenal of democracy in this war; that role awaited it in the next global conflict, two decades later.

Wilson Steps Down from Olympus

Woodrow Wilson had helped to win the war. What role would he now play in shaping the peace? Expectations ran extravagantly high. As the fighting in Europe crashed to a close, the American president towered at the peak of his popularity and power. No other man had ever occupied so dizzy a pinnacle as moral leader of the world. Wilson also had behind him the prestige of victory and the economic resources of the mightiest nation on earth. But at this fateful moment, his sureness of touch deserted him, and he began to make a series of tragic fumbles.

Under the slogan "Politics is adjourned," partisan political strife had been kept below the surface during the war crisis. Hoping to strengthen his hand at the Paris peace table, Wilson broke the truce by personally appealing for a Democratic victory in the congressional elections of November 1918. But the maneuver backfired when voters instead returned a narrow Republican majority to Congress. Having staked his reputation on the outcome, Wilson went to Paris as a diminished leader. Unlike all the parliamentary statesmen at the table, he did not command a legislative majority at home.

Wilson's decision to go in person to Paris to help make the peace infuriated Republicans, who saw it as flamboyant grandstanding. He further ruffled Republican feathers when he neglected to include a single Republican senator in his official peace delegation. The logical choice was the new chairman of the Senate Committee on Foreign Relations, slender and aristocratically bewhiskered Henry Cabot Lodge of Massachusetts, a Harvard Ph.D. But including Lodge would have been problematic for the president. The senator's mind, quipped one critic, was like the soil of his native New England: "naturally barren but highly cultivated." Wilson loathed him, and the feeling was hotly reciprocated. An accomplished author, Lodge had been known as "the scholar in politics" until Wilson came on the scene. The two men were at daggers drawn, personally and politically.

Hammering Out the Treaty

Woodrow Wilson, the great prophet arisen in the West, received tumultuous welcomes from the masses of France, Britain, and Italy late in 1918 and early in 1919. But the realistic statesmen of Italy and France were determined that Wilsonian idealism should not disrupt their fine-spun imperialistic plans.

The Paris Conference of great and small nations fell into the hands of an inner clique, known as the "Big Four." Wilson, representing the richest and freshest great power, more or less occupied the driver's seat. He was joined by Vittorio Orlando of Italy, David Lloyd George of Britain, and cynical, hard-bitten Georges Clemenceau of France, the seventy-eight-year-old "organizer of victory" known as "the Tiger."

Speed was urgent when the conference opened on January 18, 1919. Europe seemed to be slipping

Wilson in Dover, England, 1919 *Hailed by many Europeans in early 1919 as the savior of the Western world, Wilson was a fallen idol only a few months later, when his own countrymen repudiated the peace treaty he had helped to craft.*

into anarchy; the red tide of communism was licking westward from V. I. Lenin's revolutionary Russia.

Wilson's ultimate goal was a world parliament to be known as the League of Nations, but he first bent his energies to preventing any cynical parceling out of the former colonies and protectorates of the vanquished powers. He forced through a compromise between naked imperialism and Wilsonian idealism, in which the victors received conquered territory only as trustees of the League of Nations. But in practice this half-loaf solution was little more than the old prewar colonialism, thinly disguised.

Wilson envisioned a League of Nations consisting of an assembly with seats for all nations and a council to be controlled by the great powers. He gained a signal victory over the skeptical Old World diplomats in February 1919, when they agreed to make the League Covenant, Wilson's brainchild, an integral part of the final peace treaty.

On a quick trip to America, Wilson discovered that certain Republican senators, led by Senator Lodge, were sharpening their knives. To them the League was either a useless "sewing circle" or an overpotent "superstate." Their hard core was composed of a dozen or so isolationists, led by Senators William Borah of Idaho

and Hiram Johnson of California, who were known as the "irreconcilables" or "the battalion of death."

Thirty-nine Republican senators or senators-elect—enough to defeat the treaty—proclaimed that the Senate would not approve the League of Nations in its existing imperfect form. These difficulties delighted Wilson's Allied adversaries in Paris. They were now in a stronger bargaining position because Wilson would have to beg them for changes in the League Covenant that would safeguard the Monroe Doctrine and other U.S. interests dear to the senators.

As soon as Wilson was back in Paris, hardheaded Premier Clemenceau pressed French demands for the German-inhabited Rhineland and the Saar Valley, a rich coal area. Faced with fierce Wilsonian opposition to this violation of self-determination, France settled for a compromise whereby the Saar basin would remain under the League of Nations for fifteen years and then a popular vote would determine its fate.* In exchange for dropping its demands for the Rhineland, France got a security treaty in which both

---

* The Saar population voted overwhelmingly to rejoin Germany in 1935.

Britain and America pledged to come to its aid in the event of another German invasion. The French later felt betrayed when the pact was quickly pigeonholed by the U.S. Senate, which shied away from all entangling alliances.

Wilson's next battle was with Italy over Fiume, a valuable seaport inhabited by both Italians and Yugoslavs. When Italy demanded Fiume, Wilson insisted that the seaport go to Yugoslavia and appealed over the heads of Italy's leaders to the country's masses. The maneuver fell flat. The Italian delegates went home in a huff, and the Italian populace turned savagely against Wilson.

Another crucial struggle was with Japan over China's Shantung peninsula and the German islands in the Pacific, which the Japanese had seized during the war. Japan was conceded the strategic Pacific islands under a League of Nations mandate,* but Wilson fiercely opposed Japanese control of Shantung as a violation of self-determination for its 30 million Chinese residents. But when the Japanese threatened to walk out, Wilson reluctantly accepted a compromise whereby Japan kept Germany's economic holdings in Shantung and pledged to return the peninsula to China at a later date. The Chinese were outraged by this imperialistic solution, while Clemenceau jeered that Wilson "talked like Jesus Christ and acted like Lloyd George."

Wilson's Battle for Ratification

The completed Treaty of Versailles was handed to the Germans for their forced signature in June 1919—almost literally on the point of a bayonet. Loud and bitter cries of betrayal burst from their throats—charges that Adolf Hitler would soon reiterate during his meteoric rise to power in Germany.

Wilson, of course, was guilty of no conscious betrayal. But he had been forced to compromise away some of his less cherished Fourteen Points in order to salvage the more precious League of Nations. He was much more like the mother who had to throw her sickly younger children to the pursuing wolves to save

her sturdy firstborn. Greeted a few months earlier with frenzied acclaim in Europe, Wilson was now a fallen idol, condemned alike by disillusioned liberals and frustrated imperialists. He was keenly aware that some unjust provisions had been forced into the treaty. But he was hoping that a potent League of Nations, led by America, would iron out the inequities.

The loudly condemned treaty actually had much to commend it. Not least among its merits was its liberation of many oppressed peoples, such as the Poles, from the yoke of imperial dynasties. Wilson's critics to the contrary, the settlement was almost certainly a fairer one because he had gone to Paris.

Returning to America, Wilson found the Treaty of Versailles and the League of Nations being showered with abuse from all sides. Isolationists raised a whirlwind of protest against entanglement in a newfangled "League of Notions." Rabid Hun-haters, regarding the pact as not harsh enough, voiced their discontent. Principled liberals, like the editors of the *Nation*, thought it too harsh—and a gross betrayal to boot. German-Americans, Italian-Americans, Irish-Americans, and other "hyphenated Americans" complained loudly that the peace settlement was not sufficiently favorable to their native lands.

Despite mounting discontent, a strong majority of the people still seemed favorable to the treaty, with the "Wilson League" firmly riveted as Part I. At this time—early July 1919—Senator Lodge had no real hope of defeating the Treaty of Versailles. His strategy was merely to amend it in such a way as to "Americanize," "Republicanize," or "senatorialize" it.

Lodge effectively used delay to muddle and divide public opinion. He read the entire 264-page treaty aloud in the Senate Foreign Relations Committee and held protracted hearings in which people of various nationalities aired their grievances. With the treaty bogged down in the Senate, Wilson decided to go to the country in a spectacular speechmaking tour. Physicians and friends warned the increasingly frail president against making the strenuous trip. But he declared that he was willing to die, like the soldiers he had sent into battle, for the sake of the new world order.

The presidential tour that began in September 1919 got off to a rather lame start in the Midwest, where German-American influence was strong and two hostile "irreconcilable" senators, Borah and Johnson, trailed Wilson and spoke against the treaty

---

* In due time the Japanese illegally fortified these islands—the Marshalls, Marianas, and Carolines—and used them as bases against the United States in World War II.

in the same cities a few days later. But the Rocky Mountain region and the Pacific Coast, areas that had elected Wilson in 1916, welcomed him with heart-warming outbursts. The high point—and the break-ing point—of the return trip came at Pueblo, Colorado, on September 25, 1919. Wilson, with tears coursing down his cheeks, pleaded for the League of Nations as the only real hope of preventing future wars. That night he collapsed from physical and ner-vous exhaustion.

Wilson was whisked back in the "funeral train" to Washington, where several days later a stroke para-lyzed one side of his body. During the next few weeks he lay in a darkened room in the White House, as much a victim of the war as the unknown soldier buried at Arlington. For seven and a half months he did not meet with his cabinet.

Defeat Through Deadlock

Senator Lodge, coldly calculating, was now at the helm. After failing to amend the treaty outright, he came up with fourteen formal reservations to protect American sovereignty and guard Congress's war-declaring power against the League. Wilson, hating Lodge, saw red at the mere suggestion of the Lodge reservations, which he insisted "emasculated" the entire pact.

Although too feeble to lead, Wilson was still strong enough to obstruct. When the day finally came for voting in the Senate, he sent word to all true Democrats to vote *against* the treaty with the odious Lodge reservations attached. Loyal Democrats in the Senate, on November 19, 1919, blindly did Wilson's bidding. Combining with the "irreconcilables," mostly Republicans, they rejected the treaty with the Lodge reservations appended, 55 to 39.

The nation was so shocked at this outcome that the Senate was forced to vote a second time in March 1920. There was only one possible path to success. Unless the Senate approved the pact with the Lodge reservations, the entire document would be rejected. But the sickly Wilson signed the treaty's death warrant by again sending word to all loyal Democrats to vote down the treaty with the obnoxious Lodge reservations attached. On a fateful March 19, 1920, the treaty netted a simple majority but failed to get the necessary two-thirds majority by a count of 49 yeas to 35 nays.

What defeated the treaty? The Lodge-Wilson personal feud, traditionalism, isolationism, disillu-sionment, and partisanship all contributed to the confused picture. But Wilson himself must bear a substantial share of the responsibility. He asked for all or nothing—and got nothing.

The "Solemn Referendum" of 1920

Wilson's own pet solution for the deadlock was to set-tle the treaty issue by appealing to the people for a "solemn referendum" in the presidential election of 1920. This was sheer folly, for a true mandate on the League in the noisy arena of politics was clearly an impossibility.

Gathering in Chicago in June 1920, jubilant Republicans devised a masterfully ambiguous plat-form that could appeal to both pro-League and anti-League sentiment in the party. As the leading presidential contestants jousted with one another, a group of Senate bosses, meeting rather casually in the historic "smoke-filled" Room 404 of the Blackstone Hotel, informally decided on affable, malleable Sena-tor Warren G. Harding of Ohio as the candidate. To run with the "folksy," back-slapping former newspaper editor, the party nominated frugal, grim-faced Gover-nor Calvin ("Silent Cal") Coolidge of Massachusetts.

Meeting in San Francisco, Democrats nominated earnest Governor James M. Cox of Ohio, who strongly supported the League. His running mate was assis-tant navy secretary Franklin D. Roosevelt, a young, handsome, vibrant New Yorker.

Democratic attempts to make the campaign a referendum on the League were thwarted by Senator Harding, who issued muddled and contradictory statements on the issue from his front porch. Pro-League and anti-League Republicans both claimed that Harding's election would advance their cause, while the candidate suggested that if elected he would work for a vague Association of Nations—a league but not *the* League.

With newly enfranchised women swelling the vote totals, Harding was swept into power with a prodigious plurality of over 7 million votes—16,143,407 to 9,130,328 for Cox. The electoral count was 404 to 127. Eugene V. Debs, federal prisoner number 9653 at the Atlanta Penitentiary, rolled up the largest vote ever for the left-wing Socialist party—919,799.

Public desire for a change found vent in a resounding repudiation of "high and mighty" Wilsonianism. People were tired of professional highbrowism, star-reaching idealism, bothersome do-goodism, moral overstrain, and constant self-sacrifice. Eager to lapse back into "normalcy," they were willing to accept a second-rate president—and they got a third-rate one.

Although the election could not be considered a true referendum, Republican isolationists successfully turned Harding's victory into a death sentence for the League. Politicians increasingly shunned the League as they would a leper. When the legendary Wilson died in 1924, admirers knelt in the snow outside his Washington home. His "great vision" of a league for peace had died long before.

The Betrayal of Great Expectations

America's spurning of the League was tragically shortsighted. The Republic had helped to win a costly war, but it foolishly kicked the fruits of victory under the table. Whether a strong international organization would have averted World War II in 1939 will always be a matter of dispute. But there can be no doubt that the orphaned League of Nations was undercut at the start by the refusal of the mightiest power on the globe to join it. The Allies themselves were largely to blame for the new world conflagration that flared up in 1939, but they found a convenient justification for their own shortcomings by pointing an accusing finger at Uncle Sam.

The ultimate collapse of the Treaty of Versailles must be laid, at least in some degree, at America's doorstep. This complicated pact, tied in with the four other peace treaties through the League Covenant, was a top-heavy structure designed to rest on a four-legged table. The fourth leg, the United States, was never put into place. This rickety structure teetered for over a decade and then crashed in ruins—a debacle that played into the hands of German demagogue Adolf Hitler.

The United States, as the tragic sequel proved, hurt its own cause when it buried its head in the sands. Granted that the conduct of its Allies had been disillusioning, it had its own ends to serve by carrying through the Wilsonian program. It would have been well advised to forthrightly assume its war-born responsibilities and resolutely play the role of global leader that had been thrust upon it. In the interests of its own security, if for no other reason, the United States should have used its enormous strength to shape world-shaking events. Instead, it permitted itself blithely to drift toward the abyss of a second and even more bloody international disaster.

Chronology

1915	Council of National Defense established.
1917	Germany resumes unrestricted submarine warfare. Zimmermann note. United States enters World War I. Espionage Act of 1917.
1918	Wilson proposes the Fourteen Points. Sedition Act of 1918. Battle of Château-Thierry. Second Battle of the Marne. Meuse-Argonne offensive. Armistice ends World War I.
1919	Paris Conference and Treaty of Versailles. Wilson's pro-League tour and collapse. Eighteenth Amendment (prohibition of alcohol) passed.
1920	Final Senate defeat of Versailles Treaty. Nineteenth Amendment (woman suffrage) passed. Harding defeats Cox for presidency.

VARYING VIEWPOINTS

Woodrow Wilson: Realist or Idealist?

As the first president to take the United States into a foreign war, Woodrow Wilson was obliged to make a systematic case to the American people to justify his unprecedented European intervention. His ideas have largely defined the character of American foreign policy ever since—for better or worse.

"Wilsonianism" comprises three closely related principles: (1) The era of American isolation from world affairs has irretrievably ended. (2) The United States must infuse its own founding political and economic ideas—including democracy, the rule of law, free trade, and national self-determination (or anticolonialism)—into the international order. (3) American influence can eventually steer the world away from rivalry and warfare toward a cooperative and peaceful international system, maintained by the League of Nations or, later, the United Nations.

Whether that Wilsonian vision constitutes hard-nosed realism or starry-eyed idealism has excited scholarly debate for nearly a century. "Realists," such as George F. Kennan and Henry Kissinger, insist Wilson was anything but realistic. They criticize the president as a naive, impractical dreamer who failed to understand that the international order is, and always will be, an anarchic, unruly arena, outside the rule of law, where only military force can effectively protect the nation's security. In a sharp critique in his 1950 study, *American Diplomacy,* Kennan condemned Wilson's vision as "moralism-legalism." In this view, Wilson dangerously threatened to sacrifice American self-interests on the altar of his admirable but ultimately unworkable ideas.

Wilson's defenders, including conspicuously his principal biographer, Arthur S. Link, disagree with that assessment. They argue that Wilson's idealism was a kind of higher realism, recognizing that armed conflict on the scale of World War I could never again be tolerated and that some framework of peaceful international relations simply had to be found.

Some leftist scholars, such as William Appleman Williams, argue that Wilson was a realist of another kind: a subtle and wily imperialist whose stirring rhetoric cloaked a grasping ambition to make the United States the world's dominant economic power. Sometimes called "the imperialism of free trade," this strategy allegedly sought to decolonialize the world and open up international commerce, not for the good of peoples elsewhere, but to create a system in which American economic might would prevail.

Still other scholars, especially John Milton Cooper, Jr., emphasize the absence of economic factors in shaping Wilson's diplomacy. Isolationism, so this argument goes, held such sway over American thinking precisely because the United States had such a puny financial stake abroad—no hard American economic interests were mortally threatened in 1917, or for a long time thereafter. In these circumstances, Wilson—and the Wilsonians who came after him, such as Franklin D. Roosevelt—had no choice but to appeal to abstract ideals and high principles. The "idealistic" Wilsonian strain in American diplomacy, in this view, may be an unavoidable heritage of America's historically isolated situation. If so, it was Wilson's genius to make practical use of those ideas in his bid for popular support of his diplomacy.

For further reading, see the Appendix. For web resources, go to **http://college.hmco.com.**

American Life in the "Roaring Twenties"

1919–1929

*America's present need is not heroics but healing;
not nostrums but normalcy; not revolution
but restoration; . . . not surgery but serenity.*

WARREN G. HARDING, 1920

Bloodied by the war and disillusioned by the peace, Americans turned inward in the 1920s. Shunning diplomatic commitments to foreign countries, they also denounced "radical" foreign ideas, condemned "un-American" lifestyles, and clanged shut the immigration gates against foreign peoples. They partly sealed off the domestic economy from the rest of the world and plunged headlong into a dizzying decade of homegrown prosperity.

The boom of the golden twenties showered genuine benefits on Americans, as incomes and living standards rose for many. But there seemed to be something incredible about it all, even as people sang,

> My sister she works in the laundry,
> My father sells bootlegger gin,
> My mother she takes in the washing,
> My God! how the money rolls in!

New technologies, new consumer products, and new forms of leisure and entertainment made the twenties roar. Yet just beneath the surface lurked widespread anxieties about the future and fears that America was losing sight of its traditional ways.

Seeing Red

Hysterical fears of red Russia continued to color American thinking for several years after the Bolshevik (Communist) revolution of 1917, which spawned a tiny Communist party in America. Tensions were heightened by an epidemic of strikes that convulsed the Republic at war's end, many of them the result of high prices and frustrated union-organizing drives. Upstanding Americans jumped to the conclusion that labor troubles were fomented by bomb-andwhisker Bolsheviks. A general strike in Seattle in 1919, though modest in its demands and orderly in its methods, prompted a call from the mayor for federal troops to head off "the anarchy of Russia."

The big "red scare" of 1919–1920 resulted in a nationwide crusade against left-wingers whose Americanism was suspect. Attorney General A. Mitchell Palmer, who "saw red" too easily, earned the title "Fighting Quaker" for his excess of zeal in rounding up suspects. When a bomb shattered both Palmer's nerves and his Washington home in June 1919, the "Fighting Quaker" was dubbed the "Quaking Fighter." Late in December 1919, a shipload of 249 alleged alien radicals was deported on the *Buford* ("Soviet Ark") to the "workers' paradise" of Russia. Hysteria was revived in September 1920 when a still-unexplained bomb blast in Wall Street killed thirty-eight people and wounded several hundred others.

Various states joined the pack in the outcry against radicals. In 1919–1920 a number of legislatures passed criminal syndicalism laws. These antired statutes outlawed even the *advocacy* of violence to secure social change. Critics protested that mere words were not criminal deeds, that there was a great gulf between throwing fits and throwing bombs, and that "free screech" was for the nasty as well as the nice. Violence was done to traditional American concepts of free speech as IWW members and other radicals were vigorously prosecuted. The hysteria went so far that in 1920 five members of the New York legislature, all lawfully elected, were denied their seats simply because they were Socialists.

The red scare was a godsend to conservative businesspeople, who used it to break the backs of the fledgling unions. Labor's call for the "closed," or all-union, shop was denounced as "Sovietism in disguise." Employers, in turn, hailed their own antiunion campaign for the "open" shop as "the American plan."

Anti-redism and antiforeignism were reflected in a notorious case regarded by liberals as a "judicial lynching." Nicola Sacco, a shoe-factory worker, and Bartolomeo Vanzetti, a fish peddler, were convicted in 1921 of the murder of a Massachusetts paymaster and his guard. The jury and judge were prejudiced in some degree against the defendants because they were Italians, atheists, anarchists, and draft dodgers.

Liberals and radicals the world over rallied to the defense of the two immigrants doomed to die. The case dragged on for six years until 1927, when the condemned men were electrocuted. Communists and other radicals were thus presented with two martyrs in the "class struggle," while many American liberals hung their heads.

Hooded Hoodlums of the KKK

A new Ku Klux Klan, spawned by the postwar reaction, mushroomed fearsomely in the early 1920s. Despite the familiar sheets and hoods, it more closely resembled the antiforeign "nativist" movements of the 1850s than the antiblack nightriders of the 1860s. It was antiforeign, anti-Catholic, antiblack, anti-Jewish, antipacifist, anticommunist, anti-internationalist, anti-evolutionist, anti-adultery, and anti–birth control. It was also pro–Anglo-Saxon, pro–"native" American, and pro-Protestant. In short, the besheeted Klan betokened an extremist, ultraconservative uprising against many of the forces of diversity and modernity that were transforming American culture.

The reconstituted Klan spread with astonishing rapidity, especially in the Midwest and the "Bible Belt" South. At its peak in the mid-1920s, it enrolled about 5 million dues-paying members and wielded potent political influence. The Klan's most impressive displays were "konclaves" and huge flag-waving

Parade of Forty Thousand Ku Klux Klansmen in Washington, 1925

parades. The chief warning was the blazing cross. The principal weapon was the bloodied lash, supplemented by tar and feathers.

This reign of hooded horror, so repulsive to the best American ideals, collapsed rather suddenly in the late 1920s. Decent people at last recoiled from the orgy of ribboned flesh and terrorism, and scandalous embezzling by Klan officials resulted in a congressional investigation. The bubble was punctured when the movement was exposed, not as a crusade, but as a vicious racket based on a $10 initiation fee. The KKK was an alarming manifestation of the intolerance and prejudice plaguing people anxious about the dizzying pace of social change in the 1920s.

Stemming the Foreign Flood

Isolationist America of the 1920s, ingrown and provincial, had little use for the immigrants who began to flood into the country again as peace settled soothingly on the war-torn world. Some 800,000 stepped ashore in 1920–1921, about two-thirds of them from southern and eastern Europe (see "Makers of America: The Poles," pp. 446–447). The "one hundred-percent Americans," shuddering at the sight of this resumed "New Immigration," once again cried that the famed poem at the base of the Statue of Lib-

erty was all too literally true: they claimed that a sickly Europe was indeed vomiting on America "the wretched refuse of its teeming shore."

Congress temporarily plugged the breach with the Emergency Quota Act of 1921. This stopgap legislation was soon replaced by the Immigration Act of 1924. Quotas for foreigners were cut from 3 percent of persons of each nationality living in the United States to 2 percent. The national-origins base was shifted from the census of 1910 to that of 1890, when comparatively few southern Europeans had arrived.* The purpose was clearly to freeze America's existing ethnic composition, which was largely northern European. A flagrantly discriminatory section of the Immigration Act of 1924 slammed the door absolutely against Japanese immigrants. Exempt from the quota system were Canadians and Latin Americans.

The quota system effected a pivotal departure in American policy. Immigration henceforth dwindled to a mere trickle. Quotas thus caused America to sac-

---

* Five years later the Immigration Act of 1929, using 1920 as the quota base, virtually cut immigration in half by limiting the total to 152,574 a year. In 1965 Congress abolished the national-origins quota system.

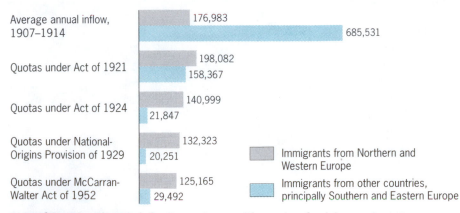

Annual Immigration and the Quota Laws *The national-origins quota system was abolished in 1965. Legislation in that year capped the level of immigration at 170,000 per year but made exceptions for children, spouses, and parents of persons already arrived. It also restricted immigration from any single country to 20,000 people per year. The immigration laws were again significantly revised in 1986 (see p. 618).*

The Poles

The Poles were among the largest immigrant groups to respond to industrializing America's call for badly needed labor after the Civil War. Between 1870 and World War I, some 2 million Polish-speaking peasants boarded steamships bound for the United States. By the 1920s, when antiforeign feeling led to restrictive legislation that choked the immigrant stream to a trickle, Polish immigrants and their American-born children began to develop new identities as Polish-Americans.

The first Poles to arrive in the New World had landed in Jamestown in 1608 and helped to develop that colony's timber industry. Over the ensuing two and a half centuries, scattered religious dissenters and revolutionary nationalists also made their way from Poland to America. During the Revolution about one hundred Poles, including two officers recruited by Benjamin Franklin, served in the Continental army.

Poland disappeared as an independent nation in the late 1700s, and many Polish patriots looked to America as a model of liberty. But the Polish hopefuls who poured into the United States in the late nineteenth century came primarily to stave off starvation and to earn money to buy land. Known in their homeland as *za chlebem* ("for bread") emigrants, they belonged to the mass of central and eastern European peasants who had been forced off their farms by growing competition from large-scale, mechanized agriculture. An exceptionally high birthrate among the Catholic Poles compounded this economic pressure, creating an army of the land-poor and landless. With wages in the United States more than eight times higher than in Poland, the American magnet was irresistible.

Many Polish immigrants were also lured by glowing letters from friends and relatives already living in the United States. The first wave of Polish immigrants had established a thriving network of self-help and fraternal associations, organized around Polish Catholic parishes. Often Polish-American entrepreneurs helped their European compatriots make travel arrangements or find jobs in the United States. One of the most suc-

Polish Coal Miners, c. 1905 *It was common practice in American mines to segregate mining crews by ethnicity and race.*

cessful of these, the energetic Chicago grocer Anton Schermann, is credited with "bringing over" a hundred thousand Poles and causing the Windy City to earn the nickname the "American Warsaw."

Most of the Poles arriving in the United States in the late nineteenth century headed for booming industrial cities such as Buffalo, Pittsburgh, Detroit, Milwaukee, and Chicago. In 1907 four-fifths of the men toiled as unskilled laborers in coal mines, meatpacking factories, textile and steel mills, oil refineries, and garment-making shops. Although married women usually stayed home and contributed to the family's earnings by taking in laundry and boarders, children and single girls often joined their fathers and brothers on the job.

When an independent Poland was created after World War I, few Poles chose to return to their Old World homeland. Instead, like other immigrant groups in the 1920s, they redoubled their efforts to integrate into American society. Polish institutions like churches and fraternal organizations, which had served to perpetuate a distinctive Polish culture in the New World, now facilitated the transformation of Poles into Polish-Americans. When Poland was absorbed into the Communist bloc after World War II, Polish-Americans clung still more tightly to their American identity, pushing for landmarks like Chicago's Pulaski Road to memorialize their culture in the New World.

rifice something of its tradition of freedom and opportunity, as well as its future ethnic diversity.

The Immigration Act of 1924 marked the end of an era—a period of virtually unrestricted immigration that in the previous century had brought some 35 million newcomers to the United States, mostly from Europe. The immigrant tide was now cut off, but it left on American shores by the 1920s a patchwork of ethnic communities separated from the larger society and from each other by language, religion, and customs. Many Italians, Jews, Poles, and others lived in isolated enclaves with their own houses of worship, newspapers, and theaters. Efforts to organize labor unions repeatedly foundered on the rocks of ethnic rivalries—often played upon by cynical employers. Ethnic variety thus undermined class and political solidarity in America.

The Prohibition Experiment

One of the last peculiar spasms of the progressive reform movement was prohibition, loudly supported by crusading churches and by many women. The arid new order was authorized in 1919 by the Eighteenth Amendment (for text, see the Appendix), as implemented by the Volstead Act passed by Congress later that year. Together these laws made the world "safe for hypocrisy."

The legal abolition of alcohol was especially popular in the South and the West. Southern whites were eager to keep stimulants out of the hands of blacks, lest they burst out of "their place." In the West, prohibition represented an attack on all the vices associated with the ubiquitous western saloon: public drunkenness, prostitution, and crime. But despite the overwhelming ratification of the "dry" amendment, strong opposition persisted in the larger eastern cities. For many "wet" foreign-born people, sociability was built around drinking in beer gardens and corner taverns. Yet most Americans assumed that prohibition had come to stay.

But prohibitionists were naive in the extreme. They overlooked the tenacious American tradition of strong drink and of weak control by the central government, especially over private lives. They forgot that the federal authorities had never satisfactorily enforced a law that the majority of the people—or a strong minority—were hostile to. Lawmakers could not legislate away a thirst.

Prohibition simply did not prohibit. The old-time corner saloons were replaced by thousands of "speakeasies," each with a tiny grilled window through which the thirsty spoke softly before the barred door was opened. Hard liquor, especially the cocktail, was drunk in staggering volume by both men and women. Largely because of the difficulties of transporting and concealing bottles, beverages of high alcoholic content were popular. Foreign rum-runners operating from the West Indies had their inning, and countless cases of liquor also leaked down from Canada. "Home brew" and "bathtub gin" became popular, as law-evading adults engaged in "alky cooking" with toy stills. The worst of the home-made "rotgut" produced blindness, even death.

Yet the "noble experiment" was not entirely a failure. Bank savings increased, and absenteeism in industry decreased, presumably because of the newly sober ways of formerly soused barflies. On the whole, probably less alcohol was consumed than in the days before prohibition, though strong drink continued to be available. As a legendary tippler remarked, prohibition was "a darn sight better than no liquor at all."

Prohibition also spawned shocking crimes. The lush profits of illegal alcohol led to bribery of the police, many of whom were induced to see and smell no evil. Violent wars broke out in the big cities between rival gangs seeking to corner the rich market in booze. Rival triggermen used their sawed-off shot-guns and chattering "typewriters" (machine guns) to "erase" bootlegging competitors who were trying to "muscle in" on their "racket." In the gang wars of the 1920s in Chicago, about five hundred mobsters were murdered.

Chicago was by far the most spectacular example of lawlessness. In 1925 "Scarface" Al Capone, a grasp-ing and murderous booze distributor, set off six years of gang warfare that netted him millions of blood-spattered dollars. He zoomed through the streets in an armor-plated car with bulletproof windows.

Gangsters rapidly moved into other profitable and illicit activities: prostitution, gambling, and nar-cotics. Racketeers even invaded the ranks of local labor unions as organizers and promoters. Organized crime had come to be one of the nation's most gigan-tic businesses. By 1930 the annual "take" of the underworld was estimated to be from $12 billion to $18 billion—several times the income of the Wash-ington government.

Monkey Business in Tennessee

Education in the 1920s continued to make giant bootstrides. More and more states were requiring young people to remain in school until age sixteen or eighteen, or until graduation from high school. The proportion of seventeen-year-olds who finished high school almost doubled in the 1920s, to more than one in four.

The most revolutionary contribution to educa-tional theory during these years was made by mild-mannered Professor John Dewey, who served on the faculty of Columbia University from 1904 to 1930. By common consent one of America's few front-rank philosophers, he set forth the principles of "learning by doing" that formed the foundation of so-called progressive education, with its greater "permissive-ness." He believed that the workbench was as essen-tial as the blackboard and that "education for life" should be a primary goal of the teacher.

Science also scored wondrous advances in these years. A massive public health program, launched by the Rockefeller Foundation in the South in 1909, had virtually wiped out the ancient affliction of hook-worm by the 1920s. Better nutrition and health care helped to increase the life expectancy of a newborn

The Fundamentalist Outcry, 1925 *Radicalism and sci-ence are both condemned.*

infant from fifty years in 1901 to fifty-nine years in 1929.

Yet both science and progressive education in the 1920s were subjected to unfriendly fire from Fundamentalists. These old-time religionists charged that the teaching of Darwinian evolution was destroying faith in God and the Bible while contributing to the moral breakdown of youth in the jazz age. Numerous attempts were made to secure laws prohibiting the teaching of evolution, "the bestial hypothesis," in the public schools, and three southern states adopted such measures. The trio included Tennessee, in the heart of the so-called Bible Belt South, where evangelical religion was especially robust.

The stage was set for the memorable "Monkey Trial" at the hamlet of Dayton, Tennessee, in 1925. A likable high school biology teacher, John T. Scopes, was indicted for teaching evolution. Batteries of newspaper reporters, armed with notebooks and cameras, descended on the quiet town to witness the spectacle. Scopes was defended by nationally known attorneys, while former presidential candidate William Jennings Bryan, an ardent Presbyterian Fundamentalist, joined the prosecution. Taking the stand as an expert on the Bible, Bryan was made to appear foolish by the famed criminal lawyer, Clarence Darrow. Five days after the trial was over, Bryan died of a stroke, no doubt brought on by the heat and strain.

This historic clash between theology and biology proved inconclusive. Scopes, the forgotten man of the drama, was found guilty and fined $100. But the supreme court of Tennessee, while upholding the law, set aside the fine on a technicality.* The Fundamentalists at best won only a hollow victory, for the trial cast ridicule on their cause. Yet even though increasing numbers of Christians were coming to reconcile the revelations of religion with the findings of modern science, Fundamentalism, with its emphasis on literal reading of the Bible, remained a vibrant force in American spiritual life. It was especially strong in the Baptist Church and in the rapidly growing Churches of Christ, organized in 1906.

---

*The Tennessee law was not formally repealed until 1967.

The Mass-Consumption Economy

Prosperity—real, sustained, and widely shared—put much of the "roar" into the twenties. The economy kicked off its war harness in 1919, faltered a few steps in the recession of 1920–1921, and then sprinted forward for nearly seven years. Both the recent war and Treasury Secretary Andrew Mellon's tax policies favored the rapid expansion of capital investment. Ingenious machines, powered by relatively cheap energy from newly tapped oil fields, dramatically increased the productivity of the laborer. Assembly-line production was so advanced at Henry Ford's famed Rouge River plant near Detroit that a finished automobile emerged every ten seconds.

Great new industries suddenly sprouted forth. Supplying electrical power for the humming new machines became a giant business in the 1920s. Above all the automobile, once the horseless chariot of the rich, now became the carriage of the common citizen. By 1930 Americans owned almost 30 million cars. The nation's deepening "love affair" with the automobile headlined a momentous shift in the character of the economy. American manufacturers seemed to have mastered the problems of production; their worries now focused on consumption. Could they find the mass markets for the goods they had contrived to spew forth in such profusion?

Responding to this need, a new arm of American commerce came into being: advertising. By persuasion and ploy, allure and sexual suggestion, advertisers sought to make Americans chronically discontented with their paltry possessions and want more, more, more.

Sports became big business in the consumer economy of the 1920s. Ballyhooed by the "image makers," home-run heroes like George H. ("Babe") Ruth were far better known than most statesmen. In 1921 a Jersey City crowd paid more than a million dollars to watch heavyweight champion Jack Dempsey knock out challenger George Carpentier—the first in a series of million-dollar "gates" in the golden 1920s.

Buying on credit was another innovative feature of the postwar economy. "Possess today and pay tomorrow" was the message directed at buyers.

Once-frugal descendants of Puritans went ever deeper into debt to own all kinds of newfangled marvels—refrigerators, vacuum cleaners, and especially cars and radios—now. Prosperity thus accumulated an overhanging cloud of debt, and the economy became increasingly vulnerable to disruptions of the credit structure.

Putting America on Rubber Tires

A new industrial revolution slipped into high gear in America in the 1920s. Thrusting out steel tentacles, it changed the daily lives of the people in unprecedented ways. Of all the technological inventions of the era, the automobile cut the deepest track. It heralded an amazing new industrial system based on assembly-line methods and mass-production techniques.

Americans adapted rather than invented the gasoline engine; Europeans can claim the original honor. By the 1890s a few daring American inventors and promoters, including Henry Ford and Ransom E. Olds (Oldsmobile), were developing the infant automotive industry. By 1910 sixty-nine car companies rolled out a total annual production of 181,000 units. Soon an enormous industry sprang into being, as Detroit became the motorcar capital of America.

It was the lean and silent Ford, more than anyone else, who put America on rubber tires. This ill-educated, multimillionaire mechanic was socially and culturally narrow; "history is bunk," he once testified. But he devoted himself with one-track devotion to the gospel of standardization and erected an enormous personal empire on the cornerstone of his mechanical genius. After two early failures, he grasped and applied fully the techniques of assembly-line production and standardization—"Fordism." He is supposed to have remarked that the purchaser could have his Model T car in any color he desired—just as long as it was black.

The high and hideous "Tin Lizzie" was cheap, rugged, and reasonably reliable, though the ride was rough and clattering. Customers flocked to buy Fords in phenomenal numbers. In 1914 the "Automobile Wizard" turned out his 500,000th Model T. By 1930 his total had risen to 20 million. By 1929, when the great bull market collapsed, 26 million motor vehicles were registered in the United States. This figure, averaging 1 for every 4.9 Americans, represented far more automobiles than existed in all the rest of the world.

The impact of the self-propelled carriage on various aspects of American life was tremendous. A gigantic new industry emerged, dependent on steel but displacing steel from its kingpin role. Employing directly or indirectly about 6 million people by 1930, it was a major pillar of the nation's prosperity. Thousands of new jobs, moreover, were created in supporting industries like rubber, glass, and fabrics, to say nothing of thousands of service stations and garages. America's standard of living, responding to this infectious vitality, rose to an enviable level.

Zooming motorcars were agents of social change. At first a luxury, they rapidly became a necessity. Essentially devices for needed transportation, they soon developed into a badge of freedom and equality—a necessary prop for self-respect. Women were further freed from their dependence on men. Isolation among the sections was broken down, and the less attractive states lost population at an alarming rate. Buses made possible the consolidation of schools and to some extent of churches. Virtuous home life partially broke down as joyriders of all ages forsook the parlor for the highway. And what might young people get up to in the privacy of a closed-top Model T? An Indiana juvenile judge voiced parents' worst fears when he condemned the automobile as "a house of prostitution on wheels." The motorcar even aided and abetted the crime wave of the 1920s and 1930s by enabling gangsters to make quick getaways.

Yet no sane American would plead for a return of the old horse and buggy, complete with fly-breeding manure. The automobile contributed notably to improved air and environmental quality, despite its later notoriety as a polluter. Life might be cut short on the highways, and smog might poison the air, but the automobile brought more convenience, pleasure, and excitement into people's lives than almost any other single invention.

Humans Develop Wings

Gasoline engines also provided the power that enabled humans to fulfill their age-old dream of sprouting wings. After near-successful experiments by others with heavier-than-air craft, the Wright brothers, Orville and Wilbur, performed "the miracle at Kitty Hawk," North Carolina. On a historic day—December 17, 1903—Orville Wright took aloft a feebly engined plane that stayed airborne for twelve seconds and 120 feet. Thus the air age was launched by two obscure bicycle repairmen.

Airplanes—once "flying coffins" for stuntmen—were first used with marked success for a serious purpose during the Great War of 1914–1918. Shortly thereafter private companies began to operate passenger lines with airmail contracts, which were in effect a subsidy from Washington. The first transcontinental airmail route was established from New York to San Francisco in 1920.

In 1927 modest and skillful Charles A. Lindbergh, the so-called Flyin' Fool, electrified the world with the first solo west-to-east conquest of the Atlantic. Seeking a prize of $25,000, the lanky stunt flier courageously piloted his single-engine plane, the *Spirit of St. Louis,* from New York to Paris in a grueling thirty-three hours and thirty-nine minutes.

Lindbergh's exploit swept Americans off their feet. Fed up with the cynicism and debunking of the jazz age, they found in this wholesome and handsome youth a genuine hero. "Lucky Lindy" received an uproarious welcome in the "hero canyon" of lower Broadway, as eighteen hundred tons of ticker tape and other improvised confetti showered upon him. His achievement—it was more than a "stunt"—did much to dramatize and popularize flying while giving a strong boost to the infant aviation industry.

The impact of the airplane was tremendous. The floundering railroads received another sharp setback through the loss of passengers and mail. A lethal new weapon was given to the gods of war with the coming of city-busting aerial bombs. The Atlantic Ocean was shriveling to about the size of the Aegean Sea in the days of Socrates, while isolation behind ocean moats was becoming a bygone dream.

The Radio and Film Revolutions

The speed of the airplane was far eclipsed by the speed of radio waves. Guglielmo Marconi, an Italian, invented wireless telegraphy in the 1890s, and his brainchild was used for long-range communication during World War I.

Next came the voice-carrying radio, a triumph of many minds. A red-letter day was posted in November 1920, when the Pittsburgh station KDKA broadcast the news of the Harding landslide.

The radio not only created a new industry but added richness to the fabric of American life. More joy was given to leisure hours, and the nation was better knit together. Advertising was further perfected as an art.

Crude filmmaking first developed in the 1890s. But the real birth of the movie came in 1903, when the first story sequence reached the screen. This breathless melodrama—*The Great Train Robbery*—was featured in the five-cent theaters, popularly called "nickelodeons." Spectacular among the first full-length classics was D. W. Griffith's *The Birth of a Nation* (1915), which glorified the Ku Klux Klan of Reconstruction days and defamed both blacks and northern carpetbaggers.

A fascinating industry was thus launched. Hollywood, California, quickly became the movie capital of the world, for it enjoyed a maximum of sunshine and other advantages. The motion picture really arrived during the World War of 1914–1918, when it was used as an engine of anti-German propaganda.

A new era began in 1927 with the success of the first "talkie"—*The Jazz Singer*, starring the white performer Al Jolson in blackface. The age of the "silents" was ushered out as theaters everywhere were wired for sound. About the same time, reasonably satisfactory color films were being produced.

Movies eclipsed all other new forms of amusement in the phenomenal growth of their popularity. Movie "stars" commanded much larger salaries than the president of the United States, in some cases as much as $100,000 for a single picture.

Critics bemoaned the vulgarization of popular taste wrought by the technologies of radio and movies, but the effects of the new mass media were not all negative. Much of the rich diversity of immigrant cultures was lost, as children, especially, turned away from Grandma's storytelling to the downtown movie theater or "Amos 'n' Andy." But the standardization of tastes and language hastened entry into the

American mainstream—and set the stage for the emergence of a working-class political coalition that, for a time, would overcome the divisive ethnic differences of the past.

The Dynamic Decade

Far-reaching changes in lifestyles and values paralleled the dramatic upsurge of the economy. The census of 1920 revealed that for the first time most Americans no longer lived in the countryside but in urban areas. Women continued to find new opportunities for employment in the cities, though they tended to cluster in a few low-paying jobs (such as retail clerking and office typing) that quickly became classified as "women's work." An organized birth control movement, led by fiery feminist Margaret Sanger, openly championed the use of contraceptives. Alice Paul's National Woman's party began in 1923 to campaign for an Equal Rights Amendment to the Constitution. To some defenders of traditional ways, it seemed that the world had suddenly gone mad.

Even before the war, one observer thought the chimes had "struck sex o'clock in America," and the 1920s witnessed what many old-timers thought was a veritable erotic eruption. Advertisers exploited sexual allure to sell everything from soap to car tires. Once-modest maidens now proclaimed their new freedom as "flappers" in bobbed tresses and dresses. Young women appeared with hemlines elevated, stockings rolled, breasts taped flat, cheeks rouged, and lips a "crimson gash" that held a dangling cigarette. Thus did the flapper symbolize a yearned-for and devil-may-care independence (some said wild abandon) in American women.

Justification for this new sexual frankness could be found in the recently translated writings of Dr. Sigmund Freud. This Viennese physician appeared to argue that sexual repression was responsible for a variety of nervous and emotional ills. Thus not pleasure alone, but health, demanded sexual gratification and liberation.

Many taboos flew out the window as sex-conscious Americans let themselves go. As unknowing Freudians, teenagers pioneered the sexual frontiers. Glued together in syncopated embrace, they danced to jazz music squeaking from phonographs. In an earlier day a kiss had been the equivalent of a proposal of marriage. But in the new era exploratory

King Oliver's Creole Jazz Band, Early 1920s *Joseph ("Joe") King Oliver arrived in Chicago from New Orleans in 1918. His band became the first important black jazz ensemble and made Chicago's Royal Garden Cafe a magnet for jazz lovers. Left to right: Honoré Dutrey, trombone; Baby Dodds, drums; King Oliver, cornet; Lil Hardin, piano; Bill Johnson, banjo; and Johnny Dodds, clarinet. Kneeling in the foreground is the young Louis Armstrong, playing a trombone.*

young folk sat in darkened movie houses or took to the highways and byways in automobiles. There the youthful "neckers" and "petters" poached upon the forbidden territory of each other's bodies.

If the flapper was the goddess of the "era of wonderful nonsense," jazz was its sacred music. With its virtuoso wanderings and tricky syncopation, jazz moved up from New Orleans along with migrating blacks during World War I. Tunes like W. C. Handy's "St. Louis Blues" became instant classics as the wailing saxophone became the trumpet of the new era. Blacks such as Handy, "Jelly Roll" Morton, and Joseph ("Joe") King Oliver gave birth to jazz, but the entertainment industry soon spawned all-white bands—notably Paul Whiteman's. Caucasian impresarios cornered the profits, though not the creative soul, of America's most native music.

A new racial pride also blossomed in the northern black communities that grew so rapidly during and after the war. Harlem in New York City, counting some 100,000 African-American residents in the 1920s, was one of the largest black communities in the world. Harlem sustained a vibrant, creative culture that nourished poets like Langston Hughes, whose first volume of verse, *The Weary Blues*, appeared in 1926.

Harlem in the 1920s also spawned a charismatic leader, Marcus Garvey. Jamaica-born Garvey founded the United Negro Improvement Association (UNIA) to promote the resettlement of American blacks in Africa. His Black Star Steamship Company and other enterprises failed financially, and Garvey himself was convicted of fraud in 1927 and deported by a nervous United States government. But the race pride that Garvey inspired among his 4 million UNIA followers helped them gain self-confidence and self-reliance. His example proved important to the later founding of the Nation of Islam (Black Muslim) movement.

Literary Liberation

Likewise in literature, an older era seemed to have ground to a halt with the recent war. By the dawn of the 1920s, most of the custodians of an aging genteel culture had died—Henry James in 1916, Henry Adams in 1918, and William Dean Howells (the "dean of American literature") in 1920. A few novelists who had been popular in the previous decades continued to thrive, notably the well-to-do, cosmopolitan New Yorker Edith Wharton and the Virginia-born Willa Cather, esteemed for her stark but sympathetic portrayals of pioneering on the prairies.

But in the decade after the war, a new generation of writers burst on the scene. Many of them hailed from ethnic and regional backgrounds different from that of the Protestant New Englanders who traditionally had dominated American cultural life. The newcomers exhibited the energy of youth, the ambition of excluded outsiders, and, in many cases, the smoldering resentment of ideals betrayed. They bestowed on American literature a new vitality, imaginativeness, and artistic quality.

A patron saint of many young authors was H. L. Mencken, the "Bad Boy of Baltimore." In the pages of his green-covered monthly *American Mercury*, Mencken assailed marriage, patriotism, democracy, prohibition, Rotarians, and the middle-class American "booboisie." The South he contemptuously dismissed as "the Sahara of the Bozart" (a bastardization of *beaux arts*, French for the "fine arts"), and he scathingly attacked do-gooders as "Puritans." Puritanism, he jibed, was "the haunting fear that someone, somewhere, might be happy."

The war had jolted many young writers out of their complacency about traditional values and literary standards. With their pens they probed for new codes of morals and understanding, as well as fresh forms of expression. F. Scott Fitzgerald, a handsome Minnesota-born Princetonian then only twenty-four years old, became an overnight celebrity when he published *This Side of Paradise* in 1920. The book became a kind of Bible for the young. It was eagerly devoured by aspiring flappers and their ardent wooers, many of whom affected an air of bewildered abandon toward life. Catching the spirit of the hour (often about 4 a.m.), Fitzgerald found "All gods dead, all wars fought, all faiths in man shaken." He followed this melancholy success with *The Great Gatsby* (1925), a brilliant evocation of the glamour and

F. Scott Fitzgerald and His Wife, Zelda *They are shown here in the happy, early days of their stormy marriage.*

cruelty of an achievement-oriented society. Theodore Dreiser's masterpiece of 1925, *An American Tragedy*, explored much the same theme through the story of a pregnant working girl murdered by her socially ambitious young lover.

Ernest Hemingway, who had seen action on the Italian front in 1917, was among the writers most affected by the war. He responded to pernicious propaganda and the overblown appeal of patriotism by devising his own lean, word-sparing but word-perfect style. In *The Sun Also Rises* (1926) Hemingway told of disillusioned, spiritually numb American expatriates in Europe. In *A Farewell to Arms* (1929) he crafted one of the finest novels in any language about the war

experience. A troubled soul, he finally blew out his brains with a shotgun blast in 1961.

Other writers turned to a critical probing of American small-town life. Sherwood Anderson dissected various fictional personalities in *Winesburg, Ohio* (1919), finding them all in some way warped by their cramped psychological surroundings. Sinclair Lewis, a hotheaded, heavy-drinking writer from Sauk Centre, Minnesota, sprang into prominence in 1920 with *Main Street*, the story of one woman's unsuccessful war against provincialism. In *Babbitt* (1922) he affectionately pilloried George F. Babbitt, a prosperous, vulgar, middle-class real estate broker who slavishly conformed to the respectable materialism of his group. The word *Babbittry* was quickly coined to describe his all-too-familiar lifestyle.

William Faulkner, a dark-eyed, pensive Mississippian, penned a bitter war novel, *Soldier's Pay*, in 1926. He then turned his attention to a fictional chronicle of an imaginary, history-rich Deep South county. In powerful books like *The Sound and the Fury* (1929) and *As I Lay Dying* (1930), Faulkner peeled back layers of time and consciousness from the constricted souls of his ingrown southern characters.

Nowhere was innovation in the 1920s more obvious than in poetry. Ezra Pound, a brilliantly erratic Idahoan who deserted America for Europe, rejected what he called "an old bitch civilization, gone in the teeth," and proclaimed his doctrine: "make it new." Pound strongly influenced Missouri-born and Harvard-educated T. S. Eliot, who took up residence in England. In "The Waste Land" (1922) Eliot produced one of the most impenetrable but influential poems of the century. Robert Frost, a San Francisco–born poet, wrote hauntingly about his adopted New England.

On the stage, Eugene O'Neill, a New York dramatist and Princeton dropout of globe-trotting background, laid bare Freudian notions of sex in plays like *Strange Interlude* (1928). A prodigious playwright, he wrote more than a dozen productions in the 1920s and won the Nobel Prize in 1936.

O'Neill arose from New York's Greenwich Village, which before and after the war was a seething cauldron of writers, painters, musicians, actors, and other artists. After the war, a black cultural renaissance also took root uptown in Harlem, led by such gifted writers as Claude McKay, Langston Hughes, and Zora Neale Hurston, and by jazz artists like Louis Armstrong and Eubie Blake. In an outpouring of creative expression called the Harlem Renaissance, they proudly exulted in their black culture and argued for a "New Negro" who was a full citizen and a "social equal" to whites.

Architecture also married itself to the new materialism and functionalism. Long-range city planning was being intelligently projected, and architects such as Frank Lloyd Wright were advancing the theory that buildings should grow from their sites and not slavishly imitate Greek and Roman importations. The machine age outdid itself in New York City, where in 1931 it thrust upward the cloud-brushing Empire State Building, 102 stories high.

Wall Street's Big Bull Market

Signals abounded that the economic joyride might end in a crash; even in the best years of the 1920s several hundred banks failed annually. This something-for-nothing craze was well illustrated by real estate speculation, especially the fantastic Florida boom that culminated in 1925. Numerous underwater lots were sold to eager purchasers for preposterous sums. The whole wildcat scheme collapsed when the peninsula was devastated by a hurricane.

The stock exchange provided even greater sensations. Speculation ran wild, and an orgy of boom-or-bust trading pushed the bull market to dizzying peaks as Wall Street gamblers gored one another and fleeced greedy lambs. The stock market became a veritable gambling den.

As the 1920s lurched forward, everybody seemed to be buying stocks "on margin"—that is, with a small down payment. Barbers, stenographers, and elevator boys cashed in on "hot tips" picked up while on duty. One valet was reported to have parlayed his wages into a quarter of a million dollars. Rags-to-riches Americans eagerly worshiped at the altar of the ticker-tape machine. So powerful was the intoxicant of quick profits that few heeded the voices raised in certain quarters to warn that this kind of tinsel prosperity could not last forever.

Little was done by Washington to curb money-mad speculators. In the wartime days of Wilson, the national debt had rocketed from the 1914 figure of $1,188,235,400 to the 1921 peak of $23,976,250,608. Conservative principles of money management pointed to a diversion of surplus funds to reduce this financial burden.

The burdensome taxes inherited from the war were especially distasteful to Secretary of the Treasury Mellon, as well as to his fellow millionaires. Their theory was that such high levies forced the rich to invest in tax-exempt securities rather than in factories that dispensed prosperous payrolls. The Mellonites also argued, with considerable persuasiveness, that high taxes not only discouraged business but also brought a smaller net return to the Treasury than moderate taxes.

Seeking to succor the "poor" rich people, Mellon helped engineer a series of tax reductions from 1921 to 1926. Congress followed his lead by repealing the excess-profits tax, abolishing the gift tax, and reducing excise taxes, the surtax, the income tax, and estate taxes. In 1921 a wealthy person with an income of $1 million had paid $663,000 in income taxes; in 1926 the same person paid about $200,000. Mellon's spare-the-rich policies thus shifted much of the tax burden from the wealthy to middle-income groups.

Mellon, lionized by conservatives as the "greatest secretary of the treasury since Hamilton," remains a controversial figure. True, he reduced the national debt by $10 billion—from about $26 billion to $16 billion. But foes of the emaciated multimillionaire charged that he should have bitten a larger chunk out of the debt, especially while the country was pulsating with prosperity. He was also accused of indirectly encouraging the bull market. If he had absorbed more of the national income in taxes, there would have been less money left for frenzied speculation. His refusal to do so typified the single-mindedly probusiness regime that dominated the political scene throughout the postwar decade.

Chronology

1903 Wright brothers fly the first airplane.
First story-sequence motion picture.

1919 Eighteenth Amendment (prohibition)
ratified.
Volstead Act.
Seattle general strike.
Anderson publishes *Winesburg, Ohio*.

**1919–
1920** "Red scare."

1920 Radio broadcasting begins.
Fitzgerald publishes *This Side of Paradise*.
Lewis publishes *Main Street*.

1921 Sacco-Vanzetti trial.
Emergency Quota Act of 1921.

1922 Lewis publishes *Babbitt*.
Eliot publishes "The Waste Land."

1923 Equal Rights Amendment (ERA) proposed.

1924 Immigration Act of 1924.

1925 Scopes trial.
Florida real estate boom.
Fitzgerald publishes *The Great Gatsby*.
Dreiser publishes *An American Tragedy*.

1926 Hughes publishes *The Weary Blues*.
Hemingway publishes *The Sun Also Rises*.

1927 Lindbergh flies the Atlantic solo.
First talking motion pictures.
Sacco and Vanzetti executed.

1929 Faulkner publishes *The Sound and the Fury*.
Hemingway publishes *A Farewell to Arms*.

For further reading, see the Appendix. For web resources, go to **http://college.hmco.com**.

33

The Politics of Boom and Bust

1920–1932

We in America today are nearer to the final triumph over poverty than ever before in the history of any land. We have not yet reached the goal—but . . . we shall soon, with the help of God, be in sight of the day when poverty will be banished from this nation.

HERBERT HOOVER, 1928

Three Republican presidents—Warren G. Harding, Calvin Coolidge, and Herbert Hoover—steered the nation on its roller-coaster ride through the 1920s, a thrilling ascent from the depths of post–World War I recession to breathtaking heights of prosperity, followed by a terrifying crash into the Great Depression. In a retreat from progressive reform, Republicans sought to serve the public good less by direct government action and more through cooperation with big business. Some corrupt officials served themselves as well, exploiting public resources for personal profit. Meanwhile, the United States abandoned its brief international fling during World War I and resumed with a vengeance its traditional foreign policy of military unpreparedness and political isolationism.

The Republican "Old Guard" Returns

Warren G. Harding, inaugurated in 1921, *looked* presidential. With erect figure, broad shoulders, high forehead, bushy eyebrows, and graying hair, he was one of the best-liked men of his generation. An easygoing, warm-handed backslapper, he exuded graciousness and love of people. Yet the amiable, smiling exterior concealed a weak, inept interior. With a mediocre mind, Harding quickly found himself beyond his depth in the presidency. "God! What a job!" was his anguished cry on one occasion.

Harding, like Grant, was unable to detect moral halitosis in his evil associates, and he was soon

457

surrounded by his poker-playing, shirt-sleeved cronies of the "Ohio gang." Harding hated to hurt his friends' feelings by saying no, and designing political leeches capitalized on this weakness. He "was not a bad man," said one Washington observer. "He was just a slob." Admitting his own scant mental furnishings, Harding appointed to his cabinet strong figures like Charles Evans Hughes (secretary of state), Andrew W. Mellon (secretary of the treasury), and Herbert Hoover (secretary of commerce). But his cabinet also included such corrupt characters as the scheming anticonservationist Albert B. Fall (secretary of the interior) and Attorney General Harry M. Daugherty, a small-town lawyer and a big-time crook.

Well intentioned but weak willed, Harding was a perfect "front" for enterprising industrialists. A McKinley-style old order settled heavily back into place at war's end, crushing the reform seedlings that had sprouted in the progressive era. This new Old Guard hoped to improve on the old business doctrine of laissez-faire. Their plea was not simply for government to keep hands off business but for government to help guide business along the path to profits. They subtly and effectively achieved their ends by putting the courts and the administrative bureaus into the safekeeping of fellow stand-patters.

The Supreme Court was a striking example of this trend. Harding lived less than three years as president, but he appointed four of the nine justices. In the first years of the 1920s, the Supreme Court axed progressive legislation. It killed a federal child-labor law, stripped away many of labor's hard-won gains, and rigidly restricted governmental intervention in the economy. In the landmark case of *Adkins* v. *Children's Hospital* (1923), the Court reversed its own reasoning in *Muller* v. *Oregon* (see p. 407) and invalidated a minimum-wage law for women. Its strained ruling was that because females now had the vote (Nineteenth Amendment), they could no longer be protected by special legislation. The contradictory premises of the *Muller* and *Adkins* cases framed a debate over gender differences that would continue for the rest of the century: Were women sufficiently different from men that they merited special legal and social treatment, or were they effectively equal in the eyes of the law and therefore undeserving of special protection and preferences?

Corporations, under Harding, could once more relax and expand. Antitrust laws were often ignored, circumvented, or feebly enforced by friendly prosecutors in the attorney general's office. The Interstate Commerce Commission, to single out one agency, came to be dominated by members who were sympathetic to the managers of the railroads.

Big industrialists, striving to lessen competition, now had a free hand to set up trade associations. Cement manufacturers, for example, would use these agencies to agree upon standardization of product, publicity campaigns, and a united front in dealing with the railroads and labor. Although many of these associations ran counter to the spirit of existing antitrust legislation, their formation was encouraged by Secretary of Commerce Herbert Hoover. His sense of engineering efficiency was shocked by the waste resulting from cutthroat competition.

The Aftermath of War

Wartime government controls on the economy were swiftly dismantled. The War Industries Board disappeared with almost indecent haste. With its passing, progressive hopes for more government regulation of big business evaporated.

Washington likewise returned the railroads to private management in 1920. The Esch-Cummins Transportation Act of 1920 encouraged private consolidation of the railroads and obligated the federal Interstate Commerce Commission to guarantee their profitability.

Labor, suddenly deprived of its wartime crutch of friendly government support, limped along badly in the postwar decade. The Railway Labor Board, a successor body to the wartime labor boards, ordered a wage cut of 12 percent in 1922, provoking a two-month strike. It ended when Attorney General Harry Daugherty, who fully shared Harding's big-business bias, clamped on the strikers one of the most sweeping injunctions in American history. Unions wilted in this hostile political environment, and membership dropped by nearly 30 percent between 1920 and 1930.

Needy veterans were among the few nonbusiness groups to reap lasting gains from the war. In 1921

Congress created the Veterans Bureau to operate hospitals and provide vocational rehabilitation for the disabled. The American Legion, founded in Paris in 1919 by Colonel Theodore Roosevelt, Jr., became known for its militant conservatism and aggressive lobbying for veterans' benefits. It pressed fervently for "adjusted compensation" to make up for the wages veterans had "lost" while in uniform. Harding vetoed one such bill in 1922, but in 1924 Congress passed the Adjusted Compensation Act over President Calvin Coolidge's veto. It gave every former soldier a paid-up insurance policy due in twenty years—adding about $3.5 billion to the total cost of the war.

America Seeks Benefits Without Burdens

Isolation was enthroned in Washington during the Harding administration. With the Senate "irreconcilables" holding a hatchet over its head, the U.S. government continued to regard the League of Nations as a thing unclean.

But disarmament was one international issue on which Harding set isolationism aside and seized the initiative. He was prodded by businesspeople unwilling to dig deeper into their pockets for money to finance the ambitious naval building program started during the war. A deadly contest was shaping up with Britain and Japan, which watched with alarm as the oceans filled with American vessels. Public agitation in America, fed by worries about British and Japanese cooperation in the Pacific, brought about the headline-making Washington Disarmament Conference in 1921–1922. The double agenda included naval disarmament and the situation in East Asia.

At the outset, Secretary of State Charles Evans Hughes dramatically proposed a ten-year "holiday" on construction of battleships, and even the scrapping of some of the huge dreadnoughts already built or being built. He suggested that the scaled-down navies of America and Britain should enjoy parity in battleships and aircraft carriers, with Japan on the small end of a 5-5-3 ratio.

The conference's Five-Power Naval Treaty of 1922 embodied Hughes's ideas on ship ratios, but only after face-saving compensation was offered to the Japanese. The British and the Americans both conceded that they would refrain from fortifying their East Asian possessions, including the Philippines. The Japanese were not subjected to such restraints in their possessions. In addition, a Four-Power Treaty bound Britain, Japan, France, and the United States to preserve the status quo in the Pacific—another concession to the Japanese. Finally, the Washington Conference gave chaotic China—"the sick man of East Asia"—a shot in the arm with the Nine-Power Treaty of 1922, whose signatories agreed to nail wide open the Open Door in China.

The Hardingites boasted of this globe-shaking achievement in disarmament, but their satisfaction was somewhat illusory. No restrictions had been placed on small warships, and the other powers churned ahead with the construction of cruisers, destroyers, and submarines, while penny-pinching Uncle Sam lagged dangerously behind. Ominously, the American people seemed content to rely for their security on words and wishful thinking rather than weapons and hardheaded realism.

A similar sentimentalism welled up later in the decade, when Americans clamored for the "outlawry of war." The Kellogg-Briand Pact, declaring war illegal, was signed by Coolidge's secretary of state Frank B. Kellogg and the French foreign minister Aristide Briand in 1928 and was ultimately ratified by sixty-two nations. It was delusory in the extreme. Lacking both muscles and teeth, the pact was a diplomatic derelict virtually useless in a showdown. Yet it accurately—and dangerously—reflected the American mind in the 1920s, which was all too ready to be lulled into a false sense of security. This mood took even deeper hold in the ostrichlike neutralism of the 1930s.

Hiking the Tariff Higher

A comparable lack of realism afflicted foreign economic policy in the 1920s. Businesspeople, shortsightedly obsessed with the dazzling prospects in the prosperous home market, sought to keep that market to themselves by flinging up insurmountable tariff walls around the United States. Congress passed the Fordney-McCumber Tariff Law of 1922, which boosted schedules from the average of 27 percent under Wilson's Underwood Tariff of 1913 to an average of 38.5 percent.

The high-tariff course thus charted by the Republican regimes set off an ominous chain reaction. European producers felt the squeeze, for the American tariff walls prolonged the postwar chaos. Impoverished Europe needed to sell manufactured goods to the United States, particularly if it hoped to achieve economic recovery and to pay its huge war debt to Washington. America needed to give foreign nations a chance to make a profit so that they could buy U.S. manufactured articles and repay debts. International trade, Americans were slow to learn, is a two-way street.

Erecting tariff walls was also a game that two could play. The American example spurred European nations, throughout the feverish 1920s, to pile up higher barriers themselves. The whole vicious circle further deepened the international economic distress, providing one more rung on the ladder by which Adolf Hitler scrambled to power.

The Stench of Scandal

The loose morality and get-rich-quickism of the Harding era manifested themselves spectacularly in a series of scandals. Early in 1923 the head of the Veterans Bureau, Colonel Charles R. Forbes, was caught with his hand in the till and later convicted of fraud. An appointee of the gullible Harding, he and his accomplices looted the government to the tune of about $200 million, chiefly in connection with the building of veterans' hospitals.

Most shocking of all was the Teapot Dome scandal, an affair that involved priceless naval oil reserves at Teapot Dome (Wyoming) and Elk Hills (California). In 1921 the slippery secretary of the interior, Albert B. Fall, induced his careless colleague, the secretary of the navy, to transfer these valuable properties to the Interior Department. Harding indiscreetly signed the secret order. Fall then quietly leased the lands to oilmen Harry F. Sinclair and Edward L. Doheny, but not until he had received a bribe ("loan") of $100,000 from Doheny and about three times that amount in all from Sinclair.

Teapot Dome, no tempest in a teapot, finally came to a whistling boil. Details of the crooked transaction leaked out in March 1923. Fall, Sinclair, and Doheny were indicted in 1924. Fall was found guilty of taking a bribe and sentenced to one year in jail. The two bribe givers were acquitted, though Sinclair served time in jail for "shadowing" jurors and for refusing to testify before a Senate committee.

Still more scandals erupted. Persistent reports about the underhanded doings of Attorney General

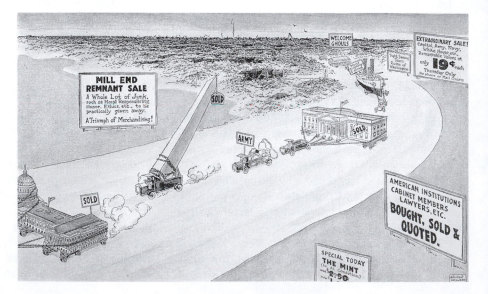

The Harding Scandals
This 1924 cartoon satirizing the misdemeanors of the Harding administration shows the sale of the Capitol, the White House, and even the Washington Monument.

Daugherty brought a Senate investigation in 1924 of the illegal sale of pardons and liquor permits. Forced to resign, the accused official was tried in 1927 but released after a jury twice failed to agree on a verdict. During the trial, Daugherty hid behind the trousers of the now-dead Harding by implying that persistent probing might uncover crookedness in the White House.

Harding was mercifully spared the full revelation of these iniquities. Just as the scandals were breaking, he died in San Francisco on August 2, 1923, of pneumonia and thrombosis.

The brutal fact is that Harding simply was not a strong enough man for the presidency—as he himself privately admitted. Such was his weakness that he tolerated people and conditions that subjected the Republic to its worst disgrace since the days of President Grant.

"Silent Cal" Coolidge

News of Harding's death was sped to Vice President Coolidge, then visiting at his father's New England farmhouse. By the light of two kerosene lamps the elder Coolidge, a justice of the peace, used the old family Bible to administer the presidential oath to his son.

Cash Register Chorus *Business croons its appreciation of "Coolidge prosperity."*

This homespun setting was symbolic of Coolidge. Quite unlike Harding, the stern-faced Vermonter, with his thin nose and tightly set lips, embodied the New England virtues of honesty, morality, industry, and frugality. His dour visage prompted the acerbic observation that he had been "weaned on a pickle."

Coolidge seemed to be a crystallization of the commonplace. Painfully shy, he was blessed with only mediocre powers of leadership. He would occasionally display a dry wit in private; but his speeches, delivered in a nasal New England twang, were invariably boring. A staunch apostle of the status quo, he became the "high priest of the great god Business." He believed that "the man who builds a factory builds a temple" and that "the man who works there worships there." Coolidge "luck" held during his five and a half prosperity-blessed years.

Ever a profile in caution, Coolidge slowly gave the Harding regime a badly needed moral fumigation. Teapot Dome had scalded the Republican party badly, but so transparently honest was the vinegary Vermonter that the scandalous oil did not rub off on him.

Frustrated Farmers

Sun-bronzed farmers were squarely in a boom-or-bust cycle in the postwar decade. While the fighting had raged, they had raked in money, hand over gnarled fist; but peace ended high farm prices.

Machines also threatened to plow the farmer under an avalanche of his own overabundant crops. The gasoline-engine tractor was working a revolution on American farms. This steel mule was to cultivation and sowing what the McCormick reaper was to harvesting. Blue-denimed farmers could sit on their chugging mechanical chariots and harrow many acres in a single day. But such improved efficiency and expanded agricultural production helped to pile up more price-dampening surpluses. A withering depression swept through agricultural districts in the 1920s, when one farm in four was sold for debt or taxes.

Schemes abounded for bringing relief to the hard-pressed farmers. A bipartisan "farm bloc" from the agricultural states coalesced in Congress in 1921 and succeeded in driving through some helpful laws.

Noteworthy was the Capper-Volstead Act, which exempted farmers' marketing cooperatives from antitrust prosecution. The farm bloc's favorite proposal was the McNary-Haugen Bill, pushed energetically from 1924 to 1928. It sought to keep agricultural prices high by authorizing the government to buy up surpluses and sell them abroad. Government losses were to be made up by a special tax on the farmers. Congress twice passed the bill, but frugal Coolidge twice vetoed it. Farm prices stayed low, and the farmers' political temperatures stayed high, reaching fever pitch in the election of 1924.

A Three-Way Race for the White House in 1924

Self-satisfied Republicans, chanting "Keep cool and keep Coolidge," nominated "Silent Cal" for the presidency at their convention in Cleveland in the simmering summer of 1924. Squabbling Democrats had more difficulty choosing a candidate when they met in New York's sweltering Madison Square Garden. Reflecting many of the cultural tensions of the decade, the party was hopelessly split between "wets" and "drys," urbanites and farmers, Fundamentalists and Modernists, northern liberals and southern stand-patters, immigrants and old-stock Americans. Deadlocked for an unprecedented 102 ballots, the convention at last turned wearily, sweatily, and unenthusiastically to John W. Davis. A wealthy Wall Street lawyer, the polished nominee was no less conservative than cautious Calvin Coolidge.

The field was now wide open for a liberal candidate, and white-pompadoured Senator Robert ("Fighting Bob") La Follette of Wisconsin sprang forward to lead a new progressive grouping. He gained the endorsement of the American Federation of Labor and enjoyed the support of the Socialist party, but his major constituency was the price-pinched farmers. La Follette's new Progressive party, only a shadow of the robust progressive coalition of prewar days, called for government ownership of railroads and relief for farmers, lashed out at monopoly and antilabor injunctions, and urged a constitutional amendment to limit the Supreme Court's power to invalidate laws passed by Congress.

La Follette turned in a respectable showing, polling nearly 5 million votes. But "Cautious Cal" and the oil-bespattered Republicans slipped easily back into office, overwhelming Davis, 15,718,211 votes to 8,385,283. The electoral count stood at 382 for Coolidge, 136 for Davis, and 13 for La Follette, all from his home state of Wisconsin.

Presidential Election of 1924 (showing popular vote by county) *Notice the concentration of La Follette's votes in the old Populist strongholds of the Midwest and the mountain states. His ticket did especially well in the grain-growing districts battered by the postwar slump in agricultural prices.*

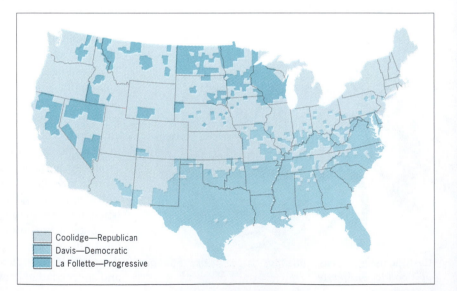

Coolidge—Republican
Davis—Democratic
La Follette—Progressive

Foreign-Policy Flounderings

Isolation continued to reign in the Coolidge era. Despite presidential proddings, the Senate proved unwilling to allow America to adhere to the World Court—the judicial arm of the still-suspect League of Nations. Coolidge only halfheartedly—and unsuccessfully—pursued further naval disarmament after the loudly trumpeted agreements worked out at the Washington Conference in 1922.

A glaring exception to the United States' inward-looking indifference to the outside world in the 1920s was the armed interventionism in the Caribbean and Central America. American troops were withdrawn (after an eight-year stay) from the Dominican Republic in 1924, but they remained in Haiti from 1914 to 1934. President Coolidge in 1925 briefly removed American bayonets from troubled Nicaragua, where they had glinted intermittently since 1909, but in 1926 he sent them back, five thousand strong, and they stayed until 1933. American oil companies clamored for a military expedition to Mexico in 1926 when the Mexican government began to assert its sovereignty over oil resources. Coolidge kept cool and defused the Mexican crisis with some skillful diplomatic negotiating. But his tough tactics elsewhere bred sore resentments south of the Rio Grande, where angry critics loudly assailed "*yanqui* imperialism."

Overshadowing all other foreign-policy problems in the 1920s was the knotty issue of international debts, a complicated tangle of private loans, Allied war debts, and German reparations. The key knot in the debt tangle was the $10 billion that the U.S. Treasury had loaned to the Allies during and immediately after the war. Uncle Sam held their IOUs—and he wanted to be paid. The Allies, in turn, protested that they had held up a wall of flesh and bone against the common foe until America the Unready had entered the fray. America, they argued, should write off its loans as war costs, just as the Allies had been tragically forced to write off the lives of millions of young men. And the final straw, protested the Europeans, was that America's postwar tariff walls made it almost impossible for them to sell the goods to earn the dollars to pay their debts.

Unraveling the Debt Knot

America's tightfisted insistence on getting its money back helped to harden the hearts of the Allies against conquered Germany. The French and the British demanded that the Germans make enormous reparations payments, totaling some $32 billion, as compensation for war-inflicted damages. The Allies hoped to settle their debts to America with the money received from Germany. The French, seeking to extort lagging reparations payments, sent troops into Germany's industrialized Ruhr Valley in 1923. Berlin responded by permitting its currency to inflate astronomically. At one point in October 1923, a loaf of

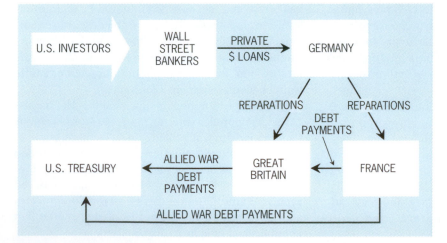

Aspects of the Financial Merry-Go-Round, 1921–1933 *Great Britain, with a debt of over $4 billion to the U.S. Treasury, had a huge stake in proposals for inter-Allied debt cancellation, but France's stake was even larger. Less prosperous than Britain in the 1920s, and more battered by the war, which had been fought on its soil, France owed nearly $3.5 billion to the United States and additional billions to Britain.*

bread cost 480 million marks, or about $120 million in preinflation money. German society teetered on the brink of mad anarchy, and the whole international house of financial cards threatened to flutter down in colossal chaos.

The fact that the Allied debt was linked to reparations was partly recognized in the Dawes Plan of 1924. Negotiated largely by Charles Dawes, about to be Coolidge's running mate, it rescheduled German reparations payments and opened the way for further American private loans to Germany. The whole financial cycle became still more complicated as U.S. bankers loaned money to Germany, Germany paid reparations to France and Britain, and the former Allies paid war debts to the United States. Clearly the source of this monetary merry-go-round was the flowing well of American credit. When that well dried up after the great crash in 1929, the tangled jungle of international finance quickly turned into a desert.

The United States never did get its money, but it harvested a bumper crop of ill will. Throughout Europe Uncle Sam was caricatured as Uncle Shylock, greedily whetting his knife for the last pound of Allied flesh. The bad taste left in American mouths by the whole sorry episode contributed powerfully to the storm-cellar neutrality legislation passed by Congress in the 1930s.

The Triumph of Herbert Hoover in 1928

Poker-faced Calvin Coolidge, the tight-lipped "Sphinx of the Potomac," bowed out of the 1928 presidential race when he announced, "I do not choose to run." His logical successor was super-Secretary (of Commerce) Herbert Hoover. He was nominated on a platform that clucked contentedly over both prosperity and prohibition.

Still-squabbling Democrats nominated Alfred E. Smith, the wisecracking, glad-handing governor of New York. "Al (cohol)" Smith was soaking wet on prohibition, abrasively urban, and Roman Catholic in an overwhelmingly Protestant—and unfortunately prejudiced—land. Many dry, rural, and Fundamentalist Democrats gagged on his candidacy, and they saddled Smith with a dry running mate and a dry platform.

Radio figured prominently in this campaign for the first time, and it helped Hoover more than Smith. The New Yorker had more personal sparkle, but he could not project it through the radio. Iowa-born Hoover, with his double-breasted dignity, came out of the microphone better than he went in.

Chubby-faced, ruddy-complexioned Herbert Hoover, with his painfully high starched collar, was a living example of the American success story, and an intriguing mixture of two centuries. As a poor orphan boy who had worked his way through Stanford University, he had absorbed the nineteenth-century copybook maxims of industry, thrift, and self-reliance. As a fabulously successful mining engineer and businessman, he had honed to a high degree the efficiency doctrines of the progressive era.

A small-town boy from Iowa and Oregon, he had traveled and worked abroad extensively. His experiences there had further strengthened his faith in American individualism, free enterprise, and small government.

As befitted America's newly mechanized civilization, Hoover was the ideal businessperson's candidate. A self-made millionaire, he recoiled from anything suggesting socialism, paternalism, or "planned economy." Yet as secretary of commerce, he had exhibited some progressive instincts. He endorsed labor unions and supported federal regulation of the new radio industry. He even flirted for a time with the idea of government-owned radio, similar to the British Broadcasting Corporation (BBC).

Despite the best efforts of Hoover and Smith, below-the-belt tactics were employed by their lower-level campaigners. Religious bigotry raised its hideous head over Smith's Catholicism. A whispering campaign claimed that "A vote for Al Smith is a vote for the Pope" and that the White House, under Smith, would become a branch of the Vatican.

Hoover triumphed in a landslide. He bagged 21,391,993 popular votes to 15,016,169 for his embittered opponent, while rolling up an electoral count of 444 to 87. A huge Republican majority was returned to the House of Representatives. Tens of thousands of dry southern Democrats—"Hoovercrats"—rebelled against Al Smith. Hoover carried all the Border States and five states of the former Confederacy, the first Republican candidate to disrupt the solid South.

President Hoover's First Moves

Prosperity in the late 1920s smiled broadly as the Hoover years began. Soaring stocks on the bull market continued to defy the laws of financial gravity. But two immense groups of citizens were not getting their share of the riches flowing from the national cornucopia: the unorganized wage earners and, especially, the disorganized farmers.

Hoover's administration, in line with its philosophy of promoting self-help, responded to the outcry of the farmers with the Agricultural Marketing Act. Passed by Congress in June 1929, it was designed to help the farmers help themselves, largely through producers' cooperatives. A Federal Farm Board also lent half a billion dollars to farm organizations seeking to buy, sell, and store agricultural surpluses.

Farmers also clutched at the tariff as a possible straw to keep their heads above the water of financial ruin. But the Hawley-Smoot Tariff of 1930, which started out as a modest measure to assist farmers, acquired more than a thousand amendments and turned into the highest protective tariff in the nation's peacetime history. The average duty was raised from 38.5 percent to nearly 60 percent. To angered foreigners, the Hawley-Smoot Tariff seemed like a declaration of economic warfare. It widened the yawning trade gaps and plunged both America and other nations deeper into the terrible depression that had already begun. It forced the United States further into the bog of economic isolationism, thus playing directly into the demagogic hands of Adolf Hitler.

The Great Crash Ends the Golden Twenties

When Herbert Hoover confidently took the presidential oath on March 4, 1929, America's productive colossus—stimulated by the automobile, radio, movie, and other new industries—was roaring along at a breathtaking speed that suggested a permanent plateau of prosperity. Prices on the stock exchange continued to spiral upward and create a fool's paradise of paper profits. A few prophets of disaster sounded warnings, but they were drowned out by the mad chatter of the ticker-tape machine.

A catastrophic crash came on "Black Tuesday," October 29, 1929, when 16,410,030 shares of stock were sold in a save-who-may scramble. Wall Street became a wailing wall as gloom and doom replaced boom. Losses, even in blue-chip securities, were unbelievable. By the end of 1929—two months after the initial crash—stockholders had lost $40 billion in paper values, or more than the total cost of World War I to the United States.

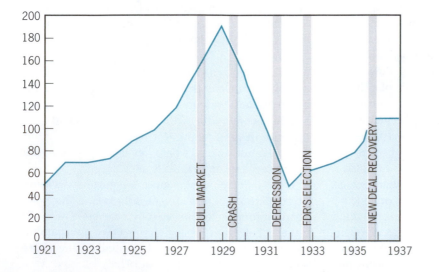

Index of Common Stock Prices (1926 = 100)

The Great Crash of 1929 *The stock-market collapse caused fear to run like wildfire through the financial world. These anxious depositors lined up outside a New York bank, clamoring to withdraw their deposits before the bank failed. Such "runs" on banks actually sped the downward economic spiral.*

The stock-market collapse heralded a business depression, at home and abroad, that was the most prolonged and withering in American or world experience. No other industrialized nation suffered so severe a setback. By the end of 1930, more than 4 million workers in the United States were jobless; two years later the figure had about tripled. Hungry and despairing workers pounded pavements in search of nonexistent jobs ("We're firing, not hiring"). When employees were not discharged, wages and salaries were often slashed.

The misery and gloom were incalculable, as forests of dead factory chimneys stood stark against the sky. Over five thousand banks collapsed in the first three years of the depression, carrying down with them the life savings of tens of thousands of ordinary citizens. Countless thousands of honest, hard-working people lost their homes and farms to the forecloser's hammer. Bread lines formed, soup kitchens dispensed food, and apple sellers stood shivering on street corners trying to peddle their wares for five cents.

Families felt the stress, as jobless fathers nursed their guilt and shame at not being able to provide for their households. Breadless breadwinners often blamed themselves for their plight, despite abundant evidence that the economic system, not individual initiative, had broken down. Mothers meanwhile nursed fewer babies as hard times reached even into the nation's bedrooms, precipitating a decade-long dearth of births. As cash registers gathered cobwebs, the song "My God, How the Money Rolls In" gave way to "Brother, Can You Spare a Dime?"

The Horn of Plenty Runs Dry

What caused the Great Depression? One basic explanation was overproduction by both farm and factory. Ironically, the depression of the 1930s was one of abundance, not want. It was the "great glut" or the "plague of plenty."

The nation's ability to produce goods had clearly outrun its capacity to consume or pay for them. Too much money was going into the hands of a few wealthy people, who invested it in factories and other agencies of production. Not enough was going into salaries and wages, where revitalizing purchasing power could be more quickly felt.

This already bleak picture was further darkened by economic anemia abroad. Britain and the European continent had never fully recovered from the upheaval of World War I. A drying up of international trade, moreover, had been hastened by the short-sighted Hawley-Smoot Tariff of 1930.

By 1930 the depression had become a national calamity. Through no fault of their own, a host of industrious citizens had lost everything. The insidious effect of all this dazed despair on the spirit was incalculable and long lasting. Hitherto the people had grappled with raw wilderness, harsh weather, and other physical obstacles. But the depression was a baffling wraith they could not grasp. Panhandlers begged for food or "charity soup." In extreme cases "ragged individualists" slept under "Hoover blankets" (old newspapers), fought over the contents of garbage cans, or cooked their findings in old oil drums in tin-and-paper shantytowns cynically named "Hoovervilles." The very foundations of America's social structure trembled.

Hoover's exalted reputation as a wonder worker and efficiency engineer crashed about as dismally as the stock market. The perplexed president was impaled on the horns of a cruel dilemma. As a deservedly famed humanitarian, he was profoundly distressed by the widespread misery about him. Yet as a "rugged individualist," deeply rooted in an earlier era of free enterprise, he shrank from the heresy of government handouts. Convinced that industry, thrift, and self-reliance were the virtues that had made America great, he feared that a government doling out doles would weaken, or perhaps destroy, the national fiber.

The president at last worked out a compromise between the old hands-off philosophy and the "soul-destroying" handouts then being used in Britain. He would assist the hard-pressed railroads, banks, and rural credit corporations, in the hope that if financial health were restored at the top of the economic pyramid, unemployment would be relieved at the bottom on a trickle-down basis.

Early in 1932 Congress, responding to Hoover's belated appeal, established the Reconstruction Finance Corporation (RFC). With an initial working capital of half a billion dollars, this agency became a

Home Relief Station, by Louis Ribak, 1935–1936 *Destitute and despairing, millions of hard-working Americans like these had to endure the degradation and humiliation of going on relief as the pall of depression descended over the land.*

government lending bank that provided indirect relief to insurance companies, banks, agricultural organizations, railroads, and even struggling state and local governments. But to preserve individualism and character, there would be no loans to individuals from this "billion-dollar soup kitchen."

"Pump-priming" loans by the RFC were of widespread benefit, but the organization was established many months too late for maximum usefulness. Projects that it supported were largely self-liquidating, and the government as a banker actually profited to the tune of many millions of dollars. Giant corporations so obviously benefited from this assistance that the RFC was dubbed—rather unfairly—"the millionaires' dole."

Hoover's administration also provided some indirect benefits for labor. After stormy debate, Congress passed the Norris–La Guardia Anti-Injunction Act in 1932, and Hoover signed it. The measure outlawed "yellow dog" (antiunion) contracts and forbade the federal courts to issue injunctions to restrain strikes, boycotts, and peaceful picketing.

The truth is that Herbert Hoover, despite criticism of his "heartlessness," did inaugurate a significant new policy. In previous panics the masses had been forced to "sweat it out." Slow though Hoover was to abandon this nineteenth-century bias, by the end of his term he had traveled a long way toward government assistance for needy citizens—a road that Franklin Roosevelt would travel much farther.

Many veterans of World War I were numbered among the hard-hit victims of the depression. They began to agitate for the premature payment of the deferred "adjusted compensation" (see p. 459) voted by Congress in 1924 and payable in 1945. Thousands of impoverished veterans, both of war and of unemployment, prepared to move on Washington, there to demand of Congress the immediate payment of their entire bonuses. The "Bonus Expeditionary Force," which mustered about twenty thousand men, converged on the capital in the summer of 1932. These supplicants promptly set up unsanitary public camps on vacant lots—a gigantic "Hooverville."

Following riots that cost two lives, Hoover ordered the army to evacuate the unwanted guests. The eviction was carried out by General Douglas MacArthur with bayonets and tear gas in the inglorious "Battle of Anacostia Flats." The veterans' shanty-town was put to the torch, a few of the former soldiers were injured, and an eleven-month-old "bonus baby" allegedly died from exposure to tear gas.

This brutal episode brought down additional abuse on the once-popular Hoover, who by now was the most loudly booed man in the country. Cynics sneered that the "Great Engineer" had in a few months "ditched, drained, and damned the country." The existing panic was unfairly branded "the Hoover depression." In truth, Hoover had been oversold as a superman—and the public grumbled when his magician's wand failed to produce rabbits. The time was ripening for the Democratic party—and Franklin D. Roosevelt—to cash in on Hoover's calamities.

Japanese Aggression

The Great Depression, which brewed enough distress at home, added immensely to difficulties abroad. Militaristic Japan stole the East Asian spotlight. In September 1931 the Japanese imperialists, noting that the Western world was badly mired down in depression, lunged into Manchuria. Alleging provocation, they rapidly overran the coveted Chinese province and proceeded to bolt shut the Open Door in the conquered area.

Peaceful peoples were stunned by this act of naked aggression. Numerous indignant Americans, though by no means a majority, urged strong measures, ranging from boycotts to blockades. Possibly a tight blockade by the League of Nations, backed by the United States, would have brought Japan sharply to book. But the League was handicapped in taking two-fisted action by the nonmembership of the United States. Washington flatly rebuffed initial attempts in 1931 to secure American cooperation in applying economic pressures.

Washington decided in the end to fire only paper bullets at the Japanese aggressors. The so-called Stimson Doctrine, crafted by Secretary of State Henry L. Stimson and proclaimed in 1932, declared that the United States would not recognize any territorial acquisitions achieved by force. Righteous indignation would substitute for vigorous initiatives. But there was no real sentiment for stronger measures among a depression-ridden people who remained strongly isolationist during the 1930s.

Chronology

1919 American Legion founded.

1920 Esch-Cummins Transportation Act.

1921 Veterans Bureau created.

1922 Five-Power Naval Treaty.
Four-Power and Nine-Power Treaties on
East Asia.

1923 *Adkins* v. *Children's Hospital.*
Teapot Dome scandal.
Harding dies; Coolidge assumes
presidency.

1924 Adjusted Compensation Act for veterans.
Dawes Plan for international finance.
U.S. troops leave the Dominican Republic.
Coolidge wins three-way presidential
election.

1926 U.S. troops occupy Nicaragua.

1928 Kellogg-Briand Pact.
Hoover defeats Smith for presidency.

1929 Stock-market crash.

1930 Hawley-Smoot Tariff.

1931 Japanese invade Manchuria.

1932 Reconstruction Finance Corporation (RFC)
established.
Norris–La Guardia Anti-Injunction Act.
"Bonus Army" dispersed from Washington.

For further reading, see the Appendix. For web resources, go to **http://college.hmco.com.**

34

The Great Depression and the New Deal

1933–1939

The country needs and . . . demands bold, persistent experimentation. It is common sense to take a method and try it. If it fails, admit it frankly and try another. But above all, try something.

FRANKLIN D. ROOSEVELT, CAMPAIGN SPEECH, 1932

Voters were in an ugly mood as the presidential campaign of 1932 neared. Countless factory chimneys remained ominously cold, while more than 11 million unemployed workers and their families sank ever deeper into the pit of poverty.

Hoover, sick at heart, was renominated by the Republican convention in Chicago without great enthusiasm. The rising star in the Democratic firmament was Governor Franklin Delano Roosevelt of New York, a fifth cousin of Theodore Roosevelt. Like the Rough Rider, he was born to a wealthy New York family, graduated from Harvard, was elected as a kid-gloved politician to the New York legislature, served as governor of the Empire State, was nominated for

the vice presidency (though not elected), and served capably as assistant secretary of the navy.

FDR: Politician in a Wheelchair

Infantile paralysis, while putting steel braces on Franklin Roosevelt's legs, put additional steel into his soul. Until 1921, when the dread disease struck, young Roosevelt—tall, athletic, and handsome—impressed observers as charming and witty yet at times a superficial and arrogant "lightweight." But suffering humbled him; courageously fighting his way back from complete helplessness to a hobbling

470

mobility, he schooled himself in patience, tolerance, compassion, and strength of will. He once remarked that after trying for two years to wiggle one big toe, all else seemed easy.

Another of Roosevelt's great personal and political assets was his wife, Eleanor. The niece of Theodore Roosevelt, she was Franklin Roosevelt's distant cousin as well as his spouse. Tall, ungainly, and toothy, she overcame the misery of an unhappy childhood and emerged as a champion of the dispossessed—and ultimately as the "conscience of the New Deal." She was to become the most active First Lady in history. Through her lobbying of her husband, her speeches, and her syndicated newspaper column, she powerfully influenced the policies of the national government. Always, she battled for the impoverished and the oppressed. At one meeting in Birmingham, Alabama, she con-

founded local authorities and flouted the segregation statutes by deliberately straddling the aisle separating the black and white seating sections. Sadly, her personal relationship with her husband was often rocky due to his occasional infidelity. Condemned by conservatives and loved by liberals, she was one of the most controversial—and consequential—public figures of the twentieth century.

Roosevelt's political appeal was amazing. His commanding presence and his golden speaking voice, despite a sophisticated accent, combined to make him the premier American orator of his generation. He could turn on charm in private conversations as one would turn on a faucet. As a popular depression governor of New York, he had sponsored heavy state spending to relieve human suffering. Though favoring frugality, he believed that money, rather than humanity, was expendable. He revealed a deep concern for the plight of the "forgotten man"—a phrase he used in a 1932 speech—although he was assailed by the rich as a "traitor to his class."

Exuberant Democrats met in Chicago in June 1932 and speedily nominated Roosevelt, who flew daringly through stormy weather to Chicago to accept the nomination in person. He electrified the delegates and the public with these words: "I pledge you, I pledge myself to a new deal for the American people."

Roosevelt Routs Hoover in 1932

In the campaign that followed, Roosevelt consistently preached a New Deal for the "forgotten man," but he was annoyingly vague and somewhat contradictory. Many of his speeches were ghostwritten by the "Brains Trust" (popularly the "Brain Trust"), a small group of reform-minded intellectuals. They were predominantly youngish college professors who, as a kind of informal cabinet, later authored much of the New Deal legislation. Roosevelt rashly promised a balanced budget and berated heavy Hooverian deficits. All this was to make ironic reading in later months.

Hoover had been swept into office on the rising tide of prosperity; he was swept out by the receding tide of depression. The flood of votes totaled 22,809,638 for Roosevelt and 15,758,901 for Hoover;

Eleanor Roosevelt (1884–1962) *America's most active First Lady, she commanded enormous popularity and influence during FDR's presidency. Here she emerges, miner's cap in hand, from an Ohio coal mine.*

the electoral count stood at 472 to 59. In all, the loser carried only six rock-ribbed Republican states.

One striking feature of the election was a distinct shift of blacks from the Republican party of Lincoln to the Roosevelt camp. Beginning with the election of 1932, they became, notably in the great urban centers of the North, a vital element in the Democratic party.

Defeated and repudiated, Hoover remained president during four long months, until March 4, 1933. But he was helpless to embark on any long-term policies without Roosevelt's cooperation. In two meetings with Roosevelt on the war-debt issue, Hoover tried to bind his successor to an anti-inflationary policy that would have made impossible many of the later New Deal experiments. But Roosevelt refused to assume responsibility without authority and airily remarked to the press, "It's not my baby."

With Washington deadlocked, the vast and vaunted American economic machine clanked to a virtual halt. One worker in four tramped the streets, feet weary and hands idle. Banks were locking their doors all over the nation as people nervously stuffed paper money under their mattresses.

FDR and the Three Rs: Relief, Recovery, and Reform

Great crises often call forth gifted leaders, and the hand of destiny tapped Roosevelt on the shoulder. On a dreary inauguration day, March 4, 1933, his vibrant voice provided the American people with inspirational new hope. He denounced the "money changers" who had brought on the calamity, and he declared that the government must wage war on the Great Depression as it would wage war on an armed foe. His clarion note was, "Let me assert my firm belief that the only thing we have to fear is fear itself."

Roosevelt moved decisively. Now that he had full responsibility, he boldly declared a nationwide bank holiday, March 6–10, as a prelude to opening the banks on a sounder basis. He then summoned the overwhelmingly Democratic Congress into special session to cope with the national emergency. For the so-called Hundred Days (March 9–June 16, 1933), members hastily ground out an unprecedented basketful of remedial legislation.

Roosevelt's New Deal program aimed at three R's—relief, recovery, and reform. Short-range goals were relief and immediate recovery, especially in the first two years. Long-range goals were permanent recovery and reform of current abuses, particularly those that had produced the boom-and-bust catastrophe. The three-R objectives often overlapped and got in one another's way. But amid all the topsy-turvy haste, the gigantic New Deal program lurched forward.

Firmly ensconced in the driver's seat, President Roosevelt cracked the whip. A green Congress so fully shared the panicky feeling of the country that it was ready to rubber-stamp bills drafted by White House advisers. More than that, Congress gave the president extraordinary blank-check powers: some laws expressly delegated legislative authority to the chief executive.

Roosevelt was delighted to exert executive leadership. He was inclined to do things by intuition—off the cuff. He was like the quarterback, as he put it, whose next play depends on the outcome of the previous play. So desperate was the mood of an action-starved public that any movement, even in the wrong direction, seemed better than no movement at all.

The frantic Hundred Days Congress passed many essentials of the New Deal's three R's, though important long-range measures were added in later sessions. These reforms owed much to the legacy of the pre–World War I progressive movement. Many of them were long overdue, sidetracked by World War I and the Old Guard reaction of the 1920s. The New Dealers, sooner or later, embraced such progressive ideas as unemployment insurance, old-age insurance, minimum-wage regulations, conservation and development of natural resources, and restrictions on child labor. Many of these forward-looking measures had been adopted a generation or so earlier by the more advanced countries of western Europe. In the area of social welfare, the United States, in the eyes of many Europeans, remained a backward nation.

Roosevelt Tackles Money and Banking

Banking chaos cried aloud for immediate action. Congress pulled itself together and in an incredible eight hours had the Emergency Banking Relief Act of

Principal New Deal Acts During Hundred Days Congress, 1933*
(items in parentheses indicate secondary purposes)

Recovery	Relief	Reform
FDR closes banks, March 6, 1933		
Emergency Banking Relief Act, March 9, 1933		
(Beer Act)	(Beer Act)	Beer and Wine Revenue Act, March 22, 1933
(CCC)	Unemployment Relief Act, March 31, 1933, creates Civilian Conservation Corps (CCC)	
FDR orders gold surrender, April 5, 1933		
FDR abandons gold standard, April 19, 1933		
(FERA)	Federal Emergency Relief Act, May 12, 1933, creates Federal Emergency Relief Administration (FERA)	
(AAA)	Agricultural Adjustment Act (AAA), May 12, 1933	
(TVA)	(TVA)	Tennessee Valley Authority Act (TVA), May 18, 1933
		Federal Securities Act, May 27, 1933
Gold-payment clause repealed, June 5, 1933		
(HOLC)	Home Owners' Refinancing Act, June 13, 1933, creates Home Owners' Loan Corporation (HOLC)	
National Industrial Recovery Act, June 16, 1933, creates National Recovery Administration (NRA), Public Works Administration (PWA)	(NRA, PWA)	(NRA)
(Glass-Steagall Act)	(Glass-Steagall Act)	Glass-Steagall Banking Reform Act, June 16, 1933, creates Federal Deposit Insurance Corporation

*For later New Deal measures, see p. 483.

Roosevelt Speaks on Radio, 1932   *FDR's smooth, confident radio voice made him seem like an intimate friend to millions of distressed Americans during the Great Depression, especially when he delivered his "fireside chats."*

1933 ready for Roosevelt's busy pen. The new law invested the president with power to regulate banking transactions and foreign exchange and to reopen solvent banks.

Roosevelt, the master showman, next turned to the radio to deliver the first of thirty "fireside chats." As some 35 million people hung on his soothing words, he gave assurances that it was now safer to keep money in a reopened bank than "under the mattress." Confidence returned with a gush, and the banks unlocked their doors.

The Hundred Days Congress also buttressed public reliance on the banking system by enacting the memorable Glass-Steagall Banking Reform Act. This measure provided for the Federal Deposit Insurance Corporation, which insured individual deposits up to $5,000 (later raised).

Roosevelt moved swiftly elsewhere on the financial front, seeking to protect the melting gold reserve and to prevent panicky hoarding. He ordered all private holdings of gold to be surrendered to the Treasury in exchange for paper currency and then took the nation off the gold standard.

The goal of Roosevelt's "managed currency" was inflation, which he believed would relieve debtors'

burdens and stimulate new production. Roosevelt's principal instrument for achieving inflation was gold buying. He instructed the Treasury Department to purchase gold, ratcheting the dollar price of gold up from $21 an ounce in 1933 to $35 an ounce in 1934, a price that held for nearly four decades. This policy did increase the amount of dollars in circulation, as holders of gold cashed it in at the newly elevated prices, although "sound-money" critics gagged on the "baloney dollar." The gold-buying scheme came to an end in February 1934, when FDR returned the nation to a limited gold standard for the purposes of international trade only. Thereafter (until 1971), the United States pledged itself to pay foreign bills, if requested, in gold at the rate of one ounce of gold for every $35 due.

Creating Jobs for the Jobless

Overwhelming unemployment clamored for prompt remedial action. One of every four workers was jobless when FDR took his inaugural oath—the highest level of unemployment in the nation's history. Roosevelt had no hesitancy about using federal money to assist the unemployed and at the same time to "prime the pump" of industrial recovery. (A farmer has to pour a little water into a dry pump to start the flow.)

The Hundred Days Congress responded to Roosevelt's spurs when it created the Civilian Conservation Corps (CCC). This agency provided employment in fresh-air government camps for about 3 million uniformed young men. Their useful work included reforestation, fire fighting, flood control, and swamp drainage. The recruits were required to help their parents by sending home most of their pay. Both human resources and natural resources were thus conserved.

The first major effort of the new Congress to grapple with the millions of adult unemployed was the Federal Emergency Relief Act. Its chief aim was immediate relief rather than long-range recovery. The resulting Federal Emergency Relief Administration (FERA) was handed over to zealous Harry L. Hopkins, a painfully thin, shabbily dressed, chain-smoking New York social worker who had earlier won Roosevelt's friendship and who became one of his most influential advisers. Hopkins's agency finally granted about $3 billion to the states for direct dole payments or preferably for wages on work projects.

Immediate relief was also given to two large and hard-pressed special groups by the Hundred Days Congress. One section of the Agricultural Adjustment Act (AAA) made available many millions of dollars to help farmers meet their mortgages. Another law created the Home Owners' Loan Corporation (HOLC). Designed to refinance mortgages on nonfarm homes, it ultimately assisted about a million badly pinched households while simultaneously bailing out mortgage-holding banks.

Harassed by the continuing plague of unemployment, FDR himself established the Civil Works Administration (CWA) under Hopkins's direction late in 1933. Designed to provide temporary jobs during the cruel winter emergency, it employed tens of thousands of jobless people in leaf raking and other make-work tasks. The CWA served a useful purpose, although it was heavily criticized as "boondoggling."

Direct relief from Washington to needy families helped pull the nation through the ghastly winter of 1933–1934. But the disheartening persistence of unemployment and suffering demonstrated that emergency relief measures must be not only continued but supplemented.

A Day for Every Demagogue

One danger signal was the appearance of various demagogues, notably a magnetic "microphone messiah," Father Charles Coughlin, a Catholic priest in Michigan who began broadcasting in 1930 with the slogan "Social Justice." His anti–New Deal harangues to some 40 million radio fans finally became so anti-Semitic, fascistic, and demagogic that he was silenced in 1942 by his ecclesiastical superiors.

Also notorious among the new brood of agitators were those who capitalized on popular discontent to make pie-in-the-sky promises. Most conspicuous of these individuals was Senator Huey P. ("Kingfish") Long of Louisiana, who used his abundant rabble-rousing talents to publicize his "Share Our Wealth" program, which promised to make "Every Man a King." Every family was to receive $5,000, supposedly at the expense of the prosperous. Fear of Long's

becoming a fascist dictator ended when he was shot by an assassin in the Louisiana state capitol in 1935.

Another Pied Piper was gaunt Dr. Francis E. Townsend of California, a retired physician whose savings had recently been wiped out. He attracted the trusting support of perhaps 5 million "senior citizens" with his fantastic plan, which nonetheless spoke to earthly need. Each oldster sixty years of age or over was to receive $200 a month, provided that the money was spent within the month. One estimate had the scheme costing one-half of the national income.

Partly to quiet the groundswell of unrest produced by such crackbrained proposals, Congress authorized the Works Progress Administration (WPA) in 1935. The objective was employment on useful projects. Launched under the supervision of the ailing but energetic Hopkins, this remarkable agency ultimately spent about $11 billion on thousands of public buildings, bridges, and hard-surfaced roads. It also controlled crickets in Wyoming and built a monkey pen in Oklahoma City. Critics sneered that WPA meant "We Provide Alms." But the fact is that over a period of eight years nearly 9 million persons were given jobs, not handouts.

Agencies of the WPA also found part-time occupations for needy high school and college students and for such unemployed white-collar workers as actors, musicians, and writers. John Steinbeck, future Nobel Prize novelist, counted dogs in his California county. Cynical taxpayers condemned lessons in tap dancing, as well as the painting of scenes on post office walls. But much precious talent was nourished, self-respect was preserved, and more than a million pieces of art were created, many of them publicly displayed.

A Helping Hand for Industry and Labor

A daring attempt to stimulate a nationwide comeback was initiated when the Hundred Days Congress authorized the National Recovery Administration (NRA). This ingenious scheme was by far the most complex and far-reaching effort by the New Dealers to combine immediate relief with long-range recovery and reform. Triple-barreled, it was designed to assist industry, labor, and the unemployed.

Individual industries—over two hundred in all— were to work out codes of "fair competition," under which hours of labor would be reduced so that employment could be spread over more people. A ceiling was placed on the maximum hours of labor; a floor was placed under wages to establish minimum levels.

Labor, under the NRA, was granted additional benefits. Workers were formally guaranteed the right to organize and bargain collectively through representatives *of their own choosing*—not through hand-picked agents of the company's choosing. The hated "yellow dog," or antiunion, contract was expressly forbidden, and certain safeguarding restrictions were placed on the use of child labor.

Industrial recovery through the NRA would be at best painful, for its "fair competition" codes called for self-denial by both management and labor. Patriotism was aroused by mass meetings and huge parades, which included 200,000 marchers on New York City's Fifth Avenue. A handsome blue eagle was designed as the symbol of the NRA, and merchants subscribing to a code displayed it in their windows with the slogan "We Do Our Part." Such was the enthusiasm for the NRA that for a brief period there was a marked upswing of business activity.

But the high-flying eagle gradually tumbled to earth. Too much self-sacrifice was expected of labor, industry, and the public for such a scheme to work. Critics began to brand the NRA "Nuts Running America," symbolized by what Henry Ford called "that damn Roosevelt buzzard."

Complete collapse was imminent when, in 1935, the Supreme Court shot down the dying eagle in the *Schechter* "sick chicken" decision. The learned justices unanimously held that Congress could not "delegate legislative powers" to the executive. They further declared that congressional control of interstate commerce could not properly apply to a local fowl business, like that of the Schechter brothers in Brooklyn. Roosevelt was incensed by this "horse and buggy" interpretation of the Constitution, but actually the Court helped him out of a bad jam.

The same act of Congress that hatched the NRA eagle also authorized the Public Works Administration (PWA), likewise intended both for industrial recovery and for unemployment relief. The agency was headed by acid-tongued Harold L. Ickes, a former bull mooser. Long-range recovery was the primary purpose of the new agency, and in time over $4 billion was spent on some thirty-four thousand projects, which included public buildings, highways, and parkways.

One spectacular PWA achievement was the Grand Coulee Dam on the Columbia River—the largest structure erected by humans since the Great Wall of China. In the depths of the depression, the towering dam seemed the height of folly. It made possible the irrigation of millions of acres of new farmland—at a time when the government was desperately trying to reduce farm surpluses. It created vast amounts of electrical power—in a region with little industry and virtually no market for additional power. But with the outbreak of World War II and then postwar prosperity, the dam would come to seem a stroke of genius, transforming the entire region with abundant water and power.

Special stimulants aided the recovery of one segment of business—the liquor industry. The Hundred Days Congress legalized and taxed "light" wine and beer (3.2% alcohol), providing new employment and federal revenue. Prohibition was officially repealed by the Twenty-first Amendment late in 1933 (see the Appendix)—and the saloon doors swung open.

Paying Farmers Not to Farm

Ever since the war-boom days of 1918, farmers had suffered from low prices and overproduction, especially in grain. During the depression, conditions became desperate as innumerable mortgages were foreclosed, corn was burned for fuel, and embattled farmers tried to prevent shipment of crops to glutted markets. In Iowa several volatile counties were placed under martial law.

A radical new approach to farm recovery was embraced when the Hundred Days Congress established the Agricultural Adjustment Administration (AAA). Through "artificial scarcity" this agency was to establish "parity prices" for basic commodities. "Parity" was the price set for a product that gave it the same real value, in purchasing power, that it had enjoyed during the period from 1909 to 1914. The AAA would eliminate price-depressing surpluses by paying growers to reduce their crop acreage.

Unhappily, the AAA got off to a wobbly start. It was begun after much of the cotton crop for 1933 had been planted, and balky mules, trained otherwise, were forced to plow under countless young plants. Several million squealing pigs were purchased and slaughtered. Much of their meat was distributed to persons on relief, but some of it was used for fertilizer. This "sinful" destruction of food, at a time when thousands of citizens were hungry, increased condemnation of the American economic system by many left-leaning voices. The much-criticized AAA was itself plowed under in 1936 by the Supreme Court, which declared its regulatory taxation provisions unconstitutional.

The New Deal recovered from this blow by passing the Soil Conservation and Domestic Allotment Act (1936), which paid subsidies to farmers if they planted soil-conserving crops, like soybeans, or let their land lie fallow. The Second Agricultural Adjustment Act (1938) permitted parity payments if farmers observed acreage restrictions on commodities such as cotton and wheat. Other provisions of the new AAA were designed to give farmers not only a fairer price but a more substantial share of the national income. Both goals were partially achieved.

Dust Bowls and Black Blizzards

Nature meanwhile had been providing some unplanned scarcity. Late in 1933 a prolonged drought struck the states of the trans-Mississippi Great Plains. Rainless weeks were followed by furious, whining winds, while the sun was darkened by millions of tons of powdery topsoil torn from homesteads in Texas, Kansas, Colorado, Arkansas, and Oklahoma—an area soon dubbed the "Dust Bowl." Despondent citizens sat on front porches with protective masks on their faces, watching the farms swirl by. Some victims of the Dust Bowl disaster predicted the end of the world or the second coming of Christ.

Burned and blown out of the Dust Bowl, tens of thousands of refugees fled their ruined acres (see "Makers of America: The Dust Bowl Migrants," pp. 478–479). In five years about 350,000 Oklahomans and Arkansans—"Okies" and "Arkies"—trekked to southern California in "junkyards on wheels." The dismal story of these human tumbleweeds was realistically portrayed in John Steinbeck's best-selling novel *The Grapes of Wrath* (1939), which proved to be the *Uncle Tom's Cabin* of the Dust Bowl.

Zealous New Dealers, sympathetic toward these desperate soil-tillers, made various efforts to relieve their burdens. The Frazier-Lemke Farm Bankruptcy Act, passed in 1934, made possible a suspension of mortgage foreclosures for five years; a revised version was upheld by the Supreme Court. In 1935 the president set up the Resettlement Administration to help farmers move to better land. And more than 200 million young trees were successfully planted on the bare prairies as windbreaks by the young men of the Civilian Conservation Corps.

Native Americans also felt the far-reaching hand of New Deal reform. Commissioner of Indian Affairs John Collier ardently sought to reverse the forced-assimilation policies in place since the Dawes Act of 1887 (see p. 363). The Indian Reorganization Act of 1934 (the "Indian New Deal") encouraged tribes to establish local self-government, helped stop the loss of Indian lands, and revived tribes' interest in their identity and culture. Seventy-seven tribes refused to organize under its provisions, though nearly two hundred did establish tribal governments.

Reforming Business and Creating Public Power

Reformist New Dealers were determined from the outset to curb the "money changers" who had played fast and loose with gullible investors before the Wall Street crash of 1929. The Hundred Days Congress passed the "Truth in Securities Act" (Federal Securities Act), which required promoters to transmit to the investor sworn information regarding the soundness of their stocks and bonds. In 1934 Congress took further steps to protect the public against fraud, deception, and inside manipulation. It authorized the Securities and Exchange Commission (SEC), which was designed as a watchdog administrative agency. Stock markets henceforth were to operate more as trading marts and less as gambling casinos.

New Dealers likewise directed their fire at public utility holding companies, those supercorporations.

The Dust Bowl Migrants

Black dust clouds rolled across the southern Great Plains in the 1930s, darkening the skies above a landscape already desolated by the Great Depression. Its soil depleted by erosion, exhausted by overintensive farming, and parched by drought, the prairie of Oklahoma, Arkansas, and northern Texas became a dust bowl. The thirsty land offered up neither crops nor livelihood to the sturdy people whose forebears had staked out homesteads there. The desiccated earth exhaled only black dust and a dry wind that blew hundreds of thousands of people—the so-called Okies and Arkies—out of the Dust Bowl forever.

They headed mainly for California. Some piled aboard buses or hopped freight trains. But most journeyed in their own autos, cramming their meager possessions into old jalopies and sputtering down the highway. But unlike the aimless, isolated Joad family of John Steinbeck's classic novel *The Grapes of Wrath*, most Dust Bowl migrants knew where they were headed. Although many had lost everything in the depression, they had relatives or friends who had migrated to California before the crash and had sent back word about its abundant promise.

But when the Okies neared California, they were greeted with a billboard posted by the state of California proclaiming "NO JOBS in California . . . If YOU are looking for work—KEEP OUT." Still, they refused to believe that the depression could sully the Golden State's bright luster. Some went to California cities, but many of them favored the San Joaquin Valley, the southern part of central California's agricultural kingdom. The migrants chose it for its familiarity. The valley shared much in common with the southern plains—arid climate, cotton growing, newfound deposits of oil, and abundant land.

During the 1930s the San Joaquin Valley also proved all too familiar in its poverty. Food, shelter, and clothing were scarce; the winter months, without work and without heat, proved nearly unendurable for the migrants. John Steinbeck, writing in a San Francisco newspaper, exposed the tribulations of the Dust Bowl refugees: "First the gasoline gives out. And without gasoline a man cannot go to a job even if he could get one. Then the food goes. And then in the rains, with insufficient food, the children develop colds."

Eventually, the Farm Security Administration—a New Deal agency—set up camps to house the Okies. A fortunate few purchased land and erected make-

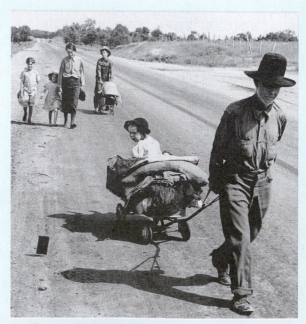

An Okie Family Hits the Road in the 1930s

shift homes, creating tiny "Okievilles" or "Little Okla-homas." Most Okies eventually escaped the uncertainty of seasonal farm labor, securing regular jobs in defense industries. But the "Okievilles" remained to form the bedrock of a still-thriving subculture in California—one that has brought the Dust Bowl's country and western music, pecan pie, and evangelical religion to the Far West.

When Chicagoan Samuel Insull's multibillion-dollar financial empire crashed in 1932, citizens rebelled against such pyramided layers of big business. The Public Utility Holding Company Act of 1935 delivered a "death sentence" to this type of bloated growth.

The sprawling electric-power industry also attracted the fire of New Deal reformers. Within a few decades it had risen from nothingness to a behemoth with an investment of $13 billion. Operating as a monopolistic public utility, it affected the pocketbooks of millions of consumers who had to pay for the vitally needed service. Ardent New Dealers accused the utility giant of gouging the public with excessive rates, especially since it owed its success to having secured, often for a song, priceless waterpower sites from the public domain.

The tempestuous Tennessee River provided New Dealers with a rare opportunity. With its tributaries, the river drained a badly eroded area about the size of England containing some 2.5 million of the most poverty-stricken people in America. The federal government already owned valuable properties at Muscle Shoals, where it had erected plants for needed nitrates in World War I. By developing the hydroelectric potential of the entire area, Washington could combine the immediate advantage of putting thousands of people to work with a long-term project for reforming the power monopoly.

An act creating the Tennessee Valley Authority (TVA) was passed in 1933 by the Hundred Days Congress. This far-ranging enterprise was largely a result of the steadfast vision and unflagging zeal of Senator George W. Norris of Nebraska, after whom one of the mighty dams was named. From the standpoint of "planned economy," the TVA was by far the most revolutionary of all New Deal schemes.

New Dealers pointed with pride at the amazing achievements of the TVA. The gigantic project brought to the area not only cheap power but full employment, low-cost housing, abundant cheap nitrates, restoration of eroded soil, reforestation, improved navigation, and flood control.

Exulting New Dealers agitated for parallel enterprises in the valleys of the Columbia, Colorado, and Missouri Rivers. Hydroelectric power from federally built dams would drive the growth of the urban West, and the waters they diverted would nurture agriculture in the previously bone-dry western deserts. But conservative reaction against the "socialistic" New Deal confined the TVA's brand of federally guided resource management and comprehensive regional development to the Tennessee Valley.

Housing Reform and Social Security

The New Deal had meanwhile framed sturdy new policies for housing construction. To speed recovery and improve homes, Roosevelt set up the Federal Housing Administration (FHA) as early as 1934. The building industry was to be stimulated by small loans to householders. So popular did the FHA prove to be that it was one of the few "alphabetical agencies" to outlast the age of Roosevelt.

Congress bolstered the program in 1937 by authorizing the United States Housing Authority (USHA)—an agency designed to lend money to states or communities for low-cost construction. Although units for about 650,000 low-income people were started, new building fell tragically short of needs. New Deal efforts to expand the project collided with brick-wall opposition from real estate promoters, builders, and landlords ("slumlords"), to say nothing of anti–New Dealers who attacked what they considered down-the-rathole spending. Nonetheless, for the first time in a century the slum areas in America ceased growing and even shrank.

Incomparably more important was the success of New Dealers in the field of unemployment insurance and old-age pensions. Their greatest victory was the Social Security Act of 1935—one of the most complicated and far-reaching laws ever to pass Congress. To cushion future depressions, the measure provided for federal-state unemployment insurance. To provide security for old age, specified categories of retired workers were to receive regular payments from Washington, ranging from $10 to $85 a month (later raised) and financed by a payroll tax on both employers and employees. Provision was also made for the blind, the physically handicapped, delinquent children, and other dependents.

Social Security was largely inspired by the example of some of the more highly industrialized nations of Europe. The United States government was finally recognizing its responsibility for the economic welfare of its citizens in an urban industrial economy. By 1939 over 45 million persons were eligible for Social Security benefits, and in subsequent years further categories of workers were added and the payments to them were periodically increased.

A New Deal for Unskilled Labor

The NRA blue eagles, with their call for collective bargaining, had been a godsend to organized labor. As New Deal expenditures brought some slackening of unemployment, labor began to feel more secure and hence more self-assertive. A rash of walkouts occurred in the summer of 1934, including a paralyzing general strike in San Francisco that was broken only when outraged citizens resorted to vigilante tactics.

When the Supreme Court axed the blue eagle, a Congress sympathetic to labor unions undertook to fill the vacuum. The fruit of its deliberations was the Wagner, or National Labor Relations, Act of 1935. This trailblazing law created a powerful new National Labor Relations Board for administrative purposes and reasserted the right of labor to engage in self-organization and to bargain collectively through representatives of its own choice. The Wagner Act proved to be one of the real milestones on the rocky road of the U.S. labor movement.

Under the encouragement of a highly sympathetic National Labor Relations Board, a host of unskilled workers began to organize themselves into effective unions. The leader of this drive was beetle-browed, domineering, and melodramatic John L. Lewis, boss of the United Mine Workers. In 1935 he succeeded in forming the Committee for Industrial Organization (CIO) within the ranks of the skilled-craft American Federation of Labor. But skilled workers, ever since the days of the ill-fated Knights of Labor in the 1880s, had shown only lukewarm sympathy for the cause of unskilled labor, especially blacks. In 1936, following inevitable friction with the CIO, the older federation suspended the upstart unions associated with the newer organization.

Undaunted, the rebellious CIO moved on a concerted scale into the huge automobile industry. Late in 1936 the workers resorted to a revolutionary technique known as the sit-down strike: they refused to leave the factory buildings of General Motors at Flint, Michigan, and thus prevented the importation of strikebreakers. Conservative respecters of private property were scandalized. The CIO finally won a resounding victory when its union, after heated negotiations, was recognized by General Motors as the sole bargaining agency for its employees.

Roosevelt's "Coddling" of Labor

Unskilled workers now pressed their advantage. The United States Steel Corporation, previously an impossible nut for labor to crack, averted a costly strike when it voluntarily granted rights of unionization to its CIO-organized employees. But the "little steel" companies fought back savagely. Citizens were shocked in 1937 by the Memorial Day massacre at the plant of the Republic Steel Company in South Chicago, where police fire killed several picketers.

A better deal for labor continued when Congress, in 1938, passed the memorable Fair Labor Standards Act (Wages and Hours Bill). Industries involved in interstate commerce were to set up minimum-wage and maximum-hour levels. The eventual goals were forty cents an hour (later raised) and a forty-hour workweek. Labor by children under sixteen was for-

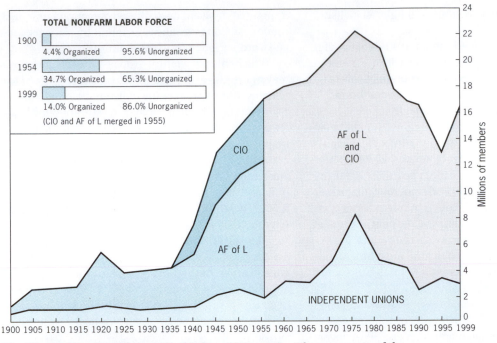

TOTAL NONFARM LABOR FORCE

1900	4.4% Organized	95.6% Unorganized
1954	34.7% Organized	65.3% Unorganized
1999	14.0% Organized	86.0% Unorganized

(CIO and AF of L merged in 1955)

The Rise and Decline of Organized Labor, 1900–1999 *The percentage of the total labor force that was organized increased until 1954, and it has declined ever since. (Source: Bureau of Labor Statistics.)*

bidden under any circumstances; under eighteen, if the occupation was dangerous. These reforms were bitterly though futilely opposed by many industrialists, especially by those southern textile manufacturers who had profited from low-wage, low-age labor.

In later New Deal days, labor unionization flourished; "Roosevelt wants you to join a union" was the rallying cry of professional organizers. The president received valuable support at ballot-box time from labor leaders and many appreciative working men and women. One mill worker remarked that Roosevelt was "the only man we ever had in the White House who would know that my boss is an s.o.b."

The CIO surged forward, breaking completely with the AF of L in 1938. On that occasion the Committee for Industrial Organization was formally reconstituted as the Congress of Industrial Organizations (the new CIO), under the high-handed presidency of John L. Lewis. By 1940 the CIO could claim about 4 million members in its constituent unions, including some 200,000 blacks.

Landon Challenges "the Champ" in 1936

As the presidential campaign of 1936 neared, the New Dealers were on top of the world. They had achieved considerable progress, and millions of "reliefers" were grateful to their bountiful government. The exultant Democrats renominated Roosevelt on a platform squarely endorsing the New Deal.

Hard pressed to find someone to run against "the Champ" Roosevelt, the Republicans finally settled on the colorless but homespun and honest governor of Kansas, Alfred M. Landon. Landon himself was a moderate who accepted some New Deal reforms, although not the popular Social Security Act. But the Republican platform vigorously condemned the New Deal for its radicalism, experimentation, confusion, and "frightful waste." Backing Landon, ex-president Hoover called for a "holy crusade for liberty," echoing the cry of the American Liberty League, a group of wealthy conservatives organized to fight "socialistic" New Deal schemes.

Such rhetoric provided a made-to-order target for FDR. Angry enough to stretch sheet iron, Roosevelt took to the stump to denounce "economic royalists" who "hide behind the flag and the Constitution." "I welcome their hatred," he proclaimed.

A landslide overwhelmed Landon as the demoralized Republicans carried only two states, Maine and Vermont. The popular vote was 27,752,869 to 16,674,665; the electoral count was 523 to 8—the most lopsided in 116 years. Democratic majorities were again returned to Congress. Jubilant Democrats could now claim more than two-thirds of the seats in the House and a like proportion in the Senate.

The battle of 1936, perhaps the most bitter since Bryan's in 1896, partially bore out Republican charges of class warfare. Even more than in 1932, the needy economic groups were lined up against the so-called greedy economic groups. CIO units contributed generously to FDR's campaign chest. Many left-wingers turned to Roosevelt as the customary third-party protest vote sharply declined. Blacks, several million of whom had also appreciated federal relief, had by now largely shaken off their traditional allegiance to the Republican party. To them, Lincoln was "finally dead."

FDR won primarily because he appealed to the "forgotten man," whom he never forgot. Roosevelt in fact had forged a powerful and enduring coalition of the South, blacks, urbanites, and the poor. He proved especially effective in marshaling the support of the multitudes of "New Immigrants"—mostly Catholics and Jews who had swarmed into the great cities since the turn of the century. These once-scorned newcomers, with their now-numerous sons and daughters, had at last come politically of age. In the 1920s, one out of every twenty-five federal judgeships went to a Catholic; Roosevelt appointed Catholics to one out of every four.

Conflict over the Court

Bowing his head to the sleety blasts, Roosevelt took the presidential oath on January 20, 1937, instead of the traditional March 4. The Twentieth Amendment to the Constitution had been ratified in 1933 (see the Appendix). It swept away the postelection lame duck session of Congress and shortened by six weeks the awkward period before inauguration.

Flushed with victory, Roosevelt interpreted his reelection as a mandate to continue New Deal reforms. But in his eyes the cloistered old men on the supreme bench, like fossilized stumbling blocks, stood stubbornly in the pathway of progress. In nine major cases involving the New Deal, the Roosevelt administration had been thwarted seven times. The Supreme Court was ultraconservative, and six of the nine oldsters in black were over seventy. As luck would have it, not a single member had been appointed by FDR in his first term.

Roosevelt—his "Dutch up"—viewed with mounting impatience what he regarded as the obstructive conservatism of the Court. Some of these Old Guard appointees were hanging on with a senile grip, partly because they felt it their patriotic duty to curb the "socialistic" tendencies of that radical in the White House.

To overcome such obstructionism, Roosevelt suddenly announced, early in 1937, a scheme to expand the Supreme Court. He bluntly asked Congress for legislation to add a new justice to the Supreme Court for every member over seventy who would not retire. The maximum membership could then be fifteen.

Congress and the nation were promptly convulsed over the scheme to "pack" the Supreme Court with a "dictator bill," which one critic called "too damned slick." Franklin "Double-crossing" Roosevelt was savagely condemned for attempting to break down the delicate checks and balances among the three branches of the government.

The Court had meanwhile seen the ax hanging over its head. Whatever his motives, Justice Owen J. Roberts, formerly regarded as a conservative, began to vote on the side of his liberal colleagues. "A switch in time saves nine" was the classic witticism inspired by this change. By a five-to-four decision, the Court, in March 1937, upheld the principle of a state minimum wage for women, thereby reversing its stand on a different case a year earlier. In succeeding decisions, the Court, more sympathetic to the New Deal, upheld the National Labor Relations Act (Wagner Act) and the Social Security Act.

Later Major New Deal Measures, 1933–1939 (items in parentheses indicate secondary purposes)

Recovery	Relief	Reform
(CWA)	FDR establishes Civil Works Administration (CWA), November 9, 1933	
Gold Reserve Act, January 30, 1934, authorizes FDR's devaluation, January 31, 1934		
		Securities and Exchange Commission (SEC) authorized by Congress, June 6, 1934
(Reciprocal Trade Agreements)	(Reciprocal Trade Agreements)	Reciprocal Trade Agreements Act, June 12, 1934
		Indian Reorganization Act, June 18, 1934
(FHA)	National Housing Act, June 28, 1934, authorizes Federal Housing Administration (FHA)	(FHA)
(Frazier-Lemke Act)	Frazier-Lemke Farm Bankruptcy Act, June 28, 1934	
(Resettlement Administration)	FDR creates Resettlement Administration, April 30, 1935	
(WPA)	FDR creates Works Progress Administration (WPA), May 6, 1935, under act of April 8, 1935	
(Wagner Act)	(Wagner Act)	(Wagner) National Labor Relations Act, July 5, 1935
		Social Security Act, August 14, 1935
		Public Utility Holding Company Act, August 26, 1935
(Soil Conservation Act)	Soil Conservation and Domestic Allotment Act, February 29, 1936	
(USHA)	(USHA)	United States Housing Authority (USHA) established by Congress, September 1, 1937
(Second AAA)	Second Agricultural Adjustment Act, February 16, 1938	
(Fair Labor Standards)	(Fair Labor Standards)	Fair Labor Standards Act (Wages and Hours Bill), June 25, 1938
		Reorganization Act, April 3, 1939
		Hatch Act, August 2, 1939

With these changes under way, Congress refused to endorse the Court-packing scheme, and Roosevelt suffered his first major legislative defeat at the hands of his own party. Yet in losing this battle, Roosevelt incidentally won his campaign. The Court, as he had hoped, became markedly more friendly to New Deal reforms. Furthermore, a succession of deaths and resignations enabled him to make nine appointments to the tribunal.

Yet in a sense FDR lost both the Court battle and the war. He so aroused conservatives of both parties in Congress that few New Deal reforms were passed after 1937, the year of the fight to "pack" the Supreme Court. With this catastrophic miscalculation, he squandered much of the political goodwill that had carried him to such a resounding victory in the 1936 election.

The Twilight of the New Deal

Roosevelt's first term, from 1933 to 1937, did not banish the depression from the land. Unemployment stubbornly persisted in 1936 at about 15 percent, down from the grim 25 percent of 1933 but still miserably high. Despite the inventiveness of New Deal programs and the billions of dollars in "pump priming," recovery had been dishearteningly modest, though the country seemed to be inching its way back to economic health.

Then, in 1937 the economy took another sharp downturn, a surprisingly severe depression-within-a-depression that the president's critics quickly dubbed the "Roosevelt recession." In fact, government policies *had* caused the nosedive, as Social Security taxes began to bite into payrolls and as the administration cut back on spending out of continuing reverence for the orthodox economic doctrine of the balanced budget.

Only at this late date did Roosevelt at last frankly and deliberately embrace the recommendations of the British economist John Maynard Keynes. Now, in April 1937, FDR announced a bold program to stimulate the economy by planned deficit spending. Although the deficits were still relatively small, this abrupt policy reversal endorsing "Keynesianism" marked a turning point in the government's relation to the economy.

Facing an increasingly conservative Congress, Roosevelt successfully backed only a few reform measures like the 1939 Hatch Act prohibiting federal employees from active political campaigning. By 1939 the New Deal had clearly lost most of its early momentum. Magician Roosevelt could find few dazzling new reform rabbits to pull out of his tall silk hat. In the congressional elections of 1938 the Republicans, for the first time, cut heavily into the New Deal majorities in Congress, though failing to gain control of either house.

The international crisis that came to a boil in 1938–1939 shifted public attention away from domestic reform and no doubt helped save the political hide of the Roosevelt "spendocracy." The New Deal, for all practical purposes, had shot its bolt.

New Deal or Raw Deal?

Foes of the New Deal condemned its alleged radicalism, incompetence, confusion, and cross-purposes. New Dealers conceded some weaknesses but defended their record as a necessary and effective response to the depression.

To some conservatives, the New Deal was a radical attempt to make America over in a Bolshevik-Marxist image. They condemned "Rooseveltski" for bringing to Washington "crackpot" college professors, leftist "pinkos," and outright communists. The Hearst newspapers lambasted

> The Red New Deal with a Soviet seal
> Endorsed by a Moscow hand,
> The strange result of an alien cult
> In a liberty-loving land.

Other critics accused Roosevelt of bringing too many bright young Jewish leftists to Washington ("The Jew Deal"), or even asserted that Roosevelt himself was Jewish ("Rosenfeld").

More widespread was the charge that the New Deal brought bureaucracy, waste, and a welfare-state mentality that undermined the old American virtues of individualism, thrift, self-reliance, and limited government. The federal government, with its hundreds of thousands of employees, became incomparably the largest single business in the country, as the states faded farther into the background. Promises of bud-

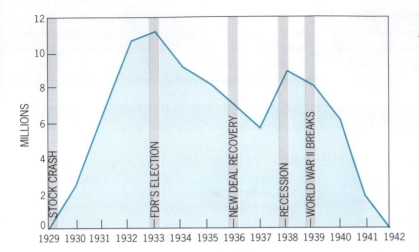

Unemployment, 1929–1942 *The cold figures can only begin to suggest the widespread human misery caused by mass unemployment. One man wrote to a newspaper in 1932: "I am forty-eight; married twenty-one years; four children, three in school. For the last eight years I was employed as a Pullman conductor. Since September, 1930, they have given me seven months of part-time work. Today I am an object of charity. . . . My small, weak, and frail wife and two small children are suffering and I have come to that terrible place where I could easily resort to violence in my desperation."*

get balancing were forgotten as the national debt skyrocketed from $19,487,000,000 in 1932 to $40,440,000,000 by 1939. Critics charged that the lavish benefactions of the "handout state" were turning once self-reliant Americans into relief-seeking loafers with wishbones larger than their backbones.

Hardheaded businesspeople, mostly Republicans, bitterly attacked what they saw as the New Deal's governmental oppression and regimentation, its class warfare, and Roosevelt's one-man rule. Private enterprise, they charged, was being stifled by a "planned economy" and "creeping socialism."

The most damning indictment of the New Deal was that it failed to cure the depression. Despite some $20 billion poured out in six years of deficit spending and lending, many economists believed that better results would have been achieved by much greater deficit spending. The New Deal, some believed, merely administered aspirin, sedatives, and Band-Aids, with the result that in 1939 millions of dispirited men and women were still unemployed. Not until World War II increased the national debt from $40 billion in 1939 to $258 billion in 1945 was the unemployment headache solved.

New Dealers staunchly defended their record. Admitting imperfection, they argued that the bureaucratic inefficiency and waste were trivial in view of the immense sums spent and the obvious need for haste. The New Deal, they insisted, relieved a crisis by demonstrating that the Washington regime was to be used, not feared. The collapse of America's economic system was averted; a fairer distribution of the national income was achieved; and the citizens were enabled to regain and retain their self-respect.

Though hated by business tycoons, FDR should have been their patron saint, so his admirers claimed. He deflected popular resentments against business and may have saved the American system of free enterprise. Roosevelt's quarrel was not with capitalism but with capitalists; he purged American capitalism of some of its worst abuses so that it might be saved from itself. He may even have headed off a more radical swing to the left by a mild dose of what was mistakenly condemned as "socialism." The head of the American Socialist party, when once asked if the New Deal had carried out the Socialist program, reportedly replied that it had indeed—on a stretcher.

Roosevelt, like Jefferson, provided reform without a bloody revolution—at a time in history when some foreign nations were suffering armed uprisings and many Europeans were predicting either communism or fascism for America. He was upbraided by the left-wing radicals for not going far enough and by the right-wing radicals for going too far. Choosing the middle road, he has been called the greatest American conservative since Hamilton. He was in fact Hamiltonian in his espousal of big government, but he was Jeffersonian in his concern for the "forgotten man." Demonstrating anew the value of powerful presidential leadership, he exercised that power to relieve the erosion of the nation's greatest physical resource—its people. He helped preserve democracy in America at a time when democracies abroad were disappearing down the sinkhole of dictatorship. And in playing this role he unwittingly girded the nation for its part in the gruesome war that loomed on the horizon—a war in which democracy the world over would be at stake.

Chronology

1932	Roosevelt defeats Hoover for presidency.
1933	Bank holiday.
	Emergency Banking Relief Act.
	Hundred Days Congress enacts HOLC, AAA, NRA, PWA, and TVA.
	Federal Securities Act.
	Glass-Steagall Banking Reform Act.
	CWA established.
	Twentieth Amendment (changed calendar of congressional sessions and date of presidential inauguration).
	Twenty-first Amendment (prohibition repealed).
1934	Securities and Exchange Commission authorized.
	Indian Reorganization Act.
	FHA established.
	Frazier-Lemke Farm Bankruptcy Act.
1935	WPA established.
	Wagner Act.
	Resettlement Administration.
	Social Security Act.
	Public Utility Holding Company Act.
	Schechter "sick chicken" case.
	CIO organized.
1936	Soil Conservation and Domestic Allotment Act.
	Roosevelt defeats Landon for presidency.
1937	USHA established.
	Roosevelt announces "Court-packing" plan.
1938	Second AAA.
	Fair Labor Standards Act.
1939	Hatch Act.

VARYING VIEWPOINTS

How Radical Was the New Deal?

The Great Depression was both a great calamity and a great opportunity. How effectively Franklin Roosevelt responded to the calamity and what use he made of the opportunity are the two questions that have animated historical debate about the New Deal.

Some historians have denied that there was much of a connection between the depression and the New Deal. Arthur M. Schlesinger, Jr., for example, who believes in "cycles" of reform and reaction in American history, has written that "there would very likely have been some sort of New Deal in the 1930s even without the Depression." But most of the first generation of historians who wrote about the New Deal (in the 1940s, '50s, and early '60s) agreed with Carl Degler's judgment that the New Deal was "a revolutionary response to a revolutionary situation." In this view, though Roosevelt never found a means short of war to bring about economic recovery, he shrewdly utilized the stubborn economic crisis as a means to enact sweeping reforms.

Some leftist scholars writing in the 1960s, however, notably Barton J. Bernstein, charged that the New

Deal did not reach far enough. This criticism echoed the socialist complaint in the 1930s that the depression represented the total collapse of American capitalism, and that the New Deal muffed the chance truly to remake American society. A bolder Roosevelt, these historians argue, might have acted to redistribute wealth, improve race relations, and bring the giant corporations to heel. Instead, say these critics, the New Deal simply represented a conservative holding action to shore up a sagging and corrupt capitalist order.

Those charges against the New Deal stimulated another generation of scholars in the 1970s, '80s, and '90s to look closely at the concrete institutional, attitudinal, and economic circumstances in which the New Deal unfolded. Historians including James Patterson, Alan Brinkley, Kenneth Jackson, Harvard Sitkoff, and Lizabeth Cohen—sometimes loosely referred to as the "constraints school"—conclude that the New Deal offered just about as much reform as circumstances allowed and as the majority of Americans wanted. The findings of these historians are impressive: the system of checks and balances limited presidential power; the disproportionate influence of southern Democrats in Congress stalled attempts to move toward racial justice; the federal system, in fact, inhibited all efforts to initiate change from Washington; and most important, a majority of the American people at the time wanted to reform capitalism, not overthrow it.

The best proof of the soundness of that conclusion is probably the durability of the political alliance that Roosevelt assembled. The great "New Deal coalition" that dominated American politics for nearly four decades after Roosevelt's election in 1932 represented a broad consensus in American society about the legitimate limits of government efforts to shape the social and economic order. William Leuchtenburg offered the most balanced historical assessment in his description of the New Deal as a "half-way revolution," neither radical nor conservative but accurately reflecting the American people's needs and desires in the 1930s—and for a long time thereafter.

For further reading, see the Appendix. For web resources, go to **http://college.hmco.com**.

35

Franklin D. Roosevelt and the Shadow of War

1933–1941

The epidemic of world lawlessness is spreading. When an epidemic of physical disease starts to spread, the community approves and joins in a quarantine of the patients in order to protect the health of the community against the spread of the disease. . . . There must be positive endeavors to preserve peace.

FRANKLIN D. ROOSEVELT, CHICAGO QUARANTINE SPEECH, 1937

Americans in the 1930s tried to turn their backs on the world's problems. Their president at first seemed to share these views. The only battle Roosevelt fought was against the depression. America had its own burdens to shoulder, and the costs of foreign involvement, whether in blood or treasure, simply seemed too great.

But as the clouds of war gathered over Europe, Roosevelt eventually concluded that the United States could no longer remain aloof. Events gradually brought the American people around to his way of thinking: no nation was safe in an era of international anarchy, and the world could not remain half-enchained and half-free.

Roosevelt's Early Foreign Policies

Roosevelt's initial foreign policy was intended to serve his schemes for domestic recovery. This was first demonstrated by his actions at the London Economic Conference in the summer of 1933. Sixty-six nations had gathered to attack the depression by stabilizing national currencies. But Roosevelt, unwilling to subordinate his gold-juggling policies to an international agreement that might tie his hands, torpedoed the conference with an explosive message that scolded the delegates for even trying to stabilize currencies. Whether the conference could have arrested the worldwide economic slide is debatable, but Roosevelt's every-man-for-himself attitude plunged the planet even deeper into economic crisis. Roosevelt also plunged the world deeper into narrow isolationism and extreme nationalism—a trend that played directly into the hands of power-mad dictators.

Roosevelt matched isolationism from Europe with withdrawal from Asia. With the descent into hard times, American taxpayers were eager to throw overboard their expensive tropical liability in the Philippines. Congress passed the Tydings-McGuffie Act in 1934, which provided for the independence of the Philippines in 1946 but threatened to leave the islands economically prostrate. American isolationists rejoiced once again, and Japanese militarists calculated that they had little to fear from inward-looking America.

Closer to home, Roosevelt inaugurated a refreshing new era in relations with Latin America. He proclaimed in his inaugural address: "I would dedicate this nation to the policy of the Good Neighbor." He renounced the policies of armed intervention that had accompanied the corollary to the Monroe Doctrine devised by his cousin Theodore Roosevelt. Accordingly, in 1934 the United States withdrew the last marines from Haiti and in 1936 relaxed its grip on Panama. When the Mexican government seized Yankee oil properties in 1938, Roosevelt successfully resisted business pressure to intervene and eventually thrashed out a settlement in 1941. These earnest acts of friendliness paid rich dividends in goodwill among the peoples to the south and made Roosevelt a hero in Latin America.

Taken together, Roosevelt's noninvolvement in Europe and withdrawal from Asia, along with his brotherly embrace of his New World neighbors, suggested that the United States was giving up its ambition to be a world power and would content itself instead with being merely a regional power, its interests and activities confined exclusively to the Western Hemisphere.

Impulses Toward Isolationism

Post-1918 chaos in Europe, followed by the Great Depression, spawned the ominous spread of totalitarianism—the notion that the individual was nothing and the state was everything. The Communist Soviet Union led the way, with the crafty and ruthless Joseph Stalin finally emerging as dictator. Blustery Benito Mussolini, a swaggering Fascist, seized the reins of power in Italy during 1922. And Adolf Hitler, a fanatic with a toothbrush mustache, plotted and harangued his way into control of Germany in 1933 with liberal use of the "big lie."

Jut-jawed Mussolini, seeking both glory and empire in Africa, brutally attacked Ethiopia in 1935 with bombers and tanks. But Hitler was the most dangerous dictator because he combined tremendous power with impulsiveness. A frustrated Austrian painter, with hypnotic talents as an orator and leader, he led the Nazi party to power in Germany by making political capital of the Treaty of Versailles and the country's depression-spawned unemployment. In 1936 the Nazi Hitler and the Fascist Mussolini allied themselves in the Rome-Berlin Axis.

International gangsterism was likewise spreading in East Asia, where imperial Japan was on the make. Like Germany and Italy, Japan was a so-called have-not power. Like them, it resented the ungenerous Treaty of Versailles. Like them, it demanded additional space for its teeming millions, cooped up in their crowded island nation. Determined to find a place in the Asian sun, Tokyo terminated the Washington Naval Treaty in 1934 and in the following year accelerated Japan's construction of giant battleships.

Isolationism, long festering in America, received a strong boost from these alarms abroad. Though disapproving of the dictators, Americans still believed that their encircling seas conferred a kind of mystic immunity. They were continuing to suffer the disillusionment born of their participation in World War I, which they now regarded as a colossal blunder. They likewise nursed bitter memories of the ungrateful and defaulting debtors. As early as 1934 a spiteful Congress had passed the Johnson Debt Default Act, which prevented debt-dodging nations from borrowing further from the United States.

As the gloomy 1930s lengthened, an avalanche of lurid articles and books condemning the munitions manufacturers as war-fomenting "merchants of death" poured forth from American presses. A Senate committee headed by Senator Gerald Nye of North

Dakota was appointed in 1934 to investigate the "blood business." By sensationalizing evidence regarding America's entry into World War I, the senatorial probers tended to shift the blame away from the German submarine onto the American bankers and arms manufacturers. Because the munitions makers had obviously made money out of the war, many a naive citizen leaped to the illogical conclusion that these scavengers had *caused* the war in order to make money. This kind of reasoning suggested that if the profits could only be removed from the arms traffic—"one hell of a business"—the country could steer clear of any future world conflict.

Responding to overwhelming popular pressure, Congress made haste to legislate the nation out of war. Action was spurred by the danger that Mussolini's Ethiopian assault would plunge the world into a new bloodbath. The Neutrality Acts of 1935, 1936, and 1937, taken together, stipulated that when the president proclaimed the existence of a foreign war, certain restrictions would automatically go into effect: no American could legally sail on a belligerent ship, sell or transport munitions to a belligerent, or make loans to a belligerent.

Such storm-cellar neutrality proved to be tragically shortsighted. Through its neutrality laws, America served notice that it would make no distinction between brutal aggressors and innocent victims. By striving to hold the scales even, it actually overbalanced them in favor of the dictators, who had armed themselves to the teeth. By declining to use its vast industrial strength to aid its democratic friends and defeat its totalitarian foes, America helped goad the aggressors along their blood-spattered path of conquest.

The Spanish Civil War of 1936–1939—a proving ground and dress rehearsal in miniature for World War II—was an especially painful object lesson in the folly of neutrality-by-legislation. Spanish rebels, who rose against the left-leaning republican government in Madrid, were headed by fascistic General Francisco Franco. Generously aided by his fellow conspirators Hitler and Mussolini, he undertook to overthrow the established Loyalist regime, which in turn was assisted on a smaller scale by the Soviet Union. This pipeline from communist Moscow offended many Americans, especially Roman Catholics.

In accordance with previous American practice, the Loyalist government should have been free to purchase desperately needed munitions from the United States. But Congress, with the encouragement of Roosevelt and with only one dissenting vote, amended the existing neutrality legislation so as to apply an arms embargo to both Loyalists and rebels.

Uncle Sam thus sat on the sidelines while Franco, abundantly supplied with arms and men by his fellow dictators, strangled the republican government of Spain. The democracies, including the United States, were so determined to stay out of war that they helped to condemn a fellow democracy to death. In so doing they further encouraged the dictators to take the dangerous road that led over the precipice to World War II.

Appeasing Japan and Germany

Sulfurous war clouds had meanwhile been gathering in tension-taut East Asia. In 1937 the Japanese militarists, at the Marco Polo Bridge near Beijing (Peking), touched off the explosion that led to a full-dress invasion of China. In a sense this attack was the curtain raiser of World War II.

Roosevelt declined to invoke the recently passed neutrality legislation by refusing to label the so-called China incident an officially declared war. If he had put the existing restrictions into effect, he would have cut off the tiny trickle of munitions on which the Chinese were desperately dependent. The Japanese, of course, could continue to buy mountains of war supplies in the United States.

In Chicago—unofficial isolationist "capital" of America—President Roosevelt delivered his sensational "Quarantine Speech" in the autumn of 1937. Alarmed by the recent aggression of Italy and Japan, he called for "positive endeavors" to "quarantine" the aggressors—presumably by economic embargoes. The speech triggered a cyclone of protest from isolationists and other foes of involvement; they feared that a moral quarantine would lead to a shooting quarantine. Startled by this angry response, Roosevelt retreated and sought less direct means to curb the dictators.

America's isolationist mood intensified in December 1937 when Japanese aviators bombed and sank an American gunboat, the *Panay*, in Chinese waters. In the days of 1898, when the *Maine* went down, this outrage might have provoked war. But after Tokyo apologized and paid an indemnity, Americans breathed a sigh of relief.

Adolf Hitler meanwhile grew louder and bolder in Europe. In 1935 he had openly flouted the Treaty of Versailles by introducing compulsory military service in Germany. The next year he boldly marched into the demilitarized German Rhineland, likewise contrary to the detested treaty, while France and Britain looked on in an agony of indecision. Lashing his following to a frenzy, Hitler undertook to persecute and then exterminate the Jewish population in the areas under his control. In the end, he wiped out about 6 million innocent victims, mostly in gas chambers (see "Makers of America: Refugees from the Holocaust," pp. 492–493). Calling upon his people to sacrifice butter for guns, he whipped the new German air force and mechanized ground divisions into the most devastating military machine the world had yet seen.

What Next? 1938 *The western European democracies looked on helplessly as Nazi Germany swallowed up Austria and part of Czechoslovakia in 1938. Hitler's juggernaut seemed unstoppable.*

Suddenly, in March 1938, Hitler bloodlessly occupied German-speaking Austria, his birthplace. The democratic powers, wringing their hands in despair, prayed that this last grab would satisfy his passion for conquest. But like a drunken reveler calling for madder music and stronger wine, Hitler could not stop. Intoxicated by his recent gains, he began to make bullying demands for the German-inhabited Sudetenland of neighboring Czechoslovakia.

British and French leaders, eager to appease Hitler, frantically arranged a conference with Hitler and Mussolini at Munich, Germany, in September 1938, where they consented to Hitler's demand. Europeans and Americans alike hoped that these concessions would bring "peace in our time." Indeed, Hitler publicly promised that the Sudetenland "is the last territorial claim I have to make in Europe."

"Appeasement" of the dictators, symbolized by the ugly word *Munich*, turned out to be merely surrender on the installment plan. It was like giving a cannibal a finger in the hope of saving an arm. In March 1939, scarcely six months later, Hitler suddenly erased the rest of Czechoslovakia from the map, contrary to his solemn vows. The democratic world was again stunned.

Hitler's Belligerency and U.S. Neutrality

Joseph Stalin, the sphinx of the Kremlin, was a key to the peace puzzle. When efforts to secure a mutual defense treaty with Britain and France fell through in the summer of 1939, the Soviet Union astounded the world by signing, on August 23, 1939, a nonaggression treaty with the German dictator. The notorious Hitler-Stalin pact meant that, contrary to hopes of wishful thinkers in western Europe, the two dictators would not bleed each other to death, but rather join hands to share the spoils.

With the signing of the Nazi-Soviet pact, World War II was only hours away. Hitler now demanded from neighboring Poland a return of the areas wrested from Germany after World War I. Failing to secure satisfaction, he sent his mechanized divisions crashing into Poland at dawn on September 1, 1939. Honoring their commitments, Britain and France promptly declared war. But they were powerless to

Refugees from the Holocaust

Fed by Adolf Hitler's genocidal delusions, anti-Semitism bared its fangs in the 1930s, spreading across Europe as Nazi Germany seized Austria and Czechoslovakia. Eluding the jackboots of Hitler's bloodthirsty SS (*Schutzstaffel*, an elite military and police force), Jews tried to flee from the Nazi juggernaut. Some succeeded, including the world's premier nuclear physicist, Albert Einstein, the Nobel laureate whose plea to Franklin Roosevelt helped initiate the top-secret atomic bomb project; the philosopher Hannah Arendt; the painter Marc Chagall; and the composer Kurt Weill. In all, some 150,000 Jews fled the Nazi Third Reich for America in the 1930s—a tiny fraction of the millions of Jews who eventually came under Hitler's heel. Why did America not make room for more?

For one thing, those exiled luminaries who managed to make it out of Germany found a divided Jewish community in America. On the one hand, prosperous German Jews who had established themselves in America in the nineteenth century had little in common with later-arriving Jews from eastern Europe and feared stirring an outburst of anti-Semitism if they advocated further immigration. On the other hand, less influential organizations of eastern European Jews struggled to pressure the Roosevelt administration to rescue Europe's Jews. This internal discord undermined the political effectiveness of the American Jewish community in the face of the refugee dilemma.

Other factors also kept America's doors shut against Jews seeking refuge in the United States. The restrictive American immigration law of 1924 set rigid national quotas and made no provisions for seekers of asylum from racial, religious, or political persecution. The Great Depression made it impossible to provide employment for workers already in the United States, much less make room in the job line for newcomers.

Many Jews and non-Jews alike, including Congressman Emmanuel Celler and Senator Robert Wagner, both of New York, lobbied Roosevelt's government to extend a welcoming hand to Jews seeking asylum—to no avail. In 1941 Congress rejected a Wagner bill to bring twenty thousand German-Jewish children to the United States outside the quota restrictions.

Albert Einstein Arriving in America, 1933 *Sadly, the United States admitted only a trickle of refugees from Nazism, while some 6 million European Jews died.*

Once the United States entered the war, the State Department suppressed early reports of Hitler's plan to exterminate all European Jewry. After the Führer's sordid "final solution" became more widely known in America, the War Department rejected pleas to bomb rail lines leading to the gas chambers. Military officials maintained that a raid on death camps like Auschwitz would divert essential military resources and needlessly extend the war. Thus only a lucky few escaped the Nazi terror, while 6 million died in one of history's most ghastly testimonials to the human capacity for evil.

aid Poland, which was quickly divided between Hitler and his partner in crime, Stalin. Long-dreaded World War II was now fully launched, and the long truce of 1919–1939 came to an end.

Americans were overwhelmingly anti-Nazi and anti-Hitler, but they were desperately determined to stay out of war; they were not going to be "suckers" again. Neutrality promptly became a heated issue in the United States. Britain and France urgently needed American airplanes and weapons, but the Neutrality Act of 1937 raised a sternly forbidding hand. Roosevelt summoned Congress into special session, and after hectic debate it came up with the makeshift Neutrality Act of 1939. This law provided that henceforth the European democracies might buy American war materials, but only on a "cash-and-carry" basis— that is, they would have to pay for munitions in cash and transport them in their own ships.

Despite its defects, this unneutral neutrality law clearly favored the democracies against the dictators—and was so intended. Because the British and French navies controlled the Atlantic, the European aggressors could not send their ships to buy America's munitions. The United States not only improved its moral position but simultaneously helped its economic position. Overseas demand for war goods brought a sharp upswing from the recession of 1937–1938 and ultimately solved the decade-long unemployment crisis (see the chart on p. 485).

The Fall of France and the Destroyer Deal (1940)

The months following the collapse of Poland, while France and Britain marked time, were known as the "phony war." An ominous silence fell on Europe as Hitler shifted his victorious divisions from Poland for a knockout blow at France. Inaction during this anxious period was relieved by the Soviets, who wantonly attacked neighboring Finland in an effort to secure strategic buffer territory.

An abrupt end to the "phony war" came in April 1940 when Hitler, again without warning, overran his weaker neighbors, Denmark and Norway. Hardly pausing for breath, the next month he attacked the Netherlands and Belgium, then struck a paralyzing blow at France. By late June, France was forced to surrender, but not until Mussolini had pounced on its rear for a jackal's share of the loot. In a pell-mell but successful evacuation from the French port of Dunkirk, the British managed to salvage the bulk of their shattered army. The crisis providentially brought forth an inspired leader in Prime Minister Winston Churchill, the bulldog-jawed orator who nerved the British to fight off the fearful air bombings of their cities.

France's sudden collapse shocked Americans out of their daydreams. Stouthearted Britons, singing "There'll Always Be an England," were all that stood between Hitler and the death in Europe of constitutional government. If Britain went under, Hitler would have at his disposal the workshops, shipyards, and slave labor of western Europe. He might even have the powerful British fleet as well. This frightening possibility, which seemed to pose a dire threat to American security, steeled the American people to a tremendous effort.

Roosevelt moved with electrifying energy and dispatch. He called upon an already debt-burdened nation to build huge airfleets and a two-ocean navy, which could also check Japan. Congress, jarred out of its apathy toward preparedness, within a year appropriated the astounding sum of $37 billion, more than the total cost of fighting World War I. Congress also passed a conscription law on September 6, 1940, America's first peacetime draft.

As the Battle of Britain raged in the air over the British Isles, debate intensified in the United States over what foreign policy to embrace. Before the fall of France in June 1940, Washington had generally observed a technical neutrality. But now the wisdom of neutrality seemed increasingly questionable.

Supporters of aid to Britain formed propaganda groups, the most potent of which was the Committee to Defend America by Aiding the Allies. The isolationists, both numerous and sincere, were by no means silent. Determined to avoid bloodshed at all costs, they organized the America First Committee. Their basic philosophy was "the Yanks are not coming," and their most effective speechmaker was the famed aviator Colonel Charles A. Lindbergh, who, ironically, had narrowed the Atlantic in 1927.

Britain was in critical need of destroyers, for German submarines were again threatening to starve it out with attacks on shipping. Roosevelt moved boldly when, on September 2, 1940, he agreed to transfer to Great Britain fifty old destroyers left over from World War I. In return, the British promised to hand over to the United States eight valuable defensive base sites, stretching from Newfoundland to South America. These strategically located outposts were to remain under the Stars and Stripes for ninety-nine years.

Shifting warships from a "neutral" United States to a belligerent Britain was, beyond question, a flagrant violation of neutral obligations. But public-opinion polls demonstrated that a majority of Americans were determined to provide the battered British with "all aid short of war."

FDR Shatters the Two-Term Tradition (1940)

In the midst of this crisis came the distracting presidential election of 1940. The Republican convention in Philadelphia was miraculously swept off its feet by Wendell L. Willkie, a colorful German-descended Indiana public utilities corporation executive who was a complete novice in politics. With the galleries in Philadelphia wildly chanting "We Want Willkie," the delegates finally accepted this magnetic political upstart as the only candidate who could possibly beat Roosevelt. The outspoken Willkie was opposed not so much to the New Deal as to its extravagances and inefficiencies. Democratic critics branded him "the rich man's Roosevelt" and "the simple barefoot Wall Street lawyer."

Roosevelt delayed to the last minute the announcement of his decision to challenge the sacred two-term tradition. Despite what he described as his personal yearning for retirement, he avowed that in so grave a crisis he owed his experienced hand to the service of his country and humanity.

With the country already badly split between interventionists and isolationists, Willkie might have widened the breach dangerously by a violent attack on Roosevelt's aid-to-Britain policies. But the Republican candidate refrained from assailing the president's interventionism and accepted the essential premises of an internationalist foreign policy. Willkie campaigned hard against Rooseveltian "dictatorship" and the third term. Roosevelt, busy at his desk with important problems, stayed close to the White House and generally ignored Willkie. But in a speech in Boston he emphatically declared, "Your boys are not going to be sent into any foreign wars"—a pledge that later came back to plague him.

Roosevelt triumphed, although Willkie ran a strong race. The electoral count was 449 to 82. The popular vote was much closer—27,307,819 to 22,321,018.

Congress Passes the Landmark Lend-Lease Law

By late 1940 embattled Britain was nearing the end of its financial tether; its credits in America were being rapidly consumed by insatiable war orders. But Roosevelt, who had bitter memories of the wrangling over the Allied debts of World War I, was determined, as he put it, to eliminate "the silly, foolish, old dollar sign." He finally hit on the scheme of lending or leasing American arms to the reeling democracies. When the shooting was over, to use his comparison, the guns and tanks could be returned, just as one's next-door neighbor would return a garden hose once the threatening fire was put out. But isolationist Senator

Robert Taft retorted that lending arms was like lending chewing gum: "You don't want it back." Who wants a chewed-up tank?

The lend-lease bill, patriotically numbered 1776, was entitled "An Act Further to Promote the Defense of the United States." The underlying concept was "Send guns, not sons" or "Billions, not bodies." America, so President Roosevelt promised, would be the "arsenal of democracy." It would send a limitless supply of arms to the victims of aggression, who in turn would finish the job and keep the war on their side of the Atlantic. Isolationists assailed the lend-lease scheme as "the blank-check bill." Isolationist Senator Burton Wheeler called it "the new triple-A [Agricultural Adjustment Act] bill"—a measure designed to "plow under every fourth American boy." Nevertheless, lend-lease was finally approved in March 1941 by sweeping majorities in both houses of Congress.

Lend-lease was one of the most momentous laws ever to pass Congress; it was a challenge hurled squarely into the teeth of the Axis dictators. America eventually sent about $50 billion worth of arms and equipment—much more than the cost to the country of World War I—to those nations fighting aggressors. By its very nature, lend-lease marked the abandonment of any pretense of neutrality. It was no destroyer deal arranged privately by Roosevelt. The bill was universally debated, over drugstore counters and cracker barrels, from California to Maine; and the sovereign citizens at last spoke through convincing majorities in Congress. Lend-lease had the somewhat incidental result of gearing U.S. factories for all-out war production. The enormously increased capacity thus achieved helped to save America's own skin when, at long last, the shooting war burst around its head.

Hitler himself evidently recognized lend-lease as an unofficial declaration of war. Until then, Germany had avoided attacking U.S. ships; memories of America's decisive intervention in 1917–1918 were still fresh in German minds. But after the passing of lend-lease there was less point in trying to curry favor with the United States. On May 21, 1941, the *Robin Moor*, an unarmed American merchant ship, was torpedoed and destroyed by a German submarine in the South Atlantic, outside a war zone. The sinkings had started, but on a limited scale.

U.S. Destroyers and Hitler's U-Boats Clash

Lend-lease shipments of arms to Britain on British ships were bound to be sunk by German wolf-pack submarines. If the intent was to get the munitions to Britain, not to dump them into the ocean, the freighters would have to be escorted by U.S. warships. Britain simply did not have enough destroyers. The fateful decision to convoy was taken in July 1941. Roosevelt issued orders to the U.S. Navy to escort

Main Flow of Lend-Lease Aid (width of arrows indicates relative amount) *The proud but desperate British prime minister, Winston Churchill, declared in early 1941: "Give us the tools and we will finish the job." Lend-lease eventually provided the British and other Allies with $50 billion worth of "tools."*

lend-lease shipments to Iceland. The British would then shepherd them the rest of the way.

Inevitable clashes with submarines ensued on the Iceland run, even though Hitler's orders were to strike American warships only in self-defense. In September 1941, the U.S. destroyer *Greer*, provocatively trailing a German U-boat, was attacked by the undersea craft, without damage to either vessel. Roosevelt then proclaimed a shoot-on-sight policy. On October 17 the escorting destroyer *Kearny*, while engaged in a battle with U-boats, lost eleven men when it was crippled but not sent to the bottom. Two weeks later the destroyer *Reuben James* was torpedoed and sunk off southwestern Iceland, with the loss of more than one hundred officers and men.

Neutrality was still inscribed on the statute books but not in American hearts. In August 1941, Roosevelt met secretly with Prime Minister Churchill on a warship off the foggy coast of Newfoundland. There they signed the Atlantic Charter, affirming the rights of peoples to choose their own form of government and proposing a "permanent system of general security" (a new League of Nations). Isolationists protested the Atlantic Charter between belligerent Britain and "neutral" America, but in fact the nation was no longer neutral. Hitler's invasion of the Soviet Union in June 1941 made the Nazi dictator's global ambitions even clearer. Congress, responding to public pressures and confronted with a shooting war in the North Atlantic, voted in mid-November 1941 to pull the teeth from the now-useless Neutrality Act of 1939. Merchant ships could henceforth be legally armed, and they could enter the combat zones with munitions for Britain. Americans braced themselves for wholesale attacks by Hitler's submarines.

Surprise Assault at Pearl Harbor

The blowup came not in the Atlantic, but in the faraway Pacific. This explosion should have surprised no close observer, for Japan, since September 1940, had been a formal military ally of Nazi Germany—America's shooting foe in the North Atlantic.

Japan's position in East Asia had grown more perilous by the hour. It was still mired down in the costly and exhausting "China incident," from which it could extract neither honor nor victory. Its war machine was fatally dependent on immense shipments from the United States of steel, scrap iron, oil, and aviation gasoline. Such assistance to the Japanese aggressor was highly unpopular in America. But Roosevelt had resolutely held off an embargo, lest he goad the Tokyo warlords into a descent on the oil-rich but defense-poor Dutch East Indies (present-day Indonesia).

Washington, late in 1940, finally imposed the first of its embargoes on Japan-bound supplies. This blow was followed in mid-1941 by a freezing of Japanese assets in the United States and a cessation of all shipments of gasoline and other sinews of war. As the oil gauge dropped, the squeeze on Japan grew steadily more nerve-racking. Japanese leaders were faced with two painful alternatives. They could either knuckle under to the Americans or break out of the embargo ring by a desperate attack on the oil supplies and other riches of Southeast Asia.

Final tense negotiations with Japan took place in Washington during November and early December of 1941. The State Department insisted that the Japanese clear out of China, but to sweeten the pill offered to renew trade relations on a limited basis. Japanese imperialists, after waging a bitter war against the Chinese for more than four years, were unwilling to lose face by withdrawing at the behest of the United States. Faced with capitulation or continued conquest, they chose the sword.

Officials in Washington, having "cracked" the top-secret code of the Japanese, knew that Tokyo's decision was for war. But the United States, as a democracy committed to public debate and action by Congress, could not shoot first. Roosevelt, misled by Japanese ship movements in the western Pacific, evidently expected the blow to fall on British Malaya or on the Philippines. No one in high authority in Washington seems to have believed that the Japanese were either strong enough or foolhardy enough to strike Hawaii.

But the paralyzing blow struck Pearl Harbor, while Tokyo was deliberately prolonging negotiations in Washington. Japanese bombers, winging in from distant aircraft carriers, attacked without warning on the

The Battleship *West Virginia*,
Blown Up at Pearl Harbor

"Black Sunday" morning of December 7, 1941. It was a date, as Roosevelt told Congress, "which will live in infamy." About three thousand casualties were inflicted on American personnel; many aircraft were destroyed; the battleship fleet was virtually wiped out when all eight of the craft were sunk or otherwise immobilized; and numerous small vessels were damaged or destroyed. Fortunately for America, the three priceless aircraft carriers happened to be outside the harbor.

The next day an angered Congress, with only one dissenting vote, declared that war had been "thrust" upon the United States. When Japan's allies, Germany and Italy, also declared war on December 11, 1941, the challenge was accepted by Congress the same day. The unofficial war was now official.

Japan's hara-kiri gamble in Hawaii paid off only in the short run. True, the U.S. Pacific fleet was largely destroyed or immobilized, but the sneak attack aroused and united America as almost nothing else could have done. To the very day of the blowup, a strong majority of Americans still wanted to keep out

of war. But the bombs that pulverized Pearl Harbor blasted the isolationists into silence. The only thing left to do, growled isolationist Senator Wheeler, was "to lick hell out of them."

But Pearl Harbor was not the full answer to the question as to why the United States went to war. This treacherous attack was but the last explosion in a long chain reaction. Following the fall of France, Americans were confronted with a devil's dilemma. They desired above all to stay out of the conflict; yet they did not want Britain to be knocked out, nor Japan's menacing conquests to overspread East Asia. To keep Britain from collapsing, the Roosevelt administration felt compelled to extend the unneutral aid that invited attacks from German submarines. To keep Japan from expanding, Washington undertook to cut off vital Japanese supplies with embargoes that invited possible retaliation. Rather than let democracy die and dictatorship rule supreme, most citizens were evidently determined to support a policy that might lead to war. It did.

Chronology

1933   FDR torpedoes the London Economic
Conference.
FDR declares Good Neighbor policy toward
Latin America.

1934   Tydings-McDuffie Act provides for Philippine
independence on July 4, 1946.

1935   Mussolini invades Ethiopia.
U.S. Neutrality Act of 1935.

1936   U.S. Neutrality Act of 1936.

**1936–
1939**   Spanish Civil War.

1937   U.S. Neutrality Act of 1937.
Panay incident.
Japan invades China.

1938   Hitler seizes Austria.
Munich conference.

1939   Hitler seizes all of Czechoslovakia.
Nazi-Soviet pact.
World War II begins in Europe with Hitler's
invasion of Poland.
U.S. Neutrality Act of 1939.

1940   Hitler invades Denmark, Norway, the
Netherlands, and Belgium.
Fall of France.
United States invokes first peacetime draft.
Battle of Britain.
Bases-for-destroyers deal with Britain.
FDR defeats Willkie for presidency.

1941   Lend-Lease Act.
Hitler attacks the Soviet Union.
Atlantic Charter.
Japan attacks Pearl Harbor.

36

America in World War II

Never before have we had so little time in which to do so much.

FRANKLIN D. ROOSEVELT, 1942

The United States was plunged into the inferno of World War II with the most stupefying and humiliating military defeat in its history. In the dismal months that ensued, the democratic world teetered on the edge of disaster.

Japan's fanatics forgot that whoever stabs a king must stab to kill. A wounded but still potent American giant pulled itself out of the mud of Pearl Harbor, grimly determined to avenge the bloody treachery. "Get Japan first" was the cry that rose from millions of infuriated Americans, especially on the Pacific Coast. These outraged souls regarded America's share in the global conflict as a private war of vengeance in the Pacific, with the European front a kind of holding operation.

But Washington, in the so-called ABC-1 agreement with the British, had earlier and wisely adopted the grand strategy of "getting Germany first." If America diverted its main strength to the Pacific, Hitler might crush both the Soviet Union and Britain and then emerge unconquerable in Fortress Europe. But if Germany was knocked out first, the combined Allied forces could then be concentrated on Japan, and its daring game of conquest would be up. Meanwhile, just enough American strength would be sent to the Pacific to prevent Japan from digging in too deeply.

The get-Germany-first strategy was the solid foundation on which all American military strategy was built. But it encountered much unwarranted criticism from two-fisted Americans who thirsted for revenge against Japan. Aggrieved protests were also registered by shorthanded American commanders in the Pacific and by Chinese and Australian allies. But President Roosevelt, a competent strategist in his own right, wisely resisted these pressures.

The Allies Trade Space for Time

Given time, the Allies seemed bound to triumph. But would they be given time? True, they had on their side the great mass of the world's population, but the wolf is never intimidated by the number of the sheep.

Time, in a sense, was the most needed munition. Expense was no limitation. The overpowering problem confronting America was to retool itself for all-out war production, while praying that the dictators would not meanwhile crush the democracies. Haste was all the more imperative because the highly skilled German scientists might turn up with unbeatable secret weapons, including rocket bombs and perhaps even atomic arms.

America's task was far more complex and back-breaking than during World War I. It had to feed, clothe, and arm itself, as well as transport its forces to regions as far separated as Britain and Burma. More than that, it had to send a vast amount of food and munitions to its hard-pressed allies, who stretched all the way from the USSR to Australia. Could the American people, reputedly "gone soft," measure up to this herculean task? Was democracy "rotten" and "decadent," as the dictators sneeringly proclaimed?

The Shock of War

National unity was no worry, thanks to the electrifying blow by the Japanese at Pearl Harbor. Prewar controversies melted away, while millions of Italian-Americans and German-Americans loyally supported the nation's war program. In contrast to World War I, when the patriotism of millions of immigrants was hotly questioned, World War II actually speeded the assimilation of many ethnic groups into American society. Immigration had been choked off for almost two decades before 1941, and America's ethnic communities were now composed of well-settled members, whose votes were crucial to Franklin Roosevelt's Democratic party. Consequently, there was virtually no governmental witch-hunting of minority groups, as had happened in World War I.

A painful exception was the plight of some 110,000 Japanese-Americans, concentrated on the Pacific Coast (see "Makers of America: The Japanese," pp. 502–503). The Washington top command, fearing that they might act as saboteurs for Japan in case of invasion, forcibly herded them together in internment camps in 1942, though about two-thirds of them were American-born U.S. citizens. This brutal precaution was both unnecessary and unfair, as the loyalty and combat record of Japanese-Americans proved to be admirable. But a wave of post–Pearl Harbor hysteria, backed by the long historical swell of anti-Japanese prejudice on the West Coast, temporarily robbed many Americans of their good sense—and their sense of justice. The internment camps deprived these uprooted Americans of dignity and basic rights; the internees also lost hundreds of millions of dollars in property and forgone earnings. The wartime Supreme Court in 1944 upheld the constitutionality of the Japanese relocation in *Korematsu* v. *U.S.* But more than four decades later, in 1988, the U.S. government officially apologized for its actions and approved the payment of reparations of $20,000 to each camp survivor.

The war prompted other changes in the American mood. Many programs of the once-popular New Deal were wiped out by the conservative Congress elected in 1942, and even President Roosevelt declared in 1943 that "Dr. New Deal" was going into retirement, to be replaced by "Dr. Win-the-War." The era of New Deal reform was over.

World War II was no idealistic crusade, as World War I had been. The Washington government emphasized action rather than propaganda. According to opinion polls during the war, a majority or near-majority of citizens confessed to having "no clear idea what the war is about." All Americans knew was that they had a dirty job on their hands and that the only way out was forward. They went about their bloody task with astonishing efficiency.

Building the War Machine

The war crisis made the drooping American economy snap to attention. Massive military orders—over $100 billion in 1942 alone—almost instantly soaked up the idle industrial capacity of the still-lingering Great Depression. Orchestrated by the War Production

Board, American factories poured forth an avalanche of weaponry: 40 billion bullets, 300,000 aircraft, 76,000 ships, 86,000 tanks, and 2.6 million machine guns.

Farmers, too, rolled up their sleeves and increased their output. The armed forces drained the farms of workers, but heavy new investment in agricultural machinery and improved fertilizers more than made up the difference. In 1944 and 1945, blue-jeaned farmers hauled in record-breaking billion-bushel wheat harvests.

These wonders of production also brought economic strains. Full employment and scarce consumer goods fueled a sharp inflationary surge in 1942. The Office of Price Administration eventually brought ascending prices under control with extensive regulations. Rationing held down the consumption of critical goods such as meat and butter, though some "black marketeers" and "meatleggers" cheated the system. The War Labor Board (WLB) imposed ceilings on wage increases.

Labor unions, whose memberships grew from about 10 million to more than 13 million workers during the war, fiercely resented the government-dictated wage ceilings. Despite the no-strike pledges of most major unions, a rash of labor walkouts plagued the war effort. Threats of lost production through strikes became so worrisome that Congress, in June 1943, passed the Smith-Connally Anti-Strike Act, which authorized the federal government to seize and operate tied-up industries. Under the Smith-Connally Act, Washington took over the coal mines and, for a brief period, the railroads. Yet work stoppages accounted for less than 1 percent of the total working hours of the United States' wartime laboring force.

Manpower and Womanpower

The armed services enlisted nearly 15 million men in World War II—and some 216,000 women, who were employed for noncombat duties. Best known of these "women in arms" were the WAACS (army), WAVES (navy), and SPARS (Coast Guard).

Despite draft exemptions for key categories of industrial and agricultural workers, military needs left the nation's farms and factories so drained of personnel that new workers had to be found. An agreement with Mexico in 1942 brought thousands of Mexican agricultural workers, called *braceros*, across the border to harvest the fruit and grain crops of the West. The *bracero* program outlived the war by some twenty years, becoming a fixed feature of the agricultural economy in many western states.

Even more dramatic was the march of women onto the factory floor. More than 6 million women took up jobs outside the home; over half of them had never before worked for wages. Many of them were mothers, and the government was obliged to set up some three thousand day-care centers to care for "Rosie the Riveter's" children while Rosie drilled the

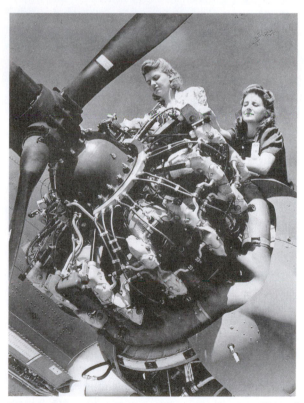

War Workers *More than 6 million women—3 million of them homemakers who had never before worked for wages—entered the work force during World War II. In contrast to the experience of women workers in World War I, many of these newly employed women continued as wage workers after the war ended.*

The Japanese

In 1853 the American commodore Matthew Perry sailed four gunboats into Japan's Uraga Bay and demanded that the nation open itself to diplomatic and commercial exchange with the United States. Within two decades of Perry's arrival, Japan's new "Meiji" government had launched the nation on an ambitious program of industrialization and militarization designed to make it the economic and political equal of the Western powers.

As Japan rapidly modernized, its citizens increasingly took ship for America. A steep land tax drove more than 300,000 Japanese farmers off their land. In 1884 the Meiji government permitted Hawaiian planters to recruit contract laborers from among this displaced population. By the 1890s many Japanese were sailing beyond Hawaii to the ports of Long Beach, San Francisco, and Seattle.

Between 1885 and 1924, roughly 200,000 Japanese migrated to Hawaii, and around 180,000 more ventured to the U.S. mainland. They were a select group: because the Meiji government saw overseas Japanese as representatives of their homeland, it strictly regulated emigration. Thus Japanese immigrants to America arrived with more money and better education than their European counterparts.

Women as well as men migrated. The Japanese government, wanting to avoid the problems of an itinerant bachelor society that it observed among the Chinese in the United States, actively promoted women's migration. Although most Japanese immigrants were young men in their twenties and thirties, thousands of women also ventured to Hawaii and the mainland as contract laborers or "picture brides," so called because their courtships had consisted exclusively of exchanges of photographs with their prospective husbands.

In Hawaii most Japanese labored on the vast sugar cane plantations. On the mainland they initially found migratory work on the railroads or in fish, fruit, or vegetable canneries. A separate Japanese economy of restaurants, stores, and boardinghouses soon sprang up in cities to serve the immigrants' needs.

From such humble beginnings, many Japanese—particularly those on the Pacific Coast—quickly moved into farming. In the late nineteenth century, the spread of irrigation shifted California agriculture from grain to fruits and vegetables, and the invention of the refrigerated railcar opened hungry new markets in the East. The Japanese, with centuries of experience in intensive farming, arrived just in time to take advantage of these developments. By 1940 Japanese farmers produced most of the state's strawberries, beans, and tomatoes.

But the very success of the Japanese proved a lightning rod for trouble. On the West Coast, Japanese

Japanese-American Evacuees, 1942 *This farm family in Los Angeles County was "relocated" shortly after this photograph was taken.*

502

immigrants had long endured racist barbs and social segregation. Increasingly, white workers and farmers, jealous of Japanese success, pushed for immigration restrictions. Bowing to this pressure, President Theodore Roosevelt in 1908 negotiated the "Gentlemen's Agreement," under which the Japanese government voluntarily agreed to limit emigration. In 1913 the California legislature denied Japanese immigrants already living in the United States the right to own land.

Legally barred from becoming citizens, Japanese immigrants (the *Issei*, from the Japanese word for "first") became more determined than ever that their American-born children (the *Nissei*, from the Japanese word for "second") would reap the full benefits of their birthright. Japanese parents encouraged their children to learn English, to excel in school, and to get a college education. Many Nissei grew up in two worlds, a fact they often recognized by Americanizing their Japanese names. Although education and acculturation did not protect the Nissei from the hysteria of World War II, those assets did give them a springboard to success in the postwar era.

fuselage of a heavy bomber or joined the links of a tank track. When the war ended, Rosie and many of her sisters wanted to keep on working and often did. The war thus foreshadowed an eventual revolution in the roles of women in American society.

Yet the war's immediate impact on women's lives has frequently been exaggerated. The great majority of women—especially those with husbands present in the home or with small children to care for—did not work for wages in the wartime economy but continued in their traditional roles. In both Britain and the Soviet Union, a far greater percentage of women were pressed into industrial service as the gods of war laid a much heavier hand on those societies than they did on the United States. The main result of wartime experience for women appeared to be not economic liberation but the postwar rush into suburban domesticity and the mothering of the "baby boomers," who were born by the tens of millions in the decade and a half after 1945. America was destined to experience a revolution in women's status later in the postwar period, but that epochal change was only beginning to gather momentum in the war years.

The war also proved to be a demographic cauldron, churning and shifting the American population. Many of the 15 million men and women in uniform, having seen new sights and glimpsed new horizons, chose not to go home again at war's end. War industries sucked people into boomtowns like Los Angeles, Detroit, Seattle, and Baton Rouge. California's population grew by nearly 2 million. The South experienced especially dramatic changes. The states of the old Confederacy received a disproportionate share of defense contracts, including nearly $6 billion of federally financed industrial facilities. Here were the origins of the postwar blossoming of the "Sunbelt."

Despite this economic stimulus in the South, some 1.6 million blacks left the land of their past enslavement to seek jobs in the war plants of the West and North. Forever after, race relations constituted a national, not a regional, issue. Explosive tensions developed over employment, housing, and segregated facilities. Black leader A. Philip Randolph, head of the Brotherhood of Sleeping Car Porters, threatened a massive "Negro March on Washington" in 1941 to demand equal opportunities for blacks in war jobs and in the armed forces. Roosevelt's response was to issue an executive order forbidding discrimination in defense industries. In addition, the president established the Fair Employment Practices Commission (FEPC) to monitor compliance with his edict.

Blacks were also drafted into the armed forces, though they were generally assigned to service groups rather than combat units. But in general the war helped to embolden blacks in their long struggle for equality. Membership in the National Association for the Advancement of Colored People (NAACP) shot up almost to the half-million mark, and a new militant organization, the Congress of Racial Equality (CORE), was founded in 1942.

The northward migration of African-Americans accelerated after the war, thanks to the advent of the mechanical cotton picker—an invention whose

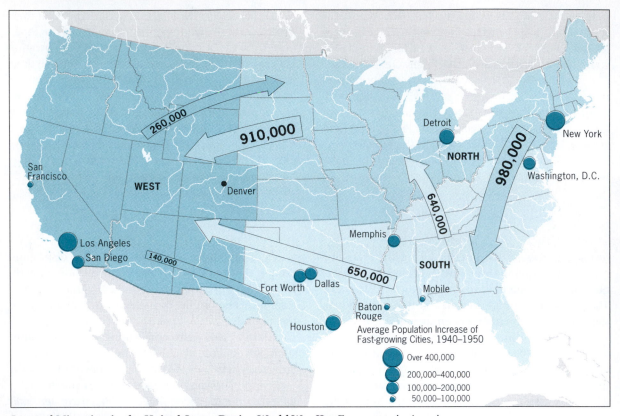

Internal Migration in the United States During World War II   *Few events in American history have moved the American people about so massively as World War II. The West and the South boomed, and several war-industry cities grew explosively. Some 1.3 million migrants from the South were blacks. (Source: United States Department of Labor, Bureau of Labor Statistics.)*

impact rivaled that of Eli Whitney's cotton gin. Overnight, the Cotton South's historic need for cheap labor disappeared. Their muscle no longer required in Dixie, some 5 million black tenant farmers and sharecroppers headed north in the three decades after the war. Within a single generation, a near-majority of African-Americans gave up their historic homeland and their rural way of life. By 1970 half of all blacks lived outside the South, and *urban* had become almost a synonym for *black*.

The war also prompted an exodus of Native Americans from the reservations. Thousands of Indian men and women found war work in the major cities, and thousands more answered Uncle Sam's call to arms. More than 90 percent of Indians resided on reservations in 1940; four decades later almost half lived in cities.

The sudden rubbing against one another of unfamiliar peoples produced some distressingly violent friction. In 1943 young "zoot-suit"–clad Mexicans and Mexican-Americans in Los Angeles were viciously attacked by Anglo sailors who cruised the streets in taxicabs, searching for victims. At almost the same time, an even more brutal race riot that killed twenty-five blacks and nine whites erupted in Detroit.

Holding the Home Front

Despite these ugly episodes, Americans on the home front suffered little from the war, compared with the peoples of the other fighting nations. By war's end much of the planet was a smoking ruin. But in America the war invigorated the economy and lifted the country out of a decade-long depression. The gross national product vaulted from less than $100 billion in 1940 to more than $200 billion in 1945. Corporate profits approximately doubled during the war. Despite wage ceilings, overtime pay fattened pay envelopes. On December 7, 1944, the third anniversary of Pearl Harbor, Macy's department store rang up the biggest sales day in its history. Americans had never had it so good—and they wanted it a lot better.

The hand of government touched more American lives more intimately during the war than ever before. The war, perhaps even more than the New Deal, pointed the way to the post-1945 era of big-government interventionism. Millions of men and women worked for Uncle Sam in the armed forces or defense industries, and their personal needs were cared for by government-sponsored housing projects, day-care facilities, and health plans. The Office of Scientific Research and Development channeled hundreds of millions of dollars into university-based scientific research, establishing the partnership between the government and universities that underwrote America's technological and economic leadership in the postwar era.

The flood of war dollars—not the relatively modest rivulet of New Deal spending—at last swept the plague of unemployment from the land. War, not enlightened social policy, cured the depression. As the postwar economy continued to depend dangerously on military spending for its health, many observers looked back to the years 1941–1945 and saw the origins of a "warfare-welfare state."

The conflict was phenomenally expensive. The wartime bill amounted to more than $330 billion—ten times the direct cost of World War I and twice as much as all previous federal spending since 1776. Despite an expanded income tax and higher tax rates, only about two-fifths of the war costs were paid from current revenues. The remainder was borrowed. The national debt skyrocketed from $49 billion in 1941 to $259 billion in 1945.

The Rising Sun in the Pacific

Early successes of the efficient Japanese militarists were breathtaking: they realized that they would have to win quickly or lose slowly. Simultaneously with the assault on Pearl Harbor, the Japanese launched widespread and uniformly successful attacks on various bastions in the Pacific and East Asia. These included the American outposts of Guam, Wake, and the Philippines, as well as Hong Kong and British Malaya, with its critically important supplies of rubber and tin.

Nor did the Japanese stop there. The soldiers of the emperor, plunging into the snake-infested jungles of Burma, cut the famed Burma road. This was the route over which the United States had been trucking a trickle of munitions to the armies of Jiang Jieshi (Chiang Kai-shek), the Chinese generalissimo who was resisting the Japanese invader in China. Thereafter, intrepid American aviators were forced to fly a handful of war supplies to Jiang "over the hump" of the towering Himalaya Mountains from the India-Burma theater of operations. Meanwhile, the Japanese had lunged southward against the oil-rich Dutch East Indies, which speedily fell to the assailant.

In the Philippines, General Douglas MacArthur's resistance effectively slowed the Japanese advance for five months. Twenty thousand American troops and a larger force of Filipinos withdrew to a strong defensive position at Bataan, near Manila, where they held off violent Japanese attacks until April 9, 1942. The eloquent and egotistical MacArthur himself was ordered to depart secretly for Australia but proclaimed as he departed, "I shall return." The battered remnants of his army were treated with vicious cruelty in the infamous eighty-mile Bataan death march to prisoner-of-war camps. The island fortress of Corregidor, in Manila harbor, held out until May 6, 1942, when it surrendered and left Japanese forces in complete control of the Philippine archipelago.

Japan's High Tide at Midway

The aggressive warriors from Japan, making hay while the Rising Sun shone, pushed relentlessly southward. They invaded the turtle-shaped island of New Guinea, north of Australia, and landed on the Solomon Islands, from which they threatened Australia itself. Their onrush was finally checked by a crucial naval battle in the Coral Sea, in May 1942. An American carrier task force, with Australian support, inflicted heavy losses on the victory-flushed Japanese. For the first time in history, the fighting was all done by carrier-based aircraft.

United States Thrusts in the Pacific, 1942–1945 *American strategists had to choose among four proposed plans for waging the war against Japan:*
1. Defeating the Japanese in China by funneling supplies over the Himalayan "hump" from India
2. Carrying the war into Southeast Asia (a proposal much favored by the British, who could thus regain Singapore)
3. Heavy bombing of Japan from Chinese air bases
4. "Island-hopping" from the South Pacific to within striking distance of the Japanese home islands
The fourth strategy, favored by General Douglas MacArthur, was the one finally emphasized.

★ Major battle sites
⎯ Limit of Japanese conquest
▦ Japanese-held areas
← U.S. thrusts

Japan next undertook to seize Midway Island, more than a thousand miles northwest of Honolulu. From this strategic base, it could launch devastating assaults on Pearl Harbor and perhaps force the weakened American Pacific fleet into destructive combat. A critical naval battle was fought near Midway from June 3 to 6, 1942. Admiral Chester W. Nimitz, a high-grade naval strategist, directed a smaller but skillfully maneuvered carrier force against the powerful invading fleet. The fighting was all done by aircraft, and the Japanese broke off action after losing four vitally important carriers.

Midway was a pivotal victory. Combined with the Battle of Coral Sea, the U.S. success at Midway halted Japan's juggernaut. But the thrust of the Japanese into the eastern Pacific did net them America's fog-girt islands of Kiska and Attu in the Aleutian archipelago, off Alaska. This easy conquest aroused fear of an invasion of the United States from the northwest. Much American strength was consequently diverted to the defense of Alaska.

Yet the Japanese imperialists, overextended in 1942, suffered from "victory disease." Their appetites were bigger than their stomachs. If they had only dug in and consolidated their gains, they would have been much more difficult to dislodge.

American Leapfrogging Toward Tokyo

Following the heartening victory at Midway, the United States for the first time was able to seize the initiative in the Pacific. In August 1942 American ground forces gained a toehold on Guadalcanal Island, in the Solomons, in an effort to protect the lifeline from America to Australia through the Southwest Pacific. After several desperate sea battles for naval control of the area, the Japanese troops evacuated Guadalcanal in February 1943.

American and Australian forces, under General MacArthur, meanwhile had been hanging on grimly to the southeastern tip of New Guinea, the last buffer protecting Australia. Aided by American naval forces, MacArthur eventually fought his way westward through the tropical jungle hells and completed the conquest of New Guinea by August 1944.

The U.S. Navy, with marines and army divisions doing the meat-grinder fighting, had meanwhile been "leapfrogging" the Japanese islands in the Pacific. Rather than proceed on a broad front and reduce Japanese outposts on their flank, as old-fashioned strategy dictated, the new American strategy of island-hopping called for bypassing the most heavily fortified Japanese posts, capturing nearby islands and setting up airfields on them, and then neutralizing the enemy bases through heavy bombing. Deprived of essential supplies from the homeland, Japan's outposts would slowly wither on the vine—as they did.

With Admiral Nimitz skillfully coordinating the efforts of naval, air, and ground units, the American attacks achieved brilliant success. In May and August 1943, Attu and Kiska in the Aleutians were easily retaken. In November 1943 "Bloody Tarawa" and Makin in the Gilbert Islands fell after suicidal resistance, and key outposts in the Marshall Islands succumbed after savage fighting in January and February 1944. The conquest of Guam and other islands in the Marianas in July and August 1944 provided airfields for America's new B-29 superbombers to carry out round-trip bombing raids on Japan's home islands. With these unsinkable aircraft carriers now available, virtual around-the-clock bombing of Japan began in November 1944.

The Allied Halting of Hitler

Early setbacks for America in the Pacific were paralleled in the Atlantic. Hitler had entered the war with a formidable fleet of ultramodern submarines, which ultimately operated in "wolf packs" with frightful effect. During ten months of 1942 more than five hundred merchant ships were lost. Not until the spring of 1943 did the Allies clearly gain the upper hand against the U-boat.

The turning point of the land-air war against Hitler came late in 1942. The British, who had launched a thousand-plane raid on Cologne in May, were joined by the American air force in cascading bombs on German cities. The Germans under Marshal Erwin Rommel—the "Desert Fox"—had driven eastward across the hot sands of North Africa into Egypt, perilously close to the Suez Canal. A breakthrough would have spelled disaster for the Allies. But late in October 1942, British general Bernard Montgomery delivered a withering attack at El Alamein, west of Cairo. With the aid of several hundred hastily shipped American Sherman tanks, he speedily drove the enemy back to Tunisia, more than 1,000 miles away.

On the Soviet front, the unexpected successes of the red army gave a new lift to the Allied cause. In September 1942 the Russians halted the German steamroller at rubble-bestrewn Stalingrad, graveyard of Hitler's hopes. In November 1942 the resilient Russians unleashed a crushing counteroffensive, which was never seriously reversed. A year later, Stalin had regained about two-thirds of the blood-soaked Soviet motherland wrested from him by the German invader.

A Second Front from North Africa to Rome

Soviet losses were already staggering in 1942; millions of soldiers and civilians lay dead, and Hitler's armies had laid waste a vast territory equivalent in the United States to the area from Chicago to the Atlantic seaboard. Small wonder that Kremlin leaders clamored for a second front to divert the German strength westward.

Many Americans, including FDR, were eager to begin an invasion of France in 1942 or 1943. They feared that the Soviets might make a separate peace with Germany, as they had in 1918, and leave the Western Allies to face Hitler's fury alone. But British military planners, remembering their appalling losses in France in 1914–1918, preferred to attack Hitler's Fortress Europe through the "soft underbelly" of the

World War II in Europe and North Africa, 1939–1945

Mediterranean. Faced with British boot-dragging, the Americans reluctantly agreed to postpone a massive invasion of Europe.

An assault on French-held North Africa was a compromise second front. The highly secret attack, launched in November 1942, was headed by a gifted and easy-smiling American general, Dwight D. ("Ike") Eisenhower. The joint Allied operation, ultimately involving some 400,000 men, was highly successful. After savage desert fighting, the remnants of the German-Italian army were finally trapped in Tunisia and surrendered in May 1943.

At Casablanca, in newly occupied French Morocco, President Roosevelt met with Winston

Churchill in January 1943 to plan new blows. The Big Two agreed to step up the Pacific war, invade Sicily, increase pressure on Italy, and insist on "unconditional surrender" by the enemy. Designed to reassure the ultrasuspicious Soviets, who professed to fear separate Allied peace negotiations, "unconditional surrender" proved to be one of the most controversial moves of the war. The main criticism was that it steeled the enemy to fight to a last-bunker resistance, while complicating the problems of postwar reconstruction.

Allied forces, victorious in Africa, now turned against the not-so-soft underbelly of Europe. Sicily fell in August 1943 after sporadic but sometimes bitter resistance. Shortly before the conquest of the island, Mussolini was deposed, and Italy surrendered unconditionally soon thereafter.

But if Italy dropped out of the war, the Germans did not drop out of Italy. Hitler's well-trained troops stubbornly resisted the Allied invaders now pouring into the toe of the Italian boot. "Sunny Italy" proceeded to belie its name, for in the snow-covered and mud-caked mountains of its elongated peninsula occurred some of the filthiest, bloodiest, and most frustrating fighting of the war. After a touch-and-go assault on the Anzio beachhead, Rome was finally taken on June 4, 1944. But painful fighting continued in northern Italy, and not until May 2, 1945, did several hundred thousand Axis troops in Italy lay down their arms. While the Italian second front opened the Mediterranean and diverted some German divisions from the blazing Soviet and French battle lines, it also may have delayed the main Allied invasion of France by many months—allowing more time for the Soviet army to advance into Eastern Europe.

D-Day: June 6, 1944

The Soviets never ceased to clamor for an all-out second front. Plans for a major Allied invasion were finally settled at a conference of Stalin, Churchill, and Roosevelt in Teheran, Iran, held from November 28 to December 1, 1943. The Soviets agreed to launch attacks on Germany from the east simultaneously with the prospective Allied assault from the west.

Preparations for the cross-channel invasion of France were gigantic. Britain's fast-anchored isle virtually groaned with munitions, supplies, and troops, as nearly 3 million fighting men were readied. Because the United States was to provide most of the Allied warriors, the overall command was entrusted to an American, General Eisenhower.

French Normandy, less heavily defended than other parts of the European coast, was pinpointed for the invasion assault. On D-Day, June 6, 1944, the enormous operation, which involved some forty-six hundred vessels, unwound. Stiff resistance was encountered from the Germans, who had been misled by a feint into expecting the blow to fall farther north.

The Allied beachhead, at first clung to with fingertips, was gradually enlarged, consolidated, and reinforced. After desperate fighting, the invaders

Allies Landing in Normandy, June 6, 1944   *Nine-foot ocean swells on invasion day made loading the assault landing craft, such as the one pictured here, treacherous business. Many men were injured or tossed into the sea as the bathtublike amphibious vessels bobbed wildly up and down alongside the troop transports. As the vulnerable boats churned toward the beach, some officers led their tense, grim-faced troops in prayer. One major, recalling the remarkable Battle of Agincourt in 1415, quoted from Shakespeare's* Henry V: *"He that outlives this day, and comes safe home / Will stand a tip-toe when this day is named."*

finally broke out of the German iron ring that enclosed the Normandy landing zone. Most spectacular were the lunges across France by American armored divisions, brilliantly commanded by blustery and profane General George S. ("Blood 'n' Guts") Patton. The retreat of the German defenders was hastened when an American-French force landed in August 1944 on the southern coast of France and swept northward. With the assistance of the French "underground," Paris was liberated in August 1944.

Allied forces rolled irresistibly toward Germany. The first important German city (Aachen) fell to the Americans in October 1944, and the days of Hitler's "thousand-year Reich" were numbered.

FDR: The Fourth-Termite of 1944

The presidential campaign of 1944 came awkwardly as the awful conflict roared to its climax. Victory-starved Republicans nominated short, mustachioed, and dapper Thomas Dewey, the popular governor of

New York. A former prosecutor, Dewey was only forty-two years old, causing one veteran New Dealer to sneer that the candidate had cast his diaper into the ring. To offset Dewey's mild internationalism, the convention nominated for the vice presidency a strong isolationist, Senator John Bricker of Ohio.

FDR, aging under the strain but still the "indispensable man," was nominated by acclamation for a fourth term. The scramble for the vice-presidential plum turned into a free-for-all. Roosevelt's third-term vice president, former agriculture secretary Henry A. Wallace, was a committed liberal who desired renomination. Conservative Democrats developed a "ditch Wallace" movement that gained tremendous momentum and finally won Roosevelt's blessing. The vice-presidential nomination then went to smiling and self-assured Senator Harry S Truman of Missouri, who had recently attained national visibility by conducting an investigation of wasteful war expenditures.

A dynamic Dewey took the offensive in the campaign, proclaiming in his beautiful baritone voice that it was "time for a change" after "twelve long years" of New Dealism. In the closing weeks of the campaign, Roosevelt left his desk for the stump. He was eager to show himself, even in chilling rains, to spike well-founded rumors of failing health.

Democrats relied heavily on the new Political Action Committee of the CIO, which provided union funds and campaign workers. Roosevelt, as customary, won a sweeping victory: 432 to 99 in the Electoral College, 25,606,585 to 22,014,745 in the popular totals. Elated, he quipped that "the first twelve years are the hardest."

The Last Days of Hitler

By mid-December 1944, the month after Roosevelt's fourth-term victory, Germany seemed to be wobbling on its last legs. The Soviet surge had penetrated eastern Germany. Allied aerial "blockbuster" bombs, making the "rubble bounce" with around-the-clock attacks, were falling like giant explosive hailstones on cities, factories, and transportation arteries. The German western front seemed about to buckle under the sledgehammer blows of the United States and its allies.

Hitler then staked everything on one last throw of his reserves. Secretly concentrating a powerful force, he hurled it, on December 16, 1944, against the thinly held American lines in the heavily befogged and snow-shrouded Ardennes Forest. Caught off guard, the outmanned Americans were driven back, creating a deep "bulge" in the Allied line. The ten-day penetration was finally halted after the 101st Airborne Division had stood firm at the vital bastion of Bastogne. The commander, Brigadier General A. C. McAuliffe, defiantly answered the German demand for surrender with one word: "Nuts." Reinforcements were rushed up, and the last-gasp Hitlerian offensive was at length bloodily stemmed in the Battle of the Bulge.

In March 1945, forward-driving American troops reached Germany's Rhine River, where, by incredibly good luck, they found one strategic bridge undemolished. Pressing their advantage, General Eisenhower's troops reached the Elbe River in April 1945. There, a short distance south of Berlin, American and Soviet advance guards dramatically clasped hands.

The conquering Americans were horrified to find blood-bespattered concentration camps, where the German Nazis had engaged in scientific mass murder of "undesirables," including an estimated 6 million Jews. The Washington government had long been informed about Hitler's campaign of genocide against the Jews and had been reprehensibly slow to take steps against it—such as bombing rail lines that carried the victims to the camps. But until the war's end, the full dimensions of the "Holocaust" were not known. When the details were revealed, the whole world was aghast.

The vengeful Soviets, clawing their way forward from the east, reached Berlin in April 1945. After desperate house-to-house fighting, followed by an orgy of pillage and rape, they captured the bomb-shattered city. Adolf Hitler, after a hasty marriage to his mistress, committed suicide in an underground bunker on April 30, 1945.

Tragedy had meanwhile struck the United States. President Roosevelt, while relaxing at Warm Springs, Georgia, suddenly died from a massive cerebral hemorrhage on April 12, 1945. Leaderless citizens discussed the future anxiously, as bewildered, unbriefed Vice President Truman took the helm.

A Nazi Death Camp   *These gaunt survivors of the Nazi concentration camp at Evensee, Austria, greeted their liberators from the U.S. 3rd Army on May 7, 1945. Scanty food and wretched sanitation claimed almost as many lives in the death camps as the horrid gas chambers. Although the world had some knowledge of these conditions before the war's end, the full revelation of Hitler's atrocities as the Allies overran Germany in the spring of 1945 stunned and sickened the invading troops.*

On May 7, 1945, what was left of the German government surrendered unconditionally. May 8 was officially proclaimed V-E Day—Victory in Europe Day—and was greeted with frenzied rejoicing in the Allied countries.

Japan Dies Hard

Japan's rickety bamboo empire meanwhile was tottering to its fall. American submarines—"the silent service"—were sending the Japanese merchant marine to the bottom so fast they were running out of prey. All told, these underseas craft destroyed 1,042 ships, or about 50 percent of Japan's entire life-sustaining merchant fleet.

Giant bomber attacks were more spectacular. Launched from Saipan and other captured Marianas, they were reducing the enemy's fragile cities to cinders. The massive fire-bomb raid on Tokyo, March 9–10, 1945, was annihilating. It destroyed over 250,000 buildings, gutted a quarter of the city, and killed an estimated 83,000 persons—a loss comparable to that later inflicted by atomic bombs.

General MacArthur was also on the move. Completing the conquest of jungle-draped New Guinea, he headed northwest for the Philippines, en route to Japan, with six hundred ships and 250,000 men. In a scene well staged for the photographers, he splashed ashore at Leyte Island, on October 20, 1944, keeping the promise he had made at Bataan two and a half years earlier. Manila was taken in March 1945, but the Philippines were not finally conquered until July, after bitter fighting against holed-in Japanese, who took a toll of over 60,000 American casualties.

Japan's navy—still menacing—was at last subdued in the gigantic clash at Leyte Gulf (October 23–26, 1944). Japan was through as a sea power. With American fleets now commanding the western Pacific, a steel vise was tightening mercilessly around Japan. In March 1945 the tiny, strategic island of Iwo Jima was captured in a desperate assault that cost over four thousand American dead. The island of Okinawa, well defended by Japanese soldiers fighting with incredible courage from caves, was finally taken in June 1945 after fifty thousand American casualties and far heavier Japanese losses. The American navy, which covered the invasion of Okinawa, sustained severe damage when

Japanese suicide pilots began crashing their bomb-laden planes onto the decks of the invading fleet, sinking over thirty ships and damaging scores more.

The Atomic Bombs

Strategists in Washington were meanwhile planning an all-out invasion of the main islands of Japan—an invasion that presumably would cost hundreds of thousands of American (and even more Japanese) casualties. Tokyo, recognizing imminent defeat, had secretly sent peace feelers to Moscow, which had not yet entered the East Asian war. But bomb-scorched Japan still showed no outward willingness to surrender unconditionally to the Allies.

The Potsdam conference, held near Berlin in July 1945, sounded the death knell of the Japanese. There President Truman, new on the job, met in a seventeen-day parley with Joseph Stalin and the British leaders. The conferees issued a stern ultimatum to Japan: surrender or be destroyed. American bombers showered the dire warning on Japan in tens of thousands of leaflets, but no encouraging response was forthcoming.

America had a fantastic ace up its sleeve. Early in 1940, after Hitler's wanton assault on Poland, Roosevelt was persuaded by American and exiled scientists, notably German-born Albert Einstein, to push ahead with preparations for unlocking the secret of an atomic bomb. Congress, at Roosevelt's blank-check request, blindly made available nearly $2 billion.

The huge atomic project was pushed feverishly forward, as American know-how and industrial power were combined with the most advanced scientific knowledge. Much technical skill was provided by British and refugee scientists, who had fled to America to escape the torture chambers of the dictators. Finally, in the desert near Alamogordo, New Mexico, on July 16, 1945, the experts detonated the first awesome and devastating atomic device.

With Japan still refusing to surrender, the Potsdam threat was fulfilled. On August 6, 1945, a lone American bomber dropped one atomic bomb on the city of Hiroshima, Japan. In a blinding flash of death, followed by a mushroom-shaped cloud, about 180,000 persons were left killed, wounded, or missing. Some 70,000 of them died instantaneously. Sixty thousand more soon perished from burns and radiation disease.

Two days later, on August 8, Stalin entered the war against Japan, exactly on the deadline date previously agreed upon with his allies. Soviet armies speedily overran the depleted Japanese defenses in Manchuria and Korea in a six-day "victory parade" that involved several thousand Russian casualties. Stalin was evidently determined to be in on the kill, lest he lose a voice in the final division of Japan's holdings.

On August 9, American aviators dropped a second atomic bomb on the city of Nagasaki. The explosion took a horrible toll of about eighty thousand people killed or missing. The Japanese nation could endure no more. On August 10, 1945, Tokyo sued for peace on one condition: that Hirohito, the bespectacled Son of Heaven, be allowed to remain on his throne as nominal emperor. Despite their "unconditional surrender" policy, the Allies accepted this condition on August 14, 1945. The formal surrender took place on the battleship *Missouri* on September 2, 1945.

The Allies Triumphant

World War II proved to be terribly costly. American forces suffered some 1 million casualties, about one-third of which were deaths. Compared with other wars, the proportion killed by wounds and disease was sharply reduced, owing in part to the use of blood plasma and "miracle" drugs, notably penicillin.

America was fortunate in emerging with its mainland virtually unscathed. Much of the rest of the world was utterly destroyed and destitute. America alone was untouched and healthy—oiled and muscled like a prize bull, standing astride the world's ruined landscape.

This complex conflict was the best-fought war in America's history. Though unprepared for it at the outset, the nation was better prepared than for the others, partly because it had begun to buckle on its armor about a year and a half before the war officially began. In the end the United States showed itself to be resourceful, tough, adaptable—able to accommodate itself to the tactics of an enemy who was relentless and ruthless.

American military leadership proved to be of the highest order. A new crop of war heroes emerged in brilliant generals like Eisenhower, MacArthur, and George Marshall (chief of staff) and in imaginative admirals like Nimitz. President Roosevelt and Prime

Minister Churchill, kindred spirits, collaborated closely in planning strategy. "It is fun to be in the same decade with you," FDR once cabled Churchill.

Industrial leaders were no less skilled, for marvels of production were performed almost daily. Assembly lines proved as important as battle lines; and victory went again to the side with the most smokestacks. The enemy was almost literally smothered by bayonets, bullets, bazookas, and bombs. Hitler and his Axis co-conspirators had chosen to make war with machines, and the ingenious Yankees could ask for nothing better. They demonstrated again, as they had in World War I, that the American way of war was simply

more—more men, more weapons, more machines, more technology, and more money than any enemy could hope to match. From 1940 to 1945, the output of American factories was simply phenomenal.

Hermann Goering, a Nazi leader, had sneered, "The Americans can't build planes—only electric iceboxes and razor blades." Democracy had given its answer, as the dictators, despite long preparation, were overthrown and discredited. It is true that an unusual amount of direct control was exercised over the individual by the Washington authorities during the war emergency. But the American people preserved their precious liberties without serious impairment.

Chronology

1941	The United States declares war on Japan. Germany declares war on the United States. Randolph plans black march on Washington. Fair Employment Practices Commission (FEPC) established.
1942	Japanese-Americans sent to internment camps. Japan conquers the Philippines. Battle of the Coral Sea. Battle of Midway. United States invades North Africa. Congress of Racial Equality (CORE) founded.
1943	Allies hold Casablanca conference. Japanese driven from Guadalcanal. Allies invade Italy. Teheran conference
1944	*Korematsu* v. *U.S.* D-Day invasion of France. Battle of Marianas. Roosevelt defeats Dewey for presidency.
1944–1945	Battle of the Bulge.
1945	Roosevelt dies; Truman assumes presidency. Germany surrenders. Battles of Iwo Jima and Okinawa. Potsdam conference. Atomic bombs dropped on Hiroshima and Nagasaki. Japan surrenders.

VARYING VIEWPOINTS

World War II: Triumph or Tragedy?

After World War II ended in 1945, many historians were convinced that the tragedy could have been averted if the United States had awakened earlier from its isolationist illusions. These scholars condemned the policies and attitudes of the 1930s as a "retreat from responsibility." Much of the historical

writing in the postwar period contained the strong flavor of medicine to ward off another infection by the isolationist virus.

This approach fell into disfavor during the Vietnam War in the 1960s, when many U.S. policymakers defended their actions in Southeast Asia by making dubious comparisons to the decade before World War II. Some scholars responded by arguing that the "lessons" of the 1930s—especially about the need to avoid "appeasement" and to take quick and decisive action against "aggressors"—could not properly be applied to any and all subsequent situations. Ho Chi Minh, they pointed out, was not Hitler, and Vietnam was not Nazi Germany.

Most recent writing has tended to avoid finding lessons for posterity in America's entry into World War II. Attention has focused instead on the wisdom or folly of specific policies, such as Washington's hard line toward Tokyo throughout 1941, when the possibility of a negotiated settlement with Japan perhaps existed. P. W. Schroeder's *The Axis Alliance and Japanese-American Relations, 1941* makes that point with particular force.

No decision of the war era has provoked sharper controversy than the atomic bombings of Japan in August 1945. Lingering moral questions about the nuclear incineration of Hiroshima and Nagasaki have long threatened to tarnish the crown of military victory. America is the only nation ever to use an atomic weapon in war; and some critics have claimed to find elements of racism in the fact that the bombs were dropped on people of a nonwhite race. The fact is, however, that Germany surrendered before the bombs were ready; if the war in Europe had lasted just a few months longer, some German city would probably have suffered the fate of Hiroshima.

Some scholars, notably Gar Alperovitz, have further charged that the atomic holocausts at Hiroshima and Nagasaki were not the last shots of World War II but the first salvos in the emerging Cold War. Alperovitz argues that the Japanese were already defeated in the summer of 1945 and were in fact attempting to arrange a conditional surrender. President Truman ignored those attempts and unleashed his horrible new weapons, so the argument goes, not simply to defeat Japan but to frighten the Soviets into submission to America's will and to keep them out of the final stages of the war—and postwar reconstruction—in Asia.

Could the use of the atomic bombs have been avoided? As Martin J. Sherwin's studies have shown, few policymakers at the time seriously asked that question. American leaders wanted to end the war as quickly as possible. Intimidating the Soviets might have been a "bonus" to using the bomb against Japan, but influencing Soviet behavior was never the primary reason for the fateful decision. American military strategists had always assumed the atomic bomb would be dropped as soon as it was available. That moment came on August 6, 1945. Yet misgivings and remorse about the atomic conclusion of World War II have plagued the American conscience ever since.

For further reading, see the Appendix. For web resources, go to **http://college.hmco.com**.

PART SIX

MAKING MODERN AMERICA

---◁▷---

1945 to the Present

World War II broke the back of the Great Depression in the United States and also ended the century-and-a-half-old American tradition of isolationism in foreign affairs. Alone among the warring powers, the United States managed to emerge from the great conflict physically unscarred, economically healthy, and diplomatically strengthened. Yet if Americans faced a world full of promise at the war's end, it was also a world full of dangers, none more disconcerting than Soviet communism. These two themes of promise and menace mingled uneasily throughout the nearly five decades of the Cold War era, from the end of World War II in 1945 to the collapse of the Soviet Union in 1991.

At home, unprecedented prosperity in the postwar quarter-century nourished a robust sense of national self-confidence and fed a revolution of rising expectations. Invigorated by the prospect of endlessly spreading affluence, Americans in the 1940s, '50s, and '60s had record numbers of babies, aspired to ever-higher standards of living, generously expanded the welfare state (especially for the elderly), widened opportunities for women, welcomed immigrants, and even found the will to grapple at long last with the nation's grossest legacy of injustice, its treatment of African-Americans. With the exception of Dwight Eisenhower's presidency in the 1950s, Americans elected liberal Democratic presidents (Harry Truman in 1948, John F. Kennedy in 1960, and Lyndon Johnson in 1964). The Democratic party, the party of the liberal New Deal at home and of an activist foreign policy abroad, comfortably remained the nation's majority party. Americans trusted their government and had faith in the American dream that their children's lives would be richer than their own lives had been. Anything and everything seemed possible.

The rising curve of expectations, propelled by economic growth, ascended through the 1950s. It peaked in the 1960s, an exceptionally stormy decade during which faith in government, in the wisdom of American foreign policy, and in the American dream itself began to sour. Lyndon Johnson's "Great Society" reforms, billed as the completion of the unfinished work of the New Deal, foundered on the rocks of fiscal limitations and stubborn racial resentments. Johnson, the most ambitious reformer in the White House since Franklin Roosevelt, eventually saw his presidency destroyed by the furies unleashed over the Vietnam War.

When economic growth flattened in the 1970s, the horizon of hopes for the future seemed to sink as well. The nation entered a frustrating period of stalled expectations, increasingly rancorous racial tensions, disillusion with government, and political stalemate, although in one important area idealism survived. As "second-wave feminism" gathered steam, women burst through barriers that had long excluded them from male domains, from the factory floor to the U.S. Army to the Ivy League. Not content with private victories, they also called on the government for help—to ensure women equal opportunity as workers, fair treatment as consumers, and the right to choose an abortion.

With the exceptions of Jimmy Carter in the 1970s and Bill Clinton in the 1990s, Americans after 1968 elected conservative Republicans to the White House (Richard Nixon in 1968 and 1972, Ronald Reagan in 1980 and 1984, George Bush in 1988, and George W. Bush in 2000), but they continued to elect mostly Democratic congresses. As the twenty-first century dawned, a newly invigorated conservative Republican party was bidding to achieve long-term majority status, while the Democratic party teetered on a tightrope between its liberal policies and the conservative demands of the day for tax cuts and welfare reform.

Abroad, competition with the Soviet Union, and after 1949 with communist China as well, colored every aspect of America's foreign relations and shaped domestic American life too. Unreasoning fear of communists at home unleashed the destructive force of McCarthyism in the 1950s—a modern-day witch hunt in which careers were capsized and lives ruined by reckless accusations of communist sympathizing. The FBI encroached on sacred American liberties in its zeal to uncover communist "subversives."

The Cold War remained cold, in the sense that no shooting conflict broke out between the great-power rivals. But the United States did fight two shooting wars, in Korea in the 1950s and in Vietnam in the 1960s. Vietnam, the only foreign war in which the United States was defeated, cruelly convulsed American society, ending not only Lyndon Johnson's presidency but the thirty-five-year era of the Democratic party's political dominance as well. Vietnam also touched off the most vicious inflationary cycle in American history, and it embittered and disillusioned an entire generation.

Uncle Sam in the Cold War era also built a fearsome arsenal of nuclear weapons, great air and missile fleets to deliver them, a two-ocean navy, and, for a time, a large army raised by conscription. Whether the huge expenditures necessary to maintain that gigantic defense establishment stimulated or distorted the economy was long a controversial question. When the Cold War ended, Americans turned their attention in the 1990s to developing the potential of a new "global economy." But as the twenty-first century dawned, a terrorist assault on American soil required a new turn to issues of national defense and international security.

37

The Cold War Begins

1945–1952

America stands at this moment at the summit of the world.

WINSTON CHURCHILL, 1945

The American people, 140 million strong, cheered their nation's victories in Europe and Asia at the conclusion of World War II. But when the shouting faded away, many Americans began to worry about their futures. Four fiery years of global war had not entirely driven from their minds the painful memories of twelve desperate years of the Great Depression. Still more ominously, victory celebrations had barely ended before America's crumbling relations with its wartime ally, the Soviet Union, threatened a new and even more terrible international conflict.

Postwar Economic Anxieties

The decade of the 1930s had left deep scars. Joblessness and insecurity had dampened the marriage rate. Babies went unborn as pinched budgets and sagging self-esteem wrought a sexual depression in American bedrooms. The war had banished the blight of depression, but grim-faced observers warned that peace would bring the return of hard times.

The faltering economy in the initial postwar years threatened to confirm the worst predictions of the doomsayers who foresaw another Great Depression. Real gross national product (GNP) slumped sickeningly in 1946 and 1947 from its wartime peak. With the removal of price controls, prices giddily levitated by 33 percent in 1946–1947. An epidemic of strikes swept the country. During 1946 alone some 4.6 million laborers laid down their tools, fearful that soon they would barely be able to afford the autos and other goods they themselves were manufacturing.

The growing muscle of organized labor deeply annoyed many conservatives. They had their revenge against labor's New Deal gains in 1947, when a

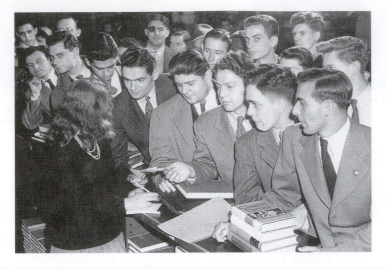

The GI Bill *Financed by the federal government, thousands of World War II veterans crowded into college classrooms in the 1940s. Here a fresh crop of ex-soldier students lays in supplies for the new term.*

Republican-controlled Congress (the first in fourteen years) passed the Taft-Hartley Act over President Truman's vigorous veto. Labor leaders condemned the Taft-Hartley Act as a "slave-labor law." It outlawed the "closed" (all-union) shop, made unions liable for damages resulting from jurisdictional disputes, and required union leaders to take a noncommunist oath.

The Democratic administration meanwhile took steps of its own to forestall an economic downturn. It sold war factories and other government installations to private businesses at fire-sale prices. It secured passage in 1946 of the Employment Act, which created a three-member Council of Economic Advisers to provide the president with data and recommendations to "promote maximum employment, production, and purchasing power."

Most dramatic was the passage of the Servicemen's Readjustment Act of 1944—better known as the GI Bill of Rights, or the GI Bill. Enacted partly out of fear that the employment markets would never be able to absorb 15 million returning veterans at war's end, the GI Bill made generous provisions for sending the former soldiers to school. In the postwar decade, some 8 million veterans advanced their educations at Uncle Sam's expense. The majority attended technical and vocational schools, but colleges and universities were crowded to the blackboards as more than 2 million ex-GIs stormed the halls of higher learning. The total eventually spent for education was some

$14.5 billion in taxpayer dollars. The act also enabled the Veterans Administration (VA) to guarantee about $16 billion in loans for veterans to buy homes, farms, and small businesses. By raising educational levels and stimulating the construction industry, the GI Bill powerfully nurtured the robust and long-lived economic expansion that eventually took hold in the late 1940s—and that profoundly shaped the entire history of the postwar era.

The Long Economic Boom, 1950–1970

Gross national product began to climb haltingly in 1948. Then, beginning about 1950, the American economy surged onto a dazzling plateau of sustained growth that was to last virtually uninterrupted for two decades. America's economic performance became the envy of the world. National income nearly doubled in the 1950s and almost doubled again in the 1960s, shooting through the trillion-dollar mark in 1973. Americans, some 6 percent of the world's people, were enjoying about 40 percent of the planet's wealth. Nothing loomed larger in the history of the post–World War II era than this fantastic eruption of affluence. It did not enrich all Americans, and it did not touch all people evenly, but it transformed the lives of a majority of citizens and molded the agenda of politics and society for at least two generations.

As the gusher of prosperity poured forth its riches, Americans drank deeply from the gilded goblet. Millions of depression-pinched souls sought to make up for the sufferings of the 1930s. They determined to "get theirs" while the getting was good. A people who had once considered a chicken in every pot the standard of comfort and security now hungered for two cars in every garage, swimming pools in their backyards, vacation homes, and gas-guzzling recreational vehicles. The size of the "middle class," defined as households earning between $3,000 and $10,000 a year, doubled from pre–Great Depression days and included 60 percent of the American people by the mid-1950s. By the end of that decade, the vast majority of American families owned their own cars and washing machines, and nearly 90 percent owned a television set—a gadget invented in the 1920s but virtually unknown until the late 1940s. In another revolution of sweeping consequences, almost 60 percent of American families owned their own homes by 1960, compared with less than 40 percent in the 1920s.

Of all the beneficiaries of postwar prosperity, none reaped greater rewards than women. More than ever, urban offices and shops provided them with a bonanza of employment as the service sector of the economy dramatically outgrew the old industrial and manufacturing sectors. Women accounted for one-quarter of the American work force at the end of World War II, and for nearly half the labor pool five decades later. Yet even as women continued their march into the workplace in the 1940s and 1950s, popular culture glorified the traditional feminine roles of homemaker and mother. The clash between the demands of suburban housewifery and the realities of employment eventually sparked a feminist revolt in the 1960s.

What propelled this unprecedented economic explosion? The Second World War itself provided a powerful stimulus. While other countries had been ravaged by years of fighting, the United States had used the war crisis to fire up its smokeless factories and rebuild its depression-plagued economy. America had almost effortlessly come to dominate the ruined global landscape of the postwar period.

Ominously, much of the glittering prosperity of the 1950s and 1960s rested on the underpinnings of colossal military budgets, leading some critics to speak of a "permanent war economy." The economic

Agribusiness *Expensive machinery of the type shown here made most of American agriculture a capital-intensive, phenomenally productive big business by the 1990s—and sounded the death knell for many small-scale family farms.*

upturn of 1950 was fueled by massive appropriations for the Korean War, and defense spending accounted for some 10 percent of the GNP throughout the ensuing decade. Pentagon dollars primed the pumps of high-technology industries such as aerospace, plastics, and electronics, and also financed much of the scientific research and development that spurred the economy.

Cheap energy also fed the economic boom. American and European companies that controlled the flow of abundant petroleum from the Middle East kept their prices low, and Americans consequently doubled their consumption of the seemingly inexhaustible oil in the quarter-century after the war. Anticipating a limitless future of low-cost fuels, they flung out endless ribbons of highways, installed air conditioning in their homes, and spread electrical cables everywhere to activate the tools of workers on the factory floor.

With the forces of nature increasingly harnessed in their hands, workers chalked up spectacular gains in productivity—the amount of output per hour of work. In the two decades after the outbreak of the Korean War in 1950, productivity increased at an average rate of more than 3 percent per year. Gains in productivity were also enhanced by the rising educational level of the work force. By 1970 nearly 90 percent of the school-age population were enrolled in educational institutions—a dramatic contrast with the opening years of the century, when only half of this age group had attended school. Better educated and better equipped, American workers in 1970 could produce nearly twice as much in an hour's labor as they had done in 1950. Productivity was the key to prosperity. Rising productivity in the 1950s and 1960s virtually doubled the average American's standard of living in the postwar quarter-century.

The Smiling Sunbelt

The convulsive economic changes of the post-1945 period shook and shifted the American people, amplifying the population redistribution set in motion by World War II. As immigrants and westward-trekking pioneers, Americans had always been a people on the move, but they were astonishingly footloose in the postwar years. For some three decades after 1945, an average of 30 million persons changed residences every year. Families especially felt the strain, as distance divided parents from children, and brothers and sisters from one another. One sign of this kind of stress was the phenomenal popularity of advice books on child-rearing, especially Dr. Benjamin Spock's *The Common Sense Book of Baby and Child Care*. First published in 1945, it instructed millions of parents during the ensuing decades in the kind of homely wisdom that was once transmitted naturally from grandparent to parent, and from parent to child.

Especially striking was the growth of the "Sunbelt"—a fifteen-state area stretching in a smiling crescent from Virginia through Florida and Texas to Arizona and California. This region increased its population at a rate nearly double that of the old industrial zones of the Northeast (the "Frostbelt"). A Niagara of federal dollars accounted for much of the Sunbelt region's new prosperity, even though southern and western politicians led the cry against government spending. By the 1990s the South and West were annually receiving some $125 billion more in federal funds than the Northeast and Midwest. Northeasterners and their allies from the hard-hit region of the Ohio Valley tried to rally political support with the sarcastic slogan "The North shall rise again."

These dramatic shifts of population and wealth further broke the historic grip of the North on the nation's political life. Every occupant of the White House elected from 1964 until the end of the century hailed from the Sunbelt, and the region's congressional representation rose as its population grew. With their devotion to unregulated economic growth, the Sunbelters were redrawing the Republic's political map.

The Rush to the Suburbs

In all regions, America's modern migrants—if they were white—fled from the cities to the burgeoning new suburbs (see "Makers of America: The Suburbanites," p. 522). Government policies encouraged this momentous movement. Federal Housing Authority

The Suburbanites

Few images evoke more vividly the prosperity of the postwar era than aerial photographs of sprawling suburbs. Neat rows of look-alike tract houses, each with driveway and lawn and here and there a backyard swimming pool, came to symbolize the capacity of the economy to deliver the "American dream" to millions of families.

Suburbanization was hardly new. Well-off city dwellers had beaten paths to leafy outlying neighborhoods since the nineteenth century. But after 1945 the steady flow became a stampede. The baby boom, new highways, government guarantees for mortgage lending, and favorable tax policies all made suburbia blossom.

Who were the Americans racing to the new postwar suburbs? People of all kinds found their way to suburbia, heading for neighborhoods that varied from the posh to the plain. Yet for all this diversity, the overwhelming majority of suburbanites were white and middle-class. In 1967 sociologist Herbert Gans published *The Levittowners*, describing one of the tract developments built by William and Alfred Levitt outside Philadelphia. He discovered that suburban families were predominantly third- or fourth-generation Americans with some college education and at least two children. Men tended to work in either white-collar jobs or upper-level blue-collar positions. Women usually worked in the home, so much so that suburbia came to symbolize domestic confinement for feminists of the 1960s and 1970s.

The house itself became more important than ever as postwar suburbanites built their leisure lives around television, home improvement projects, and barbecues on the patio. Family life became more privatized, in contrast to the neighborly city habits of visiting on the front stoop or strolling to local stores. Life in the suburbs depended on the automobile, as parents jumped behind the wheel to shuttle children, groceries, and golf clubs to and fro. Drive-through restaurants and drive-in movies sprang up, and roadside shopping centers edged out downtowns as places to shop. Meanwhile, the new interstate highway system enabled breadwinners to live far from their jobs and still commute to work, whether downtown or in other distant suburbs.

Wherever they worked, suburbanites turned their backs on the city and its problems. They fought to maintain their independent municipalities, with pastoral names like Elmwood Park and Maple Grove Village, as secluded retreats with their own taxes, schools, and zoning restrictions designed to keep out public housing and the poor. With a majority of Americans living in suburbs by the 1980s, cities lost their political clout. Bereft of state and federal aid, cities festered with worsening social problems: poverty, drug addiction, and crime.

Middle-class African-Americans began to move to the suburbs in substantial numbers by the 1980s. But even that migration failed to alter dramatically the racial divide of metropolitan America, as black suburbanites tended to settle in largely black suburbs within white-majority counties. By the end of the twentieth century, suburbia as a whole was more racially diverse than at midcentury. But old patterns of urban "white flight" and residential segregation endured.

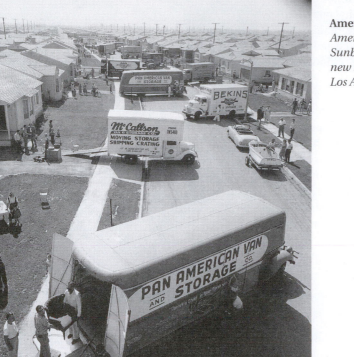

America on the Move, 1953   *Millions of Americans migrated to the suburbs and the Sunbelt in the years after World War II. Here a new housing development has just opened near Los Angeles.*

(FHA) and Veterans Administration (VA) home-loan guarantees made it more economically attractive to own a home in the suburbs than to rent an apartment in the city. Tax deductions for interest payments on home mortgages provided additional financial incentive. And government-built highways that sped commuters from suburban homes to city jobs further facilitated this mass migration. By 1960 one of every four Americans dwelt in suburbia, and the same leafy neighborhoods held more than half the nation's population as the century neared its end.

The construction industry boomed in the 1950s and 1960s to satisfy this demand. Pioneered by innovators such as the Levitt brothers, whose first "Levittown" sprouted on New York's Long Island in the 1940s, builders developed efficient new techniques for constructing mass-produced housing. Critics wailed about the esthetic monotony of the suburban "tract" developments, but eager homebuyers nevertheless moved into them by the millions.

"White flight" to the green suburbs left the inner cities—especially in the Northeast and Midwest—black, brown, and broke. Migrating blacks from the South filled up the urban neighborhoods abandoned by the departing white middle class. Taxpaying businesses fled with their affluent customers from downtown shops to suburban shopping malls.

The Postwar Baby Boom

Of all the upheavals in postwar America, none was more dramatic than the "baby boom"—the huge leap in the birthrate in the decade and a half after 1945. Confident young men and women tied the nuptial knot in record numbers at war's end and began immediately to fill the nation's empty cradles. They thus touched off a demographic explosion that added more than 50 million bawling babies to the nation's population by the end of the 1950s. The soaring birthrate finally crested in 1957 and was followed by a deepening birth dearth. By 1973 fertility rates had dropped below the point necessary to maintain existing population figures. If the trend persisted, only further immigration would lift the U.S. population above its 1998 level of some 268 million.

This boom-or-bust cycle of births begot a bulging wave along the American population curve. As the oversize postwar generation grew to maturity, it was destined—like the fabled pig passing through the python—to strain and distort many aspects of American life. Elementary-school enrollments, for example, swelled to nearly 34 million pupils in 1970. Then began a steady decline as the onward-marching age group left in its wake closed schools and unemployed teachers.

Truman: The "Gutty" Man from Missouri

Presiding over the opening of the postwar period was the "accidental president"—Harry S Truman. "The moon, the stars, and all the planets" had fallen on him, he remarked when he was called upon to shoulder Roosevelt's awesome burdens of leadership. Trim and owlishly bespectacled, with graying hair and a friendly, toothy grin, Truman was called "the average man's average man." The first president in many years without a college education, he had farmed, served as an artillery officer in France during World War I, and failed as a haberdasher. He then tried his hand at precinct-level Missouri politics, through which he rose from a judgeship to the U.S. Senate. Though a protégé of a notorious political machine in Kansas City, he had managed to keep his own hands clean.

The problems of the postwar period were staggering, and the firm-mouthed new president initially approached his tasks with humility. Gradually gaining confidence to the point of cockiness, he evolved from a shrinking pipsqueak into a scrappy little cuss. A smallish man thrust suddenly into a giant job, Truman permitted designing old associates of the "Missouri gang" to gather around him and, like Grant, was stubbornly loyal to them when they were caught with cream on their whiskers. On occasion, he would send critics hot-tempered and profane "s.o.b." letters. Most

What Next? 1946 *This cartoon expresses the feeling of many Americans that their new president was overwhelmed, even bamboozled, by his job.*

troubling, in trying to demonstrate to a skeptical public his decisiveness and power of command, he was inclined to go off half-cocked or stick mulishly to a wrongheaded notion.

But if Truman was sometimes small in the small things, he was often big in the big things. He had down-home authenticity, few pretensions, rock-solid probity, and a lot of that old-fashioned character trait called moxie. Not one to dodge responsibility, he placed a sign on his White House desk that read, "The buck stops here." Among his favorite sayings was, "If you can't stand the heat, get out of the kitchen."

Yalta: Bargain or Betrayal?

Vast and silent, the Soviet Union continued to be the great enigma. The conference in Teheran in 1943, where Roosevelt had first met Stalin on a man-to-man basis, had done something to clear the air, but much had remained unresolved—especially questions about the postwar fates of Germany, Eastern Europe, and Asia.

A final fateful conference of the "Big Three" had taken place in February 1945 at Yalta. At this former tsarist resort on the relatively warm shores of the Black Sea, Stalin, Churchill, and the fast-failing Roosevelt reached momentous agreements. Stalin agreed that Poland, with revised boundaries, should have a representative government based on free elections—a pledge he soon broke. Bulgaria and Romania were likewise to have free elections—a promise also flouted. The Big Three further announced plans for fashioning a new international peacekeeping organization—the United Nations.

The most controversial decisions at Yalta concerned Moscow's entry into the war against Japan. Uncertain of the untested atomic bomb, and expecting frightful American casualties in the projected assault on Japan, the Americans were willing to offer inducements to the Soviets to enter the Asian war and pin down Japanese troops in Manchuria and Korea.

Horse trader Stalin was in a position at Yalta to exact a high price. He agreed to attack Japan within three months after the collapse of Germany, and he later redeemed this pledge in full. In return, the Soviets were promised the southern half of Sakhalin Island, Japan's Kurile Islands, and railroad and industrial concessions in China's Manchuria.

As it turned out, Moscow's muscle was not necessary to knock out Japan. Critics charged that Roosevelt had sold Jiang Jieshi (Chiang Kai-shek) down the river and contributed to his overthrow by the Chinese communists four years later. Roosevelt's defenders countered that Stalin's mighty red army could have secured much more of China and that the Yalta conference really set limits to his ambitions. Apologists for Roosevelt also noted that Soviet troops had already occupied much of Eastern Europe and a war to throw them out was unthinkable.

The fact is that the Big Three at Yalta were not drafting a comprehensive peace settlement; at most they were sketching general intentions and testing one another's reactions. In the case of Poland, Roosevelt admitted that the Yalta agreement was "so elastic that the Russians can stretch it all the way from Yalta to Washington without ever technically breaking it." More specific understandings among the wartime allies—especially the two emerging superpowers, the United States and the Soviet Union—awaited the arrival of peace.

The United States and the Soviet Union

History provided little hope that the United States and the Soviet Union would reach cordial understandings about the shape of the postwar world. Mutual suspicions were ancient, abundant, and deep. Communism and capitalism were historically hostile social philosophies. The United States had refused officially to recognize the Bolshevik revolutionary government in Moscow until 1933. America had also aroused Soviet suspicions by its delays in opening a second front against Germany, by freezing its ally out of the project to develop atomic weapons, and by abruptly terminating vital lend-lease aid in 1945 and spurning Moscow's plea for a $6 billion reconstruction loan.

Different visions of the postwar world also separated the two superpowers. Stalin aimed above all to guarantee the security of the Soviet Union by establishing friendly governments along its western border, especially in Poland. By maintaining an extensive Soviet sphere of influence in Eastern and Central Europe, the USSR could protect itself and consolidate its revolutionary base as the world's leading communist country.

To many Americans, that "sphere of influence" looked like an ill-gained "empire." They remembered the earlier Bolshevik call for world revolution and doubted whether Stalin's emphasis on "spheres" could be reconciled with Franklin Roosevelt's Wilsonian dream of a decolonized, demilitarized, and democratized world, with a strong international organization to oversee the global peace.

Even the ways in which the United States and the Soviet Union resembled each other were troublesome. Both countries had been largely isolated from world affairs before World War II. Both nations also had a history of conducting a kind of "missionary" diplomacy—of trying to export to all the world the political doctrines precipitated out of their respective revolutionary origins.

Unaccustomed to their great-power roles, America and the USSR suddenly found themselves staring eyeball-to-eyeball over the prostrate body of battered Europe—a Europe that had been the traditional center of international affairs. In these circumstances, some kind of confrontation was virtually unavoidable. In a fateful progression of events, marked often by misperceptions as well as by genuine conflicts of interest, the two powers provoked each other into a tense standoff known as the "Cold War." Enduring four and a half decades, the Cold War not only shaped Soviet-American relations, but overshadowed the entire postwar international order.

Shaping the Postwar World

Despite these obstacles, the United States did manage at war's end to erect some of the structures that would support Roosevelt's vision of an open world. Meeting at Bretton Woods, New Hampshire, in 1944, the Western Allies established the International Monetary Fund (IMF) to encourage world trade and the International Bank for Reconstruction and Development (World Bank) to promote economic growth in war-ravaged and underdeveloped areas. In contrast to its behavior after World War I, the United States took the lead in creating these important international bodies.

Meeting in San Francisco in April 1945, representatives from fifty nations at the United Nations Conference fashioned a charter that strongly resembled the old League of Nations Covenant. It featured a Security Council dominated by the "Big Five" powers (the United States, Britain, the USSR, France, and China), each of whom had the right of veto, and a General Assembly that could be controlled by smaller countries. The U.S. Senate overwhelmingly approved the document on July 28, 1945.

The United Nations had some gratifying initial successes. It helped preserve peace in Iran, Kashmir, and other trouble spots. It played a large role in creating the new Jewish state of Israel. The U.N. Trusteeship Council guided former colonies to independence. Through such arms as UNESCO (United Nations Educational, Scientific, and Cultural Organization), FAO (Food and Agricultural Organization), and WHO (World Health Organization), the U.N. brought benefits to peoples the world over.

But it proved far less successful in controlling the fearsome new technology of the atom. The Soviets rejected an American proposal in 1946 for a U.N. agency to prevent the manufacture of nuclear weapons. The atomic clock ticked ominously on for the next forty-five years, shadowing all relations between the Soviet Union and the United States and casting a pall over the future of the human race.

The Problem of Germany

Hitler's ruined Reich posed especially thorny problems for all the wartime Allies. They agreed only that the cancer of Nazism had to be cut out of the German body politic, which involved punishing Nazi leaders for war crimes. The Allies tried twenty-two top culprits at Nuremberg, Germany, during 1945–1946 for crimes against the laws of war and humanity. Justice, Nuremberg-style, was harsh. Twelve of the accused Nazis swung from the gallows, and seven were sentenced to long jail terms.

Beyond punishing the top Nazis, the Allies could agree on little about postwar Germany. Some American Hitler-haters wanted to deindustrialize Germany, while the Soviets sought to extract enormous reparations from the Germans. Both these desires clashed headlong with the reality that an industrial, healthy German economy was indispensable to the recovery of Europe. The Americans soon came to appreciate that fact, but the fearful Soviets resisted all efforts to revitalize Germany.

Along with Austria, Germany had been divided at war's end into four military occupation zones, each assigned to one of the "Big Four" powers (France, Britain, America, and the USSR). Before long, it was apparent that Germany would remain indefinitely divided. West Germany eventually became an independent country, wedded to the West. East Germany, along with other Soviet-dominated Eastern European countries, became nominally independent "satellite" states bound to the Soviet Union. Eastern Europe virtually disappeared from Western sight behind the "iron curtain" of secrecy and isolation for more than four decades.

With Germany split in two, there remained the problem of the rubble heap known as Berlin. Lying deep within the Soviet zone (see map on p. 528), this

Witnesses for the Prosecution, 1945

Moscow's hard-line policies in Germany, Eastern Europe, and the Middle East wrought a psychological Pearl Harbor. Any remaining goodwill from the period of comradeship-in-arms evaporated in a cloud of dark mistrust. "I'm tired of babying the Soviets," Truman remarked privately in 1946, as attitudes on both sides began to harden frostily.

Truman's piecemeal responses to various Soviet challenges took on intellectual coherence in 1947 with the formulation of the "containment doctrine." Crafted by a brilliant young diplomat and Soviet specialist, George F. Kennan, this concept held that Russia, whether tsarist or communist, was relentlessly expansionary. But the Kremlin was also cautious, Kennan argued, and the flow of Soviet power into "every nook and cranny available to it" could be stemmed by "firm and vigilant containment."

Truman embraced Kennan's advice when he formally and publicly adopted a "get-tough-with-Russia" policy in 1947. His first dramatic move was triggered by word that heavily burdened Britain could no longer bear the financial and military load of defending Greece against communist pressures. If Greece fell, Turkey would presumably collapse and the strategic eastern Mediterranean would pass into the Soviet orbit.

The president went before Congress on March 12, 1947, and requested support for what came to be known as the Truman Doctrine. Specifically, he asked for $400 million to bolster Greece and Turkey, which Congress quickly granted. More generally, he declared that "it must be the policy of the United States to support free peoples who are resisting attempted subjugation by armed minorities or outside pressures"—a sweeping and open-ended commitment of vast and worrisome proportions.

Critics then and later charged that the Truman Doctrine committed the United States to back "anticommunist" despots, needlessly polarized the world into pro-Soviet and pro-American camps, and unwisely construed the Soviet threat as primarily military in nature. Apologists for Truman have explained that it was Truman's fear of a revived isolationism that led him to exaggerate the Soviet threat and to cast his message in the charged language of a holy global war against godless communism—a description of the Cold War that straitjacketed future policymakers who would seek to tone down Soviet-American competition and animosity.

beleaguered isle in a red sea had been broken, like Germany as a whole, into sectors occupied by troops of each of the four victorious powers. In 1948 the Soviets abruptly choked off all rail and highway access to Berlin, evidently reasoning that the Allies would be starved out.

Berlin became a hugely symbolic issue for both sides. The Americans organized a gigantic airlift in the midst of hair-trigger tension. For nearly a year American pilots ferried thousands of tons of supplies to the grateful Berliners. The Soviets, their bluff dramatically called, finally lifted their blockade in May 1949. In the same year the governments of the two Germanies, East and West, were formally established. The Cold War had icily congealed.

Crystallizing the Cold War

A crafty Stalin also probed the West's resolve at other sensitive points, including oil-rich Iran. In 1946 he broke an agreement to remove his troops from Iran's northernmost province. Truman sent off a stinging protest, and the Soviet dictator backed down.

Postwar Partition of Germany   *The city of Berlin, deep inside the Soviet zone (later East Germany), was also divided into four zones of occupation.*

A threat of a different sort loomed in Western Europe—especially France, Italy, and Germany. Still suffering from the hunger and economic chaos spawned by the war, these key nations were in grave danger of being taken over from the inside by Communist parties that could exploit these hardships. Truman responded boldly. On June 5, 1947, Secretary of State George C. Marshall offered American financial assistance for European economic recovery. The democratic nations of Europe enthusiastically accepted the life-giving Marshall Plan at a Paris conference in July 1947. Marshall offered the same aid to the Soviet Union and its allies, but nobody was surprised when the Soviets denounced the "Martial Plan" as one more capitalist trick.

The U.S. Congress at first balked at the Marshall Plan's proposal for spending $12.5 billion over four years in sixteen cooperating countries. But a Soviet-sponsored communist coup in Czechoslovakia finally awakened the legislators to reality, and they voted the initial appropriations in April 1948. Truman's Marshall Plan was a spectacular success. American dollars pumped reviving blood into the economic veins of the anemic Western European nations. Within a few years, an "economic miracle" drenched Europe in prosperity. The Communist parties in Italy and France lost ground, and these two keystone countries were saved from the westward thrust of communism.

A resolute Truman made another fateful decision in 1948. Access to Middle Eastern oil was crucial to European recovery and, increasingly, to the U.S. economy. Yet the Arab oil countries adamantly opposed the creation of the Jewish state of Israel in the British mandate territory of Palestine. Defying Arab wrath and his own State and Defense Departments, Truman officially recognized the state of Israel on the day of its birth, May 14, 1948. Truman's policy of strong support for Israel would vastly complicate U.S. relations with the Arab world in the decades ahead.

America Begins to Rearm

The Cold War, the struggle to contain Soviet communism, was not war, yet it was not peace. The standoff with the Kremlin banished the dreams of tax-fatigued Americans that tanks could be beaten into automobiles.

The Soviet menace spurred the unification of the armed services as well as the creation of a huge new national security apparatus. Congress in 1947 passed the National Security Act, creating the Department of

Defense. The uniformed heads of each service were brought together as the Joint Chiefs of Staff. The National Security Act also established the National Security Council (NSC) to advise the president on security matters and the Central Intelligence Agency (CIA) to coordinate the government's foreign fact-gathering. In the same year, Congress resurrected the military draft, providing for the conscription of selected young men from nineteen to twenty-five years of age. The forbidding presence of the Selective Service System played a major role in shaping young people's educational, marital, and career plans in the following quarter-century. One shoe at a time, a war-weary America was reluctantly returning to a war footing.

The Soviet threat was also forcing the United States into a defensive military alliance with the democracies of Western Europe. On April 4, 1949, twelve nations signed the North Atlantic Treaty, which pledged the signatories to regard an attack on one as an attack on all. Over last-ditch isolationist opposition, the U.S. Senate ratified the treaty on July 21, 1949, by a vote of 82 to 13.

The formation of the North Atlantic Treaty Organization (NATO) marked a dramatic departure from American diplomatic convention and a significant step in the militarization of the Cold War. NATO became the cornerstone of all Cold War American policy toward Europe. With good reason, pundits summed up NATO's threefold purpose: "to keep the Russians out, the Germans down, and the Americans in."

Reconstruction and Revolution in Asia

Reconstruction in Japan was simpler than in Germany, primarily because it was largely a one-man show. The occupying American army, led by General Douglas MacArthur as a kind of Yankee *mikado*, implemented his program for the democratization of Japan with stunning success. The Japanese cooperated to an astonishing degree. They saw that good behavior and the adoption of democracy would speed the end of occupation—and it did. A MacArthur-dictated constitution, adopted in 1946, paved the way for a phenomenal economic recovery that within a few decades made Japan one of the world's mightiest industrial powers.

If Japan was a success story for American policy-makers, the opposite was true in China, where a bitter civil war had raged for years between Nationalists and communists. Washington had halfheartedly supported the Nationalist government of Generalissimo Jiang Jieshi in his struggle with the communists under Mao Zedong (Mao Tse-tung). But ineptitude and corruption within the generalissimo's regime eroded his people's confidence and enabled the communist armies to sweep to victory late in 1949. Jiang was forced to flee with the remnants of his force to the island of Taiwan.

The collapse of Nationalist China was a depressing defeat for America and its allies in the Cold War. At one fell swoop nearly one-fourth of the world's population—some 500 million people—was swept into the communist camp. The Republicans charged that President Truman and his British-appearing secretary of state, Dean Acheson, had "lost China." Democrats heatedly replied that when a regime has forfeited the support of its people, no amount of outside help will save it. Truman, the argument ran, did not "lose" China because he never had China to lose.

More bad news came in September 1949, when President Truman shocked the nation by announcing that the Soviets had exploded an atomic bomb—approximately three years earlier than many experts had thought possible. To outpace the Soviets in nuclear weaponry, Truman ordered the development of the "H-bomb" (hydrogen bomb)—a city-smashing device many times more lethal than the atomic bomb. The United States exploded its first hydrogen device on a South Pacific atoll in 1952, despite warnings from some scientists that the H-bomb was so powerful that "it becomes a weapon which in practical effect is almost one of genocide." Not to be outdone, the Soviets exploded their first H-bomb in 1953, and the nuclear arms race entered a perilously competitive cycle. Nuclear "superiority" became a dangerous and elusive dream, as each side tried to outdo the other in the scramble to build more destructive weapons. But if the Cold War were to blaze into a hot war, there might be no world left for the communists to communize or the democracies to democratize: this chilling thought constrained both camps, and peace through mutual terror brought a shaky stability to the superpower standoff.

Ferreting Out Alleged Communists

One of the most active Cold War fronts was at home, where a new anti-red chase was in full cry. In 1947 Truman launched a massive "loyalty" program. A Loyalty Review Board investigated more than 3 million federal employees, some three thousand of whom either resigned or were dismissed, none under formal indictment.

Individual states likewise became intensely security-conscious. Loyalty oaths in increasing numbers were demanded of employees, especially teachers. The gnawing question for many earnest Americans was, Could the nation continue to enjoy traditional freedoms in a Cold War climate?

In 1949 eleven communists were convicted of advocating the overthrow of the American government under the Smith Act of 1940 and sent to prison. In 1948 Congressman Richard M. Nixon, a member of the House Un-American Activities Committee (HUAC), led the chase after Alger Hiss, a prominent ex–New Dealer and a distinguished member of the "eastern establishment." Accused of being a communist agent in the 1930s, Hiss dramatically confronted his chief accuser before the committee and denied everything. But Hiss was caught in embarrassing falsehoods, convicted of perjury in 1950, and sentenced to five years in prison.

Was America really riddled with Soviet spies? It now seems unlikely. But for many ordinary Americans, the hunt for communists was not just about fending off the military threat of the Soviet Union. Unsettling dangers lurked closer to home. While men like Nixon and Senator Joseph McCarthy led the search for communists in Washington, conservative politicians at the state and local levels discovered that all manner of real or perceived social changes—including declining religious sentiment, increased sexual freedom, or agitation for civil rights—could be tarred with a red brush. Anticommunist crusaders ransacked school libraries for "subversive" books and drove debtors, drinkers, and homosexuals, all alleged to be security risks, from their jobs.

Some Americans, including President Truman, realized that the red hunt was turning into a witch hunt. In 1950 Truman vetoed the McCarran Internal Security Bill, which authorized the president to arrest and detain suspicious persons during an "internal security emergency." But the congressional guardians of the Republic's liberties enacted the bill over Truman's veto.

The stunning success of Soviet scientists in developing an atomic bomb was attributed by many to the cleverness of communist spies in stealing American secrets. In 1951 two American citizens, Julius and Ethel Rosenberg, were convicted of "leaking" atomic data to Moscow. Their sensational trial and eventual electrocution in 1953, combined with sympathy for their two orphaned children, began to sour some sober citizens on the excesses of the red-hunters.

Democratic Divisions in 1948

Attacking high prices and "High-Tax Harry" Truman, the Republicans had won control of Congress in the congressional elections of 1946. Their prospects had seldom looked rosier as they gathered in Philadelphia to choose their 1948 presidential candidate. They noisily renominated warmed-over New York governor Thomas E. Dewey, still as debonair as if he had stepped out of a bandbox.

Also gathering in Philadelphia, Democratic politicos looked without enthusiasm on their hand-me-down president and sang "I'm Just Mild About Harry." But their "dump Truman" movement collapsed when war hero Dwight D. Eisenhower refused to be drafted. The peppery president, unwanted but undaunted, was then chosen in the face of vehement opposition by southern delegates. They were alienated by his strong stand in favor of civil rights for blacks, who now mustered many votes in the big-city ghettoes of the North.

Truman's nomination split the party wide open. Embittered southern Democrats from thirteen states, like their "fire-eating" forebears of 1860, met in their own convention, in Birmingham, Alabama, with Confederate flags brashly in evidence. Amid scenes of heated defiance, these "Dixiecrats" nominated Governor J. Strom Thurmond of South Carolina on a States' Rights party ticket.

To add to the confusion within Democratic ranks, former vice president Henry A. Wallace threw his hat into the ring. Having parted company with the administration over its get-tough-with-Russia policy, he was nominated at Philadelphia by the new Progressive party—a bizarre collection of disgruntled former New Dealers, starry-eyed pacifists, well-meaning liberals, and communist-fronters.

Wallace, a vigorous if misguided liberal, assailed Uncle Sam's "dollar imperialism" from the stump. This so-called Pied Piper of the Politburo took an apparently pro-Soviet line that earned him drenchings with rotten eggs in hostile cities. But to many Americans, Wallace raised the only hopeful voice in the deepening gloom of the Cold War.

With the Democrats deeply split three ways and the Republican congressional victory of 1946 just past, Dewey's victory seemed assured. Succumbing to overconfidence engendered by his massive lead in public-opinion polls, the cold, smug Dewey confined himself to dispensing soothing-syrup trivialities like "Our future lies before us."

The seemingly doomed Truman, with little money and few active supporters, had to rely on his "gut-fighter" instincts and folksy personality. Traveling the country by train to deliver some three hundred "give 'em hell" speeches, he lashed out at the Taft-Hartley "slave labor" law and the "do-nothing" Republican Congress while whipping up support for his program of civil rights, improved labor benefits, and health insurance. "Pour it on 'em, Harry!" cried increasingly large and enthusiastic crowds as the pugnacious president rained a barrage of verbal uppercuts on his opponent.

On election night the *Chicago Tribune* ran off an early edition with the headline "DEWEY DEFEATS TRUMAN." But in the morning it turned out that "President" Dewey had embarrassingly snatched defeat from the jaws of victory. Truman had swept to a stunning triumph, to the complete bewilderment of politicians, pollsters, prophets, and pundits. Even though Thurmond took away 39 electoral votes in the South, Truman won 303 electoral votes, primarily from the South, Midwest, and West. Dewey's 189 electoral votes came principally from the East. The popular vote was 24,179,345 for Truman, 21,991,291 for Dewey, 1,176,125 for Thurmond, and 1,157,326 for Wallace. To make the victory sweeter, the Democrats regained control of Congress as well.

Truman's victory rested on farmers, workers, and blacks, all of whom were Republican-wary. Republican overconfidence and Truman's lone-wolf, never-

say-die campaign also won him the support of many Americans who admired his "guts." No one wanted him, someone remarked, except the people.

Smilingly confident, Truman sounded a clarion note, in the fourth point of his inaugural address, when he called for a "bold new program" ("Point Four"). The plan was to lend U.S. money and technical aid to underdeveloped lands to help them help themselves. Truman wanted to spend millions to keep underprivileged peoples from becoming communists rather than to spend billions to shoot them after they had become communists. This farseeing program was officially launched in 1950, and it brought badly needed assistance to impoverished countries, notably in Latin America, Africa, the Middle East, and East Asia.

At home, Truman outlined a sweeping "Fair Deal" program in his 1949 message to Congress. It called for badly needed housing, full employment, a higher minimum wage, better farm price supports, new TVAs, and an extension of Social Security. But most of the Fair Deal fell victim to congressional opposition from Republicans and southern Democrats. The only major successes came in raising the minimum wage, providing for public housing in the Housing Act of 1949, and extending old-age insurance to many more beneficiaries in the Social Security Act of 1950.

The Korean Volcano Erupts (1950)

Korea, the Land of the Morning Calm, heralded a new and more ominous phase of the Cold War—a shooting phase—in June 1950. When Japan collapsed in 1945, Soviet troops had accepted the Japanese surrender north of the thirty-eighth parallel on the Korean peninsula, and American troops had done likewise south of that line. Both superpowers professed to want reunification of Korea, but, as in Germany, each helped to set up rival regimes above and below the parallel. When the Soviets and Americans withdrew in 1949, the entire peninsula was a bristling armed camp.

Secretary of State Acheson seemed to wash his hands of the dispute early in 1950, when he declared that Korea was outside the essential United States defense perimeter in the Pacific. But when North Korean army columns rumbled across the thirty-eighth parallel on June 25, 1950, and shoved the South Koreans southward into a tiny defensive area around Pusan, President Truman sprang quickly into the breach. The invasion seemed to provide devastating proof of a fundamental premise in the "containment doctrine" that shaped Washington's foreign policy: that even a slight relaxation of America's guard was an invitation to communist aggression somewhere.

The Korean invasion also provided the occasion for a vast expansion of the American military. Truman's National Security Council had recommended in a document of 1950 (known as National Security Council Memorandum Number 68, or NSC-68) that the United States should quadruple defense spending. Buried at the time, NSC-68 was resurrected by the Korean crisis. Truman now ordered a massive military buildup, well beyond what was necessary for the immediate purposes of the Korean War. Soon the United States had 3.5 million men under arms and was spending $50 billion per year on the defense budget—some 13 percent of the GNP.

Truman took full advantage of a temporary Soviet absence from the United Nations Security Council to obtain a unanimous condemnation of North Korea as an aggressor. The Council also called upon all U.N. members, including the United States, to "render every assistance" to restore peace. Two days later, without consulting Congress, Truman ordered American armed forces under General Douglas MacArthur to support South Korea. Officially, the United States was simply participating in a United Nations "police action," but in fact the United States made up the bulk of the U.N. contingents.

The Military Seesaw in Korea

Rather than fight his way out of the southern Pusan perimeter, MacArthur launched a daring amphibious landing behind the enemy's lines at Inchon. This bold gamble, on September 15, 1950, succeeded brilliantly; within two weeks the North Koreans had scrambled back behind the "sanctuary" of the thirty-eighth parallel. Truman's avowed intention was to restore South Korea to its former borders, but the pursuing South Koreans had already crossed the thirty-eighth parallel, and there seemed little point in permitting the North Koreans to regroup and come again. The U.N. General Assembly tacitly authorized a crossing by MacArthur, whom President Truman ordered northward, provided that there was no intervention in force by the Chinese or Soviets.

The Americans thus raised the stakes in Korea, and in so doing they quickened the fears of another potential player in this dangerous game. The Chinese communists had publicly warned that they would not sit idly by and watch hostile troops approach the strategic Yalu River boundary between Korea and

June 25, 1950 *Sept. 14, 1950* *Nov. 25, 1950* *July 27, 1953*

The Shifting Front in Korea

China. But MacArthur pooh-poohed all predictions of an effective intervention by the Chinese and reportedly boasted that he would "have the boys home by Christmas."

MacArthur erred badly. In November 1950 hordes of Chinese "volunteers" fell upon his rashly overextended lines and hurled the U.N. forces reeling back down the peninsula. The fighting then sank into a frostbitten stalemate on the icy terrain near the thirty-eighth parallel.

An imperious MacArthur, humiliated by this rout, pressed for drastic retaliation. He favored a blockade of the China coast and bombardment of Chinese bases in Manchuria. But Washington policy-makers, with anxious eyes on Moscow, refused to enlarge the already costly conflict. The chairman of the Joint Chiefs of Staff declared that a wider clash in Asia would be "the wrong war, at the wrong place, at the wrong time, and with the wrong enemy." Europe, not Asia, was the administration's first concern; and the USSR, not China, loomed as the more sinister foe.

Two-fisted General MacArthur felt that he was being asked to fight with one hand tied behind his back. He sneered at the concept of a "limited war" and insisted that "there is no substitute for victory." When the general began to take issue publicly with presidential policies, Truman had no choice but to remove the insubordinate MacArthur from command (April 11, 1951). The imperious war hero, a legend in his own mind, returned to the United States to an uproarious welcome, while Truman was condemned as a "pig," an "imbecile," a "Judas," and an appeaser of "Communist Russia and Communist China."

In July 1951 truce discussions began in a rude field tent near the firing line but were almost immediately snagged on the issue of prisoner exchange. Talks dragged on unproductively for nearly two years—while men continued to die.

Chronology

1944	Servicemen's Readjustment Act (GI Bill). Bretton Woods economic conference.
1945	Spock publishes *The Common Sense Book of Baby and Child Care.* Yalta conference. United Nations established.
1945–1946	Nuremberg war crimes trials in Germany.
1946	Employment Act creates Council of Economic Advisers. Iran crisis.
1947	Truman Doctrine. Marshall Plan. Taft-Hartley Act. National Security Act creates Department of Defense, National Security Council (NSC), and Central Intelligence Agency (CIA).
1948	United States officially recognizes Israel. Hiss case begins. Truman defeats Dewey for presidency.
1948–1949	Berlin crisis.
1949	NATO established. Communists defeat Nationalists in China.
1950	American economy begins postwar growth. McCarthy red hunt begins. McCarran Internal Security Act passed by Congress over Truman's veto.
1950–1953	Korean War.
1951	Truman fires MacArthur. Rosenbergs convicted of treason.
1952	United States explodes first hydrogen bomb.
1957	Postwar peak of U.S. birthrate.
1973	U.S. birthrate falls below replacement level.

VARYING VIEWPOINTS

Who Was to Blame for the Cold War?

Whose fault was the Cold War? And, for that matter, who should get credit for ending it? For two decades after World War II, American historians generally agreed that the aggressive Soviets were solely responsible for causing the Cold War. This "orthodox" or "official" appraisal squared with the traditional view of the United States as a virtuous, innocent land with an idealistic foreign policy. This point of view also justified America's Cold War containment policy, which cast the Soviet Union as an aggressor that must be confined by the ever-vigilant United States. America supposedly had only defensive intentions and no expansionary ambitions of its own.

In the 1960s a vigorous revisionist interpretation flowered, powerfully influenced by disillusion over U.S. involvement in Vietnam. The revisionists stood the orthodox view on its head. The Soviets, they argued, had only defensive intentions at the end of World War II; it was the Americans who behaved provocatively by brandishing their new atomic weaponry. Some of these critics pointed an accusing finger at President Truman, alleging that he abandoned Roosevelt's conciliatory approach to the Soviets and adopted a bullying attitude, emboldened by the American atomic monopoly. More radical revisionists like Gabriel and Joyce Kolko even claimed to have found the roots of Truman's alleged belligerence in long-standing American policies of economic imperialism—policies that eventually resulted in the tragedy of Vietnam.

In the 1970s a "postrevisionist" interpretation emerged that is widely agreed upon today. Historians such as John Lewis Gaddis and Melvyn Leffler poohpooh the economic determinism of the revisionists while frankly acknowledging that the United States did have vital security interests at stake in the post–World War II era. The postrevisionists analyze the ways in which inherited ideas (like isolationism) and the contentious nature of post–World War II domestic politics, as well as miscalculations by American leaders, led a nation in search of security into seeking not simply a sufficiency but a "preponderance" of power. The American overreaction to its security needs, these scholars suggest, exacerbated U.S.-Soviet relations and precipitated the four-decade-long nuclear arms race that formed the centerpiece of the Cold War.

In the case of Vietnam, the postrevisionist historians focus not on economic necessity but on a failure of political intelligence, induced by the stressful conditions of the Cold War, that lent credibility to the dubious domino theory. The domino theory held that the fall of even one country to communism would bring communist control of all Southeast Asia or even Hawaii. Misunderstanding Vietnamese intentions, exaggerating Soviet ambitions, and fearing to appear "soft on communism" in the eyes of their domestic political rivals, American leaders plunged into Vietnam, sadly misguided by their own Cold War obsessions. Most postrevisionists, however, still lay the lion's share of the blame for the Cold War on the Soviet Union. The great unknown, of course, is the precise nature of Soviet thinking in the Cold War years. Were Soviet aims predominantly defensive, or did the Kremlin incessantly plot world conquest? Was there an opportunity for reconciliation with the West following Stalin's death in 1953? Should Mikhail Gorbachev or Ronald Reagan be remembered as the leader who ended the Cold War? With the opening of Soviet archives, scholars are eagerly pursuing answers to such questions.

For further reading, see the Appendix. For web resources, go to **http://college.hmco.com**.

38

The Eisenhower Era

1952–1960

Every warship launched, every rocket fired signified . . .
a theft from those who hunger and are not fed, those
who are cold and are not clothed.

DWIGHT D. EISENHOWER, APRIL 16, 1953

In President Dwight D. Eisenhower, the man and the hour met. Americans yearned for a period of calm, in which they could pursue without distraction their new visions of consumerist affluence. The nation sorely needed a respite from twenty years of depression and war. Yet the American people unexpectedly found themselves in the early 1950s dug into the frontlines of the Cold War abroad and dangerously divided at home over the explosive issues of communist subversion and civil rights. They longed for reassuring leadership. "Ike" seemed ready both to reassure and to lead.

The Advent of Eisenhower

Democratic prospects in the presidential election of 1952 were blighted by the military deadlock in Korea,

Truman's clash with MacArthur, war-bred inflation, and whiffs of scandal from the White House. Dispirited Democrats, convening in Chicago, nominated a reluctant Adlai E. Stevenson, the witty, eloquent, and idealistic governor of Illinois.

Republicans enthusiastically chose General Dwight D. Eisenhower on the first ballot. As Ike's running mate the convention selected California senator Richard M. Nixon, who had distinguished himself as a relentless red-hunter.

Eisenhower was already the most popular American of his time, as "I Like Ike" buttons everywhere testified. Striking a grandfatherly, nonpartisan pose, Eisenhower left the rough campaigning to Nixon, who relished pulling no punches. The vice-presidential candidate lambasted his opponents with charges that they had cultivated corruption, caved in on Korea, and coddled communists. He particularly blasted the intellectual ("egghead") Stevenson as "Adlai the appeaser," with a "Ph.D. from [Secretary of State] Dean Acheson's College of Cowardly Communist Containment."

Nixon's own place on the Republican ticket was in jeopardy when reports surfaced of a secret "slush fund" he had tapped while in the Senate. But he rescued himself with a self-pitying televised speech in which he referred to the family cocker spaniel Checkers. The maudlin "Checkers speech" demonstrated the awesome political potentialities of television. Soon even Eisenhower reluctantly appeared in the short televised "spots" that amounted, one critic observed, to "selling the President like toothpaste." These televised campaign advertisements marked the beginnings of a new era in which politicians could bypass the traditional political party organizations and go straight to the voters.

The outcome of the presidential election of 1952 was never really in doubt. Given an extra prod by Eisenhower's last-minute pledge to go personally to Korea to end the war, the voters massively declared for Ike. He garnered 33,963,234 votes to Stevenson's 27,314,992. He cracked the solid South wide open, ringing up 442 electoral votes to 89 for his opponent. Ike not only ran far ahead of his ticket but pulled enough Republicans into office on his military coattails to ensure GOP control of the new Congress by a paper-thin margin.

True to his campaign pledge, president-elect Eisenhower undertook a flying three-day visit to Korea in December 1952. But even a glamorous Ike could not immediately budge the peace negotiations off dead center. Seven long months later, after Eisenhower had threatened to use atomic weapons, an armistice was finally signed but was repeatedly violated in succeeding decades.

The brutal and futile fighting had lasted three years. About fifty-four thousand Americans lay dead, joined by more than a million Chinese, North Koreans, and South Koreans. Tens of billions of American dollars had been poured down the Asian sinkhole. Yet this terrible toll in blood and treasure bought only a return to the conditions of 1950; Korea remained divided at the thirty-eighth parallel. Americans took what little comfort they could from the fact that communism had been "contained" and that the bloodletting had been "limited" to something less than

full-scale global war. The shooting had ended, but the Cold War remained frigidly frozen.

As a military commander, Eisenhower had cultivated a leadership style that self-consciously projected an image of sincerity, fairness, and optimism. Ike thus seemed ideally suited to soothe the anxieties of troubled Americans, much as a distinguished and well-loved grandfather brings stability to his family. He played this role well as he presided over a decade of shaky peace and shining prosperity. Yet critics charged that he unwisely hoarded the "asset" of his immense popularity, rather than spend it for a good cause (especially civil rights), and that he cared much more for social harmony than for social justice.

The Rise and Fall of Joseph McCarthy

One of the first problems Eisenhower faced was the swelling popularity and swaggering power of an anticommunist crusader, Wisconsin senator Joseph R. McCarthy. McCarthy had crashed into the limelight in February 1950 when he accused Secretary of State Dean Acheson of knowingly employing 205 Communist party members. Pressed to reveal the names, McCarthy later conceded that there were only 57 genuine communists and in the end failed to root out even one. McCarthy's Republican colleagues nevertheless realized the usefulness of this kind of attack on the Democratic administration. Ohio senator John Bricker reportedly said, "Joe, you're a dirty s.o.b., but there are times when you've got to have an s.o.b. around, and this is one of them."

McCarthy's rhetoric grew bolder and his accusations spread more wildly after the Republican victory in 1952. McCarthy saw the red hand of Moscow everywhere. Incredibly, he even denounced General George Marshall, former army chief of staff and ex–secretary of state, as "part of a conspiracy so immense and an infamy so black as to dwarf any previous venture in the history of man."

McCarthy flourished in the seething Cold War atmosphere of suspicion and fear. He was neither the first nor the most effective red-hunter, but he was surely the most ruthless, and he did the most damage to American traditions of fair play and free speech. The careers of countless officials, writers, and actors were ruined after "Low-Blow Joe" had "named" them, often unfairly, as communists or communist sympathizers. Politicians trembled in the face of such onslaughts, especially when opinion polls showed that a majority of the American people approved of McCarthy's crusade.

Eisenhower privately loathed McCarthy but publicly tried to stay out of his way. Trying to appease the brash demagogue from Wisconsin, Eisenhower allowed him, in effect, to control personnel policy at the State Department. One baleful result was severe damage to the morale and effectiveness of the professional foreign service. In particular, McCarthyite purges deprived the government of a number of Asian specialists who might have counseled a wiser course in Vietnam in the fateful decade that followed.

McCarthy finally bent the bow too far when he attacked the U.S. Army. The embattled military men fought back in thirty-five days of televised hearings in the spring of 1954. The political power of the new broadcast medium was again demonstrated as up to 20 million Americans watched in fascination while a boorish, surly McCarthy cut his own throat by parading his essential meanness and irresponsibility. A few months later the Senate condemned him for "conduct unbecoming a member." Three years later McCarthy died unwept and unsung. But "McCarthyism" passed into the English language as a label for the dangerous forces of unfairness and fear that a democratic society can unleash only at its peril.

Desegregating the South

America counted some 15 million black citizens in 1950, two-thirds of whom still made their homes in the South. There they lived bound by the iron folkways of a segregated society. A rigid set of antiquated rules known as "Jim Crow" laws governed all aspects of their existence, from the schoolroom to the restroom.

Blacks everywhere in the South not only attended segregated schools but were compelled to use separate public toilets, drinking fountains, restaurants, and waiting rooms. Trains and buses had "whites only" and "colored only" seating. Only about 20 percent of eligible southern blacks were registered to vote, and fewer than 5 percent in some Deep South states such as Mississippi and Alabama.

Where the law proved insufficient to enforce this regime, vigilante violence did the job. Six black war veterans, claiming the rights for which they had fought overseas, were murdered in the summer of 1946. A Mississippi mob lynched black fourteen-year-old Emmett Till in 1955 for allegedly leering at a white woman. It is small wonder that a black clergyman declared that "everywhere I go in the South the Negro is forced to choose between his hide and his soul."

In his notable book of 1944, *An American Dilemma*, Swedish scholar Gunnar Myrdal had exposed the contradiction between America's professed belief that all men are created equal and its

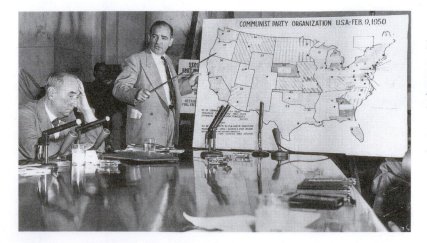

Exposing "Reds" *Senator McCarthy makes a point at the army-McCarthy hearings in 1954 while army counsel Joseph Welch ponders a reply. McCarthy declared in a speech in 1951: "Let me assure you that regardless of how high-pitched becomes the squealing and screaming of those left-wing, bleeding-heart, phony liberals, this battle is going to go on."*

sordid treatment of black citizens. There had been token progress in race relations since the war—Jack Roosevelt ("Jackie") Robinson, for example, had cracked the racial barrier in big-league baseball when the Brooklyn Dodgers signed him in 1947. But for the most part, the national conscience still slumbered, and blacks still suffered.

Increasingly, however, African-Americans refused to suffer in silence. The war had generated a new militancy and restlessness among many members of the black community (see "Makers of America: The Great African-American Migration," pp. 540–541). The National Association for the Advancement of Colored People (NAACP) had for years pushed doggedly to dismantle the legal underpinnings of segregation and now enjoyed some success. In 1944 the Supreme Court ruled the "white primary" unconstitutional,

thereby undermining the status of the Democratic party in the South as a white persons' club. And in 1950 NAACP chief legal counsel Thurgood Marshall (himself later a Supreme Court justice) wrung from the high court a ruling that separate professional schools for blacks failed to meet the test of equality.

On a chilly day in December 1955, Rosa Parks, a college-educated black seamstress, made history in Montgomery, Alabama. She boarded a bus, took a seat in the "whites only" section, and refused to give it up. Her arrest for violating the city's Jim Crow statutes sparked a yearlong black boycott of the city buses and served notice throughout the South that blacks would no longer submit meekly to the absurdities and indignities of segregation.

The Montgomery bus boycott also catapulted to prominence a young pastor at Montgomery's Dexter Avenue Baptist Church, the Reverend Martin Luther King, Jr. Barely twenty-seven years old, King became a champion of the downtrodden and disfranchised. His oratorical skill, his passionate devotion to biblical and constitutional conceptions of justice, and his devotion to the nonviolent principles of India's Mohandas Gandhi thrust him to the forefront of the black revolution that soon pulsed across the South—and across the rest of the nation.

Beginnings of the Civil Rights Revolution

In 1946 President Harry Truman commissioned a report on blacks entitled "To Secure These Rights." Following the report's recommendations, Truman in 1948 ordered an end to segregation in federal civil service and the armed forces. Yet Congress stubbornly resisted passing civil rights legislation, and Truman's successor, Dwight Eisenhower, showed no real interest in the racial issue.

It was the Supreme Court that assumed civil rights leadership, as Chief Justice Earl Warren, former governor of California, shocked traditionalists with his active judicial intervention in previously taboo social issues. Publicly snubbed and privately criticized by President Dwight Eisenhower, Warren persistently led the Court to address urgent issues that the president and Congress attempted to avoid.

The Face of Segregation   *These women in the segregated South of the 1950s were compelled to enter the movie theater through the "Colored Entrance." Once inside, they were restricted to a separate seating section, usually in the rear of the theater.*

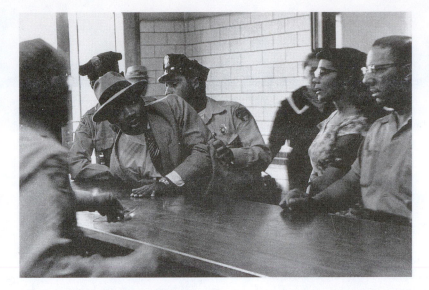

Martin Luther King, Jr., and His Wife, Coretta, Arrested   *King and his wife were arrested for the first time in Montgomery, Alabama, in 1955 while organizing a bus boycott.*

The unanimous decision of the Warren Court in *Brown* v. *Board of Education of Topeka, Kansas* in May 1954 was epochal. In a forceful opinion, the learned justices ruled that segregation in the public schools was "inherently unequal" and thus unconstitutional. The uncompromising sweep of the decision startled conservatives like an exploding time bomb, for it reversed the Court's earlier declaration of 1896 in *Plessy* v. *Ferguson* (see p. 315) that "separate but equal" facilities were allowable under the Constitution. That doctrine was now dead. Desegregation, the justices insisted, must go ahead with "all deliberate speed."

The Border States generally made reasonable efforts to comply with this ruling, but in the Deep South diehards organized "massive resistance" against the Court's attack on the sacred principle of "separate but equal." Throughout the South, white citizens' councils, sometimes with fire and hemp, thwarted attempts to make integration a reality. Ten years after the Court's momentous ruling, fewer than 2 percent of the eligible blacks in the Deep South states were sitting in classrooms with whites.

President Eisenhower remained reluctant to promote integration. He shied away from employing his vast popularity and the prestige of his office to educate white Americans about the need for racial justice. He complained that the Supreme Court's decision in *Brown* v. *Board of Education* had upset "the customs and convictions of at least two generations of Americans," and he steadfastly refused to issue a public statement endorsing the Court's conclusions. "I do not believe," he explained, "that prejudices, even palpably unjustifiable prejudices, will succumb to compulsion."

But in September 1957 Ike was forced to act. Arkansas governor Orval Faubus mobilized the National Guard to prevent nine black students from enrolling in Little Rock's Central High School. Confronted with a direct challenge to federal authority, Eisenhower sent troops to escort the children to their classes.

Blacks meanwhile continued to take the civil rights movement into their own hands. Martin Luther King, Jr., formed the Southern Christian Leadership Conference (SCLC) in 1957. It aimed to mobilize the vast power of black churches on behalf of black rights. The churches were the largest and best-organized black institutions that had been allowed to flourish in a segregated society.

More spontaneous was the "sit-in" movement launched on February 1, 1960, by four black college freshmen in Greensboro, North Carolina. Without a detailed plan or institutional support, they demanded service at a whites-only Woolworth's lunch counter. The following day, eighty-five students joined in; by the end of the week, a thousand. The sit-

The Great African-American Migration

So many black southerners took to the roads during World War II that local officials could not keep track of the migrants passing through the towns. Black workers on the move—a vast population with no addresses and no telephone numbers—crowded into boardinghouses, camped out in cars, and clustered in the juke joints of roadside America en route to a new, uncertain future in northern and western cities.

Southern cotton fields and tobacco plantations had yielded but slender sustenance to African-American farmers, most of whom labored as tenants and sharecroppers. The Great Depression had been yet another setback, with many tenants evicted from their land as a result of New Deal farm programs that paid farmers to remove acreage from production. With few other opportunities in the depression-ravaged country, dispossessed former sharecroppers toiled as seasonal farm laborers or found themselves without work, without shelter, and without hope for the future.

The spanking new war plants and busy shipyards of the South offered little solace to African-Americans. In 1940 and 1941 the labor-hungry war machine soaked up white unemployment but commonly denied jobs to southerners with the "wrong" skin color. Fed up with such injustices, many African-Americans headed for shipyards, factories, foundries, and fields north of the Mason-Dixon line, where their willing hands found waiting work in abundance.

Angered by the racism that drove their people from the South, black leaders pressured President Roosevelt into declaring that "there shall be no discrimination in the employment of workers in defense industries or government because of race, creed, color, or national origin." This executive order was but a tenuous, rudimentary step; still, many African-Americans were heartened to see a presidential response to their protests. The war experience emboldened the civil rights movement, adding momentum and tactical knowledge to the cause. NAACP leader Walter White concluded that the war "immeasurably magnified the Negro's awareness of the disparity between the American profession and practice of democracy."

Detroit Race Riot, 1943 *A black passenger is dragged from a streetcar.*

By war's end, many African-Americans made new homes in the North and Far West, shifting the heart of America's black community from southern plantations to northern cities. There they competed for scarce housing in overcrowded slums and paid outrageous rents to secure a foothold in the few neighborhoods of northern cities that would admit them.

The entire nation was now grappling with the evil of racism, as bloody World War II–era riots in Detroit, New York, and other cities tragically revealed. The trek to northern cities was an economic boon for most African-Americans, but it did not end the intractable national problem of black poverty. Black teenage unemployment, a scourge to this day, dates from World War II. Southern farms, though providing the barest subsistence, had been all too generous in dispensing work to all members of the family—work not so readily found by African-American youth in today's decaying northern cities.

in movement rolled swiftly across the South, swelling into a wave of wade-ins, lie-ins, and pray-ins to compel equal treatment in restaurants, transportation, employment, housing, and voter registration. In April 1960 southern black students formed the Student Non-Violent Coordinating Committee (SNCC, pronounced "snick") to give more focus and force to these efforts. Young and impassioned, SNCC members would eventually lose patience with the more stately tactics of the SCLC and the even more deliberate legalisms of the NAACP.

Eisenhower Republicanism at Home

Balding, sixty-two-year-old General Eisenhower had entered the White House in 1953 pledging his administration to a philosophy of "dynamic conservatism." Above all, he strove to balance the federal budget and guard the Republic from what he called "creeping socialism." Eisenhower supported the transfer of control over offshore oil fields from the federal government to the states. Ike also tried to curb the TVA by encouraging a private power company to build a generating plant to compete with the massive public utility spawned by the New Deal. His secretary of health, education, and welfare condemned free distribution of Salk antipolio vaccine as "socialized medicine."

Eisenhower responded to the Mexican government's worry that illegal Mexican immigration to the United States would undercut the *bracero* program of legally imported farmworkers inaugurated during World War II (see p. 501). In a massive roundup of illegal aliens, as many as a million Mexicans were apprehended and returned to Mexico in 1954.

In yet another of the rude and arbitrary reversals that have long afflicted the government's relations with Native Americans, Eisenhower sought to cancel the tribal preservation policies of the "Indian New Deal," in place since 1934 (see p. 477). He proposed to "terminate" the tribes as legal entities and to return to the assimilationist goals of the Dawes Severalty Act (see p. 363). But most Indians resisted termination, and the policy was abandoned in 1961.

Eisenhower Republicans obviously could not unscramble all the eggs that had been fried by New Dealers and Fair Dealers for twenty long years. Eisenhower pragmatically accepted and thereby legitimated many New Dealish programs. During his presidency, Social Security benefits were extended and the minimum wage was raised to a dollar an hour. In a public works project that dwarfed anything the New Deal had ever dreamed of, Ike backed a $27 billion plan to build forty-two thousand miles of sleek, fast, interstate highways. The construction of these modern, multilane roads created countless construction jobs and speeded the suburbanization of America.

Ike's Foreign Policies

Mere "containment" of communism was condemned in the 1952 Republican platform as "negative, futile, and immoral." Incoming secretary of state John Foster Dulles promised not merely to stem the red tide but to "roll back" its gains and "liberate captive peoples." At the same time, the new administration promised to balance the budget by cutting military spending.

How were these two contradictory goals to be reached? Dulles answered with a "policy of boldness" in early 1954. Eisenhower would relegate the army and navy to the back seat and build up an air fleet of superbombers with city-flattening nuclear bombs. These fearsome weapons would be equipped to inflict "massive retaliation" on the Soviets if they got out of hand. At the same time, Eisenhower sought a thaw in the Cold War through negotiations with the new Soviet leaders who came to power after dictator Joseph Stalin's death in 1953.

In the end, the touted "new look" in foreign policy proved illusory. The new Soviet premier, Nikita Khrushchev, rudely rejected Ike's call in 1955 for "open skies" over both the Soviet Union and the United States. In 1956 the Hungarians rose up against their Soviet masters and felt betrayed when the United States refused their desperate appeals for aid. The crushed Hungarian uprising revealed the truth that America's mighty nuclear sledgehammer was too heavy a weapon to be used in such a confined crisis.

Western Europe, thanks to the Marshall Plan and NATO, seemed reasonably secure by the early 1950s, but East Asia was a different can of worms. In Vietnam and elsewhere, nationalist movements had fought for years to throw off the yoke of French colonialism. But Cold War events dampened the dreams of anticolonial Asian peoples. Their leaders—including Ho Chi Minh—became increasingly communist while the United States became increasingly anticommunist. By 1954 American taxpayers were financing nearly 80 percent of the costs of a bottomless French colonial war in Vietnam. The United States' share amounted to about $1 billion a year.

Despite this massive aid, French forces continued to crumble under guerrilla pressure. In March 1954 a key French garrison was trapped hopelessly in the fortress of Dienbienphu. The new "policy of boldness" was now put to the test. Secretary Dulles, Vice President Nixon, and the chairman of the Joint Chiefs of Staff favored intervention with American bombers to help bail out the beleaguered French. But Eisenhower, wary about another war in Asia soon after Korea, held back.

Dienbienphu fell to the nationalists, and a multination conference at Geneva roughly halved Vietnam at the seventeenth parallel. The victorious Ho Chi Minh in the north consented to this arrangement on the assurance that Vietnam-wide elections would be held within two years. In the south a pro-Western government under Ngo Dinh Diem was soon entrenched in Saigon. The Vietnamese never held the promised elections, primarily because the communists seemed certain to win, and Vietnam remained a dangerously divided country.

Eisenhower promised economic and military aid to the autocratic Diem regime, provided that it undertook certain social reforms. Change came at a snail's pace, but American aid continued as communist guerrillas heated up their campaign against Diem. The Americans had evidently backed a losing horse but could see no easy way to call off their bet.

Cold War Crises

The United States had initially backed the French in Vietnam in part to win French approval of a plan to rearm West Germany. Despite French fears, the Ger-

East Asia, 1955–1956

mans were finally welcomed into the NATO fold in 1955. In the same year, the Eastern European countries and the Soviets signed the Warsaw Pact, creating a red military counterweight to the newly bolstered NATO forces in the West.

Despite these hardening military lines, the Cold War seemed to be thawing a bit in 1955. In May the Soviets rather surprisingly agreed to end their occupation of Austria. A summit conference in Geneva, Switzerland, in July produced little progress on the burning issues, but it bred a conciliatory "spirit of Geneva" that caused a modest blush of optimism to pass over the face of the Western world.

Violent events late in 1956 ended the post-Geneva lull. When the liberty-loving Hungarians struck for their freedom, they were ruthlessly overpowered by Soviet tanks while the Western world looked on in horror.

Fears of Soviet penetration in the Middle East also heightened Cold War tensions. The government of Iran, supposedly influenced by the Kremlin, began to resist the power of the gigantic Western companies that controlled Iranian petroleum. In response, the American Central Intelligence Agency (CIA) engineered a coup in 1953 that installed the youthful shah of Iran as a kind of dictator. Though successful in the short run in securing Iranian oil for the West, the American intervention left a bitter legacy of resentment among many Iranians. More than two decades later, they took their revenge on the shah and his American allies (see p. 581).

The Suez crisis proved far messier than the swift strike in Iran. President Nasser of Egypt, an ardent Arab nationalist, had obtained tentative offers of American and British aid to build a dam on the Nile, but when Nasser began to flirt openly with the communist camp, Secretary of State Dulles dramatically withdrew the dam offer. Nasser promptly regained face by nationalizing the Suez Canal, owned chiefly by British and French stockholders.

Nasser's action placed a razor's edge at the jugular vein of Western Europe's oil supply. America's apprehensive British and French allies, coordinating their blow with one from Israel, staged a joint assault on Egypt late in October 1956. But under sharp pressure from the United States, including a threat to withhold U.S. oil supplies, the French and British resentfully withdrew their troops.

The Suez crisis marked the last time in history that the United States could brandish its oil weapon.

As recently as 1940, the United States had produced two-thirds of the world's oil, but by 1948 America had become a net oil importer. Its days as an "oil power" clearly were numbered as the economic and strategic importance of the Middle East oil region grew dramatically.

The U.S. president and Congress proclaimed the Eisenhower Doctrine in 1957, pledging U.S. military and economic aid to Middle Eastern nations threatened by communist aggression. The real threat to U.S. interests in the Middle East, however, was not communism but nationalism. The Arab countries increasingly resolved to reap for themselves the lion's share of the enormous oil wealth that Western companies pumped out of the scorching Middle Eastern deserts. In a portentous move, Saudi Arabia, Kuwait, Iraq, and Iran joined with Venezuela to form the Organization of Petroleum Exporting Countries (OPEC). In the next two decades, OPEC's stranglehold on the Western economies would tighten.

Round Two for Ike

The election of 1956 was a replay of the 1952 contest, with President Eisenhower pitted once more against Adlai Stevenson. Democrats were hard-pressed to find issues with which to attack the genial general in a time of prosperity and peace, and the voters made it clear that they still liked Ike. Eisenhower piled up an enormous majority of 35,590,472 popular votes to Stevenson's 26,022,752; in the Electoral College the vote was even more unbalanced at 457 to 73. But Eisenhower's victory was a distinctly personal one: he failed to win for his party either house of Congress.

In fragile health, Eisenhower began his second term as a part-time president. Critics charged that he had his hands on his golf clubs, fly rod, and shotgun more often than on the levers of power.

A key area in which the president bestirred himself was labor legislation. Congressional investigations revealed scandalous revelations of gangsterism in unionist high echelons, especially the Teamsters Union. The AF of L-CIO had already expelled the Teamsters for choosing leaders like tough-fisted James R. Hoffa, who was later convicted for jury tampering, served part of his sentence, and disappeared— evidently the victim of the gangsters whom he had apparently crossed. Even labor's friends agreed that the house of labor needed a thorough housecleaning. Eisenhower persuaded Congress in 1959 to pass the Landrum-Griffin Act, which was designed to bring labor leaders to book for financial shenanigans and to prevent bullying tactics. The law also prohibited "secondary boycotts" and certain kinds of picketing.

Soviet scientists astounded the world on October 4, 1957, by lofting into orbit around the globe a beep-beeping "baby moon" (*Sputnik I*), weighing 184 pounds. A month later they topped their own ace by sending aloft a larger satellite (*Sputnik II*), weighing 1,120 pounds and carrying a dog. This amazing scientific breakthrough shattered American self-confidence and seemed to show that the nation had taken a back seat in scientific achievement. The military implications of these satellites were also sobering. If the Soviets could fire heavy objects into outer space, they certainly could reach America with intercontinental ballistic missiles (ICBMs).

"Rocket fever" swept the nation. Eisenhower established the National Aeronautics and Space Administration (NASA) and directed billions of dollars to missile development. After humiliating and well-advertised failures—notably the Vanguard missile, which blew up on national television just a few feet above the ground—in February 1958 the United States managed to put into orbit a grapefruit-sized satellite weighing 2.5 pounds. By the end of the decade, several satellites had been launched, and the United States had successfully tested its own ICBM.

The *Sputnik* success led to a critical comparison of the American educational system—already under fire as too easygoing—with that of the Soviet Union. A strong move developed in the United States to replace "frills" with solid subjects—to substitute square roots for square dancing. Congress rejected demands for federal scholarships, but late in 1958 the National Defense and Education Act (NDEA) authorized $887 million for loans to needy college students and grants to improve instruction in science and languages.

The Continuing Cold War

The fantastic race toward nuclear annihilation continued unabated. Humanity-minded scientists urged that nuclear tests be stopped before the atmosphere became so polluted as to produce generations of deformed mutants. The Soviets, after completing an intensive series of exceptionally "dirty" tests, proclaimed a suspension in March 1958 and urged the Western world to follow. Beginning in October 1958, Washington did halt both underground and atmospheric testing. But attempts to regularize such suspensions by proper inspection sank on the reef of mutual mistrust.

Thermonuclear suicide seemed nearer in July 1958, when both Egyptian and communist plottings threatened to engulf Western-oriented Lebanon. After its president had called for aid under the Eisenhower Doctrine, the United States boldly landed several thousand troops and helped restore order without taking a single life.

The burly Nikita Khrushchev, Stalin's successor, was eager to meet with Eisenhower and pave the way for a "summit conference" with Western leaders. Since November 1958, Khrushchev had been demanding that the Western powers pull their troops out of West Berlin within six months. Despite grave misgivings as to any tangible results, the president invited the blustery Soviet leader to America in 1959. Arriving in New York, Khrushchev appeared before the U.N. General Assembly and dramatically resurrected the Soviet proposal of complete disarmament. But he offered no practical means of achieving this end.

A result of this tour was a meeting at Camp David, the presidential retreat in Maryland. Khrushchev emerged saying that his ultimatum for the evacuation of Berlin would be extended indefinitely. The relieved world gave prayerful but premature thanks for the "spirit of Camp David."

The Camp David spirit quickly evaporated when the follow-up Paris "summit conference," scheduled for May 1960, turned out to be a fiasco. Both Moscow and Washington had publicly taken a firm stand on the burning Berlin issue, and neither could risk a public backdown. Then, on the eve of the conference, an American U-2 spy plane was shot down deep in the heart of Russia. After bungling bureaucratic denials in Washington, "honest Ike" took the unprecedented step of assuming personal responsibility. Khrushchev stormed into Paris filling the air with invective, and the conference collapsed before it could get off the ground. The concord of Camp David was replaced with the grapes of wrath.

What's So Funny? 1960 *Premier Khrushchev gloats over "Ike's" spying discomfiture.*

Cuba's Castroism Spells Communism

Latin Americans bitterly resented Uncle Sam's lavishing of billions of dollars on Europe while doling out only millions to the poor relations to the south. They also chafed at Washington's habit of intervening in Latin American affairs. For example, a CIA-directed coup ousted a leftist government in Guatemala in 1954, but Washington supported bloody dictators who claimed to be combating communists.

Most ominous to U.S. policymakers was the communist beachhead in Cuba. Iron-fisted Cuban dictator Fulgencio Batista had encouraged huge investments of American capital, and Washington had given him some support. But early in 1959 black-bearded Fidel Castro engineered a revolution ousting Batista, denounced the Yankee imperialists, and began to expropriate valuable American properties in pursuing a land-distribution program. Washington, finally losing patience, released Cuba from "imperialistic slav-

ery" by cutting off the heavy U.S. imports of Cuban sugar. Castro retaliated with further wholesale confiscations of Yankee property and in effect made his left-wing dictatorship an economic and military satellite of Moscow. An exodus of anti-Castro Cubans headed for the United States, especially Florida. Nearly 750,000 arrived between 1960 and 1990. Washington broke diplomatic relations with Cuba early in 1961.

Americans talked seriously of invoking the Monroe Doctrine before the Soviets set up a communist base only ninety miles from their shores. Khrushchev angrily proclaimed that the Monroe Doctrine was dead and indicated that he would shower missiles on the United States if it attacked his good friend Castro.

Kennedy Challenges Nixon for the Presidency

Republicans approached the 1960 presidential campaign with Vice President Richard Nixon as their heir apparent. The "old" Nixon had been a no-holds-barred campaigner, especially in assailing Democrats and left-wingers. The "new" Nixon who appeared in 1960 was represented as a mature, seasoned statesman. Nixon gained stature with his global travels. He was nominated on the first ballot at the Republican convention in Chicago; his running mate was the patrician Henry Cabot Lodge, Jr., of Massachusetts.

By contrast, the Democratic race for the presidential nomination started as a free-for-all. John F. Kennedy—a tall, youthful, dark-haired, and tooth-flashing millionaire senator from Massachusetts—won impressive victories in the primaries. He then scored a first-ballot triumph in Los Angeles over his closest rival, Senator Lyndon B. Johnson, the Senate majority leader from Texas. A disappointed South was not completely appeased when Johnson accepted second place on the ticket.

Bigotry inevitably showed its snarling face. Senator Kennedy was a Roman Catholic, the first to be nominated since Al Smith's ill-starred campaign in 1928. Smear artists revived the ancient charges about the Pope's controlling the White House. Kennedy pointed to his fourteen years of service in Congress, denied that he would be swayed by Rome, and asked if some 40 million Catholic Americans were to be condemned to second-class citizenship from birth.

**Presidential Election of 1960
(with electoral vote by state)**
*Kennedy owed his hairbreadth
triumph to his victories in
twenty-six of the forty largest
cities—and to Lyndon Johnson's
strenuous campaigning in the
South, where Kennedy's Catholic
religion may have been a hotter
issue than his stand on civil
rights.*

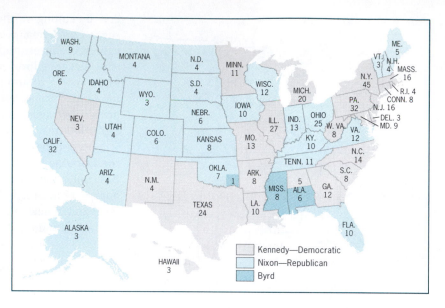

Kennedy's Catholicism aroused misgivings in the Protestant Bible Belt South, which was ordinarily Democratic. "I fear Catholicism more than I fear communism," declaimed one Baptist minister in North Carolina. But the religious issue largely canceled itself out. If many southern Democrats stayed away from the polls because of Kennedy's Catholicism, northern Democrats in unusually large numbers supported Kennedy because of the bitter attacks on their Catholic faith.

Kennedy charged that the Soviets, with their nuclear bombs and circling *Sputniks*, had gained on America in prestige and power. Nixon replied that the nation's prestige had not slipped, although Kennedy was causing it to do so by his unpatriotic talk. A series of television debates between the contestants may have tipped the scales. Nobody "won" the debates, but Kennedy held his own with the more experienced Nixon. The debates demonstrated the importance of image in a television age. Many viewers found Kennedy's glamour and vitality far more appealing than Nixon's tired and pallid appearance.

Kennedy squeezed through by the rather comfortable margin of 303 electoral votes to 219, but with a breathtakingly close popular margin of only 118,574 votes out of over 68 million cast. Like Franklin Roosevelt, Kennedy ran well in the large industrial cen-ters, where he had strong support from workers, Catholics, and African-Americans. (He had solicitously telephoned the pregnant Coretta King, whose husband, Martin Luther King, Jr., was then imprisoned in Georgia for participating in a sit-in.) Despite losing a few seats, the Democrats swept both houses of Congress by wide margins.

An Old General Fades Away

President Eisenhower continued to enjoy extraordinary popularity to the final curtain. Despite Democratic gibes about "eight years of golfing and goofing," of "putting and puttering," Eisenhower was universally admired and respected for his dignity, decency, sincerity, goodwill, and moderation.

Pessimists had predicted that Eisenhower would be a seriously crippled lame duck during his second term, owing to the barrier against reelection erected by the Twenty-second Amendment, ratified in 1951 (see the Appendix). In truth, he displayed more vigor, more political know-how, and more aggressive leadership during his last two years as president than ever before.

America was fabulously prosperous in the Eisenhower years, despite pockets of poverty and unemployment, recurrent recessions, and perennial farm problems. To the north the vast St. Lawrence water-way project, constructed jointly with Canada and completed in 1959, had turned the cities of the Great Lakes into bustling ocean seaports.

"Old Glory" could now proudly display fifty stars. Alaska and Hawaii both attained statehood in 1959. Alaska, though gigantic, was thinly populated and economically underdeveloped, but these objections were overcome in a Democratic Congress that expected Alaska to vote Democratic. Hawaii had ample population (largely of Asian descent), advanced democratic institutions, and more acreage than Rhode Island, Delaware, or Connecticut. As the first noncontiguous states to join the Union, Alaska and Hawaii helped turn America's face toward the Pacific and East Asia.

Though a crusading general, Eisenhower as pres-ident mounted no moral crusade for civil rights. This was perhaps his greatest failing. Yet he had done far more than grin away problems and tread water. As a Republican president, he had further woven the reforms of the Democratic New Deal and Fair Deal into the fabric of national life. As a former general, he had exercised wise restraint in his use of military power and had soberly guided foreign policy away from countless threats to peace. He had ended one war and avoided all others. As the decades length-ened, appreciation of him grew.

Changing Economic Patterns

The continuing post–World War II economic boom wrought wondrous changes in American society in the 1950s. Prosperity triggered a fabulous surge in home construction: one of every four homes stand-ing in America in 1960 had been built in the 1950s.

More than ever, science and technology drove economic growth. The invention of the transistor in 1948 sparked a revolution in electronics, especially in computers. The first electronic computers in the 1940s were massive machines, but eventually per-sonal computers contained more computing power than room-size earlier models. Computer giant Inter-national Business Machines (IBM) became the proto-type "high-tech" corporation in the dawning "information age."

The nature of the work force was also changing. A sort of quiet revolution was marked in 1956, when "white-collar" workers for the first time outnumbered "blue-collar" workers, signaling the passage from an industrial to a postindustrial era. Keeping pace with that fundamental transformation, organized labor withered as a percentage of the labor force, after peaking at about 35 percent in 1954.

The surge in white-collar employment opened special opportunities for women. Postwar culture developed a "cult of domesticity" celebrating the con-ventional female roles of wife and mother, portrayed on television programs like "Ozzie and Harriet" and "Leave It to Beaver." But it did so without irony. Much of middle-class America really did live in suburban households with a working husband and a wife who did not work outside the home.

But exploding employment opportunities in the 1950s, including 30 million new clerical and service jobs filled largely by women, unleashed a groundswell of social and psychological change that mounted to tidal-wave proportions in the decades that followed. Feminist Betty Friedan gave focus and fuel to women's feelings in 1963 when she published *The Feminine Mystique*, a runaway best-seller and a classic of the modern women's movement. Friedan spoke in rousing accents to millions of able, educated women who were already working for wages but also struggling against the guilt and frustration of trying to live up to the feminine "ideal" as defined by the post-war "cult of domesticity."

Consumer Culture in the Fifties

The 1950s witnessed a huge expansion of the middle class and the blossoming of a consumer culture. Diner's Club introduced the plastic credit card in 1950, and four years later the first McDonald's hamburger stand opened in San Bernardino, California. Also in 1955, Disneyland opened its doors in Anaheim, Cali-fornia. These innovations—easy credit, high-volume "fast-food" production, and new forms of recreation—were harbingers of an emerging new lifestyle of afflu-ence that was in full flower by the decade's end.

Crucial to the development of that lifestyle was the rapid rise of the new technology of television.

Only 6 TV stations were broadcasting in 1946; a decade later 442 stations were operating. TV sets were rich people's novelties in the 1940s, but 7 million sets were sold in 1951. By 1960 virtually every American home had one, in a stunning display of the speed with which new technologies can pervade and transform modern societies. By the mid-1950s advertisers annually spent $10 billion to hawk their wares on television, while critics fumed that the wildly popular new mass medium was degrading the public's esthetic, moral, political, and educational standards.

Even religion capitalized on the powerful new electronic pulpit. "Televangelists" like the Baptist Billy Graham, the Pentecostal preacher Oral Roberts, and the Roman Catholic Fulton J. Sheen took to the airwaves to spread the Christian gospel. Television also catalyzed the commercialization of professional sports, as viewing audiences that once numbered in the stadium-capacity thousands could now be counted in the couch-potato millions.

Sports also reflected the shift in population toward the West and South. In 1958 baseball's New York Giants moved to San Francisco and the Brooklyn Dodgers abandoned Flatbush for Los Angeles. Those moves touched off a new westward movement—of sports franchises. Shifting population and spreading affluence led eventually to substantial expansion of the major baseball leagues and the principal football and basketball leagues as well.

Popular music was also dramatically transformed in the 1950s. The chief revolutionary was Elvis Presley, a white singer born in 1935 in Tupelo, Mississippi. Fusing black rhythm and blues with white bluegrass and country styles, Elvis created a new musical idiom known forever after as rock and roll. Rock was "crossover" music, carrying its heavy beat and driving rhythms across the cultural divide that separated black and white musical traditions. Listening and dancing to it quickly became a kind of religious rite for the millions of baby boomers coming of age in the 1950s.

Traditionalists were repelled by Presley, and they found much more to upset them in the affluent decade. Movie star Marilyn Monroe, with her ingenuous smile and mandolin-curved hips, helped to popularize—and commercialize—new standards of sensuous sexuality. So did *Playboy* magazine, first published in 1955. As the decade closed, Americans were well on their way to becoming free-spending consumers of mass-produced, standardized products advertised on the electronic medium of television and often sold for their alleged sexual allure.

Many critics lamented the implications of this new consumerist lifestyle. Harvard sociologist David Riesman criticized the postwar generation as con-

The King *Rock superstar Elvis Presley greets a group of adoring fans in the 1950s.*

formists in *The Lonely Crowd* (1950), as did William H. Whyte, Jr., in *The Organization Man*. Harvard economist John Kenneth Galbraith questioned the relation between private wealth and the public good in a series of books beginning with *The Affluent Society* (1958). The postwar explosion of prosperity, Galbraith claimed, had produced a troublesome combination of private opulence amid public squalor. Americans had televisions in their homes but garbage in their streets. They ate rich food but breathed foul air. Galbraith's call for social spending to match private purchasing proved highly influential in the 1960s.

Sociologist Daniel Bell, in *The Coming of Post-Industrial Society* (1973) and *The Cultural Contradictions of Capitalism* (1976), found even deeper paradoxes of prosperity. The hedonistic "consumer ethic" of modern capitalism, he argued, might undermine the older "work ethic" and thus destroy capitalism's very productive capacity. Collusion at the highest level of the military-industrial complex was the subject of *The Power Elite* (1956), an influential piece of modern muckraking by radical sociologist C. Wright Mills, who became a hero to New Left student activists in the 1960s.

The Life of the Mind in Postwar America

America's affluence in the heady post–World War II decades was matched by a mother lode of literary gems. In fiction writing some of the prewar realists continued to ply their trade, notably Ernest Hemingway in *The Old Man and the Sea* (1952). A Nobel laureate in 1954, Hemingway was dead by his own duck gun in 1961. John Steinbeck, another prewar writer who persisted in graphic portrayals of American society, such as *East of Eden* (1952) and *Travels with Charley* (1962), received the Nobel Prize for literature in 1962, the seventh American to be so honored.

Curiously, World War II did not inspire the same kind of literary outpouring that World War I had. Searing realism, the trademark style of war writers in the 1920s, characterized the earliest novels that portrayed soldierly life in World War II, such as Norman Mailer's *The Naked and the Dead* (1948) and James Jones's *From Here to Eternity* (1951). But as time passed, realistic writing fell from favor. Authors tended increasingly to write about the war in fantastic and even psychedelic prose. Joseph Heller's *Catch-22* (1961) dealt with the improbable antics and anguish of American airmen in the wartime Mediterranean. A savage satire, it made readers hurt when they laughed.

The dilemmas created by the new mobility and affluence of American life were explored by Pennsylvania-born John Updike in books like *Rabbit, Run* (1960) and *Couples* (1968), and by Massachusetts-bred John Cheever in *The Wapshot Chronicle* (1957) and *The Wapshot Scandal* (1964).

Younger poets were also coming to the fore during the postwar period. Pacific northwesterner Theodore Roethke wrote lyrically about the land until his death by drowning in Puget Sound in 1963. Robert Lowell, descended from a long line of patrician New Englanders, sought to apply the wisdom of the Puritan past to the perplexing present in allegorical poems like *For the Union Dead* (1964). Troubled Sylvia Plath crafted the moving verses of *Ariel* (published posthumously in 1966) and a disturbing novel, *The Bell Jar* (1963), but her career was cut short when she took her own life in 1963. Anne Sexton produced brooding autobiographical poems until her death by apparent suicide in 1974. Another brilliant poet of the period, John Berryman, ended it all in 1972 by leaping from a Minneapolis bridge onto the frozen bank of the Mississippi River. Writing poetry seemed to be a dangerous pursuit in modern America. The life of the poet, it was said, began in sadness and ended in madness.

Playwrights were also active. Tennessee Williams wrote a series of searing dramas about psychological misfits struggling to hold themselves together amid the disintegrating forces of modern life. Noteworthy were *A Streetcar Named Desire* (1947) and *Cat on a Hot Tin Roof* (1955). Arthur Miller brought to the stage searching probes of American values, notably *Death of a Salesman* (1949) and *The Crucible* (1953), which treated the Salem witch trials as a dark parable warning against the dangers of McCarthyism. Lorraine Hansberry offered an affecting portrait of African-American life in *A Raisin in the Sun* (1959). In the 1960s Edward Albee exposed the rapacious underside of middle-class life in *Who's Afraid of Virginia Woolf?* (1962).

Books by black authors also made the best-seller lists, beginning with Richard Wright's chilling portrait of a black Chicago killer in *Native Son* (1940). Ralph Ellison depicted the black individual's quest for personal identity in *Invisible Man* (1952), one of the most haunting novels of the postwar era. James Baldwin won plaudits as a novelist and essayist, particularly for his sensitive reflections on the racial question in *The Fire Next Time* (1963). Black nationalist LeRoi Jones, who changed his name to Imamu Amiri Baraka, crafted powerful plays like *Dutchman* (1964).

Many southern writers grasped the torch after William Faulkner died in 1962. Robert Penn Warren immortalized Louisiana politico Huey Long in *All the King's Men* (1946). Flannery O'Connor wrote perceptively of her native Georgia, and Virginian William Styron confronted the harsh history of his home state in a controversial fictional representation of an 1831 slave rebellion, *The Confessions of Nat Turner* (1967).

Especially bountiful was the harvest of books by Jewish novelists. Some critics quipped that a knowledge of Yiddish was becoming necessary to understanding much of the dialogue presented in modern American novels. J. D. Salinger painted an unforgettable portrait of a sensitive, upper-class, Anglo-Saxon adolescent in *Catcher in the Rye* (1951), but other Jewish writers found their favorite subject matter in the experience of lower- and middle-class Jewish immigrants. Bernard Malamud rendered a touching portrait of a family of New York Jewish storekeepers in *The Assistant* (1957). Chicagoan Saul Bellow contributed masterful sketches of Jewish urban and literary life in *The Adventures of Augie March* (1953) and *Herzog* (1962). Bellow became the eighth American Nobel laureate for literature in 1977.

Chronology

1952   Eisenhower defeats Stevenson for presidency.

1953   CIA-engineered coup installs shah of Iran.

1954   French defeated in Vietnam.
Army-McCarthy hearings.
Brown v. *Board of Education.*
CIA-sponsored coup in Guatemala.

1955   Montgomery bus boycott begins; emergence of Martin Luther King, Jr.
Warsaw Pact signed.
AF of L merges with CIO.

1956   Soviets crush Hungarian revolt.
Suez crisis.
Eisenhower defeats Stevenson for presidency.

1957   Little Rock school desegregation crisis.
Southern Christian Leadership Conference (SCLC) formed.
Eisenhower Doctrine.
Soviet Union launches *Sputnik* satellite.

1958   U.S. troops sent to Lebanon.
NDEA authorizes loans and grants for science and language education.

1958–1959   Berlin crisis.

1959   Castro leads Cuban revolution.
Landrum-Griffin Act.
Alaska and Hawaii attain statehood.

1960   Sit-in movement for civil rights begins.
U-2 incident sabotages Paris summit.
OPEC formed.
Kennedy defeats Nixon for presidency.

For further reading, see the Appendix. For web resources, go to **http://college.hmco.com**.

The Stormy Sixties

1960–1968

*In the final analysis it is their war. They are the ones
who have to win it or lose it . . . the people of Vietnam.*

JOHN F. KENNEDY, SEPTEMBER 1963

Complacent and comfortable as the 1950s closed, Americans elected in 1960 a young, vigorous president who pledged "to get the country moving again." Neither the nation nor the new president had any inkling, as the new decade opened, of just how action-packed it would be both at home and abroad. The 1960s would bring a sexual revolution, a civil rights revolution, the emergence of a "youth culture," a devastating war in Vietnam, and the beginnings, at least, of a feminist revolution. By the end of the stormy sixties, many Americans would yearn nostalgically for the comparative calm of the fifties.

Kennedy's New Frontier

Hatless and topcoatless in the 22°F chill, John F. Kennedy delivered a stirring inaugural address on January 20, 1961. Tall, elegantly handsome, speaking crisply and with staccato finger jabs at the air, Kennedy personified the youth, glamour, and vitality of the new administration. The youngest president ever elected, he assembled one of the youngest cabinets, including his thirty-five-year-old brother, Robert, as attorney general. "Bobby," the president quipped, would find "some legal experience" useful when he began to practice law.

From the outset Kennedy inspired high expectations, especially among the young. His challenge of a "New Frontier" quickened patriotic pulses. He brought a warm heart to the Cold War when he proposed the Peace Corps, an army of idealistic and mostly youthful volunteers, to bring American skills to underdeveloped countries.

Kennedy came into office with fragile Democratic majorities in Congress. Southern Democrats threatened to team up with Republicans and ax New Frontier proposals such as medical assistance for the aged and increased federal aid to education.

Another vexing problem was the economy. Kennedy had campaigned on the theme of revitalizing the economy after the recessions of the Eisenhower years. His administration helped negotiate a noninflationary wage agreement in the steel industry in early 1962. The assumption was that the companies, for their part, would keep the lid on prices. But almost immediately, steel management announced significant price increases, thereby seemingly demonstrating bad faith. The president erupted in wrath, remarking that his father had once said that "all businessmen were sons of bitches." He called the "big steel" men onto the Oval Office carpet and unleashed his Irish temper. Overawed, the steel operators backed down.

The steel episode provoked fiery attacks by big business on the New Frontier, but Kennedy soon appealed to believers in free enterprise when he announced his support of a general tax-cut bill. He chose to stimulate the economy by slashing taxes and putting more money directly into private hands. When he announced his policy before a big-business group, one observer called it "the most Republican speech since McKinley."

Kennedy also promoted a multibillion-dollar project to land an American on the moon. When skeptics objected that the money could best be spent elsewhere, Kennedy "answered" them in a speech at Rice University in Texas: "But why, some say, the moon? . . . And they may well ask, why climb the highest mountain? Why, thirty-five years ago, fly the Atlantic? Why does Rice play Texas?" Twenty-four billion dollars later, in 1969, two American astronauts triumphantly planted human footprints on the moon's dusty surface.

Rumblings in Europe

A few months after settling into the White House, the new president met Premier Nikita Khrushchev at Vienna in June 1961. The tough-talking Soviet leader adopted a belligerent attitude, threatening to cut off Western access to Berlin. Though visibly shaken, the president refused to be bullied. The Soviets backed off from their most bellicose threats but suddenly began to construct the Berlin Wall in August 1961. A barbed-wire-and-concrete barrier, the "Wall of Shame" looked to the free world like a gigantic enclosure around a concentration camp. The Wall stood for almost three decades as an ugly scar symbolizing the post–World War II division of Europe into two hostile camps.

Kennedy meanwhile turned his attention to Western Europe, now miraculously prospering after the Marshall Plan and the growth of the Common Market, a trading union of six Western European nations formed in 1957. He finally secured passage of the Trade Expansion Act in 1962, authorizing tariff cuts of up to 50 percent to promote trade with the countries of the Common Market (later called the European Union).

But not all of Kennedy's ambitious designs for Europe were realized. American policymakers were dedicated to an economically and militarily united "Atlantic Community," with the United States the dominant partner. But they found their way blocked by towering, stiff-backed Charles de Gaulle, president of France. De Gaulle deemed the Americans unreliable in a crisis, so he tried to preserve French freedom of action by developing his own small atomic force. Despite the perils of nuclear proliferation or Soviet domination, de Gaulle demanded an independent Europe, free of Yankee influence.

Foreign Flare-ups and "Flexible Response"

Special problems for U.S. foreign policy emerged from the worldwide decolonization of European overseas possessions after World War II. Many of the new nations emerging from once-colonial Asia and Africa were critical of U.S. foreign policy, while some became battlegrounds between the noncommunist and the communist worlds.

Sparsely populated Laos, freed of its French colonial overlords in 1954, was festering dangerously by the time Kennedy came into office. The Eisenhower administration had drenched this jungle kingdom with dollars but failed to cleanse the country of an aggressive communist element. A red Laos, many observers feared, would be a river on which the influence of communist China would flood into all of Southeast Asia.

As the Laotian civil war raged, Kennedy's military advisers seriously considered sending in American troops. But the president found that he had insufficient forces to put out the fire in Asia and still honor his commitments in Europe. Kennedy thus sought a diplomatic escape hatch in the fourteen-power Geneva conference, which imposed a shaky peace in Laos in 1962.

These "brushfire wars" intensified the pressure for a shift away from Secretary Dulles's dubious doctrine of "massive retaliation." Kennedy felt hamstrung by the knowledge that in a crisis he had the Devil's choice between humiliation or nuclear incineration. With Defense Secretary Robert McNamara, he pushed the strategy of "flexible response"—that is, developing an array of military "options" that could be precisely matched to the scope and importance of the crisis at hand. To this end, Kennedy increased spending on conventional military forces and bolstered the Special Forces ("Green Berets")—an elite anti-guerrilla outfit trained to survive on snake meat and to kill with scientific finesse.

"Backbone" *The United States supports South Vietnam.*

Stepping into the Vietnam Quagmire

The doctrine of "flexible response" seemed sane enough, but it contained lethal logic. It potentially lowered the level at which diplomacy would give way to shooting. It also provided a mechanism for a progressive, and possibly endless, stepping-up of the use of force. Vietnam soon presented a grisly demonstration of these pitfalls.

The corrupt, right-wing Diem government in Saigon, despite a deluge of American dollars, had ruled shakily since the partition of Vietnam in 1954. Anti-Diem agitators noisily threatened to topple the pro-American government from power. In a fateful decision late in 1961, Kennedy ordered a sharp increase in the number of "military advisers" (U.S. troops) in South Vietnam.

American forces allegedly entered Vietnam to foster political stability—to help protect Diem from the communists long enough to allow him to enact basic social reforms favored by the Americans. But the Kennedy administration eventually despaired of the reactionary Diem and encouraged a successful coup against him in November 1963. Ironically, the United States thus contributed to a long process of political disintegration that its original policy had meant to prevent. Kennedy still told the South Vietnamese that it was "their war," but he had made dangerously deep political commitments. By the time of his death, he had ordered more than fifteen thousand American men into the far-off Asian slaughterpen. A graceful pullout was becoming increasingly difficult.

Cuban Confrontations

Although the United States regarded Latin America as its backyard, its southern neighbors feared and resented the powerful "Colossus of the North." In 1961 Kennedy extended the hand of friendship with the Alliance for Progress (*Alianza para el Progreso*), hailed as a Marshall Plan for Latin America. But results were disappointing; there was little alliance and even less progress. American handouts had a negligible impact on Latin America's immense social problems.

President Kennedy also struck below the border with the mailed fist. He had inherited from the Eisenhower administration a CIA-backed scheme to topple Fidel Castro from power by invading Cuba with anticommunist exiles. On a fateful April 17, 1961, some twelve hundred exiles landed at Cuba's Bay of Pigs. When the invasion bogged down, the bullet-riddled band of anti-Castroites surrendered. President Kennedy assumed full responsibility for the failure, remarking that "victory has a hundred fathers, and defeat is an orphan."

The Bay of Pigs blunder, along with continuing American covert efforts to assassinate Castro and overthrow his government, naturally pushed the Cuban leader even further into the Soviet embrace. Wily Chairman Khrushchev lost little time taking full advantage of his Cuban comrade's position just ninety miles off Florida's coast. In October 1962 aerial photographs from American spy planes revealed that the Soviets were secretly and speedily installing nuclear-tipped missiles in Cuba.

Kennedy and Khrushchev now began a nerve-racking game of "nuclear chicken." The president, on October 22, 1962, ordered a naval "quarantine" of Cuba and demanded immediate removal of the threatening weaponry. He also served notice on Khrushchev that any attack on the United States from Cuba would be regarded as coming from the Soviet Union and would trigger nuclear retaliation against the Russian heartland. For an anxious week, Americans waited while Soviet ships approached the patrol line established by the U.S. Navy off Cuba. The world teetered breathlessly on the brink of global atomization.

In this tense eyeball-to-eyeball confrontation, Khrushchev finally flinched. On October 28 he agreed to a partially face-saving compromise, by which he would pull the missiles out of Cuba. The United States in return agreed to end the quarantine and not invade the island.

Fallout from the Cuban missile crisis was considerable. A disgraced Khrushchev was ultimately hounded

out of the Kremlin and became an "unperson." Kennedy, apparently sobered by the appalling risks he had just run, pushed harder for a nuclear test-ban treaty with the Soviet Union. After prolonged negotiations in Moscow, a pact prohibiting trial nuclear explosions in the atmosphere was signed in late 1963.

Most significant was Kennedy's speech at American University, Washington, D.C., in June 1963. The president urged Americans to abandon a view of the Soviet Union as a Devil-ridden land filled with fanatics and instead to deal with the world "as it is, not as it might have been had the history of the last eighteen years been different." Kennedy thus tried to lay the foundations for a realistic policy of peaceful coexistence with the Soviet Union. Here were the modest origins of the policy that later came to be known as *détente* (French for "relaxation").

The Struggle for Civil Rights

Kennedy had campaigned with a strong appeal to black voters, but he proceeded gingerly to redeem his promises. Although he had pledged to eliminate racial discrimination in housing "with a stroke of the pen," it took him nearly two years to find the right pen. Civil rights groups meanwhile sent thousands of pens to the White House in an "Ink for Jack" protest against the president's slowness.

Political concerns stayed the president's hand on civil rights. Elected by a wafer-thin margin and with shaky control over Congress, Kennedy needed the support of southern legislators to pass his economic and social legislation, especially his medical and educational bills. But events soon scrambled these careful calculations.

After the wave of sit-ins that surged across the South in 1960, groups of Freedom Riders fanned out to end segregation in facilities serving interstate bus passengers. A white mob torched a Freedom Ride bus near Anniston, Alabama, in May 1961, and Attorney General Robert Kennedy's personal representative was beaten unconscious in another anti–Freedom Ride riot in Montgomery. When southern officials proved unwilling or unable to stem the violence, Washington dispatched federal marshals to protect the Freedom Riders.

Freedom Ride, 1961   *Rampaging whites near Anniston, Alabama, burned this bus carrying an interracial group of Freedom Riders on May 14, 1961.*

Reluctantly but fatefully, the Kennedy administration had now joined hands with the civil rights movement. For the most part, the relationship between Martin Luther King, Jr., and the Kennedys was a fruitful one. Encouraged by Robert Kennedy, SNCC and other civil rights groups inaugurated a Voter Education Project to register the South's historically disfranchised blacks.

Integrating southern universities threatened to provoke wholesale slaughter. Some desegregated painlessly, but the University of Mississippi ("Ole Miss") became a volcano. A twenty-nine-year-old air force veteran, James Meredith, encountered violent opposition when he attempted to register in October 1962. In the end President Kennedy was forced to send in four hundred federal marshals and three thousand troops to enroll Meredith in his first class—in colonial American history.

In the spring of 1963, Martin Luther King, Jr., launched a campaign against discrimination in Birmingham, Alabama, the most segregated big city in America. Although they constituted nearly half the city's population, blacks made up fewer than 15 percent of the city's voters. Previous attempts to crack

rigid racial barriers had produced more than fifty cross burnings and eighteen bomb attacks since 1957. "Some of the people sitting here will not come back alive from this campaign," King advised his organizers. Events soon confirmed this grim prediction. Watching developments on television screens, a horrified world saw peaceful civil rights marchers repeatedly repelled by police with attack dogs and electric cattle prods. Most fearsome were the high-pressure water hoses directed at the civil rights demonstrators. They delivered water with enough force to knock bricks loose from buildings or strip bark from trees at a distance of one hundred feet. Water from the hoses bowled little children down the street like tumbleweed.

Jolted by these vicious confrontations, President Kennedy delivered a memorable televised speech to the nation on June 11, 1963. He called the situation a "moral crisis" and pleaded for new civil rights legislation to protect black citizens. On the very night of that stirring appeal, a white gunman shot down Medgar Evers, a Mississippi civil rights worker. In August, Martin Luther King, Jr., led 200,000 black and white demonstrators on a peaceful "March on

Washington" in support of the proposed civil rights legislation. Still the violence continued. In September 1963 an explosion blasted a Baptist church in Birmingham, killing four black girls who had just finished their Sunday school lesson called "The Love That Forgives."

The Killing of Kennedy

Violence haunted America in the mid-1960s and stalked onto center stage on November 22, 1963. While riding in an open limousine in downtown Dallas, Texas, President Kennedy was shot in the head by a concealed rifleman and died within seconds. As a stunned nation nursed its grief, the tragedy grew still more unbelievable. The alleged assassin, a furtive figure named Lee Harvey Oswald, was himself shot to death in front of the television cameras by a self-appointed avenger, Jack Ruby. So bizarre were the events surrounding the two murders that even an elaborate official investigation conducted by Chief Justice Warren could not quiet all doubts and theories about what had really happened. Vice President Johnson, sworn in as president on a waiting airplane in Dallas, managed a dignified and efficient transition, pledging continuity with his slain predecessor's policies.

For several days, the nation was steeped in sorrow. Not until then did many Americans realize how fully their young, vibrant president and his captivating wife had cast a spell over them. Chopped down in his prime after only slightly more than a thousand days in the White House, Kennedy was acclaimed more for the ideals he had enunciated and the spirit he had kindled than for the concrete goals he had achieved. He had laid one myth to rest forever—that a Catholic could not be trusted with the presidency of the United States.

In later years revelations about Kennedy's womanizing and allegations about his involvement with organized crime figures tarnished his reputation. But despite those accusations, his vigor, charisma, and idealism made him an inspirational figure for the generation of Americans who came of age in the 1960s—including Bill Clinton, who as a boy briefly met President Kennedy and was himself elected president in 1992.

The LBJ Brand on the Presidency

The torch passed to craggy-faced Lyndon Baines Johnson, a Texan who towered 6 feet, 3 inches. As the Senate majority leader in the Eisenhower years, Johnson developed into a master wheeler-dealer. He could move political mountains or checkmate opponents as the occasion demanded, using what came to be known as the "Johnson treatment"—a flashing display of backslapping, flesh-pressing, and arm-twisting that overbore friend and foe alike.

As president, Johnson quickly shed the conservative coloration of his Senate years to reveal the latent liberal underneath. Seeking to carry on his predecessor's legacy, Johnson rammed Kennedy's stalled tax-cut and civil rights bills through Congress and added proposals of his own for a billion-dollar "War on Poverty."

Johnson's nomination by the Democrats in 1964 was a foregone conclusion. He had dubbed his popular domestic program the "Great Society"—a sweeping set of New Dealish economic and welfare measures aimed at transforming the American way of life. Public support for LBJ's antipoverty war was aroused by Michael Harrington's *The Other America* (1962), which revealed that in affluent America 20 percent of the population—and over 40 percent of the black population—suffered in poverty.

The Republicans, convening in San Francisco, nominated box-jawed Senator Barry Goldwater of Arizona, a bronzed and bespectacled champion of rock-ribbed conservatism. The American stage was thus set for a historic clash of political principles.

Goldwater's forces had galloped out of the Southwest to ride roughshod over the moderate Republican "eastern establishment." Goldwater attacked the federal income tax, the Social Security system, the Tennessee Valley Authority, civil rights legislation, the nuclear test-ban treaty, and, most loudly, the Great Society. His fiercely dedicated followers proclaimed, "In Your Heart You Know He's Right," which prompted the Democratic response, "In Your Guts You Know He's Nuts." Goldwater warmed right-wing hearts when he announced that "extremism in the defense of liberty is no vice. And moderation . . . in the pursuit of justice is no virtue."

Johnson cultivated the contrasting image of a resolute statesman by seizing upon the Tonkin Gulf episode early in August 1964. Unbeknownst to the American public or Congress, U.S. Navy ships had been cooperating with South Vietnamese gunboats in provocative raids along the coast of North Vietnam. Two of these American destroyers were allegedly fired upon by the North Vietnamese on August 2 and 4, although exactly what happened remains unclear. Later investigations strongly suggested that the North Vietnamese fired in self-defense on August 2 and that the "attack" of August 4 never happened. Johnson later wisecracked, "For all I know, the Navy was shooting at whales out there."

Johnson nevertheless promptly called the attacks "unprovoked" and moved swiftly to make political hay out of this episode. He ordered a "limited" retaliatory air raid against the North Vietnamese bases, loudly proclaiming that he sought "no wider war"—thus implying that the truculent Goldwater did. Johnson also used the incident to spur congressional passage of the all-purpose Tonkin Gulf Resolution. With only two dissenting votes in both houses of Congress the lawmakers virtually abdicated their war-declaring powers and handed the president a blank check to use further force in Southeast Asia.

The towering Texan rode to a spectacular victory in November 1964. The voters were herded into Johnson's column by fondness for the Kennedy legacy, faith in Great Society promises, and fear of Goldwater. A stampede of 43,129,566 Johnson votes trampled the Republican ticket, with its 27,178,188 supporters. The tally in the Electoral College was 486 to 52. Goldwater carried only his native Arizona and five other states—all of them, significantly, in the racially restless South. Johnson's record-breaking 61 percent of the popular vote swept lopsided Democratic majorities into both houses of Congress.

The Great Society Congress

Johnson's huge victory temporarily smashed the conservative coalition of southern Democrats and northern Republicans. A wide-open legislative road stretched before the Great Society programs, as the president skillfully ringmastered his two-to-one Democratic majorities. Congress poured out a flood of legislation, comparable only to the output of the New Dealers in the Hundred Days Congress of 1933, as Johnson at last delivered on long-delayed Democratic promises of social reform.

Besides a greatly expanded War on Poverty, other landmark laws flowed from Johnson's "hip-pocket Congress." Medicare for the elderly became a reality in 1965. Although it was a bitter pill for the American Medical Association to swallow, the system was welcomed by millions of older Americans who were being pushed into poverty by skyrocketing medical costs.

A tireless Johnson also prodded the Congress into creating two new cabinet offices: the Department of Transportation and the Department of Housing and Urban Development (HUD). He named the first black cabinet member in the nation's history, noted economist Robert C. Weaver, to be secretary of HUD.

Great Society programs came in for rancorous political attack in later years. Conservatives charged that poverty could not be papered over with greenbacks, yet the poverty rate did decline measurably in the ensuing decade. Medicare dramatically reduced poverty among America's elderly, and antipoverty programs like Project Head Start sharply improved the educational performance of underprivileged youth. Lyndon Johnson was not fully victorious in the war against poverty, but he did win several noteworthy battles.

Battling for Black Rights

In Johnson's native South, the walls of segregation were crumbling, but not fast enough for long-suffering African-Americans. The Civil Rights Act of 1964 gave the federal government more muscle to enforce school desegregation orders and to prohibit racial discrimination in all kinds of public accommodations and employment. But the problem of voting rights remained. In Mississippi, which had the largest black minority of any state, only about 5 percent of eligible blacks were registered to vote. The lopsided pattern was similar throughout the South. Ballot-denying devices like the poll tax, literacy tests, and bare-faced intimidation still barred black people from the political process.

Beginning in 1964, opening up the polling booths became the chief goal of the black movement in the South. The Twenty-fourth Amendment, ratified in January 1964, abolished the poll tax in federal elections (see the Appendix). Blacks joined hands with white civil rights workers—many of them student volunteers from the North—in a massive voter-registration drive in Mississippi during the "Freedom Summer" of 1964. Singing "We Shall Overcome," they zealously set out to soothe generations of white anxieties and black fears.

But events soon blighted bright hopes. In late June 1964, one black and two white civil rights workers disappeared in Mississippi. Their badly beaten bodies were later found buried beneath an earthen dam. In August an integrated "Mississippi Freedom Democratic Party" delegation was denied its seat at the national Democratic convention.

Early in 1965 Martin Luther King, Jr., resumed the voter-registration campaign in Selma, Alabama. State troopers with tear gas and whips assaulted King's peaceful demonstrators. A Boston Unitarian minister was killed, and a few days later a white Detroit woman was shotgunned to death by Klansmen on the highway near Selma.

As the nation recoiled in horror before these violent scenes, President Johnson, speaking in soft southern accents, delivered a compelling address on television. What happened in Selma, he insisted, concerned all Americans, "who must overcome the crippling legacy of bigotry and injustice." Then, in a stirring adaptation of the anthem of the civil rights movement, the president concluded: "And we shall overcome." Following words with deeds, Johnson speedily shepherded through Congress the landmark Voting Rights Act of 1965, signed into law on August 6. It outlawed literacy tests and sent federal voter registrars into several southern states.

The passage of the Voting Rights Act, exactly one hundred years after the conclusion of the Civil War, climaxed a century of awful abuse and robust resurgence for African-Americans in the South. The act did not end discrimination and oppression overnight, but it placed an awesome lever for change in blacks' hands. Black southerners now had power and began to wield it without fear of reprisals. In the following decade, for the first time since emancipation, African-Americans began to migrate into the South.

Black Power

The Voting Rights Act of 1965 marked the end of an era in the troubled history of the black movement—the era of civil rights campaigns, focused on the South, led by peaceable moderates such as Martin Luther King, Jr. Just five days after President Johnson signed the new voting law, a bloody riot erupted in Watts, a black ghetto in Los Angeles. The week-long violence left thirty-one blacks and three whites dead, more than a thousand people injured, and hundreds of buildings charred and gutted.

Increasingly, more militant voices began to be heard in the black movement. Deepening division among black leaders was highlighted by the career of Malcolm X, a brilliant Black Muslim preacher who trumpeted black separatism and inveighed against the "blue-eyed white devils." In early 1965, after he had begun to preach a more conciliatory message, he was cut down by black gunmen while speaking to a large crowd in New York City.

The moderation of Martin Luther King, Jr., came under heavy fire from younger black radicals, such as Trinidad-born Stokely Carmichael of the Student Non-Violent Coordinating Committee (SNCC). Carmichael urged the abandonment of peaceful demonstrations and instead promoted "Black Power."

The phrase "Black Power" unsettled many whites. Some Black Power advocates insisted that they simply intended the slogan to describe a broad-front effort to exercise the political and economic rights gained by the civil rights movement. But other African-Americans, recollecting previous black nationalist movements like that of Marcus Garvey earlier in the century (see p. 453), breathed a vibrant separatist meaning into the concept of Black Power. They emphasized African-American distinctiveness, shed their "white" names for new African identities, and demanded black studies programs in colleges and universities.

Shortly after the civil rights movement achieved its greatest successes, city-shaking riots erupted in the black ghettoes. A bloody outburst in Newark, New Jersey, in the summer of 1967, took twenty-five lives. In Detroit, Michigan, federal troops restored order after forty-three people died in the streets. Black rioters torched their own neighborhoods, attacking police officers, and even firefighters, who had to battle both flames and mobs chanting, "Burn, baby, burn."

These outbursts angered many white Americans, who threatened to retaliate with their own "backlash" against ghetto arsonists and killers. Inner-city anarchy baffled many northerners, who had considered racial problems a purely "southern" question. But black concerns had moved north—as had nearly half the nation's black people. In the North the Black Power movement now focused less on civil rights and more on economic demands. Black unemployment, for example, was nearly double that for whites. These oppressive problems seemed even less likely to be solved peaceably than the struggle for voting rights in the South.

Despair deepened when the magnetic and moderate voice of Martin Luther King, Jr., was forever silenced by a sniper's bullet in Memphis, Tennessee, on April 4, 1968. A martyr for justice, he had bled and died against the peculiarly American thorn of race. The killing of King cruelly robbed the American people of one of the most inspirational leaders in their history—at a time when they could least afford to lose him. This outrage triggered a nationwide orgy of ghetto-gutting and violence that cost over forty lives.

Rioters noisily made news, but thousands of other blacks quietly made history. Their voter registration had shot upward, and by the late 1960s there were several hundred black elected officials in the Old South. Cleveland, Ohio, and Gary, Indiana, had elected black mayors. By 1972 nearly half of southern black children sat in integrated classrooms. Actually, more schools in the South were integrated than in the North. About a third of black families had risen economically into the ranks of the middle class—though an equal proportion remained below the "poverty line." King left a shining legacy of racial progress, but he was cut down when the job was far from completed.

Combating Communism in Two Hemispheres

Violence at home eclipsed Johnson's legislative triumphs, whereas foreign flare-ups threatened his political life. Discontented Dominicans rose in revolt against their military government in April 1965. Johnson speedily announced that the Dominican Republic was the target of a Castrolike coup by "Communist conspirators," and he dispatched some 25,000 American troops to restore order. But the evidence of a communist takeover was fragmentary at best. Johnson was widely condemned, at home and in Latin America, for his temporary reversion to the officially abandoned "gunboat diplomacy."

About the same time, Johnson was floundering deeper into the monsoon mud of Vietnam. Viet Cong guerrillas attacked an American air base at Pleiku, South Vietnam, in February 1965. The president immediately ordered retaliatory bombing raids against military installations in North Vietnam and for the first time ordered attacking U.S. troops to land. By the middle of March 1965, the Americans had "Operation Rolling Thunder" in full swing—regular full-scale bombing attacks against North Vietnam. Before 1965 ended, some 184,000 American troops were slogging through the jungles and rice paddies of South Vietnam searching for guerrillas.

Johnson had now taken the first fateful steps down a slippery path. He and his advisers believed that a fine-tuned, step-by-step escalation in American force would drive the enemy to defeat with a minimum loss of life. But the enemy matched every increase in American firepower with more men and more wiliness in the art of guerrilla warfare.

The South Vietnamese themselves were meanwhile becoming spectators in their own war, as the fighting became increasingly Americanized. Corrupt and collapsible governments succeeded each other in Saigon with bewildering rapidity. Yet American officials continued to talk of defending a faithful democratic ally. Washington spokespeople also defended the action as a test of Uncle Sam's "commitment" and of the reliability of his numerous treaty pledges to resist communist encroachment. Persuaded by such panicky thinking, Johnson steadily raised the military stakes in Vietnam. By 1968 he had poured more than half a million troops into Southeast Asia, and the annual bill for the war was exceeding $30 billion. Yet the end was nowhere in sight.

Vietnam Vexations

America could not defeat the enemy in Vietnam but seemed to be defeating itself. World opinion grew increasingly hostile; the blasting of an underdevel-

Vietnam and Southeast Asia, 1954–1975

oped country by a mighty superpower struck many critics as obscene. Several nations expelled American Peace Corps volunteers. Haughty Charles de Gaulle, ever suspicious of American reliability, ordered NATO off French soil in 1966.

Overcommitment in Southeast Asia also tied America's hands elsewhere. Capitalizing on American distractions in Vietnam, the Soviet Union expanded its influence in the Mediterranean area, especially in Egypt. Tiny Israel stunned the Soviet-backed Egyptians in a devastating Six-Day War in June 1967. The Middle East was becoming an ever more dangerously

packed powder keg that the war-plagued United States was powerless to defuse.

Domestic discontent also festered as the Vietnamese entanglement dragged on. Antiwar demonstrations had begun on a small scale with campus "teach-ins" in 1965, and gradually these protests mounted to tidal-wave proportions. As the long arm of the military draft dragged more and more young men off to the Asian slaughterpen, resistance stiffened. Thousands of draft registrants fled to Canada; others publicly burned their draft cards. Hundreds of thousands of chanting marchers filled the streets of

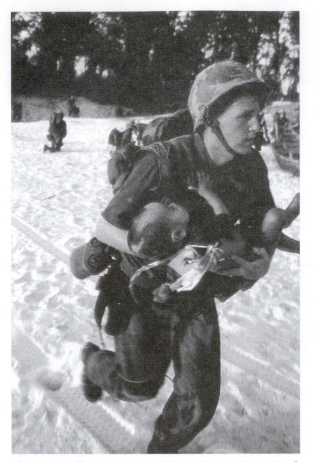

The Agony of War, 1965 *A U.S. marine carries a South Vietnamese baby to safety. The child was wounded by American jets during the opening stages of a military operation at Cape Batangan, Vietnam.*

war. Gradually the public came to feel that it had been lied to about both the causes and the "winnability" of the war. A yawning "credibility gap" opened between the government and the people. New flocks of antiwar "doves" were hatching daily.

By early 1968 the brutal and futile struggle had become the longest and most unpopular foreign war in the nation's history. Casualties, killed and wounded, already exceeded 100,000. More bombs had been dropped on Vietnam than on all enemy territory in World War II. Evidence mounted that America had been entrapped in an Asian civil war, fighting against highly motivated rebels who were striving to overthrow an oppressive regime. Yet Johnson clung to his basic strategy of stepping up the pressure bit by bit. He stubbornly assured doubting Americans that he could see "the light at the end of the tunnel." But to growing numbers of Americans, it seemed that Johnson was bent on "saving" Vietnam by destroying it.

Vietnam Topples Johnson

Hawkish illusions that the struggle was about to be won were shattered by a blistering communist offensive launched in late January 1968, during Tet, the Vietnamese New Year. At a time when the Viet Cong were supposedly licking their wounds, they suddenly and simultaneously mounted savage attacks on twenty-seven key South Vietnamese cities, including the capital, Saigon. Although eventually beaten off with heavy losses, they demonstrated anew that victory could not be gained by Johnson's strategy of gradual escalation. With an increasingly insistent voice, American public opinion demanded a speedy end to the war. Opposition grew so vehement that President Johnson could feel the very foundations of government shaking under his feet.

American military leaders responded to the Tet attacks with a request for 200,000 more troops. The size of the request staggered many policymakers. Former secretary of state Dean Acheson advised Johnson that "the Joint Chiefs of Staff don't know what they're talking about."

Meanwhile, Senator Eugene J. McCarthy of Minnesota was sharply challenging the president from

New York, San Francisco, and other cities. Many Americans felt pangs of conscience at the ghastly spectacle of their countrymen burning peasant huts and blistering civilians with ghastly napalm.

Opposition in Congress to the Vietnam involvement centered in the influential Senate Committee on Foreign Relations, headed by Senator J. William Fulbright of Arkansas. A constant thorn in the side of the president, he staged a series of widely viewed televised hearings in 1966 and 1967, during which prominent personages aired their views, largely anti-

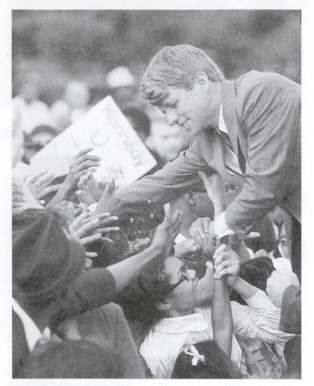

Robert F. Kennedy Campaigning for the Presidency, 1968 *Wrapped in the Kennedy family mystique and exuding his own boyish charm, Kennedy excited partisan crowds to wildly adulatory outpourings.*

within his own party for the 1968 Democrat presidential nomination. McCarthy, a sometime poet and devout Catholic, gathered a small army of antiwar college students who helped him gain an incredible 42 percent of the Democratic vote in the New Hampshire presidential primary on March 12. Four days later, Senator Robert F. Kennedy of New York, the murdered president's younger brother and by now himself a "dove" on Vietnam, threw his hat into the ring. The charismatic Kennedy, heir to his fallen brother's mantle of leadership, stirred a passionate response among workers, African-Americans, Hispanics, and young people.

These startling events abroad and at home were not lost on LBJ. In a bombshell address on March 31, 1968, he announced that he would freeze American troop levels and scale down the bombing. He also startled his vast audience by firmly declaring that he would not be a candidate for the presidency in 1968.

Johnson's "abdication" had the effect of preserving the military status quo. The United States could thus maintain the maximum acceptable level of military activity in Vietnam with one hand, while trying to negotiate a settlement with the other. North Vietnam shortly agreed to negotiations in Paris, but progress was glacially slow, as prolonged bickering developed over the very shape of the conference table.

The Presidential Sweepstakes of 1968

Summer in 1968 was one of the hottest political seasons in the nation's history. Johnson's heir apparent for the Democratic nomination was Vice President Hubert Humphrey. Loyally supporting LBJ's Vietnam policies through thick and thin, he received the support of the White House–dominated party apparatus. Senators McCarthy and Kennedy meanwhile dueled in several state primaries, with Kennedy's bandwagon gathering ever-increasing speed. But on June 5, 1968, on the night of an exciting victory in the California primary, Kennedy was shot to death by a young Arab immigrant.

Antiwar forces, deprived by an assassin of their leading candidate, streamed into Chicago for the Democratic convention in August 1968. Mayor Richard Daley responded by arranging for barbed-wire barricades around the convention hall, as well as thousands of police and National Guard reinforcements. Some militant demonstrators baited the officers in blue as "pigs" and hurled bags of filth at police lines. As people the world over watched on television, the exasperated "peace officers" broke into a "police riot," clubbing and manhandling innocent and guilty alike. Acrid tear gas fumes hung over the city even as Humphrey steamrollered to a first-ballot nomination. The Humphrey forces blocked the dovish McCarthyites' attempt to secure an antiwar platform plank and rammed through their own declaration that armed force would be relentlessly applied until the enemy showed more willingness to negotiate.

Scenting victory over the divided Democrats, the Republicans convened in plush Miami Beach, Florida, and nominated former vice president Richard Nixon, who arose from his political grave to win the nomination. As a "hawk" on Vietnam and a right-leaning middle-of-the-roader on domestic policy, Nixon pleased the Goldwater conservatives and was acceptable to party moderates. He appealed to southern whites and to the "law and order" element when he tapped as his running mate Maryland governor Spiro T. Agnew, noted for his tough stands against dissidents and black militants. The Republican platform called for victory in Vietnam and a strong anti-crime policy.

Adding color and confusion to the campaign was the third-party candidacy of former Alabama governor George C. Wallace. Wallace attacked "pointy-headed bureaucrats" and taunted hecklers as "bums" who needed a bath. He also called for prodding blacks back into their place. He and his running mate, former air force general Curtis LeMay, also proposed smashing the North Vietnamese to smithereens by "bombing them back to the Stone Age."

Between the positions of the Republicans and the Democrats on Vietnam, there was little choice. Both candidates were committed to keeping on with the war until the enemy would settle for an "honorable peace," which seemed to mean an "American victory." The millions of "doves" had no place to roost, and many refused to vote at all. Humphrey, scorched by the LBJ brand, went down to defeat as a prisoner of his chief's policies.

Nixon, who had lost a cliffhanger to Kennedy in 1960, won one in 1968. He garnered 301 electoral votes with 43.4 percent of the popular tally (31,785,480), compared with 191 electoral votes and 42.7 percent of the popular votes (31,275,166) for Humphrey. Wallace won an impressive 9,906,473 popular votes and 46 electoral votes, all from five states of the Deep South, four of which the Republican Goldwater had carried in 1964.

The Obituary of Lyndon Johnson

Talented but tragedy-struck Lyndon Johnson returned to his Texas ranch in January 1969 and died

Presidential Election of 1968 (with electoral vote by state)
George Wallace won in five states and denied a clear majority to either of the two major-party candidates in twenty-five other states. A shift of some fifty thousand votes might have thrown the election into the House of Representatives, giving Wallace the strategic bargaining position that he sought.

there four years later. His party was defeated, and his "me-too" Hubert Humphrey was repudiated. Yet Johnson's legislative leadership for a time had been remarkable. No president since Lincoln worked harder or did more for civil rights. None showed more compassion for the poor, blacks, and the ill educated.

But by 1966 Johnson was already sinking into the Vietnam quicksands. Great Society programs began to wither on the vine as soaring war costs sucked tax dollars into the military machine. Johnson promised guns and butter but could not deliver both. Ever-creeping inflation blighted the prospects of prosperity, and the War on Poverty met resistance as stubborn as the Viet Cong and eventually went down to defeat. Great want persisted alongside great wealth.

The Southeast Asian quagmire engulfed Johnson's noblest intentions. Committed to some degree by his two predecessors, he chose to defend the American foothold and enlarge the conflict rather than be run out. He was evidently persuaded by his brightest advisers, both civilian and military, that a "cheap" victory was possible and would be achieved by massive aerial bombing and large, though limited, troop commitments. His decision not to escalate the fighting further offended the "hawks," and his refusal to back off altogether antagonized the "doves." Like the Calvinists of colonial days, luckless Lyndon Johnson was damned if he did and damned if he did not.

The Cultural Upheaval of the 1960s

The struggles of the 1960s against racism, poverty, and the war in Vietnam had momentous cultural consequences. The decade came to be seen as a watershed dividing two distinct eras in values, morals, and behavior.

Everywhere in 1960s America a negative attitude toward all kinds of authority began to take hold. Disillusioned by the discovery that American society was not free of racism, sexism, imperialism, and oppression, many young people lost their traditional moral rudders. Neither families nor churches nor schools seemed to be able to define values and shape behav-

The "Free Speech Movement," Berkeley, California, December 4, 1964 *Student leader Mario Savio addresses a crowd at the University of California at Berkeley. The Free Speech Movement marked the first of the large-scale student mobilizations that would rock campuses across the country throughout the rest of the 1960s.*

ior with the certainty of shared purpose that many people believed had once existed. This upheaval even churned the tradition-bound Roman Catholic church, among the world's oldest and most conservative institutions. Clerics abandoned their Roman collars and the Latin Mass; folk songs replaced Gregorian chants; and meatless Fridays became ancient history. No matter what the topic, conventional wisdom and inherited ideas came under fire. "Trust no one over thirty" was a popular sneer of rebellious youth.

Skepticism about authority had deep historical roots in American culture, and it had even bloomed in the supposedly complacent and conformist 1950s. "Beat" poets such as Allen Ginsberg and iconoclastic novelists like Jack Kerouac had voiced dark disillusion with the materialistic pursuits of "establishment" culture in the Eisenhower era. In movies like *Rebel Without a Cause* (1955), the attractive young actor James Dean expressed the restless frustration of many young people.

The disaffection of the young reached crisis proportions in the tumultuous 1960s. One of the first organized protests against established authority broke out at the University of California at Berkeley in 1964, in the so-called Free Speech Movement. Leader Mario Savio, condemning the impersonal university "machine" more tied to corporate interests than humane values, urged his fellow students to "put your bodies upon the gears and upon the wheels . . . and you've got to make it stop." But in only a few years, the clean-cut Berkeley activists and their sober-minded sit-ins would seem downright quaint. Fired by outrage against the war in Vietnam, some sons and daughters of the middle class became political rebels, while others turned to mind-bending drugs, tuned in to "acid rock," and dropped out of "straight" society. Others "did their own thing" in communes or "alternative" institutions. *Patriotism* became a dirty word. Beflowered women in trousers and long-haired men with earrings heralded the rise of a self-conscious "counterculture" vehemently opposed to traditional American ways.

The 1960s also witnessed a "sexual revolution," though its novelty and scale are often exaggerated.

Without doubt, the introduction of the birth-control pill in 1960 made unwanted pregnancies much easier to avoid and sexual appetites much easier to satisfy. The Mattachine Society, founded in Los Angeles in 1951, was a pioneering advocate for gay rights, and by the 1960s, gay men and lesbians were demanding sexual tolerance. A brutal attack on gay men by off-duty police officers at New York's Stonewall Inn in 1969 powerfully energized gay and lesbian militancy. Widening worries in the 1980s about sexually transmitted diseases like genital herpes and AIDS (acquired immunodeficiency syndrome) finally slowed, but did not reverse, the sexual revolution.

Launched in youthful idealism, many of the decade's reform movements sputtered out in violence and cynicism. Students for a Democratic Society (SDS), once at the forefront of the antipoverty and antiwar campaigns, had by decade's end spawned an underground terrorist group called the Weathermen. Peaceful civil rights demonstrations had given way to blockbusting urban riots. What started as apparently innocent experiments with drugs such as marijuana and LSD had fried many youthful brains and spawned a loathsome underworld of drug lords and addicts.

Strait-laced guardians of respectability denounced the self-indulgent romanticism of the "flower children" as the beginning of the end of modern civilization. Sympathetic observers hailed the "greening" of America—the replacement of materialism and imperialism by a new consciousness of human values. But the upheavals of the 1960s could be largely attributed to three *P*'s: the youthful population bulge, protest against racism and the Vietnam War, and the apparent permanence of prosperity. As the decade flowed into the 1970s, the flower children grew older and had children of their own, the civil rights movement fell silent, the war ended, and economic stagnation blighted the bloom of prosperity. Young people in the 1970s seemed more concerned with finding jobs in the system than with tearing the system down. But if the counterculture had not managed fully to replace older values, it had weakened their grip, perhaps permanently.

Chronology

1961   Berlin crisis and construction of the Berlin Wall.
        Bay of Pigs.
        Alliance for Progress.
        Kennedy sends "military advisers" to South Vietnam.

1962   Pressure from Kennedy results in a rollback of steel prices.
        Laos neutralized.
        Cuban missile crisis.

1963   Anti-Diem coup in South Vietnam.
        Civil rights march in Washington, D.C.
        Kennedy assassinated; Johnson assumes presidency.

1964   Twenty-fourth Amendment (abolishing poll tax in federal elections) ratified.
        "Freedom Summer" voter registration in the South.
        Tonkin Gulf Resolution.
        Johnson defeats Goldwater for presidency.
        "War on Poverty" begins.
        Civil Rights Act.

1965   Great Society legislation.
        Voting Rights Act.
        U.S. troops occupy Dominican Republic.

1965–   Race riots in U.S. cities.
1968   Escalation of the Vietnam War.

1967   Six-Day War between Israel and Egypt.

1968   Tet offensive in Vietnam.
        Martin Luther King, Jr., and Robert Kennedy assassinated.
        Nixon defeats Humphrey and Wallace for presidency.

1969   Astronauts land on moon.

VARYING VIEWPOINTS

The Sixties: Constructive or Destructive?

The 1960s were convulsed by controversy, and they have remained controversial ever since. Conflicts raged in that turbulent decade between social classes, races, sexes, and generations. More than three decades later, conservative Republicans worked to repudiate the government activism of the sixties and uphold the "traditional values" that sixties culture supposedly trashed. Liberal Democrats, in contrast, continued to press such sixties causes as affirmative action for women and minorities, protection for the environment, an expanded welfare state, and sexual tolerance.

Four issues dominate historical discussion of the 1960s: the civil rights struggle; the Great Society's War on Poverty; the Vietnam War and the antiwar movement; and the emergence of the counterculture. Most scholars praise the civil rights achievements of the 1960s, but they disagree over the mid-sixties turn away from nonviolence to separatism and Black Power. The Freedom Riders and Martin Luther King, Jr., find much more approval in most history books than do Malcolm X or the Black Panther party. But some scholars, notably William L. Van Deburg in *New Day in Babylon: The Black Power Movement and*

American Culture, 1965–1975 (1992), argue that the "flank effect" of radical Black Power advocates like Stokely Carmichael actually enhanced the bargaining position of moderates like Dr. King.

Johnson's War on Poverty has liberal defenders in scholars like Allen Matusow (*The Unraveling of America*, 1984) and John Schwarz (*America's Hidden Success*, 1988). Schwarz demonstrates, for example, that Medicare and Social Security reforms virtually eliminated poverty among America's elderly. But the Great Society also provoked strong criticism from writers such as Charles Murray (*Losing Ground*, 1984) and Lawrence Meade (*Beyond Entitlements*, 1986). As those conservative critics see the poverty issue, to use a phrase popular in the 1960s, the Great Society was "part of the problem, not part of the solution." In their view, the War on Poverty did not simply fail to eradicate poverty among the so-called underclass; it actually deepened the dependency of the poor on the welfare state and even generated a multigenerational "cycle" of poverty.

For many young people of the 1960s, the antiwar movement protesting America's policy in Vietnam provided an initiation into politics and an introduction to "movement culture," with its sense of community and shared purpose. But scholars disagree over the movement's real effectiveness in checking the war. Writers like John Lewis Gaddis (*Strategies of Containment*, 1982) explain America's eventual withdrawal from Vietnam essentially without reference to the protesters in the streets. Others, like Todd Gitlin (*The Sixties: Years of Hope, Days of Rage*, 1987), insist that mass protest was the force that finally pressed the war to a conclusion.

Debate over the counterculture not only pits liberals against conservatives but also pits liberals against radicals. A liberal historian like William O'Neill (*Coming Apart*, 1971) might sympathize with what he considers some of the worthy values pushed by student activists, such as racial justice, nonviolence, and the antiwar movement, but he also claims that much of the sixties "youth culture" degenerated into hedonism, arrogance, and social polarization. In contrast, younger historians such as Michael Kazin and Maurice Isserman argue that cultural radicalism and political radicalism were two sides of the same coin. Many young people in the sixties made little distinction between the personal and the political. As Sara Evans demonstrates in *Personal Politics* (1980), "the personal was the political" for many women.

Critics may argue over the "good" versus the "bad" sixties, but there is no denying the degree to which that tumultuous time, for better or worse, shaped the world in which we now live.

40

The Stalemated Seventies

---cȝo---

1968–1980

In all my years of public life, I have never obstructed justice. People have got to know whether or not their president is a crook. Well, I'm not a crook; I earned everything I've got.

RICHARD NIXON, 1973

As the 1960s lurched to a close, the fantastic quarter-century economic boom of the post–World War II era also showed signs of petering out. By increasing their productivity, American workers had doubled their average standard of living in the twenty-five years since the end of World War II. Now, fatefully, productivity gains slowed to the vanishing point. The entire decade of the 1970s did not witness a productivity advance equivalent to even one year's progress in the preceding two decades. At the new rate, it would take five hundred more years to bring about another doubling of the average worker's standard of living. The median income of the average American family stagnated in the two decades after 1970 and, in fact, would have declined had not working wives' wages come to the rescue. The rising baby-boom generation faced the depressing prospect of a living standard that would be lower than that of their parents. As the postwar wave of robust economic growth crested by the early 1970s, at home and abroad the "can do" American spirit gave way to an unaccustomed sense of limits.

Sources of Stagnation

What caused the sudden slump in productivity? Some observers cited the increasing presence in the work force of women and teenagers, who typically had fewer skills than male adult workers and were less likely to take the full-time, long-term jobs by which skills might be developed. Other commenta-

The Nixon Wave *During Richard Nixon's presidency, Americans experienced the first serious inflation since the immediate post–World War II years. The inflationary surge grew to tidal-wave proportions by the late 1970s, when the consumer price index rose at annual rates of more than 10 percent.*

tors blamed declining investment in new machinery, the heavy costs of compliance with government-imposed safety and health regulations, and the general shift of the economy from manufacturing to services, where productivity gains were allegedly more difficult to achieve.

The Vietnam War also precipitated painful economic distortions. The disastrous conflict in Southeast Asia drained tax dollars from needed improvements in education, deflected scientific skill and manufacturing capacity from the civilian sector, and touched off a sickening spiral of inflation. Sharply rising oil prices in the 1970s also fed inflation, but its deepest roots lay in government policies of the 1960s—especially Lyndon Johnson's insistence on simultaneously fighting the war in Vietnam and fund-ing the Great Society programs at home, all without a tax increase to finance the added expenditures. The cost of living more than tripled in the dozen years following Richard Nixon's inauguration, in the longest and steepest inflationary cycle in American history.

Other weaknesses in the nation's economy were also laid bare by the abrupt reversal of America's financial fortunes in the 1970s. The competitive advantage of many American businesses had been so enormous after World War II that they had small incentive to modernize plants and seek more efficient methods of production. The defeated German and Japanese people had meanwhile scratched their way out of the ruins of war and built wholly new factories with the most up-to-date technology and management techniques. By the 1970s their efforts paid handsome rewards, as they came to dominate industries like steel, automobiles, and consumer electronics—fields in which the United States had once been unchallengeable.

The poor economic performance of the 1970s hung over the decade like a pall. It frustrated both policymakers and citizens who keenly remembered the growth and optimism of the quarter-century after World War II. But now a stalemated, unpopular war and a stagnant, unresponsive economy heralded the end of the self-confident postwar era. With it ended the liberal dream, vivid since New Deal days, that an affluent society could spend its way to social justice.

Nixon "Vietnamizes" the War

Inaugurated on January 20, 1969, Richard Nixon urged the American people, torn with dissension over Vietnam and race relations, to "stop shouting at one another." Yet the new president seemed an unlikely conciliator of the clashing forces that appeared to be ripping apart American society. Solitary and suspicious by nature, Nixon could be brittle and testy in the face of opposition. He also harbored bitter resentments against the "liberal establishment" that had cast him into the political darkness for much of the preceding decade. Yet Nixon brought one hugely valuable asset with him to the White House—his broad knowledge and thoughtful expertise in foreign affairs.

The first burning need of American foreign policy was to quiet the public uproar over Vietnam. President Nixon's announced policy—called "Vietnamization"—was to withdraw the 540,000 U.S. troops in South Vietnam over an extended period. The South Vietnamese—with American money, weapons, training, and advice—could then gradually take over the burden of fighting their own war. The so-called Nixon Doctrine thus evolved. It proclaimed that in the future, Asians and others would have to fight their own wars without the support of large bodies of American ground troops.

Nixon sought not to end the war but to win it by other means, without the further spilling of American blood. But even this much involvement was distasteful to the American "doves," many of whom demanded a withdrawal that was prompt, complete, unconditional, and irreversible. Antiwar protesters staged a massive national Vietnam moratorium in October 1969, as nearly 100,000 people jammed Boston Common and some 50,000 filed by the White House carrying lighted candles.

Undaunted, Nixon launched a counteroffensive by appealing to the "silent majority" who presumably supported the war. Though ostensibly conciliatory, Nixon's approach was in fact deeply divisive. His intentions soon became clear when he unleashed tough-talking Vice President Agnew to attack the "nattering nabobs of negativism" who demanded quick withdrawal from Vietnam. Nixon himself in 1970 sneered at the student antiwar demonstrators as "bums."

By January 1970 the Vietnam conflict had become the longest in American history and, with some 40,000 killed and over 250,000 wounded, the third most costly foreign war in the nation's experience. Especially in the war's early stages, African-Americans were disproportionately represented in the army and accounted for a disproportionately high share of combat casualties. Black and white soldiers alike floundered through booby-trapped swamps and steaming jungles, often unable to distinguish friend from foe among the Vietnamese peasants. Drug abuse, mutiny, and sabotage dulled the army's fighting edge.

Domestic disgust with the war was further deepened in 1970 by revelations that in 1968 American troops had massacred innocent women and children in the village of My Lai. Increasingly desperate for a quick end to the demoralizing conflict, Nixon widened the war in 1970 by ordering an attack on Vietnam's neighbor, Cambodia.

"Cambodianizing" the Vietnam War

Without consulting Congress, Nixon suddenly ordered American forces on April 29, 1970, to invade Cambodia, which was officially neutral but had long been used as a staging area by the North Vietnamese and Viet Cong. Angry students nationwide responded to the Cambodian invasion with rock throwing, window smashing, and arson. At Kent State University in Ohio, jumpy members of the National Guard fired into a noisy crowd, killing four and wounding many more; at Jackson State College in Mississippi, the highway patrol killed two students.

Nixon withdrew the American troops from Cambodia after only two months. But in America the invasion deepened the bitterness between "hawks" and "doves," as right-wing groups physically assaulted leftists. Disillusionment with "whitey's war" increased ominously among African-Americans in the armed forces. The Senate (though not the House) overwhelmingly repealed the Gulf of Tonkin blank check that Congress had given Johnson in 1964 and sought ways to restrain Nixon.

In the spring of 1971, mass rallies and marches once more erupted from coast to coast. New combustibles fueled the fires of antiwar discontent in June 1971, when the *New York Times* published a top-secret Pentagon study of America's involvement in the Vietnam War. These Pentagon Papers, "leaked" to the *Times* by former Pentagon official Daniel Ellsberg, laid bare the blunders and deceptions of the Kennedy and Johnson administrations, especially the provoking of the 1964 North Vietnamese attack in the Gulf of Tonkin.

Nixon's Détente with Beijing and Moscow

As the antiwar firestorm flared ever higher, Nixon concluded that the road out of Vietnam ran through

Beijing and Moscow. He perceived that tensions between the Chinese and the Soviets afforded the United States an opportunity to play off one antagonist against the other and to enlist the aid of both in pressuring North Vietnam into peace. Nixon's thinking was reinforced by his bespectacled and German-accented national security adviser, Dr. Henry Kissinger, who in 1969 began negotiating secretly with North Vietnamese officials in Paris while preparing the president's path to Beijing and Moscow.

Nixon, heretofore an uncompromising anticommunist, startled the nation with his historic journey to China in February 1972, which paved the way for improved relations between Washington and Beijing. Nixon next traveled to Moscow in May 1972 to play his "China card" in a game of high-stakes diplomacy in the Kremlin. The Soviets, hungry for American foodstuffs and alarmed over the possibility of intensified rivalry with an American-backed China, were ready to deal.

Nixon's visits ushered in an era of *détente*, or relaxed tensions, with the two communist powers and produced several significant agreements. First was the great grain deal of 1972, by which the food-rich United States agreed to sell the Soviets at least $750 million worth of wheat, corn, and other grain. More importantly, the two superpowers agreed to an antiballistic missile (ABM) treaty, which limited each nation to two clusters of defensive missiles. Another significant pact was the SALT (Strategic Arms Limitations Talks) agreement to freeze the numbers of long-range nuclear missiles for five years.

These accords, both ratified in 1972, constituted a long-overdue first step toward slowing the arms race. Yet even though the ABM treaty forbade elaborate defensive systems, the United States forged ahead with the development of "MIRVs" (multiple independently targeted reentry vehicles), designed to overcome any defense by "saturating" it with large numbers of warheads, several to a rocket. Predictably, the Soviets proceeded to "MIRV" their own missiles, and the arms race ratcheted up to a still more perilous plateau, with over sixteen thousand nuclear warheads deployed by both sides in the 1980s.

Nixon's détente diplomacy did, to some extent, de-ice the Cold War. Moreover, by checkmating and co-opting the two great communist powers, the pres-

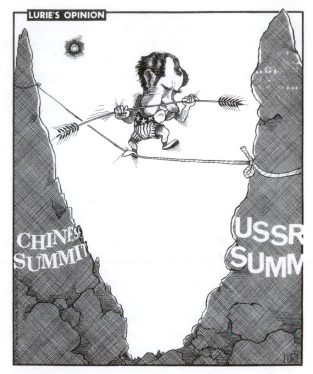

Balancing Act *Nixon treads delicately between the two communist superpowers in 1973, holding some of the wheat with which he enticed both into détente.*

ident had cleverly set the stage for America's exit from Vietnam. But the concluding act in that wrenching tragedy still remained to be played.

Nixon on the Home Front

Nixon had lashed out during the campaign at the "permissiveness" and "judicial activism" of the Supreme Court presided over by Chief Justice Earl Warren. Following his appointment in 1953, the jovial Warren had led the Court into a series of decisions that drastically affected sexual freedom, civil rights, criminal law, the practice of religion, and the structure of political representation. The decisions of the Warren Court reflected its deep concern for the individual, no matter how lowly.

In *Griswold* v. *Connecticut* (1965), the Court struck down a state law that prohibited the use of contraceptives. The Court proclaimed (critics said "invented") a "right of privacy" that soon provided the basis for decisions protecting women's abortion rights. Other controversial decisions were the cases of *Escobedo* (1964) and *Miranda* (1966), which gave accused criminals the right to remain silent, and a set of decisions in 1962 and 1963 prohibiting required prayers and Bible readings in public schools based on the First Amendment separation of church and state. Because these divisive decisions affected stubborn social problems, the Court came under relentless criticism, the bitterest since New Deal days.

Fulfilling campaign promises, President Nixon undertook to change the Court's philosophical complexion. Taking advantage of several vacancies, he sought appointees who would strictly interpret the Constitution, cease "meddling" in social and political questions, and not coddle radicals or criminals. The Senate in 1969 speedily confirmed his nomination of white-maned Warren E. Burger of Minnesota to succeed the retiring Earl Warren as chief justice. Before the end of 1971 the Court counted four conservative Nixon appointments out of nine members.

Yet Nixon was to learn the ironic lesson that many presidents have learned about their Supreme Court appointees: once seated on the high bench, the justices are fully free to think and decide according to their own beliefs, not according to the president's expectations. The Burger Court that Nixon shaped proved reluctant to dismantle the "liberal" rulings of the Warren Court; it even produced the most controversial judicial opinion of modern times, the *Roe* v. *Wade* decision in 1973, which legalized abortion (see pp. 579, 593).

Surprisingly Nixon presided over significant expansion of the welfare programs that conservative Republicans routinely denounced. He approved increased funds for entitlements like Food Stamps, Medicaid, and Aid to Families with Dependent Children (AFDC), and he added a generous new program, Supplemental Security Income (SSI), to aid the indigent, blind, and disabled. Nixon also signed legislation in 1972 guaranteeing automatic Social Security cost-of-living increases to protect the elderly against the ravages of inflation. Ironically, this "indexing" actually helped to fuel the inflationary fires.

Amid much controversy, Nixon inaugurated his so-called Philadelphia Plan in 1969 to compel construction trade unions to hire more African-Americans. Soon extended to all federal contracts, the Philadelphia Plan required employers to meet hiring quotas or to establish "set-asides" for minority contractors. Nixon's policy went beyond earlier definitions of "affirmative action" to confer privileges on certain groups. While opening broad employment and educational opportunities for minorities and women, this approach opened a Pandora's box of protest from critics who assailed "reverse discrimination" created by executive orders and unelected courts.

Among other legacies of the Nixon years was the creation in 1970 of the Environmental Protection Agency (EPA) and a companion body, the Occupational Safety and Health Administration (OSHA). Their births climaxed two decades of mounting concern for the environment. Inspired in part by author Rachel Carson's enormously influential *Silent Spring* (1962), the environmental movement pushed through the Clean Air Act of 1970, the Endangered Species Act of 1973, and similar laws. As a result, the ensuing decades saw notable progress in cleaning up befouled air, water, and waste sites. Congress also stopped funding any more of the huge irrigation projects that had damaged much of the arid West over the preceding half-century.

Elected as a minority president, with only 43 percent of the vote in 1968, Nixon devised a clever but cynical plan—called the "southern strategy"—to achieve a solid majority in 1972. Appointing conservative Supreme Court justices, soft-pedaling civil rights, and opposing school busing to achieve racial balance were all part of the scheme.

The Nixon Landslide of 1972

As fate would have it, the war in Vietnam, not domestic issues, dominated the presidential campaign of 1972. Nearly four years had passed since Nixon had promised, as a presidential candidate, to end the war and "win" the peace. Yet in the spring of 1972 the fighting escalated anew to alarming levels when the North Vietnamese, heavily equipped with foreign tanks, burst through the demilitarized zone separating the two Vietnams. Nixon reacted promptly by

The Watergate Scandal **573**

launching massive bombing attacks on strategic centers in North Vietnam, including Hanoi, the capital. Gambling heavily on Soviet and Chinese forbearance, he also ordered the dropping of contact mines to blockade the principal harbors of North Vietnam.

The continuing Vietnam conflict spurred the rise of South Dakota senator George McGovern to the 1972 Democratic nomination. McGovern's promise to pull the remaining American troops out of Vietnam in ninety days earned him the backing of the large antiwar element in the party. But his appeal to racial minorities, feminists, leftists, and youth alienated the traditional working-class backbone of his party. Moreover, the discovery, shortly after the convention, that McGovern's running mate, Missouri senator Thomas Eagleton, had undergone psychiatric care forced Eagleton's removal from the ticket and virtually doomed McGovern's candidacy.

Nixon's campaign emphasized that he had wound down the "Democratic war" in Vietnam from some 540,000 troops to about 30,000. His candidacy received an added boost just twelve days before the election when the high-flying Dr. Kissinger announced that "peace is at hand" in Vietnam and that an agreement would be settled in a few days.

Nixon won the election in a landslide. His lopsided victory encompassed every state except Massachusetts and the nonstate District of Columbia. He piled up 520 electoral votes to 17 and a popular majority of 47,169,911 votes to 29,170,383. Nixon's claim that the election gave him an unprecedented mandate for his policies was weakened by Republican election losses in both House and Senate.

The dove of peace, "at hand" in Vietnam just before the balloting, took flight after the election. After the fighting on both sides had again escalated, Nixon launched a furious two-week bombing of North Vietnam. This merciless pounding resulted in substantial losses of America's big B-52 bombers, but it drove North Vietnamese negotiators to agree to cease-fire arrangements on January 23, 1973, nearly three months after peace was prematurely proclaimed.

Nixon hailed the face-saving agreement as "peace with honor," but the boast rang hollow. The United States was to withdraw its remaining 27,000 or so troops and could reclaim some 560 American prisoners of war. The North Vietnamese were allowed to keep some 145,000 troops in South Vietnam, where they still occupied about 30 percent of the country. This shaky "peace" was in reality little more than a thinly disguised American retreat.

Watergate Woes

Nixon's electoral triumph was soon sullied by the so-called Watergate scandals. On June 17, 1972, some two months before his renomination, five men were arrested inside the Watergate office complex in Washington with electronic "bugging" equipment in their possession. They were working for the Republican Committee for the Re-election of the President—popularly known as CREEP—which had managed to raise tens of millions of dollars, often by secretive, unethical, or unlawful means. CREEP had also engaged in a "dirty tricks" campaign of espionage and sabotage, including faked documents, directed against Democratic candidates in the campaign of 1972.

The Watergate break-in was only the tip of an iceberg in a slimy sea of corruption that made the Grant and Harding scandals look almost respectable. The scandal in Washington also provoked the improper or illegal use of the Federal Bureau of Investigation and the Central Intelligence Agency. Even the Internal Revenue Service was called upon by Nixon's aides to audit or otherwise harass political opponents and others who had fallen into disfavor. A White House "enemies list" turned up that included innocent citizens who were to be hounded or prosecuted in various ways. In the name of national security, Nixon's aides had authorized a burglary of the files of Dr. Daniel Ellsberg's psychiatrist, so great was the determination to convict the man who had "leaked" the Pentagon Papers. This was the most notorious exploit of the White House "plumbers unit," created to plug up leaks of confidential information.

A select Senate committee, headed by the aging Senator Sam Ervin of North Carolina, conducted a prolonged and widely televised series of hearings in 1973–1974. John Dean III, a former White House lawyer with a remarkable memory, testified glibly and at great length about the aim of top echelons in the White House, including the president, to obstruct justice by covering up the Watergate break-in. But the committee then had only the unsupported word of Dean against weighty White House protestations of innocence.

A bombshell exploded before Senator Ervin's committee in July 1973 when a former presidential aide reported that President Nixon himself had installed bugging equipment in the White House. Nixon's conversations, in person or on the telephone, had been recorded on tape without notifying the other parties that electronic eavesdropping was taking place.

Now Dean's sensational testimony could be checked against the White House tapes, and the Senate committee could better determine if the president or his accuser was telling the truth. But for months Nixon flatly refused to produce the taped evidence. He took refuge behind various principles, including separation of powers and executive privilege.

The anxieties of the White House deepened when Vice President Spiro Agnew was forced to resign in October 1973 for taking bribes or "kickbacks" from Maryland contractors. President Nixon himself was now in danger of being removed by the impeachment route, so Congress invoked the Twenty-fifth Amendment (see the Appendix) to replace Agnew with a twelve-term congressman from Michigan, Gerald ("Jerry") Ford.

Ten days after Agnew's resignation came the "Saturday Night Massacre" (October 20, 1973). Archibald Cox, a Harvard law professor appointed as a "special prosecutor" by Nixon in May, issued a subpoena for relevant tapes and other documents from the White House. Nixon thereupon ordered the firing of Cox and then accepted the resignations of the attorney general and the deputy attorney general because they refused to carry out the order.

The Secret Bombing of Cambodia and the War Powers Act

As if Watergate were not enough, the constitutionality of Nixon's continued aerial battering of Cambodia came under increasing fire. In July 1973 America was shocked to learn that the U.S. Air Force had already secretly conducted some thirty-five hundred bombing raids against North Vietnamese positions in Cambodia. They had begun in March 1969 and continued for some fourteen months prior to the open American incursion in May 1970. The most disturbing feature of these sky forays was that, while they were going on, American officials, including the president, were avowing that Cambodian neutrality was being respected. Countless Americans began to wonder what kind of representative government they had if they were fighting a war they knew nothing about.

Defiance followed secretiveness. After the Vietnam cease-fire in January 1973, Nixon openly carried on his large-scale bombing of communist forces in order to help the rightist Cambodian government. This stretching of presidential war-making powers met furious opposition from the public and from a clear majority of both houses of Congress, which repeatedly tried to stop the bombing by cutting off appropriations. But Nixon's vetoes of such legislation were always sustained by at least one-third plus one vote in the House. Finally, with appropriations run-

Nixon, the Law-and-Order Man

ning short, Nixon agreed to a compromise in June 1973 whereby he would end the Cambodian bombing six weeks later and seek congressional approval of any future action in that bomb-blasted country.

Congressional opposition to the expansion of presidential war-making powers by Johnson and Nixon led to the War Powers Act in November 1973. Passed over Nixon's veto, it required the president to report to Congress within forty-eight hours after committing troops to a foreign conflict or "substantially" enlarging American combat units in a foreign country. Such a limited authorization would have to end within sixty days unless Congress extended it for thirty more days.

Compelling Nixon to end the bombing of Cambodia in August 1973 was but one manifestation of what came to be called the "New Isolationism." The draft had ended in January 1973, although it was retained on a standby basis. Future members of the armed forces were to be well-paid volunteers—a change that greatly eased tensions among youth.

The Arab Oil Embargo and the Energy Crisis

Adding to Nixon's problems, the long-rumbling Middle East erupted anew in October 1973, when the rearmed Syrians and Egyptians unleashed surprise attacks on Israel. Kissinger, who had become secretary of state in September, hastily flew to Moscow in an effort to restrain the Soviets, who were supplying the attackers. Believing that the Kremlin was poised to fly combat troops to the Suez area, Nixon placed America's nuclear forces on alert and ordered a gigantic airlift of nearly $2 billion in war materials to the Israelis. This assistance helped save the day, as the Israelis brilliantly turned the tide and threatened Cairo until American diplomacy brought about an uneasy cease-fire.

America's policy of backing Israel against its oil-rich neighbors exacted a heavy penalty. Late in October 1973, the Arab nations suddenly clamped an embargo on oil for the United States and other countries supporting Israel. Americans had to suffer through a long, cold winter of lowered thermostats and speedometers. Lines of automobiles at service stations lengthened as tempers shortened and a business recession deepened.

The "energy crisis" suddenly energized a number of long-deferred projects. Congress approved a costly Alaska pipeline and a national speed limit of fifty-five miles per hour to conserve fuel. Agitation mounted for heavier use of coal and nuclear power, despite the environmental threat they posed.

The five months of the Arab "blackmail" embargo in 1974 clearly signaled the end of an era—a period of cheap and abundant energy. American oil production peaked in 1970 and then began an irreversible decline. Blissfully unaware of their dependence on foreign suppliers, Americans, like revelers on a binge, had more than tripled their oil consumption since the end of World War II. The number of automobiles increased two and a half times between 1949 and 1972.

By 1974 America was addicted to oil and extremely vulnerable to any interruption in supplies. That stark fact colored the diplomatic and economic history of the 1980s and 1990s. The Middle East loomed ever larger on the map of America's strategic interests, until the United States in 1990 at last found itself pulled into a shooting war with Iraq to protect its oil supplies (see p. 597).

The Middle Eastern sheiks had approximately quadrupled their price for crude oil after lifting the embargo in 1974. Huge new oil bills wildly disrupted the U.S. balance of international trade and added fuel to the raging fires of inflation. Various sectors of the economy, including Detroit's carmakers, began their slow, grudging adjustment to the rudely dawning age of energy dependency. But full reconciliation to that uncomfortable reality was a long time coming.

The Unmaking of a President

Political tribulations added to the nation's cup of woe in 1974. The continuing impeachment inquiry cast damning doubts on Nixon's integrity. Responding at last to the House Judiciary Committee's demand for the Watergate tapes, Nixon agreed in the spring of 1974 to the publication of "relevant" portions of the tapes, declaring that these would vindicate him. But substantial sections of the wanted tapes were missing, and Nixon's frequent obscenities were excised with the phrase "expletive deleted."

Confronted with demands for the rest of the material, Nixon flatly refused. On July 24, 1974, the president suffered a disastrous setback when the Supreme Court unanimously ruled that "executive privilege" gave him no right to withhold from the special prosecutor portions of tapes relevant to criminal activity. Skating on thin ice over hot water, Nixon reluctantly complied.

The House Judiciary Committee pressed ahead with its articles of impeachment. The key vote came late in July 1974, when the committee adopted the first article, which charged obstruction of "the administration of justice," including Watergate-related crimes. Two other articles were later approved by the committee, accusing Nixon of abusing the powers of his office and showing contempt of Congress by ignoring lawful subpoenas for relevant tapes and other evidence.

On August 5, 1974, Nixon finally made public three subpoenaed tapes of conversations with his chief aide on June 23, 1972. One of them had him giving orders, six days after the Watergate break-in, to use the CIA to hold back an inquiry by the FBI. Now Nixon's own tape-recorded words convicted him of having been an active party to the attempted cover-up, in itself the crime of obstructing justice. More than that, he had solemnly told the American people on television that he had known nothing of the Watergate cover-up until about nine months later.

The public backlash proved to be overwhelming. Republican leaders in Congress concluded that the guilty and unpredictable Nixon was a loose cannon on the deck of the ship of state. They frankly informed the president that his impeachment by the full House and removal by the Senate were foregone conclusions and that he would do best to resign.

Left with no better choice, Nixon choked back his tears and announced his resignation in a dramatic television appearance on August 8, 1974. In his Farewell Address, Nixon admitted having made some "judgments" that "were wrong" but insisted that he had always acted "in what I believed at the time to be the best interests of the nation." Unconvinced, countless Americans would change the song "Hail to the Chief" to "Jail to the Chief."

The nation had survived a wrenching constitutional crisis, which proved that the impeachment machinery forged by the Founding Fathers could work when public opinion overwhelmingly demanded that it be implemented. The principles that no person is above the law and that presidents must be held to strict accountability for their acts were strengthened. The United States of America, on the eve of its two-hundredth birthday as a Republic, had given an impressive demonstration of self-discipline and self-government to the rest of the world.

The First Unelected President

Gerald Rudolph Ford, the first man to be made president solely by a vote of Congress, entered the besmirched White House, in August 1974, with serious handicaps. He was widely—and unfairly—suspected of being little more than a dim-witted former college football player. President Johnson had sneered that "Jerry" was so lacking in brainpower that he could not walk and chew gum at the same time. Worse, Ford had been selected, not elected, vice president, following Spiro Agnew's resignation in disgrace. The sour odor of illegitimacy hung about this president without precedent.

Then, out of a clear sky, Ford granted a complete pardon to Nixon for any crimes he may have committed as president, discovered or undiscovered. Democrats were outraged, and lingering suspicions about the pardon cast a dark shadow over Ford's prospects of being elected president in his own right in 1976.

Ford at first sought to enhance the so-called détente with the Soviet Union that Nixon had crafted. In July 1975 President Ford joined leaders from thirty-four other nations in Helsinki, Finland, to sign several sets of historic accords. One group of agreements officially wrote an end to World War II by finally legitimizing the Soviet-dictated boundaries of Poland and other Eastern European countries. In return, the Soviets signed a "third basket" of agreements, guaranteeing more liberal exchanges of people and information between East and West and protecting certain basic "human rights." The Helsinki accords kindled small dissident movements in Eastern Europe and even in the USSR itself.

Western Europeans cheered the Helsinki conference as a milestone of détente. But in the United States critics increasingly charged that détente was proving to be a one-way street, with American grain and technology flowing across the Atlantic to the USSR and little of comparable importance flowing back. Moscow also continued its human rights violations, including clamping tight restrictions on Jewish emigration.

Despite these difficulties, Ford at first clung stubbornly to détente. But the American public's fury over Moscow's double-dealing so steadily mounted that by the end of his term the president was refusing even to pronounce the word *détente* in public. The thaw in the Cold War was threatening to prove chillingly brief.

Defeat in Vietnam

Early in 1975 the North Vietnamese gave full throttle to their long-expected drive southward. President Ford urged Congress to vote still more weapons for Vietnam. But his plea was in vain, and without the crutch of massive American aid, the South Vietnamese quickly and ingloriously collapsed.

The dam burst so rapidly that the remaining Americans had to be frantically evacuated by helicopter, the last of them on April 29, 1975. Also rescued were about 140,000 South Vietnamese, most of them so dangerously identified with the Americans that they feared a bloodbath by the victorious communists. Ford compassionately admitted these people to the United States, adding further seasoning to the melting pot. Eventually some 500,000 arrived (see "Makers of America: The Vietnamese," pp. 578–579).

America's longest, most frustrating war thus ended, not with a bang but a whimper. In a technical sense the Americans had not lost the war; their client nation had. The United States had fought the North Vietnamese to a standstill and had then withdrawn its troops in 1973, leaving the Vietnamese to fight their own war, with generous shipments of costly American aircraft, tanks, and other munitions. The estimated cost to America was $118 billion in current outlays, along with some 56,000 dead and 300,000 wounded. The people of the United States had in fact provided just about everything, except the will to win—and that could not be injected by outsiders.

Technicalities aside, America had in fact lost the war and more. It had lost face in the eyes of foreign-

Passing the Buck *A satirical view of where responsibility for the Vietnam debacle should be laid.*

The Vietnamese

At first glance, the towns of Westminster and Fountain Valley, California, seem to resemble other California communities nearby. Tract homes line residential streets; shopping centers flank the busy thoroughfares. But these are no ordinary American suburbs. Instead, they make up "Little Saigons," vibrant outposts of Vietnamese culture in the contemporary United States.

Before South Vietnam fell in 1975, few Vietnamese ventured across the Pacific. Only in 1966 did U.S. immigration authorities even designate "Vietnamese" as a separate category of newcomers, and most early immigrants were the wives and children of U.S. servicemen. But as the communists closed in on Saigon, many Vietnamese, particularly those who had worked closely with American or South Vietnamese authorities, feared for their future. Gathering together as many of their extended-family members as they could assemble, thousands of Vietnamese fled for their lives. In a few hectic days in 1975, some 140,000 escaped before the approaching gunfire, a few dramatically clinging to the bottoms of departing helicopters. Another 60,000 less fortunate refugees escaped at the same time over land and sea to Hong Kong and Thailand, where they waited nervously for permission to move on.

To accommodate the refugees, the U.S. government set up camps across the nation. Arrivals were crowded into army barracks affording little room and less privacy. These were boot camps not for military service but for assimilation into American society. A rigorous program trained the Vietnamese in English, forbade children from speaking their native language

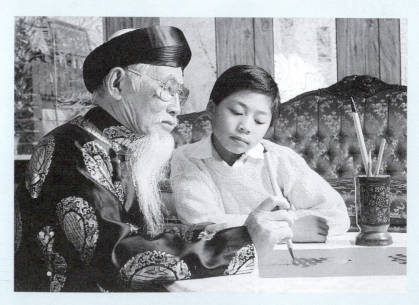

Preserving the Past *A Vietnamese-American boy learns classical calligraphy from his grandfather.*

in the classroom, and even immersed them in American slang. Many resented this attempt to mold them and strip them of their culture.

Their discontent boiled over when authorities prepared to release the refugees from camps and board them with families around the nation. The resettlement officials had decided to find a sponsor for each Vietnamese family—an American family that would provide food, shelter, and assistance for the refugees until they could fend for themselves. But the Vietnamese people cherish their traditional extended families—grandparents, uncles, aunts, and cousins living communally with parents and children. The refugees were dispersed to Iowa, Illinois, Pennsylvania, New York, Washington, and California. But as soon as they could, they relocated, hastening to established Vietnamese enclaves around San Francisco, Los Angeles, and Dallas.

Soon a second throng of Vietnamese immigrants pushed into these Little Saigons. Fleeing from the ravages of poverty and from the oppressive communist government, these stragglers had crammed themselves and their few possessions into little boats, hoping to reach Hong Kong or get picked up by friendly ships. Eventually, many of these "boat people" reached the United States. Usually less educated than the first arrivals and receiving far less resettlement aid from the U.S. government, they were, however, more willing to start at the bottom. Today these two groups total more than half a million people. Differing in experience and expectations, the Vietnamese share a new home in a strange land. Their uprooting is an immense, unreckoned consequence of America's longest war.

ers, lost its own self-esteem, lost confidence in its military prowess—and lost much of the economic muscle that had made possible its global leadership since World War II. Americans reluctantly came to realize that their power, as well as their pride, had been deeply wounded in Vietnam and that recovery would be slow and painful.

Feminist Victories and Defeats

By the time the army limped home from Vietnam, most of the protests of the 1960s, including the antiwar movement, had long since splintered and stalled. One major exception to this stood out: although they had their differences, American feminists showed vitality and momentum. They won legislative and judicial victories and provoked an intense rethinking of gender roles. (On the roots of this movement, see "Makers of America: The Feminists," p. 582).

Thousands of women marched in the Women's Stride for Equality on the fiftieth anniversary of woman suffrage in 1970. In 1972 Congress passed Title IX of the Education Amendments, prohibiting sex discrimination in any federally assisted educational program. This act created opportunities for girls' and women's athletics at schools and colleges, giving birth to a new "Title IX generation" that would professionalize women's sports in the 1980s and 1990s. The Equal Rights Amendment (ERA) to the Constitution won congressional approval in 1972. It declared, "Equality of rights under the law shall not be denied or abridged by the United States or by any State on account of sex." Twenty-eight states quickly ratified the amendment. With only ten more states needed, hopes rose that the ERA would soon be the law of the land.

Even the Supreme Court seemed to be on the movement's side. In *Reed* v. *Reed* and *Frontiero* v. *Richardson* (1973), the Court challenged sex discrimination in legislation and employment. And in the landmark case of *Roe* v. *Wade* (1973), the Court struck down laws prohibiting abortion, arguing that a woman's decision to terminate a pregnancy was protected by the constitutional right of privacy.

But the feminist movement soon faced a formidable backlash. In 1972 President Nixon vetoed a proposal to set up nationwide public day care, saying it would weaken the American family. The Catholic Church and the religious right organized a powerful grassroots movement to oppose the legalization of abortion. And in the bitterest defeat for many feminists, conservative forces led by spokeswoman Phyllis Schlafly orchestrated a campaign that stopped the ERA. In 1979 Congress extended the deadline for ratification, but the amendment died in 1982, three states short of success.

The Seventies in Black and White

Although the civil rights movement had fractured, race remained an explosive issue in the 1970s. The Supreme Court in *Milliken* v. *Bradley* blind-sided school integrationists when it ruled that desegregation plans could not require students to move across school-district lines. The decision effectively exempted suburban districts from shouldering any part of the burden of desegregating inner-city schools, forcing all the problems of desegregation into the least prosperous districts. Boston and other cities were shaken to their foundations, as the poorest, most disadvantaged elements of the white and black communities were pitted against one another in school desegregation plans.

Affirmative action programs also remained highly controversial. White workers denied advancement and white students refused college admission cried "reverse discrimination," charging that race or ethnic background was now outweighing ability in employment or admissions. In 1978 the Supreme Court upheld the claim of one white Californian, Allan Bakke, that he had been denied admission to medical school because of a program that favored minority students. In its tortured decision, the Court ordered the University of California at Davis to admit Bakke and said that preference in admissions could not be based on ethnic or racial identity alone. Yet at the same time, the Court said that racial factors might be taken into account in a school's overall admissions policy. Critics of the *Bakke* decision, including dissenting black justice Thurgood Marshall, warned that denial of racial preferences might sweep away years of civil rights progress. But many conservatives cheered the decision as affirming the principle that justice is colorblind.

Inspired by the civil rights movement, Native Americans in the 1970s gained remarkable power

through using the courts and well-planned acts of civil disobedience. But while blacks had fought against segregation, Indians used the tactics of the civil rights movement to assert their status as separate semisovereign peoples. Indian activists captured the nation's attention by seizing the island of Alcatraz in 1970 and the village of Wounded Knee, South Dakota, in 1972. In the case of *United States* v. *Wheeler*, the Supreme Court declared that Indian tribes possessed a "unique and limited" sovereignty, subject to the will of Congress but not to individual states.

The Bicentennial Campaign and the Carter Victory

America's two-hundredth birthday, in 1976, fell during a presidential election year—a fitting coincidence for a proud democracy. Gerald Ford energetically sought nomination for the presidency in his own right and won the Republican nod at the Kansas City convention.

The Democratic standard-bearer was fifty-one-year-old James Earl Carter, Jr., a dark-horse candidate who galloped out of obscurity during the long primary-election season. A former Georgia governor who insisted on humble "Jimmy" as his first name, this born-again Baptist touched many people with his down-home sincerity. Untainted by ties with a corrupt and cynical Washington, Carter ran against the memory of Nixon and Watergate as much as he ran against Ford. His most effective campaign pitch was his promise that "I'll never lie to you."

Carter squeezed out a narrow victory on election day, with 51 percent of the popular vote. The electoral count stood at 297 to 240. The winner swept every state except Virginia in his native South. Especially important were the votes of African-Americans, 97 percent of whom cast their ballots for Carter.

Carter enjoyed hefty Democratic majorities in both houses of Congress. Hopes ran high that the stalemate of the Nixon-Ford years between a Republican White House and a Democratic Capitol Hill would now be ended. At first Carter enjoyed notable political success, as Congress granted his requests to create a new cabinet-level Department of Energy and to cut taxes by some $18 billion in 1978. But Carter's honeymoon did not last long. An inexperienced outsider, he had campaigned against the Washington "establishment," and he never quite made the transition to being an insider himself. He repeatedly rubbed congressional fur the wrong way, and critics charged that he isolated himself in a shallow pool of fellow Georgians.

Carter's Humanitarian Diplomacy

As a committed Christian, President Carter displayed from the outset an overriding concern for "human rights" as the guiding principle of his foreign policy. In the African nations of Rhodesia (later Zimbabwe) and South Africa, Carter and his eloquent United Nations ambassador, Andrew Young, championed the oppressed black majority.

The president's most spectacular foreign-policy achievement came in September 1978 when he invited President Anwar Sadat of Egypt and Prime Minister Menachem Begin of Israel to the presidential retreat at Camp David, Maryland, in an attempt to prevent another blowup in the misery-drenched Middle East. Skillfully serving as go-between, Carter persuaded the two visitors to sign an accord (September 17, 1978) that held considerable promise of peace. Israel agreed in principle to withdraw from territory conquered in the 1967 war, and Egypt in return promised to respect Israel's borders. Both parties pledged themselves to sign a formal peace treaty within three months.

Carter achieved further diplomatic success by resuming full diplomatic relations with China in 1979. He also concluded two treaties turning over complete ownership and control of the Panama Canal to the Panamanians by the year 2000.

Despite these dramatic accomplishments, trouble stalked Carter's foreign policy. Overshadowing all international issues was the ominous reheating of the Cold War with the USSR. Détente fell into disrepute as thousands of Cuban troops, assisted by Soviet advisers, appeared in Angola, Ethiopia, and elsewhere in Africa to support revolutionary factions. Arms-control negotiations with Moscow stalled in the face of this Soviet military meddling.

Economic and Energy Woes

Adding to Carter's mushrooming troubles was the failing health of the economy. A stinging recession during Gerald Ford's presidency had temporarily slowed inflation, but virtually from the moment of Carter's inauguration, prices resumed their dizzying ascent, driving the inflation rate well above 13 percent by 1979. The soaring bill for imported oil pushed America's balance of payments deeply into the red (an unprecedented $40 billion in 1978).

The "oil shocks" of the 1970s taught Americans a painful but necessary lesson: they could never again seriously consider a policy of economic isolation, as they had tried to do between the two world wars. For most of American history, foreign trade had accounted for no more than 10 percent of gross national product (GNP), but huge foreign-oil bills drove that figure upward so that, by century's end, some 27 percent of GNP depended on foreign trade. Unable to dominate international trade and finance as they once had, Americans would have to master foreign languages and study foreign cultures if they wanted to prosper in the rapidly globalizing economy.

Yawning deficits in the federal budget, reaching nearly $60 billion in 1980, further aggravated the U.S. economy's inflationary ailments. The elderly and other Americans living on fixed incomes suffered from the shrinking dollar. People with money to lend pushed interest rates ever higher, hoping to protect themselves from being repaid in badly depreciated dollars. The "prime rate" (the rate of interest that banks charged their very best customers) vaulted to an unheard-of 20 percent in early 1980. The high cost of borrowing money shoved small businesses to the wall and strangled the construction industry.

Carter diagnosed America's economic disease as stemming primarily from the nation's costly dependence on foreign oil. Unfortunately, his legislative proposals in April 1977 for energy conservation ignited a blaze of indifference among the American people, who had already forgotten the long gasoline lines of 1973.

Events in Iran jolted Americans out of their complacency about energy supplies in 1979. The imperious Mohammed Reza Pahlevi, installed as shah of Iran with help from America's CIA in 1953, had long

MAKERS OF AMERICA

The Feminists

A well-to-do housewife and mother of seven, Elizabeth Cady Stanton (1815–1902) was an unlikely revolutionary. Yet this founding mother of American feminism devoted seven decades of her life to the fight for women's rights.

Young Elizabeth Cady drew her inspiration from the fight against slavery. When she and her new husband, abolitionist Henry Stanton, attended the World Anti-Slavery Convention in London, she was insulted that women were forced to sit in a screened-off balcony above the convention floor. Stanton went on to organize the Seneca Falls Convention in 1848. There she presented her Declaration of Sentiments, which proclaimed that "all men *and women* are created equal" and demanded women's rights to own property, enter the professions, and vote. Encountering a mountain of hostility to her cause, Stanton died before seeing her dream of woman suffrage realized in the Nineteenth Amendment (1920). Yet by imagining women's emancipation as an expansion of America's founding principles of citizenship, Stanton charted a path that other feminists would follow a century later.

Historians use the terms "first wave" and "second wave" to distinguish the women's movement of the nineteenth century from that of the late twentieth century. The woman most often credited with launching the "second wave" is Betty Friedan (b. 1921). Friedan, a suburban housewife who had seen her mother sacrifice her own career to raise a family, wrote the best-seller *The Feminine Mystique* to expose the quiet desperation of millions of housewives trapped in the "comfortable concentration camp" of the suburban home. In 1966 Friedan cofounded the National Organization for Women (NOW), the chief political arm of second-wave feminism.

Just as first-wave feminism grew out of abolitionism, the second wave drew ideas, leaders, and tactics from the civil rights movement of the 1960s. Civil rights workers and feminists alike focused on equal rights.

Second-wave feminism also had an avowedly radical wing, supported by younger women eager to challenge almost every traditional male and female gender role and to take the feminist cause to the streets. Among these women was Robin Morgan, a civil rights activist in organizations like the Congress of Racial Equality (CORE) and SNCC (Student Non-Violent Coordinating Committee). Women in the movement who protested gender discrimination met ridicule, as in SNCC leader Stokely Carmichael's retort that "the only position for women in SNCC is prone." Morgan went on to found WITCH (Women's International Terrorist Conspiracy from Hell), made famous by its protest at the 1968 Miss America pageant in Atlantic City, New Jersey.

As the contrast between WITCH and NOW suggests, second-wave feminism was a remarkably diverse movement. Feminists in the late twentieth century disagreed over many issues—from pornography and marriage to how much to expect from government, capitalism, and men. Some feminists placed a priority on gender equality, whereas others defended a feminism of gender difference.

Still, beyond these differences feminists had much in common. Most advocated the right to choose abortion and regarded the law as a key weapon against gender discrimination. By century's end radical and moderate feminists alike could take pride in a host of achievements that had changed the landscape of gender relations. Yet, like Elizabeth Cady Stanton, second-wave feminists also shared the burden of understanding that the goals of genuine equality would take more than a lifetime to achieve.

ruled his oil-rich land with a will of steel. His repressive regime was finally overthrown in January 1979 in a violent revolution spearheaded by Muslim fundamentalists. The crippling upheavals of the revolution soon spread to Iran's oil fields. As Iranian oil supplies stopped flowing, shortages appeared, petroleum prices rose steeply, and Americans once more found themselves waiting impatiently in long lines at gas stations or buying gasoline only on specified days.

As the oil crisis deepened, President Carter sensed the rising temperature of popular discontent. In July 1979 he retreated to Camp David, where he remained largely out of public view for ten days. Like a royal potentate of old summoning the wise men of the realm for their counsel in a time of crisis, Carter called in over one hundred leaders from all walks of life to give him their views. The nation anxiously awaited the results of these extraordinary deliberations.

When he finally came down from the mountaintop on July 15, 1979, Carter stunned and perplexed the nation by chiding his fellow citizens for falling into a "moral and spiritual crisis" and for being too concerned with "material goods." A few days later, the president let drop another shoe when he fired four cabinet secretaries and circled the wagons of his Georgia advisers more tightly about the White House. Critics began to wonder aloud whether Carter, the professed man of the people, was losing touch with the popular mood of the country.

Foreign Affairs and the Iranian Imbroglio

Hopes for a less dangerous world rose slightly in June 1979, when President Carter met with Soviet leader Leonid Brezhnev in Vienna to sign the long-stalled SALT II agreements, limiting the levels of lethal strategic weapons in the Soviet and American arsenals. But conservative critics of the president's defense policies, still deeply suspicious of the Soviet Union, unsheathed their long knives to carve up the SALT treaty when it came to the Senate for debate in the summer of 1979.

Political earthquakes in the petroleum-rich Persian Gulf region finally buried all hopes of ratifying the SALT II treaty. On November 4, 1979, a howling mob of rabidly anti-American Muslim militants stormed the United States embassy in Teheran, Iran, and took all of its occupants hostage. World opinion hotly condemned the diplomatic felony in Iran, while Americans agonized over both the fate of the hostages and the stability of the entire Persian Gulf region, so dangerously close to the Soviet Union. The Soviet army then aroused the West's worst fears on December 27, 1979, when it blitzed into the mountainous nation of Afghanistan, next door to Iran, and appeared to be poised for a thrust at the oil-jugular of the gulf.

President Carter reacted vigorously to these alarming events. He slapped an embargo on the export of grain and high-technology machinery to the USSR, called for a boycott of the upcoming Olympic Games in Moscow, and requested that young people (including women) be made to register for a possible military draft. Proclaiming that the United States would "use any means necessary, including force," to protect the Persian Gulf against Soviet incursions, Carter grimly conceded that he had misjudged the Soviets. The SALT treaty became a dead letter in the Senate. Meanwhile, the Soviet army met unexpectedly stiff resistance in Afghanistan and became bogged down in a nasty guerrilla war that came to be called "Russia's Vietnam."

The Iranian hostage crisis was Carter's—and America's—bed of nails. The captured Americans languished in cruel captivity, while the nightly news broadcasts showed humiliating scenes of Iranian mobs burning the American flag and spitting on effigies of Uncle Sam.

Carter at first tried to apply economic sanctions and the pressure of world opinion against the Iranians. But the president's frustration grew as the political upheaval in Iran rumbled on. Carter at last ordered a daring rescue mission. A highly trained commando team penetrated deep into Iran's sandy interior, but when equipment failures prevented some members of the team from reaching their destination, the mission had to be scrapped. As the commandos withdrew, two of their aircraft collided, killing eight of the would-be rescuers.

The disastrous failure of the rescue raid proved anguishing for Americans. The episode seemed to underscore the nation's helplessness and even incompetence in the face of a mortifying insult to the national honor. The stalemate with Iran dragged on throughout the rest of Carter's term, providing an embarrassing backdrop to the embattled president's struggle for reelection.

Chronology

1970   Nixon orders invasion of Cambodia.
Kent State and Jackson State incidents.
Environmental Protection Agency (EPA)
    created.
Clean Air Act.

1971   Pentagon Papers published.

1972   Nixon visits China and the Soviet Union.
ABM and SALT I treaties ratified.
Nixon defeats McGovern for presidency.
Equal Rights Amendment passes
    Congress.
Title IX of Education Amendments passed.

1973   Vietnam cease-fire and U.S. withdrawal.
Agnew resigns; Ford appointed vice
    president.
War Powers Act.
Arab-Israeli war and Arab oil embargo.
Endangered Species Act.
Frontiero v. *Richardson.*
Roe v. *Wade.*

1973–
1974   Watergate hearings and investigations.

1974   Nixon resigns; Ford assumes presidency.
First OPEC oil-price increase.

1975   Helsinki accords.
South Vietnam falls to communists.

1976   Carter defeats Ford for presidency.

1978   Egyptian-Israeli Camp David agreement.
United States v. *Wheeler.*

1979   Iranian revolution and oil crisis.
SALT II agreements signed (never ratified by
    Senate).
Soviet Union invades Afghanistan.

1979–
1981   Iranian hostage crisis.

41

The Resurgence of Conservatism

—◦◦◦—

1980–2002

It will be my intention to curb the size and influence of the federal establishment and to demand recognition of the distinction between the powers granted to the federal government and those reserved to the states or to the people.

RONALD REAGAN, INAUGURAL ADDRESS, 1981

"It's morning in America" was the slogan of Republican candidate Ronald Reagan in his 1980 presidential campaign. Certainly the 1980s were a new day for America's conservative right. Census figures confirmed that the average American was older than in the stormy sixties and much more likely to live in the South or West, the traditional bastions of the "Old Right," where many residents harbored suspicions of federal power. The conservative cause drew added strength from the emergence of a "New Right" movement, partly in response to the countercultural protests of the 1960s. Spearheading the New Right were evangelical Christian groups such as the Moral Majority, dedicated believers who enjoyed startling success as political fund-raisers and organizers.

Many New Right activists were far less agitated about economic questions than about cultural concerns—the so-called social issues. They denounced abortion, pornography, homosexuality, feminism, and especially affirmative action. They championed prayer in the schools and tougher penalties for criminals. Together, the Old and New Right added up to a powerful political combination, devoted to changing the very character of American society.

The Election of Ronald Reagan, 1980

Ronald Reagan was well suited to lead the gathering conservative crusade. Reared in a generation whose values were formed well before the upheavals of the 1960s, he naturally sided with the New Right on social issues. In economic and social matters alike, he denounced the activist government and failed "social engineering" of the 1960s. Just as his early political hero, Franklin Roosevelt, had championed the "forgotten man" against big business, the Republican Reagan championed the "common man" against big government. He aimed especially to win over from the Democratic column working-class and lower-middle-class white voters by implying that the Democratic party had become the exclusive tool of its minority constituents.

Though Reagan was no intellectual, he drew on the ideas of a small but influential group of thinkers known as "neoconservatives." Their ranks included Norman Podhoretz, editor of *Commentary* magazine, and Irving Kristol, editor of *The Public Interest*. Reacting against what they saw as the excesses of 1960s liberalism, the neoconservatives championed free-market capitalism liberated from government restraints, and they took tough, harshly anti-Soviet positions in foreign policy. They also questioned liberal welfare programs and affirmative-action policies and called for reassertion of traditional values of individualism and the centrality of the family.

An actor turned politician, Reagan enjoyed enormous popularity with his crooked grin and "aw-shucks" manner. The son of an impoverished Irish-American father from a small Illinois town, Reagan started out in radio sports announcing in the 1930s. He became a B-grade Hollywood star in the 1940s and helped purge communists from the Screen Actors Guild as the organization's president in the 1950s. In 1954 he became a spokesman for the General Electric Corporation and began preaching a conservative, antigovernment line. Reagan's skill in promoting the conservative cause inspired a group of wealthy California businessmen to help him launch his political career as governor of California from 1966 to 1974.

By 1980 the Republican party was ready to challenge the Democrats' hold on the White House. Bedeviled abroad and becalmed at home, Jimmy Carter's administration struck many Americans as bungling and befuddled. Carter's inability to control double-digit inflation was especially damaging. Frustrated critics bellyached loudly about the Georgian's alleged mismanagement of the nation's affairs.

Disaffection with Carter's apparent ineptitude ran deep even in his own Democratic party, where an "ABC" (Anybody But Carter) movement gathered steam. The liberal wing found their champion in Senator Edward Kennedy of Massachusetts, the last survivor of the assassin-plagued Kennedy brothers. He and Carter slugged it out in a series of bruising primary elections, while delighted Republicans decorously proceeded to name Reagan their presidential nominee. In the end Kennedy's candidacy fell victim to the country's conservative mood and to lingering suspicions about a 1969 automobile accident on Chappaquiddick Island, Massachusetts, in which a young woman assistant was drowned when Kennedy's car plunged off a bridge. A badly battered Carter, his party divided and in disarray, was left to do battle with Reagan.

The Republican candidate proved to be a formidable campaigner. Using his professional acting skills to great advantage, Reagan attacked the incumbent's fumbling performance in foreign policy and the Democratic party's "big-government philosophy." Galloping inflation, sky-high interest rates, and a faltering economy also put the sitting president on the defensive. Carter countered ineffectively with charges that Reagan was a trigger-happy cold warrior who might push the country into nuclear war.

Carter's spotty record in office was no defense against Reagan's popular appeal. On election day the Republican rang up a spectacular victory, bagging over 51 percent of the popular vote, while 41 percent went to Carter and 7 percent to independent candidate John Anderson. The electoral count stood at 489 for Reagan and 49 for Carter, who was the first elected president to be unseated since Herbert Hoover in 1932. Equally startling, the Republicans gained control of the Senate for the first time in twenty-five years. Leading Democratic liberals who had been "targeted" for defeat by well-heeled New-Right groups went down like dead timber in the conservative windstorm that swept the country.

Carter showed dignity in defeat. An unusually intelligent, articulate, and well-meaning president, he had been hampered by his lack of managerial talent and badly buffeted by events beyond his control,

The New Right Wing *Republican conservatives scored a double victory in 1980, winning control of both the White House and the Senate. Aided by conservative Democratic "boll weevils," they also dominated the House of Representatives, and a new era of conservatism dawned in the nation's capital.*

such as the soaring price of oil, runaway inflation, and the galling insult of the continuing hostage crisis in Iran. Though unsuccessful in the White House, Carter earned much admiration in later years for his humanitarian and human rights activities. He received the Nobel Peace Prize in 2002.

The Reagan Revolution

Reagan's arrival in Washington was triumphal. The Iranians contributed to the festive mood by releasing the hostages on Reagan's Inauguration Day, January 20, 1981, after 444 days of captivity. The new president, a hale and hearty sixty-nine-year-old, was devoted to fiscal fitness. A major goal of Reagan's political career was to reduce the size of the government by shrinking the federal budget and slashing taxes. Years of New Deal–style tax-and-spend programs, Reagan jested, had created a federal government that reminded him of the definition of a baby as a creature who was all appetite at one end, with no sense of responsibility at the other.

By the early 1980s, this antigovernment message was finding a receptive audience. In the two decades since 1960, federal spending had risen from about 18 percent of gross national product to nearly 23 per-

cent. After four decades of advancing New Deal and Great Society programs, a strong countercurrent took hold. Californians staged a "tax revolt" in 1978 (known by its official ballot title of "Proposition 13") that slashed property taxes and forced painful cuts in government services. The California "tax quake" jolted other state capitals and rocked even Washington, D.C. Ronald Reagan rode this political shock wave to presidential victory in 1980 and proceeded to rattle the "welfare state" to its very foundation.

With near-religious zeal, Reagan set out to persuade Congress to legislate his smaller-government policies into law. He proposed a new federal budget that necessitated cuts of some $35 billion, mostly in social programs like Food Stamps and federally funded job-training centers. Reagan worked naturally in harness with the Republican majority in the Senate, while in the Democratic House he enterprisingly wooed a group of mostly southern conservative Democrats (dubbed "boll weevils"), who abandoned their own party's leadership to follow the president.

Then on March 20, 1981, a deranged gunman shot the president as he was leaving a Washington hotel. A .22-caliber bullet penetrated beneath Reagan's left arm and collapsed his left lung. With admirable courage and grace, and with impressive physical resilience for a man his age, Reagan seemed to recover rapidly from his violent ordeal. Twelve days after the attack, he walked out of the hospital and returned to work. When he appeared a few days later on national television to address the Congress and the public on his budget, the outpouring of sympathy and support was enormous.

The Battle of the Budget

Swept along on a tide of presidential popularity, Congress swallowed Reagan's budget proposals, approving expenditures of some $695 billion. To hit those financial targets, drastic surgery was required, and Congress plunged its scalpel deep into Great Society–spawned social programs. Reagan's triumph amazed political observers, especially defeated Democrats. The new president had descended on Washington like an avenging angel of conservatism. He sought nothing less than the dismantling of the welfare state and the reversal of the political evolution of the preceding half-century. Reagan's impressive performance demonstrated the power of the presidency with a skill not seen since Lyndon Johnson's day.

Reagan hardly rested to savor the sweetness of his victory. The second part of his economic program called for deep tax cuts, amounting to 25 percent across-the-board reductions over a period of three years. Thanks largely to Reagan's skill as a television performer and the continued defection of the "boll weevils" from the Democratic camp, the president again had his way. In August 1981 Congress approved a set of far-reaching tax reforms that lowered individual tax rates, deeply slashed federal estate taxes, and created new tax-free savings plans for small investors. Reagan's "supply-side" economic advisers assured him that the combination of budgetary discipline and tax reduction would stimulate new investment, boost productivity, and foster dramatic economic growth.

But at first supply-side economics seemed to be a beautiful theory mugged by a gang of brutal facts, as the economy slid into its deepest recession since the 1930s. Unemployment reached nearly 11 percent in 1982, businesses folded, and several bank failures jolted the nation's entire financial system. The automobile industry, once the brightest jewel in America's industrial crown, reported losses in the hundreds of millions of dollars.

Ignoring the yawping pack of Democratic critics who charged that the president's budget cuts favored only the well-to-do, Reagan and his economic advisers serenely waited for their supply-side economic policies ("Reaganomics") to produce the promised results. The supply-siders seemed to be vindicated when a healthy economic recovery finally got under way in 1983. Yet the economy of the 1980s was not uniformly sound. For the first time in the twentieth century, income gaps widened between the richest and the poorest Americans. The poor got poorer and the very rich grew fabulously richer, while middle-class incomes largely stagnated. Symbolic of the new income stratification was the emergence of "yuppies," or young urban professionals, who sported Rolex watches and BMW sports cars. Though numbering only about 1.5 million people, yuppies showcased the values of materialism and the pursuit of wealth that came to symbolize the high-rolling 1980s.

Some economists located the sources of the economic upturn neither in the president's budget cuts and tax reforms nor in the go-get-'em avarice of the yuppies, but in his massive expenditures for the military. Reagan cascaded a budget of nearly $2 trillion onto the Pentagon in the 1980s, asserting the need to close the "window of vulnerability" in the armaments race with the Soviet Union. Ironically, this conservative president thereby plunged the government into a red-ink bath of deficit spending that made the New Deal look downright stingy. Federal budget deficits topped $100 billion in 1982, and the government's books were nearly $200 billion out of balance in every subsequent year of the 1980s. Massive government borrowing to cover these deficits kept interest rates high, and high interest rates in turn elevated the value of the dollar to record altitudes in international money markets. The soaring dollar dealt crippling blows to American exporters as the American international trade deficit reached a record $152 billion in 1987. The masters of international commerce and finance for a generation after World War II, Americans suddenly became the world's heaviest borrowers in the global economy of the 1980s.

Reagan Renews the Cold War

Hard as nails toward the Soviet Union in his campaign speeches, Reagan saw no reason to soften up after he checked in at the White House. He immediately warned that the Soviets were "prepared to commit any crime, to lie, to cheat" in pursuit of their goals of world conquest. In a later speech he characterized the Soviet empire as "the focus of evil in the modern world."

Reagan believed in negotiating with the Soviets—but only from a position of overwhelming strength. Accordingly, his strategy for dealing with Moscow was simple: by enormously expanding U.S. military capabilities, he could threaten the Soviet leaders with a fantastically expensive new round in the arms race. Desperate to avoid economic ruin, Kremlin leaders would come to the bargaining table and sing Reagan's tune.

This strategy resembled a riverboat gambler's ploy. It wagered the enormous sum of Reagan's defense budgets on the hope that the other side would not call Washington's bluff and initiate a new cycle of arms competition. Reagan played his trump card in this risky game in March 1983 when he announced his intention to pursue a high-technology missile defense system called the Strategic Defense Initiative (SDI), popularly known as "Star Wars." The plan called for orbiting battle stations in space that could fire laser beams or other forms of concentrated energy to vaporize intercontinental missiles on liftoff. Most scientists considered this an impossible goal, but the deeper logic of SDI lay in its fit with Reagan's overall Soviet strategy. By pitching the arms contest onto a stratospherically high plane of technology and astronomical expense, it would further force the Kremlin's hand.

Relations with the Soviets nose-dived in late 1981 when the government of Poland, needled by a popular union movement called "Solidarity," clamped martial law on the troubled country. Seeing the heavy fist of the Kremlin inside this Polish iron glove, Reagan imposed economic sanctions on Poland and the USSR alike.

Dealing with the Soviet Union was additionally complicated by the inertia and ill health of the aging oligarchs in the Kremlin, three of whom died between late 1982 and early 1985. Relations grew even more tense when the Soviets, in September 1983, blasted from the skies a Korean airliner, plummeting hundreds of civilians, including many Americans, to their deaths in the frigid Sea of Okhotsk. By the end of 1983, all arms-control negotiations with the Soviets were broken off. The deepening chill in the Cold War was further felt in 1984, when USSR and Soviet-bloc athletes boycotted the Olympic Games in Los Angeles.

Troubles Abroad

The volatile Middle Eastern pot continued to boil ominously. Israel badly strained its bonds of friendship with the United States by continuing to allow new settlements to be established in the occupied territory of the Jordan River's West Bank. Israel further raised the stakes in the Middle East in June 1982 when it invaded neighboring Lebanon, seeking to suppress once and for all the guerrilla bases from which Palestinian fighters harassed beleaguered Israel. The Palestinians were bloodily subdued, but Lebanon, already pulverized by years of episodic civil war, was plunged into armed chaos.

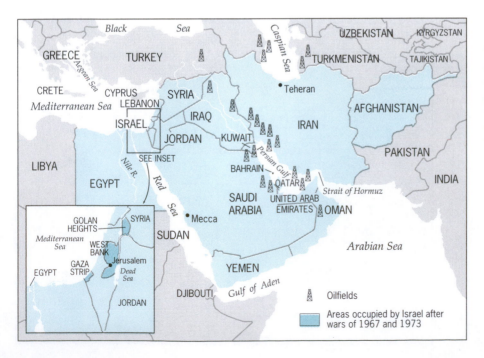

The Middle East *A combination of political instability and precious petroleum resources has made the region from Egypt to Afghanistan an "arc of crisis."*

President Reagan was obliged to send American troops to Lebanon in 1983 as part of an international peacekeeping force, but their presence did not bring peace. A suicidal bomber crashed an explosives-laden truck into U.S. Marine Corps barracks on October 23, 1983, killing more than two hundred marines. President Reagan soon thereafter withdrew the remaining American troops, miraculously suffering no political damage from this horrifying and humiliating attack. His mystified Democratic opponents began to call him a "Teflon president," to whom nothing hurtful could stick.

Central America, in the United States' own backyard, also rumbled menacingly. A leftist revolution had deposed the long-time dictator of Nicaragua in 1979. President Carter had tried to ignore the anti-American rhetoric of the revolutionaries, known as "Sandinistas," and to establish good diplomatic relations with them. But Reagan took their words at face value and hurled back at them some hot language of his own.

He accused the Sandinistas of turning their country into a forward base for Soviet and Cuban military penetration of all of Central America. Brandishing photographs taken from high-flying spy planes,

administration officials claimed that Nicaraguan leftists were shipping weapons to revolutionary forces in tiny El Salvador, torn by violence since a coup in 1979. Reagan sent military "advisers" to prop up the pro-American government of El Salvador. He also provided covert aid, including the CIA-engineered mining of harbors, to the "contra" rebels opposing the anti-American Sandinista government of Nicaragua.

Reagan flexed his military muscles elsewhere in the turbulent Caribbean as well. In a dramatic display of American might, in October 1983 he dispatched a heavy-firepower invasion force to the island of Grenada, where a military coup had killed the prime minister and brought Marxists to power. Swiftly overrunning the tiny island, American troops vividly demonstrated Reagan's determination to assert the dominance of the United States in the Caribbean, just as Theodore Roosevelt had done.

Round Two for Reagan

A confident Ronald Reagan, bolstered by a buoyant economy at home and by the popularity of his muscu-

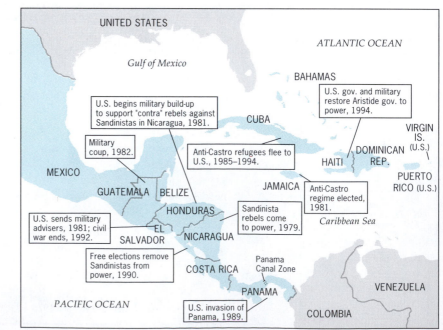

Central America and the Caribbean *This region of historic importance to the United States experienced dramatic political upheavals in the 1970s, 1980s, and 1990s.*

lar posture abroad, handily won the Republican nomination in 1984 for a second White House term. His opponent was Democrat Walter Mondale, who made history by naming as his vice-presidential running mate Congresswoman Geraldine Ferraro of New York. She was the first woman ever to appear on a major party presidential ticket. But even this dramatic gesture could not salvage Mondale's candidacy. On election day Reagan walked away with 525 electoral votes to Mondale's 13, winning everywhere except in Mondale's home state of Minnesota and the District of Columbia. Reagan also overwhelmed Mondale in the popular vote—52,609,797 to 36,450,613.

Shrinking the federal government and reducing taxes had been the main objectives of Reagan's first term; foreign-policy issues dominated the news in his second term. The president soon found himself contending for the world's attention with a charismatic new Soviet leader, Mikhail Gorbachev, installed as chairman of the Soviet Communist party in March 1985.

Gorbachev was personable, energetic, imaginative, and committed to radical reforms in the Soviet Union. He announced two policies with remarkable, even revolutionary, implications. *Glasnost,* or "openness," aimed to ventilate the secretive, repressive stuffiness of Soviet society by introducing free speech and a measure of political liberty. *Perestroika,* or "restructuring," was intended to revive the moribund Soviet economy by adopting many of the free-market practices—such as the profit motive and an end to subsidized prices—of the capitalist West.

Both *glasnost* and *perestroika* required that the Soviet Union shrink the size of its enormous military machine and redirect its energies to the civilian economy. That requirement, in turn, necessitated an end to the Cold War. Gorbachev accordingly made warm overtures to the West, including an announcement in April 1985 that the Soviet Union would cease to deploy intermediate-range nuclear forces (INF) targeted on Western Europe, pending an agreement on their complete elimination. He pushed this goal when he met with Ronald Reagan at their first of four summit meetings, in Geneva in November 1985. A second summit meeting in Reykjavik, Iceland, in October 1986 broke down in stalemate, but at a third summit in Washington, D.C., in December 1987, the

two leaders at last signed the INF Treaty, banning all intermediate-range nuclear missiles from Europe.

Reagan and Gorbachev capped their new friendship in May 1988 at a final summit in Moscow. There President Reagan, who had entered office condemning the "evil empire" of Soviet communism, warmly praised Gorbachev. Reagan, the consummate cold warrior, had been flexible and savvy enough to seize a historic opportunity to join with the Soviet chief to bring the Cold War to a kind of conclusion. For this, history would give both leaders high marks.

The Iran-Contra Imbroglio

Two foreign-policy problems seemed insoluble to Reagan: the continuing captivity of a number of American hostages seized by Muslim extremist groups in bleeding, battered Lebanon; and the continuing grip on power of the left-wing Sandinista government in Nicaragua. The president repeatedly requested that Congress provide military aid to the contra rebels fighting against the Sandinista regime. Congress repeatedly refused, and the administration grew increasingly frustrated, even obsessed, in its search for a means to help the contras.

Unbeknownst to the American public, some Washington officials saw a possible linkage between the two thorny problems of the Middle Eastern hostages and the Central American Sandinistas. In 1985 American diplomats secretly arranged arms sales to embattled Iran, then fighting a war with neighboring Iraq, in return for Iranian aid in obtaining the release of American hostages held by Middle Eastern terrorists. At least one hostage was eventually set free. Meanwhile, money from the payment for the arms was diverted to the contras. These actions brazenly violated a congressional ban on military aid to the Nicaraguan rebels—not to mention Reagan's repeated vow that he would never negotiate with terrorists.

News of these secret dealings broke in November 1986 and ignited a firestorm of controversy. President Reagan claimed he was innocent of wrongdoing and ignorant about the activities of his subordinates, but a congressional committee condemned the "secrecy, deception, and disdain for the law" displayed by administration officials and concluded that "if the president did not know what his national security advisers were doing, he should have."

The Iran-contra affair cast a dark shadow over Reagan's record in foreign policy, tending to obscure the president's achievement in establishing a new relationship with the Soviets. Although the several Iran-contra investigations presented damaging revelations of Reagan's weaknesses and laziness as a chief executive, he remained among the most popular and beloved presidents in modern American history.

Reagan's Economic Legacy

Ronald Reagan had taken office vowing to invigorate the American economy by rolling back government regulations, lowering taxes, and balancing the budget. He did ease many regulatory rules, and he pushed major tax-reform bills through Congress in 1981 and 1986. But a balanced budget remained grotesquely out of reach. The combination of tax reduction and huge increases in military spending opened a vast "revenue hole" of $200 billion in annual deficits. In his eight years in office, President Reagan added nearly $2 trillion to the national debt—more than all his predecessors combined.

The staggering deficits of the Reagan years assuredly constituted a great economic failure. And because foreign lenders, especially the Japanese, financed so much of the Reagan-era debt, the deficits virtually guaranteed that future generations of Americans would have to either work harder than their parents or lower their standard of living, or both, to pay their foreign creditors.

But if the deficits represented an economic failure, they also constituted, strangely enough, a kind of political triumph. By making new social spending both practically and politically impossible, the deficits achieved one of Reagan's paramount goals: slowing the growth of government and blocking or even repealing the social programs launched in the era of Lyndon Johnson's Great Society. They achieved, in short, Reagan's highest political objective: the containment of the welfare state. Ronald Reagan thus ensured the long-term perpetuation of his values to a degree that few presidents have managed to achieve. For better or worse, the consequences of "Reaganomics" would be large and durable.

The Religious Right

Religion pervaded American politics in the 1980s. Especially conspicuous was a coalition of conservative evangelical Christians known as the religious right. In 1979 the Reverend Jerry Falwell, an evangelical minister from Lynchburg, Virginia, founded a political organization called the Moral Majority. Falwell preached with great success against sexual permissiveness, abortion, feminism, and the spread of gay rights. In its first two years, the Moral Majority registered between 2 million and 3 million voters. Using radio, direct-mail marketing, and cable TV, "televangelists" reached huge audiences in the 1980s, collected millions of dollars, and became aggressive political advocates of conservative causes.

Members of the religious right were sometimes called "movement conservatives," a term that recalls the left-wing protest movements of the 1960s. In many ways the religious right of the 1980s was a reflection of, or an answer to, sixties radicalism. Feminists in the 1960s declared that "the personal was political." The religious right did the same. What had in the past been personal matters—gender roles, homosexuality, and prayer—became the organizing ground for a powerful political movement. Like advocates of multiculturalism and affirmative action, the religious right practiced a form of "identity politics." But rather than defining themselves as Hispanic voters or gay voters, they declared themselves Christian or pro-life voters. The New Right also mimicked the New Left in some of its tactics. If the left had consciousness-raising sessions, the right had prayer meetings. If protesters in the 1960s blocked entrances to draft offices, protesters in the 1980s blocked entrances to abortion clinics.

Several leaders of the religious right fell victim to financial or sexual misconduct in the latter part of the decade. But such scandals would not shake the faith of America's conservative Christians or diminish the new political clout of activist, evangelical religionists.

Conservatism in the Courts

If the budget was Reagan's chief weapon in the war against the welfare state, the courts became his principal instrument in the "culture wars" demanded by the religious right. By the time he left office, Reagan had appointed a near-majority of all sitting federal judges. Equally important, he had named three conservative-minded justices to the U.S. Supreme Court. They included Sandra Day O'Connor, a brilliant, public-spirited Arizona judge. When she was sworn in on September 25, 1981, she became the first woman to ascend to the high bench in the Court's nearly two-hundred-year history.

Reaganism repudiated two great icons of the liberal political culture: affirmative action and abortion. The Court showed its newly conservative colors in 1984, when it decreed, in a case involving Memphis fire fighters, that union rules about job seniority could outweigh affirmative-action concerns in guiding promotion policies in the city's fire department. In two cases in 1989 (*Ward's Cove Packing* v. *Antonia* and *Martin* v. *Wilks*), the Court made it more difficult to prove that an employer practiced racial discrimination in hiring and made it easier for white males to argue that they were the victims of reverse discrimination. Congress passed legislation in 1991 that partially limited the effects of these decisions.

The contentious issue of abortion also reached the Court in 1989. In the case of *Roe* v. *Wade* in 1973, the Supreme Court had prohibited states from making laws that interfered with a woman's right to an abortion during the early months of pregnancy. For nearly two decades, that decision had been the bedrock principle on which "pro-choice" advocates built their case for abortion rights. It had also provoked bitter criticism from Roman Catholics and various "right-to-life" groups, who wanted a virtually absolute ban on all abortions. In *Webster* v. *Reproductive Health Services*, the Court in July 1989 did not entirely overturn *Roe*, but it seriously compromised *Roe*'s protection of abortion rights. By approving a Missouri law that imposed certain restrictions on abortion, the Court signaled that it was inviting the states to legislate in an area in which Roe had previously forbidden them to legislate.

Right-to-life advocates were at first delighted by the *Webster* decision. But the Court's ruling also galvanized pro-choice organizations into a new militancy. Bruising, divisive battles loomed as state legislatures across the land confronted abortion. This painful cultural conflict over the unborn was also part of the Reagan era's bequest to the future.

The Abortion Wars
Pro-choice and pro-life demonstrators brandish their beliefs. By the beginning of the twenty-first century, the debate over abortion had become the most morally charged and divisive issue in American society since the struggle over slavery in the nineteenth century.

Referendum on Reaganism in 1988

Republicans lost control of the Senate in the off-year elections of November 1986. Hopes rose among Democrats that the "Reagan revolution" might be showing signs of political vulnerability at last. The newly Democratic majority in the Senate flexed its political muscle in 1987 when it rejected Robert Bork, the president's ultraconservative nominee for a Supreme Court vacancy. Democrats also relished the prospect of making political hay out of both the Iran-contra scandal and the allegedly unethical behavior that tainted an unusually large number of Reagan's "official family."

Disquieting signs of economic trouble also seemed to open political opportunities for Democrats. The double mountain of deficits—the federal budget deficit and international trade deficit—continued to mount ominously. Falling oil prices blighted the economy of the Southwest, slashing real estate values and undermining hundreds of savings and loan (S&L) institutions. The damage to the S&Ls was so massive that a federal rescue operation was eventually estimated to carry a price tag of well over $500 billion. A wave of mergers, acquisitions, and leveraged buyouts washed over Wall Street, leaving many brokers and traders megarich and many companies saddled with megadebt. A cold spasm of fear struck the money markets on "Black Monday," October 19, 1987, when the leading stock-market index plunged 508 points—the largest one-day decline in history. This crash, said *Newsweek* magazine, heralded "the final collapse of the money culture . . . , the death knell of the 1980s." But as Mark Twain famously commented about his own obituary, this announcement proved premature.

Hoping to cash in on these ethical and economic anxieties, a pack of Democrats—dubbed the "Seven Dwarfs" by derisive Republicans—chased after their party's 1988 presidential nomination. Black candidate Jesse Jackson, a rousing speechmaker who hoped to forge a "rainbow coalition" of minorities and the disadvantaged, campaigned energetically. But the Democratic nomination in the end went to the coolly cerebral governor of Massachusetts, Michael Dukakis. Republicans nominated Reagan's vice president, George Bush, who ran largely on the Reagan record of tax cuts, strong defense policies, toughness on crime, opposition to abortion, and a long-running if hardly robust economic expansion. Dukakis made little headway exploiting the ethical and economic sorespots and came across to television viewers as almost supernaturally devoid of emotion. On election day the voters gave him just 40,797,905 votes to 47,645,225 for Bush. The Electoral College count was 111 to 426.

George Bush and the End of the Cold War

George Herbert Walker Bush was born with a silver spoon in his mouth. His father had served as a U.S. senator from Connecticut, and young George enjoyed a first-rate education at Yale. After service in World War II, he amassed a modest fortune in the oil business in Texas. His deepest commitment, however, was to public service; he left the business world to serve briefly as a congressman and then held various posts in several Republican administrations, including emissary to China, ambassador to the United Nations, director of the Central Intelligence Agency, and vice president. He capped this long political career when he was inaugurated as president of the United States in January 1989, promising to work for "a kinder, gentler America."

In the first months of the Bush administration, the communist world commanded the planet's fascinated attention. Everywhere in the communist bloc it seemed, astoundingly, that the season of democracy had arrived.

In China hundreds of thousands of prodemocracy demonstrators thronged Beijing's Tiananmen Square in the spring of 1989. But in June of that year, China's aging and autocratic rulers brutally crushed the prodemocracy movement. Tanks rolled over the crowds, and machine-gunners killed hundreds of protesters. World opinion roundly condemned the bloody suppression of the Chinese prodemocracy demonstrators. President Bush joined in the criticism. Yet despite angry demands in Congress for punitive restrictions on trade with China, the president insisted on maintaining normal relations with Beijing.

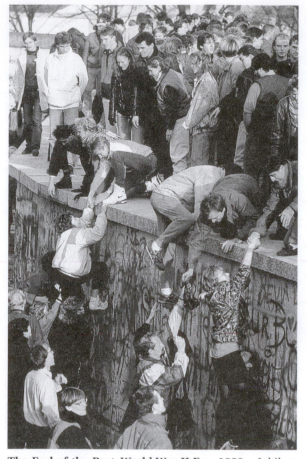

The End of the Post–World War II Era, 1989   *Jubilant Berliners partied atop the hated Berlin Wall in December 1989, dramatically symbolizing the end of the Cold War division of Germany.*

Stunning changes also shook Eastern Europe. Long oppressed by puppet regimes propped up by Soviet guns, the region was revolutionized in just a few startling months in 1989. The Solidarity movement in Poland led the way when it toppled Poland's communist government in August. With dizzying speed, communist regimes collapsed in Hungary, Czechoslovakia, East Germany, and even hyperrepressive Romania. In December 1989, jubilant Germans danced atop the hated Berlin Wall, symbol of the division of Germany and all of Europe into two armed and hostile camps. The Wall itself soon came down, heralding the imminent end of the forty-five-year-long Cold War. With the

approval of the victorious Allied powers of World War II, the two Germanies, divided since 1945, were at last reunited in October 1990.

Most startling of all were the changes that swept the heartland of world communism, the Soviet Union. Mikhail Gorbachev's policies of *glasnost* and *perestroika* had set in motion a groundswell that surged out of his control. Old-guard hard-liners, in a last-gasp effort to preserve the tottering communist system, attempted to dislodge Gorbachev with a military coup in August 1991. With the support of Boris Yeltsin, president of the Russian Republic (one of several republics that composed the Union of Soviet Socialist Republics), Gorbachev foiled the plotters. But in December 1991 Gorbachev resigned as president, and the Soviet Union dissolved into fifteen sovereign republics, with Russia the most powerful state and Yeltsin the dominant leader. To varying degrees, all the new governments in the former Soviet republics repudiated communism and embraced democratic reforms and free-market economies.

The demise of the Soviet Union wrote a definitive finish to the Cold War era. More than four decades of nail-biting tension between the two nuclear superpowers, the Soviet Union and the United States, evaporated when the USSR dismantled itself. With the Soviet Union swept into the dustbin of history and communism all but extinct, Bush spoke hopefully of a "new world order," in which democracy would reign and diplomacy would take the place of weaponry. But the disintegration of the Soviet Union posed new questions. Who would control the formidable Soviet nuclear arsenal and enforce arms-control agreements with the United States?

Throughout the former Soviet empire, waves of nationalistic fervor and long-suppressed ethnic and racial hatred rolled across the vast land as communism's roots were wrenched out. A particularly nasty conflict erupted in 1991, when the Chechnyan minority tried to declare their independence from Russia. Ethnic warfare flared in other former communist countries as well, notably in misery-drenched former Yugoslavia, racked by vicious "ethnic cleansing" against minorities. The cruel and paradoxical truth stood revealed that the calcified communist regimes of Eastern Europe, whatever their sins, had at least bottled up the ancient ethnic antagonisms that

The legend reads:

- Communist regimes overthrown since 1989
  - Rise of Solidarity in Poland, 1980.
  - Czechoslovakia broken into Czech Republic and Slovakia in 1993.
- Soviet Union, dissolved in 1991 and replaced by Commonwealth of Independent States
- Yugoslavia, dissolved in civil war, 1991–1992

Gorbachev assumes power, 1985; Moscow coup fails, Boris Yeltsin declared President of Russia, 1990; USSR dissolved, 1991.

Fall of Berlin Wall, 1989; Germany unified, 1990.

Chechnya declares independence, 1991; Russia attacks 1994.

The Breakup of Yugoslavia

U.S. troops join NATO peacekeeping forces, Dec. 1995.

The End of the Cold War Changes the Map of Europe

were the region's peculiar curse and that now erupted in all their historical fury.

Refugees from the strife-torn regions flooded into Western Europe. The sturdy German economy, the foundation of European prosperity, wobbled under the awesome burden of absorbing technologically backward, physically decrepit East Germany. The Western democracies, which for more than four decades had feared the military *strength* of the Eastern bloc, now saw their well-being threatened by the social and economic *weakness* of the former communist lands.

The end of the Cold War also proved a mixed blessing for the United States. With the Soviet threat canceled, Americans might resort to their traditional isolationism. The Soviet-American rivalry, with its demands for high levels of military preparedness, had also sustained huge sectors of the American economy such as aerospace. The Pentagon in 1991 closed thirty-four military bases and canceled a $52 billion order for a navy attack plane, and more cancellations followed. Unemployment soared in southern California and other areas that had once been deluged with Pentagon dollars. The problems of weaning the U.S. economy from its decades of dependence on defense spending tempered the euphoria of Americans as they welcomed the Cold War's long-awaited finale.

The Persian Gulf War

Sadly, the end of the Cold War did not mean the end of all wars. President Bush flexed the United States' still-intimidating military muscle in tiny Panama in December 1989, when he sent airborne troops to capture dictator and drug lord Manuel Noriega.

Still more ominous events in the summer of 1990 severely tested Bush's dream of a democratic and peaceful new world order. By August, Saddam Hussein, the brutal and ambitious ruler of Iraq, sent his armies to overrun Kuwait, a tiny, oil-rich desert sheikdom on Iraq's southern frontier. Oil fueled his aggression. Financially exhausted by its eight-year war with Iran that had ended in stalemate in 1988, Iraq needed Kuwait's oil to pay its huge war bills. Saddam's larger design was iron-fisted control over the entire Persian Gulf region. With his hand thus firmly clutching the world's economic jugular vein, he dreamed of dictating the terms of oil supplies to the industrial nations, and perhaps of totally extinguishing the Arabs' enemy, Israel.

On August 2, 1990, Saddam's army roared into Kuwait. The speed and audacity of the invasion were stunning, but the world responded just as swiftly. The United Nations Security Council unanimously condemned the invasion on August 3 and demanded the immediate and unconditional withdrawal of Iraq's troops. In November the Security Council delivered an ultimatum: Saddam must leave Kuwait by January 15, 1991, or U.N. forces would "use all necessary means" to expel his troops. For perhaps the first time in the post–World War II era, the U.N. seemed to be fulfilling its founders' dreams that it could preserve international order by putting guns where its mouth was. It also put them where the world's critical oil supply was.

In a logistical operation of astonishing complexity, meanwhile, the United States spearheaded a massive international military deployment on the sandy Arabian peninsula. As the January 15 deadline approached, some 539,000 U.S. soldiers, sailors, and pilots—many of them women and all of them members of the new, post-Vietnam, all-volunteer American military—had swarmed into the Persian Gulf region. They were joined by nearly 270,000 troops, pilots, and sailors from twenty-eight other countries in the coalition opposed to Iraq. When all diplomatic efforts to resolve the crisis failed, the U.S. Congress voted on January 12, 1991, to approve the use of force.

On January 16, 1991, the United States and its U.N. allies unleashed a hellish air war against Iraq. For thirty-seven days, warplanes pummeled targets in occupied Kuwait and in Iraq itself. Iraq responded to this pounding by launching several dozen "Scud" short-range ballistic missiles against military and civilian targets in Saudi Arabia and Israel. These missile attacks claimed several lives but did no significant military damage.

Yet if Iraq made but a feeble military response to the air campaign, the allied commander, the beefy and blunt American general Norman ("Stormin' Norman") Schwarzkopf, took nothing for granted. Saddam, who had threatened to wage "the mother of all battles," had the capacity to inflict awful damage. Iraq had stockpiled tons of chemical and biological weapons, including poison gas and the means to spread epidemics of anthrax.

Saddam's tactics also included ecological warfare as he released a gigantic oil slick into the Persian Gulf to forestall amphibious assault and ignited hundreds of oil-well fires whose smoky plumes shrouded the ground from aerial view. Faced with these horrifying tactics, Schwarzkopf's strategy was starkly simple: soften the Iraqis with relentless bombing, then suffocate them on the ground with a tidal-wave rush of troops and armor.

On February 23 the dreaded and long-awaited land war began. Dubbed "Operation Desert Storm," it lasted only four days—the "hundred-hour war." With lightning speed the U.N. forces penetrated deep into Iraq, outflanking the occupying army in Kuwait and blocking the enemy's ability either to retreat or to reinforce. Allied casualties were amazingly light whereas much of Iraq's remaining fighting force was quickly destroyed or captured. On February 27 Saddam accepted a cease-fire, and Kuwait was liberated.

Most Americans cheered the war's rapid and enormously successful conclusion. The war had nevertheless failed to dislodge Saddam Hussein from power. When the smoke cleared, he had survived to menace the world another day. The perpetually troubled Middle East knew scarcely less trouble after "Desert Storm" had ceased to thunder, and the United States, for better or worse, found itself more deeply ensnared in the region's web of mortal hatreds and intractable conflicts.

Bush on the Home Front

In his inaugural address, George Bush had pledged that he would work for a "kinder, gentler America." He redeemed that promise in part when he signed the Americans with Disabilities Act (ADA) in 1990, a landmark law prohibiting discrimination against the

43 million U.S. citizens with physical or mental disabilities. The president also signed a major water projects bill in 1992 that put the interests of the environment ahead of agriculture, especially in California's heavily irrigated Central Valley.

The new president continued to aggravate the explosive "social issues" that had so divided Americans throughout the 1980s, especially the nettlesome questions of affirmative action and abortion. Bush challenged the legality of college scholarships targeted for racial minorities, and he only grudgingly approved a watered-down civil rights bill in 1991 that was designed to make it easier for employees to prove discrimination in hiring and promotion.

Most provocatively, in 1991 Bush nominated for the Supreme Court the conservative African-American jurist Clarence Thomas, a stern critic of affirmative-action policies. Thomas's nomination was loudly opposed by labor, civil rights, and women's organizations. Reflecting irreconcilable divisions over affirmative action and abortion, the Senate Judiciary Committee concluded its hearings with a divided 7-to-7 vote and forwarded the matter to the Senate without a recommendation.

Then, just days before the Senate was scheduled to vote in early October 1991, a press leak revealed that Anita Hill, a University of Oklahoma law professor, had accused Thomas of sexual harassment. The Senate Judiciary Committee was forced to reopen its hearings. For days, a prurient American public sat glued to their television sets as Hill graphically detailed her charges of sexual improprieties and Thomas angrily responded. In the end, by a 52-to-48 vote, the Senate narrowly confirmed Thomas as the second African-American ever to sit on the supreme bench (Thurgood Marshall was the first). While many Americans hailed Hill as a heroine for her role in raising the issue of sexual harassment, Thomas maintained that her unproved allegations amounted to "a high-tech lynching for uppity blacks who in any way deign to think for themselves, to do for themselves."

The furor over Clarence Thomas's confirmation suggested that the social issues that had helped produce three Republican presidential victories in the 1980s were losing some of their electoral appeal. Many women, enraged by the all-male judiciary committee's behavior in the Clarence Thomas hearings,

grew increasingly critical of the president's uncompromising stand on abortion. A "gender gap" opened between the two political parties, as pro-choice women grew increasingly cool toward the strong anti-abortion stand of the Republicans.

Still more damaging to President Bush's political health, the economy sputtered and stalled almost at the outset of his administration. By 1992 the unemployment rate exceeded 7 percent, while the federal budget deficit continued to mushroom, topping $250 billion in each year of Bush's presidency. In a desperate attempt to stop the hemorrhage of red ink, Bush and Congress agreed in 1990 to a budget that included $133 billion in new taxes.

Bush's 1990 tax and budget package added up to a political catastrophe. In his 1988 presidential campaign, Bush had belligerently declared, "Read my lips—no new taxes." Now he had flagrantly broken that campaign promise.

The uncontrolled budgetary crisis and the stagnant economy congealed into a lump of disgust with all political incumbents. Disillusion thickened in 1991 when it was revealed that many members of the House of Representatives had written thousands of bad checks from their accounts in a private House "bank." Unprecedented numbers of officeholders declined to seek reelection, and a movement to impose term limits on elected officials gained strength in many states.

Bill Clinton: The First Baby-Boomer President

The slumbering economy, the widening gender gap, and the rising anti-incumbent spirit spelled opportunity for Democrats, frozen out of the White House for all but four years since 1968. In a bruising round of primary elections, Governor William Jefferson Clinton of Arkansas weathered blistering accusations of womanizing and draft evasion to emerge as his party's standard-bearer, with Senator Albert Gore of Tennessee as his vice-presidential running mate.

Clinton claimed to be a "new" Democrat, chastened by his party's long exile in the political wilderness. Clinton and other centrist Democrats attempted to point their party away from its traditional antibusiness, dovish, champion-of-the-underdog orientation. Clinton campaigned especially vigorously on promises to stimulate the economy, reform the welfare system, and overhaul the nation's scandalously expensive and inefficient health-care apparatus.

Trying to wring one more win out of the social issues that had underwritten the presidential victories of Reagan and Bush, the Republican convention in Houston dwelled stridently on "family values" as it renominated George Bush and Vice President J. Danforth Quayle for a second term. A tired Bush attacked Clinton's character and tried to take credit for the end of the Cold War. But fear for the economic problems of the future swayed more voters than pride in the foreign policies of the past. The purchasing power of the average worker's paycheck had actually declined during Bush's presidency.

Reflecting pervasive economic unease and the virulence of the throw-the-bums-out national mood, nearly 20 percent of voters cast their ballots for independent presidential candidate H. Ross Perot, a bantam-weight, jug-eared Texas billionaire who made a boast of the fact that he had never held any public office. With a record turnout of voters on election day, the final tallies gave Clinton 43,728,275 popular votes and 370 in the Electoral College. Bush polled 38,167,416 popular and 168 electoral votes. Perot won no electoral votes but did gather 19,237,247 in the popular count—the strongest showing for an independent or third-party candidate since Theodore Roosevelt ran on the Bull Moose ticket in 1912. Democrats also racked up clear majorities in both houses of Congress, which seated near-record numbers of new members, including thirty-nine African-Americans, nineteen Hispanic-Americans, seven Asian-Americans, one Native American, and forty-eight women. In Illinois Carol Moseley-Braun became the first African-American woman elected to the U.S. Senate, where she joined five other women in the largest female contingent ever in the upper chamber.

Women also figured prominently in President Clinton's cabinet, including the first female attorney general, Janet Reno, and former Wisconsin University president Donna Shalala, who became secretary of health and human services. Vowing to shape a government that "looked like America," Clinton appointed several ethnic and racial minority members to his cabinet contingent, including former San Antonio mayor Henry Cisneros at Housing and Urban Development and an African-American, Ron Brown, as secretary of commerce. Clinton also seized the opportunity in 1993 to nominate Ruth Bader Ginsburg to the Supreme Court, where she joined Sandra Day O'Connor to make a pair of women justices.

Clinton's Ups and Downs

Badly overestimating his electoral mandate for liberal reform, the young president made a series of costly blunders upon entering the White House. He first stirred controversy by advocating an end to the ban on gays and lesbians in the armed forces. Faced with ferocious opposition, he had to settle for a "don't ask, don't tell" policy that meant no official acknowledgment of gay and lesbian soldiers and sailors.

Even more damaging to Clinton's political standing was the fiasco of his attempt to reform the nation's health-care system. In a dramatic innovation, the president put his wife, Hillary Rodham Clinton, in charge of a task force to redesign the medical-service industry. The committee unveiled its stupefyingly complicated plan in October 1993. It was virtually dead on arrival in Congress. Its principal architect, the First Lady was doused with a torrent of abuse. Having entered the White House as a full political partner with her husband, she assumed a less visible though still active public profile, and in 2000 was elected a United States senator from New York.

Clinton had better luck with a deficit-reduction bill in 1993, which combined with an increasingly buoyant economy to shrink the federal deficit to its lowest level in more than a decade. By 1998 Clinton's economic policymakers had ceased to fret about the rapacious deficit monster, and Congress had begun to argue over how to spend projected federal budget surpluses.

Clinton induced the Congress in 1993 to pass a gun-control law, the "Brady Bill," named for presidential aide James Brady, severely wounded in the assassination attempt on President Ronald Reagan in 1981. In 1994 Clinton also pushed through a $30 billion anticrime bill that included a ban on many assault weapons.

With these measures the government struggled to hold the line against an epidemic of violence that rocked American society in the 1990s. The World Trade Center in New York City was bombed in 1993. That same year federal agents stormed the Waco, Texas, compound of the fundamentalist Branch Davidians, resulting in many deaths, including women and children. On the second anniversary of the Waco assault, a bomb destroyed a federal office building in Oklahoma City, taking 169 lives. In July 1998 a lone gunman killed two policemen inside the U.S. Capitol building itself. These episodes brought to light a secretive underground of paramilitary private "militias" and fervent antigovernment activists often armed to the teeth.

Even many law-abiding citizens shared to some degree in the antigovernment attitudes that drove a few people to murderous extremes. Thanks largely to the disillusionment spawned by Vietnam and Watergate, the confidence in government that came naturally to the World War II generation was in short supply at century's end. Reflecting that pervasive disenchantment with politics, some twenty-four states had imposed term-limit restrictions on elected officials by the late 1990s, though the Supreme Court ruled in 1995 that such laws could not apply to federal officeholders.

Clinton's failed initiatives and widespread antigovernment sentiment offered conservative Republicans a golden opportunity in 1994, and they seized it aggressively. Led by outspoken Georgia representative Newt Gingrich, conservatives offered voters a "Contract with America" that promised an all-out assault on budget deficits and radical reductions in welfare programs. Their campaign succeeded fabulously, as Republicans picked up eleven governorships, eight Senate seats, and fifty-three seats in the House, giving them control of both chambers of Congress for the first time in forty years.

But if President Clinton had overplayed his mandate for liberal reform in 1993, the congressional Republicans now proceeded to overplay their mandate for conservative retrenchment. The new Republican majority did achieve one long-standing conservative goal by restricting "unfunded mandates"—federal laws that imposed new obligations on state and local governments without providing new revenues. And in 1996 the new Congress achieved a major conservative victory when it compelled a reluctant Clinton to sign the Welfare Reform Bill, which made deep cuts in welfare grants and required able-bodied welfare recipients to find employment. Democrats howled with pain at the president's alleged betrayal of his party's heritage. But Clinton's acceptance of welfare reform became part of his shrewd political strategy of accommodating the electorate's conservative mood by sidestepping to his right.

President Clinton was at first stunned by the magnitude of the Republican congressional victory in 1994. But many Americans gradually came to feel that the Gingrich Republicans were bending the bow too far. In a tense confrontation between the Democratic president and the Republican Congress, the federal government actually had to shut down for several days at the end of 1995, until a budget package was agreed upon. These outlandishly partisan antics bred a backlash that helped President Clinton rebound from his condition as a political dead duck.

As the Republicans slugged it out in a noisy round of presidential primaries in 1996, Clinton's reelection campaign raised spectacular sums of money—some of it, investigations later revealed, from questionable sources. The eventual Republican standard-bearer was Kansas senator Robert Dole, a decorated World War II veteran who ran a listless campaign. Clinton, buoyed by a healthy economy and by his artful trimming to the conservative wind, breezed to an easy victory, with 45,628,667 popular votes to Dole's 37,869,435. The Reform party's egomaniacal leader, Ross Perot, ran a sorry third, picking up less than half the votes he had garnered in 1992. Clinton won 379 electoral votes, Dole only 159. But Republicans retained control of Congress.

Clinton Again

As Clinton began his second term—the first Democrat since Franklin Delano Roosevelt to be reelected—he again composed a diversified cabinet, but the heady promises of far-reaching reform with which he had entered the White House four years earlier were no longer heard. Still facing Republican majorities in both houses of Congress, he proposed only modest legislative goals, even though soaring tax revenues generated by the prosperous economy produced in 1999 a balanced federal budget for the first time in three decades.

Clinton cleverly managed to put Republicans on the defensive by claiming the political middle ground on contentious welfare and affirmative-action issues. He now warmly embraced the landmark Welfare Reform Bill of 1996 that he had initially been slow to endorse.

Juggling the political hot potato of affirmative action, Clinton pledged to "mend it, not end it." When voters in California in 1996 approved Proposition 209, prohibiting affirmative-action preferences in government and higher education, the number of minority students in the state's public universities temporarily plummeted. A federal appeals court decision, *Hopwood* v. *Texas,* had similar effects in Texas. Clinton criticized these broad assaults on affirmative action but stopped short of trying to reverse them, aware that public support for affirmative action, especially among white Americans, had diminished since the 1970s. In California and elsewhere, Clinton-style Democrats increasingly sought ways to aid the economically disadvantaged, including minorities, while avoiding the minefield of racial preferences.

Clinton's major political advantage continued to be the roaring economy, which by 2000 had sustained the longest period of growth in American history. While unemployment crept down below 4 percent and businesses scrambled madly for workers, inflationary pressure remained remarkably low. An economic crisis in late 1997 plunged Southeast Asia and South Korea into financial turmoil, arousing fears of a global economic meltdown. But despite volatility in the stock market, the United States surged ahead, fueled by new Internet businesses and other high-tech and media companies. The economic "Asian flu" caused only a few sniffles for the robust American economy.

Prosperity did not make Clinton immune to controversy over trade policy. During his first term, Clinton had displayed political courage by supporting the North American Free Trade Agreement (NAFTA), creating in 1993 a free-trade zone encompassing Mexico, Canada, and the United States. Clinton took another step in 1994 toward a global free-trade system when he vigorously promoted the creation of the World Trade Organization (WTO), a cherished goal of free-trade advocates since the end of the Second World War. But simmering discontent over trade policy boiled over in 1999 during WTO meetings in Seattle, where the streets filled with protesters railing against what they viewed as the human and environmental costs of "globalization." The trade talks fizzled in Seattle, with Clinton taking a hefty share of the blame.

Money spurred controversy of another sort in the late 1990s. Campaign finance reform, long smoldering as a potential issue, suddenly flared up after the 1996 presidential campaign. Congressional investigators revealed that the Clinton campaign had milked many improper sources for funds, including contributors who paid to stay overnight in the White House and foreigners who were legally prohibited from giving to American campaigns. Both Republicans and Democrats had grown dependent on vast sums to finance television ads for their candidates, and Clinton did little more than pay lip-service to the cause of campaign finance reform. But a few mavericks in both parties proposed to eliminate the corrupting influence of big donors. Senator John McCain of Arizona made campaign finance reform a centerpiece of his surprisingly strong, though ultimately unsuccessful, bid for the Republican presidential nomination in the 2000 campaign.

Two domestic issues inspired Clinton in his second term to act boldly: the fights *against* big tobacco and *for* gun control. In 1998 Clinton put his weight behind a proposed legal settlement whereby tobacco firms would give the states $358 billion to offset the public-health costs of smoking in exchange for immunity from further state and federal litigation. The deal collapsed, but the Clinton administration then turned to the courts in hopes of forcing the tobacco industry to reimburse the federal government for dollars it had spent since the 1950s on smokers' health.

Clinton's focus on gun control had a tragic impetus. On an April morning in 1999, two students at Columbine High School in Littleton, Colorado, killed twelve fellow students and a teacher in the deadliest of a series of school shootings that had shaken the nation since the mid-1990s. Debate flared over the origins of this epidemic of school violence. Some observers blamed the violence of Hollywood and video games, others the failings of parents. But the culprit that attracted the most sustained political attention was guns. Clinton engaged in a pugnacious debate with the pro-gun National Rifle Association over the need to toughen gun laws. A "Million Mom March" in Washington in May 2000 demonstrated the growing public support for new anti-gun measures.

Problems Abroad

The end of the Cold War robbed the United States of the basic principles on which it had conducted foreign policy for nearly half a century, and the Clinton administration groped for a diplomatic formula to replace anticommunism as the guiding mechanism in America's foreign affairs. The Cold War's finale also shook a number of skeletons loose from several government closets. Sensational revelations that Central Intelligence Agency double agents had sold secrets to the Soviets during the Cold War years, causing the execution of American agents abroad, demonstrated that the ghost of Cold War past still cast its frosty shadow over official Washington.

Absorbed by domestic issues, President Clinton at first seemed uncertain and even amateurish in his conduct of foreign policy. He followed his predecessor's lead in dispatching American peacekeeping troops to Somalia but quietly withdrew them after Somali rebels killed more than a dozen Americans in late 1993. Burned in Somalia, Washington stood on the sidelines when ethnic violence in Rwanda killed half a million people. A similar reluctance afflicted policy toward Haiti, where democratically elected president Jean-Bertrand Aristide had been deposed by a military coup in 1991. Clinton at last committed twenty thousand American troops to restore Aristide to the Haitian presidency in 1994.

Clinton also did an about-face on his China policy. He had denounced George Bush in 1992 for not imposing economic sanctions on China as punishment for Beijing's wretched record of human rights abuses. But after taking office, Clinton's awareness of China's economic importance to the United States led him to backpedal on his criticism of the Beijing regime. By 2000 Clinton was crusading to make China a full-fledged trading partner of the United States.

Clinton's approach to the tormented Balkans in southeastern Europe showed a similar initial hesitation, followed eventually by his assumption of a leadership role. In the former Yugoslavia, as vicious ethnic conflict raged through Bosnia, the Washington government dithered until finally deciding to commit American troops to a NATO peacekeeping contingent in late 1995. When Serbian president Slobodan Milosević in 1999 unleashed a new round of "ethnic cleansing" in the region, this time against ethnic Albanians in the province of Kosovo, U.S.-led NATO forces launched an air war against Serbia. The bombing campaign at first failed to stop ethnic terror, as refugees flooded into neighboring countries, but it eventually forced Milosević to accept a NATO peacekeeping force in Kosovo. With ethnic reconciliation still an elusive dream in the Balkans, Washington accepted the reality that American forces had an enduring role as peacekeepers in the region.

The Middle East remained a major focus of American diplomacy. In 1993 Clinton presided over a historic White House meeting in which Israeli prime minister Yitzhak Rabin and Palestinian Liberation Organization leader Yasir Arafat agreed in principle on self-rule for the Palestinians within Israel. But hopes flickered low two years later when Rabin fell to an assassin's bullet. Clinton and his second-term secretary of state, Madeleine Albright, spent the rest of the 1990s in an unsuccessful attempt to broker a settlement between Israelis and Palestinians. In the Clinton administration's final weeks in office, a last-ditch American proposal for a comprehensive peace collapsed in failure. The bitter fallout and mutual recriminations soon set off a new round of Israeli-Palestinian violence that again inflamed the Middle East.

In Iraq, Saddam Hussein continued his game of hide-and-seek with United Nations inspectors monitoring the Iraqi weapons program. When the chief U.N. inspector reported in 1998 that Iraq was out of compliance with U.N. rules, America and Britain launched air strikes against Iraqi weapons factories and warehouses. That same year the United States also conducted missile attacks against alleged terrorist sites in Afghanistan and Sudan in retaliation for terrorist bombings that killed over two hundred peo-

Clinton's Middle East Peace Initiatives   *In the last year of his presidency, President Clinton pushed hard for a resolution of the Palestinian-Israeli stalemate, hoping to deliver long-sought peace in the Middle East and secure his reputation as an international peacemaker. Despite extensive meetings with Palestinian leader Yasir Arafat and Israeli prime minister Ehud Barak, neither goal was accomplished, and tragically, tensions in the area only escalated.*

ple at the U.S. embassies in Kenya and Tanzania. In his final year as president, Clinton stepped up his efforts to leave a legacy as an international peacemaker. He sought to bring peace to Northern Ireland and the Korean peninsula, and between nuclear-armed India and Pakistan. Although the guiding principles of foreign policy in the post–Cold War era remained elusive, Clinton had become a stalwart opponent of the minority factions in both parties that yearned for a new isolationism.

Scandal and Impeachment

President Clinton had ample cause for concern about his lasting reputation, since scandal had dogged him from the beginning of his presidency. Allegations of flagrant wrongdoing, reaching back to his prepresidential days in Arkansas, included a failed real estate investment known as the Whitewater Land Corporation. The Clintons' role in that deal prompted the appointment of a federal special prosecutor to investigate. Suspicions were especially aroused by the death from apparent suicide in 1993 of White House counsel and close Clinton associate Vincent W. Foster, Jr., who had handled the Clintons' legal and financial affairs. The president's loose ethics and womanizing even found fictional expression in a runaway 1996 best-selling book, *Primary Colors.*

But all the previous scandals were overshadowed when allegations broke in January 1998 that Clinton had engaged in a sexual affair with a young White House intern, Monica Lewinsky, and then lied about it when he testified under oath in a civil lawsuit. The lawsuit had been brought by an Arkansas woman, Paula Jones, who charged that then-governor Clinton had sexually harassed her when she was a state employee. The Supreme Court had unanimously agreed to permit the case to go forward in May 1997, ruling that being sued in a civil case would not "significantly distract" the president from his duties.

The accusation that Clinton had lied under oath in the Jones case about his sexual affair with Lewinsky presented a stunning windfall to the special prosecutor, Kenneth Starr, originally appointed to investigate the Whitewater deal. Like Captain Ahab pursuing the whale Moby Dick, Starr had relentlessly tracked Clinton's steps for years, spending $40 million but never succeeding in finding evidence against the president himself. Clinton, now suddenly caught in a legal and political trap, delivered vehement public denials that he had engaged in "sexual relations" with "that woman." After maintaining his innocence for eight months, Clinton was finally forced to acknowledge an "inappropriate relationship." In September 1998 Starr presented to the House of Representatives a stinging report charging Clinton with eleven possible grounds for impeachment, all related to the Lewinsky matter.

Led by its fiercely anti-Clinton Republican majority, the House quickly cranked up the rusty machinery of impeachment. After a nasty partisan debate, the House Republicans in December 1998 eventually passed two articles of impeachment against the president: perjury before a grand jury and obstruction of justice. Crying foul, the Democratic minority charged that, however deplorable Clinton's personal misconduct, sexual transgressions did not rise to the level of "high crimes and misdemeanors" prescribed as grounds for impeachment in the Constitution (see Art. II, Sec. IV in the Appendix). The House Republican managers (prosecutors) of impeachment, led by Illinois congressman and House Judiciary Committee chairman Henry Hyde, claimed that perjury and obstruction were grave public issues and that nothing less than "the rule of law" was at stake.

As cries of "honor the Constitution" and "sexual McCarthyism" filled the air, the nation debated whether the president's peccadilloes amounted to high crimes or low follies. Most Americans apparently leaned toward the latter conclusion. In the 1998 midterm elections, voters reduced the House Republicans' majority, causing fiery House Speaker Newt Gingrich to resign his post. Incredibly, Clinton's job approval rating remained high and even rose throughout the long impeachment ordeal. Though Americans held a low opinion of Clinton's slipshod personal morals, most liked the president's political and economic policies and wanted him to stay in office. Kenneth Starr's stock in public opinion fell accordingly.

In January and February 1999, for the first time in one hundred and thirty years the nation witnessed an impeachment proceeding in the U.S. Senate. Dusting off ancient precedents from Andrew Johnson's trial, the one hundred solemn senators heard arguments and evidence in the case, with Chief Justice William Rehnquist presiding. With the facts widely known and the two parties' political positions firmly locked in, the trial's outcome was a foregone conclusion. On the key obstruction of justice charge, five northeastern Republicans joined all forty-five Democratic senators in voting not guilty. The fifty Republican votes for conviction fell far short of the constitutionally required two-thirds majority. The vote on the perjury charge was forty-five guilty, fifty-five not guilty.

Clinton's Legacy

With the impeachment trial over, a weary nation yearned for Washington to move on to other business. Vowing to serve "until the last hour of the last day of my term," Clinton spent what remained of his presidency seeking to secure a legacy for himself as an effective leader and a moderate reformer. He protected major new wilderness areas, promoted a "patients' bill of rights" to improve health care, and won congressional approval for hiring 100,000 new teachers and 50,000 more police officers.

Beyond the obvious stain of impeachment, Clinton's legacy was bound to be a mixed one for his country and his party. He came to office in 1992 determined to make economic growth his first priority, and in this domain he surely succeeded. Benefiting from global expansion, the country achieved near-full employment by decade's end, poverty rates inched down, and median income reached new highs.

Yet by governing successfully as a "New Democrat" and avowed centrist, Clinton did more to consolidate than reverse the Reagan-Bush revolution against New Deal liberalism that had for half a century provided the compass for the Democratic party and for the nation. As a brilliant communicator Clinton kept alive a vision of social justice and racial harmony. But as an executive he discouraged people from expecting government ro remedy ills. By setting such a low standard for his personal conduct, he replenished the sad reservoir of public cynicism about politics that Vietnam and Watergate had created a generation before. Controversy even trailed Clinton out the White House door when the departing president issued several executive pardons that gave at least the appearance of rewarding political backers and donors.

The Bush-Gore Presidential Battle

Like Dwight Eisenhower in the 1950s, Clinton regarded the election of his vice president as a further means of ensuring his own legacy. Clinton's loyal vice president, Al Gore, easily won the Democratic party's presidential nomination in 2000. Trying to loosen up the somewhat formal personal bearing that many Americans found off-putting, Gore also faced the tricky challenge of associating himself with Clinton-era prosperity while detaching himself from Clinton-era scandal. Trying to distance himself from Clinton's peccadilloes, he chose as his running mate Connecticut senator Joseph Lieberman, an outspoken critic of Clinton during the Lewinsky affair and the first Jew nominated to a national ticket by a major party. Meanwhile, Ralph Nader's Green party threatened to siphon off environmentalist votes from the pro-environment Gore.

The Republican nominee, George W. Bush, had catapulted to party prominence on the strength of his family name and his popularity as the two-term governor of Texas. Though untested on the national stage, he organized a formidable campaign with his promise to "restore dignity to the White House"—a thinly veiled attack on Clinton's personal failings. As his running mate Bush chose former congressman and defense secretary Dick Cheney, lending the ticket a much-needed aura of experience. Styling himself a "compassionate conservative," "George W." (or "dubbya") promised to bridge the gap between moderates and conservatives in the Republican party.

The campaign focused on how the federal government should spend the projected $2 trillion surplus over the coming decade. True to the Republican creed of smaller government, Bush championed across-the-board tax cuts, school vouchers, "faith-based" initiatives to serve the poor, and reforms to permit individual workers to invest part of their Social Security taxes in private retirement accounts. Gore advocated instead a more modest tax cut targeted at the middle and lower classes, and he proposed to use most of the surplus to reduce or eliminate the national debt, shore up Social Security, and expand Medicare.

The election turned out to be an epochal cliffhanger. Not since the Hayes-Tilden election of 1876 had the electoral mechanisms ground their gears so badly before yielding a definite conclusion. In the pivotal state of Florida, the vote was so close that the law compelled a recount. When the second tally confirmed Bush's paper-thin margin of victory, Democrats successfully petitioned the Florida

Supreme Court for hand recounts in several contested counties. Crying foul, Republicans fought back by getting the Florida-dominated legislature to name a set of pro-Bush electors, regardless of the vote retabulating under way.

The Bush campaign also pursued another strategy by taking its case to the U.S. Supreme Court. There, with the eyes of an increasingly restive nation riveted on the proceedings, the nine justices broke into a bare-knuckle judicial brawl. Five bitterly divisive weeks after election day, the presidential campaign of 2000 finally ended when the High Court's five most conservative members ruled in Bush's favor. They reasoned that the lack of uniform standards for evaluating disputed ballots meant that the hand counts violated the Fourteenth Amendment's "equal protection" clause. Speaking for the minority, Justice John Stevens wrote scathingly that the Court's decision jeopardized "the nation's confidence in the judge as an impartial guardian of the rule of law."

The Supreme Court ruling gave Bush the victory but also cast a cloud of illegitimacy over his presidency. Bush's final official margin of victory in Florida was only 537 votes out of 6 million cast. With Florida's 25 electoral votes narrowly falling into Bush's column, he won the Electoral College by a slim margin of 271 votes to 267 for Gore. Bush's popular vote of 50,456,169 fell short of Gore's 50,996,116, making Bush the first president since Benjamin Harrison to win the presidency while losing the popular count. Bush also faced an even fifty-fifty party split in the Senate and a slender ten-vote GOP majority in the House.

The fiasco of the 2000 election severely tested American democracy, but in the end the system earned a passing grade. The nation's two-century-old electoral machinery might have shown its age, but it managed to wheeze and clank its way to a peaceful resolution of one of the most ferociously contested presidential races ever. Despite all the partisan maneuvering, no credible charges of serious chicanery or outright corruption wafted up out of the election's cauldron of controversy. And however unsettling the U.S. Supreme Court's intervention might have been, both sides relied on lawyers and judges, not generals, to resolve the contest, and no serious constitutional crisis emerged. The foresight of

Presidential Election of 2000 (with electoral vote by state)
Although Democratic vice president Albert Gore won the popular election for president by half a million votes, George W. Bush's contested five-hundred-vote advantage in Florida gave him a slight lead in the Electoral College. The 2.7 million popular votes won by Green party candidate and consumer activist Ralph Nader almost surely deprived Gore of victory, casting Nader in the role of spoiler. Bush's failure to win the popular vote inspired critics to protest at his inauguration with placards reading "Hail to the Thief."

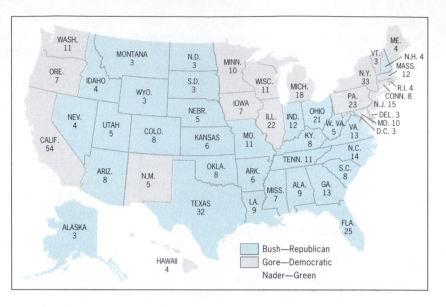

the Founders in crafting a system of elections and courts stood reaffirmed, though the imbroglio unquestionably demonstrated the need for modernized balloting procedures.

A New Bush in the White House

George Walker Bush took the oath as the forty-third president under a cloud of suspicion and doubt. The disputed photo-finish election and the Supreme Court's intervention left some voters still questioning the outcome and Bush's right to the office. Protesters at the inaugural ceremony held signs reading "Re-Elect Gore in 2004."

To build public confidence and ease concern about his own lack of experience, especially in foreign affairs, Bush appointed a heavyweight cabinet loaded with veterans of previous Republican administrations. General Colin Powell, military architect of the Persian Gulf War for Bush's father, was named the first African-American secretary of state. Russian expert Condoleezza Rice, an African-American woman,

became national security adviser. Donald Rumsfeld, defense secretary under Gerald Ford, returned for a second stint at the Pentagon. Bush's unflappable and widely experienced vice president, Dick Cheney, took an unusually active role in national security matters.

The Bush team's first steps in foreign affairs reflected an apparent "go-it-alone" strategy of pursuing America's interests without much regard for opinion elsewhere. Bush quickly renounced American participation in the Kyoto "global warming" treaty and other international environmental efforts. He also proposed developing a unilateral "national missile defense" system to shield America from nuclear attack, a project that stirred objections from Russia and some U.S. allies. In the Middle East the administration backed off from trying to broker peace between Israel and the Palestinians, in hopes that the parties would have to learn to deal with each other on their own.

In domestic affairs Bush declared that he wanted to reach out to political opponents and soften the sharp partisanship of the Clinton years and the 2000 election. The president's easy manner and Texas informality won him many friends. But the closely divided Congress, including an even fifty-fifty split in the Senate (with vice president Cheney's tie-breaking vote giving Republicans control) made cooperation difficult.

Bush's first major initiative, an enormous tax cut that would almost entirely eliminate the budget surpluses projected for the decade 2000–2010, quickly became a bone of contention. Claiming that the president's reductions were too heavily weighted toward upper- and middle-income taxpayers, Democrats also warned that the huge cuts would make future spending for baby-boomers' Social Security and Medicare retirement benefits almost impossible. But Bush, insisting that the budget surpluses belonged to the people and not the government, skillfully garnered enough support to push the ten-year, $1.35 trillion measure through Congress in June 2001. As a first installment on the cut, most American taxpayers happily cashed a rebate check from Uncle Sam.

A Bush proposal to steer federal social service spending toward "faith-based" programs sponsored by religious groups met strong objections and soon bogged down in failure. Less controversial was the president's proposal for education reform, long a favorite Bush cause and a centerpiece of his 2000 campaign. The new law provided for greatly increased federal funding to the states in exchange for expanded testing of students and monitoring of local schools' academic progress. The long-stalled cause of curbing corrupt financing of political campaigns was suddenly revived by the scandalous 2000 election. A Campaign Finance Reform Act that banned "soft money" was finally passed by Congress and somewhat reluctantly signed by President Bush in March 2002.

Bush's reliance on the Republicans' control of Congress to advance his agenda suffered a surprising blow in June 2001, when Vermont senator James Jeffords suddenly jumped off the Republican ship and declared himself an independent. Control of the Senate thus passed to the Democrats, who began promoting a "patients' bill of rights" and stalling Bush's judicial appointments.

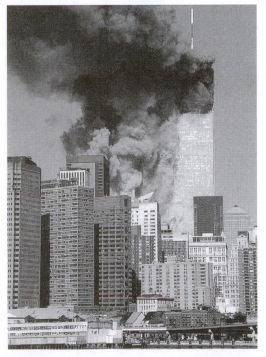

Chronology of Terror   *The first hijacked plane hit the north World Trade Center tower at 8:45 A.M. New York time on September 11, 2001. Eighteen minutes later, a second plane hit the south tower, which collapsed at 10:05 A.M. (shown here). Twenty-three minutes later, the north tower also came down. In the frantic minutes after the first impact, thousands of people were evacuated from the two buildings by rescue workers, many of whom lost their own lives.*

September 11, 2001

On a crystal-clear early fall morning, September 11, 2001, suicidal terrorists slammed two hijacked airliners, loaded with passengers and jet fuel, into the twin towers of New York City's World Trade Center. They flew a third plane into the military nerve-center of the Pentagon, near Washington, D.C., killing 189 people. Heroic passengers forced another hijacked aircraft to crash in wooded rural Pennsylvania, killing all 44 aboard but depriving the terrorists of a fourth weapon of mass destruction.

As the two giant New York skyscrapers thunderously collapsed, some three thousand innocent victims perished, including peoples of many races and faiths from more than sixty countries, as well as hundreds of New York's police and fire department rescue workers. It was the worst single-day toll of violent death in American history since the Civil War battle of Antietam. A stunned nation blossomed with flags, as grieving and outraged Americans struggled to express their sorrow and solidarity in the face of catastrophic terrorism.

The murderous events of that September morning reanimated American patriotism. They also dramatically ended a historical era. For nearly two centuries, the United States had been spared from foreign attack against its homeland. All but unique among modern peoples, that degree of national security had undergirded the values of openness and individual freedom that defined the distinctive character of American society. Now American security and American liberty alike were imperiled.

Making War on Terrorism

President Bush responded with a sober but stirring address to Congress nine days later. His solemn demeanor and the gravity of the situation helped to dissipate the cloud of illegitimacy that had shadowed his presidency since the disputed election of 2000. Warning that the struggle against terrorism would be long and messy, he pledged, "We will not tire, we will not falter, and we will not fail" until "we bring our enemies to justice, or bring justice to our enemies."

While emphasizing his respect for the Islamic religion and Muslim peoples, Bush identified the principal enemy as Osama bin Laden, head of a shadowy terrorist network known as Al Qaeda. A wealthy extremist exiled from his native Saudi Arabia, bin Laden was associated with earlier attacks on American embassies in East Africa and on a U.S. naval vessel in Yemen. He had taken refuge in landlocked Afghanistan, ruled by an extremist Islamic fundamentalist party, the Taliban. (Ironically, the United States had indirectly helped bring the Taliban to power when it supported religious rebels resisting the Soviet invasion of Afghanistan in the 1980s.) Bin Laden was known to harbor bitter resentments against the United States for its economic embargo against Saddam Hussein's Iraq, its military presence on the sacred soil of the Arabian peninsula, and its support for Israel's hostility to Palestinian nationalism. Bin Laden also fed on worldwide resentment of America's enormous economic, military, and cultural power. Ironically, America's most conspicuous strengths had made it a conspicuous target.

When the Taliban refused to hand over bin Laden, Bush ordered a massive military campaign against Afghanistan. Within three months, American forces and Afghani rebels had overthrown the Taliban and organized a new regime in the capital, Kabul. Remaining Taliban and Al Qaeda fighters fled to the country's towering mountains and remote caves, where American forces fought to flush them out and capture or confirm the death of the elusive bin Laden.

The campaign in Afghanistan impressively demonstrated the wallop and sophistication of American air power and "smart," precision-guided munitions. But it remained an open question whether in the long run America's high-tech arsenal would prove effective against foes so treacherous, zealous, and determined—foes who sought not simply to destroy the United States but to demoralize it, perhaps to corrupt its very soul.

In the weeks after September 11, belief spread that the suicide plane attacks might be only the beginning of a wider assault on the United States. While the rubble from New York's "Ground Zero" was still smoldering, a handful of Americans died after receiving letters contaminated with the deadly respiratory disease, anthrax. The culprits who sent the anthrax letters were not found, but the gnawing fear spread that biological warfare might be the next threat facing the American people. There was also concern that bin Laden and Al Qaeda could be connected to numerous underground terrorist "cells," which might have possession of biochemical or even nuclear weapons.

Confronted with this unconventional, diffuse menace, antiterrorism experts called for new tactics of "asymmetrical warfare," employing not just traditional military muscle, but innovative intelligence gathering, economic reprisals, infiltration of suspected organizations, and even assassinations. The new war against terror also compelled the Bush administration to back away from the unilateralist foreign policies it had pursued in its early months and seek antiterrorist partners around the globe, as evidenced by the surprisingly warm relationship that emerged after September 11 between the United States and its former adversary, Russia.

Domestic and Foreign Consequences

The terrorists' blows diabolically coincided with the onset of a recession. The already gathering economic downdraft worsened as edgy Americans shunned air travel and the tourist and convention industries withered. The heart of American finance and communications, New York's Lower Manhattan, had been dealt a terrible economic as well as physical blow, and the whole surrounding region suffered from unemployment and business relocation.

The economy coughed and sputtered as it tried to get back on the road to recovery in 2002. Travel and consumer spending returned to near-normal levels, but the impact of the terrorist attacks remained severe. A wave of corporate bankruptcies and scandals, led by the collapse of the giant Enron energy company, added to unemployment and Wall Street's woes. Massive emergency appropriations for security and aid to devastated New York made talk of how to spend budget surpluses seem like ancient history.

The terrorist assault, and the reaction to it, also challenged America's practice of civil liberty. In the anxious atmosphere immediately after the attacks, Congress rammed through the USA-Patriot Act, permitting extensive telephone and e-mail surveillance and authorizing the detention and deportation of immigrants suspected of terrorism. The Justice Department meanwhile rounded up hundreds of immigrants and resident aliens and held them without habeas corpus (formal charges in an open court). Several hundred Al Qaeda and Taliban fighters suspected of terrorism were also brought from Afghanistan and imprisoned at the American base at Guantanamo Bay, Cuba. The Bush administration called for trying suspected terrorists before military tribunals, where the usual rules of evidence and procedure did not apply. Public opinion polls showed Americans sharply divided on whether the terrorist threat fully warranted such drastic encroachments on America's cherished civil liberties.

As the first wave of fear passed, Americans vowed not to "let the hijackers win" by turning to repression and intolerance. Despite the fact that all the hijackers were Arabs from the violence-wracked Middle East, the proud American traditions of toleration generally fared well in the wake of September 11. With a few ugly exceptions, Americans displayed respect for their Arab-American fellow citizens and most government officials tried to guard minority civil and religious rights. In many communities and schools, concerned citizens even sought ways to learn more about their Arab-American neighbors and the faith of Islam, so badly distorted by murderous terrorists.

A new outburst of conflict between Israel and the Palestinians complicated American strategy in the troubled Middle East. Responding to suicide bombers, the Israeli army invaded Palestinian territories in March 2002 and assaulted Yasir Arafat's headquarters. The U.S. government tried to resume its mediating role, with little effect.

President Bush meanwhile vigorously pursued what he called the "axis of evil" in the world—Iran, chief state sponsor of terrorism; North Korea, with its rogue nuclear weapons program; and especially Saddam Hussein's Iraq—as the next phase of the fight against terrorism. At Bush's urging, Congress passed a resolution in September 2002 authorizing the president to wage war against Iraq whenever necessary. The United Nations Security Council also passed an American-backed resolution requiring complete elimination of all Iraq's weapons of mass destruction, with the clear threat of military action if Saddam Hussein did not comply.

Bush's political hand was strengthened by Republican gains in the 2002 mid-term elections. He successfully persuaded Congress to create a new cabinet department of homeland security that would pull together the previously scattered federal agencies concerned with protecting America's citizens.

Chronology

1980 Reagan defeats Carter for presidency.

1981 Iran releases American hostages.
"Reaganomics" spending and tax cuts passed.
Solidarity movement in Poland.
O'Connor appointed to Supreme Court (first woman justice).

1981–1991 United States aids antileftist forces in Central America.

1982 Recession hits U.S. economy.

1983 Reagan announces SDI plan (Star Wars).
U.S. marines killed in Lebanon.
U.S. invasion of Grenada.

1984 Reagan defeats Mondale for presidency.

1985 Gorbachev comes to power in Soviet Union.
First Reagan-Gorbachev summit meeting, in Geneva.

1986 Iran-contra scandal revealed.
Second Reagan-Gorbachev summit meeting, in Reykjavik, Iceland.

1987 508-point stock-market plunge.
Third Reagan-Gorbachev summit meeting, in Washington, D.C.; INF Treaty signed.

1988 Fourth Reagan-Gorbachev summit meeting, in Moscow.
Bush defeats Dukakis for presidency.

1989 Chinese government suppresses prodemocracy demonstrators.
Webster v. *Reproductive Health Services*
Eastern Europe throws off communist regimes.
Berlin Wall torn down.

1990 Iraq invades Kuwait.
East and West Germany reunite.
Americans with Disabilities Act (ADA).

1991 Persian Gulf War.
Thomas appointed to Supreme Court.
Gorbachev resigns as Soviet president.
Soviet Union dissolves.

1992 Twenty-seventh Amendment (prohibiting congressional pay raises from taking effect until an election seats a new session of Congress) ratified.
Clinton defeats Bush and Perot for presidency.

1993 NAFTA signed.

1994 Republicans win majorities in both houses of Congress.

1996 Welfare Reform Bill becomes law.
Clinton defeats Dole for presidency.

1998 Clinton-Lewinsky scandal.
U.S. and Britain launch military strikes against Iraq.
House of Representatives impeaches Clinton.

1999 Senate acquits Clinton on impeachment charges.
Kosovo crisis; NATO warfare with Serbia.
Protest in Seattle against World Trade Organization.

2000 "Million Mom March" against guns, in Washington, D.C.
U.S. normalizes trade relations with China.
Bush wins presidency in Electoral College, although Gore takes popular vote.

2001 Bush tax-reduction package enacted.
Terrorists attack New York City and Washington, D.C., toppling World Trade Center towers and killing over 3,000 Americans and others.
U.S. launches war on Al-Qaeda terrorist organization and Taliban regime in Afghanistan.

2002 U.S. and allies help form new regime in Afghanistan.
Palestinian-Israeli conflict escalates.
Congress passes Iraq war resolution.
United Nations passes Iraq disarmament resolution.

VARYING VIEWPOINTS

Where Did Modern Conservatism Come From?

Ronald Reagan's elections surprised many historians. Reflecting a liberal political outlook that is common among academic scholars, they were long accustomed to understanding American history as an inexorable unfolding of liberal principles, including the quests for economic equality, social justice, and active government. In progressive histories of the early twentieth century like those of Charles and Mary Beard, conservatives were portrayed as rich, privileged elites bent on preserving their wealth and power.

Even the New Left revisionists of the 1960s, while critical of the celebratory tone of their progressive forebears, were convinced that the deep currents of American history flowed leftward. But whether they were liberal or revisionist, most scholars writing in the first three post–World War II decades dismissed conservatives as fringe wackos—paranoid McCarthyites or racist demagogues who, in the words of liberal critic Lionel Trilling, trafficked only in "irritable mental gestures which seem to resemble ideas." Such an outlook is conspicuous in books like Daniel Bell, ed., *The Radical Right* (1963), and Richard Hofstadter, *The Paranoid Style in American Politics* (1965).

But what flowed out of the turbulent decade of the 1960s was not a strengthened liberalism but a revived conservatism. Reagan's success compelled a reexamination of the tradition of American conservatism and the sources of its resurgence.

Historians including Leo Ribuffo and Alan Brinkley have argued that characters once dismissed as irrational crackpots or colorful irrelevancies—including religious fundamentalists and depression-era figures like Huey Long and Father Charles Coughlin—articulated values deeply rooted and widely shared in American culture. These conservative spokespersons, whatever their peculiarities, offered a vision of free individuals, minimal government, and autonomous local communities that harkened back to the "civic republicanism" in the era of young nationhood.

Modern conservatism is also a product of the recent historical past. Scholars like Thomas Sugrue have shown that economic stagnation from the 1970s into the 1990s made Americans insecure about their futures and receptive to new political doctrines. At the same time, as commentator Kevin Phillips has stressed, "social issues" like sexual liberation, abortion on demand, women's rights, and race relations sharply challenged traditional beliefs. Finally, the failure of government policies in Vietnam, runaway inflation in the 1970s, as well as the disillusioning Watergate episode, cast doubt on the legitimacy and even the morality of "big government."

Many modern conservatives, including pundit George Will, stress the deep historical roots of American conservatism. In their view, as Will once put it, it took sixteen years to count the ballots from the 1964 (Goldwater versus Johnson) election, and Goldwater won after all. But that argument is surely overstated. Goldwater ran against the legacy of the New Deal and was overwhelmingly defeated. Reagan ran against the consequences of the Great Society and won decisively. Many conservatives, in short, apparently acknowledge the legitimacy of the New Deal and the stake that many middle-class Americans feel they have in its programs of Social Security, home mortgage subsidies, farm price supports, and similar policies. But they reject the philosophy of the Great Society with its more focused attack on urban poverty and its vigorous support for affirmative action. Modern conservatism springs less from a repudiation of government per se and more from a disapproval of the particular priorities and strategies of the Great Society. The different historical fates of the New Deal and the Great Society suggest the key to the rise of modern conservatism.

For further reading, see the Appendix. For web resources, go to **http://college.hmco.com**.

The American People Face a New Century

As our case is new, so we must think anew and act anew. We must disenthrall ourselves, and then we shall save our country.

ABRAHAM LINCOLN, 1862

More than two hundred years old as the twenty-first century dawned, the United States was both an old and a new nation. It boasted one of the longest uninterrupted traditions of democratic government of any country on earth. Indeed, it had pioneered the techniques of mass democracy and was, in that sense, the oldest modern polity. As one of the earliest countries to industrialize, America had also dwelled in the modern economic era longer than most nations.

But the Republic was in many ways still youthful as well. Innovation, entrepreneurship, and risk-taking—all characteristics of youth—were honored national values. The twenty-first century began much as the twentieth had, with American society being rejuvenated by fresh waves of immigrants, full of energy and ambition. The U.S. economy, despite problems, was generating new jobs at a rate of some 2 million per year. The whole world seemed to worship the icons of American culture—downing soft drinks and donning blue jeans, listening to rock or country music, even adopting indigenous American sports such as baseball and basketball. In the realm of consumerism, American products appeared to have Coca-Colonized the globe.

The history of American society also seemed to have increased global significance as the third millennium of the Christian era opened. Americans were a pluralistic people who had struggled for centuries to achieve tolerance and justice for many different religious, ethnic, and racial groups. Their historical experience could offer valuable lessons to the rapidly internationalizing planetary society that was emerging in the new century.

In politics, economics, and culture, the great social experiment of American democracy was far from completed as the United States faced its future. Much history remained to be made as the country entered its third century of nationhood. But men and women make history only within the framework bequeathed to them by earlier generations. For better or worse, they march forward along time's path bearing the burdens of the past. Knowing when they have come to a truly new turn in the road, when they can lay part of their burden down, and when they cannot, or should not—all this constitutes the kind of wisdom that only historical study can engender.

Economic Revolutions

When the twentieth century opened, United States Steel Corporation was the flagship business of America's industrial revolution. A generation later, General Motors, annually producing millions of automobiles, became the characteristic American corporation, signaling the historic shift to a mass consumer economy that began in the 1920s and flowered fully in the 1950s.

The post–World War II era inaugurated the fast-paced "information age," when the storing, organizing, and processing of data became an industry in its own right. By century's end, the rapid emergence of Microsoft Corporation and the phenomenal growth of the Internet heralded an explosive communications revolution. Americans now rocketed down the "information superhighway" toward the uncharted terrain of an electronic global village.

The communications revolution was full of both promise and peril. Ordinary citizens could gain access to information once available only to privileged elites. Businesspeople instantaneously girdled the planet with transactions of prodigious scope and serpentine complexity. By the late 1990s a "dot-com" explosion of new commercial ventures quickly expanded the market (and the stock-market stakes) for entrepreneurs leading the way in making the Internet a twenty-first-century electronic mall, library, and entertainment center rolled into one.

But the very speed and efficiency of the new communications tools threatened to wipe out entire occupational categories. Postal delivery people, travel agents, booksellers, bank tellers, stockbrokers, and other kinds of workers whose business it was to mediate between product and client worried that they might find themselves rendered obsolete in the era of the Internet. As the computer made possible "classrooms without walls," even teachers, whose job was essentially to mediate between students and various bodies of knowledge, wondered whether they might end up as roadkill on the information superhighway.

Increasingly, scientific research was the engine that drove the economy, and new scientific knowledge posed new social and moral dilemmas. Early genetic discoveries, for instance, had yielded new strains of high-yield, pest-resistant crops, but also threatened the fragile ecological balance of the wondrous biosphere. As technical mastery of biological and medical techniques advanced, unprecedented ethical questions clamored for resolution. Should the human gene pool itself be "engineered"? What principles should govern the allocation of human organs for lifesaving transplants? What rules should guide efforts to clone human beings—or should such efforts not even be attempted?

Affluence and Inequality

Americans were still an affluent people as the twenty-first century opened. Median household income declined somewhat in the early 1990s but rebounded by 2000 to about $42,000. Yet even those Americans with incomes below the government's official poverty level (defined in 2001 as $18,000 for a family of four) enjoyed a standard of living higher than that of two-thirds of the rest of humankind.

But Americans were no longer the world's wealthiest people, as they had been in the quarter-century after World War II. Citizens of several other countries enjoyed higher average per capita incomes, and many nations boasted more equitable distributions of wealth. In another unsettling reversal of long-term trends in American society, during the last two decades of the twentieth century the rich got much

Two Nations? *While decaying neighborhoods and the sad legions of the homeless blighted American urban life in the closing decades of the twentieth century, affluent Americans took refuge in gated communities like this one in the Brentwood section of Los Angeles.*

richer while the poor got an ever-shrinking share of the pie. The richest 20 percent of Americans in the early 2000s raked in nearly half of the nation's income, whereas the poorest 20 percent received just over 4 percent of national income. The gap between rich and poor began to widen in the 1980s and widened further in the following decade. Between 1968 and 2000 the share of the nation's income that flowed to the top 20 percent of its households swelled from 40 percent to 48 percent. Even more striking, in the same period the top 5 percent of income receivers saw their share of the national income grow from about 15 percent to more than 20 percent.

Widening inequality could be measured in other ways as well. Chief executives in the 1970s typically earned 41 times the income of the average worker in their corporations; by the early 2000s they earned 245 times as much. At the same time some 34 million people, 12.7 percent of all Americans (8.2 percent of whites, 26.1 percent of African-Americans, and 25.6 percent of Hispanics), remained mired in poverty—a depressing indictment of the inequities afflicting an affluent and allegedly egalitarian republic.

What caused the widening income gap? Some critics pointed to the tax and fiscal policies of the Reagan and Bush years, which favored the wealthy and penalized the poor. But deeper-running historical currents probably played a more important role. Among the most conspicuous causes were intensify-ing global competition; the shrinkage in high-paying manufacturing jobs for semiskilled and unskilled workers; the greater economic rewards commanded by educated workers in high-tech industries; the decline of unions; the rising tide of relatively low-skill immigrants; and the increasing tendency of educated men and women to marry one another, creating households with very high incomes.

The Feminist Revolution

All Americans were caught up in the great economic changes of the late twentieth century, but no group was more profoundly affected than women. When the twentieth century opened, women made up about 20 percent of all workers. Over the next five decades they increased their presence in the labor force at a fairly steady rate, except for a temporary spurt during World War II. Then, beginning in the 1950s, women's entry into the workplace accelerated dramatically. By the 1990s nearly half of all workers were women, and the majority of working-age women held jobs outside the home. Most astonishing was the upsurge in employment of mothers. In 1950, 90 percent of mothers with children under the age of six did not work for pay. But by the 2000s, a majority of women with children as young as one year old were wage earners. Women brought home the bacon and cooked it, too.

Beginning in the 1960s, many all-male strongholds—including Yale, Princeton, West Point, and even, belatedly, southern military academies like the Citadel and Virginia Military Institute—opened their doors to women. Women in the 1990s were piloting commercial airliners, orbiting outer space, governing states and cities, and writing Supreme Court decisions.

Yet despite those gains, many feminists remained frustrated. Women continued to receive lower wages, on average 76.5 cents on the dollar in 1999 compared with men doing the same full-time work, and they tended to concentrate in a few low-prestige, low-paying occupations (the "pink-collar ghetto"). Although they made up more than half the

Women's World: Something Old, Something New   *By the year 2000, revolutionary changes in the economy and in social values had opened new career possibilities to women, while not fully relieving them of their traditional duties as mothers and homemakers. Dramatic changes in race relations and the redefinition of gender roles in the 1980s and 1990s transformed even tradition-bound institutions like the U.S. Military Academy at West Point, New York, as this gathering of cadets suggests. Women's athletics came into their own in the wake of the feminist revolution. In 1999 the U.S. Women's World Cup Soccer Team brought home the trophy to a nation suddenly enthralled with women's soccer.*

population, women in the 2000s accounted for only 30 percent of lawyers and judges (up from 5 percent in 1970) and 24 percent of physicians (up from 10 percent in 1970). Overt sexual discrimination explained some of this occupational segregation, but most of it seemed attributable to the greater burdens of parenthood on women than on men. Women were far more likely than men to interrupt their careers to bear and raise children, and even to choose less demanding career paths to allow for fulfilling those traditional roles. Discrimination and a focus on children also helped account for the persistence of a "gender gap" in national elections. Women continued to vote in greater numbers than men for Democratic candidates, who were often perceived to be more willing to favor government support for health and child care, education, and job equality.

As the revolution in women's status rolled on in the 2000s, men's lives changed as well. Some employers provided paternity leave in addition to maternity leave, in recognition of the shared burdens of the two-worker household. Traditional female responsibilities such as cooking, laundry, and child care spilled over to men. Recognizing the new realities of the modern American household, Congress passed a Family Leave Bill in 1993, mandating job protection for working fathers as well as mothers who needed to take time off work for family-related reasons.

Fading Families and Aging Citizens

The nuclear family, once prized as the foundation of society and the nursery of the Republic, suffered heavy blows in postwar America. By the 1990s one out of every two marriages ended in divorce. Seven times more children were affected by divorce than at the turn of the century, and kids who commuted between separated parents were becoming commonplace.

Traditional families were not only falling apart at an alarming rate but also increasingly slow to form in the first place. The proportion of adults living alone tripled in the five decades after 1950, and by the 2000s about one-third of women age twenty-five to twenty-nine had never been married. In the 1960s, 5 percent of all births were to unmarried women, but four decades later one out of four white babies, one out of three Hispanic babies, and two out of three

The Modern Family Tree   *High divorce rates and the increasing numbers of "blended families" in modern American society could often be confusing.*

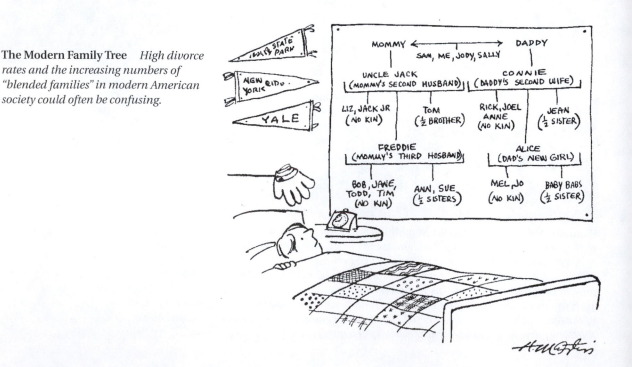

African-American babies were born to single mothers. Every fourth child in America was growing up in a household that lacked two parents. The collapse of the traditional family contributed heavily to the pauperization of many women and children, as single parents (usually mothers) struggled to keep their households economically afloat.

Child-rearing, the family's foremost function, was being increasingly assigned to "parent-substitutes" at day-care centers or schools—or to television, the modern age's "electronic babysitter." Estimates were that the average child by age sixteen had watched up to fifteen thousand hours of TV—more time than was spent in the classroom.

Born and raised without the family support enjoyed by their forebears, Americans were also increasingly likely to be lonely in their later years. Most elderly people in the 1990s depended on pension plans and government Social Security payments, not on their loved ones, for their daily bread. The great majority of them drew their last breaths not in their own homes but in hospitals and nursing facilities. From youth to old age, the role of the family was dwindling.

Americans were living longer than ever before. A person born at the dawn of the twentieth century could expect to survive less than fifty years, but a white male born in 2002 could anticipate a life span of about seventy-seven years. His white female counterpart would probably outlive him by about five years. (The figures were slightly lower for nonwhites, reflecting differences in living standards, especially diet and health care.) The census of 1950 recorded that women for the first time made up a majority of Americans, thanks largely to greater female longevity. Miraculous medical advances lengthened and strengthened lives. Noteworthy were the development of antibiotics after 1940 and Dr. Jonas Salk's discovery in 1953 of a vaccine against a dreaded crippler, polio.

Longer lives spelled more older people. One American in eight was over sixty-five years of age in 2000, and projections were that one of every five would be in the "sunset years" by 2050, as the median age rose toward forty. This aging of the population raised a host of political, social, and economic questions. Elderly people formed a potent electoral bloc that aggressively lobbied for government favors and achieved real gains for senior citizens. Poverty declined dramatically among those over sixty-five, while the percentage of children in poverty stood at about 15 percent in 2000.

These triumphs for senior citizens also brought fiscal strains, especially in the Social Security system, established in 1935 to provide income for retired workers. When Social Security began, most workers continued to toil after age sixty-five. By century's end only a small minority did (about 15 percent of men and 8 percent of women), and a majority of the elderly population relied primarily on Social Security checks for their living expenses. Contrary to popular mythology, Social Security payments to retirees did not simply represent reimbursement for contributions that the elderly had made during their working lives. In fact, the payments of current workers into the Social Security system funded the benefits of the current generation of retirees. By the early 2000s those benefits had risen so high, and the ratio of active workers to retirees had dropped so low, that drastic adjustments were necessary.

At the beginning of the new century, as the huge wave of post–World War II baby boomers approached retirement age, it seemed that the "unfunded liability"—the difference between what the government promised to pay to the elderly and the taxes it expected to take in—might eventually rise above $7 trillion, a sum that threatened to bankrupt the Republic unless drastic reforms were adopted. Yet because of the electoral power of older Americans, Social Security reform remained the "third rail" of American politics, which public figures dared not touch. A war between the generations loomed in the twenty-first century as payments to the nonworking elderly threatened to soak up fully half the working population's income by about 2040.

The New Immigration

Newcomers flooded into modern America. They washed ashore in waves that numbered nearly a million persons per year in the 1980s and 1990s—the heaviest inflow of immigrants in America's experience. In striking contrast to the historic pattern of immigration, Europe contributed far fewer people than did the countries of Asia and Latin America.

What prompted this new migration to America? The truth is that the newest immigrants came for many of the same reasons as the old. They typically left countries where populations were growing rapidly and where agricultural and industrial revolutions were shaking people loose from old habits of life—conditions almost identical to those in nineteenth-century Europe. They came to America, as previous immigrants had done, in search of jobs and economic opportunity.

The Southwest, from Texas to California, felt the immigrant impact especially sharply, as Mexican migrants concentrated heavily in that region. By the turn of the century Latinos made up nearly one-third of the population in Texas, Arizona, and California and almost 40 percent in New Mexico—amounting to a demographic *reconquista* of the lands lost by Mexico in the war of 1846.

The size and geographic concentration of the Hispanic population in the Southwest had few precedents in the history of American immigration. Most previous groups had been so thinly scattered across the land that they had little choice but to learn English and make their way in the larger U.S. society, however much they might have longed to preserve their native language and customs. But it seemed possible that Mexican-Americans might succeed in creating a truly bicultural zone in the booming southwestern states.

Some old-stock Americans worried about the capacity of the modern United States to absorb these new immigrants. The Immigration Reform and Control Act of 1986 attempted to choke off illegal entry by penalizing employers of undocumented aliens and by granting amnesty to many of those already here. Anti-immigrant sentiment flared especially sharply in California in the wake of an economic recession in the early 1990s. California voters approved a ballot initiative that attempted to deny benefits, including education, to illegal immigrants, and in 1998 the state passed another measure to end bilingual education in California schools. Congress in 1996 had already restricted access to welfare even for legal immigrants.

Yet the fact was that foreign-born people accounted for only about 11 percent of the American population in 2000—a far smaller proportion than the historical high point of nearly 15 percent recorded in the census of 1910—and a number that suggested the society's ability to take in newcomers was far from exhausted. Somewhat inconsistently, critics charged both that immigrants robbed citizens of jobs and that they dumped themselves on the welfare rolls at the taxpayers' expense. But studies showed that immigrants took jobs scorned by Americans and that they paid more dollars in taxes (withholding and Social Security taxes, as well as sales taxes) than they claimed in welfare payments. A more urgent worry was that unscrupulous employers might take cruel advantage of immigrant workers, who often had scant knowledge of their legal rights.

Ethnic Pride

Thanks both to continued immigration and to their own high birthrate, Hispanic-Americans were becoming an increasingly important minority (see "Makers of America: The Latinos," pp. 620–621). The United States by 2000 was home to about 35 million Latinos. They included some 20 million Chicanos, or Mexican-Americans, mostly in the Southwest, as well as more than 3 million Puerto Ricans, chiefly in the Northeast, and 1 million Cubans, mostly in Florida.

Flexing their political muscles, Latinos elected mayors of Miami, Denver, and San Antonio. After years of struggle, the United Farmworkers Organizing Committee (UFWOC), headed by soft-spoken and charismatic César Chávez, succeeded in improving working conditions for the mostly Chicano "stoop laborers" who followed the cycle of planting and harvesting across the American West. Latino influence seemed likely to grow, as suggested by the increasing presence of Spanish-language ballots and television broadcasts. Hispanic-Americans, newly confident and organized, became the nation's largest ethnic minority, outnumbering even African-Americans, in the early twenty-first century. Indeed, by the first decade of the new century, the Chicano population of America's largest state, California, equaled the Anglo population, making the state a patchwork of minorities with no single ethnic majority.

Asian-Americans also made giant strides. By the 1980s they were America's fastest-growing minority. Their numbers nearly doubled in that decade alone, thanks to heavy immigration, and continued to swell in the new twenty-first century. Once feared and hated as the "yellow peril" and consigned to the most menial and degrading jobs, citizens of Asian ancestry were now counted among the most prosperous of Americans. The typical Asian-American household enjoyed an income nearly 20 percent greater than that of the typical white household.

Indians, the original Americans, shared in the general awakening of "cultural nationalism." The 1990 census counted some 1.5 million Native Americans, half of whom had left their reservations to live in cities. Meanwhile, unemployment and alcoholism had blighted reservation life.

Cities and Suburbs

America's "alabaster cities" of song and story grew more sooty and less safe in the closing years of the twentieth century. Crime was the great scourge of urban life. The rate of violent crimes committed in cities reached an all-time high in the drug-infested 1980s, then leveled off in the early 1990s. The number of violent crimes even began to decline substantially in many areas after 1995. Nevertheless, murders, robberies, and rapes remained shockingly common not only in cities but in suburbs and rural areas as well. America imprisoned a larger fraction of its citizens than almost any other country in the world, and some desperate citizens resorted to armed vigilante tactics to protect themselves.

The migration from cities to the suburbs was so swift and massive that by the mid-1990s a majority of Americans made such communities their home. With the ending of the nation's brief "urban age" that had begun in the 1920s, many observers saw a new fragmentation and isolation of American life. Entire suburban neighborhoods, usually containing economically and racially homogeneous populations, walled themselves off behind elaborate security systems in "gated communities." In these safe but segregated enclaves, the sense of a larger and inclusive national community might prove hard to sustain.

By the beginning of the twenty-first century, some major cities exhibited signs of renewal. Commercial redevelopment gained ground in cities such as New York, Boston, Chicago, and San Francisco. Well-to-do residents reclaimed once-fashionable neighborhoods and sent real estate values soaring. But these latter-day urban homesteaders did little to make cities new centers of residential integration. Cities remained as divided by wealth and race as the suburban social landscape surrounding them.

Minority America

Racial and ethnic tensions exacerbated the problems of American cities. These stresses were especially evident in Los Angeles, which, like New York a century earlier, was the nation's magnet for minorities, especially immigrants from Asia and Latin America. When in 1992 a mostly white jury exonerated white Los Angeles police officers who had been videotaped ferociously beating a black suspect, the minority neighborhoods in South Central Los Angeles erupted in rage. Arson and looting laid waste entire city blocks, and scores of people were killed. Some black rioters vented their anger against white police by attacking Asian shopkeepers, who in turn formed armed patrols to protect their property.

The Los Angeles riots vividly testified to black skepticism about the American system of justice. Just three years later, again in Los Angeles, the televised spectacle of former football star O. J. Simpson's murder trial fed white disillusionment with the state of race relations. After months of testimony that seemed to many to point to Simpson's guilt, the jury acquitted Simpson, presumably because certain Los Angeles police officers involved in the case had been shown to harbor racist sentiments. In a later civil trial, another jury unanimously found Simpson liable for the "wrongful deaths" of his former wife and another victim. The reaction to the Simpson verdicts revealed the yawning chasm that separated white and black America, as most whites continued to believe Simpson guilty, while a majority of African-Americans told pollsters that the original not-guilty verdict was justified.

American cities have always held an astonishing variety of ethnic and racial groups, but in the late twentieth century, minorities made up a majority of the population of many American cities, as whites fled to the suburbs. More than three-quarters of African-Americans lived in cities at the twentieth century's end, whereas only about one-quarter of whites did. The most desperate black ghettos, housing a hapless "underclass" in the inner core of the old industrial

The Latinos

Today Mexican food is handed through fast-food drive-up windows in all fifty states, Spanish-language broadcasts fill the airwaves, and the Latino community has its own telephone book, the *Spanish Yellow Pages.* Latinos send representatives to Congress and mayors to city hall, record hit songs, paint murals, and teach history. Hispanic-Americans, among the fastest-growing segments of the U.S. population, include Puerto Ricans, frequent voyagers between their native island and northeastern cities; Cubans, many of them refugees from the communist dictatorship of Fidel Castro, concentrated in Miami and southern Florida; and Central Americans, fleeing the ravages of civil war in Nicaragua and El Salvador.

But the most populous group of Latinos derives from Mexico. The first significant numbers of Mexicans began heading for *El Norte* ("the North") around 1910, when the upheavals of the Mexican Revolution stirred and shuffled the Mexican population into more or less constant flux. Their northward passage was briefly interrupted during the Great Depression, when thousands of Mexican nationals were deported. But immigration resumed during World War II, and since then a steady flow of legal immigrants has passed through border checkpoints, joined by countless millions of their undocumented countrymen and countrywomen stealing across the frontier on moonless nights.

For the most part, these Mexicans came to work in the fields, following the ripening crops northward to Canada through the summer and autumn. Others gathered in the cities of the Southwest—El Paso, Los Angeles, Houston, and San Bernardino. There they found regular work, even if racial discrimination often confined them to manual labor. Houses may have been shabby in the barrios, but these Mexican neighborhoods provided a sense of togetherness, a place to raise a family, and the chance to join a mutual-aid society. Such societies, or *Mutualistas,* sponsored baseball leagues, helped the sick and disabled, and defended their members against discrimination.

Mexican immigrants lived so close to the border that their native country acted like a powerful magnet, drawing them back time and time again. Mexi-

Chicana Pride   *A Mexican-American girl celebrates her cultural heritage at the Texas Folklife Festival in San Antonio.*

cans frequently returned to see relatives, and relatively few became U.S. citizens. In addition, the Mexican government sometimes intervened to discourage Mexicans from becoming citizens of their adopted country by promoting Mexicanization programs among the immigrants, including parades to observe *Cinco de Mayo* ("Fifth of May"), celebrating Mexico's defeat of a French army in 1862. Since World War II, the American-born generation has carried on the fight for political representation, economic opportunity, and cultural preservation.

Fresh arrivals from Mexico and from other Latin American nations daily swell the Hispanic communities across America. As the United States entered the twenty-first century, it was taking on a pronounced Spanish accent.

cities, were especially problematic. Successful blacks who had benefited from the civil rights revolution of the 1950s and 1960s followed whites to the suburbs, leaving in the old ghetto a residue of the poorest poor. Without a middle class to sustain community institutions like schools and small businesses, the inner cities, plagued by unemployment and drug addiction, seemed bereft of leadership, cohesion, resources, and hope.

The abandoned underclass, heavily composed of blacks and other minorities, represented a social failure that eluded any known remedy. But other segments of the African-American community had clearly prospered in the wake of the civil rights gains of the 1950s and 1960s, although they still had a long hill to climb before reaching full equality. By the 1990s about 40 percent of blacks were counted in the middle class (defined as enjoying family income greater than $25,000 per year). The number of black elected officials had risen above seven thousand, including more than a thousand in the Old South, some two dozen members of Congress, and the mayors of several large cities. Voting tallies demonstrated that successful black politicians were moving beyond isolated racial constituencies and into the political mainstream by appealing to a wide variety of voters. In 1989 Virginians, only 15 percent of whom were black, elected L. Douglas Wilder as the first African-American state governor. In 1994 voters in Illinois made Carol Mosely-Braun the first African-American woman elected to the U.S. Senate.

Single women headed over half of black families, almost three times the rate for whites. Many of those African-American women, husbandless and jobless, necessarily depended on welfare to feed their children. As social scientists increasingly emphasized the importance of the home environment for success in school, it became clear that many fatherless, impov-

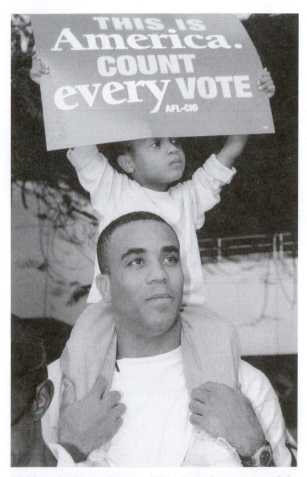

Making the Votes Count *Ever since the passage of the Voting Rights Act, African-Americans have become a more important part of the political equation, especially in key states that often decide presidential elections. This father and daughter are calling for a complete vote count in the disputed 2000 presidential contest in Florida. Many Florida blacks complained that election officials had disproportionally disqualified their votes and unfairly turned them away from the polls, resurrecting the kind of obstacles that long had kept blacks from voting in the South.*

erished African-American children seemed consigned to suffer from educational handicaps that were difficult to overcome. Black youths in the 1990s still had about one year less schooling than whites of the same age and were less than half as likely to earn college degrees. As the American economy became ever more driven by new applications of computers and biotechnology, these disadvantages were bound to widen the racial gap of employment opportunity. The political assault against affirmative action in California and elsewhere only compounded the obstacles to advanced training for many young African-Americans.

The Life of the Mind

Despite the mind-sapping chatter of the "boob tube," Americans in the late twentieth century read more, listened to more music, and were better educated than ever before. By 2000 colleges were awarding about a million degrees a year. The expanding ranks of educated people lifted the economy to more advanced levels while creating consumers of "high culture." Americans annually made some 300 million visits to museums in the 1990s and patronized about a thousand opera companies and fifteen hundred symphony orchestras—as well as countless popular music groups.

What Americans read said much about the state of American society at the dawn of the new century. Among the most striking developments in American letters was the rise of authors from once-marginal regions and ethnic groups coming into their own. Reflecting the general population shift westward, the West became the subject of a particularly rich literary outpouring. Larry McMurtry lovingly recollected the end of the cattle-drive era in *Lonesome Dove* (1985). Raymond Carver penned understated and powerful stories about working-class life in the Pacific Northwest, and Annie Dillard recreated the gritty frontier history of that same region. David Guterson penned a moving tale of interracial anxiety and affection in the World War II–era Pacific Northwest in *Snow Falling on Cedars* (1994). Norman MacLean, a former English professor, left two unforgettable accounts of his boyhood in Montana: *A River Runs Through It* (1976) and *Young Men and Fire* (1992).

African-American authors and artists also increasingly made their mark. Playwright August Wilson retold the history of black Americans in the twentieth century, with special emphasis on the psychic costs of the northward migration (*Fences*, 1985; *Joe Turner's Come and Gone*, 1988; *Jitney*, 1978). Alice Walker gave fictional voice to the experiences of black women in her hugely popular *The Color Purple* (1982). Toni Morrison wove a bewitching portrait of maternal affection in *Beloved* (1987) and in 1993 became the first African-American woman to win the Nobel Prize for literature. Native American authors like Kiowa N. Scott Momaday (*House Made of Dawn*, 1968) and Blackfoot James Welch (*Fools Crow*, 1986) also achieved literary recognition.

Asian-American authors flourished as well. Maxine Hong Kingston imaginatively reconstructed the lives of the earliest Chinese immigrants in *The Woman Warrior* (1976) and *China Men* (1980). Jhumpa Lahiri's *Interpreter of Maladies* (1999) explored the sometimes painful relationship between immigrant Indian parents and their American-born children. The older European migration continued to hold literary appeal as well, notably with Frank McCourt's memories of an Irish and American childhood, captured in *Angela's Ashes* (1996).

Women writers and women's themes forged to the fictional forefront as the feminist movement advanced. Jane Smiley modeled her searing narrative of a midwestern farm family on Shakespeare's *King Lear* in *A Thousand Acres* (1991) and followed up with a hilarious spoof on university life in *Moo* (1995). E. Annie Proulx won widespread acclaim with her comic yet tender portrayal of a struggling family in *The Shipping News* (1993). The rising interest in feminist and African-American themes revived the popularity of the 1930s writer Zora Neale Hurston, especially her naturalist novel *Their Eyes Were Watching God*, first published in 1937.

New York City became the art capital of the world after World War II, as well-heeled Americans supported a large number of painters and sculptors. The open and tradition-free American environment seemed especially congenial to the experimental mood of much modern art. Jackson Pollock pioneered abstract expressionism in the 1940s and 1950s, flinging paint on huge canvas flats stretched on his studio floor. Realistic representation went out the window as artists like Pollock and Willem de Kooning strove to create "action paintings" that made the viewer a creative participant in defining the painting's meaning. Pop artists in the 1960s, notably Andy Warhol, canonized on canvas everyday items of consumer culture, such as soup cans. Sculptors like Claes Oldenburg also incorporated into their work objects like cardboard boxes and giant, pillow-soft telephones.

On the stage, playwright David Mamet analyzed the barbarity of American capitalism in plays like *Glengarry Glen Ross* and *American Buffalo,* in which he crafted a kind of poetry from the sludge of American slang. Mamet also made savage sport of feminism and "political correctness" in *Oleanna,* a biting satire about a woman student and her professor. The AIDS epidemic inspired Tony Kushner's sensationally inventive *Angels in America,* a broad-ranging commentary, alternately hilarious and touching, about the condition of American life at century's end. Film, the most characteristic American art form, continued to flourish, especially as a wave of younger filmmakers like George Lucas, Steven Spielberg, Spike Lee, and the Coen brothers, as well as the innovative documentary artist, Ken Burns, made their influence felt.

Architecture also benefited from the building boom of the postwar era. Old master Frank Lloyd Wright produced strikingly original designs, as in the round-walled Guggenheim Museum in New York. Eero Saarinen, the son of a Finnish immigrant, contributed a number of imaginative structures, including two Yale University residential colleges that evoked the atmosphere of an Italian hill town. Chinese-born I. M. Pei designed numerous graceful buildings on several college campuses, as well as the John F. Kennedy Library in Boston. Philip Johnson artfully rendered huge edifices intimate in structures like New York City's Seagram Building and the New York State Theater at Lincoln Center in Manhattan. "Postmodernists" such as Robert Venturi and Michael Graves, inspired by the decorative details of earlier historical styles, rejected the spare functionalism that had dominated modern architecture for much of the century. Frank Gehry achieved international acclaim with his bold Guggenheim Museum in Bilbao, Spain, and with the California Aerospace Museum in Los Angeles.

The American Prospect

The American spirit pulsed with vitality as the twenty-first century commenced, but grave problems continued to plague the Republic. Women still fell short of first-class economic citizenship, and American society groped for ways to adapt the traditional family to the new realities of women's work outside the home. A whole generation after the civil rights triumphs of the 1960s, full equality remained an elusive dream for countless Americans of color. The scourge of drug abuse afflicted all sectors of U.S. society but wreaked its cruelest damage in the tortured underclass neighborhoods of the inner city.

Powerful foreign competitors challenged America's premier economic status. The alarming redistribution of wealth and income threatened to turn America into a society of haves and have-nots, mocking the ideals of democracy and breeding seething resentments along the economic frontier that divided rich from poor.

Environmental worries clouded the country's future. Coal-fired electrical generating plants helped form acid rain and probably contributed to the greenhouse effect, an ominous warming in the planet's temperature. The unsolved problem of radioactive waste disposal hampered the development of nuclear power plants. The planet was being drained of oil, and disastrous accidents like the grounding and subsequent oil spill of the giant tanker *Exxon Valdez* in 1989 in Alaska's pristine Prince William Sound demonstrated the ecological risks of oil exploration and transportation at sea.

Some Americans, soured on the false satisfactions of wealth and anxious to set the globe on the path to ecological stability, welcomed the prospect of a "no-growth" economy. But enlarging the economic pie had historically been the American way of satisfying the appetites of virtually all people for a richer life.

As the human family grows at an alarming rate on a shrinking globe, new challenges still face America and its historical beliefs. The task of cleansing Spaceship Earth of its abundant pollutants—including nuclear weapons—is one urgent mission confronting the American people in the opening years of the twenty-first century. Another is seeking ways to resolve the ethnic and cultural conflicts that erupted with renewed virulence around the globe in the wake of the Cold War's end. At the same time, new opportunities beckon in outer space and on inner-city streets, at the artist's easel and in the concert hall, at the inventor's bench and in the scientist's laboratory, and in the unending quest for social justice, individual fulfillment, and international peace.

The terrorist attack on America on September 11, 2001, posed another and quite unprecedented challenge to the United States. Shielded for over two centuries against assaults on its soil, it would now have to preserve its security in a world made smaller by global communication and transportation, without altering its fundamental democratic values and way of life. In meeting that challenge, the world's oldest republic remained resilient and resourceful. Born as a revolutionary force in a world of conservatism, the United States stood in the twenty-first century as a conservative force in a world of revolution. It had held aloft the banner of liberal democracy in a world wracked by revolutions of the right and left, including fascism, Nazism, and communism. Yet through it all, much that was truly revolutionary also remained a part of America's liberal democratic heritage, as its people pioneered in revolutions against colonialism, racism, sexism, ignorance, and poverty.

The challenges facing Americans, at home and abroad, are formidable, but so is the Republic. As the sun rose on the twenty-first century, the people of the United States still aspired to live up to Lincoln's conviction that they and their heritage represented "the last best hope of earth."

Time for Action *As Americans entered the twenty-first century, the movement to save precious environmental resources rose higher on the national and international agenda. This cartoon highlights the urgency of stopping the often heedless exploitation of trees and forests, and the need to secure nature's bounty for future generations.*

THE 21ST CENTURY

arcadio

For further reading, see the Appendix. For web resources, go to **http://college.hmco.com.**

Appendix

SUGGESTED READINGS

CHAPTER 1

PRIMARY SOURCE DOCUMENTS

Hernán Cortés's *Letters from Mexico** have been translated into English by A. R. Pagden (1971). Bartolomé de Las Casas, *Thirty Very Judicial Propositions** (1552), and Juan Gines de Sepulveda, *The Second Democrates** (1547), reflect the Spanish *conquistadores'* efforts to understand the native peoples of the New World. See also Las Casas's *The Destruction of the Indies* (1542). *The Broken Spears: The Aztec Account of the Conquest of Mexico,** edited by Miguel Leon-Portilla (1962), is an anthology of texts compiled from indigenous sources. Olaudah Equiano, *Equiano's Travels** (1789), is a fascinating account by an African in the New World in the eighteenth century.

SECONDARY SOURCES

Brian M. Fagan reviews the sketchy evidence concerning the earliest humans to arrive in the Americas in *The Great Journey: The Peopling of Ancient America* (1987). For more on the pre-Columbian history of the Americas, see Norman Hammond, *Ancient Maya Civilization* (1982); Brian M. Fagan, *Kingdoms of Gold, Kingdoms of Jade: The Americas Before Columbus* (1991); and Stuart J. Fiedel, *Prehistory of the Americas* (1992). Immanuel Wallerstein, *The Modern World System: Capitalist Agriculture and the Origins of the European World in the Sixteenth Century* (1974), provides a theoretical overview of the international economic background of European colonization. African history is sketched in J. D. Fage, *A History of West Africa* (1969), and John Thornton, *Africa and Africans in the Making of the Atlantic World, 1400–1680* (1992).

A fascinating brief synthesis of early European contact with the Americas is J. H. Elliott, *The Old World and the New, 1492–1650* (1970). Alfred Crosby discusses *The Columbian Exchange: Biological and Cultural Consequences of 1492* (1972). A marvelously illustrated volume portraying the impact of America on the European imagination is Hugh Honour, *The New Golden Land* (1975). See also Stephen Greenblatt, *Marvelous Possessions: The Wonders of the New World* (1991), and Herman J. Viola and Carolyn Margolis, *Seeds of Change: Five Hundred Years Since Columbus* (1991). D. W. Meinig presents a geographical overview of immigration in *The Shaping of America: A Geographical Perspective on 500 Years of History. Atlantic America, 1492–1800* (1986). Patricia Seed compares different forms of European conquest in *Ceremonies of Possession* (1995).

Nathan Wachtel presents the Indians' view of the Spanish conquest in *The Vision of the Vanquished* (1977). The spread of Spanish America northward is traced in Philip Wayne Powell, *Soldiers, Indians and Silver: The Northward Advance of New Spain, 1550–1600* (1952); Edward H. Spicer, *Cycles of Conquest: The Impact of Spain, Mexico and the United States on the Indians of the Southwest, 1533–1960* (1962); Andrew L. Knaut, *The Pueblo Revolt of 1680: Conquest and Resistance in Seventeenth-Century New Mexico* (1997); Ramon A. Gutierrez, *When Jesus Came the Corn Mothers Went Away* (1991); and David J. Weber's masterful synthesis, *The Spanish Frontier in North America* (1992).

CHAPTER 2

PRIMARY SOURCE DOCUMENTS

Richard Hakluyt, *Divers Voyages Touching the Discovery of America and the Islands Adjacent,** edited by J. W. Jones (1850), supplied the rationale for the establishment of English colonies in North America. John Smith, "Generall Historie of Virginia," in *Travels and Works of Captain John Smith,** edited by Edward Arber (1910), is the account of the amazing, vain man who steered Jamestown through its precarious first few years.

SECONDARY SOURCES

The immediate English background of colonization is colorfully presented in Peter Laslett, *The World We Have Lost* (1965), and in Carl Bridenbaugh, *Vexed and Troubled Englishmen, 1590–1642* (1968). Contact between Indian and European cultures is handled in Colin G. Calloway, *New Worlds for All: Indians, Europeans, and the Remaking of America* (1997); and James Axtell, *The Invasion Within: The Contest of Cultures in Colonial America* (1985). James Merrell, *The Indian's New World* (1989), describing the wrenching experiences of the Catawba Indians, is the best

---

* An asterisk indicates that the document, or an excerpt from it, can be found in Thomas A. Bailey and David M. Kennedy, eds., *The American Spirit: United States History as Seen by Contemporaries,* 10th ed. (Boston: Houghton Mifflin, 2002).

ethnohistorical account of a single tribe for the early period. See also Daniel K. Richter, *The Ordeal of the Longhouse: The Peoples of the Iroquois League in the Era of European Colonization* (1992), and Richard D. White, *The Middle Ground: Indians, Empires, and Republics in the Great Lakes Region, 1650–1815* (1991). The Chesapeake region has recently received much fresh attention, especially in Aubrey C. Land et al., *Law, Society, and Politics in Early Maryland* (1977); Lois Green Carr et al., eds., *Colonial Chesapeake Society* (1988); Lois Green Carr et al., *Robert Cole's World: Agriculture and Society in Early Maryland* (1991); Philip D. Morgan, *Slave Counterpoint: Black Culture in the Eighteenth-Century Chesapeake and Lowcountry* (1998); and James Horn, *Adapting to a New World: English Society in the Seventeenth-Century Chesapeake* (1994).

The role of slavery in early colonial society is examined perceptively in Edmund S. Morgan, *American Slavery, American Freedom* (1975). See also Winthrop Jordan's monumental *White over Black* (1968); Peter Wood's account of South Carolina, *Black Majority* (1974); and Ira Berlin's overview, *Many Thousands Gone: The First Two Centuries of Slavery in North America* (1998). Gary Nash analyzes relations among all three races in *Red, White, and Black: The Peoples of Early America* (1974), as do Daniel H. Usner, Jr., in *Indians, Settlers, and Slaves in a Frontier Exchange Economy: The Lower Mississippi Valley Before 1783* (1992), and Timothy Silver, in *A New Face on the Countryside: Indians, Colonists, and Slaves in South Atlantic Forests, 1500–1800* (1990).

CHAPTER 3

PRIMARY SOURCE DOCUMENTS

John Winthrop, "A Modell of Christian Charity" (1630), in *The American Primer,* edited by Daniel Boorstin, outlines the goals of the Puritan errand into the wilderness. Winthrop's "Speech on Liberty"* (1645), in his *History of New England* (1853), established the colony's fundamental political principles. William Bradford, *Of Plymouth Plantation,* edited by Samuel E. Morison (1952), is a rich contemporary account.

SECONDARY SOURCES

New England has received more scholarly attention than any other colonial region. Harry Stout, *The New England Soul: Preaching and Culture in Colonial New England* (1986), is a recent comprehensive account. A brilliant and complex intellectual history is Perry Miller's *The New England Mind* (2 vols., 1939, 1953), a work that has long been a landmark for other scholars. Sacvan Bercovitch traces the heritage of the New England temperament in *The Puritan Origins of the American Self* (1975). See also David Jaffe, *People of the Wachusett: Greater New England in History and Memory* (1999). Other interpretations of Puritanism as well as popular religious practice include Andrew Delbanco, *The*

Puritan Ordeal (1989), David Hall, *Worlds of Wonder, Days of Judgment* (1989); and Jon Butler, *Awash in a Sea of Faith: Christianizing the American People* (1990). For analyses of Puritan-Indian relations, see Francis Jennings, *The Invasion of America* (1975), and Neal Salisbury, *Manitou and Providence* (1982). For a fascinating account of some settlers' assimilation into Indian society, see John Demos, *The Unredeemed Captive: A Family Story from Early America* (1994). Areas outside New England are dealt with in Patricia Bonomi, *A Factious People: Politics and Society in Colonial New York* (1971); Richard and Mary Dunn, eds., *The World of William Penn* (1986); Oliver A. Rink, *Holland on the Hudson: An Economic and Social History of Dutch New York* (1986); and Joyce D. Goodfriend, *Before the Melting Pot: Society and Culture in Colonial New York City, 1664–1730* (1992). The essays in Michael Zuckerman, ed., *Friends and Neighbors: Group Life in America's First Plural Society* (1982), argue that the middle colonies provide the best early model for America as a whole.

CHAPTER 4

PRIMARY SOURCE DOCUMENTS

Adolph B. Benson, ed., *The America of 1750; Petar Kalm's Travels in North America* (1937), records the observations of a visiting Swedish naturalist with a keen eye for the behavior of human fauna. The first slave laws of Virginia are collected in Warren M. Billings, ed., *The Old Dominion in the Seventeenth Century** (1975), as are firsthand accounts of Bacon's Rebellion. See also George L. Burr, ed., *Narratives of the Witchcraft Cases, 1648–1706** (1914).

SECONDARY SOURCES

On life and labor in the Chesapeake, consult Thad W. Tate and David L. Ammerman, eds., *The Chesapeake in the Seventeenth Century* (1979), and Edmund S. Morgan, *American Slavery, American Freedom* (1975), which concentrates on race and class relations. Winthrop Jordan's magnificent *White over Black: American Attitudes Toward the Negro, 1550–1812* (1968) discusses the evolution of racial attitudes. Life in New England's towns and homes is scrutinized in John Demos, *A Little Commonwealth: Family Life in Plymouth Colony* (1970); Philip Greven, *Four Generations: Population, Land, and Family in Colonial Andover, Massachusetts* (1970); Kenneth Lockridge, *New England Town: Dedham* (1970); Lyle Koehler, *A Search for Power: The "Weaker Sex" in Seventeenth-Century New England* (1980); Laurel T. Ulrich, *Good Wives: Image and Reality in the Lives of Women in Northern New England, 1650–1750* (1982); Marilynn Salmon, *Women and the Law of Property in Early America* (1986); Mary Beth Norton, *Founding Mothers and Fathers* (1996); Cornelia Hughes Dayton, *Women Before the Bar: Gender, Law, and Society in Connecticut, 1639–1789* (1995); Lisa Wilson, *Ye Heart of a Man: The Domestic Life of*

Men in Colonial New England (1999); and Philip Greven, *The Protestant Temperament* (1977), which analyzes child-rearing practices. Witchcraft is the subject of Paul Boyer and Stephen Nissenbaum's *Salem Possessed* (1974) and John Demos's massive *Entertaining Satan* (1982). See also Carol F. Karlsen, *The Devil in the Shape of a Woman: Witchcraft in Colonial New England* (1987); Richard Godbeer, *The Devil's Dominion: Magic and Religion in Early New England* (1992); and Peter Charles Hoffer, *The Devil's Disciples: Makers of the Salem Witchcraft Trials* (1996). A sweeping survey that emphasizes the diversity of culture already present in seventeenth-century America is E. Brooks Holifield, *Era of Persuasion: American Thought and Culture, 1521–1680* (1989). The relationship of Indians and New England whites to their environment is the subject of William Cronon's intriguing *Changes in the Land* (1983).

CHAPTER 5

PRIMARY SOURCE DOCUMENTS

Noting the ethnic diversity of colonial American society, Michel Guillaume Jean de Crèvecoeur's *Letters from an American Farmer** (1904) and Benjamin Franklin's, "Observations on the Increase of Mankind,"* in Jared Sparks, ed., *The Works of Benjamin Franklin* (1840), respectively celebrate and express unease at that diversity. Franklin's entertaining *Autobiography** (1868) is an indispensable guide to the values and preoccupations of his time. It includes an account of George Whitefield's visit to Philadelphia during the Great Awakening.

SECONDARY SOURCES

Social history is painted with broad strokes in James Henretta, *The Evolution of American Society, 1700–1815* (1973), and Daniel Boorstin, *The Americans: The Colonial Experience* (1958). Richard Hofstadter takes a snapshot of colonial America in *America in 1750* (1971). Colonial immigration in general is covered in Ida Altman and James Horn, eds., *"To Make America": European Emigration in the Early Modern Period* (1991). British immigrants are considered in Bernard Bailyn, *The Peopling of British North America* (1986), and German immigrants in Marianne S. Wokek, *Trade in Strangers: The Beginnings of Mass Migration to North America* (1999). James Kettner describes *The Development of American Citizenship, 1608–1870* (1978). Large-scale economic patterns are traced in John J. McCusker and Russell R. Menard, *The Economy of British America, 1607–1789* (1991), and in Alice H. Jones, *The Wealth of a Nation to Be: The American Colonies on the Eve of the Revolution* (1980). Relations between blacks and whites are documented in Mechal Sobel, *The World They Made Together: Black and White Values in Eighteenth-Century Virginia* (1987), and William D. Piersen, *Black Yankees: The Development of an Afro-American Subculture in Eighteenth-Century New England* (1988).

The toiling classes are probed in Gary B. Nash, *The Urban Crucible: Social Change, Political Consciousness, and the Origins of the American Revolution* (1979), and Rhys Isaac, *The Transformation of Virginia, 1740–1790* (1982). Nash and Isaac link social conflict to the Great Awakening, as does Richard L. Bushman, *From Puritan to Yankee: Character and Social Order in Connecticut, 1690–1765* (1967). Patricia Bonomi also emphasizes religious conflict as a promoter of revolutionary ideology in *Under the Cope of Heaven: Religion, Society, and Politics in Colonial America* (1986), as do the essayists in Ronald Hoffman and Peter J. Albert, eds., *Religion in a Revolutionary Age* (1994). Religious revivalism is chronicled in Edwin S. Gaustad, *The Great Awakening in New England* (1957); David S. Lovejoy, *Religious Enthusiasm in the New World: Heresy to Revolution* (1985); and Susan Juster, *Disorderly Women: Sexual Politics and Evangelicalism in Revolutionary New England* (1994). Cultural history is imaginatively presented in Howard M. Jones, *O Strange New World: American Culture in the Formative Years* (1964). Comprehensive is Henry May, *The Enlightenment in America* (1976). The colonists' sometimes heroic dedication to education is portrayed by Lawrence Cremin, *American Education: The Colonial Experience, 1607–1783* (1970); and the general social implications of the early educational system are studied in James Axtell, *School upon a Hill* (1974). Colonial politics are interpreted in a most suggestive way in Bernard Bailyn, *The Origins of American Politics* (1965).

CHAPTER 6

PRIMARY SOURCE DOCUMENTS

"The Albany Plan of the Union" was the first great statement of colonial unity; "The Proclamation of 1763" forbade settlement west of the Appalachians. Both are collected in Henry Steele Commager, *Documents of American History* (1988).

SECONDARY SOURCES

The workings of the British mercantile system are detailed in Charles M. Andrews's vast *Colonial Period of American History* (4 vols., 1935–1938) and in Lawrence H. Gipson's *British Empire Before the American Revolution* (15 vols., 1936–1970). More recent works on the British Empire include John Brewer, *The Sinews of Power: War, Money, and the English State, 1688–1783* (1989), and Alison G. Olson, *Making the Empire Work: London and American Interest Groups, 1690–1790* (1992). The French colonial effort is described in George M. Wrong, *The Rise and Fall of New France* (2 vols., 1928). Calvin Martin, *Keepers of the Game* (1978), offers a provocative interpretation of the fur trade and its impact on Indian societies. Other works on the role of Indians in larger imperial struggles include Armstrong Starkey, *European and Native American Warfare, 1615–1815* (1998); Francis Jennings, *Empire of Fortune: Crowns,*

Colonies and Tribes in the Seven Years War in America (1988); Gregory Evans Dowd, *A Spirited Resistance: The North American Indian Struggle for Unity, 1745–1815* (1992); and Richard White, *The Middle Ground: Indians, Empires, and Republics in the Great Lakes Region, 1650–1815* (1991). Alan Rogers, *Empire and Liberty: American Resistance to the British Authority, 1755–1763* (1974), investigates American participation in the Seven Years' War, as does Douglas E. Leach in *Roots of Conflict: British Armed Forces and Colonial Americans, 1677–1763* (1986). Fred Anderson focuses on colonial soldiers in *A People's Army: Massachusetts Soldiers and Society in the Seven Years' War* (1984). Classic accounts are Francis Parkman's several volumes, condensed, without serious loss of flavor, in *The Battle for North America*, edited by John Tebbel (1948).

CHAPTER 7

PRIMARY SOURCE DOCUMENTS

Adam Smith's *An Inquiry into the Nature and Causes of the Wealth of Nations** (1776) is a penetrating analysis of British mercantilism. Patrick Henry's "Speech before the Virginia House of Burgesses against the Stamp Act"* (1765) was an influential statement of colonial opposition to British policy, as was John Dickinson's response to the Townshend Acts, *Letters from a Farmer in Pennsylvania* (1768). For contemporary accounts of the beginning of hostilities, see Peter Force, ed., *American Archives*, 4th Series, vol. 2* (1839). For visual sources from the period, consult the edition compiled by Donald H. Cresswell, *The American Revolution in Drawings and Prints* (1975).

SECONDARY SOURCES

Edmund S. Morgan, *The Birth of the Republic, 1763–1789* (1959), is among the best brief accounts of the Revolutionary era. It stresses the happy coincidence of the Revolutionaries' principles and their interests. Lawrence H. Gipson, *The Coming of the Revolution, 1763–1775* (1954), summarizes his 15-volume masterwork (cited in Chapter 6). A more recent attempt at synthesis is Robert Middlekauff's *The Glorious Cause: The American Revolution, 1763–1789* (1982). Two enlightening collections of essays are Jack P. Greene, ed., *The Reinterpretation of the American Revolution, 1763–1789* (1968), and Alfred F. Young, ed., *The American Revolution* (1976), which generally represents a "new left" revisionist view, a perspective also found in Edward A. Countryman, *The American Revolution* (1987), and in Alfred F. Young, ed., *Beyond the American Revolution* (1993). Bernard Bailyn's seminal *Ideological Origins of the American Revolution* (1967) stresses the importance of ideas in pushing the Revolution forward, as well as the colonists' fears of a conspiracy against their liberties. John Philip Reid, on the other hand, emphasizes legal ideas in *Constitutional History*

of the American Revolution: The Authority of Rights (1987), as does Jerrilyn Greene Marston in *King and Congress: The Transfer of Political Legitimacy, 1774–1776* (1987). On the meaning of the Revolution for African-Americans, see Sylvia R. Frey, *Water from the Rock: Black Resistance in a Revolutionary Age* (1991). Imaginative cultural history is found in Robert A. Gross, *The Minutemen and Their World* (1976). Edward A. Countryman emphasizes class conflict in *A People in Revolution: The American Revolution and Political Society in New York, 1760–1790* (1981). A psychological approach to the problem of the Revolutionary generation's assault on established authority is taken in Jay Fliegelman, *Prodigals and Pilgrims: The American Revolution Against Patriarchal Authority, 1750–1800* (1982).

CHAPTER 8

PRIMARY SOURCE DOCUMENTS

Thomas Paine's fiery *Common Sense** (1776) is the manifesto of the Revolution. "The Declaration of Independence"* (1776) is one of the foundations of American political theory. For eyewitness accounts of the war, see John C. Dann, *The Revolution Remembered* (1980). See also the "Treaty of Peace with Great Britain" (1783), in Henry Steele Commager, *Documents of American History* (1988).

SECONDARY SOURCES

The war is sketched in Don Higgenbotham's excellent military history, *The War of American Independence: Military Attitudes, Policies, and Practice, 1763–1789* (1971). On the implications of the revolutionary conflict, see John Shy, *A People Numerous and Armed: Reflections on the Military Struggle for American Independence* (1976); Charles Royster, *A Revolutionary People at War: The Continental Army and the American Character* (1980); and Mark V. Kwasny, *Washington's Partisan War, 1775–1783* (1996). Carl Becker's classic *The Declaration of Independence* (1922) is masterful; on the same subject see also Garry Wills, *Inventing America: Jefferson's Declaration of Independence* (1980), and Pauline Maier, *American Scripture: The Making of the Declaration of Independence* (1997).

General treatments of an often neglected subject are Benjamin Quarles, *The Negro in the American Revolution* (1961); Ronald Hoffman and Ira Berlin, eds., *Slavery and Freedom in the Age of the American Revolution* (1974); and Sylvia R. Frey, *Water From the Rock: Black Resistance in a Revolutionary War* (1991).

Attention to the social history of the Revolution has been largely inspired by John F. Jameson's seminal *The American Revolution Considered as a Social Movement* (1926). Jackson T. Main, *The Social Structure of Revolutionary America* (1969), takes the exploration further along the same lines, with conclusions somewhat at variance with

Jameson's. Local studies of this issue include Edward A. Countryman, *A People in Revolution: The American Revolution and Political Society in New York, 1760–1790* (1981); Gary Nash, *The Urban Crucible: Social Change, Political Consciousness and the Origins of the American Revolution* (1979); and Steven Rosswurm, *Arms, Country, and Class: The Philadelphia Militia and the "Lower Sort" During the American Revolution* (1987). For the role of Indians in the Revolutionary era, see Colin G. Calloway, *The American Revolution in Indian Country* (1995).

Women are the subject of Linda K. Kerber, *Women of the Republic: Intellect and Ideology in Revolutionary America* (1980); Mary Beth Norton, *Liberty's Daughters: The Revolutionary Experience of American Women* (1980); and Joy Day Buel and Richard Buel, Jr., *The Way of Duty: A Woman and Her Family in Revolutionary America* (1984). Michael Kammen brilliantly evokes the ways that the Revolution has been enshrined in the national memory in *A Season of Youth: The American Revolution and the Historical Imagination* (1978).

CHAPTER 9

PRIMARY SOURCE DOCUMENTS

A comparison of the text of the Articles of Confederation (1781), in Henry Steele Commager, *Documents of American History* (1988), with the Constitution* makes an intriguing study. See also Madison, Hamilton, and Jay's explanations of the Constitution in *The Federalist* papers, especially *Federalist* No. 10.* Additional primary sources may be found in Bernard Bailyn, ed., *The Debate on the Constitution: Federalist and Antifederalist Speeches, Articles, and Letters During the Struggle over Ratification* (1993). For visual sources from the period, consult the volume compiled by Donald H. Cresswell, *The American Revolution in Drawings and Prints* (1975).

SECONDARY SOURCES

John Fiske, in *The Critical Period of American History* (1888), portrayed America under the Articles of Confederation as a crisis-ridden country. His view is sharply qualified by Merrill Jensen in *The New Nation* (1950). Jack N. Rakove's *The Beginnings of National Politics* (1979) offers a history of the Continental Congress that substantially revises Jensen's work. Especially learned is Gordon S. Wood's massive and brilliant study of the entire period, *The Creation of the American Republic, 1776–1787* (1969), and his equally compelling work, *The Radicalism of the American Revolution* (1991), which documents the egalitarianism that swept revolutionary society during and after the war. For a similar argument that relies on the material culture of the era, see Richard Bushman, *The Refinement of America: Persons, Houses, Cities* (1992). See also Richard B. Morris, *The Forging of the Union, 1781–1787* (1987). An influential transatlantic per-

spective on the roots of American republicanism is J. G. A. Pocock, *The Machiavellian Moment: Florentine Political Thought and the Atlantic Republican Tradition* (1975). Edmund S. Morgan also looks at both England and America in *Inventing the People: The Rise of Popular Sovereignty in England and America* (1988).

On the Constitutional Convention, see Richard Bernstein's superb synthesis of current scholarship, *Are We to Be a Nation? The Making of the Constitution* (1987). Bernstein's work is one of a host of useful studies inspired by the bicentennial of the drafting of the Constitution. Others are Ruth Bloch, *Visionary Republic: Millennial Themes in American Thought, 1756–1800* (1986); Richard Beeman et al., eds., *Beyond Confederation: Origins of the Constitution and American National Identity* (1987); Leonard Levy, *Original Intent and the Framers' Constitution* (1988); and Jack N. Rakove, *Original Meanings: Politics and Ideas in the Making of the Constitution* (1996); and Thorton Anderson, *Creating the Constitution* (1993). For a more general interpretation of the Constitution's role in American society see Michael G. Kammen, *A Machine That Would Go of Itself* (1986). Charles A. Beard shocked conservatives with *An Economic Interpretation of the Constitution of the United States* (1913). It is seriously weakened by two blistering attacks: Robert E. Brown, *Charles Beard and the Constitution* (1956), and Forrest McDonald, *We the People: The Economic Origins of the Constitution* (1958). See also McDonald's *E Pluribus Unum: The Formation of the American Republic, 1776–1790* (1965). Jackson T. Main, *The Anti-Federalists* (1961), partially rehabilitates Beard. Gary Nash's *Race and Revolution* (1990) offers a perceptive study of controversies over race and slavery in the making of the Constitution, as do the contributors to John P. Kaminski, ed., *A Necessary Evil? Slavery and the Debate over the Constitution* (1995).

CHAPTER 10

PRIMARY SOURCE DOCUMENTS

"The Report on Manufactures" (in Daniel Boorstin, ed., *American Primer*), the last of Alexander Hamilton's messages to Congress, presented the case for the development of American industry. Thomas Jefferson expounded his views in *Notes on the State of Virginia* (1784). For further study of the Hamiltonian-Jeffersonian debate, see Henry Cabot Lodge, ed., *The Works of Alexander Hamilton** (1904), and Paul L. Ford, ed., *The Writings of Thomas Jefferson** (1985). Important salvos in the battle between national power and state sovereignty, and between Federalists and Jeffersonians, were the Virginia and Kentucky resolutions* (1798) and the reply of Rhode Island* (1799). Washington's Farewell Address* (1796) established the foundation for American attitudes about party politics and foreign policy. See also Benjamin Franklin Bache's stinging editorial on Washington's retirement, *Philadelphia Aurora** (1797).

SECONDARY SOURCES

Perceptive introductions are provided by Marcus Cunliffe's succinct *The Nation Takes Shape, 1789–1837* (1959) and Stanley Elkins and Eric McKitrick's comprehensive work, *The Age of Federalism: The Early American Republic, 1788–1800* (1993). On the Bill of Rights see Bernard Schwartz, *The Great Rights of Mankind: A History of the American Bill of Rights* (1991), and Patrick L. Conley and John P. Kaminski, eds., *The Bill of Rights and the States: The Colonial and Revolutionary Origins of American Liberties* (1992). On the use of party politics see Richard Hofstadter's thoughtful *The Idea of a Party System* (1969). For a trenchant analysis of Jeffersonianism see Joyce Appleby, *Capitalism and a New Social Order: The Republican Vision* (1984), whose analysis emphasizes the role of liberalism in American political thought, a point earlier made by Louis Hartz in *The Liberal Tradition in America* (1955). Also illuminating is Gerald Stourzh, *Alexander Hamilton and the Idea of Republican Government* (1970). See also Gordon S. Wood, *The Radicalism of the American Revolution* (1991). A comprehensive biography is James T. Flexner, *George Washington and the New Nation, 1783–1793* (1969). Consult also Forrest McDonald, *The Presidency of George Washington* (1974), and Garry Wills, *Cincinnatus: George Washington and the Enlightenment* (1984). Of special interest is Richard H. Kohn, *Eagle and Sword: The Federalists and the Creation of the Military Establishment in America, 1783–1802* (1975). On Adams, consult Page Smith, *John Adams* (2 vols., 1962), and Stephen G. Kurtz, *The Presidency of John Adams* (1957).

CHAPTER 11

PRIMARY SOURCE DOCUMENTS

Thomas Jefferson's "First Inaugural Address" (1801), in Henry Steele Commager, *Documents of American History,* echoed the themes of Washington's Farewell Address and set the tone for his presidency. Reuben G. Thwaites, ed., *Original Journals of the Lewis and Clark Expedition** (1904), chronicles the explorers' adventures. For the political flavor of the age, see the debate over the Embargo Act* (1807); for constitutional history, read the decision of John Marshall in *Marbury v. Madison** (1803). See James Madison, "War Message"* (1812), in James D. Richardson, ed., *Messages and Papers of the Presidents* (1896), vol. I, 500–504; and the protest of thirty-four Federalist congressmen, *Annals of Congress** (12 Cong., 1 sess., 2 cols. 2219–2221 [1812]). John Marshall's decision in *McCulloch v. Maryland,** 4 Wheaton 316 (1819), is a leading statement of the era's surging nationalism. Timothy Dwight offers a participant's view of the opposition to the war in *The History of the Hartford Convention** (1833).

SECONDARY SOURCES

A monument of American historical writing is Henry Adams, *History of the United States During the Administra-* *tions of Jefferson and Madison* (9 vols., 1889–1891), available in a one-volume abridgment edited by Ernest Samuels. Especially fascinating are Adams's prologue and epilogue on the United States in 1800 and 1817. A brief introduction is given in Marshall Smelser, *The Democratic Republic, 1801–1815* (1968). On the Supreme Court see R. Kent Newmyer, *The Supreme Court Under Marshall and Taney* (1986), and G. Edward White, *The Marshall Court and Cultural Change, 1815–1835* (1988). Politics are treated in a broad, imaginative context in James S. Young, *The Washington Community, 1800–1829* (1966). Noble E. Cunningham, Jr., *In Pursuit of Reason: The Life of Thomas Jefferson* (1987), is a short biography. The standard scholarly biography is Merrill D. Peterson, *Thomas Jefferson and the New Nation* (1970). Peterson has also scrutinized *The Jefferson Image in the American Mind* (1960). See also Joseph Ellis, *American Sphinx* (1997). Forrest McDonald is highly critical of his subject in *The Presidency of Thomas Jefferson* (1976). Leonard Levy debunks Jefferson's liberalism in *Jefferson and Civil Liberties* (1963). Bernard W. Sheehan examines another important aspect of policy in *Seeds of Extinction: Jeffersonian Philanthropy and the American Indian* (1973). See also Reginald Horsman, *Expansion and American Indian Policy, 1783–1812* (1967), and Gregory Evans Dowd, *A Spirited Resistance: The North American Indian Struggle for Unity, 1745–1815* (1992). Donald Jackson, *Thomas Jefferson and the Stony Mountain: Exploring the West from Monticello* (1981), captures Jefferson's fascination with the West. See also Stephen E. Ambrose's spirited biography of Meriwether Lewis, *Undaunted Courage* (1996). Doron S. Ben-Atar examines *The Origins of Jeffersonian Commercial Policy and Diplomacy* (1993). John C. Miller, *The Wolf by the Ears: Thomas Jefferson and Slavery* (1977), probes the third president's attitudes on an important question. An important work that sets the War of 1812 in a broad context of early American history is J. C. A. Stagg, *Mr. Madison's War: Politics, Diplomacy and Warfare in the Early American Republic* (1983). Also see Steven Watts, *The Republic Reborn: War and the Making of Liberal America, 1790–1820* (1987), and Donald R. Hickey, *The War of 1812: A Forgotten Conflict* (1989). On the causes of the war, Julius W. Pratt, *Expansionists of 1812* (1925), stresses western pressures; Bradford Perkins, *Prologue to War: England and the United States, 1805-1812* (1961), and Reginald Horsman, *The Causes of the War of 1812* (1961), discuss free seas; and Roger H. Brown, *The Republic in Peril, 1812* (1964), emphasizes the need for saving the republican form of government.

CHAPTER 12

PRIMARY SOURCE DOCUMENTS

Charles F. Adams, ed., *Memoirs of John Quincy Adams** (1875), offers a behind-the-scenes portrait of the creation of the Monroe Doctrine. See also the text of Monroe's public statement in James D. Richardson, ed., *Messages and Papers* *of the Presidents** (1896), vol. II, 207 ff. "The Missouri Compromise" (1819–1820), in Henry Steele Commager, *Documents of American History* (1988), reveals the dangerous sectional animosities underlying such national pride.

SECONDARY SOURCES

On the War of 1812, see the books by J.C.A. Stagg, Steven Watts, and Donald R. Hickey cited in Chapter 11. Lester D. Langley, *The Americans in the Age of Revolution, 1750–1850* (1996), takes a comparative approach to the history of the Western hemisphere. On Indian affairs and westward expansion see Dorothy Jones, *License for Empire: Colonialism by Treaty in Early America* (1982); and the works of R. David Edmunds, *The Shawnee Prophet* (1983) and *Tecumseh and the Quest for Indian Leadership* (1984). Recent treatments of Madison include Robert A. Rutland, *James Madison: The Founding Father* (1987); Drew R. McCoy, *The Last of the Fathers: James Madison and the Republican Legacy* (1989); and Jack N. Rakove, *James Madison and the Creation of the American Republic* (1990). An excellent introduction to nationalism is George Dangerfield, *The Awakening of American Nationalism, 1815–1828* (1965). See also Robert H. Wiebe's ambitious *Opening of American Society: From the Adoption of the Constitution to the Eve of Disunion* (1984). Glover Moore, *The Missouri Controversy, 1819–1821* (1953), and Charles S. Sydnor, *The Development of Southern Sectionalism, 1819–1848* (1948), place the Missouri Compromise in a broader context. On the Monroe Doctrine, the classic text is Dexter Perkins, *A History of the Monroe Doctrine* (1955). James E. Lewis, *The American Union and the Problem of Neighborhood* (1998), places the Monroe Doctrine in a new interpretive context. Ernest R. May tries to tie the doctrine to domestic politics, especially the impending election of 1824, in *The Making of the Monroe Doctrine* (1975).

CHAPTER 13

PRIMARY SOURCE DOCUMENTS

Davy Crockett, *Exploits and Adventures in Texas** (1836), is a lively description of the democratic political order of Jacksonian America. James Fenimore Cooper's *The American Democrat** (1838) offers an incisive commentary on the era's politics, while C. W. Janson, *The Stranger in America, 1793–1806** (1807), exposes the seamier aspects of American egalitarianism. On the Bank War, see Andrew Jackson, "Veto Message"* (July 10, 1832), in James D. Richardson, ed., *Messages and Papers of the Presidents* (1896), vol. II, 576 ff., and Daniel Webster's "Speech on Jackson's Veto of the U.S. Bank Bill" (1832), in Richard Hofstadter, ed., *Great Issues in American History* (1958). On the Tariff of Abominations and its implications, see the "Webster-Hayne Debate"* (1830). Webster's reply to Hayne is one of the greatest specimens of American political oratory.

SECONDARY SOURCES

A still-living classic treatise on the Jacksonian period is Alexis de Tocqueville, *Democracy in America* (1835, 1840). Edward Pessen, *Jacksonian America: Society, Personality and Politics* (rev. ed., 1978) is a good general introduction that sharply disputes Tocqueville's findings. Marvin Meyers, *The Jacksonian Persuasion* (1957), and John William Ward, *Andrew Jackson: Symbol for an Age* (1955), examine the broader cultural significance of "Old Hickory" and his supporters. Arthur M. Schlesinger, Jr., in his seminal *The Age of Jackson* (1945), stresses the support of eastern labor for Jackson, a view that comes under attack in Lee Bensen, *The Concept of Jacksonian Democracy: New York as a Test Case* (1961). On the evolution of mass-based political parties see Richard P. McCormick, *The Second American Party System* (1966), and two books by Ronald P. Formisano, *The Birth of Mass Political Parties: Michigan, 1827–1861* (1971) and *The Transformation of Political Culture: Massachusetts Parties, 1790s–1840s* (1983). Samuel Flagg Bemis, *John Quincy Adams and the Union* (1956) is the second volume of a distinguished biography. Robert V. Remini has a three-volume biography of Jackson: *Andrew Jackson and the Course of American Freedom, 1822–1832* (1981) and *Andrew Jackson and the Course of American Democracy* (1984) cover the presidential years. Remini also has a fine biography of Clay, *Henry Clay: Statesman for the Union* (1991). A masterful analysis of the period's most celebrated statesmen is Merrill D. Peterson, *The Great Triumvirate: Webster, Clay, and Calhoun* (1987).

On Van Buren see John Niven, *Martin Van Buren: The Romantic Age of American Politics* (1983). Incisive analysis can be found in Richard Hofstadter's essay on Jackson in *The American Political Tradition* (1948). See also Daniel Feller, *The Jacksonian Promise* (1995); Harry L. Watson, *Liberty and Power: The Politics of Jacksonian America* (1990); and Lawrence F. Kohl, *The Politics of Individualism: Parties and the American Character in the Jacksonian Era* (1989). On Calhoun, see John Niven, *John C. Calhoun and the Price of Union* (1988). Jackson's Indian policies are scrutinized in Ronald N. Satz, *American Indian Policy in the Jacksonian Era* (1975), and Michael P. Rogin's heavily psychoanalytic *Fathers and Children: Andrew Jackson and the Subjugation of the American Indians* (1975). See also Michael D. Green, *The Politics of Indian Removal* (1982), and Anthony Wallace, *The Long, Bitter Trail: Andrew Jackson and the Indians* (1993). For studies of the so-called civilized tribes, see Charles Hudson, *The Southeastern Indians* (1976), and William G. McLaughlin, *Cherokee Renascence in the New Republic* (1986). Daniel W. Howe provides a stimulating analysis of Jackson's opponents in *The Political Culture of the American Whigs* (1980). Also see Thomas Brown, *Politics and Statesmanship: Essays on the American Whig Party* (1985). Attempts to connect Jacksonian politics with the economic changes of the era include Harry L. Watson, *Liberty and Power* (1990), and Charles Sellers's monumental synthesis, *The Market Revolution* (1991). The color of the frothy presidential campaign of 1840 comes through in Robert G. Gunderson, *The Log-Cabin Campaign* (1957).

CHAPTER 14

PRIMARY SOURCE DOCUMENTS

Seth Luther, *An Address to the Working-Men of New England** (1833), is the eloquent appeal of an uneducated working-class labor reformer. On the transportation revolution, see John H. B. Latrobe, *Western Waters** (1871), and Mark Twain's classic *Life on the Mississippi** (1883). Lemuel Shaw's decision of 1842 in *Commonwealth* v. *Hunt,* 4 Metc. III (in Henry Steele Commager, *Documents of American History,* 1988) is regarded as the "Magna Carta of American labor organization." Thomas Dublin edited *Farm and Factory: Women's Letters, 1830–1860* (1981). Richard H. Dana, Jr.'s personal narrative, *Two Years Before the Mast* (1840), describes the romance of the clipper ships.

SECONDARY SOURCES

Charles Sellers offers a sweeping interpretation of the era in *The Market Revolution: Jacksonian America, 1815–1846* (1991). On immigration see Maldwyn Jones, *American Immigration* (1960); John Bodnar, *The Transplanted: A History of Immigrants in Urban America* (1985); Hasia Diner, *Erin's Daughters in America* (1983); and Kerby A. Miller, *Emigrants and Exiles: Ireland and the Irish Exodus to North America* (1985). For industrialism see Thomas Cochran, *Frontiers of Change: Early Industrialism in America* (1981). The laboring classes are chronicled in Bruce Laurie, *Artisans into Workers: Labor in Nineteenth-Century America* (1989). Consult also Herbert Gutman's path-breaking *Work, Culture, and Society in Industrializing America* (1976); Sean Wilentz's insightful *Chants Democratic: New York City and the Rise of the American Working Class, 1788–1850* (1984); David A. Zonderman's *Aspirations and Anxieties: New England Workers and the Mechanized Factory System, 1815–1850* (1992); and David R. Roediger, *The Wages of Whiteness: Race and the Making of the American Working Class* (1991). The experiences of women workers are the focus of Thomas Dublin, *Women at Work: The Transformation of Work and Community in Lowell, Massachusetts, 1826–1860* (1979), and Christine Stansell, *City of Women: Sex and Class in New York, 1789–1860* (1986). Mary Blewett puts the gender identities of both men and women at the center of *Men, Women, and Work: Class, Gender, and Protest in the New England Shoe Industry, 1780-1910* (1988). On the introduction of technology see David H. Hounshell, *From the American System to Mass Production, 1800–1932: The Development of Manufacturing Technology in the United States* (1984), and David F. Hawke, *Nuts and Bolts of the Past: A History of American Technology, 1776–1860* (1988). Ideological aspects of this process are described in John F. Kassen, *Civilizing the Machine: Technology and Republican Values in America, 1776–1900* (1976), and David Nye, *Consuming Power: A Social History of American Energies* (1998). The legal foundation of the market revolution is discussed in Morton Horwitz, *The Transformation of American Law, 1780–1860* (1977). Steven Hahn and Jonathan Prude, eds., *The Countryside in the Age of Capitalist Transformation: Essays in the Social History of Rural America* (1985), is a provocative look at the impact of the transportation and industrial revolutions on the countryside. See also Christopher Clark, *The Roots of Rural Capitalism: Western Massachusetts, 1780–1860* (1990), and Alan Kulikoff, *The Agrarian Origins of American Capitalism* (1992).

CHAPTER 15

PRIMARY SOURCE DOCUMENTS

Alexis de Tocqueville, *Democracy in America** (1835, 1840), has stood for over a century and a half as the classic analysis of the American character. Joseph Smith, *The Pearl of Great Price** (1829), contains an account of the Mormon leader's religious visions, which capture the religious restiveness of the age. William H. McGuffey, *Fifth Eclectic Reader* (1879), was the most popular school text of the age. On the women's movement, see the "Seneca Falls Manifesto"* (1848), which laid the foundations of the feminist movement. Catharine Beecher and Harriet Beecher Stowe, *The American Woman's Home** (1869), discusses the role of women. Stowe's classic novel, *Uncle Tom's Cabin* (1852), offers an emotional appeal against slavery and a fascinating portrait of slavery, religion, and family life in antebellum America.

SECONDARY SOURCES

A magisterial synthesis is Daniel Boorstin, *The Americans: The National Experience* (1965). Satisfying detail is found in two Russell B. Nye books: *The Cultural Life of the New Nation, 1776–1830* (1960) and *Society and Culture in America, 1830–1860* (1974). On the rise of the middle class see Karen Halttunen, *Confidence Men and Painted Women* (1982); Richard L. Bushman, *The Refinement of America: Persons, Houses, Cities* (1992); and Stuart M. Blumin, *The Emergence of the Middle Class* (1989). Sydney E. Ahlstrom, *Religious History of the American People* (1972), is sweeping. On revivalism see Nathan O. Hatch, *The Democratization of American Christianity* (1989), and Paul Johnson, *A Shopkeeper's Millennium: Society and Revivals in Rochester, New York, 1815–1837* (1978), which links revivals to economic change. Bushman describes the origins of Mormonism in *Joseph Smith and the Beginnings of Mormonism* (1984), and Leonard J. Arrington analyzes the most celebrated Mormon leader in *Brigham Young: American Moses* (1984). On the Shakers, see Stephen Stein, *The Shaker Experience in America* (1992). On reform broadly, see Ronald Walters, *American Reformers* (1978), and Robert Abzug, *Cosmos Crumbling:*

American Reform and the Religious Imagination (1994). For particular subjects consult David Rothman, *The Discovery of the Asylum* (1971), Gerald Grob, *Mental Institutions in America: Social Policy to 1875* (1973), and David Gallagher, *Voice for the Mad: The Life of Dorothea Dix* (1995); on the development of hospitals see Charles Rosenberg, *The Care of Strangers: The Rise of America's Hospital System* (1987). Women's history for this period has blossomed in a number of studies, including Carroll Smith-Rosenberg, *Religion and the Rise of the American City* (1971); Nancy Cott, *The Bonds of Womanhood: "Woman's Sphere" in New England, 1780–1835* (1977); Ellen Carol DuBois, *Feminism and Suffrage* (1978); Estelle B. Freedman, *Their Sisters' Keepers: Women's Prison Reform in America, 1830–1930* (1981); Barbara Epstein, *The Politics of Domesticity* (1981); and Nancy Hewitt, *Women's Activism and Social Change: Rochester, New York, 1822–1872* (1984). Family history is covered in Steven Mintz and Susan Kellogg, *Domestic Revolutions: A Social History of American Family Life* (1988); Jeanne Boydston, *Home and Work: Housework, Wages, and the Ideology of Labor in the Early Republic* (1990); and Carl Degler, *At Odds: Women and the Family in America from the Revolution to the Present* (1980). Studies with a cultural focus include Joseph Ellis, *After the Revolution: Profiles of Early American Culture* (1979); Larzer Ziff, *Literary Democracy: The Declaration of Cultural Independence in America* (1981); and Anne Rose, *Voices of the Marketplace: American Thought and Culture, 1830–1860* (1995). On two critically important writers, see Robert D. Richardson's excellent volumes, *Emerson: The Mind on Fire* (1995), and *Thoreau: A Life of the Mind* (1986).

CHAPTER 16

PRIMARY SOURCE DOCUMENTS

Two influential abolitionist documents are Theodore Dwight Weld, *American Slavery As It Is** (1839), and the inaugural editorial of William Lloyd Garrison, *The Liberator** (1831). Roy P. Basler, ed., *The Collected Works of Abraham Lincoln* (1933), contains the Great Emancipator's assessment of abolitionism in 1854. For southern perspectives, see James Henry Hammond's famous "Cotton Is King" speech* (*Congressional Globe*, 36 Cong., 1 sess., 961 [March 3, 1858]). Famous firsthand accounts of slavery include Frederick Douglass, *Narrative of the Life of Frederick Douglass* (1845), and Solomon Northrup, *Twelve Years a Slave* (1853). John W. Blassingame, ed., *Slave Testimony* (1977), offers a rich collection of slave narratives.

SECONDARY SOURCES

A good introduction to southern history is Clement Eaton, *A History of the Old South: The Emergence of a Reluctant Nation* (1975). Wilbur J. Cash, *The Mind of the South* (1941), is an engagingly written classic. Always incisive is C. Vann Woodward, *The Burden of Southern History* (1960). On white

politics and society see Bruce Collins, *White Society in the Antebellum South* (1985), and Bertram Wyatt-Brown, *Honor and Violence in the Old South* (1986). Important interpretations of the "peculiar institution" include Eugene Genovese, *The Political Economy of Slavery* (1965); Barbara Jeanne Fields, *Slavery and Freedom on the Middle Ground: Maryland During the Nineteenth Century* (1985); Gavin Wright, *The Political Economy of the Cotton South* (1978); and Eugene Genovese and Elizabeth Fox-Genovese, *Fruits of Merchant Capital* (1983). James Oakes questions many of Genovese's interpretations in *The Ruling Race: A History of American Slaveholders* (1982) and *Slavery and Freedom: An Interpretation of the Old South* (1990). Catherine Clinton examines *The Plantation Mistress* (1982); Elizabeth Fox-Genovese discusses southern women more generally in *Within the Plantation Household: Black and White Women of the Old South* (1988). See also Deborah Gray White, *Ar'n't I a Woman? Female Slaves in the Plantation South* (1985); Melton Alonza McLaurin, *Celia, a Slave* (1991); and Brenda E. Stevenson, *Life in Black and White: Family and Community in the Slave South* (1996). The literature on slavery and African-Americans is enormous; the best place to start is John Hope Franklin, *From Slavery to Freedom* (8th ed., 2000); see also Peter J. Parish, *Slavery: History and Historians* (1989). The modern debate on slavery began with Ulrich B. Phillips's classic *American Negro Slavery* (1918); a darker view of the same subject is found in Kenneth M. Stampp, *The Peculiar Institution* (1956). Consult also Stanley Elkins's controversial essay, *Slavery* (2nd ed., 1968), which also has interesting observations on the abolitionists. Other important studies of slavery and African-American life include John W. Blassingame, *The Slave Community* (rev. ed., 1979); Herbert Gutman, *The Black Family in Slavery and Freedom, 1750–1925* (1976); Paul David, *Reckoning with Slavery* (1976); Eugene Genovese, *Roll, Jordan, Roll* (1974); Lawrence Levine, *Black Culture and Black Consciousness: Afro-American Folk Thought from Slavery to Freedom* (1977); Albert J. Raboteau, *Slave Religion: The "Invisible Institution" in the Antebellum South* (1978); and Sterling Stuckey, *Slave Culture: Nationalist Theory and the Foundations of Black America* (1987). David B. Davis provides indispensable background to the history of abolitionism in *The Problem of Slavery in Western Culture* (1966) and *The Problem of Slavery in the Age of Revolution* (1975), as does Thomas Bender, ed., in *The Antislavery Debate* (1992). The best brief history of the abolitionists is James B. Stewart, *Holy Warriors* (1976). Ronald E. Walters emphasizes the constraints that American culture placed on the abolitionists in *The Antislavery Appeal: American Abolitionism After 1830* (1976). For provocative appraisals, see Lewis Perry and Michael Fellman, eds., *Antislavery Reconsidered: New Perspectives on the Abolitionists* (1979). See also Julie Roy Jeffrey, *The Great Silent Army of Abolitionism: Ordinary Women in the Abolitionist Movement* (1998). James B. Stewart focuses on *Wendell Phillips: Liberty's Hero* (1987). Aileen Kraditor is favorably disposed toward Garrison in *Means and Ends in*

American Abolitionism: Garrison and His Critics (1967). For a different perspective, see Shirley J. Yee, *Black Women Abolitionists: A Study in Activism, 1828–1860* (1992). Sojourner Truth is the subject of Nell Irvin Painter, *Sojourner Truth: A Life, A Symbol* (1996). The most prominent black abolitionist is portrayed in Waldo E. Martin, Jr., *The Mind of Frederick Douglass* (1984), and William S. McFeely, *Frederick Douglass* (1990).

CHAPTER 17

PRIMARY SOURCE DOCUMENTS

The colorful reminiscences of the pioneers are collected in Dale Morgan, ed., *Overland in 1846: Diaries and Letters of the California-Oregon Trail** (1963). For women's perspectives see Sandra Myres, *Ho for California! Women's Overland Diaries from the Huntington Library* (1980). The outbreak and conduct of the Mexican War come alive in the fascinating *Diary of James K. Polk,** edited by Milo Milton Quaife (1910).

SECONDARY SOURCES

A comprehensive introduction is Ray A. Billington, *Westward Expansion* (5th ed., 1982). On the ideology of expansionism, see Reginald Horsman, *Race and Manifest Destiny: The Origins of American Racial Anglo-Saxonism* (1981); Patricia Nelson Limerick, *The Legacy of Conquest: The Unbroken Past of the American West* (1987); and the early chapters of Richard D. White, *"It's Your Misfortune and None of My Own": A History of the American West* (1992). On Texas, see Frederick W. Merk, *Slavery and the Annexation of Texas* (1972) and Michael A. Morrison, *Slavery and the American West: The Eclipse of Manifest Destiny* (1997). For the Pacific region, consult Norman A. Graebner's general account, *Empire on the Pacific* (1955), and Theodore J. Karamanski, *Fur Trade and Exploration: Opening the Far Northwest, 1821–1852* (1983). On the conflict with Mexico see K. Jack Bauer, *The Mexican-American War, 1846–1848* (1974), and James McCaffrey, *Army of Manifest Destiny: The American Soldier in the Mexican War* (1992). The other side's perspective is given in Gene M. Brack, *Mexico Views Manifest Destiny, 1821–1846* (1976), and David J. Weber, *The Mexican Frontier, 1821–1846: The American Southwest Under Mexico* (1982). John H. Schroeder analyzes an important aspect of the conflict in *Mr. Polk's War: American Opposition and Dissent, 1846–1848* (1973). Robert W. Johansen uses the war to investigate American culture in *To the Halls of the Montezumas: The Mexican War in the American Imagination* (1985). Unusually colorful social history of the westward movement is provided in John Mack Faragher, *Women and Men on the Overland Trail* (1979), and John D. Unruh, Jr., *The Plains Across: The Overland Emigrants and the Trans-Mississippi West, 1840–1860* (1979). Julie Roy Jeffrey focuses on *Frontier*

Women (1979), as does Glenda Riley, in *The Female Frontier* (1988), and the contributors to Susan Armitage and Elizabeth Jameson, eds., *The Women's West* (1987).

CHAPTER 18

PRIMARY SOURCE DOCUMENTS

The *Congressional Globe* for 1850 contains the dramatic orations of a dying generation of American statesmen on the Compromise of 1850. See the speeches by Webster,* Calhoun,* and Clay (in Richard Hofstadter, ed., *Great Issues in American History,* 1958). The debate on the Kansas-Nebraska Bill can be found in the 1854 volume of the same source, which includes addresses by Stephen A. Douglas* and his Republican opponent, Salmon P. Chase.*

SECONDARY SOURCES

The best account of the events of the 1850s is David M. Potter's masterful *The Impending Crisis, 1848–1861* (1976). A concise summary of the events leading to the war is also available in the opening chapters of James M. McPherson, *Battle Cry of Freedom: The Civil War Era* (1988). Comprehensive treatments may be found in James G. Randall and David Donald, *The Civil War and Reconstruction* (rev. ed., 1969); Kenneth Stampp, ed., *The Imperiled Union: Essays on the Background of the Civil War* (1980); Richard H. Sewell, *A House Divided: Sectionalism and Civil War, 1848–1860* (1988); and William Freehling, *Road to Disunion: Secessionists at Bay, 1776–1854* (1990). On the southern view of events see Kenneth S. Greenberg, *Masters and Statesmen: The Political Culture of American Slavery* (1985), and Eugene Genovese, *The World the Slaveholders Made* (1969). The emergence of the Republican party can be studied in Eric Foner's brilliant discussion of ideology, *Free Soil, Free Labor, Free Men* (1970); William Gienapp, *The Origins of the Republican Party, 1852–1856* (1987); Michael Holt's perceptive *Forging a Majority: The Formation of the Republican Party in Pittsburgh* (1969); Paul Kleppner, *The Third Electoral System, 1853–1892: Parties, Voters and Political Cultures* (1979); and Bruce Levine, *Half Slave and Half Free: The Roots of the Civil War* (1992). Holt has developed his views in *The Political Crisis of the 1850s* (1978). Party politics are treated by Joel Silbey in his unorthodox *Partisan Imperative: The Dynamic of American Politics Before the Civil War* (1985). Richard H. Sewell, *Ballots for Freedom: Antislavery Politics in the United States, 1837–1860* (1976), is a standard work. A biographical approach is taken in Merrill Peterson, *The Great Triumvirate: Webster, Clay, and Calhoun* (1987).

CHAPTER 19

PRIMARY SOURCE DOCUMENTS

Harriet Beecher Stowe, *Uncle Tom's Cabin** (1852), and Hinton R. Helper, *The Impending Crisis of the South** (1857) are vivid and important. The Lincoln-Douglas debates* (1858) frame the issues of the 1850s and remain classics of American oratory.

SECONDARY SOURCES

For comprehensive treatments of events leading up to the Civil War, refer to Chapter 18 for the titles by David M. Potter, James M. McPherson, James G. Randall and David Donald, Kenneth Stampp, and Richard H. Sewell. Richly detailed is Allan Nevins, *The Ordeal of the Union* (2 vols., 1947). David Donald, *Charles Sumner and the Coming of the Civil War* (1960), is an outstanding biography. On the literary attack on slavery see Thomas F. Gossett, *Uncle Tom's Cabin and American Culture* (1985). Lincoln's rise is developed in Don E. Fehrenbacher, *Prelude to Greatness* (1962). On Mary Todd Lincoln, see Jean H. Baker, *Mary Todd Lincoln: A Biography* (1987). On the Buchanan administration see Kenneth M. Stampp, *America in 1857: A Nation on the Brink* (1990). On the Lincoln-Douglas debates see Harry V. Jaffa, *Crisis of the House Divided* (1959). Don E. Fehrenbacher brilliantly and thoroughly dissects *The Dred Scott Case* (1978). The final moments before fighting began are scrutinized in David M. Potter, *Lincoln and His Party in the Secession Crisis* (1942), and in Kenneth M. Stampp, *And the War Came* (1950). Stephen B. Oates paints a vivid portrait of John Brown in *To Purge This Land with Blood* (1970), as Joan Hedrick does of Harriet Beecher Stowe in *Harriet Beecher Stowe: A Life* (1994). For a broader view, see Paul Finkelman, *And His Soul Goes Marching On: Responses to John Brown and the Harpers Ferry Raid* (1995). Thomas J. Pressley reviews the copious literature about the war in *Americans Interpret Their Civil War* (1954). George Forgie offers a psychoanalytic explanation of the coming of the war in *Patricide in the House Divided: A Psychological Interpretation of Lincoln and His Age* (1979).

CHAPTER 20

PRIMARY SOURCE READINGS

The Constitution of the Confederacy (1861) makes an interesting contrast to the U.S. Constitution. Three diaries that describe life behind the Confederate lines are those of John B. Jones, published as Earl S. Miers, ed., *A Rebel War Clerk's Diary** (1958); Paul B. Barringer, *The Natural Bent** (1949); and C. Vann Woodward, ed., *Mary Chesnut's Civil War* (1981). Lincoln's Gettysburg Address* (1863) poetically proclaims the president's highest war aims, as does his Second Inaugural Address* (1865).

SECONDARY SOURCES

The best one-volume biography is Stephen B. Oates, *With Malice Toward None: The Life of Abraham Lincoln* (1977). An

excellent collection is Don E. Fehrenbacher, *Lincoln in Text and Context: Collected Essays* (1987). See also Garry Wills, *Lincoln at Gettysburg: The Words That Remade America* (1992), and David H. Donald, *Lincoln* (1995). Gerald F. Linderman examines the motivations of soldiers in *Embattled Courage: The Experience of Combat in the Civil War* (1987). Mary E. Massey presents the interesting story of women in the Civil War in *Bonnet Brigades* (1966); that topic also figures in Anne Firor Scott, *The Southern Lady* (1970). See also the essays in Catherine Clinton and Nina Silber, eds., *Divided Houses: Gender and the Civil War* (1992), and Drew Gilpin Faust, *Mothers of Invention: Women of the Slaveholding South in the American Civil War* (1996). On the Confederacy see Emory M. Thomas, *The Confederate Nation, 1861–1865* (1979), and Drew Gilpin Faust, *The Creation of Confederate Nationalism* (1988). Two useful anthologies are David Donald, ed., *Why the North Won the Civil War* (1960), and Robert P. Swierenga, ed., *Beyond the Civil War Synthesis: Political Essays on the Civil War Era* (1975). Richard E. Beringer et al. present a different viewpoint in *Why the South Lost the Civil War* (1986). The war's literary legacy is keenly analyzed in Edmund Wilson's classic *Patriotic Gore* (1962) and in Daniel Aaron's *The Unwritten War: American Writers and the Civil War* (1973). On the religious impact of the war, see Randall M. Miller et al., *Religion and the American Civil War* (1998). For a fascinating discussion of northern intellectuals and the conflict, consult George M. Fredrickson, *The Inner Civil War* (1965).

CHAPTER 21

PRIMARY SOURCE DOCUMENTS

Abraham Lincoln's reply in 1862 to Horace Greeley's "Prayer of Twenty Millions"* (*Collected Works of Abraham Lincoln*, edited by Roy P. Basler, 1953) is an early statement of the president's war aims. See also, in the same collection, the Emancipation Proclamation (1863). Reminiscences of the military struggle include Eliza Andrews, *The War-Time Journal of a Georgia Girl** (1908); *Memoirs of General William T. Sherman** (1887); and C. Vann Woodward, ed., *Mary Chesnut's Civil War* (rev. ed., 1981). See also Stephen Crane's classic war novel, *The Red Badge of Courage* (1895).

SECONDARY SOURCES

The most compelling single-volume account of the war is James M. McPherson, *Battle Cry of Freedom: The Civil War Era* (1988). Geoffrey C. Ward's *The Civil War* (1990) is beautifully illustrated. An able survey is James G. Randall and David Donald, *The Civil War and Reconstruction* (rev. ed., 1969). Other capable one-volume studies include Peter J. Parish, *The American Civil War* (1975); James M. McPherson, *Ordeal by Fire: The Civil War and Reconstruction* (1982); and Phillip S. Paludan, *"A People's Contest": The Union and the Civil War, 1861–1865* (1988). See also the multivolume study by Shelby Foote, *The Civil War* (3 vols., 1958–1974), and Allan Nevins's monumental *Ordeal of the Union* (8 vols., 1947–1971). Bruce Catton has a series of a dozen or so books on aspects of the Civil War, all readable and knowledgeable, including *A Stillness at Appomattox* (1953) and *This Hallowed Ground* (1956). Herman Hattaway and Archer Jones discuss *How the North Won* (1983). On the home front see Reid Mitchell, *The Vacant Chair: The Northern Soldier Leaves Home* (1993); William Blair, *Virginia's Private War: Feeding Body and Soul in the Confederacy, 1861–1895* (1998); and David Williams, *Rich Man's War: Class, Caste, and Confederate Defeat in the Lower Chattahoochee Valley* (1998). On the "modern" character of the war see Charles B. Royster, *The Destructive War: William Tecumseh Sherman, Stonewall Jackson, and the Americans* (1991). David P. Crook, *The North, the South, and the Powers* (1974), discusses the relationship of the combatants to England. Bell I. Wiley's descriptions of common soldiers, *The Life of Johnny Reb* (1943) and *The Life of Billy Yank* (1952), are classics.

Accounts of the black experience include Benjamin Quarles, *The Negro in the Civil War* (1953); Ira Berlin et al., *Freedom: A Documentary History of Emancipation, 1861–1867, Series II, The Black Military Experience* (1982); and Joseph Glatthaar, *Forged in Battle: The Civil War Alliance of Black Soldiers and White Officers* (1990). Emancipation is treated in Leon Litwack's powerful *Been in the Storm So Long* (1979). On the abolitionists' role in securing emancipation see James M. McPherson, *The Struggle for Equality* (1964); see also David W. Blight, *Frederick Douglass' Civil War: Keeping Faith in Jubilee* (1989). The Southern response is discussed in Robert Durden, *The Gray and the Black: The Confederate Debate on Emancipation* (1973). The two leading Civil War generals are masterfully treated in Douglas S. Freeman, *R. E. Lee* (4 vols., 1934–1935), and William S. McFeely, *Grant* (1981).

CHAPTER 22

PRIMARY SOURCE DOCUMENTS

Booker T. Washington's classic autobiography *Up from Slavery** (1901) records one freedman's experiences. Contemporary comments on Reconstruction include the laments of editor Edwin L. Godkin, *The Nation** (December 7, 1871, 364), and Frederick Douglass, *Life and Times of Frederick Douglass** (1882), as well as the debates in the *Congressional Globe** (1867–1868) between radicals such as Thaddeus Stevens and moderates like Lyman Trumbull.

SECONDARY SOURCES

Eric Foner, *Reconstruction: America's Unfinished Revolution, 1863–1877* (1988), is a superb synthesis of current scholarship. Overall accounts may be found in James G. Randall and David Donald, *The Civil War and Reconstruction* (rev.

ed., 1969), and James McPherson, *Ordeal by Fire: The Civil War and Reconstruction* (1981), perhaps the best brief introduction. Conditions in the South are analyzed in W. E. B. Du Bois's controversial classic *Black Reconstruction* (1935) and in Leon F. Litwack's brilliantly evocative *Been in the Storm So Long* (1979), a revealing study of the initial responses, by both blacks and whites, to emancipation. An excellent account of the southern economy after the war is Gavin Wright, *Old South, New South: Revolutions in the Southern Economy Since the Civil War* (1986). See also James Roark, *Masters Without Slaves: Southern Planters in the Civil War and Reconstruction* (1977). Barbara Fields looks at the Border State of Maryland in *Slavery and Freedom on the Middle Ground* (1985). William McFeely offers an excellent biography of *Frederick Douglass* (1991). On the political economy of the postbellum South see Dewey W. Grantham, *Life and Death of the Solid South* (1988), and Edward L. Ayers, *The Promise of a New South: Life After Reconstruction* (1992). Joel Williamson offers a psychological portrait of race relations in *The Crucible of Race: Black-White Relations in the American South Since Emancipation* (1984). Consult also Thomas Holt, *Black over White: Negro Political Leadership in South Carolina During Reconstruction* (1977), and Martha Hodes, *White Women, Black Men: Illicit Sex in the Nineteenth-Century South* (1997). C. Vann Woodward, *The Strange Career of Jim Crow* (rev. ed., 1974), is a classic study of the origins of segregation. His views have drawn criticism in Harold O. Rabinowitz, *Race Relations in the Urban South, 1865–1890* (1977). See also Rabinowitz's *Southern Black Leaders of the Reconstruction Era* (1982). The Freedmen's Bureau has been the subject of several studies, including Peter Kolchin, *First Freedom* (1972); Claude Oubré, *Forty Acres and a Mule: The Freedmen's Bureau and Black Land Ownership* (1978); and Donald Nieman, *To Set the Law in Motion: The Freedmen's Bureau and the Legal Rights of Blacks, 1865–1868* (1979). Nell Irvin Painter follows African-Americans who chose to leave the South altogether in *Exodusters: Black Migration to Kansas After Reconstruction* (1976). Richard N. Current rehabilitates the maligned carpetbaggers in *Those Terrible Carpetbaggers* (1988). A broad range of Reconstruction scholarship is presented in Kenneth M. Stampp and Leon Litwack, eds., *Reconstruction: An Anthology of Revisionist Writings* (1969), and Robert P. Swierenga, ed., *Beyond the Civil War Synthesis* (1975). J. Morgan Kousser and James M. McPherson, eds., *Region, Race, and Reconstruction: Essays in Honor of C. Vann Woodward* (1982), contains some intriguing essays. Eric Foner looks at emancipation in a comparative perspective in *Nothing but Freedom* (1983).

CHAPTER 23

PRIMARY SOURCE DOCUMENTS

Henry Adams penned some perceptive and sour observations on the era in his autobiographical *Education of Henry*

Adams (1907) and in his novel *Democracy* (1880). See also the classic satire by Mark Twain and Charles Dudley Warner, *The Gilded Age* (1873).

SECONDARY SOURCES

The scandal-rocked Grant era is treated with brevity in James G. Randall and David Donald, *The Civil War and Reconstruction* (rev. ed., 1969), and at greater length in William Gillette, *Retreat from Reconstruction* (1979), and James M. McPherson, *Ordeal by Fire* (1981). Southern politics is detailed in C. Vann Woodward's classic *Origins of the New South* (1951); Otto H. Olsen, *Reconstruction and Redemption in the South* (1980); Terry L. Seip, *The South Returns to Congress* (1983); Michael Perman, *The Road to Redemption* (1984); and J. Morgan Kousser, *The Shaping of Southern Politics* (1974). Brenda Stevenson traces slavery's lingering impact on post–Civil War black life and race relations in *Life in Black and White: Family and Community Life in the Slave South* (1996). The origins of racial segregation are analyzed in C. Vann Woodward, *The Strange Career of Jim Crow* (rev. ed., 1974). On the party systems see Paul Kleppner, *The Third Electoral System, 1835–1892* (1979); Morton Keller, *Affairs of State: Public Life in Nineteenth-Century America* (1977); and Richard Jensen, *The Winning of the Mid-West* (1971). Money questions are treated in Irwin Unger, *The Greenback Era* (1964); Walter T. K. Nugent, *Money and American Society, 1865–1880* (1968); and Allen Weinstein's account of the *"Crime of '73," Prelude to Populism* (1970). C. Vann Woodward sharply analyzes the Compromise of 1877 in *Reunion and Reaction* (rev. ed., 1956). California receives special attention in Alexander Saxton, *The Indispensable Enemy: Labor and the Anti-Chinese Movement in California* (1975). Labor issues are cogently discussed in Paul Krause, *The Battle for Homestead, 1880–1892: Politics, Culture, and Steel* (1992). Charles Hoffman examines *The Depression of the Nineties* (1970), an issue given much attention in David P. Thelen, *The New Citizenship: Origins of Progressivism in Wisconsin, 1885–1900* (1972). Two intriguing cultural histories of the period are Alan Trachtenberg, *The Incorporation of America: Culture and Society in the Gilded Age* (1982), and Lawrence Levine, *Highbrow/Lowbrow: The Emergence of Cultural Hierarchy in America* (1988).

CHAPTER 24

PRIMARY SOURCE DOCUMENTS

Andrew Carnegie, "Wealth,"* *North American Review* (June 1889), gives the philosophy of the Gilded Age's greatest entrepreneur. Henry Grady's Boston speech (1889), in Joel C. Harris, *Life of Henry W. Grady** (1890), dramatizes the plight of the South. Samuel Gompers penned his "Letter on Labor in Industrial Society," an open letter to Judge Peter Grossup, in 1894 (in Richard

Hofstadter, *Great Issues in American History*, 1958). William Dean Howells's novel *The Rise of Silas Lapham* (1885) treats the moral impact of the new business culture on one New England businessman and his family.

SECONDARY SOURCES

A useful survey is Samuel P. Hays's penetrating study, *The Response to Industrialism, 1885–1914* (1957). Stuart Bruchey puts the period in context in *The Growth of the Modern Economy* (1975). Business is the subject of Alfred D. Chandler, Jr., *The Visible Hand: The Managerial Revolution in American Business* (1978); Saul Engelbourg, *Power and Morality: American Business Ethics, 1840–1914* (1980); and Naomi R. Lamoreaux, *The Great Merger Movement in American Business, 1895–1904* (1985). Olivier Zunz surveys the development of corporate culture in *Making America Corporate, 1870–1920* (1990), while Scott M. Cutlip examines *The Unseen Power: Public Relations, a History* (1994). The thought and attitudes characteristic of the new industrial age are examined by Richard Hofstadter, *Social Darwinism in American Thought* (rev. ed., 1955), and Daniel T. Rodgers, *The Work Ethic in Industrial America, 1850–1920* (1978). On the railroads, see George R. Taylor and Irene D. Neu, *The American Railroad Network, 1861–1890* (1956). An important new study is David H. Bain, *Empire Express: Building the First Transcontinental Railroad* (1999). C. Vann Woodward has provided a masterful analysis in *Origins of the New South, 1877–1913* (1951), which can be profitably supplemented by Jonathan M. Wiener, *Social Origins of the New South* (1978); Edward Ayers, *The Promise of the New South: Life After Reconstruction* (1972); and Gaines M. Foster, *Ghosts of the Confederacy: Defeat, the Lost Cause, and the Emergence of the New South, 1865–1913* (1987).

On race relations in the post–Reconstruction South, see Joel Williamson, *The Crucible of Race* (1984); Howard Rabinowitz, *Race Relations in the Urban South, 1865–1890* (1978); and Neil R. McMillen, *Dark Journey: Black Mississippians in the Age of Jim Crow* (1989). Labor is the subject of Gerald Grob, *Workers and Utopia* (1961), and David Montgomery's innovative *Workers' Control in America: Studies in the History of Work, Technology, and Labor Struggles* (1979). Especially stimulating are two volumes by Herbert Gutman, *Work, Culture, and Society in Industrializing America* (1976) and *Power and Culture: Essays on the American Working Class* (1987). On female workers see David Katzman, *Seven Days a Week: Women and Domestic Service in Industrializing America* (1978); Philip Foner, *Women and the American Labor Movement* (1979); and Alice Kessler-Harris, *Out to Work: A History of Wage-Earning Women in the United States* (1982). For a discussion of labor and race, see Gerald David Jaynes, *Branches Without Roots: Genesis of the Black Working Class in the American South, 1862–1882* (1986), and Tera W. Hunter, *To Joy My Freedom: Southern Black Women's Lives and Labors After the Civil War* (1997).

CHAPTER 25

PRIMARY SOURCE DOCUMENTS

Jacob Riis, *How the Other Half Lives** (1890), is a vivid account of life in America's slums. In *A Hazard of New Fortunes* (1890), William Dean Howells penned one of the first "urban novels" in American literature. Victoria Woodhull, *The Scarecrows of Sexual Slavery** (1874), provocatively illustrates some changing ideas about women's roles. Henry James's novel *The Bostonians* (1886) vividly portrays feminists and suffragists.

SECONDARY SOURCES

The Rise of the City, 1878–1898 (1933) is a classic study by Arthur M. Schlesinger. More recent are Gunther Barth, *City People: The Rise of Modern City Culture in Nineteenth-Century America* (1980); Howard Chudacoff, *The Evolution of American Urban Society* (1975); the opening chapters of Kenneth T. Jackson, *Crabgrass Frontier: The Suburbanization of America* (1985); and Eric H. Monkkonen, *America Becomes Urban: The Development of Cities and Towns, 1780–1980* (1988). On new urban spaces and their use by city dwellers see Roy Rosenzweig and Elizabeth Blackmar, *The Park and The People: A History of Central Park* (1992); Kathy Peiss, *Cheap Amusements: Working Women and Leisure in Turn-of-the-Century New York* (1986); and David Nasaw, *Going Out: The Rise and Fall of Public Amusements* (1993). Martin Melosi, *The Sanitary City: Urban Infrastructure in America from Colonial Times to the Present* (2000), and Joel Tarr, *The Search for the Ultimate Sink: Urban Pollution in Historical Perspective* (1996), argue that waste disposal has been a key force in shaping urban politics in American history. Oscar Handlin introduced the study of immigrant communities in American cities with his *Boston's Immigrants* (rev. ed., 1959). More recent studies of the same topic include John Bodnar, *The Transplanted: A History of Immigrants in Urban America* (1985); Jon Gjerde, *From Peasants to Farmers: The Migration from Norway to the Upper Middle West* (1985); Kerby A. Miller, *Emigrants and Exile: Ireland and the Irish Exodus to North America* (1985); Donna Gabaccia, *From the Other Side: Women, Gender, and Immigrant Life in the U.S., 1820–1990* (1994); Thomas Kessner, *The Golden Door: Italian and Jewish Mobility in New York City, 1880–1915* (1977); Ronald Takaki, *Strangers from a Different Shore: A History of Asian-Americans* (1989); and Irving Howe's monumental and moving account of Jewish immigration, *World of Our Fathers* (1976). Black thought for this period is illuminated by three studies: August Meier, *Negro Thought in America, 1880–1915* (1963); Louis R. Harlan, *Booker T. Washington: The Making of a Black Leader, 1865–1901* (1972); and David Levering Lewis, *W. E. B. Du Bois: Biography of a Race, 1868–1919* (1993). For blacks in northern cities before World War I see Allan H. Spear, *Black Chicago: The Making of a Negro Ghetto, 1890–1920* (1967),

and James Borchert, *Alley Life in Washington: Family, Community, Religion, and Folklife in the City* (1980). On religion see Susan Curtis, *A Consuming Faith: The Social Gospel and Modern American Culture* (1991). On women and the family consult Carl Degler, *At Odds: Women and the Family from the Revolution to the Present* (1980); Steven Mintz, *A Prison of Expectations: The Family in Victorian Culture* (1983); Mari Jo Buhle, *Women and American Socialism, 1870–1920* (1981); Margaret W. Rossiter, *Women Scientists in America* (1982); and Rosalind Rosenberg, *Beyond Separate Spheres* (1982) and *Divided Lives* (1992). James Turner probes one aspect of the conflict between science and religion in *Without God, Without Creed: The Origins of Unbelief in America* (1985). Three fascinating studies document the rise of a "new" middle-class mentality: Burton J. Bledstein, *The Culture of Professionalism* (1976); Thomas Haskell, *The Emergence of Professional Social Science* (1977); and Stuart M. Blumin, *The Emergence of the Middle Class: Social Experience in the American City, 1760–1900* (1989).

CHAPTER 26

PRIMARY SOURCE DOCUMENTS

Black Elk Speaks, edited by John G. Neihardt (1932), is an eloquent Indian statement about the Sioux experience. Indian perspectives on the westward movement can be found in Jerome A. Greene, ed., *Lakota and Cheyenne: Indian Views of the Great Sioux Wars, 1876–1877** (1994). Theodore Roosevelt, *Hunting Trips of a Ranchman** (1885), offers the future president's views on the Indian question. Mary Lease's famous call to arms is recorded in William E. Connelley, ed., *History of Kansas, State and People** (1928). William H. Coin Harvey, *Coin's Financial School** (1894), expounded the silverite position. William Jennings Bryan's Cross of Gold speech* won him the Democratic nomination in 1896 and a hallowed place in the annals of American oratory.

SECONDARY SOURCES

Vivacious chapters appear in Ray A. Billington, *Westward Expansion* (rev. ed., 1974). Walter Prescott Webb, *The Great Plains* (1931), is a classic. Robert V. Hine, *The American West* (2nd ed., 1984), is a useful survey. Patricia Nelson Limerick traces regional themes across time in *Legacy of Conquest: The Unbroken Past of the American West* (1987). Richard White's fresh account, *"It's Your Misfortune and None of My Own": A New History of the American West* (1991), emphasizes the role of the federal government, corporations, and the market economy in the region's development and pays special attention to the twentieth century. Women in the West are discussed in Glenda Riley, *The Female Frontier: A Comparative View of Women on the Prairie and Plains* (1988), and Beverly Beeton, *Women Vote in the West: The Woman Suffrage Movement, 1869–1896* (1986). Native Americans are discussed in Robert Utley, *The Indian Frontier of* the American West, 1846–1890 (1984), and in Dee Brown's *Bury My Heart at Wounded Knee: An Indian History of the American West* (1970). Two intriguing studies of cross-cultural perception are Robert F. Berkhofer, Jr., *The White Man's Indian* (1978), and Richard Drinnon, *Facing West: The Metaphysics of Indian Hating and Empire Building* (1980). A sweeping look at Chicano history is Juan Gómez-Quiñones, *Roots of Chicano Politics, 1600–1940* (1994). David Alan Johnson explores *Founding the Far West: California, Oregon, and Nevada, 1840–1890* (1992). William Cronon explores the relationship between Chicago and the development of the "Great West" in *Nature's Metropolis* (1991), a book nicely complemented by John C. Hudson, *Making the Corn Belt* (1994). Donald J. Pisani looks at western agriculture in *From the Family Farm to Agribusiness: The Irrigation Crusade in California and the West, 1850–1931* (1984). A powerful work on the farmers' protest is Lawrence Goodwyn, *Democratic Promise* (1976), abridged as *The Populist Moment* (1978). See also Bruce Palmer, *"Man over Money": The Southern Populist Critique of American Capitalism* (1980). Richard Hofstadter's *The Age of Reform* (1955) sparked a long-running debate among historians about the nature of Populism. A more recent study is Michael Kazin, *The Populist Persuasion: An American History* (1995). Paolo Coletta's biography of *William Jennings Bryan* (3 vols., 1964–1969) is rich in detail. The election of 1896 is examined in Robert F. Durden, *The Climax of Populism: The Election of 1896* (1965), and Stanley L. Jones, *The Presidential Election of 1896* (1964). Also informative are Paul W. Glad, *McKinley, Bryan and the People* (1964), and H. Wayne Morgan, *William McKinley and His America* (1963). Keven Starr probes the cultural history of California in both *Americans and the California Dream, 1850–1915* (1973) and *Inventing the Dream: California Through the Progressive Era* (1985). Henry Nash Smith, *Virgin Land: The American West as Symbol and Myth* (1950), is a landmark study of particular interest to students of literature.

CHAPTER 27

PRIMARY SOURCE DOCUMENTS

Examples of yellow journalism include Joseph Pulitzer's *New York World* and William R. Hearst's *New York Journal.* Particularly interesting is the editorial in the *World* of February 13, 1897,* and the article by Charles Duval in the *Journal* of October 10, 1897.* "McKinley's War Message,"* in James D. Richardson, ed., *Messages and Papers of the Presidents* (1899, vol. X, 139ff.), outlines the American rationale for intervention. The anti-imperialist answer can be found in Charles E. Norton's article in *Public Opinion** (June 23, 1898, 775–776).

SECONDARY SOURCES

Main outlines are sketched in Foster Rhea Dulles, *America's Rise to World Power, 1898–1954* (1955), and in Thomas G.

Paterson, *American Foreign Policy: A Brief History* (3rd ed., 1988). Two general (and quite contrasting) interpretations of modern American foreign policy are George F. Kennan, *American Diplomacy* (1951), and William Appleman Williams, *The Tragedy of American Diplomacy* (1959). Consult also Williams's *The Roots of the Modern American Empire* (1961); Ernest R. May, *Imperial Democracy* (1961); and Walter LaFeber, *The New Empire* (1963) and *Inevitable Revolutions* (1983). On the Spanish-American War, see Frank Freidel, *The Splendid Little War* (1958), and David F. Trask, *The War with Spain in 1898* (1981). Fascinating reading is Hyman G. Rickover, *How the Battleship* Maine *Was Destroyed* (1976). Helpful studies of the opponents of expansion are Robert L. Beisner, *Twelve Against Empire: The Anti-Imperialists, 1898–1900* (1968); E. Berkley Tompkins, *Anti-Imperialism in the United States: The Great Debate, 1890–1920* (1970); and Kendrick A. Clements, *William Jennings Bryan: Missionary Isolationist* (1983). David F. Healey examines *The United States in Cuba, 1898–1902* (1963), and Leon Wolff paints a grim picture of American involvement in the Philippines in *Little Brown Brother* (1961). For more on the Philippine imbroglio see Stuart C. Miller, *"Benevolent Assimilation": The American Conquest of the Philippines, 1899–1903* (1982); Stanley Karnow, *In Our Image: America's Empire in the Philippines* (1989); and H. W. Brands, *Bound to Empire: The United States and the Philippines* (1992).

CHAPTER 28

PRIMARY SOURCE DOCUMENTS

Theodore Roosevelt's corollary* to the Monroe Doctrine, in *A Compilation of Messages and Papers of the Presidents,* vol. 16, found its first expression in 1904. The *Annual Report* of the secretary of commerce and labor for 1908 contains the "Gentlemen's Agreement"* with Japan. For the intrigue surrounding the independence of Panama and the building of the canal, see *Foreign Relations of the United States** (1903) and Theodore Roosevelt to Albert Shaw, October 10, 1903,* in *The Letters of Theodore Roosevelt,* vol. 3, edited by Elting E. Morison (1951).

SECONDARY SOURCES

Howard K. Beale describes *Theodore Roosevelt and the Rise of America to World Power* (1956). See also the work of William Appleman Williams, cited in Chapter 27. Analytical and sympathetic is John M. Blum, *The Republican Roosevelt* (new ed., 1977). An outstanding single-volume biography of TR is William H. Harbaugh, *Power and Responsibility* (rev. ed., 1975). Lewis L. Gould focuses on *The Presidency of Theodore Roosevelt* (1991), while especially good on the youthful Roosevelt is David McCulloch, *Mornings on Horseback* (1981). For the Open Door, consult Jerry Israel, *Progressivism and the Open Door: America and China, 1905–1921* (1971), and Marilyn B. Young, *The Rhetoric of Empire: Amer-*

ica's China Policy, 1895–1901 (1968). On relations with Japan see Charles E. Neu, *An Uncertain Friendship: Theodore Roosevelt and Japan, 1906–1909* (1967) and *The Troubled Encounter: The United States and Japan* (1975). Also valuable are two books by Akira Iriye, *Across the Pacific* (1967) and *Pacific Estrangement: Japanese and American Expansion, 1897–1911* (1972). James Reed discusses *The Missionary Mind and American East Asian Policy, 1911–1915* (1983). Also see William R. Hutchinson, *Errand to the World: American Protestant Thought and Foreign Missions* (1987). On the treatment of the Japanese in the United States see Ronald Takaki, *Strangers from a Different Shore* (1989). The canal issue is analyzed in Walter LaFeber, *The Panama Canal* (1978), and Richard H. Collin, *Theodore Roosevelt's Caribbean: The Panama Canal, the Monroe Doctrine, and the Latin American Context* (1990). On race relations and foreign policy, see Alexander DeConde, *Ethnicity, Race, and American Foreign Policy* (1992). On gender and imperialism, see Gail Bederman, *Manliness and Civilization* (1995), and Kristen Hoganson, *Fighting for American Manhood* (1998).

CHAPTER 29

PRIMARY SOURCE DOCUMENTS

Lincoln Steffens, *The Shame of the Cities** (1904), is an exemplary muckraking document, as is Upton Sinclair's notorious novel *The Jungle* (1906). For a less-than-gracious assessment of the muckrakers see Theodore Roosevelt, "The Man with the Muckrake,"* *Putnam's Monthly* and *The Critic*, vol. I (October 1906, 42–43). A revealing account of municipal politics is George Washington Plunkitt, *Plunkitt of Tammany Hall** (1905). See also the decision of the Supreme Court on state bakery regulations in *Lochner* v. *New York*, 198 U.S. 45 (1905). Oliver Wendell Holmes, Jr.'s thundering dissent in the *Lochner* case is reprinted in Richard Hofstadter, *Great Issues in American History* (1958).

SECONDARY SOURCES

A brief introduction is John W. Chambers, *The Tyranny of Change: America in the Progressive Era, 1900–1917* (1980). Perceptive interpretations are Samuel P. Hays, *The Response to Industrialism, 1885–1914* (1957); Robert H. Wiebe, *The Search for Order* (1967); and Richard Hofstadter, *The Age of Reform* (1955). Especially provocative are James Weinstein, *The Corporate Ideal in the Liberal State* (1968), and Gabriel Kolko, *The Triumph of Conservatism* (1963). Consult also Alfred D. Chandler, Jr., *The Visible Hand* (1977), and Morton Keller, *Regulating a New Economy: Public Policy and Economic Change in America, 1900–1933* (1990). On pure food and drugs see James Harvey Young, *Pure Food: Securing the Federal Food and Drugs Act of 1906* (1989). On progressive social work and social concerns, consult Allen F. Davis, *Spearheads for Reform: The Social Settlements and the Progressive Movement, 1890–1914* (1967); Mina Carson, *Settle-*

ment Folk: Social Thought and the American Settlement Movement, 1885–1930 (1990); James Patterson, *America's Struggle Against Poverty, 1900–1980* (1981); David B. Tyack, *The One Best System: A History of American Urban Education* (1974); and Lynn Gordon, *Gender and Higher Education in the Progressive Era* (1990). On religion see Martin E. Marty, *Modern American Religion: The Irony of It All, 1893–1919* (1986). T. J. Jackson Lears takes a different perspective in *No Place of Grace: Antimodernism and the Transformation of American Culture* (1981). On conservation see Samuel P. Hays, *Conservation and the Gospel of Efficiency* (1959); Elmo Richardson, *The Politics of Conservation* (1962); and James Penick, Jr., *Progressive Politics and Conservation* (1968). Socialism is discussed in Nick Salvatore, *Eugene V. Debs: Citizen and Socialist* (1982); James Weinstein, *The Decline of Socialism in America, 1912–1925* (1967); and Mari Jo Buhle, *Women and American Socialism, 1897–1920* (1981). On women and progressivism, see Robyn Muncy, *Creating a Fresh Dominion in American Reform* (1991); Theda Skocpol, *Protecting Soldiers and Mothers* (1992); Ellen Fitzpatrick, *Endless Crusade: Women Social Scientists and Progressive Reform* (1990); and Rosalind Rosenberg, *Beyond Separate Spheres* (1982). Jacqueline Jones focuses on black women in *Labor of Love, Labor of Sorrow: Black Women, Work, and the Family from Slavery to the Present* (1985). The Taft era is summarized in Paolo Coletta, *The Presidency of William Howard Taft* (1973). Otis Graham traces the progressive legacy in *Encore for Reform: The Old Progressives and the New Deal* (1967).

CHAPTER 30

PRIMARY SOURCE DOCUMENTS

Theodore Roosevelt's "Acceptance Speech"* at the Progressive convention of 1912, and Woodrow Wilson's collection of campaign speeches, *The New Freedom** (1913), give the substance and flavor of the critical 1912 campaign. Louis D. Brandeis, *Other People's Money and How the Bankers Use It** (1914), expresses the philosophy of a key Wilson adviser. On the *Lusitania* incident see *Foreign Relations of the United States*, 1915, Supplement (pp. 394–395, 420).

SECONDARY SOURCES

Kendrick Clements, *The Presidency of Woodrow Wilson* (1992), is an elegant synthesis of the president and his age. John M. Cooper, Jr., *The Warrior and the Priest* (1983), deftly contrasts Wilson and Theodore Roosevelt. Biographies of Wilson include August Heckscher's voluminous *Woodrow Wilson: A Biography* (1991), Arthur Link's five-volume *Wilson* (1947–1965), and John M. Blum's *Woodrow Wilson and the Politics of Morality* (1956). Particularly interesting is Alexander and Juliette George's psychological study, *Woodrow Wilson and Colonel House* (1956). For a sharply contrasting view see Edwin A. Weinstein, *Woodrow Wilson: A*

Medical and Psychological Biography (1981). The road to World War I finds comprehensive treatment in Ernest May, *The World War and American Isolation, 1914–1917* (1959). Consult also Ross Gregory, *The Origins of American Intervention in the First World War* (1971), and Patrick Devlin, *Too Proud to Fight: Woodrow Wilson's Neutrality* (1975). Mira Wilkins traces *The History of Foreign Investment in the United States to 1914* (1989). Superb biographies of prominent intellectuals include David Levy, *Herbert Croly of the New Republic: The Life and Thought of an American Progressive* (1985); Edward A. Stettner, *Shaping Modern Liberalism: Herbert Croly and Progressive Thought* (1993); and Philippa Strum, *Brandeis: Justice for the People* (1984). On Wilson's struggle over freedom of the seas, special studies of value are Thomas A. Bailey and Paul Ryan, *The* Lusitania *Disaster* (1975), and Jeffrey J. Safford, *Wilsonian Maritime Diplomacy* (1978). Social and intellectual currents are described in Henry F. May, *The End of American Innocence: A Study of the First Years of Our Own Time, 1912–1917* (1959). Michael C. Adams, *The Great Adventure: Male Desire and the Coming of World War I* (1990), is a provocative work that tries to link Victorian gender ideology to the martial enthusiasms of the early twentieth century.

CHAPTER 31

PRIMARY SOURCE DOCUMENTS

John J. Pershing, *My Experiences in the World War** (1931), recounts American fighting tactics. Woodrow Wilson's "Fourteen Points Address"* to Congress on January 8, 1918 (*Congressional Record*, 65th Cong., 2 sess., 691), defined the nation's war aims. William E. Borah, "Speech on the League of Nations" (1919), in Richard Hofstadter, *Great Issues in American History* (1958), reveals the isolationist position. Ernest Hemingway's *A Farewell to Arms* (1929) is an outstanding war novel.

SECONDARY SOURCES

The home front is emphasized in David M. Kennedy, *Over Here: The First World War and American Society* (1980). Economic mobilization is covered in Robert Cuff, *The War Industries Board* (1973), and Daniel R. Beaver, *Newton D. Baker and the American Financing of World War I* (1970). Politics is treated in Seward Livermore, *Politics Is Adjourned: Woodrow Wilson and the War Congress, 1916–1918* (1966). The abuse of civil liberties is analyzed in Harry N. Scheiber, *The Wilson Administration and Civil Liberties, 1917–1921* (1960), and Paul L. Murphy, *World War I and the Origin of Civil Liberties in the United States* (1979). Military matters are handled in Edward M. Coffman, *The War to End All Wars: The American Military Experience in World War I* (1968); Arthur E. Barbeau and Florette Henri, *Unknown Soldiers: Black American Troops in World War One* (1974); and John Whiteclay Chambers II, *To Raise an Army: The Draft Comes*

to Modern America (1987). The war experiences of women are captured in Maurine W. Greenwald, *Women, War, and Work* (1980). Works of cultural history include Stanley Cooperman, *World War I and the American Novel* (1966); Stuart Rochester, *American Liberal Disillusionment in the Wake of World War I* (1977); and Paul Fussell, *The Great War and Modern Memory* (1975). On the peace see Arthur S. Link, *Woodrow Wilson: Revolution, War, and Peace* (1979), and two studies by Thomas A. Bailey, *Woodrow Wilson and the Lost Peace* (1944) and *Woodrow Wilson and the Great Betrayal* (1945). Lloyd E. Ambrosius updates the realist critique of Wilson in *Woodrow Wilson and Wilsonian Statecraft* (1991). Consult also N. Gordon Levin, Jr., *Woodrow Wilson and World Politics* (1968); Arno J. Mayer, *Politics and Diplomacy of Peacemaking* (1967); Thomas J. Knock, *To End All Wars: Woodrow Wilson and the Quest for a New World Order* (1992); Robert H. Ferrell, *Woodrow Wilson and World War I, 1917–1921* (1985); and Lloyd C. Gardner, *Safe for Democracy: The Anglo-American Response to Revolution, 1913–1923* (1984). On Wilson's archenemy see William C. Widenor, *Henry Cabot Lodge and the Search for an American Foreign Policy* (1980). The end of this troubled period is sketched in Burl Noggle, *Into the Twenties: The U.S. from Armistice to Normalcy* (1974).

CHAPTER 32

PRIMARY SOURCE DOCUMENTS

For the fallout from the red scare see Walter Lippmann's eloquent plea for the lives of the Italian-American radicals Sacco and Vanzetti in the *New York World** (August 19, 1927). For caustic fictional versions of the decade's social conditions see the novels of Sinclair Lewis, *Main Street* (1920), *Babbitt* (1922), and *Arrowsmith* (1925).

SECONDARY SOURCES

The best introduction to the 1920s is William Leuchtenburg, *The Perils of Prosperity, 1914–1932* (1958). Also strong is Michael E. Parrish, *Anxious Decades: America in Prosperity and Depression, 1920–1941* (1992). Frederick Lewis Allen, *Only Yesterday* (1931), is an evocative recollection of the texture of life in the decade. Equally informative are Robert S. Lynd and Helen M. Lynd's classic sociological studies, *Middletown* (1929) and *Middletown in Transition* (1937). Robert K. Murray, *Red Scare* (1955), is authoritative. Immigration restriction is dealt with in John Higham, *Strangers in the Land* (1955). The standard work on the revived Klan is David M. Chalmers, *Hooded Americanism* (rev. ed., 1981). Also valuable is Kenneth T. Jackson, *The Ku Klux Klan in the City, 1915–1930* (1967), and Nancy MacLean, *Behind the Mask of Chivalry: The Making of the Second KKK* (1993), and Kathleen Blee, *Women of the Klan: Racism and Gender in the 1920s* (1991). The changing experiences of women are discussed in Winnifred Wandersee, *Women's Work and Family*

Values, 1920–1940 (1981); Lois Scharf and Joan M. Jensen, eds., *Decades of Discontent: The Women's Movement, 1920–1940* (1983); Nancy F. Cott, *The Grounding of Modern Feminism* (1987); and Phyllis Palmer, *Domesticity and Dirt: Housewives and Domestic Servants in the United States, 1920–1945* (1990). On the Scopes trial see George Marsden, *Fundamentalism and American Culture* (1980); Lawrence Levine's sensitive study of William Jennings Bryan, *Defender of the Faith* (1965); and Edward J. Larsen, *Summer for the Gods: The Scopes Trial and America's Continuing Debate over Science and Religion* (1997). On the culture of the 1920s, see Stanley Coben, *Rebellion Against Victorianism: The Impetus for Cultural Change in 1920s America* (1991), and Lynn Dumenil, *The Modern Temper: American Culture and Society in the 1920s* (1995). The "youth culture" is the subject of Paula Fass, *The Damned and the Beautiful: American Youth in the 1920s* (1977). Changing sexual attitudes are analyzed in David M. Kennedy, *Birth Control in America: The Career of Margaret Sanger* (1970), and Linda Gordon, *Woman's Body, Woman's Right: A Social History of Birth Control in America* (1976). See also Ellen Chesler, *Woman of Valor: Margaret Sanger and the Birth Control Movement in America* (1992). Gilbert Osofsky describes the background of the Harlem Renaissance in *Harlem: The Making of a Ghetto, 1890–1930* (1966). See also David Lewis, *When Harlem Was in Vogue* (1981). William M. Tuttle, *Race Riot: Chicago in the Red Summer of 1919* (1970), describes the violent side of race relations in the 1920s. The "Great Migration" of blacks to the North is described in James R. Grossman's *Land of Hope: Chicago, Black Southerners, and the Great Migration* (1989). Judith Stein, *The World of Marcus Garvey* (1986), discusses the most popular black leader of the period. Richard W. Fox and T. J. Jackson Lears have edited a fascinating collection of essays on American culture, *The Culture of Consumption: Critical Essays in American History, 1880–1980* (1983). Also see William Leach, *Land of Desire: Merchants, Power and the Rise of a New American Culture* (1993), and Warren I. Susman, *Culture as History: The Transformation of American Society in the Twentieth Century* (1984). David M. Kennedy, *Over Here: The First World War and American Society* (1980), pays special attention to the literature that emerged from the war experience.

CHAPTER 33

PRIMARY SOURCE DOCUMENTS

Herbert Hoover, *American Individualism* (1922), contains the philosophy of the man and his times. See also Hoover's "Rugged Individualism" speech (1928), in Richard Hofstadter, *Great Issues in American History* (1958). As the Great Depression descended, Hoover fought to maintain his principles in a noteworthy speech at New York's Madison Square Garden.* (*New York Times*, November 1, 1932). On foreign affairs see the "Stimson Doctrine" (1931), in Henry Steele Commager, ed., *Documents of American History* (1988).

SECONDARY SOURCES

A lively introduction to the postwar decade is Burl Noggle, *Into the Twenties: The United States from Armistice to Normalcy* (1974). On Harding see Robert K. Murray's balanced *The Harding Era* (1969) and his *Politics of Normalcy: Government Theory and Practice in the Harding-Coolidge Era* (1973). John D. Hicks presents the standard liberal interpretation of the decade in *Republican Ascendancy* (1960). Burl Noggle looks at the chief scandal of the period in *Teapot Dome* (1962). David M. Kennedy, *Over Here: The First World War and American Society* (1980), discusses postwar race relations and demobilization as well as the international economic aftermath of the war, a subject treated at greater length in Joan Hoff Wilson, *American Business and Foreign Policy, 1920–1933* (1971). Robert Cohen explores *When the Old Left Was Young: Student Radicals and America's First Mass Student Movement, 1929–1941* (1993). The complicated international financial tangle of the 1920s is deftly discussed in Herbert Feis, *The Diplomacy of the Dollar* (1950), and in the early chapters of Charles Kindleberger, *The World in Depression* (1973). The drama of the 1928 election is captured in Allan J. Lichtman, *Prejudice and the Old Politics: The Presidential Election of 1928* (1979), and in Oscar Handlin, *Al Smith and His America* (1958). The election is placed in a larger context in Samuel Lubell's classic *The Future of American Politics* (1952) and in Paul Kleppner's *Who Voted? The Dynamics of Electoral Turnout, 1870–1980* (1982). George H. Nash's multivolume biography, *The Life of Herbert Hoover* (1988), is detailed, while the best brief biography of Hoover is Joan Hoff Wilson, *Herbert Hoover, Forgotten Progressive* (1975). Brilliantly unsympathetic toward Hoover is Arthur M. Schlesinger, Jr., *The Crisis of the Old Order, 1919–1933* (1957). On the depression itself, consult John K. Galbraith's breezy *The Great Crash, 1929* (1955); Peter Temin's trenchant *Did Monetary Factors Cause the Great Depression?* (1976); Robert McElvaine, *The Great Depression* (1984); and Lester V. Chandler's comprehensive *America's Greatest Depression* (1970).

CHAPTER 34

PRIMARY SOURCE DOCUMENTS

James Agee and Walker Evans, in *Let Us Now Praise Famous Men* (1940), brilliantly evoke the misery of the depression in words and photographs. Franklin D. Roosevelt's dramatic "First Inaugural Address" (1933), in Henry Steele Commager, ed., *Documents of American History* (1988), captured the imagination of the distressed nation. Less successful was Roosevelt's "Radio Address on Supreme Court Reform" (1937), in Richard Hofstadter, *Great Issues in American History* (1982). See also Dorothy Thompson's attack on the Court plan* in the *Washington Star* (February 10, 1937). Clifford Odets' play *Waiting for Lefty* (1935) and John Steinbeck's novel *The Grapes of Wrath* (1939) exemplify the literature stimulated by the Great Depression. Robert S. McElvaine has collected a compelling set of letters in *Down and Out in the Great Depression* (1983).

SECONDARY SOURCES

A masterly summation is William E. Leuchtenburg, *Franklin D. Roosevelt and the New Deal, 1932–1940* (1963). See also Leuchtenberg's *The Supreme Court Reborn: The Constitutional Revolution in the Age of Roosevelt* (1995). Briefer and more critical of the limitations of reform is Paul Conkin, *The New Deal* (rev. ed., 1975). A detailed biography is Frank Freidel, *Franklin D. Roosevelt* (4 vols., 1952–1973). Brilliantly pro-FDR are the three volumes of Arthur M. Schlesinger, Jr., *Age of Roosevelt: The Crisis of the Old Order* (1957), *The Coming of the New Deal* (1959), and *The Politics of Upheaval* (1960). A concise biography is Frank Freidel, *Franklin D. Roosevelt: Rendezvous with Destiny* (1990). The social impact of the depression is vividly etched in Studs Terkel, *Hard Times* (1970); Ann Banks, *First Person America* (1980); and James N. Gregory, *American Exodus: The Dust Bowl Migration and Okie Culture in California* (1989). For a comprehensive portrait of New Deal America, see David M. Kennedy, *Freedom From Fear: The American People in Depression and War* (1999). Of special interest are Lois Scharf, *To Work and to Wed: Female Employment, Feminism, and the Great Depression* (1980), and *Eleanor Roosevelt: First Lady of American Liberalism* (1987). Also see Susan Ware, *Beyond Suffrage: Women in the New Deal* (1981), and Blanche Wiesen Cook, *Eleanor Roosevelt: A Life* (1992). Alan Brinkley brilliantly chronicles *Voices of Protest: Huey Long, Father Coughlin, and the Great Depression* (1982). See also his treatment of the later New Deal in *The End of Reform* (1995). Ellis Hawley, *The New Deal and the Problem of Monopoly* (1966), is a superb analysis of the conflicting currents of economic policy in the Roosevelt administration. A comprehensive assessment by several noted scholars is Harvard Sitkoff, ed., *Fifty Years Later: The New Deal Evaluated* (1985). Especially good on intellectual history are Richard H. Pells, *Radical Visions and American Dreams: Culture and Social Thought in the Depression Years* (1973), and Daniel Aaron, *Writers on the Left* (1961). A trenchant appraisal of the New Deal legacy is Steven Fraser and Gary Gerstle, eds., *The Rise and Fall of the New Deal Order* (1989).

CHAPTER 35

PRIMARY SOURCE DOCUMENTS

For background on the date that will live in infamy see *Pearl Harbor Attack: Hearings Before the Joint Committee on the Investigation of the Pearl Harbor Attack** (79 Cong., 1 sess. [1946]). Franklin D. Roosevelt's "Quarantine the Aggressors" speech (1937), in Richard Hofstadter, *Great Issues in American History* (1958), revealed what would become the goal of the president's foreign policy in succeeding years. See also

Roosevelt's "Press Conference on Lend-Lease" (1940), in *The Public Papers and Addresses of Franklin D. Roosevelt, 1940 Volume* (1941, 606–608).* For opposition to lend-lease see the speech of January 12, 1941,* by Montana senator Burton K. Wheeler (*Congressional Record*, 77 Cong., 1 sess., Appendix, 178–179). Charles A. Lindbergh elaborated the isolationist position in the *New York Times** (April 24, 1941, 12). Warren F. Kimball, ed., *Churchill and Roosevelt: The Complete Correspondence* (1984), is enlightening on many topics.

SECONDARY SOURCES

Indispensable and comprehensive is Robert Dallek, *Franklin D. Roosevelt and American Foreign Policy, 1932–1945* (rev. ed., 1995). Also strong is Kenneth S. Davis, *FDR: Into the Storm, 1937–1940, A History* (1993). A useful brief survey is John E. Wiltz, *From Isolation to War, 1931–1941* (1968). More specialized is Lloyd Gardner, *Economic Aspects of New Deal Diplomacy* (1964). Isolationism is ably handled in Manfred Jonas, *Isolationism in America, 1935–1941* (1966); Thomas Guinsburg, *The Pursuit of Isolationism in the United States Senate from Versailles to Pearl Harbor* (1982); and Robert A. Divine, *The Reluctant Belligerent* (1965). Sympathetic to the isolationists is Wayne S. Cole in *Roosevelt and the Isolationists, 1932–1945* (1983) and *Charles A. Lindbergh and the Battle Against American Intervention in World War II* (1974). On the Spanish Civil War see Douglas Little, *Malevolent Neutrality: The United States, Great Britain, and the Origins of the Spanish Civil War* (1985). On East Asia consult Dorothy Borg, *The United States and the Far Eastern Crisis of 1933–1938* (1964); P. W. Schroeder, *The Axis Alliance and Japanese-American Relations, 1941* (1958); Akira Iriye, *The Globalizing of America, 1913–1945* (1993); and Akira Iriye and Warren Cohen, eds., *American, Chinese, and Japanese Perspectives on Wartime Asia, 1931–49* (1990). Warren F. Kimball analyzes *The Most Unsordid Act: Lend Lease, 1939–1941* (1969). David L. Porter examines *The Seventy-Sixth Congress and World War II, 1939–1940* (1979). The Japanese attack on Pearl Harbor is considered in Gordon W. Prange, *At Dawn We Slept* (1981), and Michael Slackman, *Target: Pearl Harbor* (1990). A provocative analysis of the reasons (or lack of them) for U.S. entry into the conflict is Bruce Russett, *No Clear and Present Danger* (1972). See also Donald Cameron Watt, *How War Came: The Immediate Origins of the Second World War, 1938–1939* (1989).

CHAPTER 36

PRIMARY SOURCE DOCUMENTS

Vivid portraits of the fighting are found in Ernie Pyle, *Here Is Your War* (1943) and *Brave Men* (1944). On the atomic bomb consult the reactions of the *Nippon Times** (August 10, 1945), *The Christian Century** (August 29, 1945), and President Truman's justification of the bombing in *Memoirs of Harry S Truman** (1955).

SECONDARY SOURCES

See John M. Blum, *V Was for Victory: Politics and American Culture During World War II* (1976), and John W. Jeffries, *Wartime America: The World War II Homefront* (1996) for discussion of the home front. Consult also Doris Kearns Goodwin, *No Ordinary Time* (1994); William L. O'Neill, *A Democracy at War: America's Fight at Home and Abroad in World War II* (1993); Richard Polenberg, *War and Society: The United States, 1941–1945* (1972); and Harold G. Vatter, *The U.S. Economy in World War II* (1985). Studs Terkel compiled an interesting oral history of the war experience in *The Good War* (1984). On women see Susan M. Hartmann, *The Home Front and Beyond* (1982). On blacks see Neil A. Wynn, *The Afro-Americans and the Second World War* (1976), and Nicholas Lemann, *The Promised Land: The Great Black Migration and How It Changed America* (1991). The military history of the war is capably summarized in H. P. Willmott, *The Great Crusade: A New Complete History of the Second World War* (1990), and in Gerhard Weinberg's massively detailed *A World at Arms* (1994). A good introduction to wartime diplomacy is Gaddis Smith, *American Diplomacy During the Second World War* (1965). More detailed are Herbert Feis's three volumes: *Churchill, Roosevelt, Stalin* (2nd ed., 1967), *Between War and Peace: The Potsdam Conference* (1960), and *The Atomic Bomb and the End of World War II* (1966). See also John L. Gaddis, *The United States and the Origins of the Cold War, 1941–1947* (1972), and two revisionist studies that are highly critical of American policy: Gabriel Kolko, *The Politics of War: The World and United States Foreign Policy, 1943–1945* (1968), and Lloyd Gardner, *Architects of Illusion: Men and Ideas in American Foreign Policy, 1941–1949* (1970). The war in Asia is covered in Ronald H. Spector's gracefully written *Eagle Against the Sun: The American War with Japan* (1985). John W. Dower explores the racial ideas that underlay the war against Japan in *War Without Mercy: Race and Power in the Pacific War* (1986), and the war's aftermath in his award-winning *Embracing Defeat: Japan in the Wake of World War II* (1999). Paul Fussell contrasts actual combat and wartime rhetoric in *Wartime: Understanding and Behavior in the Second World War* (1989). On the atomic bomb the most comprehensive account is Richard Rhodes, *The Making of the Atomic Bomb* (1986). Also see Richard G. Hewlett and Oscar E. Anderson, Jr., *The New World* (1962); Martin J. Sherwin, *A World Destroyed: The Atomic Bomb and the Grand Alliance* (1975); and Gar Alperovitz's critiques of American nuclear strategy, *Atomic Diplomacy* (rev. ed., 1985), and *The Decision to Drop the Atomic Bomb* (1995). Paul Boyer, *By the Bomb's Early Light* (1985), analyzes the bomb's impact on the American mind.

CHAPTER 37

PRIMARY SOURCE DOCUMENTS

George F. Kennan's "long telegram,"* *Foreign Relations of the United States, 1946* (vol. 6, 1969, 696–709), outlined the containment doctrine that would form the foundation of U.S. foreign policy in the Cold War era. Harry S Truman first applied the containment doctrine when he enunciated the Truman Doctrine* (*Congressional Record,* 80 Cong., 1 sess., 1981 [1947]). On the changing postwar family consult Dr. Benjamin Spock, *Baby and Child Care** (1957).

SECONDARY SOURCES

Lucid overviews of the postwar years can be found in James Patterson, *Grand Expectations* (1996); William H. Chafe, *The Unfinished Journey: America Since World War II* (1986); John Patrick Diggins, *The Proud Decades: America in War and Peace, 1941–1960* (1988); and William O'Neill, *American High: The Years of Confidence, 1945–1960* (1986). Harold G. Vatter gives a valuable account of *The United States Economy in the 1950s* (1963). Suburbia is the subject of Kenneth T. Jackson's sweeping synthesis, *Crabgrass Frontier* (1986). On the baby boom and its implications consult Landon Y. Jones, *Great Expectations: America and the Baby Boom Generation* (1980), and Michael X. Delli Carpini, *Stability and Change in American Politics: The Coming of Age of the Generation of the 1960s* (1986). Mark Silk chronicles the role of organized religion in America since the 1940s in *Spiritual Politics: Religion and America Since World War II* (1988). On the Cold War consult John L. Gaddis, *Strategies of Containment* (1982). For an ambitious revisionist synthesis see Thomas J. McCormick, *America's Half-Century: U.S. Foreign Policy in the Cold War* (1989). Useful surveys of the diplomatic history of the period, all of them in varying degrees critical of American policy, are Stephen Ambrose, *Rise to Globalism: American Foreign Policy Since 1938* (rev. ed., 1983); Walter LaFeber, *America, Russia and the Cold War, 1945–1984* (8th ed., 1997); and Daniel Yergin, *Shattered Peace* (1977). Among the most comprehensive postrevisionist studies is Melvyn P. Leffler, *A Preponderance of Power: National Security, the Truman Administration, and the Cold War* (1992). On the first years of nuclear diplomacy, see Gregg Herken, *The Winning Weapon: The Atomic Bomb in the Cold War, 1945–1950* (1980). Korea is discussed in Callum A. MacDonald, *Korea: The War Before Vietnam* (1986); Bruce Cumings, ed., *Child of Conflict: The Korean-American Relationship, 1943–1953* (1983); and Bruce Cumings and Jon Halliday, *Korea: The Unknown War* (1988). On the red scare at home see Richard Fried, *Nightmare in Red* (1990); Ellen Schrecker, *Many Are the Crimes* (1998); as well as David M. Oshinsky, *A Conspiracy So Immense: The World of Joe McCarthy* (1983). Daniel Bell, ed., *The Radical Right* (1963), places McCarthyism in a larger context. Examinations of the impact of the Cold War on American culture include Nora Sayre, *Running Time: The Films of the Cold War* (1982); Nancy Schwartz, *The Hollywood Writers' Wars* (1982); Ellen Schrecker, *No Ivory Tower: McCarthyism and the Universities* (1986); and Richard H. Pells, *The Liberal Mind in a Conservative Age* (1985).

CHAPTER 38

PRIMARY SOURCE DOCUMENTS

Earl Warren's decision in *Brown v. Board of Education of Topeka,* * 347 U.S. 492–495 (1954), altered the course of race relations in the United States. It also sparked the opposition of one hundred southern congressmen* (*Congressional Record,* 84 Cong., 2 sess., 4515–4516, [1956]). Eisenhower's Farewell Address* (1961) warned of the dangers of the "military-industrial complex." John Kenneth Galbraith criticized the consumer culture in *The Affluent Society* * (1958). Joe McCarthy's vitriol can be found in his *McCarthyism: The Fight for America* * (1952).

SECONDARY SOURCES

The era is surveyed readably in several works, including those titles by James Patterson, William H. Chafe, John Patrick Diggins, and William O'Neill, cited in Chapter 37. Eisenhower is the subject of Stephen Ambrose's two-volume biography, *Eisenhower: Soldier, General of the Army, President-Elect, 1890–1952* (1983) and *Eisenhower: The President* (1984). See also Jeff Broadwater, *Eisenhower and the Anti-Communist Crusade* (1992), and Chester Pach and Elmo Richardson, *The Presidency of Dwight D. Eisenhower* (1991). Various aspects of foreign policy are covered in Douglas Brinkley, *Dean Acheson: The Cold War Years* (1992). For background and consequences of the Supreme Court's 1954 desegregation decision see Richard Kluger, *Simple Justice: The History of Brown v. Board of Education* (1976); Raymond Wolters, *The Burden of Brown: Thirty Years of School Desegregation* (1984); and Robert A. Margo, *Race and Schooling in the South, 1880–1950* (1990). Especially rich are Taylor Branch, *Parting the Waters: America in the King Years, 1954–1963* (1988), and David J. Garrow, *Bearing the Cross: Martin Luther King, Jr., and the Southern Christian Leadership Conference* (1986). The South before the civil rights movement is ably described in John Egerton, *Speak Now Against the Day: The Generation Before the Civil Rights Movement in the South* (1994), and Leon F. Litwack, *Trouble in Mind: Black Southerners in the Age of Jim Crow* (1998). For one man's experience of integration, see Jules Tygiel, *Baseball's Great Experiment: Jackie Robinson and His Legacy* (1983). Three excellent studies of race in northern cities are Thomas Sugrue, *Origins of the Urban Crisis* (1996); Arnold Hirsch, *Making the Second Ghetto: Race and Housing in Chicago, 1940–1960* (1983); and John T. McGreevy, *Parish Boundaries: The Catholic Encounter with Race in the Twentieth Century Urban North* (1996). On the election of 1960 see Theodore H. White's colorful *The Making of the President, 1960* (1961). For more on cultural developments during the 1950s see Lary May, ed., *Recasting America: Culture and Politics in the Age of the Cold War* (1989); Elaine May, *Homeward Bound: American Families in the Cold War Era* (1988);

Stephanie Coontz, *The Way We Never Were* (1992); Tino Balio, ed., *Hollywood in the Age of Television* (1990); David Halberstam, *The Fifties* (1993); Stephen J. Whitfield, *The Culture of the Cold War* (1991); Tom Engelhardt, *The End of Victory Culture* (1995); and Eugenia Kaledin, *Mothers and More: American Women in the 1950s* (1984). On television, see David Marc, *Demographic Vistas: Television in American Culture* (1984), and Lynn Spigel, *Make Room for TV: Television and the Family Ideal in Postwar America* (1992).

CHAPTER 39

PRIMARY SOURCE DOCUMENTS

Norman Mailer paints vivid portraits of the 1968 conventions in *Miami and the Siege of Chicago* (1968) and of the antiwar March on Washington in his *Armies of the Night* (1968). Martin Luther King, Jr.'s *Letter from Birmingham Jail* * (1963) eloquently defends the civil rights movement. The progress of the war in Vietnam is chronicled in *The Pentagon Papers* * (1971). Students for a Democratic Society (1962) and Young Americans for Freedom (1960) both issued manifestos* that suggest the political temper of the era. Stewart Alsop penned a notable editorial in *Newsweek* * in 1970 that reflects "establishment" disgust with the cultural upheavals of the decade.

SECONDARY SOURCES

The tumultuous decade of the 1960s is treated in William L. O'Neill, *Coming Apart: An Informal History of America in the 1960s* (1971); Howard Brink, *Age of Contradiction* (1998); and John Morton Blum, *Years of Discord* (1991). On Kennedy see Theodore C. Sorenson, *Kennedy* (1965), and Arthur M. Schlesinger, Jr., *A Thousand Days* (1965), both appreciative accounts by insiders. More critical is Henry Fairlie, *The Kennedy Promise* (1973). Michael Beschloss details *The Crisis Years: Kennedy and Khrushchev, 1960–1963* (1991). A splendid short biography is Bruce J. Schulman, *Lyndon B. Johnson and American Liberalism* (1994). Eric Goldman, *The Tragedy of Lyndon Johnson* (1969), is a sympathetic yet critical account of the Johnson presidency. In the same vein, with a psychoanalytic touch, is Doris Kearns, *Lyndon B. Johnson and the American Dream* (1976). Johnson's own memoir, *The Vantage Point* (1971), is marred by excessive self-justification. Equally unbalanced antidotes are Robert Caro, *The Years of Lyndon Johnson: The Path to Power* (1982) and *Means of Ascent* (1990). More revealing is *Taking Charge: The Johnson White House Tapes, 1963–1964,* edited by Michael Beschloss. For a complex portrait see Robert Dallek, *Lone Star Rising: Lyndon Johnson and His Times, 1908–1960* (1991). Two superb chronicles of the civil rights movement focusing on Martin Luther King, Jr., are the books by Taylor Branch and David J. Garrow cited in Chapter 38. The racial upheavals of the decade are discussed in

John Dittner, *Local People: The Struggle for Equal Rights in Mississippi* (1994); Harvard Sitkoff, *The Struggle for Black Equality, 1954–1992* (1993); Clayborne Carson, *In Struggle: SNCC* [Student Non-Violent Coordinating Committee] *and the Black Awakening of the 1960s* (1981); and William H. Chafe, *Civilities and Civil Rights: Greensboro, North Carolina, and the Black Struggle for Freedom* (1980). On the New Left consult two volumes by Todd Gitlin, *The Sixties: Years of Hope, Days of Rage* (1987) and *The Whole World Is Watching: Mass Media in the Making and Unmaking of the New Left* (1980); James Miller, *"Democracy Is in the Streets": From Port Huron to the Siege of Chicago* (1987); Sara Evans, *Personal Politics* (1979); and Jerry Anderson, *The Movement of the Sixties* (1995). On conservatism, see Dan Carter, *The Politics of Rage: George Wallace, the Origins of the New Conservatism and the Transformation of American Politics* (1995). On Vietnam consult Ronald Spector, *The United States Army in Vietnam* (1984); W. H. Brands, *Since Vietnam* (1996); and Stanley Karnow's encyclopedic *Vietnam: A History* (1983). Concise accounts are George Herring, *America's Longest War* (1986), and Marilyn B. Young, *The Vietnam Wars, 1945–1990* (1991). Robert S. McNamara, *In Retrospect: The Tragedy and Lessons of Vietnam* (1995), is the sorrowful apology of one of the war's principal architects for the "mistake" of Vietnam. Two works by John Lewis Gaddis shrewdly analyze the Cold War context of the Vietnam conflict: *The Long Peace* (1987) and *The United States and the End of the Cold War* (1992). In *American Genesis: A Century of Invention and Technological Enthusiasm* (1989), Thomas Hughes argues that the sixties marked the end of a century-long national love affair with technology. Also intriguing on the 1960s is Morris Dickstein, *The Gates of Eden: American Culture in the Sixties* (1977). A lucid survey of the intellectual history of the postwar era is Richard Pells, *The Liberal Mind in a Conservative Age* (1984). Changes in attitudes toward sex are scrutinized in Daniel Yankelovich, *The New Morality* (1974); Morton Hunt, *Sexual Behavior in the 1970s* (1974); and Paul Robinson, *The Modernization of Sex* (1976). A useful overview of the decade is Maurice Isserman and Michael Kazin, *America Divided: The Civil War of the 1960s* (2000).

CHAPTER 40

PRIMARY SOURCE DOCUMENTS

Richard Nixon's vision of the international order is delineated in his *RN: The Memoirs of Richard Nixon** (1978). The articles of impeachment* reported against Nixon can be found in House of Representatives Report No. 93-1305 (93 Cong., 2 sess., 1–2 [1974]). Opposing opinions on the Panama Canal treaty were voiced by Cyrus Vance and Ronald Reagan, *Hearings Before the Committee on Foreign Relations*, United States Senate (95 Cong., 1 sess., 10–15, 96–103 [1977]). An influential text of the feminist movement was Robin Morgan's anthology *Sisterhood is Powerful*.

SECONDARY SOURCES

The most comprehensive account of Nixon's early career is Stephen E. Ambrose, *Nixon: The Education of a Politician, 1913–1962* (1987). See also his *Nixon: The Triumph of a Politician, 1962–1972* (1989). Nixon's intriguing personality is examined in Garry Wills, *Nixon Agonistes: The Crisis of the Self-Made Man* (1970). A wide-ranging discussion of the home front is in Kim McQuaid, *The Anxious Years: America in the Vietnam-Watergate Era* (1989). Valuable background on U.S. foreign policy in the Nixon years can be found in David P. Calleo and Benjamin Rowland, *America and the World Political Economy* (1973). A good biography of Nixon's secretary of state is Robert D. Schulzinger, *Henry Kissinger: Doctor of Diplomacy* (1989). The background to the oil crisis is charted in Michael B. Stoff, *Oil, War and American Security* (1980). Arthur M. Schlesinger (1973) charts the growth of *The Imperial Presidency* (1973). The Watergate crisis is vividly described in two books by Carl Bernstein and Robert Woodward, *All the President's Men* (1974) and *The Final Days* (1976), and in Stanley I. Kutler, *The Wars of Watergate* (1990). Jonathan Schell, *The Time of Illusion* (1976), assesses the impact of the crisis on the nation's spirit and institutions. Robert Greene describes the Nixon and Ford administrations in *The Limits of Power* (1992). "Jerry" Ford, the first appointed president, is analyzed by his former press secretary in J. F. ter Horst, *Gerald Ford and the Future of the Presidency* (1974). For a sharply critical view see Clark Mollenhoff, *The Man Who Pardoned Nixon* (1976). On the extremes of the women's movement in the 1970s, see Alice Echols, *Daring to Be Bad: Radical Feminists in America, 1967–1975* (1989), and Susan Hartman, *The Other Feminists: Activists in the Liberal Establishment* (1998). On Jimmy Carter consult Burton Kaufman, *The Presidency of James Earl Carter* (1993), and John Dambrell, *The Carter Presidency* (1993). Sharply critical are Clark R. Mollenhoff, *The President Who Failed: Carter Out of Control* (1980), and Joseph A. Califano, Jr. (whom Carter fired from the cabinet), *Governing America: An Insider's Report from the White House and the Cabinet* (1981). On Central American policy, see Richard Fagen's, *The Nicaraguan Revolution* (1981) and Walter LaFeber's *Inevitable Revolutions: The United States and Central America* (1983). The catastrophe in Iran is described in James Bill, *The Eagle and the Lion: The Tragedy of Americans' Iranian Relations* (1987); Michael Ledeen and William Lewis, *Debacle: The American Failure in Iran* (1981); and Barry M. Rubin, *Paved with Good Intentions: The American Experience and Iran* (1980).

CHAPTER 41

PRIMARY SOURCE DOCUMENTS

The debate over "Reaganomics" can be followed in Reagan's nationally televised address of July 27, 1981* (*Weekly Compi-*

lation of Presidential Documents, vol. 17, no. 31), and in the critical response* of the New York Times (August 2, 1981). See also the comments of Budget Director David Stockman, in William Greider, The Education of David Stockman and Other Americans (1982). On arms control see the pastoral letter of the National Council of Catholic Bishops and the reply of Albert Wohlstetter in Charles Kegley and Eugene Wittkopf, eds., The Nuclear Reader (1985). On Central American policy see Reagan's remarkable speech of March 16, 1986.* The inside workings of the Iran-contra scandal can be studied in The Tower Commission Report (1987). President Bill Clinton's impeachment and trial can be followed in The Impeachment and Trial of President Clinton: The Official Transcripts from the House Judiciary Committee Hearings to the Senate Trial, edited by Merrill McLaughlin (1999).

SECONDARY SOURCES

Garry Wills, Reagan's America: Innocents at Home (1987), and Haynes Johnson, Sleepwalking Through History: America in the Reagan Years (1997), survey the Reagan era. Reagan is portrayed in Laurence Barrett, Gambling with History (1984); Fred Greenstein, The Reagan Presidency (1983); and Michael Schaller, Reckoning with Reagan (1992). Reagan's economic policies are discussed in Paul C. Roberts, The Supply-Side Revolution (1984), and are sharply criticized in David A. Stockman, The Triumph of Politics: Why the Reagan Revolution Failed (1986). The neoconservative movement is best elucidated by the writings of its leaders. See Norman Podhoretz, Breaking Ranks (1979), and Irving Kristol, Reflections of a Neoconservative (1983). For a critical view consult Peter Steinfels, The Neoconservatives (1979). Issues of special concern to the neoconservatives are treated by Charles Murray, Losing Ground (1984), an indictment of federal government social programs. Its conclusions are sharply contested by John E. Schwartz, America's Hidden Success (rev. ed., 1988). Two studies of affirmative action are Allan P. Sindler, Bakke, DeFinis and Minority Admissions (1978), and J. Harvie Wilkinson, From Brown to Bakke (1979). For more on conservatism in the last decades of the twentieth century see William C. Berman, America's Right Turn: From Nixon to Bush (1994). Kevin P. Phillips is also insightful about the implications of the conservative revival in Post-Conservative America (1982). Eugene Genovese explores The Southern Tradition: The Achievement and Limitations of an American Conservatism (1994). Useful books on the role of religion in modern politics include William Martin, With God on Our Side: The Rise of the Religious Right in America (1996); Garry Wills, Under God: Religion and American Politics (1990); Robert Wuthnow, The New Christian Right (1983); and Richard John Neuhaus, The Naked Public Square: Religion and Democracy in America (1984). On the Supreme Court see Richard L. Pacelle, Jr., The Transformation of the Supreme Court's Agenda: From the New Deal to the Reagan Administration (1991). Critical of Reagan are William Leuchtenburg, In the Shadow of FDR: From Harry Truman to

Ronald Reagan (1983); Paul D. Erickson, Reagan Speaks: The Making of an American Myth (1985); Garry Wills, Reagan's America: Innocents at Home (1987); Ronnie Duggar, On Reagan (1983); June Mayer and Doyle McManus, Landslide: The Unmaking of the President, 1984–88 (1988); and Richard Reeves, The Reagan Detour (1985). More balanced are two books by John L. Palmer, The Reagan Record (co-edited with Isabel V. Sawhill, 1984) and Perspectives on the Reagan Years (1986). Important topics in foreign policy are covered in John Ehrman, The Rise of Neoconservatism: Intellectuals and Foreign Affairs, 1945–1994 (1995); Walter LaFeber, Inevitable Revolutions (2nd ed., 1984), which discusses Central America; Robert Pastor's more probing study, Condemned to Repetition: The United States and Nicaragua (1987); and Bob Woodward, Veil: The Secret Wars of the CIA (1987). Theodore Draper details the Iran-contra affair in A Very Thin Line (1991). In The Devil We Knew: Americans and the Cold War (1993), H. W. Brands attempts to calculate how much it cost the United States to win the Cold War. The legacy of the Reagan era is the subject of Kevin P. Philips's devastating The Politics of Rich and Poor: Wealth and the American Electorate in the Reagan Aftermath (1990) and Barbara Ehrenreich's The Worst Years of Our Lives: Irreverent Notes from a Decade of Greed (1990). Bob Woodward, in The Agenda (1994) and The Choice (1996), provides inside glimpses of politics in the Clinton years. For insightful analysis by a historian, see James McGregor Burns and Georgia J. Sorenson, Dead Center: Clinton-Gore Leadership and the Perils of Moderation (1999). On the precedent-shattering First Lady, see David Brock, The Seduction of Hillary Rodham (1996). James B. Stewart, Blood Sport (1996), is especially good on Clinton's complex relationship with the media. On Clinton's impeachment, see Richard Posner, An Affair of State: The Investigation, Impeachment, and Trial of President Clinton (1999).

CHAPTER 42

PRIMARY SOURCE DOCUMENTS

Up-to-date data on income and poverty can be found at the Census Bureau's web site, http://www.census.gov/hhes/income. The classic book that launched the modern women's movement is Betty Friedan, The Feminine Mystique* (1963). For the views of a Christian conservative on the abortion issue see Ralph Reed, "We Stand at a Crossroads"* (Newsweek, May 13, 1996, 28). Statistical Abstract of the United States is an annual government publication with a wealth of information on a variety of topics, including immigration, Social Security funding, and the social and economic condition of minorities.

SECONDARY SOURCES

A useful overview of recent history is Paul Boyer, Promises to Keep: The United States Since World War II (1995). Growing income inequality is discussed in Barbara Ehrenreich, Fear *of Falling: The Inner Life of the Middle Class* (1989), and in Kevin P. Phillips, *The Politics of Rich and Poor: Wealth and the American Electorate in the Reagan Aftermath* (1990). The evolving social participation of women, and the dilemmas thereby created, are clearly spelled out in Rosalind Rosenberg, *Divided Lives* (1992), and in William H. Chafe, *The Paradox of Change: American Women in the 20th Century* (1991). See also Betty Friedan, *The Second Stage* (1981); Sylvia Ann Hewlett, *A Lesser Life: The Myth of Women's Liberation in America* (1986); Susanne M. Bianchi, *American Women in Transition* (1987); Marion Faux, *Roe vs. Wade* (1988); Jean E. Friedman et al., eds., *Our American Sisters* (1987); and Susan Faludi's provocative bestseller, *Backlash: The Undeclared War Against American Women* (1991). On the looming problems in the Social Security system see Peter G. Peterson, *Will America Grow Up Before It Grows Old?* (1996); for a provocative analysis of the leading senior citizens' lobby, the American Association of Retired Persons, consult Charles R. Morris, *The AARP: America's Most Powerful Lobby and the Clash of Generations* (1996). George J. Borjas turns an economist's critical eye on recent immigration in *Friends or Strangers* (1990). America's newest immigrants are the subjects of David M. Reimers, *Still the Golden Door: The Third World Comes to America* (1986). On Mexican-Americans see Carlos Munoz, Jr., *Youth, Identity, Power: The Chicano Movement* (1989); George J. Sanchez, *Becoming Mexican American* (1989); and Richard Rodriguez's poignant memoir, *Hunger of Memory* (1982). Asian-Americans are discussed in Bill Ong Hing, *Making and Remaking Asian America Through Immigration Policy* (1993), and in Ronald Takaki, *Strangers from a Different Shore* (1989). On blacks see Andrew Hacker, *Two Nations: Black and White, Separate, Hostile, Unequal* (1992), and Gerald David Jaynes and Robin

M. Williams, Jr., *A Common Destiny: Blacks and American Society* (1989). The problems of the cities are examined in Jon C. Teaford, *The Rough Road to Renaissance: Urban Revitalization in America, 1940–1985* (1990), and Larry Bennett, *Fragments of Cities: The New American Downtowns and Neighborhoods* (1990). Suburbs are the subject of Paul G. Lewis's *Shaping Suburbia* (1996). For penetrating analyses of the problems of the inner cities consult three studies by William J. Wilson: *The Truly Disadvantaged: The Inner City, the Underclass, and Public Policy* (1987); *Poverty, Inequality, and the Future of Social Policy* (1995); and *When Work Disappears* (1996). A probing study of the job limitations of inner-city residents who do work is Katherine Newman's *No Shame in My Game: The Working Poor in the Inner City* (1999). Welfare reform is the subject of Mary Jo Bane, *Welfare Realities* (1994). Nicholas Lemann, *The Promised Land* (1991), provides a vivid account of the welfare system and the failed promises of Lyndon Johnson's War on Poverty. The political implications of the debates over race and welfare policies are spelled out in Thomas Byrne Edsall and Mary D. Edsall, *Chain Reaction: The Impact of Race, Rights, and Taxes on American Politics* (1991). The broader cultural controversies of the era are examined in Arthur M. Schlesinger, Jr., *The Disuniting of America* (1992); Robert Hughes, *Culture of Complaint: The Fraying of America* (1993); and Henry Louis Gates, Jr., *Loose Canons: Notes on the Culture Wars* (1993). A sensitive and intriguing study of the values of modern Americans is Robert N. Bellah, *Habits of the Heart: Individualism and Commitment in American Life* (1985). See also Allan Bloom's conservative critique of modern higher education, *The Closing of the American Mind* (1987), and the rejoinder by Lawrence Levine, *The Opening of the American Mind* (1996).

Documents

Declaration of Independence
In Congress, July 4, 1776
The Unanimous Declaration of the Thirteen United States of America

[Bracketed material in color has been inserted by the authors. For adoption background, see pp. 92–93.]

When, in the course of human events, it becomes necessary for one people to dissolve the political bands which have connected them with another, and to assume, among the powers of the earth, the separate and equal station to which the laws of nature and of nature's God entitle them, a decent respect to the opinions of mankind requires that they should declare the causes which impel them to the separation.

We hold these truths to be self-evident: That all men are created equal; that they are endowed by their Creator with certain unalienable rights; that among these are life, liberty, and the pursuit of happiness; that, to secure these rights, governments are instituted among men, deriving their just powers from the consent of the governed; that whenever any form of government becomes destructive of these ends, it is the right of the people to alter or to abolish it, and to institute new government, laying its foundation on such principles, and organizing its powers in such form, as to them shall seem most likely to effect their safety and happiness. Prudence, indeed, will dictate that governments long established should not be changed for light and transient causes; and accordingly all experience hath shown that mankind are more disposed to suffer, while evils are sufferable, than to right themselves by abolishing the forms to which they are accustomed. But when a long train of abuses and usurpations, pursuing invariably the same object, evinces a design to reduce them under absolute despotism, it is their right, it is their duty, to throw off such government, and to provide new guards for their future security. Such has been the patient sufferance of these colonies; and such is now the necessity which constrains them to alter their former systems of government. The history of the present King of Great Britain is a history of repeated injuries and usurpations, all having in direct object the establishment of an absolute tyranny over these states. To prove this, let facts be submitted to a candid world.

He has refused his assent to laws, the most wholesome and necessary for the public good. [See royal veto, p. 78.]

He has forbidden his governors to pass laws of immediate and pressing importance, unless suspended in their operation till his assent should be obtained; and, when so suspended, he has utterly neglected to attend to them.

He has refused to pass other laws for the accommodation of large districts of people [by establishing new counties], unless those people would relinquish the right of representation in the legislature, a right inestimable to them, and formidable to tyrants only.

He has called together legislative bodies at places unusual, uncomfortable, and distant from the depository of their public records, for the sole purpose of fatiguing them into compliance with his measures. [e.g., removal of Massachusetts Assembly to Salem, 1774]

He has dissolved representative houses repeatedly, for opposing, with manly firmness, his invasions on the rights of the people. [e.g., Virginia Assembly, 1765]

He has refused for a long time, after such dissolutions, to cause others to be elected; whereby the legislative powers, incapable of annihilation, have returned to the people at large for their exercise; the state remaining, in the mean time, exposed to all the dangers of invasions from without and convulsions within.

He has endeavored to prevent the population [populating] of these states; for that purpose obstructing the laws for naturalization of foreigners; refusing to pass others to encourage their migration hither, and raising the conditions of new appropriations of lands. [e.g., Proclamation of 1763, p. 75]

He has obstructed the administration of justice, by refusing his assent to laws for establishing judiciary powers.

He has made judges dependent on his will alone, for the tenure of their offices, and the amount and payment of their salaries. [See Townshend Acts, p. 80.]

He has erected a multitude of new offices, and sent hither swarms of officers to harass our people and eat out their substance. [See enforcement of Navigation Laws, pp. 77–78.]

He has kept among us, in times of peace, standing armies, without the consent of our legislatures. [See p. 79.]

He has affected to render the military independent of, and superior to, the civil power.

He has combined with others to subject us to a jurisdiction foreign to our constitution, and unacknowledged by our laws, giving his assent to their acts of pretended legislation:

> For quartering large bodies of armed troops among us [see Boston Massacre, p. 80];
>
> For protecting them, by a mock trial, from punishment for any murders which they should commit on the inhabitants of these states [see 1774 Act, p. 83];
>
> For cutting off our trade with all parts of the world [see Boston Port Act, p. 83];
>
> For imposing taxes on us without our consent [see Stamp Act, p. 80];
>
> For depriving us, in many cases, of the benefits of trial by jury;
>
> For transporting us beyond seas, to be tried for pretended offenses;
>
> For abolishing the free system of English laws in a neighboring province [Quebec], establishing therein an arbitrary government, and enlarging its boundaries, so as to render it at once an example and fit instrument for introducing the same absolute rule into these colonies [Quebec Act, p. 83];
>
> For taking away our charters, abolishing our most valuable laws, and altering fundamentally the forms of our governments [e.g., in Massachusetts, p. 83];
>
> For suspending our own legislatures, and declaring themselves invested with power to legislate for us in all cases whatsoever [see Stamp Act repeal, p. 80].

He has abdicated government here, by declaring us out of his protection and waging war against us [Proclamation, p. 90].

He has plundered our seas, ravaged our coasts, burned our towns, and destroyed the lives of our people [e.g., the burning of Falmouth (Portland), p. 91].

He is at this time transporting large armies of foreign mercenaries [Hessians, p. 90] to complete the works of death, desolation, and tyranny already begun with circumstances of cruelty and perfidy scarcely paralleled in the most barbarous ages, and totally unworthy of the head of a civilized nation.

He has constrained our fellow-citizens, taken captive on the high seas [by impressment], to bear arms against their country, to become the executioners of their friends and brethren, or to fall themselves by their hands.

He has excited domestic insurrection among us [i.e., among slaves], and has endeavored to bring on the inhabitants of our frontiers the merciless Indian savages, whose known rule of warfare is an undistinguished destruction of all ages, sexes, and conditions.

In every stage of these oppressions we have petitioned for redress in the most humble terms; our repeated petitions have been answered only by repeated injury [e.g., pp. 89–90]. A prince, whose character is thus marked by every act which may define a tyrant, is unfit to be the ruler of a free people.

Nor have we been wanting in our attentions to our British brethren. We have warned them, from time to time, of attempts by their legislature to extend an unwarrantable jurisdiction over us. We have reminded them of the circumstances of our emigration and settlement here. We have appealed to their native justice and magnanimity; and we have conjured them, by the ties of our common kindred, to disavow these usurpations, which would inevitably interrupt our connections and correspondence. They, too, have been deaf to the voice of justice and of consanguinity [blood relationship]. We must, therefore, acquiesce in the necessity which denounces [announces] our separation, and hold them, as we hold the rest of mankind, enemies in war, in peace friends.

We, therefore, the representatives of the United States of America, in General Congress assembled, appealing to the Supreme Judge of the world for the rectitude of our intentions, do, in the name and by the authority of the good people of these colonies, solemnly publish and declare, That these United Colonies are, and of right ought to be, FREE AND INDEPENDENT STATES; that they are absolved from all allegiance to the British crown, and that all political connection between them and the state of Great Britain is, and ought to be, totally dissolved; and that, as free and independent states, they have full power to levy war, conclude peace, contract alliances, establish commerce, and do all other acts and things which independent states may of right do. And for the support of this declaration, with a firm reliance on the protection of Divine Providence, we mutually pledge to each other our lives, our fortunes, and our sacred honor.

[Signed by]

JOHN HANCOCK [President]
[and fifty-five others]

Constitution of the United States of America

[Boldface headings and bracketed explanatory matter and marginal comments (both in color) have been inserted for the reader's convenience. Passages that are no longer operative are printed in italic type.]

PREAMBLE

We the people of the United States, in order to form a more perfect union, establish justice, insure domestic tranquillity, provide for the common defense, promote the general welfare, and secure the blessings of liberty to ourselves and our posterity, do ordain and establish this CONSTITUTION for the United States of America.

Article I. Legislative Department

Section I. Congress

Legislative power vested in a two-House Congress. All legislative powers herein granted shall be vested in a Congress of the United States, which shall consist of a Senate and a House of Representatives.

Section II. House of Representatives

1. The people elect representatives biennially. The House of Representatives shall be composed of members chosen every second year by the people of the several States, and the electors[voters] in each State shall have the qualifications requisite for electors of the most numerous branch of the State Legislature.

2. Who may be representatives. No person shall be a Representative who shall not have attained to the age of twenty-five years, and been seven years a citizen of the United States, and who shall not, when elected, be an inhabitant of that State in which he shall be chosen.

3. Representation in the House based on population; census. Representatives and direct taxes[1] shall be apportioned among the several States which may be included within this Union, according to their respective numbers, *which shall be determined by adding to the whole number of free persons, including those bound to service for a term of years*[apprentices and indentured servants] *, and excluding Indians not taxed, three-fifths of all other persons*[slaves] .[2] The actual enumeration[census] shall be made within three years after the first meeting of the Congress of the United States, and within every subse-

See 1787 compromise, p. 112.

See 1787 compromise, p. 112.

---

[1] Modified in 1913 by the Sixteenth Amendment re income taxes (see p. 420).

[2] The word *slave* appears nowhere in the Constitution; *slavery* appears in the Thirteenth Amendment. The three-fifths rule ceased to be in force when the Thirteenth Amendment was adopted in 1865 (see p. 46 and text of amendments following).

quent term of ten years, in such manner as they shall by law direct. The number of Representatives shall not exceed one for every thirty thousand, but each State shall have at least one Representative; *and until such enumeration shall be made, the State of New Hampshire shall be entitled to choose three, Massachusetts eight, Rhode Island and Providence Plantations one, Connecticut five, New York six, New Jersey four, Pennsylvania eight, Delaware one, Maryland six, Virginia ten, North Carolina five, South Carolina five, and Georgia three.*

See Johnson trial, p. 302; Nixon trial preliminaries, pp. 575–576; and discussion of Clinton's impeachment, pp. 603–604.

4. Vacancies in the House are filled by election. When vacancies happen in the representation from any State, the Executive authority [governor] thereof shall issue writs of election [call a special election] to fill such vacancies.

5. The House selects its Speaker; has sole power to vote impeachment charges (i.e., indictments). The House of Representatives shall choose their Speaker and other officers; and shall have the sole power of impeachment.

Section III.   Senate

1. Senators represent the states. The Senate of the United States shall be composed of two Senators from each State, *chosen by the legislature thereof,*[1] for six years; and each Senator shall have one vote.

2. One-third of Senators chosen every two years; vacancies. *Immediately after they shall be assembled in consequence of the first election, they shall be divided as equally as may be into three classes. The seats of the Senators of the first class shall be vacated at the expiration of the second year, of the second class at the expiration of the fourth year, and of the third class at the expiration of the sixth year,* so that one-third may be chosen every second year; *and if vacancies happen by resignation or otherwise, during the recess of the legislature of any State, the Executive* [governor] *thereof may make temporary appointments until the next meeting of the legislature, which shall fill such vacancies.*[2]

3. Who may be Senators. No person shall be a Senator who shall not have attained to the age of thirty years, and been nine years a citizen of the United States, and who shall not, when elected, be an inhabitant of that State for which he shall be chosen.

4. The Vice President presides over the Senate. The Vice President of the United States shall be President of the Senate, but shall have no vote, unless they be equally divided [tied].

5. The Senate chooses its other officers. The Senate shall choose their other officers, and also a President *pro tempore,* in the absence of the Vice President, or when he shall exercise the office of President of the United States.

See Johnson trial, p. 302; and discussion of Clinton's impeachment, pp. 603–604.

6. The Senate has sole power to try impeachments. The Senate shall have the sole power to try all impeachments. When sitting for that purpose, they shall be on oath or affirmation. When the President of the United States is tried, the Chief Justice shall preside:[3] and no person shall be convicted without the concurrence of two-thirds of the members present.

7. Penalties for impeachment conviction. Judgment in cases of impeachment shall not extend further than to removal from office, and disqualification to hold and enjoy any office of honor, trust or profit under the United States: but the party convicted shall nevertheless be liable and subject to indictment, trial, judgment and punishment, according to law.

---

[1] Repealed in favor of popular election in 1913 by the Seventeenth Amendment.

[2] Changed in 1913 by the Seventeenth Amendment.

[3] The vice president, as next in line, would be an interested party.

Section IV.   Election and Meetings of Congress

1. Regulation of elections. The times, places and manner of holding elections for Senators and Representatives shall be prescribed in each State by the legislature thereof; but the Congress may at any time by law make or alter such regulations, except as to the places of choosing Senators.

2. Congress must meet once a year. The Congress shall assemble at least once in every year, and such meeting *shall be on the first Monday in December, unless they shall by law appoint a different day.*[1]

Section V.   Organization and Rules of the Houses

1. Each house may reject members; quorums. Each house shall be the judge of the elections, returns and qualifications of its own members, and a majority of each shall constitute a quorum to do business; but a smaller number may adjourn from day to day, and may be authorized to compel the attendance of absent members, in such manner, and under such penalties, as each house may provide.

See "Bully" Brooks case, pp. 257–258.

2. Each House makes its own rules. Each house may determine the rules of its proceedings, punish its members for disorderly behavior, and with the concurrence of two-thirds, expel a member.

3. Each House must keep and publish a record of its proceedings. Each house shall keep a journal of its proceedings, and from time to time publish the same, excepting such parts as may in their judgment require secrecy; and the yeas and nays of the members of either house on any question shall, at the desire of one-fifth of those present, be entered on the journal.

4. Both Houses must agree on adjournment. Neither house, during the session of congress, shall, without the consent of the other, adjourn for more than three days, nor to any other place than that in which the two houses shall be sitting.

Section VI.   Privileges of and Prohibitions upon Congressmen

1. Congressional salaries; immunities. The Senators and Representatives shall receive a compensation for their services, to be ascertained by law and paid out of the treasury of the United States. They shall in all cases except treason, felony and breach of the peace, be privileged from arrest during their attendance at the session of their respective houses, and in going to and returning from the same; and for any speech or debate in either house, they shall not be questioned in any other place [i.e., they shall be immune from libel suits].

2. A Congressman may not hold any other federal civil office. No Senator or Representative shall, during the time for which he was elected, be appointed to any civil office under the authority of the United States, which shall have been created, or the emoluments whereof shall have been increased, during such time; and no person holding any office under the United States shall be a member of either house during his continuance in office.

---

[1] Changed in 1933 to January 3 by the Twentieth Amendment (see p. 482 and text of amendments).

Section VII.   Method of Making Laws

See 1787 compromise, p. 113.

1. Money bills must originate in the House. All bills for raising revenue shall originate in the House of Representatives; but the Senate may propose or concur with amendments as on other bills.

Nixon, more than any predecessors, "impounded" billions of dollars voted by Congress for specific purposes, because he disapproved of them. The courts generally failed to sustain him, and his impeachment foes regarded wholesale impoundment as a violation of his oath to "faithfully execute" the laws.

2. The President's veto power; Congress may override. Every bill which shall have passed the House of Representatives and the Senate, shall, before it become a law, be presented to the President of the United States; if he approve he shall sign it, but if not he shall return it with his objections to that house in which it shall have originated, who shall enter the objections at large on their journal, and proceed to reconsider it. If after such reconsideration two-thirds of that house shall agree to pass the bill, it shall be sent, together with the objections, to the other house, by which it shall likewise be reconsidered, and if, approved by two-thirds of that house, it shall become a law. But in all such cases the votes of both houses shall be determined by yeas and nays, and the names of the persons voting for and against the bill shall be entered on the journal of each house respectively. If any bill shall not be returned by the President within ten days (Sundays excepted) after it shall have been presented to him, the same shall be a law, in like manner as if he had signed it, unless the Congress by their adjournment prevent its return, in which case it shall not be a law [this is the so-called pocket veto].

3. All measures requiring the agreement of both Houses go to President for approval. Every order, resolution, or vote to which the concurrence of the Senate and House of Representatives may be necessary (except on a question of adjournment) shall be presented to the President of the United States; and before the same shall take effect, shall be approved by him, or being disapproved by him, shall be repassed by two-thirds of the Senate and House of Representatives, according to the rules and limitations prescribed in the case of a bill.

Section VIII.   Powers Granted to Congress

Congress has certain enumerated powers:

1. It may lay and collect taxes. The Congress shall have power to lay and collect taxes, duties, imposts, and excises, to pay the debts and provide for the common defense and general welfare of the United States; but all duties, imposts and excises shall be uniform throughout the United States;

2. It may borrow money. To borrow money on the credit of the United States;

3. It may regulate foreign and interstate trade. To regulate commerce with foreign nations, and among the several States, and with the Indian tribes;

For 1798 naturalization, see p. 130.

4. It may pass naturalization and bankruptcy laws. To establish an uniform rule of naturalization, and uniform laws on the subject of bankruptcies throughout the United States;

5. It may coin money. To coin money, regulate the value thereof, and of foreign coin, and fix the standard of weights and measures;

6. It may punish counterfeiters. To provide for the punishment of counterfeiting the securities and current coin of the United States;

7. It may establish a postal service. To establish post offices and post roads;

8. It may issue patents and copyrights. To promote the progress of science and useful arts by securing for limited times to authors and inventors the exclusive right to their respective writings and discoveries;

See Judiciary Act of 1789, p. 122.

9. It may establish inferior courts. To constitute tribunals inferior to the Supreme Court;

10. It may punish crimes committed on the high seas. To define and punish piracies and felonies committed on the high seas [i.e., outside the three-mile limit] and offenses against the law of nations [international law];

11. It may declare war; authorize privateers. To declare war,[1] grant letters of marque and reprisal,[2] and make rules concerning captures on land and water;

12. It may maintain an army. To raise and support armies, but no appropriation of money to that use shall be for a longer term than two years;[3]

13. It may maintain a navy. To provide and maintain a navy;

14. It may regulate the army and navy. To make rules for the government and regulation of the land and naval forces;

See Whiskey Rebellion, p. 125.

15. It may call out the state militia. To provide for calling forth the militia to execute the laws of the union, suppress insurrections, and repel invasions.

16. It shares with the states control of militia. To provide for organizing, arming, and disciplining the militia, and for governing such part of them as may be employed in the service of the United States, reserving to the States respectively the appointment of the officers, and the authority of training the militia according to the discipline prescribed by Congress;

17. It makes laws for the District of Columbia and other federal areas. To exercise exclusive legislation in all cases whatsoever, over such district (not exceeding ten miles square) as may, by cession of particular States, and the acceptance of Congress, become the seat of government of the United States,[4] and to exercise like authority over all places purchased by the consent of the legislature of the State, in which the same shall be, for the erection of forts, magazines, arsenals, dock-yards, and other needful buildings;—and

Congress has certain implied powers:

This is the famous "Elastic Clause"; see p. 125.

18. It may make laws necessary for carrying out the enumerated powers. To make all laws which shall be necessary and proper for carrying into execution the foregoing powers, and all other powers vested by this Constitution in the government of the United States, or in any department or officer thereof.

Section IX. Powers Denied to the Federal Government

See 1787 slave compromise, p. 113.

1. Congressional control of slave trade postponed until 1808. *The migration or importation of such persons as any of the States now existing shall think proper to admit shall not be prohibited by the Congress prior to the year 1808; but a tax or duty may be imposed on such importation, not exceeding $10 for each person.*

2. The writ of habeas corpus[5] may be suspended only in case of rebellion or invasion. The privilege of the writ of habeas corpus shall not be suspended, unless when in cases of rebellion or invasion the public safety may require it.

3. Attainders[6] and ex post facto laws[7] forbidden. No bill of attainder or ex post facto law shall be passed.

---

[1] Note that the president, though he can provoke war (see the case of Polk, p. 236) or wage it after it is declared, cannot declare it.

[2] Papers issued private citizens in wartime authorizing them to capture enemy ships.

[3] A reflection of fear of standing armies earlier expressed in the Declaration of Independence.

[4] The District of Columbia, ten miles square, was established in 1791 with a cession from Virginia (see p. 123).

[5] A writ of habeas corpus is a document that enables a person under arrest to obtain an immediate examination in court to ascertain whether he is being legally held.

[6] A bill of attainder is a special legislative act condemning and punishing an individual without a judicial trial.

[7] An ex post facto law is one that fixes punishments for acts committed before the law was passed.

4. Direct taxes must be apportioned according to population. No capitation [head or poll tax], or other direct, tax shall be laid, unless in proportion to the census or enumeration herein before directed to be taken.[1]

5. Export taxes forbidden. No tax or duty shall be laid on articles exported from any State.

6. Congress must not discriminate among states in regulating commerce. No preference shall be given by any regulation of commerce or revenue to the ports of one State over those of another; nor shall vessels bound to, or from, one State, be obliged to enter, clear, or pay duties in another.

7. Public money may not be spent without congressional appropriation; accounting. No money shall be drawn from the treasury, but in consequence of appropriations made by law; and a regular statement and account of the receipts and expenditures of all public money shall be published from time to time.

8. Titles of nobility prohibited; foreign gifts. No title of nobility shall be granted by the United States: and no person holding any office of profit or trust under them, shall, without the consent of the Congress, accept of any present, emolument, office, or title, of any kind whatever, from any king, prince, or foreign state.

Section X.   Powers Denied to the States

Absolute prohibitions on the states:

1. The states are forbidden to do certain things. No State shall enter into any treaty, alliance, or confederation; grant letters of marque and reprisal [i.e., authorize privateers]; coin money; emit bills of credit [issue paper money]; make anything but gold and silver coin a [legal] tender in payment of debts; pass any bill of attainder, ex post facto,[2] or law impairing the obligation of contracts, or grant any title of nobility.

On contracts, see Fletcher v. Peck, p. 157.

Conditional prohibitions on the states:

2. The states may not levy duties without the consent of Congress. No State shall, without the consent of the Congress, lay any imposts or duties on imports or exports, except what may be absolutely necessary for executing its inspection laws: and the net produce of all duties and imposts, laid by any State on imports or exports, shall be for the use of the treasury of the United States; and all such laws shall be subject to the revision and control of the Congress.

Cf. Confederation chaos, p. 108.

3. Certain other federal powers are forbidden the states except with the consent of Congress. No State shall, without the consent of Congress, lay any duty of tonnage [i.e., duty on ship tonnage], keep [non-militia] troops or ships of war in time of peace, enter into any agreement or compact with another State, or with a foreign power, or engage in war, unless actually invaded, or in such imminent danger as will not admit of delay.

Article II.   Executive Department

Section I.   President and Vice President

1. The President the chief executive; his term. The executive power shall be vested in a President of the United States of America. He shall hold his office during the term of four years,[3] and, together with the Vice President, chosen for the same term, be elected as follows:

---

[1] Modified in 1913 by the Sixteenth Amendment (see p. 420 and amendments below).

[2] For definitions, see footnotes 6 and 7.

[3] No reference to reelection; for anti–third term Twenty-second Amendment, see text of amendments following.

See 1787
compromise,
p. 113.
See 1876 Oregon
case, p. 314.

2. The President is chosen by electors. Each State shall appoint, in such manner as the legislature thereof may direct, a number of electors, equal to the whole number of Senators and Representatives to which the State may be entitled in the Congress; but no Senator or Representative, or person holding an office of trust or profit under the United States, shall be appointed an elector.

A majority of the electoral votes needed to elect a President. *The electors shall meet in their respective States, and vote by ballot for two persons, of whom one at least shall not be an inhabitant of the same State with themselves. And they shall make a list of all the persons voted for, and of the number of votes for each; which list they shall sign and certify, and transmit sealed to the seat of government of the United States, directed to the President of the Senate. The President of the Senate shall, in the presence of the Senate and House of Representatives, open all certificates, and the votes shall then be counted. The person having the greatest number of votes shall be the President, if such number be a majority of the whole number of electors appointed; and if there be more than one who have such majority, and have an equal number of votes, then the House of Representatives shall immediately choose by ballot one of them for President; and if no person have a majority, then from the five highest on the list the said house shall in like manner choose the President. But in choosing the President the votes shall be taken by States, the representation from each State having one vote; a quorum for this purpose shall consist of a member or members from two-thirds of the States, and a majority of all the States shall be necessary to a choice. In every case, after the choice of the President, the person having the greatest number of votes of the electors shall be the Vice President. But if there should remain two or more who have equal votes, the Senate shall choose from them by ballot the Vice President.*[1]*

See Burr-Jefferson
disputed election of
1800, p. 135.

See Jefferson as vice
president in 1796,
p. 128.

3. Congress decides time of meeting of Electoral College. The Congress may determine the time of choosing the electors and the day on which they shall give their votes; which day shall be the same throughout the United States.

4. Who may be President. No person except a natural-born citizen, *or a citizen of the United States at the time of the adoption of this Constitution,* shall be eligible to the office of President; neither shall any person be eligible to that office who shall not have attained to the age of thirty-five years, and been fourteen years a resident within the United States [i.e., a legal resident].

To provide for
foreign-born like
Alexander Hamilton,
born in the British
West Indies.

5. Replacements for President. In case of the removal of the President from office or of his death, resignation, or inability to discharge the powers and duties of the said office, the same shall devolve on the Vice President, and the Congress may by law provide for the case of removal, death, resignation, or inability, both of the President and Vice President, declaring what officer shall then act as President, and such officer shall act accordingly, until the disability be removed, or a President shall be elected.

Modified by
Amendments XX and
XXV.

6. The President's salary. The President shall, at stated times, receive for his services a compensation, which shall neither be increased nor diminished during the period for which he shall have been elected, and he shall not receive within that period any other emolument from the United States, or any of them.

7. The President's oath of office. Before he enter on the execution of his office, he shall take the following oath or affirmation;—"I do solemnly swear (or affirm) that I will faithfully execute the office of the President of the United States, and will to the best of my ability preserve, protect and defend the Constitution of the United States."

---

[1] Repealed in 1804 by the Twelfth Amendment (see text of amendments following).

Section II.   Powers of the President

1. The President has important military and civil powers. The President shall be commander in chief of the army and navy of the United States, and of the militia of the several States, when called into the actual service of the United States; he may require the opinion, in writing, of the principal officer in each of the executive departments, upon any subject relating to the duties of their respective offices, and he shall have power to grant reprieves and pardon for offenses against the United States, except in cases of impeachment.[1]

See cabinet evolution, p. 121.

2. The President may negotiate treaties and nominate federal officials. He shall have power, by and with the advice and consent of the Senate, to make treaties, provided two-thirds of the Senators present concur; and he shall nominate, and by and with the advice and consent of the Senate, shall appoint ambassadors, other public ministers and consuls, judges of the Supreme Court, and all other officers of the United States, whose appointments are not herein otherwise provided for, and which shall be established by law: but the Congress may by law vest the appointment of such inferior officers, as they think proper, in the President alone, in the courts of law, or in the heads of departments.

For president's removal power, see pp. 302–303.

3. The President may fill vacancies during Senate recess. The President shall have power to fill up all vacancies that may happen during the recess of the Senate, by granting commissions which shall expire at the end of their next session.

Section III.   Other Powers and Duties of the President

Messages; extra sessions; receiving ambassadors; execution of the laws. He shall from time to time give to the Congress information of the state of the Union, and recommend to their consideration such measures as he shall judge necessary and expedient; he may, on extraordinary occasions, convene both houses, or either of them, and in case of disagreement between them, with respect to the time of adjournment, he may adjourn them to such time as he shall think proper; he shall receive ambassadors and other public ministers; he shall take care that the laws be faithfully executed, and shall commission all the officers of the United States.

For president's personal appearances, see pp. 420–421.

Section IV.   Impeachment

Civil officers may be removed by impeachment. The President, Vice President and all civil officers[2] of the United States shall be removed from office on impeachment for, and on conviction of, treason, bribery, or other high crimes and misdemeanors.

See discussion of Presidents Johnson, pp. 302–303; Nixon, pp. 575–576; and Clinton, pp. 603–604.

Article III.   Judicial Department

Section I.   The Federal Courts

The judicial power belongs to the federal courts. The judicial power of the United States shall be vested in one Supreme Court, and in such inferior courts as the Congress may from time to time ordain and establish. The judges, both of the Supreme and inferior courts, shall hold their offices during good behavior, and shall, at stated times, receive for their services a compensation which shall not be diminished[3] during their continuance in office.

See Judiciary Act of 1789, p. 122.

---

[1] To prevent the president's pardoning himself or his close associates, as was feared in the case of Richard Nixon. See pp. 575–576.

[2] I.e., all federal executive and judicial officers, but not members of Congress or military personnel.

[3] In 1978, in a case involving federal judges, the Supreme Court ruled that diminution of salaries by inflation was irrelevant.

Section II.   Jurisdiction of Federal Courts

1. Kinds of cases that may be heard. The judicial power shall extend to all cases, in law and equity, arising under this Constitution, the laws of the United States, and treaties made, or which shall be made, under their authority;—to all cases affecting ambassadors, other public ministers and consuls;—to all cases of admiralty and maritime jurisdiction;—to controversies to which the United States shall be a party;—to controversies between two or more States;—*between a State and citizens of another State;*[1]—between citizens of different States;—between citizens of the same State claiming lands under grants of different States, and between a State, or the citizens thereof, and foreign states, citizens or subjects.

2. Jurisdiction of the Supreme Court. In all cases affecting ambassadors, other public ministers and consuls, and those in which a State shall be party, the Supreme Court shall have original jurisdiction.[2] In all the other cases before mentioned, the Supreme Court shall have appellate jurisdiction,[3] both as to law and fact, with such exceptions, and under such regulations, as the Congress shall make.

3. Trial for federal crime is by jury. The trial of all crimes, except in cases of impeachment, shall be by jury; and such trial shall be held in the State where the said crimes shall have been committed; but when not committed within any State, the trial shall be at such place or places as the Congress may by law have directed.

Section III.   Treason

See Burr trial, p. 140.

1. Treason defined. Treason against the United States shall consist only in levying war against them, or in adhering to their enemies, giving them aid and comfort. No person shall be convicted of treason unless on the testimony of two witnesses to the same overt act, or on confession in open court.

2. Congress fixes punishment for treason. The Congress shall have power to declare the punishment of treason, but no attainder of treason shall work corruption of blood, or forfeiture except during the life of the person attainted.[4]

Article IV.   Relations of the States to One Another

Section I.   Credit to Acts, Records and Court Proceedings

Each state must respect the public acts of the others. Full faith and credit shall be given in each State to the public acts, records, and judicial proceedings of every other State.[5] And the Congress may by general laws prescribe the manner in which such acts, records, and proceedings shall be proved [attested], and the effect thereof.

Section II.   Duties of States to States

1. Citizenship in one state is valid in all. The citizens of each State shall be entitled to all privileges and immunities of citizens in the several States.

---

[1] The Eleventh Amendment (see text of amendments following) restricts this to suits by a state against citizens of another state.

[2] I.e., such cases must originate in the Supreme Court.

[3] I.e., it hears other cases only when they are appealed to it from a lower federal court or a state court.

[4] I.e., punishment only for the offender; none for his heirs.

[5] E.g., a marriage valid in one is valid in all.

This stipulation is sometimes openly flouted. In 1978 Governor Jerry Brown of California, acting on humanitarian grounds, refused to surrender to South Dakota an American Indian, Dennis Banks, who was charged with murder in an armed uprising.

2. Fugitives from justice must be surrendered by the state to which they have fled. A person charged in any State with treason, felony, or other crime, who shall flee from justice, and be found in another State, shall on demand of the executive authority [governor] of the State from which he fled, be delivered up, to be removed to the State having jurisdiction of the crime.

3. Slaves and apprentices must be returned. *No person held to service or labor in one State, under the laws thereof, escaping into another, shall, in consequence of any law or regulation therein, be discharged from such service or labor, but shall be delivered up on claim of the party to whom such service or labor may be due.*[1]

Basis of fugitive slave laws; see pp. 245–247.

Section III.   New States and Territories

E.g., Maine (1820); see p. 155.

1. Congress may admit new states. New States may be admitted by the Congress into this Union; but no new State shall be formed or erected within the jurisdiction of any other State; nor any State be formed by the junction of two or more States, or parts of States, without the consent of the legislatures of the States concerned as well as of the Congress.[2]

2. Congress regulates federal territory and property. The Congress shall have power to dispose of and make all needful rules and regulations respecting the territory or other property belonging to the United States; and nothing in this Constitution shall be so construed as to prejudice any claims of the United States, or of any particular State.

Section IV.   Protection to the States

See Cleveland and the Pullman strike, pp. 372–373.

United States guarantees to states representative government and protection against invasion and rebellion. The United States shall guarantee to every State in this Union a republican form of government, and shall protect each of them against invasion; and on application of the legislature, or of the executive [governor] (when the legislature cannot be convened), against domestic violence.

Article V.   The Process of Amendment

The Constitution may be amended in four ways. The Congress, whenever two-thirds of both houses shall deem it necessary, shall propose amendments to this Constitution, or, on the application of the legislatures of two-thirds of the several States, shall call a convention for proposing amendments, which, in either case, shall be valid to all intents and purposes, as part of this Constitution, when ratified by the legislatures of three-fourths of the several States, or by conventions in three-fourths thereof, as the one or the other mode of ratification may be proposed by the Congress; provided *that no amendments which may be made prior to the year one thousand eight hundred and eight shall in any*

---

[1] Invalidated in 1865 by the Thirteenth Amendment (see text of amendments following).

[2] Loyal West Virginia was formed by Lincoln in 1862 from seceded Virginia. This act was of dubious constitutionality and was justified in part by the wartime powers of the president. See p. 269.

manner affect the first and fourth clauses in the ninth section of the first article,[1] and that no State, without its consent, shall be deprived of its equal suffrage in the Senate.

Article VI. General Provisions

This pledge honored by Hamilton, p. 123.

1. The debts of the Confederation are taken over. All debts contracted and engagements entered into, before the adoption of this Constitution, shall be as valid against the United States under this Constitution, as under the Confederation.

2. The Constitution, federal laws, and treaties are the supreme law of the land. This Constitution, and the laws of the United States which shall be made in pursuance thereof; and all treaties made, or which shall be made, under the authority of the United States, shall be the supreme law of the land; and the judges in every State shall be bound thereby, anything in the Constitution or laws of any State to the contrary notwithstanding.

3. Federal and state officers bound by oath to support the Constitution. The Senators and Representatives before mentioned, and the members of the several State legislatures, and all executive and judicial officers, both of the United States and of the several States, shall be bound by oath or affirmation to support this Constitution; but no religious test shall ever be required as a qualification to any office or public trust under the United States.

Article VII. Ratification of the Constitution

See 1787 irregularity, pp. 114–116.

The Constitution effective when ratified by conventions in nine states. The ratification of the conventions of nine States shall be sufficient for the establishment of this Constitution between the States so ratifying the same.

Done in Convention by the unanimous consent of the States present, the seventeenth day of September in the year of our Lord one thousand seven hundred and eighty-seven and of the Independence of the United States of America the twelfth. In witness whereof we have hereunto subscribed our names.

[Signed by]

G⁰ WASHINGTON
Presidt and Deputy from Virginia
[and thirty-eight others]

AMENDMENTS TO THE CONSTITUTION

Amendment I. Religious and Political Freedom

For background of Bill of Rights, see pp. 121–122.

Congress must not interfere with freedom of religion, speech or press, assembly, and petition. Congress shall make no law respecting an establishment of religion,[2] or prohibiting the free exercise thereof; or abridging the freedom of speech, or of the press; or the right of the people peaceably to assemble, and to petition the government for a redress of grievances.

---

[1] This clause, re slave trade and direct taxes, became inoperative in 1808.

[2] In 1787 "an establishment of religion" referred to an "established church," or one supported by all taxpayers, whether members or not. But the courts have often acted under this article to keep religion, including prayers, out of the public schools.

Amendment II. Right to Bear Arms

The people may bear arms. A well-regulated militia being necessary to the security of a free State, the right of the people to keep and bear arms [i.e., for military purposes] shall not be infringed.[1]

Amendment III. Quartering of Troops

See Declaration of Independence and British quartering above.

Soldiers may not be arbitrarily quartered on the people. No soldier shall, in time of peace, be quartered in any house without the consent of the owner, nor in time of war, but in a manner to be prescribed by law.

Amendment IV. Searches and Seizures

A reflection of colonial grievances against the Crown.

Unreasonable searches are forbidden. The right of the people to be secure in their persons, houses, papers, and effects, against unreasonable searches and seizures, shall not be violated, and no [search] warrants shall issue but upon probable cause, supported by oath or affirmation, and particularly describing the place to be searched, and the persons or things to be seized.

Amendment V. Right to Life, Liberty, and Property

When witnesses refuse to answer questions in court, they routinely "take the Fifth Amendment."

The individual is guaranteed certain rights when on trial and the right to life, liberty, and property. No person shall be held to answer for a capital, or otherwise infamous crime, unless on a presentment [formal charge] or indictment of a grand jury, except in cases arising in the land or naval forces, or in the militia, when in actual service in time of war or public danger; nor shall any person be subject for the same offense to be twice put in jeopardy of life or limb; nor shall be compelled in any criminal case to be a witness against himself, nor be deprived of life, liberty, or property, without due process of law; nor shall private property be taken for public use [i.e., by eminent domain] without just compensation.

Amendment VI. Protection in Criminal Trials

See Declaration of Independence above.

An accused person has important rights. In all criminal prosecutions, the accused shall enjoy the right to a speedy and public trial, by an impartial jury of the State and district wherein the crime shall have been committed, which district shall have been previously ascertained by law, and to be informed of the nature and cause of the accusation; to be confronted with the witnesses against him; to have compulsory process [subpoena] for obtaining witnesses in his favor, and to have the assistance of counsel for his defense.

Amendment VII. Suits at Common Law

The rules of common law are recognized. In suits at common law, where the value in controversy shall exceed twenty dollars, the right of trial by jury shall be preserved, and no fact tried by a jury shall be otherwise re-examined in any court of the United States, than according to the rules of the common law.

---

[1] The courts, with "militia" in mind, have consistently held that the "right" to bear arms is a limited one.

Amendment VIII.   Bail and Punishments

Excessive fines and unusual punishments are forbidden. Excessive bail shall not be required, nor excessive fines imposed, nor cruel and unusual punishments inflicted.

Amendment IX.   Concerning Rights Not Enumerated

Amendments IX and X were bulwarks of southern states' rights before the Civil War.

The people retain rights not here enumerated. The enumeration in the Constitution, of certain rights, shall not be construed to deny or disparage others retained by the people.

Amendment X.   Powers Reserved to the States and to the People

A concession to states' rights, p. 124.

Powers not delegated to the federal government are reserved to the states and the people. The powers not delegated to the United States by the Constitution, nor prohibited by it to the States, are reserved to the States respectively, or to the people.

Amendment XI.   Suits Against a State

The federal courts have no authority in suits by citizens against a state. The judicial power of the United States shall not be construed to extend to any suit in law or equity, commenced or prosecuted against one of the United States by citizens of another state, or by citizens or subjects of any foreign state. [Adopted 1798.]

Amendment XII.   Election of President and Vice President

1. Changes in manner of electing President and Vice President; procedure when no presidential candidate receives electoral majority. The electors shall meet in their respective States, and vote by ballot for President and Vice President, one of whom, at least, shall not be an inhabitant of the same State with themselves; they shall name in their ballots the person voted for as President, and in distinct ballots the person voted for as Vice President, and they shall make distinct lists of all persons voted for as President, and of all persons voted for as Vice President, and of the number of votes for each, which lists they shall sign and certify, and transmit sealed to the seat of government of the United States, directed to the President of the Senate;—the President of the Senate shall, in the presence of the Senate and House of Representatives, open all the certificates and the votes shall then be counted;—the person having the greatest number of votes for President shall be the President, if such number be a majority of the whole number of electors appointed; and if no person have such majority, then from the persons having the highest numbers not exceeding three on the list of those voted for as President, the House of Representatives shall choose immediately, by ballot, the President. But in choosing the President, the votes shall be taken by States, the representation from each State having one vote; a quorum for this purpose shall consist of a member or members from two-thirds of the States, and a majority of all the States shall be necessary to a choice. And if the House of Representatives shall not choose a President whenever the right of choice shall devolve upon them, before *the fourth day of March*[1] next following, then the Vice President shall act as President, as in the case of death or other constitutional disability of the President.

Forestalls repetition of 1800 electoral dispute, p. 135.

See 1876 disputed election, p. 313.

See 1824 election, pp. 162–163.

---

[1] Changed to January 20 by the Twentieth Amendment (see text of amendment following).

2. Procedure when no vice presidential candidate receives electoral majority. The person having the greatest number of votes as Vice President shall be the Vice President, if such number be a majority of the whole number of electors appointed; and if no person have a majority, then from the two highest numbers on the list the Senate shall choose the Vice President; a quorum for the purpose shall consist of two-thirds of the whole number of Senators, and a majority of the whole number shall be necessary to a choice. But no person constitutionally ineligible to the office of President shall be eligible to that of Vice President of the United States. [Adopted 1804.]

Amendment XIII. Slavery Prohibited

For background, see pp. 280–282.

Slavery forbidden. 1. Neither slavery[1] nor involuntary servitude, except as a punishment for crime whereof the party shall have been duly convicted, shall exist within the United States, or any place subject to their jurisdiction.
2. Congress shall have power to enforce this article by appropriate legislation. [Adopted 1865.]

Amendment XIV. Civil Rights for Ex-slaves,[2] etc.

For background, see pp. 280–282.

For corporations as "persons," see pp. 333–334.

1. Ex-slaves made citizens; U.S. citizenship primary. All persons born or naturalized in the United States, and subject to the jurisdiction thereof, are citizens of the United States and of the State wherein they reside. No State shall make or enforce any law which shall abridge the privileges or immunities of citizens of the United States; nor shall any State deprive any person of life, liberty, or property, without due process of law; nor deny to any person within its jurisdiction the equal protection of the laws.

Abolishes three-fifths rule for slaves, Art. I, Sec. II, para. 3.

2. When a state denies citizens the vote, its representation shall be reduced. Representatives shall be apportioned among the several States according to their respective numbers, counting the whole number of persons in each State, excluding Indians not taxed. But when the right to vote at any election for the choice of Electors for President and Vice President of the United States, Representatives in Congress, the executive and judicial officers of a State, or the members of the legislature thereof, is denied to any of the male inhabitants of such State, being twenty-one years of age and citizens of the United States, or in any way abridged, except for participation in rebellion, or other crime, the basis of representation therein shall be reduced in the proportion which the number of such male citizens shall bear to the whole number of male citizens twenty-one years of age in such State.[3]

Leading ex-Confederates denied office. See p. 298.

3. Certain persons who have been in rebellion are ineligible for federal and state office. No person shall be a Senator or Representative in Congress, or Elector of President and Vice President, or hold any office, civil or military, under the United States, or under any State, who, having previously taken an oath, as a member of Congress, or as an officer of the United States, or as a member of any State legislature, or as an executive or judicial officer of any State, to support the Constitution of the United States, shall have engaged in insurrection or rebellion against the same, or given aid or comfort to the enemies thereof. But Congress may, by a vote of two-thirds of each house, remove such disability.

---

[1] The only explicit mention of slavery in the Constitution.

[2] Occasionally an offender is prosecuted under the Thirteenth Amendment for keeping an employee or other person under conditions approximating slavery.

[3] The provisions concerning "male" inhabitants were modified by the Nineteenth Amendment, which enfranchised women. The legal voting age was changed from twenty-one to eighteen by the Twenty-sixth Amendment.

The ex-Confederates were thus forced to repudiate their debts and pay pensions to their own veterans, plus taxes for the pensions of Union veterans, their conquerors.

4. Debts incurred in aid of rebellion are void. The validity of the public debt of the United States, authorized by law, including debts incurred for payment of pensions and bounties for services in suppressing insurrection or rebellion, shall not be questioned. But neither the United States nor any State shall assume or pay any debt or obligation incurred in aid of insurrection or rebellion against the United States, or any claim for the loss or emancipation of any slave; but all such debts, obligations, and claims shall be held illegal and void.

5. Enforcement. The Congress shall have power to enforce, by appropriate legislation, the provisions of this article. [Adopted 1868.]

Amendment XV.   Suffrage for Blacks

For background, see p. 299.

Black males are made voters. 1. The right of citizens of the United States to vote shall not be denied or abridged by the United States or by any State on account of race, color, or previous condition of servitude.

2. The Congress shall have power to enforce this article by appropriate legislation. [Adopted 1870.]

Amendment XVI.   Income Taxes

For background, see p. 420.

Congress has power to lay and collect income taxes. The Congress shall have power to lay and collect taxes on incomes, from whatever source derived, without apportionment among the several States, and without regard to any census or enumeration. [Adopted 1913.]

Amendment XVII.   Direct Election of Senators

Senators shall be elected by popular vote. 1. The Senate of the United States shall be composed of two Senators from each State, elected by the people thereof, for six years; and each Senator shall have one vote. The electors in each State shall have the qualifications requisite for electors of [voters for] the most numerous branch of the State legislatures.

2. When vacancies happen in the representation of any State in the Senate, the executive authority of such State shall issue writs of election to fill such vacancies: Provided, that the Legislature of any State may empower the executive thereof to make temporary appointments until the people fill the vacancies by election as the Legislature may direct.

3. This amendment shall not be so construed as to affect the election or term of any Senator chosen before it becomes valid as part of the Constitution. [Adopted 1913.]

Amendment XVIII.   National Prohibition

For background, see p. 447.

The sale or manufacture of intoxicating liquors is forbidden. 1. *After one year from the ratification of this article the manufacture, sale, or transportation of intoxicating liquors within, the importation thereof into, or the exportation thereof from the United States and all territory subject to the jurisdiction thereof, for beverage purposes, is hereby prohibited.*

2. *The Congress and the several States shall have concurrent power to enforce this article by appropriate legislation.*

3. *This article shall be inoperative unless it shall have been ratified as an amendment to the Constitution by the legislatures of the several States, as provided by the Constitution, within seven years from the date of the submission thereof to the States by the Congress.* [Adopted 1919; repealed 1933 by Twenty-first Amendment.]

Amendment XIX.   Woman Suffrage

For background, see pp. 433–434.

Women guaranteed the right to vote. 1. The right of citizens of the United States to vote shall not be denied or abridged by the United States or by any State on account of sex.

2. The Congress shall have power to enforce this article by appropriate legislation. [Adopted 1920.]

Amendment XX.   Presidential and Congressional Terms

Shortens lame-duck periods by modifying Art. I, Sec. IV, para. 2.

1. Presidential, vice presidential, and congressional terms of office begin in January. The terms of the President and Vice President shall end at noon on the 20th day of January, and the terms of Senators and Representatives at noon on the 3d day of January, of the years in which such terms would have ended if this article had not been ratified; and the terms of their successors shall then begin.

2. New meeting date for Congress. The Congress shall assemble at least once in every year, and such meeting shall begin at noon on the 3d day of January, unless they shall by law appoint a different day.

3. Emergency presidential and vice presidential succession. If, at the time fixed for the beginning of the term of the President, the President-elect shall have died, the Vice President-elect shall become President. If a President shall not have been chosen before the time fixed for the beginning of his term, or if the President-elect shall have failed to qualify, then the Vice President-elect shall act as President until a President shall have qualified; and the Congress may by law provide for the case wherein neither a President-elect nor a Vice President-elect shall have qualified, declaring who shall then act as President, or the manner in which one who is to act shall be selected, and such persons shall act accordingly until a President or Vice President shall have qualified.

4. The Congress may by law provide for the case of the death of any of the persons from whom the House of Representatives may choose a President whenever the right of choice shall have devolved upon them, and for the case of the death of any of the persons from whom the Senate may choose a Vice President whenever the right of choice shall have devolved upon them.

5. Sections 1 and 2 shall take effect on the 15th day of October following the ratification of this article.

6. This article shall be inoperative unless it shall have been ratified as an amendment to the Constitution by the Legislatures of three-fourths of the several States within seven years from the date of its submission. [Adopted 1933.]

Amendment XXI.   Prohibition Repealed

For background, see p. 476.

1. Eighteenth Amendment repealed. The eighteenth article of amendment to the Constitution of the United States is hereby repealed.

2. Local laws honored. The transportation or importation into any State, Territory, or Possession of the United States for delivery or use therein of intoxicating liquors, in violation of the laws thereof, is hereby prohibited.

3. This article shall be inoperative unless it shall have been ratified as an amendment to the Constitution by conventions in the several States, as provided in the Constitution, within seven years from the date of the submission thereof to the States by the Congress. [Adopted 1933.]

Amendment XXII.   Anti–Third Term Amendment

Sometimes referred to as the anti–Franklin Roosevelt amendment.

Presidential term is limited. 1. No person shall be elected to the office of President more than twice, and no person who has held the office of President, or acted as President, for more than two years of a term to which some other person was elected President shall be elected to the office of President more than once. But this article shall not apply to any person holding the office of President when this article was proposed by the Congress [i.e., Truman], and shall not prevent any person who may be holding the office of President, or acting as President, during the term within which this article becomes operative [i.e., Truman] from holding the office of President or acting as President during the remainder of such term.

2. This article shall be inoperative unless it shall have been ratified as an amendment to the Constitution by the legislatures of three-fourths of the several States within seven years from the date of its submission to the States by the Congress. [Adopted 1951.]

Amendment XXIII.   District of Columbia Vote

Designed to give the District of Columbia three electoral votes and to quiet the century-old cry of "No taxation without representation." Yet the District of Columbia still has only one non-voting member of Congress.

1. Presidential electors for the District of Columbia. The District constituting the seat of Government of the United States shall appoint in such manner as the Congress may direct:

A number of electors of President and Vice President equal to the whole number of Senators and Representatives in Congress to which the District would be entitled if it were a State, but in no event more than the least populous State; they shall be in addition to those appointed by the States, but they shall be considered for the purposes of the election of President and Vice President, to be electors appointed by a State; and they shall meet in the District and perform such duties as provided by the twelfth article of amendment.

2. Enforcement. The Congress shall have the power to enforce this article by appropriate legislation. [Adopted 1961.]

Amendment XXIV.   Poll Tax

Designed to end discrimination against blacks and other poor folk. An aspect of the civil rights crusade under President Lyndon Johnson. See pp. 557–558.

1. Payment of poll tax or other taxes not to be prerequisite for voting in federal elections. The right of citizens of the United States to vote in any primary or other election for President or Vice President, for electors for President or Vice President, or for Senator or Representative in Congress, shall not be denied or abridged by the United States or any State by reason of failure to pay any poll tax or other tax.

2. Enforcement. The Congress shall have the power to enforce this article by appropriate legislation. [Adopted 1964.]

Amendment XXV.   Presidential Succession and Disability[1]

1. Vice President to become President. In case of the removal of the President from office or of his death or resignation, the Vice President shall become President.[2]

---

[1] Passed by a two-thirds vote of both Houses of Congress in July 1965; ratified by the requisite three-fourths of the state legislatures, February 1967, or well within the seven-year limit.

[2] The original Constitution (Art. II, Sec. I, para. 5) was vague on this point, stipulating that "the powers and duties" of the president, but not necessarily the title, should "devolve" on the vice president. President Tyler, the first "accidental president," assumed not only the powers and duties but the title as well.

2. Successor to Vice President provided. Whenever there is a vacancy in the office of the Vice President, the President shall nominate a Vice President who shall take office upon confirmation by a majority vote of both Houses of Congress.

3. Vice President to serve for disabled President. Whenever the President transmits to the President pro tempore of the Senate and the Speaker of the House of Representatives his written declaration that he is unable to discharge the powers and duties of his office, and until he transmits to them a written declaration to the contrary, such powers and duties shall be discharged by the Vice President as Acting President.

4. Procedure for disqualifying or requalifying President. Whenever the Vice President and a majority of either the principal officers of the executive departments or of such other body as Congress may by law provide, transmit to the President pro tempore of the Senate and the Speaker of the House of Representatives their written declaration that the President is unable to discharge the powers and duties of his office, the Vice President shall immediately assume the powers and duties of the office as Acting President.

Thereafter, when the President transmits to the President pro tempore of the Senate and the Speaker of the House of Representatives his written declaration that no inability exists, he shall resume the powers and duties of his office unless the Vice President and a majority of either the principal officers of the executive department[s] or of such other body as Congress may by law provide, transmit within four days to the President pro tempore of the Senate and the Speaker of the House of Representatives their written declaration that the President is unable to discharge the powers and duties of his office. Thereupon Congress shall decide the issue, assembling within forty-eight hours for that purpose if not in session. If the Congress, within twenty-one days after receipt of the latter written declaration, or, if Congress is not in session, within twenty-one days after Congress is required to assemble, determines by two-thirds vote of both Houses that the President is unable to discharge the powers and duties of his office, the Vice President shall continue to discharge the same as Acting President; otherwise, the President shall resume the powers and duties of his office. [Adopted 1967.]

Gerald Ford was the first "appointed President." See pp. 574, 576.

Amendment XXVI. Lowering Voting Age

A response to the current revolt of youth. See p. 570.

1. Ballot for eighteen-year-olds. The right of citizens of the United States, who are eighteen years of age or older, to vote shall not be denied or abridged by the United States or by any State on account of age.

2. Enforcement. The Congress shall have power to enforce this article by appropriate legislation. [Adopted 1971.]

An American Profile

The United States and Its People

Population, Percentage Change, and Racial Composition for the United States, 1790–2000

Census	Population of United States	Increase over Preceding Census Number	Increase over Preceding Census Percentage	Racial Composition, Percent Distribution* White	Black	Latino	Asian
1790	3,929,214			80.7	19.3	NA	NA
1800	5,308,483	1,379,269	35.1	81.1	18.9	NA	NA
1810	7,239,881	1,931,398	36.4	81.0	19.0	NA	NA
1820	9,638,453	2,398,572	33.1	81.6	18.4	NA	NA
1830	12,866,020	3,227,567	33.5	81.9	18.1	NA	NA
1840	17,069,453	4,203,433	32.7	83.2	16.8	NA	NA
1850	23,191,876	6,122,423	35.9	84.3	15.7	NA	NA
1860	31,433,321	8,251,445	35.6	85.6	14.1	NA	NA
1870	39,818,449	8,375,128	26.6	86.2	13.5	NA	NA
1880	50,155,783	10,337,334	26.0	86.5	13.1	NA	NA
1890	62,947,714	12,791,931	25.5	87.5	11.9	NA	NA
1900	75,994,575	13,046,861	20.7	87.9	11.6	NA	0.3
1910	91,972,266	15,997,691	21.0	88.9	10.7	NA	0.3
1920	105,710,620	13,738,354	14.9	89.7	9.9	NA	0.3
1930	122,775,046	17,064,426	16.1	89.8	9.7	NA	0.4
1940	131,669,275	8,894,229	7.2	89.8	9.8	NA	0.4
1950	150,697,361	19,028,086	14.5	89.5	10.0	NA	0.4
1960†	179,323,175	28,625,814	19.0	88.6	10.5	NA	0.5
1970	203,235,298	23,912,123	13.3	87.6	11.1	NA	0.7
1980	226,504,825	23,269,527	11.4	85.9	11.8	6.4	1.5
1990	248,709,873	22,205,048	9.8	83.9	12.3	9.0	2.9
2000	281,421,906	32,712,033	13.2	82.2	12.2	11.7	3.8

* Not every racial group included (e.g., no Native Americans). Persons of Latino origin may be of any race. Data for 1980, 1990, 2000 add up to more than 100% because those who identify themselves as "Latino" could still be counted as "White."

† First year for which figures include Alaska and Hawaii.

(Source: Census Bureau, *Historical Statistics of the United States*, updated by relevant *Statistical Abstract of the United States*.)

Changing Characteristics of the U.S. Population

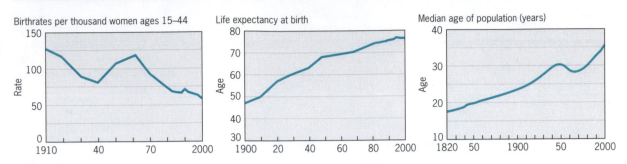

Sources: *Historical Statistics of the United States* and *Statistical Abstract of the United States,* relevant years.

Changing Lifestyles in Modern America

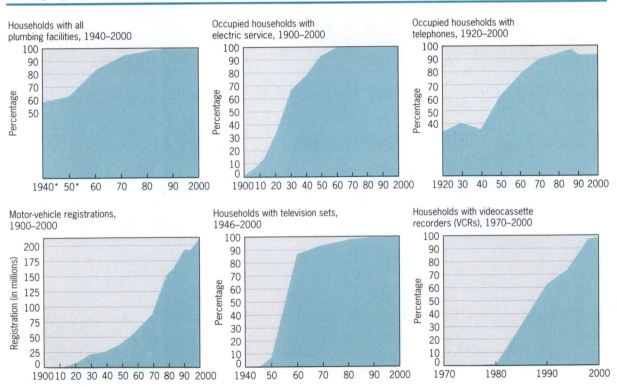

* Except for 1940 and 1950, figures are for "all plumbing facilities" (not defined in source). For 1940, figure is for flush toilet, inside structure, private use (64.7 percent had flush toilet, and private and/or shared inside structure, and 60.9 percent had installed bath or shower). For 1950, figure designates units with private toilet and bath, and hot running water (flush toilet, private or shared inside structure, is 74.3 percent; installed bathtub or shower, 72.9 percent).

Sources: *Historical Statistics of the United States* and *Statistical Abstract of the United States,* relevant years.

Characteristics of the U.S. Labor Force

Total labor force (age 16 or over, employed and unemployed seeking work)

(Area chart: Millions of persons on y-axis, 0 to 150; years 1870, 1900, 30, 70, 2000 on x-axis. Line rises from about 12 million in 1870 to nearly 150 million in 2000.)

Gender composition of labor force, 1900–2006 (percentage of men and women in civilian labor force)

(Line chart: Percentage 0 to 100 on y-axis; years 1900, 20, 40, 60, 80, 2000, 06 (projected) on x-axis. "Men" line declines from about 82% to about 53%. "Women" line rises from about 18% to about 47%.)

Top three occupational categories (rank based on total numbers) for workers age 14 and older

	farm	manual*	white collar†	service
Rank	1	2	3	
1900	farm	manual	white collar	
1920	manual	farm	white collar	
1940	manual	white collar	farm	
1960	white collar	manual	service	
1980	white collar	manual	service	
2000	white collar	manual	service	

* Manual workers = operators, fabricators, and laborers plus precision production, craft, and repair.

† White-collar workers = managerial and professional plus technical, sales, and administrative support.

Sources: *Historical Statistics of the United States* and *Statistical Abstract of the United States,* relevant years, and Department of Labor Statistics, *Handbook of Labor Statistics,* relevant years.

Leading Economic Sectors (Various Years)

Percentage of value added contributed

1849

(Pie chart)
- Manufacturing 32.1
- Construction 7.9
- Mining 1.4
- Agriculture 59.3

1899

(Pie chart)
- Construction 12.6
- Mining 4.6
- Manufacturing 49.3
- Agriculture 33.3

1949

(Pie chart)
- Trade 18.7
- Services 8.9
- Communication 1.6
- Transportation 5.7
- Finance, insurance, and real estate 10.8
- Government 8.7
- Agriculture 7.6
- Manufacturing 28.0
- Mining 3.2
- Construction 4.4

1999

(Pie chart)
- Agriculture 1.4
- Government 12.7
- Trade 16.9
- Manufacturing 17.0
- Services 20.6
- Construction 4.1
- Mining 1.5
- Communication 2.6
- Electricity, gas, and sanitation 2.6
- Finance, insurance, and real estate 19.5
- Transportation 3.2

Sources: *Historical Statistics of the United States* and *Statistical Abstract of the United States,* relevant years.

Per-Capita Disposable Personal Income in Constant (1996) Dollars, 1940–2000

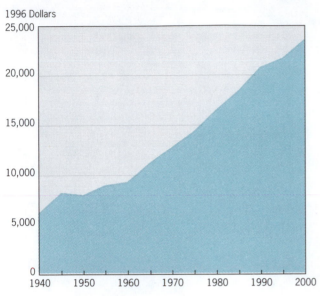

Source: *Statistical Abstract of the United States,* relevant years.

Comparative Tax Burdens (Percentage of Gross Domestic Product paid as taxes in major industrial countries, 1998)

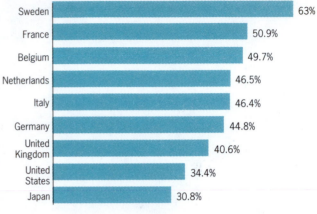

The Federal Budget Dollar and How It Is Spent, by Major Category

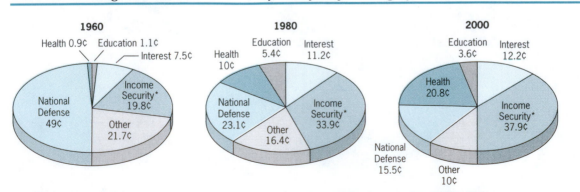

*Includes Social Security payments to the elderly and disabled, unemployment compensation, and welfare. Note the shifting emphasis in the budget from defense spending to health and income security, and to interest payments on the national debt.

The U.S. Balance of Trade, 1900–2000

Billions of dollars

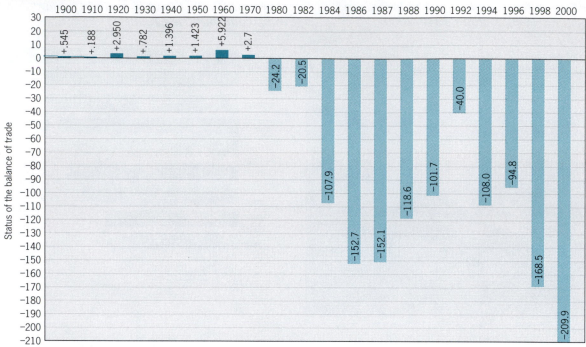

Sources: *Historical Statistics of the United States* and *Statistical Abstract of the United States,* relevant years.

Tariff Levies on Dutiable Imports, 1821–2000 (Ratio of Duties to Value of Dutiable Imports)

Sources: *Historical Statistics of the United States* and *Statistical Abstract of the United States,* relevant years.

*Gross National Product in Current and Constant 1995 Dollars**

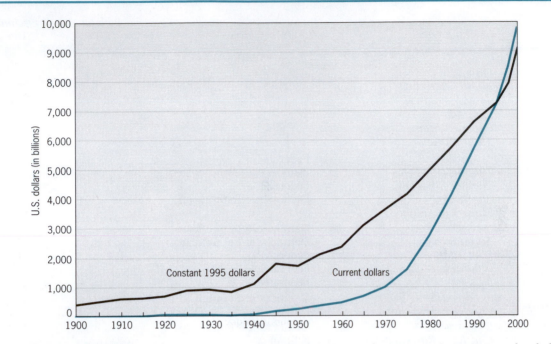

* Gross *national* product before 1960. Gross national product includes income from overseas investment, and excludes profits generated in the United States but accruing to foreign accounts. Gross *domestic* product excludes overseas profits owed to American accounts, but includes the value of all items originating in the United States, regardless of the ultimate destination of the profits. Until recent years, those factors made for negligible differences in the calculation of *national* and *domestic* product, but most economists now prefer the latter methodology.

Presidential Elections*

Election	Candidates	Parties	Popular Vote	Electoral Vote
1789	GEORGE WASHINGTON	No party designations		69
	John Adams			34
	Minor Candidates			35
1792	GEORGE WASHINGTON	No party designations		132
	John Adams			77
	George Clinton			50
	Minor Candidates			5
1796	JOHN ADAMS	Federalist		71
	Thomas Jefferson	Democratic-Republican		68
	Thomas Pinckney	Federalist		59
	Aaron Burr	Democratic-Republican		30
	Minor Candidates			48
1800	THOMAS JEFFERSON	Democratic-Republican		73
	Aaron Burr	Democratic-Republican		73
	John Adams	Federalist		65
	Charles C. Pinckney	Federalist		64
	John Jay	Federalist		1
1804	THOMAS JEFFERSON	Democratic-Republican		162
	Charles C. Pinckney	Federalist		14
1808	JAMES MADISON	Democratic-Republican		122
	Charles C. Pinckney	Federalist		47
	George Clinton	Democratic-Republican		6
1812	JAMES MADISON	Democratic-Republican		128
	DeWitt Clinton	Federalist		89
1816	JAMES MONROE	Democratic-Republican		183
	Rufus King	Federalist		34
1820	JAMES MONROE	Democratic-Republican		231
	John Q. Adams	Independent Republican		1
1824	JOHN Q. ADAMS (Min.)[†]	Democratic-Republican	108,740	84
	Andrew Jackson	Democratic-Republican	153,544	99
	William H. Crawford	Democratic-Republican	46,618	41
	Henry Clay	Democratic-Republican	47,136	37
1828	ANDREW JACKSON	Democratic	647,286	178
	John Q. Adams	National Republican	508,064	83
1832	ANDREW JACKSON	Democratic	687,502	219
	Henry Clay	National Republican	530,189	49
	William Wirt	Anti-Masonic ⎫	33,108	7
	John Floyd	National Republican ⎭		11
1836	MARTIN VAN BUREN	Democratic	765,483	170
	William H. Harrison	Whig ⎫		73
	Hugh L. White	Whig ⎪		26
	Daniel Webster	Whig ⎬	739,795	14
	W. P. Mangum	Whig ⎭		11

* Candidates receiving less than 1 percent of the popular vote are omitted. Before the Twelfth Amendment (1804), the Electoral College voted for two presidential candidates, and the runner-up became vice president. Basic figures are taken primarily from *Historical Statistics of the United States, 1789–1945* (1949), pp. 288–290; *Historical Statistics of the United States, Colonial Times to 1957* (1960), pp. 682–683; and *Statistical Abstract of the United States, 1969* (1969), pp. 355–357.

† "Min." indicates minority president—one receiving less than 50 percent of all popular votes.

Presidential Elections (Continued)

Election	Candidates	Parties	Popular Vote	Electoral Vote
1840	WILLIAM H. HARRISON	Whig	1,274,624	234
	Martin Van Buren	Democratic	1,127,781	60
1844	JAMES K. POLK (Min.)*	Democratic	1,338,464	170
	Henry Clay	Whig	1,300,097	105
	James G. Birney	Liberty	62,300	
1848	ZACHARY TAYLOR	Whig	1,360,967	163
	Lewis Cass	Democratic	1,222,342	127
	Martin Van Buren	Free Soil	291,263	
1852	FRANKLIN PIERCE	Democratic	1,601,117	254
	Winfield Scott	Whig	1,385,453	42
	John P. Hale	Free Soil	155,825	
1856	JAMES BUCHANAN (Min.)*	Democratic	1,832,955	174
	John C. Frémont	Republican	1,339,932	114
	Millard Fillmore	American	871,731	8
1860	ABRAHAM LINCOLN (Min.)*	Republican	1,865,593	180
	Stephen A. Douglas	Democratic	1,382,713	12
	John C. Breckinridge	Democratic	848,356	72
	John Bell	Constitutional Union	592,906	39
1864	ABRAHAM LINCOLN	Union	2,206,938	212
	George B. McClellan	Democratic	1,803,787	21
1868	ULYSSES S. GRANT	Republican	3,013,421	214
	Horatio Seymour	Democratic	2,706,829	80
1872	ULYSSES S. GRANT	Republican	3,596,745	286
	Horace Greeley	Democratic and Liberal Republican	2,843,446	66
1876	RUTHERFORD B. HAYES (Min.)*	Republican	4,036,572	185
	Samuel J. Tilden	Democratic	4,284,020	184
1880	JAMES A. GARFIELD (Min.)*	Republican	4,453,295	214
	Winfield S. Hancock	Democratic	4,414,082	155
	James B. Weaver	Greenback-Labor	308,578	
1884	GROVER CLEVELAND (Min.)*	Democratic	4,879,507	219
	James G. Blaine	Republican	4,850,293	182
	Benjamin F. Butler	Greenback-Labor	175,370	
	John P. St. John	Prohibition	150,369	
1888	BENJAMIN HARRISON (Min.)*	Republican	5,447,129	233
	Grover Cleveland	Democratic	5,537,857	168
	Clinton B. Fisk	Prohibition	249,506	
	Anson J. Streeter	Union Labor	146,935	
1892	GROVER CLEVELAND (Min.)*	Democratic	5,555,426	277
	Benjamin Harrison	Republican	5,182,690	145
	James B. Weaver	People's	1,029,846	22
	John Bidwell	Prohibition	264,133	
1896	WILLIAM MCKINLEY	Republican	7,102,246	271
	William J. Bryan	Democratic	6,492,559	176
1900	WILLIAM MCKINLEY	Republican	7,218,491	292
	William J. Bryan	Democratic; Populist	6,356,734	155
	John C. Woolley	Prohibition	208,914	

* "Min." indicates minority president—one receiving less than 50 percent of all popular votes.

Election	Candidates	Parties	Popular Vote	Electoral Vote
1904	THEODORE ROOSEVELT	Republican	7,628,461	336
	Alton B. Parker	Democratic	5,084,223	140
	Eugene V. Debs	Socialist	402,283	
	Silas C. Swallow	Prohibition	258,536	
1908	WILLIAM H. TAFT	Republican	7,675,320	321
	William J. Bryan	Democratic	6,412,294	162
	Eugene V. Debs	Socialist	420,793	
	Eugene W. Chafin	Prohibition	253,840	
1912	WOODROW WILSON (Min.)*	Democratic	6,296,547	435
	Theodore Roosevelt	Progressive	4,118,571	88
	William H. Taft	Republican	3,486,720	8
	Eugene V. Debs	Socialist	900,672	
	Eugene W. Chafin	Prohibition	206,275	
1916	WOODROW WILSON (Min.)*	Democratic	9,127,695	277
	Charles E. Hughes	Republican	8,533,507	254
	A. L. Benson	Socialist	585,113	
	J. F. Hanley	Prohibition	220,506	
1920	WARREN G. HARDING	Republican	16,143,407	404
	James M. Cox	Democratic	9,130,328	127
	Eugene V. Debs	Socialist	919,799	
	P. P. Christensen	Farmer-Labor	265,411	
1924	CALVIN COOLIDGE	Republican	15,718,211	382
	John W. Davis	Democratic	8,385,283	136
	Robert M. La Follette	Progressive	4,831,289	13
1928	HERBERT C. HOOVER	Republican	21,391,993	444
	Alfred E. Smith	Democratic	15,016,169	87
1932	FRANKLIN D. ROOSEVELT	Democratic	22,809,638	472
	Herbert C. Hoover	Republican	15,758,901	59
	Norman Thomas	Socialist	881,951	
1936	FRANKLIN D. ROOSEVELT	Democratic	27,752,869	523
	Alfred M. Landon	Republican	16,674,665	8
	William Lemke	Union, etc.	882,479	
1940	FRANKLIN D. ROOSEVELT	Democratic	27,307,819	449
	Wendell L. Willkie	Republican	22,321,018	82
1944	FRANKLIN D. ROOSEVELT	Democratic	25,606,585	432
	Thomas E. Dewey	Republican	22,014,745	99
1948	HARRY S TRUMAN (Min.)*	Democratic	24,179,345	303
	Thomas E. Dewey	Republican	21,991,291	189
	J. Strom Thurmond	States' Rights Democratic	1,176,125	39
	Henry A. Wallace	Progressive	1,157,326	
1952	DWIGHT D. EISENHOWER	Republican	33,936,234	442
	Adlai E. Stevenson	Democratic	27,314,992	89
1956	DWIGHT D. EISENHOWER	Republican	35,590,472	457
	Adlai E. Stevenson	Democratic	26,022,752	73
1960	JOHN F. KENNEDY (Min.)*	Democratic	34,226,731	303
	Richard M. Nixon	Republican	34,108,157	219
1964	LYNDON B. JOHNSON	Democratic	43,129,566	486
	Barry M. Goldwater	Republican	27,178,188	52
1968	RICHARD M. NIXON (Min.)*	Republican	31,785,480	301
	Hubert H. Humphrey, Jr.	Democratic	31,275,166	191
	George C. Wallace	American Independent	9,906,473	46

* "Min." indicates minority president—one receiving less than 50 percent of all popular votes.

Presidential Elections (Continued)

Election	Candidates	Parties	Popular Vote	Electoral Vote
1972	RICHARD M. NIXON	Republican	47,169,911	520
	George S. McGovern	Democratic	29,170,383	17
1976	JIMMY CARTER	Democratic	40,828,657	297
	Gerald R. Ford	Republican	39,145,520	240
1980	RONALD W. REAGAN	Republican	43,899,248	489
	Jimmy Carter	Democratic	35,481,435	49
	John B. Anderson	Independent	5,719,437	
1984	RONALD W. REAGAN	Republican	52,609,797	525
	Walter Mondale	Democratic	36,450,613	13
1988	GEORGE BUSH	Republican	47,946,422	426
	Michael Dukakis	Democratic	41,016,429	111
1992	WILLIAM CLINTON (Min.)*	Democratic	43,738,275	370
	George Bush	Republican	38,167,416	168
	H. Ross Perot	Independent	19,237,247	
1996	WILLIAM CLINTON	Democratic	45,628,667	379
	Robert Dole	Republican	37,869,435	159
	H. Ross Perot	Reform	7,874,283	
2000	GEORGE W. BUSH (Min.)*	Republican	50,456,169	271
	Albert Gore, Jr.	Democratic	50,996,116	267
	Ralph Nader	Green	2,783,728	

* "Min." indicates minority president—one receiving less than 50 percent of all popular votes.

Presidents and Vice Presidents

Term	President	Vice President
1789–1793	George Washington	John Adams
1793–1797	George Washington	John Adams
1797–1801	John Adams	Thomas Jefferson
1801–1805	Thomas Jefferson	Aaron Burr
1805–1809	Thomas Jefferson	George Clinton
1809–1813	James Madison	George Clinton (d. 1812)
1813–1817	James Madison	Elbridge Gerry (d. 1814)
1817–1821	James Monroe	Daniel D. Tompkins
1821–1825	James Monroe	Daniel D. Tompkins
1825–1829	John Quincy Adams	John C. Calhoun
1829–1833	Andrew Jackson	John C. Calhoun (resigned 1832)
1833–1837	Andrew Jackson	Martin Van Buren
1837–1841	Martin Van Buren	Richard M. Johnson
1841–1845	William H. Harrison (d. 1841) John Tyler	John Tyler
1845–1849	James K. Polk	George M. Dallas
1849–1853	Zachary Taylor (d. 1850) Millard Fillmore	Millard Fillmore

Presidents and Vice Presidents (Continued)

Term	President	Vice President
1853–1857	Franklin Pierce	William R. D. King (d. 1853)
1857–1861	James Buchanan	John C. Breckinridge
1861–1865	Abraham Lincoln	Hannibal Hamlin
1865–1869	Abraham Lincoln (d. 1865) Andrew Johnson	Andrew Johnson
1869–1873	Ulysses S. Grant	Schuyler Colfax
1873–1877	Ulysses S. Grant	Henry Wilson (d. 1875)
1877–1881	Rutherford B. Hayes	William A. Wheeler
1881–1885	James A. Garfield (d. 1881) Chester A. Arthur	Chester A. Arthur
1885–1889	Grover Cleveland	Thomas A. Hendricks (d. 1885)
1889–1893	Benjamin Harrison	Levi P. Morton
1893–1897	Grover Cleveland	Adlai E. Stevenson
1897–1901	William McKinley	Garret A. Hobart (d. 1899)
1901–1905	William McKinley (d. 1901) Theodore Roosevelt	Theodore Roosevelt
1905–1909	Theodore Roosevelt	Charles W. Fairbanks
1909–1913	William H. Taft	James S. Sherman (d. 1912)
1913–1917	Woodrow Wilson	Thomas R. Marshall
1917–1921	Woodrow Wilson	Thomas R. Marshall
1921–1925	Warren G. Harding (d. 1923) Calvin Coolidge	Calvin Coolidge
1925–1929	Calvin Coolidge	Charles G. Dawes
1929–1933	Herbert C. Hoover	Charles Curtis
1933–1937	Franklin D. Roosevelt	John N. Garner
1937–1941	Franklin D. Roosevelt	John N. Garner
1941–1945	Franklin D. Roosevelt	Henry A. Wallace
1945–1949	Franklin D. Roosevelt (d. 1945) Harry S Truman	Harry S Truman
1949–1953	Harry S Truman	Alben W. Barkley
1953–1957	Dwight D. Eisenhower	Richard M. Nixon
1957–1961	Dwight D. Eisenhower	Richard M. Nixon
1961–1965	John F. Kennedy (d. 1963) Lyndon B. Johnson	Lyndon B. Johnson
1965–1969	Lyndon B. Johnson	Hubert H. Humphrey, Jr.
1969–1973	Richard M. Nixon	Spiro T. Agnew
1973–1977	Richard M. Nixon (resigned 1974) Gerald R. Ford	Spiro T. Agnew (resigned 1973); Gerald R. Ford Nelson Rockefeller
1977–1981	Jimmy Carter	Walter F. Mondale
1981–1985	Ronald Reagan	George Bush
1985–1989	Ronald Reagan	George Bush
1989–1993	George Bush	J. Danforth Quayle III
1993–2001	William Clinton	Albert Gore, Jr.
2001–	George W. Bush	Richard Cheney

Admission of States

Order of Admission	State	Date of Admission	Order of Admission	State	Date of Admission
14	Vermont	Mar. 4, 1791	33	Oregon	Feb. 14, 1859
15	Kentucky	June 1, 1792	34	Kansas	Jan. 29, 1861
16	Tennessee	June 1, 1796	35	W. Virginia	June 20, 1863
17	Ohio	Mar. 1, 1803	36	Nevada	Oct. 31, 1864
18	Louisiana	April 30, 1812	37	Nebraska	Mar. 1, 1867
19	Indiana	Dec. 11, 1816	38	Colorado	Aug. 1, 1876
20	Mississippi	Dec. 10, 1817	39	N. Dakota	Nov. 2, 1889
21	Illinois	Dec. 3, 1818	40	S. Dakota	Nov. 2, 1889
22	Alabama	Dec. 14, 1819	41	Montana	Nov. 8, 1889
23	Maine	Mar. 15, 1820	42	Washington	Nov. 11, 1889
24	Missouri	Aug. 10, 1821	43	Idaho	July 3, 1890
25	Arkansas	June 15, 1836	44	Wyoming	July 10, 1890
26	Michigan	Jan. 26, 1837	45	Utah	Jan. 4, 1896
27	Florida	Mar. 3, 1845	46	Oklahoma	Nov. 16, 1907
28	Texas	Dec. 29, 1845	47	New Mexico	Jan. 6, 1912
29	Iowa	Dec. 28, 1846	48	Arizona	Feb. 14, 1912
30	Wisconsin	May 29, 1848	49	Alaska	Jan. 3, 1959
31	California	Sept. 9, 1850	50	Hawaii	Aug. 21, 1959
32	Minnesota	May 11, 1858			

Estimates of Total Costs and Number of Battle Deaths of Major U.S. Wars*

	Total Costs** (Millions of Dollars)	Original Costs	Number of Battle Deaths
Vietnam Conflict	352,000	140,600	47,355[†]
Korean Conflict	164,000	54,000	33,629
World War II	664,000	288,000	291,557
World War I	112,000	26,000	53,402
Spanish-American War	6,460	400	385
Civil War { Union only	12,952	3,200	140,414
Civil War { Confederacy (est.)	N.A.	1,000	94,000
Mexican War	147	73	1,733
War of 1812	158	93	2,260
American Revolution	190	100	6,824

* Deaths from disease and other causes are not shown. In earlier wars especially, owing to poor medical and sanitary practices, non-battle deaths substantially exceeded combat casualties.

** The difference between total costs and original costs is attributable to continuing postwar payments for such items as veterans' benefits, interest on war debts, etc.

[†] 1959–1990

Sources: *Historical Statistics of the United States, Statistical Abstract of the United States,* relevant years, and *The World Almanac and Book of Facts, 1986.*

Photograph Credits

Index

The United States Today

○ *Capitals of Countries*

★ *State Capitals*

PACIFIC OCEAN

Vancouver

Seattle
Olympia ★ ● Tacoma
WASHINGTON
Spokane ●

● Portland
Salem ★

OREGON

Columbia R.

ROCKY

● Missoula
★ Helena MONTANA
● Butte

Missouri R.

Yellowstone

IDAHO

★ Boise

Snake R.

WYOMING

MOUNTAINS

Cheyenne ★

Great Salt Lake
Reno ●
★ Carson City

Sacramento ★
San Francisco ●

NEVADA

Salt Lake City ★

UTAH

●Den
COLORADO

Mt. Whitney +
14,495 Ft.

CALIFORNIA

Las
Vegas ●
Hoover Dam ▬

GRAND
CANYON

Colorado R.

Los Angeles ●

ARIZONA

★ Santa Fe
● Albuquerque

NEW MEXICO

San Diego ●

Phoenix ★

● Tucson

● El Paso

Rio Grande

Hawaii inset

KAUAI
NIIHAU   OAHU
Pearl Harbor ●★   MOLOKAI
Honolulu
HAWAII   LANAI   MAUI
KAHOOLAWE

PACIFIC OCEAN

HAWAII

| 0 | 75 | 150 Mi. |
| 0 | 75 | 150 Km. |

Alaska inset

POINT BARROW   ARCTIC OCEAN

RUSSIA

ALASKA

Yukon R.

CANADA

● Nome

Fairbanks
+ Mt. McKinley
20,300 Ft.
Anchorage ●

Juneau ★

International Dateline (RUSSIA)
(UNITED STATES)

BERING SEA

KODIAK

GULF OF ALASKA

ATTU

ALEUTIAN ISLANDS

UNIMAK

MEXICO

| 0 | 250 | 500 Mi. |
| 0 | 250 | 500 Km. |